ROYAL

PIGOT AND CO.'S ROYAL NATIONAL AND COMMERCIAL DIRECTORY AND TOPOGRAPHY

OF THE COUNTIES OF

KENT SURREY SUSSEX

COMPRISING

CLASSIFIED LISTS OF ALL PERSONS IN TRADE;

AND OF

THE NOBILITY, GENTRY AND CLERGY,

RESIDENT IN THE TOWNS AND PRINCIPAL VILLAGES IN THE ABOVE COUNTIES.

AN ACCOUNT OF EVERY MODE OF CONVEYANCE BY

RAILWAY, ROAD AND WATER;

POST-OFFICE REGULATIONS, &c.

THE WORK IS EMBELLISHED WITH

BEAUTIFUL COUNTY MAPS;

UPON WHICH IS CONSPICUOUSLY LAID DOWN EVERY LINE OF RAILWAY, FOR WHICH AN ACT OF PARLIAMENT HAS BEEN OBTAINED TO THE PRESENT TIME.

September, 1839.

PUBLISHED BY J. PIGOT & CO. 59, FLEET-STREET, LONDON, AND FOUNTAIN-STREET, MANCHESTER:

And Sold by them and the following Booksellers, viz.

SIMPKIN, MARSHALL AND CO. STATIONER'S COURT; LONGMAN AND CO., AND SHERWOOD AND CO. PATERNOSTER ROW; ARTHUR VARNHAM, 61 STRAND; AND BY OTHER RESPECTABLE BOOKSELLERS: ALSO BY G. G. BENNIS, 55 RUE NEUVE ST. AUGUSTIN, AGENT FOR PARIS AND THE CONTINENT.

FACSIMILE EDITION 1993

[Ordering Details Overleaf]

PIGOT AND CO.'S
ROYAL
NATIONAL AND COMMERCIAL
DIRECTORIES

EMBELLISHED WITH BEAUTIFUL COUNTY MAPS

Facsimile Text Editions

Royal Octavo 10" x 6¼"

"May not faithful Directories of the present day be the means of preserving to after-generations 'a local habitation and a name'?"
James Pigot 1830

To order please enter amount in appropriate box/es:

Norfolk & Suffolk 1830 132 pages ISBN 0 9504069 2 9
£6.95 plus p & p: U.K. 70p, Europe & Surface Mail £1.20, Airmail £2.70.

Beds, Cambs, Herts, Lincs, Northants 1830 152 pages ISBN 0 950469 3 7
£6.95 plus p & p: U.K. 80p, Europe & Surface Mail £1.40, Airmail £3.10.

Essex, Herts, Middlesex 1839 210 pages ISBN 0 950469 4 5
£7.50 plus p & p: U.K. 90p, Europe & Surface Mail £1.50, Airmail £3.70.

Kent, Surrey, Sussex 1839 282 pages ISBN 0 9504069 5 3
£9.50 plus p& p: U.K. £1.20, Europe & Surface Mail £2.00, Airmail £4.80.

The Norwich Directory 1783 [Details Overleaf]

The Norfolk Map 1611 [Details Overleaf]

Please send the item/s as indicated.
A sterling cheque for £ .... made out to M. J. Winton is enclosed.

Name ....

Address ....

....

.... Postcode ....

Michael Winton
5 Lynn Road, Castle Rising, King's Lynn, Norfolk PE31 6AB

[Please See Overleaf]

PIGOT AND CO.'S
ROYAL
NATIONAL AND COMMERCIAL
DIRECTORY AND TOPOGRAPHY

OF THE COUNTIES OF

ESSEX HERTS
MIDDLESEX

COMPRISING

CLASSIFIED LISTS OF ALL PERSONS IN TRADE,

AND OF

THE NOBILITY, GENTRY AND CLERGY,

RESIDENT IN THE TOWNS AND PRINCIPAL VILLAGES IN THE ABOVE COUNTIES.

AN ACCOUNT OF EVERY MODE OF CONVEYANCE BY

RAILWAY, ROAD AND WATER;

POST-OFFICE REGULATIONS, &c.

THE WORK IS EMBELLISHED WITH

BEAUTIFUL COUNTY MAPS;

UPON WHICH IS CONSPICUOUSLY LAID DOWN EVERY LINE OF RAILWAY, FOR WHICH AN ACT OF PARLIAMENT HAS BEEN OBTAINED TO THE PRESENT TIME.

September, 1839.

PUBLISHED BY J. PIGOT & CO. 59, FLEET-STREET, LONDON, AND FOUNTAIN-STREET, MANCHESTER:

And Sold by them and the following Booksellers, viz.

SIMPKIN, MARSHALL AND CO. STATIONER'S COURT; LONGMAN AND CO., AND SHERWOOD AND CO. PATERNOSTER ROW; ARTHUR FARNHAM, 61 STRAND; AND BY OTHER RESPECTABLE BOOKSELLERS: ALSO BY G. G. BENNIS, 55 RUE NEUVE ST. AUGUSTIN, AGENT FOR PARIS AND THE CONTINENT.

ADDRESS.

MESSRS. PIGOT AND CO., in placing the present work in the hands of their Subscribers, have but little to address to them upon the score of novelty, or the arrangement of its contents. The most prominent feature of improvement, perhaps, will be recognized in the Provincial portion, where are introduced numerous Villages not visited by the Proprietors while compiling the same Counties, in their previous works. In Hertfordshire and Essex this augmentation is particularly apparent.

The topographical department, also, occupies a space considerably more extensive than has hitherto been devoted to this description of information. The enlargement of this section must with justice be ascribed to the value and extent of materials kindly and promptly furnished by gentlemen of the first talent and research; and to whom the best thanks of the Proprietors are due, for their obliging and valuable assistance.

Having thus briefly adverted to the principal materials forming this Directory, *the Proprietors would be wanting in gratitude did they not confess, that to the liberal patronage bestowed during their compilation, they are beholden for the means of accumulating and publishing so large and various a mass of essentially useful information.*

ESSEX.

THIS is a maritime county, bounded on the north by the counties of Suffolk and Cambridge, on the west by those of Hertford and Middlesex, on the south by the river Thames, which separates it from Kent, and on the east by the German ocean. Its figure on the sea-coast is irregular, being broken into a series of inlets and peninsulas, deeply cut in by arms of the sea, and exhibiting indelible tokens of the force and effects of that restless element. Its extent from east to west is estimated at sixty miles, and from north to south at about fifty; its circumference is computed at 225 miles, and its area comprises about 1,532 square miles, or 980,480 statute acres. In size it ranks as the tenth county in England, and in population as the fourteenth.

NAME and ANCIENT HISTORY.—At the time of the Roman Invasion this part of Britain was inhabited by the people called *Trinobantes*; an appellation connected with the situation of their country on the borders of the broad waters, principally formed by the estuary of the Thames, at a time when its embankments were few and ill constructed. In the subdivision of the island by Constantine the Great, the present county formed part of *Flavia Cæsariensis*. The origin of its name is coeval with the establishment of the kingdom of the East Saxons, of which London was the capital, and the tract comprised within the present boundaries of the county composed a considerable part; it was called *East Seaxa*—implying 'the land of the Eastern Saxons,' from its relative position to the other Saxon kingdoms. Various actions with the Danes took place in this county, as well as in most others on the east coast; one of the most memorable was fought at Assingdon (or Ashdown), near Rochford, in which King Edmund Ironside was defeated with great slaughter by the renowned Canute. One particular event, as connected with Essex, was the great rebellion of the commons, headed by Wat Tyler and Jack Straw, in the reign of Richard II. Tilbury Fort, opposite to Gravesend, is the principal protection to the Thames; in its neighbourhood Queen Elizabeth reviewed the army she had assembled to oppose the Spanish Armada, in 1588. Colchester underwent a very obstinate siege in 1648, on occasion of an insurrection of the royal adherents against the authority of the parliament, the gallant leaders of which, on the surrender of the place, were executed. The last transaction of importance in connexion with the history of Essex was the engagement off Harwich, on the 3rd June, 1665, when the Dutch fleet was defeated by the Duke of York.

SOIL, PRODUCE, MANUFACTURES and CLIMATE.—Almost every species of SOIL, from the most stubborn to the mildest loam, is to be found within the limits of Essex. This county forms part of that tract of country, on the eastern side of England, which constitutes the largest connected space of level ground in the whole island: its surface is not, however, totally flat, having many gentle hills and dales; and towards the north-west, whence most of the rivers proceed, the country rises, and presents a continued inequality of surface. The most level portion is that of the south and east hundreds; its south-west part is chiefly occupied by Epping forest and its several branches; northward the country becomes more open and uneven; the middle of Essex is in general a fine corn country, varied with moderate inequalities of surface, and sprinkled with woods. The proportion of waste land is very small; the greater part of the county is inclosed, and rendered highly productive, both in variety and quality, by the skilful management of the agriculturists. The principal PRODUCTIONS are wheat, barley, oats, beans, pease, turnips, tares, rape, mustard, rye-grass and trefoil; many acres are appropriated to hops, and a diversity of horticultural plants and roots—the latter, however, are chiefly limited to the lands contiguous to the metropolis; another product of this county is saffron, which at one period was cultivated so extensively as to originate a second appellation for a town (*Saffron* Walden), around which it flourished abundantly—a light rich soil and dry country are necessary for the successful culture of this plant. There is also a kind of treble crop cultivated, viz. coriander, carraway and teazle; the two former on account of their aromatic seeds; the latter for its prickly heads, used for the purpose of raising the nap on woollen cloths: these are all sown together, but come to maturity at different periods, and the succession of the whole crop lasts three or four years. Though this county is not particularly celebrated for its dairies, yet those in the parish of Epping and its vicinity are famous for the richness of their cream and butter—the latter mostly sent to London, where it bears a high character and price. Essex is proverbially distinguished for its calves, of which more are suckled or fattened here than in any other county. The marshy grounds, broken by arms of the sea into islands, and frequently inundated, afford fine pasturage for cattle. Fish are plentiful on the coast and in the various creeks of this county; some of the latter, near Colchester and about the Mersey island, are valuable for their fine oyster beds; these supply an article for exportation to a considerable amount, and the true breed maintain a superiority in the metropolis. The convenience of water carriage, and the goodness of the roads throughout the county, are of great advantage in transmitting its productions, and, combined with its proximity to the capital of the empire, bestow on it a commercial predominance over many other counties. The MANUFACTURES of Essex, of late years, have receded in consequence: at Colchester are some extensive silk mills, and this town also retains a share of the manufacture of baize, for which it was once very famous; Bocking, Coggeshall and Braintree likewise participate in these trades; and in the last-named town, and its neighbourhood, many of the industrious poor are supported by the making of straw plat for the London market. The CLIMATE is generally mild; but part of the eastern and southern districts of the county are subject to fogs, which originate agues; drainage and the improvement of the lands have, however, greatly diminished this evil.

RIVERS, CANALS and RAILROADS.—The principal RIVERS properly belonging to Essex are the COLNE, the BLACKWATER (or PONT), the CHELMER, the CROUCH, the INGERBOURN, the RODING and the CAM; besides these, this county partakes of other streams, which form natural boundaries, and irrigate and fertilize its borders—these are the Thames, the Lea, the Stort and the Stour. The Colne rises on the north side of the county, and in its course passes Castle Hedingham, Halstead and Colchester; it soon after expands into a wide estuary, and is navigable from the sea to within two miles of Colchester. The Blackwater has its source on the confines of Cambridgeshire, and meanders through Barking and Coggeshall; and, flowing south-east, unites with the Chelmer a little below Maldon, and then mingles with the waters of the ocean. The Chelmer has its original spring near Thaxted, and, after receiving several tributary brooks, joins the Blackwater, as before mentioned, near Maldon. The Crouch and Ingerbourn are small rivers, rising in the south side of the county, and slowly pass through a short course to the Thames. The Roding, also an inferior stream, makes a circuitous visit to Chipping Ongar and several villages, in its progress to Wanstead, Ilford and Barking; it is rendered navigable to Ilford bridge. The Cam originates from three springs near Newport, and takes a direction different from any of the former rivers: it passes Audley End, Chesterton, &c., and pursues a north course to Cambridgeshire. The Lea and the Stort constitute the west boundary of the county, separating it from Middlesex and Hertfordshire; and the Stour divides it from the county of Suffolk to the north. Other smaller streams rise in Essex, and fall either into the Thames or the ocean. The London and Cambridge CANAL passes along the north-western boundary of the county. RAILWAYS:—The EASTERN COUNTIES Railway passes by Romford, a little to the east of Brentwood; then to the west of Billericay, and through Ingatestone, on to Chelmsford; thence to within a short distance of Coggeshall, Colchester and Manningtree—when it leaves the county, and enters Norfolk on its route to Norwich. Near Colchester a branch is projected to Harwich. The THAMES HAVEN AND DOCK Railway issues from the 'Eastern Counties' at Romford, and passes to the south of Upminster and north of South Ockendon; and, running close to Stanford-le-Hope, it terminates at the Thames Haven Dock, at the distance of thirty-six miles from London, below Canvey Island.

ECCLESIASTICAL and CIVIL DIVISIONS, and REPRESENTATION.—Essex is in the province of Canterbury and diocess of London—is included in the Home circuit, and divided into the nineteen hundreds of Barstable, Becontree, Chafford, Chelmsford, Clavering, Dengie, Dunmow, Freshwell, Harlow, Hinckford, Lexden, Ongar,

Rochford, Tendring, Thurstable, Uttlesford, Waltham, Winstree and Witham, and the liberty of Havering-atte-Bower; these collectively contain one county town (Chelmsford), eighteen other market towns, 406 parishes and three parts of parishes. The whole county, previous to the operation of the reform act, sent eight members to parliament, viz. two each for Colchester, Harwich and Maldon, and two for the shire. The new act gave two additional members to the county, which it divided into two parts, named the Northern Division and the Southern Division; members to represent the former are elected at Braintree, and for the latter at Chelmsford: the polling places in addition, for the Northern Division, are Colchester, Saffron Walden and Thorpe; and for the Southern, besides Chelmsford, the poll is taken at Billericay, Romford, Epping and Maldon. The members at present sitting for the Northern Division are Sir John Tyssen Tyrrell, and Charles Gray Round, Esq.; those for the Southern Division, Thomas William Bramston and George Palmer, Esqrs.

Population, &c.—By the census for 1831 this county contained 158,881 males, and 158,352 females—total, 317,233: being an increase, since the returns made in the year 1821, of 27,809 inhabitants; and from the census of 1801 to that of 1831 the augmentation amounted to 90,796 persons. The annual value of Real Property in Essex, as assessed April, 1815, amounted to £1,556,836.

Index of Distances from Town to Town in the County of Essex.

The names of the respective towns are on the top and side, and the square where both meet gives the distance.

Town	Barking	Billericay	Braintree	Brentwood	Chelmsford	Chipping Ongar	Coggeshall	Colchester	Dunmow	Epping	Gray's Thurrock	Halstead	Harwich	Hatfield Broadoak	Maldon	Manningtree	Rochford	Romford	Saffron Walden	Thaxted	Waltham Abbey	*Distance from London.*
Barking																						7
Billericay	18																					24
Braintree	35	21																				41
Brentwood	12	6	23																			18
Chelmsford	24	9	12	11																		29
Chipping Ongar	17	12	20	7	10																	21
Coggeshall	40	26	6	26	16	27																44
Colchester	45	31	15	33	22	31	9															51
Dunmow	31	21	9	19	13	15	15	24														36
Epping	11	18	27	12	17	7	33	39	20													17
Gray's Thurrock	14	12	33	11	21	17	36	41	30	22												21
Halstead	40	27	6	29	18	26	6	14	15	34	38											47
Harwich	66	51	36	54	42	52	30	21	45	60	62	35										72
Hatfield Broadoak	25	20	14	18	12	11	20	30	8	12	29	21	50									29
Maldon	30	18	13	20	10	20	12	16	22	26	25	18	37	22								37
Manningtree	54	40	24	42	31	40	18	9	33	49	50	23	12	39	25							60
Rochford	34	15	26	21	18	28	23	29	31	33	23	29	47	30	13	36						39
Romford	7	11	29	6	17	10	32	39	24	10	12	34	60	21	27	48	26					12
Saffron Walden	36	36	20	34	27	27	26	34	13	25	46	20	55	18	34	43	45	35				42
Thaxted	37	27	12	26	19	22	19	27	3	23	37	14	48	11	25	36	37	30	8			44
Waltham Abbey	13	20	33	18	23	13	39	44	26	6	23	40	65	18	32	53	35	12	31	33		12
Witham	32	17	7	19	9	18	7	14	17	26	30	14	35	21	6	23	18	25	27	19	32	7[illegible]

AVELEY

IS a neat little village and parish in the hundred of Chafford—16 miles E. by S. from London, 10 S. from Brentwood, about 7½ S. S. E from Romford, and 4 W. by N. from Grays Thurrock; situated on a pleasant elevation. about two miles from the Thames, over which river and the country around the prospect is extensive and delightful. In the parish is Bell House, a large mansion in an agreeable park, now in the occupation of Sir Thomas Leonard, Bart.; this residence was built in the reign of Henry VIII. Amongst the privileges annexed to the manor of Aveley is one by which all persons, however elevated by rank, are excluded from entering in search of game. The church, dedicated to St. Michael, is an ancient structure with a tower; the benefice is a rectory, in the incumbency of the Rev. John Holmes. Population of the parish, in 1831, 758.

POST OFFICE, Crown and Anchor Inn, James Cook, *Post Master.*—Letters from LONDON arrive (from ROMFORD) every morning at eight, and are despatched every evening at six.

GENTRY AND CLERGY.

Joyner Henry St. John, esq. Aveley
Joyner Joseph, esq. Aveley hall
Joyner William Joseph, esq. Aveley
Leonard Sir Thomas, bart. Bell house
Vidal Mr. Charles Lewis, M.D.
White Rev. Richard, Aveley

PUBLIC HOUSES.

Crown & Anchor, James Cook
Leonard's Arms, Henry King Wennington
Ship, Edward Appleton

SHOPKEEPERS, TRADERS, &c.

Barnes William, hair dresser
Burrows Edward, grocer & draper
Burtwell Charles and George, painters and glaziers
Downe George, carpenter
Gibson William, wheelwright
Harris Henry, baker
Harvey Mary, baker
James Ruth, shopkeeper
Lee William, blacksmith
Looret Goulding, butcher
Pepper William, carpenter
Scooling John, shoe maker
Woodthorp Henry, grocer & draper

COACHES.

To LONDON, the *Perseverence* (from Horndon on the Hill) calls at the Crown and Anchor every morning at half-past eight; goes through Barking.

To HORNDON ON THE HILL, the *Perseverence* (from London) calls at the Crown and Anchor every evening at half-past nine.

VAN.

To and from LONDON & ORSETT, a *Van*, calls at the Crown and Anchor, daily.

BADDOW (GREAT),

GALLY-WOOD COMMON, SANDON AND NEIGHBOURHOODS.

GREAT BADDOW is a neat village in an extensive and extremely fertile parish of its name, and hundred of Chelmsford—two miles S. E. from Chelmsford, and 31 from London. The beauty of the country surrounding Baddow has induced a great number of genteel families to adopt this village for their residence. The church, dedicated to St. Mary, is a handsome edifice, with a tower containing a peal of sweet-toned bells. There are alms-houses for the comfortable retreat of ten poor families, and two endowed schools, one of which is for the children of dissenters. At GALLY-WOOD COMMON, a hamlet of Great Baddow, the Chelmsford races are held. Population of the parish, in 1831, 1,719.

About one mile from Baddow, in the same hundred, is the village and parish of SANDON, so called from the sandy hill on which it stands. The church is dedicated to St. Andrew; the living is a rectory, in the patronage of the president and fellows of Queen's college, Cambridge. Dr. Walton, celebrated as the editor of the 'Polyglott Bible,' was rector of this parish many years, and the remains of his wife lie interred in the church. Population of the parish, in 1831, 525.

POST OFFICE, GREAT BADDOW, James Larcher, *Post Master.*—Letters from LONDON arrive (from CHELMSFORD) every morning at six, and are despatched every evening at eight.

*** *The names without address are in* GREAT BADDOW.

GENTRY AND CLERGY.

Boggis James, esq. Baddow court
Bowers John, esq. Sandon hall
Braniston Rev. John, A. M. Vicarage
Bullen Mrs. Lucy, Vine yards
Cookson Miss, Baddow
Douglas Mrs. —, Baddow
Foaker Mr. Leonard (surgeon) Baddow
Gilson Mr. Henry S. Baddow
Greenwood Thos. esq. Baddow house
Hales Mrs. —, Woodhill
Hewitt Rev. George, Sandon
Knipe Rev. Francis, Sandon
Lewis the Misses, Baddow
M'Lachlan Mrs. —, Baddow hall
Murdock Ephraim (attorney) Baddow, and at *Chelmsford*
Pollean Mrs. —, Gallidean house
Pryor Mrs. Elizabeth
Reynolds the Misses, Pitt place
Urquhuart Alex. esq. Baddow

ACADEMIES & SCHOOLS.

Collier Amelia (ladies' boarding)
FREE GRAMMAR SCHOOL, Peter Larcher, master; Francis W. Dyer, assistant master
Gilson the Misses (ladies' boarding)
NATIONAL SCHOOL, Thos. Warner, master; Sarah Bray, mistress
Wilson the Misses (boarding)

TAVERNS & PUBLIC HOUSES.

Bear, David Daws, Gally-wood common
Bell, Joseph, Sewell
Blue Lion, William Young, Gally-wood common
Crown, Henry Ratcliff, Sandon
King's Head, James Patten
White Horse, Elizabeth Wilson

SHOPKEEPERS & TRADERS.

Bacon Thomas William, cooper
Baker John, wheelwright
Bell James and Son, grocers, &c.
Blanks Henry, boot & shoe maker
Blanks Lazarus, blacksmith
Carter Potter H. shoemaker
Clark George, shoemaker
Crabb Richard H. and Son, brewers & maltsters; house Baddow place
Dowsett Henry, baker
Duffield James, butcher
Duffield William, grocer
Dyer Francis W. assistant master at the Free Grammar School
Finch Richard, butcher
Gilson H. S. attorney, and at *Chelmsford*
Gladwin William, butcher
Goode John, well sinker
Grove Samuel James, corn dealer
Harrington Francis, baker
Harrington Thomas, watch and clock maker
Harward George, saddler
Harward John, shoemaker
Harward Samuel, hair dresser
Jackson William, carpenter & wheelwright
Kidd William P. tailor
Larcher Robert W. auctioneer and appraiser, land and estate agent, and agent for stock brokers
Martin John, saddler
Moss Thomas, bricklayer & builder
Patten John, bricklayer
Porter Anne, milliner
Porter John, shoemaker
Robinson Anne, baker
Rogers Thomas, shopkeeper
Rogers William, baker
Ruffell Ann, plumber and glazier
Sorrell James, carpenter
Taylor William, shopkeeper
Tibbeld Robert, carpenter
Turner Charles, builder
Warner Thomas, registrar of births and deaths

COACH.

To LONDON, a *Coach* (from Maldon) passes through Baddow every morning at ten, and returns every afternoon

BARKING,

WITH THE VILLAGES OF GREAT AND LITTLE ILFORD, EAST HAM AND NEIGHBOURHOODS.

BARKING, once a market town, is in the parish of its name and hundred of Becontree, seven miles from London; situated upon the banks of the river Roding, which, after flowing in two branches, unites with the Thames about two miles below the town. There is a convenient wharf and basin at Barking creek, which is navigable to Ilford for vessels of eighty tons burthen, and the neighbourhood is thus supplied with coal and timber; there is also a toll-free quay for the accommodation of the craft. The welfare of the place mainly depends upon its fishery, which employs upwards of twelve hundred men and boys, on board vessels of from forty to sixty tons, constructed with wells for preserving the fish alive until their arrival at the London market; turbot, sole and cod, taken off the coasts of Scotland and Holland, form the chief part of the cargoes: the fishery is the nursery of a hardy industrious race, who seldom fail to become excellent sailors. A considerable number of the inhabitants are also engaged in the cultivation of potatoes and other vegetables for the supply of the metropolis. An abbey, of which scarcely any remains are in existence, was founded here in 670, and for several centuries imparted a degree of consequence to Barking. Constables, and other officers of the town, are appointed at a court leet; and there is a court held under the lord of the manor, every third Saturday, for the recovery of debts under 40s. The parish church is dedicated to St. Margaret: the benefice is a vicarage, in the presentation of the college of All Souls, Oxford; the Hon. and Rev. Robert Liddell is the present incumbent. There are two chapels for dissenters; a school upon the system of Dr. Bell, in which between four and five hundred children are instructed, and another for infants. A market house, erected by order of Queen Elizabeth, was, with the market place, bestowed upon Samuel and John Jones by Charles I: the market was chartered to be holden on Saturday, but it has long been extinct; an annual fair is held, however, on the 22nd of October, chiefly for pedlery and pleasure. The parish of Barking is extensive, and divided into four wards, denominated 'Town,' 'Chadwell,' 'Ilford' and 'Ripple;' these collectively, in 1831, contained a population of 8,036.

Two miles N. W. from Barking, and in that parish, is the village, chapelry and ward of ILFORD (or GREAT ILFORD), situate on the high road to Chelmsford, and on the banks of the Roding, which separates this village from that of Little Ilford. A number of handsome houses and some good inns (the latter well supported by the great thoroughfare,) evince the respectability of this place; and a handsome church, opened in 1831, embellishes its general appearance. There is likewise a chapel of ease for the establishment; the minister of the new church is the Rev. F. Kuyvell Leighton, and the Rev. Ranson Hammond officiates in the chapel of ease. The baptists and Wesleyan methodists have their respective places of worship. An hospital, originally founded in the reign of Stephen for a prior, warden, master, two priests and thirteen lepers, is now appropriated to the use of six poor persons. The petty sessions for the division are held here every Saturday. Population of Ilford ward, 3,512.

At LITTLE ILFORD is the house of correction for the county. The church of this parish is dedicated to St. Mary. The population of Little Ilford parish is 115.

In the same hundred as Barking, not quite a mile from that town, and situated near to the Thames, is the village and parish of EAST HAM, the residence of many opulent families. From this neighbourhood the views over the opposite shore of Kent are exceedingly picturesque. The parish church, dedicated to St. Mary Magdalene, is an ancient plain structure—its interior, however, contains some curious old monuments: the benefice is a vicarage, in the patronage of the bishop of London, and incumbency of the Rev. Wm. Streatfeild. There is a school for boys and girls, conducted upon the national plan; and six alms-houses, endowed by Giles Breame, Esq. in 1621, are still maintained. Population of the entire parish, 1,543.

POST, BARKING, *Receiving-House* at William White's, Broadway.—Letters from LONDON arrive (from ILFORD) every morning at eight, noon at one, afternoon at half-past two and evening at seven, and are despatched every morning at eight, noon at one, afternoon at three and evening at seven.

POST, GREAT ILFORD, *Receiving-House* at John Gattey's.—Letters from LONDON arrive every morning at half-past seven, forenoon at eleven and afternoon at half-past two and half-past five, and are despatched every morning at nine, afternoon at one and four and evening at eight.

*** *The names are in BARKING when the town is not mentioned.*

GENTRY AND CLERGY.

Abbott Jabez, esq. East Ham
Adams Mr. Richard, East Ham
Archer Mr. John, East Ham
Balfour Mr. James, High st
Bell Rev. Henry, North st
Bourne Miss Lucy, Ilford.
Brown Mrs. Mary, Axe st
Cooke Mrs. Elizabeth, Ilford
Corney Rev. George, Barking lane
Crowe Mr. Thomas, Westbury house
Edmonds Mrs. Anne, North st
Evans Mr. Richard, Bull st
Fry Mrs. Elizabeth, East Ham
Fry John Gurney, esq. Little Ilford
Fry Joseph, jun. esq. East Ham
Fry William Storrs, esq. East Ham
Gardner Mrs. E. High st
Gilmore Lieut. John, R.N. Ilford terrace
Granger Mr. Press, Ilford
Graves Mr. Henry, Ilford
Graves Mr. James, Ilford cottage
Hackett Charles A. esq. Ilford
Hall Mrs. Margaret, Ilford
Hammond Rev. Edward Ranson, Broadway, Ilford
Harris Mr. Thomas, North st
Haslehurst Mr. William, Ilford
Hewett Mr. Scrymgeour, Bull st
Hunsden Mr. James, Ilford
Jutsum Mr. Samuel H. East Ham
King Henry, esq. East Ham
Lambert Mr. John, North st
Leighton Rev. F. Knyvett, Barking lane
Liddell the Hon. and Rev. Robert, Vicarage house
Lidderdale Mr. William, Ilford terrce
Manley Mr. John, M.D. Bull st
Martin Mrs. Elizabeth, Ilford terrace
Mead Mr. John, Barking lane
Monk Mrs. Amy, Ilford terrace
Moore Mr. Samuel, Ilford terrace
Morley Mrs. Sarah, East Ham
Parsons Mr. William, Ilford terrace
Pearce William, esq. Aldboro' Grange
Simmonds Mr. Thomas, East Ham
Sparkes Capt. John Say, Ilford terrce
Streatfeild Rev. William, Vicarage, East Ham
Streatfeild William Champion, esq. Plashett hall
Swabey Henry B. esq. East Ham
Taylor Mr. John, East Ham
Thompson Mr. John Scrafton, Ilford
Tyler Mr. Christopher, Barking lane
Tyler Mrs. Mary, Ilford
Wilkinson Mr. John, Ilford
Wincott Mr. Thomas, North st

ACADEMIES AND SCHOOLS.
Not otherwise described are Day Schools.

Beckwith Matilda, Heath st
Bruce Elizabeth (boarding), Ilford
Cooper John Henry, High st
Fenner Susannah (brdng) North st
Godfrey William Daniel (boarding) White house, Ilford
Hedger John (brdg and day) Ilford
INFANTS' SCHOOL, Bull st—Mary Crew, mistress
INFANTS' SCHOOL, Ilford—Elizabeth Slater, mistress
INFANTS' SCHOOL (parochial) High st—Ann Arnold, mistress
INFANTS' SCHOOL, Fisher st—Sarah Pynor, mistress
Lardner Francis, Ilford
Martin John, Market house buildings
Morris John, Market house
NATIONAL SCHOOL (boys and girls) High st—Richard Daniel Wilding, master; Anne Wilding, mistress
NATIONAL SCHOOL (boys and girls) East Ham—Henry Smith, master; Elizabeth Smith, mistress.
Wilmott Emma, Heath st

ATTORNEYS.

Dennes James, Ilford
Griffin Edmund (and clerk to the Board of Guardians)
Westlake George, Vine cottage, Barking lane

AUCTIONEERS, APPRAISERS, AND UNDERTAKERS.

Deeble James Thurston, Bull st
Harvey Thomas, High st, Ilford
Lambert James, High st
Oldaker William, Ilford

BAKERS.

Belchand Rebecca, Fisher st
Brown John (and biscuit) High st
Bryant William, Heath st
Claringbould Thomas, Bull st
Clark William Henry, Axe st
Collier Thomas, East Ham
Dear John, Ilford
Edwards David, Ilford
Gates William, High st
Gattey John, Ilford
Gattey Wm. Fage, Broadway, Ilford
Hart Mary, High st
Havllar Mary Alice, North st
Kelly William, East Ham
Moore Anne, Shop row
Pates Joseph, Ilford
Smorthwaite Mary, Fisher st

BLACKSMITHS.

Baker Thomas, North st
Grout Joseph
Hyde Joseph, Ilford
Kingsnorth Daniel, Ilford
Moss James, East Ham
Pearson William, Broadway
Rowland Richard, Ilford
Scrimes John, Fisher st
Ship Joseph, Town quay
Spicer John, Ripple ward
Wade and Radley, Ilford

BOOKSELLERS & STATIONRS.

Brock Benjamin, Ilford
Meek Mary Ann, Ilford
Penn Joseph (and library and news-agent) High st

BOOT AND SHOE MAKERS.

Bailey William, Axe st
Cook Edward, Ilford
Cooper David, Axe st
Coultas Thomas, Shop row
Coultas Thomas, High st
Crowest Thomas, East Ham
Deeble Henry James, Heath st
Edwards William, Heath st
Everett James, Ilford
Finch Thomas, Heath st
Fisk William, East Ham
Garrard Thomas, Shop row
Hull Charles, Ilford
Hull John, High st
Jackson William, Heath st
Jarvis James, Ilford
Lake John, High st
Macro Thomas, Ilford
Miller Luke, North st
Morris Henry Baggot, Ilford
Pigrome Charles & Benjamin, High st
Pyner Thomas, Fisher st
Reed James, Ilford
Rowland John, Ilford
Sheldrick Henry, Shop row
Wand Henry, Ilford
Wenlock Thomas, Bull st
White James Henry, North st

BREWERS.

Flint Michael, Town quay
Rose William, Ilford

BRICK MAKERS.

Kelvington William, Ilford
Thompson John Scrafton, Ilford

BRICKLAYERS.

Bosworth James, North st
Curtis and Son, High st
Curtis William, Ilford
Fullham John, Ilford
Holmes William, Axe st
Smith Charles, Ilford
Smith Henry, Ilford
Smith James, Aldborow hatch

BUILDERS.

Ashmole William, Ilford
Curtis and Son, High st
Dangerfield Henry, High st
Dangerfield James, Ilford
Suggers Robert, Heath st
Withers James, Sam's green, Ilford

BUTCHERS.

Allard William, Ilford
Barkley James, Bull st
Beadle William George, Fisher st
Beadle Wm. George, jun. Fisher st
Coppen Thomas, Ilford
Death David, Bull st
Knowles Edward, North st
Mathews John, East Ham
Mumford Thomas, Ilford
Newton William
Pearson John, Broadway
Vaines Samuel, Heath st
Wagstaff Thomas, Heath st

CARPENTRS & UNDERTAKRS.

Ashmole William, Ilford
Belcham Samuel, Heath st
Breeues George, Ilford
Dangerfield Henry, High st
Dangerfield James, Ilford
Dangerfield James, East Ham
Dowsett Samuel, Heath st
Hird David, Fisher st
Saggers Robert, Heath st
Wood William, Ilford

CHINA, GLASS, & EARTHENWARE DEALERS.

Halsey Thomas, Ilford
Webster Michael, Ilford

CHYMISTS AND DRUGGISTS.

Beal John, Ilford
Betts Robert, North st
Davies Thomas, North st
Fitt Edward, High st
Woodhouse Christopher, Ilford

COAL MERCHANTS.

Bradley William Smith, High st
Flint Michael
Kebbell John, Ilford wharf, Ilford
Laby James, Fisher st
Parsons Joseph, Town quay
Tyler and Burrell, Fisher st
Tyler Christopher, Barking lane

CORN DEALERS.

Bradley William Smith, High st
Mumford John, Ilford
Philpott James (& seedsman) Ilford
Tyler and Burrell, Fisher st

FIRE, &c. OFFICE AGENTS.

ALLIANCE, Charles Dawson, High st
COUNTY (fire) & PROVIDENT (life) Thomas Harris, High st
ESSEX ECONOMIC, William George Beadle, sen. Fisher st
ROYAL EXCHANGE, Henry Dangerfield, High st
ROYAL EXCHANGE, James Dangerfield, Ilford
SUN, Thomas Harvey, High st, Ilford

FURNITURE BROKERS.

Francis Charles, Little Ilford
Hull John, Heath st

GARDENERS & SEEDSMEN.

(See also Market Gardeners.)

Brand George, Ilford
Garnell John, Garden row, North st
Glenny Edward, Bull st
Glenny William and George, Bull st
Gooch William, Ilford
Milton Thomas and John
Palmer William, North st
Perkins John, Ilford
Pummell John, East Ham

GREENGROCERS.

Barritt John, Axe st
Brand Thomas, Ilford
Groves Ann, Heath st
Lankshear Thomas, Ilford
Milton Mary, Shop row
Pearson Ann, Heath st
Sharp Mary, Bull st

GROCERS AND DEALERS IN SUNDRIES.

Bailey William, Axe st
Brand Henry, Ilford
Brand Richard, North st
Brand Richard, sen. Ilford
Carter Ann, High st
Carter Theodore (& oilman) Heath st
Charlesworth Thomas, Fisher st
Cheek Thomas, Ilford
Cooper George, Fisher st
Crease William, Bull st
Dangerfield John, East Ham
Dore Joseph, North st
Dudley John, High st
Fisk Thomas, Wall end
Gibbard Frederick Lewis, North st
Gray Elizabeth, Shop row
Green Samuel, Ilford
Habgood William (tea dealer, cheesemonger, & oil & colourman) Ilford
Hallett Peter, Ilford
Harris Thomas, Church passage
Hawes Daniel, East Ham
Hunter Louisa, Ilford
Knowles Edward, Heath st
Knowles Edward, jun. North st
Lake John, High st
Linsdell Eleanor, Heath st
Mathews Hugh, East Ham
Porter Samuel, Fisher st
Porter Thomas, Fisher st
Pound William, Ilford
Reed Elizabeth, High st
Roberts Mary, East Ham
Sheldrick Anthony, Bull st
Stannard Wm. Broadway, Ilford
White William, Broadway
Willers Mary, Axe st
Williams Eliz. (& stamp office) Shop row

HAIR DRESSERS.

Jessett Cornelius, Ilford
Parsons William, Axe st
Penn Joseph, High st
Potter Christopher, Heath st
Taylor Joseph, Bull st

INNS.

Angel, William Ashmole, Ilford
Bull, Eliz. Parsons, High st
George, Geo. Hawkins Chalk, Broadway
Red Lion, Ann Hone, Ilford
Ship, Thomas Linsdell, Heath st

LEATHER CUTTERS AND SELLERS.

Brand Richard, North st
Crease Wm. (& grindery dealer) Bull st

LIGHTERMEN AND BARGE OWNERS.

Barritt John, Axe st
Bradley William Smith, High st
Byford William, North st

LINEN & WOOLLEN DRAPERS

Charlesworth John Oliver, Fisher st
Dawson Charles, High st
Fenton John, High st
Pummell John, East Ham
Wagstaff Mary, Heath st
Willett Robert B. Ilford

MARINE STORE DEALERS.

Burchfield Samuel
Clatworthy Harriet, High st
Dowdell Thomas
Harris Thomas, Fisher st
Wickham Henry, Shop row

MARKET GARDENERS.

Abbott Jabez, East Ham
Biggs George, Long bridge
Biggs James, Manor house
Circuit Thomas, East Ham
Glenny Edward, Bull st
Glenny William and George, Bull st
Lambert John Matthews, North st
Matthews John, East Ham
Milton Thomas, Back st
Milton Thomas and John
Palmer and Pearson, North st
Venables Daniel
Walrond and Evans, East Ham
Walrond John, East Ham

MAST, OAR, BLOCK & PUMP MAKERS.

Cross Charles, Fisher st
Horsley Luke
Horsley William, Fisher st
Spashett Jacob Henry

MILLERS.

Blakeley William, Wellington mill
Sharpe & Whitbourne, Barking mills

MILLINERS AND STRAW HAT MAKERS.

Arrow Sarah, Heath st
Belcham Elizabeth, Heath st
Bishop Sarah, Broadway, Ilford
Coultas Jemima, Shop row
Everett Catherine, Ilford
Maxwell Sarah, High st
Rennum Sarah, Heath st
Staines Sarah, Ilford

PAINTERS, PLUMBERS AND GLAZIERS.

King Philip, Bull st
Mundy Charles, Ilford
Russ Thomas, Axe st
Whitaker George, Ilford

ROPE AND LINE MAKERS.

Burchfield Samuel, Town quay
Dowdell Thomas
Soanes John and Son, Heath st

SADDLERS AND HARNESS MAKERS.

Bayley John, Ilford
Pope William, East Ham
Williers Thomas, High st
Woodhead George, Ilford

SAIL MAKERS.

Bailey John, Heath st
Forge Mary, Heath st
Gardner Edward
Harris Thomas, Fisher st
Harris Thomas, jun. Fisher st
Milton Samuel (& sacking) Heath st
Seaward Thomas, Fisher st

SHIP CHANDLERS.

Burchfield Saml. (& oilmn) Town quay
Knowles Edward, Heath st

SHIPWRIGHT.

Taylor Griffiths, Barking

SLOPSELLERS.

Hughes John, High st
Rumball Samuel, Heath st
Shelitoe Henry, Heath st
Wetherill Jas. (and tailor & outfitter) Heath st

SMACK OWNERS.

Agar Benjamin, Fisher st
Bailey John, Fisher st
Balsh Henry, Barking
Baxter Samuel, Heath st
Berry David, Heath st
Best Samuel, Fisher st
Butterfield Charles, Heath st
Butterfield William, Heath st
Chalk George, Broadway
Chalk Henry, Broadway
Davis James, Fisher st
Dowse David, Heath st
Earl Henry, Fisher st
Earl John, Fisher st
Elmer John, Fisher st
Flick William, Axe st
Forge John Wm. & Thos. Heath st
Forge Richard, High st
Forge Richard, jun. High st
Fraser Joseph, Fisher st
Frogley John, Fisher st
Frogley Nicholas, Fisher st
Gale John, Fisher st
Gale Thomas, Church gates
Gale William, Fisher st
Hale William, High st
Harris John, Axe st
Harris Joseph, Heath st
Harris Sarah, Fisher st
Harris Thomas, jun. Fisher st
Harvey John, Church gates
Hennis Edward, Heath st
Hewett Samuel, Fisher st
Horsley Luke, Fisher st
Hughes John, High st
Lake John, High st
Linsdell Thomas, Heath st
Marchent Hannibal, Fisher st
Martin Thomas, High st
Martin William, Fisher st
Milton Samuel, Heath st
Moore John, Bull st
Morgan James, Heath st
Mullett Jane, High st
Mullett Robert, High st
Pearson John, High st
Plows Thomas, North st
Pollard James, North st
Reed Joseph, Axe st
Rennum George, Heath st
Shelitoe Henry, Heath st
Smith William, Heath st
Spashett Christopher, Barking
Spashett Jacob Henry, Barking
Spicer John, Ripple ward
Stevens John, High st
Sunnaway James, Fisher st
Sunnaway John, Heath st
Taylor Henry, Heath st
Turner John, Barking
Webster John, Heath st

SURGEONS.

Allison Wm. Jeremh. Broadwy. Ilford
Davis Thomas, North st
Fayrer George, High st
Manley John, Bull st

SURVEYORS.

Harvey Thomas, High st, Ilford
Lambert James, High st, Barking

TAILORS.

Bennett Charles, Shop row
Clark John, Fisher st
Collier Richard, Barking lane
Coulling David, High st
Davie Thomas, Ilford
Harden James Smith, Ilford
Maling James, Broadway, Ilford
Moore John, Ilford
Rainbow Geo. William, North st
Spashett Anson, Ilford
Swift Thomas, Shop row
Tillett John, Ilford
Wetherill Jas. (& slopseller) Heath st
Wright John, Heath st

TAVERNS & PUBLIC HOUSES.

Blue Anchor, William Smith, Heath st
Cauliflower, Peter Reynolds, Ilford
Coach & Horses, John Glover, Little Ilford
Cock, Mary Blaker, East Ham
Duke's Head, James Carter, East Ham
Green Man, Joseph Goldacre, East Ham
Greyhound, Thomas Webb, Chadwell
Queen's Head, Ann Gray, High st
Red Lion, John Monins Hodges, North st
Rising Sun, George Lord, East Ham
Rose and Crown, John Wilson, Ilford
Still, John Ringer, Fisher st
Three Rabbits, James Othen, Little Ilford
White Horse, Thomas Castle, Ilford
White Horse, Martha Wade, East Ham

TOY DEALERS.

Deeble Henry, Heath st
Watkins Daniel, North st

WATCH & CLOCK MAKERS.

Creasy Jos. (German clock) Bull st
Moss Nathaniel, Heath st
North James, Ilford
Watkins Daniel James, North st

WHEELWRIGHTS.

Baker Thomas, North st, & at Ilford
Buttle Joseph, Ilford
Dennison William, East Ham

Miscellaneous.

Ashmole William, agent to the stamp office, Ilford
Beadle William George, registrar of births and deaths, Fisher st
Bellis Hugh, tobacco pipe maker
Chapman Joseph, turner, Ilford
Coxhead William, registrar of births and deaths, Ilford
Dennison William, parish clerk, East Ham
Elliot John, cattle salesman, East Ham
Gray John, cooper, High st
Hart Thos. & Henry, basket makers, Heath st
Hart William, veterinary surgeon, Ilford
Harvey Thomas, house & estate agent, Ilford
Hewett Samuel, fish factor, Fisher st
Hobday Edgar, tallow chandler, Axe st
House of Correction, Little Ilford—Luke Miller, governor
Joyce William, ironmonger and tin-plate worker, Broadway
Lake John, beadle, High st
Leftley James, carrier, High st
Macro Thomas, parish clerk, Ilford
Maynard Edward, carrier, Axe st
Maynard James, carrier, Axe st
Morris John, agent for the religious tract society, Market house
Pearson John, poulterer and fishmonger, Broadway
Penn Joseph, printer & bookbinder, High st
Rose Richard, maltster, Ilford
Savings' Bank, Great Ilford—William Coxhead, actuary
Savings' Bank, High st—William Coxhead, actuary
Society for Promoting Christian Knowledge, Market house buildings—John Martin, agent
Stamp Office, Shop row—Elizabeth Williams, agent
Tomlinson & Budd, pawnbrokers, High st
Tyers Robert John, spirit colour manufacturer, and at 20 Tooley st, *London*
Union Poorhouse, High st—Tunnard Sellers, governor; Eliz. Sellers, matron
White William, coach proprietor, Broadway

COACHES.

To LONDON, William White's *Coach*, from the George, every morning (Sun. ex.) at a quarter before nine, on Sunday at a quarter before eight—and Adam Kerr's *Coach*, from the same Inn, every morning (Sun. ex.) at half-past nine.
To GRAYS THURROCK, Adam Kerr's *Coach*, from the George, every evening (Sunday excepted) at five.

CARRIERS.

To LONDON, Joseph Leftley (through Eastham and Plaistow), and Edward Maynard, jun. and James Maynard (through Ilford), from their own houses, daily.

BILLERICAY,

AND THE PARISHES OF GREAT AND LITTLE BURSTEAD AND HUTTON, WITH EAST, WEST AND SOUTH HANNINGFIELDS'; STOCK AND BUTTSBURY.

BILLERICAY is a small market town, in the parish of Great Burstead and hundred of Barstable, 24 miles E. N. E. from London, 9 S. from Chelmsford, and 16 N. from Gravesend; seated upon an elevation that commands a wide and pleasing view of the surrounding country—on a clear day the coast of Kent is discernible by the naked eye, and the Nore more plainly distinguishable. At various times several articles of Roman fabrication have been found in the neighbourhood, and it is conjectured that this town occupies the site of a villa or station of that people. It is clean, tolerably well built, and consists of one main and one back street. The trade of the place, with the exception of that in corn, is inconsiderable. There are two good inns, the 'Crown' and the 'Red Lion;' the latter is the principal, and is the house of resort for persons attending the market. Lord Petre is lord of the manor, and holds courts leet and baron occasionally; at the leet court constables and other officers are appointed for the regulation of the town. On the first and third Tuesday, monthly, petty sessions are held at the market-house. A chapel of ease, dedicated to St. Mary Magdalene, stands in the centre of the town. There are places of worship for baptists, the society of friends, and independents; and a free school. The market is held, by a charter granted in 1476, on Tuesday—but of late years it has declined in importance; cattle fairs are held on 2nd August and 7th October. Population is returned with the parish of GREAT BURSTEAD, which *see*.

GREAT BURSTEAD, two miles S. S. E. from Billericay, is only noticed as being the parish of that town, and as containing the parish church, which is a neat structure, dedicated to St. Mary Magdalene, with a tower surmounted by a spire; Lord Petre is the lay rector, and the Rev. John Thomas is the vicar. A charter to hold a market here was granted to the abbey of Stratford Langthorne by Henry III, but the privilege was not long exercised. Population of the parish, in 1831, 1,977.

One mile and a half from Billericay is LITTLE BURSTEAD, composed of merely a few scattered houses and a small church; the Rev. Alfred Roberts is the rector of the living, which is in the patronage of the bishop of London. Population, 204.

In the same hundred as Billericay, two miles and a half west from that town and about three from Brentwood, situated in a hollow between the two places, is the village of HUTTON. The church is dedicated to All Saints; the benefice is a rectory, in the presentation of the dean and chapter of St. Paul's, London. The parish contained, in 1831, 381 inhabitants.

Adjoining to each other, and distinguished only by the locality of their situations, are the three parishes of HANNINGFIELD, EAST, WEST and SOUTH. The nearest of them to Billericay is about three miles, and the most distant from it about six; each has its parish church, but neither of them possess claim to particular notice. The population of the three parishes, in 1831, was 1,141.

STOCK and BUTTSBURY are parishes contiguous to each other, lying between the towns of Billericay and Chelmsford; they have each a church. The number of inhabitants in the parish of Stock, in 1831, was 619; and in that of Buttsbury, 515.

POST OFFICE, BILLERICAY, William Curtis, *Post Master*.—Letters from LONDON arrive (by mail cart from INGATESTONE) every morning at one, and are despatched every evening at half-past nine.—The delivery commences every morning at half-past seven.

**** The names without address are in* BILLERICAY.

GENTRY AND CLERGY.

Beale Mr. Thomas, East Hanningfield
Blakeley Mrs. Anne
Bower Mr. Samuel
Bridge Mrs. —, Stock
Brooksbey Rev. Thomas, A. M. Rectory, West Hanningfield
Bulwer Mr. John Elmes
Chapman Rev. James
Cross Mrs. Sarah
Cusack Mrs. Louisa
Cusack Miss —
Dale Mrs. —, Stock
Ederson Rev. Edward, Rectory, Stock
Eldridge Thomas, esq. Greenwoods
French Joseph, esq. Clock house
Hills Mr. John
Johnson Mrs. Eliza
Knightbridge Mrs. Elizabeth, Stock
Mabbs Mrs. Hannah
Mabbs Mr. James
Mabbs Mrs. Mary
Millington Mr. Charles, Stock
Moore Mr. William
Moss Mr. Wm. Buttsbury
Nottidge Rev. John, East Hanningfield
Osborne John, esq. Stock
Parnell Mrs. —, Stock
Petchey Mrs. Elizabeth
Radford John, esq.
Roberts Rev. Alfred William, Rectory, Little Burstead
Skipper Peter, esq. Hope house
Spitty Mrs. Elizabeth
Spitty Captain Thomas (magistrate) Hill house, Buttsbury
Tate Rev. James, Hutton
Thomas Rev. John, Great Burstead
Thornton Rev. John

ACADEMIES & SCHOOLS.

Burningham John (boarding & day)
Burningham Susannah (brding & day)
Hatch Sarah (day)
Johnson Elizabeth (ladies' boarding)
Mabbs Anne (day)
NATIONAL SCHOOL—William Thorn, master; Mrs. Mettleton, mistress

AGENTS.
(See also Fire, &c. Office Agents.)

Barrell John (for stamp office, and undertaker)
Oliver Thomas (for Morison's pills)
Rolph and Hills (for estates)
Ruffell William (for the provident society)

ATTORNEYS.

Johnson John Fortin
Penfold James V.
Remnant Frederick William
Shaw Geo. (& clerk to magistrates)

AUCTIONEERS.

Rolph & Hills (and estate agents)

BAKERS & FLOUR DEALERS.

Adkins John, Stock
Brown William, West Hanningfield
Collins Sarah
Moss William and John
Palmer John
Stock Thomas, East Hanningfield
Taylor Philip
Thompson William
Weld Sarah
Wood William

BLACKSMITHS & FARRIERS.

Blanks Joseph, East Hanningfield
Brown Thomas, Stock
Caton Thomas
Cockrell James
Makings Sarah
Makings William, Buttsbury
Parnell Letitia, West Hanningfield
Rushbrook William [ningfield
Shettlewood Samuel, South Han-
Shipp and Son
Steel Charles, Hutton

BOOT & SHOE MAKERS.

Allen Frederick
Bacon Thomas, East Hanningfield
Brown Samuel, Stock
Cross Charles
Dove Jesse
Drake William
Gentry Thomas
Hummerston Thomas
Markwell William
Oddy James, Stock
Reeve Samuel, Stock
Stebbing Edward
Thorp Richard
Wallden Abraham, Stock
Whistler William
Wilkin George, Hutton
Wood William
Wright John, West Hanningfield

BREWERS.

Hutson Thomas and Co
Rolph William

BRICKLAYERS.

Markwell Thomas
Mills Thomas, East Hanningfield

BUTCHERS.

Green George, West Hanningfield
Knightbridge Henry, Stock
Parnell Thomas, Stock
Richardson Daniel
Smith Thomas
Stock John
Whipps George

CARPENTERS & BUILDERS.

Curtis George
Curtis Geo. & Wm. (& brickmakers)
Curtis William
Eaton Robert, East Hanningfield
Mumford Richard
Plum William, Stock
Ruffell William

CHINA, GLASS & EARTHENWARE DEALERS.

Goslett Alfred Gweer, Stock and Buttsbury
Stock Thomas, East Hanningfield
Tunbridge John

CHYMISTS AND DRUGGISTS.

Hatch Sarah
Nix John, jun
Stedman Richard (and stationer)

COOPERS.

Davey Robert (& turner) Buttsbury
Raymond Thomas, Great Burstead

CORN FACTORS,
ATTENDING THE MARKET HOUSE.

Alexander Henry
Cross William
Gopsill Jordan, Halls and Moss
Gray Charles S.
Grove James
Meeson and Hinton
Moss William
Robinson William
Taylor Phillip
Threadgold George
Wood William

FIRE, &c. OFFICE AGENTS.

County (fire) & Provident (life) James Blatch
Economic, Crisp M. Harridge
Essex and Suffolk, William Rolph
Norwich Union, William Curtis
Phœnix, John Barrell

GARDENERS & SEEDSMEN.

Everitt John, Great Burstead
Hatch William
Heneker Henry

GROCERS AND DEALERS IN SUNDRIES.

Baker and Carter
Barrell John
Brown James, Hutton
Bull William, Stock
Cheveley James
Clarke John, Stock
Coote Sarah
Cotty John, East Hanningfield
Cross John, South Hanningfield
Dowsett Joseph, East Hanningfield
Firmin George, West Hanningfield
Gladwyn George (and earthenware dealer) [Buttsbury
Goslett Alfred Gweer, Stock and
Harris John, Great Burstead
Moore Thomas and William
Oliver Thomas
Salter Ephraim
Stock Thomas, East Hanningfield
Tunbridge John

HAIR DRESSERS.

Cockrell Charles
Root William

HORSE AND GIG OWNERS,
FOR HIRE.

Allan Henry
Cross John, Red Lion Inn
Harridge Crisp Molineux, Sun Inn
Rushbrook William
Whale William, Crown Inn

INNS.

Crown, (&posting-house) Wm. Whale
Red Lion, John Cross

IRONMONGERS.

Barrett Thomas
Gladwyn Frederick

LINEN & WOOLLEN DRAPRS.

Goslett Alfred Gweer, Stock and Buttsbury
Moore Thomas and William
Oliver Thomas (and hatter and clothier, and agent for Morison's vegetable pills)
Pyrke Henry
Tunbridge Henry

MILLERS.

Moss John, Stock
Moss William, Stock
Wood Ffinch, Billericay

MILLINERS.

Markwell Elizabeth (and library)
Sach Ann

PAINTERS, PLUMBERS, AND GLAZIERS.

Bassom James
Bassom James, jun.
Hewitt James, Stock
Humphreys James
Whipps James

SADDLERS.

Burgess George
Making George, Stock
Upson George, jun.

STRAW HAT MAKERS.

Cheveley Anne
Oliver Thomas

SURGEONS.

Carter William
D'Aranda George
Hunt James
Martin John

TAILORS AND DRAPERS.

Allan Henry George
Hewitt George, Stock
Hockley Henry, Stock
Hughes John
Smith William Henry
Stebbing Jabez and James

TAVERNS & PUBLIC HOUSES.

Bear, William Ratcliff, Buttsbury
Bell, Daniel Baker
Black Bull, Thomas Curtis
Chequers, John Cross, Hutton
Chequers, Elizabeth Dutten
Cock, Joseph Clarke, Stock
Crown Tap, Thomas Dent
Duke of York, James Nix [stead
King's Arms, Thos. Warner, Great Bur-
Old King's Head, William Jordan, Stock
Plough and Sail, Joshua Ramsay, West Hanningfield
Red Lion, John Cross
Ship, Sarah Pincham
Sun, Crisp Molineux Harridge
The Two Dukes, Robert Parker, Little Burstead
Three Compasses, George G. Mason, West Hanningfield
Three Horse Shoes, Thomas Burrell
Three Horse Shoes, Thomas Hill's, East Hanningfield
White Hart, William Punt
Windmill, Richard Mitril, East Hanningfield [field
Windmill, Mary Seward, South Hanning-

WHEELWRIGHTS.

Atherton James, Stock
Brooks William, Stock
Caton Thomas
Clark Sarah
Parker Abraham
Warner Thomas, Great Burstead
Whitebread Wm. West Hanninfield

WINE & SPIRIT MERCHANTS

Barrell John
Rolph William

Miscellaneous.

Ambrose Henry, sieve and basket maker
Barrett Thomas, watch and clock maker and hardwareman
Carter Wm. registrar of births and deaths
Clark John, maltster, Buttsbury
Crowest Thomas B. architect & surveyor
Curtis Wm. cabinet maker [sures
Curtis Wm. inspector of weights & mea-
Davan John, currier and leather cutter
Excise Office, Crown Inn—John Badcock, Colchester, collector; Joseph Jacob, supervisor [Stock
Jordan Wm. tarpawling, &c. manufacturer,
Mann Charles, coach builder
Nix Jno. sen. professor of music & dancing
Oates Thomas A. tanner [Hutton
Offin Abraham, maltster & timbermerchnt,
Pease Joseph, carrier
Porter William, pot ash manufacturer, Ramsden Heath
Rolph George, registrar of marriages
Rushbrook William, veterinary surgeon
Smith Sarah, glover and breeches maker
Stedman Richard, stationer
Union Poor House—Benjamin Granger Collis, governor

COACHES.

To LONDON, the *Telegraph*, from the Crown Inn, every morning (Sun. ex.) at a quarter before eight—and the *Despatch* (from Southend), every forenoon (Sunday ex.) at a quarter before eleven.

To SOUTHEND, the *Despatch* (from London) calls at the Crown Inn, every evening (Sunday excepted) at six.

CARRIERS.

To LONDON, Joseph Pease, from the Waggon Office, every Monday and Thursday—and — Brown, from the Chequers, every Tuesday and Friday.

To CHELMSFORD, Thomas Painter, from the Red Lion, every Monday, Wednesday and Friday—and James Joslin, every Friday.

To RAYLEIGH and SOUTHEND, — Pease's *Waggons*, every Tuesday and Friday.

BRAINTREE AND BOCKING,

WITH THE VILLAGES OF CRESSING, RAYNE, STISTED, BLACK AND WHITE NOTLEY, AND NEIGHBOURHOODS.

BRAINTREE is a considerable market town and parish in the hundred of Hinckford, 41 miles N. by E. from London and 12 N. from Chelmsford—situated on a rising ground, and connected on the north with the village of Bocking, one of the most pleasant and populous in Essex. The town itself is irregularly built, most of the streets narrow, and its general aspect indicative of an early origin: indeed the antiquity of this place is unquestionable, the site of a Roman camp being apparent close to the town, and a great number of Roman coins (from Agrippa, A. D. 37, to Honorius, A. D. 395), and even several British gold coins, and other antiques, having been found in its immediate neighbourhood. In Domesday-book the manor is denominated *Brauchtrue*, and at that time it formed part of the parish of *Raines* (now 'Rayne'), from which it was separated about the time of King John, or the commencement of the reign of Henry III, and constituted a distinct parish, for some time called Great Rayne: the manor was then held by the bishop of London, to whose see it continued attached until the reign of Edward VI. This town was formerly governed by a select vestry of twenty-four of its most influential inhabitants, but this system has long been relinquished; the justices of the division hold petty sessions here once a fortnight. Under the reform act Braintree is appointed one of the polling stations, for the northern division of the county; and under the poor law amendment act it gives name to the 'Braintree Union,' for the purposes of which a union workhouse has lately been erected, contiguous to the town, calculated to contain three hundred inmates. The principal business, exclusive of what arises from the passage of commodities between the more eastern counties and the metropolis, is the manufacture of silk, which gives employment to several hundred hands; a great quantity of straw plat is also made for the London market. The manufacture of baize was at one time of paramount importance here, but this branch is now totally extinct.

At the south side of the town, upon an elevated site, which appears to have been once occupied by a camp, stands the church, a spacious structure, dedicated to St. Michael; it consists of a nave, chancel and side aisles, and at the west end has a tower, terminated by a lofty spire cased with shingles: the church had its original foundation in the reign of Edward III, but has been materially altered, enlarged and improved since that time. The living is a vicarage, in the patronage of the Olmius family; the lay impropriator, lately, was the Earl of Winchelsea, and the Rev. Bernard Scale is the incumbent. There are places of worship for independents, baptists and Wesleyan methodists; national and infants' schools, both in Braintree and Bocking; and a school, founded and endowed by James Coker in 1702, in which a limited number of boys are instructed. Henry Smith, an alderman of London in the reign of Charles I, bequeathed £2,800. for the poor of Braintree and certain other parishes: he was a very eccentric character, and obtained the name of 'Dog Smith' from going about like a beggar, accompanied by his dog. The country around here is decidedly agricultural—the land contiguous to the town hilly, well wooded and very fertile. The market, one of the largest in Essex, is held on Wednesday, to accommodate the frequenters of which a corn exchange is in progress, in the High-street—the commodities are chiefly corn, cattle and swine; fairs, 8th May for cattle and pedlery, and (the most considerable one) 2nd October and two following days for hops and cattle. The population of Braintree parish, in 1831, was 3,422, and it has since greatly increased.

The village of BOCKING, which forms the northern suburb of Braintree, is comprised chiefly in a single street, presenting many handsome well-built houses; its trade is similar to that of Braintree. Two copyhold courts are held here: one for the manor of Bocking, of which the Rev. John Thos. Nottidge is lord; the other for the manor of Derwards Hall, possessed by the Honeywood family, of Marks Hall, in this county. This parish is peculiarly annexed to the see of Canterbury, and subject to the archbishop's jurisdiction. Between one and two miles N. W. of the principal street stands the church, a commodious edifice, conjectured to have been founded in the reign of Edward III; the benefice is a rectory, but its rector is generally co-dean of the archbishop's peculiars in Essex and Suffolk, and is styled 'dean of Bocking;' the present dean and rector is the Rev. Sir Herbert Oakeley, Bart. A meeting-house for the society of friends, and chapels for independents and methodists, are the other places of worship. There is an endowed school for thirty boys, founded by Dr. Gauden, a former rector here, and afterwards bishop of Worcester. The parish of Bocking contained, by the census of 1831, 3,128 inhabitants.

CRESSING is a village and parish in the hundred of Witham, about three miles S.E. from Braintree, situated to the east of the road leading from the latter town to Witham. The church is dedicated to All Saints—the living a vicarage, in the gift of the family of Downs. The knights templars, who at one time had a commandery here, possessed the advowson; it subsequently passed to the knights hospitallers, and reverted to the crown at the general suppression of religious houses. Population of the parish, 551.

Nearly two miles from Braintree, and in the same hundred, is the genteel village and parish of RAYNE. The church is dedicated to All Saints: the benefice is a rectory, in the presentation of the Earl of Essex; the incumbent is the Hon. and Rev. William Capel, and the present curate the Rev. Thomas Willis. The parish contained, in 1831, 320 inhabitants.

STISTED is a parish, in the same hundred as Braintree, about three miles E. N. E. from that town. It contains a church, dedicated to All Saints, and a population of about 900 inhabitants.

BLACK and WHITE NOTLEY are two parishes adjoining to each other, in the hundred of Witham; the former about two miles from Braintree, the latter between three and four. At Black Notley is the parish church (dedicated to St. Peter and St. Paul) and an endowed school. The population of this parish is 486, and that of White Notley 453.

POST OFFICE, BRAINTREE, William Sach, *Post Master*.—Letters from LONDON arrive (by mail cart) every morning at half-past four, and are despatched every evening at ten.—The box closes every evening at half-past nine, but letters are received until five minutes before ten by paying twopence with each.

*** *The streets to which the name of the town is not attached are in* BRAINTREE; *the letter* B. *to the address of other names signifies* BOCKING.

GENTRY AND CLERGY.

Albon Mr. James, Bradford st, B.
Balfour Mr. Joseph, Bradford st, B.
Barman Mrs. Great square [B.
Barnard Abraham Larkin, esq. Lyons,
Bengville Mrs. London road
Blencowe Mrs. Elizabeth, Rayne
Bloom Mary, Bradford st, Bocking
Boys Rev. Charles, Vicarage, Shalford [Notley
Brewster Mr. Sturgeon Nunn, White
Brewster William, esq. Black Notley
Bright Mrs. High st
Brunwin Rev. Martin John, Bradwell
Brunwin Milbourne Peter Carter, esq. Bradwell
Brunwin the Misses, Bradwell
Bruty Mrs. London road

Burder Jos. Davey, esq. Coggeshall rd
Carless Mrs. Charlotte, Rayne
Carter Rev. John, London road
Clarence Mrs. Great square
Claricotes Mr. John, Black Notley
Cook Mrs. Bocking end, Bocking
Corsbie Mrs. Coggeshall road, B.
Courtauld Geo. esq. Bradford st, B.
Courtauld John, esq. Church lane, B.
Courtauld Mrs. Bradford st, Bocking
Courtauld Samuel, esq. Folley house, High Garrett, Bocking
Craig Rev. Thomas, Bocking
Daking Mr. John, Church st
Davie Elizabeth, Bradford st, B.
Day Samuel Hulme, esq. High st
Dennis Rev. John, White Notley
Dixon Mrs. London road
Dobby Mrs. Great Saling
English John, esq. Rayne road, B.
Fairhead Mrs. Rachael, Stisted
Fowke Wm. esq. Groves, Gt. Saling
French Mrs. Bocking end
Garrett Mr. Saml. Panfield lane, B.
Gilson Mrs. London road
Goodrich Rev. Bartlett, Great Saling
Gordon Rev. Francis, Bradford st, B.
Grimwood Mr. Jeffrey, Temple, Cressing
Hawkes Ann, Stisted
Hobbs Mr. Wm. Durwood's hall, B.
Holmsted Mrs. London road
Hope Miss Lucy Elton, Mount cottage, Coggeshall road
Humphries Rev. Wm. Coggeshall [road
Kirby Mr. John, Bradford st, B.
Lake Mr. John, Great Saling
Marriott Richard, esq. Abbott's hall, Shalford
Myhill Mrs. London road
Nash Mrs. High st
Nottidge Rev. Edward, Black Notley
Nottidge Geo. esq. (magistrate) Bradford st, B.
Oakeley Rev. Sir Herbert, bart. [Church st, B.
Onley Charles Savill, esq. Stisted hall
Osborn Mr. Saml. Shalford
Page Rev. Robt. Lemon, Rectory, Pan-[field
Pasfield Mrs. Sarah, Bradford st, B.
Perrell Mrs. London road
Polley Mrs. Elizabeth, Church lane, [B.
Pritchard Genl. Edwd. Bradford st, B.
Pryor Rev. Richard, Little Saling
Purkis Thomas, esq. Willobys, B.
Rallings the Misses, Bradford st, B.
Rankin Mrs. Coggeshall road
Raven Mr. John, Bocking hall
Ray Mrs. Mary, Bradford st, B.
Rolfe Mrs. Ann, Rayne hall, Rayne
Rolfe Daniel Clapton, esq. Rayne
Rolfe Mrs. Emily Georgiana, Bradford st, Bocking
Rolfe Robert, esq. Rayne
Rolfe Thomas, esq. Rayne
Rolfe William, M.D. Bocking end, B.
Savill Samuel Webb, esq. (magistrate) Church lane, Bocking
Scale Rev. Bernard, Braintree
Scale Rev. John Barlow, D.D. Stisted
Sealey Mrs. London road
Smith Mrs. London road
Smith Rev. Percy, Pattiswick
Tabor John English, esq. Fenns, B.
Tabor Walter Clement, esq. Rayne
Taylor William, esq. Bradfield st, B.
Tomlinson Lieut. Robert Cosby, R.N. New st
Townsend Mrs. Great Saling
Tweed Captain, London road
Twitchett Mr. Thos. Bradford st, B.
Viall Mrs. Mary, Bradford st, B.
Wakeham Mrs. Bocking end, B.
Wakeham Rev. Perryman, Bridge
Watkins Rev. John Henry, Stisted
Williams Mr. Thos. Bradford st, B.
Willis Rev. Thomas, Parsonage, Rayne
Wood Rev. John Padge, Cressing

ACADEMIES AND SCHOOLS.

Not otherwise described are Day Schools.

Alder John (boarding) London road
BAPTISTS' SUNDAY SCHOOL, Coggeshall road—Rev. Wm. Humphries, master
Bell John, Shalford
Brown Sarah, Sandpit lane
Challis Samuel, Black Notley
CHARITY SCHOOL, Black Notley—Mrs. Brown, mistress
CHARITY SCHOOL, INDEPENDENTS' (girls), Bocking end, Bocking—Eliza Coghlan, mistress
CHARITY SCHOOL, Rayne—Eliz. Horton and Mary Peagram, mistresses
Cutts William, High st
FREE SCHOOL, INDEPENDENTS' (boys), Bocking end, Bocking—Philip Parish, master
Hart Catherine Mary (ladies' brdng.) Bocking end, Bocking
Hayward Hannah, Sandpit lane
Hicks Hannah, Coggeshall road
NATIONAL SCHOOL, Church yard—Isaac Boosey Belcher, master; Jemima Ann Coote, mistress
NATIONAL SCHOOL (boys) Church lane, B.—Thomas Carter, master
NATIONAL SCHOOL (girls) Church lane, B.—Hannah Westcott, mistrss
NATIONAL SCHOOL, Pattiswick—Elizabeth Betts, mistress
Rankin Richard, Stisted
Saltmarsh George (boarding & day) Bradford st, Bocking
Simons Henry, New st
Strait Eliza & Ann (boarding & day) Bradford st, Bocking
Swindells John, Stisted
Unwin Sarah, Coggeshall road

ATTORNEYS.

Copland John and Son (of *Chelmsford*)—at the Horn Inn, High st, every Wednesday
Craig Edward George, Mount house, Coggeshall road
Cunnington and Veley, Great square
Holmes John, Bradford st, Bocking
Jackson Henry, Bocking end
Lane Michael, New st
Smoothy Frederick (and auditor of the poor law union), Braintree

AUCTIONEERS & APPRAISRS.

Joscelyne Benjamin & Son, High st
Kirkham William Cable (and estate agent) London road
Newman Samuel, Rayne
Newman Thomas, Rayne

BAKERS.

Ager Philip, New st
Bearman Thomas, Church st, B.
Bowtell Henry, Shalford
Breed Aaron, Great square
Brown Bartholomew, Church st, B.
Brown George, High st
Butcher James, Coggeshall road
Durrant Noah, Great Saling
Emberson Joseph, Bradford st, B.
Freeborn Charles, Bradford st, B.
French William, Rayne road, B.
Gosling James, Sandpit lane
Harrington William, Swan side
Hicks John, Little Saling
Joscelyne Joseph, Bradford st, B.
Joscelyne Mary, High st
Lewsey David, Little square
Low Mary, Bocking end, Bocking
Owers William, New st
Parker Jeremiah, Church st, B.
Parker Jeremiah Pooley, Stisted
Parker William, Little square
Patten John, Church st, Bocking
Piggin Samuel, Coggeshall road
Raven William, White Notley
Sadler Robert, Cressing
Sly John, jun. Pound end
Thomas Thomas Hawkins, High st
Tyler Anthony, Bradford st, Bocking
Wooling John, High st

BANKERS.

Sparrow, Walker, and Co. High st—(draw on Barclay & Co. London)

BASKET & SIEVE MAKERS.

Collis John, High st
Goss James, New st
Ridgwell James, Panfield lane, B.

BLACKSMITHS.

Barker James, High Garrett
Barltop Reuben, New st
Bloomfield John, Rayne road
Brown William, Shalford
Bunn Jeremiah, High st
Butcher John, Panfield
Drane William, Great Saling
Eley Mary, Stisted
Eley Mary, Pattiswick
Fuller Joseph, Black Notley
Gentry Henry, Church st, Bocking
Gentry John (& whitesmith) Bradford st, Bocking
Harris James, White Notley
Hawkes Samuel, Bradford st, B.
Hempstead Thomas, Great Leighs
Hicks Hannah, Coggeshall road
Hutley Charles, Bradwell
Mortimer John, Stisted
Potter Thomas, Rayne
Smith Josiah Asaph, Church lane
Stebbing Charles, Stisted
Suckling John, Shalford
Turpin Pharoah, Little Saling
Willis William, Cressing

BOOKSELLERS & STATIONRS.

Joscelyne James (& printer & binder, and stamp distributer) High st
Martin Edward, High st
Shearcroft John Fenno (and printer) High st, and Bradford st, Bocking

BOOT AND SHOE MAKERS.

Andrews James, High st
Andrews Mordecai, Rayne
Andrews William, Rayne road, B.
Arnold John, Great Hide
Barnard William, Rayne
Bickmore Joseph, Stisted
Brock Joseph, Rayne road
Brown William, Bradford st, B.
Challis Thomas, Cressing
Coates William, Church st, Bocking
Cook Henry Polley, Coggeshall road
Cook James, Stisted
Cornell William, Shalford
Dodd Joseph, Great Saling
Eve Thomas, High st
Garrett John, High st
Goodwin James, Hide lane
Goss Isaac, White Notley
Green Joseph, Bradford st, Bocking
Hance John, Rayne
Holland Joseph, Bradford st, B.
Holmes John, Church st, Bocking
Juniper Joseph, High st
Kidds Joseph, Shalford
King Henry, Church lane, Bocking
King William, Bradford st, Bocking
Lake William, Rayne
Lambert Mary, Church st, Bocking
Payne John, Pound end
Plack James, High st
Polley William, New st
Pye John, Church st, Bocking
Rankin Thomas, Braintree bridge
Reynolds John, Panfield
Sewell Isaac, Bradford st, Bocking

BOOT, &c. MAKERS—Continued.
Strutt Martin, Great square
Totham James, Black Notley
Vale Samuel, Rayne
Wakefield Charles, Stisted
Waterman Edward, Cattle market
Wendon John, Panford lane, B.
Whipps William, Coggeshall road
Willis Martin, Panfield
Willsher William, Rayne road, B.
Wood James, High st
Wood Thomas, Bradford st, Bocking

BRAZIERS AND TIN-PLATE WORKERS.
Gentry John, Bradford st, Bocking
Knight Fredk. Rayne road, Bocking
Possell John, Square
Possell Samuel, Swan side
ShaveJas.Wharrie(&ironmngr)High st
Walford Thomas, New st

BREWERS.
Cutts John, Drury lane
Gosling Oliver & John, Bradford st, Bocking
Hodges James, Pound end
Tunbridge Samuel, New st

BRICK AND TILE MAKERS.
Tricker John,High Garrett, Bocking
Walford James, Coggeshall road
Wright Adam, Rayne road, Bocking

BRICKLAYERS, &c.
Bowtle Richard, New st
Bowtle Robert, Bradford st,Bocking
Brand Thomas, Coggeshall road
Brown John, Bradford st, Bocking
Corder John, Stisted
Hockley Robert, Pound end
Hodges Robert, Pound end
King Isaac, Church st, Bocking
Mutchgrove James, Black Notley
Watson William, New st
Willis Steel, Panfield

BUTCHERS.
Andrews Isaac, Great square
Archer William, Shalford
Bruty Thomas French, High st
Chamberlain Mary, Church st, B.
Chamberlain Stephen, Stisted
Cook William (pork) High st
Francis Frederick, Black Notley
Golding Elizabeth, High st
Golding Ruth, Sandpit lane
Golding William, Pound end
Medcalf Abraham, opposite Bank
Medcalf Elizabeth, Sandpit lane
Medcalf John, Bradford st, Bocking
Messent Thos. Isaac, Bocking end, B.
Newman Oswald Robert, Rayne
Owers William, New st
Page David, Bradwell
Parker Philip, Little square
Patten William, Church st, Bocking
Philips Wm. Henry, Bradford st, B.
Rashbrook Charles, Great square
Tiffin Alexander, White Notley

CABINET MAKERS AND UPHOLSTERERS.
Brenes Jas. Church lane, Bocking
Joscelyne Benjamin & Son, High st
Owers Thomas, Great square

CHYMISTS & DRUGGISTS.
Adams Edwd. Chas. Bocking end, B.
Boulton William, High st
Goodale John Wallett, High st

CLOTHES DEALERS.
Alston William (and hatter) High st
Archer Ann (& silversmith) High st

COACH PROPRIETORS.
Brooks Saml.(& livry stables) High st
Hayward Samuel, Rayne road, B.

CONFECTIONERS.
Brown George, High st
Low Mary, Bocking end, Bocking

COOPERS.
Andrews James, High st
Brown Stephen, Coggeshall road
Houlton Augustus, Stisted
Newman Thomas, Rayne

CORN FACTORS & DEALERS.
Buck Thomas, High st
Kidby Benjamin, Little square
Medcalf John, Bradford st, Bocking
Newman John, Rayne
Wilson Carrington, High st
Woolling John, High st

CURRIERS.
Harrison John, Great square
Nash Samuel, Swan side
Wright Daniel, High st

FIRE, &c. OFFICE AGENTS.
Argus, Edward George Craig, Coggeshall road
Essex and Suffolk, Thos. Joslin Great square
Essex Economic, Burrell & Son, Bradford st, Bocking
Phœnix & Pelican, Joseph Reeve, Bocking end, Bocking
Protestant Dissenters, Jno. Joscelyne, High st
Royal Exchange, Wm. Cable Kirkham, London rd
Suffolk and General Amicable, William Coote, High st
Sun, Augustus Portway, High st

FRUITERERS.
*Marked thus * are also Fishmongers.*
Cousins Sarah, High st
Cousins William, Cattle market
*Digby John, Great Hyde
*Martin Edward, High st
Turner James, Sandpit lane

GARDENERS & SEEDSMEN.
Barnard William, London road
Beckwith Jonas, Pound end
Brown John, London road
Brown Wm. (& nurseryman) London rd
Clark John, London road
Curtis Samuel, Bradwell
Harrington William, Swan side
Inons Christr. Chas. Coggeshall la, B.
Jolliff James, Bradford st, Bocking
Lindsell Philip, New st
Mills John, Coggeshall road
Mott Thomas, Church lane, Bocking
Rallings Edward, Bradford st, B.
Turpin Benjamin, Hoppet lane

GLASS, CHINA & EARTHENWARE DEALERS.
Brown Esther, Rayne road, Bocking
Cousins Louisa, High st
Hicks Joseph, White Notley
Smith Elizabeth, High st

GLOVERS.
Herbert Wm. (& fellmonger) Stisted
Surry Wm. (& fellmonger) High st
Taylor John (and breeches maker) Bradford st, Bocking

GROCERS & TEA DEALERS.
(See also Shopkeepers, &c.)
Adams Mary, Shalford
Blomfield John, Coggeshall road
BridgeGeo. (&tallow chandlr) High st
Byford Robert, Coggeshall road
Clayden John, High st
Davies David, High st
Gentry Charles, Bradford st, Bocking
Harrison Geo. Bradford st, Bocking
Hemmings Lucy, Little square
Hicks Joseph, White Notley
Joslin Thomas, Great square
Lake William, Rayne
Morecraft Thomas, Great Saling
Morrell William, Church st, Bocking
Nash Josiah, High st
Nunn Robert, Church st, Bocking
Parker Jeremiah Pooley, Stisted
Parmenter James, Church st, B.
Parnell Martha, Shalford
Peake Thomas, Braintree bridge
Porter Chs. (& cheesemongr) High st
Portway Augustus, High st
Wittam Sarah, Bradford st, Bocking

HEMPEN CLOTH AND MATTRESS MANUFACTURERS.
Hubbert Jos. Bradford st, Bocking
Negus George, Church lane, Bocking

INNS.
Black Lion (commercial) Jas. Bateman, Great square
Horn (commercial) Stephen Barnet, High st
White Hart (& posting) Thos. Durrant, Bocking end, Bocking

IRON FOUNDERS.
BatherWm.(& brass) Bocking end,B.
Goss Edward, Rayne

JOINERS AND BUILDERS.
Asser Jos. Panfield lane, Bocking
Atherton Thomas, Great Saling
Ayton Anthony, Cressing
BrenesJas. Coggeshall road,Bocking
Carter William, Stisted
Catley Samuel, Church st, Bocking
Coot Henry, Sandpit lane
Coote Thomas, High st
Harrington&Boosey, Bradford st, B.
Laver George, London road
Newman Samuel, Rayne
Newman Thomas, Rayne
Page James, Shalford
Porter Wm. High Garrett, Bocking
Viall Thomas, Bradford st, Bocking
Watson Charles, Coggeshall road
White John, White Notley
Wright Joseph, Black Notley
Young Isaac, Barrack yard

LINEN & WOOLLEN DRAPERS
Adams Mary, Shalford
Blomfield John, Coggeshall road
Budden Henry, High st
Davies David, High st
Joslin Thomas, Great square
Lake William, Rayne
Morecraft Thomas, Great Saling
Morrell Wm. Church st, Bocking
Nunn Robert, Church st, Bocking
Parmenter James, Church st, B.
Parnell Martha, Shalford
Piggin Joseph, High st
Piggott Abraham Legerton, High st
Portway Augustus, High st

MALTSTERS.
Firmin William, White Notley
Fitch Ebenezer, Shalford
Fitch Isaac, Shalford
Goodey Thomas, Great Leighs
Gosling John, Black Notley
Gosling Oliver & John, Bradford st, B.
Gurton Henry, White Notley
Harvey Benj. Bradford st, Bocking
Harvey Henry, New st
Hills Thomas, Black Notley
Joscelyne Jos. Bradford st, Bocking
Joyce John, Bradford st, Bocking
Lacey Richard, High st
May William, jun. Stisted
Porter Jno. Wilkin & Saml. Bradwell
Rankin Alfred, London road
Tabor John English, Church lane, B.
Taylor John and Son, Church lane
Willis Porter, Shalford

MILLERS.
Brewster Sturgeon Nunn, White Not.
Brown John, Church st, Bocking
Brown William, Cressing
Butcher Thomas, Black Notley
Evers William, Pattiswick
Green Saml. Bocking mill, Bradford st, B.
Hicks John, Little Saling
Hobbs Henry, Finch mill, Bocking
Letch Thomas, Shalford
May William, Stisted
Orphen William, Bradwell
Ridley John and William, Cressing
Rolfe Philemon, Rayne
Stammers Sarah, Stisted
Stock Sarah, Coggeshall road, Bocking

MILLINERS & DRESS MAKRS
Andrews Rebecca, High st
Barnard Sarah, Cressing
Blomfield Mrs. John, Coggeshall rd
Bloomfield Elizabeth Martha, Bradford street, Bocking
Bowtle Susannah Ellen, New st
Church Elizabeth, Shalford
Constable Mary, Swanside
Coot Mary, Sandpit lane
Gentry Phœbe, Bradford st, Bocking
Joslin Misses, Coggeshall road
King Mary Ann, Church st, Bocking
Lake Eliza, High st
Linsell & Smoothy, Rayne road, B.
Linsell Susan, New st
Medcalf Emma, Sandpit lane
Moult Sarah, Church yard
Owers Catherine, Great square
Oxbrow Ann, Drury lane
Peake Susannah, Bocking end
Piggin Elizabeth, High st
Simpson Sarah, Coggeshall road
Theobald and Newman, Great square
Ward Elizabeth and Mary, High st

PAINTERS, PLUMBERS AND GLAZIERS.
Brand Joseph, Pound end
Brasier Charles, High st [ing
Cadmore John, Rayne road, Bock-
Dodd Thos. Bocking end, Bocking
Livermore James, Drury lane
Porter James, Church st, B. [st, B.
Suckling Wm. High st, and Bradford

PERFUMERS AND HAIR CUTTERS.
Clay Mary Ann, Bradford st, B.
Coote William, High st
Spurge Edward, Church st, Bocking
Thompson Thomas, High st

POULTERERS.
Challis William, White Notley
Cook William, High st

ROPE & TWINE MAKERS.
Bagg Joseph, London road [ing
Hubbert Joseph, Bradford st, Bock-
Negus George, Church lane, Bocking

SADDLERS AND HARNESS MAKERS.
Durrant Samuel, Swan side [ing
Frost Benjamin, Bradford st, Bock-
Kirkham William Cable, London rd
Watson Joseph, High st

SHOPKEEPERS & DEALRS IN GROCERIES & SUNDRIES.
Bearman Joannah, Church st, B.
Branch James, Little Saling
Brown John, Cressing
Clark Ruth, Pound end
Coates William, Church st, Bocking
Cook Hannah, Bradwell
Currey Capel John, Great square
Cutts James, Sandpit lane
Dace William, Little Saling
Evers John, Bradwell
Hatfield Benjamin, Pound end
Hawkes Mary Ann, Bradford st, B.
Kerlogue Lucy, Cressing
Morse William, Cressing
Oddie Mary, Rayne road, Bocking
Parkinson George, Church st, B.
Peagram Joseph, Rayne
Potter James, Black Notley
Pudney John, Great Hide
Turner James, Sandpit lane
Wakefield Abraham, Hoppet lane
Willis Steel, Panfield

SILK MANUFACTURERS AND SILK THROWSTERS.
Courtauld Samuel, Taylors & Courtaulds (and crape manufacturers) Church street, Bocking
Mills and Co. Pound end
Vavasseur George, Bocking end
Walters Daniel, Pound end & *London*

STAY MAKERS.
Bailtrop Ann, London road
Goodwin Mary, Hide lane

STONE & MARBLE MASONS.
Downes John, Bradford st, Bocking
Prance Wm. Bocking end, Rayne rd

STRAW AND TUSCAN HAT MANUFACTURERS.
Asser Ann, Barrack yard
Britton Susannah, Coggeshall road
Everard Sarah, Hide lane [ing
Finch Charlotte, Rayne road, Bock-
Frost Sophia, Bradford st, Bocking
Hemmings Lucy, Little square
Lambert Phœbe, Church st, Bocking
Laver Ann & Elizabeth, London rd
Livick Mary, Bradford st, Bocking
Polley Ann, New st [ing
Sewell Elizabeth, Bradford st, Bock-
Theobald & Newman, Great square
Young Hannah, Stisted

STRAW PLAT MANUFACTURS.
Byford Robert, Coggeshall road
Sider Hannah, Sandpit lane [rd
Wakefield Jas. Bocking end, Rayne

SURGEONS.
Dixon John and Charles, High st
Harrison and Holmsted, Braintree
Harrison John Sweeting, High st
Holmsted Geo. Cook, Bradford st, B.
Ralph Stephen, Great Saling
Rolfe William, M.D. Bocking end, B.
Tweed Samuel How, Bradford st, B.

SURVEYORS.
Newman Samuel, Rayne
Newman Thomas, Rayne
Welsh Henry (taxes) London road

TAILORS & DRAPERS.
Andrews Ths. Litchfield, Coggeshll rd
Church John, Shalford
Garrett Joseph, High st.
Goose John, High st
Hasler William, Swan side
Johnson Thomas, Bradford st, B.
Pudney David, Little square
Pudney William, Little square
Pyman John, Bradford st, Bocking
Smith Henry, High st

TAVERNS & PUBLIC HOUSES.
Bell, Edmund Baldwin, Great square
Bell, John Newman, Panfield [road
Bird in Hand, Samuel Piggin, Coggeshall
Black Boy, Charles Cook, Church st, B.
Black Bull, William Joyce, Cattle market
Black Lion, Charles Stebbing, Stisted
Black Swan, Maria Patten, Rayne
Boar's Head, John Hodges, High st
Bull, John Brown, Church st, Bocking
Bull, David Page, Bradwell [st, B.
Cardinal's Cap, John Markham, Bradford
Cherry Tree, Thomas Newman, Rayne
Cock, John Wade, High street
Compasses, John Shave, Pattiswick
Cross Keys, Wm. Pashley, White Notley
Crown, Sarah Sanders, Coggeshall road
Duke's Head, John Mortimer, Stisted
Falcon, William Cook, High st
George, William Brown, Shalford
George, William Owers, New st [ley
Green Dragon, Abigail Crick, Black Not-
Green Man, Samuel Piggin, jun. New st
Hare and Hounds, James Battram, High Garrett, Bocking [rd, B.
Horse & Groom, Wm. Cartwright, Rayne
King's Head, Henry Everard, Braintree
King's Head, John Joyce, Bradford st, B.
Orange Tree, John Clarke, cattle market
Rein Deer, Jno. Wm. Tottman, Black Notley
Royal Oak, Wm. Parmenter, Church st, B.
Six Bells, Josh. Parmenter, Bradford st, B.
Spread Eagle, Jas. Brenes, Church lane, B.
Swan, James Willis, Swan side
Three Ashes, John Dobby, Cressing
Three Tuns, Martin Strutt, New st
Wheat Sheaf, William Revell, High st
White Hart, Saml. Adcock, Great Saling
White Hart Tap, Thomas Hicks, Coggeshall road, Bocking
White Lion, Jas. Underwood, Coggeshall rd
Woolpack, John Prance, Bradford st, B.

VETERINARY SURGEONS.
Challis Thomas, White Notley
Challis Thomas, jun. Black Notley
Poulton John, Bocking end, Bocking

WATCH & CLOCK MAKERS.
Lake Isaac, High st
Sach William, Swan side
Stocks John, Bocking end, Bocking
Wing Jeremiah, Great square

WHEELWRIGHTS.
Barnard John, Cressing [B.
Brookes Hannah and Son, Church st,
Bunn Jeremiah (and agricultural implement maker) High st
Butcher John, Panfield
Coney John Bentall, Stisted
Ellis James, Great Saling
Gunn Abraham, Little Saling
Harrington Thomas, Sandpit lane
Hawkes Samuel, Bradford st, B.
Hester Isaac, White Notley
Humphrey Joseph, Bradwell
Newman Samuel, Rayne
Newman Thomas, Rayne
Pudney James, Church lane
Spencer Henry, Shalford

WINE & SPIRIT MERCHANTS
Burrell Chas. Rayne road, Bocking
Goodale Jno. Wallett (British) High st
Gosling Oliver & John, Bradford st, B.
Portway Augustus, High st [ing
Reeve Joseph, Bocking end, Bock-

Miscellaneous.
Adams Edward Charles, dentist, Bocking end, Bocking [don road
Belcher Isaac Boosey, parish clerk, Lon-
Betts John, music & musical instrument seller, High street
Bianchi Nicholas, carver & gilder, High st
BIBLE SOCIETY, Church lane, Thomas Carter, agent [B.
Bowyer Samuel, supervisor, Bradford st,
Budden Henry, undertaker, High st
Daking Robert, tanner, Church lane, B.
EXCISE OFFICE, at the Horn Inn, High st
Gallafant Daniel, millwright, London rd
GAS WORKS, New st, Jos. Garrett, treasurer
Hance John, parish clerk, Rayne
Joscelyne Mary, malt, hop & sack dealer, High street
Last John, hardwareman, Bocking end
Newman Oswald Robt. wool dealer, Rayne
Parkinson Geo. parish clerk, Church st, B.
Peake Susannah, embroiderer, Bocking end
PROVIDENT SOCIETY, Bradford st, Bocking—Isaac Tyler, collector
Purl Jeffery, farrier, Bradford st, Bocking
REGISTRARS OF BIRTHS, DEATHS, &c. John Carrington, superintendent:—
Bocking District, Eli Tyler, Bradford street, Bocking.
Braintree District, Samuel Piggin, deputy, New st; and of births, deaths & marriages, Robt. C. Tomlinson, New st
Serjeant John, dyer, Sandpit lane
Smee John, coach builder, Rayne road, B.
Smith Henry, sawyer, Coggeshall road
Smith John D. gun maker, High st
Strait Robt. relieving officer, Bradford st, B.
Strutt Sarah, coal merchant, London rd
UNION WORKHOUSE, Rayne road, Bocking—John Turner, governor; Eliza Turner, matron; John Bragg, schoolmaster; Miss Turner, schoolmistress
VACCINE ESTABLISHMENT, Bocking end—Edward Charles Adams, agent
Wade John, furniture broker, High st
Warren Thos. birch broom maker, Stisted
West John, brush, clog & patten maker, High street
Wilkinson Wm. whip maker, Pound end
Wood Thos. leather cutter, Bradford st, B.
Young John, teacher of the violin, Coggeshall road

COACHES,
DAILY IMPLIES SUNDAY EXCEPTED.

To LONDON, a *Coach* (from Sudbury), calls at the White Hart, every forenoon at eleven—a *Coach* (from Bury), every afternoon at one—the *Phenomena* (from Norwich), every afternoon at three—a *Coach* (from Halstead), calls at the Horn, every morning (Monday excepted) at 7,

COACHES—*Continued.*

and on Monday at five—and the *Times* (from Norwich), calls at the Boar's Head, every Monday, Wednesday and Friday afternoon at half-past three; all go thro' Chelmsford, Ingatestone, Romford and Stratford.

To BURY, a *Coach* (from London), calls at the White Hart, every afternoon at two; goes through Sudbury.

To CHELMSFORD, the *Hope* (from Colchester), calls at the King's Head, every Monday, Wednesday and Friday morning at half-past nine.

To COLCHESTER, the *Hope* (from Chelmsford), calls at the White Hart, every Tuesday, Thursday and Saturday morning at nine; goes thro' Coggeshall.

To HALSTEAD, a *Coach* (from London), calls at the Horn Inn, every night at 8.

To NORWICH, the *Phenomena* (from London), calls at the White Hart, every forenoon at eleven—and the *Times*, calls at the Boar's Head, every Tuesday, Thursday & Saturday at the same hour.

To SUDBURY, a *Coach* (from London), calls at the White Hart, every afternoon at five; goes through Halstead.

CARRIERS.

To LONDON, — Sykes' *Waggons*, from the Pack Horse, daily (Sunday excepted); — Byford, from the King's Head, — — Mortlock, from his own house, — Howard, from the Falcon, and — Fake, from the Horse and Groom, all every Tuesday and Friday; — Newdick, from the Falcon, every Sun. Wed. and Fri. — Jarvis, from the Horse and Groom, every Monday and Friday; — Ruggle, from the same place, every Wed. & Fri. and — Potts, every Wednesday.

To BURY, — Sykes' *Waggon*, from the Wool Pack, daily—& Ruggles' *Waggon*, from the Horse and Groom, every Thursday and Saturday.

To CAMBRIDGE, — Turner, from the Horse and Groom, every Monday, Wednesday and Friday.

To CAVENDISH, — Byford's *Waggon*, from the King's Head, every Mon. & Fri.

To CHELMSFORD, — Hodge, from his house, Pound end, evry Friday.

To COLCHESTER, — Hodge, from his house, every Wednesday & Saturday.

To DUNMOW, — Hodge, from his house, every Monday.

To HALSTEAD, — Sykes, from the Wool Pack, daily—and — Howard, from the Falcon, every Tuesday & Saturday.

To NORWICH, — Newdick, & — Warlow's *Waggons*, from the Falcon, every Sunday, Wednesday and Friday.

To SUDBURY, — Sykes, from the Wool Pack, daily—and — Warlow, from the Falcon, every Thursday & Saturday.

To WITHAM, a *Mail Cart*, for parcels, from the Post Office and King's Head, every night at ten.

BRENTWOOD,

WITH THE VILLAGES OF SHENFIELD, INGRAVE, EAST HORNDON, SOUTH WEALD, GREAT AND LITTLE WARLEY AND NEIGHBOURHOODS.

BRENTWOOD is a chapelry (once a market town) in the parish of South Weald and hundred of Chafford, lying on the main road between Romford and Chelmsford—distant 6 miles from the former, 11 from the latter, and 18 N.E. from London; pleasantly situated on an eminence, and forming one street of irregularly built houses, about a quarter of a mile in length. The dilapidated town-hall and prison, which stand in this street, have been long occupied by persons in trade, subject to a covenant to repair them, should assizes ever again be held here, as they formerly were. It is a place of great thoroughfare, and several good inns are well supported; the principal ones are the 'Lion and Lamb,' the 'White Hart,' the 'Fleece' and the 'Chequers,' all excellent establishments. Courts leet and baron are held by the lord of the manor of South Weald, and the magistrates sit in petty session here weekly. The surrounding country is highly cultivated, and it is the residence of many families of respectability and consequence. The old chapel has been superseded by a handsome new one, dedicated to St. Thomas, and the former has been converted to the purposes of a school. The other places of worship are a neat Roman catholic chapel and a meeting-house for independents. The free grammar school here was founded by Sir Anthony Brown in 1537, and is open to all boys residing within three miles of Brentwood; it has an exhibition to Caius college, Cambridge. Races take place on a common near the town, but the meetings are not regular. Cattle fairs are held on the 18th July, and 15th and 16th of October. The population of Brentwood and following places is given after Warley.

About one mile N. E. by N. from Brentwood, in the hundred of Barstable, is the small village and parish of SHENFIELD. The parish church, dedicated to St. Mary, is a neat building with a lofty spire, which the eye discovers at a great distance; the benefice is a rectory, in the patronage of the Countess De Grey.

INGRAVE is a small parish, in the hundred of Barstable, distant about two miles E.S.E. from Brentwood. The houses of the village are generally well built, and its vicinity is adorned with many elegant villas. The church, dedicated to St. Nicholas, is a neat brick building, with a tower; the living is a rectory, united to that of West Horndon, in the incumbency of the Rev. Thos. Newman.

EAST HORNDON parish is between three and four miles S. E. from Brentwood, in the hundred of Barstable. Lord Petre has a seat here: the house, which is in the best style of architecture, and fitted up with superior elegance and taste, is seated on an eminence, commanding prospects as rich and varied as can well be imagined, over a country highly cultivated. The church, dedicated to All Saints, is very ancient, and comprises portions of various styles of architecture. The living is a rectory, of which Lord Brownlow and others are (or were lately) the patrons.

SOUTH WEALD is a parish and village, situated about a mile off the main road, between Romford and Brentwood, in the same hundred as the latter town, and about two miles west from it. Many opulent families have residences here; among these is 'Weald Hall,' celebrated as being the birth-place of Queen Mary. Nature has been liberal in dispensing her favours to this district; and the residents have managed their operations with such taste, as to produce one of the most beautiful and picturesque retreats in the county; the gardens, the extensive pleasure grounds and grand scenery, are objects which cannot fail to attract notice, and give delight. The church, dedicated to St. Peter, is an ancient building, with a tower and five bells; it contains some handsome monuments: the living is a vicarage, in the patronage of the Bishop of London, and incumbency of the Rev. Charles Almaric Belli. In front of the ancient hall is a chalybeate spring, possessing properties similar to those of sea water.

GREAT WARLEY is a parish and straggling village, in the same hundred as Brentwood, about three miles south therefrom. The church, dedicated to St. Mary, is an ancient brick building, with a spire; the living is a rectory, in the gift of the master and fellows of St. John's College, Cambridge. The view from Warley Gap is one of the most extensive and beautiful in the county of Essex.

LITTLE WARLEY is an adjoining parish to Great Warley, nearer Brentwood. The only object worthy of notice is 'Warley Lodge,' which is situate on a rising ground, agreeably wooded and surrounded with picturesque scenery. The church, dedicated to St. Peter, is a plain building, and stands at some distance from the village, which is very inconsiderable. In the reign of George III, a large army was encamped in this neighbourhood. The barracks, erected about thirty years ago, are extensive, but rarely now occupied.

The POPULATION of the foregoing places, according to the returns for 1831, was as follows—BRENTWOOD, 1,642; SHENFIELD, 665; INGRAVE, 402; EAST HORNDON, 438; SOUTH WEALD (exclusive of Brentwood,) 1,183; GREAT WARLEY, 424; LITTLE WARLEY, 163.

POST OFFICE, BRENTWOOD, Maria Tyler, *Post Mistress.*—Letters from LONDON arrive (by the Norwich mail), every night at half-past ten, and are despatched every morning at half-past four. The office opens for the delivery of letters at eight in the morning and closes at nine at night; but letters are received until ten by the payment of one penny with each.

**** The names without address are in* BRENTWOOD, *so are also those to which the name of a street is attached.*

NOBILITY, GENTRY AND CLERGY.

Arthur Jas. George, esq. Shenfield
Baxter Mrs. Mary, Brentwood
Bell Rev. John, Brentwood
Belli Rev. Charles Almaric, Vicarage, South Weald
Bonham Lieut.-Genl. Great Warley [place
Cawkwell Thomas, esq. Brentwood
Chittem John, esq. Heron gate
Cooper Mrs. Frances, Brentwood
Crippen Miss —, Mill hills cottage
Darvill Mrs. Ann, Brentwood
Dearsly Henry H. esq. Westbury lodge
English Sir John H. Warley house

Francis Samuel, esq. Warley franks
Gann Robert, esq. Shenfield
Gooch Col. Thomas, Shenfield place
Hanson John, esq. Wealdside house
Hawes James, esq. Great Warley
Heap Rev. Robt. Ivy house, Shenfield
Heatly Charles John, esq. Shenfield
Heatly Mrs. Mary, South Weald
Heatly Miss —, South Weald
Herringham Mrs. Mary Ann, Brentwd
Hoggat Thomas, esq. Heron gate
Hole Mrs. Susan, Brentwood
Jocelyn Henry, esq. Brentwood
Kemp Edward, esq. Brook st
Kingsland Wm. esq. Shenfield cottage
Latter the Misses, Great Warley
Leach Miss Hannah, Brentwood
Lescher Joseph Samuel, esq. Byles
Manby Mrs. Harriet, Shenfield villa
Mann Mrs. —, Brentwood
Martham Thomas John, esq. Brentwood
Moss Mrs. Ann, Brentwood
Norton Hon. and Rev. James, Heron gate cottage
Norton John, esq. Moat house
Newman Rev. Thomas, Ingrave
Offin William, esq. Brentwood
Payne Mrs. —, Brook st
Petre Right Honble. Lord, Thorndon park
Peyton George, esq. Brentwood
Phipps George, esq. Brook st
Powell Mrs. Ann, Brentwood
Pownceby Mrs. Sarah, Brentwood
Probyn Mrs. Juliana, Shenfield
Rhodes Rev. Fras. Wm. Chapel house
Richardson Thomas, esq. Heron gate
Richardson Mr. Thos. M.D. Brentwood
Sadler William, esq. Shenfield
Scott Samuel, esq. Brentwood
Searle Joseph, esq. Brentwood
Smith Jonathan, esq. Brentwood
Tasker Joseph, esq. Fitzwalter park
Thorn Mrs. Sarah, Brentwood
Tower Christr. Thos. esq. Weald hall
Tower Rev. William, How hatch
Wallis Thomas, esq. Brentwood
Walmesley Michl. esq. South Weald
Walmesley Richd. esq. Middleton hall
Whinfield Williamson, esq. Brentwd
Woollaston Henry Septimus Hyde, esq. Luptons

ACADEMIES AND SCHOOLS.

Nototherwise described are Day Schools.

Brown Sarah
Carter Martha (preparatory)
Free Grammar School, Rev. Jno. Bell, master
Mitchell Susannah (boarding)
Monkhouse James
Perry Samuel, Shenfield
Wallis — (boarding)
Williams William (boarding & day)
Wincop Miss Ann (boarding)
Zurhorst Henry (boarding)

ATTORNEYS.

Landon F. N.
Lewis Charles Carne (and coroner for the county)
Tate —, esq. (& master extraordinary in chancery)
Wall William

BAKERS.

Abrey George
Adey John, Heron gate
Burls Henry, Heron gate
Bush John
Dow John, Heron gate
Fairweather John
Marlton Thomas
Parker Samuel
Roper William
Shipman Charles, Brook st
Twinn William
Walker Thomas
Wallis Edward
Wilkinson Harriet

BANKERS.

Lemon Frederick W.
Savings' Bank, James Monkhouse, actuary

BOOKSELLERS & STATIONRS.

Brown Stephen Westwood
Perry James Hugh (& printer)
Tyler Maria

BOOT AND SHOE MAKERS.

Barker William, Shenfield
Barnes Robert
Blake William, Heron gate
Burrows William, Great Warley
Disney William
Haydon David, South Weald
Morris William
Nicholls George
Oddy James Brewster
Sayer Philip
Whilley John, Brook st
Wickwar Thomas
Wood Thomas
Wright William, Heron gate

BREWER AND MALTSTER.

Wright Thomas

BUTCHERS.

Alexander Henry
Bell James
Blatch James, Heron gate
Forster Joseph
Livermore James (pork)
Osbourn Thomas (pork)
Pattrick George, Brook st
Proud John
Sowter Thomas
Widby William, Shenfield

CARPENTERS.

Boardman William, Ingrave
Dowson William
Holliday James, Brook st
Mayhew Joseph, Brook st
Millington James
Murkin William
True James, Shenfield
White James
Winterbottom Jno. (& builder) Shenfield
Young John, Heron gate

CHYMISTS AND DRUGGISTS.

Slatter John
Thompson James (& oil & colourman)

COACH BUILDER.

Thorrowgood Thomas

CONFECTIONERS.

Abrey George
Bush John
Fairweather John
Walker Thomas
Wallis Edward

CORN DEALERS.

Barbrook Edward
Halls James

CURRIER AND LEATHER CUTTER.

Offin William

FIRE, &c. OFFICE AGENTS.

Essex, Ammon Moull
Pelican, C. C. Lewis
Phœnix, James Monkhouse
Phœnix, William Offin
Royal Exchange, William Wallis
Sun, Henry Thornton (& auctioneer)

GLOVERS.

Cove James (& woolstapler)
Haylett Elizabeth

GROCERS & TEA DEALERS.

(See also Shopkeepers, &c.)

Bacon Benjamin
Bailey Thomas (& china, &c. dealer)
Brown Stephen, Westwood
Brown William Henry
Crapnell Samuel, Heron gate
Hay William, Shenfield
Jeggo William, Great Warley
Lemon Frederick W.
Murkin William
Rickman Timothy
Smith Edward

HORSE DEALERS.

Alexander Henry
Forster John, South Weald
Simmons Robert

INNS & PUBLIC HOUSES.

Artichoke, Isaac Ray
Bell, John Bush
Boar's Head Inn, John Willard, Heron gate
Bull, Richard Phillips, Brook st
Chequers Inn, James Richards
Eagle and Child, Charles Cowles, Shenfield
Fleece Inn (commercial), Joseph Bull, Brook street
George Inn, George Augustus Hesse
Green Dragon, John Harrington, Shenfield
Green Man, William Olliff
King's Head, Joseph Elsdon
Lion & Lamb Inn (posting & commercial), George Mayling
Nag's Head, Jos. Bibbey, South Weald
Robin Hood, James Miles
Spread Eagle, William Kempster, South Weald
Swan, Thomas Wells
Thatcher's Arms, Mary Mumford, Great Warley
White Hart (posting & commercial) Ammon Moull
White Horse, James Evans
Yorkshire Grey, Robert Simmons

IRONMONGERS.

Castle John
French John William

LINEN AND WOOLLEN DRAPERS.

Bacon Benjamin
Barbrook James
Taylor Nehemiah
Tilley Thomas
Wallis Henry

MILLERS.

Moss Thomas, Brook st
Roper William
Storey John

MILLINERS AND DRESS AND STRAW HAT MAKERS.

Barnard Sarah
Carswell Mary Ann
Scarswell Elizabeth

NURSERY AND SEEDSMEN.

Breese John
Wall Isaac

PAINTERS, PLUMBERS AND GLAZIERS.

Burtwell George
Emery Edgar

SADDLERS.

Brown Samuel, Heron gate
Wallis William
White James

SHOPKEEPERS & DEALRS IN GROCERIES & SUNDRIES.

Bennett William
Boardman Ann, Ingrave
Green John, Brook st

SMITHS.

Harris — (& farrier)
Newcomb Henry (& farrier)
Newcomb John
Wingrave John

SURGEONS.

Butler Cornelius (and registrar of births and deaths)
Colborne Thomas

TAILORS.

Belchar Joseph
Burrell Thomas
Sandford William
Webster Bryant
Worth Samuel

TOY DEALERS.
Boreham Sarah
Tyler Maria

WATCH & CLOCK MAKERS.
Collis William
Higham Mary Ann

WHEELWRIGHTS.
Ashman Isaac, Heron gate
Crossingham John, Great Warley
Wood William, Shenfield
Young John, Heron gate

WINE & SPIRIT MERCHANT.
Lemon Frederick W.

Miscellaneous.
Beesley John, fishmonger
Carman Catherine, green grocer
Carswell Jonathan, hair dresser
Carver Samuel, green grocer
Curtis Robert Henry, veterinary surgeon
Dobson William, basket maker
Eayles Thos Bills, hatter and clothier
Manley Robert, stonemason
Murrell John, coach master
Overhead William, cooper
Smee William, upholsterer and cabinet maker
Stumpner John, tanner, Little Warley
Sturgeon John, fellmonger, &c.
Thorrowgood Elizabeth, upholsterer
Threader Thomas, hair dresser

COACHES,

To and from LONDON, are passing thro' almost every hour, and call either at the Lion and Lamb, or White Hart Inns.

To BURY ST. EDMUNDS, the *Old Bury* passes through every forenoon (Sunday excepted) about eleven.

To CHELMSFORD, —— French's and other *Coaches* pass through at various periods during the day.

To IPSWICH, the *Blue*, from the Lion and Lamb, every afternoon about two, & the *Shannon*, every morning about 10.

To NORWICH, the *Times*, every morning at nine.

To SOUTHEND, a *Coach* passes through during the summer months, daily.

VANS.

To LONDON, Mayling's *Spring Vans*, every Tuesday and Friday.

*** In addition to the above, other *Coaches* and *Carriers*, to and from LONDON and most parts of NORFOLK and SUFFOLK, are passing through BRENTWOOD continually.

BURNHAM,

CREEKSEA, ALTHORNE, SOUTHMINSTER, ASHELDAM, DENGIE, TILLINGHAM, BRADWELL, ST. LAWRENCE, STEEPLE AND NEIGHBOURHOODS.

BURNHAM is a port village and parish, in the hundred of Dengie, 51 miles E. by N. from London, and 19½ E.S.E. from Chelmsford, situated on the northern bank of the river Crouch, having a commodious quay. The oyster beds, both in the river and on the coast, are extremely productive, and great quantities of the fish are exported from hence to Flanders. A building, called the Belvidere, has been erected by some persons forming the oyster company, it stands near the river, and is forty-five feet in height: from its summit a most extensive and delightful prospect is commanded, embracing the Isle of Sheppy, and an expansive sea view. The White Hart here is a well-conducted commercial house. The parish church, dedicated to St. Mary, stands about a mile from the village on an elevated site, and its tower serves as a conspicuous land mark for mariners. The living is a vicarage, of which the Rev. C. A. St. John Mildmay is the incumbent. There is a place of worship for baptists, and a national school. Fairs are held on the 25th April, and 20th September, chiefly for toys. The population is given after the account of ST. LAWRENCE and STEEPLE.

About two miles N. W. by W. from Burnham is the village and parish of CREEKSEA, or *Cricksey*. The marshes are here protected from inundation by strong embankments. The church is dedicated to All Saints.

Adjoining Creeksea is the parish of ALTHORNE, the village being about four miles N. W. from Burnham. The church is dedicated to St. Andrew: the living is a vicarage, united to Creeksea, in the incumbency of the Rev. James Bruce.

SOUTHMINSTER village and parish is about three miles N. from Burnham. The parish is an agricultural one, and there are several respectable resident farmers. The church, dedicated to St. Leonard, is a cruciform structure: the living is a vicarage, in the gift of the Charterhouse, London—the Rev. Dr. Scott is the present incumbent. There is a place of worship for independents, and a national school.

About two miles N. E. from Southminster is the village of ASHELDAM, and a little further is that of DENGIE, the latter giving name to the hundred in which all the parishes before noticed are situated. They have each their parish church—that of Asheldam is dedicated to St. Lawrence, the other to St. James: the Rev. Dr. Dakins is the minister.

TILLINGHAM village and parish is about two miles N. from Dengie, and between four and five in the same direction from Burnham; the parish being bounded on the east by the German ocean. The church, dedicated to St. Nicholas, was rebuilt in 1708, and contains two monumental brasses, dated 1584: the living is a vicarage, in the gift of the dean and chapter of St. Paul's, London; the present incumbent is the Rev. George Vigne. A place of worship for baptists and four almshouses are in the village. Fairs, for toys, are held on Tuesday in Whitsun week and September 16th.

BRADWELL, or as it is designated, *Bradwell near the Sea*, is a village and parish, between two and three miles N. from Tillingham, and twelve E. from Maldon; bounded on the north by St. Peter's sand, and on the south by the Blackwater river. The church, dedicated to St. Thomas the Apostle, has a tower surmounted by a lofty spire: the living is a rectory, in the patronage of the Rev. T. Schreiber, who is the present incumbent. There is a fair for toys held on midsummer day.

ST. LAWRENCE, and STEEPLE are two small villages, situate near the road leading from Bradwell to Maldon: the former about four miles S. W. from Bradwell, and the latter about two miles from St. Lawrence. They are both agricultural parishes, and in neither is there a public house or seller of beer. There is a church belonging to each; the minister of Steeple is the Rev. Thomas T. Cresswell; that of St. Lawrence, the Rev. John Bryan Cowardine.

All the parishes above noticed are in the hundred of Dengie; the population of each is as follows, BURNHAM, 1393; CREEKSEA, 154; ALTHORNE, 352; SOUTHMINSTER, 1422; ASHELDAM, 144; DENGIE, 249; TILLINGHAM, 970; BRADWELL, 956; ST. LAWRENCE, 182; STEEPLE, 497.

POST.—Letters for all the above places brought from and are despatched to MALDON principally by light cart, and an additional penny charged on each.

GENTRY AND CLERGY.
Auger Gillson, esq. Burnham
Auger John Gillson, esq. Burnham
Badger Rev. James, Asheldam
Baird Rev. Jas. Tillingham
Baker Mr. Chas. (executors of) Creeksea
Barnes Mrs. Sarah, Burnham
Barnes Miss Sophia, Burnham
Bruce Rev. James, Vicarage, Althorne
Bygrave John, esq. Burnham wick
Cowardine Rev. John Bryan, St. Lawrence Newland
Cresswell Rev. Thomas T. Steeple
Croxon Mrs. Sarah, Creeksea lodge
Dakins Rev. Dr. Dengie
Gardner Richard, esq. Stokes hall, Althorne
Garrington Rev. John, Burnham
Grice James, esq. Asheldam hall
Hammond Rev. William, Burnham
Hawkins Jno. esq. Burnham
Hill Rev. Walter Henry, Southminster
Huddart Mrs. Hannah, Burnham
Kemp Jno. esq. Northwick, Southmnr
Kemp Samuel, esq. Creeksea hall
Ketcher Mrs. Betsey, Burnham
Ketcher W. H. esq. Ratsboro
Maldon James, esq. Dengie hall
Page Charles, esq. Southminster
Page Mrs. —, Southminster
Page William, esq. Southminster
Schreiber Rev. Thomas (magistrate) Bradwell
Spurgin Mrs. —, Southminster
Spurgin William, esq. Bradwell
Tatham Thomas James, esq. (assistant tithe commissioner) Althorne
Vigne Rev. George, Tillingham

ACADEMIES & SCHOOLS.
Not otherwise described are Day Schools.
Carter John, Bradwell
Garrington John, Burnham
Lamb Mrs. —, Burnham
Morris Jas. (bdg & day) Southminster
NATIONAL SCHOOL, Althorne—Jas. Harvey, master; Amelia Harvey, mistress
NATIONAL SCHOOL, Burnham—James Henry Shuttleworth, master; Sarah Smith, mistress
NATIONAL SCHOOL, Southminster—James Winterbon, master; Hannah Goslin, mistress
Osborne John, jun. Tillingham

BAKERS.
Belcham Mary, Southminster
Cardnell George, Steeple

Garrington Hannah, Burnham
Lawrence Benjamin, Tillingham
Lewin Hannah, Southminster
Nichols James, Tillingham
Nichols John, Bradwell
Osborne William Simpson, Tillingham
Potter William, Burnham
Smith Joseph, Althorne
Spells Edward, Southminster
Summers Jonathan, Steeple
Turner George, Bradwell
Wackrill John, Burnham
Windle James, Southminster

BASKET MAKERS.

Dennish Samuel (& cooper) Southminster
Edwards Robert, Burnham

BLACKSMITHS.

Anthony James, Althorne
Barratt Richard, Dengie
Baxter James, Tillingham
Knight George, Bradwell
Lamb John, Burnham
Munson Robert, Southminster
Newman Thomas, Althorne
Nunn George, jun, Steeple
Ramsey Jeremiah, Southminster

BOOT & SHOE MAKERS.

Austin Joseph, Ostend, Burnham
Beard John, Althorne
Bigmore William, Burnham
Clover John, Burnham
Cook Elias, Southminster
Hale Stephen, Steeple
Hawes John, Tillingham
Hews John, Bradwell
Hews Susannah, Steeple
Mason Daniel, Southminster
Newman William, Southminster
Noone Frederick Crisp(& stationer) Southminster
Page Charles, Burnham
Purkis William, Southminster
Spooner John, Steeple
Taylor John, Burnham

BRICKLAYERS.

Cook John, Southminster
Linn Joseph, Althorne
Newman William, Burnham

BUTCHERS.

Allen Samuel, Steeple
Bowerman Abraham, Southminster
Bridge John, Southminster
Croxon Edward, Burnham
Croxon Henry, Burnham
Croxon Joseph, Burnham
Francis Thomas, Althorne
Hews John, jun. Bradwell
Maskell Richard, Tillingham
Olley Edward, Southminster
Peacock Benjmn.Gaskell,Tillingham
Spurgin George, Southminster
Wood William, Ostend, Burnham

CARPENTERS.

Collins Charles, Tillingham
Collins Michael, Tillingham
Collins William, Tillingham
Gardner Christopher, Burnham
Mason Richard, Bradwell
Smith Jehu, Burnham
Stammers Wild, Southminster
Winterbon James, Southminster

CHYMISTS & DRUGGISTS.

Brown Wm. Southminstr & *Rayleigh*
Hews John, Bradwell
Hicks James Hanwell, Southminster
Osborne John, Tillingham
Ottway Thomas, Southminster

COAL MERCHANTS.

Cranmer Alexander, Burnham
Edwards William, Burnham
Garrood John, Burnham
Page William, Burnham
Richmond Isaiah, Burnham
Taylor William, Burnham

GARDENERS & SEEDSMEN.

Blunden James, Burnham
Blunden Thomas, Burnham
Camplin John, Southminster
Forlkner Thomas, Burnham
Rise Abraham, Burnham
Vice Samuel, Southminster

GROCERS & TEA DEALERS.

(See also Shopkeepers, &c.; and also Linen Drapers.)

Marked thus * are also Linen Drapers.

Bosten William, Southminster
*Hart Stephen, Tillingham
*LemereJames Henry,Southminster
*Nix Joshua Tovell, Bradwell
Nunn George,St.LawrenceNewland
*Palmer James, Tillingham
Patrick John, Southminster
Perry George, Burnham
Potter James, Southminster
*Prior John, Burnham
*Spurgin James (& fire office agent) Southminster
*Stoneham John, Burnham
Stracy James, Tillingham
*Wilson Edward, Southminster
*Wilson Isaac, Tillingham

HAIR DRESSERS.

Gardner William, Burnham
Keys George, Southminster
Philips Thomas, Burnham

INNS & PUBLIC HOUSES.

Anchor, John Sirett, Burnham
Cap & Feathers, Robert Willsmer, Tillingham
Cock, Lydia Pearson, Tillingham
George & Dragon, Samuel Gigney, Burnham
Green Man, John Woolvet, Bradwell
King's Arms, Chas. Cock, Burnham
King's Head, Ann Quay, Bradwell
King's Head, Elizabeth Willsmer, Southminster
Old Greyhound, Jas. Sexton, Creeksea
Queen's Head, Phœbe Horne, Bradwell
Rose & Crown, Mary Bridge, Southminster
Ship, Alexander Cranmer, Burnham
Star, John Willsmer, Steeple
Star and Commercial Inn, Henry Emberson, Burnham
Sun&Anchor,Susnh.Spooner,Steeple
White Hart, AnnClarke,Southminstr
White Hart and Commercial Inn, William Page, Burnham
White Horse, Thomas Baldwin, Southminster
White Horse,William Grove, Dengie

LINEN DRAPERS.

(See also Grocers, &c.)

Barnes Charles, Burnham
Miller George, Southminster

MILLERS.

Browne Henry, Mayland
Grange William, Bradwell
Lewin Hannah, Southminster
Smith Alexander, Southminster
Staggs Elisha, Burnham
Theedham Samuel, Burnham

MILLINERS AND DRESS MAKERS.

Boreham Mrs. Bradwell
Chapman M. A. Southminster
Cockett A. M. Tillingham
Grange Martha, Southminster
Stillaman Elizabeth, Southminster

OYSTER MERCHANTS.

Auger John Gillson, jun. Burnham
Clark George, Creeksea
Hawkins John, Burnham
Rogers Isaac, Burnham
Rogers Thomas, Burnham
Sweeting John, Burnham
Sweeting Labon, Burnham

PAINTERS, PLUMBERS AND GLAZIERS.

Felton William, Tillingham
Garrood George, Burnham
Winterbon John, Southminster

SADDLERS.

Dean William, Steeple
Powl Thomas, Tillingham
Poynter Joseph, Bradwell
Rumley Henry, Althorne
Smith Eleanor, Southminster
Smith John, Southminster
Stevens Robert, Burnham

SHIP OWNERS.

Edwards William, Burnham
Hawkins Mrs. Danzie, Burnham
Matthews Mary, Burnham
Richmond Isaiah, Burnham
Richmond James, Burnham
Taylor William, Burnham

SHOPKEEPRS & DEALERS IN GROCERIES & SUNDRIES.

Andrews James, Steeple
Babbs James, Bradwell
Beehag Robert, Southminster
Brocklehurst John, Burnham
Harvey Rhoda, Tillingham
Harvey William, Bradwell
Manning Jeffrey, Burnham
Mason Henry, Bradwell
Rolph James, Creeksea
Sandford Robert, Asheldam
Smith John, Southminster
Wicks Thomas, Althorne
Wood John, Steeple
Wright Mary Ann, Tillingham

SMITHS.

Ely William, Southminster
Garrood John, Burnham
Hewett John, Bradwell

STRAW HAT MAKERS.

Chapman M. A. Southminster
Hews Elizabeth, Tillingham

SURGEONS.

Quilter Henry, Southminster
Rush Isaac, Southminster

TAILORS.

Bell Thomas, Burnham
Chapman Robert, Southminster
Key William, Burnham
Moroan Robert, Bradwell
Revett John, Tillingham
Revett Sarah, Tillingham

WATCH MAKERS.

Griffis Paul, Southminster
Spencer Robert, Southminster

WHEELWRIGHTS.

Aylett John, Tillingham
Boreham Joseph, Bradwell
Ely William, Southminster
Gill Charles, Creeksea
Gill Robert, St. Lawrence Newland
Hewett John, Bradwell
Last John, Tillingham
Potter Joseph, Althorne
Stuttle Charles, Southminster

Miscellaneous.

Clark George, merchant, Creeksea
Clarke George, fruiterer, Southminster
Dowsett Sarah, glover, Southminster
GarringtonDangieS.H.sail mkr,Burnham
Harman Benjamin,maltster,Southminster
Hurrell Henry Shuttleworth, veterinary surgeon, Southminster
Osborne John, jun. deputy registrar of births and deaths, Tillingham
Parker James, barge owner, Bradwell
Pipe Benjamin, parish clerk,Southminster
Pitt John, retail brewer, Burnham
Rush Isaac, registrar of births & deaths, Southminster
Turner & Stokes, stay makers, Burnham

CHELMSFORD,

WITH THE VILLAGES OF SPRINGFIELD, BOREHAM, BROOMFIELD, GREAT AND LITTLE WALTHAM, WIDFORD AND NEIGHBOURHOODS.

CHELMSFORD, the county town of Essex, in the parish and hundred of its name, is one of established respectability, and its neighbourhood is distinguished for the number of the genteel and opulent residents. It is 29 miles N. E. from London, 22 S. W. from Colchester, and 10 W. from Maldon—situated in a beautiful valley between the Chelmer and the Cann, to which rivers, on each side of the town, the gardens of several of the houses extend; it consists of one principal street and three or four smaller ones, well paved, and lighted with gas. A handsome iron bridge bestrides the Chelmer, and an elegant one of stone crosses the Cann, connecting the town with the hamlet of MOULSHAM. A canal, navigable from hence to the Blackwater, is of considerable advantage to the place; and the Eastern Counties railway will pass through or close to Chelmsford. In the first year of the twelfth century, Maurice, bishop of London, raised this place from obscurity, by constructing a bridge of three arches over the river Cann, which has been superseded by the one before mentioned. The town is within the jurisdiction of the county magistrates, who hold petty sessions for the division twice weekly; constables and other officers are appointed at the court leet of the manor, of which Lady Mildmay is proprietor. The assizes for the county take place in Lent, July and December, the latter for the delivery of the gaol only; there are also quarterly courts of session, and a county court for the recovery of debts under 40s. The municipal and legal business of the town is transacted in the shire hall, an elegant and commodious structure of white stone, with a rusticated basement, and ornamented with handsome columns supporting a pediment: this building also comprises assembly rooms and convenient offices, and it is here that the election of members to represent South Essex is conducted. Contiguous to the hall is a neatly sculptured conduit, supplied by a spring about a quarter of a mile distant, which yields to the town excellent water. The old county gaol is a capacious well looking stone edifice, situated in the hamlet of Moulsham; adjoining the gaol is the house of correction, appropriated to the reception of female convicts. The new house of correction, on Springfield-hill, is a very extensive building, with cells for the classification of prisoners, tread-mills, workshops, &c. Though this is not a manufacturing town, its local trade is well supported by its own inhabitants, and those of the district that surrounds it; and the great thoroughfare it enjoys from its situation contributes much to its prosperity. There is a tolerable trade in corn and malt, and several large flour mills are on the banks of the Chelmer.

The church is dedicated to St. Mary: the body was rebuilt a few years since, the former having fallen down, in 1800, from the unskilfulness of some workmen, who in digging a vault undermined two of the principal pillars; it is now a fine structure, with a square embattled tower crowned with pinnacles, and surmounted by a lofty spire; and the east end of the chancel is embellished with a beautifully painted window. The benefice is a rectory, in the patronage of Lady St. John Mildmay, and incumbency of her son, the Rev. C. A. St. John Mildmay. There are two chapels for independents, one each for baptists and Wesleyan methodists, and a spacious meeting-house for the society of friends. The royal free grammar school here was founded by Edward VI, and endowed with lands situate in this county; it possesses an exhibition to Caius college, Cambridge. There are six alms-houses, founded by the Mildmay family in 1565, and others by Wm. Davis, in 1520. There are several schools for the gratuitous education of children of the humbler classes of inhabitants, on the Lancasterian and national systems; an infants' school, and charity schools for clothing and educating children of both sexes. The market is held on Friday, and is well supplied with all articles for consumption—abundantly with corn. Fairs, for cattle, take place on 12th May and 12th November. By the last returns, the population of Chelmsford, including MOULSHAM hamlet, was 5,435.

Divided only from Chelmsford by the river Chelmer is the parish of SPRINGFIELD, deriving its name, as it is said, from the many springs that rise within its limits. At this place are wharfs on the Chelmer navigation; and here is situate the new house of correction, before mentioned. The church, dedicated to All Saints, is a neat structure of some antiquity, with a tower; the living is a rectory, of which the Earl of Arran is patron. Dr. Goldsmith composed his delightful poem of the 'Deserted Village' whilst residing at a farm-house nearly opposite the village church. The population of the parish, in 1831, was 1,851.

BOREHAM is a village and parish, in the same hundred as Chelmsford, three miles E.N.E. from that town; situated in a much admired part of the county. The church, dedicated to St. Andrew, is an ancient edifice, and contains, as well as in its cemetery, some curious monuments; those in the Sussex chancel especially, to the Radclyffes, Earls of Essex, and, in the church-yard, to Lord and Lady Waltham, are deserving attention. New Hall, in this parish, belonged to Henry VIII, and the princess Mary, his daughter, resided here for several years; it afterwards came into the possession of Cromwell, and, after the restoration, became the property of the Duke of Albemarle. Since then it was purchased by some opulent Roman catholics, and is now occupied by a society of English nuns, who superintend the education of young ladies professing the Roman catholic religion. Population of the parish 991.

BROOMFIELD is a small village and parish, about two miles north of Chelmsford, in the same hundred. The church is dedicated to St. Mary; and the living, which is a perpetual curacy, is in the gift of the Bishop of London. Population 747.

GREAT and LITTLE WALTHAM are two villages and parishes; the former about five, and the latter four miles north from Chelmsford, both in the same hundred as that town. At Great Waltham, the hemp, sacking and rope manufactures, and the malting trade, are carried on, the latter to some extent. Each village has its parish church; and at Little Waltham is an endowed school, and a place of worship for independents. Great Waltham contained, in 1831, 2,013 inhabitants, and Little Waltham, at the same period, 674.

WIDFORD is an inconsiderable village, and small parish, in the hundred of Chelmsford, about a mile and a half south from that town. It contains a parish church, dedicated to St. Mary, and a population of about 160 inhabitants.

POST OFFICE, High-street, CHELMSFORD, Abjohn Joseph Stokes, *Post Master.*—Letters from LONDON arrive every night at eleven, and are despatched every morning at half-past three.—Letters from NORWICH arrive every morning at half-past three, and are despatched every night at eleven.—Letters are forwarded (by mail cart) to MALDON every morning at half-past four, and to DUNMOW at a quarter before five.

The box remains open until ten at night; but letters can be received until half-past ten by paying twopence with each, and until twelve by paying sixpence.—The delivery of the London letters commences between seven and eight in the morning.

GENTRY AND CLERGY.

Allen Mrs. Maria, Springfield
Allen William, esq. Boreham
Archer Mrs. —, Springfield
Archer Mr. Thomas, High st
Blyth Isaac, esq. Springfield
Bowser Mrs. Sarah, Springfield lane
Butterfield Thomas, esq. Boreham
Caldwell Mrs. —, King st
Chalk Mr. A. R. King st
Chalk Mr. Thomas, Duke st
Cheveley George, esq. Butlers
Cheveley Mrs. Mary, Duke st
Christy Thomas, esq. Bloomfield
Church Mrs. Sarah, Baddow lane
Clapham George, esq. Moulsham
Cleveley the Misses, Duke st
Coates Mr. George, Springfield
Coates Miss —, Springfield terrace
Crabb Miss —, King st
Dixon Mr. Robert S. King st
Durrant Mr. Thomas, Duke st
Dye Mr. Robert, Moulsham
Dyer Rev. Jas. Hardwick, Gt. Waltham
Edwards Rev. Vincent, Vicarage house, Broomfield
Embleton Miss Mary, Duke st
Finch Mrs. Hannah, Broomfield
Gerrard Mrs. Eliz. New hall, Boreham
Gosling Mrs. Elizabeth, Moulsham

Gray Rev. George, Duke st
Greenwood Mrs. Elizbth. Springfield
Greenwood Thos. esq. Baddow house
Griggs Mrs. —, Springfield
Haselfoot Robert C. esq. (magistrate) Boreham
Haselfoot Capt. William H. Boreham
Hazelfoot Mrs. —, Cottage place
Heald James, Baddow lane
Hodges Miss —, Moulsham
Hodges Thomas, esq. King st
Hodges Rev. Thomas Stephen, Little Waltham lane
Holmsted Mrs. Martha, Springfield
Howard Captain William, Duke st
Hunt Miss —, Moulsham
Hutchinson Rev. James, Duke st
King Charles, esq. Broomfield place
Knight Wm. esq. Springfield lodge
Labouchere P. C. esq. Highlands
Leake Mr. John, Springfield
Longmore Mrs. —, Duke st
Lucas William, esq. Little Waltham
Mansfield Mr. Thos. Great Waltham
Marriage Miss Caroline, Conduit sq
Marriage Francis, esq. High st
Massey Miss —, Moulsham
Mildmay Rev. C. A. St. John, Rectory
Mills Mrs. —, Coval hall
Owen Miss —, King st
Parker Charles Geo. esq. Springfield
Pearson Rev. Arthur, M.A. Springfield
Perry Mr. Isaac, Shrublands, Springfield
Porter Mrs. —, Coval cottage
Poynter Mrs. Maria, Moulsham
Prichard Mr. Octavius, Moulsham
Ray Rev. William C. Boreham
Ripton Mr. John, Springfield
Robertson Mr. Robert, Widford
Simpson Mrs. —, Chelmsford
Smith Mrs. Elizabeth, Springfield
Smith Mr. John, Great Waltham
Spencer Mr. John, Great Waltham
Staines Mrs. —, King st
Talbot Robert, esq. Springfield
Trussell Mrs. —, Moulsham
Tufnell John Joliffe, esq. Langleys
Tufnell Rev. William, Great Waltham
Tufnell Wm. Michael, esq. New st
Tyrell Rev. Charles, Boreham house
Tyrell Sir John Tyssen, M.P. Boreham house, Boreham
Wade Mr. Charles, Broomfield
Walford Rev. William, Hatfields
Warner Rev. William, Widford
Wells Mr. William Collins, Duke st
Wickrell Mr. Samuel, Moulsham
Williams Mrs. —, Duke st
Wilson James, esq. Broomfield
Wolton Mrs. Elizabeth, Springfield

ACADEMIES AND SCHOOLS.

Not otherwise described are Day Schools.

CHELMSFORD CHARITY SCHOOL, Church yd—Eliz. Wilmot, mistrss
Cornell Elizabeth (brdng.) Boreham
Dowse Catherine, High st
Francis Mary (brdng.) Cottage place
FREE GRAMMAR SCHOOL, Duke st—Rev. James Hutchinson, master
Hutchinson Rev. Jas. (brdg.) Duke st
INFANTS' SCHOOL, Church yard—Miss Basingwhite, mistress
King Mrs. (preparatory) Duke st
King Wm. Barnard (preparty.) Duke st
LANCASTERIAN SCHOOL (girls) Duke street—Margaret Tapley, mistress
NATIONAL SCHOOL (boys and girls) Springfield—Charles Owen, master; Harriet Basingwhite, mistress
NATIONAL SCHOOL (boys and girls) Church yard—John Basingwhite, master; Mrs. Street, mistress
NATIONAL SCHOOL, Little Waltham—Mrs. Edwards, mistress
NEW HALL NUNNERY & CATHOLIC SCHOOL, Boreham—conducted by the Hon. Mrs. Gerrard
Orem Charlotte and Mary Anne, Boreham
Prentice Caroline, Duke st
Taylor Ann, Moulsham
Vely and Linders, Moulsham
Watson William (brdg.) Albion house

ARCHITECTS & SURVEYORS

Fenton James, Conduit sq; house Springfield
Webb James, Springfield lane
Wilson James (of roads) Broomfield

ATTORNEYS.

Bartlett Robert (and clerk to the magistrates) Chelmsford
Brewster Robert, Conduit st
Chalk Edward S. Duke st
Copland and Son, High st
Gilson Henry Snell, Conduit st
Murdoch Ephraim, High st
Parker George Charles (and clerk of the peace, deputy vice admiral, deputy registrar of the ecclesiastical court, and clerk to the meetings of lieutenancy) Springfield green
Parkins and Gepp, New st
Wicks William, High st

AUCTIONEERS & APPRAISRS

Baker Robert, Conduit square
Clench John, Springfield lane
Cohen Jacob, Duke st
Joscelyne Benjamin, Great Waltham
Stoneham Thos. jun. Springfield lane
Wiffen George, High st
Wiffen Thomas, Moulsham

BAKERS & FLOUR DEALERS

Barnes Elisha, Springfield
Carsons Robert, Broomfield
Copeland John, jun. Springfield
Craske George, Moulsham
Craske Susannah, Duke st
Crooks Charles, Moulsham
Dodd William, High st
Doe Thomas, Springfield
Doe Thomas, Little Waltham
Emberson Jabez, Great Waltham
Eve Sarah, Boreham
Fitch Samuel, Springfield
Markham George, Moulsham
Mison Sarah, Conduit st
Palmer Thomas, Moulsham
Phillips Thomas, High st
Rolfe Joseph, Springfield
Rust Thomas, Little Waltham
Seaton Charles, Chelmsford
Smee John (and biscuit) Broomfield
Wackrill George, King st
Wackrill Thomas, Duke st

BANKERS.

Sparrow, Walford, Nottidge, Greenwood, and Tufnell, High st (draw on Barclay, Bevan & Co. *London*)
SAVINGS' BANK, High st—George Durrant, secretary

BASKET MAKERS.

Ambrose Michael, Moulsham
Ambrose Thomas, Moulsham
Terry John, Moulsham

BLACKSMITHS.

(See also Whitesmiths.)

Blanks Charles, Springfield
Blanks Thomas, Springfield lane
Candler George, Boreham
Dowe Henry, Boreham
Ford John, Widford
Hardy James, Broomfield
Harris John, Boreham
Newcomb Matthew, Little Waltham
Newman Thomas, High st
Robinson John, Great Waltham

BOOKSELLERS & STATIONRS.

Arthy Joseph, High st
Copland Alfred, High st
Dutton Thos. D. (& engrver on wood) High st
Guy Henry, High st
Shearcroft Josiah, High st

BOOT AND SHOE MAKERS.

Bedford William, Springfield
Bedwell Thomas, Great Waltham
Bennell Benjamin, Conduit st
Bennell James, High st
Bowls Joseph, Broomfield
Cable Samuel, Moulsham
Chapman James, Boreham
Eve Charles Henry, Duke st
Gosling John, Moulsham
Hill Thomas, High st
Holbrook John, Springfield
Hunt Joseph, Broomfield
Lines William, Duke st
Martin Robert, Moulsham
Monk William, Great Waltham
Overhill Joseph, Conduit st
Pulle James, Broomfield
Riddell Alfred, High st
Rumball Elizabeth, Moulsham
Saltmarsh Henry, Moulsham
Sayers John, King st
Thorogood John, Moulsham
Treadway George, Springfield
Wicks George (and leather seller) Conduit street
Wiffen Thomas, Moulsham
Wilshere Thomas, High st

BRAZIERS AND TIN-PLATE WORKERS.

Collis Samuel, High st
Dennis Thomas, High st
Horth Thomas, Moulsham
Milbank Thomas, High st
Wood George, High st

BREWERS.

Carter Henry Harridge, Springfield
Gray Chas. Stanton, Springfield lane
Ratcliff John, Baddow lane

BRICK AND TILE MAKERS.

Christy James, Broomfield
Moss Thomas & Co. Chelmsford kiln
Rippengale Smith, Moulsham
Rust William, Great Waltham
Wright George, Springfield

BRICKLAYERS.

Ayre Jeremiah, Springfield
Brown & Co. (& slaters) Duke st
Brown Samuel (& slater) Springfield
Dowsett William, Great Waltham
Lester John (& slater) King st
Moss and Son, Chelmsford
Storey James, Moulsham
White James, Moulsham

BUILDERS.

Baker William, Duke st
Hart Samuel, Moulsham
Harvey George, Springfield
Lester John, King st
Moss James and Son, Chelmsford
Pullen James, New st
Pursell Samuel, Great Waltham
Thorn Thomas, Springfield

BUTCHERS.

Butcher Robert, Duke st
Cobbin William, Moulsham
Crooks Sophia, High st
Davis James, Conduit st
Drake Thomas, Conduit st
Gladwin Henry, Moulsham
Gladwin James, Springfield
Grave John, Conduit st
Green John, Moulsham
Ive William, Moulsham
King James, Springfield
Lorkin Thomas, Chelmsford
Marriage Alfred, High st
Orton James, Moulsham

BUTCHERS—*Continued.*
Orton John, Duke st
Osborn John, Moulsham
Peacock Hannah, Springfield
Sayers John, King st
Seabrook John, Boreham
Snow Benjamin, Great Waltham
Sorrell Henry, Great Waltham
Wendon John, Conduit square
Wilson Lucking, Great Waltham

CABINET MAKERS AND UPHOLSTERERS.
Abrey Henry, High st
Bedford Henry, New st
Bull and Son, Duke st
Cohen Jacob, King st
Dowsett John, Conduit st
Myers Wolfe, High st
Overall William, High st
Turnage Samuel, Broomfield
Warner Richard, Moulsham

CARPENTERS.
Baker William, Duke st
Beardwell Thomas, Boreham
Brightwell William, Boreham
Clench John, Springfield lane
Hart Samuel, Moulsham
Harvey George, Springfield
Horsnell Thomas, Writtle
Milbank John, Little Waltham
Newcomb William, Moulsham
Pullen James, New st
Pursell Samuel, Great Waltham
Sewell Henry, Springfield

CARVERS AND GILDERS.
Braton Frank and Ernest, High st
Brown F. S. Conduit st
Ruse James, King st

CHINA, GLASS, &c. DEALERS.
Hawes John, Moulsham
Lockett John, Duke st
Newman William, Conduit square
Parker James, High st

CHYMISTS & DRUGGISTS.
Baker Wm. (and cold, warm, medicated, &c. bath proprietor) High st
Clift Mary Ann, High st
Cooper Susannah, High st
Morse Edwd. Geo. (& surgeon) High st

CLOTHES DEALERS.
Dodd John, Moulsham
Harris John, Moulsham
Marsh George Finch, High st
Myers Wolfe, High st

COACH BUILDERS.
Hart George & Samuel, Baddow lane
Maskell James, Springfield lane
Palmer Thomas, Duke st

COAL & TIMBER MERCHNTS.
Candler and Perry, Springfield
Coates George and Co. Springfield
Marriage & Leake, Springfield
Marriage Joseph, jun. Springfield
Marriage Robert, Springfield
Ridley and Son, Springfield
Wells and Perry (and lime burners) Springfield

CONFECTIONERS.
Craske Charles, Moulsham
Dodd William, High st
Drake William, High st
Mison Sarah, Conduit st
Palmer Thomas, Moulsham
Phillips Thomas, High st

COOPERS.
Boultwood Thomas, Great Waltham
Cliff William, Boreham
Crow William, Little Waltham
Hancock Edmund, Duke st
Josling Samuel, Little Waltham
Mays Jane, Moulsham

CORN & FLOUR DEALERS.
Bannister John, King st
Cottee Edward, Conduit st
Deal Abraham, Springfield lane
Finch Ephraim, Conduit st
Finch Henry (& seed) Conduit st
Keys John, Moulsham
Plum William (and rope, twine and sacking dealer) Moulsham
Scott Charles, New st

CURRIERS AND LEATHER SELLERS.
Dean Stephen James, Moulsham
Hockley William, Baddow lane
Johns William & Thomas (& leather dressers) Baddow lane
Sheppee John, High st

DYERS AND SCOURERS.
Cheeseman & Daily, Springfield lane
Tisdall Sidney, High st
Whittle John, Moulsham

FELLMONGERS.
Johns William & Thomas (& woolstaplers, & leather dressers) Baddow lane

FIRE, &c. OFFICE AGENTS.
British, Benjamin Bacon, High st
Clerical and Medical, William Baker, High st
Essex and Suffolk, James Butler, New st
Essex Economic, Edward Copland, Cottage place
Globe, Joseph Arthy, High st
Norwich Union, John Sheppee, High st
Pelican, Ths. Stoneham, jun. Springfield lane
Phœnix, Mrs. Kilham, High st
Protector, Thos. Durrant, Duke st
Royal Exchange, Hen. Guy, High st
Sun, Chalk and Co. High st
West of England, Ephraim Salter, High st
West Middlesex, Geo. Wakeling, High st

FRUITERERS & FISHMONGRS
Cohen Jacob, King st
French Thomas (and fish merchant)
Gardiner James, High st
Hawkes Samuel, Conduit st
Horner Rebecca, Conduit st
Levy Sarah, Baddow lane
Malyon John, Baddow lane
Tylor Hannah, Conduit st
Wicker George, Writtle

FURNITURE BROKERS.
Bull William and Son, Duke st
Clench John, Springfield lane
Cohen Jacob, King st
Myers Wolf, High st

GROCERS & TEA DEALERS.
(See also Tea Dealers.)
Andrews George, High st
Appleby Charles, Moulsham
Ayre Lucy, Springfield
Beardwell Thomas, Boreham
Branscombe Susan, High st
Bryant Benjamin, Springfield
Burton Zachariah, Moulsham
Buttle Richard, Duke st
Chapman Thomas, Boreham
Cooper Robert (& tobacconist) High st
Davey Susannah, King st
Deal Abraham, Springfield lane
Dodd James, Moulsham
Everitt William, High st
Finch Ephraim, Conduit st
Fuller Thomas, Duke st
Grant Thomas James, Boreham
Griggs John, Great Waltham
Hamilton John, Duke st
Hardy James, Broomfield
Hawes George C. Great Waltham
Hawes John, Moulsham
Johnson John, Conduit square
Johnson John, Great Waltham
Joslin Robert, High st
M'Donnell Mary, Boreham
Matthews Ann, Little Waltham
Nokes George, King st
Old William, Duke st
Phillips Philip, Great Waltham
Saltmarsh George, Moulsham
Smith James, Broomfield
Smith William, Great Waltham
Straight William, High st
Sutton Martin, Writtle green
Wallis John, Springfield lane
Watcham Thomas, Broomfield
Whipps William, Springfield
Wolton John Hyen, Conduit square

HABERDASHERS.
Crush Ann, High st
Ingold Mary, Conduit st
Pitson Elizabeth (& baby linen warehouse) Moulsham
Taylor John, Conduit square
Wiffen Miss, High st

HATTERS.
Darby William, High st
Hasler John, Conduit st
Marsh George Finch, High st
Myers Wolf, High st
Nicholson Henry, Conduit square
Pitt Daniel, Duke st
Rayner Henry, High st

HORSE & GIG PROPRIETORS, FOR HIRE.
Clarke George, Springfield
French Thomas, High st
Seaton Henry, Duke st
Taverner James, High st

INNS.
Bell, William Larvy, Conduit st
Black Boy, William Bacon, High st
Lion and Lamb (and posting house and fly proprietor) Henry Seaton, Duke street
Saracen's Head, George Lake, High street
White Hart, Thomas Joseph Bilton, High street

IRON AND BRASS FOUNDER.
Bewley Thomas (& agricultural implement manufacturer) Moulsham

IRON MERCHANTS.
Bewley Thomas, Moulsham
Butler and Avery, New street and Chelmer basin
Greenwood Robert (executors of), High st

IRONMONGERS.
Collis Samuel, High st
Dennis Thomas, High st
Marriage Charles, High st
Milbank Thomas, High st
Page Martin Fountain, High st
Wood George, High st

LINEN DRAPERS.
Acworth Joseph, High st
Cheveley Charles, High st
Clayton Hollis, High st
Count Charles, High st
Houghton John, High st
Johnson John, Great Waltham
Matthews Ann, Little Waltham
Nicholson Henry, High st
Palmer Richard Dudley, High st
Potter and Nicholson, High st
Sharpe Richard, High st
Smith William, Great Waltham
Taylor John, Conduit square
Wackrill and Rust, High st

MALTSTERS.
Buttle Richard, Great Waltham
Church Robert, Baddow lane
Everitt William and Charles, Great Waltham, and at *Pleshey*
Gopsill Thomas, Broomfield
Gray Charles Stanton, Springfield la
Luckin Thomas, Great Waltham
Ratcliff John, Baddow lane
Ridley Wm. and Son, Baddow lane
Samms Thomas, Little Waltham
Smith Samuel, Little Waltham

MILL & WHEELWRIGHTS.
Benton William, Springfield
Brewster John, Great Waltham
Cliff William, Boreham
Cook James, Duke st
Grout Joseph (wheelwright)
Martin Henry, Moulsham
Lucking Isaac, Boreham
Mays Abraham, Moulsham
Mecklenburgh Alfred, Moulsham
Stanaway William, Moulsham
Taylor Charles, Great Waltham

MILLERS.
Adams Samuel, Great Waltham
Cheverton Charles, King st
Child Thomas, Great Waltham
Drake —, Gallywood common
Hicks Henry, Springfield
Marriage Francis, Bishops hall mill
Marriage John, Broomfield
Marriage John, Croxton mill
Marriage Jos. jun. Moulsham mill, Baddow lane
Marriage Thomas M. Barry mills, Springfield
Marriage William & Henry (by steam and water) Broomfield mill
Mead Maria, Boreham
Pitston John, Moulsham
Portway Jno. Sandford mill, Springfield
Ratcliff John, Broomfield
Rust William, Great Waltham
Sewell Henry, Moulsham
Skill Charles, Little Waltham
Wallis Abraham, Springfield

MILLINERS & DRESS MAKRS.
Ablin Sarah, Conduit st
Alten and Woolridge, High st
Andrews Eliza, High st
Canitt Henrietta C. Moulsham
Fitch Sarah and Daughters, High st
Garrood Rebecca, High st
Hasler and Tanner, Springfield lane
Overhill Amelia, Conduit st
Palmer Eliza, High st
Phillips Anna, Baddow lane
Stevens Elizabeth, High st

MUSIC & MUSICAL INSTRUMENT DEALERS.
Bright James, Duke st
Copland Alfred, High st
Shearcroft Josiah, High st

NEWSPAPERS.
Chelmsford Chronicle (Friday) and Essex Herald (Tuesday), Chalk, Meggs & Chalk, publishers and proprietors, High st
Essex Independent (Friday), Alfred Copland, publisher, High st

NURSERY AND SEEDSMEN, AND GARDENERS.
Harris John, Broomfield
Noakes George, King st
Saltmarsh John, Moulsham
Saltmarsh Joseph, Moulsham
Sorrell Thomas, Springfield

PAINTERS, PLUMBERS AND GLAZIERS.
Dannatt Robert, Great Waltham
Farrow John, Bank st
French William, Great Waltham
Garrood Robert E. High st
Kent Henry Benjamin, High st
Sewell Edward, Moulsham
Stock William, Springfield lane
Timson James, Boreham
Whittaker Joseph, Chelmsford
Wiffen William, Broomfield

PATTEN & CLOG MAKERS.
Thorogood John, Moulsham
Wilshere Thomas, High st

PERFUMRS & HAIR CUTTERS
Bacon Benjamin, Duke st
Bond George Thomas, Conduit st
Dowsett James, Springfield
King John, High st
Lew Edwin, Moulsham
Pettit Jarvis, Duke st
Pigg Stephen, Great Waltham
Rand Joseph, Conduit house
Wade James, Conduit st
Wendon Samuel, Moulsham
Wiffen Mary Ann (and fancy repository) High st

PHYSICIANS.
Badeley John, New st
Miller Samuel, High st
Prichard Octavius, Moulsham

POULTERERS.
Dowsett James, Great Waltham
French Thomas, High st
Lewis Thomas, Moulsham
Whitney Henry, Great Waltham

PRINTERS—LETTER-PRESS.
Chalk, Meggs, and Chalk, High st
Copland Alfred, High st
Dutton Thomas D. (and engraver on wood) Conduit st
Shearcroft Josiah, High st

ROPE AND TWINE MAKERS.
Cottee Edward, Conduit st
Godfrey Henry, Moulsham
Horth Thomas, Moulsham

SADDLERS AND HARNESS MAKERS.
Ardley Thomas, Conduit square
Curtis Jno. (collar makr) Lit. Waltham
Durrant John, Conduit square
Isaac John, High st
Lawrence and Rolfe, Duke st
Martin John, Little Waltham
Osbourn James, Conduit st
Sayer James, Moulsham
Speller William, High st

SILVERSMITHS & JEWELLRS
Child Henry and Lawrence, High st
Greenhow Joseph, High st
Kelham Phillis, High st
Myers Wolf (& pawnbroker) High st
Spencer and Son, Duke st

STAY-MAKERS.
Overhill Amelia, Conduit st
Rand Violentia S. Conduit st

STONE MASONS AND STATUARIES.
Dorman and Son, Duke st
Joslin Benjamin (& slater) King st
Moss Thomas (and plasterer and modeller; manufacturer of Hamlin's mastic, and colourer in distemper) Moulsham, and at *Brentwood*
Wray George, Springfield lane

STRAW HAT MAKERS.
Chipperfield Frances, Duke st
Cooper Mary, Moulsham
Fuller Elizabeth, Springfield
Palmer Eliza, High st
Pullen Thomas, High st
Trueman Sarah, Moulsham
Winterflood Agnes, Duke st

SURGEONS.
Bird Henry, High st
Carpenter George, High st
Cremer and Son, Duke st
Gepp George Asser, High st
Gilson John, High st
Hutchinson John, Little Waltham
King Thomas, High st
Morse Edward George, High st

TAILORS.
Bennett Thomas, Conduit st
Church James, King st
Darby Ebenezer, Moulsham
Dennis Joseph, Baddow lane
Fitch Michael, High st
Gosling Richard, Moulsham
Hasler John, Conduit st
Holland John, Little Waltham
Rayner Charles, Duke st
Rayner Henry, High st
Rumball Joseph, Moulsham
Tyler Ebenezer, Conduit st
Wiffen Samuel P. Springfield lane
Winterflood Thomas, Duke st
Wornick James, Moulsham

TANNERS.
Clapham Dixon Henry, Moulsham
Sheppee John, High st

TAVERNS & PUBLIC HOUSES.
Anchor, James Saltmarsh, Moulsham
Angel, Sarah Overall, Broomfield
Bell, Henry Allen, Little Waltham
Bull, Samuel Bailey, Writtle green
Coach & Horses, Eliz. Turner, Duke st
Cock, John Playle, Boreham
Cross Keys, Zachariah Read, Moulsham
Dolphin, Elkanah Bennett, Conduit st
Duke's Head, Wm. Stock, Springfield la
General Monk's Head, James Timson, Boreham
George & Dragon, Chas. Brewster, Duke st
Golden Fleece, Joseph Piper, Duke st
Golden Lion, Augustus Stokes, Duke st
Green Man, Thos. Boultwood, Gt. Waltham
Greyhound, William Brewster, New st
Half Moon, John Webb, High st
King's Arms, Daniel Batt, Broomfield
King's Arms, John Reeve, Moulsham
King's Head, James Taverner, High st
Mason's Arms, Stephn. Goslin, Moulsham
Nelson's Head, Wm. Cobbin, Moulsham
Plough, George King, Duke st
Plough, George Treadway, Springfield
Queen's Head, Ann Puxley, High st
Red Cow, William Bruty, King st
Red Lion, John Stebbing, Boreham
Rising Sun, Sarah Rumball, Moulsham
Rose and Crown, Eleanor King, Great Waltham
Royal Oak, William Samuel Crow, Conduit st
Ship, John French, High st
Silent Woman, Francis Felton, Widford
Six Bells, John Spencer Francis, Great Waltham
Spotted Dog, Mansfield & Gee, Conduit st
Spread Eagle, James Read, Gt. Waltham
Three Cups, Ann Murrell, Springfield
Three Mariners, Thos. Arnold, Moulsham
Three Queens, Mary Wood, Moulsham
Three Tuns, Samuel James, Duke st
Two Brewers, Jas. Lamberth, Springfield
Wheat Sheaf, George Sarel, Duke st
White Hart, Francis Felton, Springfield
White Hart, Robt. Gooch, Great Waltham
White Hart, James Swain, Moulsham
White Horse, Edward Ratcliffe, Widford
Windmill, James Morrey, Great Waltham
Windmill, Susannah Thomas, Moulsham

TEA DEALERS.
Everitt William, High st
Hunter William, Baddow lane
Johnson John, Conduit square
Perkins Charles, Conduit st
Straight William, High st

TIMBER MERCHANTS.
See under Coal & Timber Merchants.

UMBRELLA MAKERS.
Bentley Thomas, High st
Rust William, Moulsham
Wright James, Duke st

UNDERTAKERS.
Acworth Joseph, High st
Bull William and Son, Duke st
Cheveley Charles, High st
Clench John, Springfield lane
Count Charles, High st
Hasler John, Conduit st
Sharpe Richard, High st
Stoneham Thomas, jun. Springfield lane
Straight Samuel, High st
Wackrill and Rust, High st

VETERINARY SURGEONS.
Baker Samuel, High st
Bright Thomas, Duke st
Gooch Samuel, Conduit square

WATCH AND CLOCK MAKERS.
Carter William, Moulsham
Child Henry and Lawrence, High st
Cowling Joseph, Moulsham

WATCH & CLOCK MAKERS —*Continued.*
Greenhow Joseph, High st
Huffmyer Martin, Conduit st
Reed George, Moulsham
Spencer and Son, Duke st

WHITESMITHS.
Bewley Thomas (and agricultural implement maker) Moulsham
Mace Robert, Duke st
Mason & Son (& spring makers) Baddow lane
Merritt Thomas, High st
Newman Benjamin (and edge-tool manufacturer) Great Waltham
Praill Joseph, Moulsham
Pudney Everard, Broomfield
Rogers John, Moulsham
Taylor William, King st
Thompson William, Moulsham

WINE & SPIRIT MERCHANTS
Butler James, New st
Carter Henry Harridge, Springfield lane
Haycock George, High st
Porter and Butler, Writtle
Wells aud Perry, Duke st

Miscellaneous.
Bartlett Robert, clerk to the Chelmsford and Blackwater Navigation Co. King st
Baths (cold, warm, &c.) High st—Wm. Baker, proprietor
Belsham Abraham, registrar of births and deaths, agent to the National Provident Institution, and accountant to the Board of Guardians, Moulsham
Biddell Henry Thomas, lithographic printer and agent to the Essex Standard
Broggi Gorlando, optician, &c. Moulsham
Chapman William, parish clerk, Boreham
Convict Gaol, Springfield—Thomas C. Neale, governor
Cooper Thomas, horse dealer, Moulsham
County Gaol, Moulsham—Thomas C. Neale, governor
County Hall, High st
Day James, lath render, Moulsham
Dispensary, Church yard—Dr. Badeley, physician; Cremer and Son, surgeons; William Newman, secretary
Excise Office, White Hart Inn, Moulsham—John Badcock (Colchester) collector; James Honey, supervisor
Felton John, sheriff's officer, Chelmsford
French Mrs. Sarah, coach proprietor, Baddow lane
Gas Works, Springfield—William Howard, clerk; Jabez Church, superintendnt
Godfrey Henry, rope and twine manufacturer, Moulsham
Green Henry, cutler, Conduit st
Hayward Geo. whiting manufactr. Springfield
Howard William, parish clerk, Duke st
Johns William, glover & parchment manufacturer, High st
Kinch Thomas, carrier, Coval terrace
Leech James H. gunsmith, Conduit st
Leslie James, assistant overseer, High st
Reader Joseph, chimney sweeper, King st
Salter Ephraim, hardwareman and rag merchant, High st
Sharpington William, parish clerk, Springfield
Spice William, eating house, Conduit st
Stamp Office, New st—Thomas Frost Gepp, distributer
Stoneham and Baker, tallow chandlers, High st
Stoneham Thomas, jun. inspector of weights and measures, Springfield lane
Stubbings Thos. parish clerk, Broomfield
Taverner Henry James, soda water and ginger beer manufacturer, High st
Tyrrell Richard, parish clerk, Gt. Waltham
Union Poorhouse, Moulsham—Robert H. Cotter, governor
Walker James, carrier, King st
Wiffen Miss, dealer in British wines, High street
Wilson Jas. surveyor of roads, Broomfield

COACHES.

To LONDON, the *Royal Mail* (from Norwich), calls at the Black Boy, every morning at half-past three, and the *Telegraph* (from Yarmouth), at a quarter past four—a *Coach* (from Maldon), calls at the Ship, every morning at half-past seven & another at eight—the *Sovereign* (from Braintree), calls at the Queen's Head, every morning at half-past eight —a *Coach* (from Coggeshall), calls at the Black Boy, every morning (Sunday excepted) at nine, and the *Wellington* (from Colchester), calls at the same Inn and the Ship, every forenoon at half-past eleven.

To LONDON, the *Bury* (from Bury St. Edmunds), calls at the Ship, and a *Coach* (from Sudbury), calls at the Black Boy, both every afternoon (Sunday excepted) at a quarter before one—the *Old Blue* (from Ipswich), calls at the same Inn at half-past one; the *Shannon* at three, and a *Coach* (from Chelmsford), calls at the Ship, at the same hour—the *Defiance* (from Colchester), calls at the Ship and the Black Boy Inns, every afternoon (Sunday excepted) at four, and the *Phenomenon* (from Norwich), calls at the latter Inn, at a quarter past four, and the *Star* (from Yarmouth), calls at the Ship, and Duke's Head, at a quarter before five.

To LONDON, the *Pilot*, from the Queen's Head, every Friday afternoon at four—a *Coach* (from Maldon), calls at the Windmill, every Monday, Wednesday & Friday morning at ten, and the *Times* (from Norwich), calls at the Queen's Head, in the afternoon of the same days at four.

The following Coaches are all from London, unless otherwise expressed.

To BRAINTREE, the *Sovereign*, calls at the Queen's Head, every afternoon (Monday excepted) at half-past six, and on Monday at half-past seven.

To BURY ST. EDMUNDS, the *Bury*, calls at the Ship, every afternoon (Sunday excepted) at a quarter before one.

To COGGESHALL, a *Coach*, calls at the Black Boy, every evening (Sunday excepted) at six.

To COLCHESTER, the *Shannon*, calls at the Black Boy, every forenoon at eleven; the *Wellington*, at half-past twelve; the *Old Blue*, every afternoon at three, and the *Defiance*, calls at the same Inn, & the *Ship*, every evening at 6.

To IPSWICH, the *Shannon*, calls at the Black Boy, every forenoon at eleven, & the *Old Blue*, every afternoon (Sunday excepted) at three.

To MALDON, a *Coach*, from the Queen's Head, every evening at half-past seven, and the *Old Maldon*, calls at the Windmill, every Tuesday, Thursday and Saturday afternoon at half-past three.

To NORWICH, the *Royal Mail*, calls at the Black Boy, every night at eleven; the *Phenomenon*, every morning at ten, and the *Times*, from the Queen's Head, every Tuesday, Thursday and Saturday morning at half-past nine.

To SAXMUNDHAM, the *Shannon*, from the Queen's Head, every forenoon (Sunday excepted) at eleven.

To SUDBURY, a *Coach*, calls at the Black Boy, every afternoon (Sunday ex.) at four.

To YARMOUTH, the *Star*, calls at the Ship & Duke's Head Inns, every morning at a quarter before ten, & the *Telegraph*, calls at the Black Boy, every night at a quarter past ten.

CARRIERS.

To LONDON, Sykes and Cooke, from the King's Head, daily; — Smith, every Monday, Wednesday and Friday— — Kinch, from Coval terrace, every Monday and Wednesday—Stanbury, Porch and Co. and — Dale and — Byford, every Tuesday and Friday and — Worlow, from the Queen's Head, same days.

To LONDON, — Johns, from Baddow lane; W. & H. Marriage, from Broomfield; — Salter, from High st; — Walker, from Duke st, and — Dixon and — Bass, every Monday and Thursday— — Jarvis and — Smith, from the King's Head, every Monday and Friday—and — Page, from the Duke's Head, every Wednesday and Friday.

To LONDON, — Samms & — Lowe, from the Queen's Head, and Broome and Co.; — Fakes, — Ablitt, — Howard, — Reeve, — Rutlle, and — Ruggles, all from the King's Head, every Friday.

To BEATFIELD, — Lowe, from the King's Head, daily.

To BENFLEET (North and South), — Wood, from the Cross Keys, every Fri.

To BILLERICAY, — Joslin, from the Cross Keys and — Poynter, from the King's Head, every Friday.

To BRAINTREE, — Hodges, from the King's Head and — Jarvis, every Wednesday and Friday.

To BURY, Stanbury and Porch, & Porch and Co.'s *Waggons*, from the Duke's Head and King's Head, every Thursday and Sunday morning.

To CAVENDISH, — Byford, from the King's Head, every Thursday & Sunday.

To CHIPPENHILL, — Page & — Moore, from the King's Head, every Thursday and Sunday.

To CHIPPING ONGAR, — Wood, from the King's Head, daily.

To COGGESHALL, — Rutlles, from the King's Head, every Wednesday & Sun.

To COLCHESTER and HARWICH, — Higgleton, from the Queen's Head, and — Moore, from the King's Head, every Tuesday and Friday.

To DEBENHAM, Broom & Winter, from the King's Head, every Thurs. & Sun.

To EYE, — Smith's *Waggons*, from the King's Head, every Wednesday & Sun.

To GREAT WALTHAM, LITTLE WALTHAM, &c. — Dowsett, from the Post office, every morning (Monday excepted) at seven.

To HADLEIGH, Stanley and Porch, — Smith, and Bennell, Deacon and Co. from the Duke's Head & King's Head, every Sunday, Wednesday, Thurs. & Fri.

To HALESWORTH, Smith's *Waggons*, from the King's Head, every Wednesday and Sunday.

To HALSTEAD, — Howard, every Thursday and Sunday.

To NORWICH, Smith's *Waggons*, from the Duke's Head, every Sun. Wed. and Friday morning—Bennell, Deacon and Co.'s *Waggons*; & Dale's *Waggons*, every Sunday and Thursday morning, and Page's, every Friday and Sunday, and Stanbury and Porch's *Waggons*, every Wednesday, Thursday, Friday and Saturday; all from the Duke's Head.

To STEBBING, — Lowe, from the King's Head, every Wednesday and Sunday.

To STOWMARKET and IPSWICH, by the carriers to *Norwich*.

To WITHAM, — Higgleton, from the Queen's Head, every Thursday & Friday, & — Moore, from the King's Head, every Tuesday & Friday. Also by the carriers to *Norwich*.

To YARMOUTH, Smith's *Waggons*, from the Duke's Head & King's Head, every Wednesday, Friday & Sunday morning —Stanbury & Porch, every Wed. Thurs. Fri. and Sat. — Page, every Fri. & Sun. and Bennell & Co.'s, and — Page, every Thursday and Sunday.

CONVEYANCE BY WATER.

To MALDON, *Lighters* (of thirty tons burden), on the river Chelmer, daily.

CHIGWELL,

CHIGWELL ROW, LAMBOURNE WITH ABRIDGE AND NEIGHBOURHOODS.

CHIGWELL is a village and parish in the hundred of Ongar, 10 miles from London. It is a beautiful rural little place, ornamented by several elegant mansions and tasteful seats; amongst the latter, Woolston Hall, the admired residence of Robert Bodle, Esq., is conspicuous. The places of worship are the parish church, a small and ancient edifice, dedicated to St. Mary, and a chapel for independents. The living of Chigwell is a vicarage, in the gift of the prebendary of St. Pancras. The free grammar school here was founded in 1629 by Samuel Harsnett, archbishop of Canterbury—William Penn, founder of the colony of Pennsylvania, received his education in this school. An annual fair is held on the 30th of September, for hiring servants. The population of the parish (including Chigwell Row), by the last census, amounted to 1,815.

CHIGWELL ROW is about one mile from the above mentioned village, and is chiefly remarkable for its beautiful woodland scenery and the respectability of its neighbourhood. There is a neat methodist chapel here.

ABRIDGE is a village in the parish of Lambourne, about two miles and a half from Chigwell and five from Epping. Edward Lockwood Perceval, Esq. is lord of the manor of Lambourne. The church is dedicated to St. Mary and All Saints: the living is a rectory, in the presentation of Corpus Christi college, Cambridge; the Rev. Robert Sutteliffe is the present incumbent. The principal charity is an endowed school in Stapleford Abbot parish, which includes in its benefits twenty children of this parish. Spencer, a *warlike* bishop of Norwich, who put down Ket's rebellion, resided in Lambourne parish; a square entrenchment, denominated 'the bishop's moat,' which encompassed his residence, still remains. The parish of Lambourne (with which the population of Abridge is returned) contained, in 1831, 778 inhabitants.

POST, CHIGWELL, *Receiving-House* at John James Hillman's.—Letters from LONDON arrive every forenoon at eleven and afternoon at five, and are despatched every morning at eight and afternoon at half-past five.

POST, CHIGWELL ROW, *Receiving-House* at William Clarke's.—Letters from LONDON arrive (by foot post from WOODFORD) every afternoon at one and evening at seven, and are despatched every morning at eight.

POST, ABRIDGE, *Receiving-House* at William Hedge's.—Letters from LONDON arrive (by mail cart) every morning at half-past seven, and are despatched every evening at six.

*** *The names without address are in* CHIGWELL; C. R. *means* CHIGWELL ROW.

GENTRY AND CLERGY.

Aldersey Richard Baker, esq. Whitehall, Chigwell Row
Aspinall Mr. Richard, Chigwell Row
Bearblock Mr. Walter, Chigwell Row
Bellin Mr. John, Chigwell Row
Bodle Robert, esq. Woolston hall
Bridger Mrs. Jane, Chigwell
Bridgman Mr. John, Chigwell
Burford Rev. William John, Chigwell
Clarke Mr. Frances, Chigwell Row
Copeland Mrs. Mary Ann, Chigwell
Dinsey Mr. John, Chigwell
Farmer Rev. Samuel, Turners
Gonpertz Rev. Richard, Abridge
Harrison Mr. Wm. Thomas, Chigwell
Hutson John, esq. Chigwell Row
Jeffries Mr. John, Chigwell
Jones Mr. John, Abridge
Lidle Mrs. —, Chigwell
Lodge Rev. Burton, Chigwell
Maitland Whitaker, esq. Chigwell
Marrell Mr. John, Chigwell Row
Mills Mr. James, Chigwell
Munn Mrs. Richard, Chigwell
Owen Henry, esq. Abridge
Percival Edward Lockwood, esq. Bishop's hall
Questell Mrs. Ann, Grange hill
Sayes Rev. Edward Lane, Chigwell
Schneider Mrs. Caroline, Chigwell
Sutteliffe Rev. Robert, Rectory, Lambourne
Tukers Mrs. Anne, Chigwell
Waddell Mr. James, Chigwell Row
Walford Joseph Green, esq. Chigwell green

ACADEMIES & SCHOOLS.

Burford Rev. Wm. John, D.D. (brdng)
FREE GRAMMAR SCHOOL, William Adams, master
Giles Sarah (preparatory) Abridge
Howell & Lake (ladies' boarding)
PAROCHIAL DISTRICT SCHOOL (girls) Chigwell Row--Jane Howe, mistrss

PROFESSIONAL PERSONS.

Rowe George Robert, physician
Savill Jonathan, architect & surveyor
Smith Henry, surgeon

INNS & PUBLIC HOUSES.

Bald Hind, Levi Grout, Grange hill
Blue Boar, William Clark, Abridge
King's Head Inn (& posting, coach proprietor & livery stables) James Oliver, Chigwell
May Pole, Mary Savill, Chigwell Row
White Hart, Chas. Trapps, Abridge

SHOPKEEPERS, TRADERS, &c.

Adlam & Son, tailors & draprs, Abridge
Baldwin Joseph, carrier
Bridgman John, fire office agent
Brown Francis, bookseller, Abridge
Bryant Richd. boot, &c. makr, Abridge
Carter Robert, parish clerk, Abridge
Cavill James, wheelwright, Abridge
Champness Thomas, auctioneer, builder and undertaker, Abridge
Chipperfield William, carrier
Clarke John, grocer, draper & tallow chandler
Clarke William, grocer and corn chandler, Chigwell Row
Crawley James, wheelwright, C. R.
Dawkins Jas. wheelwright, Grange hl
Dawkins John, tailor
Edwards George, baker
Giffin Caroline, milliner
Halls Thomas, miller and baker
Hauchett William, carrier, Abridge
Hedges Wm. grocer & draper, Abridge
Higgs Chs. carpenter & buildr, Abridge
Hillman John James, grocer & draper
Hills Thos. boot & shoe maker, C. R.
Hunter Jacob, boot & shoe maker
Isbell Jas. nursery & seedsman, C. R.
Jeffery Richard, baker and confectioner, Abridge
Jones John, carpenter, Abridge
Kirby Samuel, butcher
Knight John, shopkeeper, C. R.
Mead John, grocer, draper & clothier, Abridge
Noble Jeremiah, smith and farrier, Abridge
Noble Samnel, smith and farrier
Offin Abraham, maltster, Abridge
Oliver James Brill, corn dealer and retail brewer, Abridge
Oliver Sarah, dress maker, Abridge
Parker Elizabeth, milliner, Abridge
Partridge Daniel, carpenter, builder and undertaker, Chigwell Row
Rowe Jno. boot & shoe maker, C. R.
Savill Jonathan, builder
Savill Joseph, carpenter, builder and undertaker
Skittlethorpe John, plumber, painter and glazier, Abridge
Skeggs William, tailor, Chigwell Row
Spurge William, butcher, Abridge
Willcock William, butcher
Willson William, saddler & harness maker, Abridge
Wright Lydia, grocer and draper, Grange hill
Wright Samuel Edward, carrier
Wright Thomas, corn chandler
Young Thos. smith & farrier, Abridge

COACHES.

To LONDON, the *Mazeppa*, from the King's Head, Chigwell, and the Maypole, Chigwell Row, every morning (Sunday excepted) at eight, and on Sunday at six morning and six evening—and a *Coach* (from Chipping Ongar), calls alternately at the Blue Boar and White Hart, Abridge, every morng. at 9.

To CHIPPING ONGAR, a *Coach* (from London), calls alternately at the Blue Boar and White Hart, Abridge, every afternoon at half-past three.

CARRIERS,

FROM CHIGWELL.

To LONDON, Samuel Edward Wright, every Monday, Wednesday and Friday, and William Chipperfield and Joseph Baldwin, every Tues. Thurs. & Sat.

CHIPPING ONGAR AND NEIGHBOURHOOD.

CHIPPING ONGAR is a small market town and parish in the hundred of Ongar—21 miles N. E. from London, 10 S. W. from Chelmsford, and 7 E. from Epping; situated on an eminence on the bank of the river Roden. The appellation 'Chipping,' or *Cheping*, was conferred on it from its having formerly possessed a market of considerable celebrity, which, though not now so well attended, has of late years been reviving, and the old market-house was in consequence some time since repaired. In this place are the remains of an ancient castle; several Roman and Saxon antiquities have been found here on various occasions; extensive works may be traced round the town, and some Roman bricks have been used in the building of the church: from these circumstances it is inferred that it was a Roman station, and probably a strong hold of the Saxons before their subjugation by the Normans. The trade of the place is but inconsiderable, and there is no branch of manufactures. The magistrates hold a petty sessions here on the market day. The places of worship are the parish church and a chapel for independents. The church, dedicated to St. Martin, is a small neat structure; the benefice is a rectory, in the patronage of the Bennett family, and incumbency of the Rev. J. Tweed. The free school here was founded in 1678, pursuant to the will of Mr. Joseph King, a native of this town: about £70. per annum, the revenue of this charity, is applied to the educating and apprenticing a limited number of poor boys, teaching poor girls to read, and some other charitable purposes. The market is held on Saturday, and a fair on the 12th of October. The parish contained, in 1831, 798 inhabitants.

POST OFFICE, Hannah Maria Scruby, *Post Mistress*.—Letters from all parts arrive every morning at eight, and are despatched every evening at six.

GENTRY AND CLERGY.

Coe William, esq. Castle farm
Crewe —, esq. Shelley house
Cure Capel, esq. Blake hall
Dalby William, esq. Kelvedon commn
Dowdeswell Rev. Edw. Stanford rivers
Earle Rev. Henry, High Ongar
Edridge Rev. Charles, Marden ash
Evans William, esq. White house
Fothergill Francis, esq. Dodbrook
Gibson Rev. Edward, Fyfield
Gibson Rev. Robert, Fyfield
Gibson Mr. William (attorney) Chipping Ongar
Hurlock Brook B. esq. Chipping Ongar
Kesterman Capt. —, Stondon place
Linzee Rev. Edward, Kelvedon hall
Oldham Rev. John, Stondon
Ord Rev. Charles, Greenstead hall
Serle Rev. A. Kelvedon rectory
Stane Rev. Jno. Bramston, Forrest hall
Taylor Isaac, esq. Stanford rivers
Till Pearson, esq. Chipping Ongar
Tomlinson James, esq. Shelley hall
Tweed Rev. Jas. A.M. Chipping Ongar
Wilson Mrs. —, Chipping Ongar

ACADEMIES AND SCHOOLS.

Andrews John, Marden ash
Gidley Mary Ann & Margaret
Mott Charles
Parker John

BAKERS.

Cowee John (and confectioner)
Edwards Thomas
Starkey Henry

BOOT AND SHOE MAKERS.

Gann Rebecca
Giffin George
Hancock William
Hurrell Benjamin
Wood John

BUTCHERS.

Carter Elias
Cooper John
Cowee Thomas
Perry Edmund

CARPENTERS.

Noble Richard (and builder)
Phillpotts Daniel

CORN CHANDLERS.

Fordham John Porter
Loud Jas Jenkin (& coal merchant)

GREENGROCERS.

Dobbs Thomas
Playl Jeremiah

GROCERS & TEA DEALERS.

(See also Shopkeepers, &c.)

Boyer Francis
Hopkins James
Jackson Alexander

HAIR DRESSERS.

Kemp Thomas
Sturdy Henry

INNS & PUBLIC HOUSES.

Anchor, Francis Brown
Bull Inn (and excise office) Thomas Rowlinson
Cock, Robert Thomas
Crown Inn, Francis Leete (& licensed horse and chaise proprietor)
King's Head, Elizabeth Rawlings
Lion Inn, Henry Sturdy
Two Brewers, Isaac Ward
White Horse, John Snow

LINEN DRAPERS.

Boyer William (and wine and spirit merchant)
Haslam Charles
Watts James (and stationer)

MILLINERS AND DRESS MAKERS.

Taylor Martha
Wood and Sweetingbourg (and stay makers)

PLUMBERS AND GLAZIERS.

Collins Nathaniel
Nottage James

SADDLERS.

Parker William (& harness maker)
Silcock Jonathan

SHOPKEEPERS.

Cooper Richard
Sammes Edward (and builder)

SURGEONS.

Holt Astley
Peake John
Potter Frank and John

TAILORS.

Cowee Thomas
Darby William
Playl Jeremiah, jun.

WATCH & CLOCK MAKERS.

Freedman Mark
Turner John

WHEELWRIGHTS.

Barltrop Ammon (and smith)
Cook Nathaniel

Miscellaneous.

Blewitt Charles, miller, High Ongar
Bright Charles, veterinary surgeon
Carter John Alexander, supervisor
Clements Stephen, carrier
EXCISE OFFICE, Bull Inn
GAS WORKS, Charles Gidley, superintendent
Haslam James, auctioneer & appraiser
Mitchell Mary Ann, leather cutter
Moss Edward, bricklayer
Mott Charles, bookseller
Oliver Richard, farrier
Parker S. & C. toy & fancy repository
Rand William, brick maker
Reynolds Thomas, salesman
Saltmarsh John, blacksmith
SAVING'S BANK, open every Saturday from 1 till 2—John Gidley, clerk
Spurgin Joseph C. chymist, druggist and dentist
Wood Mary Ann and Hannah, straw hat makers
Wright John, furnishing ironmonger

COACH.

To LONDON, a *Coach*, from the Lion, every morning (Sunday excepted) at 8.

CARRIERS.

To LONDON, Jas. Jenkin Loud's *Vans*, every Monday and Thursday evening, to the Kent & Essex yard, Whitechapel, and Stephen Clement's *Waggons*, every Tues. & Fri. to the Three Nuns, Aldgate.

COGGESHALL AND NEIGHBOURHOOD.

COGGESHALL, or GREAT COGGESHALL, is a market town and parish in the Witham division of the hundred of Lexden—about 47 miles N. E. of London, by the road through Braintree and 44 through Witham, 18 N. E. of Chelmsford, and 13 S. W. of Nayland, Suffolk. It stands partly upon the low ground on the north side of the Blackwater, and partly upon the slope of an agreeable hill which rises upon the same side. Morant asserts that the town owes its existence to an abbey founded at Little Coggeshall; but other antiquaries ascribe its origin to the Romans, and contend that it is the *Canonium* of Antonius: the fact of Roman coins and other relics of that nation having been found in the neighbourhood is adduced in support of the latter opinion; and though these antiques cannot determine the designation of the place, yet they confirm the supposition of its having been a Roman station. Cole, a Saxon, was proprietor of the manor in the reign of Edward the Confessor; and it subsequently devolved to King Stephen, who founded an abbey here for Cistertian monks. The remains of a bridge of three arches, erected by the same monarch, are still to be seen at a short distance from the ruins of the abbey. Great Coggeshall is in the dutchy of Lancaster; the coroner is appointed by letters patent, and is entitled to exclusive jurisdiction: the dutchy extends to, and includes, in the county of Essex, Great and Little Coggeshall, Braintree, Bocking and about two hundred other places. Great Coggeshall had in former ages a guild, called 'the fullers' and new drapers' guild;' the guild-hall stood on what is now termed the Market-hill. The woollen and clothing trade, and particularly the production of a superior kind of baize, designated 'Coggeshall whites,' formerly gave celebrity to this town: these branches are not now attended to; they have been superseded by the manufacture of silk, which for many years has been carried on to a considerable extent, and at present employs numerous hands. Amongst several good inns, the 'White Hart' is distinguished as an excellent commercial house. The lord of the manor, Peter Du Cane, Esq. of Braxted Lodge, holds a court baron annually on Whit-Monday.

Coggeshall formerly comprised the parishes of Great and Little Coggeshall, now consolidated—the latter is at this time only a hamlet to the former. The parish church, dedicated to St. Peter, is a spacious handsome structure, with a large square tower; the benefice is a vicarage, in the patronage of the lord of the manor and incumbency of the Rev. Henry Eley, M. A. There is a chapel each for independents, baptists, Wesleyan methodists and the society of friends. Several munificent bequests benefit the poor of the parish; they are derived from estates, the principal of which are in Suffolk, and produce upwards of £360. a year; and there are other minor charities. Some years since a philosophical society was established here, by several individuals of superior talent; it continues to maintain a high character, and the monthly lecture meetings are respectably attended. This neighbourhood is embellished by many elegant seats; the country is highly cultivated, but from its flatness, and the absence of wood, the views are not of the most attractive order. The market, abundantly supplied with corn, &c. is held on Thursday; and there is an annual fair, for cattle and toys, on Whit-Tuesday. The parish of Great Coggeshall contained, in 1831, 3,227 inhabitants; at that census LITTLE COGGESHALL was returned as a separate parish, with a population of 455.

POST OFFICE, Samuel Sprague, *Post Master*.—Letters from all parts arrive every morning at seven in summer and at eight in winter, and are despatched every morning at nine.

GENTRY AND CLERGY.

Andrews Mrs. Mary, Church st
Archer Mr. John, Upr. Stoneham st
Baker Mrs. —, East st
Banks Mr. William, Bridge st
Barrett Mrs. —, Little Coggeshall
Batt Thomas, the Gravel
Corder Mrs. James, Church st
Corder Miss Jane, the Gravel
Corder Mr. Joseph, Market hill
Eley Rev. Henry, Vicarage
Everett Mrs. —, Church st
Godfrey Mrs Maria Bradshaw, Church st
Godfrey the Misses, Church st
Goodson Mr. William, Mount house
Hall John, esq. Crouch house
Hanbury Henry, esq. Holfield grange
Hanbury Osgood, esq. Holfield grange
Hunt Jno. Newton, esq. Stoneham st
Mayhew John, esq. Church st
Mayhew William, esq. East st
Mayhew Wm. jun. esq. the Cottage
Newman Charles, esq. Scripps, Little Coggeshall
Pattison Mrs. Eliz. Church st
Pattison Fisher Unwin, esq. Market end
Pazey Mrs. —, Little Coggeshall
Peed Anthony, esq. Little Coggeshall
Sadler Thomas, esq. Stoneham st
Skingley Chas. Jos. esq. Colchester rd
Skingley Mrs. —, Colchester road
Sprague Miss —, East st
Stevens Mrs. —, Church st
Swinborne the Misses, East st
Unwin Branston, esq. Stoneham st
Unwin Fisher, esq. Church st
Unwin Stephen, esq. East st
Unwin Stephen, jun. esq. East st
White Mrs. —, West st
White Richard Meredith, esq. High fields

ACADEMIES AND SCHOOLS.

Not otherwise described are Day Schools.

Cook Emma, Stoneham st
Corder Elizabeth, Bridge st
Crosby Sarah, Vain lane
Evans Theophilus, Church st
FREE GRAMMAR SCHOOL, Market hill—Henry Emery, master
Heward Miss (boarding) East st
Hume Ann, Stoneham st
LANCASTERIAN SCHOOL, Ephraim Evans, master
Moss Thomas, Church st
NATIONAL SCHOOL, East st—Henry Emery, jun. master
Seaman Misses (boarding & day) the Gravel

ATTORNEYS.

Mayhew John (and coroner for the dutchy of Lancaster, and secretary to the Great Coggeshall gas company) Church st
Sadler and Peed, Stoneham st
Waylen Samuel, Church st

AUCTIONEERS & APPRAISRS

Seaborn Robert, Church st
Surridge Joseph Smith, East st

BAKERS.

Bonner Isaac, Church st
Clark Sarah, Church st
Dawes William, Church st
Denney Alfred, the Gravel
Edwards James, Little Coggeshall
Lawrence James, Church st
Mount John, Church st
Prior Nehemiah, Church st
Seaborn Robert, Church st
Simmons Jeremiah, Stoneham st
Warren John, the Gravel

BANKERS.

Sparrow, Walford & Co. (branch of Braintree bank) East st—(draw on Barclay, Bevan and Co. London)

BLACKSMITHS.

Anthony William, East st
Baxter Thomas, Bridge st
Dalton Michael, Stoneham st
Love William, East st

BOOKSELLERS & STATIONRS

Doubleday Henry & Eliz. Market end
Gardner Matthias, Church st

BOOT AND SHOE MAKERS.

Alger John, the Gravel
Anthony Isaac, Church st
Beckwith William, East st
Birkin John, East st
Cardinal Christopher, Little Coggeshall
Emery Jubal, East st
Evans Robert, Market end
Fairs Samuel, Church st
Johnson Edward, Church st
Johnson James, Stoneham st
Smee Edmund, Church st
Till William, Market end
Willsher Habakkuk, Church st

BREWERS.

Beard Geo. Isaac & Wm. Church st
Gardner William, Little Coggeshall
Skingley Samuel, Little Coggeshall
Unwin Fisher & Branston, Stonehm st

BRICK MAKERS.

Allen Lewis, West st
Denney Joseph, East st

BRICKLAYERS.

Denney Joseph, East st
Turner William, Stoneham st

BUTCHERS.

Browning Richard, East st
Clark James, Church st
Goodey William, East st
Hills Francis, Church st
Hills Joseph, Little Coggeshall
Kirkham John, Church st

CABINET MAKERS AND FURNITURE BROKERS.

Bridge Susannah (and upholsterer) Market hill
Leaper Daniel (and upholsterer and paper stainer) East st
Rout William, East st

CARPENTERS.

Beard Geo. Isaac & Wm. Church st
Buag James, West st
Ely John, Stoneham st
Gardner Matthias, Church st
Leaper Daniel, East st
Spurgin Michael, East st

CHINA, GLASS, &c. DEALERS.

Doubleday William, Market end
Knight John, Church st

CHYMISTS & DRUGGISTS.

Denney William (& dealer in British wines) Church st
Pridgeon William, Market end

CLOTHES DEALERS.

Alsop Matthew, East st
Seamans Joshua George (and hatter) Church st
Smee Edmund, Church st

COAL DEALERS.

Johnson Jas. (& cowkeeper) Stoneham st
Newman Chas. (& ironfounder) Litt. Coggeshall
Unwin Stephen Fisher & Stephen (& woolstaplers & seed mrchts) East st

CONFECTIONERS.

Lawrence James, Church st
Woodward Lucy (& toy dealr) Church st

COOPERS.

Brasier Samuel, Market end
Wheeler Thomas, the Gravel

CORN FACTORS & DEALERS.

Appleford William, West st
Fairhead Abraham, West st
Johnson Edward, West st
Lufkin John, Stoneham st
Seaborn Robert, Church st
Skingley Samuel, Little Coggeshall

CURRIERS.

Sach Samuel, Bridge st
Swinburn William & Thos. East st

FIRE, &c. OFFICE AGENTS.

ALLIANCE, Wm. Dawes, Church st
ESSEX and SUFFOLK, Anthony Peed, Stoneham st
ESSEX ECONOMIC, Henry Cordran, East st
NORWICH UNION, Frederick Causton, Market end
ROYAL EXCHANGE, John Kirkham, Church st
SUFFOLK and GENERAL COUNTRY, William Doubleday, Market end

FISHMONGERS.

Harris Samuel, Stoneham st
Simmons James, Church st

GARDENERS & SEEDSMEN.

Bright Edward, Church st
Evans Thomas, Market hill
Hills Harry, Church st
King John, West st
King William, West st
Polley Samuel, West st
Raven Nathaniel, Church st
Redgrift John, West st
Ruffle Mary, Church st
Smith Charles, Church st
Wood William, West st

GREENGROCERS.

Anthony Isaac, Church st
Leaper Maria, East st
Plastow William, East st
Pudsey Henry, West st

GROCERS AND TEA DEALERS

Bell Rd. (& cheesemongr) Stonehm st
Dawes William, Church st
Denney Joseph, East st
Doubleday William, Market end
Franklin John, Market end
Herbert John & William, Church st
Moore and Son, Church st
Potter William, Stoneham st
Prior Nehemiah, Church st
Redgrift John, West st

INNS.

Chapel (commercial & excise office) George William Terry, Market hill
Fleece, John Richmond, West st

INNS—*Continued.*
King's Arms, William Gardner, Little Coggeshall
White Hart and Commercial Inn, William Lamprell, Market end

IRONMONGERS.
Beard Joseph, Church st
Willet Thomas (& brazier) East st

LACE MANUFACTURER.
Banks John Byng (and tambour worker) Bridge street, and Lawrence lane, Cheapside, *London*

LINEN & WOOLLEN DRAPRS.
Denney Joseph, East st
Doubleday William, Market end
Kettle Thos. (& hatter) Market hill
Moore and Son, Church st
White Sophia Elizabeth (and haberdasher) East street

MALTSTERS.
Beard George Isaac & Wm. Church st
Evans Thomas (and hop merchant) the Gravel
Gardner William, West st
Newman Charles, Bridge st
Skingley Samuel, Little Coggeshall
Unwin Fisher and Branston, Stoneham st and Little Coggeshall

MILLERS.
Appleford William, jun. the Gravel and at *Feering*
Barnard Abraham, Little Coggeshall
Lewsey James, Stoneham st

MILLINERS & DRESS MAKRS.
Cooper Susannah, Church st
Deadman Ann, Church st
Johnson Sarah and Myra (and lace workers) Market hill
White Sophia Elizabeth, East st

PERFUMERS & HAIR CUTTRS.
Kent Elijah, East st
Ready Thomas, Church st
Rowland Daniel, Church st
Rowland Samuel, the Gravel
Spurge William, Church st

PLUMBERS, PAINTERS AND GLAZIERS.
Brasier Abigail, West st
Causton Robert, Market end
Hersom Samuel, East st

SADDLERS.
Durrant Samuel, Market hill
Evans Sarah, East st
Kirkham William, Bridge st

SILK MANUFACTURERS AND THROWSTERS.
Beckwith William, Back lane
Hall John, Crouch factory, and Abby mills, Little Coggeshall
Westmacott, Goodson & Co. Gravel factory

STRAW HAT MAKERS.
Alger Phœbe, the Gravel
Cooper Susannah, Church st
Lawrence Fredk. Upper Stoneham st
Leaper Lucy, Stoneham st
Poulton Louisa, East st
Rout Maria, East st

SURGEONS.
Giles Harold, Market hill
Nott & Reilly, the Gravel house
Strowger Samuel Bradley, Church st

TAILORS AND DRAPERS.
Choate John, Market hill
Clemance Sarah (& hatter) East st
Cox Samuel, Church st
Denney Benjamin, Church st
Herbert John & William, Church st
Sprague Alfred, Bridge st
Whisley John, the Gravel

TANNERS.
Allen Lewis, West st
Swinborne William and Thomas, East st and at *Witham*

TAVERNS & PUBLIC HOUSES.
Bird in Hand, Ebenezer Bennet, East st
Black Boy, Ann Wallis, Church st
Black Horse, Samuel Crabb, Stoneham st
Bull, William Francis, Church st
Greyhound, Adam Eavery, Church st
Hare & Hounds, Jno. Turner, Lit. Coggeshll
Red Lion, John Cleveland, Market hill
Swan, Abraham Tyler, East st [end
White Hart Tap, Elijah Clarke, Market
Wool Pack, Sarah Buck, Church st

WATCH & CLOCK MAKERS.
Ambrose William, East st
Knight John, Church st
Wire Samson, Market hill

WHEELWRIGHTS.
Leaper Ephraim & Steph. the Gravel
Snell Shadrach, Little Coggeshall
Wheeler Thomas, the Gravel

WOOLSTAPLERS.
Unwin Stephen Fisher and Stephen (& coal & seed merchants) East st

Miscellaneous.
Bate William, surveyor and architect, Stoneham street
Cox John, parish clerk, Church st
Crabb Samuel, porkman, Stoneham st
EXCISE OFFICE, Bradford st—Samuel Bowyer, supervisor
Freeman George, coach proprietor, East st
Hunt John Newton, conveyancer, Upper Stoneham st
Kent Elijah, shopkeeper, East st
Mount William, basket maker, Market end
Pilgrem Charles, coach builder, West st
Pilkington David, gun maker, Stoneham st
Poulton Thos. veterinary surgeon, East st
PROVIDENT SOCIETY (Coggeshall Branch) East st; Henry Emery, collector
STAMP OFFICE, East st—Henry Cordran, distributer.
Sullings John, shopkeeper, Stoneham st
Theedom Wm. shopkeeper, the Gravel
Thurga Thomas, engineer, East st

COACHES.
To LONDON, the *Fly*, from the Chapel Inn, daily
To BRAINTREE, the *Hope* (from Colchester), every Tues. Thurs. & Sat.
To COLCHESTER, the *Hope* (from Braintree), every Tues. Thurs. & Sat.

CARRIERS.
To LONDON, — Ruffell's *Waggon*, from her house, every Monday and Friday.
To BRAINTREE, — Hodges, from the Bird in Hand, every Wed. and Sat.
To COLCHESTER, — Hodges, from the Bird in Hand, every Wed. & Sat. & — Hunwick's *Van*, every Mon. Wed. & Sat.

COLCHESTER,

WITH THE VILLAGE OF LEXDEN AND NEIGHBOURHOODS.

COLCHESTER, a market town, and borough both corporate and parliamentary, having separate jurisdiction, locally in the Colchester division of the hundred of Lexden, is 51 miles N. E. from London, 22 N. E. from Chelmsford, and 18 S. W. from Ipswich. This, the most considerable town in Essex, is situated partly upon the summit and partly upon the side of a fine eminence rising from the Colne, which river washes its north and east sides, and is navigable as far as New Hythe, at the eastern extremity of the town. The Eastern Counties' Railway, on its route from London to Norwich, will pass close to Colchester. Although near the sea, yet the town is sufficiently inland to be protected from noxious damps and marine vapours; and it is remarkable for its dryness, cleanness and consequent salubrity. The early history of this place has been a source of much controversy among antiquarians, some of whom maintain that it was the Roman *Camulodunum*: of its extreme antiquity, however, no doubts are entertained, investigation having established the fact of its having been a British as well as a Roman city. Relics of Roman grandeur are here discovered in far greater numbers than in any other part of South Britain; and the strength of those portions of its fortifications which have weathered the assaults of time, convince the spectator of the vast importance of the place they were destined to defend. While the Saxon power was predominant in this country, Colchester, then known by the name of *Colon-ceaster* or *Colne-ceaster*, lost much of its importance, owing to the increasing wealth and consequence of its powerful neighbour, London, the situation of which was much more favourable for commerce. Colchester has suffered very severely by the ravages of civil war, particularly in the contest between Charles and the parliament. The town was bravely defended by the royalists; but, after an eleven weeks' siege by Fairfax, the parliamentary general, it was obliged to capitulate upon the hardest terms. Previous to the departure of Fairfax, he compelled the citizens to dismantle their fortifications, the magistrates being forced to provide the tools for that purpose: before that period, great attention had been paid to the preservation of the walls, of which at present but few remains can be traced. The castle stands upon an elevated spot to the north of the High-street, and commands a magnificent view of the valley winding to the north and east: the outer walls are tolerably perfect; they are built of an admixture of silicious and calcareous stones and Roman brick, but the latter are chiefly in large masses—fragments, as it were, of some more ancient building. Within the last twenty years Colchester has been gradually improving in its general appearance. The public buildings, erected within the above period, are the exchange, hospital and observatory: the hospital is an extensive structure, in a very healthful situation, supported by annual subscriptions, donations, &c. The theatre is a large handsome edifice, open during the winter months. The barracks are very extensive, and when occupied are of material benefit to the retail trade of the town. The borough gaol and corn market are in High-street, and the county house of correction in the Ipswich road. The moot hall, an ancient fabric, comprises the hall, the exchequer chamber and council room, and underneath is the town gaol. A literary and philosophical society, established in 1820 by a few respectable and intelligent individuals, has attained a state of great prosperity; essays on various interesting subjects are occasionally delivered. A botanical and horticultural society, founded in 1823, is liberally supported in the vicinage and throughout the county; attached to it is a comprehensive botanic garden, affording to the proprietors and subscribers a delightful treat. A medical society was instituted in 1774. There are a private subscription and some good circulating libraries, and an amateur musical society. The manufacture of baize, and extensive silk-mills, furnish employment to a great number of the inhabitants; while the oyster fishery, for which Colchester has been so long famous, occupies many others. There are some hundreds of smacks engaged in conveying to London the oysters dredged from the river, for which there is always a great demand—especially for those of Purfleet, which are found in a small creek, and are remarkable for their excellent flavour. The other branches that prominently flourish here are iron founding, the tanning and currying of leather, several breweries, two distilleries, chymical works and some corn mills. There are a number of handsome shops, and the retail trade, which is very considerable, rarely experiences depression. There are ten superior inns and hotels, and two banking houses, exclusive of a savings' bank. Colchester issues from its press three newspapers weekly, the titles of which and the days of publication will be found under the proper head. Richard I conferred the first charter of incorporation upon the inhabitants of Colchester, with many valuable privileges, particularly the exclusive fishery of the Colne between the north and west bridges; this charter has been repeatedly confirmed, and the original privileges extended, by succeeding monarchs; the last, by which the government of the town was regulated previous to the operation of the existing municipal act, was granted by George III, in 1763. The new act of 1835 vested the government in a mayor, six aldermen and eighteen councillors, with the usual assistant officers, and styled the corporate body 'the mayor and commonalty of the borough of Colchester;' the same bill divided the borough into three wards, and provided for it a commission of the peace. The corporation hold quarterly courts of session for the borough and liberties; two courts of pleas, for the recovery of debts to any amount, on Monday and Thursday; and petty sessions for the division every Saturday. The borough first sent members to parliament in the 23rd of Edward I; since which time, with occasional intermissions, it has returned two representatives: those at present sitting are Sir G. H. Smith, Bart., and Richard Sanderson, Esq.

The borough and liberties of Colchester comprise sixteen parishes, but several of the churches have disappeared; among those that remain are some handsome structures, and others of considerable antiquity. The principal church within the borough is that dedicated to St. Peter; the others are, St. Mary's at the Walls, St. James's, St. Runwald's, St. Nicholas', St. Botolph's, All Saints', St. Giles', St. Leonard's, St. Mary Magdalene's, the Holy Trinity, St. Martin's, St. Michael's, Greenstead, Lexden and Bere church—none of which require a detailed description. There are places of worship for baptists, independents, unitarians, Wesleyan methodists, and the society of friends. A grammar school, with exhibitions, founded by Henry VIII; two charity schools (in which fifty-five boys and thirty girls are educated and clothed), and others upon the national and Lancasterian systems, are the institutions for gratuitous instruction; there is also a school for children of the society of friends. For the relief of the indigent there are several charities, including alms-houses; and this is one of those towns included in the will of the late Sir Thomas Whichcote. From the most elevated points the views over the surrounding country are extensive, and embrace some picturesque and interesting scenery, including the ruins of St. John's abbey and St. Botolph's priory. Colchester has been a market town from time immemorial, but it was first chartered as such by Richard I; the market days are Wednesday and Saturday, the latter the principal: the corn market is an elegant building, and is a great ornament to High-street. Fairs are held on the 5th and 23rd of July, and 10th October. The population of the sixteen parishes (including Lexden) within the borough and liberties of Colchester, by the census for 1831, was 16,167.

About two miles east from Colchester, and included within that borough, is the genteel and delightful little village, and parish of LEXDEN—admired for its particular cleanliness, and the tasteful elegance of many of the houses. The church, dedicated to St. Leonard, is in the pointed style of architecture, and is an embellishment to this respectable village, being, perhaps, as neat an edifice for divine worship as any in the county; the living is a rectory, and the Rev. George Preston is the present incumbent. The parish contained, in 1831, 1,184 inhabitants.

POST OFFICE, 34 Head street, COLCHESTER, Henry Verlander, *Post Master*.—The office opens for the delivery of letters from all parts at seven in the morning; the box closes at ten at night, but letters are received until half-past ten by paying threepence with each, and until eleven by paying sixpence with each. The mail to and from LONDON and NORWICH, passes through about half-past one in the morning.

GENTRY AND CLERGY.

Andrews Mrs. Rebecca, 86 East hill
Appleby Miss Caroline Maria, Crouch street
Argent Jas. Underwood, esq. Greenstead
Austin Mrs. Susannah, 8 East hill
Baddeley Mrs. G. 9 East hill
Balderstone Captain Frank, R. N. 1 St. Mary's terrace East
Barker Mrs. Elisha, 21 Crouch st
Barnes John, esq. Greenstead
Bawtree Mrs. —, 16 Queen st
Bawtree Charles, esq. High st
Bawtree George, esq. Culver st
Bawtree John, esq. 17 Queen st
Bawtree Mrs. William, Lexden
Betts Miss Elizabeth, 64 High st
Bland Henry, esq. 1 St. Mary's terr. W.
Blomfield Mrs. Harriet, Berechurch
Boutflower Charles, esq. 61 Crouch st
Bridgeman Mrs. —, 18 Head st
Brock Geo. esq. 6 St. Mary's terr. East
Brooke Mrs. —, 5 St. Mary's terr. W.
Brown Bartholomew, esq. Lexden rd
Brown Mrs. Mary Anne, 7 St. Mary's terrace West
Brown Stephen, esq. Crouch st
Bull Rev. Elijah, Military road
Carr Mrs. —, North hill
Carr Rev. Samuel, High st
Chamberlain Mrs. Ananias, North hill
Chaplin John, esq. Lexden
Chignell Mrs. Mary Ann, 4 Queen st
Chisholm P. esq. High st
Clarke Thomas, esq. Beverley lodge
Clay Benjamin, esq. Greenstead
Clay John, esq. Delbridge farm
Clay Miss Maria, Greenstead
Craven Miss —, 80 East hill
Creek Thomas, esq. 14 Lexden road
Dakins Rev. John, East hill
De Horne John, esq. Lexden
Devall Peter, esq. High st
Downes Mrs. —, Church st
Duffield Rev. Matthew Dawson, Berechurch
Errington George Henry, esq. High st
Fenton William, esq. 123 High st
Freeman Mrs. —, Lexden
Frost Rev. William F. Langhan
Fyson James, East hill
Green John William Egerton, esq. 8 High st
Green Nickson, esq. Greenstead hall
Green William, esq. Stanway hall
Grimwood Thomas, esq. Lexden road
Gross Frederick, esq. 27 Culver st
Haddock Jeremiah, esq. 10 Crouch st
Halls James, esq. 9 Crouch st
Hammond Mrs. Mary, East hill
Haselfoot Captain Charles, Casina cottage, house, Lexden road
Hayward Robert, esq. St. Leonard's
Herlein Miss Louisa Anne, Head st
Hewitt Rev. Charles, Greenstead
Holman Miss Harriet, 13 Lexden rd
Holroyd Rev. James John, 9 Saint Mary's terrace West
Keeling Frederick, esq. 28 Culver st
Keeling John, esq. 1 Queen st
Keymer William, esq. 41 Head st
King Rev. Charles, Priory st
King Mrs. John, Observatory court
Lewis Mrs. Anne, 3 Queen st
Lingwood Mrs. Sarah, Head st
M'Lean Lieut-Genl. Sir John, Hythe
M'Owan Rev. Peter, Wesley place
Markham Rev. David, Great Horsley
Martin Mrs. Mary Stuart, 28 Crouch st
Mason Mrs. M. 20 Queen st
Mayhew Thomas, esq. 7 Queen st
Mersey Capt. George, Military road
Miller —, esq. St. John's green
Mills John Fletcher, esq. Lexden park
Moore William, esq. Lexden road
Morgan Rev. John Woodruff, Bourne cottage
Moy John, esq. West Stockwell st
Mustard Rev. Charles Frederick, Maidenburgh street
Mustard David, esq. Roman hill
Nicholl C. esq. 5 St. Mary's terr. East
Norman Rev. Charles, Boxted
Papelion Mrs. Eliz. Lexden Manor hse
Pattison Joshua, esq. Lexden road
Payne Alfred, esq. East hill
Pertwee Mrs. Elizbth. Sarah, Head st
Philbrick Samuel, esq. 6 Queen st
Pinton Captain —, R. N. Lion walk
Preston Rev. George, Rectory house, Lexden
Richards Wm. esq. East hill & Dedham point

GENTRY AND CLERGY
—*Continued.*

Rix Mrs. —, 72 High st [road
Roddam George, esq. M. D. Lexden
Rolle Miss Mary, 25 East hill
Round Chas. Gray, esq. M.P. Birch hall
Round George, esq. East hill
Round Rev. James Thos. Castle house
Round Mrs. Joseph, Lexden house
Ruggles Miss Maria, 8 Saint Mary's terrace West [East
Rust Rev. Scipio, 3 St. Mary's terrace
Sach Mrs. Mary, North hill
Sadler Stephen, esq. Great Horsley
Saunders Rev. John, 20 Culver st
Savage Miss Maria, Head st [East
Savill Mrs. Frances, 4 St. Mary's terr.
Savill George, esq. Whitehall
Savill Robt. Maitland, esq. London rd
Savill Wm. Carrington, esq. London rd
Scale Mrs. Henrietta, 73 High st
Shearman Mrs. Sarah, 16 Crouch st
Sheppard Mrs. Revett, 2 St. Mary's terrace East [road
Shugar William Reed, esq. Lexden
Smyth Sir Henry George, bart. M.P. Berechurch hall [Lexden rd
Smythies Francis, esq. Villa franca,
Sparling Wm. esq. 6 St. Mary's terr.
Spaull Barnrd. esq. Observatory court
Stokes George, esq. East hill
Strong Rev. Philip, Mile end
Tabor Mrs. Sarah, Priory st
Taylor Mrs. Isabella, 20 High st
Taylor Thos. esq. West Stockwell st
Tayspill Mr. Thomas, Hythe
Theobald John Hudson, esq. 65 High street [terr. West
Thorogood John, esq. 3 St. Mary's
Torriano Rev. Vicessimus, North hill
Tucker Rev. Thomas Marwood, All Saints' rectory [Lexden
Vint Henry, esq. Crescent house,
Waddell John, esq. 33 Head st
Walford L. William, esq. Head st
Walter William, esq. 35 Head st
Waterhouse Mrs. —, 52 North hill
Waterhouse Jos. esq. Military road
Webb Isaac, esq. 49 Priory st
White Thos. jun. esq. Berechurch hall
Withers Miss Lucy, 13 Lexden road
Wright Miss Elizabeth, East hill
Wright Rev. R. Marksley [West
Wynne Mrs. Mary, 10 St. Mary's terr.

ACADEMIES & SCHOOLS.

Not otherwise described are Day Schools.

Bare John Halls (day and boarding) 12 Crouch street
Bennell Elizabeth, 10 Queen st
Bugg Martha, Mile end
Chaplin and Hicks (ladies' boarding) 20 North hill
Cockrell Charlotte, East hill
Cooper James, Priory st
Cullum Mary Anne, Maidenburgh st
Duell Elizabeth, 67 East hill
Durrell Susan (day and boarding) Observatory court
Fenner Henry Nye (boarding) East Stockwell house
FREE SCHOOL, Crispin court—Louisa Boyden, mistress
Garnon Mrs. & Miss (boarding) 12 East Stockwell st
Glanfield William (boarding) 8 East Stockwell st [North hill
Green Eliz. and Mary (boarding) 19
Hayward Misses (preparatory boarding) St. John st [Lexden
Holton Harriet (preparatory) Park la.
Hubbard Saml. (boarding) 103 High st
INFANTS' SCHOOL, East st—Mary Scott, mistress
INFANTS' SCHOOL, Hythe street—Eliza Scott, mistress
INFANTS' SCHOOL, Magdalene st—Louisa Boyden, mistress
LANCASTERIAN SCHOOL (boys' and girls') Priory st—John Kinns, master; Elizabeth Durham, mistress
NATIONAL SCHOOL (boys' & girls') Maidenburgh street—John Hatch, master; M. A. Rickwood, mistress
NATIONAL SCHOOL (girls') Lexden—Elizabeth Gosling, mistress
Partridge Miss S. A. Prospect house, East hill [John st
Paxman William (boarding) 19 St.
Robertson Misses (brdg) 5 North hill
Rowe Susannah Jackson (boarding) West Stockwell st [Queen st
Sargant Charlotte (preparatory) 27
Tanner Jane (preparatory) Culver st
Thorn Mary, High st
Wilson Richard, 14 North hill
Woolmer Theophilus (boarding) St. Helen's lane

ARCHITECTS & SURVEYORS.

(*See also Surveyors.*)

Clay Edward, 58 North hill
Glover Alexander Keatle, East hill
Hayward Henry, Bank bldgs. High st
Parkins Henry, Military road
Penrie John, 13 Crouch st
Ruffell William, Queen st
Sergeant George, Queen st [hill
Sheldrake Robert Everett, 53 North

ATTORNEYS.

Abell Francis Gibbs (& superintendent registrar) Crouch st
Barnes John Stuck (& clerk of the peace) 51 North hill
Church John Henry, East hill
Church John, Henry and Edgar, 56 Crouch street
Cooper William Salmon, 76 East hill
Daniell Edward & James, Head st
Daniell James, 82 East hill
Francis William W. Trinity st
Howard William, 30 Head st
Maberley Thomas, Balkerne lane
Mason, Son, Keeling and Howard, Head st
Mason William (and clerk to magistrates & head distributer of stamps for Essex) Church st, St. Mary's
Newell Fredk. Hasell, 41 North hill
Philbrick & Savill, 25 Head st
Randell Robert Richard, 96 High st
Savill Joseph, North hill
Smythies Francis & Son, North hill
Sparling Philip S. St. John st
Sparling William (and town clerk) East hill
Wittey Samuel (& clerk to the magistrates) Queen street

AUCTIONEERS, APPRAISERS, AND HOUSE AND ESTATE AGENTS.

(*See also Estate, Land, &c. Agents.*)

Clay Edward, 58 North hill
Cobb Nathaniel (and undertaker) 19 Head st
Cousins Joseph, 17 Crouch st
Dawson William K. High st
Fenton Francis, High st
Garrard Lionel, Culver st [hill
Sheldrake Robert Everett, 53 North
Syer Martin Edward, East hill
Taylor John, High st
Williams John, East Stockwell st

BAKERS & FLOUR DEALERS.

Abbott William & Son, Greenstead
Appleby William, Boxted
Batthram Samuel, Sir Isaac's walk
Beaumont John Rootsey, Stockwell st
Beaumont Jonathan, 25 East st
Beaumont Jos. 58 West Stockwell st
Biggs Benjamin, 3 North hill
Braggs William, High st
Carter John, 17 Crouch st
Chignall Thomas, 42 St. Botolph st
Choat Joseph, Hythe st
Choat Joseph, Magdalene st
Coppin John, 35 Crouch st
Dell Robert, Stanwell st
Dennis William (biscuit) 89 High st
Ellis Richman, St. Botolph st
Fenning Daniel, Middleburgh
Fenning Robert, Hythe st
Fitch James, St. John's green
Frost William (& mealman) Lexden
Gardner James, Magdalene st
Garland John, East hill
Green Thomas, Barrack st
Gilson Thomas (biscuit) Head st
Hacklett John, 16 North hill
Humm Daniel, Magdalene st
Hunt Philip, 4 Crouch st
Isbern Thomas, East st
Johnson Samuel, Hythe st
Jolly John, 20 Long Wyre st
Maidwell James, East hill
Mays Jonathan, East hill
Miller William, St. Botolph st
Peachey James, Middleburgh
Prior Alfred John, 22 Long Wyre st
Rawlins Thomas, Magdalene st
Rouse William, 163 High st
Rowe Joseph, North st
Scott Thomas, St. John's green and Black Boy lane
Simpson George, Magdalene st
Smith Henry, Priory st
Springett Roger, Magdalene st
Vale John, Magdalene st
Wire Charles, Magdalene st
Wire Chignall, 59 East hill
Woodroffe John, Middleburgh
Wright Abraham, Culver st

BANKERS.

Mills, Bawtree and Co. 3 High st—(draw on Hankeys & Co. London)
Round, Green, Green and Pattison, 8 High st—(draw on Barnetts, Hoare & Co. London)
SAVINGS' BANK, 146 High street—William Fisher Brill, actuary

BASKET MAKERS.

Ambrose Samuel, East st
Gosling Robert, Middleburgh
Hubbard John, 96 High st
Peck Thomas, Long Wyre st
Windfield George, Middleburgh

BLACKING MANUFACTURER.

Boag James (Japan and self-polishing) 3 Crouch st

BOOKSELLERS, STATIONERS AND BOOKBINDERS.

Albin Thos. 15 High st [High st
Brackett Joshua (& newsvender) 12
Cook & Brown, 10 High st [st
Dennis George (& library) 40 High
Fenton Chas. Frederick, 51 High st
Mattacks Underwood, jun. 14 Head st
Mattacks Underwood William, Short Wyre st [Crouch st
Rudkin John (& tract depository) 5
Sergant M. A. Queen st
Totham William, 10 North hill

BOOT & SHOE MAKERS.

Bagnell Thomas, Middleburgh
Barker Samuel, Langhan
Bather William, 151 High st
Blatch William, North st
Bolton Thomas, 11 Crouch st
Bowers Hannah, East st
Bradbrook Frederick, Gt. Horsley
Bruce Daniel, Middleburgh
Bugg Jos. E. Middle row, High st
Burgess Charles, St. Botolph st
Candler William, Long Wyre st
Carter John, East hill
Carter Josiah, 58 East hill
Cockrell Mathias, East st

Cranmer Thomas, Magdalene st
Dennis David, Maidenburgh st
Dennis Jacob (& grindry warehouse) Maidenburgh st
Dennis John, Maidenburgh st
Devall John, 132 High st
Ellisdon Frances, 4 High st
Farrau Joseph, Middleburgh
Farran Samuel, West Stockwell st
Fenning James, 25 Queen st
Gilbert Jas. Crispin court, North hill
Godfrey John, Langhan
Greenleaf William, 37 Head st
Harbour Thomas, Long Wyre st
Harwood Frederick, Hythe st
Hazel James, 15 North hill
Holland William, 68 High st
Hyam John, Stockwell st
Isbern James, East st
Ives William, 9 Short Wyre st
Leech George, 33 St. Botolph st
Leech Nathaniel, 33 Long Wyre st
Lilly William, Lexden
Loyd James, 57 North hill
Nevill James A. St. Botolph st
Nunn John, 76 East hill
Potter John, Barrack st
Pummeter William, Hythe st
Roofe Charles Bell, 119 High st
Rust Samuel, Boxted
Sarls William, Magdalene st
Saward Robert, Magdalene st
Smith James, 35 Long Wyre st
Stuck John, Nicholas st
Thurston John, St. Botolph st
Thurston John, jun. Magdalene st
Warren John, Greenstead
Waterman James, Magdalene st
Webb William, Mile end
White Obadiah, 162 High st
Willes Robert, East hill
Wire James, Long Wyre st

BREECHES MAKERS AND GLOVERS.

Culpeck James, Dead lane
Emmerson Thomas, High st
Mills Henry, Magdalene lane
Mills Thomas, North st
Mills Thomas, 66 East hill
White George, Wyre st

BREWERS.

Cobbold R. and Co. North hill
Daniel Thomas, Hythe
Fenning Robert, Hythe st
Hurnard Robert, East hill
Kimber, Gross & Nicholl (& porter merchants) East hill
Osborne John Posford (and vinegar manufacturer) Botolph st
Rolfe John, Hythe st

BRICK MAKERS.

Alsten William, Mile end
Ambrose John, Hythe
Austen Richard, Mile end
Chignall William, Middleburgh
Daniel Thomas, Bergholt
Dennis Charles, Harwich road
Gall Timothy, Mile end

BRICKLAYERS, &c.

Boyden James, North st
Bullock Charles, Magdalene st
Clarke Charles, Church st
Franklin John, Magdalene st
Green John, North hill
Lissiamore Samuel, jun. 25 Culver st
MartinJno.Henry(&slater)Greenstd
Nelson Thomas, Butt lane
Pitt William, Hythe
Scovell William, East bridge
Tunmer Wm. Wesley place, Culver st
Walter James, Stockwell st
Willett Ebenezer, Hythe

BRUSH MANUFACTURERS.

Rowland Philip, Middleburgh
Smith George, Magdalene st

BUILDERS.

See under Carpenters.

BUTCHERS.

Barker John, Maidenburgh st
BarnardWilliamDaniel,35 North hill
Bear Daking, St. Botolph st
Blomfield Robert, Culver st
Cater George, Magdalene st
Chaplin William, 133 High st
Chignall James, Hythe st
Colleer Samuel, 131 High st
Cranmer William, East hill
Dennis George, High st
Dennis James, High st
Finch William, Lexden
Foster James, 127 High st
Gall Timothy (pork) Magdalene st
Goss Joseph, East st
Griggs James, Hythe
Hybart William, West Stockwell st
Isitt John, 106 High st
Ladbrook Peter, Lexden
Murray John, East hill
Nevill John, Magdalene st
Reeves George, Hythe st
Ridgley Daniel, Magdalene st
Simpson Thomas, Great Horsley
Wenden James, Magdalene st

CABINET MAKERS AND UPHOLSTERERS.

Barnes Robert, 3 St. Botolph st
BarrittJames(& appraiser) Head gate
Brown John Alexander, North st
Brown Matthew, North st
Chignall Charles, St. Botolph st
Cobb Nathaniel (and undertaker) 19 Head street
Couch William, 30 Crouch st
Cross Edmund, Magdalene st
Cross John Wainwright, 107 High st
Day William and Son, 8 Crouch st
Ellisdon Joseph, Eld lane
Fenton Francis & Charles, 51 High st
Keeble Elizabeth, Nicholas st
Shave Philip, Long Wyre st
Taylor John, 27 High st
Winch John, Priory st

CARPENTERS.

Marked thus * are also Builders.

Abbott Charles, Military road and Magdalene st
Abbott John, Magdalene st
Baker Isaac, Maidenburgh st
Bale John, 29 Queen st
Branson Samuel, Magdalene st
Bridge John, Lion walk
Chapman James, Priory st
Coe Thomas, Balkerne lane
Copping Edward, Magdalene st
Crow John, East hill
Cullum John, Maidenburgh st
Disey Samuel, Mile end
Elliott John, 14 Long Wyre st
*Everitt Charles, Lexden
Green William, 46 Crouch st
*Grimes Samuel, Duck lane
Hale William, Hythe
*Hayward Henry Hammond, Bank buildings
Hewes Matthew, North st
*Jenkin Richard, St. John st
Lingwood Isaac, St. Botolph st
Neep William, East st
Orrin James, Stockwell st
*Pitt William, East hill
Sames Thomas, Mill st
*Scott and Son, North hill
*Scott Thomas, 39 North hill
Seaman Joseph, North st
Seaman Richard, George lane
Seex John, High st
Start John, Hythe st
Ward James, Mile end

CARVERS & GILDERS.

Aggio Paul, 37 High st
Calver James, Lion walk
Lingwood Isaac, St. Botolph st

CHAIR MAKERS.

Ainsworth Thomas, Pelham st
Simmons John, East hill
Turner William, Magdalene st

CHINA, GLASS & EARTHENWARE DEALERS.

Brill & Bready, 146 High st
Cheshire Robert, 24 St. Botolph st
Gilson Samuel, East hill
Howe William, 18 Long Wyre st
Humphrey William, High st
Raven William, 52 High st

CHYMIST—MANUFACTURING

Payne Alfred, Hythe

CHYMISTS & DRUGGISTS.

Dickinson Charlotte, St. Botolph st
HarringtonThos.Rawling,16 Head st
Hitchcock Chas. Edward, 29 Head st
Hodson James, 58 High st
King John Maber, 9 High st
Leech William, 33 St. Botolph st
Manthorp Samuel, 105 High st
Meadowcroft Thomas (& soda water manufacturer) 28 High st
Smith Thomas (and soda water manufacturer) 13 High st
Spaull Bernard, 31 High st
Townson Thomas, 24 High st

CLOTHES DEALERS.

Cubit Samuel, St. Botolph st
Gershon George, 19 Short Wyre st
Hagg and Son, St. Botolph st
Hawkins George, Long Wyre st
Hyam Hyam, Queen st
Levy Mordecai, East st
Pells William, Long Wyre st

COACH BUILDERS.

Gale Joseph, Lexden
Gale William, 58 Crouch st
Ladell Christmas, East hill
Peachey James, Middleburgh
Sharman William & Henry, East st
Silvester John (and harness maker) Crouch st
Stripling Thomas, 36 North hill

COAL MERCHANTS.

Ambrose John, Hythe
Baker John, Hythe
Bawtree George and A. Hythe
Brown Samuel S. Hythe
Cooke Saml. Geo. St. John's green & Hythe
Daniels Thos. Hythe, & at *Bergholt*
Fenton William, Hythe
Frost William, Lexden
Garrard John, Hythe
Gin Thomas, Hythe
Greenwood and Knight, Hythe
Gull Daniel (& bone) Dead lane
Jackson John William, 45 East hill
Jarvis and Man, Hythe
Knight George, 165 High st
Lewis Francis, Hythe
Lewis John, Magdalene st
Mann John, Hythe
Mansfield James, Maidenburgh st
Minter Daniel, East hill
Osborne John P. St. John st
Scott John, Hythe
Smith John S. 53 East hill
Unwins Stephen, Hythe
Willett Everard, Hythe

CONFECTIONERS.

Beard John, 35 High st
Biggs Benjamin, North hill
Dennis William, 89 High st
Fairhead George, 55 High st
Filer Susannah, North hill

COOPERS.

Barnes William, St. John st
Brightman Benjamin, Priory st
Chignall Charles, Wyre st

COOPERS—*Continued.*
Correy Joseph, Magdalene st
Crainfield William, 128 High st
Hitchcock George, East st
Pressney Abithai, Middleburgh
Scott Daniel Whitlock, Middleburgh

CORK CUTTERS.
Greenfield and Son, East hill
Hale John, Magdalene st
Lubbock William, East st

CORN AND SEED DEALERS.
(See also Seed Merchants.)
Cross Charles, High st
Hewes Matthew, North st
Knight George, 165 High st
Osborne Joseph, St. Botolph st
Spaull Barnard, 31 High st

CORN MERCHANTS.
Bawtree Geo. & Co. Hythe [bridge
Brown Bartholomew, East mill, East
Brown Samuel Simons, Head st
Brown Stephen, Crouch st, & Hythe
Burleigh Robert William, New quay
Cross Charles, High st
Frost William, Lexden
Jarvis and Mann, Hythe
Knight George, High st
Lewis Francis, Hythe
Mann John, Hythe st
Osborne John P. St. Botolph st
Scott John, Hythe
Smith John Sidney, 53 East hill
Smithers Frank, Hythe
Woodroffe John, Middleburgh

CURRIERS AND LEATHER CUTTERS.
Dennis Charles Hezekiah, Maidenburgh st
Eisdell & Warmington, 60 High st
Powell Samuel, Culver st
Roberson James, 4 Long Wyre st
White Wm. Nicholas, Church passge
Whiteson William, Church alley

DISTILLERS.
Bawtree Geo. & Charles, Culver st
Savill Geo. & Co. (malt) New quay

DYERS.
Hitchcock James, St. Botolph st
Pretty Catherine, Greenstead [st
Revell Thos. (silk) 56 West Stockwell
Salmon John (silk) 120 High st
Warren Jno. Elisha, 15 St. Botolph st

ESTATE, LAND, &c. AGENTS.
(See also Auctioneers, &c.)
Clay Edward, 58 North hill
Cobb Nathaniel, 19 Head st
Creek Thomas, Lexden road
Dawson William, High st [hill
Sheldrake Robert Everett, 53 North
Taylor John, High st

FIRE, &c. OFFICES & AGENTS.
Atlas, John Pattison, Lexden road
British, Thomas Scott, 39 North hill
Clerical and Medical (life) J. H. Theobald, High st
County, John Bridge, St. Botolph st
Essex and Suffolk Equitable, Frederick Page Keeling, secretary, Corn Exchange, High street
Essex Economic, Lionel Garrard, Culver st [East hill
Globe, John William Jackson, 45
Norwich Union, George Dennis, 40 High st, and George Knight, 165 High st
Pelican (life) and Phœnix (fire), Samuel Tillett, Head st
Protestant Dissenters', Edward Wormington, High st
Royal Exchange, James William Coleman, 23 Head st
Suffolk and General County, Alfred Thorby, High st

Sun, John Enfield, High st, and at Langhan [Wyre st
West Middlesex, Jas. Saxty, Long

FISHMONGERS & OYSTER PACKERS.
Bare Elizabeth, 24 Head st
Chapman Sarah, Middle row, High st
Halls Robert (and dealer in game) top of High st [row
Nash Jas. (& dealer in game) Middle

FRUITERERS.
Bare Elizabeth, 21 Head st
Blomfield John, 114 High st
Cant George, Long Wire st
Halls Robert, High st
Parker Benjamin, St. Botolph st

FURNITURE BROKERS.
Cross John, High st
Gershon George, Wyre st
James John, 42 North hill
Nason John, 22 North hill
Orrin James, Pelham's lane
Pells William, Wyre st
Wolton Samuel, Maidenburgh st

GARDENERS & SEEDSMEN.
Baker John, Middleburgh
Bedwell Simon, East hill
Blomfield John, East hill
Brett Edward, East hill
Burridge William, Crouch st
Burrows Joseph, Magdalene st
Fenning Charles, 135 High st
Garland John, East st
Maynard Joseph, St. Botolph st
Morten William, Stockwell st
Page Henry, Hythe st
Sebberne Thomas, Balkerne hill
Shead Isaac, Priory st
Spinks Thomas, Magdalene st
Vale James, East st

GROCERS AND DEALERS IN SUNDRIES.
(See also Grocers and Tea Dealers.)
Alden William, 33 North hill
Appleby John, Boxted
Bacon Daniel, 51 East hill
Baines Sarah, Culver st
Balls Sarah, St. Botolph st
Bradbrook William, 74 East st
Byron John, 23 East st
Clover Samuel, North st
Colleer Mary Ellen, Middleburgh
Cooper John, Lexden
Dennis James, 29 Crouch st
Farrow Thomas, North st
Gall Timothy, Barrack st
Garland George, 51 East st
Gilson Daniel Page, Middleburgh
Green Robert, East st
Halls John, Hythe st [st
Haward Charles Stephen, 124 High
Knight William, Magdalene st
Mays Jonathan, East hill
Monson Daniel, Great Horsley
Moore Thomas, Barrack st
Nevill John, Magdalene st
Page John, Langhan
Raven Thomas, 16 St. John st
Robinson Robert, East Stockwell st
Rust Samuel, Boxted
Sheade Isaac, Priory st
Smith John, Mile end
Tillett Robert, Greenstead
Weatherby John, Maidenburgh st
Whiteman Robert, 40 St. Botolph st

GROCERS & TEA DEALERS.
(See also the preceding list.)
Bantock Robert, Head gate
Carr John Oliver, 11 High st
Cooper William, 1 Wyre st
Craske Robert G. 111 High st
Foster Ebenezer, 32 High st
Gardner John, Hythe st
Gilson Daniel Page, Middleburgh
Habgood James, 1 High st

Johnson John, North gate
Marshall George, 62 High st
May Abraham, Head st
Moore Thomas, Barrack st
Sach James, Hythe
Seabrook John, 47 High st
Steggell Charles, St. Botolph st
Stone Charles, 15 Crouch st
Strutt Edward, Greenstead
Tabrum & Parkes, East street, and at *Wivenhoe* [Long Wyre st
Wilmshurst Thomas, Crouch st and
Wolton Henry, 41 High st

GUN MAKERS.
Hast Philip, 118 High st
How Richard, 150 High st

HABERDASHERS.
Bower Robert, High st
Gonner John, High st
Griffin William, Botolph st
Kent Robert, High st
Kerry Robert, High st
Rayner Richard S. 36 High st
Thorn Thomas, George st
Verlander John, 136 High st

HAIR DRESSERS.
(See also Perfumers & Hair Dressers.)
Boyles Jeremiah, Magdalene st
Duell Thomas, Short Wyre st
Hibble Henry, Magdalene st
Martin John, Middle row, High st
Nunn John, Magdalene st
Richards Joseph, St. Botolph st
Swan William, East hill

HARDWAREMEN AND TOY DEALERS.
Bower Robert, High st
Ritchie Thomas, Hythe st
Salter Ephraim, High st
Secret Joseph, Hythe st
Verlander John, 136 High st

HATTERS.
Everitt Wm. (manufactr.) 91 High st
Hagg Ichabod, St. Botolph st
Jennings William, 14 High st
Nockold James, High st
Shairp George, 39 High st

HORSE & GIG PROPRIETORS—FOR HIRE.
Braggs William, High street and Sir Isaac's walk
Heard Charles, High st
Isbern Thomas, East st
Moore William, Eld lane
Roofe Charles Bell, 119 High st
Roper George, Swan Inn, High st
Shuttleworth James, High st
Smith John, High st
Ward Ebenezer, North hill

HOSIERS.
Bower Robert, 33 High st
Marsden John, 34 High st
Thorby Alfred, 23 High st
Tracy James, Long Wyre st

HOTELS, INNS AND POSTING HOUSES.
Angel, Samuel Turner, High st
Blue Posts (commercial) Geo. Strait, St. Botolph street
Fleece (commercial) Edgar Batrum Cundy, Head street
George & Commercial, John Smith, High street
Horse and Groom, Thomas Brown, Crouch street [street
King's Arms, Richd. Pargeter, Crouch
Red Lion, Charles Heard, 42 High st
Ship, John Seaborn, Head gate
Swan, George Roper, High st
Three Cups Hotel, George Chaplin, High street

IRON FOUNDERS.
Coleman Richard (and engineer) St. John street
Dearn William, St. Botolph st
Wallis Charles, 167 High st

IRONMONGERS & BRAZIERS.
Beard Benjamin, 2 St. John st
Catchpool Thomas, 122 High st
Coleman George, 21 Long Wyre st
Coleman James William, 23 Head st
Coleman Richard (& engineer) Saint John street
Dearn William, St. Botolph st
Downs Philip, East hill
Joslin George, 108 High st
Rouse William & Thomas, 57 High st
Wallis Charles, 167 High st

JEWELLRS & SILVERSMTHS.
Banister Joseph, 18 High st
Braddock Jas. (working) Middle row
Hedge Nathaniel, 95 High st
Mason Thomas, 25 High st
Mitchell Joseph, 22 High st

LIBRARIES—CIRCULATING.
Dennis George, 40 High st
Mattacks William Underwood, Short Wyre street
Totham William, 10 North hill

LIME BURNERS.
Knight George, High st and Hythe
Pannifer William, Hythe

LINEN DRAPERS.
Alden William, North hill
Barber Robert, 6 High st
Bryant Josias Hovell, 17 Head st
Chenery William Henry, 29 High st
Cobb James, 16 High st
Cole Abraham, 30 High st
Cole John, St. Botolph st
Griffin William, 5 & 6 St. Botolph st, and carpet warehouse, 13 Queen st
Kent Robert, 38 High st
Kerry Robert, 64 High st
Knight Thos. (& tea dealer) 48 High st
Salmon John, 50 High st
Seaman Elizabeth, 53 High st
Thorn Edward, George st

MALTSTERS.
Brown Barthlmw. East mill, East bdge
Cobbold R. & Co. North hill
Mann John, Hythe st
Phillips Samuel, Lexden
Pryor Robert, New quay

MILLERS.
Abbott William & Son, Greenstead
Borham Jeremiah, Harwich road
Bouthell Edward, Middle hill
Brown Bartholomew, East mill
Butcher William, Boxted
Byles Edward, Layer la Haye
Candler John, Great Horsley
Clubb Stephen, North st
Dell William R. Butt lane
Fisher William, Boxted
Grubb Jonathan, Lexden
Houlding Leonard, Military road
Poppy John, Mersey road
Scott Robert, Lexden heath
Shairp George, Mile end
Stammers Edward C. Military road
Wayley John, Langhan

MILLINERS AND DRESS MAKERS.
Barnes Ann & Catherine, High st
Beard & Clarke, 3 St. John st
Bennell Mrs. Church steps
Bryant Josias, Head st
Butler A. North hill
Cutler Mary Anne, Long Wyre st
Dennis Emma J. Maidenburgh st
Dobson Ann, St. Botolph st
Doel Mary, East hill
Dowman Alias, Wyre st
Garrad Mary, 17 Long Wyre st
Gonner & Robinson, High st
Hailes Mary, 20 St. John st
Mattocks Mary Ann, 14 Head st
O'Bree Mary, West Stockwell st
Payne Ann, Middleburgh
Pretty Maria, 13 Short Wyre st
Renton Mary, High st
Seaman Jane, 2 North hill
Slaney Mary, Middleburgh
Snape Charlotte, 80 East hill
Stone —, 15 Crouch st
Stuck Britannia, 26 Queen st
Thurston Elizabeth, Magdalene st
Turner Mary, Maidenburgh st
Wade Jane, Maidenburgh st
Ward Martha & Harriet, Crouch st
Wenlock Mary Ann, High st
Wire Mary, 2 East Stockwell st

MILLWRIGHTS.
Bowles John, Greenstead
Clubb Alfred (and brass founder) Maidenburgh street
Clubb Stephen, North st

MUSIC & MUSICAL INSTRUMENT SELLERS.
Bland Sarah, 21 Culver st
Dennis George, 40 High st
Fenton Charles Frederick, High st
Suazel Ambrose, 22 Culver st

NEWSPAPERS.
Essex & Suffolk Times (Saturday), John Bawtree Harvey, publisher, East Stockwell st
Essex, Herts & Kent Mercury (Tuesday), John Bawtree Harvey, publisher, East Stockwell st
Essex Standard (Friday), John Taylor, jun. printer and publisher, 19 High st

NURSERY AND SEEDSMEN.
Austin Edward, East hill
Bunting Isaac (& florist) Lexden rd
Cant William, St. John st
Jackson John William, 45 East hill
Morton William, West Stockwell st

OIL & COLOUR MERCHANTS.
Barrett Thos. (& varnish and lead manufacturer) Castle Bailey; house, East Stockwell st
Kent Jno. (& window glass cutter) 104 High st

PAINTERS, PLUMBERS AND GLAZIERS.
Clark William, Trinity st
Combe James Wm. 36 Long Wyre st
Farren Benjamin, St. John's green
Filer James, 28 North hill
Frost Abraham, 6 North hill
Harding Charles, 149 High st
Hawkins Benjamin, East hill
Hitchcock James, St. Botolph st
Longuehaye Wm. Edward, Head st
Mordon James Joseph, Hythe st
Seaman Joseph, North st
Spurling John, 93 High st
Strutt Hannah, Long Wyre st
Strutt Thomas, East hill

PAWNBROKERS.
Bedwell John & Robert, 63 High st
Samuel Michael, 70 High st

PERFUMERS AND HAIR CUTTERS.
Cardy Samuel, 141 High st
Faiers John, 1 High st
Gibbons George, 6 Crouch st
Mitchell Joseph, High st
Nunn John, Botolph st
Percival William Henry, 17 Head st
Tillett Robert, 148 High st
Watson Edward, 49 High st
Watson Ephraim, Crouch st

PHYSICIANS.
Maclean Allen, Crouch st
Nunn Roger, Queen st
Williams Edward, 31 High st
Wilson Edward, Head st

PORTER MERCHANTS.
Argent William, Duck lane
Blythe Daniel O. Hythe
Jarvis and Mann, Hythe
Kimber, Gross & Nicholl (& brewers) East hill Botolph st
Osborne Jno. Posford (& vinegar mnfr)

PRINTERS—LETTER-PRESS.
Dennis Geo. (& coppr-plate) 40 High st
Fenton Charles Frederick, 51 High st
Harvey John Bawtree, East Stockwell street
Totham William, 10 North hill

PROFESSORS & TEACHERS.
Austin Jno. Mears (dancing) Culver st
Glover Alex. K. (drawing) East hill
Lewis Henry (drawing) 17 East Stockwell street
Scott George (astronomy) Church lane
Thorn Henry (music) High st

SADDLERS AND HARNESS MAKERS.
Bedwell William, East hill
Brooks Abraham, Maldon road
Carpenter Jno. Foundry yard, High st
Clary Edward, 147 High st
French Philip, 75 East hill
French Philip, jun. Middleburgh
Harrington William P. Queen st
Hayward Thomas, Magdalene st
Humphrey Thomas, St. Botolph st
Mills James William, 46 High st
Mortimer John, Crouch st
Quilter Thomas Risby, Head gate
Stripling Thomas, 36 North hill

SEED MERCHANTS.
Cross Charles, High st
Knight George, 165 High st
Osborne James, St. Botolph st

SHIP OWNERS.
Baker John and Co. Hythe
Blyth Daniel O. Hythe
Brown Samuel and Co. Hythe
Cross and Mann, Hythe
Hall James, Hythe st
Jarvis and Mann, Hythe
Lewis Francis, Hythe
Murrells John, Hythe
Nunn Thomas, Hythe

SILK MANUFACTURERS.
Brown and Moy (and throwsters) Dead lane

SILK MERCERS.
(See also Linen Drapers.)
Bryant Josias Hovell, 17 Head st
Chenery Wm. Henry, 29 High st
Cole Abraham, 30 High st
Gouner & Robinson, 5 High st
Kerry Robert, 64 High st
Salmon John, 120 High st
Thorn Edward, George st

SMITHS.
Alvous Thomas, Culver st
Asten Robert (shoeing) St. John st
Bennell Joseph, Queen st
Binks John, Barrack st
Bruce William, 26 East st
Cannel John, Foundry yard, High st
Chappell Charles, 11 George st
Clarke John, Duck lane
Cole William, Boxted
Dewell Mark Dill, East hill
Downes Henry, East hill
Downes James, Magdalene st
Folgate Samuel, Langhan
Garwood James, Mile end
Lamb Thomas, Middleburgh
Mann John, Greenstead
Mann John, Hythe
Mann John, jun. Hythe
Mason William, Magdalene st
May William, 7 George st
Page Abraham, Great Horsley
Richardson John (shoeing) Culver st
Sebborn John, Boxted
Sebborn Robert, Mile end
Wenlock George, Great Horsley
White Matthew, North st

STATUARIES AND STONE AND MARBLE MASONS.
Bremer William, 18 St. John st
Lufkin George, High st
Lufkin Henry, East hill

STAY AND CORSET MAKERS.
Appleby Ann, 129 High st
Dowman Alice, Long Wyre st
Heckford Eliza, St. John st
James Charlotte, 42 North hill
Ward M. and H. Crouch st

STRAW HAT MAKERS.
Archer Mary, Trinity st
Austin Mary Ann, Middleburgh
Beckwith Sarah, Hythe st
Bennell Ann, Balkerne lane
Devall Susannah, Hythe st
Faux Elizabeth, St. Botolph st
Garrad Mary, 17 Long Wyre st
Green and Whitley, High st
Hale Sarah, Magdalene st
Hales Phillis, Magdalene st
Montagu Louisa, North st
Moss Isaac, Greenstead
Smith Caroline, Eld lane
Thorp Hannah, St. Botolph st
Watson Amelia, 49 High st

SURGEON—DENTISTS.
Mann William Paston, Head gate
Meus Thomas, Williams' walk

SURGEONS.
Allen —, Long Wyre st
Bewick Robert, West Stockwell st
Blair Charles Edward, K. C. and K. T. S., &c. East hill
Churchill James M. 2 Queen st
Johnson Walter, 40 Head st
Mann William Paston, Head gate
Norman John, Head gate
Nunn Roger Stirling, Queen st
Partridge Alderman, High st
Philbrick, Morris and Philbrick, 26 Head street
Spaull Bernard, 31 High st
Waylen William, 28 Queen st
Worts William, 30 East Stockwell st

SURVEYORS.
(See also Architects and Surveyors.)
Downes Wm. North hill & *Dedham*
Gilbert & Tayspill (and land agents) Observatory court
Lay John Sarjeant (of taxes) North hill
Parkins Joseph, Military road
Sergeant Geo. 30 Queen st
Sheldrake Robert Everett, 53 North hill

TAILORS.
(See also Tailors and Drapers.)
Allen James, Head st
Bland John, George lane
Everitt George, 81 East hill
French Joshua, St. Helen's lane
Hatfield Robert, 1 East Stockwell st
Nash George, East Stockwell st
Osbourn William, St. John's green
Peggs John, 36 Crouch st
Polyth Samuel, Culver st
Quilter William, Hythe st
Robson Thomas, 20 Culver st
Ross Andrew, St. Botolph st
Ross John, 1 Short Wyre st
Seaman Robert, 4 North hill

TAILORS AND DRAPERS.
(See also the preceding list.)
Allen James, Head st
Argent William, Duck lane
Austin Samuel, Crouch st
Balham John, Head gate
Butler William S. 21 High st
Cross William, 2 Nicholas st
Cubitt Samuel, St. Botolph st
Fenning William, East st
Fenton & Kington, 59 High st
Hagg Ichabod, St. Botolph st
King William, St. Botolph st
Martin William, 2 Crouch st
Montagu Henry, Magdalene st
Rand William, East st
Saxty John, 26 High st
Scott George, jun. 15 Head st
Seaborn Edward, Langhan
Smith Benjamin, 16 Head st
Tassie John, East hill
Watts James, 94 High st
Worts James, 27 St. John st

TALLOW CHANDLERS.
Colleer Mary Ellen, Middleburgh
Dowman John, Long Wyre st
Moore Thomas, Barrack st
Sanders John, Magdalene st
Tabrum & Parkes, East st
Wolton Henry, 41 High st

TANNERS.
Culpeck James, Dead lane
Eisdell Joseph Carter, East bridge house, East hill

TAVERNS & PUBLIC HOUSES.
Anchor, Mark Munson, Magdalene st
Barley Mow, Edward Lay, Hythe st
Bear, James Wicks, 125 High st
Bell, Francis Ward, Priory st
Berechurch Arms, Patience Biggs, Lexden
Bird in Hand, James Wellham, 28 East Stockwell st
Bishop Blaize, Edwd. Corder, West Stockwell st
Blue Boar, Peter Ingram, W. Stockwell st
Blue Posts, George Strach, Botolph st
Brewer's Arms, Wm. Cooper, Stonewell st
Buck's Horns, John Hy. Martin, Greenstead
Bugle Horn, Henry Hunt, Barrack st
Bull, Thomas Phillips, Crouch st
Castle, Susan Crickmore, High st
Castle, William Minter, North st
Chaise & Pair, Thos. Wilson, 9 North hill
Chequers, John Jocelyne, Lexden
Coach & Horses, Sarah Smith, North gate
Cock & Crown, Jeremiah Bortholomew, North st
Colchester Arms, Saml. King, Magdalene st
Cross Keys, William Begg, Culver st
Cross Keys Tap, John Hooper, 38 Long Wyre street
Crown, Sarah Bowers, Great Horsley
Crown & Punch Bowl, Ann Daniel, East st
Dog & Pheasant, James Ward, Mile end
Dolphin, James Hall, Hythe st
Duke of Wellington, Simon Day, Magdelene st
Duke of York, John Marriott, Barrack st
Duncan's Head, William Payne, Head st
Fencers, Thomas Wire, Maidenburgh st
Fleece Tap, John Hills, Culver st
Goat & Boot, William Pitt, East hill
Green Dragon, George Clare, Pelham's la
Greyhound, Joseph Appleby, St. Botolph st
Greyhound, Robert Ransdale, Langhan
Horse & Groom, Thos. Brown, Crouch st
Joiner's Arms, Elizabeth Lloyd, Trinity st
King's Arms, Thomas Fitch, Harwich rd
King's Head, Elizabeth Gurling, Lexden
Lamb, George Appleby, High st
Leathern Bottle, William Smith, Lexden
Marlborough's Head, Mary Ann Dowson, Queen st
Maltster's Arms, William Hale, Hythe New quay
Marquess of Granby, Nathan Bentall, 28 North hill
Mitre, James Folkard, East hill
Nelson's Head, John Bacon, W. Stockwell st
Neptune, William Pannefer, Hythe
Old Whalebone, Francis Malcolm, East hill
Ordnance Arms, Everard Willett, Hythe
Packet, William Fuller, Hythe st
Partridge, John Cross, Boxted
Plough, John Long, Magdalene st
Prince of Wales, Wm. Mason, Magdalene st
Queen's Head, Jas. Chamberlain, Hythe st
Red Cross, William Wade, Magdalene st
Rising Sun, William Mills, Hythe
Rose & Crown, Benjamin Smith, East st
Sawyer's Arms, Thomas Rawlins, Magdalene street
Sea Horse, Benjamin Turpin, 61 High st
Ship, Samuel Cranfield, East hill
Ship, John Seaborn, St. John st
Star and Anchor, Edward Buckingham, Stonewell street
Star & Garter, Charles Norden, East hill
Sun, Jeremiah Emmen, Maidenburgh st
Sun, Joseph Wenden, Lexden
Swan, John Murrells, Hythe st
Tailor's Arms, Jno. Overall, 10 Short Wyre st
Three Horse Shoes, Thos. Nunn, Hythe
Three Mariners, James Gardner, Magdalene street
Waggon and Horses, Jemima Godden, North hill
Waterloo, James Eustace, Magdalene st
Weaver's Arms, Geo. Jackson, Middleburgh
White Hart, James Hawes, Crouch st
White Horse, Wm. Scovell, East bridge
White Lion, Saml. Howell, Magdalene st
Wool Pack, Robt. Palmer, St. Botolph st
Yorkshire Grey, Samuel Branson, Magdalene street

TOBACCO PIPE MAKERS.
Lowthroup Elizabeth, Magdalene st
Pettitt James, 38 East st
Rand Stephen, George lane

TOBACCONISTS.
Gentry Jno. (& tea dealer) 56 High st
Gosnell John, 6 Short Wyre st
Roberson Hannah, Long Wyre st

TOY DEALERS.
See Hardwaremen & Toy Dealers.

UMBRELLA MAKERS.
Foster William, 13 North hill
Whistock James, Magdalene st

VETERINARY SURGEONS.
Cross William, Queen st
Garrard Abraham, Trinity house, Culver st
Ward Ebenezer, 59 North hill

VINEGAR MANUFACTURER.
Osborne John Posford, Botolph st

WATCH & CLOCK MAKERS.
Banister Joseph, 18 High st
Banister Thomas, St. Botolph st
Barker George F. 26 St. John st
Hedge Nathaniel, 95 High st
Jennings William, 37 Long Wyre st
Mason Thomas, 25 High st
Mitchell Jos. (& engraver) 22 High st
Shuttleworth John, 7 Crouch st
Turner Henry, 10 Short Wyre st
Wire William, 45 High st

WHEELWRIGHTS.
Ames John, St. James's
Barrett Samuel, Langhan
Cole Joseph, Langhan
Garwood James, Mile end
Green John, Great Horsley
Kiddington Robert, East st
Lee John, Magdalene st
Osborne James, East st
Ward Thomas, Maidenburgh st
Woods Henry James, East st

WHITING MANUFACTURERS.
Bloomfield John, Hythe
Willet Joseph, Greenstead

WINE & SPIRIT MERCHANTS.
Bawtree George & Charles (and rectifiers) Culver st
Kimber, Gross and Nicholl (& porter merchants and brewers) East hill
Mason James William, 49 North hill
Osborne Jno. Posford, St. Botolph st
Sallows Edward, 7 High st
Salmon Robert, High st
Smith John, High st
Smith Wm. Bolton & Son, Head st

WOOLSTAPLERS.
Miller Alex. Fordice, St. John's green
Wright William, Long Wyre st

Miscellaneous.
Avey John, trunk maker, Short Wyre st
Badcock John, collector of excise, East hill
Barnes Thos. clog, &c. maker, Long Wyre st
Barnes William, dairyman, Castle Bailey
Bennell Joseph, waggon office, Head st
Blyth Samuel, mattress maker, Culver st
Brown James & Co. rag merchants, Magdalene street
Brown John Alexander, turner, North st
Carr John, last maker, Eld lane
Cater John, dealer in birds, 65 East hill
Chaplin John, oil mills, Lexden
Clubb Stephen, flock manufacturer, Hythe
Coveney Jno. wire worker, 18 Long Wyre st
Cranfield Geo. hay dealer, Maidenburgh st
Culpeck James, fellmonger, Dead lane
Doel Mary, register office, East hill

Eisdell James Carter, ivory black manufacturer, Hythe
Farmer George, cutler, 17 St. John st
Fenning James, town crier and parish clerk, 25 Queen st
Field Wm. parish clerk, St. John's green
Folkard James, cattledealer, Mitre Tavern, East hill
Ford J. J. and Co. ginger beer manufacturers, 7 Maidenburgh st
Foster Ebenezer, dealer in British wines, 32 High street
Fox William, relieving officer for the poor law union, 53 Crouch st
Freeman William, engraver and copperplate printer, 23 Crouch st
Gull Daniel, parish clerk, Layer road
Hawkins William, timber merchant, Magdalene street
Howe William, parish clerk, Wyre st
Huggins Jeremiah, parish clerk, Culver st
Ladell Christmas, parish clerk, East hill
Mann Geo. parish clerk, Maidenburgh st
Mann Wm. parish clerk, Maidenburgh st
Philbrick Wm. parish clerk, Schere gate
Rogers William, parish clerk, Hythe
Roofe Chas. Bell, horse dealer, 119 High st
Sack James, parish clerk, Hythe
Salmon Robert, proprietor of funeral carriages, 98 High st
Sams Thomas Frederick, parish clerk, Butt road
Sarly William, parish clerk, Magdalene st
Saunders John, lathe filer, 8 North hill
Scott Daniel, parish clerk, Middleburgh
Southgate Edward, carrier, North st
Squires James, tinman, St. Botolph st
Swire Geo. dutch clock makr. St. Botolph st
Wagstaff William, parish clerk, Church la
Wallis John, chimney sweeper, Maidenburgh st
Wallis John, jun. chimney sweeper, 2 George st
Watson Ephraim, parish clerk, Balkerne la
Whitten Samuel, parish clerk, Greenstead
Willett Sarah, shipwright, Greenstead
Wittey Samuel, clerk to the magistrates, Queen street
Wyre Chignall, market clerk, East hill

Public Buildings, Offices, &c.

Assembly Rooms, at the Three Cups Hotel, High st
Borough Gaol, High st—Samuel Cardy, *governor*
Botanic Gardens, East hill—Henry Goody, *secretary;* John Brown, *curator.*
Colchester and Essex Hospital, Allen Maclean and Edward Williams, *physicians;* Alderman Partridge, William Waylen & Roger Sterling Young, *surgeons;* C. H. Macintosh, *house surgeon and apothecary;* C. E. Stuart, *secretary;* Mrs. M. Barron, *matron*
Conservative Reading Rooms, 18 Head st
Corn Exchange, High st—James Martin, *clerk*
County House of Correction, Ipswich road—William Mason, *governor*
Custom House, Hythe street:—
Collector—William John Williams
Comptroller—James Underwood Argent
Clerk—William Devall
Locker—Allison Abbott
Landing Waiter—William Probyn
Tide Surveyor—William Bull
Excise Office, John Badcock, *collector;* Richard Davies, *supervisor*
Gas Works, St. Leonard's, Hythe—William Fenton, *manager*
News Room (subscription), at the Three Cups Hotel, High st
Police Office, High st—William Rand, *inspector*
Registrars of Births, Deaths, &c.: Francis Gibbs Abel, *superintendent*, Crouch st; John Bland, 15 George street, & William Fisher Bull, 146 High st, *registrars*
Religious Tract Depository, 30 Queen st
Stamp Office, William Mason, esq. *distributer;* S. Tillett, *superintendent*
Theatre, Queen st
Union Poorhouse, Balkerne hill—James Roy, *governor*
Water Works, Balkerne lane
Weights and Measures' Office, North hill—William Reeves, *inspector*

COACHES.

To LONDON, the *Royal Mail* (from Norwich), calls at the Three Cups Hotel, every morning at twenty minutes past one; the *Wellington* (from Hadleigh), every morning at nine—the *Defiance* (from Harwich), calls at the same Inn, and the George, every afternoon at a quarter before two; and the *Star* (from Yarmouth), calls at the Three Cups, every afternoon at three.
To LONDON, the *Telegraph* (from Yarmouth), calls at the George, every morning at a quarter before two—the *Blue* (from Ipswich), calls at the Red Lion office, every forenoon (Sunday excepted) at eleven, and the *Shannon*, from the George, every day at twelve.
To BRAINTREE, the *Hope*, from the George, every Tuesday, Thursday and Saturday afternoon at four; goes thro' Coggeshall.
To CAMBRIDGE, the *Rover*, from the Red Lion, every Monday, Wednesday and Friday forenoon at eleven; goes thro' Colne, Halstead and Linton.
To HADLEIGH, the *Wellington*, from the Three Cups, every afternoon (Sunday excepted), at a quarter past three.
To HARWICH, a *Mail Cart*, from the Post Office, every morning at three.
To HARWICH, the *Le Hirondelle*, from the George, and the *Defiance* (from London), calls at the same Inn, both every night at half-past eight, and go through Manningtree.
To IPSWICH, the *Blue* (from London), calls at the Red Lion, every evening (Sunday excepted) at six.
To NORWICH, the *Royal Mail* (from London), calls at the Three Cups, every morning at half-past one.
To WATTON, the *Perseverance*, from the George, every morning at eight; goes through Thorpe.
To YARMOUTH, the *Telegraph* (from London), calls at the Three Cups, every morning at half-past one, and the *Star*, daily, at half-past twelve.

CARRIERS.

To LONDON, Bennell, Deacon & Son's *Fly Vans* and *Waggons*, from the Sea Horse Inn, and their office, Head street, every Tuesday, Wednesday and Friday at noon, and Stanbury & Porche's *Fly Vans* & *Waggons*, from the India Arms, All Saints, every Monday, Tuesday, Wednesday and Friday morning.
To BENTLEY, — Clark, from the Castle, daily.
To BOXFORD, a *Mail Cart*, from the Post Office, every morning at six.
To BRAINTREE, — Hodge, from the Bull, every Saturday.
To BRIGHTLINGSEA, — Cook, from the Swan, — Day, from the George, and — Littlewood, from the Castle, all daily.
To BURY ST. EDMUNDS, a *Mail Cart*, from the Post Office, every morning at five, and Edward Southgate's *Van*, from North street, & the Waggon & Horses, every Tuesday morning at ten; goes through Lavenham.
To CAMBRIDGE, — Clayton, from the Bull, every Saturday.
To CLACTON, — Bagley, from the Castle, every Tuesday, Thursday & Saturday.
To CLARE, — Elmer, from the Bull, every Tuesday and Saturday.
To COGGESHALL, — Unwin, from the Bull, daily.
To COPFORD, — Bartholomew, from the Horse and Groom, daily.
To DEBENHAM, — Ridings, from the Bull, every Sunday.
To DEDHAM & STRATFORD, a *Mail Cart*, from the Post Office, every morning at six, and — Folkard, from the Sea Horse, every Wednesday and Fri.
To DISS, *Waggons*, from the Bull, every Tuesday, Thursday and Saturday.
To EARLS COLNE, — Halstead, from the Bull, daily.
To EAST BERGHOLT, — Peck, from the Swan, daily.
To EAST MERSEA, — Greenleaf, from the Blue Post, every Mon. Wed. & Fri.
To ELMSTEAD, — Rea, from the Swan, daily.
To FRETING, — Almond, from the Swan, every Tuesday and Saturday.
To GREAT BENTLEY, — Lilly, from the Castle, every Monday, Wednesday and Saturday, and — Clark, from the same place, every Tues. Thurs. & Sat.
To GREAT HOLLAND, — Cunningham, from the Swan, every Tuesday, Thursday and Saturday.
To HADLEIGH, Bennell, Deacon and Sons, from Head street, daily, and — Warren, from the Lion Tap, every Wednesday and Saturday.
To HARWICH, a *Mail Cart*, from the Post Office, every morning at six—Bennell, Deacon & Sons, from Head street, daily, and — Salter, from the Swan, every Monday, Wednesday & Saturday.
To IPSWICH, Bennell, Deacon & Sons, from Head street, daily— — Garwood, from the Castle, every Tuesday, Thursday & Saturday, & — Rouse, from the Sea Horse, and — Hawkins, from the Swan, every Monday, Wed. and Friday.
To KIRBY, — Burrell, from the Sea Horse, every Tues. Thurs. and Sat.
To MALDON, — Keys, from the Bull, every Tuesday, Thursday & Saturday.
To MANNINGTREE and MISTLEY, Bennell, Deacon and Sons, from Head street, daily— — Salter, from the Swan, every Monday, Wednesday & Saturday, and — Baker, from the Swan, every Monday, Tuesday and Thursday.
To MISTLEY, — Wilton, from the Sea Horse, daily.
To NEYLAND, — Parker, from the Waggon and Horses, every Tuesday, Thursday and Saturday.
To NORWICH, — Beart, from the Castle, every Saturday.
To OAKLEY, — Cousins, from the George, every Tuesday, Wed. and Sat.
To PELDON, — Greenleaf, from the Blue Posts, every Monday, Wednesday & Fri.
To ST. OSYTH, Franklin & Minter, from the George, every Tuesday, Thurs. & Sat.
To STOKE, — Parker, from the Waggon and Horses, every Tues. Thurs. & Sat.
To STOWMARKET, — Broom, from the Bull, every Sunday.
To STRATFORD ST. MARY, — Garwood, from the Castle, — Rouse, from the Sea Horse, and — Hawkins, from the Swan, every Monday, Wed. and Fri.
To SUDBURY, a *Mail Cart*, from the Post Office, every morning at four, and — Bray, from North hill, every Tuesday and Friday.
To TENDRING, — Lilly, from the Castle, every Monday, Wednesday & Saturday.
To THORPE, — Bagley, from the Sea Horse, every Monday, Wed. and Sat.
To TOLESBURY & TOLLESHUNT, — Garrett, from the Ship, every Wednesday and Saturday.
To WATTON, Bennell, Deacon & Sons, from Head street, and — Moles, from the Swan, daily.
To WEIGHLEY, a *Mail Cart*, from the Post Office, every morning at five, and — Lilly, from the Castle, every Monday, Wednesday and Saturday.
To WEST BERGHOLT, — Clark, from the Waggon and Horses, daily.
To WEST MERSEA, — Harvey, from the Blue Posts, every Tues. Thurs. & Sat.
To WIVENHOE, — Powell, — Cole, & — Penny, from the Lamb, daily.
To WORMINGFORD, — Bray, from North hill, every Tuesday and Friday.
To YARMOUTH, — Smith, from the Bull, every Wednesday and Saturday.

CONVEYANCE BY WATER, FROM THE QUAY, HYTHE.

To LONDON, Jarvis and Mann's (late Parker & Jarvis) *Vessels*, to Wool quay; Thomas Nunn, to Nicholson's wharf; Baker & Co. to Galley quay; Samuel S. Brown, to Botolph wharf (all to Lower Thames street) every Saturday; and F. Lewis, to Fenning's wharf, London bridge, every Wednesday and Saturday.

To GAINSBOROUGH and HULL, F. Lewis' & Thomas Nunn's *Vessels*, every fortnight.

DANBURY, LITTLE BADDOW & NEIGHBOURHOODS.

DANBURY is a village and parish, in the hundred of Chelmsford, situate between that town and Maldon, about five miles distant from either place. It stands on one of the highest hills in this county, within an area of an ancient encampment, about six hundred and eighty yards in circumference, and is supposed to have obtained its name from *Danesbury*, signifying a town or fortress of the Danes. 'Danbury Place' has been the residence of many noble families, but the building is now going fast to decay. The church, from its high and exposed situation, has often suffered through storms and lightning, particularly in May, 1402, when the body and part of the chancel was destroyed. In February, 1749, the spire was struck by lightning, which consumed twenty feet of it downwards; since that time it has been repaired. The edifice is dedicated to St. John the Baptist; the living, which is a rectory, is in the incumbency of the Rev. Brook Henry Bridges. A fair, for toys, is held on the 29th of May. The parish, which is more extensive than populous, contained (including the hamlet of RUSSELLS,) in 1831, 1,060 inhabitants.

LITTLE BADDOW is a parish and village, in the same hundred as Danbury, the village being about two miles south from it. It is a place of but little note; and with the exception of a rich monument in the parish church, to the memory of Sir Henry Mildmay, Knight, and 'Tofts,' the handsome seat of General Strutt, presents no claims upon the attention of the stranger. The church is dedicated to St. Mary; the living is a discharged vicarage, in the patronage of the Strutt family. A certain number of children of the parish are clothed and educated by means of the produce of lands, bequeathed by Edward Butler in 1717; and other children are instructed in a school supported by the dissenters. The parish (including the hamlet of MIDDLE MEAD) contained, in 1831, 548 inhabitants.

POST OFFICE, DANBURY, Isaac Flory, *Post Master.*—Letters from LONDON arrive (by mail cart from Chelmsford) every morning at half-past five, and are despatched every evening at a quarter before ten.

*** *The names without address are in* DANBURY.

GENTRY AND CLERGY.

Bridges Rev. Brook Henry (magistrate) Rectory, Danbury
Bridges Rev. Thomas Pym, Danbury
Bygrave Mr. Robert, Danbury
Johnson Rev. Arthur, Little Baddow
Phillips John Robert Spencer, esq. Riffens lodge
Round John, esq. M.P. Danbury park
Strutt Major-General, Tofts house
Tomlinson Mr. Thomas (surgeon) Danbury

ACADEMIES & SCHOOLS.

INFANTS', Ann Finch, mistress
Morrell Thomas (boarding)
NATIONAL SCHOOL, Alexndr. Cocket, master
NATIONAL SCHOOL—Little Baddow, Frederick Phillips, master; Caroline Phillips, mistress

INNS AND PUBLIC HOUSES.

Bell, James Ellis
Griffin Inn, Samuel Cooper
Rodney, Mary Pullen, Little Baddow
Saracen's Head, James Crow

SHOPKEEPERS & TRADERS.

Ager Augustus, grocer and draper
Bailey Henry, baker
Barker Oswald, shoemaker
Barwell Robert, shoemaker
Bellamy Thomas, tailor
Blanks Lazarus, parish clerk, Little Baddow
Bright Edward, carpenter
Chipperfield Elijah, millwright
Crabb Jesse, carpenter
Edwards John, shopkeeper, Little Baddow
Ewers Ann, shopkeeper
Flory Isaac, grocer and draper
Flory Isaac, saddler
Francis James, butcher
Harris Robert, blacksmith
Hollingsworth Hny. grocer & draper
Hollingsworth William, baker
Jaggs Thos. carpenter, Little Baddow
Joslin Wm. plumber, painter & glazier
Joyce Thomas, baker
Lewin Benj. maltster, Little Baddow
Livermore Benj. miller, Lit. Baddow
Maddox John, blacksmith, Little Baddow
Mallett Joshua, miller
Nunn Josh. shoemaker, Lit. Baddow
Page William, shopkeeper
Pickman Richd. shoemaker [dow
Piggott John & Co. millers, Lit. Bad-
Ramsay Josiah, blacksmith
Saward Richard William, bricklayer
Simmonds Edward, butcher
Stevens John, carpenter
Thornton Daniel, parish clerk
Wilson William, baker and shopkeeper, Little Baddow

DUNMOW, GREAT AND LITTLE,

WITH THE VILLAGES OF FELSTEAD, STEBBING AND NEIGHBOURHOODS.

DUNMOW, though hitherto considered as scarcely ranking, in size, population or trade, beyond a village, is a corporate town, and entitled to hold a market on Tuesdays; the latter privilege has not for some years been exercised, but its resumption is now seriously contemplated by some spirited inhabitants of the place and neighbourhood. This town is situated on the Chelmer (one of the finest trout streams of its size in the kingdom), in the hundred of Dunmow—36 miles N. N. E. from London, and 9 E. from Bishops Stortford. It was incorporated in the 2nd and 3rd of Philip and Mary—the charter vested its government in a bailiff and twelve burgesses. The Right Hon. Henry Viscount Maynard, whose seat and beautiful park, at Little Easton, called Easton Lodge, is about two miles N. W. of Dunmow, is lord of the manor (parcel of the dutchy of Lancaster), and holds a court leet and baron annually. The town of Great Dunmow is now well lighted with gas; and a coal company has been formed, whose object is to supply the inhabitants with good fuel, at a more moderate rate than they have hitherto been able to procure it, from Chelmsford and Maldon. The principal inns at this place are the 'Saracen's Head,' the 'Star' and the 'White Lion,' all well conducted comfortable houses—the first a posting house. At Little Dunmow, about a mile and a half from hence, was a priory, now the parish church, remarkable for a curious tenure, instituted in the reign of Henry III, whereby the lord of the manor is bound to 'give a flitch of bacon to any couple who, being married a year and a day, shall swear that they have not once quarrelled or repented of their marriage.' The flitch, it is said, has been claimed by *six* couples since the reign of Henry VI—three times before the dissolution of monasteries, and three times since: the last couple recorded as successful were John Shakeshanks, woolcomber, and Ann his wife, on the 20th June, in the year 1751; once since that period, in 1832, it was demanded by a Mr. Vine and his wife (from Reading, in Berkshire), who took up their abode at the Saracen's Head inn, Great Dunmow, and continued to prosecute their claim, but the reward was evaded. The Saffron Walden and Dunmow agricultural society, established about four years since, has, however, been the medium of reinstituting the ancient practice, divested of antiquated rites and without the obligation of an oath: on the 25th of September, 1837, John Player, Esq., then mayor of Saffron Walden and a member of this society, at the annual meeting and ploughing-match, presented a gammon of bacon to Samuel and Mary Bloomfield, as a reward for having brought up a family of nine children, and placed them in respectable service, without parochial relief, during a union of forty years—and also with a copy of verses, written to commemorate the more rational revival of the prize. In 1838 the gammon was offered by N. Catlin, Esq., mayor of Saffron Walden in that year; and there is no doubt but the custom will be perpetuated. The parish church, dedicated to St. Mary, is a large ancient structure, with an embattled tower: the benefice is a vicarage, in the patronage of the bishop of London; the Rev. Henry Lewis Magendie is the present incumbent. There are places of worship for independents, baptists and the society of friends; a charity school for boys and girls, and a savings' bank: the latter, established in 1818, is of incalculable benefit to the industrious classes of the neighbourhood—it has 490 depositers, and nearly £15,000. invested monies. There are several handsome seats contiguous to Dunmow, and the surrounding country affords some pleasing prospects; the land is fertile, and more diversified by hill and dale than in many other parts of Essex. Fairs are held on the 6th of May and 8th of November. The population of Great Dunmow, in 1831, amounted to 2,462; and that of Little Dunmow to 378.

About four miles E. by S. from Dunmow, in the hundred of Hinckford, is FELSTEAD, or *Feelstead*, village and parish. Richard Lord Rich founded a free grammar school here for eighty poor boys, born in this county, which formerly attracted some notice and excited considerable interest; but—from what cause is not generally understood—there has been but one pupil upon the establishment for many years! There are alms-houses for six indigent persons, founded by the same nobleman. Upon the Chelmer, which divides this parish from that of Great Waltham, are some corn mills. The living of Felstead is a vicarage, in the presentation of the Hon. W. Pole Tilney Long Welleley, the lord of the manor; the incumbent is the Rev. Jeremiah Awdry, and his curate the Rev. G. L. Hanson. The parish contained, by the last census, 1,788 inhabitants.

STEBBING is a village and parish in the same hundred as Felstead, rather more than three miles east from Dunmow. The church, which is dedicated to St. Mary, has lately been enlarged; the benefice is a vicarage, in the patronage of the Butt family. A fair for cattle and fat lambs is held annually on the 10th of July. The population of the parish, in 1831, was 1,788.

POST OFFICE, GREAT DUNMOW, John Perry Gunn, *Post Master*.—Letters from LONDON arrive every morning at half-past six, and are despatched every evening at half-past seven.

POST, FELSTEAD, *Receiving House* at Robert Rutland's, Swan Inn.—Letters from LONDON arrive every morning at six, and are despatched every night at eight.

NOBILITY, GENTRY AND CLERGY.

Barnard Charles, esq. Marks hill
Beaumont Mrs. Bridget, Garston ldge
Blyth Thomas, esq. Little Dunmow
Chesshyre Rev. Jno. Rectory, Easton
Crocker Rev. James, Felstead
Davey Mr. William, Stebbing
Franklin Mr. John, Dunmow
Frost Rev. Richard, Dunmow
Garrard Rev. William, Dunmow
Hanson Rev. George Lowden, Vicarage, Felstead [cottage
Henniker Hon. Lady Bridget, Brook
Knight Mr. Edward (merchant) Dunmow [mow
Majendie Rev. Henry Lewis, Dun-
Mark Rev. John, Felstead
Maynard Vicount, Easton lodge
Morrison Rev. Joseph, Stebbing
Pepper Mrs. Susan B. Dunmow
Philbrick Saml. esq. Dunmow [bing
Pocklington Rev. Henry Sharpe, Steb-
Surridge Rev. Dr. Thomas, Felstead
Toke Rev. Richd. Randall, Barnstone
Willis Jas. Webb, esq. Stebbing park

ACADEMIES AND SCHOOLS.

Not otherwise described are Day Schools.

Barfield Arthur (boarding and day), and land surveyor, Dunmow
FREE GRAMMAR SCHOOL, Felstead —Rev. Dr. Thomas Surridge, master
FREE SCHOOL, Stebbing—Mary Allen, mistress [mow
Gunn Susan (boarding & day) Dun-
Moor Robert, Stebbing
NATIONAL SCHOOLS (boys' & girls') Dunmow—Chas. Barker, master; Maria Barker, mistress [stead
Surridge Rev. Dr. Thos. (brdng.) Fel-
Warner John (boarding & day) Dunmow [Felstead
Woodwards John (boarding & day)

ATTORNEYS.

Johnson William, Dunmow
Sterry William, Dunmow
Toke Nicholas (and clerk to the magistrates) Dunmow
Wade William Thomas, Dunmow

BAKERS & FLOUR DEALERS.

Banister John, Felstead
Bavin James, Stebbing
Boyton William, Stebbing
Choppin Samuel, Stebbing
Langworthy John, Dunmow
Linsell Samuel, Stebbing
Mumford Simeon, Dunmow
Parker Jno. (& confectionr) Dunmow
Tyler Philip, Dunmow
Willis Ezra, Dunmow

BASKET MAKERS.

Gosling James, Felstead
Grant James, Dunmow
Prior John, Dunmow

BLACKSMITHS.

Barker John, Stebbing
Chiles James, Dunmow
Cock Timothy, Stebbing
Drane James, Dunmow
Drane John, Stebbing
Farrow Joseph, Stebbing
Fuller James, Felstead
Fuller Robert, Little Dunmow
Fuller Sarah (& whitesmith) Felstead
Guyver and Collis, Dunmow
Parr Richard Stebbing
Young James, Dunmow

BOOKSELLER & STATIONER.

Carter Dansie (& printer, bookbinder, and news agent) Dunmow

BOOT & SHOE MAKERS.

Barker James, Felstead
Cheek Benjamin, Dunmow
French Thomas Joseph, Felstead
Glasscock John, Stebbing
Gower William, Stebbing
Joyce Thomas, Felstead
Lapworth Mordecai, Stebbing
Philpott Wm. Stebbing and Felstead
Prance William, Dunmow
Pratt William, Dunmow
Prior William, Dunmow
Pye William, Dunmow
Staines James, Stebbing

BREWERS.

Randall Richard & William, Dunmow

BRICK AND TILE MAKERS.

Medson Robert, Dunmow
Philbrick Edward S. Dunmow
Scruby John, Dunmow
Scruby William, Dunmow

BRICKLAYRS AND SLATERS.

Cock William, Dunmow
Cross Stephen, Stebbing
Cross Thomas, Stebbing
Johnson James, Dunmow
Johnson John, Dunmow
Johnson Samuel, Dunmow
Laszell Edward, Felstead

BUTCHERS.

Britton Elizabeth, Stebbing
Harrisson John, Felstead
Hasler Robert, Felstead
Taylor John, Dunmow
Taylor Robert, Dunmow
Watson George, Dunmow

CARPENTERS & JOINERS.

Franklin Samuel, Dunmow
Holgate Abraham, Dunmow
Lamprell William, Dunmow
Leech William, Dunmow
Smith William, Stebbing
White Elizabeth, Felstead
Young Sarah, Felstead

CHYMISTS AND DRUGGISTS.

Frankum Thomas, Dunmow
Piper Wm. (& news agent) Dunmow

COOPERS.

Ellis William, Felstead
Faiers John Wm. (& turner) Stebbing
Gibbons Thomas (& turner and patten maker) Dunmow
Wright Charles, Dunmow

CORN DEALERS & MEALMEN.

Burton Robert, Dunmow
Mumford Samuel, Felstead

CORN FACTORS.

Hitching Richard, Dunmow
Randall Richard & William, Dunmow

CURRIERS AND LEATHER CUTTERS.

Philbrick Edward S. Dunmow
Searl Thomas, Dunmow

FIRE, &c. OFFICE AGENTS.

ESSEX and SUFFOLK EQUITABLE, Sarah Sewell, Dunmow
ESSEX ECONOMIC, Robert Brightwen, Dunmow [Dunmow
NORWICH UNION, John Warner,
ROYAL EXCHANGE, William Collis, Dunmow [Felstead
ROYAL EXCHANGE, C. F. Phillips,
WESTMINSTER (life) and BRITISH (fire), John Perry Gunn, Dunmow

GLASS, CHINA, &c. DEALERS.

Clayton William Impey, Dunmow
Sewell Sarah, Dunmow
Willis Samuel, Dunmow

GLOVERS.

French Thomas Joseph, Felstead
Taylor Josiah, Dunmow

GROCERS & TEA DEALERS.

(See also Shopkeepers, &c.)

Barnard John (and dealer in British wines) Dunmow
Britton John James, Dunmow
Burton John (& clothier) Dunmow
Clayton William Impey, Dunmow
Linsell William, Stebbing
Phillips Cheveley Frederick, Felstead and Little Dunmow
Sewell Sarah, Dunmow
Taylor Elizabeth & Abigail, Stebbing
Turner Charles, Felstead

HAIR DRESSRS & PERFUMRS.

Gunn John Perry (& news agent and cutler) Dunmow [stead
Philpott William (& toy dealer) Fel-

HATTERS.
Collis William, Dunmow
Hockley Robert, Dunmow
Suckling & Leech, Dunmow

INNS.
Saracen's Head (commercial & posting-house) Isaac Malster, Dunmow
Star (& coach house) Mary Bennett, Dunmow
Swan (& coach office) Robert Rutland, Felstead
White Lion, Robt. Medson, Dunmow

LINEN & WOOLLEN DRAPRS.
Clayton William Impey, Dunmow
Linsell William, Stebbing
Moor Robert, Stebbing
Phillips Cheveley Frederick, Felstead
Sewell Sarah, Dunmow
Taylor Elizabeth & Abigail, Stebbing
Turner Charles, Felstead

MALTSTERS.
Barnard John, Dunmow
Barnard William, Stebbing
Bull Charles, Little Dunmow
Choppin Samuel, Stebbing
Chuck Joseph, Stebbing
Ereth William, Stebbing
Franklin William, Dunmow
Jasper Samuel, Stebbing
Linsell Robert, Stebbing
Newman Thomas, Stebbing
Randall Richard & William, Dunmow
Ridley William, Felstead
Scruby John, Dunmow

MILLERS.
Choppin Samuel, Stebbing
Dixon Joseph, Stebbing
Dixon Robert, Felstead
Hitching Richard, Dunmow
Lambert Joseph, Dunmow
Mumford Simeon, Dunmow
Ridley William, Felstead
Whitehead Joseph, Stebbing

MILLINERS.
Faires Elizabeth Ann, Stebbing
Flaxman Maria & Elizabth. Dunmow
Franksman Maria (and stamp distributer) Dunmow
Harrington Sarah, Stebbing
Piper Betsy, Dunmow
Shuttlewood Mary Ann, Stebbing

PAINTERS, GLAZIERS, &c.
Bloomfield George, Dunmow
Young John, Dunmow
Young John, Stebbing

SADDLERS & HARNESS MKRS
Mumford Elisha, Stebbing
Mumford Samuel, Felstead
Savill George, Dunmow
Wilton Henry & Co. Dunmow

SHOPKEEPERS & DEALRS IN GROCERIES & SUNDRIES.
Barker William, Felstead
Bradshaw Thomas, Dunmow
Chalk William, Little Dunmow
Crow John, Stebbing
Pigram William, Stebbing
Reynolds Sarah, Dunmow
Taylor William, Stebbing
Thorn Samuel, Dunmow
Willis Samuel, Dunmow
Wilson Elizabeth, Stebbing

STRAW HAT MAKERS.
Aylett Matilda, Dunmow
Faires Elizabeth Ann, Stebbing
Harrington Sarah, Stebbing
Prior Mary, Dunmow

SURGEONS.
Grice Joseph (and registrar of births and deaths) Dunmow
Salt Thomas, Dunmow

TAILORS AND DRAPERS.
Collis William (& hatter) Dunmow
Crawford Robert, Stebbing
Hockley Robert, Dunmow
Mason Geo. (& clothes dealer) Dunmow
Nash George, Dunmow
Smith William, Stebbing
Suckling and Leech, Dunmow
Suckling Elias, Felstead

TANNERS.
Fuller John, Dunmow
Philbrick Edward S. Dunmow

TAVERNS & PUBLIC HOUSES.
Angel & Harp, Sarah Bush, Dunmow
Bell, Elizabeth Britton, Stebbing
Bell, Josiah Wallis, Felstead
Bell, Charles Wright, Dunmow
Boar's Head, Elizabeth Bright, Dunmow
Bowling Green, Wm. Franklin, Dunmow
Chequers, James Gillett, Dunmow
Chequers, Thomas Skingle, Felstead
Flitch of Bacon, Robt. Parish, Dunmow
Green Man, William Stock, Stebbing
King's Head, Richard Andrews, Stebbing
Old King's Head, Wm. Thorn, Dunmow
Red Lion, Thomas King, Stebbing
Three Tuns, John Willett, Dunmow
White Hart, William Messent, Stebbing
White Horse, Saml. Franklin, Dunmow

TOY DEALERS.
Philpott William, Felstead
Thorn Samuel (& fruiterer) Dunmow

WATCH AND CLOCK MAKERS AND SILVERSMITHS.
Knight Charles, Dunmow
Spurge James, Dunmow

WHEELWRIGHTS.
Brewster James (and timber merchant) Dunmow
Ellis William, Felstead
Guyver and Collis, Dunmow
Ruffel Thomas, Stebbing
Wood Ezekiel, Dunmow
Young John Charles, Felstead

WINE & SPIRIT MERCHANTS
Briggs John Cavell, Dunmow
Randall Richard & Co. Dunmow

Miscellaneous.
Banister John, parish clerk, Felstead
Carter D. secretary to Coal Co. Dunmow
Cheek Benjamin, parish clerk, Dunmow
Cock Charles, parish clerk, Stebbing
Cock John, gunsmith, Dunmow
Collis Joseph, ironmonger, Dunmow
Friendly Society, Town hall, Dunmow—John Perry Gunn, secretary
Gas Works, Dunmow—Danzie Carter, secretary
Hudson Thos. veterinary surgeon, Dunmow
Leapingwell William, accountant, Town hall, Dunmow
Lowe William, poulterer, Felstead
Mumford John, auctioneer, Stebbing
Palmer James, gardener, Dunmow
Savings' Bank, Town hall, Dunmow, (open the first Tuesday in the month, from 11 till 2)—Arthur Barfield, clerk
Smith William, cabinet maker, upholsterer, and turner, Dunmow
Workhouse, Dunmow—Bartholomew Allen, governor; Cath. Allen, matron.

COACHES.
To LONDON, a *Coach*, from the Saracen's Head, Dunmow, every Mon. morn. at 5, and every other morning (Sunday excepted) at six—& the *Times* (from Clare) calls at the Star, every forenoon (Sunday excepted) at half-past eleven; both go through the Roothings, Chipping Ongar, Abridge, Chigwell & Stratford—Hayward's *Coach*, from the Swan, Felstead, every Monday morning at five, & every other morning (Sunday excepted) at seven; goes through Braintree, &c.
To CLARE, the *Times*, (from London), calls at the Star, Dunmow, every afternoon (Sunday excepted), at half-past 2.
To WALTHAM, the *Braintree Branch Coach*, from the Swan, Felstead, every Monday morning at five, and every other morning (Sunday excepted) at seven.

CARRIERS.
To LONDON, Garrett's *Waggons*, from the White Lion, Dunmow, every Fri.—— Brand, every Wed. and — Theobald's *Van*, every Thurs.—Yeulett's *Waggon*, from the Three Tuns, — Watson, from the Chequers, and — Lowes, from the Swan, Felstead, all every Mon. & Fri. — Champen, every Monday, & — Reynolds' *Waggons*, from the Star, every Wed.
To BISHOP'S STORTFORD, a *Mail Cart*, from the Saracen's Head, every morning at half-past six.
To BRAINTREE, James Lewis (from Stebbing), every Friday, and a *Cart*, from the White Lion, Dunmow, every Mon
To HAVERHILL, — Brand's *Waggons*, from the White Lion, Dunmow, every Fri.

EPPING

IS a market town and parish, in the hundred of Waltham; nearly 17 miles N. from London, and the like distance W. by S. from Chelmsford; pleasantly situate on elevated ground near the extensive forest to which it gives name, and on the direct road to Newmarket. It is surrounded by large and rich dairies, the produce of which is much esteemed in the London markets, the butter especially, and the pork and sausages are also held in high estimation. Henry John Conyers, Esq. (whose elegant mansion, 'Copt Hall,' stands about two miles from the town,) is lord of the manor, under whom courts leet and baron are held annually. Epping contains a chapel of ease (the parish church being two miles distant,) and two meeting-houses—one belonging to the independents, and the other to the society of friends. The living of Epping is a vicarage, in the gift of the lord of the manor; the Rev. H. L. Neave is the present incumbent, and the Rev. Richard Sale is the minister of the chapel of ease. The numerous walks, near and through the adjoining forest, render the neighbourhood of this small town rural and delightful; it cannot, however, boast any manufactories, or public institutions of any kind, but, being a place of considerable thoroughfare, it possesses some good inns. The celebrated and ancient 'Fairlop Oak' stood in Hainault forest, formerly a part of Epping forest; it was some years since cut down, and part of its timber now forms the beautiful carved and highly finished pulpit in the new church of St. Pancras, London: the tree, when standing, measured (at about a yard from the ground) thirty-six feet in circumference, and covered with its branches an area of three hundred feet. A fair for dairy cattle is held here on Tuesday in Whitsun week, and a large cattle fair on the 13th of November, which are well attended by graziers from the adjoining districts, also by Scotch and Welch dealers with cattle. A market is held on Friday.—The parish of Epping (which comprises the chapelry of EPPING UPLAND and the hamlet of RYHILL) contained, by the returns of 1831, 2,313 inhabitants.

POST OFFICE, John Judges, *Post Master* (and stamp distributer).—Letters from LONDON arrive every night at ten, and are despatched every morning at four.—Letters from NORWICH and intermediate places arrive every morning at four, and are despatched every night at ten.

NOBILITY, GENTRY AND CLERGY.

Abdy Rev. Charles Boyd, Thoydon Garnon Vicarage
Alcott Joseph, esq. Epping
Ashton John, esq. Wintry park
Bannister Rev. Stephen, Linsey st
Berkley Wm. esq. Coopersale hall
Collins Robert, esq. Rose cottage
Conyers Henry John, esq. Copt hall
Egerton Rev. Charles, Kendal lodge
Frankfort Right Hon. Lord Viscount, Thoydon bower
Gingell Mr. Daniel, Upland
Griffin Mrs. Margaret, Epping
Hinde Misses Louis and Charlotte, Langham lodge
Houblon Mrs. —, Newton house
Jackson Mr. John Bedson
Keys Mr. Philip, Epping
Latham John, esq. Linsey st
Linsell James, esq. Plain [hall
Marsh William Coxhead, esq. Park
Moseley John, esq. Plain
Neave Rev. Henry L. Vicarage
Patman Mr. William, Epping
Payne Mr. Isaac, Vale cottage
Reid Daniel, esq. Plain
Sale Rev. Richard, Epping
Slater Gabriel, esq. Linsey st [hall
Smyth Rev. Edw. (magistrate) Hill
Squire Mr. Thomas, Epping
Thurlow Mr. John, Plain
Towers Mrs. Fanny, Thoydon lodge
Tyrer Mr. John, Plain
[illegible]iles Mr. Edward, Epping
Whiteman John Charlemont, esq. the Grove
Williams Miss Dorothy, Plain

ACADEMIES & SCHOOLS.

Abbatt Richard (boarding)
Day Rachel (boarding)
Dunham Miss
Fowler George (day) [sey st
Jenkins Ann (boarding & day) Lin-
NATIONAL SCHOOL, Wm. Basham, master; Mary Brown, mistress
Palmer Geo. (boarding) Hill house
Smith Ann (day) [and day
Underton Ann & Hannah (boarding

ATTORNEYS.

Andrews Richard Bullock (& clerk to the magistrates)
Windus John (& clerk to the board of guardians)

AUCTIONEERS.

Champness Thomas
Haslam William
Hoy Thomas

BAKERS.

Allen Michael
Haslam Edward
Hobbins Henry (and confectio[ner)
Whipps Charles (and corn dealer)

BLACKSMITHS.

Barltrop Benjamin
Bennett Joseph
Deane Robert, Coopersale
Gilderson John

BOOT & SHOE MAKERS.

Adeane Frederick
Austin Thomas
Burgess William
Colcock Robert
Dodson Samuel
Freestone Thomas
Giffin William
Hummerstone Ann (ladies')
Ingham William
Jessup William
Pratt Richard
Turner James, Coopersale

BRAZIERS & TINMEN.

Appleton George Gross
Hoy Joseph
Hoy Thomas (and coppersmith)

BRICK MAKERS.

Champness Thomas [kiln
Harvey Robert (and potter) Wintry
Stiles John, Solomon hoppet

BRICKLAYERS.

Heath Henry
Marrable Charles

BUTCHERS.

Chapman William
Fairchild Charles [maker)
Fairchild Wm. (& porkman & sausage
Hills John (pork)
Parker Thomas
Teece Charles James
Tubman Joseph Lucas [sett
White Jonathan, North Weald, Bas-

CHYMISTS & DRUGGISTS.

Earle Joseph
Rowlands Thomas (and stationer and oil and colourman)

COOPERS.

Cowland Frederick
Wright George

CORN FACTORS & DEALERS.

Abrey John
Clarke William (dealer)
Whipp Charles

CURRIER.

Wakeling Edward (& leather cutter)

FIRE, &c. OFFICE AGENTS.

PHŒNIX, William Haslam
SUN, Benjamin Doubleday

GROCERS & TEA DEALERS.

(See also Shopkeepers, &c.)

Champness William
Clarke William (and corn dealer)
Crabb John, Coopersale
Doubleday Benjamin
Haslam William (& cheesemonger)
Hyde John, Coopersale
Maxwell James (tea dealer)
Neall Charles
Palmer John (and flour dealer)
Pollard Mary, Linsey st
Stevens Timothy
Wolton James

HORSE AND GIG OWNERS, FOR HIRE.

Basham Thomas (the Cock)
Harvey Robert (the Bell)
Palmer Joseph (the George)
Tweed George (the Thatched House)

INNS & PUBLIC HOUSES.

Bell, Robert Harvey
Black Lion, James Hammond
Chequers, Elizabeth Smith, Uplands
Cock (commercial & posting) Thos. Basham
Duke of Wellington, Geo. Jenkins
Duke of York, Charles James Teece
Epping Place (family hotel and posting House) Richard Stokes
George, Joseph Palmer
Globe, Richard Fairchild
Merry Fiddlers, Susannah Hampton
Royal Oak, Edward Clark, Plain
Sun, William Marrable
Thatched House, George Tweed
Wake Arms, Thomas Billings
White Hart, Peter Coulson
White Horse, Thomas Vince
White Lion, Henry Clark
White Swan, John Miller

IRONMONGERS.

Appleton George Gross
Doubleday Benjamin
Hoy Joseph (and house agent)

JOINERS AND BUILDERS.

Champness Samuel
Champness Thomas [maker
Dawsett Thos. (and turner and chair
Freshwater John
Harvey and Davis
Lawrence James

LINEN & WOOLLEN DRAPRS.

Adeane Frederick (and clothier)
Champness William
Haslam William
Wolton James

LOCKSMITHS AND BELL-HANGERS.

Barltrop Benjamin
Gray George

MILLINERS & STRAW HAT MAKERS.

Ditcher Ann
Lawrence Lucy
Pegrum Jane
Smith Ann

PAINTERS, &c.

Basham Ann
Clarke William and Samuel
Foster John

PERFUMERS.

Campbell John
Hallows Thomas

SADDLERS AND HARNESS MAKERS.

Crossingham William
Phipps William (and rope maker)

SHOPKEEPERS & DEALRS IN GROCERIES & SUNDRIES.

Archer Mary
Clapton Elizabeth
Hampton William
Marsh James
Smith Bonham
Warwicker Maria

SURGEONS.

Gray Thomas (and registrar of births and deaths)
Loft Thomas
M'Nab Daniel Robert

TAILORS.

Adeane Frederick
Foster William (and draper)
Haslam William
Hasler William
Mantell George (and draper)
Spencer John
Tuck Charles
Wood Jeremiah

WATCH & CLOCK MAKERS.

Clarke Charles
Pratt Charles

WHEELWRIGHTS.

Nichols William, Linsey st
Saward & Greatrex (& coach makers)

Miscellaneous.

Brown John, gardener & seedsman, Linsey street
Champness Edmund, constable & inspector of weights and measures
Champness Sarah, confectioner
Coell Thomas, maltster
EXCISE OFFICE, George Inn—Joseph Wilson Gittens, officer
Franklin Jos. glover and breeches maker
Griffiths Charles, coal dealer
Griffiths Frederick, printer, bookseller, stationer, toy dealer, tobacconist, &c.
Grimswick William, parish clerk
Hobson Aaron, statuary and mason, and *Waltham Abbey*
Ingham William, spirit merchant
Monk John, basket maker

MISCELLANEOUS—*Continued.*

Parker James, brush maker
Rogers William, professor of music
Savill Peter, parish clerk, Coopersale
SAVINGS' BANK (open the first Friday in every month, from 12 to 2)—Richard Bullock Andrews, secretary
Tanner William, miller
UNION POORHOUSE, Thoydon Garnon—Charles Littlechild, governor; Sophia Littlechild, matron

COACHES.

To LONDON, the *Royal Mail* (from Norwich), calls at the Thatched House Inn, every morning at four, and the *Epping*, from the Cock Inn, every Monday morning at seven, on other mornings (Sunday excepted) at half-past eight.

*** *Coaches* to and from BURY, CAMBRIDGE, NEWMARKET, NORWICH, BISHOPS STORTFORD, SAFFRON WALDEN, &c. pass through EPPING daily.

CARRIERS.

To LONDON, — Hollinshead, from his house, every Tuesday, Thursday and Saturday, and — Hammond, from the Black Lion, every Monday and Thursday—— Chalk's *Waggon*, from the same Inn, every Monday, Wednesday & Friday, and — Gare's *Van*, every Tuesday and Friday.

To NEWMARKET, Gare's *Van*, twice a week.

GRAYS THURROCK,

WEST THURROCK, WITH PURFLEET; LITTLE THURROCK, CHADWELL AND STIFFORD.

GRAYS THURROCK, once a market town, is in the hundred of Chafford, 21 miles E. of London and 22 S.S.W. of Chelmsford, seated on the north bank of the Thames, nearly opposite to Dartford; it consists of one street, irregularly built, extending along a small creek from the river, navigable for barges and other small craft; it derives its name from having been the property, for more than three centuries, of the noble family of Gray. Formerly this place had a good market for corn; but that of Romford gradually depressed and finally destroyed it. Brick-making is carried on extensively, and barges are kept solely for the purpose of conveying the bricks to the metropolis; there also is a considerable brewery here. The church, dedicated to Saints Peter and Paul, is a small neat edifice; the benefice is a discharged vicarage, in the patronage of the master and fellows of Pembroke college, Oxford. There is a free school in the church-yard, endowed by William Palmer in 1706. About a mile from the town, on an eminence, is Bellmont Castle, the beautiful seat of Richard Webb, Esq. Fairs for cattle are held on the 23rd of May and 20th of October. Population of the parish, in 1831, 1,248.

The village of WEST THURROCK, in the same hundred as Grays, is about one mile and a half W. from that town, situated close to the Thames. The church is dedicated to St. Clement; the living is a discharged vicarage, in the appointment of the Whitbread family. The hamlet of PURFLEET, in this parish, is seated on a gentle acclivity, commanding a romantic, interesting and extensive view over the Thames and the county of Kent. The trade in lime is carried on here to a considerable amount, and the inhabitants of the hamlet are almost entirely employed in the quarries. The excavations and caverns from which the lime and chalk have been taken are exceedingly curious and expansive. One of the largest government magazines for gunpowder is established here, under a superintendent and other officers. There is a neat chapel of ease to the parish of West Thurrock, which, including Purfleet, contains a population amounting to about 800.

About a mile east from Grays stands LITTLE THURROCK; brick-making is the principal employment of its inhabitants. The church, dedicated to St. Mary, is a plain building; the benefice is a rectory, in the gift of the Schreiber family. Population, in 1831, 302.

CHADWELL (or Chadwell St. Mary) is a small scattered village and parish in the hundred of Barstable, about two miles and a half east from Grays Thurrock, the parish being bounded on the south by the Thames. In a wood near the road leading to Stifford are some excavations, the work of an early period, popularly designated 'Danes' holes.' The church is dedicated to St. Mary; the living is a rectory, in (or was lately) the patronage of the Rev. J. P. Herringham. Tilbury Fort is partly in this parish. The population is about 200.

STIFFORD is a small village and parish in the same hundred as Grays Thurrock, nearly two miles N.W. from that town. The church is dedicated to St. Mary; the living is a rectory, in the gift of the master and fellows of Pembroke college, Oxford. Population, 274.

POST OFFICE, GRAYS THURROCK, Ann Smith, *Post Mistress.*—Letters from LONDON arrive (by mail cart from ROMFORD) every morning at nine, and are despatched every afternoon at five.

POST, PURFLEET, *Receiving-House* at the Ordnance Depôt.—Letters from LONDON arrive every morning at eight, and are despatched every afternoon at half-past five.

POST, STIFFORD, *Receiving-House* at the Dog and Partridge.—Letters from LONDON arrive every morning at a quarter past eight, and are despatched every evening at six.

GENTRY AND CLERGY.

Freeman John, esq. Stifford
Harman Benjamin, esq. Purfleet
Heberden Rev. Frederick, Vicarage, West Thurrock
Hele Rev. Henry Selby, Vicarage, Grays Thurrock
Hemmings Mr. Henry Keene, Grays [Thurrock
Ingram Thomas, esq. Stifford
Maconachie Mr. George, A.M. Orsett house, Orsett
Meeson John, esq. Grays Thurrock
Pelling Rev. Wm. Rectory, Stifford
Skinner Mr. Ambrose William, West Thurrock
Webb Richard, esq. Bellmont castle

ACADEMIES AND SCHOOLS.

FREE SCHOOL, Grays Thurrock—William Horncastle, master
Freestone John (day) Stifford
Maconachie George, A.M. (boarding) Orsett house, Orsett
White Caroline, Purfleet

BAKERS.

Boyton Thomas, Grays Thurrock
Buke William, Grays Thurrock
Burrows Thomas, Grays Thurrock
Harris James, Grays Thurrock
Sanford William, Purfleet
Steel Thomas, West Thurrock
West Robert, Little Thurrock

BARGE OWNERS AND LIGHTERMEN.

Baker Peter, Grays Thurrock
Jarvis Richard, Grays Thurrock
Middleton Jno. Wm. Grays Thurrock
Smith Ann, Grays Thurrock

BOOT AND SHOE MAKERS.

Brown George, Grays Thurrock
Coker Thomas, Grays Thurrock
Straight Walter, Grays Thurrock
Taylor Henry, Grays Thurrock

BREWERS AND MALTSTERS.

Clark John (maltster) Lit. Thurrock
Seabrooke Thomas & James, Grays brewery, Grays Thurrock

BRICK MAKERS.

Hemmings Henry Keene, Grays Thurrock
Ingram Robert, Little Thurrock

BRICKLAYERS.

Cribb Alfred, Purfleet
Osborn James, Grays Thurrock

BUILDERS.

Binder William, Orsett
Osborn James, Grays Thurrock
Talbot Robert, Grays Thurrock

BUTCHERS.

Cattaway James, Grays Thurrock
Hutchins John, Grays Thurrock
Ives Thomas, Purfleet
Jordan John, Grays Thurrock

CARPENTERS AND JOINERS.

Binder Wm. (& undertaker) Orsett
Talbot Robert (& undertaker) Grays Thurrock

COAL MERCHANTS.

Aldon James, Grays Thurrock
Baker Peter, Grays Thurrock

CORN DEALER.

Harvey Stephen (and wharfinger) Grays Thurrock

GREENGROCERS.

Argent Maple, Grays Thurrock
Wood William, Grays Thurrock

GROCERS & TEA DEALERS.

(See also Shopkeepers.)

Blaker John, Grays Thurrock
Flower William, Grays Thurrock
Sherriff James, Grays Thurrock

INNS & PUBLIC HOUSES.

Bull, James Aldon, Grays Thurrock
Bull, Abraham Turp, Little Thurrock
Dog & Partridge, Jas. Holt, Stifford
Fox & Goose, Thomas Finch, West Thurrock
King' Arms Inn, Thomas Foreman, Grays Thurrock [fleet
Purfleet Hotel, Daniel Hagan, Pur-
Rising Sun, John Urn, Middleton
Ship, Wm. Cowland, West Thurrock
Ship, Edward Dees, Little Thurrock
Theobald Arms, Jeremiah Jones, Grays Thurrock [Thurrock
White Hart, William Taylor, Grays

SHOPKEEPERS & DEALRS IN GROCERIES & SUNDERIES.

Argent Jesse, Grays Thurrock
Barns Thomas, Grays Thurrock

Barns William, Purfleet
Cowell Richard, West Thurrock
Hodgson Frances, Purfleet
Pain Martin, Little Thurrock
Schooling James, Purfleet
Summers Elizabeth, Grays Thurrock
Turp Abraham, Little Thurrock
Wheeler John, Little Thurrock
Winnett Thomas, Grays Thurrock

SMITHS.

Brookes Thomas, Grays Thurrock
Burchall John, Stifford
Wheeler John, Little Thurrock

TAILORS.

Jackson William, Grays Thurrock
Oxley John, Grays Thurrock

Miscellaneous.

The names without address are in GRAYS THURROCK.

Andrews Joseph, plumber & glazier
Barnes Chas. hair dresser & watch maker
Booker William, carrier
CHALK WORKS, Purfleet—Benjamin Harman, esq. actuary
Coker William, turner
Hewet Thomas, linen draper
Horncastle William, parish clerk
Jackson George, carrier [Thurrock
Meeson John & Thos. lime burners, Grays
Nokes Thomas, miller, West Thurrock and Stifford [Thurrock
Pain Mary Ann, straw hat maker, Little
Peck John, wheelwright, Stifford
POWDER MAGAZINE, Purfleet—Charles Wilkes, esq. store keeper; George Fortiscue, engineer and clerk of the works, and John Piper, chief clerk
Radley John, parish clerk, Orsett
West James, saddler [Purfleet
White Caroline, stationer and library,

COACHES.

To LONDON, a *Coach*, from the King's Arms, every morning (Sunday excepted) at eight; goes through Barking

VANS.

To LONDON, William Booker & George Jackson, from their own houses, Grays Thurrock, every Thursday & Saturday; go through West Thurrock, Avely, Purfleet, Rainham and Barking

CONVEYANCE BY WATER.

To LONDON, Peter Blaker's *Barges*, daily—*Steam Packets* pass also continually during the day.
To ESSEX and KENT (various parts of), Peter Blaker's *Barges*, three times a week, and oftener occasionally.

HALSTEAD,

WITH THE VILLAGES OF CASTLE AND SIBLE HEDINGHAM, EARLS COLNE, GREAT YELDHAM, PEBMARSH AND NEIGHBOURHOODS.

HALSTEAD is a flourishing market town and parish in the hundred of Hinckford, 47 miles N. N. E. from London and 12 s. from Clare, in Suffolk—situated upon the river Colne, and on the slope of a gravelly eminence. Its name originated from the salubrity of the place, our Saxon ancestors applying to it the word *hale*, which in their language, as well as in our modern tongue, bears that signification; and it still maintains its healthy character. A number of hands are here employed in the manufacture of silk and crape, and many others obtain a livelihood by making straw plat, which is in good demand. Courts leet and baron, under the lord of the manor, are held generally once a year; and petty sessions for the south division of Hinckford hundred (for which there is a house of correction here) take place every Friday. The church, dedicated to St. George, is a spacious structure, with a tower surmounted by a wooden spire, the third it has sustained—the second suffered (as Prior poetically foretold) the fate of its predecessor, both being destroyed by lightning: the living is a vicarage, in the patronage of the bishop of London; the present incumbent is the Rev. W. Adams. There are places of worship for baptists, independents and the society of friends; and a free grammar school, founded by Lady Mary Ramsey in 1594, for the education of forty boys belonging to the parishes of Halstead and Colne Engaine; the trusts of this school are committed to the governors of Christ's hospital, London. Several elegant seats adorn this neighbourhood; at Gosfield Hall, one of these mansions, the late royal family of France for some time resided. From the elevations in this part of the county the views are extensive, and present much rich and fertile scenery. A market, chiefly for corn, is held on Friday; and fairs for cattle on the 6th of May and 29th of October. In 1831 the parish of Halstead contained 4,637 inhabitants.

Four miles from the town of Halstead, and in the same hundred, is CASTLE HEDINGHAM (once a market town) village and parish; it takes its name from the contiguous castle, an edifice presenting the purest style of Anglo-Norman architecture, and which, from the massive solidity of its walls (from eleven to thirteen feet in thickness), has for six centuries withstood the operations of time and atmosphere; the hall of audience, and many other apartments, are still in so perfect a state as to excite pleasurable sensations in the mind of the inspecting antiquary. The parish church, dedicated to St. Nicholas, is a fine ancient structure, with a large chancel, containing a superb monument to the memory of John Earl of Oxford, several members of which noble family are interred in this church; and there are some other monuments to persons of distinction: the living is a lay rectory, in the presentation of Ashurst Majendie, Esq., and present incumbency of the Rev. H. D. Morgan. The hop plantations form a pleasing feature in the rich scenery of this neighbourhood. Fairs are held on the 14th of May, 25th July, 15th August and 25th October, for hops and cattle. Population, in 1831, 1,220.

About a mile distant from Castle Hedingham, and in the same hundred, is the genteel and populous village and parish of SIBLE HEDINGHAM. The church, a fabric of considerable size and antiquity, having three aisles and a chancel, with a ring of fine-toned bells, is dedicated to St. Mary: the benefice is a rectory, in the gift of Thomas Warburton, Esq.; the Rev. Charles Parr Burney, D.D. is the present incumbent. In this parish also the hop plantations are numerous.—On an estate in the occupation of Mr. John Spurgeon, builder, there were dug up, in the year 1838, a number of fossil bones, which were embedded in the gravel about fourteen feet below the surface; they have been inspected by several eminent geologists, and pronounced to be those of the mammoth, deer, &c., and are supposed to be antediluvian. An annual fair is held on Easter-Tuesday, chiefly for toys and pedlery. Population, in 1831, 2,194.

EARLS COLNE is a village and parish in the hundred of Lexden, rather more than three miles E. S. E. from Halstead, situated on the main road leading from that town to Colchester, and near to the banks of the Colne. The church, dedicated to St. Andrew, contains several monuments to the De Veres, earls of Oxford; the living is a vicarage, in the alternate patronage of the Reeve and Clarence families. A place of worship for baptists, and an ancient free school, founded by one of the earls of Oxford, are in the village. An annual fair for cattle and toys is held on the 25th of March.

Two miles from Castle Hedingham, and in the same hundred, on the road from Cambridge to Colchester, is the village and parish of GREAT YELDHAM. This neat and genteel little village contains an ancient church, dedicated to St. Andrew: the benefice is a rectory, in the patronage (or was lately) of Sir William B. Rush; the Rev. Edward William Clarke is the present incumbent. The parish contained, in 1831, 673 inhabitants.

PEBMARSH is a parish in the same hundred as Halstead, about three miles and a half N. N. E. from that town. It contains a parish church, dedicated to Saint John the Baptist; the benefice is a rectory, in the presentation of Earl Verulam. The parish, which is strictly agricultural, contains a population of about 650.

POST OFFICE, North-street, HALSTEAD, Lydia Anderson, *Post Mistress*.—Letters from LONDON arrive every morning at half-past five, and are despatched every night at nine.—Letters from CLARE and SUDBURY arrive every night at nine, and are despatched every morning at twenty minutes before six.—Letters from HAVERHILL arrive every evening at eight, and are despatched every morning at six.

A foot post leaves HALSTEAD every morning at nine with letters for PEBMARSH and ALPHAMSTONE.

POST OFFICE, CASTLE HEDINGHAM, Jeffery Carter, *Post Master*, and SIBLE HEDINGHAM, Joseph Curtis, *Post Master*.—Letters from LONDON arrive every morning at 7, and are despatched every evening at 7.

POST OFFICE, EARLS COLNE, William Tawell, *Post Master*.—Letters from LONDON arrive every morning at eight, and are despatched every evening at six.

POST OFFICE, YELDHAM, Mary Fuller, *Post Mistress*.—Letters from LONDON arrive every morning at half-past seven, and are despatched every evening at seven.

GENTRY AND CLERGY.

Adams Rev. William, Vicarage, Parsonage lane
Ager Rev. Thomas, Castle Hedingham
Alder Rev. Wm. Little Maplested
Asle Mrs. Susanh. Castle Hedingham
Balls Mr. James, Alphamstone
Barnard Edwd. Geo. esq. Gosfield hall
Bentall Mr. John, High st
Boston Henry Scott, esq. Chapel st
Brackenberry Horatio, esq. Great Yeldham
Braithwaite William, esq. Castle Hedingham
Brewster Cardinall, esq. Halsted lodge
Brewster James, esq. Maplested hall
Brewster Jos. Nunn, esq. Halsted ldge
Bull Mrs. Mary Ann, Sible Hedingham
Bullock Rev. John Frederick, Earls Colne
Carwardine Henry, esq. Priory, Earls Colne
Cay Miss Mary, High st
Clarke Rev. Edwd. Wm. Sible Hedingham
Clarryvince Rev. John, Earls Colne
Clements Rev. Wm. Colchester road
Currey Mrs. Mary, Sible Hedingham
De Tastet Firmin, esq. Ashford lodge
Edwards Richard Sharwood, esq. Colchester road
Fisher Mrs. Mary, Sible Hedingham
Fisher Rev. Thomas, Pebmarsh
Fisher William, esq. Sible Hedinghm
Fowke Mrs. Mary, Sible Hedingham
Freeborn Mr. John, Gt. Maplested
Gee Mrs. Mary, Ashford lodge
Greenwood Rev. John, Colne Engain
Griffiths Mrs. Henrietta, Castle Hedingham
Hill Robert, esq. Colne park
Hilton Mrs. Hannah, Sible Hedinghm
Hodges Rev. —, Alphamstone
Hume Rev. Edward, White Colne
Hustler Orbell, esq. High st
Jennings Thos. esq. Sible Hedingham
Johnson Rev. Benjamin, High st
Johnson Oliver, esq. Hay house
Kemp Mr. Edward, Alphamstone
Langford Rev. Robt. Sible Hedingham
Lloyd Rev. Wm. Charles, Gosfield
Lukin Mrs. Esther, Sible Hedingham
Majendie Ashurst, esq. Hedingham Castle
Martin Philip Stewart Feake, esq. Sloe farm, Halsted
May Edward, esq. Howe
May John, esq. Gosfield
Mayhew John Jeremiah, esq. Colne Engain
Mayhew Mr. Joseph, Pebmarsh
Morgan Rev. Hector Davies, Castle Hedingham
Nottage George, esq. Castle Hedingham
Nunn Philip, esq. Chapel place
Osborn Mr. John, Sible Hedingham
Partridge Mrs. Eliz. Castle Hedinghm
Prout Rev. Ebenezer, Parsonage la
Rayner Mr. William, Sible Hedingham
Reynolds Rev. David T. Earls Colne
Sayer Mr. Meshech, Earls Colne
Scale Mr. Richd. Fitzjohns, Halsted
Sewell John, esq. Chapel st
Smoothy Thomas, esq. Bois hall
Sparrow Jas. G. esq. Gosfield place
Sperling George, esq. Attwoods
Sperling James Moss, esq. High st
Sperling John, esq. Dynes hall
Sperling Rev. James, Gt. Maplested
Start Mr. John, Pebmarsh
Stebbing Mr. Wm. Vial, Pebmarsh
Steer Rev. Saml. Castle Hedingham
Stevenson Miss Eliz. Castle Hedinghm
Taylor John, esq. Sible Hedingham
Vaizey George D. esq. Star stile
Vaizey Mrs. Sarah, Star stile
Watkinson Rev. Robt. Earls Colne
Way Rev. Charles, Great Yeldham
Way John, esq. Spaynes hall
Woolmer Miss Jane, Sible Hedinghm
Wyatt Robert Burget, esq. Cut edge
Yeldham Joseph, esq. Planas farm

ACADEMIES & SCHOOLS.

Not otherwise described are Day Schools. Marked thus * are Boarding and Day.

*Baldwin Margaret, Castle Hedinghm
Cheveley John, Pebmarsh
Clements Rev. Wm. (brdng) Colchestr road
Coy Miss —, Yeldham
Evans Robert (boarding) Colchester road
Fairbank Susan, High st
Fitch Elizabeth, Earls Colne
*Flavell James, High st
FREE GRAMMAR SCHOOL, Earls Colne—Rev. Jno. Clarryvince, mstr
FREE GRAMMAR SCHOOL, High st—James Flavell, Master
FREE SCHOOL, Great Yeldham—James Laws, master
FREE SCHOOL, Gosfield—Elizabeth Beard, mistress
Honeyman Sarah, Earls Colne
*Hughes Robert C. Chapel st
INFANTS' SCHOOL, High st—Sarah Chaplin, mistress
Jefferies Sarah, Sible Hedingham
*Jephson Charles, Yeldham
*Jones J. T. P. Little Maplested
*Laws James, Yeldham
*Marson Elizabeth, Sible Hedingham
*Marson George James, Chapel st
*Nott Susanh. & Adaliza, Colchestr rd
Paxton Mary Ann (boardng) Yeldham
Percival Sarah, Castle Hedingham
Ruffle Eliza, Castle Hedingham
SCHOOL OF INDUSTRY, Earls Colne—Ann Jarman, mistress
SCHOOL OF INDUSTRY, High st—Jane Pask, mistress
*Thorne Cornelius Josiah, Earls Colne
Whybrew Ann, Great Maplested—(supported by Mrs. Gee)

ATTORNEYS.

Hustler Charles Devereux, High st
Hustler Orbell (and superintendent registrar of marriages) High st
Sewell Decimus, High st
Sperling George, High st
Sperling James Moss (& solicitor to the gas company) High st

AUCTIONEERS & APPRAISRS.

Collis Samuel (appraiser) Pebmarsh
Newman Aaron, Castle Hedingham
Savill and Son, Sible Hedingham

BAKERS.

Angier John, High st
Bowles John, White Colne
Bowles Richard, Causeway
Butcher Hannah, Chapel hill
Emberson George, North street and Parsonage lane
Garrod Thomas, Sible Hedingham
Gilby John, High st
Green John, High st
Hardy Mary, Sible Hedingham
Ingate Sarah, White Colne
King Thos. (& mealman) Greenstead green
Lee William, High st
Lee William, Castle Hedingham
Little William, High st
Mullins John, Chapel st
Redley Isaac, Castle Hedingham
Root Isaac, Castle Hedingham
Sadd Samuel, Earls Colne
Sargeant Robert, North st
Smith Joseph, High st

BANKERS.

Sparrow, Walford & Co. High st—(draw on Barclay & Co. London)

BASKET MAKERS.

Archer Robert, North st
Burder Mrs. Castle Hedingham
Cornell David, High st

BLACKSMITHS & FARRIERS.

Bowyer Samuel, Bridge st
Eldred William, Pebmarsh
Eley Jamson, High st
Farrant Henry, Castle Hedingham
Firman Thomas, Colne Engain
Goodey Samuel, Colchester road
Hawkins Henry, Gt. Maplested
Hawkins John, High st
Hayward Asa, Greenstead green
Hutton Ann, Sible Hedingham
Hutton Thomas, Yeldham
Jarman Jonth. & Thos. Colne Engaine
May Joseph, Earls Colne
Mead John, Sible Hedingham
Messent Charles, Alphamstone
Newcomb Mary, Gosfield
Rayner William, jun. North st
Smith James, North st
White Henry, Earls Colne
White Thomas Hy. Sible Hedingham

BOOKSELLERS & STATIONRS.

Carter Jeffery (and printer) Castle Hedingham
Farrant Zachariah (& stamp distributer) Earls Colne
Gilbert Henry (& printer) High st
Greenwood Robert (stationer) Market hill
Riddle Robert, North st

BOOT & SHOE MAKERS.

Arnall Stephen, Chapel st
Avis Isaiah, High st
Baldwin George, Chapel hill
Byford James, High st
Cardinall James, High st
Cracknell Richard, Gt. Maplested
Davey Daniel, North st
Davis Thomas, High st
Evans Harlow, Alphamstone
Fenner George, High st
Fitch Richard, Sible Hedingham
Gage Thomas, Colne Engain
Hammond Henry, Castle Hedingham
Jay Jonah, Castle Hedingham
Lee Samuel, Earls Colne
Levett George, Pebmarsh
Newcomb John, Gosfield
Percival George, Castle Hedingham
Prior Wm. (& leather cutter) High st
Smith Benj. (& leather cutter) High st
Smoothy John, Yeldham
Staines Thomas, High st
Stucks Joseph, High st
Thurston James, Castle Hedingham

BRASS & IRON FOUNDER.

Hayward Asa, Greenstead green

BRAZIERS AND TIN-PLATE WORKERS.

Beard James, High st
Day Robert John & Co. (& cutlers) High street

BREWERS.

Sewell Alfred, Chapel st
Walford Isaac, High st

BRICK AND TILE MAKERS.

Hilton Hannah, Sible Hedingham
Leonard William, Castle Hedingham
Linnett Joseph, Colchester road
Parish John, Sible Hedingham

BRICKLAYERS.

Bowles Richard, Causeway
Brett Joseph, Sible Hedingham
Fuller John, Yeldham
Goodey William, High st
Green John, Castle Hedingham
Hardy Joseph, Yeldham
Harrington John, Castle Hedingham
Rodgers Zachariah (and builder) Earls Colne
Wildman Robert, Bridge st
Wright Fras. (& builder) White Colne

BUTCHERS.

Allen Thomas, High st
Ames William, Sible Hedingham
Bridgeman George, Gosfield
Butcher Thomas, Colne Engain
Chamberlain Joseph, Gosfield
Dunt John, High st
Dunt William Philip, North st
Evans Jacob (pork) North st
Fairhead Thomas, Earls Colne
Farrington Robert, Sible Hedingham
Fitch Daniel, Sible Hedingham
Fitch Richard, Sible Hedingham
French John, Bridge st
French William, High st
Gallafent Robert, High st
Gatward Henry, Castle Hedingham
Gatward William, Yeldham
Hammond James, Castle Hedingham
Stuttor George, Castle Hedingham
Stuttor James, Earls Colne
Webber John, Pebmarsh

CABINET MAKERS AND UPHOLSTERERS.

Cooper Thomas, High st
Jarman James, Castle Hedingham
Newman Aaron, Castle Hedingham
Oakley James, High st

CARPENTERS & BUILDERS.

Cant Daniel, Alphamstone
Clarke Joseph, Earls Colne
Dent Samuel, High st
Hart John, Colne Engain
Hubbard Stephen, Earls Colne
Jarman Edward, Yeldham
Jarman James, Sible Hedingham
King John, High st
Rayner Abraham, Colchester road
Spurgeon John, jun. Sible Hedingham
Sudbury John, High st
Wicks Robert, Yeldham

CATTLE DEALERS.

Kemp Samuel, Sible Hedingham
Nott William, Pebmarsh

CHINA & GLASS DEALERS.

Gladwyn Ebenezer, Castle Hedinghm
Knight William, Market hill
Wilson Stewardson, High st

CHYMISTS AND DRUGGISTS.

Greenwood Robert (& cigar dealer) Market hill
Jerard John (and apothecary) Castle Hedingham
Paul Horace, High st

COAL MERCHANTS AND DEALERS.

Greenwood & Knight, North st
Haiden Edward, High st
Howard William, Parsonage land
Hubbard John, Sible Hedingham
Taylor John, Sible Hedingham

COOPERS.

Mann Thomas, Earls Colne
Purkiss George, Sible Hedingham
Purkiss Isaac, High st
Root Thomas, Sible Hedingham
Walford Isaac, High st

CORN & SEED DEALERS.

Marked thus * are also Mealmen.

Allen John, Pebmarsh
*Baker Benjamin, High st
*Lee William, High st
*Maidwell Thomas, High st
Ralling Charles, Sible Hedingham
*Robinson William, Chapel st
Rogers Joseph, Castle Hedingham

CORN & SEED MERCHANTS.

(See also the preceding list.)

Haiden Edward, High st
Hubbard John, Sible Hedingham
Sewell Isaac, High st
Smoothy Charles (& hop) the Chase, High st
Taylor John (& porter) Sible Hedingham

CURRIERS AND LEATHER CUTTERS.

Bridge Ferdinand, High st
Cardinall Thomas, North st
Farmer Titus, High st
Thorn Charles E. Sible Hedingham

FIRE, &c. OFFICE AGENTS.

British, Michael King (and news agent) High st
Essex & Suffolk Equitable (fire) James Jesup, Market hill; and Savill and Son, Sible Hedingham
Essex Economic, Ezekiel Bentall, High st; and Jeffery Carter, Castle Hedingham
Norwich Union, F. H. Cawston, Earls Colne
Protestant Dissenters' & General Life & Fire Assurance Co. John Sherring, High st
Royal Exchange, Henry Sutton, High st
Suffolk and General Country, Robert Greenwood, Market hill
Union, James Moss Sperling, High st

GARDENERS & SEEDSMEN.

Barnes Barney, Earls Colne
Brown James, Earls Colne
Cook Jeremiah, High st
Cook John, North st
Fairbank James, Parsonage lane
Fairbank John, High st
Flack Charles, Sible Hedingham
Flack John, Sible Hedingham
London John, Earls Colne
Root William, Town garden

GLOVERS.

Knipp William, High st
Scotcher James (& fellmonger, and woolstapler) Great Yeldham

GROCERS & TEA DEALERS.

(See also Shopkeepers, &c.; and also Tea Dealers.)

Austin Robert, Earls Colne
Bentall Ezekiel, High st
Bishop Thomas, Sible Hedingham
Bourne Thomas N. Earls Colne
Bowtell Thomas, Yeldham
Dix Francis, North st
Farrant Zachariah, Earls Colne
Gladwyn Ebenezr. Castle Hedingham
Harvey Matthew B. High st
Jesup James, Market hill
Lee James, Pebmarsh
Lee William, High st
Nott Samuel, Sible Hedingham
Nott Samuel, jun. Sible Hedingham
Paine George, Castle Hedingham
Silvester William, Alphamstone
Spurgeon John, Sible Hedingham
Stedman Robert, Earls Colne

HAIR CUTTERS.

Avis Isaiah, High st
Clark Thomas, Earls Colne
Heckford Edward, Sible Hedingham
Milnes James (and perfumer, and toy dealer) High st
Rowland Elisha, North st
Smith George, Castle Hedingham
Spurge Harriet (& perfumer) High st

HOP PLANTERS.

Braithwaite Wm. Castle Hedingham
Hobbs Bedo, Nightingale hall, Earls Colne
Hubbard John (and hop merchant) Sible Hedingham
Johnson Oliver, Earls Colne
King Isaac, Castle Hedingham
Leonard William, Castle Hedingham
Myall Richard, Castle Hedingham
Osborn John, Sible Hedingham
Pudney Robert James, Earls Colne
Seymour William, Sible Hedingham
Taylor John (and hop merchant) Sible Hedingham

INNS.

Bell (and posting house) Ambrose Mason, Castle Hedingham
George (& posting house, and family hotel) Market hill
Royal Oak, Charles Colebrook, High st

IRONMONGERS.

Beard James (and brazier) High st
Day Robert John and Co. (and importers of bar iron) High st
Jarman James, Castle Hedingham

LINEN DRAPERS, &c.

Austin Robt. Earls Colne
Bentall Ezekiel (& stamp distributer) High st
Bourne Thomas N. Earls Colne
Bowtell Thomas, Yeldham
Dennis William, Sible Hedingham
Dix Francis, North st
Gladwyn Ebenezer, Castle Hedingham
Harvey Matthew B. High st
Houghton Jas. (& haberdasher) High st
Jesup James, Market hill
Lee James, Pebmarsh
Nott Samuel, Sible Hedingham
Nott Samuel, jun. Sible Hedingham
Paine George, Castle Hedingham
Parlett Susannah & Elizabeth, High st
Silvester William, Alphamstone
Spurgeon John, Sible Hedingham
Stedman Robert, Earls Colne
Tawell and Son, Earls Colne
Tweed John, Yeldham

LOCKSMITHS AND BELL-HANGERS.

Johnson John (& whitesmith) High st
Rayner William, jun. (& gunsmith) North st

MALTSTERS.

Brown Isaac, Colne Engaine
Butcher George, Parsonage lane
Cardy John, Castle Hedingham
Creffield Thomas, Pebmarsh
Gardiner Peter, Earls Colne
Hayward Elizabeth, Castle Hedinghm
Hubbard John, Sible Hedingham
Joscelyn John, Pebmarsh
Nunn James Hardy, Yeldham
Osborn John, Sible Hedingham
Sewell Benjamin, High st
Sewell Joseph, Chapel st
Smoothy Charles, the Chase, High st
Taylor John, Sible Hedingham
Walford Isaac, High st
Weybrew Woodford, Castle Hedingham
Whitlock Francis, Yeldham
Woodward James, Earls Colne

MARINE STORE DEALERS.

King William, Sible Hedingham
Maskell Joseph, Market hill

MILLERS.

Amey Henry, Sible Hedingham
Dell Richard Latimer, Earls Colne
Dow Thomas, Castle Hedingham
Ely Robert, Sible Hedingham
Emson Robt. West Tower mill, North st
Greenwood Oliver, Langley mill
Legeaton Thomas, Sible Hedingham
Livesey Zachariah, Pebmarsh
Mansfield Geo. Castle Hedingham
Mumford Edward, Great Maplested
Nott Samuel, Alphamstone
Ruffle John, Box mill, Halsted
Ruffle Wm. Castle Hedingham
Sewell Isaac, East Tower mill, High st

MILLINERS & DRESS MAKRS.

Avis Amy, High st
Elliston Martha, Bridge st
Firmin Sarah & Susanh. Colchester road
Gallifant Mary, High st
Ling Sarah and Mary, High st
Murray Emily, High st
Spiller Mary, High st
Wright Mary Ann, High st

PAINTERS, PLUMBERS AND GLAZIERS.

Cawston Frederick H. Earls Colne
Coates Harriet, High st
Coates Samuel, High st
Dansie Richard, Castle Hedingham
Farrow William, Sible Hedingham
Hopkins William (and ornamental painter) High st
King Thomas, Bridge st
King Thomas, Greenstead green
Patten George, Colchester road
Smith Henry, Earls Colne
Wilson Richard S. Sible Hedingham
Wilson Stewardson, High st

SADDLERS AND HARNESS MAKERS.

Ardley Benjamin, Gosfield
Crisp Sarah, Pebmarsh
Gilby Mary, Earls Colne
King William, Sible Hedingham
Maskell Joseph, Market hill
Quilter Edward, High st
Rogers James, Castle Hedingham
Smith Robert, Castle Hedingham
Smith William, High st
Staines Elizabeth, High st

SHOPKEEPERS & DEALRS IN GROCERIES & SUNDRIES.

Andrews Jane, High st
Angier John, High st
Beckwith William, High st
Cable Benjamin, Parsonage lane
Cardy John, Castle Hedingham
Cook George, Bridge st
Cooper John, High st
Cooper Simon, Chapel hill
Coward Grace, Gosfield
Cowell Samuel, Gosfield
Cressall Henry, Chapel st
Dowsett Mary, Yeldham
Goldston James, North st
Hart James, Colne Engaine
Harvey Mary, Sible Hedingham
Ingate Sarah, Earls Colne
Kemp John, Bridge st
King Elizabeth, High st
Osborn Sarah, Colne Engaine
Rayner James, North st
Rogers George, Castle Hedingham
Smith Daniel, Earls Colne
Smith Joseph, High st
Snell Maria, High st
Wilding John, Chapel hill

SILK, &c. MANUFACTURERS.

Courtauld, Taylor & Co. (crape manufrs. & silk throwsters) Causeway
Gibson Thos. Field, Parsonage lane
Jones and Foyster (stay lace) Parsonage lane
Paul Horace (shawl) High st
Rodick E. L. & H. Pebmarsh

STRAW HAT MAKERS.

Allen Elizabeth, High st
Alston Sarah, High st
Cardinall Caroline, Bridge st
Dunt Susannah, Chapel st
Fitch Rosanna, Sible Hedingham
May Ann, Earls Colne
Springate Mary Ann, Earls Colne

STRAW PLAT DEALERS.

Basham Lydia, Castle Hedingham
Cooper Simon, High st
Gatward Samuel, Castle Hedingham
Sherring John, High st

SURGEONS.

Duncan Sinclair, Chapel house
Fitch Frederick, Sible Hedingham & Yeldham
Gilson and Rodick, High st
Harvey George, Castle Hedingham
Rodick Septimus, High st
Seymour William, Sible Hedingham
Taylor John Cornelius, M. D. Chapel house, Halsted
Taylor John Polley, Earls Colne

SURVEYORS AND ESTATE AGENTS.

Myall Richard, Castle Hedingham
Savill and Son, Sible Hedingham

TAILORS.

Marked thus * are also Woollen Drapers.

*Basham George, Castle Hedingham
Berring Robert, Yeldham
*Bridge Ferdinand, High st
Brown William, High st
*Eminson William, Earls Colne
*Freeborn James, Castle Hedingham
Harrington Jas. Castle Hedingham
Harris Thomas, Chapel st
Jeggs Joseph, Gosfield
*King Michael, High st
King William, High st
*Mason William, Castle Hedingham
*Nott John, Sible Hedingham
*Sale George, Castle Hedingham
Samson Jesse, High st
*Sherring John, High st
*Sutton Hy. (& furnishing undertakr) [High st
*Tawel & Son (& hatters) Earls Colne
*Wenden Henry, White Colne
Young Robert, Earls Colne

TALLOW CHANDLERS.

Bishop Thomas, Sible Hedingham
Wing Thos. (& melter) Earls Colne

TAVERNS & PUBLIC HOUSES.

Angel, Eliz. Hayward, Castle Hedingham
Angel, James Webb, Bridge st
Bell, David Simpson, Sible Hedingham
Bird in Hand, Tim. Gozzard, Chapel hill
Black Horse, John Root, Sible Hedingham
Bull, Joseph Ward, Bridge st
Cock, James Thurston, Castle Hedinghm
Dog, William Rayner, North st
Five Bells, Thos. Butcher, Colne Engaine
George, George Maldon, Earls Colne
Green Man, Thos. Chamberlain, Gosfield
Griffin, George Butcher, Parsonage lane
Hare & Hounds, Jos. Davey, Greenstead green
King's Arms, Robert Goodram, North st
King's Head, Benjamin Ardley, Gosfield
King's Head, Daniel Balls, jun. Pebmarsh
King's Head, Nebemiah Davey, Colchestr rd
King's Head, Geo. Hunt, Castle Hedinghm
Lamb, William Butler, Sible Hedingham
Lamb, Robert Gallafent, High st
Plough, John Beavis, Greenstead green
Red Cow, Thomas Draper, Box Mill lane
Rose & Crown, Stephen Spencer, High st
Ship, Thomas Davey, High st
Swan, Charles Ralling, Sible Hedingham
Three Crowns, William Moye, High st
Three Sugar Loaves, William Root, Sible Hedingham
White Hart, Ann Chaplin, Earls Colne
White Hart, William Gooch, Yeldham
White Hart, Wm. W. F. Warner, High st
White Horse, Richd. Fitch, Sible Hedinghm
White Lion and Blue Boar, Joseph Milne, Earls Colne
Windmill, Samuel Nott, Alphamstone

TEA DEALERS.

Elliston Joseph, Bridge st
M'Cartney George, High st

TIMBER MERCHANTS.

Davey Thomas, Garden lane
Walford Isaac, High st

VETERINARY SURGEONS.

Hawkes Thos. Baines, Colchester rd
Hutton Thomas, Yeldham
Messent Charles, Alphamstone
Wallis William Sheppard, High st

WATCH & CLOCK MAKERS.

Jacob Robert, High st
Knight William, Market hill

WHEELWRIGHTS.

Beards Thomas, Gosfield
Belsham William, Greenstead green
Chapman Josiah, Yeldham
Coe Zachariah, Earls Colne
Deal Isaac, Great Maplested
Dixey John, Alphamstone
Goodey James, High st
Goodey Samuel, Colchester road
Griggs William (coach) Bridge st
Hawkins George, Castle Hedingham
Jarman John & Thos. Colne Engaine
Jarvis Barnabas, Yeldham
Lee James, Pebmarsh
Nash Robert, Castle Hedingham
Wheeler Alfred, White Colne
Willis Thomas, Sible Hedingham

WINE & SPIRIT MERCHANTS.

Day Robert John and Co. (and importers) High st
Gatward William (spirit) Yeldham

Miscellaneous.

Archer Elizabeth, basket maker, High st
Baker Benjamin, parish clerk, High st
Bartrupp Reuben, parish clerk, Yeldham
Bishop Thos. parish clerk, Sible Hedingham
Brown James, parish clerk, Earls Colne
Cardinall Jas. collector of rates, High st
Cardinall Thos. relieving officer, Bridge st
Carter Jeffery, parish clerk, Castle Hedingham
Cross James, attorney's clerk, High st
EXCISE OFFICE, White Hart, High st—John Meryett, officer, Chapel st
GAS WORKS, Rosemary lane—Greenwood and Knight, proprietors
Goodey James, chair maker, High st
HOUSE OF CORRECTION, Bridge street—George Wright, keeper; Ann Marson, matron
Hustler Orbell, clerk to the magistrates and chief constable of the hundred of Hinchford
Hutchins John, dyer & scourer, High st
Patten William, horse dealer, White Colne
Pettit William Cole, pawnbroker & clothes salesman, High st
REGISTRARS OF BIRTHS, DEATHS, &c. Arbell Hustler, superintendent, High st; Gilson & Rodick, High st, & Frederick Fitch, Sible Hedingham, registrars
Riddle Robt. rag & paper mrchnt. North st
Shead Elizabeth, stay maker, High st
Smith Barron, flock manufactr. Chapel st
Smith Daniel, jun. general dlr. Earls Colne
Spencer John R. tanner, High st
Stuck Thomas, cattle dealer, Bridge st
Wicker Tobias, fishmonger, Bridge st
Willis Thos. coach makr. Sible Hedingham
WORKHOUSE, High st—Thos. Johnson, governor; Elizabeth Johnson, matron
WORKHOUSE, Sible Hedingham—Francis Sewell, master; Mary Sewell, matron

COACHES.

To LONDON, the *Halstead*, from the Royal Oak, every Monday morning at four, and other mornings (Sunday excepted) at six, and the *Sudbury*, every forenoon (Sunday excepted) at a quarter before eleven—the *Old Bury* (from Bury St. Edmunds), calls at the Bell, Castle Hedingham, every day (Sunday excepted) at twelve—the *Phenomena* (from Norwich), calls at the Royal Oak, every afternoon at a quarter past two, and the *Times*, calls at the Rose and Crown, every Monday, Wednesday and Friday at three; all go thro' Braintree, Chelmsford, Ingatestone, Brentwood, &c.

To BURY ST. EDMUNDS, the *Old Bury* (from London), calls at the Bell, Castle Hedingham, every afternoon (Sunday excepted) at three; goes thro' Sudbury and Long Melford.

To CAMBRIDGE, the *Red Rover* (from Colchester), calls at the George Hotel, every Monday, Wednesday and Friday afternoon at one; goes thro' Haverhill and Linton.

To COLCHESTER, the *Red Rover* (from Cambridge), calls at the George Hotel, every Tuesday, Thursday and Saturday afternoon at one; goes through Earls Colne and Fordham.

To NORWICH, the *Phenomena* (from London), calls at the Royal Oak, every day at twelve, and the *Times*, calls at the Rose & Crown, every Tuesday, Thursday and Saturday, at the same hour; both go thro' Sudbury, Long Melford, Bury St. Edmunds, Ixworth, Bottesdale, Eye, Diss, Scole, &c.

CARRIERS.

To LONDON, — Newdick, from the Rose and Crown, every Sunday, Wednesday and Friday— — Fakes and — Wharlow, from the same Inn, and — Howard, from his house, High street, every Tuesday and Friday, and — Ruggles, from the Rose and Crown, every Friday.

To and from LONDON, BURY ST. EDMUNDS, CLARE, &c. *Waggons* call at the Bell Inn, Castle Hedingham, daily.

To BURY ST. EDMUNDS, — Sykes, from the Rose and Crown, daily.

To CAMBRIDGE, Robert Clayton, from the King's Arms, every Sunday morng.

To CLARE, a *Mail Cart*, from the Post Office, every morning at a quarter past five; goes through Sudbury.

To COLCHESTER, — Clayton, from the King's Arms, every Friday morning, and Edward Howard, from his house, Parsonage lane, every Monday, Tuesday, Thursday and Friday.

To WITHAM, a *Mail Cart*, from the Post Office, every evening at nine; goes thro' Braintree.

HARLOW,

WITH THE VILLAGE OF SHEERING AND NEIGHBOURHOODS.

HARLOW is a respectable and neat little town in the parish and hundred of its name, 23 miles N. from London, 7 N. from Epping, and the like distance S. from Bishops Stortford; situated on the Newmarket road, a little above the valley of the Stort, which flows about a mile to the north of it, and separates the counties of Essex and Herts. This town formerly possessed a market and a considerable share of trade, especially in the manufacture of woollens; the former is discontinued, and the latter has long been unworthy of notice--malting is now the only business of any importance. Petty sessions for the division are held at Harlow every Monday. In the early part of the last century the church was destroyed by fire; the present edifice, a more beautiful one, its windows embellished with stained glass, subsequently compensated for the calamity: it is dedicated to St. Hugh; the benefice is a vicarage, in the appointment of the Marquess and Marchioness of Bute, the possessors of the manor; the present incumbent is the Rev. Charles Miller, M.A., and his curate the Rev. Geo. Edward Bruxner. The other places of worship are a chapel of ease, dedicated to St. Mary Magdalene (three miles distant), and one for a baptist congregation. The principal charities comprise a free school, conducted upon the British and Foreign system, for two hundred children of both sexes—others upon the national plan, and some alms-houses. A short distance south-east from Harlow is the parish of HIGH LAVER, venerated by the philosophic visiter as containing in its cemetery a plain marble tomb enclosing the remains of the exalted Locke. Fairs, May 13th, September 9th and November 28th: the September fair (for horses and cattle), which is very celebrated, and termed 'Harlow-bush' fair, is held on a common about two miles from Harlow, and is throngly attended by horse-dealers, graziers and farmers. The population of the parish is about 2,200.

In the same hundred as Harlow, three miles N. E. from that town, on the mail road to Chelmsford, is the village and parish of SHEERING. The church is dedicated to St. Mary—the living a rectory, in the gift of the dean and canons of Christ church, Oxford. Population of the parish, in 1831, 547.

POST OFFICE, High-street, HARLOW, Thomas Penn, *Post Master*.—Letters from LONDON arrive every night (Sunday excepted) at eleven, and are despatched every morning at four.—Letters from NORWICH and intermediate places arrive every morning at four, and are despatched every night at eleven.

GENTRY AND CLERGY.

Arkwright Rev. Joseph, Mark hall
Awcock Mr. Richard, Sheering
Bishop John, esq. Howesham hall
Brown Rev. Edw. Rectory, Sheering
Bruxner Rev. Geo. Edw. Potter st
Chaplin Mrs. Elizabeth, High st
Chaplin Frederick, esq. Mulberry green
Finch Rev. Thomas, High st
Gipps Rev. John, Potter st
Glasscock Mr. James, Sheering
Glyn Mrs. Henrietta Elizabeth, Dorrington house
Hankin Michael, High st
Malin Miss Martha, High st
Miller Rev. Charles, Vicarage
Mumford Mrs. Elizabeth, High st
Pavitt Peter, esq. Sheering hall
Perry Mrs. Maria Jane, Moor hall
Pollett Thomas, esq. New house
Risdon Wm. esq. Kingsmore house
Sims Rev. Henry, Rectory, Parndon
Sims William, esq. Hubbard hall
Stone Mrs. Elizabeth, Mulberry green
Turner Mrs. Mary, High st
Ward Plumer, esq. Gilston park
Willson John, esq. Potter st
Wright the Misses Barbara and Hannah, Mulberry green

ACADEMIES & SCHOOLS.

Chew Lucy (brdng. & day) Potter st
FAWBERT AND BARNARD'S CHARITY SCHOOL, London road—Richard Blackwell, master; Maria M. Hill, mistress
FREE SCHOOL, Sheering—Abigail Press, mistress
Jones John (brdng. & day) High st
Jones Martha and Eliza (boarding and day) High st
Kent William (boarding) Potter st
Lodge Louisa (boarding) High st
NATIONAL SCHOOL, Churchgate st—Eliza Winger and Lucy Reddington, mistresses
NATIONAL SCHOOL, Potter st—Sarah Whitehead, mistress

AUCTIONEERS & APPRAISRS.

Goodwin Edmund (and estate agent and land surveyor) High st
Pool John, Potter st

BAKERS & FLOUR DEALERS.

Aylett William, Latton st
Borham William, Churchgate st
Bridgman James, High st
Glasscock Ann (& confectioner) High st
Glasscock Ths. (& corn factor) High st
Grimwood William, Mulberry green

BLACKSMITHS & FARRIERS.

Bowtell Thomas, Mulberry green
Debman Benjamin, Potter st
Hutchin James, Sheering
Hutchin John, Market place
Hutchin John, jun. High st
Pluckrose James, Netteswell cross

BOOT AND SHOE MAKERS.

Bayman James, Market place
Hutson William, Churchgate st
Parsons John, Potter st
Patmore William, Sheering
Pool John, Potter st
Rumble Charles, High st
Sanders Henry, High st
White Charles, High st
Young John, Sheering

BREWER.

Chaplin Thomas, High st

BRICK MAKERS.

Prior Henry, Harlowbury
Wright John, Harlow mill

BUTCHERS.

Brown John, Potter st
Fitch Edward, Potter st
Gladwin William, Netteswell cross
May Thomas, High st
Prior William, High st
Rattee John, Sheering
Smith Francis, Potter st

COAL MERCHANTS.

Barnard John, Harlow mill
Death Jones, Parndon mill
Death William, Burnt mill
Glasscock Thomas, High st

FIRE, &c. OFFICE AGENTS.

ESSEX ECONOMIC—Thomas Glasscock, High st
NORWICH UNION, John Jones, High street
ROYAL EXCHANGE, John Pool, Potter street

GLASS, CHINA, &c. DEALERS.

Girling Henry, High st
Perry James, Churchgate st

GROCERS & TEA DEALERS

(See also Shopkeepers, &c.)

Awcock John, Sheering
Borham Ann, Potter st
Dyer Ann (tea dealer) High st
Girling Henry, High st
Moult George, High st
Perry Edward, Mulberry green
Perry James, Churchgate st
Savill George, Potter st
Smith Francis, Potter st
Thurgood Mary, Netteswell cross
Whittaker David, High st
Witherly Ann, Churchgate st

INNS.

George, George Crane (commercial and posting house) High st
Green Man, Ann Cook, Mulberry green

IRONMONGERS.

Humphreys John, High st
Hutchin John, Middle row

JOINERS & BUILDERS.

Glasscock John, Sheering
Humphreys John (undertaker and appraiser) High st
Izard John, Potter st
Sharp William, High st and at *Sawbridgeworth*
Smith William, Potter st

LINEN & WOOLLEN DRAPERS.

Awcock John, Sheering
Carr Elizabeth, High st
Girling Henry, High st
Moult George, High st
Perry Edward, Mulberry green
Perry James, Churchgate st
Witherly Ann, Churchgate st

MALTSTERS.
Barnard John, Churchgate st, and at *Sawbridgeworth*
Barnard John, Harlow mill
Barnard John, Sheering
Barnard William, Harlowbury
Chaplin Thomas, High st
Goodwin George, High st
Holmes James, Netteswell cross
Parris Richard, Sheering

MILLERS.
Barnard Charles, Latton mill
Barnard John, Harlow mill
Barnard John, Sheering
Death Jones, Parndon mill
Death William, Burnt mill
Death William, Hunsdon mill
Grange William, Potter st
Phillips Joseph, Potter st

MILLINERS & DRESS MAKRS.
Bignell Sarah, Middle row
Judd Mary, Market place
Whittaker Miss, High st

PAINTERS, PLUMBERS AND GLAZIERS.
Deards George, Middle row
Nottage Susannah, Market place

PERFUMRS & HAIR CUTTERS
Archer Samuel, High st
Bignell William, Middle row

SADDLERS.
Francis Francis (and rope maker) Market place
Monk Henry, Churchgate st

SHOPKEEPERS & DEALRS IN GROCERIES & SUNDRIES.
Aylett William, Latton st
Bayman James, Market place
Dedman James, Churchgate st
Mead William, Sheering
Tyser Richard, Potter st

STRAW HAT MAKERS.
Brown Rachael, Sheering
Field Elizabeth, Market place
Hutchin Ann, Back st
Whittaker Rebecca, High st

SURGEONS.
Dobson James Stuart, High st
Haylock Thomas Busick, Church end

TAILORS AND DRAPERS.
Lambert Charles, Potter st
Scott Benjamin, Churchgate st
Whittaker Joseph, High st

TAVERNS & PUBLIC HOUSES.
Bush Fair House, Thomas Houghton (and keeper of the assembly rooms and west Essex archery house) Bush fair
Crown, John Garrett, Sheering
Crown, John Perry, Market place
George IV, William Cook, Potter st
Greyhound, James Holmes, Netteswell cross
Horns & Horse Shoes, William Grange, Potter st
King's Head, Edward Fitch, Potter st
Marquess of Granby, Thos. May, High st
Old Cock, James Foster, Sheering
Queen's Head, Benj. Billings, Churchgate st
Red Lion, Joseph Chipperfield, Potter st
Sun and Whalebone, Jas. Casidy, Potter st
White Horse, Thomas Smith, Potter st

WHEELWRIGHTS.
Cannon John, High st
Chapman Thomas, Sheering
Collin James, High st
Smith James, Potter st

WOOLSTAPLER.
Chaplin Philip (and corn and seed dealer) High st

Miscellaneous.
Bentley Thomas, millwright, High st
Chew John, registrar of births & deaths, Potter st
Ekins Shadrach S. cabinet maker, upholsterer and wire worker, Churchgate st, and at *Sawbridgeworth*
Excise Office, at the Marquess of Granby, High st—Matthew Hopkin, officer
Foreman John, attorney, Churchgate
Goodwin George, overseer, High st
Morris Joseph, professor of music, High st
Newton Francis, parish clerk, High st
Parrish John, rake and hurdle maker, Mulberry green
Pollett Christiana, wine merchant, Potter st
Pratt William, watch maker, High st
Prior Jane, bricklayer, Market place
Spurgin Frederick William, chymist and druggist, & dealer in home-made wines, High st, and at *Dedham*
Tadgell James, parish clerk, Sheering
Whittaker David, bookseller, High st
Wright James, cooper, Mulberry green

COACHES.
To LONDON, the *Royal Mail*, the *Magnet* and the *Telegraph* (from Norwich), calls at the George, every morning, and *Coaches* from Bury, Cambridge, Haverhill, Holt, Norwich, Swaffham and Saffron Walden, call at the same Inn, every day (Sunday excepted) & a *Coach*, from the Green Man and George Inns, every Monday morning at half-past six, other mornings (Sunday excepted) at eight.
To BURY SAINT EDMUNDS, CAMBRIDGE, HAVERHILL, HOLT, SWAFFHAM, SAFFRON WALDEN, &c. *Coaches* (from London), call at the George Inn, daily.
To NORWICH, the *Royal Mail*, the *Magnet* and the *Telegraph* (from London), call at the George Inn, every night.

CARRIERS.
To LONDON, John Nash, from his house, every Monday & Thursday, and Joseph Clarke, every Wednesday and Friday.
*** *Waggons* & *Vans*, to and from LONDON, NORWICH, BURY ST. EDMUNDS, HAVERHILL, &c. pass thro' HARLOW, daily.

CONVEYANCE BY WATER.
To and from LONDON, BISHOPS STORTFORD, *Barges* call at Harlow bridge wharf, frequently.

HARWICH,

WITH THE PARISHES OF DOVER COURT, RAMSEY AND NEIGHBOURHOODS.

HARWICH is a market town and sea-port, and borough both parliamentary and corporate, having separate jurisdiction, locally in the hundred of Tendring; 72 miles N. E. by E. from London, 21 E. by N. from Colchester, and 12 S. E. from Ipswich, in Suffolk; seated on a point of land, washed upon the east by the German ocean, and upon the north by an estuary formed by the junction of the united streams of the Orwell and the Stour with the sea—an estuary memorable for an action fought between the British and Danish fleets in the year 884. The town, according to Camden, derives its name from *Herewic*, signifying in the Saxon, what it was originally, a 'strong hold,' having likewise been a Roman station, and, if an opinion may be founded upon the many Roman antiques discovered in its vicinity, one of considerable importance. Subsequent to the Norman conquest it rose in consequence, and its prosperity received another impulse from the ruin of Orwell, a town which tradition states to have stood upon a shoal called the 'West Rocks.' Harwich obtained the charter constituting it a borough and market town from Edward II; James I and Charles II confirmed its more ancient privileges, and granted others. Under the new municipal act the borough is governed by a mayor, four aldermen and twelve councillors, and the corporate body is styled 'the mayor and burgesses of the borough of Harwich;' the same act conferred upon the borough a commission of the peace. This place first sent members to parliament in the 17th of Edward III, but discontinued till the 12th of James I, since which time it has uninterruptedly been represented; the present members are the Right Hon. John Charles Herries and Capt. Alexander Ellice, R. N. A court of pleas for the recovery of debts not exceeding £100. is entitled to be holden for the borough, but it is rarely resorted to. The present lord of the manor is Nathaniel Garland, esq. The guildhall is a modern erection; under it is a prison for the borough, but used chiefly for prisoners previously to their committal to the county gaol. The naval yard is a very fine and commodious establishment; several third-rates, besides merchantmen of considerable burthen, have been built in it. The harbour is deep, and sufficiently spacious for the accommodation of a large fleet. There are two handsome lighthouses, and a large martello tower on which ten guns are mounted. A number of smacks belonging to this place are engaged in the north sea fishery. Ship-building, and other employments connected with maritime affairs, form the source of support to a great portion of the population; in addition to which a numerous class are employed in dredging for cement stone, which is found very plentifully outside the harbour, and at present constitutes a prominent branch of business in the town. This part of the coast being peculiarly well adapted for sea-bathing, Harwich is much resorted to by visiters in the season: the air is clear and healthy, and in no situation can the sea-breezes be more satisfactorily enjoyed; in summer, when in most places the intense heat is too powerful for the out-door exercise of the valetudinarian, it is here tempered by the aeriel currents from the ocean, and the atmosphere is rendered at once refreshing and invigorating. A favourite promenade for the fashionable visitants is the esplanade, to the east of the town; and the scenery up the river is an inducement to many delightful excursions.

In the thirteenth century Roger Bigod, Earl of Norfolk, founded the old church, dedicated to St. Nicholas. This gave place to a spacious and elegant structure, erected in 1821, chiefly of brick, with stone buttresses and steeple—its appearance, on the whole, is neat & attractive. The mother church stands at Dover Court: the living is a consolidated vicarage, in the gift of the crown; the Rev. Samuel N. Bull is the vicar, and the officiating minister at Dover Court is the Rev. Wm. Bull. There are places of worship for baptists, independents and Wesleyan methodists; a free school, founded in 1724 by Humphrey Parsons, Esq.; another, upon the national system; and several alms-houses, in West-street. The market days are Tuesday and Friday; fairs (each continuing three days) on the 1st of May and 18th October. The population of the borough of Harwich (including the two parishes of St. Nicholas and Dover Court), by the returns for 1831, was 4,297.

The parish of DOVER COURT, forming part of the borough of Harwich, contains about 1,900 acres of rich arable and meadow land; its surface has been much diminished by the inroads of the sea, which is still making gradual encroachments upon its southern part. The inhabitants are principally engaged in agriculture, and others partake in the labour of raising cement stone, which is carried on upon the sea border of this parish. The church is dedicated to All Saints, and is situated on the north side of the road leading to Harwich. An annual fair takes place here on Whit-Monday.

The village and parish of RAMSEY is in the same hundred as Harwich, about three miles from that town. The chief proprietor of the land is Nathaniel Garland, Esq., whose mansion, called Michaelstow Hall, after the name of the manor in which it is situated, is in this parish. This gentleman has added about 1,500 acres to his property by embankments on the river Stour. Mrs. Garland supports a school here for the education of girls; and there is another, endowed by a Mr. Smith, for the instruction of twelve boys. The parish church and a methodist chapel are the places of worship; the benefice is a vicarage, in the appointment of the crown. A fair is held on the 15th of April. Population, 708.

POST OFFICE, Hanover-square, HARWICH, William Baggott Nalborough, *Post Master.*—Letters from LONDON and all parts arrive every morning at seven, and are despatched every evening at eight.—Letters for the North, posted on Saturday, are forwarded by a cross post, and arrive one day sooner at their place of destination than if sent through London.—Letters are despatched (by penny post) to DOVER COURT, RAMSEY and GREAT and LITTLE OAKLEY every morning at half-past seven.

POST, DOVER COURT, *Receiving-House* at John Baldwin's.—Letters from HARWICH arrive every morning at eight, and are despatched every evening at five.

POST, RAMSEY, *Receiving-House* at Dinah Ellis's.—Letters from HARWICH arrive every morning at nine, and are despatched every afternoon at four.

GENTRY AND CLERGY.

Adeney Rev. John, Ramsey
Bailey Mr. John, M.D. Church st
Billingsley Samuel, jun. esq. West st
Bowness Captain, King's Quay st
Bull Rev. Saml. Nevil, King's Quay st
Bull Rev. William, King's Quay st
Chapman Edward, esq. Church st
Clarke Charles, esq. West st
Cobbold Thomas, esq. King's Quay st
Cox Anthony, esq. King's Quay st
Dean George, esq. (mayor) King's Head st
Garland Nathaniel, esq. Michaelstow hall, Ramsey
Graham George, esq. King's Quay st
Hammond Capt. Thomas, Church st
Heseltine Samuel, esq. Church st
Hewett Captain, R.N. King's Quay st
Hordle Rev. William, Hanover square
Morgan Captain (inspecting commander) Church st
Parry Col. Dore Albert, Esplanade
Rickard Samuel, esq. Harwich
Runnacles Captain A. King's Quay st
Runnacles Harcourt, esq. Bath side
Sansum John, esq. King's Quay st
Tylden Lieut.-Col. William Burton, Government house
Vigis Rev. Everit, Bath side
Winter Robert, esq. King's Quay st
Wordsworth C.F.F. esq. Dover Court

ACADEMIES AND SCHOOLS.

Birch John, King's Quay st
Bishop Emma, St. Austin's lane
Cook Mary, West st
CORPORATION FREE GRAMMAR SCHOOL, King's Quay st—Rev. Samuel N. Bull, master
Freshfield Caroline Bullard, King's Head st
Hatt Joseph Bridge, Hanover square
Hempson Nathaniel, Ramsey
Lash Samuel, West st
NATIONAL SCHOOL (for boys) Esplanade—Richd. Read Barnes, master
NATIONAL SCHOOL (for girls) King's Quay st—Susannah Grigson, mistress
Norster Abraham, Dover Court
Nunn Mary Ann, West st
Ratford Hannah, Ramsey
Sansum Henrietta, King's Head st

AGENTS.

(See also Fire, &c. Office Agents.)

Billingsley & Co. (for Lloyds, and shipping and commercial, and insurance brokers) Bath side
George Thomas (general shipping and commercial agent, and dealer in anchors, chain cables, & cordage) King's Head court
Mayor Samuel, sen. (Trinity) Wellington place
Ranfield William (ship) West st
Read Jacob (to Francis and White, cement manufacturers, *Nine Elms, Surrey)* West st
Sansum John (shipping) King's Quay street

ATTORNEYS.

Chapman Edward (and town clerk) Church st
Cox Anthony, jun. West st
Sansum John, King's Quay st

AUCTIONEERS & APPRAISRS.

Hast & Hales, Church st
Johnson Matthew, King's Quay st
Miall William John, West st
Trundle Charles, Market st

BAKERS.

Butcher John, St. Austin's lane
Clark John, West st
Ellis William, King's Head st
Grigson William, King's Head st
Grove Thomas, Market st
Howe Jacob, Church st
Lucas William, Ramsey
Pimm Henry John, King's Head st
Turner Joseph, Hanover square
Webber Edward, Church st

BANKERS.

Cox Anthony and Anthony, jun. King's Quay st (draw on Williams, Deacon & Co. London)

BLACKSMITHS.

Marked thus * are also Farriers.

Broom James, Bath side
*Campion Ann, Ramsey
Dore James G. (& bellhanger) West st
Elliss Dinah, Ramsey
Everett John, West st
*Everett Sarah, Dover Court
*Gold John, Ramsey
Webber Edward, Church lane

BLOCK, MAST, &c. MAKERS.

Davison John (and boat builder) Bath side
Nalborough Philip & Robert, Bath side
Tovell Richard (& boat builder) Bath side

BOOKSELLRS & STATIONERS.

Saxby Job (and stamp distributer) Church st
Trundle Charles, Market st

BOOT & SHOE MAKERS.

Abbot William, Dover Court
Cook John, Market st
Deex Samuel, Ramsey
Deex William, Church st
Hart Isaac, Market street
Hart Joseph, West st
Lewis William, Church st
Norster Abraham, Dover Court
Precious Abraham, King's Head st
Rayson John, West st
Sansum John, King's Head st
Smith John, Ramsey
Spaull William, Market st
Thompson John, Ramsey
Veale Phœbe, Hanover square
Ward William, West st
Webb Jonathan, Market place
Webb Joseph, King's Quay st

BRICK & TILE MAKERS AND LIME BURNERS.

Fuller Edward, Dover Court
Wilding John, Dover Court

BRICKLAYRS & PLASTERERS

Crane Adam, Ramsey
Crane James, West st
Fuller Edward (and builder) West st
Graham John, King's Quay st
Wilding Thomas, Dover Court

BUTCHERS.

Durrant James, Market st
Durrant Joseph Harman, Church st
Ennels Thomas, King's Quay st
Gooding John, Market st
Gray William (pork) Church lane
Josselyn Francis, Dover Court
Weaver John, Ramsey

CARPENTERS.

Clark Benjamin, Ramsey
Girling George, Bath side
Graham Samuel, Bath side
Hast Philip (and builder) Bath side
Hast William, West st
Newton Saml. (& builder) Bath side
Sharman John, Ramsey
Starling John, Dover court

CEMENT MANUFACTURERS—ROMAN.

Alder William, Market place
Read Jacob (agent to Francis & White, of *Nine Elms, Surrey)* West st

CHYMISTS AND DRUGGISTS.

Bolton Benjamin Cooper, Church st
Nunn William (druggist) West st
Thompson Thomas, King's Head st

COAL MERCHANTS.

Billingsley and Co. Bath side
George Thomas, King's Head st
Randfield William, West st
Salter Jas. (& potato) King's Quay st
Stevens Francis, Market place
Stiles Chas. (& potato) King's Quay st

CONFECTIONERS.

Clark John, West st
Clark Susanna, Market st
Grigson William, King's Head st

CONSULS.
Billingsley & Co. (vice) Bath side
Sansum John (for the Netherlands and Hanover, and vice for Sweden, Norway and the United States of America) King's Quay st

COOPERS.
Naylor Abraham, Currant's lane
Pain James, West st
Warn John, King's Head st

FIRE, &c. OFFICE AGENTS.
Essex and Suffolk Equitable, Edward Chapman, Church st
Medical, Clerical and General (life) Thos. George, King's Head st
Norwich (life) Edward Chapman, Church st
Phœnix (fire) & Pelican (life) Richd. Read Barnes, Wellington place
Royal Exchange, Benj. Goodwin, Wellington place
Shipping Assurance, Thos. George, King's Head st

FISHMONGERS.
Marchant John, King's Quay st
Ragen William, King's Quay st
Stiles Charles, King's Quay st

FURNITURE BROKERS.
Bannocks Philip, Church st
Cook William, Market place
Howgego William, King's Head st

GREENGROCERS.
Fryatt Ann, King's Quay st
Spooner Daniel, King's Quay st

GROCERS & TEA DEALERS.
(See also Shopkeepers, &c.)
Bishop Richard, King's Head st
Butcher William, King's Quay st
Grice William, Church st
Salmon Eliza, Market st
Spaull William, Market st
Webber Edward, jun. Church st

HAIR CUTTERS.
Coker John, Church st
Pyeman James, Ramsey
Salter William, Market st
Saxby Job, Church st
Spooner Daniel, King's Quay st
West Jacob, West st

INNS.
Great White Horse, William Rumsey, Dover Court
New Bell, Grace Beeston, Market place
Spread Eagle, Mary Joyce, West st
Three Cups (and posting house) Ann Bull, Church st
White Hart, Isaac Nicholls, West st

LINEN DRAPERS, &c.
Dickerson Thomas G. Market st
Hansford Francis, Market st
Nalborough William and Co. (and hatters, woollen drapers and tea dealers) Hanover square

LODGING HOUSES.
Bailey James, Bath side
Bannocks Philip, Church st
Blackett John, West st
Bridge Ann, Dover Court
Crisp Elizabeth, Dover Court
Gosnell Robert, Wellington place
Hart Elizabeth, West st
Hucks Eliza Ann, Hanover square
Iblett Francis, Wellington place
Jordan Judith, West st
Mayor William, King's Quay st
Skinner Harriet, West st
Stevens Francis, Hanover square

MARINE STORE DEALERS.
Cole James, King's Head st
Forster Samuel, Castlegate st
Mechen James, West st
Ragen William, Castlegate st
Read Jacob, West st
Stiles Charles, King's Quay st
Tovell Richard, Bath side
Webber Edward, West st

MARKET GARDENERS.
Bull James, Ramsey
Chisnall John, Dover Court
Chisnall William, Dover Court
Durrant Jeremiah, Dover Court
Meddows Richard, Dover Court
Smith John, Dover Court

MILLINERS & DRESS MAKRS
Baker Joannah, Church st
Davies Jane, Market place
Jones Eliza and Alicia, Church st
Lancaster Eliz. St. Austin's lane
May Sarah, St. Austin's lane

NOTARIES.
George Thomas, King's Head st
Sansum John, King's Quay st

PLUMBERS, PAINTERS AND GLAZIERS.
Cottingham Lewis (and proprietor of Shelder's patent fountain pump) King's Quay st
Hucks Philip, Church st
Lloyd Abraham, Ramsey
Whittingham Thos. Hordle, Market st

SAIL MAKERS.
Forster Samuel, Castlegate st
Powell Richard, Church st

SHIP CHANDLERS.
Butcher William, King's Quay st
Salter James, King's Quay st

SHOPKEEPERS & DEALRS IN GROCERIES & SUNDRIES.
Banham Isaac, Market st
Benneworth Richard, Market st
Bickmore James, Church st
Broom Robert, Dover Court
Butcher John, St. Austin's lane
Cole James, King's Head st
Cooper Elizabeth, Ramsey
Deex Sarah, West st
Farr Thomas, Church st
Hardwick Charles, Dover Court
Harriss Charles, Dover Court
Hilling Sarah, Dover Court
King Lydia, King's Head st
Lucas William, Ramsey
Pain Joseph, West st
Penkiss Elizabeth, Church lane
Rowland Joseph, Dover Court
Salmon Francis, West st
Salter James, King's Quay st
Skeet Shadrach, Ramsey
Thornton Mary, King's Head st
Ward Mary, Ramsey
Webber Edward, Church st
Whipp Sarah, Castlegate st
Whitley Sarah, King's Head st

STONE MERCHANTS.
Etherden John, King's Quay st
Read Jacob, Church st
Wakefield Thomas, West st

STRAW HAT MAKERS.
Dixon Hephziba, West st
Hansell Sarah, Hanover square
Nalborough Eliza & Eliz. Church st
Pain Fanny, West st

SURGEONS.
Bailey John, M.D. Church st
Bird John, Church st
Freshfield Philip, King's Head st
Hart Francis Freeling, Church lane

TAILORS.
Bellamy Thos. (& draper) Church st
Cousins Isaac, West st
Hart Edward, King's Quay st
Johnson Matthew (& draper) King's Quay st

TAVERNS & PUBLIC HOUSES.
Angel, Ann Rowland, King's Quay st
Castle, John Weaver, Ramsey
Coach & Horses, Eliz. Lucas, Hanover sq
Duke's Head, Margaret Feller, Church st
Glove, John Etherden, King's Quay st
Half Moon, Jos. Hunwicks, St. Austin's la
Harwich Packet, Edward Webber, Customhouse lane court
King's Arms, William Leopard, Dover court
King's Head, Sarah Waight, Market st
New Swan, Wm. Haxell, King's Head st
Privateer, William Ragen, King's Quay st
Royal Oak, Thomas Denney, Market st
Royal Oak, Mary Osborn, Dover court
Trafalgar, Robert Brown, Dover court
William the Fourth, James Pain, West st

WATCH & CLOCK MAKERS.
Skinner William, West st
Trundle Charles (and toy dealer) Market st

Miscellaneous.
Argent Mary Ann, stay maker, Bath side
Baths (medicated & vapour), West st—William Nunn
Baths (warm, cold & shower) Bath side—Robert Waller, manager
Benneworth John, town crier, West st
Billiard Rooms, King's Head st
Borough Goal, Church st—William Burton, goaler
Butcher John, sawyer, Bath side
Carter Joseph, collector of geological specimens, Dover court
Crickman Robert, cabinet maker, King's Quay st
Dore Jas. Golding, ironmonger, Church st
Etherden Jno. shipwright, King's Quay st
Excise Office, Three Cups, Church st
Gooch John, stone and marble mason, Bath side
Graham Geo. ship builder, King's Quay st
Gosnal Robert, clerk of the market, Wellington place
Harris Harman, registrar of births & deaths
Hatt Jonathan, wheelwright, Dover court
Hiblett Francis, parish clerk, Wellington pl
House of Correction, Church st—John Benneworth, keeper
Jordan Abraham, saddler, West st
News and Reading Rooms (Subscription), Esplanade
Ogilvie John, working jeweller, Dover ct
Pain Joseph, artist & library, West st
Pattrick John, corn miller, Dover court
Pearson Isaac, gunsmith & cutler, King's Quay street
Rawlings John, bookbinder, Market st
Reid Jane, dyer & scourer, Bath side
Royal Ordnance Depôt, Esplanade—Dore Albert Parry, esq. store keeper
Smith Richard James, brazier & tinman, King's Quay st
Town Hall, Church street—William Burton, keeper
Work House, King's Quay st—Thomas Leech, governor; Hannah Leech, governess.

CUSTOM HOUSE, WEST STREET.
Collector—Robert Welch
Comptroller—Frederick Freshfield
Coast Waiter and *Tide Surveyor*—Isaac Seggers
Principal Coast Officer at Mistley & Manningtree—Samuel Mayor, jun.
Principal Coast Officer at Thorpe and Walton—Robert Tabrom

COACH.
To LONDON, a *Coach*, from the Three Cups, every morning at ten; goes thro' Manningtree and Colchester.

CARRIER.
To COLCHESTER, Robert Salter, from the Spread Eagle, West street, every Monday, Wednesday, Thursday and Saturday; goes through Manningtree.

CONVEYANCE BY WATER.
To LONDON, the *Albion* and *Ipswich Steam Packets*, sail (from Ipswich) every Monday & Thursday morning, calling off Harwich.
To DOVER, the *Sarah Trader*, occasionally, James Harris, master, Noah's Ark, Bank side.
To IPSWICH, the *Albion Steam Packet* (from London), calls off Harwich, every Wednesday and Saturday evening, and the *Ipswich*, every Tuesday and Friday evening.
To IPSWICH, John Runnacles & Harvey Manning's *Wherries*, daily.
To MANNINGTREE, a *Wherry*, daily.
To SHOTLEY GATE and COLNESS, *Ferry Boats* may be obtained at any hour.

HATFIELD BROAD-OAK, TAKELEY

AND NEIGHBOURHOODS.

HATFIELD BROAD-OAK is a village and parish, in the hundred of Harlow, 29 miles E. from London, 16 S.E. from Hertford, 5 N.N.E. from Sawbridgeworth, and 7 S.E. from Bishops Stortford, situate about midway between Harlow and Dunmow. It derives its adjunctive from a very large spreading oak in the parish, and its ancient appellation, *Hatfield Regis*, from its having been a royal chase in the days of king Harold. In times past this was a market town; but that advantage, and its consequence in the scale of towns, have passed away together. The church, dedicated to St. Mary, is a handsome building, of some antiquity, but the exact date of its erection does not appear; that it was built prior to the 11th century is, however, ascertained, by certain mementos of departed greatness within its walls. The living is a vicarage, in the gift of the master and fellows of Trinity College, Cambridge; the Rev. T. F. Hall is the incumbent. Here are, besides, three meeting-houses for dissenters, two national schools and several almshouses. To the east of the church stood a priory, founded in the reign of Henry III, for black monks, by Robert de Vere, third Earl of Oxford; his effigy lies in the chancel of the church: the coat of mail is admirably executed. No remains of the priory are now to be seen, its site having been converted into a garden. In the vicinity of this village commences the rich district of the ROOTHINGS or *Rodings*, comprehending eight adjoining parishes. The general appearance of the country is flat; but there are still some pleasing variations in the scenery, especially on the north-west side of the parish, where is a fine forest of about eight miles in circumference, embosomed in which is a beautiful little lake. Hatfield has a large lamb fair on the 5th of August. This parish is divided into four townships, respectively named Brumsend Quarter, Heath Quarter, Town Quarter and Wood-row Quarter: these collectively contained, in 1831, 1,825 inhabitants.

TAKELEY is a village and parish, in the hundred of Uttlesford, about four miles north from Hatfield, on the road to Thaxted. It contains a parish church and a place of worship for independents: the living is a vicarage, in the patronage of the bishop of London. Population of the parish, in 1831, 1099.

POST, *Receiving-House* at James Kay's, who conveys letters to and from SAWBRIDGEWORTH for various parts every day (Sunday excepted); likewise a *Receiving-House* at James Aylett's, who conveys letters to and from BISHOPS STORTFORD for other parts every Wednesday and Friday.

NOBILITY, GENTRY, AND CLERGY.

Berry Rev. Cornelius, Heath
Budd Rev. Henry, Parsonage, White Roothing
Caporn Rev. James (vicar) Takeley
Cocks Thomas, esq. Hatfield
Glyn Rev. Thomas Clayton, Gladwin
Hall Rev. Thomas Francis, Vicarage, Hatfield
Hanson Rev. John, Brewer's end
Houblon John Archer, esq. Hallinbury place
Lowndes Thomas, esq. Barrington [hall
Parris George, esq. White house
Roden Right Hon. Earl of, Hyde hall
Selvin John Thomas, esq. Down hall
Willson John Malyon, esq. Fitz John

SCHOOLS.

NATIONAL, Hatfield—Richard Pulmer, master; Ruth Aylett, mistress
NATIONAL, Forest—Mary Clayton, mistress

BAKERS.

Parker Judith, Hatfield
Read Philip, Hatfield
Tizley Charles, Hatfield

BLACKSMITHS.

Brown Charles, Takeley
Cowell Edmund, Takeley
Hesler John, White Roothing
Serl Richard, Heath
Stock Elizabeth, Hatfield

BOOT & SHOE MAKERS.

Childs Joseph, Heath
Cockett John, Hatfield
Cook James, Brewer's end
Newell John, White Roothing
Smith James, Hatfield
Speller Robert, Takeley
Wybrew Francis, Hatfield

BRAZIERS & TIN-MEN.

Clark James (& ironmonger) Hatfield
Clark John, Hatfield

BRICKLAYERS & BUILDERS.

Barker Nathaniel, Hatfield
Dawkins Thomas, White Roothing

BUTCHERS.

Blatch Elizabeth, Heath
Clarke Thomas, White Roothing
Flack Thomas, Takeley
Judd Joseph, Hatfield
Mead George, Hatfield
Mumford James, Hatfield

GARDENERS & SEEDSMEN.

Willey James, Brewer's end
Woolley John, Heath

GROCERS & DRAPERS.

(See also Shopkeepers, &c.)

Awcock John, Hatfield
French William, White Roothing
Pamphilion Mary, White Roothing
Rouse John, Takeley
Viney Robert, Hatfield [Heath
Whitham John (draper & corn dealer)

JOINERS & BUILDERS.

Bacon Joseph, White Roothing
Bacon Samuel (& millwright) White Roothing [Roothing
Bacon Wm. (and millwright) White
Bird Edward, Takeley
Bird John, Takeley

MALTSTERS.

Parris Edward, White Roothing
Sullins Peter, Hatfield

MILLERS.

Andrews Thomas, Hatfield
Davey Ephraim, Hatfield
French William, White Roothing
Piper Isaac, Takeley

MILLINERS AND DRESS MAKERS.

Rawlings Sarah, Hatfield
Simpson Jane, Hatfield

SADDLERS.

Brown George, Heath
Burnett John, Hatfield
Porter John, Hatfield

SHOPKEEPERS & DEALRS IN GROCERIES & SUNDRIES.

Bird Edward, Takeley
Blatch Frances, Hatfield
Boatman John, Hatfield
Read Philip, Hatfield
Sach James, Takeley
Willey Isaac, Takeley
Wood James, Hatfield

SURGEONS.

Cocks Thomas (& registrar of births and deaths) Hatfield
Gear Isaac, White Roothing

TAILORS & DRAPERS.

Boatman Samuel, Hatfield
Lambert Thomas, Takeley
Tall John, Hatfield
Willson Thomas, White Roothing

TAVERNS & PUBLIC HOUSES.

Cock, Peter Sullins, Hatfield [field
Duke of Wellington, Chas. Edwards, Hat-
Green Man, Thomas Choppin, Takeley
Old Stag, Susannah Staines, Heath
Plume of Feathers, John Button, Hatfield
Rein Deer, John Spiller, Takeley
Whalebone, Wm. Bacon, White Roothing
White Horse, Elizabeth Mann, Heath

WHEELWRIGHTS.

Bird Nathaniel, Hatfield
Hudson Joseph, Hatfield
Wentworth Richard, Heath
Willey Isaac, Takeley

Miscellaneous.

The names without address are in Hatfield.

Aylett Thomas, cooper [ing
Baker Joseph, horse breaker, White Rooth-
Boatman John, plumber, &c.
Burton Robert, surveyor
Button John, tallow chandler
Hubbard Robert, excise officer
King George, veterinary surgeon
Mackenzie George, hair dresser
Marriott Charles, parish clerk
Mumford James, corn dealer
Norris John, basket maker, Heath
Rouse John, china, &c. dealer, Takely
Sullins Peter, fire office agent
Warren Robert, clothes dealer, Takeley

COACH.

To LONDON, a *Coach*, from the Cock, every Monday morning at five, & every other morning (Sun. excepted) at eight.

CARRIERS.

To LONDON, — Watson's *Waggons*, from the Duke of Wellington, every Monday & Friday, and — Mead, from his house, Hatfield, every Monday and Thursday.
To GREAT EASTON, — Watson's *Waggons*, from the Duke of Wellington, every Wednesday and Sunday.

HORNCHURCH, UPMINSTER AND CORBETS TAY.

HORNCHURCH is a village and parish, in the liberty of Havering-atte-Bower, 14 miles E. by N. from London, two S. W. from Romford, and about four miles and a half from the river Thames. It is a place unimportant to the commercial traveller, and to the curious stranger it possesses but little worth his detention. The church, dedicated to St. Andrew, is an ancient structure, with a handsome spire, about one hundred and seventy feet in height, and from its elevated site may be seen at a great distance. At the chancel end of the church is a piece of carved work of a bullock's head, the horns of which are gilt: the appearance of this figure is attempted to be accounted for by the custom, arising out of a charter granted by Henry II, which takes place every Christmas day, of wrestling for a boar's head; but why the head of the latter animal has obtained a preference over the former is not explained. The living is a vicarage, in the patronage of the warden and fellows of New College, Oxford; the present incumbent is the Rev. Daniel George Stacy. The parish of Hornchurch is rather extensive, containing about 6,500 acres of land, and a population, in 1831, of 2,186 inhabitants.

UPMINSTER is a village and parish, in the hundred of Chafford, situate about one mile from Hornchurch. The church, dedicated to St. Lawrence, is a neat ancient building with a spire, the greater part of which is covered with ivy. The living is a rectory, of which the Rev. John Rose Holden is the incumbent. There is also a place of worship for independents. In this vicinity are many elegant residences, some of which are adorned with beautiful plantations. 'Upminster Hall,' the manor house, formerly belonging to the abbots of Waltham, is an old building, but its situation commands extensive and delightful prospects. Population of the parish, in 1831 (including CORBETS TAY, an inconsiderable hamlet) 1,033.

POST OFFICE, HORNCHURCH, William Frost, *Post Master.*—Letters from ROMFORD arrive (by mail cart) every morning at seven, and are despatched every evening at seven.

POST OFFICE, UPMINSTER, Robert Lee, *Post Master.*—Letters from ROMFORD arrive every morning at a quarter past seven, and are despatched every evening (Sunday ex.) at half-past six, and on Sundays at six.

GENTRY AND CLERGY.

Bankin Mr. John, Upminster North
Bartlett Mrs. Elizabeth, Hornchurch
Bearblock Mr. James, Lillypot house
Bearblock Mr. John, Hornchurch hall
Bearblock Mr. Peter, Hornchurch
Benton Mr. Samuel, Hornchurch
Boyce Mr. Thomas, Upminster
Branfield Edward Champion, esq. Upminster
Brett Mr. James, Hornchurch
Brittan Mrs. Anne, Hornchurch
Calls Mr. William, Hornchurch
Clarke Chas. esq. Suttons, Hornchrch
Clayton Rev. George, Hornchurch
Clayton Rev. John, Gaines
Hammond Mr. Saml. Hoppey hall.
Hammond Mr. Saml. jun. Park cottge
Hammond Mr. William, Upminster
Holden Rev. John Rose, Upminster
Johnson Thomas, esq. Gaines lodge
Lee Mr. Joseph, Upminster
Mashiter Thomas, esq. Hornchurch
Masser Mrs. Mary, Hornchurch
Newman Richard, esq. Hornchurch
Peade Benjamin, esq. Acton house
Penney Rev. William, Fox hall, Corbets Tay
Shepherd Mr. W. Upminster
Stacey Rev. Daniel George, Vicarage, Hornchurch
Sterry Wasey, esq. Hill house, Upminster
Tabrum Mr. Wm. M.D. Upminster
Thompson Mr. Chas. Hornchurch
Townsend Mrs. Eliz. Hornchurch
Truston William, esq. Hornchurch
Wedlake Mr. Thomas, Hornchurch

ACADEMIES & SCHOOLS.

Garnham Charlotte, Hornchurch
Garnham Henry, Hornchurch
Marshall Alexander, Hornchurch
Saunders John (brding.) Corbets Tay
Townsend Mrs. Hornchurch
Wilkin Jane, Hornchurch

BAKERS.

Hobbs William, Hornchurch
Springett Abraham, Hornchurch
Steel John, Hornchurch
Stevens James, Hornchurch
Turpin Thomas, Hornchurch
Woodward Charles, Upminster

BOOT & SHOE MAKERS.

Aldous John, Hornchurch
Allen Alfred, Hornchurch
Franklyn John, Hornchurch
Harvey William, Hornchurch
Lazell William, Corbets Tay
Parker George, Hornchurch
Rowe George, Hornchurch
Spooner Isaac, Upminster

BUTCHERS.

Barwell Robt. & Chas. Hornchurch
Gate Thomas, Hornchurch
Oakes Edward, Upminster
Simpson Ralph, Hornchurch
Smith Mary, Hornchurch
Turner Thomas, Hornchurch
Ward Mary, Corbets Tay

CARPENTERS.

Cove Charles (and builder and brick and tile maker) Hornchurch
Dockrill James, Hornchurch
Sarrell James, Corbets Tay
Stevens George, Hornchurch
Wilson Thomas, Upminster

GROCERS AND DEALERS IN SUNDRIES.

Brett John Goodall, Hornchurch
Franklyn John, Hornchurch
Holmes William, Hornchurch
Kemp George, Hornchurch
Lee Robert, Upminster
May Isaac, Hornchurch
Ward Mary, Hornchurch
Wenn William, Hornchurch

HAIR DRESSERS.

Finch Charles, Hornchurch
Frost William, Hornchurch

INNS & PUBLIC HOUSES.

Bell, Thomas Clarke, Upminster
Bull Inn, Aaron Martin, Hornchurch
Cherry Tree, Geo. Barr, Hornchurch
Cricketers, Sarah Bront, Hornchurch
Crooked Billet, Jas. Squires, Hornch
Crown, Joseph Brewer, Hornchurch
George and Dragon, Jas. Godsalve, Corbets Tay
Harrow, John Cole, Hornchurch
Huntsman and Hounds, John Mansfield, Corbets Tay
King's Head, Jane Buckland, Hornchurch
Spencer's Arms, Thos. Woolf, Hornch
White Hart, John Bowton, Hornch

MILLERS.

Bearblock Walter & Jno. Hornchurch
Nokes Thomas, Upminster

SMITHS AND FARRIERS.

Cressey Joseph, Hornchurch
Drayton John, Hornchurch
Eldred John, Upminster
Gates Edward, Hornchurch
Idle Edmund, Corbets Tay
Wheatley Robert, Hornchurch

SURGEONS.

Quennell Robert Wm. Hornchurch
Tabrum William, M.D. Upminster

TAILORS.

Martin Robert, Hornchurch
Miller John, Hornchurch
Oxley George, Hornchurch
Oxley Jesse, Upminster

WHEELWRIGHTS.

Manning Isaac, Hornchurch
Wheatbread John, Corbets Tay

Miscellaneous.

The following names are in HORNCHURCH.
Alsop Robert, carrier
Archer Thomas, glover
Brett John G. agent for the imperial fire and life office
Bridge George, hurdle maker
Bright & Beardwell, fellmongers
Crabb John, gardener & seedsman
Gage Elizabeth, milliner & dress maker
Garnham Mary, stay maker
Grant & Yarnold, leather dressers & glovers
Harvey Robert, fishmonger
Jarvis John, bricklayer
Martin & Son, plumbers, painters & glaziers
Page William, greengrocer
Pendish Sarah, coal dealer
Quennell Robert William, registrar of births and deaths
Stricklett Thomas, gardener
Thompson Charles, bookkeeper
Wedlake Thomas, iron and brass founder and agricultural implement maker
West Sophia, saddler
Woodfine Thomas, brewer and maltster

COACHES.

To LONDON, a *Coach*, from the Bull, every morning at half-past eight and every Sunday evening at half-past four; both go through Romford.
To SOUTH OCKENDON, a *Coach*, from the Bull, every evening at seven.

CARRIERS.

To LONDON, Robert Alsop, from his house, Hornchurch, Tuesday & Friday.

INGATESTONE, FRYERNING, MARGARETTNG,

MOUNTNESSING AND NEIGHBOURHOODS.

INGATESTONE, once a market town, but now only recognized as a village, is in the hundred of Chelmsford, situated on the main road between that town and Brentwood—six miles S. W. from the former, five N. E. from the latter, and 23 N. E. from London. The church, dedicated to the Virgin Mary, is an ancient structure of brick, standing in the centre of the village, and contains some superb monuments to the Petre family; the living is a rectory, in the patronage of Lord Petre and incumbency of the Rev. John Lewis. The ancient mansion of the noble family just mentioned is in the vicinity of Ingatestone, and is an antique but irregular pile; their modern residence, a very splendid one, is at West Thorndon. A fair for cattle, held on the 1st of December, is tolerably well attended. Population, in 1831, 789.

About one mile from Ingatestone, in the same hundred, is the village and parish of FRYERNING. The church, dedicated to St. Mary, stands on an elevation which commands a wide range of prospect; it is an ancient edifice, with a tower containing five bells: the benefice is a vicarage, in the presentation of the warden and fellows of Wadham College, Oxford; the present incumbent is the Rev. George Price. The inhabitants, chiefly employed in agriculture, number about 700.

MARGARETTING is a village and parish in the same hundred as Ingatestone, nearly two miles from that town. The village is remarkably pleasant, and there are several fine seats in the parish. A house called Killigrew's Farm is recorded to have been the frequent resort of Henry VIII. The church, a small neat fabric, with a spire, is dedicated to St. Margaret: the living is a discharged vicarage, in the patronage of several persons, and in the present incumbency of the Rev. Wm. Jesse. Population, in 1831, 545.

In the same hundred as the preceding villages, about two miles from Ingatestone, is MOUNTNESSING, a village agreeably situated on a rising ground, surrounded by diversified and pleasing scenery, embellished by several elegant residences. Its small church, dedicated to St. Giles, stands about a mile and a half from the village; the benefice is a discharged vicarage, in the presentation of the family of Bramston. Population, about 800.

POST OFFICE, INGATESTONE, John Whichford, *Post Master*.—Letters from LONDON arrive (by the Norwich mail) every night (Sunday excepted) at half-past ten, and are despatched every morning at a quarter past four.—A mail cart arrives from ROCHFORD every evening at ten, and is despatched every night at twelve.

GENTRY & CLERGY.

Arnold Miss, Ingatestone
Cliff Mr. Robert, Grange
Diney John, esq. the Hyde
Hedgley Mr. James, Margaretting
Holcomb Chas. Thos. esq. Millgreen house
Jesse Rev. William, Margaretting
Langley Mr. John, Margaretting
Lewis Rev. John, Ingatestone
Main Mr. Mazenett, Ingatestone
Nicholas Thomas, esq. Mountnessing
Price Rev. George, Ingatestone
Straight George, esq. Peacocks, Margaretting

ACADEMIES & SCHOOLS.

INFANTS' SCHOOL, Margaretting—Sarah Brooks, mistress
Tabrum John (preparatory) Ingatestone
Webber Amelia (ladies' boarding) Ingatestone
Wright William (boardng) Margaretting

BAKERS.

Dew James, Ingatestone
Gosling William, Mountnessing
Humblin John E. Ingatestone
Justice John, Margaretting
Palmer Wm. (& biscuit) Ingatestone
Raven Thomas, Ingatestone

BOOT & SHOE MAKERS.

Cable John, Fryerning
Dennis John, Ingatestone
Jeffery William, Ingatestone
Steward Robert, Mountnessing
Thompson Henry, Fryerning

BRICKLAYERS.

Cross William, Mountnessing
Dennis John, Ingatestone

BUTCHERS.

Archer James, Margaretting
Childs Jas. Ipswich Arms, Ingatestone
Finch William, Margaretting
Harrington John, Ingatestone
Nunn James, Fryerning
Tibbald John, Ingatestone

CARPENTERS.

Cross William, Mountnessing
Dowsing William, Fryerning
Earee Thomas (and builder) Margaretting
Frewer Richard, Ingatestone
Hardy Robert, Margaretting
Palmer Emanuel (and bricklayer) Mountnessing

FIRE, &c. OFFICE AGENTS.

ATLAS, Thos. Earee, Margaretting
ESSEX and ECONOMIC, John Self (and maltster) Ingatestone

GROCERS & DRAPERS.

Cant Daniel, Fryerning
Cross William, Mountnessing
Dixey William, Fryerning
Finch John, Fryerning
Hogg John, Ingatestone
Justice Henry, Margaretting
Langrish Anthony, Fryerning
Moore Robert, Mountnessing
Smith William, Fryerning
Whichcord John (and stationer) Ingatestone

INNS & PUBLIC HOUSES.

Anchor, William Nunn, Ingatestone
Bell, Richard Spinks, Ingatestone
Bull, John Spight, Margaretting
Crown, Geo. Jno. Deane, Ingatestone
Eagle, John Outten, Margaretting
George and Dragon, Joseph Snow, Mountnessing
Ipswich Arms, James Childs, Ingatestone
New Inn, John Self, Ingatestone
Red Lion, Edward Curtis, Margaretting
Royal Oak, Wm. Miles, Fryerning
Ship, Daniel Dennis, Ingatestone
Spread Eagle, Jno. Tabor, Ingatestone

PLUMBERS AND GLAZIERS.

Farrow Emily, Fryerning
Gardiner Henry, Fryerning

SADDLERS, &c.

Perry William, Fryerning
Woolley George, Fryerning

SEEDSMEN.

Hogg Alex. (& nurserymn) Fryerning
Hogg Benjamin, Fryerning

SMITHS & FARRIERS.

Clay George, Fryerning
Hewett George, Ingatestone
Richardson Ann, Fryerning
Speekman Samuel, Mountnessing
Waters George, Fryerning

SURGEONS.

Butler Cornelius, Ingatestone
Carpenter John, Fryerning
Lewis Richard, Ingatestone

TAILORS.

Hockley Ebenezer, Fryerning
Jarvis John, Fryerning

Miscellaneous.

Agness Joseph, miller, Mountnessing
Arnold Francis, gardener, Ingatestone
Brock William, hair dresser, Fryerning
Cable John, parish clerk, Ingatestone
Cable Lucy, milliner, Fryerning
Clay Sarah, straw hat maker, Fryerning
Clayton Henry, land agent and surveyor, Ingatestone
Overhead Webb, cooper, Fryerning
Talbot Robert, corn chandler, Fryerning
Thompson Edw. wheelwright, Fryerning
Welton William, veterinary surgeon, Fryerning and Ingatestone
Whichcord John, watchmaker and hardwareman, Ingatestone

COACHES,

To and from LONDON, and towns in the counties of Suffolk and Norfolk, pass through Ingatestone daily, some of them calling at the Eagle.

CARRIERS.

To and from LONDON, and towns in the counties of Suffolk and Norfolk—carriers pass through Ingatestone daily.
To CHELMSFORD, John Hunt, from his house, Ingatestone, every Tuesday, Wednesday, Friday and Saturday

KELVEDON, FEERING, RIVENHALL, MESSING,

INWORTH, GREAT AND LITTLE TOTHAM, LAYER MARNEY AND NEIGHBOURHOODS.

KELVEDON, a large and respectable village in the parish of its name and hundred of Witham, is 41 miles N. E. from London, 10 S. W. from Colchester, and three S. from Coggeshall; situated on the high road leading to London, Colchester, Chelmsford, Witham, and other towns on the main line of communication between the metropolitan county and that of Suffolk—and consequently enjoying a thoroughfare on which may be said principally to depend its prosperity, and the support of several public houses for the accommodation of travellers; the principal Inns are the 'Swan,' the 'Star and Fleece' and the 'Angel.' The Right Hon. Lord Western is lord of Church Hall manor; Felix Hall, his residence, about a mile distant, is a beautiful seat, with an extensive park, surrounded by tasteful plantations: the lord of Kelvedon manor is the Bishop of London. The church, dedicated to St. Mary, is a neat structure, with a tower and spire; the benefice is a vicarage, in the patronage of the see of London, and present incumbency of the Rev. Charles Dalton. The independents have a chapel, and the society of friends a meeting-house. A small free school, and alms-houses for eight poor families, comprise the charities. At Easter a fair is held for pleasure and pedlery. The Witham union includes this parish, which contained, in 1831, 1,463 inhabitants.

FEERING, a village, the parish of which is separated from that of Kelvedon by the Blackwater, is more extensive than populous, and chiefly occupied by opulent farmers. The church is dedicated to All Saints; the living is a discharged vicarage, in the gift of the bishop of London. Population of the parish, 735.

RIVENHALL is a parish also adjoining to Kelvedon, in the same hundred. The church is dedicated to St. Mary and All Saints: the benefice is a rectory, in the patronage of Lord Western and incumbency of the Rev. John Lewis, of Ingatestone; the Rev. Bradford Dean Hawkins is the present minister. Population, 653.

Between four and five miles south from Kelvedon, and rather more than that distance north from Maldon, is the parish and village of GREAT TOTHAM, in Thurstable hundred. The church, dedicated to St. Peter, is situated towards the centre of the parish, and is an ancient building, with a spire; the living is a discharged vicarage, in the presentation of W. P. Honeywood, Esq. From 'Cock-a-Beaver's Hill,' between this village and Braxted, may be contemplated one of the finest prospects in the county. The population, in 1831, was 696.

The parish of LITTLE TOTHAM is contiguous to Great Totham and Messing, and possesses nothing to invite the tourist or the man of business. Its ancient church is dedicated to All Saints; the living is a perpetual curacy, annexed to the rectory of Goldhanger. At the last census the population amounted to 306.

About three miles from Kelvedon, in the Witham division of Lexden hundred, is the small village and parish of MESSING. The church, dedicated to All Saints, is a neat edifice, adorned with a handsome window of stained glass, and some monuments worthy of inspection, particularly one to Sir William de Messing, the founder of the church: the benefice is a vicarage, in the gift of the Earl of Verulam; the Rev. Thomas Henderson is the incumbent. On the 25th of July an annual fair for pleasure and pedlery is held on Tiptree heath, where horse-racing likewise takes place. The parish, in 1831, contained a population of 775.

INWORTH parish is contiguous to that of Messing, in the same division and hundred—the village being about a mile and a half S.E. from Kelvedon. The church, dedicated to All Saints, is deserving of some notice from the antiquary for its small porch, composed of flints and Roman bricks, evidently constructed at an early period: the living is a rectory, in the presentation of the Poynder family. Population, in 1831, 443.

LAYER MARNEY is a small village and parish in the hundred of Winstree, between five and six miles east from Kelvedon, chiefly occupied by agriculturists. The church, dedicated to the Virgin Mary, is a stately structure with a tower; the interior is ornamented with a beautiful screen, and there are several monuments that will gratify the curious. The living is a rectory, in the patronage of Quintin Dick, Esq. M. P. for Maldon, who has lately purchased the manor from the representatives of the late Matthew Corseller, Esq., by whose family it had been possessed for several centuries; the Rev. Alfred Gibson Utterson is the present incumbent. The great entrance tower or gateway of Layer Marney Hall, erected by Sir Henry Marney in the year 1500, is still standing; from its summit a fine commanding view is obtained, extending over the country to the sea-coast. The population, at the last census, was 275.

POST OFFICE, KELVEDON, Ann Crampin, *Post Mistress.*—Letters from LONDON arrive every night at half-past twelve, and are despatched every morning at seven in summer and eight in winter.—Letters may be posted as late as nine at night.

GENTRY AND CLERGY.

Allaker Mr. Thomas, Kelvedon
Baker Mrs. —, Kelvedon
Bateman Mrs. —, Birch
Baxendale Mrs. —, Kelvedon
Bickmore Mr. Thos. Luke, Kelvedon
Brewer Mr. James, Kelvedon
BrownCapt.Jno.Thos.Great Totham
Bullen Mr. Henry, Kelvedon
Cantley the Misses, Kelvedon
Catling Mrs. Fanny, Kelvedon, and Hoo hall, *Suffolk*
Clapham Geo.esq.Hoo hall, Rivenhall
Clark Robert, esq. Little Totham
Cole George, esq. Kelvedon
Corder Mr. William, Bury, Feering
Corsellis Mrs. —, Kelvedon
Cubbage Miss —, Kelvedon
Dalton Rev. Charles (magistrate), Vicarage, Kelvedon
Dalton Rev. William Brown, Kelvedon
De Horne Mr. George, Gt. Totham
Docwra Anna, Kelvedon
Docwra Mr. Wm. Kelvedon
DrummondRev.Robt.Vicarage,Feering
Elvy Lieut. George, R. N. Kelvedon
Emson Mrs. —, Kelvedon
Everett Mr. Joseph, Feering
Franklin Lieut. John, R. N. Kelvedon
Freeman Mr. Robert, Kelvedon
Frodsham Miss —, Birch
Frost Mrs. —, Kelvedon
Gower Rev.Thos.Foote, Gt. Totham
Grant Thomas, esq. Inworth
Griggs John, esq. Messing
Guy Mr. Robert, Kelvedon
Hallward Rev. W. Easthorp
Harrison Miss —, Kelvedon
Hart Lieut. Benj. R. N. Kelvedon
Hawkins Miss —, Kelvedon
Hawkins Rev.Bradford Dean, Rivenhall
Haywood Mr. Robert, Kelvedon
Helen Mrs. —, Birch
Henderson Rev. Thomas, Vicarage, Messing
Humphreys Miss —, Kelvedon
Hunwick Rev. Francis, Kelvedon
Hutley Mr. John, Rivenhall
Hutley Mrs. —, Rivenhall
Impey William, esq. Kelvedon
Jacobs William, esq. Kelvedon hall
Johnson Abraham, esq. Parsonage, Messing
Knights Mr. James, Kelvedon
Lee Mr. Charles Boyse, Kelvedon
Lungley Smith, esq. Church hall
Marchant Rev. Wm. Layer Breton
Moore Mr. Nathaniel, Rivenhall
Nolan Mrs. —, Kelvedon
Raven Mr. William, Feering
Round Chas. Gray, esq. M. P. Birch hall
Smith Paul Kneller, esq. Rivenhall pl
Sutton Rev. Robert, Parsonage, Layer Breton
Taylor Saml.esq. Hill house, Messing
Turner Mr. Charles, Great Totham
Unwin Jordan, esq. Ewell hall
Utterson Rev. Alfred Gibson, Layer Marney
Wallace Mrs. S. Kelvedon
Waller Rev. Richard, Rectory, Birch
Webbdale the Misses, Kelvedon
Western Right Hon. Lord, Felix hall
Wix Rev. Samuel, Rectory, Inworth
Wood Philip Whittle, Kelvedon
Woodward Mr. Richd. A. Warrens, Feering
Wright John, esq. Birch hall, Messing
Wright John Sterling, esq. Birch

ACADEMIES.

Not otherwise described are Day Schools.

Brewer Elizabeth, Kelvedon
CHARITY SCHOOL, Layer Breton—Joseph Firmin, master
Eley John, Kelvedon
Eley Maria, Kelvedon
Eley Miss, Easthorp
FREE GRAMMAR SCHOOL, Maldon road—John Fuller, master
Groom Sarah, Inworth
KELVEDON SCHOOL (boys', boarding) Joseph Paul, master
NATIONAL SCHOOL, Great Totham—Richard Jolliffe, master
Piercy the Misses (boarding) Kelvedon
Serjeant Frances, Messing
South James, Layer Breton

ATTORNEYS.

Bickmore Thomas Luke, Kelvedon
Bullen Henry, Kelvedon

BAKERS.

Barleyman James, Kelvedon
Birdseye John, Kelvedon
Bowles Henry, Birch
Cheek James, Kelvedon
Digby James, Birch
Green George, Messing
Haward Philip, Inworth
Hughes Wm. Tiptree heath, Messing
Hutley Jonathan, Layer Marney
Johnson William, Kelvedon
Pye James, Kelvedon
Royce John, Birch

BLACKSMITHS.

Beckwith Thos. Silver end, Rivenhall
Dowsett William, Messing
Hampshire William, Inworth
Haward Philip, Inworth
Humphrey Robert, Kelvedon
Hutley Charles, Easthorp
Hutley Jonathan, Layer Marney
Hutley Susannah, Feering
Hutley Thomas, Layer Marney
Hutley William, Layer Breton
May John, Tiptree heath, Messing
Munson Isaac, Birch
Suckling John, Rivenhall
Tunmer James, Kelvedon

BOOT AND SHOE MAKERS.

Chamberlain David, Birch
Cooper John, jun. Messing
Denney Benjamin, Kelvedon
Dow William, Birch
Harris William, Kelvedon
King Samuel, Kelvedon
Little Samuel, Birch
Mayhew James, Rivenhall
Osborn Robert, Messing
Osborn Robert, Kelvedon
Potter Isaac, Great Totham
Potter Samuel, Feering
Richardson William, Messing
Ruggles John, Great Totham
Trowles John, Layer Marney

BREWERS.

Fuller John, Kelvedon
Rush Hayward Henry, Gt. Totham

BRICK MAKERS.

Banham Robert, Inworth
Chaplin William, Inworth

Cottee James, Great Totham
Larkin William, Great Totham
Whitehead Mark, Great Totham

BRICKLAYERS.

Chaplin William, Inworth
Shephard Aaron, Kelvedon
Siggers William, Kelvedon
Woodward William, Birch

BUTCHERS.

Dennis John, Inworth
Frost William, Messing
Martin William, Kelvedon
Revett Benjamin, Kelvedon
Revett Townsend, Kelvedon
Tiffin Charles, Birch

DRESS MAKERS.

Cook Sarah, Kelvedon
Sarjeant Frances, Messing
Taylor Hannah, Birch

DRUGGISTS.

Stribling John (and basket maker) Kelvedon
Wyatt Mary, Kelvedon

GARDENERS, &c.

Abbott Richard, Kelvedon
Archer James, Kelvedon
Archer Thomas, Kelvedon
Church Thos. (& seedsman) Feering
Fitch Isaac (& seedsman) Gt. Totham

GROCERS & DRAPERS.

(See also Shopkeepers, &c.)

Anger John, Tiptree heath, Messing
Anthony William, Layer Breton
Archer Samuel, Kelvedon
Banks Margaret, Kelvedon
Beckwith Thos. Silverend, Rivenhall
Blackborn Ann, Rivenhall
Clayton Allen Francis, Kelvedon
Davey George, Layer Marney
Day William, Kelvedon
Denney Chas. (& china dealer) Messing
Eley Thomas, Easthorp
Fuller John, Kelvedon
Good George, Messing
Hicks Henry, Feering
Holloway Edward, Layer Breton
Hughes Wm. Tiptree heath, Messing
Hulley Jonathan, Layer Marney
Martin Samuel, Birch
Osborn Robert, Kelvedon
Trowles John, Easthorp
Wager James, Little Totham

INNS.

Angel (commercial & posting) David Hume, Kelvedon
Star and Fleece, Benj. Revett, Kelvedon
Swan, Thomas Wood, Kelvedon

JOINERS AND CARPENTERS.

Abbott William, Inworth
Baker John, Kelvedon
Barleyman William, Feering
Beckwith Thos. Silver end, Rivenhall
Braddy Jeremiah, Kelvedon
Bull John, Rivenhall
Bull William, Rivenhall
Cottee James, Great Totham
Dudley Frederick, Messing
Gentry George, Great Totham
Hutton Thomas, Birch
Little James, jun. Layer Breton
Martin Thomas, Inworth
Sach William, Inworth
Siggers William (& builder) Kelvedon
Wager John, Rivenhall

MALTSTERS.

Allaker George, Gt. Totham
Baker Jos. Bennett, Kelvedon & Feering
Brown James, Messing
Cranmer Thomas, Church st, Kelvedon
Duffield John, Birch
James William, Feering
Quilter Thomas, Feering
Rumble Charles, Kelvedon
Rush Hayward Henry, Messing and Great Totham
Siggers William, jun. Kelvedon
Stebbing George, Easthorp

MILLERS.

Appleford William, Feering
Digby James, Birch
Docwra Joseph, Maldon road, Kelvedon
Everett Cowlin, Kelvedon & Feering
Goody Thomas, Great Totham
Green Charles William, Litt. Totham
Royce John, Birch
White Charles, Kelvedon
Whitehead Mark, Great Totham

PAINTERS, PLUMBERS AND GLAZIERS.

Burfield Robert, Messing
Causton Robert, Kelvedon
Fuller and Mills, Kelvedon
Siggers Thomas, Kelvedon

SADDLERS, &c.

King William, Kelvedon
Polley William, Messing
Siggers John, Kelvedon

SHOPKEEPERS & DEALRS IN GROCERIES & SUNDRIES.

Banton Thomas, Birch
Grange Mary, Feering
Heard Benjamin, Tiptree heath
Hutton Charles, Birch
Woodward William, Birch

STRAW, &c. HAT MAKERS.

Cook Sarah, Kelvedon
Patten Mary, Birch
Polley Joseph, Kelvedon
Serjeant Frances, Messing
Taylor Hannah, Birch

SURGEONS.

Patmore Joseph Phillips, Kelvedon
Varenne Ezekiel George, Kelvedon

SURVEYORS.

Ash Christopher (roads) Kelvedon
Raven William (land) Feering

TAILORS.

Abbott Wm. Tiptree heath, Messing
Barleyman Chas. (& draper) Kelvedon
Bird James, Church st, Kelvedon
King George, Kelvedon
Palmer Francis, Great Totham
Robinson Henry, Kelvedon
Sansum Samson, Kelvedon
Skinner James Smith (and breeches maker) Kelvedon

TAVERNS & PUBLIC HOUSES.

Anchor, William Chaplin, Inworth
Angel, John Duffield, Birch
Bell, Joseph Burton, Feering
Bull, Thomas Barrett, Great Totham
Compasses, Isaac Greengrass, Gt. Totham
Fox, Abraham Bilney, Rivenhall
Hare & Hounds, Edwd. Holloway, Layer Breton
King's Head, Danl. Colf, Kelvedon
King's Head, Saml. Ely, Tiptree heath, Messing
Maypole, Mark Cottee, Great Totham
Queen's Head, James Hall, Messing
Ship, Jos. Emmerson, Inworth
Western Arms, Thos. Beckwith, Silver end, Rivenhll
White Hart, Eliz. Westcoate, Kelvedon
White Horse, Edward Quy, Little Totham
White Horse, Charles Brown, Birch

VETERINARY SURGEONS.

Gayfer Henry, Kelvedon
Oddy George (farrier) Layer Marney
Poulton William, Kelvedon

WHEELWRIGHTS.

Beckwith Thos. Silver end, Rivenhall
Belchem Thomas, Feering
Cook James, Kelvedon
Cooper John, Messing
Cottee James, Great Totham
Cowlin Thos. Tiptree heath, Messing
Everett William, Layer Marney
Grout William, Great Totham
Howard Thomas, Inworth
Simpson Geo. Tiptree heath, Messing
Wager John, Rivenhall
Wheeler Edmund, Church st, Kelvedon

Miscellaneous.

Aikin & Co. mnfctrng. chymists, Gt. Totham
Barbrook Wm. parish clerk, Great Totham
Barleyman William, parish clerk, Feering
Brown Jas. dealer in marine stores, Messng
Bundock John, parish clerk, Layer Breton
Christmas Thomas, parish clerk, Easthorp
Cottee Jas. timber merchant, Gt. Totham
Davis Rebecca, clothes dealer, Kelvedon
Day Sarah, confectioner, Kelvedon
Day William, corn dealer, Kelvedon
Dennis James, parish clerk, Inworth
Eley John, parish clerk, Kelvedon
Eley Joseph, registrar of births, deaths & marriages, stationer, printer, bookbinder, and agent to the Chelmsford Chronicle and Essex Herald, Kelvedon
Everett Thomas, parish clerk, Messing
EXCISE OFFICE, Kelvedon — Nuthall Spanton, officer.
Fuller John, fire office agent, Kelvedon
Gunn Hezekiah, fishmonger, Kelvedon
Hunwick William, hair dresser, Kelvedon
Hutley Jon. parish clerk, Layer Marney
Matthews Samuel, glover, &c. Kelvedon
Mayn Benjamin, watch maker, Kelvedon
Mayn Geo. Thurston, cooper, Kelvedon
Moore Edward, carrier, Feering
Rawlinson Jno. parish clerk, Litt. Totham
Slyth James, pastry cook, Kelvedon
Smith St John, artist, Church st, Kelvedon
Surridge Jos. Smith, auctioneer, Feering
Tame William, parish clerk, Rivenhall
Webdale Gustavus Wm. artist, Kelvedon
Willsher James, parish clerk, Birch

COACHES.

To & from LONDON, COLCHESTER, and parts of SUFFOLK, &c. *Coaches* pass thro' Kelvedon daily, the greater number of which call at the King's Head.
To COGGESHALL, a *Coach*, from the King's Head, every morning.

CARRIERS.

To LONDON, — Smith's *Waggons*, from the Angel, every Monday & Friday.
To CHELMSFORD, — Higgleston, from his house, Kelvedon, every Tuesday & Friday.
To COLCHESTER, — Smith's *Waggons*, from the Angel, every Sunday & Wednesday, — Higgleston, from his house, Kelvedon, and — Moore, from Feering, every Wednesday and Saturday.

LOUGHTON AND NEIGHBOURHOODS.

LOUGHTON is a village and parish in the hundred of Ongar, about twelve miles from London, five s. from Epping and the like distance s. e. from Waltham Abbey, situated on the main road to Epping. The houses, generally speaking, are irregularly scattered, without any regard to uniformity of arrangement; yet there are several handsome private residences in the village and its vicinage. The country around is well cultivated, and the scenery beautifully rural. Wm. Whittaker Maitland, Esq., of Chigwell, is lord of the manor. The church, dedicated to St. Nicholas, was rebuilt some years since; the benefice is a rectory, of which the gentleman just named is patron; the venerable Archdeacon Hamilton is the incumbent, and the Rev. Septimus Pope, M.A., his curate: the edifice stands at an inconvenient distance from the village. There is a place of worship for baptists, and a school conducted upon the national system. The parish contained, in 1831, 1,269 inhabitants.

POST, *Receiving-House* at Joseph Barton's, tailor.—Letters from LONDON arrive every morning at eight and noon at half-past twelve, and are despatched every morning at eight and afternoon at three.

GENTRY & CLERGY.

Appleton Mr. —, Golden Hill house
Brawn Rev. Samuel, Loughton
Carroll Sir George, Loughton
Davidson John, esq. Loughton
Finlaison John, esq. Loughton
Gingell Mr. —, Loughton Hall farm
Gould Mr. George, Loughton
Gould Mr. Isaac, Loughton
Hamilton the Venerable Archdeacon, Loughton
King William, esq. Loughton
Lane Charles, esq. Loughton
Messenger William, esq. Loughton
Nicholson John, esq. Buckhurst hill
Pearce Mrs. Sarah, Debden green
Philby Mrs. Ann, Golden hill
Pope Rev. Septimus, M.A. Victoria row
Powell Mrs. Sophia, Bench house
Read Henry, esq. Buckhurst hill
Sheeres Mr. Lewis, Loughton lodge
Skerritt Mr. Thomas, Loughton
Smith Mrs. —, Golden Hill cottage
Turner Mr. —, Warren lodge
Turner Mrs. Mary, Loughton

PROFESSIONAL PERSONS.

Campion George, auctioneer, surveyor & estate agent, Albion lodge
Godfrey John, academy
Harding Philip, surgeon & registrar of births and deaths

INNS & PUBLIC HOUSES.

Crown, James Eaton
Feathers, Richard Fuller
King's Head, Esther Davies
Roebuck, Henry Frost

SHOPKEEPERS & TRADERS.

Allard John, boot & shoe maker
Barton Joseph, tailor
Bolton Henry, butcher
Chinnery Jasper, plumber, painter & glazier
Dawkins Thomas, tailor
Dimmock Ann, shopkeeper
Dove Thomas, carpenter
Eley Mary Ann, grocer
Ellis James, potter, Golden hill
Enever John, carpenter
Enever William Roger, smith and farrier
Fuller James, butcher
Gower John, shopkeeper
Grant Eliz. mistress of national school
Grout James, parish clerk
Habgood James, corn factor
Heath Comfort, grocer & tea dealer
Heath Noah, bricklayer
Hills Joseph, shopkeeper
Hills Osborn, carpenter & builder
King John, carpenter
King William, retail brewer & corn factor
Maynard Daniel, master of national school
Page Jonathan, baker
Radley William, smith & farrier
Searle Thomas, veterinary surgeon
Spruzen Sarah, shopkeeper
Vernon James, boot & shoe maker
Wallis James, plumber & grocer
Wallis Robert, grocer & draper
Warren Jeffrey, wheelwright
Welham Sarah, shopkeeper
Wilks Joseph, wheelwright, & smith and farrier
Wright Josiah, wheelwright

COACHES,

To and from LONDON, EPPING, &c. pass through every morning & afternoon.

CARRIERS.

To LONDON, William Thompson, every Monday, Wednesday, Thursday and Saturday—and John Johnson, every Monday, Tuesday, Thursday and Saturday.

LOW LEYTON, LEYTONSTONE & NEIGHBOURHOODS.

LOW LEYTON is a village, and with Leytonstone constitutes the parish of St. Mary's Leyton, in the hundred of Becontree. The first-named village is about five miles and a half from Shoreditch church, London, eight w. by s. from Romford, and two from Stratford, situate on high ground, on the right of the Epping road; agreeably wooded, and watered by the Lea river. Like many other rural places, so near the metropolis, it is the residence of a number of opulent families. There are two manors in the parish of Leyton, viz. Leyton Grange and Ruckholts. The parish church, dedicated to St. Mary, is a brick edifice, containing the monuments of many eminent persons; amongst which are those of Charles Goring, Earl of Norwich, Sir John Strange, Sir William Hicks and John Strype; the latter person renowned for his antiquarian researches, and who, though never inducted, held this vicarage during the space of sixty-eight years, by a special license from the bishop of London. The present vicar is the Rev. Charles Henry Laprimaudaye, and the Rev. Charles John Laprimaudaye is the curate. The other places of worship are, a chapel of ease (at Leytonstone), and two others for independents and Wesleyan methodists. In the parish are eight almshouses, an endowed free-school and others on the national plan. The population of the entire parish, by the census for 1831, was 3,323.

LEYTONSTONE is a short distance from Low Leyton, and in the account of the latter place we have mentioned all that is necessary to be said of this village. The pursuits of its inhabitants, which are agricultural, and its situation and aspect, partake of the same character; and its population is included in the returns for the parish of Low Leyton.

POST OFFICE, LOW LEYTON, Susan Munns, *Post Mistress*.—Letters from LONDON arrive every morning at nine and twelve and every evening at six, and are despatched every morning at nine and half-past twelve and afternoon at four.

POST, LEYTONSTONE, *Receiving-House* at Elizabeth Johnson's.—Letters from LONDON arrive every morning at eight and half-past ten, and afternoon at half-past two and a quarter past five, and are despatched every morning at half-past ten, afternoon at half-past one and half-past four, and evening at eight.

GENTRY AND CLERGY.

Abbott Mr. William, Low Leyton
Baker Mrs. Ann, Leytonstone
Barclay Mr. Rawlinson, Forest place
Barclay Robert, esq. Knotts green
Bignell Thomas, esq. Low Leyton
Brooks Thos. esq. Leytonstone house
Capper Samuel, esq. Low Leyton
Chadsey Mr. John, Leytonstone
Charrington Nichls. esq. Leytonstone
Clarke Miss, Knotts green
Clement Jas. Kinloch, Leytonstone
Copeland Mr. William, Low Leyton
Cotton Benjamin, esq. Leytonstone
Cotton Miss Mary, Low Leyton
Cotton William, esq. Wallwood house
Daubuz Lewis Chas. esq. Low Leyton
Daubuz Mrs. Magdalene, Low Leyton
Davies Robert, esq. Knotts green
Davies William, esq. Manor house
Dorman Charles, esq. Leytonstone
Doxat John A. esq. Phillibrook house
Fallows Mr. Thomas Gray, Salter's buildings
Gale Mr. James, Leytonstone
Gibbern Mr. Low Leyton
Golden Edward, esq. Holloway down, Leytonstone
Goldie Mr. James, Forest place
Gore Mr. Edward, Salter's buildings
Gore John, esq. Hetlow house
Graham Robt. esq. Buckstone house
Green Mrs. Ann, Leytonstone
Hadden James, esq. Low Leyton
Hall William, esq. Low Leyton
Hanson Mrs. —, Forest place
Hayes Mr. John, Low Leyton
Hibbert John, esq. Syborn's corner
Hubbard Rev. Thomas, Leytonstone
Hutchinson Mr. Jno. Salter's buildgs
Innis Mrs. Anna, Knotts green
Innis Mr. James, Forest place
Innis Robert Hugh, esq. Knotts green
James Mrs. Mary, Forest place
Laprimaudaye Rev. Charles Henry, Low Leyton
Laprimaudaye Rev. Charles John, Low Leyton
Laugher Thomas T. esq. Low Leyton
Lesley Mr. John, Leytonstone
Levin Mrs. —, Capper st
Marshall Mr. John, Leytonstone
Masterman John, esq. Low Leyton
Masterman Thos. esq. Knotts green
Masterman Wm. esq. Low Leyton
Miles William, esq. Low Leyton
Morini Mr. Henry, Salter's buildings
Mouat Mr. John, Royal lodge
Niblet Mrs. Eliza, Leytonstone
Nind Benjamin, esq. Leytonstone
Nind Benjamin Wharton, esq. Leytonstone
Olding Stephen, esq. Low Leyton
Oliver Samuel, esq. Forest lodge
Oswell Mrs. E. Leytonstone
Patterson Mr. Thomas, Low Leyton
Pavitt Mr. William, Leytonstone
Potts Mr. Thomas, Leytonstone
Powell Mr. John, Leytonstone
Privat Mrs. Ann Maria, Forest place
Radcliffe the Misses, Leytonstone
Reeves James, esq. Low Leyton
Rhodes William, esq. Grange house
Robinson William Robert, esq. Forest house
Seal Mr. William, Leytonstone
Simms Mr. Jacob, Leytonstone
Simms Mr. John, Leytonstone
Solly Isaac, esq. Leyton house
Stait Mr. William Edward, Low Leyton
Turner Rev. George, Low Leyton
Venton Mr. Thomas, Low Leyton
Windle Miss Mary, Leytonstone

ACADEMIES & SCHOOLS.
FREE SCHOOL, Low Leyton—Wm. Acton Evans, master
Greig John G.(brdng.) Leytonstone
Kibble Elizabeth (day) Leytonstone
Morris Georgiana (bdg) Forest place
NATIONAL SCHOOL, Leytonstone—Henry John Emerson, master
NATIONAL SCHOOL, Low Leyton—William Walker, master
SCHOOL OF INDUSTRY, Low Leyton—Eleanor Barker, mistress

BAKERS.
Andrew Sarah, Low Leyton
Dobbin Henry, Leytonstone
Griffin Philip, Low Leyton
Macomie John, Leytonstone
Nash Samuel, Low Leyton

BLACKSMITHS.
Easton Thomas, Leytonstone
Hopkins Mary, Leytonstone
Skelton and Son, Low Leyton
Williams Charles, Salter's buildings

BOOT & SHOE MAKERS.
Fuller Ebenezer, Low Leyton
Furness Robert, Low Leyton
Gibbard Benjamin Wm. Low Leyton
Plumb William, Leytonstone
Renwick Edward, Leytonstone
Sanders Isaiah, Low Leyton
Thurling George, Low Leyton
White Thomas, Low Leyton
Windley Charles, Leytonstone

BRICKLAYERS.
Arber Benjamin, Leytonstone
Brett Anthony, Low Leyton
Johnson & Munt (& buildrs) Low Leyton
Mann George, Leytonstone
Morphett Jno. (& buildr) Low Leyton
Munt George, Leytonstone
Munt Samuel, Low Leyton

BUTCHERS.
Dawson Rebecca, Leytonstone
Emery Joseph, Low Leyton
Ives John, Low Leyton
Toll Thomas, Low Leyton
Warwick William, Leytonstone

CARPENTERS, BUILDERS, AND UNDERTAKERS.
Cheesman John, Low Leyton
Lucking William, Low Leyton
Marshall John, Low Leyton
Parsingham Sarah, Low Leyton
Pennyfeather Charles, (and cabinet maker & auctioneer) Leytonstone
Scarlett John & William, Leytonstone
Wildsmith Benjamin, Leytonstone

COAL MERCHANTS.
Addison John, Low Leyton
Bullpitt Henry, Low Leyton
Mantz William C. Low Leyton
Saunders Thomas and George, Essex wharf, Lea bridge

CORN DEALERS.
Bullpitt Henry, Low Leyton
Griffin Philip, Low Leyton
Hagger Joseph, Leytonstone
Mantz William C. Low Leyton
Payze Richd. (& miller) Leytonstone

FIRE, &c. OFFICE AGENTS.
IMPERIAL (fire & life) Charles Pennyfeather, Leytonstone
PALLADIUM (life) & PHŒNIX (fire) John Addison, Low Leyton

GROCERS & SHOPKEEPERS.
Amess Elizabeth, Low Leyton
Berry Robert, Low Leyton
Bowman Wm. Joseph, Leytonstone
Brett Joseph, Low Leyton
Bush Thomas, Leytonstone
Butcher Sarah, Low Leyton
Durman Thomas, Low Leyton
Hurry Isaac, Low Leyton
Jenkins John, Low Leyton
Johnson Elizabeth, Leytonstone
Keeling Joseph (& stamp distributer) Leytonstone
King Kemuel (tea dealer) Leytonstone
Markby William, Leytonstone
Munn Susan, Low Leyton
Phillips Sarah, Low Leyton
Smith Richard, Low Leyton
Strange Elizabeth, Leytonstone
Williams John, Leytonstone
Wilson John, Leytonstone
Wright John, Leytonstone

HAIR DRESSERS.
Turner John, Low Leyton
Whitham James, Leytonstone

HORSE & GIG OWNERS FOR HIRE.
(See also Livery-stable Keepers.)
Briggs William, Low Leyton
Wright William, Low Leyton

INNS & PUBLIC HOUSES.
Crown, Samuel Nice, Leytonstone
Green Man, Thomas Barford, Leytonstone
King's Head, Edward Freeman, Low Leyton
Lion & Key, Sml. Cooper, Low Leyton
Old Bell, Thos. Squires, Leytonstone
Plough and Harrow, John Phillipps, Leytonstone
Red Lion, William Amer, Leytonstone
Rose & Crown, George Grant, Low Leyton
Three Blackbirds, John Wright, Low Leyton

LIVERY-STABLE KEEPERS.
Amer William, Leytonstone
Barford Thomas (Green Man) Leytonstone
Clarke Joseph, Low Leyton
Freeman Edward (King's Head) Low Leyton
Nice Samuel (Crown) Leytonstone
Watson Edward, Low Leyton
Wright John, Low Leyton

MILLINERS AND DRESS AND STRAW HAT MAKERS.
Arber Sarah, Leytonstone
Barker Louisa, Leytonstone
Gibbard Elizabeth, Low Leyton
Griffin Elizabeth, Low Leyton
Hills Caroline & Esther, Low Leyton
Martin Ann, Leytonstone
Wilson Ann, Leytonstone

NURSERY & SEEDSMEN.
Fraser Finley, Low Leyton
Green Edw. (gardener) Low Leyton
Hill Charlotte, Leytonstone
Vale James, Leytonstone

PAINTERS, PLUMBERS, AND GLAZIERS.
Fordham Robert, Low Leyton
Hepworth John James, Leytonstone
Turner John B. Low Leyton
Whittaker George, Leytonstone

SADDLERS.
Markby Joseph, Low Leyton
Markby William, Low Leyton

SURGEONS.
Brealey Richard, Low Leyton
Collins Robert (& registrar of births and deaths) Low Leyton
Mackenzie Stephen, Leytonstone

TAILORS.
Hills William, Low Leyton
Hopkins James, Low Leyton
Miles John, Leytonstone
Pearce Thomas, Low Leyton
Southcott John, Low Leyton
Sumner William, Low Leyton

VETERINARY SURGEONS.
Easton Thomas, Leytonstone
Skelton and Son, Low Leyton

WHEELWRIGHTS.
Bale Thomas, Leytonstone
Mayhew Mark, Low Leyton
Ralling George, Low Leyton
York William, Leytonstone

Miscellaneous.
Binder Samuel, parish clerk, Leytonstone
Braithwaite Sidney, brewer, Low Leyton
Burrell Thomas, cattle-dealer, Low Leyton
Evans Wm. Acton, parish clk. Low Leyton
Fickling William, draper, Low Leyton
Hills Mark, cooper, Low Leyton
Knott George, tea-dealer & stationer, Low Leyton
Lamb Wm. chief constable of *Becontree*, Leytonstone
Morris William, artist, Low Leyton
POLICE STATION, Leytonstone—Charles Whitman, horse patrol
Powell William, toy dealer, Low Leyton
Reeves Robert, cow-keeper, Low Leyton
Richardson Samuel, clerk to the West Ham union, Low Leyton
Sheen Samuel, undertaker, Leytonstone
Teague Joseph, statuary, Leytonstone
Turner John S. iron and tin-plate worker, Leytonstone
Wiggins Thos. watchmaker, Leytonstone
Wilson Jno. surveyor of roads, Low Leyton

COACHES.
To LONDON, R. Wragg's *Coaches*, from the Three Blackbirds, Low Leyton, every morning at nine and eleven, afternoon at three and five, and evening at seven—*Coaches* (from Wanstead), call at the Green Man, Leytonstone, every morning (Sunday excepted) at a quarter before nine—*Coaches* (from Woodford and Epping), call at the same house, every morning (Sunday excepted) at half-past nine—*Coaches* (from Harlow), every forenoon (Sunday excepted) at a quarter past eleven, and *Coaches* (from Clare), every afternoon (Sun. excepted) at three.
To CLARE, *Coaches* (from London), call at the Green Man, Leytonstone, every afternoon (Sunday excepted) at half-past three
To EPPING and WOODFORD, *Coaches* (from London), call at the Green Man, every afternoon at half-past five.
To WANSTEAD, *Coaches* (from London), call at the Green Man, every day at twelve, and afternoon at three and four.

CARRIERS.
To LONDON, Wm. Cole, from Low Leyton, & Joseph Wright, from Leytonstone, daily (Sunday excepted.)

MALDON,

WITH THE VILLAGES OF GOLDHANGER, HEYBRIDGE, LANGFORD, PURLEIGH, LATCHINGDON, MUNDON, SNOREHAM AND NEIGHBOURHOODS.

MALDON is a market town, port, and corporate and parliamentary borough, with separate jurisdiction, locally in the hundred of Dengie—37 miles N. E. from London, 16 S. S. W. from Colchester, and 10 E. from Chelmsford; situated upon the slope of an eminence which rises to the south-west of the estuary of the Blackwater (the *Idumanum* of the Romans). The first historical notice we have of this town is in the year 913, when the elder Edward encamped here. The earliest charter it received appears to have been conferred by Henry II; Queen Mary, in 1553, granted a second, by which its government was regulated until the new municipal act vested it in a mayor, four aldermen, twelve councillors and the usual assistant officers, and gave to the corporate body the title of 'the mayor, aldermen and capital burgesses and commonalty of Maldon;' it likewise provided for the borough a commission of the peace. This place has sent members to parliament from the reign of Edward III to the present time; the mayor is the returning officer, and the present representatives are Quintin Dick and John Round, Esqrs. The corporation are lords of the manor. Courts of quarter session are regularly holden on the days before those for the county; petty sessions for the hundred of Dengie weekly, and a court of record for pleas of debt to any amount. The town-hall is an ancient fabric of brick, and the custom-house is a small neat edifice composed of the same material. Maldon does not possess any manufactures worth notice, but it enjoys a good local trade, and its imports and exports are considerable: the former comprise coal, iron, tin, deals, &c.; the latter, flour, pease, beans, wheat, oats and salt. A productive fishery on the Blackwater belongs to the corporation; and oysters of superior quality, called 'Wallfleet oysters,' are abundant here. The harbour is convenient; at spring tides the channel has a sufficient draught of water for vessels of from 150 to 200 tons; the colliers, however, remain in the deep water below the town, and lighters are employed to bring up their cargoes. A canal from Heybridge to Chelmsford passes within a mile of the town. The custom of 'borough English,' by which the *youngest*, and *not the eldest* son succeeds to the burgage tenement of his father, is still in practice at this place.

The borough of Maldon includes the three parishes of All Saints, St. Peter and St. Mary: the two first, however, have long been consolidated, and on the site of St. Peter's church is the grammar school, with a library over it; but the church-yard continues to be appropriated to the use of the parish. All Saints' is the principal church, and is an ancient spacious structure, with a square tower, surmounted by an equilateral triangular spire. St. Mary's, a large pile with a massive tower (supposed to have been originally founded in the tenth century), stands in the lower part of the town; both church and tower were rebuilt in the reign of Charles I. The living of the united parishes of All Saints and St. Peter is a vicarage, of which the Rev. C. Mathews is patron and incumbent; St. Mary's is a peculiar of the dean and chapter of Westminster—Rev. R. L. Bridge incumbent. The charities are the grammar school, as above, founded by Ralph Breeder, and further endowed with a scholarship at Christ's college, Cambridge, by Dr. Plume, who left an estate to keep in repair for ever the grammar school and library; the latter, containing about 5,000 volumes, chiefly divinity, was founded by the same generous benefactor for the use of the clergy and others in the town and neighbourhood of Maldon: in addition to other charitable bequests, he likewise founded a lecture, to be delivered every Wednesday from Lady-day to Michaelmas in All Saints' church, by clergymen who are appointed for that purpose; and also endowed the Plumean professorship in the university of Cambridge. The market, a good one for corn, is held on Saturday; fairs are on Lady-day, May 1st, and September 13th and 14th. The borough of Maldon, including the three parishes, contained, in 1831, 3,831 inhabitants.

About four miles from Maldon, on the Colchester road, and in the hundred of Thurstable, is GOLDHANGER village and parish. The church, dedicated to St. Peter, is a strongly built edifice, with a tower. The parish, which is bounded on the south by the Blackwater river, contains some salt-works. A small fair or revel is held here, for toys, &c., on Whit-Monday. The population of the parish, by the last returns, was 496.

HEYBRIDGE is a village and parish in the same hundred as Goldhanger, about one mile from Maldon, on the Colchester road. Its name is said to be derived from an old bridge of five arches, through which a principal branch of the river, that now passes at some distance, in former ages took its course. The church is dedicated to St. Andrew; the benefice is a vicarage, in the gift of the dean and chapter of London. The general employment of the inhabitants of the parish is agricultural; their number, in 1831, amounted to 1,064.

Adjoining to Heybridge, in the same hundred, is the small parish and village of LANGFORD—noticed chiefly as having in its locality Langford Hall, a beautiful mansion, surrounded by a finely wooded park, once the property of the celebrated Dr. William Harvey. The church is dedicated to St. Giles; the living is a rectory, in the patronage of Mrs. Wescombe. Population, 273.

PURLEIGH is a village and parish in the same hundred as Maldon, four miles south from that town. The village, which is neat, contains a handsome spacious church, with an embattled tower of flint and stone: it is dedicated to All Saints, and the benefice is a rectory annexed to the provostship of Oriel college, Oxford; the Rev. Robert Walker is the present incumbent. There is a charity school for boys and girls. Population of the parish, in 1831, 1,044.

LATCHINGDON, MUNDON and SNOREHAM are villages and parishes in the same hundred as Maldon, extending from three to six miles S. E. from that town. The two former have each a church; the Rev. Charles Owen is incumbent for the parish of Latchingdon, and the Rev. Coventry Payne for that of Mundon. Population in 1831:—LATCHINGDON, with the hamlet of LAWLING, 451; MUNDON, 273; and SNOREHAM, 225 inhabitants.

POST OFFICE, MALDON, John Polley, *Post Master.*—Letters from CHELMSFORD arrive (by mail cart) every morning at six, and are despatched every evening at nine.—The box opens every morning at seven and closes every evening at half-past eight; but letters are received until nine by paying one penny with each.

GENTRY AND CLERGY.

Alsop Mr. Robert, Maldon
Baker Mr. Benjamin, M. D. Maldon
Barker Mrs. Sarah, Heybridge
Bickmore Robert, esq. Maldon
Blackbone William, esq. Maldon
Bridge Rev. Robert Lee, Maldon
Bright Miss —, Maldon
Bright Edward, esq. (mayor) Maldon
Burls Rev. Robert, Maldon
Bygrave George, esq. Maldon
Clift Samuel, esq. Lawling hall
Coape Henry, esq. Maldon
Cole Mrs. —, Langford
Cousins Mr. —, Woodham Mortimer lodge
Dawson William, esq. Maldon
Drake Mrs. —, Maldon
Dunn Rev. Salisbury, A. M. Maldon
Driffeld Rev. Joseph, Maldon
Dyke Mrs. —, Maldon
Evans Mrs. —, Maldon
Green Mrs. —, Maldon
Hammond Mrs. —, Maldon
Hammond Mr. William, Maldon
Joscelyne Mrs. —, Maldon
Kemp Mrs. —, Maldon
Lee Rev. Edward, Goldhanger
Martham John, esq. Mundon
Mathews Rev. Charles, Maldon
Morrell Rev. R. P. Woodham Mortimr
Nash Mr. Samuel, Maldon
Owen Rev. Charles, Latchingdon
Parke Capt. —, Heybridge
Parker Mr. Christopher C. Woodham Mortimer place
Pattison Joseph, esq. Maldon
Pattison Capt. Joseph (magistrate & deputy lieutenant for the county) Maldon
Phillips Mr. William, Maldon
Pond William, esq. Maldon
Poynter Mrs. —, Maldon
Robinson Mrs. —, Maldon
Rogers Mrs. —, Maldon
Rush Mr. John, Maldon
Solly Richard, esq. Mundon hall
Stothard Mrs. —, Maldon
Tanfield Richard, esq. Maldon
Taylor Mr. Samuel, Heybridge
Thomas Miss —, Maldon
Tunmer Mr. —, Maldon
Walker Rev. Robert, Purleigh
Waring Mrs. —, Heybridge
Watts Mrs. —, Maldon
Wells Mrs. —, Maldon
Wescomb Mrs. —, Langford grove
Whitehead Mrs. —, Maldon

ACADEMIES AND SCHOOLS.
Not otherwise described are Day Schools.

Bright Rebecca (boarding and day) Maldon
CHARITY SCHOOL, Latchingdon—John Glasscock, master
CHARITY SCHOOL, Purleigh—John Borrett, master; Mary Ann Sly, mistress
Collis Mira, Heybridge
Enever Martha, Purleigh
GRAMMAR SCHOOL, Maldon—Rev. Salisbury Dunn, A. M. master
LANCASTERIAN SCHOOL, Maldon—— Poole, master; — Poole, mistrss
May Misses (boarding & day) Maldon
NATIONAL SCHOOL, Maldon—Geo. Dandridge Bridge, master; Mary Cooke, mistress
Nichols Robert, Maldon
Polley Jesse (preparatory) Maldon
Quin Hannah (brdng & day) Maldon
Reynolds Amey, Maldon
Sladden Lavinia (boarding) Maldon
Sutton Sarah, Maldon
Trussell James, Purleigh
Wilmshurst Misses (boardg) Maldon
Wrake Sarah (boarding & day) Heybridge

ATTORNEYS.

Codd William (and county coroner, and town clerk) Maldon
Codd William, jun. (and clerk to the trustees of the Essex turnpikes, to the magistrates of Dengie division, & commissioners of taxes) Maldon
Crick John & William, Maldon
Digby George Wyatt, Maldon
Hance William Lawrence, Maldon
Lawrence William, Maldon
Wright William, Maldon

AUCTIONEERS.

Herbert & Hurrell, Maldon & Heybridge
May Alfred (& estate agent) Maldon

BAKERS.

Beckwith David, Maldon
Bretton Joseph, Maldon
Brewer Joseph, Purleigh
Chaplin Caleb, Goldhanger
Coote Charles, Maldon
Cross Stephen, Heybridge
Death William, Maldon
Harridance Samuel, Maldon
Harvey Thomas, Maldon
Herbert James, Maldon
Houghton Charles, Snoreham
Mitson John, Heybridge
Raven George, Purleigh
Rumsey Elizabeth, Maldon
Sayer Edward, Purleigh
Stow Louisa, Maldon
Worraker Charles, Heybridge
Yell Charles, Heybridge

BANKERS.

Sparrow, Walford, Nottidge and Co. (Branch)—(draw on Barclay and Co. London)—John West, agent
SAVINGS' BANK, Maldon—George D. Bridge, clerk

BASKET MAKERS.

Beckett Robert, Maldon
Smith John, Maldon

BOOKSELLERS, STATIONERS AND PRINTERS.

Herbert Henry, Maldon
Pettit Richard (stationer) Maldon
Youngman Philip Henry (and subdistributer of stamps) Maldon

BOOT & SHOE MAKERS.

Ayes Samuel Porter, Maldon
Bale John, Maldon
Balls John, Maldon
Barnard William, Maldon
Boyten Thomas, Heybridge
Bulley William, Maldon
Clapton John, Maldon
Clark John, Maldon
Clark Samuel, Maldon
Clarke Samuel, Maldon
Collis William, Heybridge
Everard John, Maldon
Genllond Benjamin, Maldon
Gepp John, Maldon
Hammond William, Maldon
Harridance James, Maldon
Hitch Thomas, Snoreham
Keys George, Purleigh
Keys Joseph, Purleigh
Livermore Thomas, Maldon
Loker William, Maldon
Marlar John, Maldon
Mason Daniel, Maldon
Matham William, Purleigh
Miles William, Maldon
Orrell William, Maldon
Polley Samuel, Maldon
Quilter William, Maldon
Ramplee Thomas, Heybridge
Reynolds Matthias, Latchingdon
Sealey Arthur, Goldhanger
Steward Thomas, Maldon
Willson Ambrose, Purleigh
Worraker Thomas, Basin, Heybridge

BREWERS.

Pitcairn John, Maldon
Syrett Frances, Maldon

BRICKLAYERS.

Barker Francis, Maldon
Baxter Robert, Maldon
Baxter Samuel, Maldon
Baxter William, Maldon
Cook William, Purleigh
Hurricks Samuel, Maldon
Palmer James, Heybridge
Turner John, Purleigh

BUTCHERS.

Allen John, Maldon
Anstey James, Heybridge
Burchell John, Maldon
Cranies Robert Josiah, Maldon
Croxon Chas. (& salesman) Purleigh
Finch and Wade, Maldon
King William, Goldhanger
Lamb Richard, Maldon
Limner Hannah, Maldon
Mayhew Samuel, Heybridge
Raymond John, Maldon
Raymond Thomas, Maldon
Upson James, Latchingdon
Willis Peter, Maldon
Worraker Charles, Heybridge

CABINET MAKERS.

Beale James, Maldon
Cotte James, Maldon
Hodgson John, Maldon
Orrell Stephen, Maldon
Stratford George, Maldon

CARPENTERS.

Ardley Abrhm. Simpson, Goldhanger
Bickmore Stephen, Heybridge
Cannom Samuel, Maldon
Cook John, Maldon
Emberson and Harvey, Langford
Emberson William, Langford
Gepp and Seamans, Maldon
Hayward Henry, Maldon
Hodgson John, Maldon
Kemp Robert, Purleigh
Montague Daniel (and boat builder) Basin, Heybridge
Orrell John (& turner) Maldon
Rawlinson Samuel, Goldhanger
Sadd John, jun. Maldon
Webber George, Maldon

CHINA, &c. DEALERS.

Heard John, Maldon
Moses Moses, Maldon

CHYMISTS & DRUGGISTS.

Aikin Arthur Jennings, Maldon
Fearnley Richard, Maldon
Lee John, Maldon

CLOTHES DEALERS.

Lee John Maldon
Moses Israel, Maldon
Nathan Barned & Jacob, Maldon
Seamens Joshua, Maldon
Sizer Joseph, Maldon

COACH BUILDERS.

Williams Thomas, Maldon
Woodfine Charles, Maldon

COAL MERCHANTS.

Belsham Daniel & Son, Heybridge
Bentall William, Heybridge
Coates George, Maldon & *Chelmsford*
Eve Henry William, Maldon
Johnson & Clapham, Heybridge
Miles Barnard, Maldon
Payne John & Son, Maldon
Piggot & Son, Langford
Polley John, jun. Maldon
Puplett Daniel, Maldon
Ridley William, Heybridge
Rush Henry Hayward, Heybridge
Sadd John & Son, Maldon
Sparks William (dealer) Maldon

CONFECTIONERS.

Harridance Henry, Maldon
Harvey Thomas, Maldon

COOPERS.

Beckett Joshua, Maldon
Orrell John, Maldon
Spencer Robert, Maldon

CORN MERCHANTS AND DEALERS.

Babbs Elizabeth (dealer) Maldon
Cornell John (dealer) Maldon
Eve Henry Westow, Maldon
Harridance & Wright, Maldon
Harvey Thomas (dealer) Maldon
Payne John & Son, Maldon
Polley John, jun. Maldon
Ridley William, Heybridge
Sadd John & Son, Maldon
Ward George Gepp, Heybridge
Webber Robert Partridge (dealer) Heybridge

CURRIERS AND LEATHER CUTTERS.

Felton William, Maldon
Smith Robert, Maldon

FIRE, &c. OFFICE AGENTS, AT MALDON

BRITISH, John Augustus Bygrave
ESSEX ECONOMIC, Hen. Harridance
ESSEX EQUITABLE, Alfred May
GLOBE, Henry Herbert
IMPERIAL, Henry May
PHŒNIX (fire) and PELICAN (life), Arthur Jennings Aiken
ROYAL EXCHANGE, John Sadd and Son
UNION, John Polley

FISHMONGERS.

Miller John, Maldon
Payne James, Maldon
Stebbens William, Maldon
Ward James Walter, Maldon

GARDENERS & SEEDSMEN.

Brown William, Maldon
Copping Joseph, Maldon
Gill Thomas, Maldon
Heard William, Maldon
Stratford Elizabeth, Maldon
Stratford James, Maldon
Stratford William, Maldon
Unwin Samuel, Maldon

GLOVRS & BREECHES MAKRS

Dibdin Joseph, Maldon
Matthews William, Maldon
Matthews William Thomas, Maldon
Wallace William, Maldon

GROCERS & TEA DEALERS.

(See also Shopkeepers, &c.)

Bygrave and Son, Maldon
Cross Stephen, Heybridge
Dudley Daniel, Maldon
Horton Susannah, Maldon
Lemere James Henry (and importer of salt) Maldon
May Henry, Maldon
Potter Thomas, Maldon
Smith Tamer, Maldon
Theobald Samuel, Purleigh
Wilmshurst John, Maldon

HAIR CUTTERS.

Ely William Waylen, Maldon
Miles Edward, Maldon
Miles John, Maldon
Pettit Richard (& perfumer) Maldon
Wright Thomas, Maldon

HATTERS.

Bentall Josiah, Maldon
Bulley Richard, Maldon
Martin John, Maldon

INNS & PUBLIC HOUSES.

Anchor, Joseph Rayner, Maldon
Bell, Cranmer Harris, Purleigh
Blue Boar, Mary Shynn, Maldon
Chelmer, John Going, Basin, Heybridge
Chequers, Geo. Cowell, Goldhanger
Chequers, William Damson, Maldon
Crown, Henry Whitmore, Heybridge

INNS, &c — *Continued.*

Duke of Wellington, Mary Cranis, Maldon
Half Moon, Henry Everard, Maldon
Jolly Sailor, Edward Tovee, Basin, Heybridge
King's Head, Samuel Fuller (commercial and posting) Maldon
Queen Adelaide, William Newman, Maldon
Queen's Head, Francis Syrett, Maldon
Red Lion, Eliz. Taylor, Snoreham
Rose & Crown, Jas. Barker, Maldon
Royal Oak, John Jenkins, Woodham Mortimer
Ship, Edward Everard, Maldon
Ship and Anchor, Barnard Miles, Maldon
Spread Eagle, John Smith, Maldon
Swan Inn, Reuben Cottee, Maldon
Victoria, William Keys, Heybridge
Welcome Sailor, Chas. Tanner, Maldn
White Hart, James Cook, Hazeleigh
White Hart, Richd. Richbell, Maldon
White Horse, John Deeks, Mundon
White Horse (posting & commercial) William Hickford, Maldon
White Lion, Henry Gepp, Maldon

IRON FOUNDERS.

Bentall William, Heybridge
Gymer Thomas, Maldon

IRONMONGERS.

Hewes Stephen (and nail maker) Maldon
Knight Edward (& tinman) Maldon
Rayner Thomas, Maldon

LINEN, &c. DRAPERS.

Bentall Josiah, Maldon
Cross Stephen, Heybridge
Humpherys Edward, Maldon
Lemere James Henry, Maldon
Wilmshurst John, Maldon
Wyllie Thomas, Maldon

MALTSTERS.

Belsham James, Goldhanger
Busbridge Alfred, Maldon
Eve Henry Westow, Maldon
Grimwood Charles, Goldhanger
Rush Henry, Heybridge

MILLERS.

Belsham James, Goldhanger
Dixon Benjamin and Robert Walker, Blue mills
Green Charles William, Heybridge
Havers Robert, Maldon
Marrige Robert, Hoe mill, Woodham Walter
Piggot and Son, Langford
Raven William, Purleigh
Spight Daniel, Woodham Mortimer
Ward George Gepp, Heybridge
Ward Joseph, Beeleigh mills, Maldon

MILLINERS & DRESS MAKRS.

Blythe Dorcas and Maria, Maldon
Burchell Mary Ann, Maldon
Cook Mrs. Maldon
Farrow M. Maldon
Howe Catherine, Heybridge
Hurring Catherine, Maldon
Mountford Mary, Maldon
Nelson Ann, Maldon
Newman M. Maldon

PILOTS.

Austin Giles, Maldon
Forman James, Maldon
Handley Abraham, Maldon
Morris William, Maldon
Payne James, Maldon

PLUMBERS & PAINTERS.

Furlong James, Purleigh
Hawkes Samuel, Maldon
Hearn William, Maldon
Joslin William, Maldon
Stannard James, Maldon

SADDLERS.

Edwards James, Maldon
Ellis John, Latchingdon
Greatrix Thomas, Maldon
Jay Thomas, Maldon
Palmer Charles, Maldon

SALT MERCHANTS, &c.

Bright Edward, Maldon
Worraker Thos. (salt-works) Basin, Heybridge

SHIP AGENTS.

Busbridge Egbert, Maldon
Everard Edward, Maldon

SHIP OWNERS.

Harridance and Wright, Maldon
Miles Barnard, Maldon
Payne John and Son, Maldon
Sadd John and Son, Maldon
Sadd John, jun. Maldon

SHIPWRIGHTS.

Abbott Benjamin, Maldon
Porter James, Maldon
Williamson James, Maldon

SHOPKEEPERS & DEALRS IN GROCERIES & SUNDRIES.

Abley Sarah, Maldon
Braisted William Robert, Maldon
Bridge James, Mundon
Brooks Edmund, Purleigh
Brown William, Maldon
Cottis John, Purleigh
Doubleday William, Maldon
Emberson William, Langford
Freeman Joseph, Maldon
Halls Elizabeth, Langford
Horton Mrs. Maldon
Houghton Charles, Snoreham
Hubbard John, Latchingdon
Huby William, Basin, Heybridge
King William, Goldhanger
Marlar Charlotte, Maldon
Mayhew Samuel, Heybridge
Pretty John, Maldon
Reynolds Amey, Maldon
Russell William, Snoreham
Sayer Edward, Purleigh
Skinner Sarah, Heybridge

SMITHS & FARRIERS.

Abbott John, Goldhanger
Brown Joseph, Maldon
Bruce Thomas, Maldon
Burchell Samuel, Mundon
Collis James, Heybridge
Cook William, Goldhanger
Fowler John, Maldon
Gepp William, Maldon
Gill William, Maldon
Harris John, Purleigh
Harris Thomas, Snoreham
Hawkes Elizabeth, Purleigh
Kemp Samuel, Purleigh
Pretty John, Maldon
Stockings Samuel, Goldhanger
Warren Joseph, Heybridge
Wood George, Langford
Wright Sampson, Maldon

STRAW HAT MAKERS.

Alexander M. Goldhanger
Burchell William, Maldon
Lawson Mary Ann, Maldon
Lawson Sophia, Maldon
Porter Hannah, Maldon
Thurston and Moss, Heybridge
Tring Elizabeth, Heybridge
Ward Mary, Maldon

SURGEONS.

May George and Son, Maldon
Thorp John and Son, Maldon
Tomlinson James Francis, Maldon

TAILORS.

Ashley James, Maldon
Brown John, Maldon
Bulley Richard, Maldon
Holland John, Maldon
Huxter John, Maldon
Lawson Francis, Maldon
Martin John, Maldon
Moses Israel, Maldon
Newbold Charles, Purleigh
Pitcairn David, Maldon
Sizer Joseph, Maldon
Uxter John, Maldon
Woolley William, Maldon

TALLOW CHANDLER.

Bright Edward (and soap-maker) Maldon

TEA DEALERS.

Purkis Thomas, Maldon
Wilson Robert, Maldon

TIMBER MERCHANTS.

Coates George, Maldon & *Chelmsford*
Puplett Daniel, Maldon
Sadd John, jun. Maldon

VETERINARY SURGEONS.

Elstow Tunmer, Maldon
May Charles, Maldon

WATCH & CLOCK MAKERS.

Jeffries Elizabeth, Maldon
Pepper Henry, Maldon
Wright Sampson, Maldon

WHEELWRIGHTS.

Bickmore Stephen, Heybridge
Cooper Henry, Mundon
Cowland John, Snoreham
Deadman William, Heybridge
Franklin William, Purleigh
Harvey Joseph, Maldon
Playle William, Purleigh

WHITING MANUFACTURERS.

Baxter William, Maldon
King Isaac, Maldon

WINE & SPIRIT MERCHANTS

Bygrave John Augustus, Maldon
Dawson William (and beer) Maldon
May and Son, Maldon

Miscellaneous.

Adams Thomas, rope maker, Maldon
Ardley Abraham Simpson, parish clerk, Goldhanger
Bartlem Thomas, superintendent of the navigation, Heybridge
BATHS, Maldon—William Morris, proprietor
Bentall William, agricultural implement maker, Heybridge
Blanks William, gun maker, Maldon
Bray Thos. dealer in British wines, Maldon
Carr William, stone mason, Maldon
CHELMSFORD PROVIDENT SOCIETY, (branch)—William Quilter, Maldon, and Matthias Reynolds, Latchingdon, collectors.
Chipperfield Daniel, parish clerk, Maldon
Dunnett Jno. tobacco pipe maker, Maldon
EXCISE OFFICE, at the King's Head Inn, Maldon—Edward Honeywood, supervisor.
French Geo. coach & waggon proprietor, Maldon
GAS WORKS, Maldon—John Orrell, secretary.
Goring Joseph, sail maker, Basin, Heybridge
Greenwood Robt. iron merchant, Maldon
Hance Edward, registrar of births and deaths, Maldon
Lawson Frances, furniture broker, Maldon
Lee John, hardwareman and haberdasher, Maldon
LIBRARY, Maldon—Rev. Chas. Matthews, librarian
MALDON UNION (for 32 parishes)—John Beale, master; Mary Ann Beale, mistress
May Henry, merchant, Maldon
Mayhew Samuel, parish clerk, Heybridge
Nelson Ann, stationer & toy dealer, Maldon
Parker Christopher, brick maker, Woodham Mortimer
Sadd John, surveyor, Maldon
SOCIETY FOR PROMOTING CHRISTIAN KNOWLEDGE, Maldon—Rev. William Holland, secretary
Stokes Lydia, stay maker, Maldon
Thompson Daniel, millwright, Maldon
Verlander Joseph, druggist and marine store dealer, Maldon

CUSTOM-HOUSE, AT MALDON.

Collector and Tide Surveyor, Wm. Barker
Collector's Clerk, James Lewis
Notary, Egbert Busbridge

COACHES,

FROM THE KING'S HEAD, MALDON.

To LONDON, the *Telegraph*, every Monday, Wednesday, and Friday morning, at ten, and another *Coach* every Monday morning at five, and every other morning (Sunday excepted) at six; both go thro' Chelmsford, Ingatestone, Brentwood, and Romford.

To BURNHAM, the *Telegraph*, every Tuesday, Thursday, and Saturday afternoon, at five.

CARRIERS.

To LONDON, George French's *Van*, from his office, every Friday at twelve—and Sorrell's *Waggon*, from the Swan Inn, every Tuesday and Friday afternoon.

To BRADWELL, William Creasey, from the Swan Inn, every Monday, Thursday and Saturday afternoon at three

To BURNHAM, William Keys, from the Swan Inn, every Monday, Thursday, and Saturday.

To COLCHESTER, Wm. Keys, from the Swan Inn, every Wednesday and Saturday morning.

To TOLLESBURY, Banyard, from the Swan Inn, every Monday, Thursday, and Saturday.

To WITHAM, Agar's *Van*, from the Ship Inn, daily.

CONVEYANCE BY WATER.

To LONDON, John Payne & John Sadd and Son, every Saturday.

MANNINGTREE,

WITH THE VILLAGES OF MISTLEY, DEDHAM, LANGHAM, ARDLEIGH & NEIGHBOURHOODS.

MANNINGTREE is a market town and parish in the hundred of Tendring—60 miles N. E. from London, 12 S. from Ipswich (Suffolk), and 12 W. from Harwich; situated on the road from the last-named town to the metropolis, and on the southern bank of the Stour, which river was made navigable from hence to Sudbury, in Suffolk, in the reign of Queen Anne. Maud de Clare, Countess of Hereford and Gloucester, bestowed the manor on a nunnery of the order of St. Augustine, at Canon Leigh, in Devonshire; after the dissolution, Manningtree (then called *Many Tree*, or *Scidinghoo*, in the grant,) was given by Henry VIII to Sir John Rainsworth. The town, which is irregularly built, has been much improved in its external aspect within the last thirty years: its market, however, has not kept pace with this apparent prosperity; on the contrary, the benefits resulting from it to the town have declined—the chief business now existing is in malt, corn, coal and timber, in which branches there are several respectable establishments. Petty sessions for the division are holden alternately at Manningtree, Mistley, Thorpe and Great Bromley, on Mondays; and a court baron is held annually for the manors of Manningtree and Mistley. The church, erected in 1616, has received additional sittings by the society for the enlargement of churches and chapels. In the church is a neat mural monument to the memory of Thomas Osmond, a protestant martyr, who suffered death by burning, in the reign of the intolerant Mary, for refusing to attend the celebration of mass at Easter. The living is a perpetual curacy, in the patronage of the rector of Mistley; the present curate is the Rev. James Salisbury, M.A. There are places of worship for baptists, independents and Wesleyan methodists, and a national school for children of both sexes. The country around is pleasant, with an agreeable succession of hill and dale; the land is in a very superior state of cultivation, and some of the finest corn in the kingdom is produced from it. It has been stated as a remarkable fact, that there are only three oak trees growing in this parish. The market is on Thursday, and a fair for toys and pleasure on the Friday in Whitsun week. The parish contained, in 1831, 1,237 inhabitants.

In the same hundred as Manningtree, about half a mile from that town, on the Harwich road, is the genteel village and parish of MISTLEY. The river Stour is navigable at the village, where are convenient quays and warehouses for corn, malt and coal, in which articles considerable business is carried on. The church, consecrated in 1785, and dedicated to St. Mary, is a neat structure, with a handsome chancel: the benefice, a discharged rectory, is in the presentation of Lady Rigby; the incumbent is the Rev. Henry Thompson, and his present curate the Rev. Thomas Collingwood Hughes. A statute and pleasure fair is held on the 8th of August. Population of the parish, at the last census, 876.

DEDHAM, formerly a market town, at present ranks only as one of the most respectable Essex villages: it is in the hundred of Lexden, about three miles and a half from Manningtree, and, like that town, situate in a picturesque valley, on the river Stour, possessing the same advantages of navigable communication with Harwich. The clothing trade at one time flourished here; that branch has become wholly extinct, and the place is now solely remarkable for the number of genteel residences in its vicinity. The church is a spacious and very elegant edifice, with a fine chancel, an organ and eight sweet-toned bells: the benefice is a vicarage, the right of presentation being in the chancellor of the dutchy of Lancaster; the incumbent is the Rev. Robert Marratt Miller, D.D. There is also a rich lectureship attached to this church, in the appointment of twenty-four trustees; the present lecturer is the Rev. William Milton Hurlock. The independents have a place of worship here; and there is a free school, chartered by Queen Elizabeth in 1575, for boys, natives of Dedham and Great Bromley, endowed with an exhibition of the value of £60. per annum. An assembly-room is well supported by the gentry of the neighbourhood. The market was appointed to be held on Tuesdays; but many years have passed away since the privilege of holding it was exercised: a fair for toys takes place on Easter-Tuesday. The population, in 1831, was 1,770.

About two miles from, and in the same hundred as Dedham, is the village and parish of LANGHAM, containing the church, dedicated to St. Mary, and a baptist chapel. The parish, which is bounded on the north by the river Stour, contained, in 1831, 821 inhabitants.

ARDLEIGH is a village and parish in the same hundred as Manningtree, rather more than four miles S. W. from that town, on the road to Colchester. It contains the parish church, dedicated to St. Mary, and a chapel for Wesleyan methodists. Population, in 1831, 1,545.

POST OFFICE, MANNINGTREE, Thomas Taylor, *Post Master*.—Letters from LONDON, &c. arrive (by mail cart from Colchester) every morning at five, and are despatched every night at half-past nine.—The box closes at nine at night.

POST, DEDHAM, *Receiving-House* at John Barker's.—Letters from LONDON, &c. arrive every morning at seven, and are despatched every evening at seven.—The box closes at a quarter before seven evening.

NOBILITY, GENTRY AND CLERGY.

Ambrose John, esq. Mistley
Anderton Edward, esq. Lawford
Bishop Rev. Henry, Ardleigh
Blyth Daniel, esq. Langham
Blyth Thomas, esq. Langham
Borthwick Mrs. —, Ardleigh
Borthwick Mrs. General, Ardleigh
Borthwick the Misses, Ardleigh
Brown Lieutenant Colonel, Dedham
Carrington Benjamin, esq. Ardleigh
Constable Abram, esq. Dedham
Cousens John, esq. Manningtree
Cox Richard Waite, esq. Lawford
Davey Miss —, Dedham
De Couffon Rev. Claudius Maria, Dedham
Downes William, esq. Dedham
Dunn Rev. Jas. Salisbury, Manningtree
Elton Mrs. Hannah Maria, Dedham
Elton Jacob, esq. Ardleigh
Everard Mrs. —, Dedham
Ewen Thos. Lestrange, esq. Dedham
Eyre Rev. Charles, Dedham
Folkard William, esq. Manningtree
Fox John, Dedham
Freeman William, esq. Dedham
Frost Rev. William Bird, Langham
Gould the Misses, Dedham hall
Green Edward Henry, esq. Lawford
Harris Philip, esq. Lawford
Howard Mrs. Hannah, Manningtree
Hughes Rev. Thomas Collingwood, Bradfield
Hurlock Rev. James Thomas, D.D. Dedham
Hurlock Rev. Wm. Milton, Dedham
Manning Alderman, esq. Dedham
Martin William, esq. Dedham
Maude Wm. Jemmett, esq. Langham
May Mr. —, Manningtree
Merry Miss —, Dedham
Miller Rev. Robt. Marratt, D.D. Dedham
Monteith James, esq. Mistley
Moore Jno. esq. Stour lodge, Bradfield
Mule William, esq. Dedham
Mumford Rbt. esq. Great Reeds, Dedham
Nichols the Misses, Wix
Norman Edward, esq. Mistley
Norman Mrs. Eliz. Manningtree
Norman Francis, esq. Manningtree
Norton Rev. John, Langham hall
Nunn Carrington, esq. Little Bromley
Nunn the Misses, Mistley
Nunn Thomas, esq. Lawford house

NOBILITY, GENTRY AND CLERGY—*Continued.*

Nunn Wm. esq. Netherhall, Bradfield
Page Robert, jun. esq. Mistley
Page Thomas, esq. Mistley
Pilkington Right Hon. Lady, Dedham
Reeve Edward, esq. Dedham
Rivers Right Hon. Lord, Mistley hall
Sadler Major, Lawford [ham
Sadler William Stebbing, esq. Lang-
Sawyer Miss —, Ardleigh
Silke William, esq. Mistley
Smith Martha, Manningtree
Stevens Rev. John, Manningtree
Taylor Rev. George, D. D. Dedham
Trew Rev. John, Dedham
Ward Joseph, esq. Dedham cottage
Webb William, esq. Manningtree
Whaley Nathaniel, esq. Dedham
Whitfield Rev. Wm. Brett, Lawford
Wilkinson Mrs. —, Dedham
Wratislaw John, esq. Dedham

ACADEMIES AND SCHOOLS.

Not otherwise described are Day Schools.

Alloway John, Manningtree
Barrell John, Langham
Byles Elizabeth, Langham [leigh
Carrington Misses (brdng & day) Ard-
Charity School (girls') Lawford—Maria Harris, mistress
Charity School (girls') Mistley park—Mary Bunnis, mistress
Free Grammar School, Dedham—Rev. George Taylor, master
Frostick Mary, Mistley
Hitchcock Mary Ann & Caroline (brdg & day) Hill house, Manningtree
Hollick Ebenezer, Dedham
Manningtree & Mistley National School, William Smith, master; Jane Proome, mistress
National School (boys' & girls') Dedham—Mrs. Cole & Mrs. Seden, mistresses [Dedham
Platten Corder (boarding and day)
Salmon Sarah, Ardleigh
Sargent Mary Ann, Langham
Seargeant Susannah, Ardleigh
Simson Ellen Maria (boarding and day) Dedham

ATTORNEYS.

Ambrose John & John Thos. Mistley & Manningtree [Hadleigh
Barstow Thos. John, Dedham and
Firmin Harcourt, Dedham
Hitchcock Saml (& registrar of births, deaths & marriages) Manningtree

AUCTIONEERS.

Cook Edward, Stratford St. Mary's
Goodwin Robert, Manningtree
Goodwin Robert, jun. Manningtree

BAKERS.

Balls William, Bradfield
Cant William, Lawford
Cant William, Manningtree
Cook John, Manningtree
Daniel George, Dedham
Finch Charles, Dedham
Finch William, Mistley
Hurring Thomas, Mistley [tree
Long John (& corn dealer) Manning-
Lowe John, Manningtree
Mecklenburgh John, Dedham
Page William, Dedham
Paskell Thomas, Manningtree
Rivers John, Manningtree
Spooner John, Lawford
Tweed Robert, Bradfield
Vince William, Dedham

BANKERS.

Alexander and Co. Manningtree—(draw on Barnetts, Hoare & Co.)
Nunn & Co. Manningtree—(draw on Barnetts, Hoare & Co. London)

BASKET MAKERS.

Barker Mrs. —, Dedham
Pittock James, Manningtree
Ralph William, Manningtree
Vice James, Manningtree

BLACKSMITHS.

Bird Hannah, Dedham
Bond Thomas, Ardleigh
Borrett William (farrier) Lawford
Clarke Samuel, Manningtree
Disney Wm. & John, Mistley [tree
Downes Edwd. (& white) Manning-
Eade John, Mistley
Felgate Samuel, Langham
Frostick James, Mistley
Lord James, Mistley
Marshall John, Langham
Pettitt Daniel, Dedham
Poppy Jeremiah, Dedham
Sargeant William, Ardleigh
Sherman John, Bradfield
Smith George, Ardleigh
Towler Robert, Manningtree
Unwin Thomas, Lawford
Wade James, Bradfield
Whitaker John, Ardleigh

BOOT & SHOE MAKERS.

Ainger James, Mistley
Arnold Joseph, Manningtree
Bacon Charles, Ardleigh
Bacon James, Ardleigh
Bacon John, Ardleigh
Baker Samuel, Manningtree
Baker William, Dedham
Barker James, Ardleigh
Barker Samuel, Langham
Barton Harvey, Ardleigh
Beaston James, Manningtree
Blundell Robert, Dedham
Bones John, Ardleigh
Bull George, Ardleigh
Buss William, Ardleigh
Cant James, Bradfield
Cant Robert, Lawford
Carter Jonathan, Manningtree
Davey Edgar, Manningtree
Davey Susannah, Manningtree
Goden Robert, Dedham
Gosling John, Manningtree
Hayward John, Manningtree
Jerman James, Manningtree
Long Samuel, Manningtree
Marratt George, Dedham
Norfolk William, Ardleigh
Randall Henry, Dedham
Spink George, Bradfield
Strutt Robert, Lawford
Waller James, Ardleigh
White George, Mistley
Windle James, Dedham

BRAZIERS.

Ames Isaac, Dedham
Disney William, Manningtree
Harris William (& bell-hanger) Manningtree
Whisley Samuel, Dedham

BREWERS.

Alston Edward & Daniel Constable, Manningtree

BRICKLAYERS.

Atkin John, Dedham
Bones John, Lawford
Candler Benjamin, Manningtree
Downs Allan, Ardleigh
Hawes Thos. (& slater) Manningtree
Howell Charles, Dedham
Howell Hugh, Dedham
Howlett William, Ardleigh
James William, Ardleigh
Seaborn William, Langham [ham
Webb Joseph (& lime burner) Lang-
Whymark William, jun. Mistley

BUTCHERS.

Bacon James, Langham
Biggs James Bell, Ardleigh
Boggins John, Dedham
Bruce Thomas, Dedham
Cant Henry, Manningtree
Cook James, Mistley
Diaper William, Dedham
English James, Bradfield
Green Thomas, Manningtree
Green William, Manningtree
Ham Charlotte, Dedham
Hart George, Dedham
Long John, jun. Manningtree
Mott James, Manningtree
Page Samuel, Lawford
Payne James, Lawford
Rivens Robert, Manningtree
Simons William, Langham

CABINET MAKERS.

Curtis Anthony, Mistley
Griffiths Robert, Dedham
Paskell John, Mistley
Self Robert, Manningtree

CARPENTERS & BUILDERS.

Marked thus * are also Undertakers.

Barber John, Lawford
*Capon Robert, Manningtree
Church James, Dedham
Clark Joseph, Dedham
Cooper Samuel, Dedham
*Curtis Anthony, Mistley
Durrant Stephen, Mistley
Francis Samuel, Ardleigh
Godfrey James, Langham
Goodwin Robert, Manningtree
*Goodwin Robert, jun. (and upholsterer) Manningtree
Manning Thomas, Lawford
Masterson James, Bradfield
Page William, Lawford
Paskell John, Mistley
Saunders Nathaniel, Dedham
Seaborn Samuel, Langham
Seargeant Samuel, Ardleigh
Tweed Abraham, Bradfield
Whitey John, Langham
Whitaker John, Ardleigh
White Alexander, Dedham
Wilden James, Bradfield

CATTLE SALESMEN.

Bruce Thomas, Dedham
Page John, Langham
Payne James, Lawford

CHYMISTS & DRUGGISTS.

Spurgin Frederick William, Dedham
Vince John (and dealer in British wines) Dedham
Winter Susannah, Manningtree

COACH BUILDERS.

Alexander Isaac, Manningtree
Neville William & Co. Manningtree

COAL MERCHANTS.

Berry James, Manningtree
Brown William & Co. Manningtree
Constable Abraham, Mistley & Dedham, Cataway and East Bergholt
May John, Manningtree
Norman Edward, Manningtree
Page Robert & Son, Manningtree
Shansfield William (and salt works) Manningtree
Tovell Samuel, Mistley
Whymark William, jun. Mistley

CONFECTIONERS.

Finch Charles, Dedham
Finch William, Mistley
Rivers John, Manningtree
Vince William, Dedham

COOPERS.

Hitchcock Enoch, Dedham
Naylor John, Manningtree
Vice James, Manningtree

CORN MERCHANTS.

Alston Edward & Daniel Constable, Manningtree
Berry James, Manningtree
Enfield William (& seed) Langham

Norman Edward, Manningtree
Page Robert & Son, Manningtree

CURRIERS.

Green John Box, Manningtree
Palmer Charles, Mistley
Palmer Mary, Manningtree

EARTHENWARE DEALERS.

Cook James, Mistley
Hitchcock Ebenezer, Dedham
Ralph William, Manningtree

FIRE, &c. OFFICE AGENTS.

Essex and Suffolk Equitable, Thomas Scrivener, Manningtree
Essex Economic, William Angel (& clerk to the board of guardians, & superintendent registrar) Manningtree
Norwich Union, William Angell, Manningtree
Phœnix, Susannah Winter, Manningtree, and Robert Kay, Dedham
Royal Exchange, J. W. Webber (& auditor to the Tendring union) Manningtree
Suffolk & General County Amicable, William Booth, Dedham
Sun, John Enfield, Langham
Yorkshire, Samuel Hitchcock

FRUITERERS AND GREENGROCERS.

Arthy Sarah, Lawford
Cant James, Manningtree
Savell James, Manningtree

GARDENERS.

Belstead Thomas, Dedham
Bruce John Golding, Dedham
Cant Charles, Manningtree
Folkard William, Dedham
Nevill George, Lawford

GROCERS & DRAPERS.

(See also Shopkeepers, &c.)

Barber Benjamin, Dedham
Booth William, Dedham
Grave William, Manningtree
Harvey Samuel, Manningtree
Paskell Susan, Manningtree
Scott William (& worsted manufacturer) Dedham
Shansfield William, Manningtree
Spurgeon Clement, Bradfield
Stopes Aylmor (and cheesemonger) Manningtree
Swinborne John (& tallow chandler) Dedham
White John, Dedham
Wright James, Mistley

HAIR DRESSERS AND PERFUMERS.

Hempson Amis, Mistley
Ray Robert, Dedham
Saxby William, Manningtree
Viall George, Manningtree

INNS—COMMERCIAL, &c.

Marlborough Head, James Ransom, Dedham
Mistley Thorn, Isaac Churchyard Dowsing, Mistley
Packet Inn, John Slark, Manningtree
Rose & Crown, William Parmenter, Manningtree
Sun (& posting) Joseph Catchpole, Dedham

MALTSTERS.

Alston Edward & Daniel Constable, Manningtree
Littlebury William, Dedham
May John, Manningtree
Norman Edward, Manningtree
Page Robert and Son, Manningtree
Parsons William, Dedham

MILLERS.

Back William, Stratford St. Mary's
Beckwith Henry, Bradfield
Berry James, Langham
Berry James, Manningtree
Blyth John, Langham
Cocksedge Nathan, Bradfield
Constable Abram, Dedham and *East Bergholt*
May James, Lawford and Mistley
Morgan William Henry, Lawford
Mortimer John, Ardleigh
Wakeley Jonathan, Ardleigh
Warren Zachariah, Ardleigh
Whiley Charles, Langham

MILLINERS & DRESS MAKRS.

Bruce Elizabeth, Dedham
Goodwin Maria, Manningtree
Kerridge Louisa, Mistley
Long Maria, Dedham
Luckey Mary, Dedham
Mason Caroline and Matilda, Manningtree
Moor Ann, Mistley

PILOTS.

TO MISTLEY HARBOUR.

Ateen Benjamin
Ateen John
Ateen Robert
Bardale William
Honibal Thomas
Moor John
Saville Richard, Manningtree
Thompson James, Manningtree

PLUMBERS, PAINTERS AND GLAZIERS.

Finch James, Manningtree
Finch Robert, Manningtree
Hawkins John, Ardleigh
Howard Nathaniel, Dedham
Mason John Simpson, Manningtree
Parsons William, Manningtree
Rice Joseph, Dedham

SADDLERS AND HARNESS MAKERS.

Bloom Edward, Bradfield
Bloom James, Lawford
Luen Robert, Ardleigh
Orriss Thomas, Ardleigh
Shoobridge Elizabeth, Dedham
Turpin Robert, Manningtree

SAIL MAKER.

Moor John, jun. Mistley

SHIP OWNERS.

Berry James, Manningtree
Chissell Charles, Manningtree
Howard George, Manningtree
Howard James, Manningtree
Long Benjamin, Mistley
May John, Manningtree
Page Robert and Son, Manningtree
Tovell Charles, Mistley
Tovell George Randfield, Mistley
Tovell Samuel (& merchant) Mistley

SHOPKEEPERS & DEALRS IN GROCERIES & SUNDRIES.

Ainger James, Mistley
Angier Charles, Bradfield
Barber Benjamin, Dedham
Barrell Samuel, Langham
Barrett William, Lawford
Bready Thurston, Ardleigh
Bryant William, Langham
Cant Jacob, Dedham
Cant William, Lawford
Eade Elizabeth, Manningtree
Emmeny John, Langham
Everett Hezekiah, Bradfield
Fish David, Manningtree
Francis John, Manningtree
Gaymer Susannah, Mistley
Harris Joseph, Wix
Hempson Amis, Mistley
James William, Ardleigh
Lott James, Bradfield
Mauldon Hannah, Langham
Page Mary Ann, Langham
Ray Robert, Dedham
Russell Elizabeth, Manningtree
Scowen William, Wix
Seaborn Samuel, Langham
Smith John, Ardleigh
Spooner John, Lawford
Watts Elizabeth, Manningtree
White John, Dedham

STRAW HAT MAKERS.

Bailey Ann, Manningtree
Bruce Eliz. Dedham
Burrows Saml. (& haberdasher) Manningtree
Hayward Susannah, Manningtree

SURGEONS.

Bidwell Wm. & Henry H. Dedham
Smith James Henry, Manningtree
Thompson and Gooch, Manningtree

TAILORS AND DRAPERS.

Barker John, Dedham
Carter Jonathan, Manningtree
Disney John, Mistley
Downing Benjamin, Manningtree
Downing Robert, Manningtree
Ham William, Dedham
Perryman Charles, Langham
Salmon Thomas, Ardleigh
Seaborn Edward, Langham
Spooner John, Lawford
Watts Thomas, Manningtree
Whisley Robert, Dedham
Whisley Robert, jun. Dedham
White James, Ardleigh
White William, Dedham

TANNERS, FELLMONGERS & WOOL MERCHANTS.

Page Joseph & Son, Manningtree

TAVERNS & PUBLIC HOUSES.

The Names without Address are in Manningtree.

Anchor, Edward Martin, Dedham
Ardleigh Crown, Mark Scott, Ardleigh
Cock, John Sizer
Cross, Mary Howe, Mistley
Fox & Hounds, John Whitaker, Ardleigh
Greyhound, Robert Ransdale, Langham
Gun, William Burrows, Dedham
King's Arms, Jonathan Bull, Lawford
King's Head, Richard Herlock
King's Head, Thos. Seargeant, Ardleigh
Lamb, John Arnold, Dedham
Plough, Sarah Cutting, Bradfield
Red Lion, William Blyth
Red Lion, Mary Vince, Ardleigh
Rose & Crown, Nathaniel Saunders, Dedham
Three Compasses, Robt. Blundell, Dedham
Waggon, John Jessop, Wix
Wherry, John Moor, Mistley
White Hart, Nathaniel Dale
White Hart, George Lowe, Wix

TIMBER MERCHANTS AND DEALERS.

Brown William & Co. Manningtree
Whitaker John, Ardleigh

WATCH & CLOCK MAKERS.

Ambrose Unice, Dedham
Barker George (& working jeweller) Dedham
Watkins Martha (and silversmith) Manningtree

WHEELWRIGHTS.

Bedford John, Ardleigh
Cole Joseph, Langham
Francis Samuel, Ardleigh
Kerridge Robert, Mistley
Osborn Mary, Dedham
Osborn William, Dedham
Rayner William, Langham
Rymer John, Ardleigh
Whitaker John, Ardleigh
White Alexander, Dedham

WINE & SPIRIT MERCHANTS

Alston Edward & Daniel Constable, Manningtree
Webb Charles Baker, Manningtree
Winter Susannah (British wine) Manningtree
Witheal George, Dedham

Miscellaneous.

Assembly Rooms, Dedham—T.L. Ewen, esq. treasurer; Benj. Cole, superintendent
Baker Whitmore, veterinary surgeon, Dedham hall
Baker William, brick maker, Dedham
Bendall David, ironfounder and agricultural implement maker, Lawford
Burrows Charles, turnery dealer, Lawford
Carter Jonathan, hatter, Manningtree

MISCELLANEOUS—*Continued.*

COAST OFFICE CUSTOMS, John Moor & Samuel Tovell, agents; Samuel Mayor, principal coast officer
Cole Benjamin, parish clerk, Dedham
Dearn & Baxter, ironmongers, Mistley
Downes William, surveyor, Dedham
Downing Benj. parish clerk, Manningtree
EXCISE OFFICE, Packet Inn—Benjamin Payne, supervisor
Felgate Samuel, edge tool maker, Dedham
Hines Sarah, patten & clog maker, Lawford
Howe Thomas, turner, Manningtree
Sambell Benjamin Olver, district constable, Mistley
Scrivener Thomas, undertaker, Manningtree
Sharman Henry, florist, Dedham
Spurling Wm. porter merchant, Mistley
Taylor John, parish clerk, Lawford
Thompson Jas. fishmonger, Manningtree
Tovell George Randfield, barbour master, Mistley
Watts Thomas, bookseller, stationer and printer, Manningtree
Whymark William, parish clerk, Mistley

COACH.

To LONDON, the *Defiance* (from Harwich), calls at the White Hart, every day at twelve; goes through Colchester, Chelmsford and Brentwood.
To HARWICH, the *Defiance* (from London), calls at the White Hart, every night at ten.

CARRIERS.

To LONDON, Broom & Winter's *Waggons*, from the Marlborough Head, Dedham, every Wednesday and Saturday.
To COLCHESTER, a *Mail Cart*, every night at half-past nine, to meet the Mail from Norwich to London.
To COLCHESTER, Benjamin Cant, from his house, every Tuesday, Wednesday, Friday and Saturday—Samuel Baker, from his house, and James Wilson, from Mistley, every Monday, Tuesday, Thursday and Saturday—Robert Salter, from the Rose and Crown, every Monday, Wednesday, Thursday and Saturday—J. Porch, from the King's Head, every Tuesday and Friday—and John Folkard, from the Sun, Dedham, every Wednesday and Saturday.
To HARWICH, a *Mail Cart*, from the Cock, every morning at five.
To IPSWICH, William Blyth, from the Red Lion, every Tuesday, Thursday, Friday and Saturday—Robert Salter, from the Rose and Crown, and John Townsend, from the King's Head, every Tuesday and Friday—and Thomas Tye, from the Packet Inn, every Tuesday.
To LONG MELFORD, Winter's *Waggon*, from the White Hart, every Tuesday and Friday night.
To STOWMARKET, Broom & Winter's *Waggons*, from the Marlborough Head, Dedham, every Wednesday & Saturday.

CONVEYANCE BY WATER.

To LONDON, goods from Mistley quay (by way of Harwich) are forwarded by the following regular trading vessels:—the *Sarah Ann*, *Telegraph*, *Sisters*, *Albion*, *Lovely Nancy*, *Two Brothers*, *Little John*, *Manningtree Packet*, *Deborah*, *Traveller*, *Lark*, *Lydia*, *Friends*, *Increase*, *Good Intent* (sloop), *Good Intent* (schooner), *Friendship*, *General Elliott*, *Mary* and the *Despatch*.
To HARWICH, the *Sally Passage Boat*, for passengers, daily, to meet the London packets—John Moor, captain & owner.

NEWPORT, WITH STANSTEAD-MOUNTFITCHET
AND NEIGHBOURHOODS.

NEWPORT, or NEWPORT POND, is a flourishing but irregularly built village, formerly a market town, in the parish of its name and first division of Uttlesford hundred—39 miles N. from London, 9 N. from Bishops Stortford, 17 S.S.E. from Cambridge, and 3 S.W. from Saffron Walden. It is pleasantly situated in a fertile valley, on the west side of the small river Cam, which rises at Little Henham, about four miles hence. The market here was at one time of consequence; the place likewise derived some importance from its free grammar school, which, it is said, still possesses considerable endowments: this establishment was founded by Joyce Franckland and William Saxie in 1586; and its revenues are derived from a portion of the great tithes of Banstead, in the county of Surrey—from the rents of two houses in Distaff-lane, London, and a cottage at Hoddesdon, Hertfordshire; the entire producing upwards of £200. per annum. The church, dedicated to St. Mary, is a handsome edifice, with a lofty tower crowned with embattled turrets; the living is a vicarage, in the gift of the crown, and present incumbency of the Rev. Edward G. Monk. An annual fair, called 'colt fair,' from the number of Welch and Scotch ponies brought to it for sale, is held on the 17th November and following day. The parish contained, in 1831, 914 inhabitants.

STANDSTEAD-MOUNTFITCHET is a village and parish, partly in the hundred of Uttlesford, and extending into that of Clavering—three miles N.E. from Bishops Stortford, which is the nearest post town. Its name is derived from *stane*, a 'street,' and from the castle erected by William de Gernen, surnamed Montfichet. The parish includes two manors, viz. Bentfield Bury, and Stanstead and Burnells: William Gosling, Esq. is lord of the former; and E. Fuller Maitland, Esq. is proprietor of the latter, and patron of the living. The church, dedicated to St. Mary, and situated in Stanstead park, was some years since repaired and enlarged by the church commissioners; the benefice is a vicarage, of which the Rev. Josias Torriano is the present incumbent. There are two chapels for dissenters, a meeting-house for the society of friends, and three free schools, chiefly supported by voluntary subscriptions. An annual fair, for cattle and toys, is held on the 1st of May and following day. The parish, including the hamlet of BENFIELD (the population of which amounted to 505) contained, according to the last census, 1,560 inhabitants.

POST OFFICE, NEWPORT, Thomas Osborne, *Post Master.*—Letters from LONDON arrive every morning at half-past eight, and are despatched every evening at half-past seven.

POST, STANSTEAD-MOUNTFITCHET, *Receiving-House* at the Bell Inn.—Letters from LONDON arrive every morning at half-past seven, and are despatched every night at half-past eight.

GENTRY AND CLERGY.

Bedford Rev. Josiah, Stanstead
Bell William Nassau, esq. Newport
Canning Rev. Thomas, Vicarage, Elsenham
Chamberlayne Major, Orford house, Stanstead
Clayton Rev. Wm. John, Stanstead
Crosdaile Mrs. Harriet, Hargrave lodge
Grover Mrs. Isabella, Stanstead
Hawkes Wm. Robt. esq. Pines hill
Hopkins Rev. James, Newport
Maylin the Misses, Stanstead
Monk Rev. Edward Goold, Vicarage, Newport
Pinchback Rev. Thomas, Stanstead
Probert Mr. Thomas (attorney) Newport and *Saffron Waldon*
Redford Rev. Josiah, Stanstead
Robinson John, esq. Wendon
Rush George, esq. Elsenham hall
Scott Thomas, esq. Wendon
Smyth Wm. Chas. esq. Shotgrove hall
Torriano Rev. Josiah, Vicarage, Stanstead
Tuffnell Jolliffe, esq. Sim house, Stanstead
Welsh Mrs. Ann, Pines hill
White Mr. Mordaunt, Stanstead
Wolfe R. B. esq. Woodhall, Arksden

ACADEMIES & SCHOOLS.

Not otherwise described are Day Schools.

Bailey Isabella (brdg. & day) Newport
Bedford Rev. Josiah, Stanstead
FREE GRAMMAR SCHOOL, Newport—Rev. Edwd. Goold Monk, master
INFANTS' SCHOOL, Stanstead—Jane Jones, mistress
Morgan Mrs. (brdg. & day) Stanstead
NATIONAL SCHOOL, Stanstead—William Sealey, master
Philpott William, Stanstead
Redford Rev. Josiah, Stanstead
Sapsed Mary Ann, Newport
Sawkins Rachel, Stanstead
WELSH'S CHARITY SCHOOL, Stanstead—Margaret Witney, mistress

AUCTIONEERS.

Nockolds & Son (and estate agents) Stanstead

BAKERS.

Hayden James, Stanstead
Parratt Elizabeth, Newport
Preston James, Stanstead
Sanders Samuel, Stanstead
Snow Samuel, Stanstead
Stiles Henry, Newport

BLACKSMITHS.

Barron John, Stanstead
Brand Thomas, Newport
Brett Thomas, Stanstead
Brett William, Stanstead
Gagger Elizabeth, Newport
Hayden James, Stanstead

BOOT & SHOE MAKERS.

Bailey Charles, Newport
Harris Daniel, Stanstead
Johns and Son, Newport
Plasted John, Stanstead
Sawkins Thomas, Stanstead
Searle Joseph, Newport

BRICKLAYERS.

Peacock John, Stanstead
Snow John, Stanstead
Trott William, Newport

BUTCHERS.

Hawks Charles, Newport
Laird Edward, Stanstead
Mascall Thomas, Newport
Smith Robert, Stanstead

CARPENTERS.

Day James Capp, Newport
Debnam Robert, Newport
Levey Thomas, Stanstead
Sanders John, Stanstead
Sanders John, jun. Stanstead
Tripp Richard, Stanstead
Wedd Joseph, Newport

CLOTHES DEALERS.

Levey David, Stanstead
Peacock Sarah, Stanstead

COOPERS.
Levy William, Stanstead
Thompson William, Newport
Wedd Joseph, Newport

CORN DEALERS.
Buck Philip, Newport
Canning William, Stanstead

GARDENERS & SEEDSMEN.
Bailey Jonas, Newport
Hutley James, Stanstead
Knowles John, Newport

GROCERS & DRAPERS.
(See also Shopkeepers, &c.)
Brocklehurst George, Stanstead
Chipperfield George (and druggist) Newport
Day Samuel Papspill, Stanstead
Gurson Benjamin Thomas (& worsted manufacturer) Newport
Sanders Samuel, Stanstead
Seamer John, Stanstead

HAIR DRESSERS.
Osborne John, Stanstead
Osborne Thomas, Newport

INNS & PUBLIC HOUSES.
The names without address are in STANSTEAD.
Bell, George Clark [Newport
Coach and Horses, Maregt. Marking,
Hercules, George Fennell, Newport
King's Arms, George Pryer
Old Bell, Robert Smith
Rose and Crown, George Bird
Rose and Crown, Thomas Mascall, Newport
Star, John Edwick, Newport
Three Colts, Sophia Sanders
Three Tuns, Robt. Debnam, Newport

MALTSTERS AND CORN MERCHANTS.
Clark Joseph, Newport
Hicks Charles and Edward (and coal merchants) Stanstead
Parris William, Stanstead
Woodley Matthew, Stanstead

MILLERS.
Felsted John, Stanstead
Howard Adam, Widdington mill
Phillips John, Bentfield mill
Salmon Henry, Wendon mill
Smith Thomas, Stanstead

PAINTERS, PLUMBERS, AND GLAZIERS.
Johns William, Newport
Lilly John, Newport
Ratcliff Henry, Stanstead
Ratcliff John, Stanstead

SADDLERS.
Giffin John, Stanstead
Newell Joseph, Newport
Speller Newman, Stanstead

SHOPKEEPERS & DEALRS IN GROCERIES & SUNDRIES.
Belsham Joseph, Newport
Crane Thomas Osborn, Newport
Hayden James, Stanstead
Searle Joshua, Newport

STRAW HAT MAKERS.
Johns Sarah, Newport
Norman Elizabeth, Newport
Osborne Mary, Newport
Rumbell Mary, Stanstead

SURGEONS.
Brook Henry, Newport
Brook William, Stanstead
Welch George (& registrar of births and deaths) Stanstead
Welch Samuel, Stanstead

SURVEYORS—LAND.
Nockolds & Son (and estate agents) Stanstead
Wedd Joseph, Newport

TAILORS & DRAPERS.
Atkin John, Stanstead
Hesler James, Newport
Jackson Henry, Stanstead
Paul Thomas, Stanstead
Say George, Stanstead
Watson Kidman, Newport

WATCH MAKERS.
Debnam Charles (and dealer in cutlery) Newport
Sanders William, Stanstead

WHEELWRIGHTS.
Bedlow William, Stanstead
Buck Benjamin, Newport

Miscellaneous.
Bailey Jonas, nurseryman, Newport
Beckwith Hy. veterinary surgeon, Newport
Clark William, horse dealer, Stanstead
HOUSE OF CORRECTION, Newport—John Mead, keeper
Pigram James, fellmonger and glover, Stanstead
Ratcliff Sarah, stationer, Stanstead
Raven Joseph, brewer, Stanstead
Scott Thomas, parish clerk, Stanstead
Traylen Christopher, relieving officer and registrar of births and deaths, Newport
Tyler John, brick maker, Stanstead
Witney Joseph, fishmonger, Stanstead

COACHES.
To and from LONDON, CAMBRIDGE, NEWMARKET, &c. pass thro' Newport and Stanstead-Mountfitchet frequently during the day.

CARRIERS.
To LONDON, Thomas Trott's *Van*, every Tuesday, and Samuel Lambkin's *Cart*, both from Newport; go through Stanstead and Bishops Stortford.

*** Besides the above, there are *Waggons* and *Vans* to and from NEWMARKET, CAMBRIDGE, &c. which pass thro' Newport and Stanstead daily.

OCKENDON (SOUTH & NORTH) & NEIGHBOURHOODS.

SOUTH OCKENDON is a small village and parish in the hundred of Chafford—8 miles S. S. E. from Romford, 4 N. from Grays Thurrock, and 3 S. from Upminster. Though the village is respectable, it possesses no attractions for the tourist or man of business. The parish church is dedicated to St. Nicholas; the living is a rectory, in the patronage (or was lately) of G. Leith, Esq. There is also a chapel for independents in this place. The parish contained, in 1831, 816 inhabitants.

NORTH OCKENDON is in the same hundred as the village just noticed, about a mile distant from it. The only object of the least interest here is the church, which is dedicated to St. Mary Magdalene: the edifice is nearly covered with ivy, and presents an ornament in unison with this little rural locality; the benefice is a rectory, in the gift of Sir Charles Halse, Bart. The number of inhabitants, by the last returns, was 294—being a *decrease*, since 1821, of 31 persons.

POST OFFICE, SOUTH OCKENDON, Henry Smith, *Post Master.*—Letters from LONDON arrive (by way of ROMFORD) every morning at eight, and are despatched every evening at six.

POST OFFICE, NORTH OCKENDON, John Elliott, *Post Master.*—Letters from LONDON arrive every morning at half-past seven, and are despatched every evening at half-past five.

*** *The names are in* SOUTH OCKENDON *when the place is not mentioned.*

GENTRY AND CLERGY.
Barker Mr. James, South Ockendon
Brown Mr. Edward (surgeon) South Ockendon
Eve Rev. Henry, Rectory, South Ockendon
Francis Samuel, esq. Stifford
Freeman Button, esq. Stifford
Hand Rev. Thomas, Bulphan fell
Ingram Mr. Jno. Stifford [Ockendn
Jorderson Mr. Wm. (surgeon) South
Lloyd Edward, esq. South Ockendon
Ludby Rev. John, Cranham
May Mr. William, Molands hall
Paling Rev. John, Stifford
Priddon Rev Wm. North Ockendon
Sturgeon Thomas B. esq. South Ockendon
Swaby Rev. Stephen, North Ockendon

INNS & PUBLIC HOUSES.
Dog & Partridge, James Holt, Stifford
King's Head, William Clarke
Red Lion, Samuel Sweeting
White Horse, Wm. Clark, Nrth Ockendon

SHOPKEEPERS, TRADERS, &c.
Attwell Elizabeth, shopkeeper
Beard David, baker
Briggs John, painter and glazier
Burchell James, blacksmith, North Ockendon
Cole William, parish clerk, North Ockendon
Davey Abraham, carpenter
De Ville William, bricklayer
Elsdon John, wheelwright
Elsdon Wm. wheelwright
Folkes Jas. shopkeeper, Nrth. Ockendon
Fordham James, butcher
Good James, grocer and draper
Holland Geo. baker, North Ockendn
Kirkham Josiah, saddler
Meam Enock, shopkeeper, N. Ockendon
Pain William, blacksmith
Poston James, butcher
Smith Henry, grocer and draper
Sweeting Samuel, carpenter
Thurgood Lawrence, shoemaker
West Saml. grocer, &c. N. Ockendon

COACH.
To LONDON, Thomas Boyce's *Coach*, from the Red Lion, every morning, at half-past seven, goes through Romford and Ilford.

CARRIER.
To LONDON, Abraham Coe's *Waggon*, daily.

ORSETT AND HORNDON-ON-THE-HILL.

ORSETT is a village and parish in the hundred of Barstable, 12 miles S. E. from Romford, 9 S. S. E. from Brentwood, and about 3½ N. N. E. from Grays Thurrock, and close to the line of the Thames Haven railway. The best system of agriculture is practiced in this part of the county, and the fertile soil amply rewards the industry of the farmer. The village has an obvious claim to the notice of the antiquary, as in its neighbourhood are the well-defined remains of an entrenchment enclosing four or five acres; the manor house of Orsett, too, has survived the vicissitudes of upwards of three centuries and a half. The church is dedicated to Saint Giles and All Saints; the living is a rectory, in the presentation of the bishop of London. The methodists have a place of worship in the parish; and in the village is an endowed school, founded by Edward Anson, Esq., for educating and clothing fourteen boys; also a respectable boarding academy for young gentlemen. The entire of this parish contained, in 1831, 1,274 inhabitants.

HORNDON-ON-THE-HILL is a village and parish in the same hundred as Orsett, about two miles north therefrom, and a short distance north of the line of the Thames Haven railway. The church, dedicated to St. Peter, is a very old fabric; the benefice is a discharged vicarage, in the patronage of the dean and chapter of St. Paul's, London. The wool fairs, held here in June and July, have long been declining, and at present are of no importance. Population of the parish, in 1831, 511.

POST OFFICE, George Inn, ORSETT, James Ramplee, *Post Master.*—Letters from LONDON arrive (from ROMFORD) every morning at nine, and are despatched every afternoon at five.

GENTRY AND CLERGY.

Baker Mrs. Jane, Orsett
Bennett Rev. George Peter, Orsett
Corbet Mr. David (surgeon) Orsett
Maconachie Mr. Geo. A.M. Orsett hse
Spitty Mr. Wm. Horndon
Usko Rev. John Fredk. Rectory, Orsett

ACADEMIES.

Maconachie George, A.M. (gent's. boarding) Orsett house
NATIONAL SCHOOL, Orsett—Charles Wright, master
Wright Charles, Orsett

INNS & PUBLIC HOUSES.

Bell, William Jeffereys, Horndon
Crown, Mary Fletcher, Orsett
George, James Ramplee, Orsett
King's Arms, Benj. Lewis, Baker st
Old Cock, Robert Partridge, Orsett
Swan, Charles Robinson, Orsett

SHOPKEEPERS & TRADERS.

The names without address are in ORSETT

Andrews Thomas, painter & glazier, Horndon
Barnes William, hair dresser
Binder Wm. builder and undertaker
Bridge James, carpenter, Horndon
Brumhead Eliza & Ann, shopkeepers
Clark Golden, shopkeeper
Corbet David, surgeon and registrar of births and deaths
Finch George Carlow, wheelwright
Fordham Thomas, butcher
Freeman James, shopkeeper
Freeman James, boot & shoe maker
Hallam Thos. blacksmith, Horndon
Hockley John, blacksmith
Jackson George, governor of Union Workhouse
James Richard, miller
Jarvis Thomas, butcher
Kirkham James, butcher, Horndon
Lee Thomas, butcher
Mead Thomas, shoemaker
Meekings Ambrose, saddler, &c.
Mott John, tailor, Horndon
Newman Thos. shoemaker, Horndon
Oackley Thomas, blacksmith
Packman Harrison, shopkeeper
Philpott Ratcliffe, carpenter
Radley John, parish clerk
Sanders Jas. painter & glazier, Baker st
Sanford Thomas, butcher
Schooling Robert, shoemaker
Smith Thomas, grocer, draper, and fire office agent
Spurgen John, bricklayer
Tirrell Pratt, grocer, Horndon
Wade James, butcher
Wallis John, baker and corn dealer
Wollings James, miller and baker

COACHES.

To LONDON, the *Perseverance*, from Horndon-on-the-Hill, calls at the George Inn, every Tues. Wed. Thus. & Saturday mornings, at a quarter before eight: goes through Stifford, Aveley, Rainham and Barking, and every Monday & Friday morning at a quarter before seven, through Grays Thurrock and Purfleet.

To HORNDON-ON-THE-HILL, the *Perseverance*, from London, calls at the George Inn, every evening at seven.

RAYLEIGH,

HADLEIGH, HOCKLEY, HAWKWELL, RETTENDON, RUNWELL, SOUTH BENFLEET, THUNDERSLEY, CANVEY ISLAND AND NEIGHBOURHOODS.

RAYLEIGH is a village and parish in the hundred of Rochford, situated between Billericay and Rochford, distant 10 miles S. E. from the former and 5 east from the latter, 16 E. by S. from Brentwood, 14 S. S. E. from Chelmsford, and 35 E. by N. from London. The remains of Rayleigh castle, a fortress erected by Swene, the Dane, in the eighth century, present their time-worn features at the upper end of the town; they are environed by a deep ditch, and an entrenchment, with a rampart, are still sufficiently developed to exhibit the art of fortification possessed by the Scandinavians at that period; the site of the castle is a lofty mount, from the summit of which there is an extensive and pleasant prospect over the surrounding country. The church, dedicated to the Holy Trinity, occupies a moderately elevated position; the living is a rectory, in the gift of the Bristow family. There is a chapel for baptists here. A market was formerly held on Saturday, but it has been discontinued many years; an annual fair for cattle, on Trinity-Monday, is still frequented. [The population of the several places is given after CANVEY ISLAND.]

In the same hundred as Rayleigh, three miles south of that place, is the village and parish of HADLEIGH. Hadleigh castle, stated to have been erected in the reign of Henry III by Hubert de Burgh, Earl of Kent, stood about half a mile from the village, near the summit of a hill, from which a very extensive prospect is obtained; the ruins, chiefly consisting of two dilapidated circular towers, are mantled with moss and ivy; from the massiveness of the walls, which are nine feet in diameter, it is apparent that it must have been a structure of great strength, and that it was of considerable magnitude is equally obvious. The parish church, an ancient edifice with a spire, is dedicated to St. James; the benefice is a discharged rectory, in the presentation of the rector and fellows of Lincoln college, Oxford.

HOCKLEY, likewise in the same hundred as Rayleigh, two miles from the village of that name, is an agreeable village and extensive parish, the latter bounded on the north by the navigable river Crouch. The church, dedicated to St. Peter, stands upon an eminence, about half a mile from the village; it is a plain building, with a massive tower and small spire; Wadham college possesses the presentation to the living.

Adjoining to Hockley is the parish and village (if so it may be termed) of HAWKWELL; the latter is composed of a few houses, scattered over a level locality. The church, dedicated to St. Mary, has an unassuming exterior, and its interior presents nothing attractive: the benefice is a rectory.

Four miles N. N. W. from Rayleigh, in the hundred of Chelmsford, is the small village and parish of RETTENDON—a name said to have been applied to it by the Saxons on account of the badness of the roads in its vicinage. The church, dedicated to All Saints, is a neat structure, with a tower supporting a spire; the living is a rectory, in the gift of the bishop of Ely.

In the same hundred as Rettendon, five miles N.W. of Rayleigh, is the village and parish of RUNWELL; a famous well (formerly in this parish), from which issued a running stream, is said to have originated the name. The Crouch river is navigable from the sea to this place. The church, dedicated to St. Mary, is an ancient fabric, with a tower and diminutive spire; the benefice is a rectory, in the patronage of Vicessimus Knox, Esq.

SOUTH BENFLEET, a village and parish in the hundred of Barstable, is pleasantly situated about three miles from the Thames, and four S. W. by S. from Rayleigh. The church, dedicated to St. Mary, is of ancient erection, with a tower; the living is a discharged vicarage, in the presentation of the dean and chapter of Westminster. Hadleigh bay runs up between this place and Canvey Island, and is navigable for small craft; the other creeks penetrating from the Thames round Benfleet have an established fame for their good oysters, which are highly estimated in the metropolis.

About two miles from Rayleigh and the like distance from Hadleigh, partly in Rochford hundred and partly in that of Barstable, is the small hamlet and parish of THUNDERSLEY. The church, dedicated to St. Peter, is of considerable antiquity, and occupies an elevated position; the benefice is a discharged vicarage, in the appointment of the Rev. G. Hemming.

CANVEY ISLAND is a chapelry, partly in the parishes

of North and South Benfleet, Bowers Gifford, Laindon, Pitsea and Vange, in the hundred of Barstable, and partly in the parishes of Leigh, Prittlewell and Southchurch, in the hundred of Rochford; situated between Benfleet and the Thames, near the mouth of the latter, and encompassed by branches from that river, but there is a passage over the strand at low water. The island is about five miles in length and two in breadth, comprising about 3,600 acres. Several of the inhabitants are engaged in fishing, and there are many flocks of sheep fed on the island. The chapel is dedicated to St. Catherine: the benefice is a perpetual curacy, in the gift of the rector of Laindon—but divine service is generally performed by the minister of South Benfleet. A fair is held upon the island on the 25th of June.

The POPULATION of the foregoing parishes, by the last returns, was as follows:—RAYLEIGH, 1,339; HADLEIGH, 365; HOCKLEY, 777; HAWKWELL, 329; RETTENDON, 671; RUNWELL, 341; SOUTH BENFLEET, 533; THUNDERSLEY, 526; CANVEY ISLAND contains fifty or sixty houses, but its population is returned with the several parishes in which it is situated.

POST OFFICE, RAYLEIGH, William Pissey, *Post Master.*—Letters from INGATESTONE arrive (by mail cart) every morning at three, and are despatched every night (Sunday expected) at eight, on Sunday they are despatched one hour earlier.

POST OFFICE, HADLEIGH, George Lloyd, *Post Master.*—Letters from ROCHFORD arrive (by foot post) every morning at half-past eight in summer and at nine in winter, and are despatched every afternoon (Sunday excepted) at four, on Sunday they are despatched one hour earlier.

GENTRY AND CLERGY.

Baker Mr. Samuel, Hawkley hall
Belcham Mrs. Mary, Rayleigh
Borrodell Mr. James, Rettendon common
Brewitt Thomas, esq. Down hall, Rayleigh
Brown James Attridge, esq. Hockley
Burkin Mr. Thomas, Rayleigh
Byas Wheatley, esq. Dawes heath, Thundersley
Cleeve Henry, esq. Rettendon
Fairhead Mr. George, Rayleigh
Ford Miss Mary Ann, Rayleigh
Harding Rev. William, Hockley
Higham Mr. Samuel, Park farm, Hadleigh
Hill Mr. John, Hockley hall
Kemble Thomas, esq. Runwell
Lamprell John, esq. White House farm, Rayleigh
Mee Edward, esq. Rayleigh
Moore Mr. James, Rettendon
Nash Mrs. South Benfleet
Nash Thomas, esq. Runwell hall
Page John, esq. Turrett house, Rayleigh
Pertwee Mr. William, Rettendon
Phelps Rev. John, South Benfleet
Pilkington Rev. James, Rayleigh
Prentice Golding Nehemiah, esq. Rayleigh
Richens George, esq. Runwell
Smith Rev. Francis, Rayleigh
Smith Mr. William, Hockley
Tuckwell Thomas, esq. Runwell
Turner Mrs. Susannah, Hockley
Tyrrell James, esq. Hadleigh
Wallington Rev. Charles, Hawkwell
Watherston Rev. J. P. Hadleigh
Williams Mr. Joseph, Runwell
Wood Mr. Jonathan, Hadleigh
Wood Mr. Jonathan, jun. Hadleigh

ACADEMIES AND SCHOOLS.
Not otherwise described are Day Schools.

Baldwin Mary, Thundersley
Bell John, Rayleigh
Fitch Mary Elizabeth, Rayleigh
Freeman Sarah, South Benfleet
Gyant Sarah Blenell, Hadleigh
Hill Honor, Hawkwell
Pilkington and Uwins (gentlemen's boarding and day) Rayleigh
Potter William, South Benfleet
RAYLEIGH CHARITY SCHOOL (boys' and girls') James Rox, master; Ann Bell, mistress
Salisbury Alice, South Benfleet

AUCTIONEERS.

Markwell Joseph (and land-agent and cooper) Rayleigh
Rod James, Rayleigh

BAKERS.

Brewer Thomas, Rayleigh
Britton George, Rayleigh
Cracknell Thomas, Hawkwell
Davey William, Rayleigh
Eckworth Elizabeth, Rayleigh
Fairs Samuel, South Benfleet
French William, South Benfleet
Greenham William, Hadleigh
Lloyd George, Hadleigh
Parker Noble, jun. Hockley
Scudder Thomas, Rayleigh
Smith John, Rayleigh
South Samuel, Battles bridge

BLACKSMITHS.

Bowyer Jonathan, Rayleigh
Chapman Joseph, Rayleigh
Clarke Isaac, Rettendon
Edwards John, Rayleigh
Freeman William, South Benfleet
Gibbs George, Hadleigh
Linggood William, Rayleigh
West Philip, Hockley

BOOT AND SHOE MAKERS.

Blakeley Edward, South Benfleet
Bone Samuel, Battles bridge
Brewitt Henry, South Benfleet
Coller Paul, Rayleigh
Crow John, Hockley
Finch Thomas, Rayleigh
Foot Samuel, Rayleigh
Foster John, Hadleigh
Foster John, Rayleigh
Garratt James, South Benfleet
Grigson Abraham, Rayleigh
Hammond John, Rayleigh
Mansfield Thomas, South Benfleet
Marsh Abraham, Battles bridge
Peek Abraham, Rayleigh
Rod James, Rayleigh
Summers William, Hadleigh

BRICKLAYERS.

Custerton James, Rayleigh
Prentice Joseph, Rayleigh
Smith John Thomas, Rayleigh
Storey William, Battles bridge

BUTCHERS.

Ager William, Battles bridge
Baldwin Thomas, Hadleigh
Belcham William, Rayleigh
Boston Frederick, Rayleigh
Carver Thomas, Hockley
Cracknell Thomas, Hawkwell
Turner Philip, Hawkwell
Watts Daniel, Rayleigh
Webster William, Rayleigh

CARPENTERS.

Bone William, Battles bridge
Daines Simon, South Benfleet
Hawkins James, Thundersley
Haylock William, South Benfleet
Sneezum James, Rayleigh
Stearns Jeremiah, Rayleigh
Stearns Samuel, Rayleigh
Wagstaff Thomas, Rayleigh

CHYMISTS & DRUGGISTS.

Brown William, Rayleigh and *Southminster*
Kernot George Noyce (and oilman) Rayleigh

COACH MAKERS.

Croxen William Henry, Rayleigh
Witham Henry, Rayleigh

COAL MERCHANTS.

Galton Henry, Battles bridge
Meeson and Hinton, Battles bridge

CONFECTIONERS.

Croxon Elias, Rayleigh
Foot Samuel, Rayleigh

FARRIERS.

Williams John, Rayleigh
Williams William, Rayleigh

FIRE, &c. OFFICE AGENTS.

BRITISH, Charles Syer, Rayleigh
ESSEX ECONOMIC, Samuel Count, Rayleigh
ESSEX EQUITABLE, Geo. Belcham, Rayleigh
LICENSED VICTUALLERS, Jas. Rod, Rayleigh

GROCERS & TEA DEALERS.
(See also Shopkeepers, &c.)

Bishop Thomas, Rayleigh
Bornes William, Battles bridge
Count Samuel, Rayleigh
Greenham William, Hadleigh
Lucking William, Rayleigh
Porter Peter, Hawkwell
Prentis Henry Wood, Rayleigh
Sopwith William, South Benfleet
Syer Charles, Rayleigh

INNS & PUBLIC HOUSES.

Anchor, Mary Lockwood, Hadleigh
Bell, Jno. Wright, Rettendon commn
Blue Anchor, Mary Lockwood, South Benfleet
Bull, George Peach, Hockley
Castle, John Pike, Hadleigh
Crown, Robert Cole, Hadleigh
Crown Inn, Neville Syer, jun. Rayleigh
Drover's Arms, Henry Finch, Rayleigh
Golden Lion (commercial & posting) Neville Syer, Rayleigh
Half Moon, Mary Yell, Rayleigh
Hawk, Edward Mann, Battles bridge
Hoy, Mary Potter, South Benfleet
Lobster Smack, William Finch, Canvey Island
Quart Pot, Robert Raven, Runwell
White Hart, William Eckworth, Thundersley
White Hart, Stephen Parr, Hawkwell
White Horse, Jno. Wagstaff, Radleigh

IRONMONGERS.

Bossi Paul, Rayleigh
Cook Henry, Rayleigh

LINEN DRAPERS.

Belcham George, Rayleigh
Bornes William, Battles bridge
Lucking William, Rayleigh
Pissey William, Rayleigh
Syer Charles, Rayleigh

MILLERS.

Meeson and Hinton, Battles bridge
Myhill William, Rettendon common
Ruffle Benjamin, Rayleigh

MILLINERS.

Gouldstone Sarah, Rayleigh
Gyant Sarah Blenell, Hadleigh
Redgrave Mary, Rayleigh

SADDLERS.

Brown Thomas, Rayleigh
Noone John Loten, Rayleigh

SHOPKEEPERS & DEALRS IN GROCERIES & SUNDRIES.

Blatch John, South Benfleet
Crow John, Hockley
Glasscock James, Rayleigh
Kendall Ann, Rettendon common
Livermore Sarah, Hawkwell
Lloyd George, Hadleigh
Parker Noble, Hockley
Poole Robert Thorby, Hawkwell
Prentice Joseph, Rayleigh
Raven Robert, Runwell
Savill William, Rettendon common
Sneezum James, Rayleigh

SURGEONS.

Asplin Jonas, M.D. Rayleigh
Bradley Thomas, Hadleigh
Byass Thomas James, Rayleigh
Digby Edward, Rayleigh
King Robert, Rayleigh

TAILORS.

Codlin Charles, Rayleigh
Coish William, Rayleigh
Coller Peter, Rayleigh
Count Charles (and draper) Rayleigh
Guy Thomas, South Benfleet
Miller Thomas, Rayleigh

WATCH MAKERS.

Kemp George Firman, Rayleigh
Long Samuel, Rayleigh

WHEELWRIGHTS.

Blakeley Francis, South Benfleet
Cloppen John, Hadleigh
Clarke Isaac, Rettendon
Croxon William Henry, Rayleigh
Pask George, Rayleigh
Savill Samuel, Hockley

Miscellaneous.

Adey Thomas, plumber, Rayleigh
Cross Wm. brewer & maltster, Rayleigh
Dale William, fruiterer, Rayleigh
Dennis Samuel, clothes dealer, Rayleigh
EXCISE OFFICE, Golden Lion, Rayleigh —Joseph Jacobs, supervisor
Fairhead Thomas, gardener & seedsman, Rayleigh
Finch Samuel, basket maker, Rayleigh
Flattery Edward, marine store dealer, Thundersley
Howard George, barge owner, South Benfleet
Jacobs Joseph, supervisor, Rayleigh
Johnson Jas. hurdle maker, Thundersley
Laver Robert, beast salesman, S. Benfleet
Linggood Thomas, whitesmith, Rayleigh
Low Algernon & Wm. curriers, Rayleigh
Mayhew Geo. veterinary surgeon, Rayleigh
Murrell John, glover, Rayleigh
Noone Charles Clark, stationer and hair dresser, Rayleigh
Peach George, brick maker, Hockley
Prentice Mary, straw hat maker, Rayleigh
Rolph Rebecca, leather seller and corn chandler, Rayleigh
Rule Ann, nursery keeper, Hockley
Warren Joseph, iron founder, Rayleigh

COACHES.

To LONDON, the *Despatch* (from Southend) calls at the Golden Lion, Rayleigh, every morning at nine; goes through Billericay, Brentwood, Romford, &c.

To SOUTHEND, the *Despatch* (from London) calls at the Golden Lion, Rayleigh, every evening at seven.

CARRIERS.

To LONDON, Edward Brown's *Waggon*, every Tuesday and Friday afternoon—and Joseph Pease's *Van*, every Monday and Thursday afternoon.

To CHELMSFORD, John Brittan's *Van*, every Friday morning.

To ROCHFORD, Joseph Pease's *Van* every Wednesday & Saturday afternoon

ROCHFORD,

WITH THE VILLAGES OF EASTWOOD, ASHINGDON, CANEWDON, PAGLESHAM, AND GREAT AND LITTLE STAMBRIDGE AND NEIGHBOURHOODS.

ROCHFORD is a market town and parish, giving name to a hundred, 39 miles E. from London and 5 E. from Rayleigh; situated on the small river Roche (from which it is said to derive its name), and within a mile of the Broomhill river, communicating with the navigable Crouch and the Thames. Rochford Hall, a short distance to the west of the town, was the residence, or, as some historians state, the birth-place of Ann Boleyn, one of the unfortunate queens of Henry VIII: it is an ancient fabric of large dimensions, the greater part of which was destroyed by fire about seventy years ago, and for a long period remained in a ruinous condition; at length, however, it was completely repaired and improved, and at present is a handsome residence, in the occupation of John Lodwick, Esq. magistrate. The market house, a wooden edifice, standing in the centre of the town, is now chiefly appropriated to the storage of wool. The magistrates for the hundred sit here every alternate Thursday, and occasionally more frequently, for general business. The church, dedicated to St. Andrew, situated nearly half a mile west of the town, is a structure more commodious than splendid, with a lofty square tower: in 1827 a gallery was erected, and new sittings added, by the society for the enlargement of churches and chapels; and in 1828 the building received repair and its general appearance improved. The living is a rectory, in the patronage of the Hon. W. T. L. P. Wellesley. There is a place of worship for independents. The charities comprise schools upon the national and other approved systems, and alms-houses for six indigent persons. The family of Nassau, which became extinct upon the demise of the late nobleman of that name in 1830, took the title of earl from Rochford. The market is held on Thursday, and the fairs on the Tuesday and Wednesday in Easter week for toys, &c., and on the Wednesday and Thursday after Michaelmas-day for toys, and articles required by tailors, glovers, &c. The parish contained, in 1831, 1,256 inhabitants—the population having increased only *twenty-eight* in the preceding thirty years.

EASTWOOD parish adjoins that of Rochford, the village being situated about a mile and a half from that town. The church is dedicated to St. Lawrence and All Saints; the living is a vicarage, in the presentation of the crown. [The population of this and the following parishes is given after STAMBRIDGE.]

ASHINGDON is a small village and parish in the same hundred as Rochford, rather more than two miles north from that town. The church, dedicated to St. Andrew, is a small plain building; the benefice is a rectory, in the patronage of Josiah Nottidge, Esq.

CANEWDON, a village and parish in the same hundred as the preceding places, is rather more than three miles N.N.E. from Rochford, situated on the Canewdon creek, issuing from the Crouch river. Canute the Dane kept his court here, from which circumstance the name of the place is supposed to have been derived. The situation of the village is elevated and pleasant—the prospects extensive and diversified; and there are several handsome residences in the parish. The church, dedicated to St. Nicholas, is a large structure, with a massive tower at its western end; the living is a vicarage, in the gift of the bishop of London.

PAGLESHAM, in the same hundred, is about four miles N.E. by E. from Rochford. The parish includes the western part of Wallasea island; on the north runs the Crouch, and on the south the Bromhill, both navigable. Several persons are here engaged extensively in the oyster fishery. The church is dedicated to St. Peter; the living is a rectory, in the gift of the see of London.

GREAT and LITTLE STAMBRIDGE are parishes in the same hundred as Rochford, extending from a mile and a half to two miles from that town. They have each their parish church—the livings are both rectories; that of Great Stambridge is in the patronage of the charter-house, and Little Stambridge in that of the crown.

The POPULATION of the foregoing places, by the returns at the last census, was as follows:—EASTWOOD, 531; ASHINGDON, 98; CANEWDON, 675; PAGLESHAM, 450; GREAT STAMBRIDGE, 405; LIT. STAMBRIDGE, 105.

POST OFFICE, ROCHFORD, Thomas White, *Post Master.*—Letters from INGATESTONE arrive (by mail cart) every morning at five, and are despatched every evening (Sunday excepted) at seven, on Sunday they are despatched at six.

GENTRY AND CLERGY.

Atkinson Rev. William, Canewdon
Attridge Mrs. Susannah, Eastwood
Barlow Rev. Edward Wm. Rochford
Blakeley Mr. James, Eastwood
Browning Mr. Charles, Paglesham
Coe Henry, esq. South hall, Pagleshm
Crick Mrs. Sarah, Eastwood
Digby Mrs. —, Rochford
Dowler John, esq. Ashingdon
Dyer Charles, esq. Canewdon hall
Fawcett Rev. Jas. Grisdale, Rochford
Fenwick Mrs. —, Canewdown
Fisk Thos. esq. Church hall, Pagleshm
Gardiner Rev. William, Rochford
Hayward Mrs. and Misses, Rochford
Hickinbotham Mr. Jno. Litt. Stambrdg
Kebbell Mrs. —, Stroud green, Rochfd
Kersteman Miss —, Canewdon
Kersteman Col. Loftman (magistrate) Canewdown
Keys Jas. esq. Little Stambridge hall
Keys William, esq. Ashingdon
Lodwick Mrs. Eliza, Canewdon
Lodwick John, esq. (magistrate) Rochford hall
Marsh Thomas Hurst, esq. Rochford

Merryfield Thos. esq. Great Daggetts
Mew Mr. John, Canewdon
Mew Mr. William, Canewdon
Penny Rev. Edward Henry, Great Stambridge
Rolph James, esq. Pound house, Paglesham [Paglesham
Stebbing Thomas, esq. West hall,
Temple Rev. Ebenezer, Rochford
Thorn Mrs. Nelly, Rochford
Walker Mrs. Mary, Eastwood
Warden Mrs. —, Canewdon
Wood Mr. James, Great Stambridge
Wren Wm. Weld, esq. Eastwoodbury
Wyatt Mrs. —, Rochford

ACADEMIES & SCHOOLS.

Not otherwise described are Day Schools.

Allen Ann (boarding & day) Rochford
Beckwith Ann, Rochford
Brady Betsy, Rochford
British Charity School, Rochford—Eli Beckwith, master
British Charity School, Canewdon—Stephen Clay, master; Ann Clay, mistress
National School, Rochford—Jno. Popplewell, master; Phœbe Popplewell, mistress
Richardson Thomas, Rochford

ATTORNEYS.

Comport and Gregson, Rochford
Swaine William (& clerk to the magistrates) Rochford
Wood George, Rochford

AUCTIONEERS & APPRAISRS.

Jackson William Henry, Rochford
Quy William (and surveyor and house and estate agent) Rochford

BAKERS & FLOUR DEALERS.

Appleton Henry, Rochford
Clark William, Rochford
Coe John, Rochford
Fairchild George, Paglesham
Harris William, Canewdon
Harvey William & James, Rochford
Ling Abraham, Rochford
Marsh Thomas, Great Stambridge
Potten John William, Canewdon
Say Samuel, Eastwood

BANKER.

Giles James, Rochford—(draws on Sir R. C. Glyn and Co. London)

BOOT AND SHOE MAKERS.

Banyard James, Rochford
Livens William, Paglesham
M'Durmid Thomas, Rochford
Mann Henry, Rochford
Mouwl Thomas, Canewdon
Nash George, Great Stambridge
Newman John, Rochford
Prentice William, Paglesham
Pryke James, Rochford
Sexton James, Paglesham
Shepherd Thomas, Great Stambridge
Spooner Daniel, Rochford
Turner George, Rochford
White John, Rochford
Wood Henry, Rochford

BRICKLAYERS.

Carter Charles & William (& stone masons) Rochford
Kemp and Johnson, Rochford

BUTCHERS.

Horsnell Charles, Rochford
Scott James, Canewdon
Sexton James, Paglesham
Stock Joseph, Rochford
Thorn John, Rochford
Turner Robert, Rochford
Warren Joseph, Great Stambridge

CARPENTERS & BUILDERS.

Allen Mary Ann, Rochford
Arnold George, Rochford
Hart John, Canewdon
Mascall Mary, Rochford
Robinson John, Great Stambridge

COAL MERCHANTS.

Tabor & Rankin, Little Stambridge
Wade Saml. (& lime burner) Canewdn

CONFECTIONERS.

Lancaster William, Rochford
Scott Thos. (& stationer) Rochford

COOPERS.

Clark John, Great Stambridge
Livermore James, Rochford

CORN DEALERS.

Hawley William (& stamp distributer) Rochford
Wade Samuel, Canewdon

DRUGGISTS.

Kernot William Pearce, Rochford
Raynham William (and veterinary surgeon) Rochford

FIRE, &c. OFFICE AGENTS.

Essex Economic, William Pearse Kernot, Rochford [Rochford
London Insurance, William Quy,
Norwich Union, Jas. Giles, Rochfrd
Phœnix, Chas. Richardson; & Wm. Hawley, Rochford [Rochford
Royal Exchange, Thomas White,

GROCERS, TEA DEALERS, &c.

(See also Shopkeepers, &c.)

Gillingham Wm. White (and tallow chandler & china dealer) Rochford
Harris William, Canewdon
Hawley Wm. (& chandler) Rochford
James and Burchell, Canewdon
Le'Grys William, Rochford [ford
M'Durmid Ths. (& china dealr) Roch-
Marsh Thomas, Great Stambridge
Mills Elizabeth, Paglesham
Mills Margaret, Rochford

HAIR DRESSERS.

Noone Elijah George, Rochford
Richardson Charles, Rochford
Smith John, Rochford

HOP GROWER.

Stebbing Thomas, Paglesham

INNS & PUBLIC HOUSES.

Anchor, Isaac Pond, Canewdon
Anchor, Samuel Saunders, South Fambridge [Canewdon
Chequers, Henry William Slade,
Cherry Tree, Samuel Offerd, Little Stambridge
Crown, Thomas Smith, Rochford
Ferry Boat, Wm. Allen, Canewdon
Horse & Groom, Wm. Sorrell, Eastwd
King's Head, Mary Wilson, Rochford
Marlborough Head, Stephen Piper, Rochford
New Ship, Charles Bailey, Rochford
Old Ship, Robert Bright, Rochford
Plough & Sail, Geo. Fairchild, Paglshm
Punch Bowl, Henry Hall, Paglesham
Royal Oak, Benj. Threadgold, Great Stambridge [wood
Three Ashes, John Gladwell, East-
Vernon's Head, Ts. Hy. Ford, Rochford

IRONMONGERS.

Jackson William Henry, Rochford
Quy William (and cabinet maker and upholsterer) Rochford

LINEN & WOOLLEN DRAPRS.

Bentall and Marsh, Rochford
James and Burchell, Canewdon
Le'Grys William, Rochford
Richardson William, Rochford
Winterbon Geo. (& clothier) Rochford

MILLERS.

Potton John William, Canewdon
Tabor & Rankin, Little Stambridge

MILLINERS.

Harvey Mrs. Isaac, Rochford
M'Durmid Mary, Rochford
Mann Mrs. Henry, Rochford
Wilson Hannah, Rochford

NURSERY AND SEEDSMEN.

Boosey James, Eastwood
Mills Margaret, Rochford

OYSTER MERCHANTS.

Browning George Fuller, Paglesham
Wendon John, Great Stambridge
Wiseman James, Paglesham
Wiseman James, jun. Paglesham

PAINTERS, PLUMBERS AND GLAZIERS.

Asby Robert, Rochford
Burgess James, Rochford

SADDLERS.

Burrows George, Rochford
Foster Susannah, Rochford
Turner John, Great Stambridge
Wiggins Thomas, Stroud green

SHOPKEEPERS & DEALRS IN GROCERIES & SUNDRIES.

Arnold Ann, Rochford
Miller Mary, Paglesham
Sexton James, Paglesham
Wiggins Elizabeth, Rochford

SMITHS & FARRIERS.

Bacon Charles, Canewdon
Bowton Richard, Ashingdon
Clark Isaac, Rochford
Codlin Elizabeth, Canewdon
Codlin George, Rochford
Snell William, Paglesham
Whittingham Wm. Great Stambridge
Whittingham Wm. jun. Gt. Stambridge

STRAW HAT MAKERS.

Beard Sarah, Paglesham
Blanks Thomas, Rochford
Wilder Ann, Rochford

SURGEONS.

Fairchild James, Rochford
Grabham John, Rochford
Green John, Rochford
Harridge Edward, Rochford

TAILORS.

Aylett John, Rochford
Harridge William, Rochford
Ranson James, Rochford
Raymond John, Rochford
Roff Thomas, Rochford
Whitaker James, Rochford

WATCH & CLOCK MAKERS.

Carter Charles, Rochford
Furner Francis, Rochford
Gullock Philip Hoare, Rochford

WHEELWRIGHTS.

Arnold George, Rochford
Freeman William, Rochford
Whittingham Wm. jun. Gt. Stambridge

Miscellaneous.

Beckwith Eli, bookbinder, Rochford
Bishop Jas. dealr in marine stores, Rochford
Blanks William, gun maker, Rochford
Brady Patrick, tea dealer, Rochford
Bruce Samuel, millwright, Eastwood
English John, brewer, Little Stambridge
Giles James, bill broker, Rochford
Kemp William, boat builder, Paglesham
Marsh George, deputy registrar of births and deaths, Rochford
Murrell Joseph, glover, Rochford
Salmon Thomas, high constable, Rochford
Salmon Thomas, wine & spirit merchant, Rochford [Rochford
Topsfield William, basket & sieve maker,
Townsend Barnabas, pot ash mkr. Rochford
Union Workhouse, Rochford—William Clayton, master; Mary Clayton, mistress
Wiseman Elijah, sail maker, Paglesham

COACHES.

To LONDON, the *Despatch* (from Southend) calls at the King's Head, every morning (Sunday excepted) at half-past eight; goes thro' Rayleigh, Billericay, Brentwood, Romford and Ilford

To SOUTHEND, the *Despatch* (from London) calls at the King's Head, every evening at eight.

VANS.

To LONDON, Edward Brown, from his house, every Tuesday and Friday morning at eleven—and Joseph Pease, from the Vernon's Head, every Monday and Thursday morning at eight.

To CHELMSFORD, George Minter, every Tuesday and Friday morning at five.

ROMFORD,

WITH THE VILLAGES OF HARE STREET, DAGENHAM, HAVERING-ATTE-BOWER, RAINHAM, WENNINGTON AND NEIGHBOURHOODS.

ROMFORD is a populous market town in the liberty of Havering-atte-Bower, about 12 miles N. E. from London; situated on the main road leading to Chelmsford, Colchester, Harwich, Ipswich, Norwich and Yarmouth, and consequently is a place of great thoroughfare. The earliest notice we find of this manor is in a record dated 1299, at which period it belonged to Adam de Cretinge, of whom Henry de Winchester, a jewish proselyte, held it. The town consists chiefly of one long and spacious street, which is well paved, and lighted with gas. The market-house stands near the centre of the town, as also does the court-house or town-hall, in which are held the quarter sessions for the liberty. The Eastern Counties' railway passes close to the town, and from this locality will issue the Thames Haven and Dock railway. Romford, Hornchurch and Havering constitute the liberty of Havering-atte-Bower. Edward the Confessor granted it a charter, and vested the government in a high steward, a deputy steward and one justice of the peace; these are elected by the inhabitants of the liberty, and exercise magisterial authority; they are a corporate body, and have the privilege of trying every class of offences, treason not excepted—but this extensive right has not recently been assumed. The sessions are held on the Friday after the county quarter sessions. Romford is a polling station at the election of members to represent the southern division of the county. This is not a manufacturing town, nor does it possess any peculiar commercial advantages; but its abundant and well attended market, added to its thoroughfare situation, renders its local business flourishing.

The church (or more correctly chapel, for it is under Hornchurch,) is dedicated to the Virgin Mary and Edward the Confessor; of the latter there is a full-length portrait in the east window of the chancel: the living is in the nature of a vicarage, in the patronage of the warden and fellows of New college, Oxford. The other places of worship are for independents and Wesleyan methodists. A school for sixty boys and thirty girls, and alms-houses for six poor men and the like number of women (the latter founded by Roger Reed), are the most noted charities; the parishes of Romford, Hornchurch and Dagenham have the alternate right of nomination to the alms-houses, as vacancies occur. The market is held on Wednesday, and a fair on the 24th of June for horned cattle and horses. The parish, at the census of 1831, contained 4,294 inhabitants.

About a mile from Romford, on the main road to Chelmsford, is HARE STREET, a hamlet to the former town. Many families of distinction reside in the surrounding district, the soil of which is remarkably rich and productive. Hare Hall is an elegant mansion of Portland stone, and on the opposite side of the road is Gidea Hall, a capacious square brick structure, in the occupation of Mrs. Alice Black.

Two miles and a half from Romford, between that town and the Thames, near to the high road leading from Barking to Rainham, and in the hundred of Becontree, is the village and parish of DAGENHAM. The Thames, in the winter of 1703, made a most destructive breach on this parish, and laid one thousand acres of valuable land, in the levels adjoining its banks, under water: a new embankment was subsequently constructed, at an expense of £40,472.; of this sum the original contract allowed only £25,000, but £15,000. were afterwards added by parliament, and the spirited contractor, Captain Perry, supplied the deficiency. The church, dedicated to St. Peter and St. Paul, was thoroughly repaired, and the windows and angles of the tower faced with brick, in 1800; it is a very handsome edifice: the benefice is a vicarage, of which the Rev. Thomas Lewis Fanshawe is the patron and incumbent. In 1828 Mr. William Ford endowed a free school here for thirty boys and twenty girls. The population of the parish, in 1831, amounted to 2,118.

HAVERING-ATTE-BOWER is a village in the parish and liberty of its name, and in a district celebrated in monkish legends. In a most delightful situation, commanding rich and extensive prospects, are the remains of an ancient palace, the erection or repair of which tradition ascribes to the Confessor. The church, dedicated to St. John the Evangelist, is very ancient, with a steeple of wood of singular appearance; it originally was the chapel of the palace: the living is a perpetual curacy, in the gift of Charles Ellis Heaton, Esq.; the Rev. R. Rowland Faulkner is the present incumbent. Mrs. Anne Tipping, in 1724, founded and endowed a charity school here, which in 1827 was rebuilt and enlarged by voluntary subscriptions. The Saxon kings included the liberty of Havering-atte-Bower in their personal demesnes, and it received many marks of distinction from the Norman dynasty: hence this district became possessed of some peculiar privileges, which Henry IV embodied in a charter, and succeeding monarchs confirmed. The number of inhabitants in this parish, according to the census of 1831, was only 332, but the entire liberty contained 6,812.

RAINHAM, a village and parish in Chafford hundred, near the river Thames, is about five miles south from Romford—the parish bounded on the west and south by extensive marshes. The church, dedicated to Saint Helen and Saint Giles, is an ancient building, and contains a few monuments of some antiquity, in the Norman style; the living is a vicarage, of which Major J. C. G. Crosse is the patron. In 1779 a charity school was founded here for the instruction of poor children. The population, by the last returns, consisted of 671 persons.

In the same hundred as Rainham, about midway between that place and Purfleet, lies the small village and parish of WENNINGTON. In the parish are continuous marshes, stretching southward and westward to the Thames. The church is dedicated to St. Peter; the benefice is a rectory, in the presentation of the bishop of London.

POST OFFICE, Market place, ROMFORD, William Henry Attwell, *Post Master.*—Letters from LONDON arrive (by the twopenny post) every forenoon (Sunday excepted) at half-past eleven and evening at six, and are despatched every morning at nine and afternoon at four; also letters from LONDON arrive (by the NORWICH mail) every night at half-past nine, and are despatched every morning at five.—Letters from CHIPPING ONGAR arrive (by mail cart) every night at eight, and are despatched every morning at six.—Letters from HORNDON-ON-THE-HILL and GRAYS THURROCK arrive (by mail cart) every evening at seven, and are despatched every morning at half-past six.—Letters from DAGENHAM arrive every evening at seven, and are despatched every morning at half-past six.

POST, RAINHAM, *Receiving-House* at Robert Ennever's.—Letters from ROMFORD arrive every forenoon at eleven, and are despatched every afternoon at two.

GENTRY AND CLERGY.

Anderson Major Jas. Havering grange
Andrews Wm. esq. Gothic lodge
Arnold Mr. Jon. Whalebone cottage
Barnes Jno. esq. Round hse. Havering
Black Mrs. Alice, Gidea hall
Burbrow Mr. Alexander, North st
Button Mr. Philip, Wennington
Cock Mrs. Lydia, Romford
Collier Mr. Pratt, Romford
Crosse Major John C. G. Berwick hse. Rainham [Rainham
Crosse Rev. John Godfrey, Vicarage,
Delamare Mr. John, Collier row lane
Delamare Mrs. John, Hornchurch la
Delamare Mrs. Peter, Romford
Fanshawe Henry, esq. Parglocs
Fanshawe Rev. John, Parglocs
Fanshawe Rev. Thos. Lewis, Parglocs
Faulkner Rev. Richd. Rowland, Parsonage, Havering [vering
Field Robert, esq. Pergo park, Ha-
Grant Rev. Anthony, Vicarage house
Graves Col. Benj. Shrubbery cottage
Higgs Mrs. Mary, Market place
Ind Edward, esq. Isbury lodge
Ind Edward Vipaud, esq. Romford
Last Mr. Joseph, North st
Mackintosh Hugh, esq. Marshalls
Martin Mr. William, Hare st
Mashiter Octavius, esq. Priests
Neave Sir Thomas, Dagenham park
Orbell Mrs. Eliz. Hare st [bone hse
Peacock Jno. Pickering, esq. Whale-
Reynolds Richard, esq. Hare st
Richardson Captain, London road
Robinson Edwd. esq. Havering bower
Rogers John, esq. Bedford
Taylor Mrs. —, North st

Tolbutt Mrs. —, Romford
Tolbutt Edward, esq. Romford
Tolbutt Wm. esq. Hornchurch lane
Turner Mr. John, Romford
Tweed Mrs. Mary, Hornchurch lane
Tyler Mrs. Susannah, Dagenham
Warren Wm. esq. Hampden house
White Captain Thos. Dagenham

ACADEMIES AND SCHOOLS.
Not otherwise described are Day Schools.
Axon Elizabeth (infants) Romford
CHARITY SCHOOL (boys & girls) Dagenham—Thomas Cutler, master; Anne Bridge, mistress
Fallover John, Hornchurch lane
Griggs Henry (boarding) Regent house [Romford
Hambleton Mrs. & Miss (boarding)
INFANTS' SCHOOL, Romford—Elizabeth Axon, mistress
NATIONAL SCHOOL (boys and girls) Romford—Oswald Adams, master; Sarah Adams, mistress
Peachey Frances, North st
Sage Anne (boarding) Romford
Trott Emma (boarding) Romford
Ward John R. Market place
Warwick Eliz. (brdg & day) North st

ATTORNEYS.
Collin Henry, North st
Griffin and Surridge (& clerks to the Romford and Orsett Unions) Market place
Sterry Wasey (& clerk of the peace & coroner) Romford
Wadeson Samuel James, Romford
Ward Alfred, Market place

AUCTIONEERS & APPRAISRS
Collier Stephen, High st
Collis George, Market place
Dawson William, Romford
Matthews Samuel J. P. High st

BAKERS.
Belchar James, Market place
Boyton Joseph, Dagenham
Cooper Richard, Rainham
Fisher Charles, Havering
Gentry Mark, Rainham
Goodwin William, Romford
Ingram Charles, Romford
Langham Lewis, Market place
Mitchell James, Dagenham
Mumford Joseph, Market place
Parker James, Romford
Price Charles, Market place
Ray Thomas, High st
Steele John, Romford
Taylor John, Havering

BANKERS.
Johnson Thomas and Co. High st—(draw on Sir Richd. Carr, Glyn & Co. and Whitmore, Wells & Co.)
SAVINGS' BANK, Romford—William Andrews, esq. treasurer; Samuel James Wadeson, secretary; Oswald Adams, actuary

BOOKSELLERS & STATIONRS
Marked thus * are also Letter-press Printrs
*Bridge Samuel, Market place
*Harvey Charles, Romford
Redin Thomas, High st [place
Staines Geo. Thos. (& library) Market
*Tooke Jas. (& news agent) Romford

BOOT & SHOE MAKERS.
Aldous John, Romford
Baker James, High st
Bevis John, Market place
Black Isaac, Romford
Dowsett William, Dagenham
Ennever Robert, Rainham
Farrow James, Dagenham
Farrow John, Rainham
Finch Joshua, Market place
Gillman George, North st
Grout Nathan, Rainham
Hale Henry, Romford
Hirst Thomas, Dagenham
Hornstead John, High st
Manning John, Hare st
Marridge John, Rainham
Mead John, Market place
Minnis William, High st
Mumford William, Havering
Piggott Charles, Market place
Potipher Edward, Romford
Wheatley William, Market place
Wood William, High st

BRAZIERS & TIN-PLATE WORKERS.
Collis George, Market place
Hodson Harry Farncombe, High st

BRICKLAYRS & PLASTERERS
Curtis Robert, North st
Marrable James, Romford
Moore Joseph, Romford
Paveley Robert, Romford
Stafford James, Dagenham

BUTCHERS.
Abrey Daniel, Havering
Axon John (pork) Romford
Axon William (pork) Romford
Collier Louisa, Market place
Collier Thomas, Romford
Couzens Thomas, Dagenham
Ennever Thomas, Rainham
Finch John, Romford
Mayhew Samuel, Rainham
Mitchell James, Dagenham
Nichols Thos. (pork) Market place
Poston William John, High st
Rayner William, Romford
Smith Edward, Market place
Smith Henry, Dagenham
Sorrell Henry, Hare st
Sorrell William, Romford
Spurge Jas. jun. Hornchurch lane
Spurge Joseph, North st

CABINET MAKERS.
Clube Ann, Romford
Collier Stephen, Romford

CARPENTERS.
Bartlett & Son (& builders) North st
Collins John, Romford
Curtis Robert, North st
Death John, Rainham
Dykes Wm. and Elizabeth, North st
Everett John, Rainham
Gardner Samuel, Havering
Hammond Samuel Adams, Romford
Holgate Benjamin, Dagenham
White Thomas, North st

CHEESEMONGERS.
Ellis William, Romford
Savill Charles, High st

CHYMISTS AND DRUGGISTS.
Macarthy James (& soda water and ginger beer manfr.) Market place
Redin Thomas, High st
Sewell Edward, Market place

COACH BUILDERS.
Laver William, Romford
Strutt Mary, Romford

COAL MERCHNTS. & DEALRS.
Daldy Edward Mee (and maltster) Rainham
Freshwater Daniel, Romford
Higgs John, High st
Kershaw Jeremiah, High st

COOPERS & BASKET MAKERS
Dykes Wm. and Elizabeth, North st
Starkey Diana, Market place

CONFECTIONERS.
Dodd Henry, North st
Higgs John, High st
Mundy George, Market place
Parker James, Romford

CORN CHANDLERS.
Green Matthew, Hare st
Higgs John, High st
Langham Lewis, Market place
Mumford Joseph, Market place

FIRE, &c. OFFICE AGENTS.
ALLIANCE, Wm. Cook, Market place
COUNTY, William Ellis, High st
ESSEX ECONOMIC, William Henry Attwell, Market place [High st
ESSEX EQUITABLE, John Higgs,
GUARDIAN, Robert Surridge, High st
NORWICH UNION, Edward Sewell, Market place
PHŒNIX, Jno. Bartlett, North st, and Alfred Ward, Market pl [High st
ROYAL EXCHANGE, Stephen Collier,
SUN, John Delamare, North st

FISHMONGRS & FRUITERERS
Bailey John, Romford
Bolster Richard, Romford
Brower John, Romford
Brown John, Romford
Clarance Adolphus, Market place
Howe Mary, Romford
Lovely James, High st
May Emma, Hornchurch lane
Moore Joseph, Market st

FURNITURE BROKERS.
Clube Anne, Market place
Dykes Wm. and Elizabeth, North st

GARDENERS & SEEDSMEN.
Attewell John and James, Romford
Lewsey Thomas, London road

GROCERS & TEA DEALERS.
(See also Shopkeepers, &c.)
Busby James, Market place
Clarke William, Dagenham
Dodson and Higgs, Market place
Ellis Wm. (& tallow chandler) High st
Hollinsworth Chas. Chevin, Romford
Payne Henry, Rainham
Revill Sarah, High st
Rorison Thos. (tea dealer) North st
Savill Charles, High st

HAIR DRESSERS.
Andrews George, High st
Keys James, High st
Keys John, Market place
March George, Market place
Parker Charles, Rainham

HATTERS & CLOTHES DELRS
Black Isaac, Romford
Bray Joseph, Market place
Pedder Daniel, Market place

INNS & PUBLIC HOUSES.
Angel, George Beal, Rainham
Bell, John Ennever, Rainham
Blucher's Head, Samuel Adams Hammond, Market place
Bull, Elizabeth Jones, Market place
Bull, George Kittle, Dagenham
Chequers, Joseph Scales, Dagenham
Coach and Bell Inn, Richard Carter, High st [Market place
Cock and Bell, Shadrach Parker,
Compasses, Edward Finch, Romford
Cross Keys, Thos. Hirst, Dagenham
Dolphin Inn, James Merrington, Market place [church lane
Fox & Hounds, Jas. Spurge, Horn-
Golden Lion, Noah Dunnett, High st
King's Arms, Robt. Neal, Market place
King's Head, Henry Orbell, Market pl
Lamb, Nathl. Brown, Market place
Leonard's Arms, George Frith, Wennington [lane
Liberty Arms, George Sears, Dog
New Mill, Louisa Humsden, Romford
Old Windmill & Bells, William Sawyer, Market place [ing
Orange Tree, Thomas Clark, Haver-
Phœnix, Thomas Howell, Rainham
Rose and Crown, William Morley, Dagenham
Ship, Charlotte Humphreys, Hare st
Star, Thomas Read, High st

INNS, &c.—Continued.
Sun, Frederick Belsey, London road
Swan, John Bowton, Market place
Unicorn, William Sweeting & Son, Hare st
White Hart, Richard Sharpe, Hare st
White Hart Inn, Henry and George Taverner, High st
Woolpack, Elizabeth Holdaway, High st

IRONMONGERS AND WHITESMITHS.
Collis George, Market place
Hodson Harry Farncombe (& copper smith, bell-hanger, brazier & gas fitter) High st
Starnes James, High st

LAND & ESTATE AGENTS.
Collier Stephen, High st
Collis George, Market place
Twyford Thomas Waters (and surveyor) Romford

LINEN DRAPERS.
Bonnington & Waghorn, High st
Ellis John Ping (and silk mercer) Market place
Hebblewhite Frederick, Market place
Hunter William, High st
Phillips Cheveley, High st
Shipton John, Market place
Smith Michael, Market place
White Ann, High st

MILLERS.
Clark James, Hornchurch lane
Collier Edward, Romford
Collier John, Collier row
Collier Pratt, jun. London road
Payes and Bigg, Mark's gate

MILLINERS & DRESS MAKRS.
Bonnington & Waghorn, High st
Day Sarah, Dagenham
Gentry Jane, North st
Littlechild Sarah & Caroline, Market place
Skinner Elizabeth, Market place
White Ann, High st

MUSIC TEACHERS.
Lucas Charles, Hornchurch lane
Tipper John Ely, Romford

PAINTERS, PLUMBERS AND GLAZIERS.
Poulter Samuel, Romford
Rooke Ash, Hornchurch lane
Seymour George, Romford
Whitaker William Thomas, High st

PRINTERS—LETTER-PRESS.
See Booksellers.

SADDLERS AND HARNESS MAKERS.
Chase Mary, Dagenham
Draper Charles, High st
Mead & Son, Hornchurch lane
Playl Thomas, Havering
West Edward Seed, Dagenham

SHOPKEEPERS & DEALRS IN GROCERIES & SUNDRIES.
Beard John, Wennington
Cleaver William, Havering
Enever Ann, Romford
Enever Robert, Dagenham
Golding Joseph, Romford
Hill John, Rainham
Holmes Sarah, North st
Kershaw Geo. (& eating house) Romford
Kittle William, Dagenham
Nichols Thomas, Market place
Sackett James, Dagenham
Taylor Richard, Hare st
Waters Charlotte, Dagenham

SMITHS AND FARRIERS.
Bennett John, Havering
Cresey George, Dagenham
Hasten John, Dagenham
King William, Rainham
Lutman John, Wennington
Parker Robert, Hornchurch lane
Pearson Charles Andrew, Dagenham
Staines William, Hare st
Strutt Mary, Romford
Wheatley James, Romford
Wheatley Octavius, Rainham

STAY MAKERS.
Dawson Louisa Ann, Romford
Rooke Ash, Hornchurch lane

STRAW HAT MAKERS.
Collett Eliza, Romford
Dawson Louisa Ann, Romford
Hornstead Lydia, Romford
Littlechild John, Market place
Staff Elizabeth, North st
Wall Martha, Market place

SURGEONS.
Bowers Robert Arnold, Market place
Butler Charles, Market place
Sewell and Collin, North st
Sewell George, Romford

TAILORS.
Anderson Mark, Romford
Barlow John, Romford
Byatt John, High st
Cook Samuel, Romford
Edney William, High st
Ouzman Richard, Romford
Sawyer Thomas Fennell, North st
Southy Samuel, High st
Worth Richard, High st

WATCH & CLOCK MAKERS.
Attwell William Henry (& jeweller) Market place
Bennett James, Romford
Kistler Andreas, Romford

WHEELWRIGHTS.
Cobb John, Havering
Hasten John, Dagenham
Laver William, Romford
Strutt Mary, Romford
Vanderour Abraham, Rainham

WINE & SPIRIT MERCHANTS
Carter Richard, High st
Merrington James, Market place

Miscellaneous.
Attwell William Henry, fancy bazaar, Market place
Boyce Elizbth. horse & gig owner for hire, Romford
Brown Joseph, tripe dresser, Romford
Carter John, millwright, Romford
Chapel John, carrier, Romford
Clifton Henry, dyer & scourer, Romford
Collett Thomas, coach proprietor, Romford
Collier Stephen, timber merchant, Romford
Cook Wm. glass & earthenware dlr. Romford
Daniels William, machine maker, Romford
Day William, eating house, Market place
EXCISE OFFICE, Sun Inn, Romford—Thomas Albon Carter, supervisor
Fletcher Saml. pawnbroker, Market place
Flood Edward, news agent, Hornchurch la
Fredman Isaac, toy dealer, Romford
Gardner Saml. brick & tile makr, Havering
GAS WORKS, Hornchurch lane—George Martin Bell, proprietor
Ind & Smith, brewers, Romford
Lake James, umbrella makr, Gray's square
Lexford Henry, carrier, Romford
Nichols Thomas, parish clerk, Market place
Orbell George, horse dealer, Romford
Packer Anthy. whip & thong mkr. Romford
Rooke Ash, glass cutter, Hornchurch lane
Rorison Thomas, tea dealer, North st
Savill Chas. dealer in British wines, High st
Smith James, currier and leather cutter, Market place
Southy Samuel, glover & breeches maker, High st
Sparkes Thos. veterinary surgeon, Romford
STAMP OFFICE, Market place—James Macarthy, agent
Starnes James, gun maker, High st
Strutt Henry, tobacco pipe maker, Romford
Sturdy Wm. statuary & mason, Romford
Tolbutt Edward, corn inspector, Romford
Turner Ann, eating house, Romford
UNION POORHOUSE, Romford—Benjmn. Goode Miller, governor
Viall John, yarn spinner, Dagenham
Workman William, town crier, Gray's sq
Wynn John, dlr in marine stores, Havering

COACHES.

All call at or go from the White Hart except the Mail.

To LONDON, the *Royal Mail* (from Norwich) calls at the Post Office, every morning at five—a *Coach*, every morning at half-past eight, except Sunday, when it goes at six—the *Ockendon*, every morning (Sunday excepted) at nine—and another *Coach*, every afternoon (Sunday excepted) at half-past two, and on Sunday at five.

To BURY ST. EDMUNDS, a *Coach*, every forenoon (Sun. excepted) at eleven.

To CHELMSFORD, a *Coach*, every forenoon at half-past eleven, and evening at a quarter past five.

To COLCHESTER, a *Coach*, every morning at half-past ten.

To HARWICH, a *Coach*, every afternoon at a quarter before four.

To MALDON, a *Coach*, every Tuesday, Thursday and Friday afternoon at one.

To NORWICH, the *Royal Mail* (from London) calls at the Post Office, every night at half-past nine.

CARRIERS.

To LONDON, John Chapel, from his house, and Henry Lexford, from his house, every Tuesday, Thursday and Saturday—and William Stephenson, from his house, every Tuesday & Thurs.

*** Besides the above, there are other *Coaches* and *Carriers* to and from LONDON and certain places in ESSEX, NORFOLK and SUFFOLK, which pass thro' Romford daily, & call at the White Hart.

SAFFRON WALDEN,

WITH THE VILLAGES OF GREAT AND LITTLE CHESTERFORD, ASHDON, DEBDEN, LITTLEBURY, RADWINTER AND NEIGHBOURHOODS.

SAFFRON WALDEN is an ancient and respectable market and corporate town and parish, having separate jurisdiction, locally in the hundred of Uttlesford—42 miles N. from London, 27 N. W. from Chelmsford, 14 S. S. E. from Cambridge, 12 N. from Bishops Stortford, and about a mile off the main road to Cambridge, on a dry chalky soil. Dr. Stukeley thus describes the situation of the town:—'A narrow tongue of land shoots itself out like a promontory, encompassed with a valley, in the form of a horse-shoe, enclosed by distant and delightful hills; on the bottom of the tongue, towards the east, stand the ruins of the castle, and on the top or extremity the church, the greater part of which is seen above the surrounding houses.' From its massive remains the castle appears to have been a fortress of uncommon strength; its foundation was laid, shortly after the conquest, by Geoffrey de Magheville, whose grandson obtained for the town many important privileges, among which was the removal of the market hither from Newport. The name of this place is evidently derived from *Weald* and *Den*, signifying a 'woody vale,' and the term *Saffron* from the profusion of that plant formerly cultivated hereabout. The town contains several good streets, and a spacious market-place displays a neat town-hall; some of the houses have a very ancient aspect, but of late years many handsome ones have been erected; a new cattle-market also has been formed, and other improvements effected. Edward VI, in 1549, first incorporated Saffron Walden: its government, under the provisions of the municipal act passed in 1835, is vested in the town council, consisting of four aldermen and twelve councillors, out of whom one is chosen mayor; the recorder is a magistrate for the borough—so also is the mayor for the time being, as well as the past mayor; the two latter are included with others in the commission of the peace conferred by the new act, which also styles the corporate body 'the mayor and aldermen of the town of Saffron Walden, in the county of Essex.' The quarter sessions are held four times in a year, at which the recorder presides; a court of record sits for the recovery of small debts; and the Right Hon. Lord Braybrooke, lord of the manors of Chipping Walden and Brooke Walden, holds a court leet annually in June. Saffron Walden is a polling station at the election of members for North Essex. There are numerous respectable establishments here in the malting trade; also several others in the hop business, and in the neighbourhood are many corn mills. There are three principal inns, one of which is a good posting house.

The church, dedicated to the Holy Trinity, is a spacious and elegant specimen of English architecture, and comprises a nave, chancel and side aisles; the windows are ornamented with mullions and tracery, and between several are carved niches for statues; it has a very fine tower, surmounted by a needle spire of beautiful symmetry; and, viewed as a whole, it is considered one of the lightest and most elegant churches in the kingdom. In the south aisle is a monument to Lord Chancellor Audley; there are many others in the church, but they present nothing attractive. The benefice is an endowed vicarage, in the patronage of Lord Braybrooke, and incumbency of the Rev. Nicholas Bull. The independents, general baptists, unitarians, Wesleyan methodists, and society of friends, have their respective places of worship. The alms-houses founded by Edward VI have recently been rebuilt: the revenue of this charity has been much improved during the mastership of Thomas Smith, Esq.; it at present amounts to nearly £1,000. per annum, and yields sustenance, habitation and comfort to thirty poor men and women: the affairs of the charity are now under the control of fifteen trustees appointed by the court of chancery, as well as the other charities formerly under the management of the corporation. The free grammar school was founded in the fifteenth century by John Leche, vicar; it is now conducted upon the national plan, and educates about one hundred and fifty boys: there is another school for girls, similarly conducted. A horticultural society possesses the patronage of many scientific and opulent residents of the town and neighbourhood; and in 1835 a museum was opened—it originated with the late Jabez Gibson, Esq., and is supported by subscription; the collection is annually increasing in value and interest, and its zoological specimens are of great rarity. The market is held on Saturday; fairs, the Saturday before Midlent Sunday and the 1st of November: the toy fair formerly holden at Audley End on the 5th of August is now held on Walden common, about the 3rd of the month, for lambs, &c.; the two others are large fairs for horses and cattle; a great cattle fair is likewise held at Newport, about two miles distant, on the 17th November. The population of the town and parish, in 1831, was 4,762.

In the same hundred as Saffron Walden, four miles north from that town, is GREAT CHESTERFORD (or, as it was formerly called, *Chesterford Magna)*, a village situated upon the confines of Cambridgeshire, washed upon the west by the waters of the Granta, which here form the boundary of that county and Essex; it is a place of great antiquity, and, from the numerous Roman vestiges found here, is believed to have been a military station of that people. The church, dedicated to All Saints, is an ancient and spacious structure; the living is a discharged vicarage, with the rectory of LITTLE CHESTERFORD annexed, in the alternate presentation of the crown and the Marquess of Bristol. An annual fair is held on the first Friday in July. Population of Great Chesterford, 873; Little Chesterford, 211.

One mile west from Saffron Walden, in the same hundred as that town, is the small village and parish of LITTLEBURY; the village is situated on the main road to Cambridge and London, and consequently is a considerable thoroughfare, which supports a good inn, the 'Queen's Head.' The church is dedicated to the Holy Trinity; the benefice is in the patronage of the bishop of Ely. Population of the parish, in 1831, 875.

RADWINTER is in the hundred of Freshwell, five miles from Saffron Walden. Fairs are held here on Easter-Tuesday and Whit-Tuesday. Population, 819.

Four miles east of Saffron Walden, in the same hundred as Radwinter, is the village and parish of ASHDON. The village contains the parish church, a neat and commodious edifice, and a population of 1,103 inhabitants. There are fairs on Easter-Monday and Whit-Monday.

Three miles and a half south-east from Saffron Walden, in the hundred of Uttlesford, is DEBDEN village and parish. The small but elegant church, of Gothic architecture, which stands in the village, cannot fail to attract the observation of the stranger, who will also be gratified by a view of Debden Hall, a fine mansion, with a grand portico of Ionic columns. A fair is held on the first of June. Population, in 1831, 985.

POST OFFICE, Butter market, SAFFRON WALDEN, Jane Spicer, *Post Mistress.*—Letters from LONDON arrive every morning at half-past six in summer and at half-past seven in winter, and are despatched every night at nine.—Letters from CAMBRIDGE and the North arrive (by mail cart) every morning at nine, and are despatched every evening at six.—Besides the above, bags are made up and forwarded to LITTLEBURY at the same time as those for LONDON, to the following places:—BISHOPS STORTFORD, HARLOW, EPPING, NEWMARKET, BURY, BRANDON, THETFORD and NORWICH.

POST, LITTLEBURY, *Receiving-House* at Mary Green's.—Letters from LONDON arrive every morning at half-past one, and are despatched every morning at two.

NOBILITY, GENTRY, AND CLERGY.

Allen Mr. Joseph, Church st
Andrews Thomas, esq. Hempstead
Archer Lewis, esq. Little Church st
Archer Mrs. Mary Ann, High st
Braybrooke Right Hon. Lord, Audley house
Bromley Rev. Henry, Clavering
Bull Rev. Henry, Littlebury
Bull Rev. Nicholas, Vicarage
Bullock Rev. John, Radwinter
Burrell Hon. Lindsay, Debden park
Carr Rev. J. A. Hadstock
Carver Rev. J. W. Sampford
Catlin Mrs. Martha, High st
Catlin Nathaniel, esq. Bridge st
Chapman Rev. Benedick, Ashdon
Clarke Mr. Turner Poulter, Rope farm
Clayden Mr. John, Bird's farm
Clayden Mr. John, Littlebury
Cornwell Mrs. Francis, High st
Cottingham R. M. J. esq. Great Chesterford
Fiske Charles, esq. Fairy Croft
Fiske John, esq. Castle hall
Fiske Mrs. Mary, Bridge st
Fiske Rev. Robert, Elmdon
Fiske Samuel, esq. Farmadine
Forster Rev. Luke, Gold st
Gibson Mrs. Ann, Hill st
Gibson Miss Mary, High st
Gibson Wyatt George, esq. High st
Gorthorn Mr. Thomas, Hill st
Green Henry, esq. Chesterford
Green Mr. Joseph Markes, High st
Griffinhoofe Rev. Thomas, Arkesden
Harris Joseph, esq. Littlebury
Haylock Charles, esq. Ashdon
King Hon. and Rev. Richard Fitzgerald, Great Chesterford
Mapletoft William, esq. Audley end
Martin Captain —, Clavering
Middleton the Misses, High st
Monk Rev. T. Newport
Nash Peter, esq. Great Chesterford
Player John, esq. Market place
Player Rev. John, King st
Probert Thomas, esq. Newport
Raymond Rev. —, Wimbish
Robinson Stephen, esq. Market st
Sampson Mr. John, Gt. Chesterford
Shepherd Mrs. —, Gold st
Spicer Mr. Cornell, Westley farm
Spicer Mr. Waite, London road
Totten Rev. William Jurin, Debden
Walker Rev. Matthew, Gold st
Wilkinson Rev. Josiah, Bailey's lane
Wolfe Richard Birch, esq. (magistrate) Wood hall, Arkesden

ACADEMIES AND SCHOOLS.
Not otherwise described are Day Schools.
Bird Betsy, Castle st
Fincham Mary, Horn lane
FREE SCHOOL, Ashdon—Richard Ruse, master

ACADEMIES, &c.—*Continued.*
FREE SCHOOL, Audley end—Charlotte Smith, mistress
Frye Emma, Church st
FryeThos. (boarding &day) Church st
Harris Susannah (bdg. & day) High st
INFANTS' SCHOOL, Abbey lane—Elizabeth Rumsey, mistress
Jones William Taylor (boarding and day) Walden common
Mansfield Timothy, Debden
Mark Ann and Jane (boarding and day) Church st
NATIONAL SCHOOL, Great Chesterford—Rev. Robert King, master
NATIONAL SCHOOL (boys) Castle st—William Drew, master
NATIONAL SCHOOL (girls) Museum street—Emma Briggs, mistress
Pursey William, East st
Stackwood Wm. (bdg. & day) Bridge st
Turner Sarah, Great Chesterford
Werren Susannah, Gold st
Wilkinson Rev. Josiah (boarding and day) Bailey's lane
Wright Maria, Gold st

ARCHITECT.
Goldsmith Cassius, 1, Castle st

ATTORNEYS.
Collin Joseph Thomas, Church st
Fiske and Good, High st
Master Charles Fessier (and town-clerk) High st
Probert Thos. King st, and at *Newport*
Thurgood and Son, High st

AUCTIONEERS & APPRAISRS
Dunn Hannibal, Market street
Nockolds Martin (and estate agent) High st
Paul Robert, Market place
Thurgood Robert Driver (and stamp distributer & estate agent) High st
Ward Matthew (appraiser) High st

BAKERS.
Adams James, Butter market
Camp William, London road
Green Thomas, Ashdon
Hodson James, Castle st
Legerton John (gingerbread) High st
Mascall James, Radwinter
Mason William, Great Chesterford
Onion William, Great Chesterford
Parker James, Church st
Parratt James, Radwinter
Player James Edmund, High st
Rule Reuben, Market hill
Watson Charles, Queen st
White Francis, Castle st

BANKERS.
Gibsons & Co. Market hill—(draw on Drewett and Fowler, London)
Savings' Bank, Market hill (open on Fridays from 12 till 2)—Jephtha Miller, secretary

BLACKSMITHS & FARRIERS.
Barker Charles, Sewers end
Barnes William S. Butter market
Boatman John, Debden
Bunton William, Radwinter
Butcher John, Castle st
Green Josiah, Ashdon
Green Thomas, Ashdon
Green Thomas and John, Littlebury
Jeffrey Dean, Great Chesterford
Kent Nehemiah, Great Chesterford
Rider William, Church st
Spicer Richard, George lane
Spicer William, George lane
Willett Samuel, Ashdon

BOOKSELLERS, STATIONERS AND BOOKBINDERS.
Hart Henry (and stamp distributer) Market st
Low Mary (and toy dealer) High st
Pursey William (bookbinder) East st
Youngman George (and printer and library) Market place

BOOT AND SHOE MAKERS.
Baron Charles, Market place
Brand Joseph & Chas. Butter market
Brand William, Abbey lane
Cowell Robert, Audley end
Cox Benjamin, Gold st
Cox William, Castle st
Hall Henry, Ashdon
Hammond John, Great Chesterford
Hayles John, Market st
Holgate John, Debden
Jeffrey Charles, Castle st
Jeffrey Nathaniel, Castle st
Johns Daniel, Debden
Love Charles, Butter market
Mascall Robert, Radwinter
Mascall William, Radwinter
Nichols William A. Church st
Pratt John, Castle st
Rice Thomas, Great Chesterford
Savil John, High st
Sherrin George, Great Chesterford
Spink John C. Butter market
Suckling John, Littlebury
Wilson Simon, High st

BRAZIERS AND TIN-PLATE WORKERS.
Kiddell George, Butter market
Paul Robert (& wire-worker) Market place
Peachey William, Butter market
Spicer Matthew, Butter market

BREWERS.
Taylors and Co. High st

BRICKLAYERS.
Ketteridge William, Ashdon
Orbell James, Great Chesterford
Orbell William, Great Chesterford
Porter Stephen, Radwinter
Ward Joseph, Castle st
Ward William, Waldon common
Wright John, Littlebury

BUILDERS.
Abraham William, Littlebury
Bird Thomas, London road
Erswell Charles, Hill st
Granger James, Bridge st
Ward Joseph, Castle st
Ward William, Waldon common

BUTCHERS.
Adams William, Church st
Archer James, Castle st
Bacon James, Debden
Brewer William (pork) Bridge st
Debney Thomas, Butter market
Duke Ann, Littlebury
Gatward Henry, Church st
Gatward William, Littlebury
Lagden William, Ashdon
Mansfield James, Debden
Mascall Charles, Radwinter
Mascall Edward, Ashdon
Page Robert, Radwinter
Player John, Church st
Porter Bird, High st
Spicer Seamer (& dealr in game) Market st
Waldock Samuel, Great Chesterford
Wills Thomas, Hill st

CABINET MAKERS AND UPHOLSTERERS.
Dunn Hannibal, Market st
Paul Robert, Market place
Smart Jonathan, High st

CARPENTERS.
Abraham William, Littlebury
Bird Thomas, London road
Cro Thomas, Ashdon
Douglas John, Castle st
Downham Henry, Radwinter
Erswell Charles, East st
Green William, Ashdon
Hagger Jeremiah, Great Chesterford
Thomason James, Debden
Ward William, Church st

CHINA, GLASS, & EARTHENWARE DEALERS.
Rickard Mary, Hill st
Rogers Henry, Market place

CHYMISTS & DRUGGISTS.
Burch Robert (and dentist) High st
Burrows Henry (and oil and colourman) Market place
Low William, High st
Miller Jephtha, Market hill

COACH BUILDERS.
Kent William, High st
Rider William, Church st

CONFECTIONERS.
Player James Edmund, High st
Rule Reuben, Market hill

COOPERS.
Unwin and Patient, Museum st
Willis John, Castle st

CORN FACTORS.
Legerton Thomas (and seedsman) Church st
Middleditch William, Market st
Searle Jno. (& seedsman) Market hill
Stokes Edward, jun. High st
White Francis, High st

CURRIERS AND LEATHER CUTTERS.
Nichols Charles, High st
Wilkins Charles Barnes, High st

DYERS & SCOURERS.
Harris Ebenezer, High st
Overton Thomas, Great Chesterford

FIRE, &c. OFFICE AGENTS
COUNTY (fire) & PROVIDENT (life) Robert D. Thurgood, High st
ESSEX & SUFFOLK EQUITABLE, Wm. S. Barnes, Butter market
ESSEX ECONOMIC, John Emson, Market place
MUTUAL BENEFIT, Thomas Patient, Museum st
NORWICH UNION, Robert Paul, Market place
PHŒNIX, Hannibal Dunn, Market st; and William Stackwood, Bridge st
ROYAL EXCHANGE, John Leverett, Market place
SUFFOLK and GENERAL COUNTRY, George Youngman, Market place
SUN, Martin Nockolds, High st

GROCERS & TEA DEALERS.
(See also Shopkeepers, &c.; and also Tea Dealers.)
Bailey Winnifred, Audley end
Day, Robson and Co. King st
Duke George, High st
Dunn Henry, Butter market
Emson John and Son, Market place
Hardwick Thomas (and fruiterer) Market hill
Haylock William, Butter market
Leverett John, Market place
Rogers Henry (and cheesemonger) Market place
Spicer William, Great Chesterford
Wiseman William, Market place

GUN MAKERS.
Furlong John, Church st
Perkins William, Bridge st

HATTERS.
Leverett Jno. Market place
Richardson Jno. (& manufr.) Market place
Thompson Matthew, Market place
Tokelove John (& manufr.) Gold st

HOP MERCHANTS.
Emson and Son, Market place
Gibsons and Clarke, High st
Wiseman William, Market place

INNS.
Crown (and posting house) Owen H. Edwards, Gt. Chesterford
Queen's Head, John Westley, Littlebury

Rose and Crown (and posting house) William Leverett, Market place
Sun (and excise office) Jos. Scruby, Market hill
White Horse, Richd. Smoothy, Market place

IRONMONGERS.

Barnes William S. (and gas fitter) Butter market
Dunn Hannibal (and agent for Ransome's agricultural implements) Market st
Kent Jos. (& cutler & patten maker) Market st
Paul Robert, Market place
Spicer Matthew, Butter market

LIME BURNERS.

Bird Thomas, London road
Richardson Joseph, Thaxted road

LINEN AND WOOLLEN DRAPERS.

Beard Thomas and Samuel, High st
Burrows William, Market st
Day, Robson and Co. King st
Duke George, High st
Dunn Henry, Butter market
Emson John and Son, Market place
Hailes Mary & Martha, Gt. Chesterfrd
Humphreys James, Butter market
Leverett John, Market place
Spicer William, Great Chesterford
Wiseman William, Market place

MALTSTERS.

Catlin Nathl. (& corn mercht) High st
Clark John, High st
Clark Joseph, Castle st
Clarke Joshua, High st
Edwards Owen H. Gt. Chesterford
Gibsons and Clarke, High st
Hawkes and Co. High st
Jennings Reginald, High st
Kent Philip, Little Chesterford
King Thomas, Gold st, & Littlebury
Paul Robert, Market place
Porter Charles, Gold st
Rickard Phillis, Castle st
Robinson Nathaniel, Littlebury
Smith James, Debden
Stokes Edward, jun. High st
Taylors and Co. High st

MILLERS.

Bewsher and King, Littlebury
Hardy John, Ashdon
Living Josiah, Great Chesterford
Middleditch William, Long lane
Mynott John, Sewers end
Reeve Thomas, Debden
Ruse John, Ashdon
Ruse William, Radwinter
Sampson Elizabeth, Gt. Chesterford
Saward Joseph, Radwinter
Searle John, Copt hall
Sparrow Elizabeth, Ashdon

MILLINERS & DRESS MAKRS

Butterfield Isabella, Market place
Crush Elizabeth, High st
Giblin Eliza and Mary Ann, Market place
Kent Elizabeth, Church st
Kent Martha, High street
Porter Mary, King st
Raven Harriet, High st
Rickard Mary, Hill st

PAINTERS, PLUMBERS AND GLAZIERS.

Bunten Robert, Church st
Cowell Steward, Great Chesterford
Durrant Joseph, King st
Smith William, Great Chesterford
Ward Matthew, High st

PERFUMRS & HAIR CUTTERS

Barratt William, Castle st
Butterfield Geo. Thos. and Henry (& news agents) Market st
Howard Jas. (& news agent) Market place
Howard William, Church st
Smith Thomas, Church st

SADDLERS AND HARNESS MAKERS.

Archer Henry, Ashdon
Carter Thomas, Church st
Samuel John, Butter market
Stokes Edward, High st
Wedd James, Market st
Whitby Thomas, Great Chesterford

SHOPKEEPERS & DEALRS IN GROCERIES & SUNDRIES.

Abraham Mary, Littlebury
Andrews William, Gt. Chesterford
Archer William, Castle st
Bacon James, London road
Bard James, Great Chesterford
Barry Francis, High st
Bates Jeremiah, High st
Bunten John, Radwinter
Burdett Godfrey, Castle st
Cade Charles, Radwinter
Carrington Amelia, Gold st
Cass John, Debden
Chapman Edward, Little Chesterford
Claydon Sarah, Radwinter
Cowell Sarah, Ashdon
Cowell Steward, Great Chesterford
Cro Jane, Ashdon
Garwood James, Littlebury
Granger Thomas, Bridge st
Gunson Elizabeth, Gold st
Housden Charles, Ashdon
Hunt Samuel, Queen st
Kemp William, Great Chesterford
Kettle John, Castle st
Mansfield James, Debden
Martin Joseph, Debden
Mascall Charles, Radwinter
Miller James, Church st
Potter Thomas, Debden
Richardson Harriet, Debden
Richardson John, Littlebury
Rushforth John, Debden
Sargent John, Ashdon
Searle John, Little Chesterford
Shaul James, Castle st
Stacey Daniel, Littlebury
Swan Samuel, Radwinter
Ward Silvanus, Castle st
Weeden Ann, Great Chesterford
Wesson James, Church st
Wright John, Littlebury

STRAW HAT MAKERS.

Crush Elizabeth, High st
Crussell Frances, Church st
Glover Mary Ann, Castle st
Hailes Mary & Martha, Gt. Chesterford
Jones Mary, High st
Parnwell Matilda, Bridge st
Redhead Susannah, Church st
Wright Ann, Castle st

SURGEONS.

Browne Thomas, High st
Fiske and Jones, Farmadine
Spurgin Thomas, Church st

SURVEYORS.

King John and Son, Castle st
Nockolds Martin, High st
Ward Wm. (& architect) Walden common

TAILORS.

Marked thus * are also Drapers.

Bryant George, Museum st
*Burrows William, Market st
Danns Edward, Great Chesterford
Housden James, Bridge st
Housden James, jun. Castle st
*Kemp William and Joseph (and glovers) High street
*Kight Maria and Amelia, King st
Monk James, Debden
*Redhead William, Market hill
Reynolds John, Radwinter
Seaman Joseph, Little Chesterford
Silk Thomas, Bridge st
Speller Chas. (& clothes dealer) Butter market
Wesson James, Church st
*Wright Samuel M. Ashdon

TAVERNS & PUBLIC HOUSES.

Compasses, Charles Erswell, Hill st
Cross Keys, Mary Ackland, High st
Crown and Thistle, James Arbell, Great Chesterford
Duke of York, Samuel Hills, London rd
Eight Bells, William Perkins, Bridge st
Falcon, Josiah Green, Littlebury
Fox, Edward Mascall, Ashdon
George, William Spicer, George lane
Green Dragon, John Neville, Market hill
Greyhound, Emma Smith, High st
Hoops, Allen Hopwood, Market st
King's Arms, William Child, Market hill
Old Castle, John Douglas, Castle st
Plough, John Chapman, Radwinter
Plough, William Mason, Gt. Chesterford
Queen's Head, James Day, High st
Red Lion, James Parratt, Radwinter
Rose & Crown, William Woodall, Ashdon
Ship, Daniel Johns, Debden
White Hart, James Savill, Debden
White Horse, Thomas Shildrick, Great Chesterford
White Horse, Samuel Willett, Ashdon

TEA DEALERS.

Burrows Henry, Market place
Carnes William, Church st
Marshall John, Church st
Nott Mary Ann and Lydia, Butter market

TURNERS.

Smart Jonathan, High st
Unwin and Patient, Museum st

VETERINARY SURGEONS.

Bainbridge George, Church st
Rule James (and horse dealer) Bailey's lane

WATCH & CLOCK MAKERS.

Gatward Thomas, High st
Kent John (& silversmith & jeweller) High st

WHEELWRIGHTS.

Barrett John, Ashdon
Chapman John, Radwinter
Hagger Jeremiah, Great Chesterford
Hills Samuel, London road
Kent William, High st
Rushforth John, Debden
Rushforth Robert, Sewers end
Stackwood John, Littlebury
Swan James, Radwinter

WINE & SPIRIT MERCHANTS

Miller Jephtha, Market hill
Starling James, Church st

Miscellaneous.

Baines Henry, rope maker, Butter market
Brand Robert, grindery warehouse, Butter market
Chater William, nurseryman, Walden common
Debnam William, parish clerk, Great Chesterford
Emson John, brick maker, Radwinter
Frye John Thomas, professor of music, Church street
Gas Works, Thaxted road—R. W. Ward, superintendent, Commons end
Haylock Henry, farmer and brick maker, Ashdon
Horton Richard, land steward, Audley end
House of Correction, High street—Samuel Francis, keeper
Kent Joseph, clerk of the market and constable for the borough, Market st
Latten John, supervisor of excise, High st
Legerton Thomas, dealer in British wines, Church street
Low William, coach proprietor, High st
Mascall Robert, parish clerk, Radwinter
Monk James, parish clerk, Debden
Museum, Castle hill—Joshua Clarke, honorary curator, High st; Saml. Kent Barnes, sub-curator, Butter market
Poole Robt. basket maker, Butter market
Procter William, registrar of births and deaths, Queen street
Rider William, iron founder, Church st
Ruse William, parish clerk, Ashdon
Salmon William, parish clerk, Littlebury
Smart David, chair maker, Castle st
Smith Thomas, tanner, Horn lane
Spink John C. fishmonger, Butter market

MISCELLANEOUS—*Continued.*

Thurgood Robert Driver, superintendent registrar of marriages, and clerk to the board of guardians, High st

Union Workhouse, East st—George Birkmyre, governor; Ann Birkmyre, matron [common

Ward Richard W. stone mason, Walden

Warren Edward, parish clerk, Castle st

COACHES.

To LONDON, the *Walden*, from Low's house, High street, and the Rose and Crown, every Monday morning at a quarter past four, other mornings (Sunday excepted) at six—and the *Telegraph* (from Haverhill) calls at Tredgett's office, Hill street, and the Rose and Crown, every Monday, Wednesday and Friday morning at ten.

To HAVERHILL, the *Telegraph* (from London) calls at Tredgett's office, Hill st, and the Rose and Crown, every Tuesday, Thursday and Saturday afternoon at half-past three.

*** Other *Coaches* to and from LONDON, BURY, CAMBRIDGE, FAKENHAM, HOLT and NORWICH pass through Great Chesterford and Littlebury daily.

CARRIERS.

To LONDON, — Chalk, from the Cross Keys, every Monday, Wednesday and Friday; — Gore, every Tuesday and Friday; — Adams, from his house, Gold street, — Tilbrook, from the Greyhound, and — Trott, from the Sun, every Monday; — Parish, from his house, Gold st, every Tuesday; and — Cockerton, from the Greyhound, every Friday.

To CAMBRIDGE, — Claydon, from his house, Hill street, every Wednesday and Saturday morning.

To THAXTED, — Ragell, from Claydon's house, Hill street, every Saturday afternoon.

*** *Waggons* and *Vans* to and from LONDON, BRANDON, BURY, NEWMARKET, SWAFFHAM, THETFORD, WATTON, &c. pass through Great Chesterford and Littlebury daily.

ST. OSYTH AND BRIGHTLINGSEA.

ST. OSYTH (anciently called *Cice* or *Chich*) is an extensive parish and village, in the hundred of Tendring, 13 miles S.S.E. from Colchester. It derives its name from St. Osyth, daughter of Redwald, king of East Anglia, who, having made a vow of virginity, fixed upon this spot as her place of retirement, and founded a church and nunnery, which were afterwards plundered by the Danes, who murdered the founderess. In the beginning of the twelfth century, Belmeis, bishop of London, founded a priory for Augustine canons on the supposed site of the nunnery. The remains comprise a capacious court-yard, with a commanding Gothic porch entrance, on which are emblazoned the arms of its former possessors; the gateway having two towers or posterns, and to the east are three other towers, one of which is more lofty than the rest. Frederick Nassau, Esq. is the present possessor of this eminently interesting edifice. Upon a creek, or arm of the Colne, which divides into two branches, and are navigable for small craft, are wharfs. At the south-eastern extremity of the parish is a martello tower, erected for the defence of this part of the coast, and now used as a signal station. The church is large, and of the construction of former ages; it has a ring of six bells; and in the chancel are many monuments to the memory of the Lords D'Arcy and their wives. The living is a donative, in the gift of Frederick Nassau, esq.; the present incumbent is the Rev. Frederick Sterkey. The land about here is well suited to the business of the agriculturist, highly cultivated and very fertile; and its marsh grounds equally serviceable for grazing. The views are extensive, embracing pleasing sea-coast and inland scenery. The parish contained, in 1831, 1,583 inhabitants.

BRIGHTLINGSEA is a village and parish, in the same hundred as St. Osyth, about 4 miles N.W. from that village, and about 3 by water from Wivenhoe. The parish forms a peninsula, by means of the Colne on the west, and an arm or creek projecting from that river on the east. The oyster trade is carried on here to a great extent, giving employment to the chief part of the inhabitants. Brightlingsea is a member of the cinque-port town of Sandwich. Dorrien Magens, Esq. is the lord of the manor. The church, dedicated to All Saints, which stands about a mile and a half N. E. of the village, is a very fine old edifice, and the chancel contains a splendid monument to the memory of Lady Magens. The living is a discharged vicarage, in the patronage of the bishop of London; the Rev. William Latten is the present incumbent. There are two chapels for dissenters, and a free-school for the education of sixteen boys. A small pleasure fair is held here in July. Population of the parish, in 1831, 1,784.

POST OFFICE, ST. OSYTH.—Letters from LONDON arrive (from COLCHESTER) every Tuesday, Friday and Saturday morning at ten, and are despatched the same afternoons at two.

POST OFFICE, BRIGHTLINGSEA.—Letters from FRETING arrive (by foot post) every forenoon at eleven, and are despatched every morning at eight.

GENTRY AND CLERGY.

Latten Rev. William, Brightlingsea
Nassau Fred. esq. St. Osyth Priory
Sterkey Rev. Frederick, St. Osyth

ACADEMIES & SCHOOLS.

Burgess Ann, St. Osyth
Crampin Samuel, St. Osyth
Ling Ruth, St. Osyth
Lott John, Brightlingsea
Rudlin John, Brightlingsea
Slowgrove Mary, St. Osyth
Woodman Woodville (and librarian) Brightlingsea

BAKERS.

Bagley William, Brightlingsea
Carter William, St. Osyth
Coppin Samuel, Brightlingsea
Jessemen John, Brightlingsea
Jessup Thomas, Brightlingsea
Riches Nathaniel, Brightlingsea
Tranham Thomas, Brightlingsea

BLACKSMITHS.

Hanby John, St. Osyth
Hubbard John, Brightlingsea
Minter William, Brightlingsea
Wells Jonathan, St. Osyth

BOOT & SHOE MAKERS.

Clarey William, Brightlingsea
Coppin James, Brightlingsea
Dunnett William, St. Osyth
Glendining James, St. Osyth
Riches Thomas, Brightlingsea
Sealey John, St. Osyth
Sharp James, Brightlingsea
Vince William, Brightlingsea
Waltham Samuel, St. Osyth

BUTCHERS.

Bond James, Brightlingsea
Gardener George, St. Osyth
Nicholson Isaac, St. Osyth
Norman James, St. Osyth

CARPENTERS & BUILDERS.

Demaid James, St. Osyth
Whatsham James, St. Osyth

COAL & CORN MERCHANTS.

Pilbrow Thomas, St. Osyth
Thompson Peter, St. Osyth

GROCERS & DRAPERS.

Brooks William, Brightlingsea
Bryant John, Brightlingsea
Dunnerton John, Brightlingsea
Forster Ebenezer, Brightlingsea
Griggs Hazel, Brightlingsea
Lilly James, St. Osyth
March George, Brightlingsea
Newcombe Robt. & Jas. St. Osyth
Ormes John, Brightlingsea
Sealey John, St. Osyth
Wilson John and Son, St. Osyth

MALTSTERS.

Blomfield Robt. (& brewer) St. Osyth
Thompson Peter, St. Osyth
Tracy Thomas, Brightlingsea

MILLERS.

Dean James, St. Osyth
Mayhew Mark, St. Osyth
Ransom G. D. Brightlingsea

OYSTER MERCHANTS,
AT BRIGHTLINGSEA.

Ames Abraham
Barnes John
Brastead William
Everitt John Burgess
Francis William
Griggs Hazell
How James
Jeffries Thomas John
Jolly William
Martin Samuel
Maskell William
Noble John
Root John
Salmon Joseph
Stammers John
Tranham John
Woolvett Joseph
Woolvett Saml.

PAINTERS, PLUMBERS AND GLAZIERS.

Jay George and Jacob, St. Osyth
Rand John, Brightlinsea

SADDLERS.

Blowers Edward, St. Osyth
Salmon Thomas, St. Osyth

SAIL MAKERS.

Sadler Thomas, Brightlingsea
Went John, Brightlingsea

SHIP OWNERS.

Pilbrow Thomas, St. Osyth
Summerson Thomas, Brightlingsea

SURGEONS.

Fletcher Moses, Brightlingsea
Linton William, St. Osyth
Scarnell Samuel Finch, St. Osyth

TAILORS & DRAPERS.

Carter Abraham, St. Osyth
Dunnett James, St. Osyth
Ormes John, Brightlingsea
Ormes William, Brightlingsea
Wade S. Brightlingsea

TAVERNS & PUBLIC HOUSES.

Anchor, James Harrington, Brightlingsea
Flag, Thomas Carey, St. Osyth
King's Arms, Ann Last, St. Osyth
King's Head, Wm. Francis, Brightlingsea
Red Lion Inn, James Norman, St. Osyth
Ship, William Allatson, Brightlingsea
Ship Inn, Martin Cook, St. Osyth

Swan, John Thos. Harmer, Brightlingsea
Wellington, Thomas Jessup, Brightlingsea
White Hart, Samuel Beach, St. Osyth
White Lion, George Griggs, Brightlingsea

Miscellaneous.

Allatson William, watch and clock maker, Brightlingsea
Barber James, hair-dresser, Brightlingsea
Chaplin James, shopkeeper, St. Osyth
Coe William, shopkeeper, St. Osyth
Cook James, nursery & seedsman, St. Osyth
Co-operative Society for the Sale of Provisions, Draperies, &c.—George March, actuary, Brightlingsea
Cowell John, bricklayer, St. Osyth
Floughgrove William and John, wheelwrights, St. Osyth
Gilders William, shopkeeper, St. Osyth
Glendinning Jas. tinplate-workr, St. Osyth
Nevill Thos. parish clerk, Brightlingsea
Noble John, cowkeeper and dairyman, Brightlingsea
Page Joseph, bricklayer, St. Osyth
Rudlin Henry H. tea-dealer, Brightlingsea
Stammers John, jun. smack-owner, Brightlingsea
Wilson John, agent to the Phœnix fire-office, St. Osyth

CARRIERS.

FROM BRIGHTLINGSEA.

To COLCHESTER, John Cook & Geo. Day, daily, and Nathaniel Littlewood, every Monday, Wednesday, and Friday.

SOUTHEND AND PRITTLEWELL,

WITH THE VILLAGES OF SOUTHCHURCH, NORTH AND SOUTH SHOEBURY, LEIGH AND NEIGHBOURHOODS.

SOUTHEND is a modern and genteel little watering place and hamlet in the parish of Prittlewell, 42 miles east from London and four south from Rochford—situated on the acclivity of a well-wooded hill, near the sea; the air is esteemed dry and salubrious, and the water, notwithstanding its mixture with the Thames, preserves its clear and saline qualities. For a considerable time back it has acquired a great portion of celebrity as a bathing place, and in the summer months is much frequented by the inhabitants of the metropolis on account of its delightful situation. There are now a large number of lodging-houses, most of them erected in a very superior style; and the terrace which receives the name of New Southend, is a handsome pile, commanding an extensive view of the river Thames and the coast of Kent, including the Nore, &c. There are also baths, libraries, an elegant hotel, assembly-rooms and a small theatre, which, together with the walks and rides in the vicinage, contribute to the relaxation and enjoyment of its many respectable visitants. There is a place of worship for independents, and a chapel of ease under Prittlewell is about to be erected.

PRITTLEWELL is a charming village, and with Milton forms a parish in the hundred of Rochford—situated between that town and Southend, three miles from the former and one and a half from the latter. The village is neatly built, and has a good church, dedicated to St. Mary, with a handsome tower containing six sweet-toned bells; the benefice is a vicarage, in the patronage of the bishop of London. The free school here was endowed in 1727, for instructing sixteen boys in reading, writing and arithmetic. The country around is fertile and pleasant, the inhabitants being chiefly devoted to agriculture. A fair for toys, &c. is held on the 15th of July. The population of the whole parish, Southend included, in 1831, amounted to 2,266 persons.

About one mile from Southend and four from Rochford is SOUTHCHURCH, a small village and parish. The parish is bounded on the south by the Thames, where are considerable oyster-beds. The village contains the church, a neat edifice with a spire; the living is a rectory, in the incumbency of the Rev. Charles Chisolm. The inhabitants, mostly agriculturists, amount to 401.

NORTH and SOUTH SHOEBURY (the Saxon *Schoebirig)* are two villages and parishes—the former about three miles, and the latter about two and a half from Southend. The remains of considerable Danish fortifications or entrenchments are visible in these parishes, and several antique urns, apparently Roman, have been dug or ploughed up. Government has here a preventive station, and on Shoebury Ness stands a signal station. The mansion now occupied by Christopher Parsons, Esq. was formerly an occasional residence of the late Princess Charlotte of Wales. Each parish has its church, both of which are ancient structures. The population of North Shoebury, in 1831, amounted to 226, and that of South Shoebury to 202—the latter having precisely doubled its number within the preceding thirty years.

LEIGH is an ancient village and parish in the hundred of Rochford, four miles west from Southend. The parish borders upon the Thames, and includes an island called Leigh Marsh, with the east end of Canvey Island, where there is a prolific oyster creek. The principal occupation of the inhabitants is oyster dredging and the collection of shrimps, from nine hundred to a thousand gallons of the latter being sent from hence weekly to the London markets. The residents are supplied with water from three excellent springs. The boundary-stone marking the jurisdiction of the lord mayor of London, as conservator of the river Thames, is about a mile and a half to the eastward of this village, on a stone bank a little below high-water mark, and is annually visited in form by the lord mayor and corporation. There is a small custom-house at Leigh. The church, dedicated to St. Clement, stands upon an eminence, and, being covered with ivy, presents a venerable and pleasing appearance: the benefice is a rectory, in the presentation of the bishop of London; the present incumbent is the Rev. Robert Eden, who has erected a very handsome residence, in the most approved English style of architecture. There are three schools here, for boys, girls and infants, supported by the beneficence of the Hon. Lady Sparrow. The parish contained, in 1831, 1,254 inhabitants.

POST OFFICE, SOUTHEND, Thomas Thorn, *Post Master.*—Letters from INGATESTONE arrive (by mail cart) every morning at a quarter before seven, and are despatched every evening (Sunday excepted) at a quarter before six—on Sunday they are despatched one hour earlier.

POST OFFICE, PRITTLEWELL, Thomas Bell, *Post Master.*—Letters from INGATESTONE arrive (by mail cart) every morning at half-past six, and are despatched every evening (Sunday excepted) at six—on Sunday they are despatched one hour earlier.

NOBILITY, GENTRY AND CLERGY.

Allen Stephen, esq. Chalkwill hall, Prittlewell
Arnold Mr. John, Prittlewell
Barnes Mr. Anthony, Southend
Bazeley Mrs. Agnes, Southend
Benton Saml. esq. North Shoebury
Carr Mr. Thomas, Prittlewell
Chisolm Rev. Chas. (dean of Rochford hundred & magistrate) Southchurch
Cole Mrs. Sarah, Southend
Copps Mrs. —, Southend
Cummings Rev. Jos. E. North Shoebury
Curlewis Lieut. —, R.N. South Shoebry
Daines Mr. John, Southchurch
Dines Mr. John, Southchurch
Eden Rev. Robert, Leigh
Festing Capt. B. Morton, R.N. Southnd
Fletcher Rev. Richard, Southend
Foley Mrs. General, Southend
Gilson John, esq. Southend
Heard Mrs. —, Prittlewell
Heygate Miss —, Southend
Heygate James, esq. Southend
Heygate Sir Wm. bart. Southend
Hickinbotham Mr. Jos. South Shoeby
Hills Mr. George, Southend
Hills Mr. Joseph, Southend
Hudson Thomas Beaumont, esq. Southend
Kilworth Mr. Edward, Southchurch
Kilworth Mr. Thomas, Southchurch
King Lieut. —, R.N. South Shoebury
King Wm. Hy. esq. South Shoebury
Lacell Mr. John, Southchurch
Lacell Mrs. Sarah, Southend
Lamprell Mr. Edw. Leigh
Leroux Mr. Medford Geo. M.D. Southchrch
Lewis Mrs. Sarah, Southend
Lewsley Mr. Samuel, Southend
Linggood Mrs. Ann, Southend
Napping Mr. Christr. Dale, South Shoebury hall
Nolan Rev. Doctor Frederick, Prittlewell
O'Reilly John, esq. Milton Halmet, Prittlewell
Parsons Christopher, esq. Lawn, Southchurch
Parsons Edward, esq. Southend
Parsons Mrs. —, North Shoebury
Patterson Capt. John, Pier, Southend
Pissey Mr. John, Southchurch wick
Poynter Saml. esq. North Shoebury
Robinson Mrs. —, Southend
Robjent Mr. James, North Shoebury
Scallon Capt. Robt. R. N. Prittlewell
Scratton Jno. esq. Priory, Prittlewell
Scratton John Bayntun, esq. Milton hall, Prittlewell
Scratton Robert, esq. Southend
Shairpe Lady, Southend
Shaw Samuel, esq. Southend

NOBILITY, GENTRY AND CLERGY—*Continued.*

Silva Emanuel, esq. Southend
Silversides Mr. William, Southend
Stallibras Frederick, esq. Southchurch hall
Strutt Major General William Goodday, Tofts Danbury and Southend
Swaine Mr. William (attorney) Milton Hamlet, Prittlewell
Sylvester Mrs. Margaret, Southend
Tabor James, esq. Earl's hall, Prittlewell
Taylor Edmund, esq. Southend
Vanderzee George, esq. South Shoebury cottage
Wade Mrs. Lydia, Prittlewell
Watts Mr. Samuel, South Shoebury
White Rev. Andrew, Southend
Wright George, esq. Southend
Wright Romley, esq. Southend
Yorke Rev. Philip Wyne, South Shoebury

ACADEMIES AND SCHOOLS.

Boosey Miss (day), Prittlewell
FREE SCHOOL, Prittlewell—Thomas Hussey, master
LADY SPARROW'S SCHOOLS (for boys, girls and infants), Leigh—John Drewett, master; E. Chatteries, mistress, and Miss Theobald, mistress of infant's school
Laver Mary Eliza (boarding & day), Southend
Middleton Ann, Prittlewell
Walker Mrs. Maria (boarding and day), Southend
Walker William Henry (boarding & day), Belle vue house, Southend

BAKERS.

Barber Charles (and confectioner), Southend
Barnard George, Leigh
Bragg Thomas, Prittlewell
Browning Thomas, Southend
Dawson William, Prittlewell
Garrard Alfred Lucas, Prittlewell
Gillson John, Leigh
Lovitt John, Southend
Million Henry, Southend
Price Mary, Prittlewell
Price Peter, Prittlewell
Pritchard Joseph, Southend
Salmon John, Prittlewell
Surridge Henry, Leigh
Surridge John, Leigh
Thompson John Bayley, Leigh

BLACKSMITHS.

Alp James, North Shoebury
Bradley John, Southend
Chapman Edward, Leigh
Clark Francis, Southchurch
Gibbs James, Southend
Joscelyne William, Leigh
Lindsell Thomas (and wheelwright) Prittlewell
Whittingham Joseph, Prittlewell

BOAT AND BARGE OWNERS.

Ingram Thomas, Southend
Martin Mark, Leigh

BOAT BUILDERS.

Bandock Thomas, Leigh
Cadman Joseph, Southend
Maddams Edward, Southend
Peters and Daniels, Southend

BOOKSELLERS, STATIONERS AND LIBRARIANS.

Bragg George, Prittlewell
Tarry Ann (and perfumer) Southend

BOOT & SHOE MAKERS.

Bedwell John, Southend
Clay Stephen, Prittlewell
Deer Joseph, Prittlewell
Deer William, Southend
Dowsett Christopher, Southend
Dowsett Henry, Prittlewell
Garrard Edward, Prittlewell
Gray William, Prittlewell
Havers John, Southend
Page Benjamin, Leigh
Partridge Thomas, Leigh
Robinson John, Leigh
Willison John, Leigh

BREWERS.

Lazarus, Meyer and Co. Southend

BRICKLAYERS.

Gusterson William, Prittlewell
Unwin Henry William, Prittlewell

BUTCHERS.

Francis George, Prittlewell
Hart William, Prittlewell
Hay Arthur, Leigh
Osborne Joseph, Leigh
Perkins William, Southend
Surridge Abraham, Leigh
Surridge John, Leigh
Thorn Thomas, Southend
Turmidge Thomas, Leigh

CARPENTERS.

Bell Giles, Prittlewell
Bragg Samuel, Prittlewell
Bragg William, Prittlewell
Coolbear James, Southend
Scott Jas. (& timber merchnt) Southend

COAL MERCHANTS.

Bragg Thomas, Prittlewell
Million Henry (& corn dealer) Southend
Pritchard Joseph, Southend

FIRE, &c. OFFICE AGENTS.

PHŒNIX, William Henry Walker, Southend
ROYAL EXCHANGE, Thomas Thorn, Southend

GROCERS AND TEA DEALERS

(See also Shopkeepers, &c.)
Marked thus * are also Drapers.

Bell Giles, Prittlewell
*Bell Isaac, Prittlewell
Bragg George, Prittlewell
Carter Thomas, Prittlewell
Clark Thomas, Southend
*Fox William, Southend
*James Lewis, Leigh
*Le' Grys William, Leigh
*Livermore Catherine, Prittlewell

HAIR DRESSERS.

Barnes Thomas Knight, Leigh
Dowsett John, Prittlewell
Whitfield Henry, Southend

HOUSE AGENTS.

Thorn Thomas, Southend
Walker William Henry, Southend

INNS, HOTELS & PUBLIC HOUSES.

Bell, John Joscelyne, Leigh
Blue Boar Inn, Mary Whale, Prittlewell
Castle Inn, John Blakely, Southend
Crooked Billet, Henry Frost, Leigh
Hope Inn (commercial and posting) Susan Brasier, Southend
King's Head, William Foster, Leigh
King's Head, Charlotte Saunders, Prittlewell
Peter Boat, Arthur Hay, Leigh
Royal Hotel (posting house & billiard rooms) Henry Choules, Southend
Ship Hotel (commercial & posting) Charles Woosnam, Southend
Ship Inn, Samuel Bridge, Leigh
Smack, Samuel Fairchild, Leigh
Spread Eagle, Evan Hart, Prittlewell
White Horse, Jos. Webb, Southchurch

MILLERS.

Tabor and Rankin, Prittlewell
Watson James, Prittlewell

MILLINERS & DRESS MAKERS

Garrard Sophia, Prittlewell
Jemson Catherine, Southend

PLUMBERS, PAINTERS & GLAZIERS.

Garon John, Prittlewell
Morton William, Southend

POULTERERS.

Culham James, Southend
Dixson George, Southend

RECTIFIERS.

Lazarus, Meyer & Co. Leigh

SADDLERS AND HARNESS MAKERS.

Bell Thomas, Prittlewell
Goodman John, Prittlewell

SHOPKEEPERS & DEALRS IN GROCERIES & SUNDRIES.

Chapman Edward, Leigh
Lamb Charles, Leigh
Little William, Leigh
Pavitt George, Leigh
Robjent Samuel, North Shoebury
Smith Alfred, Southend
Staff George, Southend
Surridge John, Leigh
Thompson John Bayley, Leigh
Walker Samuel, Southend
Weidner Elizabeth, Southend

STRAW HAT MAKERS.

Garrard Sophia, Prittlewell
Jemson Catherine, Southend
Salmon Eliza, Prittlewell
Way M. and A. Southend

SURGEONS.

Bradley Nathaniel, Leigh
Sheehy Michael, Southend
Sopwith Henry, Southend & Prittlewell

TAILORS.

Glass James, Southend
Stoker John, Southend
Stoker William, Prittlewell

Miscellaneous.

BATHS (warm), Ship Hotel, Southend—Charles Woosnam, proprietor
Bell Stephen Asser, private tutor, South Shoebury
CUSTOM HOUSE, Leigh—William Henry King, collector, tide surveyor and coast waiter
Garon William, currier, Prittlewell
Graffe George, linen draper, Southend
Hussey Thomas, parish clerk, Prittlewell
Kernot William & Co. chymists & druggists, Southend
Lewin Benjamin, hosier & glover, Prittlewell
Montague David, cement manufacturer, potter, & brick maker, Leigh
Mountain John, coach proprietor, Southend
Price William, nursery and seedsman, Southend
Ray Charles, fruiterer & curiosity dealer, Southend
Sheehy Michael, registrar of births and deaths, Southend
Steward Henry, clothes dealer, Leigh
Trower William, watch & clock maker, Prittlewell
Wilder John, cow keeper, Southend

COACHES.

To LONDON, the *Despatch*, from the Ship Hotel, every morning (Sunday excepted) at a quarter before eight; goes through Prittlewell, Rochford, Rayleigh, Billericay, &c.

VAN.

To LONDON, Joseph Pease's *Van*, from the Hope, every Thursday morning at seven, and Saturday evening at seven; goes thro' Prittlewell, Rochford, Rayleigh, Billericay, &c.

CONVEYANCE BY WATER.

To LONDON, *Steam Packets*, during the season, daily (Sunday excepted), and George & James Vanderword's *Sailing Vessels*, every Saturday.

STRATFORD, WEST HAM, PLAISTOW
AND NEIGHBOURHOODS.

STRATFORD, or STRATFORD LANGTHORNE, is a populous hamlet and ward in the parish of West Ham and hundred of Becontree, about three miles from Whitechapel church, London. The river Lea separates this county from Middlesex, but the communication is maintained by means of Bow-bridge: on the Lea are extensive flour-mills, and many manufacturing establishments, silk and calico print-works, breweries, distilleries, chymical works, &c., some of which are upon a very extensive scale. Stratford has of late years been greatly improved, and its general appearance materially heightened by the new church, an admirable Gothic structure, situated in the Broadway. There are places of worship for independents, Wesleyan methodists and Roman catholics. In the parish of West Ham are several schools for gratuitous education: the revenue of one of these (for the parish generally) amounts to upwards of £3,000., derived from benefactions; and another, founded by Mrs. Bonnell in 1761, is likewise well endowed. There are also some alms-houses. An abbey for monks of the Cistertian order was founded at Stratford in 1135, and richly endowed, by William de Montfichet; the ruins still preserved (contiguous to the church) comprise a brick gateway and an ornamented arch. The land here is extremely fertile, well wooded, and the scenery pleasing; great numbers of the inhabitants are engaged in agriculture, which the vicinity of Stratford to the metropolis renders a profitable pursuit. (Population returned with the parish.)

About four miles from London is the village of WEST HAM, in the populous parish of its name, which is divided into four wards, respectively denominated All Saints, Church Street, Plaistow and Stratford. It is favoured by being the residence of numerous opulent and respectable families, some of whom have very handsome mansions; and in the neighbourhood are several tasteful seats. A market, for which a charter was obtained by Richard de Montfichet (a descendant of William) in 1253, has long been discontinued; but the resumption of the right would be of great advantage to the parish and adjoining district. All Saints, the parochial church, is a spacious edifice, with a tower at its west end seventy-four feet high; and its general appearance is indicative of great antiquity. In the church-yard are interred the remains of George Edwards, Esq., whose acquirements in natural history were highly estimated. There are some fine monuments in the church, to the memory of several literary and civil characters; and a curious Gothic tomb in the wall. The celebrated and unfortunate Dr. Dodd was a resident and lecturer of this parish. The living of West Ham is a vicarage, in the patronage of the crown; the Venerable Archdeacon Jones is the present incumbent. The population of the parish, in 1831, amounted to 11,580.

The village of PLAISTOW is four miles and a half from London, and is so intimately connected with the places before described as to require but brief notice. A very handsome chapel of ease, in the Gothic style, was completed in 1830, at an expense of £4,800., of which sum the parliamentary commissioners contributed £2,300. The independents and Wesleyan methodists have their respective places of worship; and there is a well endowed school, named after the liberal benefactor, Mr. Oliver. The living of Plaistow is a district incumbency, in the presentation of the vicar of West Ham. The population is returned with the parish.

POST OFFICE, Broadway, STRATFORD, John Gibson, *Post Master.*—Letters from LONDON arrive (by the Norwich mail) every night at half-past eight, and (by the twopenny post) every day at twelve noon, at three afternoon, and evening at six, and are despatched every morning at half-past nine, afternoon at one and half-past four and night at half-past eight.

POST OFFICE, Church street, WEST HAM, James Coles, *Post Master.*—Letters from LONDON arrive every morning at eight, noon at half-past twelve and evening at six, and are despatched every morning at a quarter past nine, and afternoon at half-past one and half-past four.

POST OFFICE, PLAISTOW, Hannah Eames, *Post Mistress.*—Letters from LONDON arrive every morning at half-past eight, afternoon at one and evening at half-past six, and are despatched every morning at nine, and afternoon at one and four.

*** *The names are in* STRATFORD *when the village is not mentioned.*

GENTRY AND CLERGY.

Allcard Mr. John, Stratford green
Anderson Mrs. Elizabeth, Plaistow
Anderson Mr. Jas. F. Stratford green
Archer Mr. John, Stratford grove
Austin Mr. William, Stratford green
Baker —, esq. West Ham abbey
Banneytyre Rev. Charles, West Ham
Batger Mr. John, Stratford green
Beale Mrs. Plaistow
Bell Mrs. —, Catherine, Plaistow
Bell Mr. Luke, Plaistow
Bernard Mr. John, Plaistow
Blood Mr. Thomas, Plaistow
Bond Mrs. Sarah, Plaistow
Bosanquet Rev. Edw. Stanley, Plaistow
Brady Mr. Antonio, Stratford green
Bristow Capt. Henry, Stratford green
Brookes Mr. John, Stratford green
Brown Mr. Thomas, Upton place
Brushfield Mr. Benjamin, Plaistow
Buck Mr. Frederick, West Ham
Burgh Mr. James, Stratford green
Buxton —, esq. Upton
Campbell Mrs. West Ham
Carter Mrs. Alice, Upton place
Catterton Mr. Wm. M. Upton place
Cheape Mr. Henry, Stratford green
Clarke Mrs. Harriet, Plaistow
Clarke Mr. William G. Plaistow
Cohn Mrs. Jane, 3 Surinam terrace
Cohn Mr. John, 3 Surinam terrace
Cooke Mr. Thomas, West Ham
Cort Mr. Conningsby, Stratford green
Court Miss Lucy, Stratford grove
Court Miss Mary Ann, Stratford grove
Crawley Mr. Alfred, Plaistow
Cresswell Rev. William, Broadway
Curtis Charles, esq. Plaistow
Delaway Mrs. Mary, 9 Vicarage terr
Dodds Mrs. Jane, West Ham lane
Drane Mr. John, Upton place
Driver Mr. Samuel, Plaistow
Eaton Mrs. Susannah, Stratford green
Edwards Mr. Geo. Maryland point
Emblem Rev. John, West Ham lane
Ferdinando Mr. Thomas, West Ham
Fowler Mr. William, West Ham
Fox Mr. Henry, Plaistow
Franks Mr. William, Stratford green
Fry Joseph, esq. Upton
Gowar Mr. Raydin, 2 Surinam terr
Gray Mr. John, Stratford grove
Greenwood Mrs. Rebecca, 17 Upton pl
Gregory Mr. Jno. S. 7 Essex bldngs.
Griffin Mr. Daniel, West Ham
Griffiths Mrs. West Ham
Gunson Mr. Henry, West Ham
Gurney Samuel, esq. Upton
Haden Mr. George, Upton place
Hamilton Mr. Stratford grove
Harris Capt. Alex. Stratford green
Harris Mr. James, Stratford green
Harrison Mr. Phinney, Plaistow
Hasluck Mr. Samuel, Stratford green
Higden Mrs. Mary, Magdalene point
Hinchcliff Mr. Chamberlain, Stratford grove
Hirons Mrs. Sarah, Maryland point
Hitchen Mr. Thomas, Stratford green
Holden Mrs. Anne, High st
Homer Mr. Thomas, 25 Upton place
Honey Mrs. Maria, 8 Vicarage terrace
Hubbard Mr. John, Stratford grove
Hudson Mrs. 26 Upton place
Huthwaite Mr. Stoken, Stratford grn
Ireland Mr. Thomas, Plaistow
Jefferies Mr. William, West Ham
Jenkins Mr. John, Plaistow
Jeremy Mr. Alfred, Stratford grove
Jones the Venerable Archdeacon, Stratford green
Joyce Mr. Thomas, Plaistow
Kilner Miss Eliza, Maryland point
Kilner Miss Francis, Maryland point
Knowles Mr. John, Stratford grove
Lack Mrs. Elizabeth, Plaistow
Lart Mr. John, Stratford green
Legg Mr. Jabez, Stratford green
Leicester Joseph, esq. Upton
Lennox Mr. Thomas, Plaistow
Leshey Mr. William, West Ham
Ligins Mr. John Wheatley, Plaistow
Liverton Mr. Thomas, West Ham
Lulman Mr. Thomas, Upton place
Lunn Mr. Thomas, West Ham
Manby Mr. Wm. Stratford grove
Marsh Mr. Samuel, Stratford green
Marshall Miss, West Ham
Marten Mr. Charles, Plaistow
Martin Mr. James, Plaistow
Martin Robt. Humphreys, esq. Plaistow
Masterman Mr. John, Plaistow
Miller Capt. George, 5 Vicarage terr
Moates Mr. William, Stratford grove

GENTRY AND CLERGY—*Contd.*

Morgan Mr. Daniel, Stratford green
Mount Mrs. Jane, 1 Vicarage terrace
Mundy Mr. Jno. Church st, West Ham
Nockells Mr. William, Print ground
Nutt Mr. David, Stratford green
Oliver Mr. Thomas, Broadway
Parker Mrs. Judith, Broadway
Pealler Mr. Samuel, Stratford green
Pedley Mr. Joseph, Broadway
Pelly John Henry, esq. Upton
Perry Mr. Richard Samuel
Pooght Mr. George, West Ham abbey
Raws Mr. Richard, Stratford grove
Renn Mrs. —, West Ham
Robinson Mr. Alfred, Plaistow
Robinson Mr. Jon. Stratford grove
Rogers Mrs. Rebecca, West Ham
Schode Mr. —, Plaistow
Seale Mr. Joshua, Plaistow
Seale the Misses, Plaistow
Sewell Mr. Thomas, Plaistow
Shaw Mr. Thomas, West Ham lane
Sheppard John, esq. Upton
Sheppard Mrs. Sarah, Plaistow
Smith Mrs. Mary, Maryland point
Somes Mrs. Sarah, Stratford green
Spenser Mr. James, Plaistow
Spooner Mr. John, Plaistow
Taylor Mr. John, Stratford green
Taylor Mr. Samuel, Stratford green
Tebb Mr. Richard, West Ham
Temple Rev. William, Plaistow
Thompson Mrs. Stratford green
Thompson Captain, Plaistow
Train Mrs. Frances, Maryland point
Tucker John, esq. West Ham abbey
Tuit Captain James, 15 Upton place
Turner Mr. George, Plaistow
Tweedle Mr. Jacob, Plaistow
Wainhouse Miss, Plaistow
Walmsley Mr. Stratford green
Ward Mrs. Anne, Plaistow
Warmington Mr. John, Plaistow
Warren Mr. Robert, 3 Vicarage terr
Watts Mrs. Anne, Plaistow
Webb Mr. James, Plaistow
Webster Mr. James, West Ham
Westlake Mr. John, Plaistow
Whalley Mr. Robt. 10 Vicarage terr
Wilkins Mr. Thomas, 18 Upton place
Wilson Mr. George, Stratford green
Wilton Mr. Henry, Plaistow
Wilton Mr. John, 4 Vicarage terrace
Wood Mrs. Sarah, Maryland point
Woodward Rev. John, Carnarvon hall
Woollett Mr. Joseph, West Ham lane

ACADEMIES AND SCHOOLS.

Not otherwise described are Day Schools.

Ashby Charles, West Ham lane
Ault Henry (brding.) 8 Upton place
Baker Elizabeth, Channel Sea terrace
Berryman Sarah, High st
BONNELL'S CHARITY SCHOOL (girls) West Ham—Elizabeth Miles
BRITISH AND FOREIGN SCHOOL SOCIETY, Plaistow—Anne Raynor, mistress
BRITISH SCHOOL (boys) Little North st—Matthew Cape Witty, master
Carpenter Thomas (boarding & day) West Ham
CHARITY SCHOOL (girls) West Ham—Sarah Blackburn, mistress
Cooper Mary and Eliza (boarding) Stratford grove
Coppell Eliza, High st
Farrow Harriet, Angel lane
Ferguson Elizabeth (boarding & day) Upton place
Freeman John (boarding) High st
Gibbs Elizabeth (boarding) 6 Vicarage terrace
GRAMMAR SCHOOL, Broadway—Rev. W. Cresswell, master
Herden John William (boarding) Maryland point
Hunter Sarah Jane (brdg.) Stratford green
INFANTS' SCHOOL (Gurney's) Plaistow—Harriet Harper, mistress
INFANTS' SCHOOL, Marsh—Caroline Hodierne, mistress
INFANTS' SCHOOL, West Ham—Mary Anne Hodierne, mistress
Jones Misses (brdng) Maryland point
Mason Mrs. E. Plaistow
Miller Mary and Elizabeth, 3 Upton place
NATIONAL SCHOOL (boys and girls) Stratford—Joseph Usher, master; Miss Lancaster, mistress
NATIONAL SCHOOL (boys) West Ham—Geo. Henry Lovegrove, master
Perry Sarah, Chapel st
Philp Elizabeth (brdng.) West Ham
Scrivener Anne Mitchell (boarding) 9 Upton place
Strange Stephen, Fisher's yard
Taylor Sarah, Stratford grove
Todd Robert, Plaistow
Tovey Rebecca, High st
White Sarah Anne (brdg.) Stratford hall
Woodcock Anne, Maryland point
Woodcock Sarah Anne and Eliza (boarding) Stratford green

ATTORNEYS.

Dacre George, Stratford green
Hilleary Robert G. A. and G. E. Broadway
Martin George, West Ham
Otway and Allen (and solicitors for the Thames & Oxford Steam Tow Company) Stratford grove, and 10 Austin friars, *London*
Taylor James, 3 Clement's terr, West Ham

AUCTIONEERS & APPRAISRS

Asals James, Broadway
Deane William H. (& estate agent) 6 Surinam terrace
White John, West Ham

BAKERS.

Bullock Thomas, Waterworks row
Champion Henry, West Ham
Clark William, High st
Dare Philip, High st
Dee William, Broadway
Dow James, High st
Fireash John, High st
Frost Giles, Church st, West Ham
Gentry John, Broadway
Heighton William, High st
Lambrith Edward, Plaistow
M'Cash William, Broadway
Mackness Robert, High st
Mayhew Philip, Plaistow
Noad John, High st
Noble Thomas, Prospect place, West Ham
Pain Oliver, Broadway
Raynor William, Plaistow
Rowley Jonas, West Ham
Stubbs Richard, Maryland point
Surry Timothy, Plaistow

BASKET MAKERS.

Bayley John, High st
Burton John, Broadway
Mackay Thomas, Plaistow

BOOKSELLERS & STATIONRS.

Crick Susanh. (& library) Broadway
Morris Septimus (& library) Broadwy
Rogers Richard, Broadway
Showell Jas. (and stamp distributer) Broadway
Vandrant Charles (and stamp distributer) Langthorne place

BOOT AND SHOE MAKERS.

Abbott John, West Ham
Allen James, High st
Ball John, High st
Bibbing James, West Ham
Bush John, Stratford green
Craddock William, Broadway
Creighton Edwd. John, West Ham
Debney James, Maryland point
Eapps John, West Ham lane
Gallifent Pool, Plaistow
Gower Reuben, High st
Grainger John, New st
Greenwood Joseph, High st
Griffiths William, Angel lane
Hillman Joseph, High st
Holbrook William, Chapel place
Hollorn William, High st
Honey John, High st
Hudson Henry, West Ham
Hull John, Plaistow
Jones Thos. Allen's buildings, Broadway
Lamplugh John, High st
Lushey John, Prospect place, West Ham
Murray Jas. Chapel place, West Ham
Norris John, West Ham abbey
Palser John, Bridge place
Pigrome Jeremiah & Edmund, Plaistow
Porter Wm. Prospect pl. West Ham
Presland John, Broadway
Reynolds Jeremiah, High st
Sadler Henry, Broadway
Scearfe William, Maryland point
Short John, High st
Skinner William, High st
Smart James, West Ham lane
Stracey George, West Ham
Thompson Philip, Waterworks row
Twigg Adam, Broadway
Williams John, Waterworks row
Wright William, High st

BRAZIERS AND TIN-PLATE WORKERS.

Fletcher Frederick, Broadway
Little Burgess, Broadway
Miles William, Broadway
Page George, Broadway

BREWERS.

Gray & Dacre (and maltsters) West Ham lane
Jennings Richard, Plaistow
Woodman Wm. Lake, Angel lane

BRICKLAYRS & PLASTERERS

Cocks James, Plaistow
Heath William, High st
Hopkins Henry, High st
Hopkins William, Broadway
Kemplay David, High st
Smith Charles, West Ham
Wright Musgrave Fitch, Chapel st

BUILDERS.

Bantock John, Broadway
Curtis and Son, Broadway, and at Barking and West Ham
Fisher John H. and Son, High st
Fisher John Holwill, Plaistow
Rivett Jas. Chapel st, & at West Ham
Woodcock John, High st

BUTCHERS.

Bright Edward, Plaistow
Butcher Robert, High st
Ferguson William, Chapel st
Gee Joseph, Broadway
Gee William, Broadway
Gibling William, West Ham
Herbert William, Waterworks row
Hurley Abraham, High st
Lowe Thomas, East st
May Abraham, Broadway
Mee Samuel, Waterworks row
Pipe John, Prospect pl. West Ham
Robinson William, Broadway
Shipston Francis, Broadway
Vause Robert, Plaistow

CABINET MAKERS AND UPHOLSTERERS.

Hawkins John, Broadway
Maddison Charles, Broadway
Martin Frederick, Stratford grove

CARPENTRS & UNDERTAKRS
Bantock John, Broadway
Dalby James, West Ham
Devenish John, Plaistow
Dowsett —, Plaistow
Dyer John, West Ham [West Ham
Dyer Thos. (& turner) Prospect place,
Fisher John H. and Son, High st
Gosling John, Waterworks row
Mitchell James, High st [Ham
Rivett James, Chapel st & at West
Tovey John, High st
Turner Richard, Plaistow
Underwood William, East st
Wenham William, High st

CHEESEMONGERS
(See also Grocers and Tea Dealers.)
Avery Thomas, High st
Barnard James, Broadway
Batley Joseph, High st
Hudson Anthony, High st
Moore Thomas, Broadway
Prime Benjamin, Broadway
Rowlay John, Broadway
Wilson Henry and Co. Broadway

CHINA, GLASS, &c. DEALERS.
Churchland Edward, Broadway
Hatherill Elizabeth, Broadway
Maguire William, Broadway
Newton William, High st

CHYMISTS AND DRUGGISTS.
Huxley John Holden (operative and dispensing) High st
Kennedy Angus, Broadway
Moss Joseph, Broadway
Nicholson Samuel, High st
Rees Joseph, Broadway
Scatton Samuel, Plaistow

CHYMISTS--MANUFACTRNG.
Bouglinval & Nyren, Marshgate lane
Crane Henry Samuel, and at Tom's coffee house, Cornhill, *London*
Howard, Gibson & Co.
Neuman John Paul, High st
Pitchford John & Co.

CLOTHES DEALERS.
Donnithorn William, High st
Ife John, Plaistow [way
Levy Hyman, Allen's bldngs. Broad-
Stepto James, High st
Williams David, West Ham lane
Worley Charles, High st

COACH BUILDERS.
Farrant and Son, High st
Gowar Stephen and James H. (and harness makers) Broadway
Hancock Walter (steam) High st

COACH PROPRIETORS.
Bish Henry, Stratford
Covell Samuel, Plaistow
Crump George, West Ham lane
Hancock Walter, High st [place
Neale William Henry, Langthorne

COAL DEALERS.
Carter James, West Ham lane
Grant Christopher, High st
Staines Samuel, High st
Woodland Benjamin, Plaistow

COAL MERCHANTS.
Bigg Thomas, Maryland point
Burling James, High st
Gibson John Ralph, High st
Meeson Thomas and Richard, near Bow bridge
Tanner Charles William, Stratford wharf, High st

COLOUR & VARNISH MANUFACTURERS.
Harrison, Layman, & Co. (& patent ink and blacking manufacturers) Stratford; colour works, near Bow bridge, *London*
Hopcraft Robert (colour) Stratford

CONFECTIONERS & PASTRY COOKS.
Barber John, Broadway
Brickell Elias, High st [High st
Volckman John & Sons (wholesale)

COOPERS.
Burton John, Broadway & West Ham
Franks Edward, High st
Siveyer John, West Ham lane

CORN DEALERS.
Clark William, High st
Coleby William, High st
Dee William, Broadway
Gentry John, Broadway
Gwalter Richard, Plaistow
Mayhew Philip, Plaistow
Moss Francis, High st
Pain Oliver, Broadway
Surry Timothy, Plaistow
Tanner Charles, Broadway
Tanner Charles William, Stratford wharf, High st
Woodland Benjamin, West Ham

CURRIERS AND LEATHER CUTTERS.
Crossley Jonas, High st
Jones Charles (and grindery warehouse), High st

DAIRYMEN.
Curtis John, High st
Fisher William, South st
Peck Matthew, Langthorne place
Purkis John, High st
Robey Joseph, Bridge st
Rogers John, West Ham
Sharp James, Chapel st
Willis Thomas, Broadway

DYERS & SCOURERS.
Elliott William, 3 High street and 6 Goswell road
Symons John, High st

EMERY AND GLASS CLOTH MANUFACTURERS.
Barsham and Lonsdale (patent) and 41 Threadneedle st, *London*

FIRE, &c. OFFICE AGENTS.
ALLIANCE, John Stevens, West Ham
COUNTY (fire) & PROVIDENT (life) Septimus Morris, Broadway

FRUITERERS AND GREENGROCERS.
Balley William George, High st
Chapman Rebecca, Broadway
Covell Sarah, Broadway
Dench William, Langthorne place
Ellis Charles, High st
Felgate George, Chapel st
Fuller Robert, High st
Hall Joseph, Channel Sea crescent
Hutley Elizabeth, High st
Lamprell Joseph, High st
Lincoln Phœbe, Broadway
Moss Thomas, High st
Short George, Broadway
Short Robert, High st
Turner John, West Ham
Wells James, High st
Wiseman Benjamin, High st
Wood James, West Ham lane

FURNITURE BROKERS.
Asals James, Broadway
Carder John, High st
Davies Esther, High st
Levy Hyman, High st
Wenham William, High st

GROCERS & TEA DEALERS.
Marked thus * are also Cheesemongers.
(See also Shopkeepers, &c.)
*Allen Anne, High st
*Avery Thomas, High st
*Baldey William, West Ham
Barnard James, Broadway
Batley Joseph, High st
*Benton Benjamin, Plaistow
*Catton Benjamin, Plaistow
*Coles James, West Ham
Croxford Arthur (& dealer in British wines) 12 and 13 Upton place
Eames Hannah, Plaistow
Gregory John, West Ham lane
*Hollick Samuel, Broadway
Hopkins William, High st
Hudson Anthony, High st
Lee Henry, Stratford green
Moore Thomas, Broadway
Scatton Samuel, Plaistow
Prime Benjamin, Broadway
Rowlay John, Broadway
Stubbs Richard, Maryland point
*Taylor William, High st
Wilson Henry, Broadway
Winnill William Hill, High st
Woodland Benjamin, West Ham

HAIR DRESSRS & PERFUMRS
Craddock John, Broadway
Gilvray John, Plaistow
Moss James, High st
Nunn Samuel, Broadway
Pancoast Michael, Stratford green
Robertson Adam, Church st, W. Ham
Scotchmer John, High st
White James, Broadway

HATTERS.
Glazbrook Mary, Broadway
Story Christopher, Bridge place

INNS AND PUBLIC HOUSES.
Abbey Arms, Thos. Kerry, Plaistow
Adam and Eve, Robert Birdsall, West Ham abbey
Angel, Mary Ann Brain, West Ham
Angel, William Good, Broadway
Bird-in-Hand, Alexander M'Gregor, High st
Black Lion, Joseph Duck, Plaistow
Blue Boar, William May, High st
Cart & Horses, Thomas Bigg, Maryland point
Coach & Horses, Jno. Bright, Plaistow
Coach and Horses, James Chapman, Broadway
Crown, Leabon Rout, West Ham
Eagle & Child, Henry Ellis Moseley, West Ham [High st
Fox & Hounds, Henry Harmsworth,
George, Mary Blaker, Broadway
GreenGate, Wm. Robt. Trott, Plaistow
Green Man, Margaret Bird, High st
Half Moon, Charles Pugh, West Ham
Harrow, Robert Martin, High st
King of Prussia, Geo. Griff, Broadway
King's Head, Wm. Lamb, West Ham
King's Head Inn, Robert Francis Beeton, Broadway
Old Black Bull, Susannah Carter, Broadway [tow
Old Greyhound, Rich. Turner, Plais-
Spotted Dog, William Vause, Upton
Swan, Geo. Tuting Evered, Broadway
Three Pigeons, Wm. Hinchley, Stratford green [st
Two Brewers, William Bugg, High
Unicorn, Thomas Pickett, West Ham
White Swan, Robert Augustine Ion, West Ham abbey
Yorkshire Gray, Joseph Cowland, High st [West Ham
Yorkshire Gray, Benjamin Grout,

IRONMONGERS.
Fletcher Frederick, Broadway
Little Burgess, Broadway
Page George, Broadway

JEWELLERS AND SILVERSMITHS.
Isaacs Barnett, High st
Lamb Richard, Broadway
Radford Thomas, Broadway

LINEN DRAPERS.
Bilton John and Co. Broadway
Hickes Richard Turner, High st

LINEN DRAPERS—*Continued.*
King Susannah, Balaam st, Plaistow
Lancaster Abraham, Broadway
Maguire William, Broadway
Stevens John, Broadway
Stewart John, Plaistow

LIVERY STABLE KEEPERS.
Beeton Robt. King's Head, Broadway
Bish Henry, High st
Crump George, West Ham lane
Mayhew Philip, Plaistow
Neale Wm. Henry, Langthorne place

MARINE STORE DEALERS.
Coster John, Ham lane [point
Laney William, Frances st, Maryland
Lifford Daniel, West Ham lane
Smith John, near Bow bridge
Williams William, High st

MILLERS.
Cooper Jno. Abbey mills, West Ham
Leeder James, Stratford, and at *Exning, Suffolk* [ford green
Sadler William, Pigeon mills, Strat-

MILLINERS & DRESS MAKRS.
Allen Frances, Chapel st
Asals Emma, High st
Baker Sarah, High st
Beck Harriet, Waterworks row
Burford Catherine, High st
Craddock Eliza, Broadway
Emblem Elizabeth, High st
Fisher Mary, Maryland point
Hudson Sarah, West Ham
Kirkham Eliza, High st
M'Cormick Henrietta, Broadway
Maguire Hannah, Broadway
Nuttman Phœbe, Chapel st
Pritchard Sarah, West Ham lane
Read Anne, West Ham lane
Russell Frances, Angel lane
Wildey Jane, Langthorne place
Willis Anne, Broadway
Wing Mary Anne, Allen's buildings, Broadway

NURSERYMEN, &c.
Bigg William, West Ham [point
Bunney George Hockley, Maryland
Garvie William, Maryland point
Hill Peter, West Ham
M'Pherson Robert & Son, Plaistow

OIL & COLOURMEN.
Croxford Arthur, 12 & 13 Upton place
Dalton John, High st
West Thomas, Broadway

PAWNBROKERS.
Isaacs Barnet, High st
Radford Thomas, Broadway

PLUMBERS, PAINTERS AND GLAZIERS.
Gilson Henry, Prospect place, West Ham
Gore William, Broadway
Greaves Robert, Broadway
Hepworth Thomas, High st
Johnson Edward, High st
Maywood Johannah, Plaistow
Perfect Huntley, Plaistow
Wilson John, High st
Woodland Benjamin, West Ham

POULTERERS AND PORK BUTCHERS.
Knight Henry, High st
Knight John, West Ham lane
Knight William, High st
Nichols Henry, Broadway
Root Joseph, Broadway
Thornton James, Broadway

SADDLERS AND HARNESS MAKERS.
Moase James, High st
Palmer William, High st
Sayer John, High st
Scott John, High st

SHOPKEEPERS & DEALRS IN GROCERIES & SUNDRIES.
Akhurst Harriet, Church st, West Hm
Allen Jno. Frances st, Maryland point
Allen Mary, Frances st, Marylnd point
Bailey Jonathan, West Ham lane
Barclay Elizabeth, West Ham
Bone Jane, High st
Cable Thomas, Plaistow
Clements Anne, High st
Cox Anthony, Farringdon place
Ford John, West st
Golding George, Marsh
Goodrich Thomas, South st
Hand James, West Ham
Hawes Henry, High st
Hayward Charles, High st
Hope Sarah, Maryland point
Jarvis John, Farringdon place
Keymer Mary Ann, Faringdon place
Marrion Thomas, West Ham
Morris John, West Ham
Osborn John, Angel lane
Palmer Joseph, West Ham abbey
Penn John, Stratford green
Perkins George, New st
Phripp Stephen, Chapel st
Purser Henry, Plaistow
Rand John, Prospect pl, West Ham
Robinson Henry, Broadway
Sharples John, Prospect pl, West Ham
Taylor Richard, West Ham
Walls Anne, South st
Weeham Elizabeth, Maryland point
Wiseman Wm. Cornelius, High st
Wisker Wm. Prospect pl, West Ham
Wort Jane, Plaistow
Yoe Henry, Plaistow
Yoe John, Plaistow

SILK & CALICO PRINTERS
Brown & Sedgwick (silk) Stratford
Burford David and Ephraim (calico) Print grounds
Tucker John (silk) West Ham abbey, and 10 Trump st, *London*

SLATERS.
Catley, Cullum & Catley, Meeson's Lime wharf, Stratford
Palmer William, High st
Pratt George, High st

SMITHS & FARRIERS.
Beckwith William, High st
Bish Henry, High st [point
Clift James (& whitesmith) Maryland
Easton Thomas, High st
Mace George, West Ham
Moss James, Plaistow
Reeves William, West Ham
Smith George, Langthorne place

STAY & CORSET MAKERS.
Collingwood Elizabeth, High st
Neal Ann, Broadway
Thompson Ann, High st

STRAW HAT MAKERS.
M'Cormick Henrietta, Broadway
Maythorn and Clapton, High st
Rogers Jane, High st
Willis Anne, Broadway

SURGEONS.
Beale John Evans, Plaistow
Kennedy Angus, Broadway
Maiden and Elliot, Stratford green
Staines Richard, Stratford grove
Vallance James Thomas, Broadway
Vincent Edward, Stratford green

TAILORS.
Biddle George, High st
Carret John, West Ham
Dangerfield James, Broadway
Derrick Henry, Chapel st
Gillman Joseph, 1 Surinam terrace
Gitland John, Balaam st, Plaistow
Hezell John, East st
Jones Samuel, Broadway
Lorking William, High st
Moss John, New st
Read Thomas, West Ham lane
Rudall Samuel, Plaistow
Shales Sarah and John, Broadway
Smith Samuel, Chapel st
Tarrant Richard, Broadway
Tyler Joseph, Maryland point

TALLOW CHANDLERS.
West Thos. (and oilman) Broadway
Wilton John (and melter) Broadway

TANNER.
Moline Edward, Angel lane, and 8 Billiter st, *London*

TIMBER MERCHANTS.
Burling James, High st
Curtis and Son, Broadway
Geere Thomas, High st
Gibson John Ralph, High st
Palmer William (and slate) High st

TOBACCONISTS.
Dowler Hannah, Broadway
Hand James, West Ham
Hatherill Elizabeth, Broadway
Smith John James, High st

TOY DEALERS.
Eames Benjamin, Broadway
Showell James, Broadway
Vandraut Chas. Langthorne

VETERINARY SURGEONS.
Easton Thomas, High st
Moss James, Plaistow

WATCH AND CLOCK MAKERS.
Ashdown Charles, Broadway
Golledge Richard, 5 Surinam terrace
Hodierne William Harvey, Church street buildings, West Ham
Lamb Richard, Broadway
Wayland Henry, Broadway [way
Wing Mark, Allen's buildings, Broad-

WHEELWRIGHTS.
Burrell William, Plaistow
Farrant and Son, High st
Fordham James, Turnpike row
Stonard William, Plaistow
Straight William, Plaistow

Miscellaneous.
Bailey Wm. Geo. potato dealer, High st
Beale John Evans, registrar of births and deaths, for West Ham, &c. Plaistow
Biggs William, working cutler, Broadway
Chapness John, bookkeeper, West Ham
Churchland Edward, sponge and rug manufacturer, Broadway
CONGREVE ROCKET FACTORY, West Ham marshes; office 14 Lombard st, *London* [bridge
Cossington John, lighterman, near Bow
Craddock Eliza, servant's register office, Broadway
French John, cattle salesman, Plaistow
Gingell James, hay salesman, Angel lane
Golledge Richard, parish clerk, 5 Surinam terrace [Ham lane
Gregory John, stamp distributer, West
Haines Edward, yest dealer, High st
Hancock Walter, engineer, High st
Hett James Keir & Co. vinegar makers, West Ham
HORSE PATROL POLICE STATION, Maryland point—William Holt and David Johnson, officers
Humphreys Chas. coach painter, High st
Hutchinson James, clerk, 2 Vicarage terr.
Jay Alexander, professor of dancing, Stratford green [place
Jones Wm. professor of music, 30 Upton
Lambert Geo. Smith, bellhanger, Stratford
Lawes Algernon, horse dealer, Stratford
Lenty Wm. chimney sweeper, Broadway
Maguire William, dealer in British wines, Broadway [st
Matthews Wm. furniture japanner, High
Maybank William, lighterman, High st
Meeson Thomas & Richard, lime burners, near Bow bridge
Mundy Stephen, relieving officer, High st
Mure James & Co. distillers, Three Mills, West Ham, and *Bromley, Middlesex*
Murphy James Patrick, tar & turpentine distillers, Marshgate lane

Newton William, dealer in building materials, Bridge place
Pratt George, stone mason, High st
Rake Thomas, clerk, 7 Vicarage terrace
Rees Joseph, dentist, High st
Richardson Samuel, clerk to the West Ham Union, Stratford
Richardson William, inspector of the police horse patrol, 27 Upton place
Rogers Richd. carver & gilder, Broadway
Rogers Thomas, French polisher, High st
Russell Susannah, floor cloth manufacturer, West Ham
SAVING'S BANK, West Ham—Septimus Morris, actuary, Broadway
Sawyer Jonathan, eating-house, Broadway
Smith George, locksmith and bellhanger, Langthorne place
Stevens Jno. commission agent, WestHam
Thodey William, printer, Plaistow
Thorn Widow & Sons, chimney sweepers, &c. West Ham
Turner & Montague, Roman cement manufacturers, Farringdon wharf, & brick and tile makers, Leigh
UNION POORHOUSE, West Ham—Thomasin Foster, matron
Vallance James Thos. registrar of births & deaths for Stratford District, Broadwy
Vandrant Charles, engraver and copperplate printer, Langthorne place
Wackett Jno. dealer in building materials, Bridge place
White James, musical instrument seller and music tuner, Broadway
Wilkins Richard, brush maker, High st
Wood Robt. carrier, Church st, West Ham
Woodward Richard, engraver to calico printers, Mount st

COACHES.

To LONDON, *Omnibusses* and *Coaches*, from the King's Head and principal Inns, every quarter of an hour during the day; and *Coaches* to and from all parts of ESSEX, NORFOLK & SUFFOLK pass through almost hourly.

CARRIERS.

To LONDON, James Cotton, John Good, William Layman, Thomas Nickelson, John Osborne, Noah Shipman & Jacob Bates, from Plaistow, daily; also *Waggons* to and from NORFOLK & SUFFOLK are passing through continually.

THAXTED,

WITH THE VILLAGES OF GREAT BARDFIELD, BROXTED, FINCHINGFIELD, GREAT AND LITTLE SAMPFORD AND NEIGHBOURHOODS.

THAXTED, once a market town, is in the parish of its name and hundred of Dunmow, 44 miles N. N. E. from London and 19 N. N. W. from Chelmsford—situated on the main road from the latter town to Cambridge, and on the eastern bank of the river Chelmer. Many Roman coins have been found in Thaxted parish; and a beautiful amphora (in the possession of Mr. Clarence, surgeon, of this place,) was dug up near the town not many years since. Thaxted received a charter from Queen Mary, which was confirmed by Elizabeth—but rendered nugatory either by the fears or the poverty of the corporate officers, who, on being served with a *quo warranto* in the reign of James II, deemed it prudent to retire from their offices in silence. The present lord of the manor is Sir Thomas Smyth, Bart., who holds a customary court once in every two years. The church, dedicated to the Virgin Mary (to St. Lawrence, some assert), is a structure of great amplitude and elegance: the entire fabric is embattled, and supported by strong buttresses, terminated by canopied niches; its length is one hundred and eighty-three feet, and its breadth (inside) eighty-seven; the west end is surmounted by a noble tower and spire, of exactly corresponding height with the length of the church—the tower containing eight sweet-toned bells. The benefice is a vicarage, in the gift of the Right Hon. Henry Lord Maynard. and incumbency of the Rev. Thomas Jee. There are chapels for independents, baptists and the society of friends; a free grammar school for the education of thirty boys, founded by Thomas Yardley; and other charities, left by the same person, for the benefit of the poor: likewise alms-houses, the gift of the late Sir Thos. Smyth, Bart. The guildhall, situate in Town-street, is rather an imposing edifice, now the property of the parish, and appropriated to the uses of a school. The market, formerly held on Friday, has been discontinued for many years; there are two fairs—one on the Monday before Whit-Monday, the other on the 10th August, for cattle, &c. Population of the parish, in 1831, 2,293.

Five miles E. by S. from Thaxted, in the hundred of Freshwell and parish of its own name, is the village of GREAT BARDFIELD—once a market town, but at present scarcely recognizable as such; Tuesday, the day on which the market is entitled to be held, presenting very little to distinguish it from the other days of business. The church is dedicated to St. Mary; the living is a vicarage, in the presentation of the lord of the manor. Population, at the last census, 1,029.

BROXTED is a village and parish in the same hundred as Thaxted, about three miles S. W. from that town; it contains a parish church, and about 700 inhabitants.

FINCHINGFIELD village is in the same hundred as Bardfield, between two and three miles south therefrom. Many hop plantations are in this parish, and the land is exceedingly productive. The places of worship are the parish church, dedicated to St. John the Baptist, and a chapel for independents: the living of Finchingfield is a vicarage, of which the Rev. James Westerman is the incumbent. An alms-house for poor widows, a school with a small endowment, and an apprenticeship fund, are the charities connected with this parish—the population of which amounts to 2,101.

GREAT SAMPFORD and LITTLE SAMPFORD are two small villages and adjoining parishes, in the same hundred as the two preceding places—the former about four miles N. by E. from Thaxted, the latter not so distant. Each parish contains its church, and in Great Sampford is a baptist chapel. General Eustace, of Little Sampford, is lord of both manors. A fair is annually held on Whit-Monday, for toys, &c. Great Sampford parish contained, in 1831, 800 inhabitants; and that of Little Sampford, 423.

POST OFFICE, Town street, THAXTED, Samuel Newell, *Post Master.*—Letters from LONDON arrive (by foot post from DUNMOW) every morning at half-past nine, and are despatched every afternoon at half-past four.

POST OFFICE, BARDFIELD, James Fuller, *Post Master.*—Letters from BRAINTREE arrive (by foot post) every morning at a quarter before nine, and are despatched every evening at half-past five.

POST OFFICE, FINCHINGFIELD, Thomas Darby, *Post Master.*—Letters from BRAINTREE arrive (by foot post) every morning at half-past eight, and are despatched every evening at five.

GENTRY AND CLERGY.

Aldrich Rev. Stephen, Park st
Awdry Rev. Charles, Little Sampford
Brand Mrs. Mary, Town st
Bristow Rev. James, Bardfield
Brown Rev. John, Broxted
Brice John Ruggles, esq. Spaines hall, Finchingfield
Byatt Rev. Thomas, Mill end
Carver Rev. Jeremiah Wolsey, Great Sampford
Chaplin Mrs. Mary, Town st
Christie Rev. George, Finchingfield
Clark Rev. John, Mill end
Eustace General Sir William Cornwallis, Little Sampford hall
Fitch Mr. Abraham, Town st
Hill Mrs. Sarah, Watling st
Jee Rev. Thomas, Vicarage, Thaxted
M'Adam Sir James, Tindon end
Sewell Rev. Joshua, Town st
Stock Mrs. Rebecca, Town st
Westerman Rev. Jas. Finchingfield
Windham Mrs. Cath. Mary, Town st
Woodley Mrs. —, Town st

ACADEMIES & SCHOOLS.

Not otherwise described are Day Schools.

Adams Elizabeth, Great Sampford
Barnard Mary Ann & Sarah, Town st
Clark Rev. John, Mill end
FREE SCHOOL, Bardfield—Jane Wicks, mistress
FREE SCHOOL, Finchingfield—Wm. Nye, master
FREE SCHOOL, Town st—Jas. Frye, master; Frances Freeman, mistress
Frye James, Town st
Fuller Sarah, Bardfield
Ruse Misses (boarding) Bardfield
Wenden Miss (boarding) Bardfield

ATTORNEY.

Townley John (& registrar of births and deaths) Park st

AUCTIONEERS & APPRAISRS.

Cole William, Newbiggin
Franklin Robert, Park st
Haslam Thomas Frederick, Town st

BAKERS.

Ballard Thomas, Bardfield
Barnard Samuel, Mill end
Barnard Samuel, Finchingfield
Bell William Josiah, Newbiggin
Cutts Isaac, Finchingfield
Day Thomas, Newbiggin
Garnham Hereford, Finchingfield
Messent Daniel, Bardfield
Stone Nathaniel, Town st
Tarrant Thomas, Mill end
Tyler Nathan, Mill end
Webb Lawrence Hill, Town st

BLACKSMITHS & FARRIERS.

Barker Joseph, Bardfield
Barltrop Moses, Broxted
Farrant James, Mill end

BLACKSMITHS & FARRIERS —Continued.
Goldstone Joseph, Great Sampford
Hardy Cornelius, Finchingfield
Humphreys John (and veterinary surgeon) Finchingfield
Sturgeon Samuel, Mill end
Turner James, Newbiggin
Turner James, Orange st
Turner John, Finchingfield
Turpin James, Great Sampford
Young William (and iron founder) Bardfield

BOOT & SHOE MAKERS.
Dodd John, Town st
Dodd Samuel, Bardfield
Dodd Thomas, Finchingfield
Everett Daniel, Great Sampford
Everett John, Town st
Everett Stephen, Mill end
Everett Thomas, Newbiggin
Everett Thomas, Orange st
Freeman George, Watling st
Mascall Edmund, Great Sampford
Mumford John, Bardfield
Mumford Thomas, Great Sampford
Nevill Samuel, Newbiggin
Ramsey James, Town st
Redgwell Jereboam, Town st
Ridgwell Elias, Little Sampford
Rolph James, Mill end
Turner John, Finchingfield

BRICK & TILE MAKERS.
Nodes John, Bardfield
Webb John, Park st

BRICKLAYERS.
Betts John, Finchingfield
Bowtle Robert, Bardfield
Grout John, Mill end
Moore Abraham, Bardfield
Moore John, Bolford st
Moore Thomas, Great Sampford
Moore William, Great Sampford
Wright Thomas, Bolford st

BUTCHERS.
Barnard William, Newbiggin
Freeborn John, Finchingfield
Gateward Martin, Finchingfield
Hills Lawrence, Town st
King John, Bardfield
Mascall Martin, Great Sampford
Wenden Joseph, Town st

CABINET MAKERS AND UPHOLSTERERS.
Cocke George, Town st
Cole William, Newbiggin

CARPENTERS & BUILDERS.
Cocke George, Town st
Cocke George, jun. Great Sampford
Davies William, Bolford st
Gray George, Bolford st
Gray James, Little Sampford
Gray William, Great Sampford
Martin John & Wm. Finchingfield

COOPERS.
Darby Thomas, Finchingfield
Unwin Thomas, Newbiggin

CORN DEALERS.
Cornell Joseph, Town st
Cowell William, Newbiggin
Fitch Robert, Town st
Willis James (& factor) Mill end

FIRE, &c. OFFICE AGENTS.
Essex Economic, Josiah Beddall, Finchingfield
Norwich Union, Robert Franklin, Park st; and Daniel George Paine, Finchingfield
Royal Exchange, James Frye, Town st

GARDENERS.
Bayford Charles (& clothes dealer) Bolford st
Fitch Nathaniel, Great Sampford
Palmer Charles, Newbiggin

GROCERS & TEA DEALERS.
(See also Shopkeepers, &c.)
Barltrop Moses, Broxted
Barnard Abraham, Town st
Baynes John, Newbiggin
Beddall Josiah, Finchingfield
Byatt Thomas (tea dealer) Mill end
Fuller James, Bardfield
Gilder James, Great Sampford
Haslam Thomas Frederick (& druggist) Town st
Moss Henry, Mill end
Paine Daniel George, Finchingfield
Ruffle William, Great Sampford
Simms Josiah, Finchingfield
Smith James, Bardfield
Woolley Thomas, Town st

HAIR DRESSERS.
Freeman William, Town st
Frye Philemon, Watling st
Spurge Richard, Bardfield

IRONMONGERS.
Davies William, Bolford st
Ruffle William, Great Sampford

LINEN DRAPERS.
Barltrop Moses, Broxted
Barnard Abraham, Town st
Baynes John, Newbiggin
Beddall Josiah, Finchingfield
Fuller James, Bardfield
Gilder James, Great Sampford
Haslam Thomas Frederick, Town st
Moss Henry, Mill end
Paine Daniel George, Finchingfield
Ruffle William, Great Sampford
Simms Josiah, Finchingfield
Smith James, Bardfield

MALTSTERS.
Fitch Robert, Town st
Franklin & Webb, Watling st
Leonard Thomas, Broxted
Messent Thos. (& corn factor) Bardfield
Nodes John, Bardfield

MILLERS.
Barnard Abraham, Sibley green
Barnard Samuel, Finchingfield
Davey Charles, Broxted
Francis Thomas, Cutler's green
Harrod William, Great Sampford
Letch Edward, Finchingfield
Pettit John, Great Sampford
Reynolds Thomas, Little Sampford
Salmon Joseph, Newbiggin
Webb John, Park st

MILLINERS & DRESS MAKRS.
Bunting Charlotte Yorke, Town st
Byatt Susan, Newbiggin
Fitch Charlotte, Newbiggin
Hart Eliza, Finchingfield
Lee Maria, Finchingfield
Thurston Emma, Bardfield
Ward Jane, Watling st
Waters Sarah, Finchingfield

PLUMBERS, &c.
Beckwith Thomas, Bardfield
Button Thomas Martin, Newbiggin
Dodd Thomas, Finchingfield
Lilly William, Newbiggin
Noon William, Bardfield

SADDLERS.
Goldstone James, Bardfield
Newell Samuel (and rope maker) Watling st
Newell Thomas, Great Sampford
Turner John, Bardfield

SHOPKEEPERS & DEALRS IN GROCERIES & SUNDRIES.
Barnard Mary & Sarah, Town st
Barnard Samuel, Mill end
Barker John, Town st
Barrett Samuel, Newbiggin
Bowtle James, Finchingfield
Halls Mary, Great Sampford
Hutt Mark, Park st
Lacey Amos, Newbiggin
Mumford Thomas, Bardfield
Richardson Elizabeth, Town st
Salmon Sarah, Mill end
Smith Angelo Willis, Cutler's green
Turner John, Bardfield
Unwin William Henry, Bardfield

STRAW HAT MAKERS.
Cole Eliza, Bardfield
Faircloth Sarah, Bardfield
Moss Sarah, Mill end
Thedham Sarah, Mill end
Turner Matilda, Finchingfield

STRAW PLAT DEALERS.
Linsell Joseph, Finchingfield
Smith Lewis, Finchingfield

SURGEONS.
Barnes Thomas Buxton, Park st
Clarence & Marsh, Watling st
Owen William Boyes, Finchingfield
Spurgeon Branwait, Bardfield

SURVEYORS.
Cocke George, Town st
Frye James (& bookseller) Town st
Haslam Thomas Frederick, Town st

TAILORS.
Marked thus * are also Drapers.
*Barnard Thomas, Mill end
*Baynes John, Newbiggin
Brown John, Bardfield
Byatt George, Newbiggin
Fox Robert, Bardfield
Holland Peter, Newbiggin
*Moss Henry, Mill end
Porter Thomas, Great Sampford
Reynolds Edward, Great Sampford
Smith Richard, Bardfield
*Smith Richard Marshall (& clothier, and furniture broker) Bardfield
Waters Thomas, Finchingfield

TAVERNS & PUBLIC HOUSES.
Anchor, James Wisbey, Newbiggin
Bull, Edmund Mascall, Great Sampford
Cock, Robert Cocke, Great Sampford
Cock, Thomas Newell, Town st
Fighting Cock, John Speakman, Little Sampford
Fox and Hounds, Joseph Salmon, Newbiggin
Green Man, Mary Webb, Finchingfield
King's Head, Chas. Bunting, Watling st
Red Lion, Thos. Burton, Great Sampford
Red Lion, Sarah Gibbons, Finchingfield
Rose & Crown, James Bush, Mill end
Saracen's Head, John Grout, Mill end
Star, John Bond, Mill end
Sun, William Sargent, Mill end
Swan, Franklin & Webb, Watling st
Three Tuns, Thos. Darby, Finchingfield
Vine, Thomas Newman, Bardfield
Vine, Thomas Woolley, jun. Watling st
White Hart, Thomas Norris, Bardfield

VETERINARY SURGEONS.
Malyon Cole, Great Sampford
Walford William, Bardfield
Ward Thomas Hutton, Watling st

WATCH & CLOCK MAKERS.
Knight Charles, Mill end
Philpot John, Bardfield
Turner Charles, Finchingfield
Webb Lawrence Hill, Town st

WHEELWRIGHTS.
Barker John, Finchingfield
Doe William, Finchingfield
Guyver George, Mill end & Broxted
Philpot William, Little Sampford
Prentice John, Bardfield
Rantell John, Watling st
Turner James, Newbiggin
Willis Samuel, Finchingfield

Miscellaneous.
Andrews James, excise officer, Watling st
Andrews Mordecai, worsted manufacturer, Park st
Barker Saml. dealer in British wines, Park st
Bunting Matthew, cattle dealer, Orange st
Chaffer Daniel, fellmonger, Town st
Chaffer Elijah, glover & breeches maker, Town street
Chaffer John, wool dealer, Orange st
Clark Thomas, coal dealer, Mill end
Cooper George, millwright, Mill end

Franklin William, tanner, Back lane
Freeman William, parish clerk, Town st
Gray Wm. parish clerk, Great Sampford
Haslam Wm. stamp distributer, Town st
Johnson Abraham, vestry clerk, Little Sampford
Lee Samuel, basket maker, Finchingfield
Martin William, parish clerk, Finchingfield
Mascall Chas. poulterer, Great Sampford
Salmon Edmund, cattle dealer, Newbiggin
Slater Thos. fishmonger, Great Sampford
Turner John, poulterer, Finchingfield
WORKHOUSE, Newbiggin—Northey Rowland, governor; Priscilla Rowland, matrn

COACHES.

To LONDON, the *Clare* (from Clare), calls at George Paine's, Finchingfield, every morning (Sunday excepted) at half-past ten in summer, and at the same time on Monday, Wednesday and Friday in winter; goes through Bardfield, Dunmow, Chipping Ongar, Abridge, Chigwell, Woodford Bridge and Stratford.

To CLARE, the *Clare* (from London), calls at George Paine's, Finchingfield, every afternoon (Sunday excepted) at four in summer, and at the same hour on Tuesday, Thursday and Saturday in winter.

CARRIERS.

To LONDON, William Bowtle, from his house, Thaxted, every Monday; — Harrison, from Great Sampford, every Tuesday; George Yulet and John Reynolds, from Finchingfield, every Wednesday; John Yulet, every Friday; and — Garrett's *Waggon*, from the Cock, same day.

To SAFFRON WALDEN, John Turner, from Thaxted, every Wednesday & Sat.

To STEEPLE BUMPSTEAD, — Garrett's *Waggon*, from the Cock Inn, Thaxted, every Monday.

THORPE-LE-SOKEN, KIRBY-LE-SOKEN,

WALTON-LE-SOKEN, GREAT AND LITTLE OAKLEY AND NEIGHBOURHOODS.

THORPE-LE-SOKEN is a market village and parish in the hundred of Erpingham, 63 miles N. E. from London, 12 E. from Colchester, and somewhat more than 9 miles S.S.E. from Manningtree. The parish comprises about 2,800 acres, chiefly very excellent corn land. A creek or arm of the sea runs up to Landermere, a hamlet in this parish, where there is a convenient wharf for vessels that sail occasionally with corn for London. The lord of the manor, who is styled the 'lord of the liberty, franchise, dominion and peculiar jurisdiction of the Soken,' appoints a commissary for ecclesiastical purposes, who is also coroner within the limits of the manor; he holds a court in Thorpe church annually, and the lord holds his court annually, on St. Ann's day, at Kirby: the present owners of the manor are the executors of the late Benjamin Chapman, Esquire. The 'Tendring Hundred Agricultural Association' held their first meeting (which is intended to be annual), for the show of cattle and agricultural implements, at Thorpe, on the 1st of June, 1838. The church, dedicated to St. Mary, has within these few years been enlarged. This parish, with the adjoining ones of Kirby and Walton, form the liberty and peculiar of the 'Soken,' and one benefice, of which the Rev. William Burgess is the present patron and incumbent. A small customary market is held on Wednesday, and there are fairs on the Monday before Whit-Sunday and the 29th September. The parish contained, in 1831, 1,173 inhabitants.

KIRBY-LE-SOKEN is a parish adjoining to that of Thorpe, in the hundred of Tendring. What may be termed the village (two parallel lines or streets, about half a mile from each other,) is about three miles from Thorpe. The land is considered very good, and the crops of corn are usually abundant. The church, which is dedicated to St. Michael, was nearly all taken down and rebuilt in 1833; the benefice forms part of the peculiar of the 'Soken,' as before mentioned, of Thorpe. A fair is held on July 26th, and another in August, the latter for lambs. Population of the parish, 972.

WALTON-LE-SOKEN is a parish in the same hundred and adjoining to that of Kirby—forming a promontory, called 'the Naze,' bounded on three sides by the sea, which is unceasingly making inroads among the cliffs, wherein are found a great variety of fossils, shells, and antediluvian animal remains; the shore abounds with pyrites, and nodules of argillaceous clay, which, when they have acquired firmness, are collected and conveyed to London and Harwich for making Roman cement. The beach, composed of a fine, level, firm sand, affords a delightful promenade and superior facilities for bathing. Of late years the parish has become the resort of a considerable number of genteel visiters, including respectable families, for whose accommodation an excellently conducted hotel (the Porto Bello) has been provided, together with a number of lodging-houses. Many of the dwellings present peculiar neatness and taste, particularly those erected by Mr. Penrice, architect, of Colchester. Opposite the hotel, on the beach, is a convenient pier of wood, upwards of two hundred feet in length, perfectly eligible for the landing and embarking of passengers. A square tower, eighty feet high, stands upon the most elevated ground in the parish, and forms a guide to shipping entering the harbour of Harwich. About forty years since, the ancient church, dedicated to All Saints, was entirely swept away by the sea, which had been long previously encroaching upon the land; and in 1804 a small new church was erected, which was subsequently enlarged. This parish is included, as already stated, in the consolidated benefice of 'Soken.' An annual regatta is held here, which is numerously and respectably attended. The population, in 1831, was 469, but since that period it has greatly increased.

GREAT OAKLEY is a parish in the same hundred as Walton, situate north-west therefrom, and contiguous to an inlet of the German ocean, opposite to Pewit island. This parish was the scene of a bloody conflict between King Ethelwolf and the Danes. A castle of considerable strength once stood here, and the remains of the keep and moat are still to be seen. The church is dedicated to All Saints; the living, which is a rectory, is in the gift of the master and fellows of St. John's college, Cambridge. Population of the parish, 1,118.

LITTLE OAKLEY, an adjoining parish on the north of that last-mentioned, is about four miles and a half S.W. from Harwich, bounded on the east by the ocean. It contains the parish church, and 244 inhabitants.

POST OFFICE, THORPE-LE-SOKEN, William Lake, *Post Master.*—Letters from COLCHESTER arrive every morning at half-past seven, and are despatched every evening at half-past six.

POST OFFICE, WALTON-LE-SOKEN, William Daniels, *Post Master.*—Letters from COLCHESTER arrive every morning at eight, and are despatched every evening at six.

POST, KIRBY-LE-SOKEN, *Receiving-House* at John Daniels'.—Letters from COLCHESTER arrive every morning at half-past seven, and are despatched every evening at a quarter past six.

POST, GREAT OAKLEY, *Receiving-House* at Elizabeth Salter's.—Letters from HARWICH arrive every morning at ten, and are despatched every afternoon at four.

GENTRY AND CLERGY.

Baldock Miss Anna, Terrace, Walton
Beaumont Mrs. —, Terrace, Walton
Beaumont Miss Mary Ann, Terrace, Walton
Blunt Rev. John James, Gt. Oakley
Bull Jas. Allen, esq. Gt. Oakley hall
Burgess Rev. William, Thorpe
Burmester Rev. Geo. Little Oakley
Daniel Mrs. Lydia, Thorpe
Dunker Andrew, esq. Thorpe cottage
Fenn Rev. Warwell, L. L. B. Kirby
Foaker Jeremiah, esq. Kirby
Harrison Rev. Benjamin, Beaumont
Jenner Rev. Stephen, B. A. Walton
King Mrs. Eliz. Comarkhouse, Walton
Leake Mr. John Martin, Thorpe hall
Mason William, esq. Landermere hall, Thorpe
Pertwee James, esq. Thorpe park
Rough Mrs. Elizabeth, Thorpe lodge
Wright Wm. Polden, esq. New hall, Thorpe

ACADEMIES & SCHOOLS.

Not otherwise described are Day Schools

Allen John, Great Oakley
Bacon Mary (boarding) Thorpe
Benneworth Charlotte, Thorpe
Burrell William, Walton
Cousins Sarah, Great Oakley
Crampin Henry, Great Oakley
Dudgeon Margaret, Walton
INFANTS' SCHOOL, Walton
Pratt Miss, Beaumont
Savage Elizabeth (boarding) Kirby
Seaman Shadrach (boarding) Thorpe
Webb Isaac, Thorpe

AGENTS.

Barndon John (estate agent and appraiser) Terrace, Walton
Blyth Edward (estate, &c. and to the Essex and Suffolk Insurance Company) Thorpe

ATTORNEY.

Spurling Henry (& registrar of births and deaths for the Thorpe district) Thorpe

AUCTIONEERS & APPRAISERS.

Blyth Edward, Thorpe
Holby James, Thorpe

BAKERS.

Bloice John, Thorpe
Carter Thomas, Great Oakley
Carter William, Walton
Cowie Susan, Great Oakley
Day Daniel, Thorpe
Hughes Joseph, Kirby
Pyman John, Walton

BATHS, WARM, COLD AND SHOWER.

Aldrich Edmund, Bath House Inn, Beach, Walton
Kent Benj. (& subscription news and reading and billiard rooms) Family Hotel, Crescent, Walton
Simey Sarah (warm&shower) Beach, Walton

BAZAARS.

Barnden John (and news and reading rooms) Terrace, Walton
Gilson Misses (and library) Crescent, Walton
Woolston Jas. (and fancy fair) Crescent, Walton

BLACKSMITHS.

Abbs George, Thorpe
Claxon James, Great Oakley
Garrod Isaac, Walton
Howard William, Kirby
Lawrance Samuel (and farrier) Great Oakley
Mussett John, Thorpe
Randall William, Great Oakley
Riddlesdell Thomas, Kirby
Riddlesdell Thos. (& farrier) Walton
Triggs Henry, Great Oakley
Wilson John, Thorpe

BOOT AND SHOE MAKERS.

Butler Olding, Walton
Candler Jesse, Walton
Cole Thomas, Great Oakley
Cowey John, Great Oakley
Keeble Sarah, Great Oakley
Lappage and Co. Thorpe
Rayner Nathan, Great Oakley
Sherman Benjamin, Walton
Smith Joseph, Great Oakley
Thompson Robert, Thorpe
Webb James Leech, Kirby
Wells Henry, Thorpe

BRAZIERS AND TINMEN.

Clide Thomas, Great Oakley
Harris William, Great Oakley
Shead George, Thorpe

BRICKLAYERS.

Atkins William (and slater) Walton
Barton Joseph (and builder) Walton
Finch William, Great Oakley
Gifford William, Thorpe
Young Edmund, Great Oakley

BUILDERS.

Barnden John, Terrace, Walton
Salmon Joseph, Beaumont

BUTCHERS.

Bundock Thomas, Kirby
Cooper Edward, Great Oakley
Hempson Philip, Thorpe
Hubbard Benjamin, Walton
Low George, Kirby
Nicholson James, Thorpe
Smith John, Kirby
Thomas James, Walton
Warren William, Beaumont

CARPENTERS.

Angier Robert, Great Oakley
BarndenJno. (& buildr) Terrace, Walton
Collins John, Great Oakley
Hanger Abraham, Great Oakley
Lilley John, Thorpe
Simey George, Walton,
Wilson John, Kirby

COAL MERCHANTS.

Archer John, Walton
Pearson William, Thorpe
Salmon Joseph, Beaumont

CONFECTIONERS.

Pyman John, Walton
Theobald Charlotte, Thorpe
Ward Susan, Walton

COOPERS.

Hempson William, Thorpe
Smith Joseph, Great Oakley
Wilson John, Kirby

CORN MERCHANTS.

Archer John, Walton
Holly James, Thorpe
Pattrick George, Thorpe
Pearson William, Landermere wharf, Thorpe

EATING & COFFEE ROOMS.

Clark Samuel, Walton
Ward Samuel, Walton

GLOVERS.

Bates John (and breeches maker) Thorpe
Carpenter Mark (& fellmonger) Great Oakley

GROCERS & TEA DEALERS.

(See also Shopkeepers, &c.)

Bloice John, Thorpe
Devereux James, Walton
Hawes Michael, Thorpe
Lott Henry, Kirby
Moss John Robert, Great Oakley
Salmon Benjamin, Great Oakley
Wilson William, Thorpe
Worters John, Thorpe

HAIR CUTTERS.

Chisnall John, Thorpe
Jeffery Daniel, Thorpe
Lake William, Thorpe
Mann Robert, Great Oakley
Ward Samuel, Walton

INNS.

Bath House, Edmund. Aldrich, Beach, Walton
Bell, William Bagley, Thorpe
Hotel (and posting house) Benjamin Kent, Crescent, Walton
Maid's Head, Sarah Tungatt, Thorpe
Porto Bello, John Palmer, Walton

LINEN DRAPERS, &c.

Bloice John, Thorpe
Daniels William, Walton
Devereux James, Walton
Hawes Michael, Thorpe
Lott Henry, Kirby
Palmer Samuel, Walton
Salmon Benjamin, Great Oakley
Wilson William, Thorpe
Worters John, Thorpe

LODGING HOUSES.

Atkins Wm. Esmeralda pl. Walton
Barton S. C. Esmeralda pl. Walton
Burrell Wm. Sidmouth pl. Walton
Cross John W. Saville row, Walton
Hewett Wm. Esmeralda pl. Walton
Millions Mrs. Sidmouth pl. Walton
Simey Saml. Esmeralda pl. Walton
Skipper Peter, Esmeralda pl. Walton
Spratling John, Walton

MALTSTERS.

Hughes Jos. (& spirit merchnt) Kirby
Rayner John, Great Oakley
Salmon Joseph, Great Oakley

MARKET GARDENERS.

Barton William, Kirby
Haldon John, Little Oakley
Peck John, Thorpe
Smith John, Thorpe
Smith Samuel, Great Oakley

MILLERS.

Archer John, Walton
Bugg Samuel, Great Oakley
Pattrick George, Thorpe
Wilson John, Kirby

PAINTERS, PLUMBERS, &c.

Claxton Charles, Great Oakley
Frost Simon, Thorpe

SADDLERS.

Bloom William, Kirby
Blowers John, Thorpe and Kirby
Blowers Richard, Great Oakley
Cole John, Thorpe

SHOPKEEPERS & DEALERS IN GROCERIES & SUNDRIES.

Barton Samuel Crooks, Walton
Campion George, Little Oakley
Clark James, Great Oakley
Daniels John, Kirby
Daniels William, Walton
Day Richard, Kirby
Finch William, Great Oakley
Frost Sarah, Thorpe
Hunt Henry, Thorpe
Shead George, Thorpe
Smith Hannah, Great Oakley
Sorrell Benjamin, Beaumont

STRAW HAT MAKERS.

Harvy Mary, Thorpe
Peacher Mary, Thorpe
Simey Elizabeth, Walton

SURGEONS.

Manthorp Daniel Levett, Thorpe and Walton
Osmond and Son, Thorpe and Walton

TAILORS.

Burling Edward, Walton
Cousins Edward, Great Oakley
Saunders Jonathan, Great Oakley
Theobald Thomas, Thorpe, Kirby and Great Oakley

TAVERNS & PUBLIC HOUSES.

Greyhound, John Smith, Kirby
King's Head, Jacob Manning, Thorpe
May Bush, Henry Cecksedge. Gt. Oakley
Red Lion, George Low, Kirby
Ship, John Palmer, Kirby
Swan, John Manning, Beaumont
Swan, James Salmon, Great Oakley
Three Cups, William Cousins, Gt. Oakley
ThreeHorseShoes, Wm. Warren, Beaumont

VETERINARY SURGEON.

Lines William, Thorpe

WHEELWRIGHTS.

Allsop James, Great Oakley
Burgess William, Kirby
Lewis Thomas, Thorpe
Lilley John, Thorpe
Mean James, Kirby

Miscellaneous.

Archer William, millwright and machine maker, Great Oakley
Baker Simon, parish clerk, Thorpe
Barton Joseph, brick & tile maker & lime burner, Walton
Brooke Daniel, cabinet maker and upholsterer, Thorpe
Burling Frances, milliner & dress maker, Walton
Clark John, horse dealer, Thorpe
Hubbard Daniel, basket maker, Thorpe
Ledger Edmund, chymist, Thorpe
Lewis George, coach maker, Thorpe
Raggett James, watch and clock maker, silversmith, jeweller & optician, Thorpe, Walton and Great Oakley
Sizer Robert, harness maker, Gt. Oakley
Stebbin P. relieving officer, Red house, Beaumont
Wilson Wm. stamp distributer, Thorpe
WORKHOUSE, Thorpe—Jas. Holby, governor; Maria Holby, governess
Worters John, tallow chandler, Thorpe

COACHES.

To COLCHESTER, a *Coach*, from Kent's Hotel and the Porto Bello Inn, Walton, every morning at 8, & evening at six—and a *Coach*, from Walton, every evening at half-past seven.

CARRIERS.

To COLCHESTER, Isaac Moles & Peter Burrell, from Walton and back, daily; and Henry Hunt, from Thorpe, daily; through Tendring, Great Oakley, &c.
To HARWICH, Robt. Salter, from Great Oakley and back, daily
To IPSWICH, Thos. Tye, from Thorpe and back, daily

CONVEYANCE BY WATER.

STEAM PACKETS.

To LONDON, the *Albion* and *Ipswich*, (from Ipswich), call off Walton, every Monday and Thursday; and from London to Ipswich, every Tuesday, Wednesday, Friday and Saturday.

TILBURY FORT, WEST TILBURY, EAST TILBURY,

STANFORD-LE-HOPE, MUCKING AND CORRINGHAM.

TILBURY FORT is a strong and regular fortification, which entirely commands the navigation of the river Thames: it is distant six miles from Grays Thurrock, 16¼ S.S.W. from Brentwood, and 14 S. from Billericay. It does not contain anything worthy of notice besides the barracks, and the fortress here referred to.

WEST TILBURY, about two miles from Tilbury Fort, is a small village, situated on an eminence, opposite to Gravesend, with which town, and the interior of Kent, there is a constant traffic, by means of ferryboats, for the conveyance of passengers, cattle, carriages, &c. It was, at an early period, called *Tillaburgh*, and was then of much more importance than at present.

EAST TILBURY, four miles from Tilbury Fort, is bounded on the north east by the Thames, where, at a point called the Hope, is a battery for the defence of the river.

STANFORD-LE-HOPE is six miles from Grays Thurrock, one mile and a half from Horndon-on-the-Hill, and a short distance to the north of the Thames Haven and Dock Railway.

MUCKING is about four miles from Tilbury Fort, bounded on the east by the river Thames.

CORRINGHAM is about two miles from Stanford-le-Hope, situated between Tilbury Fort and Canvey Island; it consists of but a few houses and a church, which is an ancient building, with a wooden spire.

The above, with the exception of Tilbury Fort, are small villages, in parishes of their respective names, all in the hundred of Barstable, each containing its parish church. The POPULATION of the parishes, by the returns for 1831, is as follows:—WEST TILBURY, 276; EAST TILBURY, 245; STANFORD-LE-HOPE, 330; MUCKING, 212; and CORRINGHAM, 234 inhabitants.

POST OFFICE, King's Head, WEST TILBURY, Edward Travis, *Post Master.*—Letters from LONDON arrive (from ROMFORD) every forenoon at half-past 11, and are despatched every afternoon at a quarter before 1.

GENTRY AND CLERGY.

Armstrong Rev. William, Rectory, Stanford-le-Hope
Asplin Mr. Joseph, West Tilbury
Lloyd Rev. Logan, Rectory, E. Tilbury
Newing Mrs. Anne, West Tilbury
Osborn Rev. Peter, West Tilbury
Radford Dr. Thos. Stanford-le-Hope

PUBLIC HOUSES.

Bull, Mary Anne Moore, Corringham
Cock, James Nathaniel Dale, Stanford-le-Hope
Cross Keys, John Ennever, Chadwell
Crown, Philip Jaggs, Mucking
George and Dragon, Henry Rumball, Muckingford
King's Head, Edward Travis, West Tilbury
King's Head, Anne Eliza Osborne, Stanford-le-Hope
Ship, Richard Archbold, E. Tilbury
World's End & Ferry House, Wm. Creed, Tilbury Fort

SHOPKEEPERS, TRADERS, &c.

Archbold Rchard, parish clerk, East Tilbury
Atkinson Oliver, shopkeeper, East Tilbury
Bath Benjn. parish clerk, W. Tilbury
Bearman William, parish clerk, Stanford-le-Hope
Chapman Anne, smith, East Tilbury
Clark James, wheelwright, Stanford-le-Hope
Crampton Wm. Jas. shopkeeper and beer-seller
Cruswell George, boot & shoe makr, Corringham
Dale James Nathaniel, shopkeeper, Stanford-le-Hope
Eastwood James, wheelwright, Chadwell
Freeman John, smith, Corringham
Gentry Wm. shopkeeper, Stanford-le-Hope
Goodchild Rev. Thomas Wm. East Tilbury
Grover Richard, shopkeeper & shoe maker, West Tilbury
Harris John, miller, East Tilbury
Harris William, baker, West Tilbury
Herriday Samuel, shopkeeper, Corringham
Jaggs George, shoemaker, Stanford-le-Hope
Jaggs Philip, shopkeeper, Mucking
James Joseph and Richard, millers, West Tilbury
Knowles John, smith, Stanford-le-Hope
Newin Anne, school, West Tilbury
Palmer Thomas, tailor, W. Tilbury
Pelt Joshua, shopkeeper, E. Tilbury
Petchey William, smith, Muckingford
Quinton Henry, shopkeeper, East Tilbury
Ranson John, smith & farrier, West Tilbury
Scott Richard, boot & shoe maker, Corringham
Travis Edwd. wheelwright & smith, W. Tilbury

ORDNANCE DEPOT,
TILBURY FORT.

Major Kelly, *commandant*
William Eagle, esq. Gravesend, *storekeeper*

TOLLESHUNT DARCY, TOLLESHUNT KNIGHTS,

TOLLESHUNT MAJOR AND TOLLESBURY.

TOLLESHUNT DARCY is a village and parish in the hundred of Thurstable, situated on the road betwixt Maldon and Colchester—between six and seven miles N. E. from the former, and ten S. W. from the latter town; the parish is bounded on the south-east by the Blackwater river. The church is dedicated to St. Nicholas; the living is a discharged vicarage, in the patronage (or was until lately) of the family of Rebow. This is one of the fourteen parishes in Essex whose poor are benefited by the munificence of Henry Smith, Esq.

TOLLESHUNT KNIGHTS and TOLLESHUNT MAJOR are adjoining parishes to the preceding one. They have each their parish church: that of Knights is dedicated to All Saints, and its benefice a rectory, in the gift of the crown; that of Major to St. Nicholas, and is a vicarage, in the presentation of the Jegon family.

TOLLESBURY village and parish is in the same hundred as the three preceding places, eight miles E. N. E. from Maldon: the parish has that of Tolleshunt Major on the north, and the Blackwater river on the south, with which it communicates by means of the Southfleet, a navigable creek. The church is dedicated to St. Mary; the living is a vicarage, in the patronage of Sir W. B. Rush. There is a place of worship here for independents.

The POPULATION of these parishes, in 1831, was—DARCY, 690; KNIGHTS, 374; MAJOR, 478; TOLLESBURY, 1,066.

POST OFFICE, TOLLESHUNT DARCY, Isaac Hardy, *Post Master.*—Letters from MALDON arrive (by light cart) every forenoon (Monday excepted) at eleven, and are despatched every afternoon at four.

GENTRY AND CLERGY.

Carwardine Rev. Charles W. Tolleshunt Knights
Dixon Richard, esq. Brook hall, Tolleshunt Knts
Knight Mr. Thomas, Beckingham hall, Tolleshunt Major
Watkins Roger, esq. Tolleshunt Darcy
Wells Rev. —, Tollesbury
Wilkin Chas. esq. Tolleshunt Knights

Names without address are in Tolleshunt Darcy.

PROFESSIONAL PERSONS.

Dawson John, surgeon
Everard Edward, boarding and day academy
Whitfield Edward, surgeon

PUBLIC HOUSES.

Bell, Robert Sadler, Beckingham
King's Head, Wm. Payne, Tollesbury
Lion, William Gray
Plough & Sail, William Frost, Tollesbury
Queen's Head, Frederick Woodward
Rose & Crown, James Kettle, Tolleshunt Knights

SHOPKEEPERS & TRADERS.

Alden Wm. shopkeeper, Tollesbury
Banham Rbt. shopkeeper & carpenter
Banyard John, shopkeeper, Tollesbury
Blaxall James, baker
Bolton Thomas, shoe maker, Tollesbury
Bowles Wm. shopkeeper, Tollesbury
Brewer Henry, grocer & tea dealer
Cooper Thomas, wheelwright
Cox Thomas, parish clerk, Tollesbury
Dudley Thos. blacksmith, Tolleshunt Major
Ely Thomas, wheelwright, Tolleshunt Knights
Fen George, shoe maker
Gardner William, carpenter & retail brewer
Godson John, shoe maker, Tollesbury
Grout Abraham, wheelwright, Tolleshunt Major
Harvey William, baker, Tollesbury
Horsenall William, baker, Tolleshunt Major
Ludgater Samuel, glover
Ludgater Samuel, jun. tailor
Martin Edward, shoe maker
Martin Hannah, blacksmith
Neville Thos. blacksmith, Tollesbury
Nott Mrs. shopkeeper, Tollesbury
Page Orbel, blacksmith & wheelwright
Payne William, butcher, Tollesbury
Peake Jas. miller, Tolleshunt Knights
Polley George, baker
Polley William Thomas, saddler, &c.
Seabrook Richard, butcher
Strutt Ambrose, plumber, &c.
Walford John, shopkeeper, Tollesbury
White Wm. grocer & wine merchant
Woodyard Frederick, shopkeeper & bricklayer
Woodyard Frederick, jun. carpenter

WAKERING (GREAT & LITTLE) AND FOULNESS.

GREAT WAKERING is a village and parish in the hundred of Rochford, about four miles and a half E.N.E. from Southend and six S.E. from Rochford—situated at the mouth of the Thames, nearly opposite to the Isle of Sheppey, and has a small haven. The places of worship are the parish church, dedicated to St. Nicholas, and a chapel for independents: the living is a vicarage, in the patronage of the bishop of London. The population of the parish, in 1831, amounted to 834.

LITTLE WAKERING parish is contiguous to that of Great Wakering on the north and north-east; in the latter quarter is Potton island, belonging to the parish. The church is dedicated to St. Mary; the benefice is a vicarage, of which the governors of St. Bartholomew's hospital, London, are patrons. Population, in 1831, 297.

The island and parish of FOULNESS lies to the north-east of the Wakerings, nine miles E. by N. from Rochford, upon the eastern extremity of Rochford hundred, encompassed by branches of the sea—the only passage to it being by the sands at low water, the distance over which is about six miles. The island is about twenty miles in circumference, comprising about six thousand acres, near the centre of which is a small church, dedicated to St. Mary; the living, which is a discharged rectory, is in the presentation of the Earl of Winchelsea. Courts leet and baron are occasionally held by the lord of the manor; and there is a fair, for toys, on the 10th of July. Population of the island, 630.

POST OFFICE, GREAT WAKERING, Charles Gardner, *Post Master.*—Letters arrive every morning at half-past eight, and are despatched every afternoon (Sunday excepted) at half-past four—on Sunday they are despatched at half-past three.

*** *The names without address are in* GREAT WAKERING.

GENTRY AND CLERGY.

Asplin Charles, esq. Wakering hall
Bannister Francis, esq. Barling
Cause Mr. William, Little Wakering
Crump Mr. Samuel, Little Wakering
Deeley Mrs. —, Barling
Dodson Rev. Edwd. Great Wakering
Fenn Mrs. —, Barling
Hartley Rev. James Bishop, Barling
Hickinbotham Mr. John, Potton Island
Hudson Thos. Beaumont, esq. Barling hall
Jacobs Rev. Isaac, Great Wakering
Jennings Mr Withers, Wakering wick
Knight Rev. James, Foulness
Lambert Mr. John, Barling
Miller Mr. Chas. (surgeon) Gt. Wakering
Reave Joseph, esq. Barling
Rumble Mr. Thomas, Gt. Wakering
Stratton Rev. Ths. (magistrate) Sutton
Tabor Edward, esq. Sutton hall
Walton Mr. Thomas, Shoplin
Wedd Alfred, esq. Great Wakering

PUBLIC HOUSES.

Anchor, John Lusey
Bell, Tanmer Potter
Castle, William Freeman, Little Wakering
George & Dragon, Jno. Allen, Foulness
King's Head, Wm. Guiver, Foulness
Red Lion, Mary Wesney
White Hart, John Rivers

SHOPKEEPERS & TRADERS.

Adams John, boot maker
Ayton James, saddler
Ballinger Jon. baker & shopkeeper, Foulness
Beard Thomas, butcher
Belton Danl. wheelwright & butcher
Bennewith Henry, wheelwright
Bloss Robert, gardener and seedsman, Little Wakering
Boreham John, saddler
Brown Wm. shopkeeper, Barling
Bullock & Hindes, grocers & drapers
Burgess Eliz. milliner & dress maker, Lit. Wakering
Burgess Jno. bricklayer & plasterer, Lit. Wakering
Catmull James, carpenter
Cousins Robert, blacksmith
Crick Mary, shopkeeper
Ellis Abraham, wheelwright
Faulkner Samuel, boot maker, Little Wakering
Francis Isaac, carpenter
Freeman William, shopkeeper, Little Wakring
Fuller Chas. boot maker, Lit. Wakring
Gardner James, boot maker
Gascoigne Joseph, bricklayer
Gilson Abraham, baker
Goodson Thomas, boot maker
Harris William, grocer and draper
Harvey Joseph, baker
Howard William, barge owner
Jackson Emma, baker
Jackson Mary, milliner & dress maker
Kernot William Pearce, distiller of essential oils, Barling
Leeks Charles, shopkeeper
Norden Alexander, blacksmith
Price Samuel, hurdle maker, smith and wheelwright, Little Wakering
Sheed Daniel, nurseryman
Smith John, baker
Smith Thomas, bricklayer
Springett Wm. linen draper & clothier
Springett Wm. linen draper, Foulness
Stow James, baker
Sumner Edwin, high constable, Little Wakering
Thornton Jas. blacksmith and shopkeeper, Foulness
Threadgold John, baker
Vince Charlotte, milliner & straw hat maker
Westhorpe Wm. grocer & slopseller
Whale Jno. bootmaker & shopkeeper
Whitaker Wm. grocer and draper
Wilson Lucy, shopkeeper, Lit. Wakrng
Wyborn Meller, boot maker
Wyborn Robert, boot maker

WALTHAM ABBEY

AND HAMLETS, WITH THE VILLAGE OF NAZEING AND NEIGHBOURHOODS.

WALTHAM ABBEY is a market town in the parish of its name (or Holycross,) and hundred of Waltham—12 miles N. from London, and the like distance S.S.E. from Hertford; situated on the banks of the river Lea, which here separates into several streams, and divides the counties of Essex and Herts. The town, which is irregularly built, lies to the left or west of the main road leading from the metropolis to Cambridge. The abbey, by which this place attained so much celebrity, was originally founded by Tovy or Tovius, who was standard-bearer to the famous Canute; it was afterwards refounded by Earl Harold, who endowed it, and constituted it a college, consisting of a dean and eleven secular canons belonging to the Augustine order. Upon the dissolution of this abbey, a grant of its site, for the term of thirty-one years, was given to Sir Anthony Denny, whose widow purchased the reversion in fee, from Edward VI, for above £3,000. The only remains of the abbey which have survived the shocks of time are the ruins of the gateway that led into the abbey yard, the bridge by which it is approached, some dilapidated walls, and the church, the architecture of which evinces its erection to have been long antecedent to that of the rest. Notwithstanding its mutilated condition, this once magnificent pile still furnishes the architect and the antiquary with many beautiful and interesting specimens of the Norman style; the pillars supporting the arches which divide the body from the side-aisles are very massive, like those of Durham cathedral. The trade of this place is not so prosperous as it was some years back: the branches connected with manufactures comprise pin making, and silk throwing and silk printing, but they are not so extensive as formerly; several breweries, flour-mills and malt-kilns are the other prominent establishments of business. Gunpowder mills, belonging to government, which in time of war employ from four to five hundred persons, are situated here.

The church, dedicated to the Holy Cross and Saint Lawrence (and which comprises the nave only of the old abbey church), is a spacious structure in the Norman style, with a tower of later erection; it contains a Lady chapel, and several interesting monuments and ancient memorial tablets: the living is a perpetual curacy, or donative, of which certain trustees are patrons; the Rev. J. L. Capper is the present officiating minister. There are places of worship for baptists and Wesleyan methodists; a free school, founded by the Leverton family; and Green's alms-houses for eight poor widows. The market is held on Tuesday; the fairs on the 14th May and 25th September, for cattle, and 26th September for hiring servants. The parish of Waltham Abbey (including the hamlets of HOLYFIELD, SEWARDSTONE and UPSHIRE) contained, in 1831, 4,104 inhabitants.

HIGH BEACH hamlet, distant about two miles from Waltham Abbey, and situated close to Epping forest, is particularly to be noticed for the number of tasteful seats and elegant villas in its neighbourhood, as well as for the extensive prospects and delightful picturesque scenery which may be enjoyed on every side.

NAZEING, a parish and village, the latter a respectable little place, is between four and five miles north from Waltham Abbey; it contains a church, dedicated to All Saints, but possessing nothing besides worthy of particular mention. Population of the parish, 757.

POST OFFICE, High Bridge street, WALTHAM ABBEY, Eliza Allsup, *Post Mistress*.—Letters from LONDON arrive every morning at eight and afternoon at one and four, and are despatched every day at twelve, afternoon at a quarter before three and evening at a quarter past seven.

GENTRY AND CLERGY.

Allen Matthew, esq. M. D. Fair mead, High Beach
Arabin William St. Julian, esq. High Beach
Banbury William, esq. Warlies park
Bazett Mrs. Sarah, Sewardstone lodge
Bury Frederick, esq. St. Leonard's, Nazeing
Buttress John Josiah, esq. Sewardstone
Capper Rev. John Lewis, Parsonage
Cockburn Rt. Hon. Sir Geo. High Beach
Collins Edward, esq. Nazeingbury
Colvin Beale B. esq. Holy field
Connop Newell, jun. esq. Honey lands
Conyers J. H. esq. Copt hall
Hargreaves Rev. James, Paradise row
Hood Rev. Geo. Vicarage, Nazeing
Jessopp Mr. Joseph, Waltham Abbey
Kettlewell Thomas, esq. Fair mead lodge, High Beach
Lovell George, esq. Waltham Abbey
Messenger Rbt. Benj. esq. High Beach
Moody Col. Thomas, High Bridge st
Palmer George, esq. Nazeing
Parnell John, esq. Paradise cottage
Preston Charles, esq. Sewardstone
Preston Miss Harriet, Sewardstone
Shearmear Capt. Fredk. Waltham hall
Silvester Lady D. M. Sewardstone
Smith Mr. Thomas, East end
Sotheby Capt. Charles, Manor house, High Beach
Sotheby Mrs. Hans, Manor cottage, High Beach
Steevens Francis, esq. Copt hall green
Taylor Jefferys, esq. Austey house, High Beach
Thomas William Kent, esq. Sewardstone
Usborne Thomas, esq. Gillwell house, Sewardstone
Walford William, esq. High Beach
Whitehead Miss —, Warley cottage
Woollard Mrs. Mary, Market place
Wright James, esq. Waltham Abbey

ACADEMIES & SCHOOLS.

Gibbs Ann (day) High Bridge st
LEVERTON'S SCHOOL, High Bridge street—William Leggatt, master; Martha Leggatt, mistress
Pugh Edward (day) Sewardstone st
Tyler Edward (day) High Bridge st

ATTORNEYS.

Allsup James, High Bridge st
Jessopp Joseph (and clerk to the magistrates) High Bridge st
Parnell Jno. Jessop, Paradise cottage

AUCTIONEERS & APPRAISRS.

Davis Robert Kirkup, East end
Pryor Charles (& estate agent) Sun st

BAKERS.

Crean George (biscuit) Sun st
Hicks William, Sun st
Paul Daniel, Sewardstone st
Reed John, High Bridge st
Reed Thomas, High Bridge st
Reed William, High Bridge st
Sayer William, High Bridge st

BOOKSELLERS & STATIONRS.

Brackett John (& library) Sun st
Marshall James Ainsworth, High Bridge street

BOOT AND SHOE MAKERS.

Beckwith James, Malting yard
Carr James, Sun st
Hunt Charles, Green yard
Johnston Eliz. (& toy dealer) Sun st
Larman James, Sun st
Pegrum William, Holy field
Upton Joseph, Market place
Woodbridge William, High Bridge st

BREWERS.

Chatteris Thomas, Sun st
Death Frances, Sun st
King William & Thomas, Nazeing

BRICKLAYERS.

Sibthorp William, Sun st
Sinkwell Thomas, Sewardstone
Wiggs William, Sun st

BUTCHERS.

Bigg Harriet, High Bridge st
Carr Charles, High Bridge st
Dugard William, Market place
Harknett James, High Beach
Paine John, Sun st
Sibthorp Charles, Sun st
Sinkwell Thomas, Sewardstone
Sturgeon Thomas, High Bridge st
Want Samuel (pork) Sewardstone st
Watts John, Sewardstone st

CARPENTERS, BUILDERS & UNDERTAKERS.

Clark John Mullins, High Bridge st
Franks Edward, Sewardstone st
Whitley John, High Bridge st

CHINA AND EARTHENWARE DEALERS.

Barwick James, Market place
Burrell Lydia, High st
James Isaac (& glass) Sun st

CHYMISTS AND DRUGGISTS.

Marshall James Ainsworth (and tea dealer) High Bridge st
Mayhew Anthony (& dentist) Sun st

CLOTHES DEALERS.

Anderson Elizabeth, Sun st
Dyer William, High Bridge st
Pugh Samuel Boys, Sun st

COAL & CORN MERCHANTS.

Clark William, High Bridge st
Clayden John, Nazeing
Mitchell John, High Bridge st
Smith Thomas, Market place
Webster William (& miller) Sun st

COAL DEALERS.

Aylin Jeremiah, Sun st
Larman Joseph, Rome land
Smith Peter, High Bridge st
Woodbridge John, Paradise row

CORN & FLOUR DEALERS.

Bates Richard, Sun st
Carr James, High Bridge st
Hicks William, Sun st
Jones Edward, High Bridge st
Pegrum James, Nazeing
Watson William, Nazeing
Webster William, Sun st
Wray John, Sun st

FIRE, &c. OFFICE AGENTS.

LONDON (fire & life) John Mayhew (& stamp distributer) East end
NORWICH UNION, Anthony Woodrouffe, East end
PHŒNIX (fire) and PELICAN (life) Charles Pryor, Sun st

FISHMONGERS.

Copperthwaite Henry, Market place
Turner Joseph, High Bridge st

FURNITURE BROKERS.

Beall James, High Bridge st
Dyer William, Sun st

GROCERS & TEA DEALERS.

Marked thus * are also Cheesemongers.
(See also Shopkeepers, &c.)

Barwick James, Market place
*Bates William John, Sun st
Benton Richard, Nazeing
Burrell Lydia, High Beach
Clark John Mullins, High Bridge st
*Denby Walter (& tallow chandler) Sun street
*Imms Richard, High Bridge st
*James Isaac, Sun st
*Rickett James, Market place
Thompson John (& tallow chandler) Green yard
Wood John, High Bridge st
Wray John, Sun st

INNS.

Cock (commercial), Henry Quire Alger, High Bridge st
Ship, Frances Death, Sun st

IRONMONGERS & BRAZIERS.

Marsh John, High Bridge st
Richardson Wm. (furnishing) Sun st

LINEN DRAPERS.

Buck William, Market place
Denby Walter (& hatter) Sun st
Higgs James and Thomas, Sun st
Pugh Saml. Boys (& hatter) Sun st
Sedgwick William, Sun st

LIVERY STABLE KEEPERS.

Alger Henry Quire, Cock Inn, High Bridge st
Death Frances, Ship Inn, Sun st

MALT, & HOP DEALERS AND MALTSTERS.

Chapman Thomas, Abbey farm
Chatteris Thomas, Sun st
Jones Edward, High Bridge st
Upton Joseph, Market place

MILLERS.

Jones Edward, High Bridge st
Pegrum James, Nazeing
Webster William, Sun st

MILLINERS AND DRESS AND STRAW HAT MAKERS.

Allsup Eliza, High Bridge st
Barker Mary, Market place
Bigg Miriam, High Bridge st
Clark Sarah, High Bridge st
Thompson Mary, High Bridge st
Wright Harriet, Green yard

PERFUMERS, &c.

Dench Thomas (and fishing tackle dealer) Market place
Law Matthew, Sun st

PHYSICIAN.

Allen Matthew (and private lunatic asylum) Fair Mead, and Leopard Hill lodge, High Beach

PLUMBERS, PAINTERS AND GLAZIERS.

Copeland Robert, Sun st
Goff Sarah, East end
Nicholls Samuel, High Bridge st
Rudge Richard, High Bridge st
Smith William (and paper hanger) High Bridge street

SADDLERS.

Johnson Mary, Sun st
Judd William, Sun st
Phillipson Robert, Sun st

SHOPKEEPERS & DEALRS IN GROCERIES & SUNDRIES.

Argent Thomas, Nazeing
Bride John, Sewardstone
Cook James, Sun st
Light John, Market place
Mears Joseph, Nazeing
O'Brien James, High Bridge st

SILK THROWSTERS.

Buttress John Josiah and Son, Sewardstone mill

SMITHS AND FARRIERS.

Cook Thomas, Sun st
Greatorex Thomas, High Beach
Green Thomas, Sun st
Lowe Thomas, Nazeing
Powell Philip, Sewardstone

STONE & MARBLE MASONS.

Hobson Aaron, High Bridge st
Smith Peter, High Bridge st

SURGEONS.

Brown John, Sun st
Hilton Frederick, East end
Hilton Robert (to the honourable board of ordnance) East end
Wheble Edwin, Rome land

SURVEYORS.

Davis Robert Kirkup, East end
Pryor Chas. (& estate agent) Sun st

TAILORS.

Everett Charles, Sun st
Phipps William, Market place

TAVERNS & PUBLIC HOUSES.

Angel, Jeremiah Aylin, Sun st
Coach & Horses, John Clayden, Nazeing
Crooked Billet, William Watson, Nazeing
Crown, George & Thomas Want, Broxtorn bridge, Nazeing
Green Dragon, Mary Hasler, Market place
Green Man, Elijah Fordham, Farm hill
Greyhound, John Reffell, Sun st
Harp, Isaac Baker, High Bridge st
King Harold's Head, Richard Benton, Nazeing
King's Arms, William Clarke, High Bridge st
King's Oak, Jas. Phillipson, High Beach
New Inn, Richard Tuckwell, Sun st
Owl, John King, High Beach
Red Lion, William Argent, Market place
Royal Oak, Thos. Sinkwell, Sewardstone
Sun, Joseph Larman, Sun st
Three Compasses, William Kenuerley, Sewardstone street
Three Tuns, John Carr, Market place
White Horse, Fanny Smith, Sun st
White Lion, Wm. Perry Warner, Sun st

WATCH & CLOCK MAKERS.

Ellison William, High Bridge st
Pratt John, Sewardstone st

WHEELWRIGHTS.

Pegram James, Sewardstone
Worton John, Sun st

Miscellaneous.

Abrey William, confectioner, Sun st
Austen Thomas, superintendent of the machinery of Her Majesty's flour mills, High Bridge st
Beard George, clog & patten maker, Sun st
BILLIARD ROOMS, at the Cock Inn
Boards Thomas, bottle dealer, Market pl
Carr William, parish clerk, Church yard
Carter David, greengrocer, High Bridge st
Clark John, fellmonger, glover and tawer, High Bridge st
Cook James, cow leech and farrier, Sun st
Durnford and Co. pin manufacturers, Rome land
EXCISE OFFICE, Ship Inn, Sun st—John Muthlingham, suprvisr. Sewardstone st
King Thos. market gardener, Church yard
Littler Edmd. silk printer, High Bridge st
Lovell George, storekeeper of Her Majesty's small arms department at Enfield lock, High Bridge st
Mayhew John, registrar of births and deaths, East end
Maynard Wm. umbrella maker, Church yard
Pardoe Thomas, brush & patten maker, High Bridge st
Rapley John, timber dealer, High Bridge st
Rowley Jas. sausage maker, High Bridge st
Smith James, parish clerk, Nazeing
Thompson Ebenezer, printer and bookbinder, Sewardstone st
Thompson Henry, pattern designer, High Bridge st
Turner John, basket maker, Green yard
Ware William, sawyer, Fountain row

ROYAL GUNPOWDER MANUFACTORY.

Commanding Engineer—Col. Thos. Moody
Deputy Storekeeper, James Wright, esq.
Superintendent of the Machinery—Thos. Austen
Master Worker—Hugh Jones
First Clerk—Thomas Littler
Second Clerk—David Wilkie
Clerk of the Works—John Baker

COACHES.

To LONDON, John Pratten's *Coach*, from East end, calling at the Cock, High Bridge st, every morning at eight, except Sunday, when it calls at six in the morning and five in the evening.

CARRIERS.

To LONDON, Fanny Elizabth. Presland, from the White Horse, Sun st, every Monday, Tuesday and Friday.

CONVEYANCE BY WATER.

To LONDON, William Clark's, John Mitchell's & William Webster's *Barges*, from their wharfs, High Bridge street, three times a week.

WALTHAMSTOW AND NEIGHBOURHOOD.

WALTHAMSTOW is a delightful village, in the hundred of Becontree, about 6½ miles N. E. from St. Paul's, London, and 3 from Stratford; situate upon the borders of Epping forest, in a very extensive parish, which includes five manors, viz., the manor of the Rectory, that of Walthamstow-Tony, Walthamstow-Frances, Higham Benstead, and Salsbury Hall. The name of *Waltham* is purely Saxon, signifying 'a dwelling in a wood,' and indeed is perfectly applicable to this parish, which might be compared to what the ancients called 'a rural city.' Country seats, farms, houses and cottages, are so blended together—and the paths, encompassed with trees and hedges, are so beautifully romantic—that no surprise can be manifested that so many opulent and respectable families reside in this healthy district. The river Lea forms the western boundary of the parish; on this stream is the manufactory of the 'British Copper Company.' The places of worship are, the parish church, dedicated to St. Mary; the chapel of ease of St. John's, at Chapel end, and two chapels for independents and unitarians. The church, which stands on an eminence, is a spacious Gothic structure, and appears to have been built in or about the twelfth century; the two aisles, however, are of more recent date, and two galleries were added in 1807. There are a considerable number of monuments that ornament the interior, some of which are of great beauty; amongst these a supurb one of white marble, with figures as large as life, to Sigismond Trafford, his wife and infant, will particularly excite admiration. The living of Walthamstow is a vicarage, of which the Rev. William Wilson is the patron and incumbent, and his present curate is the Rev. J. N. Dalton. The free grammar school here was founded and endowed by Sir George Monoux, Knight, in 1527, who likewise endowed thirteen almshouses with rents arising from houses and lands; six other alms-houses for widows of decayed tradesmen were endowed by Mrs. Mary Squires. There are besides a proprietory grammar school, infants', and national schools, and one supported by the congregation of independents. The parish contained, in 1831, 4,258 inhabitants.

POST OFFICE, Whipp's cross, William Southgate, *Post Master.*—Letters from LONDON arrive every morning at half-past seven, forenoon at eleven, afternoon at three and evening at six, and are despatched every morning at nine, afternoon at one and a quarter past four.

Letter Boxes at William Dacomb's, Wood street, and at John Cock's, Marsh street.

NOBILITY, GENTRY AND CLERGY.

Allen Mr. Richard, Hoe st
Badams Mr. George, Wood st
Barclay Ford, esq. Walthamstow
Barker Robert, esq. Whipp's cross
Barr Mr. Thomas, Marsh st
Barrow Thomas, esq. Marsh st
Bedford Miss Ann, Hoe st
Bedwell Mr. Francis, Salter's buildngs
Benett Mr. George, Wood st
Berthon the Misses, Wood st
Blicke William, esq. Marsh st
Bourdillion James, esq. Grove place
Bracher Mr. Richard, Whipp's cross
Branfill Mr. Benjamin, Wood st
Bright Mrs. Elizabeth, Church lane
Brown Mr. George, Marsh st
Burrell Mr. Charles, Markhouse lane
Caley Miss —, Marsh st
Careless Miss —, Marsh st
Charlton Mr. Adam, Higham hill
Clarke Matthew, esq. Clay st
Clarke Mr. William, Hale end
Cogan Rev. Eleazer, Higham hill hse
Collard Mrs. Elizabeth, Shearnhall st
Cook Mrs. Henry, Grove lane
Cook Mrs. Sarah, Bellevue house
Corbett Mr. Archibald, Marsh st
Corbyn John, esq. Wood st
Cotesworth Robert, esq. Marsh st
Dalton Rev. John Neale, Vicarage
Danvers Edward Fuller, esq. Salter's buildings
Danvers Mr. Henry, Wood st
Davis Miss —, Salter's buildings
Degrand Mr. Jas. Vincent, Chapel end
Dobrie Harry, esq. Hoe st
Drake William Walker, esq. Marsh st
Dubree Mr. Bonomy, Shearn hall
Duncan Mr. Peter, Marsh st
Durzant James M. B. esq. Shearn hall lodge
Farish Mrs. Hannah, Church end
Foulger John, esq. Hoe st
Forster Edward, esq. Hale end
Freeman Mr. Charles, Church end
Freeman Rev. Joseph, Church end
Gadsden Mr. Henry, Marsh st
Gore Robert, esq. Castle house
Gosling John, esq. Elm house
Goss Miss —, Clay st
Greaves William, esq. Church end
Hall Mrs. Ann, West grove
Hall Miss Ann Gloyne, West grove
Hall James, esq. Marsh st
Hankey Wm. Alexander, esq. Hoe st
Harris Jos. Owen, esq. Salter's bldgs
Harris Richard, esq. Wyatt lane
Helme James, esq. Wood st
Helme Robert, esq. Wood st
Hill Mrs. —, Salter's buildings
Hindman Mr. Josiah, Shearnhall st
Janson Alfred, esq. Hoe st
Jury Mr. James, Marsh st
Laprimaudaye the Misses Sarah and Catherine, Marsh st
Lemert Mr. George, Salter's buildings
Loxham Robert, esq. Hale end
Massey Honourable George, Marsh st
Masterman Ths. esq. Salter's buildings
Morley John, esq. Salter's buildings
Morton John, esq. Clay st
Nesbit Mr. John, Church hill
Niblock Miss —, Clay st
Nicholls Rev. Benjmn. Elliott, Greenleaf lane
Noel Honorable and Rev. Baptist W. Hale end
Petty Edward, esq. Mark house
Price Mrs. Elizabeth, West grove
Secretan Mr. Philip, Hoe st
Short Rev. William, Salter's buildings
Sinnott Mr. —, Higham hill
Stephenson Mrs. —, Shearnhall st
Stubbins Benjamin, esq. Wyatt lane
Thompson Mr. Charles, Vine house
Thorpe Mr. Joseph, Marsh st
Thorpe Mr. Robert, Grove place
Todhunter Mr. Benjamin, Haggerlane
Truman Joseph, esq. Grosvenor house

Turner Mr. John Guttredge, Church la
Vigne Henry, esq. Church hill
Vigne Thomas, esq. Hoe st
Waite Rev. Thomas, Church end
Warner Edward, esq. West grove
Washington Mrs. Amy, Greenleaf lane
Webb Mr. William, Salter's buildings
Wigram Edw. esq. Clay st [house
Wigram Lady Eleanor, Walthamstow
Wigram Octavius, Prospect house
Williams Daniel Hunt, esq. Walthamstow [ings
Wilmot Mr. Sinnott, Salter's build-
Wilson Thomas, esq. Marsh st
Wilson Rev. William, Grove lane
Woodward Miss Eliz. Grove cottage

ACADEMIES & SCHOOLS.

Benson William (brdng) Vine house
Courtney Charlotte (boarding & day) Marsh st
FOREST PROPRIETORY GRAMMAR SCHOOL—Rev. Thos. Dry, master
FREE SCHOOL, Marsh street—Ann Knight, mistress
Gollop Lucy (day) Wood st
INFANTS' SCHOOL, Church end—Eliza Martin, mistress
Milford Mrs. and the Misses (boarding) Walthamstow
MONOUX GRAMMAR SCHOOL, Church yard—Rev. Ths. Waite, head master
NATIONAL SCHOOL, Church end—Robert Matthews, master; Emlyn Tope, mistress
Penn Hannah (preparatory) Marsh st
Sorrell Harriet (boarding and day) Grove house

BAKERS.

Bailey Robert, Wood st
Brockley David (biscuit) Wood st
Cheffins Paul, Shearnhall st
Lewis Isaac, Wood st
Rudd David, Marsh st
Wesley William, Marsh st

BOOKSELLERS & STATIONRS.

Cox Thomas (& toy dealer) Wood st
Penn Francis, Marsh st

BOOT & SHOE MAKERS.

Berry Thomas, Wood st
Boffee Samuel, Marsh st
Bowman William, Marsh st
Broadhurst Thomas, Wood st
Carter Thomas, Wood st
Challis William, Marsh st
Evans Thomas, Marsh st
Potter Joshua, Chapel end
Renwick Henry, Church end
Smith John, Marsh st
Smith Samuel, Wood st
Turner John, Church lane
Whiffen John, Wood st
Wilson John, Church end

BRICKLAYERS.

How James, Wood st
Turner Esther, Marsh st

BUILDERS.

How James, Wood st
Lucking Wm. Wright, Church end
Saltwell Richard, Marsh st
Turner Esther, Marsh st

BUTCHERS.

Boltwood Mary, Marsh st
Bradshaw John, Marsh st
Chalk Sarah, Marsh st
Mitchell William, Wood st
Pledger Henry, Wood st
Proye Peter, Wood st

CABINET MAKERS AND UPHOLSTERERS.

Waller John, Wood st
Williams Henry, Wood st

CARPENTRS & UNDERTAKRS

Cosser George, Hale end
Lucking William Wright, Church end
Moore John, Whipp's cross
Pledger James, Wood st
Roberts William, Marsh st
Saltwell Richard, Marsh st

CORN-DEALERS.

Casborn John (& earthenware dealr) Wood st
Turner and Budd, Wood st
Wragg Robert, Marsh st

FIRE, &c. OFFICE AGENTS.

GUARDIAN, James How, Wood st
PHŒNIX, Samuel Lilley, Marsh st
ROYAL EXCHANGE, William Wright Lucking, Church end

FURNITURE BROKERS.

Butterworth John, Market st
Waller John, Wood st

GROCERS.

Marked thus * are also Cheesemongers.
(See also Shopkeepers, &c.)

*Aylett Matthew, Marsh st
*Claridge George, Marsh st
*Dacomb William, Wood st
*Hobson Robert (and earthenware dealer) Marsh st
*Laver William, Wood st [Marsh st
*Lilley Samuel (& tallow chandler)
Stainer Ann, Chapel end
*Turner and Budd, Wood st
Wright Samuel (tea) Forest bldngs

HAIR DRESSERS.

Boffee Thomas, Marsh st
Cross Charles, Wood st
Wright William, Wood st

HORSE AND GIG OWNERS, FOR HIRE.

Boffee Thomas, Marsh st
Clark Joseph, Marsh st
Warr William, Wood st
Wragg Robert, Marsh st

IRONMONGERS.

Sinfield John, Wood st
Turner James (& tinman) Marsh st

LACE MENDERS & CLEANRS.

Bailey Sophia, Church end
Poole Mary, Church lane

LINEN, &c. DRAPERS.

Cock John, Marsh st [*brook*
Clarke Ebenzr. Marsh st, & *Snares-*
Dacomb William, Wood st
Embleton Sarah, Marsh st
Hicks John, Marsh st
Hobson Robert, Marsh st
Turner and Budd, Wood st

LIVERY STABLE KEEPERS.

Orme John, Duke's Head, Wood st
Wilson Richard, Chequers, Marsh st
Wragg Robert, Marsh st

LOCKSMITHS AND BELL HANGERS.

Corsham Samuel, Marsh st
Sinfield John, Wood st

MILLINERS AND DRESS AND STRAW HAT MAKERS.

Evans Sarah, Wood st
Hill Caroline, Wood st
Jeffries Caroline, Wood st
Linsell Susan, Wood st
Noyes Mary Ann, Marsh st

MUSIC TEACHERS.

Bird George (& music seller) Marsh st
Mullinex Henry, Marsh st

NURSERY, SEEDSMAN, AND FLORIST.

James Pamplin (and new ground workman) Wood st, & Lea Bridge road, *Leyton*

PAINTERS, PLUMBERS, &c.

Penn Francis, Marsh st
Watkins Harry, Marsh st
Webber Charles (and paper hanger) Wood st
Wincey John Charles, Wood st

SADDLERS.

Fenn John, Marsh st
Giffin —, Marsh st
Randall Elizabeth, Wood st
Speller Charles, Wood st

SHOPKEEPERS & DEALRS IN GROCERIES & SUNDRIES.

Burrows Eleanor, Marsh st
Chipperton James, Chapel end
Embleton Sarah, Marsh st
Saltwell Richard, Marsh st
Savill Elizabeth, Marsh st
Taylor William, Church end
Whiffen John, Wood st
Woodard Isaac, Wood st
Wright William, Wood st

SMITHS & FARRIERS.

Barltrop Jonathan, Marsh st
Evans Richard, Marsh st
Nicholls James, Wood st
Sinfield John, Marsh st
Turner Henry (and veterinary surgeon) Marsh st

SURGEONS.

Blicke William, M.D. Marsh st
Browne John Dallisson, Wood st
Solly Thomas, Marsh st

TAILORS.

Clarke Thomas, Marsh st
Fesenmeyer Sebastian, Marsh st
Hicks John, Marsh st
Smith Zachary, Wood st
Stock Samuel, Wood st
Taylor William, Church end
York William, Marsh st

TAVERNS & PUBLIC HOUSES.

Chequers, Richard Wilson, Marsh st
Coach & Horses, Wm. Wiltshire, Marsh st
Cock, Joseph Willson, Marsh st
Crooked Billet, Wm. Naldrett, Chapel end
Duke's Head, John Orme, Wood st
Ferry Boat, Wm. Hewes, Hilleyer's ferry
Nag's Head, Joshua Brookes, Church end

WHEELWRIGHTS.

Clinker and Chapman, Marsh st
Vale Robert & Son (& coach makers) Wood st
Wren James, Chapel end

Miscellaneous.

Coe John, parish clerk, Wood st
Dyer William, poulterer, Marsh st
Gollop John, market gardener and coal dealer, Wood st
Grant Alice, fancy worsted dealer, Wood st
Hollely William, fishmonger, Marsh st
How Jas. stone & marble m[illegible], Wood st
Humphreys John, surveyor, [illegible]uctioneer & estate agent, Church end [bldgs.
Jordan George, market gardener, Salter's
Markham Thos. umbrella maker, Wood st
Maynard Robert, parish beadle, Wood st
Pledger Thomas, cowkeeper, Wood st
POLICE STATION, Church end—Thomas Godwin, serjeant [Marsh st
Putnam Norris, watch and clock maker,
Robarts Robert, cooper, Wood st
Ruggles James, sawyer, Wood st
SOCIETY FOR PROMOTING CHRISTIAN KNOWLEDGE—depository at Robert Matthews', Church end
Stoker John, confectioner, Wood st
Taylor Samuel, chymist & druggist and agent for Bett's brandy, Wood st
Trapps George, greengrocer, Wood st
Williams, Foster & Co. copper manufacturers, Marsh st
WORKHOUSE, Church end—John Britain, governor; Mary Britain, matron
Wragg Robert, coach proprietor, Marsh st

COACHES.

To LONDON, Robert Wragg's *Coaches*, from his house, Marsh st, calling at the Cock & the Duke's Head, every morning (Sunday excepted) at 8, 9 & 10; afternoon 2 and 5, and evening at 7; on Sunday morning at eight and nine, and evening at six, seven and eight.

CARRIERS.

To LONDON, Richard Milsom & Elizabeth Vickery, from Wood st. Richard Wilson, from Marsh st, & William Robinson, from the Crooked Billet, Chapel end, daily.

WANSTEAD AND NEIGHBOURHOOD.

WANSTEAD is a genteel and interesting little village, in the parish of its name, and hundred of Becontree; six miles from Whitechapel Church, London, two from Stratford, and one from Leytonstone, delightfully situated on the margin of Waltham forest, on the main road from London to Cambridge. But a comparatively few years since, it was famous for possessing one of the most splendid and extensive mansions that this country could boast—"Wanstead House"—erected in 1715, by the Tylney family; and every descendant from the ancient stock added something to enrich, extend, or embellish it. The last of this family, in lineal descent, who occupied this princely edifice, was Miss Tylney Long; she married the Hon. W. T. L. P. Wellesley, who, in 1822, caused the mansion to be pulled down, and its materials sold in lots under the hammer; together with the costly furniture, the valuable antiques, &c.; since which time, the beautiful and extensive park that surrounded the building has been let for the grazing of cattle. The lady did not many years survive the scattering of these interesting heir-looms, and the destruction of her house—she died in 1825, leaving two children.

The church (dedicated to St. Mary) is a modern building, remarkable for its neatness and simplicity; it contains a nave and two aisles; the chancel is enriched with a beautifully painted window; the living is a rectory, in the gift of the Hon. W. T. L. P. Wellesley, who is also lord of the manor. Here is a charity school, founded by Miss Long, for twenty boys and twenty girls; the endowment is vested in trustees. The parish of Wanstead contained, in 1831, 1,403 inhabitants.

POST, *Receiving-House* at Thos. Gooke's.—Letters from LONDON arrive every morning at eight, afternoon at three and evening at seven, and are despatched every morning at nine and afternoon at a quarter before four.

GENTRY AND CLERGY.

Andrews William, esq. Wanstead
Barber Captain James, Wanstead
Bardon the Misses, Wanstead place
Barlow John, esq. Wanstead
Bingley Mr. Henry, Snaresbrook
Birch William, esq. Wanstead
Brown James, esq. Snaresbrook
Chapman Abel, esq. Snaresbrook
Chapman Jonathan, esq. Mall
Dettmar Mrs. —, Wanstead
Dobson Thomas, esq. Wanstead
Dosseter Mr. Thomas, Lake house
Doxat Lewis, esq. Snaresbrook
Dubois Mrs. —, Snaresbrook
Hair Mr. Michael, Wanstead
Heaphy Mr. John, Snaresbrook
Hewetson Mr. Henry, Wanstead
Hill the Misses, Snaresbrook
Hodgson Thomas, esq. Wanstead
Ivory Mr. Richd. Forest gate
Jennings Mr. David, Snaresbrook cottage
Knight Mr. Joseph, Wanstead cottage
Lennox John, esq. Snaresbrook
Middleton Boswell, esq. Bush gate
Morgan the Misses, Wanstead
Morrisson James, esq. Snaresbrook
Paris Archibald, esq. Wanstead
Plaxton Mr. Thomas, Canal farm
Plaxton Mr. William, Forest gate
Rushout Hon. Anne, Grove
Saunders Mr. John, Snaresbrook
Scholey George, esq. Snaresbrook
Scratton Mrs. —, Snaresbrook
Smith Colonel James, Snaresbrook
Sparring Mr. James, Wanstead
Waite Mrs. Elizabeth, Snaresbrook
Welch Mrs. Snaresbrook
Wells Thomas, esq. Holloway down
Wigram Money, esq. Wood house
Wigram Rev. Wm. Pitt, Wanstead
Willis Mr. Arthur, Wanstead
Wilson Miss Ann, Snaresbrook
Wright Mr. William, Wanstead

PROFESSIONAL PERSONS.

Chalcroft Richmond, boarding school
Coudell Alfred, schoolmaster
Franklin Arthur, surgeon

INNS & PUBLIC HOUSES.

George, Edward Dyer, Wanstead
Spread Eagle, Edward Whitfield, Snaresbrook
Thatched House, Sarah Renwick, Wanstead

SHOPKEEPERS & TRADERS.

Barker Thomas, tax collector
Brown Jas. plumbr, glazier, & painter
Clarke Ebenezer, grocer, draper, corn and coal merchant, and job master, Snaresbrook
Claydon James, shopkeeper
Clement John, fishmonger
Cocket William, shoemaker
Coles Henry, baker
Cooke Thomas, grocer and draper
Dalladay James, shoemaker
Halestrap Jas. shopkeeper, Wanstead
Hammond Henry, baker
Hart Thomas, butcher, Wanstead
Matthews James, shopkeeper
Mears James, plumber, &c
Merwood Mary, dress maker
Michell John, tailor
Pegler John, plumber, painter, &c.
Pegler Peter, parish clerk
Pepper Mary, milliner
Russell William, shoe maker
Scales James, blacksmith
Shephard Thos. bricklayer & builder
Slater Mary Ann, shopkeeper
Smith Wm. shoemaker, Wanstead
Smith Wm. jun. shoemakr, Wanstead
Wildsmith Benjamin, builder
Willoughby John, plumber, &c.
Withers John, carpenter
Yardly Daniel, tailor and draper

COACHES.

To LONDON, Barnard & Green's *Coaches*, from their office, every morning (Sunday excepted) at nine, and afternoon at half past five—and Sunday morning eight, and evening at six.

CARRIERS.

To LONDON, John Welton, from his house, George lane, every morning (Sunday excepted) at nine.

WICKFORD, BOWERS GIFFORD, PITSEA, RAWRETH AND NEIGHBOURHOODS.

WICKFORD is a small village and parish in the hundred of Barstable, situated in a hollow between Billericay and Rayleigh, about six miles distant from either place. As regards trade, Wickford is destitute of interest, nor does it present anything to gratify curiosity. The church, a small edifice, stands on elevated ground, at a short distance from the village; the living is a rectory, in the patronage of R. B. De Beauvoir, Esq. The population of the parish, in 1831, amounted to 402.

BOWERS GIFFORD is a parish in the same hundred as Wickford, bounded on the south by Holly and East Havens, creeks that are navigable to the Thames. The village church, dedicated to St. Margaret, stands about four miles and a half south-west from Rayleigh: the living is a rectory, in the patronage (or lately was) of John Carter, Esq. Population of the parish, by the returns of 1831, 231.

PITSEA is also an inconsiderable parish, in the same hundred as Wickford, about five miles south from that village. It contained, at the last census, 276 inhabitants.

RAWRETH parish is in the hundred of Rochford, three miles N. W. from Rayleigh, and about the like distance E. from Wickford. The church here, dedicated to St. Nicholas, has within these few years been enlarged; the living is a rectory, in the gift of the master and fellows of Pembroke college, Cambridge. Population, 321.

POST OFFICE, WICKFORD, Moses Miller, *Post Master*.—Letters from INGATESTONE arrive (by mail cart) every morning at two, and are despatched every night (Sunday excepted) at half-past eight—on Sunday they are despatched one hour earlier.

GENTRY AND CLERGY.

Abrey Mr. Daniel, Pitsea
Archer Mr. David, Wickford
Bayley Mr. Charles, Bowers Gifford
Bell Mr. Thomas, Wickford
Berens Rev. Edward R. Wickford
Blakeley Mr. Thos. Bowers Gifford
Brewitt John, esq. Wickford
Brunwin Mr. Samuel, Wickford
Cleave Henry, esq. Rawreth hall
Grout Mr. John, Rawreth
Grout Mr. William, Rawreth
Hanney Rev. James, Bowers Gifford
Nottidge Rev. John, Wickford
Sparks Mr. James, Pitsea
Talbot Mr. Robert R. Pitsea
Thackthwaite Mr. Colchester (surgeon, and registrar of births and deaths) Wickford
White Rev. John Calcutta, Rawreth

INNS & PUBLIC HOUSES.

Bull, William Green, Pitsea
Carpenters' Arms, Robert Phillips, Rawreth
Castle (and posting) John Jeffries, Wickford
Gun, William Doe, Bowers Gifford

SHOPKEEPERS & TRADERS.

Adey Aaron, shopkeeper & butcher, Wickford
Bailey Charles, saddler, Bowers
Bowdle Wm. wheelwright, Pitsea
Carter Rebecca, straw hat maker, Wickford
Clark William, bricklayer, Wickford
Crooks Thomas, blacksmith, Pitsea
Crow Joseph, shoemaker, Wickford
Franklin Benj. butcher, Wickford
Freeman Wm. carpenter, Pitsea
Frost Robert, shoemaker, Rawreth

Grout Robert, miller, Pitsea
Hart Charles, shopkeeper, Rawreth
Large Samuel, retail brewer, Bowers
Larrett Jas. shopkeeper, Wickford
Mace Sarah, blacksmith, Bowers
Miller Moses, shopkeeper, Wickford
Moyse John, boot maker, Wickford
North Jno. plumber & glazier, Wickfd
Read Sarah, shopkeeper, Bowers
Reed Thomas, blacksmith, Wickford
Rushbrook William, veterinary surgeon, Wickford
Salmon Geo. Maskell, baker, Wickford
Woollard Wm. wheelwright, Wickfd

COACHES AND VANS.

To LONDON, a *Coach* (from Southend), passes through Wickford, every morning (Sunday excepted), at ten—and a *Van* passes through (from Rochford), every Monday and Thursday afternoon.
To ROCHFORD, a *Van* (from London), passes through Wickford, every Wednesday and Saturday afternoon.
To SOUTHEND, a *Coach* (from London), passes through Wickford, every evening (Sunday excepted), at half-past six.

WIGBOROUGH (GREAT & LITTLE), FINGRINGHOE,

LANGENHOE, MERSEA ISLAND AND PELDON.

GREAT and LITTLE WIGBOROUGH are two parishes in the hundred of Winstree, lying between Maldon and Colchester, from which latter town Great Wigborough is distant about eight miles. The church, which is dedicated to St. Stephen, stands on a considerable eminence, and is distinguished at a great distance. This parish is bounded on the south by the Blackwater. The church at Little Wigborough is dedicated to Saint Nicholas. The livings of both parishes are rectories.

The parish of FINGRINGHOE lies to the south-east of the Wigboroughs, on the road to Colchester, about four miles and a half from that town—bounded on the east by the navigable Colne. The church is dedicated to St. Andrew; the benefice is a discharged vicarage, in the presentation of the Firmin family.

LANGENHOE village is situated to the south-west of Fingringhoe, about three miles therefrom; and this parish, like that of Fingringhoe, has the river Colne on its eastern side. The church is dedicated to St. Andrew—the living is a rectory, in the gift of Earl Waldegrave.

EAST and WEST MERSEA are two parishes comprised in the island of Mersea, nine miles south by east from Colchester—bounded on the north and west by the Mersea channel, on the east by the Colne, and on the south by the Blackwater river. With the main land the island is connected, at low water, by a causeway. The church of East Mersea, dedicated to St. Edmund, has a square stone tower, which serves as a landmark to the mariner approaching the coast; the benefice is a rectory, in the patronage of the crown. The church of West Mersea, dedicated to St. Peter and St. Paul, is a structure by no means inelegant; the living is a vicarage, of which Mrs. Simpson is (or was) the patroness.

PELDON parish is about five miles and a half south by west from Colchester—bounded on the south-east by the Mersea channel, which separates it from Mersea island. The church is dedicated to St. Mary, and the benefice, which is a rectory, is in the same patronage as that of Langenhoe.

All the above-mentioned parishes are in the hundred of Winstree. The population, in 1831, was as follows:—GREAT WIGBOROUGH, 434; LITTLE WIGBOROUGH, 123; FINGRINGHOE, 542; LANGENHOE, 146; EAST MERSEA, 300; WEST MERSEA, 847; PELDON, 424.

GENTRY AND CLERGY.

Atkinson Rv. Christr. Gt. Wigborough
Barnes Thomas, esq. Langenhoe
Cooper Thomas, esq. Langenhoe hall
Harris Rev. James, Wigborough
Mayes Mr. James, Peldon
Norman Mr. John (surgeon) West Mersea
Polley Mr. John, Peldon

PUBLIC HOUSES.

King's Head, Joseph Runicle, Great Wigborough
Lion, Elizabeth Horn, Langenhoe
Rose, John Green, Peldon
Whalebone, Mary Stone, Fingringhoe
White Hart, James Sayers, Mersea Island

SHOPKEEPERS & TRADERS.

Balls Joseph, grocer, West Mersea
Chapman John, shoemaker, West Mersea
Cook John, wheelwright, Peldon
Cooper George, miller, Peldon
Hall David, shopkeeper, Great Wigborough
South Elizabeth, grocer, Great Wigborough
Sparrow Richd. carpenter & wheelwright, Great Wigborough
Sparrow Wm. blacksmith, Peldon
Stammers Edwd. miller, Fingringhoe
Stammers Jos. maltster, Abberton
Williams Wm. carpenter, &c. Peldon
Wright Jos. baker, Gt. Wigborough
Wright Wm. parish clerk, Wigboro'

WITHAM,

WITH GREAT AND LITTLE BRAXTED, FAULKBOURN, HATFIELD PEVERELL, ULTING, WICKHAM BISHOPS AND NEIGHBOURHOODS.

WITHAM is a small market town in the parish and hundred of its name, situated near the confluence of the Braine stream with the Blackwater river, on the main road from London to Colchester, Harwich, &c., 37 miles N. E. by E. from the metropolis. The town, consisting chiefly of one long street, has an agreeable aspect, and the houses are of neat construction. The manufacture of baize was at one time carried on here extensively, but it has entirely ceased for several years, and the principal trade now is that which arises from the requisite supply of the inhabitants and a respectable vicinage, together with its great thoroughfare: the latter advantage tends to support three good inns. The county magistrates hold petty sessions for the division in Witham every Tuesday; and constables, and other officers for the town, are appointed at the manorial courts of Peter Du Cane, Esq. About three quarters of a mile from hence is a chalybeate spring, formerly of considerable repute, and visited by many, but now totally neglected. On the south side of Cheping hill, about half a mile north of the town, are the traces of a Roman camp; and the church, but more particularly the tower, is in a great measure constructed of Roman bricks—Mr. Gough and some other authorities are of opinion that Witham occupies the site of the military station *Canonium*. The church, dedicated to St. Nicholas, which stands on Cheping hill before mentioned, is a neat structure, in the later style of English architecture, and contains several ancient monuments; the benefice is a vicarage, in the patronage of the bishop of London, and incumbency of the Rev. John Newman. There are places of worship for baptists, the society of friends, independents and Roman catholics. The charities comprise two schools upon the national plan, several alms-houses, and some minor benefactions to the poor. This being the centre, under the present poor-law, of a union of eighteen parishes, the union poor-house is established here. The market is held on Tuesday, and the fairs on the Monday before Whit-Sunday and the 14th of September. Witham parish, in the year 1831, contained 2,735 inhabitants.

Three miles from Witham, in the same hundred, is the small village of GREAT BRAXTED, situated on an eminence in the parish of its name. Near the village, in a fine park, with an extensive prospect in front, stands the beautiful residence of Peter Du Cane, Esq. The church, dedicated to All Saints, is an ancient edifice, about one mile from the village. The parish, which is more extensive than populous, contained, in 1801, 502 inhabitants; but in 1831 the number was only 471, shewing a decrease of 31 in the preceding thirty years.

Adjoining the above is the parish of LITTLE BRAXTED, composed of about eight hundred acres of land, with a population of only ninety-two persons; it contains, however, a small church, dedicated to St. Nicholas.

FAULKBOURN is about three miles from Witham, on the Braintree road. Faulkbourn Hall, a stately fabric, the residence of Jonathan Bullock, Esq., was erected about the time of Henry II, and is the only object that can reward curiosity in this locality. The church is dedicated to St. Germanus. Population, 160.

Situated betwixt Chelmsford and Witham, between two and three miles S. S. W. from the latter town, is the village of HATFIELD PEVERELL. The parish, which is extensive, is embellished by several seats and handsome residences. The church, dedicated to St. Andrew, was enlarged some few years since; the living is a vicarage, in the incumbency of the Rev. Coventry Payne. The population, in 1831, amounted to 1,313 persons.

ULTING is a parish adjoining to Hatfield on the south, in which direction it is bounded by the Chelmer and Blackwater navigation. The church is dedicated to All Saints; the living, a discharged vicarage, is in the presentation of R. Nicholson, Esq. Population, 158.

WICKHAM BISHOPS is in the hundred of Thurstable, situated between Maldon and Witham—distant from the former three miles and a half, and from the latter two and a half. Wickham '*Bishops*' is so called from having formerly been a residence for the bishops of London; and at this day the greater part of the parish is possessed by the prelate of that see. The number of inhabitants, by the last census, was 549.

POST OFFICE, WITHAM, William Garrett, *Post Master.*—Letters from LONDON arrive every night at twelve, and are despatched every morning at seven.—Letters from SUDBURY, &c. arrive every night at eleven, and are despatched every morning at seven.—Letters are despatched to CLARE (by cross post, leaving bags at BRAINTREE, HALSTEAD and SUDBURY) every morning at three.—The box closes every night at ten, but letters are received until eleven by paying sixpence with each.

GENTRY AND CLERGY.

Aldridge Edward B. esq. Witham
Allaker William, esq. Hatfield
Beadel Mr. Pitt, Hatfield Peverell
Boyfield Mrs. —, Witham
Bretnall Robert, esq. Cheping hill
Bright the Misses, Witham
Bullock Jonathan, esq. Faulkbourn hall
Burgess Rev. Robert B. Faulkbourn [parsonage
Cutts John, esq. Cheping hill
Du Cane Rev. Henry, Grove, Witham
Du Cane the Misses, Witham
Du Cane Peter, esq. Braxted lodge
Dyer Miss —, Witham
Eaton Mrs. —, Cheping hill
Edwards George, esq. Cheping hill
Gower Rev. Thomas Foote, Totham
Granger Mrs. —, Witham
Granger Mr. William, Wickham
Grimwood Jas. esq. Hatfield Peverell
Hastings William, esq. Cheping hill
Herring Rev. Thos. Great Braxted
Hunt Mrs. —, Witham
Ives Samuel, esq. Witham
Jarvis Mrs. —, Witham [Peverell
Johnson Abraham, esq. Hatfield
Leigh Rev. Thos. Wickham Bishop
Lowe Mrs. —, Witham
Luard William Wright, esq. (magistrate) Witham
Manby Rev. William, Cheping hill
Newman Rev. John, Cheping hill
Osborne Mr. John, Witham
Payne Rev. Coventry, Hatfield Peverll
Philbrick Mr. John, Witham
Pryke William, esq. Cheping hill
Robinson Rev. Richard, Witham
Rush Captain —, Little Braxted
Shaen the Misses, Witham
Shaen Samuel, esq. (magistrate) Hatfield Peverell
Sims Mrs. —, Witham
Smith Mrs. —, Witham
Smith Mr. Thomas, Wickham hall
Talbot Misses Eliz. & Louisa, Witham
Townsend Capt. —, Hatfield Peverell
Walford John Edw. esq. Cheping hill
Walford Rev. Wm. Hatfield Peverell
Walker the Misses, Witham
Ward Mr. —, Hatfield Peverell
Wright Mrs. —, Wickham place
Wright Peter, esq. (magistrate) Hatfield priory

ACADEMIES & SCHOOLS.

BRITISH SCHOOL (boys' and girls') Witham—William Edmund Clark, master; Susannah Aves, mistress
Houghton Mary Ann and Harriet (boarding & day) Witham
Howard Miss, Witham
Johnson Misses (day) Witham
NATIONAL SCHOOL, Witham—Wm. Wade, master; Eliza Wade, mistrss
Spaull Sarah (boarding) Witham
Steele Isabella (boarding) Witham

ATTORNEYS.

Banks Edward Wilson, Witham
Blood Joseph Howell, Witham
Pattison and Cutts, Witham
Thomasin James Henry, Witham

AUCTIONEERS & APPRAISRS.

Beadel James (and architect and surveyor) Witham
Cook John, Cheping hill

BAKERS & CORN DEALERS.

Collis Christr. Annett, Cheping hill
Deadman Robert, Wickham
Dowsett William, Hatfield Peverell
Ely Thomas, Witham
Fairhead David, Witham
Hubbard Elizabeth, Witham
Lake Mrs. Cheping hill
Larkin Robert, Great Braxted
Sayer Joseph, Witham
Shelley Uriah, Hatfield Peverell
White George, Witham

BANKERS.

Mills, Bawtree and Co. (branch of Colchester) Witham—(draw on Hankeys & Co. London)
SAVINGS' BANK, Witham (open Tuesday)—Rev. Charles Dalton, secretry

BOOKSELLERS & STATIONRS.

Knight & Turner, Witham

BOOT & SHOE MAKERS.

Abbott David, Cheping hill
Aves James, Hatfield Peverell
Bather Absalom, Witham
Boutwood James, Witham
Brand Joseph, Witham
Bridge Samuel, Wickham
Cornwell James, Cheping hill
Dunsdon Alfred, Witham
Hansell David, Hatfield Peverell
Harvey James, Witham
Lemon Samuel, Witham
Mann James, Hatfield Peverell
Sayer Alfred, Witham
Simpson William, Witham
Wood Philip, Witham

BRICKLAYERS.

Chalk Joseph, Witham
Cooke Francis, Witham
Ellis Robert, Wickham
Harrison Theodorus, Witham
Page William, Witham
Taverner James, Hatfield Peverell
Wright Richard, Witham

BRUSH MANUFACTURER.

Thomasin James (& painting brush, mop, mop yarn, and patten and clog maker) Witham

BUTCHERS.

Barwell Charles, Witham
Barwell Edmund, Witham
Barwell Henry, Witham
Belcher James Thomas, Witham
Franklin Thomas, Witham
Pavitt William, Hatfield Peverell
Rust William, Witham
Warren James, Witham
Webb Isaac, Hatfield Peverell

CABINET MAKERS AND UPHOLSTERERS.

Coote John, Cheping hill
Cottee Benjamin, Witham
Cottee John & George, Witham

CARPENTERS & BUILDERS.

Agar Edward, Witham
Barker Thomas, Witham
Mortimer Hugh, Witham
Warren Thomas, Wickham

CLOTHES DEALERS.

Nott Joseph, Witham
Payne Richard, Witham
Theobald Thomas, Witham

COOPERS.

Branwhite Bloss, Cheping hill
Cooper John, Witham
Norton John Neave, Witham

CURRIERS.

Buchanan John, Witham
Potto Firmin, Witham

FIRE, &c. OFFICE AGENTS.

ESSEX & SUFFOLK EQUITABLE, Jas. Catchpool, Witham [Witham
ESSEX ECONOMIC, John Philbrick,
GLOBE, James Beadel, Witham
NORWICH UNION, Wm. Nash, Withm
STANDARD OF ENGLAND, Edward Wilson Banks, Witham

GARDENERS.

Fuller Robert, Cheping hill
Rule Fredk. (& seedsman) Witham

GROCERS & TEA DEALERS.

(See also Shopkeepers.)

Agar Edward, Witham
Butcher Joseph, Cheping hill
Butler Thomas and Son, Witham
Candler William, Wickham [ham
Hicks Marven (& cheesemonger) Wit-
Hubbard Elizabeth, Witham
King Robert, Witham
Nott Joseph, Witham
Scott James, Witham

INNS, AT WITHAM.

Blue Posts Hotel (& posting) William Goldsmith [Nunn
Spread Eagle (commercial) Sarah
White Hart (commercial) John Cook

IRONMONGERS & BRAZIERS.

Gardner Francis, Witham
Sanders Josiah Martin, Witham

LINEN & WOOLLEN DRAPRS.

Butcher Robert, Cheping hill
Butler Thomas and Son, Witham
King Robert, Witham
Smith Edward, Witham
Tracy William, Witham

MALTSTERS.

Catchpool James, Witham
Ellis George, Hatfield Peverell
Grimwood Wm. (execrs. of) Witham

MILLERS.

Copland Frederick, Little Braxted
Dixon Benjamin & Robert Walker, Wickham Bishops
Johnson Abraham, Great Braxted
Piper Daniel Harvey, Cheping hill
Shoobridge Thos. Hoffgard, Witham
Warren Thomas, Hatfield Peverell

MILLINERS & DRESS MAKRS.

Chappell Sarah, Witham
Foster Miss, Witham
Gardner Elizabeth, Witham
Harwood Sarah, Witham
Hazell Mary, Witham
Smith Mrs. Edward, Witham

PERFUMERS AND HAIR DRESSERS.

Cottis William & Son, Witham
Rowe George, Witham
Walford Cornelius, Witham

PLUMBERS, PAINTERS, AND GLAZIERS.

Elmy Benj. John & Henry, Witham
Elmy Sarah and William, Witham
Eve William, Hatfield Peverell
Lewis Charles, Witham

SADDLERS & COLLAR MAKRS.

Curtis Mary, Cheping hill
Polley Edward Thomas, Witham
Smith James, Wickham
Thorne Samuel, Witham
Warwicker Isaac, Witham

SHOPKEEPRS & DEALERS IN GROCERIES & SUNDRIES.

Agar Edward, Witham
Brand John, Witham
Brand Joseph, Witham
Chalk Joseph, Witham
Cotton John, Witham
Dale James, Cheping hill
Johnson James, Hatfield Peverill
Lake Elizabeth, Cheping hill
Lungley James, Hatfield Peverell
Mortimer Hugh, Witham
Nott Joseph, Witham
Shelley John, Hatfield Peverell
Shelley William, Witham
Simpson Thomas, Witham
Turpin Thomas, Hatfield Peverell

SMITHS.

Blanks Edward, Cheping hill
Chappell Chas. (&bellhangr) Witham
Firmin William, Wickham
Fuller Henry, Witham
Fuller Nehemiah, Witham
Harris Joseph, Hatfield Peverell
Horsnell John, Hatfield Peverell
Ives Samuel, Witham

SPIRIT MERCHANTS.

Green Robert Styleman, Witham
Harrison Francis (& wine) Hatfield Peverell
Nash William, Witham

STAY MAKERS.

Butcher Mary, Cheping hill
Walford Lucy, Witham

STRAW HAT MAKERS.

Davey Sarah, Witham
Eve Julia, Hatfield Peverell
Garrett Eliza, Witham
Harwood Sarah, Witham

SURGEONS.

Dixon and Proctor Witham
Tomkin Thomas (and private lunatic establishment) Witham

TAILORS AND DRAPERS.

Abbot James, Great Braxted
Ely Thomas, jun. Witham
Gardner John, Witham
Garrard John, Witham
Garrett Thomas, Witham
Pond William, Hatfield Peverell
Prior William Nehemiah, Witham

TAVERNS & PUBLIC HOUSES.

Angel, James Turner, Witham
Buck, Thomas Baker, Great Braxted
Chequers, William Borret, Wickham
Crown, Martha Riley, Hatfield Peverell
Fleece, William Page, Witham
George, William Cousins, Witham
Green Man, Thos. Wendon, Little Braxted
King's Head, Thos. Wiggett, Cheping hill
Red Lion, Robert Dennis, Witham
Rising Sun, Theodorus Harrison, Witham
Swan, Charles Page, Witham
Swan, Thomas Rance, Hatfield Peverell
Waggon & Horses, John Mann, Witham
Wellington, Eliz. Kirkham, Hatfield Pev
White Horse, Joseph Argent, Cheping hill
Woolpack, Christopher Annett Collis, Cheping hill

TIMBER MERCHANTS.

Cottee James (dealer) Gt. Braxted
Wood Thomas, Cheping hill

VETERINARY SURGEONS.

Cowell William, Hatfield Peverell
Ottway William, Wickham
Spink William, Witham
Wakelin Robert, Witham

WATCH & CLOCK MAKERS.

Allatson William, Witham
Holden Benjamin John (& jeweller) Witham
Wright Richard, Witham

WHEELWRIGHTS.

Chipperfield Saml. Hatfield Peverell
Fleuty William, Witham
Murrells William, Great Braxted
Newman James, Hatfield Peverell
Spooner Benjamin, Wickham

Miscellaneous.

The names without address are in Witham.

Barnard James, parish clerk, Wickham
Chappell Barnard, millwright, Witham
Collis Christopher Annett, brewer, Cheping hill
Cornelius Cornelius, basket maker, Witham
Cunnington Robert, clerk to the magistrates, commissioner of taxes & stamp distributer, Witham
Dace William, parish clerk, Cheping hill
GAS WORKS, Thomas Butler, treasurer
Green John, cutler, Witham
Lewis Sarah, glass & china dealer, Witham
Matthews James, fellmonger and woolstapler, Witham
Nash Wm. registrar of births, &c. Witham
Nash William, druggist, Witham
Payne Richard, furniture broker, Witham
Perry William, coach maker, Witham
Pyman Thos. chymist & druggist, Witham
Savill John, fishmonger, Witham
Scott James, china, &c. dealer, Witham
Theobald Thos. general broker, Witham
Thorpe Thos. parish clerk, Little Braxted
UNION POORHOUSE, London rd. Witham —Robert Dodd, master; Sarah Dodd, matron
Warwicker Isaac, marine store dealer, Witham
Whitaker Mary, toy dealer, Witham
White Henry Lawshall, corn factor, Witham

COACHES.

To LONDON, the *Royal Mail* (from Norwich), calls at the Post Office, and the *Telegraph* (from Yarmouth), calls at the Spread Eagle, every morning at half-past two—the *Old Blue* (from Saxmundham), calls at the Spread Eagle, every afternoon at one, the *Shannon*, every afternoon at half-past one, and the *Wellington* (from Colchester), every alternate morning at half-past ten—the *Defiance* (from Colchester), calls at the White Hart, every afternoon at three, and the *Wellington*, every alternate morning at half-past ten—and the *Fly* (from Coggeshall), calls at the Angel, every Monday morning at seven, and every other morning (Sunday excepted) at eight; all go thro' Chelmsford, Ingatestone, Romford and Stratford.

To COGGESHALL, the *Fly* (from London), calls at the Angel, every evening (Sunday excepted) at seven.

To COLCHESTER & HARWICH, the *Defiance* (from London), calls at the White Hart, every evening at seven, and the *Wellington*, calls at the White Hart and Spread Eagle, every alternate afternoon at two.

To IPSWICH, the *Shannon* (from London), calls at the Spread Eagle, every morning at twelve.

To NORWICH, the *Royal Mail* (from London), calls at the Post Office, every night at twelve.

To SAXMUNDHAM, the *Old Blue* (from London), calls at the Spread Eagle, every afternoon at four.

To YARMOUTH, the *Star*, from the Spread Eagle, every morning at eleven, and the *Telegraph*, from the same Inn, every night at 11; both go thro' Ipswich.

CARRIERS.

To LONDON, James Dale's *Waggon*, from his house, Cheping hill, every Tuesday & Friday morning, and Charles Page's *Vans*, from his house, Witham, every Wednesday and Friday morning.

Carriers are also passing thro' Witham, to and from LONDON, COLCHESTER and most parts of SUFFOLK, daily.

WIVENHOE, ALRESFORD AND THORRINGTON.

WIVENHOE is a village and parish, in the Colchester division of the hundred of Lexden, four miles S. E. from Colchester and about nine S. S. W. from Manningtree; agreeably situated on the acclivity and summit of an eminence on the north bank of the navigable river Colne. This place is considered the port to Colchester; it posseses a custom-house establishment, with a convenient quay: from the latter the noted Colchester oysters are shipped for the London and other markets. Independent of the oyster fishery (which materially declined during the seasons of 1837 and 1838), it is a place of but little business. The importation of coals lately, and which is now carried on rather extensively, has, in some measure, contributed to the revival of its trade. The church, dedicated to St. Mary, is a large and rather handsome structure: the living, which is a discharged rectory, is in the gift of N. C. Corsellis, Esq. the lord of the manor. Population, in 1831, 1,714.

ALRESFORD is a small village and parish, in the hundred of Tendring, two miles S. E. of Wivenhoe; containing a parish church and 297 inhabitants.

THORRINGTON village and parish is in the same hundred as Alresford, two miles S. E. from it. It contains a church, dedicated to St. Mary Magdalene, and a chapel for Wesleyan methodists. The living is a rectory, with that of Frating annexed, in the gift of the master and fellows of St. John's College, Cambridge. Population of the parish 431.

POST OFFICE, WIVENHOE, Sarah Pratt, *Post Mistress.*—Letters from LONDON arrive (by mail cart from COLCHESTER) every morning at seven in winter and five in summer, and are despatched every evening at half-past seven in winter and eight in summer.

NOBILITY, GENTRY AND CLERGY.

Allen Rev. Jno. Taylor, A.M. Alresford
Chamberlain John Green, esq. (agent for Lloyds) Wivenhoe
Corsellis Nicholas Cæsar, esq. Wivenhoe hall
Frost William Stutter, esq. Thorrington hall
Havens Mr. Philip (surgeon) Wivenhoe
Ind Rev. James, Wivenhoe
Mason Mrs. Elizabeth, Wivenhoe
Pigott Captain —, Wivenhoe house
Rebow General Francis Slater, Wivenhoe park
Smith Benjamin, esq. Wivenhoe

SCHOOLS.

Caston Edward, Wivenhoe
NATIONAL SCHOOL, Wivenhoe—James Powell, master; Elizabeth Powell, mistress

BAKERS.

Carrington John (and flour dealer) Wivenhoe
Chapman Mary (& biscuit) Wivenhoe
Franks William, Wivenhoe
White Henry, Wivenhoe

BLACKSMITHS.
Baxter William, Alresford
Catt Edmund, Wivenhoe
Rodwell John, Thorrington
Sommers John, Wivenhoe

BOOT AND SHOE MAKERS.
Chamberlain George, Wivenhoe
Harden Thomas, Wivenhoe
Hayward Jonathan, Thorrington
Sanford John, Wivenhoe
Watchand Samuel, Wivenhoe

BUILDERS.
Barton Joseph, Alresford
Turpin Thomas, Wivenhoe

BUTCHERS.
Blyth Isaac, Wivenhoe
Corder Thomas, Wivenhoe
Richardson John, Thorrington
Ridgley William, Wivenhoe

GROCERS AND DRAPERS.
(See also Shopkeepers, &c.)
Cooper Samuel, Alresford
Moore James, Wivenhoe
Tabrum and Parkes, Wivenhoe, and East street, *Colchester*
Wells John, Alresford

HORSE DEALER.
Cousens John (& importer of foreign horses) Pound farm, Thorrington

MILLERS.
Pyman John, Wivenhoe
Smith John, Wivenhoe

OYSTER MERCHANTS.
Chamberlain Geo. (& coal) Wivenhoe
Heath William, Wivenhoe
Sanford Thomas (& coal) Wivenhoe

PUBLIC HOUSES.
The names without address are in Wivenhoe.
Anchor, William Henry Roberts
Black Boy, Thomas Harvey
Falcon, Thomas Turpin
Flag, Abraham William Abbott
Greyhound, Samuel Wade
Horse and Groom, Edward William Schofield
Lion, Thomas Wade, Thorrington
Pointer, Frederick Wade, Alresford
Rose & Crown, John Mills
Ship at Launch, Geo. Chamberlain

SHIP OWNERS.
Chamberlain George, Wivenhoe
Chamberlain John Green, esq. Wivenhoe
Harvey Thomas (and ship builder), Wivenhoe
Sanford Thomas, Wivenhoe

SHOPKEEPERS & DEALRS IN GROCERIES & SUNDRIES.
Hardy John, Wivenhoe
Polley John, Wivenhoe
Potter Margaret, Thorrington

TAILORS.
Ross Andrew, Wivenhoe
Rust James, Wivenhoe

WHEELWRIGHTS.
Plumb Ruth, Wivenhoe
Wade Thomas W. Thorrington

Miscellaneous.
All in WIVENHOE.
Abbott Abraham, carpenter
Barrell John, parish clerk
Bromly Nathaniel, brewer & maltster
Browne Wm. rope, cable and twine maker
Durrell David, sail maker
Elsworthy Jno. mast, block & pump maker
Jolliffe William, gardener & seedsman
Lufkin Robert, hair dresser
Pitt Benjamin, bricklayer & plasterer
Saints Caroline, milliner & straw hat mkr
Sanford Edwd. painter, plumber & glazier

CARRIERS.
To COLCHESTER, Daniel Cole, John Powell & Jas. Penny, from Wivenhoe daily

CONVEYANCE BY WATER.
To LONDON, Gainsborough and Hull, *Vessels* from the Quay, Wivenhoe, weekly, and oftener occasionally.

WOODFORD, CHINGFORD & NEIGHBOURHOODS.

WOODFORD is a village, in the parish of Woodford St. Mary and hundred of Becoutree; eight miles N.N.E. from London, and the like distance S. S. W. from Epping. This is one of the most delightful villages within the like distance of the Metropolis: the air is good—the views beautiful and extensive; and the rides and walks, through the woody and umbrageous scenery, render it an enchanting place of retreat to the long pent-up citizen: its charms are, indeed, appreciated by many opulent families; and the villas and grounds on all sides, which are tastefully interspersed amongst the rural glades, heighten the general effect of the natural beauties that here abound. Amongst the seats that ornament Woodford and its immediate vicinity may be particularly named, 'Woodford Hall,' Wm. Cox, Esq.; 'Woodford Grove,' Mrs. Elizabeth Mildred; 'Higham,' Jeremiah Harman, Esq.; 'Gwyn House,' Robert Ramsey, Esq.; and 'Claybury Hall,' John Mills, Esq. Woodford and its charming vicinity have long been deservedly celebrated for the number and excellence of the establishments for the education of youth of both sexes: these seminaries are of the most respectable and efficient kind; while the situations they occupy are acknowledged to be eminently conducive to the health of the pupil. Some few years since a new road, communicating with the Metropolis, was opened from the upper part of the village; it passes through the forest into the Leigh Bridge road. The church, dedicated to St. Mary, is a handsome structure, erected in 1817, on the site of the former church: it is faced with cement, and its interior is very clean, and neatly fitted up for the accommodation of the respectable congregation that assembles within its walls: at its eastern end is a fine painted window; and in the church, as well as in its cemetery, are many very handsome monuments; amongst which is a beautiful Corinthian column of marble, forty feet in height, erected to the memory of the family of Godfrey; also a tomb, with a column entirely clothed with ivy. In the church yard is a yew tree of extraordinary dimensions, its boughs shadowing a circumference of about 180 feet. There are places of worship for independents and Wesleyan methodists; and in April, 1837, a neat Gothic chapel was opened at Buckhurst Hill, adjoining Woodford. The benefice of Woodford is a rectory, of which the Rev. W. Parr Phillips is the incumbent, and his present curate the Rev. H. Rickards; the Rev. Thomas Stanton is the minister of Buckhurst Hill chapel, upon the presentation of the bishop of London. There is a national school for children of both sexes; and the parish has the privilege of sending two boys for gratuitous education to the schools founded by Archbishop Harsnett at Chigwell, as also that of presenting two boys to Christ's hospital, London. The parish contained, in 1831, 2,548 inhabitants.

CHINGFORD is a village and parish in the hundred of Waltham, situated a short distance to the north-west of Woodford, near the border of Epping forest; and the parish is bounded on the west by the river Lea and the county of Middlesex. Although the habitations of Chingford are totally destitute of uniformity in construction and arrangement, yet it is a pleasing and respectable rural village, and with its church presents a correct illustration of the picturesque and beautiful: this unostentatious structure, clothed in its verdant and venerable garb of ivy, stands on an eminence, and, though antique and even sombre in aspect, adds a feature that perfects the beauty of the landscape; the edifice is dedicated to All Saints; the living, a rectory, is in the patronage of J. Heathcote, Esq., and incumbency of the Rev. R. B. Heathcote. Population, 963.

POST OFFICE, WOODFORD, George Liddell, *Post Master* (and stamp distributer.) Letter boxes at Ann Hoyes', Woodford row, and Elizabeth Jeffries', Woodford bridge.—Letters from LONDON arrive every forenoon at eleven, afternoon at three and evening at six and nine, and are despatched every morning at nine, afternoon at one and four and night at eight.

POST, CHINGFORD, letter box at Charles Garrod's.—Letters arrive every afternoon at one and evening at seven, and are despatched every morning at eight and afternoon at half-past three.

GENTRY & CLERGY.
Adams Mr. John, Smith's villa
Ainslie Sir Robert, Ink's green
Bingley Mr. John, Woodford
Bingley Robert, esq. Higham lodge
Birch John Richard, esq. Woodford
Bridger Mr. James, Woodford
Bruhl George, esq. Cherrydown farm
Bryant John, esq. Chingford hall
Budd Thomas, esq. Nightingale hall
Chapman Abel, esq. Woodford
Cloves Peter, esq. Rookery
Cotton Mrs. Ann Maria, Hope lodge, Woodford bridge
Cox William, esq. Woodford hall
Dowding Richard, esq. Green
Doxat Lewis, esq. Woodford
Duley Mr. George, Bridge
Foster Edward, esq. Ivy house
Foster Edwd. jun. esq. Mill cottage
Geike Miss Sarah, Smith's villa
Gibb Mr. David, Woodford
Gilbert Mr. Matthew, Forest
Gilbert Mr. William, Forest
Godfrey Mrs. Cath. B. Prospect house
Goode Mr. William Henry, Flee hall
Gore John, esq. Harts
Graves Mr. Frederick, Woodford
Guillemard John, esq. Green
Gurson Mr. William, Wells
Hallett Mr. Richard, Wells
Harman Jeremiah, esq. Higham house
Heathcote Rev. Rbt. Boothby, Chingfd

Heatley Richard, esq. George lane
Herron Mrs. Phillis, Woodford
Hill James, esq. Caroline mount
Humphreys Mr. Jos. Chingford farm
Knowles Mr. John, Woodford
Lewis Thomas, esq. Ray house
Mallard Peter, esq. Woodford
Mildred Daniel, esq. Hale end
Mildred Mrs. Elizabeth, the Grove
Mildred Frederick, esq. Woodford
Mildred Henry, esq. Woodford
Mills John, esq. Claybury hall
Mohon Mr. John, Woodford bridge
Moseley Mrs. Mary, Turret house
Mure James, esq. Woodford
Oliver Mrs. Catherine, Woodford
Parlett William, esq. Bath cottage
Pearse Brice, esq. Monkham
Peppercorn James, esq. Green
Phillips Rev. William Parr, Woodford rectory
Podmore Mr. Arthur, Bald Stag gate
Popplewell Miss Ann, Woodford
Ramsey Robert, esq. Gwyn house, Bridge
Reynolds Abraham Edmund, esq. Green
Rickards Rev. Hely, Green
Saunders Mr. John, Woodford
Smart John, esq. Manor house
Stanton Rev. Thomas, Green
Stewart Alexander, esq. Grove house
Vine Thomas, esq. Woodford wells
Waite Mrs. Elizabeth, Hope lodge
Walton William, esq. Little Friday hill
Webb Mr. Benjamin, Woodford
Wood Mrs. Frances, Woodford
Wood Jno. esq. Mount echo, Chingford

ACADEMIES & SCHOOLS.

Boarding when not otherwise described.

Clarke Dorothy (preparatory) Green
Cooke Robert, Ray lodge
Foyle Charlotte, Nottingham villa
Gibbins Ths. Salway house, Woodford
Hallett Selby, Grove house, Woodford
Hodgkins Mary M. (day) Row
NATIONAL SCHOOL, Chingford—John Abrey, master; Elizabeth Nutting, mistress
NATIONAL SCHOOL, Woodford—David Wilkinson, master; Sarah Wilkinson, mistress
Partridge John (boarding and day) Eagle house, Green
Robson William, Chingford lodge
Rutland Mary, Green
Stevens Francis Worrall, Woodford house

BAKERS.

Archer Samuel, Woodford
Boulter Thomas, Woodford
Coote William, Wells
Holwell Abraham, Row
Johnson Robert, Bridge
Saltwell William, Bridge
Stubbins John, Wells
Turner Joseph, Chingford green

BASKET MAKERS.

Bywater William, Wells
Wells John, Bridge

BOOT AND SHOE MAKERS.

Brown William, Woodford bridge
Cason William, Grove row
Cooler John, Green
Cox Henry, Wells
Cox John, Inman's row
Cox Thomas, Chingford green
Enness Samuel, Bridge
Enness William, Woodford bridge
Mead Joshua, Woodford
Oliver John, Wells
Perrin Job, Grove row
Perrin John, Wells
Pluckrose Charles Henry, Bridge
Porter William, Horn lane
Riley John, Row
Scott Henry, Woodford
Wheeler John, Chingford

BRAZIERS & TINMEN.

Ayton William, Chingford
Rogers Edward Thomas (and stove and range manufactr.) Woodford
Watson Samuel, Row

BRICKLAYRS & PLASTERERS

Asbey Robert, Row
Fletcher Samuel, Woodford
Heath William, Chingford
Lowe Thomas, Grove row
Shephard Francis, Bridge
Shephard Joseph, Woodford bridge
Willson John, Chingford

BUTCHERS.

Brooker Henry, Woodford bridge
Fladgate Arthur, Woodford
Frearson Joseph, Chingford green
Irons William, Wells
Nunn William (pork) Green
Parker Wm. (pork) Chingford hatch
Robinson Samuel, Chingford green
Symonds Mary, Green

CARPENTERS & BUILDERS.

Francis William, Woodford
Hartshorne William, Chingford
M'Narrin Jos. Chingford bridge
Messer Jas. (& undertaker) Woodford
Morter John and James, Row
Noble George Richard and Richard (and undertakers) Woodford, and Woodford bridge

CHINA, GLASS, &c. DEALERS.

Dixon Saveal, Row
Fuller James, Woodford
Jeffries Elizabeth, Bridge
Wiggins William, Wells

CORN DEALERS.

Coote William, Wells
Holwell Abraham, Row
Johnson Robert, Bridge
Liddle George, Woodford
Parrish Gilbert, Grove row
Shepard William, Wells
Turner Joseph, Chingford green
Wiggins William, Wells

FIRE, &c. OFFICE AGENTS.

GUARDIAN, Wm. Francis, Woodford
ROYAL EXCHANGE, Selby Hallett, Grove house, Woodford
SUN, Geo. Richd. Noble, Woodford

GROCERS & TEA DEALERS.

(See also Shopkeepers, &c.)

Abdy Hannah, Chingford green
Carter Edwin, Wells
Dixon Saveal, Row
Doolittle Mary, Row
Fox Lucy, Woodford bridge
Fuller James, Woodford
Garrod Charles, Chingford green
Jeffries Elizabeth, Bridge
Liddle George, Woodford
Messer James, Woodford bridge
Pooley Thomas, Chingford hatch
Scarlett Thomas Hyem (and Italian warehouse) Woodford
Trotter Jane, Woodford bridge
Wiggins William, Wells

HORSE AND GIG OWNERS, FOR HIRE.

Grove Richard, Prospect cottage
Hill Francis, Inman's row

INNS AND PUBLIC HOUSES.

Bald Stag, Minors Acock, Forest
Bull & Crown, Jos. Finch, Chingfrd grn
Castle Inn (and posting house) Alfred Critcher, Woodford
Crown and Crooked Billet, James Linnett, Woodford bridge
George, Thomas Back, Woodford
King's Head, Robt. Goldacre, Chingfrd
Three Jolly Wheelers, Sarah Vincent, Woodford bridge
White Hart Inn (commercial and family) Edwin Stokes, Woodford
White Hart, Thomas Radley, Bridge
Woodford Wells Inn, Thos. Rounding, Wells

LINEN DRAPERS.

Carter Edwin (and woollen) Wells
Dixon Saveal, Row
Jeffries Elizabeth, Bridge
Liddle George, Woodford

LIVERY STABLE KEEPERS.

Critcher Alfred, Castle, Woodford
Stokes Edwin, White Hart, Woodford

LOCKSMITHS AND BELL-HANGERS.

Rogers Edward Thomas, Woodford
Watson Saml. (& whitesmith) Row

MILLINERS & DRESS MAKRS.

Chipperfield Frances (and straw hat maker) Row
Gunn Ann (& straw hat maker) Grove row
Hodgkins Mary M. Row

PLUMBERS, PAINTERS, &c.

Brown Jas. Woodford, & at *Wanstead*
Chinnery John, Woodford bridge
Chinnery Robert, Woodford
Chinnery Thomas, Row
Cox Henry, Row
Shepherd Samuel, Grove row
Turner John, Row, and at *Leyton*

POULTERERS.

Nunn William, Green
Parker William, Hatch

SADDLERS.

Miller George, Chingford green
Palmer John, Woodford bridge
Speller Charles, Woodford
Whitman Richard, Row

SHOPKEEPERS & DEALRS IN GROCERIES & SUNDRIES.

Allen William, Chingford
Bailey William, Chingford
Deemer Edward, Bridge
Ellis Stephen, Chingford
Emmerson John, Green
Hillman Elizabeth, Wells
Hubble John, Bridge
Lee John Thomas, Chingford
Shephard Joseph, Bridge
Smith Joseph, Chingford hatch
Swygart Joseph, Green
Ward William, Bridge

SMITHS AND FARRIERS.

Arnill William, Wells
Herbert Edward, Chingford
Matthews Joseph, Chingford
Priest James, Green
Radley Elizabeth, Bridge
Radley Henry, Woodford
Rainbird Samuel, Row
Rogers Edward Thomas, Woodford

SURGEONS.

Cary William Henry, Woodford
Davies and Bunce, Wells
Morgan Thomas, Woodford

SURVEYORS.

Noble George Richard (and estate agent) Woodford
Vaux Thomas, Bridge

TAILORS.

Allen William, Chingford green
Dixon Sarah (and draper) Row
Harris William (and draper) Row
Nichols James, Row
Rackham Marcus, Woodford bridge
Sawyer Thomas, Woodford
Sutton Cornelius, Woodford bridge

VETERINARY SURGEONS.

Rounding William, Wells
Webb Thomas, Woodford

WHEELWRIGHTS.

Broad Saml. (& coach maker) Wells
Bryan Peter, Forest
Clarke Simon, Woodford
Enever Joseph, Chingford green
Harwood Mary, Bridge
Vale John, Chingford hatch

Miscellaneous.

Abrey John, parish clerk, Chingford
ASSEMBLY & CONCERT ROOMS, White Hart Inn, Woodford
Bates Francis, professor of music, Woodford
Bayley Geo. forest keeper, Woodford green
Bean Joseph, sail maker, grove row
Burrell Wm. cattle dealer, Chingford green
Clark Ann, haberdasher and stamp distributer, Woodford row
Clark Joseph, cooper, Woodford
Dixon Amelia, toy dealer, Row
Dorward David, parish & vestry clerk & registrar of births and deaths for Walthamstow district, Woodford row
Eckford James, bookseller & binder, Grove
Hill Francis, horse breaker, Inman's row
Jessop Joseph, gunsmith, Chingford hatch
Knight Frederick, ornamental & heraldic publisher, Chingford green
Lee John Thos. glass grinder, Chingford
LequentreAlphonso, miller, Chingfrd mills
Linton Wm. Jas. engraver, Woodford green
Moss William, hair cutter, Green
Neate James, dairyman, Horn lane
Noble Geo. Richd. auctioneer, Woodford
Pike Christopher John, attorney, Bridge
Powter John, fishmonger, Wells
Rayment William, gardener, Green
Ridley Thomas, watch maker, Row
Riley Thomas, dyer & scourer, Green
WORKHOUSE, Woodford wells—Thomas Horn, governor; Mary Horn, matron

COACHES.

To LONDON, Rounding and Barnard's *Coaches*, from the Woodford Wells Inn, calling at the Castle and White Hart, every morning (Sunday ex.) at eight, nine and ten, afternoon at five and evening at half-past six, and on Sunday at seven in the morning and seven in the evening—and Jane Pettengill's *Coach*, from her office, Woodford row, calls at the King's Head, Chingford & the George, Woodford, every morning (Sunday excepted) at eight, and on Sunday at seven in the morning and six in the evening.

Coaches to and from LONDON, CHIGWELL, CHIPPING ONGAR, CLARE, DUNMOW, &c. call at the White Hart, Woodford bridge; also to and from LONDON, EPPING, HARLOW, BISHOPS STORTFORD, SAFFRON WALDEN, CAMBRIDGE, NEWMARKET, NORWICH, BURY, &c. pass through Woodford daily.

CARRIERS.

To LONDON, Houghton & Jordan, from Woodford, daily—and — Hubble, from Woodford bridge, every Tuesday, Thursday and Saturday.

Besides the above, there are *Waggons* and *Vans* to and from LONDON, EPPING, HARLOW, BISHOPS STORTFORD, SAFFRON WALDEN, CAMBRIDGE, NEWMARKET, NORWICH, BURY, &c. pass through Woodford, daily.

WRITTLE AND ROXWELL.

WRITTLE is a village and parish in the hundred of Chelmsford, about two miles and a half w. by s. from that town; it formerly was a market town, but has long been divested of that consequence, together with its trade, by the prosperity of Chelmsford; it still, however, maintains its rank amongst the most respectable villages in this district, and is the residence of many opulent families. At a short distance from the town are the remains of a palace, erected by King John in 1211. A remarkable custom, denominated 'leppe and lasse,' is established in the manor of Writtle, by which every cart traversing a certain part of it called Greenbury (except it belong to a nobleman) must pay 4*d.* to the lord of the manor. The present possessor of the manor is Lord Petre, of Thorndon Hall. The parish is very extensive—it is computed to be sixty-one miles in circumference. The church, dedicated to All Saints, is an ancient structure, and consists of a nave, chancel and side aisles, with an embattled tower at the western end; in 1802 a loud crash announced to the inhabitants the fall of the tower; it has, however, been rebuilt, and furnished with six excellent bells and a handsome clock. The living is in the peculiar jurisdiction of the court of Writtle with Roxwell annexed, and in the patronage of the warden and fellows of New college, Oxford; the Rev. Thomas Penrose is the present incumbent.

ROXWELL formerly ranked only as a hamlet to Writtle, but it is now a distinct parish, except as to the peculiar jurisdiction. A place of worship for independents, alms-houses for six poor persons, and a national school, are in Writtle; and at Roxwell there is another school, conducted upon the same system. A pleasure fair is held in Writtle on Whit-Monday. Population of Writtle, 2,348; that of Roxwell, 847.

POST, WRITTLE.—Letters from CHELMSFORD arrive (by foot post) every morning at eight.

GENTRY AND CLERGY.

Barnes Mr. John, Writtle
Bramston Thomas William, esq. M.P. Skreens, Roxwell
Bullock Miss Charlotte, Writtle
Christie —, esq. Boyton hall, Roxwell
Clarke Mr. George Adams, Writtle
Henderson Rev. John, Writtle
Murdock Mr. Ephraim, Writtle
Penrose Rev. Thos. Vicarage, Writtle
Shuckburgh Rev. Chs. Verney, Roxwll
Smith Mrs. Elizabeth, Writtle

ACADEMIES AND SCHOOLS.

Dawson Thomas (boarding) Writtle
NATIONAL SCHOOL (boys) Writtle—John Winders, master
NATIONAL SCHOOL, Roxwell—Wm. Bright, master; Sarah Wybrow, mistress
Rutter — (gent.'s boarding) Roxwll

INNS & PUBLIC HOUSES.

Bull, Samuel Bailey, Writtle green
Chequers, Ruth Horsnell, Roxwell
Cock & Bell Inn, Jos. Hunt, Writtle
Hare & Hounds, Sarah Cheek, Roxwll
Rose & Crown, Saml. Jas. Lucking, Writtle
Star, Robert C. Brazier, Writtle

SHOPKEEPERS & TRADERS.

The names without address are in Writtle.

Bailey John, grocer and draper
Blyth William, butcher
Boosey Robert, miller
Brazier Edward, butcher
Brazier John, wheelwright
Brazier Robert C. butcher
Brewster Wm. flour & meal dealer
Bright William, baker, Roxwell
Brown John, boot and shoe maker
Brown William, shoemaker
Burr Charles, grocer and draper
Carpenter Daniel, maltster
Clarke Robert, baker
Collicott Thomas, tailor
Cooch Jos. maltster & miller, Roxwell
Cooch William, grocer, Roxwell
Gray Michael, shoemaker
Hains George, blacksmith
Hardy Samuel, shopkeeper & baker
Harper Hartley, tailor, Roxwell
Harris George, blacksmith
Horsnell Thomas, carpenter
Hunt Thomas, tailor and draper
Judd Jas. parish clerk, Roxwell
Lambith Henry (executors of late) brewer and maltster
Livermore Robert bricklayer and parish clerk
Lowe John, flour dealer
Lucking Samuel James, baker
Monk William, carpenter
Oddy William, shoemaker, Roxwell
Pearson William, shoemaker
Phillips and Bretnall, brewers
Poole James, carpenter
Poole James, china, glass, &c. dealer
Porter and Butler, wine and spirit merchants, and at *Chelmsford*
Potter Elizabeth, painter, plumber and glazier
Richards James, saddler
Saltwell Mary, shopkeeper, Roxwell
Simons Thomas, butcher
Sorrell Jas. hair dresser & toy dealer
Summerfield Joseph, painter, plumber and glazier
Sutton Martin, grocer & tea dealer
Wicker George, greengrocer and fishmonger
Wilks George, shoemaker
Wood Joseph, wheelwright

CARRIER.

To LONDON, John Curtis, from his house, every Friday.

HERTFORDSHIRE

IS an inland county, of an extremely irregular form, and its boundaries are of the like character. Its most distant extremities lie in a direction nearly north-east and south-west; its shortest, south-east and north-west. Upon the north it is bounded, for a few miles, by the county of Cambridge, and its north-eastern angle also meets the latter county; for a considerable distance it is bounded on the east by Essex, and its southern boundary is formed (with some palpable indentions) by Middlesex; upon the western side are the counties of Bucks and Bedford—the latter county likewise extending to and meeting Cambridgeshire on the north. Some difficulty exists in ascertaining with precision the dimensions of Hertfordshire: measured, however, from Royston, upon its N. N. E. confines, to the extremity of its most southerly indenture with Bucks, its length is about thirty-six miles; and its greatest breadth, taken in an oblique direction, from Bishops Stortford on the east, to Berkhampstead, upon the confines of Buckinghamshire, on the south-west, is about thirty miles: but its medium length may be grossly estimated at thirty miles, and its breadth at twenty-five miles. Its ambit is calculated at somewhat between one hundred and thirty and one hundred and forty miles, and the government returns state the area to comprise five hundred and twenty-eight square miles, or 337,920 statute acres. In size it ranks as the thirty-fifth county in England, and in population as the thirty-fourth.

NAME and ANCIENT HISTORY.—The origin of this county's appellation has never been satisfactorily traced; it is, however, conceded by respectable authorities to be derived from the chief town in the shire, 'Hertford'—under which head we shall impart the most accredited information upon the subject. Previous to the invasion of the Romans, Hertfordshire, with the adjoining counties of Essex, Bedford and Buckingham, constituted the territory of the *Cassii, Trinobantes* and *Cattieuchlatii*, over whom Cassievellaunus reigned—making, as some are inclined to think, Verulam his chief place of residence. When the Romans, under the conduct of Julius Cæsar, made their first descent upon the shores of Britain from the opposite coast of conquered Gaul, the several nations (or tribes) who at that time occupied the south-eastern part of the island summoned their forces to repel the invaders: unavailing, however, were the desperate efforts made by these undisciplined, though gallant natives, to oppose the veteran and well marshalled legions of Rome, flushed with recent triumphs, and headed by a general whom they idolized, and who had never experienced a defeat; the inefficacy of further resistance was felt by the British commander, and he was compelled to bow before the victor. Upon the final subjugation of the southern parts of the island, and their division into districts or governments, Hertfordshire constituted a portion of one of these, to which, in compliment to the first conqueror of the country, was given the name of *Flavia Cæsariensis*. When the more domestic misfortunes of Rome obliged her to withdraw her forces from the distant provinces, their domination in this country was succeeded by that of the Saxons—another race of invaders, who divided the country into a number of kingdoms or principalities; at which time the county of Hertford was unequally apportioned between the kingdom of the East Saxons and that of Mercia, the *Ermine-street* being conjectured to have constituted the boundary. At Berkhampstead William the Conqueror took the oath to maintain the laws of Edward the Confessor. At Wheathampstead the barons concentrated their forces against Edward II. In 1381 Richard II, accompanied by his chief justice Tresilian, came to St. Albans with a numerous guard, and caused to be executed a number of insurgents brought from Hertford gaol, who were engaged in Wat Tyler's rebellion. In the wars of 'the Roses,' three most important battles were fought within the confines of the county, viz.: at St. Albans, in 1455, when Henry VI was wounded and made prisoner; in 1465, in the same neighbourhood, when Margaret of Anjou was defeated by the Earl of Warwick; and in 1468, the decisive battle of Barnet, in which the Earl of Warwick was slain, with, it is recorded, ten thousand of his army. It was at Theobalds, in this county, that Charles I received the petitions of both houses of parliament; and then departed to put himself at the head of his army.

SOIL and CLIMATE, PRODUCE and MANUFACTURES.—The SOILS of this county mix and run into each other in a very remarkable manner, so that they cannot be traced and named with any great certainty: the prevailing ones are loam and clay; the former is met with in almost all its gradations, and is more or less intermingled with flints, or sand. The vales through which the rivers or brooks take their course are composed of a rich sandy loam, with the exception of a small quantity of peat, or marshy moor. The principal clay district is on the north-east or Essex side; yet even here the upper surface is in general a strong wet loam. The only parts where the soils may be considered sterile are in the parishes of North Holt and North Mimms, and the lower part of that of Hatfield; but these, of late years, have been much improved under the management of the agriculturist. The chalky soil prevails generally on the northern side of the county; but indeed the basis of the whole county is chalk, either more or less pure, though the depths at which it is found vary. The CLIMATE of Hertfordshire is considered as most salubrious, and the air is generally mild; to delicate constitutions its temperature has been pronounced soothing and efficacious. These advantages, with the general beauty of the country, the goodness of the roads, and the almost uninterrupted fertility of the soil, have been the means of making this county a favourite residence, and inducing great numbers of wealthy persons to purchase lands for building villas—thereby causing estates to multiply in a manner unknown in the distant counties. The general aspect of Hertfordshire is extremely pleasant; and though its eminences are not enough elevated, nor its vales sufficiently depressed and broken, to claim a decisive character of picturesque or romantic beauty, yet its surface is so diversified as to constitute a considerable degree of fine scenery. The northern part is the most hilly; and a range of high ground stretches out from the neighbourhood of Kings Langley towards Berkhampstead and Tring, which in many parts overlooks a great extent of country; another elevated ridge commences at St. Albans, and proceeds in a north direction; the south line is also sufficiently high to embrace some extensive prospects. Most of the country is enclosed; and the enclosures being principally live hedges, intermixed with flourishing timber, have a verdant and agreeable effect: independent of the wood thus distributed in hedge-rows, large quantities of very fine timber are grown in the parks and grounds belonging to the numerous seats of the nobility and gentry, which are spread over every part of the county, and give animation to almost every view. By far the greatest proportion of Hertfordshire is under tillage—as a corn county, it is considered one of the first in England: the produce in wheat, barley and oats is very considerable; large quantities of turnips are also grown, and artificial grasses cultivated to a very great extent. The meadows are very productive in many parts, and the various streams that intersect the land are extremely favourable to irrigation. In the south-west corner of the county are many orchards; apples and cherries, which always find a ready market in London, are their principal produce. The quantity of waste lands is but inconsiderable—many acres of these are appropriated as sheep down. As the land in this county is chiefly arable, live stock has become an object of inferior regard: the Suffolk breed is considered the best; the sheep are mostly ewes of the South Down and Wiltshire kinds. The horses are of various breeds, but the Suffolk appears to have the preference. The chief MANUFACTURES of Hertfordshire, at one time, were cotton and silk; the former has much declined, nor is the latter carried on extensively. When the article was more worn than of late years, Berkhampstead employed many female hands in making black lace; but the principal occupation of the labouring females, in most parts of the county, is platting straw for hats, bonnets, &c. A very considerable quantity of malt is made in various districts of this shire; there are also many flour mills and lime kilns, and paper is manufactured in several of the towns.

RIVERS and MINERAL SPRINGS, CANALS and RAILWAYS.—The principal RIVERS of Hertfordshire are the LEA and the COLNE; these two are composed of many inferior streams, most of whose sources lie within the county. The Lea rises near Leagrave, in Bedfordshire—enters Hertfordshire near Bower Heath, and pursues a direction nearly from north-west to south-east, to its conflux with the Stort about a mile east of Hoddesdon; and flowing through Broxbourn, Wormley and Cheshunt, finally quits the county near Waltham Abbey. The Colne is formed by the union of several small streams, one of which rises at Kix or Kits End, in Middlesex; these unite in the vicinity of North Mimms, and flow by and give name to London-Colney, Colney Park and Colney Street; and being increased near the latter place by the Verulam or Meuse river from St. Albans, it subsequently passes Watford and Rickmansworth, when it enters Middlesex, and forms the boundary between that county and Bucks. The names of the other chief tributary streams are the Maran, or *Mimerum*, which rises near Frogmore, and, with the Beane, which originates near Cromer, joins the Lea near Hertford; the Rib, whose source is near Buntingford, and the Quin, from Biggin, mingle together, and add to the waters of the Lea: from these rivers united the inhabitants of the metropolis derive a leading necessary of life, conveyed to them by the NEW RIVER. The Ash falls into the Lea near Ware; the Stort rises in Essex, and is navigable from Bishops Stortford to its junction with the Lea; and the Gade stream, in conjunction with another, enriches the Colne. Several of the small streams that unite to form the Rhee (a chief branch of the Cam,) likewise have their origin in this county, in the neighbourhood of Ashwell. The few MEDICINAL SPRINGS rising in this county are chiefly chalybeate: these are confined to the south part, and the principal is near the race-ground on Barnet common; others rise on Northaw common, and another at Cattley, in Northaw parish. Some incrustating springs have been known near Clothall, in the north part of the county. CANALS:—The Grand Junction canal enters this county above Berkhampstead, and follows the course of the Gade to Rickmansworth, and from thence the course of the Colne till it leaves Hertfordshire. An act was obtained for the formation of another canal, from St. Albans, to join the Grand Junction below Cashiobury park; but subscriptions failing, the design was abandoned. RAILWAYS:—The Northern and Eastern railway, on its route to Cambridge, runs close to Waltham Cross, and within a quarter of a mile east of Hoddesdon; then on to the right of Sawbridgeworth; and, leaving Bishops Stortford a little to the left or west, and Saffron Walden to the right or east, it pursues nearly the course of the mail road to Cambridge. Branches connecting Ware and Hertford with the main line also are projected. The London and Birmingham railway runs to Watford—then to the well-known station of Boxmoor, which is within a mile and a half west of Hemel Hempstead; and, running close to Berkhampstead, passes about four miles to the south of St. Albans, and one mile and a half north of Tring. From the latter town a branch has been constructed to Aylesbury, in Buckinghamshire.

ECCLESIASTICAL and CIVIL DIVISIONS, and REPRESENTATION.—Part of Hertfordshire is in the diocess of Lincoln, and part of it in that of London—the whole being within the province of Canterbury. It is included in the home circuit, and divided into eight hundreds, viz. Braughin, Broadwater, Cashio, Dacorum, Edwinstree, Hertford, Hitchin and Pirton, and Odsey: these collectively contain one county town (Hertford); two boroughs (Hertford and St. Albans), fourteen other market towns, and one hundred and thirty-one parishes and four parts of parishes. The whole county returns seven members to parliament, namely, two each for the boroughs of Hertford and St. Albans, and three for the shire. The representatives at present sitting for the county are Viscount Grimston, Rowland Alston, Esq., and Abel Smith, Esq. The election of county members is held at Hertford; and the polling stations, in addition to that town, are Bishops Stortford, Buntingford, Hatfield, Hemel Hempstead, Hoddesdon and Stevenage.

POPULATION, &c.—By the census for 1831 Hertfordshire contained 71,395 males, and 71,946 females—total 143,341: being an increase, since the returns made in the year 1821, of 13,627 inhabitants; and from the census of 1801 to that of 1831 the augmentation amounted to 45,764 persons. The annual value of Real Property in this county, as assessed April, 1815, amounted to £571,107.

Index of Distances from Town to Town in the County of Hertfordshire.

The names of the respective towns are on the top and side, and the square where both meet gives the distance.

	Baldock	Barnet (Chipping)	Berkhampstead	Bishops Stortford	Hatfield	Hemel Hempstead	Hertford	Hitchin	Hoddesdon	Redbourn	Rickmansworth	St. Albans	Stevenage	Tring	Ware	*Distance from London.*
Baldock																37
Barnet (Chipping)	26															11
Berkhampstead	25	18														26
Bishops Stortford	21	26	36													30
Hatfield	18	9	17	22												19
Hemel Hempstead	22	14	4	32	11											24
Hertford	18	12	24	14	7	18										21
Hitchin	5	23	15	26	15	19	16									34
Hoddesdon	22	12	27	16	10	21	4	21								17
Redbourn	15	14	8	31	9	5	16	14	20							25
Rickmansworth	29	12	10	38	16	9	23	26	26	13						18
St. Albans	18	10	9	27	5	6	12	14	15	4	11					21
Stevenage	6	20	19	23	12	16	12	4	16	12	23	12				31
Tring	27	23	5	41	20	8	27	22	30	12	14	15	23			31
Ware	17	14	26	12	9	20	2	15	4	18	25	15	11	29		21
Watford	25	9	11	34	12	8	20	21	22	11	3	7	19	15	22	15

BALDOCK,

WITH THE VILLAGE OF ASHWELL AND NEIGHOURHOODS.

BALDOCK is a market town and parish, in the hundred of Broadwater, 37 miles N. from London, 18 N. by W. from Hertford, 21 S.S.W. from Cambridge, and eight S.S.E. from Biggleswade, in Bedfordshire. It is a neat, open, and well-built town, situated in a fertile valley, surrounded by chalky hills; the north road from London to Edinburgh passing through it, and the ancient Roman road, called the *Ickneild-street*, running along its north side, and forming a boundary to the town. A little way to the south of the town are the remains of a Roman and Danish encampment; from this circumstance, and that of its being on a Roman road, it would appear that Baldock has been a place of some note in ancient times. The present lord of the manor is Adolphus Meetkerke, Esq.; and his steward is Mr. Samuel Veasey, of this town. Constables and other officers are appointed at the court leet, and the county magistrates hold a petty session on the first Monday monthly. The malting, brewing, and straw-plat trades are the principal branches here: of the first there are some large establishments, and the last furnishes employment to numerous females in the town and neighbourhood. This is, besides, a place of considerable thoroughfare to the north of England, and some good inns here afford requisite accommodation to the posting or commercial traveller. The town is now well lighted with gas, from works erected in 1837.

The church, which is dedicated to St. Mary, and

situated in the centre of the town, is a beautiful and spacious structure, adorned with a handsome tower and spire; and within the church are several monuments, interesting to the curious. The living is a rectory, in the patronage of the crown; the present rector is the Rev. John Smith. There are places of worship for methodists, independents, and the society of friends; and schools, for gratuitous education, under the church and dissenting establishments; also, almshouses, and some other minor charities. The day for holding the market has been changed several times: it takes place now on Friday, but it is of very trifling importance to trade, except for that in straw plat. The fairs are—the 7th of March, the last Thursday in May, 5th of August, 2nd and 3rd of October, and the 11th of December, for horses, cattle, cheese, &c. By the government returns for 1831, the parish contained 1,704 inhabitants.

ASHWELL is a village and large parish, in the hundred of Odsey, four miles N.N.E. from Baldock. The remains of a Roman camp and burial place have lately been discovered here; and some earthenware vases, coins, &c. have also been dug up. The church, dedicated to St. Mary, is a spacious stone structure, with a tower at its western end, 122 feet high, surmounted by a neat spire of 55 feet. The interior of the church is neat, with some fine carvings in oak, particularly a beautiful screen that separates the nave from the chancel. The living is a vicarage, in the patronage of the Bishop of London, and incumbency of the Rev. Henry Morice, A.M. The other places of worship are chapels for the society of friends, methodists, and independents. The free school here, originally founded by Henry Colbron, in 1681, is now supported by the Merchant Tailors' Company, of London; the number of scholars is about 40. There are alms-houses for six poor persons, and an apprenticeship fund. The population of the parish, in 1831, was 1,072.

POST OFFICE, High street, BALDOCK, William Stocken, *Post Master* (and general newspaper agent.)—Letters from LONDON arrive (by the Glasgow mail) every night at twelve, and are despatched (by the Hull and Lincoln mail) every morning at two.—Letters from the North arrive every morning at half-past one, and are despatched every night at twelve.

GENTRY & CLERGY.

Blackburne Rev. Thomas, Clothall rectory
Chatfield Rev. Allen William, Stotfold, *Beds.*
Cooch Mrs. Kitty, High st
Donne Rev. Benjn. Weston vicarage
Edwards Rev. Samuel Valentine, Newnham vicarage
Fitz-John Robt. esq. White Horse st
Fossey Mrs. Edey Edith, High st
Fowler Rev. William, High st
Gall Mrs. Ann, the Elms, Baldock
Goldsmith Mrs. Sarah, High st
Hampson Edward, esq. High st
Haydon Mr. Josiah, White Horse st
Herbert Mrs. White Horse st
Ind Mrs. Mary, White Horse st
Lafont Rev. Jno. Hinxworth rectory
Logsdon Mrs. Eliz. White Horse st
Mills Samuel, esq. Radwell Bury
Morice Rev. Henry, Ashwell vicarage
Norris Wm. Jno. esq. Radwell house
Oliver Mrs. Fanny, Norton st
Peacock Mrs. Ann, High st
Pryor Mrs. Elizabeth, High st
Pym Rev. Wm. Wollaston, Willian rectory
Roe Henricus Octavius, esq. Retreat, Weston
Smith James, esq. Bygrave
Smith Rev. John, Baldock rectory
Spencer Rev. Charles John, Radwell
Thompson William, esq. Ashwell
Trash Fred. Chas. esq. M.D. Hitchin st
Tuck Rev. —, Wallington rectory
Watson Rev. J. B. Norton vicarage

ACADEMIES AND SCHOOLS.

BRITISH, Norton st—Joseph Lofts, master
Frost —, (day) Hitchin st
MERCHANT TAILORS' SCHOOL, Ashwell—John Thomas, master
NATIONAL SCHOOL, High st—Edwd. Hankin, master; Sophia Seymour, mistress
Pryor Sarah (day and boarding) Norton st
Troup Miss (day) White Horse st

ATTORNEYS.

Veasey Samuel (and clerk to the magistrates, to the commissioners of the Ivel navigation, and to the turnpike trusts) High st
Wade George de Vins, High st

BAKERS & FLOUR DEALERS.

Davies William, Norton st
Day William, Hitchin st
Freshwater Mary, White Horse st
Heath George, High st
Horn Frederick, High st
Howard Ann, Stotfold
Jermyn William, Norton st
Lunnis George, Ashwell
Porter Charles, Ashwell
Strickland John, Ashwell

BANKERS.

Wells, Hogg, and Lindsell (branch) High street—(draw on Barnett, Hoares, & Co. London)

BLACKSMITHS.

Bloom Jno. (& ironfoundr) Hitchin st
Bryant William, Ashwell
Edwards Benjamin, Ashwell
Pack James, Ashwell
Packton John, Ashwell
Swain George, White Horse st
Theobalds Jesse, High st

BOOKSELLERS & STATIONRS

Tranter Joseph, High st
Warren John (and printer and publisher) White Horse st, & *Royston*

BOOT & SHOE MAKERS.

Clarke Thomas, Weston
Emery George, Hitchin st
Fossey John, High st
Goodchild Turner, Hitchin st
Leonard Henry, Norton st
Lovell William, White Horse st
Oliver Joseph, Norton st
Pestell Henry S. High st
Smith William Z. High st
Street John, Norton st
Strickland John, Ashwell
Trolley John, White Horse st
Trolley William, High st
Waldock John, Ashwell

BRAZIERS AND TIN-PLATE WORKERS.

Pryor Charles, White Horse st
Pryor George (& gasfitter) Norton st

BREWERS.

Fordham Edward, Ashwell
Penn Wm. Oliver, White Horse st
Pryor John and Morris, High st
Steed John, Norton st

BRICKLAYERS.

Bailey Peter, Ashwell
Bentley William (& plasterer) White Horse street
Farr James, White Horse st
Farr John Evered (and builder) Hitchin st
Jackson William, White Horse st
Monk Joseph, White Horse st

BUTCHERS.

Castle Kezia (pork) Norton st
Day Robert, High st
Edwards Thomas, Ashwell
Kitchener John, Ashwell
Kitchener Joseph, White Horse st
Logsdon Joseph, White Horse st
Thody William, Norton st
Tinger James, Ashwell
West Sarah, High st

CABINET MAKERS AND UPHOLSTERERS.

Rickerby John (and paper hanger) White Horse st
Seymour George, White Horse st

CARPENTERS & JOINERS.

Atkins Edward, Ashwell
Farr John Evered, Hitchin st
Picking Thomas, Ashwell
Potter William, White Horse st
Richardson Elizabeth (and furniture broker) High st
Rickerby John (and builder) White Horse st
Scott John, High st

CHINA & GLASS DEALERS.

Brown Crowther, High st
Raban Jno. (& tea dealer) Hitchin st

CHYMIST & DRUGGIST.

Brown Crowther, High st

CONFECTIONERS.

Day William, Hitchin st
Fryer William, Norton st

FIRE, &c. OFFICE AGENTS.

COUNTY (fire) & PROVIDENT (life), William Stocken, High st
NORWICH UNION, William Oliver Penn, White Horse st
PHŒNIX, Joseph Tranter, High st; and James Newbery, High st

GLOVERS.

Craft Philip, High st
Hankin John, High st
Ison Josiah, Hitchin st

GROCERS AND DEALERS IN SUNDRIES.

Brown Crowther, High st
Christy George William, Ashwell
Clarke Samuel, Norton st
Edwards William, Ashwell
Fryer William, Norton st
Horn Frederick, High st
Howard Ann, Stotfold
Oliver George, High st
Pestell Henry S. High st
Routledge Henry, High st
Ward William, Norton st
Westrope John, Ashwell

INNS.

George (commercial) Edward Smith, Hitchin st
Rose & Crown, Robert Bloom, White Horse st
White Horse (commercial & posting, & excise office) Frederick Archer, White Horse st

IRONMONGERS.

Dear William, White Horse st
Pryor Charles, White Horse st

LINEN & WOOLLEN DRAPRS, HOSIERS, &c.

Christy George William, Ashwell
Edwards William, Ashwell

LINEN & WOOLLEN DRAPRS, HOSIERS, &c.—Continued.
Oliver George (and hatter) High st
Routledge Henry (& hatter) High st
Westrope John, Ashwell

MALTSTERS.
Bowman Ann, Ashwell
Folbigg William, High st
Fordham Edward, Ashwell
Lawrence Edward, White Horse st
Pryor John and Morris, High st
Pryor Vickris, Hitchin st
Steed John, Norton st
Westrope Thomas, Ashwell

MILLERS.
Cane William, Radwell mill
Fordham John George, Stotfold mill, and Ashwell
Gurney John, Norton mill
Iredale Frances, Bygrave mill
Kitchener John, Ashwell
Long Seth, Windmill, Ashwell
Waldock George, Astwick and Stotfold, *Bedfordshire*

MILLINERS & STRAW HAT MAKERS.
Burrows Ann, Norton st
Carter Ann, White Horse st
Gudgin Mary, Norton st
Newbery Marshall, White Horse st
Richardson Hannah, High st
Scott Sarah, Hitchin st

PLUMBERS, PAINTERS, AND GLAZIERS.
Hopwood Henry, High st, & Ashwell
Thody Samuel, High st

SADDLERS.
Bacon William, Ashwell
Carter William, White Horse st
Hankin Thomas, High st
Sheppard Henry, White Horse st

SEEDSMEN.
Troup John (and gardener) White Horse st
Wylie James, Newton st

SURGEONS.
Inverarity Robert, Hitchin st
Marshall Frederick, Hitchin st
Sharpe George Brereton, Hitchin st
Tindale Edward, Ashwell

TAILORS.
Cane George, White Horse st
Craft Matthew, High st
Craft Philip, High st
Edwards Charles, Ashwell
Garrard William, Ashwell
Gentle William, High st
Gingell George (& hatter & clothier) White Horse st
Hankin John, High st
Lewis Thomas, Norton st

TAVERNS & PUBLIC HOUSES.
Angel, Susan Webster, High st
Black Lion, Wm. Hide, Stotfold, *Bedfordshire*
Bull's Head, Ann Baldock, Norton st
Bull's Head, George Bird, Ashwell
Chequers, Jas. Seymour, White Horse st
Chequers, Charles Waldock, Stotfold
Cock, Clark Gailor Cooper, High st
Crown & Anchor, Philip Saunderson, High st
Horse Shoes, James Page, High st
Orange Tree, George Studman, Willian
Plough, Elizabeth, Payne, Stotfold
Plume of Feathers, William Dear, White Horse st
Rose and Crown, William Flint, Ashwell
Saracen's Head, John Seymour, White Horse st
Sun, Elizabeth Goodchild, White Horse st
Three Tuns, Ann Bowman, Ashwell
White Lion, John Little, High st

WATCH & CLOCK MAKERS.
Carter John, Ashwell
Harvey Thos. (& toy dealer), High st
Raban Jno. (& toy dealer), Hitchin st

WHEELWRIGHTS.
Bloom John, Hitchin st
Pitty James, Ashwell
Simkins John, Norton st
Thorne Abraham, Ashwell
Thorne Samuel, Ashwell

WHITING MANUFACTURERS.
Day William, High st
Saunders Benjamin, Pond lane

WIRE WORKERS.
Farr John Evered, Hitchin st
Scott John, High st

Miscellaneous.
Dear Wm. hair dresser, White Horse st
GAS WORKS, Baldock—George de Vins Wade, secretary
Goldsmith James, corn dealer, High st
Hine Thomas, farmer, Newnham
Plyer William, farmer, Berry farm, Stotfold
Reynolds John, veterinary surgeon, Pepper alley
Seymour George, tea dealer, White Horse st
Smith John, registrar & relieving officer, White Horse st
Thurgood William, cooper, Hitchin st
Tranter Joseph and John, wine and spirit merchants, High st
Westrope John, farmer, Ashwell

COACHES,
Calling at or going from the Rose & Crown, unless otherwise expressed.

To LONDON, the *Royal Mail* (from Glasgow), and the *Royal Mail* (from Lincoln & Hull), call at the Post Office, every morning at two; go thro' Stevenage, Welwyn & Barnet—the *Highflyer* (from York), every forenoon (Sunday excepted) at eleven—the *Express* (from Lincoln), every morning at ten—the *Union* (from Leeds), at a quarter past twelve—the *Rockingham*, every morning at half-past three—and the *Perseverance* (from Boston), calls at the George, every afternoon (Sunday excepted) at three.
To LONDON, — Kershaw's *Coach*, every Monday & Friday morning at half-past five, and every Tuesday, Wednesday, Thursday & Saturday at half-past eight—a *Coach* (from Oundle), every Monday, Wednesday & Friday at twelve—and the *Regent* (from Stamford); every Tuesday, Thursday & Sat. afternoon at two

The following Coaches are all from LONDON.

To BOSTON, the *Perseverance*, calls at the George, every Tuesday, Wednesday, Thurs. & Saturday forenoon at eleven, and every Mon. & Fri. night at eleven.
To GLASGOW, the *Royal Mail*, calls at the Post Office, every night at eleven.
To LEEDS, the *Rockingham*, every night at half-past eight—and the *Union*, at half-past ten.
To LINCOLN, the *Express*, every night at eight.
To LINCOLN & HULL, the *Royal Mail*, calls at the Post Office, every night at 12.
To OUNDLE, a *Coach*, every Tuesday, Thursday and Saturday, at twelve.
To STAMFORD, the *Regent*, every Mon. Wed. and Fri. noon, at half-past twelve.
To YORK, the *Highflyer*, every forenoon (Sunday excepted) at eleven.

CARRIERS.
To LONDON, Jackson & Co's *Waggons*, from the George, daily—John Little's, from his house, High st, every Tuesday and Friday—a *Waggon*, from the Chequers, every Monday and Saturday—Woodward's, from the same place, every Friday—and George Petty's, from the George, every Tuesday.
To HITCHIN, William Manning, from the George, every Tuesday & Friday.
To LEEDS, Jackson and Co's *Waggons*, from the George, daily
To ST. NEOTS, — Woodward, from the Chequers, every Sunday—and another *Waggon*, every Thursday.

BERKHAMPSTEAD,

WITH THE VILLAGE OF NORTHCHURCH AND NEIGHBOURHOODS.

BERKHAMPSTEAD, or GREAT BERKHAMPSTEAD, is a market town and parish, in Dacorum hundred; 26 miles N.W. by W. from London, and 5 S.E. from Tring; situated upon the main road leading from London to Aylesbury—upon the banks of the Grand Junction canal, and close to the line of the London and Birmingham railway. Berkhampstead is supposed by some writers to have been a Roman station; from the name, however, it appears to be of Saxon origin, its designation having been *Berghamstedt*, or 'the town among the hills,' which accords well with its local situation. In this place the kings of Mercia often resided and kept their court, and some of the walls of their castle are still standing at the end of Castle street. 'Berkhampstead place,' the seat of the Honorable Miss Grimstone, in this parish, was formerly occupied by the first and second Charles during their infancy. Formerly lace making and the manufacture of wooden ware was carried on extensively here, but have become nearly, if not entirely, extinct. Brewing, malting, and the making of straw plat are the present existing branches. Petty sessions are held here once a fortnight, at the 'King's Arms Inn;' and courts baron and leet annually, for the 'Honour and Borough' of Berkhampstead. The church, dedicated to St. Peter, is a beautiful pile of architecture, cruciform, with a tower rising from the intersection; within the church are two chapels, and some interesting monuments. The living is a rectory, in the gift of the Crown, and incumbency of the Rev. John Crofts. The baptists, and those of Lady Huntingdon's connexion, have each a chapel, and the society of friends a meeting-house. Two excellent charity schools are established here, a parochial school of industry, and another conducted upon the national plan. There are almshouses for six poor widows, erected and endowed by John Sayer, Esq. in 1684; besides other minor charities, by which the poor of this parish are benefited. The poet Cowper was born in this parish in 1731. The market, held on Saturday, is chiefly for corn, but indifferently attended; the fairs are on Shrove-Tuesday, Whit-Monday, and October 12th—they are toy and pleasure fairs, but are, like the markets, unimportant as regards advantage to the town. In 1831 the number of inhabitants in Berkhampstead parish was 2,369.

NORTHCHURCH is a village, in the parish of Berkhampstead St. Mary, contiguous to the above town. It is pleasantly situate on the high road to Tring, and respectably inhabited. The population of the parish amounted, in 1831, to 1,156 persons.

POST OFFICE, High street, BERKHAMPSTEAD, George Scott, *Post Master*.—Letters from LONDON arrive every afternoon at one and night at ten, and are despatched every morning at four and noon at twelve.—Letters from the North arrive every morning at four, and are despatched every night at nine.

NOBILITY, GENTRY AND CLERGY.

Browne Rev. Jas. Caulfield, High st
Compigne Mr. —, High st
CooperAstleyPaston,esq.Northchrch
Crofts Rev. John, Rectory house
Deacon Sir Charles, K. C. B. High st
Dorrien Thomas, esq. Haresfoot
Dorrien Thos. jun. esq. King's hill
Duncombe Wm. esq. Northchurch
Dupré Rev. Thomas, Church yard
Eeles Mr. John, High st
Field Mr. James, High st
Foster Rev. H. B. High st
Fountain Mr. Richard, High st
Grimstone the Honourable Miss, Berkhamstead place
Hill Miss Sarah, High st
Howes Miss Sarah, Northchurch
Hyde John esq. High st
Minific Mrs. —, High st
Moore Frank, esq. Northchurch
Norris Mr. Stephen, High st
Nugent Miss Elizabeth, High st
Pechell Mrs. Sarah, High st
Seymour Sir John Hobart, Rectory, Northchurch
Smith Augustus, esq. Ashlin's hill
Smith James, esq. Ashlin's hill
Squire Mr. Thos. High st
Sutton Robt. esq. Rossway, Northchurch
Williams Mr. Samuel, High st

ACADEMIES & SCHOOLS.

BOURNE'S CHARITY SCHOOL, High st —Wm. Fenteman, master; Mary Ann Bourne, mistress
Cutforth Sarah (English and French boarding) High st
Dell Mary (boarding) High st
GRAMMAR SCHOOL, Church yard— Rev. Thomas Dupré, master
Green Mary Ann (boarding) High st
NATIONAL SCHOOL, High st—Saml. Crew, master; Eliz. Trott, mistress
PAROCHIAL SCHOOL OF INDUSTRY, High st—Robert Gamble, master; Willowes Gamble, mistress
Spicer Elizabeth (boarding) High st

ATTORNEYS.

Duncombe James, Woodcock hill, Northchurch
Williams Henry, Gossom lodge, Northchurch

BAKERS & FLOUR DEALERS.

Austin Charity, High st
Clare James, High st
Clarke Charles, High st
Gadsden John, Northchurch
Halsey William, High st
Rushworth Thomas, High st
Sear William, High st
Sutton Mary (& confectioner) High st

BANKERS.

AYLESBURY BRANCH BANK, High st —(draws on Praed and Co. London)—Richard Woodman, agent

BLACKSMITHS.

Bligh Thomas, High st
Bunn James, High st
Nash James, High st
Pocock Obadiah, High st

BOAT BUILDER.

Hatton John, Wharf, High st

BOOKSELLERS & STATIONRS

Hobbs Joseph, High st
Scott George, High st

BOOT & SHOE MAKERS.

Harris James, High st
Hurst Benjamin, High st
Hurst Thomas, High st
Loader John Shepard, High st
Margrave George, Castle st
Margrave Mark, High st
Norris William, Northchurch
Putnam James, Grubs lane
Riley Charles, Northchurch
Tomlin John, High st
Tompkins James, High st
Underwood Robert, High st

BREWERS.

Foster James, High st
Mills John and Son, High st
Tomlin William, High st

BRICK & LIME BURNER.

Howard John, Woodcock hill, Northchurch

BRICKLAYRS & PLASTERERS

Bird William, Back lane
Holloway Stephen, High st
Skinner John, High st

BUTCHERS.

Austin Joseph, High st
Johnson John, High st
King John (and fishmonger) High st
King William, High st
Timson Thomas, High st
Tompkins Francis, High st
Tompkins John, Northchurch
Tompkins Sarah, High st
Tompkins William, High st

CARPENTERS & JOINERS.

Costin John, Back lane
Gomm Joseph, High st
Goodman Joseph, High st
Harris Edward, High st
Hawkins Wm. (and cabinet maker) High st
Kendall Charles John, High st
King Thomas, Northchurch
Matthews Thomas, Castle st

CHYMISTS AND DRUGGISTS.

Irish Thomas Cowling, High st
Jones Charles, High st

COACH BUILDERS.

Austin James, High st
Pethybridge John, High st

COAL DEALERS.

Collins Chas. (& wharfinger) Wharf
Harris Richard, Castle st
Hatton John, Wharf, High st
Tompkins John (and wharfinger) Castle st wharf

COOPERS & VAT MAKERS.

Brinkman Thomas, High st
Underwood Samuel, Grubs lane

FARRIERS.

Massey Thos. (& cow leech) High st
PrudamesChas. (&cow leech) High st

FIRE, &c. OFFICE AGENTS.

COUNTY (fire) Thos. Martin and Son, High st
PHŒNIX, Jos. Hobbs, High st
PROVIDENT, Thos. Martin & Son, High st

GROCERS AND DEALERS IN SUNDRIES.

Allum John, High st
Austin Jas. (& tallow chandler) High st
Bunn John, High st
Duncombe David, High st
Faulkner Thomas, High st
Harris Edward, High st
Hazell Wm. (and fruiterer) High st
Hill Jesse, Northchurch
Holliman John, High st
Kidd William, High st
Lawrence James, Northchurch
Mallard Samuel, Northchurch
Margrave Geo. (& draper) Castle st
Osborn James, Northchurch
Prior Ann (and fruiterer) High st
Putnam John, High st
Rickard Jno. (& china & glass dealer) High st
Sear William, High st
Sewell James, Castle st
Shannon William, Castle st
Skinner John, High st
Tompkins John, Northchurch
Woodman Richard (& tallow chandler) High st

HAIR DRESSERS.

Bartlett John, High st
De Fraine William, High st

INNS.

King's Arms (& posting) John Page, High st
Red Lion, Mary Bailey, High st
Swan, James Foster, High st

IRONMONGERS.

Miller Frederick (and furnitune broker) High st
Prudames Amelia, High st

LAND SURVEYOR.

Scott George, High st

LINEN & WOOLLEN DRAPRS.

Allum John, High st
Baker Ann, High st
Elliman James, High st
Hill William, Northchurch
Martin Thomas and Son, High st
Woodman Richard, High st

MALTSTERS.

Foster James, High st
Mills John and Son, High st
Tomlin William, High st

MILLERS.

Cook George, Water lane
Littleboy Sarah, Lower mill

MILLINERS AND DRESS MAKERS.

Davie Sarah, High st
Hobbs Sarah, High st
Rickard Elizabeth, High st

PLUMBERS, PAINTERS AND GLAZIERS.

Bailey Charles, High st
Hallifax William, High st
Hunt William, Northchurch

SADDLERS, &c.

Butterfield Joseph, High st
Heading William, High st

SURGEONS.

Brown Thomas, High st
Hilder Henry Hugh, High st
Steel Richard, High st
Whately Thomas, High st

TAILORS.

Abbey James, High st
Clarke George, High st
Grove Joseph, High st
Pitkin Joseph, High st
Pitkin Thomas, High st
Scott Thomas, Northchurch
Whitehorn Gad, High st

TAVERNS & PUBLIC HOUSES.

Bell, Elizabeth Christie, High st
Chaff Cutter, Richard Tebboth, High st
Crooked Billet, Robt. Rance, Northchurch
Five Bells, Stephen Holloway, High st
George, Martha Manton, Northchurch
Goat, John Siret, High st
Grey Mare, Saml. Bedford, Northchurch

TEACHER OF LANGUAGES & MATHEMATICS.

Scott George, High st

TURNERS & SHOVEL MAKRS.

Foster Martha (turner) Back lane
Grove Joseph, Castle st
Howard Thomas, High st
Meek Samuel, Castle st

WHEELWRIGH'

Holliday John, High st
King William, High st

Miscellaneous.

Allen John, brazier, High st
Baldwin Joseph, carrier, High st
Bedford Francis, rope mat maker, High st
Cox Wm. French polisher & paintr. High st
Deal Wm. poulterer & fishmonger, High st
Fry James, stone mason, High st
Harris Richard, flour dealer, Castle st
Key William, timber merchant, High st
King John, fruiterer, High st
Lane Henry & Son, nurserymen, High st
Leaper Thomas, bellhanger, High st
Miller Frederick, pawnbroker, High st
Shortnall Francis, rope maker, High st
UNION POORHOUSE, High st—Ths. Rickard, governor; Mary Frowde, mistress

MISCELLANEOUS—*Continued.*
Weedon Joseph, basket maker, High st
Wood Jas. smith & wire worker, High st
Wood Thomas, watch maker, High st
Young James, gardener, High st

COACH.

Calling at the Red Lion.

To LONDON, the *Dispatch* (from Aylesbury), every morning (Sun. excepted), at half-past nine; goes through Watford, Stanmore and Edgeware.

To AYLESBURY, the *Dispatch* (from London), every evening (Sun excepted), at half-past six; goes through Northchurch and Tring.

RAILWAY CONVEYANCE.

To LONDON, *Trains*, daily (Sunday excepted) eight minutes past eight morning, eighteen minutes before twelve forenoon, and twelve minutes past five afternoon.

SUNDAY TRAINS,

Eight minutes past eight morning and twelve minutes past six evening.

To BIRMINGHAM, *Trains*, thirty-three minutes past ten morning, thirty-three minutes past three afternoon, & thirty-three minutes past six evening.

SUNDAY TRAINS,

Thirty-three minutes past nine morning and thirty-three minutes past six eveng.

CARRIERS.

To LONDON, John King & Sarah Willis, from their houses, every Tues. & Friday, and James Austin, every Friday.

To AMERSHAM and WINDSOR, John Chapman's *Cart*, from the Swan Inn, every Wednesday.

BISHOPS STORTFORD AND NEIGHBOURHOOD.

BISHOPS STORTFORD is a respectable market town and parish, in the hundred of Braughin; 30 miles N.N.E. from London, 31 S.S.W. from Newmarket, 26 S.S.E. from Cambridge, 14 E.N.E. from Hertford, and 15 N. from Epping. It derives its name from having been given by William the Conqueror to the Bishop of London, and also from its situation on the Stort and its former ford. This river (now crossed by two bridges) is navigable from hence until it joins the Lea at Roydon, in Essex, and is, throughout that distance, the boundary line of the two counties. Stortford appears to have been of some consequence in the early ages: the Conqueror erected here Watymore Castle, and the remains of the keep are still to be seen on the east side of the town. The form of the town is that of a cross, the principal streets crossing each other at right angles; its appearance has rapidly improved of late years; the town is lighted with gas, and the inhabitants are well supplied with water. A spacious and handsome corn exchange and public market, including coffee and assembly rooms, magistrates' chamber, &c., was erected in 1828; the building is of the Grecian Ionic order, and is well adapted to its several purposes. Most of the shops and dwellings, also, evince the spirit and prosperity of their inhabitants. This was formerly a representative borough, but it has not exercised the elective franchise since the reign of Edward III. The town is within the jurisdiction of the county magistrates, who hold petty sessions, every fortnight, in a room in the Corn Exchange, where also the general business of the town is transacted. Bishops Stortford is a polling station at the election of county members. The staple of the place is malt and other grain, immense quantities of which are annually supplied to the metropolis, by the navigable canal; there are also three very extensive breweries, and several flour mills. The town possesses some good inns, both posting and commercial: the principal are the 'George,' in North-street, and the 'Crown,' in Hockerill.

The parish church, dedicated to St. Michael, is an elegant edifice, not many years since repaired and beautified at a considerable expense. It comprises a nave, chancel, and aisles, and is adorned with a lofty tower and spire; in the tower is an excellent ring of ten bells. Within the church are many ancient monuments, and the general interior is deservedly admired for its neatness. It also contains an elegantly fitted-up and spacious room, for the reception of the books formerly belonging to an old and extinct grammar school. Over the north door is the figure of St. Michael, casting the old serpent out of heaven. The living is a vicarage, in the presentation of the precentor of St. Paul's cathedral; and the present incumbent is the Rev. Charles Spencer, to whom the inhabitants of this parish are much indebted for bringing into activity sundry charities which had long lain dormant. The baptists and independents, who compose a large and respectable portion of the inhabitants, have a handsome chapel each; and the Wesleyan methodists and society of friends have also places of worship. The charities comprise a national school and Sunday schools, well supported and attended; some alms-houses, and numerous bequests for the benefit of the poor, in supplying bread and clothing, and apprenticing children. There are many handsome residences in this vicinity: one that will arrest the attention is Hallingbury Place, the seat of John Archer Houblon, Esq. near to the town; the beauty of the park, and the diversified and picturesque scenery in the adjoining forest, call forth the admiration of the lovers of rural nature. That, also, of Thomas Wilby, Esq. Wind hill, is deserving of notice. The market, held on Thursday, is a good one for corn, swine, poultry, and other commodities for domestic consumption. There are three fairs, viz. on Holy Thursday, the Thursday after Trinity Sunday, and the 11th of October, for horses and cattle. The population of the parish, by the census for 1831, was 3,958.

POST OFFICE, North street, James Hillatt Summers, *Post Master.*—Letters from LONDON arrive (by the Norwich and Newmarket mail) every night at eleven, and are despatched every morning at three.—Letters from WARE and the North arrive every night at eight, and are despatched every morning at seven.—Letters from all parts of ESSEX & SUFFOLK arrive every morning at eight, & are despatched every evening at six.

GENTRY & CLERGY.
Bangham Miss —, Wind hill
Beaumont Mrs. Sarah, North st
Bird Mr. John, Wind hill
Bouchier Rev. Chas. Spencer, Great Hallingbury
Chaplin Rev. William, Water lane
Clements James, esq. Hockerill
Frere George, esq. Twyford house
Greata Miss —, Apton cottage
Horsley Mrs. —, Garston green
Houblon John Archer, esq. Hallingbury place
Johns E. B. esq. Wind hill lodge
Johnson Mrs. —, Wallberry
Norris Mrs. Sarah, Wind hill
Pennington Rev. Ths. Thorley rectory
Pritchett Rev. Chas. Litt. Hallingbury
Spencer Rev. Charles, Church yard
Starling George Augustus, esq. M. D. Wind hill
Stock Mrs. Rosanna, High st
Tufnell John Jolliffe, esq. Threem hall priory
Wilby Thomas, esq. Wind hill

ACADEMIES & SCHOOLS.
Not otherwise described are Day Schools.
Bass Sarah (brding) Bishops Stortford
Bates William, South st
Boutle John, Back lane
Browne Mary (boarding) Wind hill
Fitch Elizabeth, Church st
Kent James (boarding) Apton field
Miller William, Wind hill
NATIONAL SCHOOL, Bishops Stortford—Thomas Venimore, master; Susan Sarah Venimore, mistress
Perry Ann (for music) Bridge st

ATTORNEYS.
Fiske Samuel, Hockerill
Gee William, High st
Leete John, North st
Phipps George, Hockerill
Taylor and Johnstone, Market place

AUCTIONEERS & APPRAISRS.
Cheffins William (and surveyor and estate agent) North st
Slater John, Bridge st
Summers Jas. Hillatt (& estate agent) North st

BAKERS & FLOUR DEALERS.
Beverly Joseph, Hockerill
Clarke Sarah, Back lane
Coote James, Hockerill
Davey Thomas, Bishops Stortford
Ettridge Michael, North st
Tucker Henry, South st
Tucker James, New town

BANKERS.
Gibson and Co. (branch of Saffron Walden) Bridge street—(draw on Drewett and Fowler, London)—William Taylor, agent

BARGE OWNERS.
Jennings Reginald, South st
Miller Benjamin, South st
Miller David, South st
Taylor John and Son, Bridge st

BLACKSMITHS.
Bush Thomas, Market place
Chandler Jane, Church st
Perry Edward, Bridge st
Sell Richard (and white) South st

BOOKSELLERS & STATIONRS
Barnard Richard, South st
Bradfield Thos. (& printer) Bridge st
Mullinger John Morse (and printer) North st

BOOT & SHOE MAKERS.
Anderson William, Back lane
Blackaby James, Church st
Gossugh Thomas, Dell lane
Pannell William, Hockerill
Petty James, North st
Seymour George, Bridge st
Thurgood Thomas, South st

Tucker William Scruby, South st
Waterman Thomas, North st

BRAZIERS AND TIN-PLATE WORKERS.

Nind John Newton, South st
Summers and Sworder, North st

BREWERS.

Hawkes, Nash and Co. North st
Newman William, South st
Percival Robert, Hockerill
Tucker John, South st

BRICK & TILE BURNERS.

Glasscock Joseph, South st
Prior Richard, North st
Snow John Henry, North st

BRICKLAYERS.

Bartlett Samuel, New town
Ball Sarah, Wind hill
Glasscock Jos. (& builder) South st
Snow John Henry, North st

BUTCHERS.

Barber John, South st
Christy William, Church st
Finch Augustine, Hockerill
Fitch Samuel Haiden, Church st
Gilson Edward, Market place
Nottage Mary, North st
Petts Joseph, Dell lane
Phillips John, South st
Prance Benjamin, North st
White George, South st

CABINET MAKERS AND UPHOLSTERERS.

Slater John, Bridge st
Summers and Sworder, North st
Thurgood Thomas (and furniture broker) South st

CARPENTERS.

Marked thus * are also Builders.

Bangham John, Bridge st
*Cheffins Elizabeth, North st
Cornwell William, South st
*Nash and Skipp, Back lane
*Perry George & Son, South st [st
Seymour Geo. (& boat builder) South
Warner Saml. (& paper hangr) Hockrill

CHINA & GLASS DEALERS.

Palmer William, Bridge st
Phillips James, North st

CHYMISTS & DRUGGISTS.

Bruce Joseph, Church st
Eddy and Jennings, North st
Odams James, North st
Slater John High st

COACH & HARNESS MAKERS.

Perry and Hunt, Hockerill
Tyler William and Son, Hockerill

COACH PROPRIETORS.

Gilby Henry, Wind hill
Percival Robert, Hockerill

COAL & CORN MERCHANTS.

(See also Corn Dealers.)

Case and Patmore, Bridge st
Jennings Reginald, South st
Miller Benjamin, South st
Miller David, South st
Miller Joshua, South st

COOPERS.

Bangham John, Bridge st
Nash and Skipps, Back lane

CORN DEALERS.

(See also Coal and Corn Merchants)

Cole Robt. (& hop and seed) High st
Parmenter William, Hockerill
Pavitt Joseph and Peter, South st

CURRIERS AND LEATHER CUTTERS.

Jolly William & Margaret, North st
Waterman Thomas, North st

FIRE, &c. OFFICE AGENTS.

County (fire) and Provident (life) John Slater, Bridge st [South st
London Union, Henry Jennings,
National Endowment, Jas. Sanders, North st
Phœnix, John Taylor & Son, Bridge st, and Thos. Sparling, Wind hill
Royal Exchange, George Perry, jun. South st [street
Sun, James Hillatt Summers, North

FISHMONGERS.

Carter James, Hockerill
Franklin James, Market place

GROCERS & TEA DEALERS.

(See also Shopkeepers, &c.; and also Tea Dealers.)

Clarke James, Water lane
Cole Robert, High st
Dodd James (and draper) North st
Everard James, Market place
Heath Joseph, South st
Mumford Burton, South st
Phillips James, North st
Slater George, Bridge st
Wenden Samuel, High st

HAIR DRESSERS.

Clark Thomas, Palmer's lane
Copsey John (and registry office for servants) North st
Cowel William, Hockerill
Hodgkin Dinah, South st
Mackenzie James, North st

HORSE DEALERS.

Heskin Thomas, Hockerill
Heskin Thomas, jun. Hockerill
Polley John, Back lane

INNS.

Chequers, Sarah Glasscock, North st
Crown (commercial & posting) Robt. Percival, Hockerill
George (family hotel, posting house, commercial inn and excise office) James Goodwin, North st

IRONMONGERS.

Nind John Newton (and smith and bell hanger) South st
Summers and Sworder, North st

LINEN & WOOLLEN DRAPERS

Beard Thomas, North st
Cole Robert, High st
Heath Joseph, South st
Johnson Joseph Thomas, North st
Mumford Burton, South st
Phillips Edwin, North st

MALTSTERS.

Marked thus * are also Factors.

Baynes John, Hockerill
Case and Patmore, Bridge st
Cornwell John Carter, Bridge st
*Daniels William, Bridge st
Fairman Joseph, Bridge st
Hawkes, Nash and Co. North st
*Jennings Reginald, South st
Miller Joshua, South st
*Nash Frederick, South st
Newport William, Hockerill
*Taylor John and Son, Bridge st
Taylor Joseph, jun. North st
Woodley Matthew, Hockerill

MILLERS.

Barnard John, South mill
Bird Thos. (steam mills) South st
Canning John Cater, Parsonage mill
Daniels William, Bridge st
Davey Thomas, Bishops Stortford
Quire James, Twyford mill

MILLINERS AND DRESS MAKERS.

Johnson Joseph Thomas, North st
Perry Mary, South st
Shea Esther, North st
Smith Frances, North st

NURSERY & SEEDSMAN.

Tucker John, South st

OIL AND COLOURMAN.

Nind John Newton, South st

PLUMBERS, PAINTERS AND GLAZIERS.

Cooper Henry, Wind hill
Fordham Josiah, South st
Kent Samuel, Hockerill
Perry Benjamin, North st
Perry Samuel, Church st

PORTER DEALERS.

Heath Joseph and Son (Dublin porter stores) Market place

SADDLERS AND HARNESS MAKERS.

Game Samuel, Hockerill
Harvey Edward, South st
Petty Thomas, Market place

SHOPKEEPERS & DEALRS IN GROCERIES & SUNDRIES.

Beverly William, Hockerill
Cass William, New town
Hughes James, New town
Thurgood Thos. (& draper) South st
Turner Thomas, Hockerill
Tyler Benjamin, Hockerill

SLATERS.

Glasscock Thomas (and slate merchant) South st
Reed James (and patentee for the improved method of joining slate and stone) South st

STAY MAKERS.

Lane Sarah, Back lane
Thorby Lydia, Market st

STONE & MARBLE MASONS.

Glasscock Thos. (& builder) South st
Reed James, South st

STRAW HAT MAKERS.

Kidd Elizabeth, High st
Shea Esther, North st
Young and Reed, South st

SURGEONS.

Alger Jno. Speller (& registrar) High st
Scarr Renforth Thomas, Wind hill
Tweed and Cribb, North st

SURVEYORS.

Cheffins Wm. (& estate agent) North st
Seymour George (to the trustees of the river Stort) South st
Weeks James (road) South lodge

TAILORS AND DRAPERS.

Ashby Charles, South st
Beadle George, South st
Greata Michael, Bridge st
Harris Jonathan, Hockerill
Heath Joseph & Son, Market place
Marshall Thomas, Church st
Searle Richard (and clothes dealer) Palmer's lane
Slater John, High st

TALLOW CHANDLERS.

Mumford Burton, South st
Palmer William, Bridge st

TAVERNS & PUBLIC HOUSES.

Anchor, Matthew Thurgood, South st
Bear's Head, Abraham Smoothy, High st
Bell, William Wells, Bridge st
Black Lion, Jane Wilkinson, Bridge st
Castle, Mary Wolston, New town
Coach & Horses, John Moore, Hockerill
Cock, Henry Goodwin, Hockerill
Curriers' Arms, Jas. Franklin, Market pl
Dog & Pot, Sarah Glasscock, Market place
Half Moon, John Woolstone, North st
Plume of Feathers, Jno. Miller, Market pl
Red Lion, Titus Ottas May, Hockerill
Rein Deer, John Sayer, South st
Star, William Bird, Bridge st
Swan, Benjamin Giffin, South st
White Horse, John Parish, North st

TEA DEALERS.

Hughan John, Palmer's lane
Thompson Robert, Hockerill
Turnbull Wm. (and coffee) South st

VETERINARY SURGEONS.

Folks Thomas, Hockerill
Titchmarsh Minott, Market place

WATCH AND CLOCK MAKERS

Pratt John, North st
Yardley Jas. (& pawnbroker) High st
Yardley Peter (& wire worker) South st

WHARFINGERS.
Jennings Reginald, South st
Taylor John and Son, Bridge st

WHEELWRIGHTS.
Newman William, South st
Smith John, North st [yard
Webb John (and smith) Black Lion

WINE & SPIRIT MERCHANTS
Goodwin James, North st
Hawke Charles, South st [st
Hawkes, Nash & Co. (spirit) North
Heath Samuel Duncon (spirit) Market place
Johnson George, North st
Pavitt Joseph & Peter, Market place
Percivall Robert, Hockerill

Miscellaneous.
Barnard Richard, dyer, &c. South st
Boulcott John, timber merchant, Bridge st
Cawley Stephen, millwright, North st
Chaplin Frederick, tanner, Water lane
Clark Thomas, patten maker, Palmer's la
Evans Thomas, gas fitter, Wind hill
Fish Henry, marine store dealer, South st
Francis Steph. relieving officer, South st
Gas Works, Bishops Stortford—Thos. Evans, secretary [Bridge st
Hughes Wm. iron founder & pump maker,
Johnstone John, superintendent registrar, Corn Exchange.
Lee Thomas, furniture broker, Church st
Liddard Geo. marine store dealer, South st
Norton Wm. rope & sack maker, Hockerill
Patmore James, livery stables, High st
Pittock Samuel, hatter, North st
Quilter Thos. shovel maker, Market place
Richards Samuel, glover, High st
Sanders James, confectioner, North st
Taylor John, clerk to the board of guardians, Market place
Tyler Fredk. carver and gilder, Hockerill
Union Workhouse, Hockerill—Samuel Stribling, mstr; Sarah Stribling, mstrss
Wade Susannah, toy dealer, &c. Market pl

COACHES.
To LONDON, the *Royal Mail* and the *Magnet* (from Norwich), call at the Crown Inn, Hockerill, every morning at half-past two—the *Times* (from Cambridge), every morning (Sunday excepted) at half-past eight, and the *Fly*, at half-past twelve—and the *Hero* (from Fakenham & Swaffham), every evening (Sunday excepted) at a quarter past five.
To LONDON, a *Coach*, from the George Hotel, every morning (Sunday excepted) at eight—and other *Coaches*, every Monday morning at five and six—the *Marquess Cornwallis* (from Bury), calls at the George Hotel, every afternoon at two—a *Coach* (from Haverhill), calls at the Chequers, every Monday, Wednesday and Friday, at twelve—and the *Telegraph* (from Norwich), calls at the Cock, every afternoon at three; all go through Sawbridgeworth, Harlow & Epping.
To BURY ST. EDMUNDS, the *Marquess Cornwallis*, from the George, every day at twelve; goes through Chesterford & Newmarket.
To CAMBRIDGE, the *Fly* (from London), calls at the Crown, every afternoon (Sunday excepted) at a quarter before two—& the *Times*, every evening (Sunday excepted) at a quarter past five; both go through Stanstead, Newport & Chesterford.
To FAKENHAM and SWAFFHAM, the *Hero*, from the Crown, every morning, at a quarter before ten; goes through Chesterford, Cambridge & Newmarket.
To HAVERHILL, a *Coach* (from London), calls at the Chequers, every Tuesday, Thursday & Saturday afternoon, at two; goes through Newport & Saffron Walden.
To NORWICH, the *Royal Mail*, (from London), calls at the Crown, every night, at half-past eleven, and the *Magnet*, at eleven—and the *Telegraph*, calls at the Cock, every morning at half-past ten; all go through Quendon, Chesterford & Newmarket
To SAFFRON WALDEN, a *Coach*, from the George Hotel, every evening (Sunday excepted) at half-past six.

CARRIERS.
To LONDON, John Mysom's *Waggons*, from his house, Hockerill, & John Crabb, from his house, North st, every Monday & Thursday; and Acorn & Bell's *Waggons*, and William Gore, from the Red Lion, every Tuesday and Friday.
To LONDON, Charles Adams, from the Cock Inn, Hockerill, and Isaac Boutell, from the Red Lion, Hockerill, every Monday—John Parish, from the Cock Inn, and John Pilgrim, from the Red Lion, every Tuesday—Samuel Fordham and Joseph Pilgrim, from the Cock Inn, and Joseph Ruse, from the Red Lion, every Wednesday; and William Cockerton & James Clements, from the Red Lion, every Friday.
To CHESTERFORD, John Pilgrim, from the Red Lion, every Thursday, and Joseph Pilgrim, from the Cock, every Fri.
To HAVERHILL, William Cockerton, from the Red Lion, every Sunday.
To LINTON, Samuel Fordham, from the Cock Inn, every Friday.
To NEWMARKET, William Gore's and Acorn & Bell's *Waggons*, from the Red Lion, every Wednesday and Saturday.
To SAFFRON WALDEN, Chas. Adams, from the Cock, every Wednesday, and John Parish, every Thursday.
To SOHAM, James Clements, from the Red Lion, every Sunday.
To SWAFFIELD, Joseph Ruse, from the Red Lion, every Friday.
To THAXTED, Isaac Boutell, from the Red Lion, every Wednesday.

CONVEYANCE BY WATER.
BY THE RIVER STORT.
To LONDON, from the wharfs of Reginald Jennings and Taylor & Son.

BUNTINGFORD AND NEIGHBOURHOOD.

BUNTINGFORD is a chapelry and neat town, formerly having a market, in the parishes of Aspeden, Layston, Throcking and Wyddial, in the hundred of Edwinstree, 31 miles N. from London, 12 N. N. E. from Hertford, 28 S. S. E. from Huntingdon, 20 S. from Cambridge, and 7 S. from Royston; pleasantly situated on a gentle acclivity close to the Rib, from a *ford*, over which river, and *Bunting*, the name of a person (who once had a forge here), it is said its appellation is derived. It is a place of but little trade: some business is done in malt and leather, and upon the river are corn mills. The county magistrates sit here in petty sessions for the division at one of the principal inns, and a septennial court leet is held for the hundred. The chapel, dedicated to St. Peter, is a commodious brick building, erected in 1626, mainly through the exertions of the Rev. Alexander Strange. The living is a perpetual curacy, in the patronage of the vicar of Layston. There are places of worship for the society of friends and independents. The principal charities comprise a free grammar school, founded by the same person who originated the chapel; and eight almshouses, founded by Seth Ward, a bishop of Salisbury, who was a native of this town. The market, granted by Henry VIII, has been entirely discontinued; and the fairs, formerly held on the 29th June and 30th November, are now but irregularly kept. The population of Buntingford is returned with the four parishes before named; these contained collectively, by the parliamentary returns for 1831, 1,972 inhabitants.

POST OFFICE, William Hampton, *Post Master*.—Letters from LONDON arrive every night at twelve, and are despatched every morning at three.—Letters from the North arrive every morning at three, and are despatched every night at twelve.

GENTRY AND CLERGY.
Bray Mrs. Elizabeth, Buntingford
Butt William, esq. Coney berry
Butt Wm. jun. esq. Cottage, Buntingfd
Edridge Mrs. Mary Ann, Buntingford
Gardner Mrs. Sybella, Aspeden
Green Mrs. Sarah, Buntingford
Greg Thomas, esq. Westmill
Holbrook James, esq. Aspeden hall
Hooper John, esq. M.D. Buntingford
Maxwell Rev. C. Wyddial rectory
Meetkirke Adolphus, esq. Julians
Mickley Miss —, Buntingford
Mickley Mrs. Sarah, Buntingford
Murray Mrs. —, Yardley berry
Papys Rev. Henry, Westmill
Skinner Rev. William, Rushden
Soames Henry, esq. Broadfield
Soames Nathaniel, esq. Yardley
Ray Rev. John, Throcking
Titchmarsh Mr. Thomas, Buntingford
Watts Wm. Henry, esq. Buntingford
Williamson William, esq. Buntingford
York Rev. Grantham, Aspeden
Young Capt. —, Buntingford
Young Rev. William, Aspeden

ACADEMIES & SCHOOLS.
Aspeden Charity School—Thos. Woodwards, master; Amey Woodwards, mistress [Dewe
Grammar School—Rev. Samuel
Infants' School, Aspeden—Mrs. Bacchus, mistress [tress
Infants' School—Mrs. Hoy, mis-
Stracey Miss (day)
Watson Ann (day and boarding)

ATTORNEYS.
Lander George
Wortham Cecil Proctor

BAKERS & FLOUR DEALERS.
Biscoe John
Burr George
Monk James
Sutton James

BLACKSMITHS.
Jackson Edward
Jordan William
King George, Aspeden
Mottram Francis

BOOT & SHOE MAKERS.
Benstead Joseph
Butler Peter
Farrington Sarah
Meredith Robert
Shaw John Thomas

BUTCHERS.
Archer Stephen
Eling William

CARPENTERS.
Meredith James
Seamer Charles
Warren Nathan (& flour dealer)

COOPERS.
Bigg John (& measure maker)
Nicholls Charles (& retail brewer)

CORN & COAL DEALERS.
Bowman Martha
Burr George
Camp Edward

DRESS MAKERS.
Dix and Waldock
Makintosh Miss

FIRE, &c. OFFICE AGENTS.
COUNTY (fire) & PROVIDENT (life), George Cook
NORWICH, James Sutton
PHŒNIX, Charles Nicholls
SUN, Sarah Mickley

GROCERS AND DEALERS IN SUNDRIES.
Anthony John, Aspeden
Bedells William (and chymist)
Geldard Sophia
Haradence James
Medcalf Thomas (& tallow chandler)
Patmore James (& draper)
Titchmarsh Thomas (& glass dealer)
Weston William

INNS.
Bell (commercial and posting, and excise office) John Sibley
George (commercial and posting) George Robinson

LINEN & WOOLLEN DRAPRS.
Dix and Waldock
Weston William (and hatter)

MILLERS.
Body William
Burr George
Chamberlain William

PLUMBERS, PAINTERS, &c.
Cook George (and paper hanger)
Houchin William

SADDLERS.
Grout William
Wright James

SURGEONS.
Gaffney George
Macklin Charles (& registrar)

TAILORS.
Bigg William (and draper)
Munt Henry (and draper)
Nicholls Thomas (and draper)
Sampson William Carter

TAVERNS & PUBLIC HOUSES.
Adam & Eve, William Hunt
Angel, William Smith
Bull, Edward Phillips
Chequers, George Milne
Crown, Joseph Wright
Fox & Duck, John Robinson
Hoops, James Winters
Red Lion, James Field, Aspeden
White Hart, John Blackley
Windmill, William Newland

WATCH MAKERS.
Read Richard
Read William

Miscellaneous.
Chamberlain Elizabeth, confectioner
Gray Charles & Henry, bricklayers
Hamilton John, ironmonger & brazier
Knight William, gardener & seedsman
Lodge James, fellmonger & glover
Lodge Thomas, wheelwright
Medcalf Thomas, glass dealer
Munns Elizabeth, straw hat maker
Nicholls Charles, hair dresser, hatter and stationer
Peggram Thomas, currier and tanner
Shepherd Richard, wheelwright
Stracey Henry, dyer
Titchmarsh Thomas, stamp distributer
UNION WORKHOUSE, Charles Dalton, governor; Louisa Dalton, mistress
Wren Richard, maltster

COACHES.
All call at the Bell Inn, except the Cambridge Star, which calls at the George.

To LONDON, the *Royal Mail*, (from Edinburgh), every morning at two, and the *Royal Mail* (from Boston), every morning at three—the *Rapid* (from Holbeach), at the same hour—the *Star* (from Cambridge), every morning at nine, and the *Telegraph*, every day at twelve—a *Coach* (from Wisbeach), every afternoon at two—the *Wellington* (from Newcastle) every afternoon at half-past three—the *Beehive* (from Cambridge), every Monday, Wednesday & Friday morning, at half-past ten, and a *Coach* (from Stamford), the same afternoons at two; all go through Ware.

The following are all from LONDON.
To BOSTON, the *Royal Mail*, every night at half-past eleven
To CAMBRIDGE, the *Telegraph*, every afternoon at two—the *Star*, every evening at seven, and the *Beehive*, every Tuesday, Thursday & Saturday at four.
To EDINBURGH, the *Royal Mail*, every night at half-past eleven; through Royston and Huntingdon.
To HOLBEACH, the *Rapid*, every night at half-past ten; through Royston and Cambridge.
To NEWCASTLE, the *Wellington*, every evening at half-past six; through Royston and Cambridge.
To STAMFORD & PETERBOROUGH, a *Coach*, every Tuesday, Thursday and Saturday at twelve; through Royston and Huntingdon.
To WISBEACH, a *Coach*, every day at twelve; thro' Royston & Cambridge.

CARRIERS.
To LONDON, John Biscoe's *Waggon*, from his house, every Tuesday & Friday—Deacon & Co.'s *Waggon*, every evening, and Deacon & Co.'s *Vans*, five times a week.
To BURY ST. EDMUNDS, Deacon & Co.'s *Vans*, five times a week.
To ELY, Deacon & Co's *Vans*, every Sunday, Wednesday and Friday.
To NORWICH, Deacon and Co.'s *Vans*, every day (Monday excepted).
To YORK, Deacon & Co.'s *Waggons*, every morning.
All Deacon & Co.'s Vans and Waggons call at their agent's, Thomas Nicholls.

CHESHUNT, WALTHAM CROSS & NEIGHBOURHOODS.

CHESHUNT is a large and populous village, in the hundred of Hertford and parish of Cheshunt St. Mary, which comprises the wards of Cheshunt Street, Waltham Cross and Woodside. The village is rather more than 12 miles from London, 8 s. from Hertford, the like distance s. E. from Hatfield, 8 s. by w. from Ware, 5 w. from Epping, and 4 N. from Enfield; situated near the course of the Lea and the line of the New river. It was in ancient days denominated *Cestrehunt;* but the most remarkable circumstance in its annals is its having been the residence of Richard Cromwell, the unambitious son of Oliver, who died here in 1712, in the eightieth year of his age. The trade of Cheshunt is limited to that in articles of immediate convenience for its inhabitants, and the opulent residents in the neighbourhood; but it is distinguished by the number of respectable academies in the village and its vicinity. Sir Geo. Beeston Prescott, Bart., is lord of the manor of Theobalds, and holds a court baron twice and a court leet once in the year. The magistrates meet in petty sessions every alternate Monday, at the 'Green Dragon,' in Churchgate. The church, dedicated to St. Mary, and erected in the reign of Henry VI, is a handsome structure; it stands about half a mile to the west of the village: the benefice is a vicarage, of which the Marquess of Salisbury is patron, and the Rev. M. Morris Preston incumbent. The other places of worship are Trinity chapel of ease, in Crossbrook-street, erected about six years ago (a neat edifice, in the curacy of the Rev. William Bolland), and meeting houses for dissenters. There are schools for gratuitous instruction under the establishment and on the national system, a free grammar school, and Cheshunt college, observable by its somewhat remarkable spire; the college was founded by the Countess of Huntingdon, for the preparation of young men for the ministry. The number of inhabitants in the entire parish, in 1831, was 5,021.

WALTHAM CROSS is a hamlet and ward in the parish of Cheshunt, and, in fact, forms a street in continuation of Crossbrook-street, Turner's-hill and Cheshunt-street—all situated on the London and Cambridge road. The Cross, from which the addition to the original name was taken, was one of those erected by Edward I on the different stations where the bearers of the remains of Eleanor, his beloved queen, had a temporary resting place, during their journey from Hardeley, in Lincolnshire (where she died) to Westminster abbey, the place of her interment; this ancient memorial having suffered much from the effects of age and weather, it was a few years since repaired, and in a great measure restored to its former style and proportions, by voluntary contributions. A Roman urn, bearing the inscription, '*Via uno Romano*,' was, about 1804, discovered beneath the spot where the 'Roman Urn' inn now stands, in Crossbrook-street, and is exhibited to the passing traveller as a decorative antique on the front of the house. A station on the line of the Northern and Eastern railway is about three hundred yards east of the cross.

POST OFFICE, WALTHAM CROSS, Joseph Hunt, *Post Master*.—Letters arrive from LONDON (by the general and by the twopenny posts) and are delivered at seven in the morning and one and half-past three in the afternoon.—Letters are despatched to LONDON at five morning, at noon and three afternoon.—There is also a penny post to the adjacent villages every morning at six.

GENTRY AND CLERGY.
Adamson Charles, esq. Brook house, Cheshunt wash
Aldersey Hayden Stephens, esq. Bury green
Batho Joseph, esq. Crossbrook st
Bethune Mrs. Margt. Douglas, Walnut-tree house, Turner's hill
Bollard Rev. William, Bury green
Bore Mr. John Pearson (attorney) Crossbrook st
Bridgman Thomas, esq. Lordship
Buchanan Wm. esq. M.D. Chalk lodge
Busk Jacob Hans, esq. Theobalds
Butler the Hon. Charles Lennox, Pengelly house
Chauncy Mrs. Amelia, Theobalds
Clarke Edward, esq. Waltham Cross
Collyer George C. esq. Churchgate
Cross Mrs. Mary, Grove house
Dyson Mr. Richard, Waltham Cross
Ewster Mr. Samuel, Churchgate
Foster Mrs. Ann, Turner's hill
Foster Rev. J. K. Churchgate
George Miss Fanny, Waltham Cross

GENTRY, &c.—Continued.
Greene Miss Eliza, Woodgreen house
Gregory Miss Clarissa, Waltham Cross
Harman Ezekiel, esq. Theobalds
Harrison William, esq. Churchgate
Hatton Miss Elizabeth, Church lane
Idle Major, Theobalds lane
Jefferson Mrs. Mary, Water lane
Johnston Charles, esq. Claremont
Kemp George, esq. M.D. Turner's hill
Kennard —, esq. Theobalds
Kerr Chas. Hy. Bellenden, Swiss cottage
Lloyd E. J. esq. Hammond cottage
Lucena Mr. Stephen Lancaster (attorney) Turner's hill
Lyde Mr. William (attorney) Churchfield
M'Cullough Mrs. —, Crossbrook st
Mayo Rev. Charles, M.A. Coles grove
Mayo Miss R. Lime cottage
Meux Sir Henry, bart. Theobalds park
Munt Matthew, esq. Beaumont
Murdoch Mr. Broomer, Broomer cottage
Northover Mr. Wm. Emm, Turnford
Parkinson Mr. John (attorney) Cheshunt st
Pearce Stewart Peter, esq. Cheshunt st
Prescott Mrs. Sarah, Bury green
Preston Rev. Matthew Morris, M.A. Vicarage, Churchgate
Relph Cuthbert, esq. Turner's hill
Russell Thomas Artemidorus, esq. Cheshunt park
Sanders John Harry, esq. Water lane
Sanders Thos. esq. M.D. Turner's hill
Saudon Mr. John Kidgell, Turner's hill
Thorpe Major Saml. K.H. Goff Oak cottage
Ward James, esq. R.A. Round croft
Westley Miss Elizabeth, Turner's hill
Wilkinson Chs. esq. Applebury cottge
Wingfield William, esq. Theobalds
Wright Job, esq. Crossbrook st
Wright Mr. John, Paradise house

ACADEMIES & SCHOOLS.
Not otherwise described are Day Schools.
Chapman Mrs. and Miss (boarding) Cheshunt st
COLLEGE OF THE COUNTESS OF HUNTINGDON, Churchgate--Jacob K. Foster, president and classical tutor; John Harris, D. D. theological tutor; Rev. Joseph Sortain, B.A. mathematical tutor
Crook Chas. (bdg. & day) Turner's hill
Dewey Mrs. Lewis (bdg.) Cheshunt st
FREE SCHOOL, Churchgate—John Gilpin, master
INFANTS' SCHOOL, Churchgate—Miss Huntley, mistress
Martin Robert, Park lane
Moore Miss (boarding) Cheshunt st
Paul Jane & Margt. (bdg) Cheshunt st
SCHOOL OF INDUSTRY, Churchgate Matilda Porter, mistress
Scott Caroline Sibel, Turner's hill
Stubert Madame (bdg) Waltham Cross
Thornton Edw. (brdg) Crossbrook st
VICARAGE SCHOOL (girls), Churchgate—Maria Stephenson, mistress
Wildsmith Mary (bdng.) Turner's hill

AUCTIONEERS & APPRAISRS.
Crawter Henry and Sons (and surveyors) Turner's hill

BAKERS & FLOUR DEALERS.
Blain George, Waltham Cross
Brown William, Waltham Cross
Butler Henry, Cheshunt st
Cartwright William, Turner's hill
Chamney Edward, Crossbrook st
Chymist Samuel, Cheshunt st
Cooper William, Cheshunt st
Green Sylvia, Waltham Cross
Hewitt John, Waltham Cross

BLACKSMITHS & FARRIERS.
Champness James (and whitesmith) Cheshunt st
Coomes William, Waltham Cross
Cordell John, Waltham Cross
Jones Edward, Waltham Cross
Pack Susan, Flamstead end
Spurr Richard, Cheshunt st
Woollard Ths. (& locksmith) Turner's hill
Wright Michael, Goff Oak

BOOKSELLERS & STATIONRS.
Aspland William (& library) Waltham Cross
Bagster Josiah S. (& binder & printer) Turner's hill
Gritten Edward (& binder, printer, and library) Cheshunt st
Hunt Joseph (& stamp distributer) Waltham Cross

BOOT & SHOE MAKERS.
Allen Thomas, Waltham Cross
Chaplin John, Crossbrook st
Crick James, Crossbrook st
Ellis Robt. (& leather cuttr.) Cheshunt st
Morris George, Turner's hill
Pigram James, Crossbrook st
Richer George, Waltham Cross
Seccull John, Waltham Cross
Tuckett Charles, Cheshunt st
Willsher Joseph, Crossbrook st
Wood John, Churchgate

BRAZIERS AND TIN-PLATE WORKERS.
Champness James, jun. (& coppersmith) Cheshunt st
Champness James Mason (& whitesmith & wire worker) Cheshunt st
Frank Francis, Cheshunt st
James Joseph, Crossbrook st

BREWERS.
Heward Henry, Waltham Cross
Walker Wm. Marsh lane, Cheshunt

BRICKLAYERS.
Cheeck John, Waltham Cross
Coomes Charles, Turner's hill
Reece James, Cheshunt st
Wiggs Thomas, Waltham Cross
Wright William, Turner's hill

BUILDERS.
Camp John & Daniel, Waltham Cross
Harris Robert, Prospect place
Yorke William, Turner's hill

BUTCHERS.
Dorman John, Waltham Cross
Gocher John, Turner's hill
Gocher William, Crossbrook st
Feast William, Waltham Cross
Hammond Chas. S. Waltham Cross
Hulls Thomas, Cheshunt st
North Daniel, Waltham Cross
Pate William, Turner's hill
Taylor Joseph, Cheshunt st
Woollard John, Waltham Cross

CABINET MAKERS AND UPHOLSTERERS.
Orange Mary and Rebecca, Turner's hill
Smith Nathaniel Alexander (fancy) Crossbrook st

CARPENTERS.
Batt John (and turner) Cheshunt st
Bowles William, Crossbrook st
Bradstock John, Waltham Cross
Camp John and Daniel (and timber merchants & undertakers) Waltham Cross
Harris Robt. (& undertaker) Prospect place
Harris William, Cheshunt st
Moxam Charles, Waltham Cross
Yorke William, Turner's hill

CHINA, GLASS, &c. DEALERS.
Dewey Lewis, Cheshunt st
Jay Frederick, Waltham Cross
Owen John, Cheshunt st
Sayer William, Waltham Cross
Seymour Thomas, Turner's hill
Windsor John W. Cheshunt st

CHYMISTS & DRUGGISTS.
Johnson William H. Cheshunt st
Redin Thomas H. Turner's hill

COACH MAKERS.
Cleaver William, Waltham Cross
Mold James, Waltham Cross
Robinson Edward, Turner's hill

COAL DEALERS.
Barber John James, Crossbrook st
Griffiths Thomas, Coal wharf
Owen John, Cheshunt st

CONFECTIONERS.
Francis Joseph, Turner's hill
Pointer Kitty, Cheshunt st

CORN DEALERS & MEALMEN.
Cooper William, Cheshunt st
Hollis Frederick, Waltham Cross

FIRE, &c. OFFICE AGENTS.
PHŒNIX, Thomas Seymour, Turner's hill; and Lewis Dewey, jun. Cheshunt st
ROYAL EXCHANGE, Joseph Hunt, Waltham Cross
SUN, Henry Crawter and Sons, Turner's hill

GROCERS & TEA DEALERS.
(See also Shopkeepers, &c.)
Blades Francis W. Waltham Cross
Dewey Lewis, Cheshunt st
Harding John S. Waltham Cross
Jay Frederick, Waltham Cross
Owen John (& oilman) Cheshunt st
Sayer William, Waltham Cross
Seymour Thomas, Turner's hill
Windsor John W. Cheshunt st

HAIR DRESSERS.
Champness Charles, Turner's hill
Davis William, Waltham Cross
Threader George, Cheshunt st

INNS.
Coach and Horses, Sarah Tasker, Crossbrook st
Falcon, Henry Heward (post master to Her Majesty) Waltham Cross
Four Swans, Elizabeth Norton, Waltham Cross
Green Dragon, Henry Thompson, Churchgate
Haunch of Venison, Benjamin Whittenbury, Cheshunt st
New Inn, George Wildbore, Waltham Cross
Roman Urn, John James Barber, Crossbrook st
White Hart, Daniel North, Waltham Cross

IRONMONGERS.
Champness James, jun. Cheshunt st
Champness James Mason (and bellhanger) Cheshunt st
Frank Francis, Cheshunt st
Woollard Thomas, Turner's hill

LINEN & WOOLLEN DRAPRS.
Death Oliver, Cheshunt st
Halfhide Samuel M. Cheshunt st
Laxton John & Co. Cheshunt st
Marsdell Rebecca, Waltham Cross
West Ezra, Waltham Cross
Wyllie Robert, Crossbrook st

MILLINERS AND DRESS MAKERS.
Bowles Charlotte, Crossbrook st
Crick Eliz. (& toy dealr) Crossbrook st
Dockrill Kesia & Sister, Turner's hill
Drury Eliz. & Charlotte, Church field
Hewitt the Misses, Waltham Cross
Parker Ann, Crossbrook st
Tasker Sarah, Crossbrook st
Tuckett Jane, Cheshunt st
West Ellen, Waltham Cross

NURSERYMEN, SEEDSMEN AND FLORISTS.
Paul Adam & Son, Cheshunt st

PLUMBERS, PAINTERS, GLAZIERS & PAPER-HANGERS.
Bames Thomas, Crossbrook st
Cheffins Lewis, Crossbrook st
Clifton Joseph, Turner's hill
Furlong Robert, Cheshunt st
Goffe John, Waltham Cross

SADDLERS AND HARNESS MAKERS.

Hammond Robert, Waltham Cross
Ives William, Cheshunt st
Mold Samuel, Cheshunt st
Wiggins Walter, Waltham Cross

SHOPKEEPERS & DEALRS IN GROCERIES & SUNDRIES.

Adams James, Turner's hill
Bayley William, Church gate
Bradstock John, Waltham Cross
Cousins William, Cheshunt st
Green Robert, Crossbrook st
Jones Jane, Waltham Cross
Linnington John, Turner's hill
Nelmes William, Cheshunt st
Pearce John, Waltham Cross
Pearce William, Crossbrook st
Stevens Samuel, Cheshunt st
Webb William, Cheshunt st

SURGEONS.

Harrold Edward, Cheshunt st
Sharpe John, Waltham Cross
Watkins Joshua, Crossbrook st

SURVEYORS.

Crawter Henry & Sons (& land, & estate agents) Turner's hill
HarrisRobt.Prospect place,Cheshunt
York William, Turner's hill

TAILORS AND DRAPERS.

Aspland William, Waltham Cross
Bull John, Cheshunt st
Colley John, Turner's hill
Gocher Samuel, Crossbrook st
Muggeridge George (and clothes dealer) Waltham Cross
Shields Joseph, Waltham Cross
Talbot Francis, Cheshunt st
Waidson William, Crossbrook st

TAVERNS & PUBLIC HOUSES.

BirdCage,CharlotteWiggs,WalthamCross
George, Hannah Sams, Turner's hill
Goff Oak, Wm. Gayler,Cheshunt common
Red Lion, John Medcalf, Cheshunt st
Rose & Crown, John Clifton, Turner's hill
Ship, Robert Parrott, Cheshunt st
White Horse, James Green, Flamstead end
Woodman, William Wackett, Hammond st
Woolpack, John Darton, Cheshunt st

VINEGAR AND BLACKING MERCHANT.

Fisher George Thomas Cheshunt, and Grosvenor basin, Wilton road, *Chelsea*

WATCH & CLOCK MAKERS.

Boultwood Thomas (and gunsmith) Turner's hill
Woollard Thomas, Cheshunt st

WHEELWRIGHTS.

Ives James, Waltham Cross
Robinson Edward, Turner's hill

Miscellaneous.

Bristow Edw. coach proprietr.Cheshunt st
Bugg William, veterinary surgeon, Turner's hill
Butcher William,cooper, Waltham Cross
Chaplin Henry, woollen rug maker, Turner's hill
Chaplin William, lath render, Crossbrook st
Coote Chas. music professor, Turner's hill
Dennant Jos. stone mason, Waltham Cross
Dewey William, dairyman, Cheshunt st
Drury James Francis,musical bell founder, Church fields
Foster Joseph, eating house, Waltham Cross
Hutchings William, stationer and tobacconist, Crossbrook st
Jordan William, fruiterer, Cheshunt st
M'Ewan Robt. tea dealer, Crossbrook st
Mole Thomas, tallow chandler & melter, Cheshunt st
Pigrum James, tanner and currier, Crossbrook st
POLICE STATION, Turner's hill—John Davies, chief officer
Sanders Richd. F. accountant, Cheshunt st

COACHES.

To LONDON, the *Royal Mail* (from Edinburgh) calls at the Haunch of Venison, Cheshunt-street, every morning at five —Bristow's *Coach*, every morning at eight and afternoon at three—Wright's *Omnibus*, from the White Hart, Waltham Cross, every morning at eight and afternoon at five—and Guiver's *Omnibus* from the Red Lion, Cheshunt, every morning at eight and afternoon at three.

*** There are many other *Coaches* from the north that pass through Cheshunt and Waltham Cross during the day.

To BOSTON, LINCOLN, EDINBURGH, &c., the *Royal Mail* passes through, every night, at a quarter past 9.

To CAMBRIDGE, *Coaches* several times a day.

To HODDESDON and WARE, *Coaches* every hour.

CARRIERS.

To LONDON, Charles Blain, from Crossbrook-street, and Robert Haynes, from Cheshunt-street, every Monday, Wednesday and Friday morning—and — Linnington, from Turner's hill, and — Richley from Cheshunt-street, ever Tuesday, Thursday, and Sat. morning.

CHIPPING BARNET, EAST BARNET, FRYERN BARNET,

WEST BARNET, WHETSTONE, COLNEY HATCH, HADLEY AND TOTTERIDGE;

Together with that part of SOUTH MIMMS *in the Town of Barnet.*

CHIPPING BARNET is a town and parish, partly in the hundred of Edmonton, Middlesex, but chiefly in Cashio hundred, and liberty of St. Albans, Hertfordshire, being intersected by the boundary of the two counties; it is 11 miles N. W. from London, 9 S. from Hatfield, and 10 S.E. from St. Albans—seated on a pleasant eminence, and popularly denominated *High* Barnet from its situation. The appellation *Chipping* or *Cheping*, signifying, in the Saxon, 'market,' had its origin from Henry II having granted to the monks of St. Albans a charter for one being held here; but it has fallen into disuse, or at least insignificance. The town formerly had an extensive common right, but the common has for some years been completely enclosed; the mineral spring, for the protection of which Mr. Owen, an alderman of London, left £1. per annum, is, however, still preserved by act of parliament: in times past it was of much celebrity, and, although now but little resorted to for medicinal purposes, is still considered equal to the waters of Tonbridge and Harrogate; its situation is only about three quarters of a mile from the town, and the walk or drive to it is remarkably pleasant. Chipping Barnet is governed by a headborough and constables: it is within the jurisdiction of a court held at St. Albans, for the recovery of debts under forty shillings; and a court leet of the lord of the manor is held at Easter. There are several good inns here, well supported by the number of travellers and coaches passing through; the 'Red Lion' is one of the best, and is the principal posting-house. Much fine hay is produced in this neighbourhood, and sent to the London market.

The church, dedicated to St. John the Baptist, stands in the centre of the town; it is a very ancient edifice, of the style of architecture that prevailed in the fifteenth century: the living is a perpetual curacy, united to the rectory of East Barnet. A new chapel of ease, having a school and dwellings attached, has recently been erected in the part now called WEST BARNET, (formerly Barnet common) at an expense of £5,000., defrayed solely by E. Durant, Esq. of High Canons, Shenley. A free school was founded here by Queen Elizabeth, and endowed by alderman Owen (above mentioned), and other benefactors, for the instruction of seven children gratis, and others of the parish for five shillings per quarter; the revenue for its support is paid by the fishmongers' company; it is conducted by twenty-four governors, who have the appointment of the master and usher. There are twelve alms-houses, in which the inmates are comfortably maintained, and some other contingencies for the indigent. There are two excellent libraries—one conducted by Mr. Cowing, the other by Mr. Thompson, booksellers, in High-street. A mechanics' institute has lately been established, under the patronage of George Byng, Esq. M.P., who is also president of an agricultural association recently formed here. A horticultural society, a mutual benefit society and a tradesman's club, are likewise well supported. A public hall was a short time since erected in Union-street, at a cost of £1,000., for the purpose of moral and scientific meetings. Fairs are held here on the 8th, 9th and 10th of April, for cattle; on the 4th, 5th and 6th September, for cattle and pleasure; and an additional fair has lately been established, in November, for the sale of stock and agricultural produce. Pony races are annually held on the last day of the September fair. [The population of this and the following places is given after TOTTERIDGE.]

EAST BARNET is a pleasant village and parish in the hundred of Cashio, Herts—situate in a valley, ten miles from London, on the right of the north-western road. The country around is fertile, and it is the residence of many respectable families. The church, dedicated to the Virgin Mary, is a small and very ancient structure; the benefice is a rectory, in the patronage of the crown, and incumbency of the Rev. Thomas Henry Elwin.

FRYERN BARNET parish and village, situated to the south of East Barnet, in the Finsbury division of the hundred of Ossulton, Middlesex, is of no importance with reference to either business or extent; the village, however, contains some handsome houses, and the environs abound with agreeable scenery. The church, dedicated to Saint James, has been partly rebuilt; the living is a perpetual curacy, in the gift of the dean and chapter of St. Paul's, London. A national school, and alms-houses for twelve aged persons, are in the village. In this parish is the hamlet of COLNEY HATCH, distinguished particularly for the number of respectable and opulent inhabitants, and tasteful residences.

WHETSTONE is a hamlet, partly in the parish of Fryern

Barnet, and partly in that of Finchley, distant one mile from the former and two from the latter. A number of coaches proceeding to London, and from the metropolis to the north, pass through this place.

The much admired village and parish of HADLEY, or MONKEN HADLEY, is in the hundred of Edmonton and county of Middlesex: in the parish, which is adjoining to that of Chipping Barnet, are the mansions of many families of the first respectability. At the north end of the village, near the 12-mile stone, stands an obelisk, called the 'Hadley High Stone,' erected in commemoration of a sanguinary battle fought on this spot, on the 14th of April, 1471, between Edward IV and Guy Earl of Warwick (to whom the title of the 'king-maker' was generally applied), in which the earl fell, with many of the nobility, and with a slaughter of his followers that was then considered almost unprecedented. The parish church, dedicated to St. Mary, is an old structure, chiefly of flint, and its site is commonly said to be more elevated than that of any other church in England; it has an embattled tower, almost wholly covered with ivy, upon which is a beacon, with the identical iron pot which contained the signal fire in times of rebellion. A little to the north of Hadley is Wrotham Park, the beautiful seat of George Byng, Esq., M. P. for Middlesex.

TOTTERIDGE is a delightful village and parish in the hundred of Cashio, situated about two miles to the south-west of Chipping Barnet. The church, dedicated to St. Andrew, stands near the centre of the village.

The POPULATION of the several parishes, according to the returns made to parliament in 1831, was as follows:—CHIPPING BARNET, 2,369 inhabitants; EAST BARNET, 547; FRYERN BARNET, 615; HADLEY, 979; and TOTTERIDGE, 595. The population of WHETSTONE and COLNEY HATCH is included in the returns for FRYERN BARNET.

POST OFFICE, High street, CHIPPING BARNET, J. P. Ward, *Post Master.*—Letters from LONDON and the North are delivered in Barnet and the villages round every morning at eight.—Letters for LONDON are despatched every morning at a quarter before nine, afternoon at a quarter before four and night at ten.—Letters for the North are despatched every evening (Sunday excepted) at half-past seven, on Sunday at seven.

C. B. *at the end of an address signifies* CHIPPING BARNET, E. B. EAST BARNET, H. HADLEY, *and* S. M. SOUTH MIMMS.

NOBILITY, GENTRY, AND CLERGY.

Aitken James, esq. Hadley
Aitken Mrs. —, Hadley
Anderson Duncan, esq. Cock fosters
Anderson Mrs. —, Cock fosters
Arrowsmith Mrs. L. Totteridge park
Barnes Lady —, Totteridge
Baxendale Joseph, esq. Whetstone
Beavan Edward, esq. Hadley
Betham Mr. Frederick, Arkley hall
Bevan David, esq. Belmont, E. B.
Bevan Robt. Cooper Lee, esq. Trent park, Enfield
Bittlestone Mr. John, Hadley green
Blane Mrs. Selina, Clock house, E.B.
Bosanquet August. Hy. esq. Osage, E.B.
Bridgett Joseph, esq. Colney Hatch
Brooks James, esq. Colney Hatch
Brown Mr. Wm. Westend cottage
Browning Thos. esq. Hadley commn
Burrows Mrs. Fras. Hadley common
Byng Geo. esq. M. P. Wrotham park
Carwick Thos. esq. Highwood hill
Cass Frederick, esq. (magistrate) Little Grove, East Barnet
Catling James, esq. East Barnet
Child Mrs. Frances, Hadley green
Clarke Sir Simon Haughton, bart. Oak hill, E.B. [Cock fosters
Cotton Hon. Harriet, Ludgrove cottg.
Cottrell Mrs. —, Hadley lodge
Crawshay Geo. esq. Colney Hatch
Creyke Mrs. —, Grove, Hadley
Crossley John, esq. Wood st, C. B.
Cuthbert Geo. esq. Colney Hatch
Dearman Mrs. —, Barnet common
Debenham Mr. Robt. Barnet commn
Dell Mr. William, High st, C. B.
Dickins James, esq. Hadley green
Dimsdale Thomas, esq. Hadley
Dowton Mr. Jeremiah, High st, C.B.
Dury Col. Alex. (magistrate) Hadley
Elwin Rev. Thos. Henry, East Barnet
Foster Robert, esq. Hadley
Fox Henry, esq. Gannick Corner
Franklyn James, esq. Totteridge
Franklyn Richard, esq. Totteridge
Franklyn Wm. Norris, esq. High st
Franks Chas. esq. Dacre lodge, E. B.
Garrow Mrs. Charlotte, The Priory, Totteridge
Goodman Mr. William, Moxon st
Green Joseph Henry, esq. F. R. S. the Mount, Hadley [Totteridge
Hall Mrs. Mary Strettell, Copped hall,
Harman Mrs. Ann, Hadley green
Harris Edwd. esq. The Folly, Hadley
Hickes Mrs. Mary Anne, Totteridge
Hopegood Andrew, esq. Hadley comn
Jackson Wm. esq. Clock house, E. B.
Johnson Miss Margaret, Hadley grn
Knott Geo. esq. Bohun lodge, E. B.
Lambert William, esq. Whetstone
Lawrence Joseph, esq. Hadley green
Lendon Rev. Abel, Totteridge
Lendon Rev. William, Totteridge
Macdowall Mrs. —, Barnet common
M'Farlane Chas. esq. Colney Hatch
Macintosh Jas. esq. Totteridge lodge
M'Kenzie Miss Eliza, Hadley [ridge
Maitland Miss Charlotte Mary, Totte-
Marr Mrs. Maria Ann, Wood st, C.B.
Marsham Mrs. Penelope Judith, Totteridge
Montagu Mrs. —, Hadley
Mountain Mrs. Sarah Ann, Whetstone
Newman Mrs. —, Whetstone
Newman Thos. esq. Hadley [C.B.
Nicholl Richd. esq. Green hill grove,
Osborne O. Delano, esq. Whetstone
Page Samuel, esq. Manor house, Hadley green [Hadley
Paris Thomas, esq. Greenwood plain,
Payne Benjamin, esq. Hadley
Pearson Charles, esq. East Barnet
Pfeil Adolph Leopold, esq. Willenhall house, East Barnet
Puget Mrs. Catherine, Totteridge
Quilter Miss Emma C. Hadley commn
Reid Andrew, esq. Lionsdown, E. B.
Reid Rev. Henry, Lionsdown, E. B.
Reid Robert, esq. Lionsdown, E. B.
Reid Wm. esq. Lionsdown, East B.
Riccard —, esq. Totteridge [E.B.
Richardson Chs. Js. esq. Everley lodge,
Rix Francis, esq. Hadley green
Robarts Nathaniel, esq. Wood st, C.B.
Rumball Sampson A. esq. Chipping B.
Schneider John, esq. Beaver hall
Scrimgeour Robert Sheddon, esq. Totteridge [ping Barnet
Sears Thomas, esq. Wood st, Chip-
Shepherd Captain T. Arkley lodge
Smith Mr. Benj. Lawn house, C. B.
Smith George, esq. Colney Hatch
Stewart Rev. Alex. Wood st, C. B.
Strong Capt. Saml. Woodlands, H.
Sykes Edward, esq. Totteridge
Thackeray Rev. John Richd. (rector) Hadley rectory
Thompson Henry, esq. Totteridge
Thorogood Jno. Chas. esq. Totteridge
Tilly Mrs. Margaret, Lawn terrace
Trotter Hon. Mrs. —, Dyrham park
Trotter Jno. esq. (magist.) Dyrham park
Ventriss Rev. Henry, Whetstone
Walker Edmund, esq. Fryern Barnet
Weale Miss Anne, Manning cottge. H.
White Charles, esq. Totteridge
Wilson Miss —, Hadley [Barnet
Wilson Thos. Mansell, esq. Chipping
Winbolt Rev. Thos. Hy. Hadley green
Wood Rev. Jas. Alx. B.A. Wood st, C.B.
Wood John, esq. Totteridge
Wood Jno. Brook, esq. Colney Hatch
Wynne Mrs. Ann, Wood st, C. B.

ACADEMIES & SCHOOLS.

Not otherwise described are Day Schools

CHARITY SCHOOL (girls') Colney Hatch—Jane Butt, mistress
CHARITY SCHOOL (boys' and girls') Whetstone—Rev. Henry Ventriss, master
Esling Simon, Whetstone
FREE GRAMMAR SCHOOL, Wood st, Chipping Barnet—Rev. Jas. Alexander Wood, master
Heady Mary, East Barnet
Hilton John, St. Albans New road
Hudson Samuel (boarding) Hadley
INFANTS' SCHOOL, Moxon st (E. Durant, esq.'s)—Wm. Schwartz, master; Eliz. Schwartz, mistress
Lean Geo. (boarding) Whetstone
Medlicott Cath. (boarding) High st
NATIONAL AND PAROCHIAL SCHOOL, Wood st, C. B.—Edward Vidler, master; Ann Treewick, mistress
NATIONAL SCHOOL, East Barnet—Mrs. Macfarlane, mistress
NATIONAL SCHOOL, Hadley—Daniel Mayo, master [Whetstone
Smith John Stantial, Terry's house,
Stevens Mrs. (brdng) Barnet commn
Stewart Rev. Alx. (brdg.) Wood st, C.B.
Sutleffe Misses (brdg.) Wood st, C. B.
UNION WORKHOUSE SCHOOL—Thos. Buckle, master; Fras. Woodcock, mistress [Totteridge
Wood and Thorogood (gent.'s brdg.)

ATTORNEYS.

Franklyn Wm. Norris (and clerk to the magistrates and the Barnet Union, and superintendent registrar) High st
George Thomas, Wood st, Chipping Barnet

AUCTIONEERS & APPRAISRS.

Attfield John, Whetstone
Attfield Wm. Poole, Hadley green
Duckworth and Taplin (and upholsterers) High st, Chipping Barnet
Leather Joseph (and house and land agent) High st, Hadley
Pippet J. G. Hadley green

BAKERS, CORN CHANDLERS AND MEALMEN.
(See also Corn Dealers.)
Finney Thos.(& biscuit) High st, H.
Gregory Geo. High st, South Mimms
Hooker William, High st
Jennings George, High st, Hadley
Matthews Benjamin, Whetstone
Porter Richard Henry, High st
Rolph William, High st
Royer George, High st, Hadley
Sheffield Archibald, Wood st
Sheffield Samuel, Hadley
Smith George, East Barnet
Smith James, Hadley
Trendall Robert, Whetstone
Wand Edward, Whetstone
Willmer William, Wood st

BANKER.
Buckland James (agent to the St. Albans, and to the London and Westminster banks) High st

BLACKSMITHS & FARRIERS.
Auton John, High st, South Mimms
Bass William, Fryern Barnet
Colley William, Totteridge
Cripps Michael, High st, Chipping B.
Cripps William, High st, Chipping B.
Dover George, Colney Hatch lane
Ford John, Whetstone
Peach Jas. High st, South Mimms
Peet James, Cock fosters
Peet William, Hadley
Peters William, Whetstone
Pratchett Edward, East Barnet

BOOKSELLERS, STATIONERS AND BOOKBINDERS
Baldock William, High st, C. B.
Cowing John James, High st, C. B.
Thompson Ann (stationer and toy dealer) High st, Chipping Barnet
Ward John Prior (and engraver and news agent) High st, Chipping B.
Wells Jos. (and news agent) High st, South Mimms
Wells Thomas (stationer and news agent) High st, Chipping Barnet

BOOT AND SHOE MAKERS.
Audsley John, Whetstone
Cannon Thos. J. St. Albans, New rd
Clemence Edward, High st
Crane John, East Barnet
Cox Charles, High st, Chipping B.
Cox James, Whetstone
Cox Jonathan, High st, S. M.
Croxton Charles, High st, Hadley
Day William, High st, Chipping B.
Evans William, Hadley green
Grant Francis, High st, S. M.
Hawkes Charles, High st, Hadley
Heron John B. Hadley
Humphrey John, High st, C. B.
Marshall William, High st, Hadley
Riley James, Totteridge
Scarfe James, High st, Hadley
Williams Henry, East Barnet

BREWERS.
Buckthorp John, Wood st
Dunger Henry, Colney Hatch
Secret Thomas, High st, Hadley
Thorpe William and Maria (& maltsters) Hadley green

BRICKLAYERS.
Anstee Richard, Wood st
Cooper James, East Barnet
Cox James, South Mimms
Gray John, Wood st
Jennings John, High st, Hadley
Peak Thomas, Wood st, Chipping B.
Peak Thomas, jun. Moxon st, C. B.
Purser John, Whetstone
Stovel John, Whetstone
Williams John, High st, Hadley
Williams Richard, Hadley green

BUILDERS.
Hill and Son (and stone masons) High st, Chipping Barnet
Markwell Alexander, High st, C. B.
Miller George Wm. High st, Hadley
Pritchard Charles, High st
Williams Richard, Hadley green

BUTCHERS.
Anderson James (pork) High st
Byford Samuel, High st, Hadley
Clayton William, High st
Crawley James (pork, and poulterer) Hadley green
Fordham John, Whetstone
Harris William, High st, Hadley
Hibbert Ralph, Hadley
Hudson George, High st
Hunt John, Whetstone
Jarvis William (pork) High st, C. B.
Kent Charles, High st, Chipping B.
Nisbet John, High st, H. and E. B.
Propstring John (pork) High st, H.
Tingey John, High st
White William, Whetstone

CARPENTERS AND UNDERTAKERS.
Bangs John, High st, H. and S. M.
Bentley John, Whetstone
Ginger William, St. Albans New rd
Goss Henry, East Barnet
Harrison Benjamin, Hadley green
Horn Henry, Whetstone
King Caleb, Whetstone
Lawrence Joseph, Hadley green
Lorkin Eli and Son, Colney Hatch
Markwell Alexander, High st, C. B.
Miller George William, High st, H.
Pritchard Charles, High st, C. B.
Sellwood Robert, East Barnet
Tubby Robert, Whetstone
Wager John, High st

CHYMISTS AND DRUGGISTS.
Lawrence Joseph P. High st, C. B.
Morse John, High st, Chipping B.
Smith James, High st, Chipping B.
Tyer George, Whetstone

CLOTHES DEALERS.
Shurts George, High st, Hadley
Shuttleworth A. & M.A. High st, C.B.
Thimbleby John, High st, Chipping B.

COACH MASTERS.
Godden Benjamin, High st, Hadley
Page Henry William, High st, Hadley
Salmon John (and post master) Albion, High st, South Mimms

COAL MERCHANTS AND DEALERS.
Bayley Thomas, High st, Hadley
Field Thos. (& hay, &c.) High st, S.M.
King James, High st, Chipping B.
Pruden James, High st, Chipping B.

COOPERS.
Brodie Richard, High st
Sherlock Alexander, High st, South Mimms
Thomas William, Whetstone

CORN DEALERS & MEALMEN.
Green William, Wood st, C. B.
Jones David, High st, Chipping B.
King James, High st, Chipping B.
Mallett John (and miller) Hadley green windmill
Pooley George & Mary Ann, High st, Hadley
Robson William, High st, Hadley
Wand Edward, Whetstone

FIRE, &c. OFFICE AGENTS.
ALLIANCE, Robt. Dixon, High st, C.B.
BRITISH, Benjamin Smith, High st, C. B.; and Wm. Rose, Whetstone
COUNTY, Jno. Hopewell, High st, C.B.
CROWN, PELICAN & PHŒNIX, Duckworth & Taplin, High st, C. B.
GENERAL BENEFIT SOCIETY, A. & I. Walker, High st, Hadley
ROYAL EXCHANGE, John Underwood, High st, S. M.
SUN, John James Cowing, High st, C. B.

FURNITURE BROKERS.
Duckworth & Taplin, High st, C. B.
Lardner Thomas, High st, C. B.

GROCERS, TEA DEALERS AND CHEESEMONGERS.
(See also Shopkeepers, &c.)
Bayley Thomas, High st, Hadley
Constable Thomas, Whetstone
Ellis James, Whetstone
Gray James, Whetstone
Harrington Benjamin, Hadley green
Hopewell John, High st, Chipping B.
Pruden James (& glass, &c. dealer) High st, Chipping Barnet
Robson William, High st, Hadley
Smith Benjamin & Son (and tallow chandlers) High st, Chipping B.
Stuchbery Hanson, Whetstone

HAIR DRESSERS.
Atwell Thomas, High st, C. B.
Cooke John (& cutler) High st, H.
Thompson Ann (& perfumer) High st, Chipping Barnet

HORSE DEALERS.
Brett James Abel, High st, C. B.
East Joshua (& mules) East Barnet

INNS.
Green Man, Jos. Richards, Whetstone
Green Man Hotel (& posting house) James Buckell, High st, South M.
Red Lion Hotel (& posting house) Charles Bryant, High st
Salisbury Arms (New) James Pepper, High st, Hadley
Salisbury Arms (Old) James Abel Brett, High st, Chipping Barnet
White Hart, Wm. Haines, High st, C.B.
Woolpack, Wm. Hill, High st, C. B.

IRONMONGERS & TIN-PLATE WORKERS.
Buckland James, High st, C. B.
Samuels Frances, Church passge, C.B.
Walker Abraham and Isaac (& zinc workers, braziers, manufacturers of Dr. Arnott's stoves, and dealers in oils & colours) High st, Hadley

LIBRARIES AND READING ROOMS.
Cowing John James, High st, C. B.
Thompson Ann, High st, Chipping B.

LINEN AND WOOLLEN DRAPERS.
Courtnall James, High st, Hadley
Parker Robert, Whetstone
Robinson Messdames, High st, C. B.
Shurts George, High st, Hadley
Smith Charles, High st, & Waterloo house, Chipping Barnet

MARINE STORE DEALERS.
Bartlett Thomas, High st, Hadley
Bennett Thomas, Wood st, C. B.
Cheek George, Wood st, C. B.
Dearman John, High st, South M.

MILLINERS & DRESS MAKRS
Batt Sarah, Hadley green
Davison Mirah, High st, Hadley
Heyward Harriet, High st, Hadley
Marshall Mary, Union st, South M.
Robinson Messdames, High st, C. B.
Smith Emma, Barnet common

NURSERY & SEEDSMEN
Cornwell George (and gardener) High st, Chipping Barnet
Cornwell William, High st, Hadley
Kemp William, High st, Hadley

PASTRY COOKS.
Lardner Thomas, High st, C. B.
Warby George, High st, South M.

PLUMBERS, PAINTERS AND GLAZIERS.
Allen Charles, Moxon st
Barnes John B. Whetstone
Cooper James, High st, Chipping B.
Ellerd Joseph, High st, Chipping B.
Farnell Charles, Whetstone

PLUMBERS, &c.—Continued.

Haswell Robert, Whetstone
Jameson William, High st, C. B.
Lucas Robert, High st, Hadley

PRINTERS—LETTER-PRESS.

Baldock William (and copper-plate printer) High st, Chipping Barnet
Cowing John James (& engraver, & paper-hanger) High st, Chipping B.

SADDLERS.

Butt James, Whetstone
Grout Charles, High st
Sharp John, High st, Hadley

SHOPKEEPERS & DEALRS IN GROCERIES & SUNDRIES.

Axford Edward, Whetstone
Barbor Edward, Barnet common
Bigg Charles, High st, South Mimms
Clark Joseph, Whetstone
Cox William, High st
Field Thomas, High st, South Mimms
Heady Esaias, Whetstone
King Samuel (& fish & fruit dealer) New road
Loader Elizabeth, Barnet common
Negus William, High st, Hadley
Page Francis, Whetstone
Randle Thomas, High st, Hadley
Royer George, High st, Hadley
Salmon William, High st
Sellwood Robert, East Barnet
Sudlow Elizabeth, Colney Hatch
Talbot Thomas, East Barnet
Taylor George, Wood st
Townsend Benjamin, New road
Wade Henry, High st
White James, Whetstone
Wilson Samuel, Totteridge

STRAW HAT MAKERS.

Anstee Sarah, High st, Hadley
Bedford Eliz. (wholesale) East Barnt
Beresford Caroline, High st, S. M.
Finney Elizabeth, High st, Hadley
Wade Ann, High st, Chipping Barnet

SURGEONS.

Baines Edward May, High st, C. B.
Hammond William, Whetstone
Humphrys John, Wood st, C. B.
Morison Walter, Wood st, C. B.
Morris Griffith, High st, Chipping B.

SURVEYORS.

Attfield John, Whetstone
Attfield William Poole (& land, and estate agent) Hadley green
Duckworth & Taplin (& land agents) High st
Miller George William (land, timber and architectural) High st, S. M.
Pippett J. G. Hadley green

TAILORS.

Bedford George, Whetstone
Bedford Jesse, East Barnet
Burgess Joseph, Whetstone
Foster Robert, High st, South Mimms
Haynes Charles, East Barnet
M'Intosh John, Union st, South M.
Priestley William, High st, South M.
Sands James, High st, South Mimms
South John, High st, Hadley
Summerfield James, High st, S. M.
Underwood John, High st, S. M.
Whiteman James, High st
Wilson Samuel, Totteridge

TAVERNS & PUBLIC HOUSES.

Angel, Thomas Dean, Kits end
Bell, John Heath, Barnet gate
Black Horse, Wm. Miller, Barnet common
Blue Anchor, Jane Taylor, Whetstone
Boar's Head, David Jones, Wood st, C. B.
Bricklayer's Arms, William Woodward, Whetstone
Bull, William Paul, High st, C. B.
Bull, Thomas Moulton, Whetstone
Bull & Butcher, Wm. Matthews, Whetstone
Bull's Head, James Cox, Kits end
Bull's Head, Chas. Hodge, Wood st, C. B.
Cat, Samuel Chandler, East Barnet
Cock, John Bangs, High st, C. B.
Cock, Charles Turner, Cock fosters
Crown, Walter Caswell, Wood st, C. B.
Duke of Wellington, Henry Read, High st, South Mimms [corner
Duke of York, John Ashkettle, Gannick
Edinburgh Castle, William Coe, High st
Green Dragon, John Stephen Racine, High st, South Mimms
Griffin, John Ely, Whetstone
Hart's Horn, Benjamin Hurring, High st, South Mimms [South Mimms
King of Prussia, John Allport, High st,
King's Head, Jas. Clark, High st, C. B.
Old Mitre, William Oliver, High st, C. B.
Orange Tree, James Hull, Totteridge
Orange Tree, Nathan Danes, Colney Hatch
Rising Sun, Joseph, Chambers, High st, South Mimms [Whetstone
Swan with two Necks, Catherine Baker,
Three Horse Shoes, Joseph Kipping, Totteridge [High stone
Two Brewers, James Jackson, Hadley
White Lion, Geo. Fraiser, New road, S. M.
Windmill, Rlph. Hibbert, Old St. Alban's rd

TOBACCONIST.

Ward John P. (and dealer in British wines) High st, Chipping Barnet

WATCH & CLOCK MAKERS.

Catchpool William (and working jeweller) St. Albans New road
Pitt William, Whetstone [Hadley
Wells Jos. (and news agent) High st,
Wells Thomas, High st, Chipping B.
Weslake William, High st, C. B.

WHEELWRIGHTS.

Child William, Moxon st, C. B.
Cooper William, Whetstone
Henning Richd. (and coach) High st
King James, St. Albans New road

WHITESMITHS.

Sharp Geo. High st, South Mimms
White John, High st, Chipping B.

WINE & SPIRIT MERCHANTS

Bower George, High st, Chipping B.
Kent Henry and Co. High st, C. B.
Smith Jas. (British) High st, C. B.
Ward J. P. (British) High st, C. B.

Miscellaneous.

Acason William, registrar of births and deaths, Barnet common
Anstee Charlotte, stay maker, High st, H.
Beattie Edward, plasterer & paper hanger, Lawn terrace, Chipping Barnet
Brunt William, currier, High st, C. B.
Cox William, horse, &c. owner for hire, High st, Chipping Barnet
Dixon Robert, collector of taxes, &c. High st, Chipping Barnet
Eyers Wm. rope maker, Barnet common
Field Mary, earthenware manufacturer, Barnet common
GAS WORKS, Mary Payne's place—Joseph Leather, superintendent
Gransby John Alexander, brick maker, Barnet common [ley
Heron John B. parish clerk, Monken Had-
Logsdon John & Sons, coach builders & harness manufacturers, High st, Hadley
Mann Peter, supervisor of excise, West end lane [Hadley
Provart Oliver, veterinary surgeon, High st,
Spragg Henry, glass and china dealer, High street, Hadley
Taplin Edward, auditor, and registrar of marriages, High st, Chipping Barnet
Teasdell Samuel, eating & coffee house, High st, Chipping Barnet [C. B.
Thimbleby John, pawnbroker, High st,
UNION WORKHOUSE, Barnet common—Benjamin Woodcock, governor; Elizabeth Woodcock, matron

COACHES.

*** *Nearly the whole of the following Coaches call at the* Salisbury Arms Inn, High st, CHIPPING BARNET. *With but few exceptions, they run six days a week. As the Railways are opened, the number of Coaches will not only be diminished on this road, but the time of those remaining will, in all probability, be altered.*

To LONDON, the *Royal Mail* (from Glasgow, Halifax, Leeds, &c.) every morning at five—and the *Second Mail* (from Leeds), every afternoon at half-past five—the *Star* (from Birmingham) the *Regent* (from Shields), and the *Star*, and the *Swallow* (from Liverpool), every morning at seven—the *Express*, & the *Rockingham* (from Leeds), at half-past seven—the *Favourite* (from Luton), at nine—the *Eclipse* (from Hertford), at half-past nine—and the *Times* (from Bedford), at twelve at noon.

To LONDON, a *Coach* (from Boston and Hull), every afternoon at half-past one—a *Coach* (from Northampton & Wellingborough), at two—another at half-past three—the *Union* (from Leeds), at four—a *Coach* (from Boston), and the *Victoria*, and the *Highflyer* (from York), at seven—and the *Defiance* (from Manchester), at eight.

To LONDON, the *Civility* (from Bedford), every Monday, Wednesday and Friday forenoon at eleven—the *Industry* (omnibus), same afternoons at three—a *Coach* (from Oundle), same days at four—and a *Coach* (from Kettering), same days at 5.

To LONDON, the *Regent* (from Stamford), every Tuesday, Thursday & Saturday evening at five—and the *Lark* (from Dunstable), on the mornings of the same days at ten—a *Coach* (from Hitchin), every Monday and Friday morning at eight, and every Tuesday, Wednesday, Thursday & Saturday, at twelve noon.

BARNET COACHES AND OMNIBUSES.

To LONDON, the *Criterion* (coach), from Godden's office, High st, every morning (Sunday excepted) at nine—& the *Wonder*, from the Old Salisbury Arms, every evening (Sunday excepted) at five, and on Sunday evening at six—Elwood's *Omnibuses*, from the Cock Inn, High st, every morning (Sunday excepted) at eight, and evening at seven, & on Sundays, at half-past seven in the morning—& Salmon's *Omnibus*, from the Albion, High st, every morning at nine.

THE FOLLOWING COACHES ARE FROM LONDON.

To AMPTHILL & BEDFORD, a *Coach*, every Tuesday, Thursday & Sat. afternoon, at half-past two; goes thro' Luton.

To BEDFORD, the *Civility*, and the *Self Defence*, every Tuesday, Thursday and Saturday afternoon, at two; go through St. Albans, Harpenden and Luton—and the *Times*, every afternoon (Sunday excepted) at three.

To BIRMINGHAM and LIVERPOOL, the *Star*, and the *Swallow*, every evening (Sunday excepted) at half-past seven.

To BOSTON, the *Old Coach*, calls at the Woolpack, High st, Barnet, every Monday and Friday night at seven, & every Tuesday, Wednesday, Thursday and Saturday morning at eight.

To BOSTON, *see* HULL and LINCOLN Coaches.

To DUNSTABLE, the *Lark*, every Tuesday, Thursday and Saturday afternoon, at half-past five.

To HERTFORD, the *Eclipse*, every afternoon (Sunday excepted) at five.

To HITCHIN, a *Coach*, every afternoon (Sunday excepted) at four.

To HULL, LINCOLN and BOSTON, a *Coach*, every afternoon, at half-past 5.

To KETTERING and UPPINGHAM, a *Coach*, every Tuesday, Thursday and Saturday night, at half-past nine.

To LEEDS, the *Express*, and the *Rockingham*, every evening (Sunday excepted) at six—and the *Union*, at seven.

To LINCOLN, *see* HULL.

To LIVERPOOL, *see* BIRMINGHAM

To LUTON, the *Industry* (omnibus), every Tuesday, Thursday and Saturday afternoon at one.—*See also* Coaches to AMPTHILL, BEDFORD and ST. ALBANS

To MANCHESTER, the *Defiance*, every evening at nine.

To NORTHAMPTON, the *Old Coach*, every afternoon (Sunday excepted) at half-past one.

To NORTHAMPTON and WELLINGBOROUGH, a *Coach*, daily (Sunday excepted) at twelve, noon.
To OUNDLE, a *Coach*, every Tuesday, Thurs. & Sat. morning at half-past eight.
To ST. ALBANS and LUTON, the *Favourite*, every evening (Sunday excepted) at seven.
To STAMFORD, the *Regent*, every Monday, Wednesday & Fri. morning at nine.
To WELLINGBOROUGH, *see* NORTHAMPTON Coach.
To YORK, the *Victoria* and the *Highflyer*, every night at half-past nine.

CARRIERS.

To LONDON, Cox's *Cart*, from Hadley, and Flitt's *Cart*, from Wood st, Barnet, every morning at eight.
The *Waggons* of the principal land carriers, to and from LONDON, BEDFORD, BIGGLESWADE, BIRMINGHAM, BOSTON, DAVENTRY, HITCHIN, LEEDS, LEICESTER, LUTON, MARKET STREET, NORTHAMPTON, NOTTINGHAM, OUNDLE, PETERBORO', POTTON, SHEFFIELD, SHEFFORD, SILSOE, STAMFORD, TORRINGTON, TOWCESTER, and WOBURN, pass regularly through Chipping Barnet and Whetstone, daily, but have no particular inns or warehouses.

ELSTREE,

OR IDLESTREE, is a small village and parish in Cashio hundred, 11 miles N. W. of London, seated upon the confines of the county of Middlesex; a turnpike road, leading to St. Albans through Edgeware, passing through the village. The village stands on elevated ground, and affords pleasing views—amongst others, that of St. Albans abbey church. At no great distance from this place is the site of a Roman station, called *Sulloniacæ:* many relics of that nation, consisting of urns, coins, Roman bricks, &c. have at various periods been found here and at Pennywells. The church, dedicated to St. Nicholas, which has been re-edified, has now a neat appearance, but its interior is destitute of any claim to particular description. In this church are interred the remains of Martha Rey, who fell a victim to the ungovernable attachment of the Rev. Jas. Hickman, by whom she was shot on the 7th of April, 1779, as she was entering her carriage after the performance at Covent-garden theatre; he was executed at the Old Bailey a few days after her interment. In the churchyard is buried Mr. Weare, who was murdered by John Thurtell at Gill's-hill cottage, parish of Aldenham, on the 24th of October, 1823. The reservoir belonging to the Grand Junction Company, and rented by the Regent Canal Company to feed their navigation, forms a delightful lake embellishment to the village. Population, 341.

POST OFFICE, Main street, James Warrall, *Post Master.*—Letters from LONDON arrive every morning at nine and afternoon at one, and are despatched every afternoon at three and evening at seven.

NOBILITY, GENTRY, AND CLERGY.

Alsop John, esq. Theobald st
Baker William, esq. Letchmore heath
Benbow Rev. John, Aldenham
Bond Benjamin, esq. Boreham wood
Boulton Chas. esq. Letchmore heath
Brough Anthony, esq. Aldenham
Bygrave John, esq. Elstree
Carter Thomas, esq. Brockley hill
Dalrymple Sir Adolphus, Dalrow
Denny Anthony, esq. Boreham wood
Franks Mr. John, Theobald st
Haworth Mrs. Euphrasia, Boreham lodge [Theobald st
Hayword Mr. Robert B. (surgeon)
Hinchliff John, esq. Aldenham park
Macready Wm. Chas. esq. Elm place
Mason Alex. W. esq. Deacon's hill
Mason Captain George, Oak lodge, Aldenham [lodge
Mason John Finch, esq. Aldenham
Morris Rev. John, D.D. rector, Elstree new rectory
Nicolls Thomas, esq. Boreham wood
Northland Right Hon. Lord, Boreham house
Oliphant Jas. esq. Aldenham grove
Perry Mr. Wm. Robt. Boreham wood
Phillimore Wm. esq. Deacon's hill
Phillimore Capt. Wm. Robt. Aldenhm
Pitt Capt. Samuel, Aldenham
Player Thos. Henry, esq. Letchmore
Richards John, esq. Boyd's hill, Aldenham [ley hill
Savary N. N. esq. Newlands, Brock-
Sills Mr. Joseph, Elstree
Stuart Wm. esq. Aldenham abbey
Timins John Fann, esq. Hill field

SCHOOLS.

ALDENHAM GRAMMAR SCHOOL, Rev. Thomas Spyers, master
SUBSCRIPTION (boys & girls), Miss H. W. Harrison, mistress

INNS & PUBLIC HOUSES.

Artichoke, Sophia Field
Crown, Wm. King, Boreham wood
Green Dragon, John Brown
Holly Bush, Witcomb Johnson
Plough, John Brooks
Red Lion (postng house) John Billings

SHOPKEEPERS & TRADERS.

Ambler William, boot & shoe maker
Bodimeade Henry, plumber & glazier
Bradshaw Sarah, linen draper
Brown Richard, boot & shoe maker
Clark Jas. grocer, & coal & corn dealr
Clark William, plumber and glazier
Eames Thomas, boot & shoe maker
Eames William, boot & shoe maker
Fitch William, brewer, Reservoir
Hall Joseph, bricklayer
Hart John, hair dresser
Harvey Jonathan, tailor
Jackson Jenny, baker
Jones Richard, wheelwright
Lane Adam, tailor
Marriott Thomas, butcher
Martin Isaac, blacksmith
Morris Edward, carpenter [wood
Morris William, bricklayer, Boreham
Olney Thomas, butcher and brewer
Orton Thomas, grocer
Pridmore Matthew, butcher
Rainbow James, shopkeeper, Boreham wood
Robertson Robert, tailor
Row and Hinson, saddlers
Stacey Chas. grocer & wheelwright
Stanford Henry, saddler
Tomlin Dorothy, baker
Wardall Thomas, butcher
Wilson William, carpenter
Young John, tailor

COACHES,

CALLING AT THE RED LION.

To LONDON, *The Favourite* (from St. Albans), every morning (Sunday excepted), at 10, and Billing's *Coach* (from Shenley), at a quarter before nine.
To ST. ALBANS, *The Favourite* (from London), every afternoon (Sunday excepted), at half-past four.
To SHENLEY, Billing's *Coach* (from London), every evening (Sunday excepted), at six.

CARRIERS.

To LONDON, Green and Drinkwater, every morning.

GREAT AND LITTLE HADHAM.

GREAT, or MUCH HADHAM, is a village and parish, in the hundred of Edwinstree; 26 miles north from Shoreditch church, London, nine miles N.E. from Hertford, and five E. from Bishops Stortford. It is situated in a fertile vale, upon the river Ash, and is a place unimportant in trade, but is the residence of many families of the highest respectability. The Bishop of London is lord of the manor, and patron of the living; the latter is a rectory, of which the Rev. Thomas Randolph is the incumbent, and also of the adjoining parish of Little Hadham; the Rev. — Hannan is the present curate. In the latter parish is a place of worship for independents. The parish church of Great Hadham is dedicated to St. Andrew; it is a handsome building with a tower, and contains some monuments deserving notice. The church at Little Hadham is not distinguished by anything of particular interest, except its situation, from which is commanded an extensive view over the surrounding country, the face of which is exceedingly pleasing, and studded with seats; amongst those in the vicinity of the village are—'Moore Place,' the residence of Sir Henry Seymour Blane, Bart.; 'Lordship House,' the residence of John Dalyell, Esq.; 'Wynches,' the residence of Mrs. Anthony; the 'Rectory,' the Rev. Thomas Randolph, &c. &c. At Great Hadham is a lunatic asylum, ably conducted. By the census for 1831, the parish of Great Hadham contained 1,268 inhabitants, and that of Little Hadham, 878.

POST OFFICE, GREAT HADHAM, Richard Woor, *Post Master.*—Letters from LONDON arrive every morning at nine, and are despatched every evening at six.

POST OFFICE, LITTLE HADHAM, Henry Cundall, *Post Master.*—Letters from LONDON arrive every morning at seven, and are despatched every evening at seven.

GENTRY AND CLERGY.

Anthony Mrs. —, Wynches [place
Blane Sir H. Seymour, bart. Moore
Chaplyn Mrs. —, Little Hadham
Dalyell John, esq. Hadham lordship
Harman Rev. —, Great Hadham
Jones the Misses, Great Hadham
Mott Mrs. Elizabeth, Great Hadham
Parry Nicholas, esq. Little Hadham
Pitcairne Mrs. —, Culver lodge
Randolph Rev. Thomas, Rectory, Great Hadham
Williams Rev. Robt. Little Hadham

ACADEMIES AND SCHOOLS.

Cooper Mary Ann, Little Hadham
FREE SCHOOL, Great Hadham—John Crook, master
FREE SCHOOLS, Lit. Hadham—Mrs. Dean and Mrs. Cooper, mistresses
Hobson Thomas, Great Hadham
SCHOOL OF INDUSTRY, Gt. Hadham—Alice Deacon, mistress

PROFESSIONAL PERSONS.

Smith & Moore, surgeons, Gt. Hadham
Smith James, surgeon, Lunatic asylum, Great Hadham [ham
Times & Mott, attorneys, Great Had-

INNS & PUBLIC HOUSES.

Angel, Henry Cundall, Lit. Hadham
Bull, Ann Ainey, Great Hadham
Fox, Edmund Gillett, Little Hadham
Red Lion (posting house) Richard Woor, Great Hadham

SHOPKEEPERS & TRADERS.

The names without address are in GREAT HADHAM.

Barker Stephen, miller, maltster, & brick maker, Little Hadham
Bawcock Thos. smith & bell hanger
Burr John, tailor
Crossingham John, saddler
Cundall Mary, milliner & dressmaker
Easton Thomas, grocer and draper
Ellcock Danl. carpenter, Lit. Hadhm
Ellcock John, grocer and brewer, Little Hadham
Fletcher John, grocer & shoemaker
Fuller Peter, cattle dealer
Fuller Thomas, butcher and brewer
Giffin Joseph, boot and shoe maker
Gillett David, grocer, Little Hadham
Gillett Fred. wheelwright, L. Hadhm
Green William, tailor [Hadham
Hale Samuel, grocer & baker, Little
Hardy William, boot & shoe maker
Harvey George, saddler, L. Hadham
Hummerstone George, butcher, Lit. Hadham
Hunt John, miller, Great Hadham
Jennings John, baker, Little Hadham
Joslyn William, carpenter & baker, Little Hadham
Knight James, butcher [Hadham
Maling Wm. boot & shoe maker, Lit.
Miller Charles, butcher
Mitchell Geo. shoemaker, L. Hadham
Mitchell Martha, grocer, L. Hadham
Moginie John, grocer and brewer, Little Hadham
Morris Thomas, carpenter
Mott John, baker and sh[illegible] Little Hadham
Orgar Sarah, smith, Little Hadham
Page Frederick, smith & bellhanger
Prior Edward, corn dealer
Randle John, grocer
Randle William, baker
Speller Andrew, plumber, &c.
Thurgood Aright, grocer and draper
Thurgood James, bricklayer
White James, grocer, Little Hadham
Wilson John, saddler
Wright Charles, nurseryman

COACH.

To LONDON, *The Times*, every morning (Sunday excepted), at seven, goes thro' Hoddesdon and Waltham Cross.

CARRIER.

To LONDON, Thomas Fuller's *Waggon*, every Tuesday and Friday.

HATFIELD AND NEIGHBOURHOOD.

HATFIELD, a market town in the parish of Bishops Hatfield and hundred of Broadwater, is 19 miles N.N.W. from London, 7 W.S.W. from Hertford, and 14 S.S.E. from Luton, in Bedfordshire—eligibly and agreeably situated on the declivity of a hill, west of the river Lea, upon the great north road, and in the midst of luxuriant pasture and corn lands. A silk factory, at the workhouse, produces the chief manufacture that the town now possesses. The Marquess of Salisbury is lord of the manor; courts leet and baron are held under him occasionally, and the county magistrates hold petty sessions here for the division. Hatfield formed, at a very remote period, part of the property of the Saxon monarchs; in 1607 it was vested in the family of the Earl of Salisbury, in exchange for Theobalds, or, as it is popularly termed, 'Tibbalds.' Hatfield House, the seat and residence of the present Marquess of Salisbury, is a noble mansion, surmounted by a tower, and, being seated on a proud eminence, commands the attention of the stranger on entering the town. About half a mile from the mansion stands a venerable oak, still called 'Queen Elizabeth's oak,' and so named from its marking the distance to which that princess was permitted to extend her walks, when a prisoner here in the reign of the bigoted and rigorous Mary. Brockett Hall, the seat of the Right Hon. Viscount Melbourn, is situated a few miles to the north of Hatfield.

The church, dedicated to St. Etheldreda, stands upon high ground; it is a handsome structure, and contains a nave, chancel and aisles, with an embattled tower at the west end. In the sepulchral chapel of the Salisbury family, on the north side of the chancel, is a fine marble monument to Robert Cecil, first Earl of Salisbury, and lord high treasurer under James I; here likewise were interred, December 20th, 1835, the mutilated remains of the Right Hon. Mary Emily, Dowager Marchioness of Salisbury, who was burnt to death in the previous month of November, in her 85th year. The benefice is a rectory, with the perpetual curacy of Totteridge attached, in the patronage of the Marquess of Salisbury; the present rector of Hatfield is the Rev. F. J. Faithful. A national school for boys, an endowed school of industry for girls, and six alms-houses, are the charitable institutions. Though rather hilly, the country around is well cultivated, and abundantly rewards the labour of the agriculturist. The market is on Thursday; fairs, for toys and pleasure, 23d of April and 18th of October. The parish contained, in 1831, 3,593 inhabitants.

POST OFFICE, Fore street, Ruth Mawe, *Post Mistress.*—Letters from LONDON arrive every night at ten, and are despatched every morning at three and afternoon at four.—Letters from the North arrive every morning at three, and are despatched every night at ten.—Letters from St. ALBANS arrive (by cross post) every morning at eight, and are despatched every day at twelve.—Letters from HERTFORD arrive (by cross post) every day at twelve, and are despatched every morning at eight.—The box closes at nine at night.

NOBILITY, GENTRY AND CLERGY.

Brampton Mrs. Elizabeth, Bush hall
Church John, esq. Woodside place
Cox Mr. Henry, Handside
Faithful Rev. Francis Joseph, rector, Parsonage house
Franks William, esq. Wood hill
Gaussen Robert S. esq. Brookman's park
Hall William, esq. Hill house
Melbourne Right Hon. Viscount, Brockett hall
Orme Rev. Robert, Essendon
Oshaldeston Thos. esq. New house
Peile Rev. Benjamin, North road
Salisbury the most Noble the Marquess of, Hatfield house
Smith Sir C. E. Bedwell park
Yorke Hon. Harriet, Woodside house
Young Benjamin, esq. Fore st

ACADEMIES & SCHOOLS.

Faithful Rev. Francis Joseph (boarding) Parsonage house
NATIONAL SCHOOL, Fore st—James Austin, master [road
Peile Rev. Benjmn. (boarding) North
Powell Mark, Fore st
Smith Thomas (writing) North road

AUCTIONEER & SURVEYOR.

Langford J. G. (and furniture broker and land agent) French Horn lane

BAKERS.

Badcock Joseph, Park st
Bradshaw George, Back st
Humphreys Jos. French Horn lane
Stones James Dunton, Park st
Thurtell Mary, Fore st

BLACKSMITHS.

Barnes William, Back st
Bunker Ebenezer, Pond hill
Swain William, French Horn lane

BOOT & SHOE MAKERS.

Austin John, Park st
Church Edward, Back st
Saunders George, North road
Stocks Thomas, Fore st
Toogood Joseph, Fore st

BREWERS & MALTSTERS.

Complin Fras. Denyer, North road
Pratchett Leonard, North road
Pryor Alfred and Co. Fore st
Sandon Charles, Fore st
Whitehead John, Bell bar

BRICKLAYERS.

Chapman James, North road
Chapman Thomas, Back st

BUTCHERS.

Dudley Jacob, Fore st
Hart John, Fore st
Simkins James, Fore st
Walby William, Park st

CARPENTERS.
Dunham Benjamin, Park st
Hall William, Park st
Webb James, Park st
Wilson Isaac, North road

FIRE, &c. OFFICE AGENTS.
Phœnix, Thomas Smith, corner of North road
Royal Exchange, John Rawley, Fore st

GROCERS & PROVISION, &c. DEALERS.
Cain Mary, Park st
Cox Stephen, Park st
Little George, Park st
Wade Wm. (and glass, &c.) Back st
Whitehead Litchfield (and cheesemonger, ironmonger and tallow chandler) Fore st

HAIR DRESSERS.
Cubis William, Fore st
Sherrell James, Fore st

INNS.
Greyhound, John Smith, Hatfield Woodside
Red Lion (commercial) Wm. Webb, North road
Salisbury Arms(posting)Chas.Townsend, Fore st

LINEN & WOOLLEN DRAPERS AND HABERDASHERS.
Chapman John, Fore st
Clark Mary Ann (& milliner) Fore st
Ewins John (and clothier & hatter) Park st
Rayley John (and hatter) Fore st

MILLERS.
Farr Edward, Witter mill
Farr Edward, Burby mill
Farr George, Hatfield mill
Roberts Thomas, Lensford mill

PLUMBERS, PAINTERS, AND GLAZIERS.
Hardum Charles, Fore st
Tayler Thomas, Fore st

SADDLERS AND HARNESS MAKERS.
Arch Samuel, Fore st
Parry William, Pond hill

STRAW HAT MAKERS.
Allen Sarah, Park st
Chapman Mary, Back st

SURGEONS.
Galbraith James, Fore st
Osbaldeston Thomas, North road
Thomas William L. North road

TAILORS & DRAPERS.
Ewins John, Park st
Hammond George, Fore st
Hankin William, Fore st
Moorcroft Benjamin, Pond hill
Wilson John, Park st

TAVERNS & PUBLIC HOUSES.
Angel, John Nightingall, Brickwall
Bull, Sarah Laugton, Stanbury
Chequers, James Clarke, Hornbeam hall
Coach & Horses, Danl. Byford, Newgate st
Crooked Billet, John Harvey, Mill green
Eight Bells, Isaac Wilson, Fore st
Horse & Groom, William Waller, Park st
One Bell, William Lowin, Fore st
Two Brewers, Edward Church, Back st
Wrestlers, William Seymour, North road

WHEELWRIGHTS.
Bunker Ebenezer, Pond hill
Hadlin Thomas, North road

Miscellaneous.
Archer James, tanner, Pond hill
Bryan William, chimney pot, &c. manufacturer, Woodside pottery
Cox Stephen, chymist & stationer, Park st
Hall Andw. watch maker, Fore st
Hickson Jos. veterinary surgeon, Batterdale
Little George, confectioner, Park st
Powell Mark, stationer & dealer in British wines and toys, Fore st
Sandon William, registrar of births, deaths and marriages, Back st
Scarborough Josh. coach proprietor, North road
Wingrave Joseph, cooper, North road
Workhouse and Silk mill, St. Albans road—J. Bridgens, governor

COACHES.
To LONDON, the *Sovereign*, from the Eight Bells, every morning at seven.
Besides the above, Coaches to and from LONDON, GLASGOW, YORK, LEEDS, BEDFORD, HITCHIN, Kettering, Oundle, St. Neots, Boston, Stamford, &c. pass thro' Hatfield daily.

CARRIERS.
To LONDON, William Parry, from Pond hill, every Tuesday and Friday, and Mrs. Tuitte, every Friday; also *Carriers and Waggons*, to and from London and the North, are passing through Hatfield constantly.

HEMEL HEMPSTEAD,

WITH BOXMOOR, THE CHAPELRIES OF BOVINGDON AND FLAUNDEN, AND THE VILLAGES OF GREAT AND LITTLE GADDESDEN AND NEIGHBOURHOODS.

HEMEL HEMPSTEAD is a populous and thriving market town in the parish of its name and hundred of Dacorum, 24 miles N.W. from London, 18 W. from Hertford and 6 W. by N. from St. Albans. By the Saxons the town was called *Henamsted* or *Hean Hempsted*, signifying 'High Hempsted;' subsequently it obtained the appellation of *Hemelam-Steole*, from which its present denomination evidently is derived. The town, which consists principally of one street, nearly a mile in length, is situated on the declivity of a hill, near the small rivers Gade and Bourn—within about a mile of the Grand Junction canal, and a mile and a half from the London and Birmingham Railway. The leading manufacture of the place is that of paper, which indeed may be considered its staple; the making of straw plat employs a considerable number of females and children, and several corn mills are in the vicinity. There are some respectable inns, both commercial and posting; among these the 'Bell' and the 'King's Arms' are particularly well regulated establishments. Henry VIII granted to the inhabitants a charter of incorporation, which was renewed by Cromwell: by this charter, still in existence, the government of the town was vested in a jury chosen from among the inhabitants, and a bailiff, elected annually. The police regulations of the place are conducted upon the improved metropolitan system, and there is a regular office at Bury Mill End.

The church, dedicated to St. Mary, is the principal ornament of the town; it is of Norman architecture, but has undergone various alterations in the progress of time; its form is that of a cross, from the intersection of which a tower rises. The interior consists of a nave, chancel, aisles and transept: the entrance at the west end presents a richly ornamented recessed arch; the mouldings are finely sculptured, the capitals all dissimilar. The tower, surmounted by a well-proportioned spire, rests upon semicircular arches, springing from large clustered pillars with square capitals, the sculpture of each of which is different. In the church are some few monuments the inspection of which will interest the visiter; it also contains an excellent organ, built by Lincoln at a cost of four hundred guineas, and two truly beautiful painted windows—that at the west end presented by Sir Aston Paston Cooper, Bart. The benefice is a vicarage, in the appointment of the dean and chapter of St. Paul's, on the nomination of the see of Lincoln; the present incumbent is the Rev. Jacob Henry Brook Mountain. There are places of worship for baptists and the society of friends, besides meeting houses in the parish and its hamlets for other religious classes. The charities comprise a general infirmary, erected and partly endowed by Sir John Sebright, Bart.; a school of industry, one upon the national system, and another for infants. The country about Hemel Hempstead is hilly, picturesque and in a high state of cultivation; and the appearance of the town, with its handsome church and beautiful lofty spire, on the approach from St. Albans, is eminently imposing. In the immediate vicinity the walks are of a most attractive description. The market (a superior one for corn) is on Thursday: a fair is held on the Thursday week after Whit-Sunday for cattle, and a statute fair on the third Monday in September; and there is a large cattle show or market on Holy Thursday. The entire parish, including the chapelries of Bovingdon and Flaunden, contained, in 1831, 6,037 inhabitants.

Boxmoor, now well known as a station on the London and Birmingham railway, is situated about one mile and a half west of Hemel Hempstead, of which town, together with Two Waters (where there are paper mills), and a number of small hamlets, it forms a populous suburb. The principal interest attached to this place arises from the views it affords of the railroad and one of its highly curious skew bridges. The Gade and the Bourne rivers here unite; the latter is locally denominated the 'warm' Bourne, from the early appearance and abundance of the trout in it—a circumstance that attracts many anglers to its banks in the fishing season, who are comfortably accommodated in the house called the 'Fishery Inn.' A new chapel of ease, and others for baptists and independents, are the places of worship here.

Bovingdon and Flaunden are chapelries and hamlets to Hemel Hempstead. The chapel of the former, dedicated to St. Lawrence, was some years since improved and embellished: in its interior is the figure of a warrior, cut in soft stone—the head bears a helmet, and at the feet is a lion *couchant*. A new chapel has been erected at Flaunden, by the Right Hon. Charles Compton Cavendish, of Latimers.

About three miles from Hemel Hempstead, and in the same hundred as that town, is the large parish and small village of GREAT GADDESDEN, or *Gaddesden Magna*, situated upon the banks of the Gade, a short distance off the road leading to Tring and Berkhampstead. In the vicinity of the village is Gaddesden Place, a modern seat of perfect elegance. The church, dedicated to St. John the Baptist, contains several monuments to the Halsey family, one of whom erected the above mansion. Population of the parish, 988.

Upon the opposite bank of the Gade lies LITTLE GADDESDEN, a large village and smaller parish than the one preceding. This parish in former ages acquired some celebrity as being the birth-place of John de Gaddesden, an eminent physician and contemporary writer with Chaucer. The beautiful seat of the Countess of Bridgwater (who has erected a splendid testimonial to the memory of the late duke) is contiguous to the village. The church, a small edifice, dedicated to Saint Peter and Saint Paul, contains several monuments, but none that can afford gratification to curiosity. The population of this parish amounts to 492 persons.

POST OFFICE, High street, HEMEL HEMPSTEAD, George Coupland, *Post Master*.—Letters from LONDON arrive every afternoon at two, and are despatched every night at half-past nine.—Letters from the North arrive every morning at six, and are despatched every night at twenty minutes before nine.

NOBILITY, GENTRY AND CLERGY.

Belch Mrs. Elizabeth, Marlowes
Bingham Rev. John Batt, Great Gaddesden
Bridgwater the Countess of, Ashridge
Brooke Miss, Vicarage, H.Hempstead
Carey Rev. Eustace, Marlowes
Cooper Sir Astley Paston, bart. Gadebridge house
Cornwall Mrs. —, Marlowes
Cranstone Mrs. Sarah, Marlowes
Davies Thomas, esq. M. D. Box lane
Dwarris Sir Fortunatus, Piccott's end
Evans Mrs. Mary Ann, Marlowes
Field Miss Fanny, Marlowes
Ford James, esq. Marlowes
Godwin Mrs. Amelia, High st
Godwin Shadrach, esq. Two Beeches
Gotch Rev. Fredk. Wm. Crouch field
Grover Mrs. Sibylla, the Bury
Halsey Rev. John F. Moore, Gaddesden park
Halsey Thomas Plumer, esq. Gaddesden place
Hamilton Rev. Wm. M. A. Marlowes
Heale —, esq. Highfield
Hopley Rev. Thomas, near High st
Horwood Miss —, Marlowes
Howard George, esq. Elm cottage, Marlowes
Howard Mrs. Sophia, Marlowes
Howard Mr. Daniel Simeon, Handpost farm
Jenks Rev. David, Little Gaddesden
Johnson Mr. William, the Lodge
Key Charles Arton, esq. M. D. the Heath, Boxmoor
M'Donogh Rev. T. M. Bovingdon vicarage
Montague the Right Hon. Lord, Bovingdon green
Mountain Rev. Jacob Henry Brooke, B. D. the Heath, Boxmoor
Napier Capt. W. H., R. N. the Lawn
Reynolds Thomas, esq. the Fishery
Rosier Daniel, esq. Marlowes
Ryder the Hon. Granville Dudley, Westbrook hay
Sandars Samuel, esq. Lockers
Smith Mr. Hugh, Bury mill end
Smith Mr. Samuel, Marlowes
Smith Thomas, esq. Bovingdon lodge
Stevenson Mrs. —, Shantock hall
Thorp Mr. George, Piccott's end
Von Dadelszen George Michael, esq. Corner hall
Warren Mr Francis, Bury mill end
Watson the Hon.& Rev.Richd. Felden
Williams Robert, esq. Marlowes
Woodman Mrs. Elizabeth, Marlowes
Yelloly Rev. John, M. A. the Lodge

ACADEMIES AND SCHOOLS.

Not otherwise described are Day Schools.

Blake Maria (brdng. & day) Queen st
Butler Charles, Marlowes
Gwillim Mary (gentlemen's preparatory) Marlowes
Hamilton Rev. William J. M. A. (gentlemen's boarding) Marlowes
Hyde Thomas, Queen st
INFANTS' SCHOOL, Queen st—Caroline Blake, mistress
Innes Margaret (brdng.) Marlowes
Jennings Mary (boarding) High st
NATIONAL SCHOOL, Pope's lane—Guy Guppy, master
Russell Ann (boarding) Marlowes
SCHOOL OF INDUSTRY (girls') Marlowes—Tryphena Robinson, mistrs

AGRICULTURAL MACHINE MAKER.

Smith James (and smith) High st

ATTORNEYS.

Day Frederick (and auditor to the Hemel Hempstead Union) Redbourn road
Smith and Grover (and clerks to the magistrates & to the Hemel Hempstead and Great Berkhampstead Unions) High st

AUCTIONEERS & APPRAISRS.

Foster Thomas, High st
Griffin John (and surveyor, valuer and estate agent) High st
Humphrey Henry, High st
Watson Alfred, High st

BAKERS & FLOUR DEALERS.

Andrew Thomas, Chapel st
Capell George, Queen st
Cassidy John, High st
Cook George, Piccott's end
Jeffs Mary, Bury mill end
Jennings Joseph, High st
Johnson Joseph, Flaunden
Marshall George, Corner hall
Mutton Robert, Two Waters
Sells Charles, High st
Sibley William, Crouch field
Smith John, Two Waters
Sweetman Ann, High st
Wells Elizabeth, High st

BANKERS.

Grover & Smith, High st—(draw on Dorrien, Magens & Co. London)

BOOKSELLERS & STATIONRS.

Beale William (stationer) High st
Girton Jos. Francis (& library) High st

BOOT AND SHOE MAKERS.

Clark John, High st
Conquer John, Corner hall
Dollamore Jas. Swan and Trout yard
Dunham George, Water end
Freeman George, Pope's lane
Hall John, High st
Hyde Joseph, High st
Martin William, Queen st
Pryor John, High st
Rogers Richard, Piccott's end
Scear Thomas, High st
Turney Daniel, Piccott's end
Weatherhead Thomas, High st

BRAZIERS AND TIN-PLATE WORKERS.

Drage William, High st
Smith John, High st

BREWERS.

Hall Mary, Pope's lane
Liddon John Wm. & Co. Bury mill end
Winter Isaac, Two Waters

BRICK MAKERS AND LIME BURNERS.

Edwin John, Leverstock green
Franklin Thomas, Bennett's end
Glover John, Marlowes

BRICKLAYERS, SLATERS, & PLASTERERS.

Castle William, Queen st
Child Henry, top of Chapel st
Durrant William, Pope's lane
Glenister Henry (& builder) Flaunden
Glover John, Marlowes
Goodson Thomas, High st
Ivory George, Great Gaddesden
Walker John, High st

BUTCHERS.

Battams John, High st
Blois Benjamin, Shambles
Burrington George, Piccott's end
Catherall David, High st
Collins Francis, High st
Collins James, High st
Collins William, Queen st
Cripps John, Bury mill end
Deacon Joseph, Two Waters
Elliott Joseph, Two Waters
Fordom Eden, Two Waters
Horn George, Little Gaddesden
Keen Joseph, Chapel st
Kinder Elizabeth, Two Waters
Reeve William, Little Gaddesden
Saunders William, High st
Saunders William, Piccott's end

CARPENTERS.

Bellamy John, High st
Cheshire James, Caroline place
Glover John, Marlowes
Groom Geo. (and builder) Marlowes
Hill John, Queen st
Horn Edward, Chapel st
Monk Thomas, Moor end
Sargent James, High st
Sear William, Piccott's end
Woodhouse John, High st

CHYMISTS & DRUGGISTS.

Beale William (and oil and Italian warehouse snd stationer) High st
Evans John, High st
Smith Jonathan K. (and stationer) High st

CLOTHES DEALERS.

Austin James, near Fishery Inn, Boxmoor
Bingham William, Queen st
Clark John, High st
Grout Robert, Queen st
Wallington Matthew, Flaunden

COAL MERCHANTS AND DEALERS.

Austin John, Fishery wharf, Boxmoor
Ebborn Thos. (& salt) St. Albans wharf
Howard George (& stone) Boxmoor
Liddall James, Albion place
Pedley Henry, Marlowes
Price James, Piccott's end

COOPERS.

Greenhill William & Son, High st
Starman William, Pope's lane
Wingrave James, High st

CORN DEALERS & MEALMEN.
Austin James, Fishery Inn, Boxmoor
Axtell William, High st
Buckingham George, Two Waters
Cooper Richard, Two Waters
Coupland George, High st
Coupland Thomas, Two Waters
Hoar James, High st
Jennings Joseph, High st
Mitchell Samuel, High st
Oakley Richard, Bury mill end
Price James (& salt) Piccott's end
Robinson William, Albion place
Sidwell George (& seed) Flaunden

CURRIERS AND LEATHER CUTTERS.
Hall John, High st
Harris William, High st
Seear Thomas, High st
Weatherhead Thomas, High st

FIRE, &c. OFFICE AGENTS.
CLERICAL and MEDICAL, Joseph Cranstone, High st
FAMILY ENDOWMENT, Frederick Day, Redbourn road
PHŒNIX, George Thorp, High st; Jos. Cranstone, High st
ROYAL EXCHANGE, John Smith, High st
SUN, John Evans (and stamp distributer) High st

FURNITURE BROKERS.
Finch Bartholomew, High st
Foster Thomas, High st
Watson Alfred (& upholsterer) High st

GROCERS, AND HOP, SEED & PROVISION DEALERS.
(See also Shopkeepers, &c.)
Austin James, Fishery Inn, Boxmoor
Birdsey John Cato (& tallow chandler) High st
Cross James, High st
Evans John, High st
Holloway Henry, Bovingdon
Johnson Joseph, Flaunden
Lea George (& tallow chandler) High st
Marshall George, Corner hall
Orchard Joseph & Francis, High st
Thorp George, High st

HAIR DRESSERS, &c.
Hudson Francis, High st
Lawrence Joseph, Queen st

INNS.
Bell, Geo. Buckingham, Two Waters
Bell (commercial & posting house) Mary Jones, High st
Bridgwater Arms, George Garrett, Little Gaddesden
Fishery Inn, James Austin, Boxmoor
King's Arms (commercial, excise office, and parcel agent to the Railway Co.) William Deacon, High st
Rose & Crown, Wm. Morris, High st
Sun, John Liddall, High st
Swan, Thomas Watson, High st
White Hart, Geo. Saunders, High st

IRONMONGERS.
Cranstone Joseph, High st
Fowler Thomas, High st
Smith John, High st

LINEN & WOOLLEN DRAPERS, MERCERS, HOSIERS, &c.
Baker and Bruton, High st
Brice Robert, High st
Eyles William, Marlowes
Partridge Ann, High st
Rolph George, High st
Sheppard William, High st
Swannell Samuel (& tea dealer) High st
Turnor John B. High st
Watson Alfred, High st

MALTSTERS.
Fowler Thomas, Bury mill end
Liddon John Wm. & Co. Bury mill end

MILLERS.
Cook Thomas, Noak mill
Littlebury Wm. Bourne end, Bovingdon
Smith John, Piccott's end
Warren Francis, Bury mill end

MILLINERS & DRESS MAKRS.
Eyles Maria, Marlowes
Harding Ann, Thorp's yard
Lane Jane, High st
Partridge Ann, High st
Taylor Amy, Halfmoon court
Rowed Elizabeth & Maria, Marlowes
Weedon S. & M. High st

NURSERY & SEEDSMEN.
Brownlees Wm. (& florist) Marlowes
King Joseph, Crouch field
King Thomas, Pope's lane
Sedwell George, Flaunden

OMNIBUS AND HORSE AND CARRIAGE OWNERS—FOR HIRE.
Deacon William, King's Arms, High st
Jones Mary, Bell, High st

PAPER MANUFACTURERS.
Dickinson John and Co. Nash mills, and at *London* & *Manchester*
Hunter William, Frogmore mill, Two Waters
Stevens John Dovey, Two Waters mill

PLUMBERS, PAINTERS, GLAZIERS & PAPER HANGERS.
Best John, Queen st
Hales Josiah, Marlowes
Pedley Mary & Sons, High st

PRINTER—LETTER-PRESS.
Buttfield William, High st

ROPE & TWINE MAKERS.
Bail John, Chapel st
Kingston William, High st

SADDLERS AND HARNESS MAKERS.
Dennis John, High st
Kingston William, High st
Lacey Nehemiah, High st
Reeve Thomas, Bovingdon
Talbot James, Queen st

SHOPKEEPERS & DEALRS IN GROCERIES & SUNDRIES.
Barnes Samuel, Piccott's end
Barnett Thomas, Albion place
Buckoke Thomas, Queen st
Capell George, Queen st
Church James, Two Waters
Freeman George, Pope's lane
Gristwood George, Boxmoor
Horn Edward, Chapel st
Reeve William, Little Gaddesden
Sells Charles, High st
Sells George, Two Waters
Smith William, Albion place
Weightman George, Two Waters

SMITHS AND FARRIERS.
Child Henry, Flaunden
Gates William, Bell Inn yard
Glenister Joseph, Corner hall
How Joseph, Piccott's end
Oldfield Frederick, Queen st
Priest James, Two Waters
Shepherd Joseph, Water end
Smith James, High st
Sutton Thomas, White Hart yard

STRAW HAT MAKERS.
Hale Elizabeth, Two Waters
Modlin Sarah, High st
Partridge Ann, High st
Weatherhead Mary, High st

STRAW PLAT DEALERS AND STRAW FACTORS.
Brundan John, Halfmoon yard
Gibbs John, High st
Grout Robert (factor) Queen st
Modlin James, High st
Smith Elizabeth, Marlowes

SURGEONS.
Bowen Henry, Marlowes
Cherrington Charles, High st
Hallett John James, Marlowes
Merry Robert, Marlowes
Ross Edward (house surgeon to West Herts Infirmary) Marlowes

SURVEYOR.
Griffin John (land and architectural) High st

TAILORS.
Marked thus * are also Drapers.
*Barker John, High st
Evans John, High st
*Eyles William, Marlowes
Lawrence James, Queen st
Lawrence James, jun. Queen st
Mallord William, High st
*Sheppard William, High st
Short Peter, High st
*Swannell Samuel, High st
*Tomlin James, Little Gaddesden

TAVERNS & PUBLIC HOUSES.
Barley Oil Bottle, Hy. Austin, Boxmoor
Bell, Henry Staines, Bovingdon
Boar's Head, Joseph Kilbey, Piccott's end
Boot, Martha Durrant, High st
Bull, Thomas Austin, Bovingdon
Cock, John Woodhouse, High st
Cock & Bottle, Geo. Chennells, Gt. Gaddesden
Compasses, Joseph Hancher, High st
Green Dragon, Henry Child, Flaunden
Half Moon, Benjamin Juffs, High st
Horse & Jockey, Ann Hall, Gaddesden row
King's Head, William Wright, High st
Lamb, Thomas Goodson, High st
Queen's Head, Jas. Holloway, Corner hall
Railway Tavern, Jeremiah Smith, Boxmoor
Red Lion, Thomas Jeffery, High st
Six Bells, Richard Oakley, Bury mill end
Swan, John Catling, Boxmoor
Three Tuns, William Smith, Nash mills

TIMBER MERCHANTS.
Griffin John (& surveyor) High st
Howard William (and lath, slate and salt) Corner hall

TOY DEALERS.
Girton Joseph Francis (& jeweller) High st
Hudson Francis, High st

VETERINARY SURGEONS.
Davison William, Queen st
How Joseph, Piccott's end

WATCH AND CLOCK MAKERS AND JEWELLERS.
Bish Edward, High st
Frowd William, High st
Varney George, High st

WHARFINGERS.
Austin John, Boxmoor
Ebborn Thomas, St. Albans wharf
Gore John, Two Waters
Howard George (& stone merchant) Boxmoor
Norris & Pedley, Boxmoor

WHEELWRIGHTS.
Bailey George, Piccott's end
Cook John, Water end
Gates William, Rose and Crown yard
Janaway John Henry (and smith) Two Waters
Oldfield Reuben, Queen st
Smith James, High st

WINE & SPIRIT MERCHANTS
Howard George (and agent for Guiness' Dublin porter & Edinburgh ale) Boxmoor
Thorpe Geo. (British wine & brandy) High st

Miscellaneous.
Barratt William, glover & legging maker, High street
Blacknell Charles, dairyman, Bury mill end
Deacon Thos. Elisha, tanner, Corner hall
Eggbear Richard, supervisor of excise, Marlowes
Fensome John, turner and plat machine maker, Piccott's end
GAS WORKS, Pope's lane—Joseph Cranstone, superintendent, High st
Harrison Thomas, fish and game dealer, Shambles
Howard D. S. farmer, Handpost farm
Humphrey Henry, registrar of births, deaths and marriages, High st

MISCELLANEOUS—*Continued.*

INFIRMARY, Marlowes—Eliza Bennett, matron
Lane Jane, stay maker, High st
Litchfield Thos. glass & china dealer, Shambles
Marshall Augustus, paper makers' wire weaver, Nash mills
Miller William, hat & cap maker, High st
POLICE STATION OFFICE, Bury mill end—William Taylor, superintendent
Pryor Thos. clog & patten maker, High st
Sweetman Sarah, fruiterer, &c. High st
UNION WORKHOUSE, Hemel Hempstead—James Frederick Leedham, governor; Mrs. E. Leedham, matron
Waller Edward, coach builder, High st
Weedon George, basket & turnery warehouse, High st
Wilsden William, confectioner, High st
Wright Jos. straw, &c. dyer, Piccott's end

CONVEYANCE BY RAILWAY.

From BOXMOOR STATION, one mile and a half from Hemel Hempstead.

To & from LONDON & BIRMINGHAM—there are five trains that pass the station each way daily (except Sunday), on Sunday three only.

. The trains (from London) arrive at Boxmoor in about an hour and a quarter from the time of starting; and those from Birmingham in about four hours and a half from the time of leaving that town. The exact time at which the carriages arrive at Boxmoor may be ascertained at the *Bell* and *King's Arms Inns*, High st, Hemel Hempstead, and at the *Fishery Inn*, Boxmoor. From the two first named houses *Omnibuses* start regularly to meet the trains.

CARRIERS—WAGGONS.

To LONDON,—Batchelor, from Bury mill end, & —Hughes, from the White Hart, High st, every Monday & Thursday afternoon, and —Claridge, and —Young, pass thro' Hemel Hempstead, every Tuesday and Friday evening.

To LEIGHTON BUZZARD,—Claridge and —Young, pass thro' Hemel Hempstead, every Sunday & Thurs. morning.

CONVEYANCE BY WATER.

To and from LONDON, and all places on the line of the Grand Junction Canal, goods are forwarded by the following wharfingers, viz. George Howard, John Austin, —Norris, and —Pedley, from Boxmoor; Thomas Ebborn, from St. Albans wharf, & John Gore, from Two Waters.

HERTFORD,

WITH THE VILLAGE OF HERTINGFORDBURY AND NEIGHBOURHOODS.

HERTFORD is a market town, and borough both corporate and parliamentary, possessing separate jurisdiction, locally in the hundred of its name—21 miles N. from London, 28 S.S.E. from Bedford, 32 S. from Cambridge, and the like distance N. by W. from Chelmsford; pleasantly situated on the river Lea, which is navigable to the town for small craft. The opinions of etymologists and historians are at variance with respect to the origin of its modern name: according to the venerable Bede it is derived from *Herud-ford*, or 'Red-ford,' an appellation acquired from a sanguinary battle fought on its site; while others deduce it from *Here-ford*, a 'military ford.' The corporate seal, however, represents *a hart in the water*, and the most prominent feature in the town's arms is *a hart couchant:* in ancient times this neighbourhood abounded with deer—and it may hence be inferred (an inference coincident with existing tradition), that its name originated from *Hart* and *ford*—imperceptibly changed to HERTFORD. So early as the reign of Alfred, considerable importance was attached to this town; the remains of a castle, erected at that period of our history, still attest the fact. From the Norman conquest down to the reign of Mary (who incorporated the town), and under subsequent sovereigns, Hertford obtained numerous privileges, most of which it still continues to enjoy; by an ordinance of Henry VI, no market within seven miles of the town was allowed to be held on the same day with Hertford market, on pain of seizure of the goods by the bailiff of the latter place. The town consists of three principal streets, meeting in the centre; these are lighted with gas from works situated on the Lea, the property of private individuals, who purchased them of the International Gas Company. The inhabitants are abundantly supplied with water from public works. The Lea is crossed by a toll-bridge; beyond this is Cow-bridge, laid over the Beane, a small river that falls into the Lea. The public buildings are the shire-hall, which stands in the market-place, comprising, in addition to the courts of law, a handsome assembly-room; very considerable improvements were effected in this building a few years since, when an excellent clock was placed in the front. The borough gaol, and the county house of correction, are seen on the road leading to Ware; and the general infirmary, a valuable institution (established in January, 1822), stands eastward of the town. Hertford has received several charters: the first from Mary—the last, previous to the municipal act of 1835, from Charles II. The late enactment placed the government of the town in the hands of a mayor, four aldermen and twelve councillors, with power to elect the usual assistant officers; it styled the corporate body 'the mayor, aldermen and commonalty of the borough of Hertford,' and conferred upon the borough a commission of the peace. The corporation have the power to hold a court of record for pleas of actions and debts under £20.: this privilege, which for some years had lain dormant, has been revived, and the sittings take place every Wednesday. The lent and summer assizes are held in the shire-hall, and the quarter sessions for the county and the borough are held in the same place every six weeks. There is a police establishment, consisting of a superintendent and four privates. This borough sent two members to parliament from the reign of Edward I to the 50th of Edward III; from that period the elections were discontinued till the time of James I, when, on petition, the ancient right was recognized and revived. The present representatives are the Hon. Wm. F. Cowper, brother to the Earl Cowper, and Viscount Mahon, son of the Earl of Stanhope. The mayor for the time being is the returning officer. The return of county members is made from this town. Hertford confers the title of marquess on the family of Seymour Conway. Two newspapers are published here—the 'Reformer' and the 'County Free Press;' they are both issued on Saturday. There are also three literary and reading institutions, namely, 'the Hertford Literary Institution and Library,' founded in 1831; 'the County Library and Reading-rooms,' formed in 1833; and the Old newsroom, in the market-place. Corn, malt and flour, of which large quantities are continually poured into the metropolitan market, are the staple commodities of Hertford; there are several breweries on a respectable scale, two oil-mills, and a considerable trade exists in coal and timber, besides a brisk general business.

Hertford comprises the united parishes of All Saints and Saint John, and the liberties of Little Amwell and Brickendon within the parish of All Saints; together with the united parishes of St. Andrew, St. Mary and St. Nicholas, in the archdeaconry of Huntingdon and diocess of Lincoln. The church of All Saints (the one most worthy of remark) is handsome and spacious, cruciform, and in the later style of English architecture, with a tower surmounted by a spire; within the church are several very ancient monuments: the living is a vicarage with that of Saint John's, in the alternate patronage of the crown and the proprietor of an estate called Balls, in this parish. St. Andrew's church is a neat edifice, with a low embattled tower surmounted by a small spire; the benefice is a rectory with the vicarage of St. Mary and St. Nicholas, in the gift of the crown. The churches of the other three parishes have long ceased to exist. There are places of worship for baptists, independents, the society of friends, Wesleyan methodists, and the Countess of Huntingdon's connexion. There are many public well supported charities: the blue-coat school (a branch of Christ's hospital) is a commodious building, affording accommodation for 420 boys and 80 girls; the senior of these are from time to time sent to the parent institution in London, as vacancies occur. The free grammar school here (now ably conducted) was founded in 1667 for the education of freemen's sons; the master, who is appointed by Lord Melbourne, is allowed to take boarders. Green and blue coat schools, and several others for gratuitous instruction, together with alms-houses and many minor charities, display the benevolent character of the inhabitants of this respectable town. Haileybury college, established in 1806 for the education of young men intended for the civil service of the East India Company, stands at a short distance from Hertford, on the London road—(for a list of the professors, &c., *see* under the head 'Public Buildings,' page 194. The weekly market is held on Saturday, when the business transacted in grain, particularly barley, is truly astonishing; much of the latter is in demand for the maltsters of Ware. There is also a number of sheep brought to the market. Fairs are held on the third Saturday before Easter, the 12th May, 5th July and 8th November, for horses, cattle, &c. At the census for 1831, the borough of Hertford (including the several parishes and the liberty of St. John without,) contained 5,247 inhabitants.

One mile and three quarters from Hertford, in the same hundred as that town, is the village of HERTINGFORDBURY. It contains the parish church, dedicated to St. Mary; and, by the last returns, the entire parish contained a population of 753 persons—being a *decrease* of twenty-six in the preceding ten years.

POST OFFICE, at the Junction of Fore street and Castle street, John Griffiths Austen, *Post Master*.—Letters from LONDON arrive every night at half-past ten, and are despatched every morning at four.—Letters from BIRMINGHAM, MANCHESTER and LIVERPOOL arrive (by cross post from St. Albans) every evening at seven, and are despatched every morning at seven.—Letters from other parts of the North arrive (by cross post from Ware) every morning at seven, and are despatched every night (Sunday excepted) at a quarter before nine—on Sunday they are despatched one hour earlier.—Letters (by penny post) are brought from and forwarded daily to HERTINGFORDBURY, BAYFORD and EPPING GREEN.

The regular delivery of LONDON letters commences at seven in the morning, but letters can be obtained the night of arrival by paying sixpence.—The office closes at ten at night.

*** The times of arrival and despatch of letters both for LONDON and places Northward will, it is anticipated, be altered and influenced by arrangements with the railways.

NOBILITY, GENTRY AND CLERGY.

Alington Henry, esq. Bailey hall
Anthony Rev. Isaac, Cowbridge
Baker Mrs. —, Bayford house
Baker Wm. Robt. esq. Bayfordbury
BaylyRev.Edw.Goodenough,Rectory
Best Capt. Wm. R. Vicarage, Bengeo
Bickersteth Rev. Edward, Watton
Birch Geo. esq. M.D. Hertingfordbury
Blake Mrs. Catherine, How green
Booker —, esq. Hertford heath
Bourchier Rev. Edward, Bramfield
Brassey George, esq. Bramfield
Byde Rev. John, Bengeo [house
Carter John Moses, esq. Cowbridge
Chambers Thos. esq. Port Vale house
Chauncey Chas. esq. Little Munden
Cherry Mrs. Mary, Fore st
Colbeck Rev. William R. Vicarage
Cowper Right Hon. Earl, Panshanger
Cowper Henry, esq. Tewin water
Cust the Hon. Captain, Ball's park
Daniell Mrs. —,Little Berkhamstead
Demain Rev. Hy. M.A. St. Andrew st
DimsdaleChas.J.esq. Essendon place
Dimsdale the Dowager Baroness, Sele cottage [place
Dimsdale the Hon. Baron, Campfield
Ellis Wynn, esq. Pensbourne park
Farquhar Sir Minto, bart. Golding
Feilde Rev. Thos. Hertingfordbury
FitzgibbonHon.Col.M.P.Warrenwood
Gilpin Rev. Barnard, Bengeo
Goodis Capt. Thos. West st [hall
Goslin Rear-Admiral Thos. Bengeo
Green Mrs. Elizabeth, Fore st
Green Thomas, esq. Port hill
Hatton Mrs. Ann, Wallfield,Castle st
Hickman Mr. Jos. Hertingfordbury
Horne Sir Wm. knt. Epping green
Hotham Hon.Capt.Geo.F.Woolmers
Hudson Wm. esq. Frogmore lodge
Hysham the Misses, North Crescent
Ibraheem the Meerza, Rose cottage, Hertford heath
Lewis —, esq. Bayfordbury farm
Lloyd the Misses, Hertingfordbury
Lloyd Rev. Thomas, Sacomb rectory
Longmore Philip, esq. (coroner, &c.) Fore st
Lucas Mr. James, Fore st
Manser Mr. William, Fore st
Medland William, esq. Castle st
Mills Thomas, esq. Tolmers
Morgan George Gould, esq. Brickendonbury house
Nicholson Geo. esq. (county treasurer, under sheriff, &c.) the Castle
Pollard Rev. John, Benington
Prescott Mrs. —, Hertingfordbury
Proctor George, esq. Bennington
Reay the Right Hon. Lord, Goldings
Roseberry the Honourable Earl of, Warren wood house
Sewell Rev. H. Little Berkhamstead
Smith Abel, esq. M.P. Watton wood hall [stead
Smith Miss Culling, Little Berkham-
SmithJno.Abel,esq.M.P.Sacomb park
Smith Thomas, esq. North road
Spence Edw.Robt.esq.North Cresent
StrattonWm.esq.Litt.Berkhamstead
Sutton George, esq. Bayford
Sworder Thomas, esq. Bull plain
Taylor MissPenelope,NorthCrescent
ThorntonClaudeGeo.esq.Marden hill
Townshend Capt. John, Ball's park
Vincent J. esq. Wore park
Woodward Mr. Joseph, Bengeo
Yeathard George, esq. Waterford

ACADEMIES & SCHOOLS.

Not otherwise described are Day Schools.

BLUE COAT SCHOOL (boys') Fore st —Rev. N. Keymer and — Coleman, esq. classical masters; Mr. G. Ludlow, writing master; Mr. R. A. Steele, steward; Mrs. S. Moore, matron
CHRIST'S HOSPITAL SCHOOL(girls') Fore st—Miss E.Thompson,mistrss
Cole James, Back st
FREE GRAMMAR SCHOOL (& boarding) Fore street—Clement Henry Cruttwell, master
GREEN COAT SCHOOL (boys') All Saints Church yard—Thos. Green, master
GREEN SCHOOL (girls') Water lane —Sarah Skerman, mistress
Mowbray Susannah, Back st
NATIONAL SCHOOL, Free School yard—William Miller, master
Nicolls William, Bull plain
Peck Ann and Eliz. Fore st [st
Poulton Wm. (brdg & day) St.Andrew
SCHOOL OF INDUSTRY, Water lane —Sarah Middleton, mistress
Taylor Wm. (ladies' & gent.'s boarding and day) Hertingfordbury
Towes Amelia Ann (boarding & day) Lombard house

ARCHITECT & ENGINEER.

Smith Thomas (and surveyor to the county of Hertford) North road, and 4 Bloomsbury square, *London*

ATTORNEYS.

Gripper and Prangley, Castle st
Medland William, Castle st
Nicholson and Longmore, Castle st
Powell and Spence, St. Andrew st
Silk George, St. Andrew st
Sworder Thomas, Bull plain

AUCTIONEERS.

Jackson Geo. (& estate agent) Fore st
Kimpton John H. and Son, Fore st

BAKERS.

Briden William, George st
Galer Henry, Butchery green
Garwood Peter, Fore st
Hogsflesh William, Castle st
Lancaster John, the Wash
Males Ephraim, West st
Manfield Thomas, Butchery green
Newman Mary, Maidenhead st
Turner William, the Wash
Whiston Hannah & G. S. Fore st
Wilkinson Thomas, Back st
Willmot Samuel, St. Andrew st
Wing George, West st
Wyman Charles, St. Andrew st

BANKERS.

Adams Samuel and Co. Fore st and *Ware*—(draw on Masterman and Co. London)
SAVINGS' BANK, Fore st—Robert Kember, secretary—(open every Wednesday from twelve to two)

BARGE OWNERS.

Adams and Co. Fore st
Andrews Samuel, jun. (and builder) Castle street
Ayres John, Priory wharf
Gripper John J. and Jasper, Gripper's wharf
Lawrence Edward and Robert, Old Cross wharf

BASKET MAKERS.

Kimpton J. S. and Son, Fore st
Wilds Henry, Fore st

BLACKSMITHS & FARRIERS.

Baker John, Old Cross
Britt James, Old Cross
Ford William, Hertingfordbury
George Henry, South lane
King Ann, Back st
Pennyfather George, Bengeo
Redman & Trott, St. Andrew st
Skerman William & James, Parliament row [Frog's hall
Wackett Jos. (and edge-tool maker)
Wells George, Fore st
Wilkinson James Fogg, Priory lane

BOOKSELLERS, STATIONERS AND BOOKBINDERS.

Austin Stephen & Son (to the East India College) Fore st
Simpson George (to the East India College) Market place
Staughton Simon (& Herts Literary Society rooms) Fore st

BOOT & SHOE MAKERS.

Adeane Henry, Mill bridge
Ansell Benjamin, Market place
Biggin John, Fore st
Brice William, Castle st
Chesher Henry, Fore st
Drew George, St. Andrew st
Grimes Thomas, Fore st
Mayers Daniel, George st
Mills James, Back st
Neal James, Fore st
Rice John, Hertingfordbury
Skerman Samuel, St. Andrew st
Terry Charles, St. Andrew st

BOOT, &c. MAKERS—Contd.
Twaddle William Christopher (manufacturer) Mill bridge
Wenham Thomas, Back st

BRAZIERS AND TIN-PLATE WORKERS.
Adams Edward, Church lane
Kiddill James (and whitesmith) the Wash
Nunn James, Fore st
Pamphilon Thomas, Fore st
Taylor Thomas, Market place

BREWERS.
Barnard Joseph, Fore st
Bentley John Hankin, Hertingfordbury
Carridge Samuel, West st
Carter John Moses, Saint Andrew street Brewery
Cater John Adams, Old Cross
Haggar George, Sele mill brewery
Hutcherson James, St. Andrew st
M'Mullen Peter, Mill bridge
Medcalf Thomas Driver, Back st
South Thomas, Back st
Wickham Edward, Mill bridge
Young Noah Robt. (extr. of) Fore st

BRICK MAKERS.
Darby George, Port vale
George William, near Jenningsbury
Trennery John. Sele wood

BRICKLAYERS.
Brown James, Fore st
Darby George, Port vale
Fordham John, Butchery green
Hutcherson James, St. Andrew st
Jefferies George, Hertingfordbury
Johnson Sarah (& plasterer) Saint Andrew street
Waller Richard (& builder) Fore st
Wilds William, Cow bridge

BUILDERS.
(See also Carpenters.)
Brown James, Fore st
Darby George, Port vale
Hutcherson James, St. Andrew st
Waller Richard, Fore st

BUTCHERS.
Farrin Robert, Bull plain
Farrow Joseph, Back st
Giles Henry, Maidenhead st
Hankin Sarah, Hertingfordbury
Hanley Sarah (pork) Fore st
Harris Robert (pork) Honey lane and the Wash
Harris Thomas, Bull plain
Hills Charles, St. Andrew st
Hills William, St. Andrew st
Hills William, jun. Castle st
Newman George, Fore st
Savill Joseph, Cow bridge
Scales Thomas, St. Andrew st
Thody William, Old Cross
Willmott Henry, Maidenhead st

CABINET MAKERS AND UPHOLSTERERS.
Clark John, St. Andrew st
Jackson George, Fore st
Kimpton John H. & Son, Fore st

CARPENTERS.
Marked thus * are also Builders.
(See also Builders.)
*Andrews Samuel, jun. Castle st
*Bentley Jesse, St. Andrew st
Bentley Jno. Hankin, Hertingfordbry
Carridge Samuel, West st
Chandler Joseph, Castle st
*Darby George, Port vale
Hinson Nathaniel, St. Andrew st
Jackson John, Back st
*Latter James Thomas, Old Cross
Nunn Robert, the Wash
Randall James, Maidenhead st
Rose John, Cow bridge
Sheffield William, Bengeo
Smith William, Butchery green
Taylor Charles, West st
*Tisoe Henry, St. Andrew st
Wenham Joseph, Priory lane

CHYMISTS & DRUGGISTS.
Haslam William, Fore st
Hughlings John Powell, Fore st
May Joseph, Market place

COACH BUILDERS.
Crawley Young, jun. Castle st
Fry George, Fore st
M'Mullen Henry, North Crescent

COACH PROPRIETORS.
Carter Charles & Co. Port vale
Carter Thomas & Co. Castle st
Staples John, Back st
Staples John, jun. Bull plain

COAL MERCHANTS & DEALRS.
(See also Corn Merchants, &c.)
Andrews Samuel, jun. Castle st
Ayres John, Priory wharf
Newton Benjamin, Mill bridge
Stocks Charles, Old Cross
Waller Richard, Fore st
Wing George, West st
Young Noah (executors of) Fore st

CONFECTIONERS.
Kidman John, St. Andrew st
Whiston Hannah and George Seymour, Fore st
Young John, St. Andrew st
Young Peter, Maidenhead st

COOPERS.
M'Mullen Peter, Mill bridge
Taylor James, St. Andrew st
Wing Thomas, Castle st

CORN MERCHANTS, CORN CHANDLERS & MEALMEN.
Marked thus * are also Coal Merchants.
(See also Millers and Mealmen.)
*Barnard Joseph, Fore st
Brown Samuel Neale and Richard, Old Cross
*Dack Sarah, Old Cross
Daines William, Fore st
Dorrington John, Stapleford
*Gripper John J. & Jasper (& salt & hops) Gripper's wharf
*Gutteridge Samuel (and seedsman) Fore st
Hinson Harriet, St. Andrew st
*Lawrence Edward and Robert, Old Cross wharf
*M'Mullen Edward, Maidenhead st
Peck Ann (flour) Fore st
*Randall James, Maidenhead st
*Wilkinson Thomas, Back st

CURRIERS AND LEATHER CUTTERS.
Gripper Charles & Co. (and manufacturers of patent engine straps) Gripper's wharf
Wenham Thomas, Back st

FELLMONGER.
(See also Tanners.)
Harris Robert, Honey lane and the Wash

FIRE, &c. OFFICE AGENTS.
ALLIANCE, William Nunn, Castle st
BRITISH (fire) and WESTMINSTER (life) Robert Kember, Fore st
BRITISH COMMERCIAL, Wm. Wilds, Cowbridge
CLERICAL and MEDICAL (life) Gripper and Prangley, Castle st
COUNTY, Jno. Lawrence & Co. Fore st
CROWN (life) Jno. Gardener, Fore st
NORWICH UNION, James Matthias Gilbertson, Fore st
PHŒNIX, Gripper & Prangley, Castle st; George Simson, Market place; William Prattchett, Bank, Fore st; James Medcalf, Fore st
ROYAL EXCHANGE, George Jackson, Fore st
SUN, Thomas Sworder, Bull plain
YORK and LONDON, Stephen Austin, jun. Fore st

FRUITERERS, &c.
Baines Richard, Old Cross
Baines William, Fore st
Camp William, Fore st
M'Lorinan Martha, Honey lane
Middleton Jno. (and slater) the Wash
Palmer William, St. Andrew st
Young Henry, Maidenhead st
Young Peter, Maidenhead st

FURNITURE BROKERS.
Clark John, St. Andrew st
Crawley Richard, West st
Drew George, St. Andrew st
Jackson George, Fore st
Kimpton John H. Fore st

GLASS, CHINA & EARTHENWARE DEALERS.
Field James & Son, Fore st
Joslin Elizbth. Parsons, Back street
Marshall Joseph, Maidenhead st

GROCERS, TEA DEALERS, &c.
(See also Shopkeepers, &c.)
Brown Saml. Neale & Rd. Old Cross
Champ Sagittary, Castle st
Davis John, Hertingfordbury
Ephgrave Joseph, St. Andrew st
Garwood Peter, Back st
Gilbertson James, Fore st
Lynott Martha, St. Andrew st
M'Mullen Edward, Maidenhead st
Medcalf James, Fore st
Rayment Edward Drury, Fore st
Searle Francis Benjamin, Market pl
Westrope Cordwell, near Bull plain

GUNSMITHS.
Gooch Thomas R. C. (and working cutler) Fore st
Gooch William, Back st
Nunn James, Fore st

HATTERS.
Davis James Warren, Market place
Judd Thomas (manufacturer and furrier) Maidenhead st
Leete Samuel, Maidenhead st
Pollard William, Market place
Rolf Charles, Fore st
Twaddle William Christopher, Millbridge

INNS.
Bull, Richard Southee (posting) Bull plain
Cross Keys, Thomas Philips, Fore st
Dimsdale's Arms, Jno. Bristow, Fore st
Falcon, Frederick Edwards, Fore st
Green Dragon, James Smith, Maidenhead st
Salisbury Arms, Henry Myall Mason, Fore st
White Hart (commercial) Robert Thomas, Market place

IRON FOUNDERS.
Isaacs Thomas, Folly yard
Wilkinson James Fogg, Priory lane

IRONMONGERS.
Folkard George, Market place
Kiddill James, the Wash
Nunn James (& furnishing) Fore st
Taylor Thomas, Market place

LAW STATIONERS.
Carter Henry Hunt, Castle st
Munday Wm. Gray. Maidenhead st

LIME BURNERS.
Brown James, Fore st
Drummond Robert Horatio (& road contractor) North Crescent

LINEN & WOOLLEN DRAPERS AND CLOTHES DEALERS.
Dear James, Maidenhead st
Gardener John, Fore st
Gilbertson James Matthias, Fore st
Gutteridge C. & F. Fore st
Pollard Joseph & Son, Market place
Sedgwick Samuel, Fore st

LIVERY STABLES.
(See also the Inns.)
Dorling Samuel (& bowling green, pleasure boat keeper, and tenant of the river Lea fishery) West st
Smith James, Castle st

MALTSTERS.
Adams Samuel, Old Cross
Barnard Joseph, Fore st
Carter John Moses, St. Andrew st
Cass John, Folly bridge and *Ware*
Cater John Adams, Old Cross
Christie & Cathro, Bull plain
Green Thomas, Porthill house
Gripper John J. & Jasper (& wharfingers) Gripper's wharf
Gripper Joseph & Son, St. Andrew st
Lawrence Edward and Robert, Old Cross wharf
Sheppard John, Park mills
Squire Henry, West st
Sworder John, Back st & *Ware*
Young Noah Robert, Fore st

MARINE STORE DEALERS.
Camp James (and rag) Back st
Crawley Richard, West st
Garwood Peter, Back st

MILLERS & MEALMEN.
Coleman Henry, Old Cross
Fordham John George and Henry, Horns mill
Grenoff Richard (county) Ware road
Haggar Thomas Neatby, Sele mill
Hitch Thomas Waller, Town mill
Hudson John, Town mill
Mason William, Dicker mill
Newman Thomas, Hertingfordbury
Palmer John Wm. Molewood mill
Sheppard John, Park mills
Squires Charles, Waterford
Wyman William, St. Andrew st

MILLINERS & DRESS MAKRS.
Clark Martha, West st
Cousins Sarah (and draper) St. Andrew st
Gilbertson James Matthias, Fore st
Grant Kitty, Old Cross
Gutteridge Cathn. & Fanny, Fore st
James Ann, Fore st
Minter Caroline, Bull plain
Nicholls & Kirkby, Maidenhead st
Petts Sarah, West st
Robins Sarah, Honey lane
Tattam Sarah, Fore st

MILLWRIGHTS.
Darby George (and engineer and machine maker) Port vale
Jordan Joseph, Hertingfordbury

NEWSPAPERS.
COUNTY PRESS (Saturday), Simon Staughton, Fore st
HERTFORD REFORMER (Saturday), Stephen Austin, jun. Fore st

NURSERY AND SEEDSMEN.
Dimsey John (and market gardener) Castle street
Francis Edward P. Hertford Nursery, North road
Hale Samuel & Daniel (and market gardeners) Ball's hill
M'Mullen Edward (seedsman) Maidenhead st
M'Mullen William, St Andrew st

OIL PRESSERS.
Fordham John, George and Henry, Horns mill
Mason William, Dicker mill

PAINTERS, PLUMBERS, GLAZIERS & PAPER HANGERS.
England Robert, St. Andrew st
Ginn Thomas, Castle st
Hancock George, West st
Hancock James, Fore st
Mowbray Susannah, Back st
Pamphilon Thomas (& brazier) Fore st
Rayment Jeremiah Joseph, the Wash
Stallibrass Sarah, Bull plain
Tisoe William, Maidenhead st

PERFUMERS AND HAIR DRESSERS.
Austin S. & Son (& library) Fore st
Carter Mary, Maidenhead st
Harding George, the Wash
Osborne Joseph, Fore st

POULTERERS.
Baines William, Fore st
Pritchett S. J. Mill bridge

PRINTERS—LETTER-PRESS.
Austin Stephen & Son (and music sellers) Fore st
Staughton Simon, Fore st

PROFESSORS & TEACHERS.
Bridgeman Charles (music) West st
Bridgeman Richd. (dancing) West st
Lequentre Adelson Julian Alexis (drawing) West st
Luppino Thomas William (organist of Ware church & Stanstead chapel) Fore street

SADDLERS AND HARNESS MAKERS.
Adkins Thomas, Fore st
Dring Thomas, St. Andrew st
Randall Samuel, the Wash
Roberts Thelwall, Market place

SHOPKEEPERS & DEALRS IN GROCERIES & SUNDRIES.
Bush William, Back st
Cousins Thomas, Old Cross
Evison Jane, Port vale
Garwood Peter, Back st
King Charles, Back st
Newton Benjamin, Mill bridge
Oakley Richard, Port hill
Tapping Joseph, St. Andrew st
Wilkinson Jane, Market place
Winfield John, Castle st

STAY & CORSET MAKERS.
Barrand Martha, Market place
Randall Eliza, Mill bridge
Reeve Lydia (and surgical) Saint Andrew street
Winters Harry, Maidenhead st

STONE & MARBLE MASONS.
Peck David (& statuary) Fore st
Smith Thomas (and statuary) St. Andrew street
Waller Richard, Fore street

STRAW HAT MAKERS.
Collins Louisa, West st
Gilbertson J. M. Fore st
Grumitt Ann, St. Andrew st
James Ann, Fore st
Nicoll Martha, St. Andrew st
Squires Ann, West st

SURGEONS, &c.
Bennington Robert, Bull plain
Colbeck Thomas & Thos. R. Fore st
Davies John, Fore st
Dickens George, St. Andrew st
Furnival John Jas. M. D. North crest
Norwood & Evans, St. Andrew st
Reilly Philip and Michael (& licenciates of Apothecaries' Halls, *London* and *Dublin*) Market place
Shillitoe Richard, Castle st
Towers George Augustus, North rd
Woodhouse John, St. Andrew st

SURVEYORS—LAND, &c.
Hollingsworth Daniel (& architect) Fore street
Kimpton J. H. & Son (& land agents) Fore st
Metcalf James, Fore st
Nunn Robert (buildings) the Wash
Sawyer Thomas, Port vale
Smith Thomas (& architect) North Crescent, & 4 Bloomsbury square, *London*
Wilds William (and building) Cow bridge

TAILORS.
Marked thus * are also Drapers.
Ashman George (and hatter) Maidenhead street
Austin John, St. Andrew st
Austin William, West st
*Cheek Thomas, Maidenhead st
Collins George, West st
Cousins James, St. Andrew st
Cousins Thomas, Old Cross
*Davis James Warren, Market place
Harris Thomas, St. Andrew st
Hill William, Castle st
Little George, Old Cross
Munnings Robert, George st
Randall Richard, Mill bridge
Reeve Oakley St. Andrew st
Rolf Charles, Fore st
Satchell James, Old Cross
Taylor Edward, West st
*Twaddle William Christopher, Mill bridge
*Wand Thomas, Market place
Webster Charles, Old Cross
Webster Maria, Mill bridge
Winters Harry, Maidenhead st

TALLOW CHANDLERS.
Gilbertson James (& oilman) Fore st
M'Mullen Edward, Maidenhead st
Rayment Edward, Fore st
Searle Francis Benjmn. Market place

TANNERS & FELLMONGERS.
(See also Fellmongers.)
Gripper Charles & Co. (and manufacturers of the patent straps) Gripper's wharf

TAVERNS & PUBLIC HOUSES.
Blackbirds, Thomas Wing, Castle st
Black Swan, Samuel Dorling, West st
Bull's Head, Charles Collins, Market place
Coffee House, James Ilott, Maidenhead st
Cold Bath, Jas. Hutcherson, St. Andrew st
Cowper's Arms, Samuel Jeans, Hertingfordbury
Crown & Thistle, Joseph Farrow, Back st
Globe, William Sheffield, Bengeo
Horns, John Green, Brickendon
Jolly Bargeman, Thos. Willborn, the Folly
Little Bell, Nathaniel Hinson, St. Andrew st
Maidenhead Inn, Robt. Hill, Maidenhead st
Old Red Cow, John Nicholson, Back st
Old Ship, Elizabeth Cook, Old Cross
Plough, William Viney, Fore st
Queen's Head, William Daines, Fore st
Ram, Elizabeth Devonshire, Fore st
Rein Deer, Richard Greenoff, Port hill
Robin Hood, Richard Hoskitt, Tunnel
Rose & Crown, Jos. Tyler, Maidenhead st
Three Tuns, Harriet Carter, St. Andrew st
Vine, Jane Wilkinson, Market place
Wheat Sheaf, John Hughes, Back st
White Horse, John Hankin Bentley, Hertingfordbury
White Lion, William Cock, Back st
White Swan, George Littleford, Fore st
Windmill, John Hollingsworth, Waterford
Woolpack, Mary Pinneberg, Old Cross

TEA DEALERS.
Edwards Jane, West st
Stevens Charles, the Wash

TIMBER MERCHANTS.
Andrews Samuel, jun. Castle st
Ayres John, Priory wharf

TOY DEALERS.
Munday William Gray (& stationer) Maidenhead st
Wand Thomas, Market place

WATCH & CLOCK MAKERS.
Bear Robert (& jeweller) Honey lane
Brodie George, Bull plain
Field James & Son (& silversmiths, &c.) Fore street
Petts William N. West st
Simson George (& silversmith and perfumer) Market place
Skerman William & James (church and turret clocks) Parliament row

WHEELWRIGHTS.
Clifford John, St. Andrew st
Crawley Young, jun. Castle st
George Henry, South lane

WHEELWRIGHTS—*Continued.*
M'Mullen Henry, North Crescent
Pennyfather George, Bengeo
Richardson John, Back st
Wilkinson James Fogg, Priory lane

WINE & SPIRIT MERCHANTS
Gripper John J. & Jasper (& ale & porter) Gripper's wharf
I'on Catherine (& porter and cider) Mill bridge
Lawrence John & Co. Fore st
M'Mullen Edward (& British wine) Maidenhead st
Smith Jas. (& agent to Barclay, Macdonald & Co. malt whisky distillers, *Scotland*) Maidenhead st
Young Noah R. Executors of (spirit) Fore street

Miscellaneous.

Booth Thomas, governor, & Sarah Booth, matron, of the Union Workhouse, Ware rd
Carter Henry Hunt, deputy registrar of births and deaths, Castle st
Chamberlain Thomas, leather gaiter, &c. maker, Parliament row [bridge
Cousens Saml. fancy worsted dealer, Mill
England William Hepworth, wire worker, Maidenhead st
Harris Robert, farmer, Priory
Hopwood Mary Sophia, matron to the Infirmary, North road
Kember Robert, clerk to the commissioners of taxes, Fore st
Middleton John, slater, the Wash
Neale Samuel, clothes warehouse & dyer, Fore street
Rayment Jeremiah Joseph, carver, gilder and printseller, the Wash
Shadbolt John, net maker, Butchery green
Simson John, registrar of births & deaths, Port vale
Sparrow George Jas. veterinary surgeon, St. Andrew st
Taylor Charles, farmer and cattle dealer, Priory farm [ket pl
Taylor Thos. clog and patten maker, Mar-

Public Buildings and Institutions.

EAST INDIA COLLEGE,
HAILEYBURY.

The Right Rev. the Bishop of London, *visiter* [*principal*
The Rev. Charles Webb Le Bas, A. M.
H. H. Wilson, esq. *visiter in the oriental department*

PROFESSORS.

Arabic—The Meerza Ibraheem [*dean*
Classical—Rev. James Amiraux Jeremie,
General Polity and Laws—William Empson, Esq. M. A. F. R. S.
Hindoo—Edward Vernon Schalch, Esq.
History—Rev. Richard Jones
Mathematics—Rev. Frederick Smith, *librarian* and *registrar*, and Rev. J. W. L. Heaviside [son, Esq.
Sanscrit and Bengalic—Frederick John-

COUNTY GAOL, Ware road—G. P. Duins, governor
GAS WORKS, King's meads—Thomas Hackney, superintendent
HERTFORD COUNTY LIBRARY & READING ROOM, Fore st
HERTFORD LITERARY AND SCIENTIFIC INSTITUTION & NEWS ROOM, Fore st
INFIRMARY, North road—George A. Towers, medical resident & secretary; Mary Sophia Hopwood, matron
NEWS & READING ROOMS (Old County), at Mr. Roberts', saddler, Market place
POLICE STATION, Parliament row—Thomas Knight, superintendent
UNION WORKHOUSE, Ware road—Thos. Booth, governor; Sarah Booth, matron.

COACHES.

To LONDON, the *Royal Mail* (from Lincoln) calls at the Salisbury Arms, every morning at a quarter before four—and the *Highflyer* (from York) calls at the Dimsdale's Arms and the White Hart Inns, every afternoon at a quarter past 1.
To LONDON, the *Times*, from the Cross Keys, every morning (Sunday & Friday excepted) at eight, and on Friday at a quarter before seven—the *Regulator*, from the Salisbury Arms, every morning (Sunday and Monday excepted) at nine, and on Monday at eight—the *Express*, from the Bull Inn, every morning (Sunday excepted) at eight—and the *Rocket*, every afternoon (Sunday ex.) at three, and on Sunday at four.
To LINCOLN, the *Royal Mail* (from London) calls at the Salisbury Arms, every night at half-past ten.
To YORK, the *Highflyer* (from London) calls at the Dimsdale's Arms, every forenoon at a quarter before twelve.

CARRIERS.

To LONDON, Edmund Fisher's *Waggons*, from Bull plain, every Monday, Tuesday, Wednesday and Thursday evening at five; through Haileybury, to the Catherine Wheel, Bishopsgate st—Thomas Wilkinson, from Back st, every Monday, Wednesday & Friday—James Fisher, every Tuesday and Friday—and — Wood's *Waggon* passes thro' (from St. Neots) every Friday.
To HITCHIN & BEDFORD, — Templar's *Van*, from the Green Dragon, every afternoon.
To ST. NEOTS, — Wood's *Waggon* passes through every Sunday morning.
To SIDLINGTON, — Mould's *Cart*, from the Queen's Head, every afternoon.
To WARE, HATFIELD & ST. ALBANS, — Tillock's *Spring Cart*, from the Green Dragon, every Monday, Wednes. & Fri.

HITCHIN,

WITH THE VILLAGES OF PRESTON, ICKLEFORD, OFFLEY, PIRTON, WHITEWELL AND NEIGHBOURHOODS.

HITCHIN is a populous market town and parish in the hundred of Hitchin and Pirton—34 miles N. N. W. of London, 16 N. W. of Hertford, and 17 S. E. of Bedford; delightfully situated on the river Hiz, at the base of a hill which shelters it from the easterly winds. The town has a high claim to antiquity, having been a place of considerable importance in the reign of Alfred, and formerly comprised in the Mercian territory. According to Norden its name is derived from a wood, called *Hitch*, which in the Saxon ages flourished at one *end* of the town. Two priories were founded here—one for nuns of the Gilbertine order, the other for White Carmelites: remnants of these religious houses are still in existence; the former, now called New Biggin, near the church—the latter towards the western extremity of the town, called the Priory, and forming part of the estate of F. P. D. Radcliffe, Esq. Many antiques have been discovered near Hitchin; among others a portable Roman altar was dug up in the orchard of the late Rev. Samuel James, M. A., in the beginning of the last century. The town is divided into three wards, namely, Bancroft, Tilehouse and Bridge, for the whole of which two constables and four headboroughs are appointed at the court leet of the lord of the manor (Wm. Wilshire, Esq.), held at Michaelmas. The county magistrates hold petty sessions here every Tuesday. The streets are for the most part spacious, partially paved, and lighted with gas; the environs are pleasant, and many noble mansions have lately been erected. As the district around is exclusively agricultural, corn, malt and flour are the principal articles of trade at Hitchin; the soil in the vicinity is peculiarly favourable to the growth of barley, of which great quantities are sold at the market—one of the best attended in the county. There are several breweries, two or three of which are upon a large scale; malting is carried on extensively, and many females are employed in making straw plat. The places of worship are the parish church, a large baptist chapel with a cemetery, two for independents, one for methodists, and a meeting-house for the society of friends. The venerable and beautiful church, situated near the centre of the town, was originally dedicated to St. Andrew; but on being rebuilt, prior to the reign of Henry VIII, it was dedicated to the Virgin Mary. It is a spacious structure of stone, chiefly in the later style of English architecture, with a low massive embattled tower, surmounted by a spire; the south porch is a splendid enriched specimen of that style. The interior is highly ornamented: on each side of the chancel is a chapel; and over the altar is a fine painting, by Rubens, of the offerings of the wise men of the east; there is also a font of singular beauty, with carvings of the twelve apostles. The benefice is a vicarage, in the disposal of Trinity college, Cambridge, and incumbency of the Rev. Henry Wiles. A free grammar school, endowed schools for boys and also girls, with infant, national and Sunday schools, benevolent bequests, apprenticeship funds, an admirably conducted dispensary, alms-houses, &c., form the principal charities. A public subscription library has been some years established, and there are several book societies. The market (toll-free) is held on Tuesday; the fairs, or rather holiday markets, are held in Easter and Whitsun weeks. Population of parish, in 1831, 5,211.

PRESTON, a small hamlet to Hitchin, has several respectable seats in its neighbourhood; it holds a charter for a fair, which is still maintained on the last Wednesday in October, when a considerable number of sheep is brought for sale; and these are the only circumstances connected with it that are worthy of notice.

About two miles north from Hitchin, in the same hundred as that town, is ICKLEFORD, a small village in the parish of its name, the etymology of which is traced from the *Ickling* or *Ickneild* street, one of the Roman roads. The church is dedicated to St. Catherine; the principal entrance is by a fine arch, in the Norman style of architecture: the living is a rectory, in the patronage of the Peers family; the present incumbent is the Rev. T. W. Thirlwall. Some degree of interest is attached to this church on account of its being the burial-place of Henry Boswell, king of the gypsies, who died in 1760, at the advanced age of 90; the remains of his wife and grand-daughter are likewise interred here. The parish contained, in 1831, 502 inhabitants.

OFFLEY (or GREAT OFFLEY) village and parish are in the same hundred as Hitchin, three miles west of that town—situated upon a commanding elevation. The church, dedicated to Saint Mary Magdalene, has a very handsome chancel; the living is a discharged vicarage, in the presentation of the Marquess of Salisbury. There is an endowed charity school here for children of both sexes. Offley Place, the manor house, a spacious and interesting edifice, was erected in this village, in 1600, by Sir Richard Spencer; and in the church is inscribed, upon black marble tablets, an account of that family. Population of the parish, in 1831, 967.

The small village of PIRTON, situated in the hundred and parish of its name, stands three miles north-west from Hitchin. The church, dedicated to St. Mary, is a neat edifice, with a square embattled tower rising from its centre; the living is united with that of Ickleford. A sheep-fair is held here on the fourth Thursday after the 10th of October. Population of the parish, 738.

WHITEWELL is a respectable village in the parish of St. Paul's Walden and hundred of Cashio, five miles and a half south from Hitchin. The church is dedicated to All Saints; the benefice is a vicarage, in the patronage of the dean and chapter of St. Paul's, London. In the parish are places of worship for baptists and independents. In 1831 the population of the parish of St. Paul's Walden amounted to 1,050 persons.

POST OFFICE, Bucklersbury, HITCHIN, John Palmer, *Post Master* (and general newspaper agent.)—Letters from LONDON arrive (by the Leeds mail) every night at a quarter before twelve, and are despatched every afternoon at half-past two and evening at eight.—Letters from the North arrive every afternoon at half-past two, and are despatched every night at a quarter before twelve.

POST, WHITEWELL, *Receiving-House* at William Eldred's.—Letters from LONDON arrive (by foot post from Welwyn) every morning (Monday excepted) at nine, and are despatched every evening at five.

NOBILITY, GENTRY AND CLERGY.

Allen Samuel, esq. Sun st
Arnold Mr. John, Ippolites
Baron John, esq. Ippolites
Baron William, esq. Bancroft st
Beckett Mrs. —, Hitchin hill
Bowyer Wm.esq.Mount pleasant hse
Bradley Mrs. Ann, Bull's corner
Burrows Mrs. —, Welbury hoo
Cammeron Rev. —, King's Walden
Cockayne Thos. esq. Ickleford house
Collison Brown, esq. New England
Curling William, esq. Bancroft st
Dacre Right Hon.Lord, Kimpton hoo
Darton Thos. Harwood, esq. Preston
Dove Mrs. Harriet, Ippolites
Drake Mrs. —, Paul's Walden
Duncombe Fredk. esq. Stagnel park
Fowler Rev. John, Kenning, B. A. Pirton
Geard Mr. Samuel Bradly, Bancroft street
Griffin Rev. Thomas, Hitchin hill
Hale William, esq. King's Walden
Hanscombe Wm. esq. Pirton grange
Hardy Rev. Charles, Whitewell
Hawkins Mr. Fredk. M.D.Bancroft st
Jeeves Mrs. Sarah, Bancroft st
Jeeves William, esq. Bancroft st
Jepps Mr. Richard, Hitchin hill
Kempton Mrs. Mary, Bancroft st
Kershaw Mrs. —, Paykes park
Lax Mrs. —, St. Ibbs bush
Lovell Peter Harvey, esq. St. Ibbs
Lucas the Misses Mary & Margaret, Tilehouse street
Lucas Rev. Richard, Tilehouse st
Lucas Mr. Thomas, Tilehouse st
Malein Miss Mary, Portmill lane
Marshall Mrs. —, Bancroft st
Oakley Richard, esq. Offley
Proctor Mrs. Ann, Tilehouse st
Radcliffe Frederick Peter Delme, esq. Hitchin priory
Read Miss Mary, Bucklersbury
Roberts Mrs. Catherine, Bancroft st
Salusbury Lady Mary Elizabeth, Offley place
Salusbury Rev. Thelwell, Offley vicarage
Sawyer Henry, Little Offley
Thirlwall Rev. T. W. B. D. Ickleford rectory
Times Miss Christiana, Bancroft st
Wiles Rev. Henry, Church yard
Wilshere Miss Ann, Bancroft st
Wilshere Mrs. Laura, Bancroft st
Wilshere Miss Mary, Bancroft st
Wilshere Thomas, esq. Bancroft st
Wilshere Wm. esq. M.P. Bancroft st

ACADEMIES AND SCHOOLS.
Not otherwise described are Day Schools.

Bristow Whiston (brdng.) Bancroft st
Brown Isaac (boarding) Bull corner
Clark Ann, Bridge st
Dunnage Letitia (brdng) Bancroft st
Emmerton Jas. (bding.) New England
FREE GRAMMAR SCHOOL, Tilehouse street—John Sugars, master
Goodwin Saml. (brdng.) Bancroft st
Hudson & Crouch (ladies' boarding) Bancroft street
INFANTS' SCHOOL, Dead st—Emma Burch, mistress
Metham Thomas, Whitewell
NATIONAL SCHOOL, Dead street—Nathaniel Brooks, master; Mary Ann Evered, mistress
NATIONAL SCHOOL, Whitewell—Ann Tomlin, mistress
Newton John, Tilehouse st
OFFLEY CHARITY SCHOOL (boys' & girls')—John Church, master; Ann Church, mistress
Pilgrim Charles Hallett, Whitewell
Sloper Sarah, Bridge st

ATTORNEYS.

Bentley William (and conveyancer) Tilehouse st
Hawkins John & William (& clerks to the magistrates) Sun st
Times Charles, Tilehouse st
Wright Septimus, Tilehouse st

AUCTIONEERS & APPRAISRS

Estwick William, Market place
Marks John, Cock st
Stanton William (and estate agent) Bull corner

BAKERS & FLOUR DEALERS.

Bates Thomas, Offley
Bonfield Samuel, Whitewell
Brown William, Cock st
Camp Mary, Whitewell
Carning William (& pork butcher) Tilehouse street
Cartwright William, Tilehouse st
Craft George, Back st
Fensom John, Bancroft st
Fox Mary, Hitchin hill
Jeeves George, Back st
Jeeves William, Back st
Kempson Thomas, Bridge st
Lane Samuel, Offley
Lewin Geo. (& biscuit) Bucklersbury
Malden John, Hitchin hill
Newton Henry, Bucklersbury
Olney Thomas, Offley
Rudd William, Ippolites
Saunders William, Whitewell
Thompson John, Market place
Topham Robert, Church yard

BANKERS.

Pierson Joseph Margattes and Son Cock st—(draw on Masterman & Co. London)
Sharples, Exton & Lucas, Cock st—(draw on Barclay, Bevan and Co.)

BASKET & SIEVE MAKERS.

Beaver George, Market place
Bullard Richard, Bancroft st
Scott Matthew, Market place

BLACKSMITHS.
(See also Whitesmiths.)

Beckingham John, Ickleford
Bowler John P. Pound lane
Bowler Samuel, Pound lane
Cousins William, Offley
Foreman Thomas, Bridge st
Foster William, Bull's corner
Lane William, Offley
Odell Jephtha, Pirton
Odell John, Bucklersbury
Odell Thomas, Bridge st
Swaine William, Preston
Thurrogood John, Offley
Tomlin John, Whitewell

BOOKSELLERS & STATIONRS.

Morgan John, Back st
Palmer John, Bucklersbury
Paternoster Charles (and music seller, binder and printer) Sun st

BOOT AND SHOE MAKERS.

Abbiss Josiah, Bucklersbury
Arnold James, Whitewell
Bates Thomas, Offley
Chalkley William, Whitewell
Clark James, Sun st
Crawley George, Back st
Ellard George, Market place
Fearey James, Tilehouse st
Foster James, Offley
Hunt David, Dead st
Law Thomas, Tilehouse st
Newman William, Biggin lane
Orsman John, Whitewell
Peters Joseph, Preston
Rooksby William, Church yard
Russell John, Church yard
Spencer Thomas, Biggin lane
Wilson Thomas, Bucklersbury
Wilson William, Sun st
Wright George, Sun st

BRAZIERS AND TIN-PLATE WORKERS.

Impey William, Dead st
Jackson James, Bridge st
Kempton John, Cock st
Langford William and Son, Sun st

BREWERS.

Cobb Edward, Bancroft st
Geard John Bradley, Bancroft st
Hill John, Whitewell
Lucas Wm. Jos. & Wm. jun. Sun st
Marshall & Pierson, Sun st
Timpson Henry Robt. (retail) Whitewell

BRICK MAKERS AND LIME BURNERS.

Jeeves Maria, Dead st
Ransom John, Silver st
Raves James, Bridge st
Sharp Abel, Maiden crofts

BRICKLAYERS.
Butterfield Abraham, Offley road
Goodship William, Pound lane
Jeeves Maria, Dead st
Pollard William, Tilehouse st
Raves James (and slater) Bridge st
Woodfield Jos. (& slater) Tilehouse st

BUTCHERS.
Atkin James, Tilehouse st
Atkin Richard, Bridge st
Bent John, Market place
Cook James, Market place
Crawley Daniel, Bancroft st
Crawley Daniel, jun. Cock st
Gascoine George, Bridge st
Gascoine William, Back st
Hall Thomas, Sun st
Hide James, Back st
Lewin William, Market place
Olney William, Offley
Poulter John, Back st
Robinson William, Preston
Saunderson Stephen, Whitewell
Spencer William, Bancroft st
Waby James, Whitewell
Walker William, Bucklersbury

CABINET MAKERS AND UPHOLSTERERS.
Estwick William, Market place
Galer Thomas (and turner) Back st
Langford William and Son, Sun st
Marks John, Cock st
Paternoster Jonathan, Bucklersbury

CARPENTERS.
Allen John, Silver st
Bowler William, Russell's slip
Carter Henry (and turner) Whitewell
Day Elizabeth, Ickleford
Joyner Daniel, Biggin lane
Lane Caleb, Bull corner
Lane Joseph, Sun st
Lane Samuel, Offley
Marks John, Cock st
Norris James, Church yard
Seymour John, Back st
Rudd Daniel, Ippolites
Toll Abraham, Whitewell
Winch James, Tilehouse st

CARVER AND GILDER.
Cooper James, Market place

CHYMISTS AND DRUGGISTS.
Perks Sarah, Cock st
Ransom Joseph, Sun st

CONFECTIONERS & PASTRY-COOKS.
Latchmore Thomas, Cock st
Milne Abigail, Cock st
Topham Robert, Church yard

COOPERS.
Bloom Robert, Bull corner
Rose Robert, Bancroft st

CORN & SEED DEALERS.
Burrows John, Market place
Chapman Michael, Market place
Clark James, Silver st
Farmer John, Sun st
Heath Thomas, Market place
Lewington Wm. (& coal) Tilehouse st
Young John, Back st

CORN, COAL, TIMBER & IRON MERCHANTS.
Pierson and Pope, Cock st

CURRIERS AND LEATHER CUTTERS.
Carr Thomas, Pound lane
Hainworth William, Bull corner
Peggram Thomas, Bucklersbury

FIRE, &c. OFFICE AGENTS.
COUNTY (fire) and PROVIDENT (life), Paternoster and Hoare, Cock st
PELICAN, Edward Clisby, Cock st
PHŒNIX, William Braund, Cock st; Edward Clisby, Cock st
ROYAL EXCHANGE, Benjamin Rider and Son, Sun st

GROCERS AND TEA DEALERS
Marked thus * are also Tallow Chandlers.
(See also Shopkeepers, &c.)
Button Elizabeth, Market place
Carter William, Bridge st
Cornell Marshall, Sun st
Crawley John (and hop merchant) Market place
*Hall William, Tilehouse st
Hardwick Thomas, Cock st
Heath Thomas, Market place
Kent James, Sun st
Latchmore Thomas, Cock st
*Lewin Luke, Cock st
Paddon George, Sun st
Shadwell Reuben, Bucklersbury
*Whitney & Paternoster, Market pl

HAIR DRESSERS.
Hawkins Richard, Market place
Impey Samuel, Bucklersbury
Impey Samuel, jun. Sun st

HATTERS.
Best George, Cock st
Rider Benjamin & Son (& clothiers) Sun st

INNS.
Angel (commercial) Thos. Lowden, Sun st
Sun (posting & commercial) Samuel Hill, Sun st
Swan (commercial) John Kershaw, Market place

IRONMONGERS.
Chapman William, Cock st
Crawley William, Market place
Gatward John, Cock st
Jackson James, Bridge st
Langford William and Son, Sun st
Rogers William, Bucklersbury

LINEN & WOOLLEN DRAPRS.
Conder George, Market place
Neal James William, Sun st
Paddon George, Sun st
Palmer Mary, Sun st
Smith and Newton, Market place
Syder James, Bucklersbury
Thompson John, Cock st

MALTSTERS.
Christy John, Bancroft st
Cobb Edward, Bancroft st
Folbigg William, Cock st
Hill John, Whitewell
Lawrence Robert, Market place
Lucas Wm. & Joseph & Wm. Sun st
Marshall and Pierson, Sun st

MILLERS & MEALMEN.
Armstrong Thomas, Portmill lane
Burr Edward, Charlton
Cox William, West mill
Nash William, Purwell mill
Priest John Crouch, Shitlington mill
Ransom Joshua, Grove mill
Rowley John, Ickleford mill
Welch Timothy, Tilehouse st
Wilmott William, Ippolites mill
Young John, Whitewell

MILLINERS & DRESS MAKRS.
Conder George, Market place
Cowley Mary, Market place
Newton Ann and Jane, Tilehouse st
Orsman Phœbe, Sun st
Palmer Mary, Sun st
Shelton Mary, Market place
Syder Elizabeth, Bucklersbury

NURSERY & SEEDSMEN.
Fells Abraham, Church yard
Hodgson Henry, Bull corner
Newton Daniel, Tilehouse st
Scrafton William, Offley road

PLUMBERS, PAINTERS AND GLAZIERS.
Baker James, Pound lane
Mackaness George, Whitewell
Newton Isaac & Son, Bucklersbury
Reynolds Anna, Church yard

SADDLERS AND COLLAR MAKERS.
Baker Thomas, Sun st
Clark Susannah, Bridge st
Cowley Robert, Sun st
Pierson James, Bucklersbury and Whitewell
Topham Sarah, Cock st
Weatherley John, Whitewell
Woodward John, Tilehouse st

SHOPKEEPERS & DEALRS IN GROCERIES & SUNDRIES.
Ambrose John, Bancroft st
Bullard Richard, Bancroft st
Camp Mary, Whitewell
Clement Samuel, Hitchin hill
Cooper James, Hollow lane
Davies Thomas, Dead st
Day John, Ickleford
Day Samuel, Ickleford
Day Squire, Back st
English Thomas, Preston
Festing Messing G. Hitchin hill
Francis John, Pirton
Furr William, Pirton
Jarvis George, Bancroft st
Milne Abigail, Cock st
Morgan Daniel, Preston
Olney James (and draper) Offley
Pursell Sarah, Offley
Reed George, Preston
Reed William, Whitewell
Reynolds James, Tilehouse st
Robinson James, Back st
Rudd Daniel, Ippolites
Saunders Martha, Whitewell
Saunders William, Whitewell

STAY MAKERS.
Button Harriet, Tilehouse st
Parker Edw. (& shoe warehouse) Sun st
Paul Thomas, Market place

STONE & MARBLE MASON.
Warren John, Dead st

STRAW HAT MAKERS.
Conder George, Market place
Dear Emma, Back st
Impey Fanny, Bucklersbury
Raban Martha, Biggin lane
Wilding Frances, Bucklersbury

SURGEONS.
Bally Archibald, Hitchin hill
Butler Thomas, Whitewell
Foster Oswald and Son, Bancroft st
Huston George Francis, Whitewell
Perks Watson, Cock st

SURVEYORS.
Pilgrim Charles Hallett, Whitewell
Wilding John, Tilehouse st

TAILORS.
Arnold William, Bucklersbury
Bates Joseph, Offley
Bellamy William (& draper) Sun st
Bentley James, Bridge st
Bentley William, Church yard
Blyuel William, Whitewell
Carrington George, Tilehouse st
Craft James (and breeches maker) Bancroft st
Elliman Ann (and clothier) Market place
Gascoine John, Back st
Groom George (and draper) Market place
Jeeves George, Back st
Jordon James, Tilehouse st
Pinnock George (and glover) Church yard
Raban Samuel, Biggin lane
Robinson George, Whitewell
Thompson John (& hatter) Cock st

TANNERS.
Keen Stephen, Bancroft st
Wellingham John & Samuel, Whitewell

TAVERNS & PUBLIC HOUSES.
Adam and Eve, John Allen, Silver st
Artichoke, Wm. Poulter, Market place
Black Horse, Ann Kingsley, London road
Boot, George Gascoine, Bridge st
Bricklayer's Arms, Abm. Butterfield, Offley road

Bull, William Camp, Ippolites
Bull, William Eldred, Whitewell
Bull's Head, John Carter, Tilehouse st
Chequers, John Young, Preston
Cock, Thomas Olney, Offley
Cock, John Platt, Cock st
Cross Keys, William Warren, Bull corner
Crown, George Sprigings, Bancroft st
Curriers' Arms, Daniel Cotton, Back st
Dial, Richard Atkin, Bridge st [hill
Duke of Wellington, Jon. Waller, Hitchin
Eagle & Child, George Johns, Whitewell
Fox, James Davis, Pirton
George, Luke Lewin, Cock st
Green Man, Mary Bates, Offley
Green Man, George Primett, Ickleford
Greyhound, Thomas Harper, London rd
Half Moon, Robert Bloom, Bull corner
Highlander, Wm. Scrafton, Offley road
King's Arms, Wm. Richardson, Bucklrsbry
King's Head, Mary White, Back st
Maidenhead, James Crouch, Whitewell
Old George, Thomas Day, Ickleford
Plough, Thomas Kempson, Bridge st
Plume of Feathers, John Chambers, Ickleford
Queen's Head, James Atkin, Tilehouse st
Red Cow, Thomas Smith, Market place
Red Hart, James Ellard, Bucklersbury
Red Lion, William Lane, Offley
Red Lion, William Lewin, Market place
Robin Hood, James Cooper, Hollow lane
Rose & Crown, John Bent, Market place
Royal Oak, Geo. Turner, London road
Shoulder of Mutton, Saml, Mayles, Pirton
Six Bells, John Burrows, Market place
Swan with Two Necks, Thos. Howard, Tilehouse st [st
Three Horse Shoes, George Bunyan, Cock
Three Moor Hens, Thos. Grant, Hitchin hill
Three Tuns, George Bailey, Tilehouse st
Trooper, Richard Bullard, Bancroft st
Two Brewers, John Gascoine, Back st
Wheat Sheaf, James Halsey, Tilehouse st
White Horse, Henry Chambers, Cock st
White Horse, Joseph Lake, Pirton
White Horse, Thomas Watson, Back st
White Lion, Daniel Crawley, Bancroft st

WATCH & CLOCK MAKERS.

Button Thomas, Tilehouse st
Field Chas. Nicholas, Market place
Gatward John, Cock st

WHEELWRIGHTS.

Carter John, Whitewell
Foster William, Bull corner
Foster William, Offley
Halsey James, Tilehouse st
Richardson Wm. Bucklersbury
Watson James, Back st
Watson Thomas, Back st

WHITESMITHS.

Goodchild James, Back st
Prudden George (and iron founder) Bucklersbury
Prudden Samuel, Cock st

WINE & SPIRIT MERCHANTS

Burton Edwd. Butterfield, Bancroft st
Lowden Thomas, Sun st
Marshall John and Augustus, Sun st

Miscellaneous.

Barrett William Lamb, fishmonger, &c. Sun st [Tilehouse st
Brown Thomas, steward to Earl de Grey,
Button Henry, tea dealer, Tilehouse st
Chambers Henry, flour dealer, Cock st
Cllsby Edward, glass, &c. dealer, Cock st
DISPENSARY, Cock st—Frederick Hawkins, physician [bury
Estwick Henry, clothes dealer, Bucklers-
FREEMASON'S LODGE (Cecil), held at the Sun Inn—Charles Times, secretary
GAS WORKS, Benge mead—John Hawkins, secretary
Gatward Frances, toy dealer, Sun st
Hall William, rope maker, Dead st
Hare Jno. furniture broker, Back st [st
Holiday Wm. veterinary surgeon, Tilehouse
Hicks Thos. cowleech, Ippolites [rian
LIBRARY, Sun st—Chs. Paternoster, libra-
Logsdon & Sons, coach builders, Bull cornr
Martin Wm. millwright, Ippolites [st
Maynard W. maltkiln plate mkr. Tilehouse
Nicholls James, fishmonger, Back st
Prudden George, gunsmith, Bucklersbury
Prudden Samuel, stove and range maker, Cock street
REGISTRAR'S OFFICE, Bancroft st—Wm. Stevens, superintendent registrar; Jas. Coleman, registrar, Hitchin hill
Ryder Benj. and Son, rag dealers, Sun st
Saunders Joseph, poulterer, Whitewell
Shelton Lavender, shoe and stay warehouse, Market place [st
Swaine William, straw plat dealer, Back
Tatham Benj. woolstapler, Bancroft st
UNION WORKHOUSE, Hitchin—Mr. Manning, governor. [Whitewell
Wellingham John and Samuel, farmers,
Whiting John, fellmonger, Market place
Winch William, coach-spring maker, Bucklersbury

COACHES.

All call at or go from the Sun unless otherwise expressed.

To LONDON, the *Royal Mail* (from Leeds) every afternoon at three—the *Times* (from Bedford) every morning (Sunday excepted) at ten—the *Uppingham* (from Kettering) every Monday, Wednesday & Friday afternoon at two—and — Kershaw's *Coach*, from the Swan, every Monday and Friday morning at six, and Tuesday, Wednesday, Thursday and Saturday morning at nine; all go through Welwyn and Hatfield.

To BEDFORD, the *Times* (from London) every evening (Sunday excepted) at a quarter past six.

To KETTERING, the *Uppingham* (from London) every Tues. Thurs. and Sat. at half-past twelve; goes thro' Bedford.

To LEEDS, the *Royal Mail* (from London) every night at half-past eleven; goes through Bedford.

CARRIERS.

To LONDON, Charles Brown's *Waggons*, every Monday, Wednesday and Friday —Samuel Cocking (from Biggleswade) and John Estwick, every Tuesday and Thursday—J. Hearn's *Waggons* (from Boston) every Sunday, Wednesday and Friday—and James Harper, every Monday and Thursday; all go from or call at the Cock Inn—William Reed, from his house, Hitchin, and Thomas Lucas, from his house, Whitewell, every Friday morning.

To LONDON (passing through Hitchin), Joseph Hickman and — Jinks, every Tuesday and Thursday—and — Lavender, every Thursday.

To BALDOCK, — Manning's *Cart*, every Tuesday and Friday.

To BEDFORD, Charles Brown's *Waggons*, every Tuesday, Thursday and Saturday—Joseph Hickman, every Tuesday and Saturday—and — Lavender's *Waggon*, every Thursday.

To BIGGLESWADE, Samuel Cocking's *Waggon*, every Thursday & Sunday.

To BOSTON, Joseph Hearn, every Tuesday, Thursday and Saturday.

To CAMBRIDGE, — Clutton's *Van*, every Tuesday and Friday; goes thro' Baldock, &c.

To LUTON, — Seabrook's *Van*, from the Sun Inn, every Tuesday & Friday.

To OUNDLE, — Jinks' *Waggons*, every Wednesday and Saturday.

HODDESDON,

WITH THE VILLAGES OF BROXBURN AND WORMLEY.

HODDESDON is a small market town and chapelry hamlet, partly in the parish of Great Amwell and partly in that of Broxburn, in Hertford hundred—17 miles N. by E. from London, 34 S. from Cambridge, and 4 S. by E. from Hertford; it occupies an elevated situation, on a line of communication between the metropolis and Cambridgeshire and the north, and from the consequent thoroughfare arises the principal support of the inhabitants, as they have neither manufactures nor any particular branch of local traffic, with the exception of a little malting business: the town, however, is the residence of many genteel families, the vicinity is highly respectable, and the country around has a most cheerful and prosperous aspect. The house and grounds of John Warner, Esq., are peculiarly attractive; the improvements pursued on the latter evince consummate judgment, and the embellishments are executed by persons of acknowledged skill and taste; the three figures brought here from Oatlands are in the first style of excellence. A small town-hall, with a tower called the 'clock-house,' and offices attached, are of recent erection. The inhabitants are supplied with excellent water from a conduit which stands in the Fore-street, the gift of Sir Marmaduke Rawdon in 1679. The Thatched House, where Izak Walton and his friend, Sir Henry Wotton, were accustomed to regale themselves after angling in the Lea, still perpetuates their memory. The chapel, originally erected in 1734, and rebuilt, in the Doric style of architecture, in 1827, is a commodious handsome structure. There are places of worship for independents and the society of friends. The principal charities are a national school for one hundred boys, and an endowed school for fifty girls—the latter founded by Mrs. Jones in 1818; and five alms-houses, provided by Richard Rich in 1440. The market day is Thursday, and a fair is held on the 29th of June. The population of the chapelry or hamlet of Hoddesdon amounted, in 1831, to 1,615 inhabitants; and with that portion of the town belonging to Amwell parish (375), presented a total of 1,990.

About one mile S. E. of Hoddesdon is the village of BROXBURN—its site a gentle acclivity, intersected by rich meadows, irrigated by the river Lea; the prospect from the church, which stands between that stream and the New river, embraces an extensive range. It is intended to erect a station-house for the Northern and Eastern railway within a quarter of a mile of the high road leading from London to Hoddesdon. The church, dedicated to St. Augustine, is spacious and handsome, with a tower surmounted by a spire; the interior is ornamented with some elegant monuments, and the font is of considerable antiquity: the living is a discharged vicarage, in the presentation of the bishop of London. The parish of Broxburn contained, in 1831 (exclusive of the chapelry of Hoddesdon), 529 inhabitants.

About two miles and a half south from Hoddesdon, in the same hundred, is the small village of WORMLEY; the New river passes through the parish, and the river Lea bounds it on the east. The church, dedicated to St. Lawrence, contains several monumental memorials, some of an early date; the edifice is entered by a Norman doorway, and the west end is surmounted by a square tower of wood. Population of the parish, in 1831, 471—being a *decrease* of twenty-one inhabitants in the preceding ten years.

POST OFFICE, Fore street, HODDESDON, George Allen, *Post Master.*—Letters from LONDON arrive every night at nine, and are despatched early in the morning.—Letters from the North arrive early in the morning, and are despatched at nine at night.

*** The completion of the Northern and Eastern Railway will effect an alteration in the post office regulations upon this line of road.

GENTRY AND CLERGY.

Auber Mrs. Catherine, Fore st
Auber Mrs. Jane, Fore st
Baker Miss Anne, Fore st
Baker Lieut.-Colonel, Norris lodge
Barnard Rev. Mordaunt, Primrose hill
Boreham Miss Elizabeth, Fore st
Bosanquet George Jacob, esq. Broxbourn park
Bounds William, esq. Wormley
Bridge Mr. Samuel Bradley, Fore st
Christie Mrs. Margaret, Fore st
Christie Peter, esq. Fore st
Clarke John, esq. Gideon house
Crowther Mrs. —, Amwell
Dampier Christr. esq. Amwell cottage
Deacon James, esq. Hailey
Downing Mrs. Mary, Fore st
East Mr. William, Hertford road
Fenner Thomas P. esq. Broxbourn
Griffin Mr. William, Fore st
Halden Mrs. J. Fore st
Hare Miss —, Wormley
Hare Charles, esq. Wormley
Hobbs Mrs. —, Fore st
Hughes Mrs. Hugh, Fore st
Keeling Mrs —, Broxbourn
Lawrence Mrs. Sybilla, Fore st
Lutyens Lewis Nich. esq. Broxbourn
M'Adam Mrs. Ann Charlotte, Fore st
Mylne Wm. Chadwell, esq. Amwell
Ottey Philip, esq. Broxbourn
Oxlade Mrs. —, Fore st
Palmer Christopher, Esq. R.N. Ware road
Palmer Edward, esq. Broxbourn
Pickthall Rev. Thos. M.A. Wormley
Robinson Robert, esq. Fore st
Searle Mr. Henry, Westfield house
Stephens Miss Sarah, Fore st
Stokes Joseph George, esq. Fore st
Tuck William, esq. Amwell house
Walker Mrs. —, Wormley
Wallace Mr. Thos. Rawdon cottage
Waller Edward, esq. Burfords
Walmsley Miss Ann, Yew house
Ware Mrs. —, Ware hill, Amwell
Warner John, esq. Warner's house, London road
Warner Mr. Robert, Fore st
Wilkes Robert, esq. Fore st
Wood Mrs. Ann, Rawdon house

ACADEMIES AND SCHOOLS.

Cooper Caroline and Jane, Fore st
Hill Francis (boarding) Broxbourn
NATIONAL SCHOOL (boys') Stanstead valley—Richard Mills, master
NATIONAL SCHOOL (girls') Fore st—Elizabeth J. Mills, mistress
Plume Mrs. F. Fore st
Wallace Thos. (brdg.) Rawdon cottage

BAKERS AND MEALMEN.

Armstrong Thos. Hoddesdon valley
England Thomas, Wormley
Haynes Daniel, Fore st
Iredale James, Wormley
Jefferies Samuel, Fore st
Stracey Daniel, Broxbourn
Williams Joseph Morgan, Fore st

BLACKSMITHS & FARRIERS.

Allen George (and white) Fore st
Allen Richard (& white) Broxbourn
Beckwith Samuel, Hoddesdon valley
Coomes Charles, Fore st
English James, Wormley

BOOKSELLERS, STATIONERS AND BOOKBINDERS.

Dickenson Geo. (& printer) Fore st
Sams Harriet & Arabella (& stamp office, library & silversmiths, Fore st
Tuffs Robert (and library) Fore st

BOOT AND SHOE MAKERS.

Allen Wilson, Wormley
Ashford James, Fore st
Aylott William, Hoddesdon valley
Betts Benjamin, Broxbourn
Blackaby John, Fore st
Griffin James, Fore st
Humphrey James, Chapel hill
Mansfield William, Wormley

BREWERS.

Christie & Cathrow (& maltsters and general merchants) Chapel hill
Widdecombe John, Fore st

BRICKLAYERS.

Allen William, Broxbourn
Andrews Henry, Fore st
Faint George, Fore st

BUTCHERS.

Aylin Thomas, Broxbourn
Boreham James (pork) Fore st
Clark Robert, Hoddesdon valley
Gocher James, Fore st
Hulls Thomas, Fore st
Humphrey Wm. Hoddesdon valley
Nottage Samuel, Wormley
Rowley Thomas, Fore st
Starling John, Broxbourn
Tuck William, Fore st

CARPENTERS.

Aylott Samuel, Stanstead valley
Cheffins George & Son (and builders) Fore st
Hampton William, Fore st
Nicholls John, Fore st
Smith Edward William, Broxbourn
Tingay Geo. (& cabinet mkr.) Fore st

CHYMISTS & DRUGGISTS.

Coulson Watson, Fore st
Sams Harriet and Arabella, Fore st

CLOTHES DEALERS.

Parker Philip, Broxbourn
Samuel Saul, Fore st

COACH BUILDER.

Perkins William Henry (& inventor, patentee and manufacturer of the regulating malting caps) Hoddesdon valley

COAL MERCHANTS.

Allen George, Fore st
Crosby William, Fore st
Williams Joseph Morgan, Fore st

CORN CHANDLERS.

Green William, Fore st
Newell Richard, Stanstead valley
Wood Susannah Ann, Fore st

FIRE, &c. OFFICE AGENTS.

COUNTY, Edward Lock, Fore st
PHŒNIX, George Allen, High st
SUN, Charles Whitley, Fore st
UNION, Caius Cheffins, Broxbourn

GROCERS AND DEALERS IN SUNDRIES.

Collins William, Fore st
Cozens Henry, Broxbourn
Davis William, Fore st
Dearsley William, Fore st
Finch Ann, Stanstead valley
Logsdon Charles, Broxbourn
Lyne Thomas, Amwell
North Elizabeth, Fore st
Pryor Joseph, Fore st
Sams William, Fore st
Waller Wm. Richard Hellings, Fore st
Wellman Thomas, Broxbourn
Wills William, Wormley
Wiseman William, Wormley

HAIR DRESSERS.

Dorrington Edward, Fore st
Sherrell James, Fore st
Smith James, Spittle brook

INNS.

Bull, Thomas Aylin, Broxbourn
Bull, Richard King (posting & commercial) Fore st
Salisbury's Arms, John Widdecombe, Fore st

IRONMONGERS.

Allen George, Fore st
Allen Richard, Broxbourn

LINEN & WOOLLEN DRAPRS.

Bell Thomas, Broxbourn
Collins William, Fore st
Lock Edward, Fore st
Tuck Christopher, Fore st

MILLERS.

Heavers John, Broxbourn mills
Manser James Poulter, Hoddesdon

MILLINERS & STRAW HAT MAKERS.

Fuller Sarah, Fore st
Pegram Esther, Fore st
Thompson Susanna, Fore st
Thorp Martha, Fore st
Wells Catherine, Fore st

PLUMBERS, PAINTERS, GLAZIERS & PAPER HANGERS.

Dunn & Hunt, Fore st
Dymock Charles, Fore st
Sams Henry, Fore st
Thorpe George, Fore st

SADDLERS.

Hunt Thomas, Fore st
Plume Edward, Fore st

SURGEONS.

Gosse William, Fore st
Horley William (and registrar of births and deaths) Fore st

TAILORS.

Cooper Mary, Wormley
King John, Chapel hill
Morrell James, Wormley
Waidson James, Fore st
Whitley Charles, Fore st

TAVERNS & PUBLIC HOUSES.

Bell, Esther Wright, Stanstead valley
Boar's Head, Chas. Perry, Stanstead valley
Crown, George and Thomas Want, Broxbourn bridge
Duke William, John Roberson, Ware road
Fox, Elizabeth Nicholls, Fore st
George, Ann Wood, Fore st
Globe, William Wiseman, Wormley
Golden Lion, William Jones, Fore st
Green Man, William Clarke, Broxbourn
Harrow, James Sams, Fore st
King William, Thos. Wellman, Broxbourn
Maidenhead, John Merison, Chapel hill
Queen's Head, Mary Ann Dunton, Fore st
Star, Mary Wiseman, Wormley
Swan, (old London and country waggon house) Samuel Wood, Fore st
White Bear, Sarah Nicholls, Broxbourn
White Horse, William Woodward, Wormley

WHEELWRIGHTS.

Gaylor Samuel, Stanstead valley
Perkins Wm. Hy. Hoddsdon valley
Sams James, Fore st
Tabraham Leonard, Broxbourn

Miscellaneous.

Cheffins Caius, auctioneer and surveyor, Broxbourn
Francis Elizabeth, confectioner, Fore st
Gillet John, marine store dealer, Duke st
Guiver Thomas, coach proprietor, Fore st
Hammond Edward, watch maker, Fore st
Jones William, fruiterer, &c. Fore st
Metheringham Benjamin, supervisor of excise, Fore st
Oakden John, glass, china, and earthenware dealer, Fore st
Phipps James, cooper, Fore st
Satchwell Thomas, tobacconist, Fore st
Squires Thomas, fishmonger, Chapel hill

COACHES.

To LONDON, the *Union*, from the Bull Inn, every morning (Sunday excepted) at eight, and on Sunday at seven—the *Times* (from Hadham) every morning (Sunday & Monday excepted) at eight, and on Monday at seven—and Guiver's *Fly* (from Roydon) every morning at 8.

To and from LONDON and the NORTH, HERTFORD, HOLBEACH, HUNTINGDON, LINCOLN, LOUTH, LYNN, PETERBOROUGH, ST. IVES, STAMFORD, WISBEACH, YORK, &c. *Coaches* pass through daily, the greater number of which call at the Bull Inn.

To HADHAM, the *Times* (from London) calls at the Bull Inn, every evening at six.

To ROYDON, Guiver's *Fly*, every evening at six.

CARRIERS—WAGGONS.

All from the Swan, Fore st, unless otherwise expressed.

To LONDON, — Kidman, — Little, — Elburn, and — Biscoe, every Tuesday and Friday; — Jordan, every Sunday and Friday; — Reynolds and — Pittey, every Tuesday; — Docwra, every Wednesday; — Gilby, every Thursday, and — Peters, every Friday.

To LONDON, Thomas Deacon, every Tuesday and Friday, and James Boreham, every Monday and Thursday, from their respective houses, Fore street.

To ASHWELL, — Pittey, every Wednesday evening.

To BALDOCK, — Little, every Wednesday aud Saturday evening.

To BASSINGBOURN and ROYSTON, — Elburn, every Sunday and Thursday evening.

To BUNTINGFORD, — Biscoe, every Wednesday and Saturday evening.

To GODMANCHESTER, — Docwra, every Thursday evening.

To MELBOURNE, — Gilby, every Friday evening.

To POTTON, — Peters, every Saturday evening.

To ROYSTON, — Reynolds, every Wednesday evening.

To ST. IVES, CHATTERIS, MARCH and WISBEACH, — Kidman, every Wednesday and Saturday evening.

To ST. NEOTS, — Jordan, every Monday and Saturday evening.

KINGS LANGLEY, ABBOTS LANGLEY

AND NEIGHBOURHOODS.

KINGS LANGLEY is a village and parish in the hundred of Dacorum—20 miles N. N. W. from London, 19 W. S. W. from Hertford, 5 N. from Watford, and 3½ S. from Hemel Hempstead. In ancient days this village was a regal residence: Henry III erected a palace here, which subsequently was the birth place of Edmund Langley, son of Edward V; these circumstances sufficiently demonstrate the origin of the present name of the place: scarcely a vestige of the once splendid abode of royalty remains—a farm-house now occupies a small portion of its site. A Dominican priory was founded here in the thirteenth century, and richly endowed; Speed states the amount of its revenues, at the period of the general dissolution, to be £150. 14*s*. 8*d*. The village, at the present day, is of comparatively trifling consideration; nevertheless it contains many respectable inhabitants, and the manufacture of paper is carried on rather extensively; there is likewise a considerable brewery, and in the vicinity are several corn mills. The church, dedicated to All Saints, is a neat structure of flint and stone, with a large embattled tower at its western end; the benefice is a vicarage, in the patronage of the bishop of Ely. The other places of worship comprise a chapel erected by a congregation of independents in 1836, and (at Chipperfield, in this parish,) a chapel of ease for the establishment and one for baptists. In 1831 the parish contained 1,423 inhabitants.

ABBOTS LANGLEY is a village and parish in the hundred of Cashio, situated a short distance to the west of the main road to St. Albans, between that town and Kings Langley, nearly two miles from the latter place; it formerly belonged to the abbey of St. Albans, and thus obtained its present designation. This parish is reputed to have been the birth-place of Adrian IV, the only Englishman who ever attained the pontifical dignity, which he enjoyed, however, but four years; in 1159 he received his death by poison, said to have been administered by a citizen of Rome, whose son he refused to create a bishop; his English name was Nicholas Breakspeare, and a farm near the village is still called 'Breakspeare farm:' as head of the church he was imperious and arrogant—a disposition that was forcibly exemplified by his refusal to invest the emperor Frederick with the imperial diadem, till that monarch had previously prostrated himself before him, and held the stirrup of his horse while he mounted. The church, dedicated to St. Lawrence, is a commodious and rather a handsome structure, having a chapel connected with it; the church contains some handsome and ancient monuments. Richard II was interred here, though his remains were subsequently exhumed and removed to Westminster. There are two free schools in the village, and at Bedmond (within the parish) is a chapel for independents. The Grand Junction canal passes through both parishes, and a view of the London and Birmingham railway can be obtained from both villages. The parish of Abbots Langley contained, in 1831, a population of 1,980 persons.

POST OFFICE, KINGS LANGLEY, John Roberts, *Post Master*.—Letters from LONDON arrive every night at a quarter before eleven, and are despatched every morning at a quarter before five.—Letters from the North arrive every morning at a quarter before five, and are despatched every night at a quarter before eleven. The delivery of letters commences every morning at eight.

*** *The letters* K. L. *signify* KINGS LANGLEY, *and* A. L. ABBOTS LANGLEY.

GENTRY AND CLERGY.

Atkinson Robert Hall, esq. Troley house, Abbots Langley
Bagot Wm. esq. Langley house, A. L.
Betts Mr. John, Kings Langley
Butt Rev. John Wm. (vicar of Kings Langley) Vicarage
Cromack Mr. Thomas, Kings Langley
Dennis Rev. Henry, Chipperfield
Dickinson Jno. esq. Blackhill house, Abbots Langley
Dutton Mrs. Mary, Kings Langley
Evans Mr. Joseph, Chipperfield
Foskett Capt. Geo. Rose hill, A. L.
Gambier Col. —, Hasle wood, A. L.
Hill Mr. Joseph, Main st, Kings L.
Jackson Mrs. —, Hill cottage, A. L.
Lefont Mrs. Jane, Barns lodge, K. L.
Lewis Rev. William, Vicarage, A. L.
Longman Chas. esq. Nash mills, A. L.
Mure James, esq. Cecil lodge, A. L.
Parsley Jno. esq. Chipperfield house, Kings Langley
Sinclair Mr. Jno. Two Waters, Kings Langley
Smith Mrs. Sarah, Abbots Langley
Solly Samuel Reynolds, esq. Serge hill, St. Stephen's
Squire Miss Dorcas, Kings Langley
Tomlin Rev. Jas. Bulstrode-Chipperfield, Kings Langley
Whittingstall Edmund Fernley, esq. Langley Bury
Wotton Mr. Richard (surgeon) Kings Langley
Wotton Mr. William, Kings Langley

ACADEMIES AND SCHOOLS.

BAGOT'S FREE SCHOOL, Abbots Langley—Cath. Wood, mistress
Brett Robert (day) Bedmond, A. L.
Jagger James (boarding & day) K. L.
NATIONAL SCHOOL, Abbots Langley—John Parker, master
SUBSCRIPTION SCHOOL (girls'), Kitters green, Abbots Langley—Sarah Taylor, mistress

BAKERS.

Dell William, Nash mills, A. L.
Eales Thomas, Chipperfield, K. L,
Gibbs David, Abbots Langley
Sutton Henry, Kings Langley
Warren Samuel, Kings Langley
Weedon William Henry, Bedmond

BLACKSMITHS.

Dell Thomas (and farrier) Kings L.
How Edmund, Bedmond, Abbots L.
King William, Abbots Langley
Monk John, Water side, Kings L.

BOOT & SHOE MAKERS.

Catlin John, Kitters green, A. L.
Gentle Philip, Chipperfield, K. L.
Payne Oliver, Bedmond, Abbots L.
Seare Henry, Kings Langley
Seare William, Kings Langley
Simmons Caleb, Chipperfield, K. L.
Sturman George, Kings Langley
Sturman Richard, Kings Langley
Trapp John, Tibbs hill, Abbots L.
Turner John, Bedmond, Abbots L.

BREWER.

Groome John Andrew, Kings Langley

BRICKLAYERS.

Bateman Wm. Kings Langley hill
Bisney Mark, Bedmond, Abbots L.
Bunker William, Tanners, Abbots L.
Harris Samuel, Bedmond, Abbots L.
Hosier William, Kings Langley
Tyers William, Kings Langley

BUTCHERS.

Jordan James, Chipperfield, K. L.
King George (pork) Abbots Langley
Leach Caroline, Kings Langley
Mead Thomas Andrew, Kings L.
Oldfield Obed, Hunton bridge
Simons Robert, Abbots Langley

CARPENTERS.
Chalk Joseph, Abbots Langley
Darvill William, Under the Heavens
Dickinson Thomas, Bedmond, A. L.
Gulstone Daniel, Bedmond, A. L.
Paine William, Kings Langley
Tyers William, Kings Langley

COAL MERCHANTS.
Monk John, Water side, Kings L.
Oldfield Obed, Hunton bridge, K. L.

GROCERS AND DEALERS IN SUNDRIES.
Biggs Henry, Chipperfield, Kings L.
Catlin John, Kitters green, A. L.
Chalk Hannah, Abbots Langley
Culley Henry, Chipperfield, K. L.
Dell William, Nash mills, Abbots L.
Dowse John, Bedmond, Abbots L.
Ellerd George, Kings Langley
Evilthrift George, Kings Langley
Gibbs John, Hunton bridge
Gilmore Hannah, Abbots Langley
Ginger William, Kings Langley
Glenister Owen, Bedmond, A. L.
Hill Joseph, Kings Langley
Ives John, Bedmond, A. Langley
Monk John, Waterside, Kings Langley
Reddall Ann, Waterside, K. Langley
Smith Thomas, Nash mills
Spicer Edward, Kings Langley
Weedon Thomas, Kings Langley
Young James, Kings Langley

MILLERS.
Carpenter John, Hunton mill, Abbots Langley
Howard Wm. Hunton mill, Abbots Langley
Kemp John, Chipperfield, K. L.
Toovey Thomas, Kings Langley mills

PAPER MAKERS.
Dickinson John and Co. Nash mills, and at *London* and *Manchester*

PLUMBERS, PAINTERS AND GLAZIERS.
Ellard George, Kings Langley
Godman Henry, Abbots Langley
Spicer Edward, Kings Langley

TAILORS.
Chalk John, Abbotts Langley
Crew William, Abbots Langley
Hill Joseph, Kings Langley
James Jos. Lewis, Kittersgreen, A.L.
Smith William, Kings Langley
Young James, Kings Langley

TAVERNS & PUBLIC HOUSES.
Bell, George Barter, Bedmond, Abbots L.
Bell, Joseph Barton, Primrose hill
Compasses, Amelia Thick, Troby bottom
Eagle, William Rose, Kings Langley
George, William Fountain, Nash mills
Jolly Boat Man, John Monk, Waterside, Kings Langley
King's Head, George King, Abbots Langley
King's Head, Obed Oldfield, Hunton bridge
Plough, Wm. Darvill, Under the Heavens
Red Lion, James Harley, Waterside, K. L.
Red Lion, Wm. Holloway, Nash mills, K. L.
Rose & Crown, Richard Osler, Leverstock green, Abbots Langley
Rose & Crown Inn, Martha Page, King's Langley
Saracen's Head, Thomas Andrew Mead, Kings Langley
Three Tuns, William Smith, Nash mills
Two Brewers, John Kemp, Chipperfield, Kings Langley
Unicorn, John Wrench, Gallows hill, Abbots Langley
White Hart, Isaac King, Bedmond, A. L

WHARFINGERS.
Monk John (and dealer in corn, salt, hay, straw, &c.) Waterside wharf, Kings Langley
Oldfield Obed, Hunton bridge wharf, Kings Langley

WHEELWRIGHTS.
Austin William, Kings Langley
Chalk George, Abbots Langley
Saunders Samuel, Bedmond, A. L.
Taylor Richard, Chipperfield, K. L.

Miscellaneous.
Baldwin Ann, straw plat dealer, Kings L.
Carvell Thomas, fishmonger, &c. Kings L.
Harley James, gardener, Waterside, K. L.
Leach Ann, dress maker, Kings Langley
Roberts John, iron founder, Kings Langley
Robinson, John, saddler, Kings Langley
Tovey Benjamin, maltster, Abbots Langley
Weedon Thos. corn dealer & mealman, K.L.
Wingfield Wm. veterinary surgeon, Sarratt

COACHES.
To LONDON, the *Royal Mail*, from the North, passes through Kings Langley, every morning at a quarter before five, and, on its rout to the NORTH, every night at a quarter before eleven.
To LONDON, the *Despatch* (from Aylesbury) passes through Kings Langley, every morning at ten, and to AYLESBURY, every evening at five.

CONVEYANCE BY RAILWAY.
To and from LONDON and BIRMINGHAM, the Railway trains pass the BOXMOOR station, one mile and a half from HEMEL HEMPSTEAD, which town see for more particular information respecting the trains, as also for waggons, &c. many of which pass through Kings Langley.

CONVEYANCE BY WATER.
To LONDON and all parts on the line of the Grand Junction canal, goods are forwarded by John Monk, Waterside wharf, and Obed Oldfield, Hunton bridge wharf, wharfingers.

MIMMS (SOUTH AND NORTH), POTTERS BAR, RIDGE,
SHENLEY AND NEIGHBOURHOODS.

SOUTH MIMMS is a village and parish in the hundred of Edmonton, Middlesex—14 miles from London, and nearly 4 miles N. N. W. from Chipping Barnet. The village is seated on the main road leading from London to Birmingham, Manchester, Liverpool, &c., and to this situation is to be attributed whatever little business is done in the place; but the majority of the inhabitants derive their support from agricultural employment. The parish church, dedicated to St. Giles, is of considerable antiquity; its tower is clothed in ivy, and the interior of the church contains a monument or two of very remote erection. The living is a discharged vicarage, in the patronage of the family of Hammond; the Rev. Thomas Price is the present incumbent. The parish contained, in 1831, 2010 inhabitants.

NORTH MIMMS is a village in the hundred of Dacorum, Hertford, two miles from South Mimms. Near the 'Maypole' inn, in this village, at a place called Water-end, is one of those natural curiosities presented by waters collected among the hills disappearing (in 'swallow-holes,' as they are termed,) with a great noise: the direction of these waters is unknown, but it is conjectured that they feed the New river stream at Amwell. The church, dedicated to St. Mary, contains some monuments and brasses with inscriptions worth perusal; amongst these is one to lord chancellor Somers, who died in 1716. The living is a discharged vicarage, in the presentation of Mr. Gaussen. In a delightful situation here is North Mimms Place, the beautiful and much admired seat of Alderman Sir William Heygate, Bart. Population of the parish, in 1831, 1,068.

About three miles from South Mimms, in that parish, is the hamlet of POTTERS BAR. A handsome chapel of ease was erected here, by subscription, in 1835, at an expense of five thousand pounds, and largely endowed by George Byng, Esq. M. P., of Wrotham Park.

About one mile from South Mimms, in the hundred of Cashio, lie the village and parish of RIDGE, watered by the river Colne. The church is dedicated to Saint Margaret; the benefice, a vicarage, is in the patronage of the Earl of Hardwick. Population of the parish, 347.

Two miles from London Colney, South Mimms and Ridge, in the hundred of Dacorum, is SHENLEY village and parish. The church, dedicated to St. Botolph, is a neat small edifice of flint and brick, containing some handsome & interesting monuments, and a good organ: the living is a rectory, in the patronage and incumbency of the Rev. T. Newcome. Population, in 1831, 1,167.

POST, SOUTH MIMMS, *Receiving-House* at Edward Walley's, Cross Keys Inn.—Letters from LONDON arrive every morning at nine and afternoon at two, and are despatched every morning at eight, afternoon at three and evening at five.

POST, NORTH MIMMS.—Letters (by foot post) are brought from and forwarded to HATFIELD every morning at nine and afternoon at three.

Receiving-Houses—POTTERS BAR, at George Pallett's, the Green Man Inn; RIDGE, at Stephen Swain's, the Old Guinea; and SHENLEY, at Thomas Hampton's, baker.—The arrival and despatch of letters for these places the same as at North Mimms.

*** *Other persons and residences belonging to the parish of* SOUTH MIMMS, *but locally situated in* CHIPPING BARNET, *will be found in the directory of that town, page* 181. *The letters* N. M. *mean* NORTH MIMMS, *and* S. M. SOUTH MIMMS.

NOBILITY, GENTRY AND CLERGY.

Barlow Mr. Nathaniel, South Mimms
Barroneau Mrs. Eliz. New lodge, S.M.
Bayles Mr. Thomas, Ridge
Brooks William, esq. Kitwell ridge
Byng George, esq. M.P. Wrotham park
Cameron David, esq. Northaw place
Carpenter William Leonard, esq. Potters Bar [Potterells
Casamajor William Charles, esq.
Davies Rev. Sml. Parsonage, Northaw
Durant Enosh, esq. High Canons, Shenley [Mimms
Fox Hny. esq. Gannick corner, South
Gaussen Robert Williams, esq. Bell bar, North Mimms
Gill Hamilton, esq. Shenley lodge
Gould Admiral Sir Davidge, K.C.B. Hawkshead, North Mimms
Hammond James, esq. Potters Bar
Hardwicke the Countess Dowager, Tittenhanger [hall, Ridge
Hearne Thos. William, esq. Deave's
Heygate Sir William, bart. North Mimms place
Hicks John, esq. Dancer's hill
Kemble Mrs. Virginia, Leggatts, N.M.
Le Blanc Thomas, esq. Nyn lodge, Northaw
Lemm Mr. Michael, Potters Bar
Lysley William Jno. esq. Mimmwood
Marryatt Charles, esq. Cedar lodge, Potters Bar [North Mimms
Marryatt Joseph, esq. Little heath,
Mead Mr. George, Chase cottage
Milton Mr. Thomas, South Mimms
Mulgrave the Dowager Countess, Brookmans, North Mimms
Newcome Rev. Thos. Shenley rectory
Oddie Henry Hoyle, esq. Colney house, Shenley [Mimms
Piggott John, esq. Knightlands, South
Price Rev. Thomas, South Mimms
Sharp Mrs. A. Clare hall, South M.
Smedley Francis, esq. Nyn, Northaw
Smith Mr. Samuel, South Mimms
Sotteby Rev. Thomas, Hans, N.M.
Trotter John, esq. (magistrate) Dyrham park, S.M. [ters Bar
Watkins Rev. Henry Geo. jun. Pot-
White Henry, esq. Porter's lodge, Shenley [South Mimms
White Thomas, esq. Dancer's hill,
Whitehead Mr. Thos. N. Ridge hill
Winter John Mico, esq. Shenley

ACADEMIES & SCHOOLS.

Alsop William (day) South Mimms
Barrenger Elizabeth (day) Shenley
Bayles Thomas (boarding) Ridge
Hawkes J.W. (boarding) Potters Bar
INFANTS' and NATIONAL SCHOOLS, South Mimms—Mr. & Mrs. Woodrow, master and mistress

BAKERS.

Chesher George, London colney
Dolamore Richard, Potters Bar
Hampton Thomas, Shenley
Messer James, North Mimms
Pridmore Ann, South Mimms
Slow Jos. (gingerbread) Potters Bar
Smith John, South Mimms

BLACKSMITHS & FARRIERS.

Bamford Wm. & Nathaniel, Bell bar
Briers John, Shenley
Giddins Thomas, South Mimms
Hall George (& locksmith) Potters Bar and Kitsend
Massey John, North Mimms
Roberts Samuel, Potters Bar
Savile Joseph, Ridge [Northaw
Thomlinson James, Cooper's lane,
Webb William, South Mimms

BOOT & SHOE MAKERS.

Arnold William, Ridge
Chesher Thomas, South Mimms
Chesher Thomas, jun. South Mimms
Denham Joseph, Potters Bar
Grange John, Shenley
Groom William, North Mimms
Hesketh John, Shenley
Holmes William, Potters Bar
Marshall Matthew, South Mimms
Sears William, South Mimms

BREWERS.

Cox James, Kitsend, South Mimms
Freeman William, Shenley
Whitehead John, Bell bar

BRICKLAYERS.

Baker William, South Mimms
Carter William, Shenley
Cowland Charles, South Mimms
Cox James, Kitsend, South Mimms
Peck William, North Mimms
Williams James Fosbury, Potters Bar
Young Richard, Potters Bar

BUTCHERS.

Carter Joseph, Potters Bar
Palmer George, Shenley
Pridmore William, South Mimms
Simkins William, Potters Bar
Tebbott George, Shenley

CARPENTERS.

Bangs John, South Mimms
Cotton and Hopwood, Potters Bar
Nash John, North Mimms
Osmond William, Shenley
Tull John, Shenley
Young Richard, Potters Bar

GROCERS AND DEALERS IN SUNDRIES.

Aser Nathaniel, Potters Bar
Bristow George, Potters Bar
Camplin Robert, South Mimms
Carter Thomas and Ann, Shenley
Clark James, South Mimms
Cooper John, Northaw
Everett William, Bell bar, North M.
Harvey Joseph, Potters Bar
Hollis William, Shenley
Marshall Matthew, South Mimms
Stephens William, South Mimms
Swain Stephen, Ridge
Tomlinson Thomas, South Mimms
Tomlinson William, Cooper's lane

INNS & PUBLIC HOUSES.

Bell, John Heath, Barnet gate
Black Horse, Charles Cowland, S.M.
Black Lion, Thomas Carter, Shenley
Bull's Head, Jas. Cox, Kitsend, S.M.
Cross Keys, Edward Walley, S.M.
Duke of Leeds' Arms, Hannah Speary, Welham green, North Mimms
Duke of York, Richard Ashkettle, Gannick corner [Bar
Green Man, George Pallett, Potters
Greyhound, Robert Goodwin, S.M.
Maypole, Jn. Massey, Water end, N.M.
Old Guinea, Stephen Swain, Ridge
Red Lion, John Bradley, South M.
Robin Hood and Little John, Henry Craft, Potters Bar [Ridge hill
Waggon & Horses, Gabriel Ellingham,
Wheat Sheaf, William Freeman, Well end, Shenley
White Hart, Richard Dawes, Bell bar
White Hart, George Wylde, S.M.
White Horse, Ann Hare, Shenley
White Horse, Thomas Langton, Potters Bar [bar
White Swan, William Anderson, Bell

PAINTER & PLUMBER.

Clark William, Potter's bar

SADDLERS AND HARNESS MAKERS.

Ellis Francis, South Mimms
Kemp Mary, Potters Bar

SURGEONS.

Ringrose John, Potters Bar
Smith Henry Bennett, Shenley hill

TAILORS.

Fusedale John (and draper) Shenley
Giles John, Bell bar
Nicholson Benjamin, Potters Bar
Roberts James, Shenley
Roberts Thomas, South Mimms
Walters Vincent, Northaw

WHEELWRIGHTS.

Briers John, Shenley
Everett William, Bell bar
Giddins Thomas, South Mimms
Nash Samuel, South Mimms
Stokes Andrew, Potters Bar
Windsor John, Potters Bar

COACHES.

To LONDON, Billing's *Coach*, from the White Horse and Wheat Sheaf Inns, Shenley, every morning (Sunday excepted) at eight; goes through Elstree and Edgware.

Several other *Coaches* and *Carriers* pass through South Mimms and Potters Bar, for which *see* BARNET, page 184.

REDBOURN, FLAMSTED, HARPENDEN
AND NEIGHBOURHOODS.

REDBOURN is a populous and respectable village and parish in the hundred of Cashio—25 miles N. W. from London, 17 W. from Hertford, and 4 N. N. W. from St. Albans: being pleasantly seated on the great northern road, it is a place of incessant thoroughfare, and consequently derives some advantage therefrom, with the steady support of several inns, the principal of which is the 'Bull,' a respectable commercial and posting establishment. In this place many females are occupied in platting straw for hats and bonnets, and malting and brewing are the chief employments of the other sex. About a mile from the village stands the church, which is approached by a fine avenue of elms; it was rebuilt in the reign of Henry VIII, but since that period has undergone many repairs and alterations; it is dedicated to St. Mary. The benefice is a vicarage, in the presentation of Lord Verulam, and present incumbency of the Rev. Lord Beauclerc; the Rev. William Wade is his curate. The other places of worship in the parish are for baptists, independents and Wesleyan methodists. A Benedictine priory, consecrated to Saint Amphibalus, and subject to the control of the abbey of St. Albans, was formerly established here. Redbourn is entitled to have a market on Friday, but the privilege has for many years been unexercised; an annual fair is held, however, on the first Wednesday after January 1. The parish, in 1831, contained 2,047 inhabitants.

About two miles from Redbourn, in the hundred of Dacorum, stands the village of FLAMSTED, situated not far from the Roman *Watling-street*, and upon the summit of a high ridge of land rising abruptly from a valley through which courses the river Ver; from its contiguity to that stream it was in ancient times designated *Verlamstedt*. The parish church, dedicated to Saint Leonard, is a commodious edifice, consisting of a nave, chancel and aisles, with a tower at its western extremity; a profusion of foliage is displayed upon the capitals of the pillars of the nave, which is divided from the chancel by an elegantly carved screen of considerable height. The benefice is a perpetual curacy, in the patronage of the master and fellows of University college, Oxford. There is a small fund for the education of children, and alms-houses for four poor persons, the latter founded by Thomas Sanders in 1669. The population of the parish, in 1831, amounted to 462.

HARPENDEN, or, according to popular contraction, *Harden*, is a village and parish in the same hundred as Flamsted; situated upon the main road leading from Luton, in Bedfordshire, to St. Albans—distant from the latter town four miles and a half, and from Redbourn two. The houses composing the village present no uniformity of arrangement, but many of them are neatly and well constructed; and the whole occupying a pleasant situation, the place has a cheerful and engaging appearance for a country residence. The church, dedicated to St. Nicholas, is of Norman architecture and cruciform, with a tower at the western end; it has a nave, chancel and transept, and contains some interesting monuments; the living is a perpetual curacy annexed to the rectory of Wheathampstead. The other places of worship are for independent and Wesleyan methodists. A grammar school for preparing pupils for the independent ministry is established here. At Nomans-land, about midway between this village and that of Sandridge, horse-races were formerly held; and the turf here has frequently been the scene of brutal pugilistic contests. A fair, or rather market, is held at Harpenden on the 16th of May, for horses and cattle. By the returns for 1831 the parish contained 1,972 inhabitants.

POST OFFICE, High street, REDBOURN, Samuel Farey, *Post Master.*—Letters from LONDON and all parts are delivered at the office at half-past seven in the morning, and are despatched at six in the evening.

POST OFFICE, HARPENDEN, Sarah Downs, *Post Mistress.*—Letters from LONDON and all parts are delivered at the office at half-past seven in the morning, and are despatched at five in the evening.

*** *The addresses to which the name of the village is not attached are in* REDBOURN.

NOBILITY, GENTRY AND CLERGY.

Bailey George, esq. Harpenden
Basil Robt.Smith,esq.Flamsted grove
Bent the Misses Ellen & Elizabeth, Harpenden
Brown Mrs. Patty, High st
Burnham Mrs. Louisa, High st
Cain Mrs. —, Beaumont hall
Ells Mrs. Elizabeth, Harpenden
Fogg John Barrett, esq. Harpenden
Frazer —, esq. Flamstedbury
Gilbert Mr. William Henry, High st
Glamis Lady Charlotte, High st
Grimstead Thomas, esq. Redbourn common
Hale Mrs. Fanny, Harpenden lodge
Harris Mr. Thomas, High st
Harrowsmith Mrs. Frances, High st
Hawkins John, esq. Bylands
Holmes Mr. Charles, Harpenden
How Mrs. —, Beech hide
Hunt Mrs.Penelope Ann,Harpenden
Johnson Rev. Edward, Harpenden
Laws Mrs. —, Rothamstead park
Laws John Bennett, esq. Rothamstead park
Oakley Richard, esq. Harpenden
Ogilvie Capt. James, Harpenden
Osborn Mr. Thomas, High st
PayneMr.Jonathan,Kinsman's green
Pocock Mrs. Sarah, Harpenden
Pugh Rev. Thomas, Elm cottage
Rutherford Mr. Peter, Harpenden common
Slack Joseph Evans, esq. Redbourn house
Smith Rev. Edward, Harpenden
Wade Rev. William, Church end
Wyatt John, esq. Harpenden
Young Mrs. Hannah, Harpenden

ACADEMIES AND SCHOOLS.

Ball Thos.& Ann,North place,High st
Lawrence Sarah, High st
Leonard Rev. Solomon (independent grammar) Harpenden
Mercier Elizabeth (brdg.) Harpenden
Slythe Sarah (day) High st
Whitehouse Jno. Redbourn common

BAKERS & FLOUR DEALERS.

Barnes Thomas, High st
Batchelor Richard, Harpenden
Bates Edmund, Harpenden
Bigg William, Church end
Dixon Charles, High st
Gilbert Daniel, High st
Missenden John, Harpenden
Saunders Jos. (& corn dealer) High st
Simons George, Harpenden

BLACKSMITHS, &c.

Arnold Thomas, Flamsted
Cheeseman Joseph, High st
Dunckley Robt. Harpenden common
Lines Joseph, Harpenden
Row James, Harpenden common
Smith Daniel, Redbournbury lane
Swain Stephen, Harpenden
Woodstock Charles, Lamb lane

BOOT & SHOE MAKERS.

Archer George, Harpenden
Archer John, Harpenden
Butler John, High st
Clark John, High st
Grace Thomas, High st
Green Henry, High st
Green Thomas, Crouch hall
Henson William, Harpenden
Huson Thomas, Harpenden
Turpin George, Flamsted
Weatherhead John, High st

BRICKLAYERS.

Doggett Joseph, Harpenden
Homan George, Harpenden lane
Lee James, Flamsted
Pratt Edward, North place, High st
Wells William, Harpenden

BUTCHERS.

Ells John, Harpenden
Farey William, Fish st
Farnell John, Harpenden
Heath George, Harpenden
Olney George, High st
Olney Martha, High st
Robertson John, Harpenden
Spacey Thomas, High st

CARPENTERS.

Adams Edward, High st
Clark John, Flamsted
Innard William, Harpenden
Neal John, High st
Reading Richard, Fish st
Robinson John, Harpenden
Thoroughgood John, High st

CORN DEALERS.

Dixon Charles, High st
Morton Thomas, Flamsted
Patmore Thos. (& coal) Harpenden
Scrivener Thos. (mealman) High st
Varney James (and coal) Harpenden

GROCERS AND DEALERS IN SUNDRIES.

Ashby John, High st
Barnes Thomas, High st
BisneyFrancis(& clothes dlr.) Fish st
Clark Wm. (& cheesemonger) High st
Hunt Wm. Cold arbour, Harpenden
Innard William, Harpenden
Knott William, Harpenden
Lewin William (and cheesemonger and druggist) Harpenden
London Edward, Church end
Lord Johannah, High st
Newman William, Flamsted
Norwood William, Flamsted
Nott William, Harpenden
Patmore Thomas, Harpenden
Pitkin Henry (and druggist) High st
Smith Daniel, High st
Stratford John, Church end
Turpin John, Flamsted
Varney James, Harpenden
Weatherhead William, Flamsted

INNS.

Bull, Thomas Dixon (posting and commercial & excise office) High st
Bull, Henry Oldaker, Harpenden
Cross Keys, James Payne, Harpenden
Red Lion, William Hooper, High st
White Hart, Jno. Tomlinson, High st
White Horse, Joseph Liley, High st

LINEN, &c. DRAPERS.

Cherry Jabez, High st
Grace Ann, High st
Osborn Elizabeth & Barbara, High st
Sandars Ann, High st

MALTSTERS & BREWERS.

Curtis James, Harpenden
House Jno. Jas. & Thos. jun. Harpenden
Oldaker Henry, Harpenden
Stevens John, Fish st

MILLERS.

Dixon Ernest, Redbourn mill
Smith Hy. Tovey, Redbournbury mill

PLUMBERS, PAINTERS AND GLAZIERS.

Best John, High st
Dunkley William, Flamsted
Dunkley William, jun. High st
Ellard James, Harpenden
Owen Charles, High st

SADDLERS.

Chase John, Harpenden
Pedder John, High st

STRAW HAT MAKERS.

Bisney Fras. (& plat dealer) Fish st
Webb Ann, High st

SURGEONS.

Kingston Francis, Harpenden
Saunders Daniel, High st
Simons William, Harpenden

TAILORS AND DRAPERS.

Cherry Jabez, High st
Childs Henry, Harpenden
Eyles John, Harpenden
Gilbert John, Harpenden
Lawrence Thomas, High st
Skillman John, High st

TAVERNS & PUBLIC HOUSES.

Bell, William Mann, Flamsted
Black Horse, John Patmore, Market st rd
Blackbird, Robert Palmer, Flamsted
Chequers, Matthew Leno, Flamsted
Chequers, Thomas Partridge, London rd
Cock, John Missenden, Harpenden
Crown, Michael Smith, High st
George, Mattw. Tomalin, jun. Harpenden
George & Dragon, Chas. Carpenter, High st
Holly Bush, Joseph Abbott, Church end
Lion & Lamb, George Pusev, High st
Prince's Head, James Dell, High st
Punch Bowl, William Seabrook, London rd
Red Lion, Matthew Tomalin, Harpenden
Running Horses, Edwd. Childs, London rd
Saracen's Head, Thos. Scrivener, High st
Tom in Bedlam, Thomas Ballard, High st

WHEELWRIGHTS.

Cole William, Fish st
Lord Johannah, High st
Wright Samuel, Harpenden

Miscellaneous.

Farey Samuel, fellmonger, &c. High st
Leedham Henry Joseph, rope maker and registrar of births & deaths, Harpenden
Payne James, clothier, &c. Harpenden
Smith Jas. lath render, Redbourn common
Smith John, fire office agent, Fish st
Swain Mary, stay maker, Harpenden
Vallance William, ironmonger & stationer, Harpenden
Warner Joseph Nelson, hair dresser, and hardware and toy dealer, High st

COACHES.

To LONDON, the *Royal Mail* (from Derby) calls at at the White Horse, every morning at half-past three—the *Swallow* (from Birmingham) calls at the Red Lion, every morning at six—the *Favourite* (from Luton) calls at the Cross Keys, Harpenden, every morning (Sunday excepted) at half-past six—the *Times* (from Dunstable) calls at the Bull, every morning (Sunday excepted) at a quarter past eight—and the *Express* (from Leeds) calls at the White Horse, every morning at half-past nine.
To LONDON, a *Coach* (from Northampton) calls at the White Hart, and one (from Wellingborough) calls at the Red Lion, every afternoon at two—the *Defiance* (from Manchester) calls at the White Horse, every afternoon at three—the *Star* (from Liverpool) calls at the Bull, every afternoon at four—and the *Self-Defence* (from Ampthill) calls at the Cross Keys, Harpenden, every Monday, Wednesday and Friday morning at half-past nine.

The following Coaches are from London.

To AMPTHILL & BEDFORD, a *Coach*, calls at the Bull, every Tuesday, Thursday and Saturday afternoon at five—and the *Self-Defence*, from the Cross Keys, Harpenden, same afternoons at half-past five.
To BIRMINGHAM, the *Swallow*, calls at the Red Lion, every evening at nine.
To DERBY and HALIFAX, the *Royal Mail*, calls at the White Horse, every night at half-past ten.
To DUNSTABLE, the *Times*, calls at the Bull, every evening at half-past seven.
To LEEDS, the *Express*, calls at the White Horse, every evening at half-past seven.
To LIVERPOOL, the *Star*, calls at the Bull, every night at a quarter before nine.
To LUTON, the *Favourite*, calls at the Cross Keys, Harpenden, every evening at half-past eight.
To MANCHESTER, the *Defiance*, calls at the White Horse, every night at ten.
To NORTHAMPTON, a *Coach*, calls at the White Hart, every afternoon at half-past three.
To WELLINGBOROUGH, a *Coach*, calls at the Red Lion, every afternoon at one.

CARRIERS—WAGGONS, &c.

To LONDON, — Clark's *Waggons* and *Carts*, pass through Redbourn, daily; — Codgbrook, every Monday, Wednesday and Friday evening; — Whitbread, — Deacon, — Stoke, and — Haydon, every Monday and Thursday, and — Shepherd, same days, and on Sunday evening; — Huckel's *Cart*, from Redbourn common-side, every Monday and Thursday; — Barnes, from the same place, and — Jeeves, from Fish st, every Thursday, and Curtis's *Van*, every Tuesday evening.
To AMPTHILL, — Whitbread, every Wednesday and Saturday morning.
To BIRMINGHAM, — Clare's *Fly Waggons*, every Wednesday and Saturday morning.
To DAVENTRY, — Shepherd, every Tuesday and Wednesday morning and Friday night.
To LUTON, — Clarke's *Waggon & Carts*, daily, and — Deacon, — Haydon, — Whitbread, and — Stoke, every Wednesday and Saturday.
To STONY STRATFORD, — Curtis's *Van*, every Friday morning.
To TOWCESTER, — Ellis' *Waggons*, every Wednesday & Saturday morning.
To WELLINGBOROUGH, — Codgbrook, every Tuesday, Thursday and Saturday morning.

RICKMANSWORTH AND NEIGHBOURHOOD.

RICKMANSWORTH is a market town and parish in the hundred of Cashio—18 miles N. W. by W. from London, 11 N. from Uxbridge, and 3 W. by S. from Watford, at which latter town is a station on the London and Birmingham railway. It is agreeably seated in a valley, near the confluence of the Colne and Gade with the Chess—rivers abounding with trout, and much resorted to by anglers; upon these streams are several paper mills, and others for grinding corn. The manufacture of straw plat, and horse-hair seating, employs numbers of the inhabitants; and the cultivation of water-cresses, in the proper season, for the metropolitan market, is a source of profit to many others. The Grand Junction canal passes at one end of the town, and affords a communication with the capital and different parts of the kingdom. In the earliest records in which this town is named, it is written *Rykemeresweearth* and *Richmeresweard*, signifying the 'rich moor meadow,' which at one time was, and still in some measure is, applicable to the quality of the land about here. The government of the town is confided to two constables and one headborough.

The church, dedicated to St. Mary, has an embattled tower of flint at its western end; some few years since the body was rebuilt of brick: over the altar is a fine window of stained glass, representing the crucifixion; it was brought originally from St. Peter's, at Rome, and cost at Paris £200. The benefice is a vicarage, in the gift of the bishop of London; the present incumbent is the Rev. Edward Hodgson. The other places of worship are chapels for baptists and independents. A national school for boys and girls, a charity school for girls, and two sets of alms-houses, are the principal charitable institutions. The number of seats and parks which present themselves, in tasteful elegance, in every direction round Rickmansworth, render the environs one continued scene of beauty. The market, for holding which on Saturday a charter was granted by Henry VIII, in the early part of his reign, for the benefit of the monastery of St. Albans, is exempt from toll, and was for a long period a considerable one; those of Watford and Hemel Hempstead, however, gradually effected its reduction, and at the present day the business transacted at it is by no means important. The fairs are held on the 20th July, for horses and cattle; second Saturday in September, for pleasure and hiring agricultural servants; and 24th November, for horses, sheep, &c. The population of the parish, in 1831, was 4,574.

POST OFFICE, RICKMANSWORTH, James Church, *Post Master.*—Letters from LONDON arrive every morning at six, and are despatched every evening at seven.—Letters from AMERSHAM and CHESHAM arrive every evening at half-past six, and are despatched every morning at seven.

NOBILITY, GENTRY AND CLERGY.

Arden Jos. esq. Rickmansworth park
Barnes John, esq. Chorley wood
Bentley Miss —, Croxley green
Const Mr. Francis, Rickmansworth
Day Thos. Brantorn, esq. Sarrat
Fellows Mr. Thomas (attorney) Rickmansworth
Finch John, esq. Red heath
Gaskell Wm. esq. Micclefield hall
Hayward James, esq. Loudwater
Hodgson Rev. Edwd. Rectory house
Howard Mrs. —, Batchworth heath
Hunt William, esq. Mill end
Larouche Capt. —, Batchworth
Muskett George Alfred, esq. M. P. Burry house
Percy Hon. Captain, Scots bridge
Perks Mrs. —, Money hill
Scrope N. esq. Chorley wood
Skidmore Mrs. Jane, Rickmanswrth
Thomson George, esq. Chorley wood
Vander Meulen Rev. —, Rickmansworth
Westminster the most noble the Marquess of, Moor park
Wilson Mr. Thos. Rickmansworth
Winstanley J. esq. Money hill house

ACADEMIES AND SCHOOLS.

Bigrave Thomas
Miles Misses (day and boarding)
NATIONAL SCHOOL—Wm. Plaistowe, master; Jemima Plaistowe, mistrss
Smith Joshua (brding.) Basing house

BAKERS & FLOUR DEALERS.

Berry Elizabeth, Batchworth
Brown Daniel, Mill end
Harris Mary, Batchworth
King Thomas, Croxley green
Plaistowe Eleanor
Sinfield Henry, Mill end
Sinfield William, Mill end
Swannell Owen, Mill end
Wallington Levi

BLACK AND WHITESMITHS.

Beeson James
Brown Zachariah, Maple cross
Corfield Charles
East Thomas, Croxley green
Thompson John
Watson Leonard (and bell hanger)

BOOKSELLERS & STATIONRS.
Church James
Turner Frederick

BOOT AND SHOE MAKERS.
Eggelton James
Ford Daniel
Gurney James
King James
Marks Joseph
Mills Joseph, Mill end
Nicholls George
Payne Richard, Mill end
Richardson James
Stockley Thomas
Temple James

BRICKLAYERS.
Ayles William (and builder)
Ebelthite Matthew
Grover James, Chorley wood lane
Robinson William

BUTCHERS.
Caffall William
Haddex John
Harris William, Batchworth
Lawrence Daniel
Payne Joseph
Swannell Henry

CARPENTERS.
Body William, Mill end
Clay Thomas (and furniture broker)
Spencer James (and builder)
Taylor Joseph (and builder)

CHYMISTS AND DRUGGISTS.
Quested William
Weaver John

COAL MERCHANTS.
Cooper John, Town wharf
Laxton John, Batchworth wharf
Payne Christopher

GROCERS AND DEALERS IN SUNDRIES.
Barnard Abraham
Benham Spencer (and stationer)
Berry Sarah, Batchworth
Bowman Daniel (and glass dealer)
Church James (and druggist)
Goodman Thomas, Croxley green
Haddex John
Lawrence Daniel
Mead William
Plaistowe Richard
Rogers Timothy
Swannell Henry (and corn, hop, and malt merchant, & tallow chandler)
Swannell Owen, Mill end
Wellings Thomas

INNS.
Bell (commercial, & booking office) John Laughton
George, John Stidolph
Swan (posting, and excise office), Edward Boraston

IRONMONGERS.
Beeson James
Watson Leonard

LIME BURNERS.
Abbee John and James (and brick and tile makers) Chorley wood
Cooper John (& brick maker) Cashio bridge
Kirby Richard, Woodcock hill

LINEN & WOOLLEN DRAPRS.
Grover Daniel
Johnson Joseph and Son
Paine Thomas
Perks James

MILLINERS & DRESS MAKRS.
Batchelor E. and S.
Bowman Judith
Jordan Elizabeth and H.
Pool Louisa
Temple Sarah

NURSERY & SEEDSMEN.
Greenus Edward Rutter
Splatt Richard, Batchworth
Stidolph John

PAPER MAKERS.
Dickinson & Longman, Batchworth
Magness Chas. & James, Mill end
Munn Lewis, Solesbridge [water
Weedon Thos. Scots bridge & Loud-

PLUMBERS, PAINTERS AND GLAZIERS.
Hailey Henry
Laughton John
Taylor James

SADDLERS.
Darvill John
Stone Matthew (and rope maker)

SURGEONS.
Ayres Thomas
Jones Charles

TAILORS.
Ainsworth Thomas
Coupland William Francis
Perks James
Richardson William
Rogers Timothy
Turner Luke
Whitmore James

TAVERNS & PUBLIC HOUSES.
Artichoke, Joseph Austin, Croxley green
Boot, James Border, Sarrat green
Cart & Horses, Joseph Beeson
Chequers, George Ward
Coach & Horses, Elizabeth Ellingham
Coach & Horses, William Branch, Batchworth heath
Coach & Horses, Lydia Southam, Croxley green
Cock, John Hubbard, Sarrat green
Cock, Hannah Stone
Cross, James Wilson, Mill end
Gate, William Dorofield, Chorley wood
King's Arms, Joseph Barnes [cross
Maple Cross, Zachariah Brown, Maple
Mines Royal Arms, John Roberts
Queen's Head, John Wyatt, Batchworth
Rose & Crown, Wm. Weatherley, Mill end
Whip & Collar, Ann Wild, Mill end
White Bear, Wm. Treadaway, Batchworth
White Horse, Wm. Pratt, Chorley wood

VETERINARY SURGEONS.
Bean William
Smith Thomas
Williamson Thomas

WHEELWRIGHTS.
Ashby John (and coach maker)
Ashby William, Mill end

Miscellaneous.
Collins Thomas, brazier, &c.
Fellows Thomas, attorney
Horne Joseph, cooper
Horwood Thomas, fishmonger
Jeffs Elizabeth, china & glass dealer
Jeffs Maria, hair dresser
Jones John, coach maker
Jordan William, watch maker & gunsmith
King Jonathan, confectioner & glass dealer
Knight John, tarpauling & sack maker
Paine Thomas, basket maker
Perry John, furniture broker
Prickett John, chair maker
Salter, Woodman & Co. brewers
Sedgwick James, gun smith, Mill end
Sedgwick John and Son, auctioneers and surveyors
Ward George, fishmonger & poulterer
Wild Thomas, tanner, Mill end
Wilson Thos. agent to the County fire office

COACHES,

To LONDON, the *Accommodation* (from Chesham) calls at the Bell Inn, every morning, at half-past seven, goes through Watford and Stanmore.

To CHESHAM, the *Accommodation* (from London) calls at the Bell Inn, every evening at half-past six.

To WATFORD RAILWAY STATION, a *Fly*, from the George, every morning at eight & evening at five, to meet the trains

CONVEYANCE BY RAILWAY.

To and from LONDON and BIRMINGHAM, a *Fly*, from the George, to the Watford station, to meet the trains, every morning and evening.

CARRIERS.

To LONDON, William Brown's *Waggon*, from his house, every Monday, Wednesday and Friday, and Edward Fry, twice a week.

ST. ALBANS,

WITH THE VILLAGE OF LONDON COLNEY AND NEIGHBOURHOODS.

ST. ALBANS, a borough, market town and liberty of itself, is locally situated in the hundred of Cashio—21 miles N. W. from London, 23 E. by S. from Aylesbury, and 12 W. by S. from Hertford. It is seated on the great thoroughfare road leading from London to the midland and northern counties, and about half a mile east of the site of the ancient city of *Verulamium*, of which, indeed, it may be considered a surviving portion. At the period of the Roman invasion Verulam was a large and populous city; many writers are of opinion that it was a place of much greater antiquity than even London itself: with the Romans it constituted a chief station, and the inhabitants had the same rights, privileges and immunities as the citizens of Rome. Towards the end of the third century its splendour began to decline; and the only remains now above ground are large fragments of uncommonly hard walls, composed of flints, Roman bricks and large tiles, cemented together with mortar so firm and adhesive that the other materials cannot be separated from it without breaking. Historians inform us that, about the time of the declination of this city, Alban, or Albanus, a famous protomartyr, for his religious principles fell a sacrifice to the malice and bigotry of his heathen fellow-citizens; having, however, subsequently embraced Christianity, they reflected upon their former crime with horror, and in expiation erected a church, which they consecrated to the memory of Albanus: Offa, a king of the Mercians, actuated by a similar zeal, many years afterwards caused a church and monastery to be founded on the spot where Albanus had been martyred, and endowed the latter place for one hundred monks of the Benedictine order; in process of time dwellings were erected in the vicinity of the monastery, from which the town took the name of St. Albans. The monastery, or, as it is now called, the 'abbey,' is certainly the most ancient and perfect structure of the kind in England: it is of the form of a cross, and from its intersection springs a square embattled tower, supported on four semicircular arches; the tower is of various styles of architecture, the dissimilarity of which is striking and perceptible at the first glance. The entire length of the abbey, including the west porch and the chapel of the Virgin, is five hundred and thirty-nine feet, being fourteen and a half feet longer than York cathedral, and only six feet shorter than that of Winchester, which latter is the longest in the kingdom; the breadth of the body of the church is seventy-four and a half feet. St. Cuthbert's screen, and the elaborately carved altar screen, are both magnificent specimens of sculpture. Many fine brasses, dedicated to the abbots, were taken away by Cromwell's soldiers; but some still remain to gratify the antiquarian. The ponderous columns of which the nave is composed, with the light and elegant architecture of the chancel and other parts of the interior, form a very imposing *coup d'œil.* A small chapel, dedicated to the Blessed Virgin, adjoining the abbey, has of late years been converted into the grammar school, founded by Edward VI, for the education of the children of those who are free of the borough. At Sopwell, no great distance from the ancient 'Holy Well,' are the ruins of a pile of brick buildings, which, according to tradition, formed a royal palace belonging to Henry VIII; some authorities, however, contend (with greater probability) that it was a nunnery, founded by abbot Geoffrey de Gorham in 1140.

Besides the abbey church there are three others, parochial, viz. St. Michael's, St. Peter's and St. Stephen's, all founded by Ulsinus, the sixth abbot, in the reign of Edred, about A. D. 948; the parish of St. Albans, and part of those of St. Michael and St. Peter, are within the borough. The living of St. Albans is a rectory, in the gift of the corporation; St. Michael's and St. Peter's are vicarages—the former in the presentation of the Earl of Verulam, the latter in that of the bishop of Ely. In St. Michael's church is a marble monument to the great Lord Francis Bacon, who died in 1626, at the age of sixty-six. Baptists, independents, Wesleyan methodists and unitarians have places of worship. The charities of the borough comprise, amongst others, several public schools and numerous alms-houses, all supported in a creditable manner; of the latter, those erected and endowed by the Duchess of Marlborough are the most conspicuous. The other public buildings are the gaol, the clock-house (a high square tower), and the town-hall; the latter is a handsome and commodious edifice, erected in 1830, at an expense of £1,200. The manufacture of straw plat employs, it is conjectured, upwards of eight hundred persons in the town and immediate neighbourhood; there is also a silk and cotton manufactory, and one for ribbons, but these branches are not extensive; there are several good breweries, some business is done in malting, and in the vicinity are a few corn mills. The inns, of which there are several respectable ones, both posting and commercial, are supported in a considerable degree by the influx of passengers; but their prosperity has suffered a material diminution from the opening of the London and Birmingham railway—one inn alone, it is said, having lost the stabling of two hundred and fifty horses since this modern mode of conveyance has been brought into operation.

St. Albans obtained its first charter of incorporation, which prescribed its form of government, about the year 1553; this was subsequently changed by Charles II; his regulations were, in their turn, superseded by the municipal act of 1835, which vested the government in a mayor, four aldermen and twelve councillors, with the usual corporate officers—styling the body 'the mayor and aldermen and burgesses of the borough of St. Albans, in the county of Hertford;' the same act conferred upon the borough a commission of the peace, under which four justices for it were appointed. The mayor presides at a court of aldermen on the first Wednesday in every month, a court of requests for recovery of debts under 40*s.* is held every Saturday; the magistrates for the liberty hold sessions quarterly, and the borough justices sit in petty session every Friday. St. Albans sends two members to parliament, the franchise having been obtained in the 35th of Edward I; the mayor is the returning officer: the present representatives are the Hon. E. Harbottle Grimstone, of Gorhambury, and George Alfred Muskett, Esq. of Rickmansworth. St. Albans confers the title of duke upon the family of Beauclerc, and the representative of the family of Grimstone enjoys the title of Earl Verulam. About a mile from the town, at OSTER HILLS, a beautiful and sequestered spot, is an establishment for the insane; it is admirably conducted, upon the humane and social principle of treating the patients as part of the family—this system being more efficiently maintained here than in other asylums where the inmates are inconveniently numerous. Ostorius, the Roman general, was slain in this locality in a conflict with the Britons. St. Albans, by charter, is privileged to hold two markets in the week, but a long time has elapsed since more than one was found necessary; this is held on Saturday, and is well supplied with general articles of provision, grain and straw plat—extraordinary quantities of the latter material are occasionally disposed of. Fairs—March 25th and 26th, for cattle and horses; October 10th, for horses, cattle and sheep; and a statute fair on the 11th October and two following days. By the returns for 1831 the population of the parishes within and without the borough of St. Albans was as follows:—The Abbey parish, 3,092; St. Michael's within the borough, 517—without, 1,010; St. Peter's within, 1,163; hamlets without, 1,810: total number of inhabitants, within and without the borough, 7,592.

About three miles S. E. from St. Albans, partly in the parish of St. Peter, at that town, in Cashio hundred, is the neat village of LONDON COLNEY, the residence of many respectable and opulent inhabitants. The chapel of ease, dedicated to St. Peter, the site for which was the gift of the Earl of Hardwicke, is a handsome modern edifice, erected for the use of the inhabitants of the parishes of St. Peter, Shenley and Ridge, at an expense of £2,700.

POST OFFICE, Verulam street, ST. ALBANS, Samuel Ward, *Post Master.*—Letters from LONDON arrive every afternoon at three and night at ten, and are despatched every morning at four.—Letters from DERBY and HALIFAX arrive every morning at four, and are despatched every night at ten.—Letters from other parts of the North arrive (by railway from the Watford station), and are despatched every night at eight.

The box closes for the North letters at seven in the evening, and for the London letters at nine.

NOBILITY, GENTRY, AND CLERGY.

Adey Danl. Goodson, esq. Fishpool st
Ames William, esq. St. Peter st
Bacon Mrs. Elizabeth, St. Peter st
Ballard Mr. William, Verulam st
Barnard Rev. Markland, Ridge
Beauclerc Rev. Lord Fredk. Vicarage
Bell John Thomas, esq. Waterside
Berner Mr. George Manfield, St. Peter's
Biddle Joseph, esq. St. German's, St. Michael's
Bowen Rev. William Mogg, D.D. St. Peter st
Brabant Mrs. Mary, Dagnall lane
Brogden Rev. James, Holywell hill
Brown James, esq. St Peter's
Brown William, esq. St. Peter's
Children Mr. Geo. London Colney
Coleman Rev. Phil. Vincnt. Market pl
Cotton Miss Sarah, St. Peter's
Crakelt Mrs. Sophia, Verulam villas
Crowther Mrs. Elizabeth, St. Peter st
Donald Rev. Andrew, M.A. St. Peter st
Dorant Mr. James Annesley, Abbey cottage
Drage Mr. William, London Colney
Durant George, esq. Chilwick hall
Eastlands Mrs. Elizabeth, Fishpool st
Faircloth Richard, esq. St. Stephen's
Fitch Mr. James, Verulam villas
Fordham Mr. Edwd. Allen, College st
Gape Thos. Foreman, esq. Fishpool st
Gosling Mrs. —, St. Peter st
Grimstone the Hon. Edw. Harbottle, M.P. Gorhambury
Hardwick the Dowager Countess of, Tittenhanger house
Harris Rev. Wm. New London road
Hayward Mr. Thos. New London road
Heath Mrs. Rosa, Verulam road
Henley Mrs. —, St. Stephen's
Henslow John, esq. St. Peter st
Howard James, esq. Windridge
Isaacs Edward, esq. St. Stephen's villa
Jenkins Rev. James, M.A. St. Peter st
Johncock Mr. Jno. New London road
Jones Mr. Samuel, Dalton house
Kingston Francis, esq. St. Peter st
Kentish Mr. Richard, St. Peter st
Leach Rev. William, M.A. St. Peter st
Le June Mr. Henry, Colney st
Lomax Capt. Joshua, Chilwick
Lowe R. G. esq. (magistrate) St. Peter street
Mason Mr. Richard, Abbey terrace
Massey Mr. Ambrose, St. Peter st

NOBILITY, &c.—*Continued.*
Muskett George Alfred, esq. M. P. Holywell [hill
Nicholson Mrs. Hannah, Holywell
Nicholson Rev. Henry, Abbey cloisters [Colney house
Oddie Henry Hoyle, esq. London
Osbaldeston Fras. esq. Abbey terrace
Parez Mr. Charles, Verulam villas
Parken W. P. esq. New London road
Piggott Mrs. Eliz. New London road
Preedy Miss Eliz. Abbey Mill lane
Read Mrs. Elizabeth, Rome lands
Russell Mrs. Sarah, Holywell hill
Sandars Mrs. Alice, St. Peter st
Searancke Mrs. Mary, Abbey terrace
Smith Stephen, esq. Kingsbury
Smith Mrs. T. St. Peter st
Smith Mr. William, New house
Southwell Rev. Marcus Richard, Colney st
Spittall Mr. Edw. New London road
Story Anthony Browne, esq. Holywell hill
Story John Samuel, esq. High st
Timperan Mr. Joseph, New Barns
TuckMr.HughCameron,St.Michael's
Upton Rev. William, College st
Verulam the Right Hon. the Earl of, Gorhambury
Wade Rev. William, St. Peter st
White Miss Elizabeth, Chequer st
Wigg Fras. esq. Frogmore, Park st
Woodhouse Mr. Daniel, St. Peter st
Young Mr. Charles, Holywell hill

ACADEMIES & SCHOOLS.
Not otherwise described are Day Schools.
Browne Mary (prepartry) College st
Clare Thomas (brdg.) Holloway hill
Crowther Jane (brdg.) St. Peter st
Donald Rev. Andrew, St Peter st
Goodland John, Dagnall lane
GRAMMAR SCHOOL, Abbey cloisters—Rev. Wm. Mogg Bowen, D.D. master
INFANTS' SCHOOL, Cross st—Harriet Henshaw, mistress [Peter's
Lomax Mrs. M. (boarding & day) St.
Mills Susan (brdg. & day) Verulam st
NATIONAL SCHOOL, Cock lane—M. A. Taylor, master
Stebbings John, Spencer st
Tyler Thomas, Holloway hill
UNION WORKHOUSE SCHOOL, Oster hill—C. J. and S. Fox, masters
UNITARIAN SCHOOL, Dagnall lane—Rev. P. V. Coleman, master
Wellingham Mr. John, Hollywell hill
Wells Eliza (preparatory) St. Peter st

ARCHITECTS & BUILDERS.
(See also Carpenters and Builders.)
Bennett Joseph, St. Peter st
Bennett William, St. Peter st
Fowell John, Fishpool st
Pew Richard, Dagnall lane

ATTORNEYS.
Ashwell George, Verulam villas
Blagg Thomas Ward, Fishpool st
Boyce Edward, St. Peter st
FaircIoth Wm. Wickham, Dagnall lane
Fairthorne Thomas, St. Peter st
Gibson Edward, St. Peter st
Lowe Richard Grove, St. Peter st
Osbaldeston Francis, Fishpool st
Story John Samuel, Holywell hill
Story J. S. & A. B. (and registrars of the Archdeaconry) Holywell hill

AUCTIONEERS & APPRAISERS.
Crawley Samuel, St. Peter st
Page John, Holywell hill
Rumball John Horner, St. Peter st

BAKERS AND MEALMEN.
Batchelor Richd. New London road
Boome Henry, London Colney
Cheshire George, London Colney
Climance William, Market place
Coles Joseph, St Peter st
Fensom Edward, Park st
Gregory William, Holywell hill
Inwood Thomas, Spicer st
Janes James, Fishpool st
Marston George, Holywell hill
Osborn Jarvis, High st
Payne William, Park st
Sanders Susannah, St. Michael's
Sturgess Thomas, Spencer st
Thackster Priscilla, Dagnall lane
Walker Thomas, Market place
Warren George, Fishpool st
Wiles Hannah, Fishpool st
Young Thomas, St. Peter st

BANKERS.
Muskett Geo. Alfred, Holywell hill —(draw on the London and Westminster bank, London)
Story John Saml. Old Bank, Market place—(draw on Sir John Lubbock and Co. London)

BASKET MAKERS.
Birch Elizabeth, St. Peter st
Birch Thomas, Spencer st

BLACKSMITHS.
Abbott Elizabeth, St. Michael's
Austin Sarah, Fishpool st
Baker William, St. Peter st
Downing Elizabeth, St. Peter st
Downing Thomas, St. Michael's
Lowe Joseph, London Colney
Martin George, Park st
Martin William, Watford road
Pinnock John, Chequer st
Wright James, Colney st

BOOKSELLERS, STATIONERS AND BOOKBINDERS.
Marked thus * are Letter-press Printers.
*Gibbs Richard (and news agent) Market place
Johnson Robert (bookbinder and paper-hanger) Holywell hill
*Langley Wm. (& lithogrphr.) High st
*Nash John Brasbridge (and library, and newspaper agent) Holywell hill
Richardson John Pitt (and library and news room) High st [hill
Smale Jas. (periodicals, &c.) Holywell

BOOT & SHOE MAKERS.
Blake Jacob (warehouse) St. Peter st
Brown Ann, Fishpool st
Chamberlain Catherine, Market place
Costin Robert, London Colney
Dickinson John, London Colney
Dickinson Joseph, London Colney
Divis William, Holywell hill
Garrod John, St. Peter st
Grange William, London Colney
Hanmer Mary, George st
Hirst Samuel, Market place
Hiskett Charles, High st
Hiskett Elizabeth, Market place
Hulks Jesse, Holywell hill
Johnson Thomas, Fishpool st
Kine James, Rome lands
Luff William, St. Peter st
Monk John, St. Michael's
Payne Joseph, St. Peter st
Robinson William, Spencer st
Taylor Joseph & Geo. Market place
Thompson William, Spencer st
White John, Dagnall lane
Wilkins Edward, Back st

BRAZIERS AND TIN-PLATE WORKERS.
Grover George, Holywell hill
Manlove Richd. & Son, Market place
Mason John, High st

BREWERS.
Foster Daniel, George st
Kent Thomas Weedon, Chequer st
Kinder Thomas, St. Peter st
Marks Thos. corner of Holywell hill
Parsons Henry, St. Peter st
Saunders Ashby, Fishpool st
Searancke Francis, Verulam road
Wildbore Samuel, Dagnall lane

BRICK MAKERS AND LIME BURNERS.
Bennett William, St. Peter st
Kinder Thomas, Sandridge Bury

BRICKLAYERS.
Bottom William, Park st
Dunham John, Fishpool st
Horsfield Benjamin, London Colney
Lines John, St. Michael's
Pew Richard, Dagnall lane
Savage Daniel, Cross st, St. Peter's
Vass James, Queen Adelaide st
Webb James, Spencer st
Webb John, Verulam st
Webb Thomas, Queen Adelaide st

BUTCHERS.
Aldridge Joseph (pork) Fishpool st
Brown William (pork) Holywell hill
Bull Mary Ann, Back st
Day John, Holywell hill
Eales John (pork) Dagnall lane
Eling Daniel, George st
Field John, Back st
Furness James, High st
Galer John (pork) Holywell hill
Gilbert James, Fishpool st [hill
Glascock H. & Son (pork) Holywell
Goodspeed Henry, Fishpool st
Hart Thomas, High st
Ives John, Portland st
Kentish Henry, Holywell hill
Kilby Harriet (pork) Holywell hill
Lovett Elizabeth, Holywell hill
Nicoll Thomas, St. Peter st
Norris Caleb, London Colney
Norris William, Market cross
Peppercorn James, St. Peter st
Smith Samuel, St. Peter st
Sutton William, London Colney
Whitbread Henry, George st
White James, Colney st

CABINET MAKERS AND UPHOLSTERERS.
Cosier Henry, High st
Haynes Edward, St. Peter st [st
Richardson Jas. Christphr. Verulam

CARPENTERS & BUILDERS.
Anderson Joseph, Park st
Bennett Joseph, St. Peter st
Bennett William, St. Peter st
Bradshaw John, Fishpool st
Cross James, London Colney
Fountain John, London Colney
Fowell John, Fishpool st
Hale William, St. Peter st
Lines John, near the Cotton mill
Mead Felix, New London road
Norris Caleb, London Colney
Owen Charles, Fishpool st
Pails William, Hollywell hill
Pew Richard, Dagnall lane
Smith William, St. Peter st

CHINA, GLASS & EARTHENWARE DEALERS.
Fowell Sarah, Market place
Galer John, Holywell hill

CHYMISTS & DRUGGISTS.
Lewis John, Chequer st
Margetts John Peck, High st
Reid John, Market place
Wheeler Frederick, High st

CLOTHES SALESMEN.
House Thomas, Market place
Maylard Thomas, Holywell hill
Plummer Wm. Bufton, Verulam st
Sullivan Cornelius, Holywell hill

COACH BUILDERS.
Saunders Joseph, Fishpool st
Wilkins George (patent axle-tree and harness manufactr.) Holywell hill
Wood John, Holywell hill

COAL MERCHANTS.

Atkins William, London Colney
Austin Sarah, St. Michael's
Eales John, Dagnall lane
Harris Wm. Grange farm, St. Peter's
Helborn James, Spicer st
Marks Thomas, corner of Holywell hill and New London road
Mason Richard, George st
Moore Thomas, Spicer st
Nicoll Thomas, St. Peter st
Raymint Thomas, St. Peter st
Ruffett Thomas, St. Peter st

CONFECTIONERS.

Burton John, Verulam st
Climance Richard, George st
Osborn Ann, High st

COOPERS.

Batten Luke, Market place
Negus Robert, Chequer st

CORN, &c. DEALERS.

Climance William, Market place
Harris William, Grange farm
Mason Richard, George st
Mills Thomas, Lamb alley
Woodward William, St. Stephen's

CURRIERS AND LEATHER CUTTERS.

Blow George, College st
Hulks Jesse, Holywell hill
Radway John, Fishpool st

FIRE, &c. OFFICE AGENTS.

British, John Mason (and stamp distributer) High st
Clerical & Medical, Wm. Langley, High st
County (fire) and Provident (life) Joseph Russell, Holywell hill
Globe, Richd. Gutteridge, St. Peter st
London Union, Charles Geard, Chequer st
Mutual Insurance, Benj. Agutter, jun. Verulam st
Norwich Union, H. J. Martin, Market place
Phœnix, William Langley, High st
Protestant Dissenters' (fire and life) Wm. Fisk, George st
Royal Exchange, Robert Brooks, High st
Sun, John H. Rumball, St. Peter st

FISHMONGERS.

Davis Thos. George, Market place
Harding Thomas, Market place

FURNITURE BROKERS.

Capel John, Market place
Parrot John, St. Peter st

GROCERS & TEA DEALERS.

(See also Shopkeepers, &c.)

Brooks Robert, High st
Causton Thos. Dilworth, Chequer st
Crawley Samuel, Market place
Dollamore John, London Colney
Edmonds John, St. Peter st
Galer John, Holywell hill
Glascock Hannah and Son, Holywell hill
Harris Thomas, Market place
Herbert Edward, Fishpool st
Hilliard Joseph, George st
Ironmonger Joseph, George st
Jenkins Joseph Jackson, High st
Kent John, Market cross
Kilby Harriet, Holywell hill
Langridge Edward, Market place
Lord Elizabeth, London Colney
Payne Edward, St. Peter st
Peacock Henry, Market place
Potter William, Holywell hill
Pridmore Sarah, London Colney
Soar Henry, St. Peter st
Steabban Isaac, Fishpool st
Tallett John Kings, Fishpool st

GUNSMITHS.

Gooch William, Back st
Woolfield Thomas, Market place

HAIR DRESSERS.

Glinister Edmund, Fishpool st
Mawbey Joseph, High st
Mawbey William, Market place
Pitkin George, Holywell hill
Rawson Jonathan, London Colney
Smith William, St. Peter st

HATTERS.

Agutter Benjamin, jun. Verulam st
Gibbs Richard, St. Peter st
Martin Henry John, Market place

INNS.

Bell, John Bradberry, St. Peter st
Blue Boar, Geo. Michell, Market pl
Bull, Richd. Tebboth, London Colney
Cross Keys, Job Bates, Chequer st
Fleur de lis, Ann Bryan, Market cross
George, Daniel Foster, George st
George, Geo. Proctor, London Colney
Golden Lion, Thomas Hoar, London Colney
Great Red Lion, Jas. Dunton, High street
Pea Hen, Thomas Marks, Holywell hill, and New London road
Swan, Wm. Atkins, London Colney
Turf Hotel (and news and billiard rooms) Thos. Coleman, Chequer st
Verulam Arms Hotel (posting house) Mary Anne Wilkins, Verulam rd
White Hart, Newman Glover, Holywell hill
Woolpack, John Page, Holywell hill

IRONMONGERS.

Geard Charles, Chequer st
Manlove Richd. & Son, Market place
Mason John, High st

LINEN & WOOLLEN DRAPERS AND HABERDASHERS.

Bennett William, High st
Brown William, High st
Cherry Jesse & Samuel, Chequer st
Fisk William, George st
Syrett Thomas, Market place
Woolley James Henry, High st

MALTSTERS.

Josceline William, London Colney
Kinder Thomas, St. Peter st
Mason Richard, George st
Parsons Henry, St. Peter st
Searancke Francis, Verulam road
Wildbore Samuel, Dagnall lane

MARINE STORE, RAG AND BOTTLE DEALERS.

Moore Thomas, Spicer st
Rogers George, Portland st
Shrimpton William, College place

MILLERS.

Beaumont George, New Barns mill
Goddard Thomas, Park st
Hollinshead Wm. St. Michael's mill
Parsons Jonathan, Shafford mill
Smith Samuel, Sopwell mills
Smith William (and oil) Prea mill, St. Michael's
Woodward Thomas, Moor mill

MILLINERS & DRESS MAKRS.

Agutter Emma, Verulam st
Bean Mary, St. Peter st
Bradshaw S. and E. Fishpool st
Brown Sarah, St. Peter st
Coleman Eliz. (warehouse) Market place
Edwards Elizabeth, Chequer st
Finch Mary and Eliz. Market cross
Hare Emily, St. Peter st
Hiskett Elizabeth, Market place
Johnson Ann, Holywell hill
Woolley Jas. H. (warehouse) High st

MUSIC TEACHERS.

Brown Fras. Michael, Holywell hill
Richardson J. P. High st

NURSERY AND SEEDSMEN AND FLORISTS.

Josling Robert, George st
Maunder Vincent, High st
Sears Thomas, Sweetbriar lane
Spriggins George, St. Michael's
Varnham Charles, Holywell hill
Watson David, New London road

PAWNBROKERS.

Capel John, Market place
Gibbs Richard, Market place

PHYSICIANS.

Hawkins John, New London road
Lydekker Richard, St. Peter's

PLUMBERS, PAINTERS, GLAZIERS & PAPER-HANGERS.

Buckland Jonathan, London Colney
Hart Thomas, Park st
Kent John Walter, Chequer st
Mason Richard, Spicer st
Perry George, Verulam st
Richardson Richard, New London road
Smith Henry, St. Peter st

POULTERERS.

Caustin Thomas Frogmore, Park st
Clark George, Fishpool st
Pratt John, Fishpool st

ROPE MAKERS.

Carter Thos. (& net, &c.) Holywell hill
Dawson George, Spencer st
Gladman William, Fishpool st
Nicoll Thomas (& sack) St. Peter st
Shrubb Saml. (& sacking) Dagnall lane

SADDLERS AND COLLAR MAKERS.

Shrubb Samuel, Verulam st
Wilson Joseph, London Colney
Winch William, London Colney
Wood John, Holywell hill
Wood Thomas, Chequer st

SHOPKEEPERS & DEALRS IN GROCERIES & SUNDRIES.

Brown William, Holywell hill
Dennis Thomas, New London road
Ghost Joseph, Spencer st
Glascock George, Sopwell lane
Gregory William, Holywell hill
Griffin Martha, George st
Hair Sarah, Fishpool st
Harding Thomas, Sopwell lane
Ives John, Portland st
Lattimore Osborn, George st
Mead Joseph, Verulam st
Monk John, St. Michael's
Moore James, Spicer st
Ross Elizabeth, St. Peter st
Savage Daniel, Cross st, St. Peter's
Thomas Henry, College place
Tillcock James, Old London road
Titmass Wm. (& pork shop) St. Peter st

STAY MAKERS.

Gooch Catherine, St. Peter st
Holt Elizabeth, Holywell hill

STONE & MARBLE MASONS.

Bennett William, St. Peter st
Gregory Abraham, Fishpool st

STRAW HAT MANUFACTRS.

Marked thus * are Wholesale.

*Allway Elizabeth, Spencer st
*Ewins Thomas, St. Peter st
Gilbert Jos. (& plat dlr.) St. Michael's
*Harrison Jacob, Fishpool st
*Henly Thomas (and purple, &c. straw dyer) Fishpool street, & 46 Goodge street, *London*
*Humbles Harriet, College st
Jones Mary Ann, Cock lane
Kentish Chas. Thos. Catherine lane
*Langley Eliz. (& boys' caps) Spencer st
*Osborn Wm. Thomas, Chequer st
Pratt Sarah, Sopwell lane
*Richards Hannah, St. Peter st
*Richardson Thomas, Holywell hill
Stapleton John (and glover) London Colney
Waddington M. (and plat) New London road
*Wingrave John, St. Peter st
*Wingrave John, jun. near Spencer st
*Wingrave Josiah, Dagnall lane

SURGEONS.

Burgess William, Albany terrace, New London road
Coales John and John, Verulam st
Kingston Francis, St. Peter st
Lewis Thomas, St. Peter st
Lipscomb John Thos. Holywell hill
Rumball James Q. (private lunatic asylum) Oster-hills
Webster Richard, High st
Woodward Charles, London Colney

SURVEYORS—LAND.

Faircloth Richard (and valuer) St. Stephen's
Godman John, Park st
Gutteridge Richard, St. Peter st
Higgs Wm. (road) London Colney
Page John, Holywell hill
Rumball John Horner, St. Peter st

TAILORS AND DRAPERS.

Agutter Benjamin, Verulam st
Bradshaw Job, George st
Carter Richard, Chequer st
Cherry Luke & Son, Chequer st and Fishpool st
Fusedale George, London Colney
House Thomas, Market place
Pursell Thomas, London Colney
Reeves Harvey, Holywell hill
Stockwell Samuel, Holywell hill
Turner Charles, George st
Ward Samuel, Verulam st
Wright James, Frogmore, Park st

TALLOW CHANDLERS.

Brooks Robert, George st
Church Mary, Back st
Payne Edward, St. Peter st

TAVERNS & PUBLIC HOUSES.

Angel, Richard Dowling, Verulam road
Black Boy, Henry Green, Waterdale
Black Horse, William Field, Colney st
Black Lion, Henry Goodspeed, Fishpool st
Boot, William Reynolds, Market place
Bull & Butcher, Thomas Davies, London Colney
Coach & Horses, Thos. Bishop, Fishpool st
Cock, Sarah Brown, Cock lane
Cock & Flower Pot, Richard Lawrence, Fishpool st
Crabtree, William Smith, St. Peter st
Cross Keys, James Wing, London Colney
Crow, Thomas Barber, Fishpool st
Crown, Jacob Lyne, Holywell hill
Dog, Joseph Smith, Back st
Falcon, Richard Reynolds, Park st
Fighting Cocks, Edw. Atkins, Round house
George, Emanuel Ing, Colney st
Goat, Edward Dolling, Sopwell lane
Green Dragon, Robt. Costin, London Colney
Green Man, Joseph Aldridge, Fishpool st
Hare & Hounds, Chas. Smith, Sopwell lane
Jolly Sailor, John Kilby, Sandridge road
King Harry VIII, Mary Hibberd, St. Stephen's
King's Arms, Thomas Young, George st
King's Head, Jas. Deayton, Market place
King's Head, Thos. James, London Colney
Lamb, Joseph Sams, Chequer st
Peacock, William Hill, Cock lane
Plough, Robert Lines, Verulam st
Portland Arms, Thomas Dell, Portland st
Post Boy, James Everett, Holywell hill
Queen Adelaide, James Vass, St. Peter st
Red Cow, William Pepworth, Colney st
Red Lion, John Dennis, Fishpool st
Red Lion, John Warren, Frogmore bridge
Red Lion (Little), Charles Wm. Bennett, High street
Robin Hood, William White, Dagnall lane
Rose & Crown, Thos. Budden, St. Michael's
Royal Oak, Thomas Bates, Fishpool st
St. Christopher, Rosanna Greaves, Back st
Six Bells, William Saunders, St. Michael's
Stag, George Dawson, Spencer st
Swan, William Deards, Dagnall lane
Traveller's Friend, Wm. Dell, Verulam rd
Trumpet, Mark De Fraine, Holywell hill
Two Brewers, James Hagger, Holywell hill
Unicorn, John Aldridge, Fishpool st
Valiant Trooper, William Brown, George st
Vine, Samuel Chapple Young, Spicer st
White Horse, Richard Bagster, Park st
White Horse, Richard Delahunt, London Colney
White Horse, Ezekiel Hobbs, St. Peter st
White Lion, William Burgoine, Sopwell la
White Lion, James Cross, London Colney
William IV, George Eames, St. Peter st
Windmill, Samuel Walker, St. Peter st
Woolpack, Winsler Wise, London Colney

TIMBER MERCHANT.

Turner Thomas, Old Brewery, Fishpool st

TOY DEALERS.

Coleman Elizabeth, Market place
Crouch William, Holywell hill
Vincent Elizabeth, Market place

VETERINARY SURGEONS.

Hale William, New London road
Silvester Francis Robert, College st

WATCH & CLOCK MAKERS.

Bradshaw Thomas, Chequer st
Crouch William, Holywell hill
Munns William, Market place

WHEELWRIGHTS.

Austin Sarah, Fishpool st
Bassill William, London Colney
Childs Jesse, St. Peter st
Cook Thomas, St. Peter st
Inwood Thomas, Frogmore, Park st
Wright William, Park st

WHITESMITHS, &c.

Childs Jesse, St. Peter st
Earle Thomas, St. Peter st

WINE & SPIRIT MERCHANTS

Jenkins Joseph J. (British wines) High st
Langridge Edward (spirit) Market place
Martin Henry John (British wines) Market place
Payne Edward (British brandy and British wines) St. Peter st
Searancke Francis (spirit) Market place

Miscellaneous.

Ablett William, clerk to the court of requests, Albion place
Arnold David, pipe maker, &c. Dagnall lane
Blake Jacob, registrar of births, marriages and deaths, St. Peter st
Brown Thomas, parish clerk, Holywell hill
Deayton John, keeper of the gaol, Abbey mill lane
Deayton Thomas, sergeant at mace, Abbey mill lane
Dupree Henry, candle wick manufacturer, St. Albans Cotton mill
Ferrari Bernard, looking-glass manufacturer, Fishpool st
Gas Works, St. Stephen's—James Peacock, manager
Godman Thomas, vestry clerk, St. Stephen's
Greenwood James, relieving officer, near Redbourn road
Harcourt Thomas, millwright & engineer, near Verulam st
Harding Francis, fruiterer & game dealer, Market place
Harkness James, tea dealer, Dagnall lane
Hayward Isaac Newton, proprietor of posting horses, New London road
Lunatic Asylum, Oster hills—James Q. Rumball, surgeon
M'Chain Kirkpatrick, travelling draper, Dagnall lane
Mawbey Wm. musical instrument seller, Market place
Monk John, parish clerk of St. Michael's, St. Michael's
Police Station Office, Back of Town hall—Joseph Douglas, superintendent
Rumball James Q. surgeon of private lunatic asylum, Oster hills
Sibley William, house, &c. agent, New London road
Union Workhouse, Oster hills—Wm. Weir, governor; Helen Weir, matron
Water Works, High st—William Langley, manager
Woollam & Co. silk mill, Abbey mill lane

COACHES.

All call at the Pea Hen unless otherwise expressed.

To LONDON, the *Royal Mail* (from Derby and Halifax) every morning at four—the *Swallow* (from Birmingham) at six—the *Favourite* (from Luton) every morning (Sunday excepted) at half-past seven—the *Express* (from Leeds) every morning at eight—the *Times* (from Dunstable) every morning (Sunday excepted) at a quarter before nine—and the *Accommodation*, from the Fleur de Lis, every morning (Sunday ex.) at nine.

To LONDON, a *Coach* (from Wellingborough) every afternoon (Sunday excepted) at one, and a *Coach* (from Northampton) at a quarter past two—the *Defiance* (from Manchester) every afternoon at half-past three, and the *Star* (from Liverpool) at four—the *New Coach* (from Bedford) every Monday, Wednesday and Friday morning at ten—and the *Civility*, on the same mornings at half-past ten.

The following Coaches are from London.

To BEDFORD, the *New Coach*, every Tuesday, Thursday and Saturday afternoon at four, and the *Civility*, at half-past four.

To BIRMINGHAM, the *Swallow*, every evening at half-past eight. [at ten.

To DERBY, the *Royal Mail*, every night

To DUNSTABLE, the *Times*, every evening (Sunday ex.) at a quarter before seven.

To LEEDS, the *Express*, every evening at half-past seven. [at eight.

To LIVERPOOL, the *Star*, every evening

To LUTON, the *Favourite*, calls at the Fleur de Lis, every evening at half-past 7.

To MANCHESTER, the *Defiance*, every night at half-past nine.

To NORTHAMPTON, a *Coach*, every afternoon (Sunday excepted) at two.

To WELLINGBOROUGH, a *Coach*, every afternoon (Sunday excepted) at half-past one.

CONVEYANCE BY RAILWAY.

To LONDON, BIRMINGHAM, &c. a *Coach*, from the Blue Boar Inn, Market place, to the Watford station, every morning at half-past seven, to meet the trains, and returns at seven at night.

CARRIERS.

To LONDON, — Clarke, from the Cock, daily; — Codgbrook, from the Bell Inn, James Humphreys, from Holywell hill, and — White, from the Parcel office, every Monday, Wednesday and Friday.

To LONDON, George Clarke, from Fishpool street, the Garforths, from Colney street, — Clare, from the Little Red Lion, — Shepherd and — Ellis, from the Great Red Lion, — Deacon, from the Cock, Haydon and Stokes, and — Whitbread, from the Windmill, all every Monday and Thursday—and — Curtis's *Van* passes through every Tues. evening.

To BIRMINGHAM, — Clare, from the Little Red Lion, every Wednesday and Saturday morning.

To DAVENTRY, — Shepherd, from the Great Red Lion, every Wednesday and Saturday morning.

To HATFIELD, HERTFORD and WARE, James Tillcock, from Old London road and the Bell Inn, every Monday, Wednesday and Fri. morning.

To LUTON, — Clark, from the Cock, every morning; — Deacon, from the same place, every Monday & Thursday morning, Haydon and Stokes, from the Windmill, every Wednesday and Saturday; and George Clark, from Fishpool street, every Monday morning.

To LUTON and AMPTHILL, — Whitbread, from the Windmill, every Wednesday and Saturday morning.

To STONY STRATFORD, — Curtis's *Van*, from the Great Red Lion, every Friday morning.

To TOWCESTER, — Ellis's *Van*, from the Great Red Lion, every Wednesday and Saturday morning.

To WELLINGBOROUGH, — Codgbrook, from the Bell Inn, every Sunday, Tuesday and Friday morning.

SAWBRIDGEWORTH,

A RESPECTABLE and populous village, in the parish of its name and hundred of Braughin, is 24 miles N.N.E. from London, 11½ E. from Hertford, and about 5 S. from Bishops Stortford—situated near the navigable river Stort, and on the line of the Northern and Eastern railway. Though deprived of the consequence formerly attached to it as a market town, this place maintains that of a prosperous village, and within the last twenty years it has considerably increased in size and population. It enjoys a trade in malt of some importance, with the facility of water conveyance by the river above mentioned; and its home trade is assisted by its local position as a continual thoroughfare for travellers: this advantage, however, must necessarily be impaired, in some degree, when the railway referred to becomes the medium of transit. The church, dedicated to St. Mary, contains several elegant monuments; one to Sir Ralph Jocelyn is rich, and merits inspection, as also does that to Sir John Leventhorpe. The benefice is a vicarage, in the incumbency of the Rev. Thos. Hutchinson. There are places of worship for independents and Wesleyan methodists. Fairs are held here on the 23rd of April and 20th of October. The parish of Sawbridgeworth contained, in 1831, 2,231 inhabitants.

POST OFFICE, Cock street, Charles Norris, *Post Master.*—Letters from LONDON arrive (by the Norwich and Newmarket mail) every night at eleven, and are despatched every morning at two.

NOBILITY, GENTRY AND CLERGY.

Alston Rowland, esq. M. P. Pisobury
Bennett Mr. Edward, London road
Bright Jno. esq. Great Providence hse
Brown Adam, esq. Fair green
Dyson Mrs. —, Bell st
Elliott Miss Margaret, Fair green
Fawcett Mrs. —, Cock st
Garratt Joseph, esq. Bell st
Hutchinson Rev. Thomas Vicarage house
Le de Spencer Hon. Lady, Hyde hall
Lord Mrs. Mary, London road
Lord Mr. Roger Rant, London road
Lyles the Misses, Spelbrook
Steevens Mr. George, London road
Stewart Rev. James, London road
Stock Mrs. Matilda, London road
Tyler Rev. Herbert, London road
Webber William, esq. Cock st
White Miss Maria, Church st
Wilson Mrs. Mary, London road

ACADEMIES.

Norris Richard (day) Bell st
Shipway James (boarding) Providence house
Whitnall Miss (boarding) Cock st

ATTORNEYS.

Sims and Unwin, Fair green
Williams Thos. Nathl. Grove lodge

BAKERS.

Billings George, Bell st
Cole Thomas (and confectioner and toy dealer) Church st
Parsons Edward, London road
Prentice Smith, Bell st

BARGE OWNERS.

Barnard John, the Mill
Whitnall William, Cock st

BLACKSMITHS.

Bush William, Bell st
Jocelyn William, London road

BOOT & SHOE MAKERS.

Brown James, London road
Camp Edward, Bell st
Clark John, Church st
Frost Mark, Bell st
Giffin Benjamin, Brook lane
Pipe Samuel, Cock st

BRICKLAYERS.

Prior William, London road
Vale John, London road

BUTCHERS.

Whitehead George, Fair green
Wright Thomas, Bell st

CARPENTERS & BUILDERS.

Burton John, Cock st
Sharp William, Cock st

COAL MERCHANTS.

Barnard John, the Mill
Barnard William, Fair green
Whitnall William, Cock st

FIRE, &c. OFFICE AGENTS.

ESSEX and SUFFOLK EQUITABLE, William Barnard, Fair green
PHŒNIX, Thos. Unwin, Fair green

GROCERS AND DEALERS IN SUNDRIES.

Marked thus * are also Drapers.

*Bacon John, Fair green
*Crawley Thos. (& ironmonger) Bell st
Farrow Samuel, Bell st
*Norris Charles, Cock st
Parsons Edward, London road
Perry William, Cock st
Smee William, London road
*Whitnall William Sherwood (and corn dealer) London road

HAIR DRESSERS.

Perry James (& patten maker) Cock st
Wright James (& bookseller) Cock st

INNS.

Bell & Feathers, Jos. Silcock, Cock st
White Lion (and excise office) John Smith, London road

MALTSTERS.

Barnard John, the Mill
Barnard Wm. (& factor) Fair green
Goodwin George, Sawbridgeworth
Parris Edward, Bell st
Parris William, Cock st
Quare Henry Thos. Hewett, Cock st

MILLERS.

Barnard John, the Mill
Edwards William, High Wites

MILLINERS & DRESS MAKRS

Chamberlain Sarah, London road
Crawley Jane, London road

NURSERY AND SEEDSMEN.

Mead John, Cock st
Rivers Thomas & Son, London road

PLUMBERS, PAINTERS AND GLAZIERS.

Bacon George, London road
Bright James, Bell st
Morris John, London road

SADDLERS.

Palmer Wm. (& leather cutter) Cock st
Silcock Joseph, Cock st
Williams William, London road

STRAW HAT MAKERS.

Clark Sarah, Church st
Mead Elizabeth, Cock st

SURGEONS.

Brickwell John, Cock st
Leech Edward (& registrar) Bell st

TAILORS AND DRAPERS.

Burges Thomas, Cock st
Perry James, Cock st

TAVERNS & PUBLIC HOUSES.

Bell, Robert Bright, Cock st
Bull, Elizabeth Ryder, London road
George the Fourth, Joshua Crow, Bell st
Greyhound, Ann Whitehead, Spelbrook
Hand & Crown, Daniel Cakebread
King of Prussia, John May, London road

WATCH MAKERS.

Pratt Thomas, Cock st
Pratt William, Church st

Miscellaneous.

Clarke Henry, fishmonger, Cock st
Emson John, horse dealer, Cock st
Emson John, jun. veterinary surgeon, Cock st
Groves Saml. Patmore, coach mkr, Londn rd
Smith James, wheelwright, London road
Wilson John, spirit merchant, Cock st

COACHES & CARRIERS.

To and from LONDON, BISHOPS STORTFORD, CAMBRIDGE, HAVERHILL and LINTON pass through daily.

CONVEYANCE BY WATER.

To LONDON, *Barges*, by the river Stort, daily.

STANDON, BRAUGHIN AND PUCKERIDGE.

STANDON is a village and parish in the hundred of Braughin, 27 miles N. from London, and 8 N. E. from Hertford, situated about a mile to the east of the high road to Cambridge. Charles II granted this place a charter for holding a market; but it does not appear to have derived any advantage from the privilege, for its exercise was but of short duration; indeed it does not seem to have been, at any time, a place of consequence with regard to trade. At the present day paper is manufactured here, and there are several corn mills on the small river Rib. The church, dedicated to Saint Mary, is a large ancient structure, with a tower on the north side; the living is a discharged vicarage, in the patronage and incumbency of the Rev. Henry Law. The baptists and Wesleyan methodists have places of worship, and there is an endowed free school. The parish contained, in 1831, 2,272 inhabitants.

About a mile and a half north of Standon is the village of BRAUGHIN, situated on the river Rib, in the parish and hundred of its name. In ancient times this was a place of some note, in the Norman survey called *Brachinges;* it was of sufficient consequence to have its name attached to a division of the county, and is said to have been a market town; of this importance, however, no trace now remains, and many ages must have passed away since its prosperity attracted any marked attention. The church, dedicated to St. Mary, may be termed a handsome edifice, with a square tower surmounted by a spire; the benefice is a vicarage, in the presentation of the family of Harvey. A place of worship for independents, and a free school, are in the parish. A pleasure fair is held on Whit-Monday. Population of the parish, in 1831, 1,266.

PUCKERIDGE is a hamlet in the parishes of Standon

and Braughin, about one mile south from the latter village: as respects business and appearance, it surpasses either of the above places, presenting some very good houses and shops, with an excellent inn and posting house. At Old Hall Green, about a mile and a half from Puckeridge, on the road to Ware, is St. Edmund's college, established for the education of the sons of the English nobility and gentry of the Roman catholic religion; it was erected in 1795, upon the expulsion of the English of that persuasion from their college at Douay by the French revolutionists. Courts baron are held here annually for the manors of Standon and Milkley; R. P. Ward, Esq. is lord of the former, and the latter is in the possession of Miss C. M. Mellish. A pleasure fair is held here on Easter Monday. The population of Puckeridge is included in the returns for Standon.

POST OFFICE, PUCKERIDGE, John Cates, *Post Master.*—Letters from LONDON arrive (by horse post from Ware) every morning at eight, and are despatched every evening at seven.

GENTRY AND CLERGY.

Cavendish Guy, esq. Standon
Chances Chas. Snell, esq. Little Munden
Chancer Nathaniel, esq. Green elm
Grigg Thomas, esq. Poles
Larkin Mr. John, Puckeridge
Law Rev. Henry, Standon
Mellish Miss C. M. Hammel's park
Packman Mr. John (surgeon) Puckeridge
Palmer Rev. —, Puckeridge
Price Rev. Wm. Great Munden
Say Rev. Francis Edward, Braughin
Stacey Mr. J. Great Munden
Watts Wm. Henry, esq. The Mount, Braughin
Woodward Rev. William Edward, Braughin

ACADEMIES & SCHOOLS.

Carter Charles William (& registrar) Puckeridge
FREE SCHOOL, Standon—Thomas Gray, master
Parr Caroline (boarding and day), Puckeridge
Shoebridge Miss (boarding & day), Puckeridge
Walker William (and registrar) Braughin
Woodward Rev. William Edward, Braughin

BAKERS.

Burr William, Standon
Clements William, Puckeridge
Gault James, Standon
Huttlestone Charles, Braughin
Keirby William, Puckeridge
Lees George, Puckeridge
Walker William, Braughin

BASKET MAKERS.

Newman John, Braughin
Whittaker Jonathan, Braughin

BLACKSMITHS.

Barron William, Standon
Barron William, Braughin
Griffin David, Puckeridge
Marchant James, Puckeridge
Mole Chamberlain, Braughin
Summerlin George, Great Munden

BOOT & SHOE MAKERS.

Aylott William, Braughin
Benn Isaac, Braughin
Clark Daniel, Standon
Clark William, Standon
Clark William, jun. Standon
Drage David, Braughin
Fairhurst George, Standon
Giffin James, Puckeridge
Knight James, Puckeridge
Lees George, Puckeridge
Marchant Francis, Braughin
Parker Henry, Standon
Reeks Mark, Puckeridge
Saunders Stephen, Standon
Smith Charles, Braughin

BRICKLAYERS.

Hagger William, Braughin
Munt William, Great Munden

BUTCHERS.

Batt Joseph, Standon
Bennett William, Standon
Lawrence —, Puckeridge
Mumford William, Coller's end
Nichol John, Puckeridge
Waldock William, Braughin

CARPENTERS.

Ginn Edward (and brick maker) Puckerdge
Hilliard Joseph, Great Munden
Lawrence Edward, Puckeridge
Lawrence Isaac, Braughin
Lawrence Samuel, Great Munden
Merchant James, Braughin
Newman Benjamin, Standon
Smith John, Puckeridge
Warner William, Puckeridge
Whittaker William, Standon

GROCERS AND DEALERS IN SUNDRIES.

Marked thus * are also Drapers.

Anderton Henry, Braughin
*Bangs Jane & Martha, Puckeridge
*Cole Thomas, Braughin
Cundall William, Standon
*Foster Michael (and hop merchant) Standon
Gillett John, Puckeridge
*Lawrence Edward, Braughin
Lawrence Samuel Great Munden
Mardlin John, Puckeridge
*Neobard James, Puckeridge
*Purdue Simon, Braughin
*Smith George, Puckeridge
Smith Sarah, Puckeridge
Smith Sarah, Great Munden
*Webster Thomas, Braughin
Whittaker William, Standon
Wyman William, Braughin

INN.

Bell (posting house) Samuel Hort, Puckeridge

MALTSTERS.

Adams Samuel, Puckeridge
Clark Thomas Prior, Braughin
Smith John and James, Standon
Smith John, jun. Braughin
Welch James, Braughin

MILLERS.

Smith John and James, Standon
Stringer Joseph, Standon

STRAW HAT AND DRESS MAKERS.

Darvin Mary, Puckeridge
Smith Elizabeth, Puckeridge

TAILORS.

Neobard James, Puckeridge
Singleton Edward, Standon
Smith Edward, Braughin
Smith George, Puckeridge

TAVERNS & PUBLIC HOUSES.

Adam and Eve, Wm. Halden, Braughin
Anchor, John Fletcher, Puckeridge
Axe and Compass, Geo. Pinman, Braughin
Bay Horse, Benjn. Hayward, Old hall green
Bear, James Merchant, Braughin
Bell, Joseph Batt, Standon
Bell, Daniel Smith, Braughin
Bird in Hand, Jeremiah Walls, Braughin
Buffalo's Head, Elizh. Bunce, Puckeridge
Bull, William Bowcock, Braughin
Chequers, William Munt, Great Munden
Crown & Falcon, John Mardlin, Puckeridge
Falcon, William Lambert, Standon
Fleece, George Nicholl, Braughin
Rising Sun, John Stringer, Puckeridge
Rose & Crown, John Newman, Braughin
White Hart, William Lagden, Puckeridge
White Lion, Benj. Boltwood, Great Munden
Windmill, Ann Gault, Standon
Woolpack, Rt. Archer Parker, Puckeridge

VETERINARY SURGEONS.

Edwards William, Puckeridge
Everett Robert, Puckeridge

WHEELWRIGHTS.

Merchant James, Puckeridge
Ridenton John Seymore, Standon

Miscellaneous.

Carter Chas. Wm. bookseller, Puckeridge
Geekie John, road surveyor, Puckeridge
Grout James, saddler, Puckeridge
Grubb James, fishmonger, Puckeridge
Houchin Jas. painter & glazier, Puckeridge
Judd James, cooper, Puckeridge
Monk John, livery stables, Puckeridge
Nicholl George, rope maker, Braughin
Pinman George, cabinet maker, Braughin
Whittaker Martha, paper maker, Standon

COACHES.

To LONDON, the *Alert*, from the Bell Inn, every Monday and Friday morning at ½ past 6, and Tuesday, Wednesday, Thursday and Saturday mornings at 7.

Besides the above, *coaches* to and from LONDON, CAMBRIDGE, PETERBORO' & YORK, pass through Puckeridge daily.

CARRIERS.

To LONDON, George Mitchell & Massey Gillett, from their houses, Puckeridge, every Tuesday and Friday

To and from LONDON, CAMBRIDGE, PETERBORO' and YORK, waggons pass through Puckeridge daily.

STANSTEAD-ABBOTS, EASTWICK, HUNSDON

AND NEIGHBOURHOODS.

STANSTEAD-ABBOTS is a village and parish in the hundred of Braughin—19 miles N. from London, about three from Hoddesdon and two from Ware; situated upon the river Lea, which passes through its centre, and here assumes a breadth commensurate with its importance as a navigable stream. This and other advantages in point of situation entitle it to rank higher as a town of trade than it really does, its staple articles being confined to malt and corn. The church, dedicated to St. James, stands upon an eminence, about a mile south-east from the village; it is of considerable antiquity, and contains some very old monuments: the benefice is a vicarage, in the incumbency of the Rev. J. W. Thomas. There are six alms-houses, and a free school, founded by Sir Edward Bash. This village is noticed in history as having within its limits a certain building, in which a plot for the assassination of Charles II was said to have been hatched; it obtained the name of the 'Rye-house Plot,' and several persons were condemned and executed as being privy to the alleged conspiracy; the old fabric in which the conspirators were sworn to have assembled is now occupied by one Godfrey, a woolcomber. At the last census the parish contained 966 inhabitants.

EASTWICK, a small village and parish in the same hundred as Stanstead, is three miles from that place, on the road to Sawbridgeworth. The neat church here, dedicated to St. Botolph, contains a monument to the memory of a knight templar, which has been frequently noticed by antiquaries. In 1831 the population of the parish was 169—being a *decrease*, in ten years, of 43.

About two miles north-east from Stanstead, in the same hundred, stands the pleasant village of HUNSDON, in the parish of its name. From the church, and other positions in the neighbourhood, some beautiful views may be obtained, including the course of the Stort to join the Lea. The church is an ancient edifice, and contains some monuments of remote date; the living is a rectory, in the incumbency of the Rev. Nicholas Calvert; the Rev. Robert Calvert is his curate. Hunsdon House, the residence of Nicholson Calvert, Esq., was in the time of Henry VIII a palace, in which the children of that monarch were educated; and, though much reduced in size, it still preserves a grand and venerable appearance. The parish contains about 600 inhabitants.

POST OFFICE, Main street, STANSTEAD-ABBOTS, Sarah Salmons, *Post Mistress.*—Letters from all parts are delivered every morning at eight, and are despatched every afternoon at five.

GENTRY AND CLERGY.

Booth Chas. esq. Netherfield house
Calvert Col. —, Hunsdon
Calvert Edmond, esq. Bonningtons
Calvert Rev. Nicholas, New Vicarage, Hunsdon
Calvert Nicholson, esq. Hunsdon hse
Calvert William, esq. Hunsdon
Curphey Major, Newlands
Dick Major, Stansteadbury house
Hankin Daniel, esq. Main st
Phelips Charles, esq. Briggens park
Pratt Mrs. —, St. Margaret's
Thomas Rev. J. W. Vicarage house, Stanstead
Ward Henry, esq. Gilstone park
Williams Miss —, Cat's hill house

INNS & PUBLIC HOUSES.

Crown, Mary Brett, St. Margaret's
Fox & Hounds, Jas. Haney, Hunsdon
George and Dragon, George Croft, St. Margaret's
Kings Arms, John Munt, Rye house
Pied Bull, James Smith (& brewer) Main street, Stanstead-Abbots
Plummer Ward's Arms, Wm. Foster, Gilstone
Plummer Ward's Arms, Jno. Holmes, Eastwick
Red Lion, Michl. Woodhouse, Main st, Stanstead-Abbots
Rose & Crown, Saml. Brazier, near the Bridge

SHOPKEEPRS, TRADERS, &c.

The letters S. A. *attached to an address mean* STANSTEAD-ABBOTS.

Allin Nathaniel and William, millers, Stanstead mills
Archer John, cattle dealer, Eastwick
Archer John, jun. cattle dealer, Mead lodge, Eastwick
Blackaby Jos. baker, Main st, S. A.
Buckland Wm. land surveyor, Eastwck
Bywater Thos. general dealer, Main st
Cain Jno. boot & shoe maker, Main st
Camp Robert, blacksmith, Gilstone
Clark Wm. grocer, &c. Main st, S.A.
Cobham Thos. and Chas. maltsters, Elm Tree
Cooper John, brewer and maltster, Main st, S. A.
Cordell Joseph, grocer, &c. Main st, S. A.
Crabb Mary, baker, Main st, S. A.
Curtis Wm. tailor, Main st, S. A.
Death Wm. miller, Hunsdon mill
Ekins William, tailor, Main st, S. A.
Evans John, grocer, &c. Eastwick
French Mrs. —, mistress of Mrs. Pratt's girl's school, St. Margaret's
Godfrey Thomas, woolcomber, Old Rye house
Gottard Edmund, general dealer, Main st, S. A.
Haney John, wheelwright and carpenter, Hunsdon
Hardy Chas. general dealer, Main st, S.A.
Hitch Thos. maltster, Barge yd. S. A.
Lawrence Edward and Robert, maltsters, corn factors, and coal, &c. merchants, Lea wharf, S. A.
Mason William, boot and shoe maker, Main st, Stanstead-Abbots
Miller John, master of Bash's chapel school, Stanstead-Abbots
Miller William, general dealer, Main st, Stanstead-Abbots
Perkins Richard, carpenter, Main st, Stanstead-Abbots
Reddington John, general dealer, Hunsdon
Roe John, wheelwright, Eastwick
Smith Benjamin, blacksmith, Main st, Stanstead-Abbots
Smith Sarah, butcher, Main st, S. A.
Soole Geo. saddler, Main st, S. A.
Suckling Henry, blacksmith, Main st, Stanstead-Abbots
Taylor Samuel Marsh warden, Main st, Stanstead-Abbots
Tween Edwd. painter, plumber, &c. Main st, S. A.
Waller Charles, bricklayer, Main st, S. A.
Waller Isaac, maltster, the Rye

COACHES.

CALLING AT THE PIED BULL.

To LONDON, the *Times* (from Hadham), every morning (Sunday excepted) at eight, and the *Fly* (from Roydon), every morning (Sun. excepted) at half-past 7.

To HADHAM, the *Times* (from London), every even. (Sun. ex.) at half-past six.

To ROYDON, the *Fly* (from London), every even. (Sun. ex.) at half-past six.

CARRIER.

To LONDON, HODDESDON, &c. Aaron Trump, from Main st, every Monday and Friday evening.

CONVEYANCE BY WATER.

To and from LONDON, &c. — Allin's and — Lawrence's *Vessels*, from their wharf, Lea side

---

STEVENAGE,

WITH THE VILLAGES OF GRAVELEY, WATTON AND NEIGHBOURHOODS.

STEVENAGE is a market town and parish in the hundred of Broadwater, 31 miles N. N. W. from London and 12 N. W. by N. from Hertford, pleasantly situated on the great north road; and consists principally of one long and rather spacious street, with two or three inferior ones. In the Saxon times it was named *Stigenhace* or *Stigenhaught*, and in Domesday-book it is written *Stevenach*. About a mile southward of the town, on the west side of the road, are six large 'barrows,' supposed to have been formed by the Danes, several battles having been fought between them and the Saxons in this county, and some fields near them still retaining the name of 'Danes-blood.' To its thoroughfare situation Stevenage is mainly indebted for whatever share of prosperity it enjoys—independent of that, it at present is a place of but little consequence. The platting of straw furnishes employment to many females in the town and its neighbourhood. Petty sessions for the division are held here, and the bishop of London holds a manorial court annually. The parish church, dedicated to Saint Nicholas, is a neat structure; it comprises a nave, chancel and side aisles, and has a square tower at its western end, surmounted by a spire; it stands on an eminence, and is approached by a fine avenue of trees. The living is a rectory, in the patronage of William Robert Baker, Esq.; the present incumbent is the Rev. George Becher Blomfield, M. A. There is a place of worship for Wesleyan methodists. The free grammar school here was founded by the Rev. Thos. Allen in the reign of Queen Mary; the master is appointed by Trinity college, Cambridge; and the present master is the Rev. J. Osborne Seager, B. A., of that college. A national school, three ancient alms-houses, and some bequests to the poor, comprise the charities. Henry Trigg, an eccentric individual, who carried on the business of grocer in this town, by his will (proved 15th October, 1724,) devised the principal part of his property to his brother, upon the condition contained in the following extract from his will:—

> "And as to my body I commit it to the west end of my *hovel*, to be decently laid there upon a floor, erected by my executor, upon the *purlin*, for the same purpose; and if my brother, George Trigg, should refuse to lay my body under my hovel, then, what I have bequeathed unto him, as all my lands and tenements, I lastly bequeath them unto my nephew, William Trigg and his heirs, for ever, upon his seeing that my body is decently laid upon there as aforesaid."

These singular directions were faithfully complied with; the corpse still remaining (or was lately) upon the rafters of the west end of the hovel. Stevenage received a charter for a weekly market and three annual fairs from James I; the market is still held on Tuesday—but, from the contiguity of other towns in which large markets are held, that of Stevenage has gone to decay, except for cattle; two of its fairs, also, are extinct—the one that is continued is holden on the 22nd of September, for cattle, pedlery, &c. The parish contained, by the returns for 1831, 1,859 inhabitants.

About two miles north from Stevenage, in the same

hundred, is the little village of GRAVELEY; the parish, which bears the same name, is likewise of small dimensions. The old Roman road leading from Verulam to Chesterfield passes through the parish. The church, dedicated to St. Mary, is a neat structure, having a square embattled tower at the west end, surmounted by a spire; the benefice is a rectory, with that of Chivesfield annexed, in the presentation of the family of Green. Population of the parish, in 1831, 331.

WATTON is a village and parish in the same hundred as Stevenage, about five miles S. E. from that town, situated on the river Beane. The church, dedicated to St. Mary and St. Andrew, is a small edifice, containing some handsome monuments, with a square embattled tower; the benefice is a rectory, in the presentation of Abel Smith, Esq., and incumbency of the Rev. Edward Bickersteth. A school upon the national plan, and one for infants, are in the village. Population of parish, 830.

POST OFFICE, STEVENAGE, Charlotte Aldham, *Post Mistress*.—Letters from LONDON arrive (by the Glasgow mail) every night at half-past eleven, and are despatched (by the Hull and Lincoln mail) every morning at half-past three.—Letters from the North arrive every morning at half-past three, and are despatched every night at half-past eleven.

*** *The names without address are in* STEVENAGE.

GENTRY AND CLERGY.

Bellamy John, esq. Gravely
Bickersteth Rev. Edw. Watton rectory
Bishop Thomas, esq. M.D. Gravely
Blomfield Rev. George Becher, Stevenage rectory
Bradberry Rev. Robert, Stevenage
Chambers Mrs. Ann, Stevenage
Crowton Robert, esq. Gravely
Fitz-John Mr. Geo. Wells (attorney) Stevenage
Gibbs Mr. William, Watton
Green John, esq. Bradbury end
Green Rev. John F. Gravely
Heathcote Unwin, esq. Sheephall bury
Hill Mrs. Mary, Watton
Leete Rev. T. T. Gravely
Pollard Rev. John, Bennington
Parkins Edward, esq. Chisfield lodge
Pryor John Izard, esq. Clay hall, Walkern
Seager Rev. J. Osborne, B.A. Stevenage
Smith Abel, esq. Watton wood hall
Smith Mr. George, Stevenage
Turner Lieut. Jellicoe, R.N. Stevenage
Whittington Richard, esq. Stevenage
Woodford Miss —, Stevenage

ACADEMIES & SCHOOLS.

Fisher Alice (day and boarding)
FREE GRAMMAR SCHOOL—Rev. J. Osborne Seager, B.A. master
INFANTS' SCHOOL, Watton—Frances Jeffery, mistress
NATIONAL SCHOOL—Oliver Whittle, master; Elizabeth Griggs, mistress
NATIONAL SCHOOL, Watton—Chas. Wood, master; Harriet Viviers, mistress
Otway Richard Septimus (day and boarding)

BAKERS & FLOUR DEALERS.

Beadle Mary M.
Moulden Simon
Moules George
Taylor William
Waldock William, Watton
Wiltshire John, Watton

BLACKSMITHS.

Beechner John, Watton
Boutell William
Bush William Aden
Prime Robert, Gravely
Saunders William, Watton
Stapleton Thomas.
Steel Thomas

BOOT AND SHOE MAKERS.

Allen William
Ansell Joseph
Chalkley John
Colley William
Craft James
Shelford William
Taylor William
Tucker Charles
Wiltshire John, Watton

BREWERS.

Hicks and Richardson
Morris Samuel, Watton

BRICKLAYERS.

Hutcherson Robert, Watton
Munsey Samuel
Munsey William

BUTCHERS.

Adkins John
Field Hannah, Watton
Field John
Field Richard, Watton
Moulden Joseph and Simon
Parrott Joseph
Titmuss Samuel
Waby Benjamin

CARPENTERS & JOINERS.

Andrews Edward, Watton
Austin William
Dorrington John and Son, Watton
Draper Benjamin
Munsey Amy
Toll Robert

COAL & CORN DEALERS.

French William
Lodgsdon William

COLLAR MAKERS.

Harvey Mary
Martin John
Odwell Thomas, Watton

GROCERS AND DEALERS IN SUNDRIES.

Ansell Joseph
Ansell Samuel
Ashwood John (and farrier)
Baron John, Watton
Bates Benjamin, Watton
Bates Joseph
Benison Townsend George
Craft Matthew, Gravely
Favell James
Field Charles
Franklin John Birdsey
French Thomas
Grove William Bell
Hebbs Joseph
Moginie Joseph, Watton
Moules James, Gravely
Parker Sophia, Watton
Poulton Edward (and plat dealer)
Ray Samuel, Watton
Taylor William

INNS—COMMERCIAL.

White Lion, Mary Stalley
White Swan (& posting) Thos. Cass

LINEN DRAPERS.

Benison Townsend George
Favell James
Franklin John Birdsey
French Thomas
Hebbs Joseph
Moginie Joseph, Watton
Ray Samuel, Watton

MALTSTERS.

Folbigg William
Newman Fredk. (& miller) Watton

MILLINERS & STRAW HAT MAKERS.

Boutell Mary
Munns Mary

PLUMBERS, PAINTERS, AND GLAZIERS.

Hughes George
Lawrance Thomas and Son, Watton
Mackaness George

SURGEONS.

Connell Thomas John
Wall William

TAILORS.

Ansell William, Watton
Deller Horatio
Jones Matthew (and hatter)
Lucas James
Poulton John

TAVERNS & PUBLIC HOUSES.

Bull, William Waldock, Watton
Chequers, Joseph Carpenter
Coach and Horses, Robert Smith
George & Dragon, James Craft, Gravely
George and Dragon, George Lawrance
George & Dragon, Geo. Lawrance, Watton
Marquess of Granby, Daniel Norman
Old Castle, John Parratt
Red Lion, Edward Waby
Unicorn, John Chalkley
Waggon & Horses, Chas. Foreman, Watton
White Hart, George Weedon
White Horse, Joseph Norton
White Horse, George Rose, Watton

WHEELWRIGHTS.

Crawley John, Watton
Mercer Thomas, Watton
Smith Robert
Titmuss Joseph

Miscellaneous.

Benison Townsend George, glass dealer
Dickins William, hair dresser
Harding William, road surveyor
Keer John, draper and clothier
Moulden William, cooper
Muncey Saml. agent to Phœnix fire office
Munns William, hair dresser
Oliver William, brazier and tinman
Rogers John, watch maker
Shrimpton John, marine store dealer
Squires Thomas, farrier

COACHES.

To LONDON, the *Royal Mail* (from Glasgow) and *Royal Mail* (from Hull and Lincoln) calls at the Post Office and Coach and Horses, every morning at 3; goes through Welwyn and Hatfield.
To BALDOCK, a *coach* (from London) every evening (Sunday excepted) at half-past seven.
To GLASGOW, the *Royal Mail*, every evening at half past eleven; goes through Baldock and Biggleswade.
To HULL and LINCOLN, the *Royal Mail*, calls at the Post Office, every night at half-past eleven.

CARRIERS.

To LONDON, John Little's *Waggons*, every Tuesday and Thursday.
Besides the above, carriers to and from LONDON, LEEDS and YORK, pass daily.

—o—

TRING,

WITH THE HAMLETS OF LONG MARSTON AND WILSTONE, AND THE VILLAGES OF ALDBURY AND WIGGINTON, AND NEIGHBOURHOODS.

TRING is a market town and parish in the hundred of Dacorum—31 miles N.W. by W. from London, 5 N.W. from Berkhampstead, and 7 E. by S. from Aylesbury, in Buckinghamshire; situated at the most westerly part of the county—the London and Birmingham railway passing within a mile and a half of the town, and the Grand Junction canal at a shorter distance; for the supply of the latter there are within the parish five large reservoirs, covering, together, an extent of nearly two hundred and fifty acres. The origin of this town is of considerable antiquity; at the division of the county by Alfred, it was considered of sufficient importance to give name to a hundred, then called *Treung*. The town consists principally of one long street, containing many well-built houses, some of which are of modern erection. The market house, which is manorial property, stands on the north side of the main street. Courts leet and baron are held annually by the lord of the manor, when two constables are appointed. Tring Park, covered with noble wood, is contiguous to the town; the mansion was erected by Charles II, for his favourite mistress, familiarly called *Nell Gwynn;* it has since been modernized, is now the property of the lord of the manor, and occupied by Thomson Hankey, Esq. Tring gave birth, in 1699, to Robert Hill, a remarkable self-taught linguist; he died in 1777. Canvass, straw plat, silk and parchment comprise the manufactures of the place: the two first-named branches have for many years been established here; that of silk, belonging to Messrs. Evans and Co., of London, employs more than three hundred hands.

The church, dedicated to St. Peter and St. Paul, situated about the centre of the town, is a spacious and handsome embattled structure, with a tower at its western end; the interior is neat, the chancel is embellished with several marble monuments, and there is a handsomely enriched font. The living is a perpetual curacy, in the gift of Christ college, Oxford, and present incumbency of the Rev. Charles Lacy. There are places of worship for baptists and independents. A free school, conducted upon the Lancasterian plan, was established in 1829 by Mr. John Hull, and is now supported by contributions. The market, held on Friday, is a large one for straw plat, and is well supplied with the ordinary articles of consumption; the fairs, for cattle and pleasure, are on Easter-Monday and Michaelmas-day. The population of the parish of Tring (including the hamlets of LONG MARSTON and WILSTONE), by the census for 1831, amounted to 3,488 persons.

About two miles and a half E.N.E. from Tring, in the same hundred, is the village of ALDBURY, pleasantly situated, in the parish of its name, at the foot of the Chiltern hills, the summits of which are covered with thick plantations. Near the village is a lofty stone monument to the noble father of inland navigation, the Duke of Bridgwater. The church, dedicated to Saint John the Baptist, is an ancient edifice, containing some interesting monumental brasses, and an altar tomb of an armed knight and his lady: the benefice is a rectory, in the patronage of the trustees of the late Earl of Bridgwater; the present incumbent is the Rev. James Galloway. Population of the parish, 457.

WIGGINTON is an adjoining parish to Aldbury, the village being situated about one mile from Tring, in a very healthy part of the county, on a gentle eminence, commanding an expansive and fine view of the country round. The church is dedicated to St. Giles; the living, which is a rectory, is in the gift of the principal and fellows of Jesus college, Oxford. By the returns made in 1831, the parish contained 536 inhabitants.

POST OFFICE, Market street, TRING, Elizabeth Montague, *Post Mistress.*—Letters from LONDON arrive (by railway) every afternoon at one and night at eleven, and are despatched every morning at four and forenoon at half-past eleven.—Letters from the North arrive (by railway) every morning at half-past five, and are despatched every night at eleven.—Letters from EDGWARE, STANMORE and WATFORD arrive every night at twelve, and are despatched every morning at three.—Letters from ST. ALBANS and HERTFORD arrive (by horse post) every morning at eight, and are despatched every evening at seven.—Letters from WENDOVER and PRINCES RISBOROUGH arrive (by horse post) every evening at a quarter past six, and are despatched every morning at a quarter past six.

GENTRY AND CLERGY.

Boyd Mrs. Frances, Dunsley
Bruce Mr. Henry, Akeman st
De Fraine Rev. Richd. Prospect place
Firth Mrs. Harriet, Market st
Galloway Rev. James, Aldbury
Glover Rev. Richard, Akeman st
Gordon Jas. Adam, esq. Aldbury
Griffin Mr. William, Aylesbury road
Hankey Thomas, esq. Tring park
Harris Mr. Henry, Maidenhead st
Kay Mrs. —, Market st
Lacy Rev. Charles, Parsonage house
Meade John, esq. Frogmore house
Norman Mr. George, Market st
Woodman Mrs. Eliz. Akeman st

ACADEMIES & SCHOOLS.

Not otherwise described are Day Schools.

Blake Jos. (day & brding.) Market st
Knight Mary Ann, Market st
Miles Elizabeth (boarding) Dunsley
NATIONAL SCHOOL, Maidenhead st —Jonathan Sharp, master
Rich Elizabeth, Market st
Young Mark, Prospect place

AGENTS—LAND & TIMBER.

Brown William (& estate) Market st
Glenister John Rolfe and Son (and estate) Market st

ATTORNEYS.

Benson Richard, Maidenhead st
Faithfull George Lockton, Market st

AUCTIONEERS & APPRAISRS.

Brown William, Market st
Glenister John Rolfe & Son, Market st
Jones Garnett (appraiser) Market st
Philby John (appraiser) Market st
Woodman Thomas, Tring grove

BAKERS.

Ashby William, Aldbury
Boyd Robert, Market st
Branson Jas. (& confectioner) Akeman st
Cross Thomas, Frogmore end
Foskett John, Frogmore end
Gregory Joseph, Long Marston
Hayward Richard, Frogmore end
Hinton Henry, Akeman st
Philbey Joseph, Wilstone
Putnam Thomas, Frogmore end
Read Richard, Long Marston
Rodwell James, Wilstone
Springwell Thomas, Brook end
Tompkins Martha, Market st
Tompkins William, Market st
Walter Thomas, Wilstone
Ware Jonathan, Akeman st

BANKERS.

Butcher Thos. and Son, Market st—(draw on Drewett and Fowler, London)

BLACKSMITHS.

Coley George, Aldbury
Goodson Thomas, Wilstone
Goodson William (and edge tool maker) Market st
Grace Sebastian, Frogmore end
Newins Thomas, Frogmore end
Pocock Richard, Wigginton

BOOKSELLERS & STATIONRS

Gates Thos. (& stamp office) Markt st
Pattisson Henry (& printer and bookbinder) Market st

BOOT AND SHOE MAKERS.

Bird Thos. Akeman st
Brandon Jno. (& leather seller) Frogmore end
Chappin Samuel, Wilstone
Coughtrey Thomas, Akeman st
Kindell Francis, Market st
Kindell John, Market st
Lake James, Market st
Moulder Joseph, Market st
Norman John Charles, Frogmore end
Poole Moses, Wigginton
Rodwell Robert, Wilstone
Waring Robert, Long Marston

BREWERS.

Amsden Thomas, Market st
Brown John, Market st
Cutler George, Frogmore end
Liddington Seabrook, Market st
Northwood Timothy, Market st
Olney William, Akeman st

BRICKLAYERS.

Burch Sarah, Bottle end
Clark Joseph, Wilstone
Mortimer John, Long Marston

BUTCHERS.

Gregory Henry, Long Marston
Hanshaw James, Dunsley
Mead John, Market st
Seaton Augustus, Market st
Somes Samuel, Long Marston
Woodman Richard, Akeman st
Wright Robert, Akeman st

CABINET MAKERS AND UPHOLSTERERS.

Griffin William, Market st
Higgs William, Aylesbury road
Jones Garnett, Market st

CANVASS MANUFACTURERS.
Cato William, Akeman st
Cutler George, Frogmore end
Olney Daniel, Dunsley
Olney William, Akeman st

CARPENTERS.
Clark Thomas, Wilstone
Griffin William, Market st
Higgs William, Aylesbury road
Honour James, Aldbury
Honour Job, Frogmore end
Jones Garnett, Market st
Osborn John, Frogmore end
Stangroom Augustus, Long Marston
Williams Moses, Frogmore end

COAL DEALERS.
Clark Thomas, Wilstone
Grover Wm. and Son, Gamnel wharf
Hanshaw James, Dunsley
Landon Thomas, Cow Roast wharf

COOPERS.
Brinkman William, Market st
Rogers Joseph, Market st

CORN DEALERS.
Cato Sarah, Frogmore end
Grace Carter, Akeman st
Grover Thomas, New mill
Putnam Thomas, Frogmore end

FIRE, &c. OFFICE AGENTS.
ALLIANCE, John Rolfe Glenister and Son, Market st
ATLAS, Henry Pattison, Market st
BRITANNIA, Geo. Lockton Faithfull, Market st
COUNTY, Thos. Elliman, Market st
MEDICAL and CLERICAL, Jno. Chapman, Market st
NORWICH UNION, Jno. Philbey, Market st
ROYAL EXCHANGE, Knight and Andrews, Market st
SUN, William Brown, Market st

GROCERS & TEA DEALERS.
(See also Shopkeepers, &c.)
Butcher Thomas & Son, Market st
Norris James, Market st
Tompkins William, Market st
Warcup Charles, Aylesbury rd
Wood Jas. (& oil & colourman) Market st

HAIR DRESSERS.
Ludgate Thomas, Market st
Norris Thomas, Market st

HATTERS.
Boyd Robert, Market st
Elliman Mary and Son, Market st
Elliman Thomas, Market st

HOP MERCHANTS.
Butcher Thomas & Son, Market st
Norris James, Market st

INNS.
Bell, Thos. Christmas, Market st.
Green Man, Jane Tompkins, Market st
Harcourt Arms (and posting house) Samuel Brown, Tring station
Plough (and posting house) William Kingsley, Market st
Rose & Crown (& posting house and excise office) Timothy Northwood, Market st

IRONMONGERS.
Clement Thos. and John (and watch makers) Market st
Limbrey John (and coppersmith and brazier) Market st
Rogers Joseph, Market st.
Tompkins Wm. (& brazier) Market st

LINEN AND WOOLLEN DRAPERS.
Elliman Mary and Son, Market st
Elliman Thomas, Market st

MALTSTERS.
Brown John, Market st
Grace Carter, Akeman st

MILLERS.
Grover James, Goldfield, near Tring
Grover Wm. & Son, Gamnel wharf

MILLINERS AND DRESS MAKERS.
Clement Ann, Akeman st
Hanshaw Maria, Dunsley
Hinton Eliz. and Mary, Market st

PLUMBERS, PAINTERS AND GLAZIERS.
Knight and Andrews, Market st
Philbey Charles, Akeman st
Philbey John, Market st

ROPE AND TWINE MAKERS.
Ashby Robert, Market st
Bull James, Market st
Sutton Mary, Market st

SADDLERS AND HARNESS MAKERS.
Ashby Robert, Market st
Bull James, Market st
Prouse William, Akeman st
Sutton Mary, Market st

SHOPKEEPERS & DEALRS IN GROCERIES & SUNDRIES.
Adams John, Frogmore end
Atkins Thomas, Wigginton
Austin Beatrice, Akeman st
Austin Elizabeth, Akeman st
Bavin Thomas, Aldbury
Bransom James, Akeman st
Clark Thomas, Wilstone
Fleet Thomas, Akeman st
Foskett John, Frogmore end
Meade Elizabeth, Long Marston
Missenden Hannah (& seed dealer) Frogmore end
Page Jesse, Akeman st
Philbey Joseph, Wilstone
Read Richard, Long Marston
Rich Sarah, Market st
Rodwell James, Wilstone
Row Fanny, Akeman st
Short Humphrey, Aldbury
Springwell Thomas, Brook end
Tompkins Mary, Market st
Walter Thomas, Wilstone
Ware Jonathan, Akeman st

SILK THROWSTERS.
Evans David & Co. Tring mills, Brook end, and 121 Cheapside, *London*

STRAW HAT MANUFACTURS.
Bailey Susan, Market st
Cheshire Jane, Akeman st
Clement Ann, Akeman st
Griffin Mary, Market st
Kindell Sarah, Market st
Moulder Elizabeth, Market st
Springall Hannah, Market st

STRAW PLAT DEALERS.
Amsden Thomas, Market st
Archer James, Market st
Fleet Thomas, Akeman st
Hall John, Aldbury
Rodwell James, Wilstone
Rodwell Thomas, Wilstone
Short Joseph, Akeman st
Smith George, Dunsley
West Samuel, Akeman st

SURGEONS.
Dewsbury Peter Richard, Market st
Moody Robt. Jeninges, Frogmore hse
Pope Edward, Market st

SURVEYORS.
Brown William, Market st
Glenister John Rolfe & Son, Market st

TAILORS.
Brittain Jesse, Akeman st
Cosier John, Frogmore end
Dancer James, Wilstone
Elliman Mary and Son, Market st
Elliman Thomas, Market st
Hill George, Aylesbury road
Prentice Hy. (& clothes dealer) Aldbury
Smith Edward, Akeman st

TALLOW CHANDLERS.
Butcher Thos. and Son, Market st

TAVERNS & PUBLIC HOUSES.
Cow Roast, Thos. Landon, Cow Roast wharf
Crown, John Nash, Long Marston
George, Thomas Clarke, Frogmore end
Greyhound, Mary Elliott, Aldbury
Half Moon, Jos. & Jas. Clark, Wilstone
Queen's Arms, John Price, near Gamnel wharf
Queen's Head, James Clark, Long Marston
Robin Hood, Ann Tompkins, Dunsley
Royal Oak, William Cato, Akeman st
Trooper, Ann Hall, Aldbury
White Hart, Jonathan Cox, Long Marston

TURNERS.
Austin James, Akeman st
Page Jesse, Akeman st
Tompkins John, Aylesbury road

WHARFINGERS.
Grover Wm. & Son, Gamnel wharf
Landon Thomas, Cow Roast wharf

WHEELWRIGHTS.
Crawley William, Akeman st
Griffin Wm. (& gig maker) Market st
Montague Harley, Long Marston
Newman Thomas, Wilstone
Richardson Thomas, Aldbury

WINE & SPIRIT MERCHANT.
Brown John, Market st

Miscellaneous.
Beal William Henry, timber merchant, Aylesbury road
Brown John, dyer, Akeman st
Chapman John, chymist & druggist, Market st
Edwin Edmund, confectioner, Market st
Gower William, fellmonger & parchment maker, Frogmore end
Holland Henry, engineer, Aylesbury rd
Norris Thomas, fruiterer, Market st
Osborn Thomas, hay dealer, Aldbury
Warcup Charles, dealer in china curiosities, Aylesbury road
Webb Paul, basket maker, Frogmore end

COACHES,

To LONDON, the *Despatch* (from Aylesbury) calls at the Rose & Crown, every morning at nine; goes through Berkhampstead.

To AYLESBURY, the *Despatch* (from London) calls at the Rose and Crown, every evening at seven.

To OXFORD, the *Courier*, every afternoon at half-past three and evening at seven; goes through Aylesbury.

RAILWAY CONVEYANCE.

To LONDON, *Trains*, daily (Sunday excepted) at six minutes before eight morning; at twenty-eight minutes after eleven forenoon; about five afternoon; and about a quarter before seven and a quarter before nine evening—the *Mail Trains* (also on Sunday) at twenty-eight minutes before one morning, and about four afternoon.

Sunday Trains.

At six minutes before eight morning, and a little before six evening,

To BIRMINGHAM, *Trains*, daily (Sunday excepted) at twenty-five minutes before ten and a quarter before eleven forenoon; at a quarter before four and twenty-five minutes before six afternoon, and at a quarter before seven evening—the *Mail Trains* (also on Sunday) at twenty-five minutes before one morning, and a quarter past ten night.

Sunday Trains.

At a quarter before ten morning, and at a quarter before seven evening.

To AYLESBURY, a *Train*, every day at twelve and evening at seven.

*** A *Coach*, from the Plough Inn, TRING, to meet all the trains, and an *Omnibus*, from the Rose and Crown.

CARRIERS.

To LONDON, William Stevens's *Cart*, from his house, Dunsley, and Joseph Hedges' *Waggons*, from the Plough Inn, every Tuesday and Friday—Parker and Co.'s *Waggons*, from the Rose & Crown Inn, every Tuesday, Thursday & Friday—and Thomas Rodwell's *Waggons*, every Wednesday and Sunday.

To AYLESBURY, Parker & Co.'s *Waggons*, from the Rose and Crown Inn, every Sunday, Thursday and Saturday—Joseph Hedges, from the Plough Inn, every Thursday and Sunday—Thomas

Rodwell, every Tuesday and Friday—and William Turner, every Saturday.

To BERKHAMPSTEAD, John Bunn, from the Plough Inn, every Monday, Friday and Saturday.

To BUCKINGHAM, Joseph Hedges' *Waggons*, from the Plough Inn, every Sunday and Thursday.

CONVEYANCE BY WATER.

To LONDON and all places on the line of the Grand Junction Canal, and goods forwarded to all other parts of the kingdom, by Grover and Son, from Gamnel wharf, and Thomas Landon, from Cow Roast wharf, daily.

WARE,

WITH THE VILLAGE OF WADESMILL AND NEIGHBOURHOODS.

WARE is a populous and flourishing market town and parish, in the hundred of Braughin—21 miles N. from London, 30 S. from Cambridge, and rather more than two miles E. N. E. from Hertford; situated in a valley, on the north-eastern side of the navigable river Lea, on the high road from London to Cambridge, &c. The town, which consists of several streets, is well supplied with water, and is in a general state of improvement. At an early period the Danes took possession of this town and fortified it; after they had been subdued and expelled, Edward I enlarged and improved it; and subsequently, in the reign of John, Ware rapidly increased in size and population, so as to compete in these respects with Hertford. A destructive inundation occurred in the year 1403, since which period sluices and weirs have been constructed, and similar accidents prevented. Adjoining to the town, and near to the river, formerly stood a Benedictine priory, now a private residence, retaining the name of 'Ware Priory;' some remains of the old structure are still to be recognized. At the north end of the town was situated another religious establishment, of the Franciscan order; this is at present occupied by Mr. Samuel Adams as a malting house. The 'great bed of Ware' (to which some reference has always been made in noticing this town), measuring twelve feet square, is still to be seen at the 'Saracen's Head' inn, and is said to have belonged to Warwick the king-maker: the bed might contain twelve persons, but certainly not 'twelve butchers and their wives,' as erroneously magnified; it has much ancient carving about it, and the date '1463' is sufficiently legible: the bed is said to have been sold, amongst other moveables belonging to Warwick, at Ware park. At the same inn is a piece of very ancient tapestry, well deserving the inspection of the curious. The principal trade is in malt and corn. There is not a place in the kingdom in which more malting business is done, and immense quantities of that article are supplied to the London breweries from this town. Some idea of the extent of this trade may be formed from the fact of there being sixty-five malthouses, with eighty-one kilns: the average duty on the malt, for three years ending Midsummer, 1838, amounted to not less than £120,000. per annum; and the trade is evidently on the increase, as four new maltings of seven kilns were erected in 1838. The town is under the superintendence of a headborough, one constable and four policemen; the county magistrates hold a petty session every alternate Tuesday, and a court baron is held annually. A well-built market-house was erected by subscription in 1827; it is supported on sixteen arches, and contains an elegant assembly-room.

The church, dedicated to St. Mary, is a commodious edifice, having a nave, chancel and three aisles, with a square embattled tower at the western end; the interior of the church was formerly highly embellished and decorated—some very perfect remains of its ancient ornaments are still displayed on the roof of the chancel. The benefice is a vicarage, with that of Thundridge annexed, in the presentation of the master and fellows of Trinity college, Cambridge. In the church-yard is a tomb-stone bearing the following inscription:—'To the memory of William Meade, M. D., who departed this life the 28th day of October, 1652, aged *one hundred and forty-eight years, nine months, three weeks and four days.*' There are places of worship for independents, Wesleyan methodists, the society of friends and Irvingites. Ware is the seat of several public charities, well supported by the benevolent; they include a lying-in charity, seventeen alms-houses, and several free schools for children of both sexes, besides bequests to a considerable amount, by which the poor are periodically benefited. The market, entitled to be holden on Tuesday, is now but little frequented—the inhabitants, maltsters and country people chiefly attending at Hertford. Two fairs are held annually, for horses and cattle, pedlery, &c.; the first on the last Tuesday in April, the second on the Tuesday before the 21st September. According to the census of 1831, the population of Ware at that period (including the hamlet of WADESMILL) amounted to 4,214 persons.

POST OFFICE, Amwell end, WARE, George Price, *Post Master.*—Letters from LONDON arrive every night at a quarter past ten, and are despatched every morning at half-past three.—Letters for BISHOPS STORTFORD, BRAUGHIN, the County of ESSEX, HATFIELD, HERTFORD, ST. ALBANS, TRING, &c. are despatched every morning at six.—The box closes at nine at night.—The general delivery of letters commences at eight in the morning.

NOBILITY, GENTRY AND CLERGY.

Adams Samuel, esq. Wadesmill road
Bond Albany Carrington, esq. Rose cottage, Amwell end
Brown Miss —, Amwell
Cass Mr. William, Baldock st
Cater Mr. William, Back st
Chauncey Nathl. esq. Little Munden
Cobham Nathaniel, esq. Baldock st
Coddington Rev. Henry, Vicarage hse.
Collier Joseph, esq. Castlebury
Crowther Mrs. —, Amwell
Dampier Rev. Wm. Jas. M.A. Baldock st
Dickinson Miss Ann, Baldock st
Elwell Rev. Fredk. Hoddesdon road
Fell Miss Mary, Baldock st
Green Edward, esq. Sprange well
Hadsley Miss Maria, Ware priory
Hanbury Mrs. Agatha, Poles
Hooper Mrs. Maria De Horne, Amwell house
King Daniel Giles, esq. Youngsbury
Lockyer Rev. John, Star lane
Marchant John, esq. Rectory house
Mylne William C. esq. Amwell
Pearce Rev. George, Bray's folly
Phelips Charles, esq. Briggin's park
Proctor Capt. Ambrose, Thunder hall
Puller Lady, Youngsbury
Squire Jos. Hooper, esq. Amwell hse.
Strafford Rt. Hon. Lord, Amwellbury
Usbourne Miss Jane, Amwell end
Vickers Mrs. Sarah, Baldock st
Ware Mrs. Major, Mount pleasant, Amwell
Wright Miss Sarah, Baldock st
Wyatt Mr. Joseph Francis, Baldock st

ACADEMIES & SCHOOLS.

Not otherwise described are Day Schools.

BRITISH SCHOOL, Star lane—Joseph Dines, master
CHARITY SCHOOL (girls') Church lane—Mary Gull, mistress
CHARITY SCHOOL (boys' and girls') Wadesmill—Geo. Harris, master; Mary Ann Mardell, mistress.
FREE GRAMMAR SCHOOL, Church yard—George Moore, master
INFANTS' SCHOOL, French Horn lane—Ann Linster, mistress
INFANTS' SCHOOL, Wadesmill—Mary Pee, mistress
Josleyn Thomas (boarding) Ware side
Malin Susan, High st
Medcalf Eliza and Martha, High st
NATIONAL SCHOOL, French Horn lane—William Wells, master
Pavey Ann, French Horn lane
Pugh Mrs. Jane, French Horn lane
Salter Edith, High st
Wiggens Mary, Mill lane

AGENTS.

(See also Fire Office Agents.)

Machon Francis (land) Kibe's lane
Ree Henry (estate) High st

ATTORNEYS.

Cobham Nathaniel (and clerk to the magistrates, and to the commissioners of lighting) Baldock st
Green James Fordham, High st
Hollingsworth John, High st
Judson Charles B. High st
Wartnaby and Dampier, (and commissioners for taking acknowledgments of deeds by married women) Baldock st

AUCTIONEERS, APPRAISERS AND HOUSE AGENTS.

Ree Henry, High st
Worpell John, High st

BAKERS.

Baker Robert, Baldock st
Ekins George, High st
Hitch Thomas Waller, High st
Page Henry, Bridge foot
Page Henry, Churchgate
Page Jonathan Brown, Bridge end
Smith John, Wadesmill
Tagg David, Amwell end

BANKERS.

Adams Samuel and Co. High st, and at *Hertford*—(draw on Masterman, Peters and Co. London)

BARGE OWNERS.

Adams Samuel, Wadesmill road
Cass John, High st
Cater William, New st
Chuck Edward, High st
Cobham Thomas, Amwell end
Cobham Wm. & Co. Hoddesdon road
Cobham William and Son, High st
Green Edward, High st
Heavers Thos. & William, Ware mill
Hitch Caleb (and builder) Baldock st
Hitch James (and builder) Star lane
Page J. C. and N. (and general merchants) High st
Sworder John, High st

BLACKSMITHS.

Brett James, Wadesmill
Pee Joseph, Wadesmill
Suckling James, Steeple end, High st
Wells Charles (and white) High st
Wells George, Blue Coat yard

BOOKSELLER, STATIONER, BINDER & PRINTER.

Batty Henry (and library, newspaper agent and paper hanger) High st

BOOT & SHOE MAKERS.

Cowler William, Wadesmill
Edwards Thomas, High st
Gates William, Back st
Goodwin John, Wadesmill
Goodwin Thomas, Back st
Hull Henry, High st
Inskip James, French Horn lane
Lawrence James, Bridge foot
Lawrence William, Baldock st
Sands George, High st
White Thomas Dennis, High st

BRAZIERS AND TIN-PLATE WORKERS.

Ree Henry, High st
Skerman John, French Horn lane
Wells Charles, High st

BREWERS.

Aylett John W. Back st
Baker Robert, Baldock st
Brown Daniel, High st
Harris John, Amwell end
Page Robert, Churchgate

BRICKLAYERS.

Hitch Caleb (& brickmkr.) Baldock st
Reason Alfred, Mill lane
Smith George Escott (& lime burner) Amwell end

BUILDERS.

Hitch Caleb (& bricklayer) Baldock st
Hitch James (& carpenter) Star lane
Mayfield John (and carpenter) Amwell road

BUTCHERS.

Adams Joseph, Kibe's lane
Brown Isaac, Back st
Brown John, High st
Fitch Zachariah, Baldock st
Long Elizabeth, High st
Marshall Martha (pork) High st
Pepper Henry, West Mill road
Ree Thomas, Wadesmill
Sams Ebenezer, Amwell end
Thorowgood Thomas, Amwell end
Thorowgood William, High st
Thorowgood Wm. jun. Baldock st
Thorpe Samuel, Bridge foot
Tween Thomas, High st

CABINET MAKERS AND UPHOLSTERERS.

Bland John, West Mill road
Ekins George, High st
Ekins Geo. (& wire worker) Back st
Hitch James, Star lane
Smart Wm. (and appraiser) High st
Webb Thomas, High st

CARPENTERS.

Francis John, French Horn lane
Griggs James, Amwell end
Hitch James (and builder) Star lane
Long Edmund, High st
Mayfield John Shepherd (& builder and undertaker) Amwell end
Smart William, High st
Webb Thomas, High st

CHINA, GLASS & EARTHENWARE DEALERS.

Giffin Samuel, Baldock st
Hobbs Ann, High st
Radmall John, Back st
Sullivan Patrick (and marine stores) Amwell end

CHYMISTS AND DRUGGISTS.

Hadley Charles, corner of Baldock st
Medcalf Mary, Market place

CLOTHES DEALERS.

Harradance James, High st
White Thomas D. High st
Williams John, Amwell end

COAL MERCHANTS AND DEALERS.

Clibbon Thomas, Hoddesdon road
Cobham William, High st
Hayden Thomas W. Back st
Machon Francis, Kibe's lane
Page Henry, Churchgate
Page J. C. and N. High st
Page Jonathan Brown, Bridge foot
Sworder John, High st

CONFECTIONERS.

Dellow William, Bourne hill
Marshall Miriam, High st
Powell James, Amwell end

COOPERS.

Page Robert, Churchgate
Powter George, Baldock st

CORN DEALERS.

(See also Millers & Mealmen.)

Allen John, Wadesmill
Hayden Thomas W. Back st
Hitch Thomas, High st
Page Henry, Churchgate
Page Jonathan B. Bridge foot

FIRE, &c. OFFICE AGENTS.

ATLAS, James F. Green, High st
LONDON & COUNTY, Benjamin Medcalf, Back st
PHŒNIX, Jas. Harradance (& stamp office) High st
PROVIDENT (life) Benjamin Medcalf, Back st
UNION ASSURANCE, Wartnaby and Dampier, Baldock st
YORK and LONDON, Richard Filbridge Cass, High st

GROCERS AND PROVISION DEALERS.

(See also Shopkeepers.)

Cass Richard Filbridge (and oils, hops and seeds) High st
Giffin Samuel, Baldock st
Hobbs Ann, High st
Hollingsworth Thomas, High st
Page Elizabeth, Amwell end
Radmall John, Back st

HAIR DRESSERS.

Campbell William, High st
Cutmore James, Baldock st
Cutmore Joseph, Bridge foot

HATTERS.

Hartland Charles, Middle row
Marks John, Amwell end
White Thomas D. High st

INNS.

Bull, Frances Brown (and posting) High st
Feathers, Frederick Evenett, Wadesmill
French Horn, Edward Birch, High st
Saracen's Head, Daniel Brown (commercial and posting) High st

IRONMONGERS.

Long Edmund, High st
Ree Henry, High st
Webb Thomas, High st
Wells Chas. (& iron founder) High st

LINEN & WOOLLEN DRAPRS, AND CLOTHES DEALERS.

Cranstone George, High st
Green Frances (and hosier) High st
Hartland Charles, High st
Matthews John, Market place
Medcalf Elizabeth, Amwell end
Stephens Samuel, High st
Worpell Ann, High st

MALTSTERS.

Marked thus * are also Malt Factors.

*Adams Samuel, Baldock st
Adams Samuel, jun. (and general merchant) Baldock st
Bell Charles, High st
Cass John, High st
Cass John & Edwd. Church, French Horn lane
*Cater William, New st
*Chuck Edward, High st
*Chuck Joseph, High st
Clark Thos. Prior, High st & Braughin
*Cobham John & Son, High st
*Cobham William, High st
*Cobham Wm. jun. & Co. Amwell end
Cowell John, French Horn lane
*Cowell John, jun. Crib st
Green Edward Haysham, High st and Sprangewell
*Green Thomas & Edward, High st
Hitch Caleb, jun. Baldock st
Hudson James, High st
Kimpton Thomas, Star lane
*Page J. C. and N. High st
Sheppard John, Ware park mill
Sworder Charles, High st
*Sworder John, High st
Waller Isaac Kimpton, High st
Whitehead Samuel, Baldock st
Wright Thomas, High st & Walkern

MILLERS & MEALMEN.

Heavers Thomas and Wm. Ware mill
Page Henry, Churchgate
Sheppard John, Ware park mill
Smith James, Wadesmill
Tween John, Ware west mill

MILLINERS AND DRESS MAKERS.

Johns Sarah and Mary (and haberdashers) Mill lane
Slade Harriet, French Horn lane
Smith Elizabeth, High st

PAINTERS, PLUMBERS AND GLAZIERS.

Cobham John, Baldock st
Heasler William, Amwell end
Skegg George, French Horn lane

ROPE, TWINE, SACK, TILT & CANVASS MANUFACTRS.

Nicoll Edward, Bridge foot
Norton William, Baldock st
Whittle Elizabeth, Baldock st

SADDLERS AND HARNESS MAKERS.

Newell Samuel, High st
Pettengell William, High st
Wilson Isaac, Bridge foot

SHOPKEEPERS & DEALRS IN GROCERIES & SUNDRIES.

Brown Nathaniel, Wadesmill
Chick Ann, French Horn lane
Isaac Joseph, Wadesmill
Lawrence Johannah, Mill lane
Martin Mary, Amwell end
Medcalf Elizabeth, Amwell end
Norris Thomas, Baldock st
Pallett George, Baldock st

Smith James, Wadesmill
Webb James, High st
Wilson Ann, Wadesmill
Worbey Johannah, Mill lane
Worpell Samuel, Baldock st

STRAW HAT MAKERS.

Gatwood Mary Ann, High st
Groom Ann, Baldock st
Welsh Ann, Baldock st

SURGEONS.

Butcher Henry, High st
Judson John H. & Son, High st
Judson John Henry, jun. High st
M'Nab William, High st
Reilly John, M. D. (and member of the Royal College of Surgeons, London) High st

TAILORS & DRAPERS.

Beadle James, Baldock st
Culver James, French Horn lane
Culver William, Market place
Ekins George, High st
Ekins John, Back st
Grapes Joseph, High st
Harradence James, High st
Marshall Thomas, High st
Piggott Ellis, Wadesmill
Powell Thomas, New st
Smith James, Wadesmill

TALLOW CHANDLERS.

Cass Richard Filbridge, High st
Hollingsworth Thomas, High st
Radmall John, Back st

TAVERNS & PUBLIC HOUSES.

Anchor, Thomas Dixon, Wadesmill
Angel, George Ginn, Star lane
Barge, Jane Ansell, Bridge foot
Bay Horse, Joseph Dyton, High st
Bell and Sun, Stephen Norfolk, Back st
Black Bull, Daniel Elliot, Wadesmill
Bull's Head, James Stamp, Baldock st
Chequers, George Patmore, Ware side
Clarendon, John Worpell, High st
Cock, David Lambert, Amwell end
College Arms, — Starlings, Haileybury
Crane, Joseph Charvill, Bridge end
Dolphin, Campbell & Wren, Land row
Fox & Goose, Samuel Soame, High st
George, William Francis, Amwell end
Harrow, Judith Jones, Kibe's lane
Hind, John Munt, Wadesmill
King's Head, Thomas Ellis, Mill lane
Red Cow, William Anderson, Cribb st
Rose & Crown, John Bland, West mill lane
Sow & Pigs, John Bowcock, Wadesmill
Spread Eagle, John Harris, Amwell end
Star, Aaron & Esther Webb, High st
Waggon & Horses, Peter Felsted, Baldock st
White Hart, James Harrison, Baldock st
White Horse, William Parker, Ware side
White Lion & Wheat Sheaf, Henry Hoy, Market place [st
White Swan, John Williams Aylett, Back
White Swan, Thomas Watson, Wadesmill

WHEELWRIGHTS.

Ives Thomas, Wadesmill
Smith Thomas, Church lane
Wells George, Blue Coat yard

WINE & SPIRIT MERCHANTS

Cass Richard Filbridge (British wines) High st
Ellis John & Son, Back st

Miscellaneous.

Bullard Henry, basket maker, Back st
Bunyan Joseph, market gardener, Hemp ground, Bourne hill
Campbell William, toy dealer, High st
Dives Joseph, stationer, Bridge foot
Edwards Panton, leather cutter and tea dealer, High st
Ekins George, stone mason, Anwell end
Fowler Nathaniel, veterinary surgeon, Church lane [High st
Gatward Benjamin, watch, &c. maker,
Griffith Christr. seedsman, &c. Baldock st
Hale Edward, woolstapler & fellmonger, Market place and Mill lane
Harradance James, registrar of marriages, High st
Harris Nathaniel, gardener, High st
Jordan James, millwright, Wadesmill
Machon Francis, parish clerk, collector of watch rates, gas superintendent, and high constable of the hundred, Kibe's lane
Moss Cath. rag & paper dealer, Amwell end
Pallett George, land surveyor, Baldock st
Piggott Ellis, parish clerk, Wadesmill
POLICE STATION, corner of the Church yard, High st [hill
Smith James, superviser of excise, Bourne
Smith William, tea dealer, High st
WARE NEWSPAPER SUBSCRIPTION SOCIETY, Town hall
Wells Charles, wire worker, weaver and whitesmith, High st
Wilkins Robert Bird, timber & slate merchant, Amwell end [High st
Wren Thomas, wood turner & fishmonger,

COACHES.

Calling alternately at the Bull & Saracen's Head unless otherwise expressed.

To LONDON, the *Royal Mail* (from Cambridge and the North) every morning at half-past three—the *Telegraph* (from Cambridge) every afternoon (Sunday excepted) at one—a *Coach* (from Wisbeach) every afternoon at half-past three, and a *Coach* (from Lynn) at a quarter before four—the *Rocket* (from Cambridge) every evening at half-past six—the *Rocket* (from Hertford) calls at the Saracen's Head, every afternoon (Sunday excepted) at half-past three, and on Sunday at half-past four—and the *Wellington* (from Newcastle-upon-Tyne) every afternoon (Monday excepted) at the same hour.

To LONDON, a *Coach*, every morning (Sunday and Monday excepted) at eight, and on Monday at six, and the *Star* (from Cambridge) same days at ten, and on Monday at nine—a *Coach* (from Puckeridge) every Monday, Wednesday and Friday morning at half-past seven —the *Bee Hive* (from Cambridge) same days at half-past twelve—and the *Defiance* (from Peterborough and Stamford) calls at the Bull, every afternoon at a quarter before four.

The following Coaches are from London.

To CAMBRIDGE, the *Telegraph*, every day (Sunday ex.) at half-past twelve—the *Rocket*, every afternoon (Sunday excepted) at half-past four—the *Star*, at six—and the *Bee Hive*, every Tuesday, Thursday & Saturday afternoon at two.

To CAMBRIDGE and the NORTH, the *Royal Mail*, every night at a quarter past ten.

To HERTFORD, the *Rocket*, calls at the Saracen's Head, every day at twelve.

To LYNN, a *Coach*, every forenoon (Sunday excepted) at a quarter before eleven.

To NEWCASTLE-UPON-TYNE, the *Wellington*, every afternoon (Sunday excepted at five.

To PETERBOROUGH and STAMFORD, the *Defiance*, calls at the Bull, every Tuesday, Thursday and Saturday morning at eleven.

To PUCKERIDGE, a *Coach*, every Monday, Wednesday and Friday evening at a quarter before seven—and a *Coach*, every Tuesday, Thursday and Saturday evening at a quarter before seven.

To WISBEACH, a *Coach*, every morning (Sunday excepted) at half-past ten.

CARRIERS.

To LONDON, William Anderson & John Pavey, from French Horn lane, every Monday, Wednesday & Friday afternoon.

To HERTFORD, HATFIELD and ST. ALBANS, James Tillcock, from the Saracen's Head, every Monday, Wednesday and Friday afternoon.

*** Besides the above, there are Carriers' *Waggons* passing through Ware to and from LONDON and places in the counties of CAMBRIDGE, SUFFOLK, NORFOLK and the North, by day and night.

CONVEYANCE BY WATER.

ON THE RIVER LEA.

To and from LONDON, goods are conveyed by the several barge owners, whose names and offices are given in the preceding page.

WATFORD,

AND ITS HAMLETS, WITH THE VILLAGES OF ALDENHAM AND BUSHEY.

WATFORD is a market town and parish (including the hamlets of Cashio, Levesdon and Oxhey), in the hundred of Cashio, or liberty of St. Albans—15 miles N. W. from London, 20 W. S. W. from Hertford, about 7 S. S. W. from St. Albans, and 3 E. by N. from Rickmansworth; pleasantly situated on a gently rising eminence, upon the river Colne, over which there is a viaduct for the London and Birmingham railway, which important line passes the town; and about a mile from it is a station, where a large hotel has lately been erected for the accommodation of passengers waiting for the trains. The Grand Junction canal passes about a mile to the west of the town; by the latter the transmission of its products and the introduction of those of other places is effected, and a water communication maintained with the metropolis and the northern counties. Watford consists of one main street, nearly a mile and a half in length, well lighted with gas from works established in 1834. The manufactures comprise silk, straw plat and paper; the malting business is extensive, and there are some corn-mills of great power and one for the manufacture of oil cake. In 1760 the lordship of this manor was vested in the family of Baron Ellesmere, who sold it to the Earl of Essex, whose family still possess it; the present earl is also patron of the living and lay impropriator of the great tithes. A court of requests, for the recovery of small debts, is held in the court-house every alternate Tuesday, and the magistrates sit on the same days. The parish church stands nearly in the centre of the town; it is a large stone edifice, having two chapels annexed, and a lofty square tower at its western end, surmounted by an hexagonal spire; the church is dedicated to St. Mary. The burial-place of the Essex family is situated upon the left side of the chancel. Amongst the monuments there are two that, from the excellence of their workmanship, attract particular attention: the first of these is to the memory of Sir Charles Morison, Knt.; the other to that of his son, Sir Charles Morison, Bart., and his lady; the latter is placed against the north wall, and both are beautiful specimens of the sculptural skill of Nicholas Stone. Other monuments, to the Clarendon and Bucknall families, embellish this church, and merit the inspection of those who are gratified by 'contemplation among the tombs.' The living is a vicarage, enjoyed by the Hon. and Rev. William Capel. There are places of worship for baptists, Wesleyan methodists, and for a congregation of Lady Huntingdon's connexion. The charities comprise two endowed schools (founded by Mrs. Fuller in 1701), in which forty boys and twenty girls are educated and partly clothed; two sets of alms-houses—one for four poor women, the other for eight; and an apprenticeship fund. A large union poor-house, capable of accommodating two hundred and fifty inmates, has recently been erected under the present poor law act. There are many handsome seats and mansions in the vicinity—Cashiobury, the seat of the Countess of Essex; theGrove,LordClarendon; Nascot House,Geo.Ricketts, Esq.; and Watford Place, Jonathan King, Esq., are generally admired. The chartered market, which is well attended, is held on Tuesday; and there is another on Saturday, for butchers' meat, &c. The fairs are on the Tuesday after Trinity-Sunday, for pleasure; 29th August, and following day, for cattle; and 9th September for pleasure and hiring servants. In 1831 the parish of Watford contained 5,293 inhabitants, of which number the 'town hamlets' reckoned 2,960.

About two miles and a half N.N.E. from Watford, and in the same hundred, is the village of ALDENHAM. The parish is extensive, and the employment of most of the inhabitants is agricultural. The church, dedicated to St. John the Baptist, is in the early English architectural style, built of flint and rubble, with a tower at its western end; the interior is remarkably neat, and enshrines some handsome monuments: the benefice is a vicarage, of which Lord Rendlesham is patron, and the Rev. Edward Benbow the present incumbent. A free school for boys and girls, and some alms-houses, are the principal charities. Population of the parish, by the returns for 1831, 1,494.

The populous village of BUSHEY is rather more than a mile from Watford, in the parish of its name and hundred of Dacorum. The church, dedicated to St. James, is a handsome structure, with a tower surmounting its western end; the living is a rectory, in the patronage of the rector and fellows of Exeter college, Oxford. There is a chapel for independents, with a Sunday school attached; and on Bushey heath, contiguous to the village, has lately been erected a neat chapel of ease, the great increase of population in the parish having rendered this measure indispensable. The prospect from the heath is grand and extensive, embracing St. Albans, Westminster Abbey, Hampton Court and Windsor, with the course of the Thames, along the borders of Surrey and Middlesex. Population, in 1831, 1,586; the number at present (1839) probably may amount to 2,300.

POST OFFICE, WATFORD, Joseph Johnson, *Post Master.*—Letters from LONDON arrive every day at twelve and evening at a quarter past nine, and are despatched every morning at four and noon at half-past twelve.—Letters from the North arrive every morning at five, and are despatched every evening at nine.

POST OFFICE, BUSHEY, William Hawkins, *Post Master.*—Letters from all parts arrive every morning at eight, and are despatched every evening at half-past six.

POST, ALDENHAM, *Receiving-House* at William Moth's.—Letters are brought from and despatched to WATFORD daily.

NOBILITY, GENTRY AND CLERGY.

Allen Mr. J. Bushey cottage
Anderton Miss —, Bushey
Appleyard Mrs. —, Bushey
Baker John Richard,esq. Letchmore heath, Aldenham
Barkley Henry,esq.Sparrows,Bushey
Benbow Rev. Edward, Vicarage, Aldenham
Berner Benjamin, esq. Watford
Bolton Charles, esq. Aldenham
Bosworth Mrs. Sarah, Watford
Buckland Mrs. —, Bushey
Burchell Harper, esq. Bushey grange
Capel the Honourable & Rev. William, Vicarage, Watford
Capel William, esq. Kytes farm
Chapman Mr. William, Bushey
Chawell Mrs. Charlotte, Aldenham
Clarendon the Earl of, Grove
Clutterbuck Mrs. Mary Ann,Watford
Clutterbuck Mrs. Sophia,Newhouse, Watford [farm
Colville General Sir Charles, Russell
Conder Josiah, esq. Watford
Cowley Philip, esq. Watford
Crawford John, esq. Watford
Dalrymple Sir Adolphus, Aldenham
Dalton Christopher, esq. Watford
Donkin Rev. Edward, Watford
Dyson Miss Sybella, Watford
Dyson Thomas Edward, esq. Tolpit, Watford [park
Essex the Countess of, Cashiobury
Evans Matthew, esq. Little Bushey
Ewer Francis, esq. Bushey
Falcon John, esq. Gaston house
Fernie Rev. Jno.Chapel house,Bushy
Field Mrs. —, Bushey
Filmer Lady, Little Bushey lodge
Foster Mr. Thomas, Bushey
Goddard Miss —, Little Bushey
Goodeson Mrs. —, Nascot cottage
Gray Hon. Mrs. —, Grove Mill house
Griffiths Mr. Thomas, Bushey
Hammond Mrs. Sarah, Watford
Harris Christr. Arthur, esq. Bushey
Hassell Mrs. Mary, Watford
Hibbert Mrs. —, Watford [hill
Hibbert Nathaniel, esq. Little Merry
Hicks Miss —, Watford
Higgs Miss —, Watford
Hinchliffe J. H. esq. Aldenham
Hodsoll Walter, esq. Rosedale cottage, Bushey
Hollingshead John, esq. Watford
Howard James, esq. Watford
Howard Mr. Robert, Fossey,Watford
Hull Rev. Edmund, Watford
Hyam W. esq. Fair Lawn lodge, Caldecot hill, Aldenham
Jackson George, esq. Bushey
Jennings Mr. Joseph, Bushey
Kilby Mrs. —. Watford
King Mrs. —, Watford
King Jonathan, esq. Watford place
Lushington Dr. Steph.Lit. Merry hill
Macready Mr. John, Aldenham
Majoribanks Campbell, esq. Bushey grove
Marshall Mr. Francis, Bushey
Marshall Wm. esq. M.P. Aldenham
Mason Captain John, Aldenham
Mason John Finch, Aldenham
Miles John, esq. Watford
Miln —, esq. Little Bushey
Monro Doctor, Bushey
Moore Mr. —, Watford
Packer Richard, esq. Bucks hill
Pearse Mrs. —, Watford
Peaumier Mrs. Sophia, Watford
Phibbs Mrs. —, Bushey
Phillimore William Robert, esq. Newberrys, Aldenham
Pitt Captain Samuel, Aldenham
Player Thos. Gregory, esq. Aldenham
Pugh Mr. Richard, Watford
Ramsay James, esq. Bushey house
Richards Mrs. Grove cottage, Bushey
Ricketts George, esq. Nascot house
Robins John, esq. Watford
Robinson William, esq. Bentley cottage, Bushey
Ryler John, esq. High Elms
Salmon Stephen, esq. Bushey
Salter David, esq. Watford
Salter Mr. Samuel, Watford
Sharp Edmund Pell, esq. Bushey
Sheval Mrs. —,Caldecot hill,Aldnhm
Smith Bailey, esq. Watford
Spires Rev. Thomas, Aldenham
Stedman Charles, esq. Watford
Stevens Thomas, esq. Little Bushey
Strong Rev. Edmund, Bushey
Stuart Lieutenant James, Bushey
Swannell Mrs. —, Watford
Thellusson Mrs. —, Aldenham
Timmins John Fam, Illfield lodge, Aldenham
Turner Mrs. —, Watford
Vaughan Baron, Eastburry
Walker Genl. Sir Frederick, Bushey
Warburton Jno. esq. M.D. Hartsbourn
Watlington Charles, esq. Aldenham
West Raphael, esq. Bushey
White Mrs. —, Watford
Wilkinson Miss Ann, Bushey
Wincer Mrs. —, Carpenters
Withers Mr. John, Bushey
Woods John, esq. Grove Mill heath
Wool Miss —, Watford

ACADEMIES & SCHOOLS.

Not otherwise described are Day Schools.

Adcock John, Watford
Anderton & Jackson (and boarding) Watford
Billing Miss(day& boarding) Watford
Bogue George (boarding) Holly grove house, Bushey
Broderick Henry, Watford
Broy William (day and boarding) Bushey
Callard Theresa (day and boarding) Bushey
Dawson Sarah, Bushey
FREE SCHOOL, Aldenham—J.Thorpe, master; Mrs. Richard, mistress
FULLER'S CHARITY SCHOOL, Watford—Thomas William Camfield, master; Ann Budget, mistress
Gareys the Misses (day & boarding) Watford
INFANT'S SCHOOL, Watford—Mary Carter, mistress
Jones Mary (boarding) Watford
Maynard Thomas (boarding) Grove house, Bushey [denham
Spires Rev. Thomas (boarding) Al-
Young William, Watford

ATTORNEYS.

Cowley Philip, jun. Watford
Goldsmith George (and master in chancery) Watford
Nicholl Thomas, Watford
Pugh Richard (and deputy clerk to the magistrates) Watford
Sedgwick John, Watford

AUCTIONEERS & APPRAISRS.

Fitch Joseph (& surveyor) Bushey
Hackman Thomas (appraiser) Bushey
Hawkins William (appraiser) Bushey
Lavender Thomas, Watford
Pugh William, Chalk hill, Bushey

BAKERS & FLOUR DEALERS.

Aldwin Chs. (& game dealer) Watford
Brace Elizabeth, Watford
Claydon Thomas, Bushey
Fowler John (biscuit) Watford
Gregory John, Watford
Gregory Joseph, Bushey
Groom Joseph, Bushey
Guildford Hannah, Bushey
Holloway Henry, Bushey heath
Holloway Sarah, Aldenham
King Jonathan John, Watford
Kingston Samuel, Aldenham
Major Richard, Watford
Payne Thomas, Watford
Rhodes Joseph, Watford
Rodwell William, Watford
Shackle Samuel, Watford
Simmonds William, Watford
Squire Ann, Watford
Tomlin Dorothy, Aldenham

BLACKSMITHS.

Beeson John, Aldenham
Beeson Wm. (and farrier) Watford
Child James (and white, and bell hanger) Watford
Franklin Thos. and Benj. Aldenham
Green and Colley, Watford
Haskell Bartholomew, Watford
Lawfort Joseph, Bushey
Martin Thomas, Aldenham
Pope John (& bell hanger) Watford
Rodwell James, Watford
Sears Samuel, Bushey
Simmons William, Watford
Timberlake William, Bushey
Vale Thomas, Bushey

BOOKSELLERS & STATIONRS.

Gittings George, Bushey
Mayes Christopher, Watford
Niddery David, Watford

BOOT AND SHOE MAKERS.

Allen William, Bushey heath
Bird James, Watford
Brown Richard, Aldenham
Butler William, Bushey
Chester John, Watford
Cook John, Watford
Cordery William, Watford
Darvil Thomas (and patten maker) Watford
Davison Thomas, Watford
Dickinson George, Aldenham
Dickinson Thomas, Aldenham
Edwards James, Watford
Fletcher John, Bushey
Gotts Samuel, Bushey
Hanshew Thomas, Watford
Hanshew Thomas, jun. Watford
Hyom and Squire, Watford
Racklyeft John, Watford
Roadnight Joseph, Watford
Stapleton John, Bushey
Stevens William, Watford
Taylor John, Watford
Taylor William, Watford
Wilson Thomas, Watford

BRAZIERS AND TINMEN.

Child Charles (and bell hanger) Watford
Duffield Mark, Bushey
Edlin Mary, Watford
Edmonds John, Watford
Rogers Thomas, Watford

BREWERS.

Dyson John, Watford
Fitch Edward, Aldenham
Toppin Thomas, Watford
Whittingstall Edmd. Fearnley, Watford

BRICKLAYERS.

Carey Jonathan (and plasterer, &c.) Watford
Chapman Thomas, Watford
Child John, Aldenham
Deacon Martin, Watford
Hill Benjamin, Aldenham
Hill James, Bushey heath
Mayes John (and slater) Watford
Pratt John, Bushey
Taylor James Henry, Watford
Wallis William, Bushey

BUTCHERS.

Ballard William James, Watford
Chapman Thomas, jun. Watford
Child John (and dairyman) Bushey
Clisby Edward, Watford
Deeley James (pork) Watford
Dodd Henry, Watford
Dracott Joseph, Watford
Dumbleton Elizabeth, Bushey
Epgrave James, Bushey
Glennerster Robert, Bushey
Gregory Isaac, Watford
Hodgson William, Watford
Hollingsworth William, Watford
How Elizabeth, Bushey
Moss James, Bushey
Robinson William, Bushey
Rogers Thomas, Watford
Russell Arthur, Watford
Saunders David, Watford
Stone Ralph, Watford
Tookey Stephen, Watford
Warrell William, Watford

CABINET MAKERS.

Capell James, Watford
Mitchell John, Watford
Pinnock John, Watford
Sparrow Phillis, Watford
Wilkinson Henry, Watford

CARPENTERS.

Marked thus * are also Builders.

Bellis Michael William, Watford
Burnell James & Richd. Aldenham
*Downer Thomas, Watford
Eames Charles, Watford
*Hawkins William, Bushey
Hodgson George, Watford
*Matthews Thomas, Bushey
Matthews William, Bushey
*Mitchell John, Watford
Richardson Alexander, Aldenham
Stone Joseph, Watford

CHYMISTS & DRUGGISTS.

Chater Jonathan (and British wine dealer) Watford
Henson Matthew (and oilman) Watford

CLOTHES DEALERS.

Elias Samuel, Watford
Young Thomas, Watford

COACH MAKERS.

Christmas Thomas, Watford
Wilkey Joseph, Watford

COAL MERCHANTS.

Cooper John, Cashio bridge, New wharf
Ebbern Thomas, Lady Capel's wharf
Howard George, Grove wharf
Rogers Joseph, Cashio bridge wharf, and Watford

CONFECTIONERS.

Abbott William, Watford
King Jonathan, Watford
Young Sarah, Watford

COOPERS AND VAT MAKERS.

Middleton William, Watford
Rogers Thomas, Watford
Woodward Thomas, Watford

CORN & SEED MERCHANTS.

Anderton George, Bushey
Harris Kennet, Watford
Rogers William, Watford

CORN CHANDLERS AND MEALMEN.

Bygrave Thomas, Watford
Catlin Henry, Watford
Cooper John, Watford
Draycott Thomas, Watford
Dyson Frederick, Watford
Fullwood James, Watford
Heath William, Bushey
Johnson George, Bushey

EARTHENWARE DEALERS.

Robertson Robert, Watford
Wilkinson Henry, Watford

FIRE, &c. OFFICE AGENTS.

County (fire) and Provident (life), George Reeve, Watford
Guardian, John Mitchell, Watford
Guardian, Wm. Hawkins, Bushey
Phœnix, Joseph Johnson, Watford
Phœnix, Bruton & Good, Watford
Protestant Dissenters', Jonathan Chater, Watford
Royal Exchange, Ths. Rogers, Watford
Sun, Dyson and Lavender, Watford
Union, John Adcock, Watford

FURNITURE BROKERS.

Brown John, Bushey heath
Capell James, Watford
Coates Thos. (& appraiser) Bushey
Egelton Ann, Bushey
Field Elisha, Watford
Hackman Thomas, Bushey

GROCERS, TEA DEALERS & CHEESEMONGERS.

(See also Shopkeepers, &c.)

Carey Jonathan, Watford
Harris Alpheus, Watford
Hawkins William, Bushey
Haws James Cooper, Watford
Healey George, Watford
Kingham Elizabeth, Watford
Perrin Thomas, Bushey
Reeve George, Watford
Wise George, Watford

HAIR DRESSERS.

Arnold Joseph, Bushey
Downer David (& stationer) Watford
Graves William, Watford
Kent Robt. (& bird stuffer) Watford
Smith Joseph, Watford

HOP MERCHANTS.

Dracott George, Watford
Wise George, Watford

INNS—POSTING, &c.

Essex Arms, Fras. Barnard, Watford
George, Catherine Humberstone, Watford
Railway Hotel, James Toovey, near the Station
Rose & Crown, Mary Rogers, Watford
Three Crowns, John Bailey, Bushey heath

IRONMONGERS.

Child Charles, Watford
Edlin Mary, Watford
Edmonds John, Watford
Rogers Thomas, Watford

LEATHER CUTTERS.

Brunt John (& currier) Watford
Davison Thomas, Watford
Wild Thomas (& tanner) Watford

LINEN & WOOLLEN DRAPRS.

Bruton and Good, Watford
Hudson William, Watford
Johnson Joseph, Watford
Turner Thomas, Bushey
Young Thomas, Watford

MALTSTERS.

Clutterbuck Thomas, Watford
Dracott George, Watford
Salter Samuel, Watford

MILLERS.

Allum Samuel, Bushey mill
Leach James & Frederick, Grove mill
Smith William (& oil cake) Watford

MILLINERS & DRESS MAKRS.
Aldwin Jane, Watford
Colley Sarah, Watford
Goodman Hannah, Watford
Holt Mary, Watford
Lewin Sarah, Bushey
Urlwin Mrs. Watford

PAPER MAKER.
Smith James (for drawing, writing and copper-plate) Hamper mills, Watford

PLUMBERS, PAINTERS AND GLAZIERS.
Aldwin William, Watford
Clarke James, Aldenham
Collins George, Bushey
Halsey William, Watford
Kingham William Frederick, Bushey
Wise & Restarick, Watford

SADDLERS AND HARNESS MAKERS.
Gaseley Joseph, Watford
Maddin Richard, Watford
Neale John, Watford
Robinson Joseph, Watford
Stanford Henry, Bushey

SHOPKEEPERS & DEALRS IN GROCERIES & SUNDRIES.
Ashby William, Bushey
Barker Thomas, Watford
Brock John, Aldenham
Claydon Thomas, Bushey
Freeman Fanny & Mary, Bushey
Galer Harriet, Watford
Glennerster John, Watford
Heath William, Bushey
Hodgson William, Watford
Holloway Henry, Bushey heath
Hopkins Christian, Watford
Johnson George, Bushey
Moth William, Aldenham
Newton John, Watford
Norris William, Watford
Parrott William, Bushey
Potton James, Watford
Prince James, Bushey
Ryder Richard, Watford
Scott William, Watford
Taylor William, Watford
Trott Ann, Bushey
Wellings Margaret Ann, Watford

SILK THROWSTERS.
Shute Thomas Rock, Watford and *Rickmansworth*
Toppin Thomas, Watford

STONE MASON.
Pigg Joseph (& marble) Watford

STRAW HAT MAKERS.
Adcock Sarah, Watford
Allen Elizabeth, Watford
Hall Ann, Bushey
Peacock Mrs. —, Watford
Sheppard Sarah, Watford

SURGEONS.
Betts George Harvey, Watford
Burke John French, Watford
Drury John, Bushey
Kemball Arthur Clark, Bushey
Pidcock John, M. D. Watford
Pidcock Spencer, Watford
Rose Clement, Watford
Ward and Sylvester, Watford

SURVEYORS AND ESTATE AGENTS.
Fitch Joseph, Bushey
Hawkins William, sen. Bushey
Lavender Thomas, Watford
Matthews Thomas, Bushey
Pugh William, Chalk hill, Bushey

TAILORS AND DRAPERS.
Adcock Daniel & Son, Watford
Armstrong William, Watford
Barnett Charles, Bushey
Butcher John, Watford
Bygrave Robert, Watford
Byway John, Bushey
Chalk William, Watford
Groom Robert, Watford
Hanshew Ambrose, Watford
Moth William, Aldenham
Robinson Robert, Aldenham
Young John, Aldenham

TAVERNS & PUBLIC HOUSES.
Those without address are in WATFORD.
Angel, Sarah Axtin
Bell, William Tyler
Bell, Ann Ginger, Bushey
Chequers, Thomas Coles
Chequers, William Nicholls, Aldenham
Coach & Horses, Wm. Mason, Aldenham
Compasses, William Goodman
Cross Keys, William Hadnutt, Aldenham
Crown, James Smith
Dog & Partridge, Joshua Southgate
Eight Bells, John Kilby
Fighting Cocks, Martin Deacon
Green Man, George Potton
Hare, William Downer, Levesden
Horns, James Nix
King's Head, Archelaus Crocker
King's Head, James Rance, Aldenham
Leathersellers' Arms (& excise office), John Tookey
Leviathan, Adam Parkinson, Watford Station
Maidenhead, James Cole
Railway Arms, John Hodgson, near the Station
Red Lion, Elizabeth Armstrong
Red Lion, Daniel Darvill, Colny butts
Red Lion, Elizabeth Weaver, Bushey
Spread Eagle, John Wilson
Swan, Edward Ginger
Three Compasses, Sarah Beaumont, Aldenham
Three Crowns, James Robinson
Three Horseshoes, Jno. Leaper, Aldenham
Three Tuns, Thomas Freeman
Two Wrestlers, Thos. Marryott, Aldenham
Wheat Sheaf, John Spencer
White Hart, George Green, Bushey
White Horse, William Denham, Bushey

TIMBER MERCHANTS.
Bellis Michael William, Watford
Eames Charles, Watford
Rogers Joseph, Watford

TOY DEALERS.
Mayes Christopher, Watford
Niddery David, Watford

TURNERS.
Eldridge William, Watford
Freeman Sarah, Bushey
Whitaker Charles, Watford

WATCH AND CLOCK MAKERS
Chapman John, Watford
Sims Richard, Watford
Wright Sampson (& jeweller) Watford

WHARFINGERS.
Cooper John, Cashio bridge New wharf
Howard Geo. Grove wharf
Rogers Joseph, Cashio bridge, Watford

WHEELWRIGHTS.
Haskell Bartholomew, Watford
Humphrey George, Watford
Jones James, Aldenham
Morgan Joseph, Bushey
Stacey Charles, Aldenham
Stone John, Watford

WINE & SPIRIT MERCHANTS
Brown George, Watford
Howard Robert, Watford
Lewin Charles, Watford

Miscellaneous.
Names without address are in WATFORD.
Bail George, dairyman, Bushey
Benford Joseph, dyer
Brown John, hurdle maker, Bushey heath
Bye Benjamin, fishmonger & poulterer
Bygrave George, fishmonger
Capell James, pawnbroker
Chapman Thomas, brick maker
Cleaver John, tripe dresser
Cleeve Henry, farmer, Bushey lodge, Watford
Cooper George, glass rivetter
Cooper George & Son, gunsmiths
Field Elisha, tallow chandler
Fowler Michael, importer of Alderney cows, Little Bushey
GAS WORKS, Watford——George Goldsmith, secretary
Harding Joseph, basket maker
Hawkins Henry, rake maker
Irish John, plasterer and paper hanger, Bushey heath
Latham Thomas, hatter
Munday Reuben, brush maker
Neale John, high constable
Nicholls Charles, farmer, Garston, Watford
Oldmeadow William, artist, Bushey
Peacock John, printer & stationer
Poulton Nathaniel, glover
REGISTRARS—John Adcock, for marriages; Nathaniel Poulton and Richard Pugh, for births and deaths
SAVING'S BANK, Watford—John Watson Walker, actuary
Simmons Thomas, cow keeper, Bushey
Smith Thomas, farmer, Aldenham
Splatt Richard, nursery and seedsman
Tidcombe & Strudwick, engineers
UNION WORKHOUSE, Colny butts—John Hilditch, master; Eliz. Hilditch, matron
Urlwin William, fellmonger
Walker John Watson, accountant, Bushey
White Mary Ann, haberdasher
Woodward James, millwright
Wright William, rope maker, Bushey

COACHES.
To LONDON, the *Despatch* (from Aylesbury) calls at the Rose & Crown, every forenoon (Sunday excepted) at eleven; goes through Stanmore—and a *Coach* (from Chesham) every morning (Sunday excepted) at eight.
To AYLESBURY, the *Despatch* (from London) calls at the Rose and Crown, every evening (Sunday excepted) at five; goes through Berkhampstead and Tring.
To CHESHAM, a *Coach* (from London) every evening (Sunday excepted) at six; through Rickmansworth and Chenies.
To RICKMANSWORTH, a *Fly*, every morning (Sunday excepted) at nine and evening at six.
To ST. ALBANS, a *Coach*, from the Railway station, every evening at half-past 5.

RAILWAY CONVEYANCE.
John Thomas Hand, *agent*, at the Station.
To LONDON, *Trains*, daily (Sunday excepted) at a quarter past four (*Mail*, daily) and eighteen minutes before nine morning; at a quarter past twelve noon; at a quarter past one and five afternoon; & at a quarter before six, quarter before eight and quarter past nine evening.

Sunday Trains.
At a quarter before nine morning; at a quarter after one afternoon, and a quarter before seven evening.
To BIRMINGHAM, *Trains*, daily (Sunday excepted) at nine and ten morning; at eleven forenoon; at twelve noon; at three afternoon; at six evening, and the *Mail Train*, every night at twenty-three minutes after nine.

Sunday Trains.
At nine morning; at twelve noon, and at six evening.

CARRIERS.
To LONDON, Wootton Clarke's *Waggon*, from his house, Bushey, every Monday, Wednesday & Saturday—William Axten's *Waggon*, and Daniel Darvell, from their houses, Watford, every Tuesday and Friday evening—James Coles, from the Maidenhead, every Tuesday, Friday and Saturday—and John Walters, every Friday.

CONVEYANCE BY WATER.
BY THE GRAND JUNCTION CANAL.
Goods consigned to Mr. Joseph Rogers, at his wharf, Cashio bridge, are forwarded to all places on the line of the above canal, as also to all parts of the kingdom.

WELWYN, CODICOTE, KIMPTON & NEIGHBOURHOODS.

WELWYN is a large and respectable village in the parish of its name and hundred of Broadwater, 25 miles N. from London and 7 N. W. from Hertford—situated on the small river Mimram, on the great north road from London to York: its position is of essential benefit to many of the inhabitants, by the traffic consequent upon the continual thoroughfare; whilst others are occupied in agricultural avocations, and a considerable number (particularly of the female sex) are employed in making straw plat. This is the place, according to tradition, at which the Danes were massacred on Hoe-Tuesday. In modern days it acquired celebrity as the residence of Dr. Young, who was rector of the parish until his death, which occurred in April, 1765; he was interred under the communion table in the church, beside his lady; a great part of his 'Night Thoughts,' and many other pieces of minor excellence, were written at Welwyn: he was the founder and endower of the free school here, which is now conducted upon the national system. The church is dedicated to St. Mary; the benefice, a rectory, is in the presentation of All Saints college, Oxford, and incumbency of the Rev. Samuel John Knight, who also is lord of the manor. The chalybeate spring in Mill-lane, formerly in high estimation, and reputed to possess qualities similar to those of the Tonbridge waters, has long since ceased to be resorted to. An annual statute fair is observed, but the period of holding it is regulated by the harvest, and the day fixed by the high constable of the hundred. The parish contained, at the census of 1831, 1,369 inhabitants.

Between one and two miles N. N. W. from Welwyn, in the hundred of Cashio and parish of its name, stands the village of CODICOTE. It formerly must have been of superior importance to what it is at the present day, having obtained from Henry III the privilege of holding a market, on Friday, and a fair on St. James's day, both of which have long been disused—the only semblance of a market, at the present day, is the attendance of persons on Thursday for sale of straw plat. The church, dedicated to St. Giles, with a chapel attached, is of some antiquity, and has an embattled tower surmounted by a spire; the living is a discharged vicarage, in the patronage of the bishop of Ely. Population, in 1831, 805.

Rather more than four miles N. W. from Welwyn, in the hundred of Hitchin and Pirton, is the village of KIMPTON. The parish church, dedicated to St. Peter and St. Paul, situated on rising ground to the north of the village, is of early foundation; it has a square embattled tower at its western end, and its interior is embellished with a fine screen of oak: the benefice is a vicarage, in the presentation of Lord Dacre. In 1831 the parish contained 944 inhabitants.

POST OFFICE, WELWYN, James Freshwater, *Post Master.*—Letters from LONDON arrive every night at five minutes before eleven, and are despatched every morning at three and afternoon at three.—Letters from the North arrive every morning at three, and are despatched every night at five minutes before eleven.

NOBILITY, GENTRY AND CLERGY.

Bassett Mr. William, Welwyn
Batten John, esq. Welwyn
Blake William, esq. Danesbury, Welwyn
Bunting Rev. Edward S. Datchworth
Clinton Henry Fynes, esq. Welwyn
Clutterbuck —, esq. Frythe
Clutton Rev. Ralph, Welwyn
Colley Mrs. Ann, Welwyn hill
Cowper the Right Hon. Earl, Pansanger
Dacre the Right Hon. Lord, Kimpton Hoo
Daring Cholmondeley, esq. Ayot, St. Lawrence
Daring Robert, esq. Lockley house
Davis Mrs. —, Codicote
Dickenson Rev. John, Tewin
Duncombe Captain —, Stagen Hoo
Ellis Mrs. —, Holly hall
Gray Mrs. Mary Augusta, Welwyn
Greenstreet Major John, Lawrence end, Kimpton
Heathcote Unwin, esq. Sheephall Bury
Jaunnard Rev. Thomas J. Parsonage, Codicote
Kemble Mrs. —, Welwyn hill
Knight Rev. Samuel John, Welwyn
Leeson the Hon. Mary, the Node
Lytton Mrs. Bulwer, Nebworth
Mansfield John, esq. Digwell house
Oakley Jas. esq. Porter's end, Kimptn
Peacock Henry, esq. Ayot cottage
Penneyfather Thomas, esq. Digswell water
Rayment Mrs. —, Welwyn hill
Sapte Francis, esq. Codicote
Smart Rev. Daniel, Welwyn
Sullivan Rev. Frederick, Kimpton
Thornton Geo. esq. Marden house, Tewin
Vincent Mr. Barker, Kimpton hall
Watson the Rev. Archdeacon, Digswell rectory
Wroe Rev. John, Welwyn
Yorke Rev. —, Little Ayot

ACADEMIES & SCHOOLS.

Fox Thomas (preparatory) Welwyn
NATIONAL SCHOOL, Kimpton—Edward Day, master
NATIONAL SCHOOL, Welwyn—John Burdett Ring, master
Otway Eliza (boarding) Welwyn
Otway William (boarding) Welwyn
Trash Misses (boarding) Welwyn

BAKERS & FLOUR DEALERS.

Crew Daniel, Kimpton
Elmer Richard, Kimpton
Lane James, Codicote
Moore John, Welwyn
Pointon Francis, Codicote
Young Henry, Welwyn

BLACKSMITHS.

Caine Elizabeth, Codicote
Caine Nathaniel, Codicote
Flindall Thomas, Welwyn
Tomalin John (and general) Kimpton
Wynn John (and farrier) Welwyn

BOOT & SHOE MAKERS.

Bigg Samuel, Codicote
Bolton Thomas, Welwyn
Clark James, Codicote
Clark William, Codicote
Clarke George, Kimpton
Lee Francis, Welwyn
Morgan James, Codicote
Smith Martin, Codicote

BREWERS & MALTSTERS.

Cass George (& corn & coal dealer) Welwyn
Hill John, Whitwell
Kingsley William, Kimpton

BRICKLAYERS.

Bailey John, Kimpton
Huckle James, Codicote
Waller Geo. (and brick maker) Digswell hill

BUTCHERS.

Barker James, Kimpton
Baron William, Welwyn
Brand George, Welwyn
Crane Susan, Codicote
Parker Joseph, Welwyn
Smith William, Codicote

CARPENTERS & JOINERS.

Batten Elizabeth, Welwyn
Blow Thomas, Welwyn
Chalkley John, Hampton
Dixon William, Codicote
Greenham Joseph, Welwyn
Prior Thomas (& builder) Welwyn
Welsh Joel, Codicote

COAL DEALERS.

Cass George, Welwyn
Elmer Richard, Kimpton

GROCERS AND DEALERS IN SUNDRIES.

Allen James, Welwyn
Bailey John, Kimpton
Baron William, Welwyn
Beale Mary, Codicote
Chalkley John, Kimpton
Chambers Joseph, Welwyn
Coleman Charles, Codicote
Crew Edward (and corn and spirit dealer) Kimpton
Drage Thomas, Welwyn
Higgs John Wells, Welwyn
Hill Elizabeth, Codicote
Pestall Louisa, Welwyn
Prior Eleanor, Welwyn
Wellingham William, Welwyn
Wilston John, Welwyn

INNS.

Duke of Wellington, Henry Ambrose, Welwyn
Rose & Crown (commercial) Joseph Brand, Old North road
White Hart (posting) Joseph Barker, Welwyn

IRONMONGERS.

Boulton George, Welwyn
Greenham Joseph, Welwyn
Wynn John, Welwyn

LINEN DRAPERS.

Batten Elizabeth, Welwyn
Crew Daniel, Kimpton
Frank Sarah (& hatter & fire office agent) Welwyn
Freshwater John (and hatter and undertaker, Welwyn
Welsh Joel, Codicote

MILLERS.

Cannon John, Welwyn
Cannon John, jun. Tewin mill
Garratt George (and farmer) Codicote mills
Hawkins William, Kimpton mill

PAINTERS, PLUMBERS AND GLAZIERS.

Deards Richard & Samuel, Welwyn
Joyner William, Welwyn
Tayler Thomas, Welwyn

SURGEONS.

Butcher John, Welwyn
Oldmeadow Henry E. Welwyn

TAILORS.

Nicholls Richard, Welwyn
Poulton Thomas, Welwyn
Sumner Charles & Son, Welwyn

TAVERNS & PUBLIC HOUSES.

Bell, William Smith, Codicote
Boot, Richard Elmer, Kimpton
Bull, Elizabeth Bigg, Codicote
Bull, Mary Biggs, Welwyn
Chequers, Richard Deards, Welwyn
Chequers, James Watson, Woolmer green
George, Mary Smith, Codicote
Goat, Alice Westwood, Codicote
Half Moon, Frederick Swain, Peter's green
Red Lion, James Cheshire, Digswell hill
Red Lion, James Huckle, Codicote
Red Lion, Richard Pedder, Woolmer green
Robin Hood, Nathnl. Cousins, Robley heath
Two Brewers, John Gray, Kimpton
Vine, George Brand, Welwyn
White Horse, John Waller, Welwyn

WHEELWRIGHTS.

Halsey John, Codicote
Medcraft George, Welwyn
Read George, Codicote
Wilston John, Welwyn
Wren William, Kimpton

Miscellaneous.

Chambers John, corn dealer, Welwyn
Clark George, clothes dealer, Welwyn
Davies Henry, land surveyor, Kimpton park
Deards George, cooper, Welwyn
Deards William and Richard, saddlers, Welwyn
Frank Livett, hair dresser, Welwyn
Freeman Charles B. watch maker, Welwyn
Garrett Samuel, fulling miller, Codicote
Goldsmith William, fellmonger & glover, Welwyn
Lawrance Philip, druggist and stationer, Welwyn
Messenger Thomas, rope, &c. maker, Welwyn
Ring John B. registrar of births & deaths, Welwyn

COACHES.

To and from LONDON, LEEDS, YORK, BOSTON, BEDFORD, HITCHIN, KETTERING, OUNDLE, ST. NEOTS, STAMFORD, &c. pass through Welwyn, daily.

CARRIERS.

To LONDON, — Brown's *Waggons*, from Welwyn, daily—and Sarah Etteridge's *Cart*, every Monday and Thursday.
To BEDFORD, — Brown's *Waggons*, daily
*** Besides the above, *Carriers* to & from LONDON, LEEDS, PETERBOROUGH, &c. pass through Welwyn, daily.

WHEATHAMPSTEAD AND SANDRIDGE.

WHEATHAMPSTEAD village and parish are in the hundred of Dacorum; the village is 24 miles N. N. W. from London, 5 N. from St. Albans, rather more than 4 miles W. S. W. from Welwyn, and 8 S. S. E. from Luton, in Bedfordshire—situated upon the navigable river Lea. Although at the present day this place presents little worthy of description, yet its name is connected with an occurrence of some importance in the fourteenth century—here it was that, in 1311, the barons confederating against Edward II concentrated their followers. Brewing and malting are the most prominent branches of business carried on in the village, and a paper mill gives employment to some hands. The parish church, dedicated to St. Helen, is an antique cruciform fabric, with a tower springing from the intersection of the transept and the nave: the living is a rectory, in the gift of the bishop of Lincoln, and present incumbency of the Rev. Geo. Thomas Prettyman, whose curate is the Rev. Joseph Douton. The independents have a chapel, and there is a school conducted upon the national system. The parish, in 1831, contained 1,666 inhabitants.

SANDRIDGE is a small village, in the parish of its name, two miles from Wheathampstead and three from St. Albans, in the hundred of Cashio. There is nothing in this vicinage to gratify the curiosity of the stranger. The church is dedicated to St. Leonard; the benefice, which is a vicarage, is in the patronage of Earl Spencer. A national school, erected in 1824, is supported by voluntary contributions—the late earl gave the ground for its site. Population of the parish, 810.

POST, WHEATHAMPSTEAD.—Letters are brought from and taken to ST. ALBANS (by foot post) daily.

GENTRY & CLERGY.

Boutel Rev. Charles, Sandridge
Clarke Mr. Robert (surgeon) Wheathampstead
Davies Rev. John, Wheathampstead
Douton Rev. Jos. Wheathampstead
Garratt Chas. Drake, esq. Lamar park
House Jno. esq. Wheathampstead hse
Kidman Mr. Thomas, Piggott's hill
Kinder Thomas, esq. Pound farm
Martin Mrs. Charlt. Marshal's wick
Prettyman Rev. George Thomas, Wheathampstead rectory

ACADEMIES AND SCHOOLS.

Douton Rev. Joseph (gentlemen's boarding) Wheathampstead
Gifkins George, Wheathampstead
NATIONAL SCHOOL, Wheathampstead—William Messer, master
NATIONAL SCHOOL, Sandridge—Dinah Mardell, mistress

BAKERS & MEALMEN.

Gregory John, Wheathampstead
Lattimore William, Wheathampstead
Parsons Jonathan, Sandridge
Sibley Thomas, Gustard wood

BLACKSMITHS.

Brown George, Wheathampstead
Ephgrave John, Sandridge
Messer John, Wheathampstead

BOOT & SHOE MAKERS.

Arnold James, Wheathampstead
Bond George, Sandridge
Grover George, Wheathampstead

BREWERS.

Lattimore Wm. H. jun. Wheathampstd
Sutton Geo. & Sons, Wheathampstead

BUTCHERS.

Chennels Amelia, Wheathampstead
Mowbray William, Wheathampstead
Mumford John, Wheathampstead

CARPENTERS.

Arnold George, Wheathampstead
Brown George, Wheathampstead
Kilby John, Gustard wood
Paull William, Sandridge

CORN MILLERS AND CORN DEALERS.

Bates Edmond, Batford mills
Bruton Edward, Wheathampstead
Lattimore William, Wheathampstead
Sutton George (and coal) Wheathampstead mills

GROCERS & TEA DEALERS.

Nash George & Sarah (& drapers & fire office agents) Wheathampstead
Sibley Edward, Gustard wood

MALTSTERS.

Dorrington John, Wheathampstead
Kinder Thomas, Sandridge
Lattimore William H. jun. Hope brewery
Sibley Henry, Wheathampstead
Sutton Geo. & Sons, Wheathampstead
Thrale Ralph, Mackray end

TAILORS.

Poulter James, Wheathampstead
Tong Thomas, Wheathampstead

TAVERNS & PUBLIC HOUSES.

Bell, Frederick Baker, Wheathampstead
Bull, William Hooper, Wheathampstead
Queen's Head, Henry Wilmot, Sandridge
Rose & Crown, John Higgins, Sandridge
Swan, Samuel Smith, Wheathampstead
William the Fourth, Cornelius Franklin, No-man's land

WHEELWRIGHTS.

Bray Robert, Wheathampstead
Lattimore John & Joseph, Sandridge

Miscellaneous.

Bray Robert, cooper, Wheathampstead
Dunham Ann, bricklayer, Wheathampstead
Grover Geo. shopkeeper, Wheathampstead
Jones Edward, paper maker, Pickford mill
Mondin Geo. poulterer, Wheathampstead
Walker William, straw plat bleacher, No-man's land
Young George, farmer, Sandridge

CARRIERS.

To LONDON, Thomas Humphreys, every Monday and Friday morning—and Geo. Munday, every Thursday evening.

MIDDLESEX.

THIS is the smallest of the counties, except one (Rutland), in England; yet it is only exceeded in its population by the largest county (York). It is one of the highest grandeur and importance in the united kingdom, as containing the metropolis of the British empire, besides the city of Westminster, and being the seat of royalty, all the departments of government, and the legislature—as also from its having within its boundaries residences belonging to the chief nobility of the land. It is bounded on the north by Hertfordshire; on the south by the river Thames, which separates it from the county of Surrey; on the west by Buckinghamshire, from which it is separated by the river Colne; and on the east by Essex, its boundary line at this part being the river Lea. In length, from south-east to north-west, it is about twenty-three miles; and in breadth it does not exceed fifteen miles: in circumference it is estimated at about one hundred miles, and its area as containing two hundred and eighty-two square miles, or 180,480 statute acres.

NAME and ANCIENT HISTORY.—The name MIDDLESEX is derived from the *Middle Saxons*—the people inhabiting it residing between the East, West and South Saxons, and those who were then called the Mercians. At the time of Cæsar's invasion of Britain the *Trinobantes* occupied this part of the island, where, according to Cæsar, they had a very strong city: their king at that time was Imanuentius, who was subsequently murdered by Cassibelan; Mandrubratius, the son of the former, saved his life by flight, and, joining Cæsar in Gaul, returned under his protection to Britain; at the same time the *Trinobantes* applied by deputies to Cæsar to defend Mandrubratius from Cassibelan's injustice, and to send him to assume the chief authority in their state; this request, upon receiving forty hostages, the politic Roman immediately complied with—and thus this tribe became the first of the British that succumbed to his ambition. In the reign of Nero, however, the *Trinobantes* conspired with the *Icenii* to shake off the Roman yoke; but Suetonius Paulinus defeated the confederacy, at the expense of much Roman, and torrents of British blood. On the extinction of the Roman dominion in this country, Vortigern, a Briton, in order to obtain his liberty from the Saxons, whose prisoner he was, gave up to them this district with others; and it was long governed by sovereigns of its own (but tributary to those of Kent or Mercia)—of whom Sibert, in 603, first embraced Christianity; Suthred, the last chief, was conquered by Egbert, and surrendered his principality to the West Saxons. All the Roman roads centered in this county, at a place called 'London Stone,' still to be seen in Cannon-street, in the city of London. This stone appears to be preserved as the *Palladium* of the city; it is, like a sacred relic, cased within freestone, with a hole left in the centre which discovers the original: superstitious respect has been paid to it at various times; amongst other occurrences attached to it is that recorded of the notorious rebel, *Jack Cade*, who, as he passed by it when he had forced his way into the city, struck his sword on 'London Stone,' saying, '*Now is Mortimer lord of this city!*' as if that had been a customary ceremony of taking possession. At Brentford, where the Brent enters the Thames, King Edmund Ironside defeated the Danes, drawn off from the siege of London, and drove them across the river: to this place, also, Charles I advanced with his army after the battle of Edgehill, and excited no little consternation among his opponents in the metropolis.

SOIL, CLIMATE and AGRICULTURAL PRODUCE.—The prevailing SOILS in Middlesex are loam and clay, or sand and gravel more or less intermixed with loamy clay. In the immediate vicinity of the capital the clay has in many parts been dug up to a considerable depth, for the composition of bricks; and almost innumerable buildings have arisen on the very spots where the land has been thus excavated. The CLIMATE in general is considered salubrious, owing to the greater proportion of the soil being naturally dry, and the less elevated districts efficiently drained, and consequently free from unwholesome exhalations. The arable lands are for the most part spread out into common fields, although above twenty thousand acres are now enclosed. The corn grown in this county is nearly confined to wheat and barley, oats and rye being but partially cultivated: the greater portion of the upland meadow and pasture lands is very productive, and in the art of hay-making the Middlesex farmers are superior to any others in the island. The banks of the Thames, Colne and Lea rivers, and generally of the smaller streams that water this county, present a series of luxuriant meadows, principally produced from a rich loamy soil; those which lie contiguous to the Thames are occupied, to an extent of many miles, by nurserymen and gardeners, who cultivate an immense quantity of fruit and vegetables for the London market. The quantity of live stock kept in this county is less, probably, than in any other, in proportion to the number of acres. Middlesex, from its undulating surface, is peculiarly suited to the purposes of agriculture, being sufficiently sloping to secure a proper drainage, without having any abrupt elevations; at the same time the inequalities of the surface contribute to health, ornament and beauty. For the most part, the ground rises from the banks of the Thames towards the north; and within a few miles of London a range of gently swelling eminences (of which Hampstead, Highgate and Muswell Hill are the chief,) protect the metropolis from the severity of the northern blasts. From these heights many pleasing and extensive prospects are obtained; and some equally comprehensive may be had from Harrow Hill, which, from rising in an almost insulated manner, forms a prominent object at the distance of several miles: this eminence is detached from a yet higher and more extensive ridge, stretching from Pinner, Stanmore, Elstree, Totteridge and Barnet to Enfield Chace. The roads throughout the county, both public and parochial, are in general good; those on the great lines of thoroughfare, for many miles around the metropolis, are incomparably excellent, and kept in repair at a vast expense: where the flatness of the surface does not admit the advantages of draining, the roads are constructed in what is termed the 'barrel' form—that is, the middle is raised as high as can be with proper regard to the safety of the vehicles passing on it, in order to prevent the water from settling on the surface, and thereby diminishing its compactness and solidity, as well as impairing its beauty.

MANUFACTURES, COMMERCE, &c.—The MANUFACTURES of this county are more numerous and varied than a superficial observer would be led to believe; the principal, however, have their seat in the metropolis, where are establishments for the manufacture of such articles of elegance and luxury as are required to be of superior workmanship, and which are not only supplied to the country, but exported to all parts of the world. In the manufacture of silk goods, in all its branches, it stands unrivalled; for the drawing of wire from all the metals, and the making of pins and needles, it has long been deservedly famous; fancy articles, in worsted, silk, and gold and silver (as laces, fringes, &c.), with beautiful and rich productions from the embroiderer's frame, are branches in which the London artizan may fearlessly challenge competition. The trade arising from the consumption of food, in the metropolis, also is immense, and influences the traffic not only of its own county, but others much more distantly situated. The breweries of London are upon a scale of unequalled magnitude, and the porter is celebrated all over Europe; the distilleries in the capital and its neighbourhood are likewise extraordinary establishments, and their produce is distributed throughout the entire kingdom. It has been computed that the total amount of property shipped and unshipped, in the port of London alone, amounts to nearly £70,000,000. sterling yearly; there are employed in the exports and imports about four thousand ships, and not less than fifteen thousand cargoes annually enter the port—these are exclusive of about five thousand vessels employed in the importation of coal alone to London; from this, conjecture may be assisted as to the immense quantity consumed of this essential article. There are between two and three thousand barges engaged in the inland trade, and twelve hundred revenue officers are constantly on duty in the port of London. Sugar refining is a business in which a great number of firms have large capitals and numerous hands employed—their establishments are to be found chiefly in the eastern part of the metropolis, Although the trade and commerce of the capital are so intimately connected, in a greater or less degree, with the prosperity of Middlesex, and, indeed, the country at large, yet other places in the county have resources within themselves of high consideration. In some towns are large bleaching and calico printing works; in others, extensive iron foundries, soaperies and distilleries; tanneries and roperies, of important consideration, are to be seen in different parishes; while paper mills, chymical works, potteries, &c., and various other manufactories of minor consequence, are occasionally met with. The entire, with the addition of its agricultural treasures, and the splendour of its two great cities, combine to render the county of Middlesex the most important and opulent, as it is the most interesting, of all other counties in the British empire.

RIVERS and MINERAL SPRINGS, CANALS and RAILWAYS.—The RIVERS of Middlesex are the THAMES, the LEA, the COLNE, the BRENT, and the NEW RIVER. The Thames, whose rise, progress, &c., have been described in the particulars of other counties, is one of the most beautiful rivers in the world; and at London its depth is sufficient, not only for the navigation of large ships, but for making its capacious channel what it really is—one of the greatest ports for trade in the universe; it abounds with a great variety of fish, and is noted for its salmon, smelts, flounders and eels. The Lea rises near Luton, in Bedfordshire, and running to Hertford and Ware, and afterwards dividing Essex from part of Hertfordshire and Middlesex, falls into the Thames below Blackwall. The Colne runs through the county of Hertford and part of Middlesex, dividing the latter county from Buckinghamshire, and falls into the Thames at Staines. The Brent, as has been mentioned, joins the Thames at Brentford. The New River is an artificial stream, brought from two springs at Chadwell and Amwell-Parva, near Ware, in Hertfordshire, for supplying the metropolis with water: this river, with all its windings, is nearly thirty-nine miles long, has forty-three sluices, and over it upwards of two hundred bridges; it is under the management of a flourishing corporation, called the New River Company; the water was brought into the basin, termed the New River Head, on Michaelmas-day, 1613. In various parts of the county are SPRINGS of MINERAL WATER, some of which were formerly in great repute for their medicinal virtues, but none of them are now much resorted to; those still visited are Bagnigge wells, St. Chad's wells and Islington spa, all which are on the northern side of the metropolis. The two principal CANALS of the county are the Grand Junction canal and the Paddington canal. The former enters Middlesex near Uxbridge; passes by Cowley and Eplingdon to the west, and Drayton, Harlington, Cranford park, Norwood and Osterley park to the east—where, intersecting the river Brent, it falls into the Thames between Brentford and Sion House. The Paddington canal branches off from the Grand Junction near Cranford, and is continued on a level the whole way to the basin at Paddington. The Regent's canal commences at a short distance above the basin, and then enters a tunnel under Maida hill, from which it emerges and skirts the northern side of the Regent's park; it then continues its course by Islington (through a tunnel), Kingsland and Hackney to Limehouse, where it terminates in an extensive basin communicating with the Thames. There is likewise a navigable canal leading from Hertfordshire along the banks of the river Lea, with which it forms a junction in the neighbourhood of Bow, from whence the united streams continue their course to Limehouse, and at that place incorporate themselves with the Thames. RAILWAYS:—This county, and that of Surrey, dividing between them the distinction of possessing within their limits the metropolis of Great Britain, have become, in consequence, the nucleus of some of the most important railroads that intersect the country. The London and Birmingham railway has its station at Euston-square, near to the new church of Saint Pancras: this important line received the sanction of parliament in the session of 1833, at a cost of nearly £73,000!—on the 20th July, 1837, it was opened to Boxmoor (about twenty-five miles), and on the 17th September the whole line was opened; its entire length is one hundred and twelve miles and a half—the longest line and greatest railway work completed in this kingdom at that period; the original estimate was two and a half millions, but the entire expense has considerably exceeded five millions. This line, in connexion with the Grand Junction, affords a rapid communication between the metropolis and Birmingham, Liverpool, Manchester, Preston, Lancaster, &c. The station of the London and Southampton railway is situated at the Nine Elms, near to Vauxhall, Lambeth; while that of the Great Western line is at Paddington: this railway was opened to Maidenhead on the 4th June, 1838. The station for the Greenwich railway is close to the foot of London-bridge, on the Surrey side of the Thames; the same locality serves for the London and Brighton railway and the Croydon railway. Amongst other lines which will originate from, or have their *termini* in the metropolis, are the South-Eastern railway, between London and Dover; the Eastern Counties' railway, running into Norfolk; the London and Blackwall railway, and the Northern and Eastern railway. The Eastern Counties' was opened as far as Romford, in Essex, on the 21st June, 1839.

ECCLESIASTICAL and CIVIL DIVISIONS, and REPRESENTATION.—The county of Middlesex is in the province of Canterbury, and diocess of London and Westminster; is included in the home circuit of the judges, and divided into the six hundreds of Edmonton, Elthorne, Gore, Isleworth, Ossulton and Spelthorne. The hundred of Ossulton is apportioned into four districts, respectively named Finsbury division, Holborn division, Kensington division, and Tower division: these hundreds and divisions collectively contain one hundred and ninety-seven parishes, two cities (London and Westminster), and six market towns. REPRESENTATION:—Previous to the passing of the reform bill Middlesex returned *eight* members to parliament, of whom two sat for the county, four for the city of London and two for Westminster. The new act created the following additional boroughs, and conferred upon them the privilege of sending two members each, viz. Finsbury, Marylebone, and the Tower Hamlets. The return of county representatives is made at Brentford; and the polling stations in addition are at King's Cross (Saint Pancras), or within half a mile thereof, Hammersmith, Bedfont, Edgware, Mile End and Uxbridge.

POPULATION, &c.—By the census for 1831 the county of Middlesex (including the city of London and those of its suburbs not in the county of Surrey, and the city of Westminster,) contained 631,493 males, and 727,048 females—total, 1,358,541, being an increase, since the returns made in the year 1821, of 214,010 inhabitants; and from the census of 1801 to that of 1831 the augmentation amounted to 540,412 persons. The total population of the METROPOLIS and its suburbs (including the city of Westminster, the borough of Southwark, certain parishes without the bills of mortality, and others in the county of Surrey), by the above returns, amounted to 1,474,069 souls—being an increase, since the year 1821, of 248,378; and from the census of 1801 to that of 1831, of 609,224 inhabitants.—The total annual value of Real Property in this county, as assessed April, 1815, amounted to £5,595,537.

Index of Distances from Town to Town in the County of Middlesex.

The names of the respective towns are on the top and side, and the square where both meet gives the distance.

	Barnet	Brentford	Edgware	Enfield	Hounslow	Southall	Staines	Uxbridge	*Distance from London.*
Barnet									11
Brentford	14								7
Edgware	4	10							8
Enfield	5	16	9						10
Hounslow	16	2	12	18					10
Southall	18	4	12	24	4				9
Staines	23	9	19	25	7	10			16
Uxbridge	15	10	11	16	9	6	9		15

ACTON, EAST ACTON AND SHEPHERD'S BUSH.

ACTON is a village and parish, in the Kensington division of the hundred of Ossulton, five miles west from London, pleasantly situated on the declivity of a gently sloping eminence, and on the main road to Oxford. This is an agricultural parish, and, with the exception of a manufactory for Lapland rugs, it enjoys no peculiar branch of trade. It is enlivened by its thoroughfare situation, and numerous genteel residences ornament its neighbourhood; but the village itself, which consists of one long street, has little to boast in appearance. The church, dedicated to St. Mary, was repaired and enlarged, at the expense of the inhabitants, in 1825; the living is a rectory, in the patronage of the Bishop of London: and the incumbency is enjoyed by the Rev. William Antrobus, who has been rector of this parish forty-three years. The almshouses of the goldsmiths' company of the city of London, at East Acton, liberally endowed for twelve poor men and the like number of poor women, form the principal charity. The company are about to erect a chapel for the use of the inmates; and there is a Lancasterian school, erected near the church. That part of the village called EAST ACTON is contiguous to the Uxbridge road, about a mile hence, and, from the beauty of its situation, is eminently qualified for a summer retreat. In a garden on Old Oak common is a mineral spring, formerly held in considerable repute. The parish of Acton contained, by the last official returns, 2,453 inhabitants.

Two miles from Acton, situated between that village and Kensington gravel-pits, is SHEPHERD'S BUSH, a hamlet to the parish of Fulham. It is an improving little place; its situation is much admired, and is the summer residence of numerous respectable families.

POST OFFICE, ACTON, William Collett, *Post Master.*—Letters from LONDON arrive every morning at seven, afternoon at one and three and evening at seven, and are despatched every morning at half-past eight and afternoon at one and three.

POST, EAST ACTON, *Receiving-House* at Thomas Barnard's, grocer.—Letters from all parts arrive (from Turnham Green) every day at twelve & evening at six, & are despatched every morning at eight & afternoon at ½ past 3.

POST, SHEPHERD'S BUSH, *Receiving-House* at Martha Rolfe's.—Letters arrive & are despatched twice a day.

GENTRY & CLERGY.

The letters S. B. means SHEPHERD'S BUSH.

Anderson Mrs. —, Acton
Antrobus Rev. Edward, jun. Acton
Antrobus Rev. William, Acton
Baker Mr. Chas. Beaumont place, S.B.
Bagster Chas. esq. Shepherd's Bush
Bridge Geo. esq. Wood house, S. B.
Biscaby Rd. esq. Oldfield lodge, Acton
Bushnan Christopher, esq. Addison terrace, S. B. [Bush
Chadwick Mrs. Mary, Shepherd's
Church Major Handy, East Acton
Coombe Boyce, esq. Acton
Cooper Mr. James, Wood place, S. B.
Cooper Mr. Thos. Shepherd's Bush
Costen Mr. Henry, Shepherd's Bush
Cranfield Miss —, Askew villa, S. B.
Croft Sir Archer, Acton
Curtis Berwick, esq. Acton
Daniel Mr. Robert, Shepherd's Bush
Davies Thomas, esq. East Acton
Disney Sir Moore, East Acton
Engleheart John Cox Dillman, esq. East Acton
Evans Robert, esq. East Acton
Gardner Mrs. —, East Acton
Geary Mr. William, Acton
Grant John, esq. Acton
Greenhald Mr. —, Shepherd's Bush
Greenland Mr. —, Lawn place, S. B.
Grillion Pier, esq. East Acton
Hall Benjamin, esq. Shepherd's Bush
Hall Mrs. —, Cumberland cottge, S.B.
Harvey William, esq. Acton
Hay Mrs. General, Beaumont pl, S.B.
Key Mrs. —, Addison terrace, S. B.
King Miss —, Wood place, S. B.
Lambert Mr. James, Acton
Leaf Mr. James, Acton [S. B.
Lewis Benjamin, esq. Addison terrace,
North Mrs. Mary, East Acton
Overy Miss —, East Acton
Parker Mr. —, Shepherd's Bush
Parker Sir Charles, East Acton
Peel Mrs. —, Acton cottage [S. B.
Piper Robt. esq. Cumberland house,
Selby Mrs. Acton [S. B.
Sharman John, esq. Poplar cottage,
South Jon. esq. Addison terrace, S. B.
Thomas Thos. esq. Shepherd's Bush
Thompson Chs. esq. Beaumont pl, S.B.
Tubbs the Misses, Acton
Vine Chas. esq. 2 Lawn place, S. B.
Wall Rev. Frederick, East Acton
Wegg Miss —, Acton [S. B.
Wattier Philip, esq. 3 Lawn place,
Whippy Mr. John, Acton
White Richard, esq. Acton
Whitrow Miss —, Lawn place, S. B.
Williams William, esq. Addison terrace, Shepherd's Bush
Winter John, esq. Acton [Acton
Wood Jas. Richd. esq. Friar's place,
Wool William, esq. Lawn lodge, S. B.

ACADEMIES & SCHOOLS.

Bard Jane (preparatory), Acton
Bard Stanislaus (preparatory), Acton
Fowler Mary Ann, Manor house seminary [Green, mistress
INFANTS' SCHOOL, Acton — Esther
Mullins Felix (boarding), Orger house, Acton [Huddle, mistress
NATIONAL SCHOOL, Acton—Frances
Read Mrs. Martha, Lawn house, S.B.
Zamora Wm. (day), Shepherd's Bush

BAKERS.

Billington William, Acton
Bluck Thomas, East Acton
Boyd Wm. Ropier, Shepherd's Bush
Clifton John, Acton
Clifton William, Acton
Farmer Daniel, Acton
Plumridge Joseph, Shepherd's Bush
Westall Thomas, Shepherd's Bush

BLACKSMITHS.

Atlee Richard, East Acton
Morris James, Shepherd's Bush
Smith John, Acton
Winning William, Acton

BOOT & SHOE MAKERS.

Andrews John, Shepherd's Bush
Ellis William, Acton
Gates Charles, Acton
Hayward William, Shepherd's Bush
Holford Henry, Acton
Lodge William, Acton
Treadaway Frederick, Acton

BRICKLAYERS.

Acton Robert James, Acton
Bailey William, Acton
Beagley Thomas, Shepherd's Bush
Rose Joseph, Acton

BUTCHERS.

Hallett James, Shepherd's Bush
May Wm. Osborn, Acton [Bush
Orchard Wm. Seagram, Shepherd's
Price Thomas, Acton

CARPENTERS.

Aldridge Thomas, Shepherd's Bush
Compton & Millward, Acton
Dorset Edward, Acton
Frethy Thos. (and appraiser), Acton
Giles Thomas (& undertaker), Shepherd's Bush
Hayward George & Son, Acton
Pritchard William, Acton
Robinson James, Acton

COAL DEALERS.

Billington William, Acton
Clifton John, Acton
Dean Joseph, Shepherd's Bush

CORN DEALERS.

Adams Ann, Acton
Billington William, Acton
Boyd William Ropier, Acton
Clifton John, Acton
Farmer Daniel, Acton

COW KEEPERS.

Barnard Thomas, East Acton
Biggs Joseph, East Acton
Butler George, Shepherd's Bush
Thatcher Joseph, Acton

DRESS MAKERS.

Tilbury Clara, Acton
Treadaway Ann, Acton

GROCERS AND DEALERS IN SUNDRIES.

Barnard Thomas, East Acton
Bright William, Shepherd's Bush
Bright Wm. jun. Shepherd's Bush
Collett William, Acton
Cookson Edward, Acton
Dean Joseph, Shepherd's Bush
Fielder Edward, Shepherd's Bush
Halsey Wm. Edwd. Shepherd's Bush
Harding Benjamin, Acton
Hilder Catherine, Shepherd's Bush
Holford Henry, Acton
Jones Susannah, Acton
Jones William, Acton
Lowe John (& druggist & fire office agent), Acton
Marke Robert, Acton
Miller John, Acton
Morgan James, Shepherd's Bush
Palmer Samuel, Acton

HAIR DRESSERS.

Brown George, Acton
Elliott James, Shepherd's Bush

LINEN, &c. DRAPERS.

Savaker Samuel, Acton
Tilbury Clara, Acton

LIVERY STABLE KEEPERS.

Oldham Martin, Acton
Wheeler Thomas, East Acton

NURSERY & SEEDSMEN.

Essex John, Acton
Plumley William, Shepherd's Bush
Scott Andrew, Shepherd's Bush

PAINTERS & GLAZIERS.

Clews Robert, Acton
Hadden Joseph (painter), Shepherd's Bush [Bush
Maynard William Smith, Shepherd's
Perry George Parker, Acton
Smith Margaret, Acton

SURGEONS.
Clubbe William, Acton
Day Henry, Acton
Salt John (& chymist), Acton

TAILORS.
Adams Elizabeth (& dyer), Acton
Barge James, Acton
Crocker Joseph, Shepherd's Bush
Smith William, Acton

TAVERNS & PUBLIC HOUSES.
Anchor, John William Maynard, Acton
Beaumont Arms, James Tapley, Shepherd's Bush
Duke of Clarence, Nathaniel Britton, Shepherd's Bush
George, Martin Oldham, Acton
Goldsmith's Arms, Thos. Wheeler, East Acton
Horse & Groom, Samuel Mill, East Acton
King's Arms, Richard Lambourn, Acton
King's Head, Arthur Kite, Acton
Mail Coach, William West, Shepherd's Bush
Princess Victoria, Samuel Douglas, Shepherd's Bush
Queen Adelaide, Simon Gowing, Shepherd's Bush
Red Lion, Thomas Ives, Acton
Wellington Arms, John Bonsall, Shepherd's Bush
White Hart, Esther Farquarson, Acton
White Horse, Jas. Butcher, Shepherd's Bush
William IV, Robert James Acton, Acton

Miscellaneous.
Adams Ann, miller, Acton
Bagster Wm. market gardener, Shepherd's Bush
Berry Richard, bookseller, stationer and printer, Acton
Biggs Joseph, cooper, Acton
Bird George & William, brick makers, Shepherd's Bush
Clutterbuck Benjamin, brick maker, Shepherd's Bush
Congreve Henry, chymist, Shepherd's Bush
Cunningham Thomas, wheelwright, Shepherd's Bush
Day Henry, saddler, Acton
Gee John Charles, Lapland rug manufacturer, Steyne mill, Acton
Harris Ann & Mary, glass & china dealers, Acton
Hirons Thomas, wheelwright, Acton
Holland Henry, coach smith, Shepherd's B.
Moore Edwd. coach maker, Shepherd's Bush
Searle Isaac, tobacco-pipe manufacturer, Shepherd's Bush
Sizmur James, brewer, Shepherd's Bush
Waite Eliza, fruiterer, &c. Shepherd's Bush
Williamson John, registrar of births and deaths, Acton

COACHES, &c.
To LONDON, Joseph Hart's *Coach* (from Wycombe) calls at the White Hart, Acton, every day (Sunday excepted) at twelve—and Thomas Ives' *Omnibuses*, six times a day—besides the above, a *Coach* (from Uxbridge) and *Omnibuses* (from Ealing) pass through continually during the day.
To EALING, HIGH WYCOMBE and UXBRIDGE, *Coaches* (from London), pass through Acton daily.

CARRIERS.
To LONDON, John Graham, from his house, Acton, daily—also by the Uxbridge and Wycombe carriers, who pass through Acton.

BRENTFORD

IS a market town, comprising OLD BRENTFORD, in the parish of Ealing and hundred of Ossulton, and NEW BRENTFORD, in the parish of Hanwell and hundred of Elthorne; seven miles s. w. from Hyde Park corner, situate on the great western road, and upon the northern bank of the Thames, which river separates it from Kew gardens on the south. It was anciently called *Brainforde*, or *Braynford;* and takes its name from a ford formerly on the river Brent, near the site of the present bridge. Brentford possesses some claim to antiquity, a battle having been fought here, in 1016, between Edmund Ironside and Canute, King of Denmark, in which the latter was defeated. A treaty of peace was concluded here betwixt Charles I and the deputies of the parliamentary forces, after the defeat of the latter, in 1642, at Edgehill. In the reign of Edward I a toll was exacted on and in aid of the 'bridge of *Braynford*.' The town is within the jurisdiction of the county magistrates, who hold a petty session for the division every alternate week. The township of New Brentford is within the manor of Boston, and for which only customary courts are held. A court of requests for the recovery of debts under 40s. is held here during the summer half year, and during the winter at Uxbridge. The parliamentary elections for the county take place in New Brentford, it being the county town; and the hustings, upon those occasions, are erected behind the market-place. It is here that the Grand Junction canal enters the Thames, from which circumstance, in addition to the great thoroughfare of the place, arises its present prosperity. The principal concerns in trade are the extensive brewery of Messrs. Hazard & Co., and the old established distillery of Messrs. Booths'; besides which there is a considerable soap manufactory. The town is well lighted with gas, as is also the road extending eastward as far as Hammersmith, thereby adding much to the consequence of the town and convenience of the neighbourhood. The principal inn and booking-house is the 'Castle,' in New Brentford.

The church (or rather chapel) of St. Lawrence, is in New Brentford; it is a neat brick structure, first erected in the reign of Richard I, and rebuilt in 1764; the walls of the interior are almost covered with monuments, and tables of donations that have from time to time been bestowed. St. George's chapel, standing in Old Brentford, and appertaining to Ealing parish, is a plain modern building, the curacy to which was at one period enjoyed by the celebrated Horne Tooke. The living of New Brentford is a perpetual curacy, in the patronage of the rector of Hanwell. There are meeting-houses for several religious denominations, and two well supported charity-schools for educating and clothing children of both sexes; there is also a dispensary, supported by subscription; an apprenticeship fund, originating with Mrs. Mary Spencer and Lord Ossulton, and a savings' bank. The market day is Tuesday; and the annual fairs are 17th, 18th and 19th May, for cattle, and 12th, 13th and 14th September, for toys and pedlery. In 1831, New Brentford contained 2,085 inhabitants,—and Ealing parish, with Old Brentford, 7,783; total, 9,868.

POST OFFICE, NEW BRENTFORD, Philip Norbury, *Post Master.*—Letters from LONDON arrive every morning at nine, forenoon at eleven, afternoon at three and evening at six, and are despatched every morning at nine and afternoon at one and four.—Letters for the West are despatched to HOUNSLOW & KINGSTON every evening at seven.

POST, OLD BRENTFORD, *Receiving-House* at Senols and Barton's, grocers.—Letters are despatched to NEW BRENTFORD every morning at a quarter before nine, afternoon at a quarter before one and a quarter before four and evening at a quarter before nine.

*** *The letters* N. B. *or* O. B. *attached to an address means* NEW BRENTFORD *and* OLD BRENTFORD.

GENTRY AND CLERGY.
Annands William, esq. Myrtle cottage, Butts
Blagg Capt. James, Butts, New B.
Booth Sir Felix, Old Brentford
Carrington Mr. —, Butts, New B.
Carrington Mrs. Eliz. Butts, N. B.
Clarke George, esq. New Brentford
Clitherow Col. James, Boston house
Crane Mrs. —, Old Brentford
Crighton Charles, esq. Brent cottage
Cross Salem, esq. Butts, New B.
Dewell Mrs. Francis, Butts, New B.
Fletcher Mrs. —, Butts, New B.
Franklin Mrs. —, Butts, New B.
Furber Charles, esq. Boston lane
Geary Rev. John, Old Brentford
Leader J. C. esq. Butts, New B.
Lewis Mrs. Julia, Butts, New B.
Morris Mrs. —, Boston road, Old B.
Oliver George, esq. Boston rd. O. B.
Platt Miss Elizabeth, Windmill lane
Powell Geo. esq. Boston road, O. B.
Reynolds Mrs. Hannah, Butts, N. B.
Rooke Mrs. Elizabeth, Butts, N. B.
Saxton Mr. William, Butts, N. B.
Shirley Mrs. —, Butts, New Brentfd
Shury Mr. Geo. Windmill hse. O. B.
Smith Mrs. S. Boston road, O. B.
Stoddart Rev. John, D.D. New Brentfd
Sturgess Wm. esq. Boston rd. O. B.
Thompson Rev. F. E. Old Brentford
Tomson Capt. —, Butts, New B.
Trimmer Jas. Rustell, esq. Old Brentfd
Trimmer Miss Maria T. New Brentford
Wilkinson Mr. Saml. Old Brentford

ACADEMIES AND SCHOOLS.
Not otherwise described are Day Schools.
Brown George, New Brentford
CHARITY SCHOOL, Butts, New Brentford—Miss Cane, mistress
Hill Joseph (private teacher), Butts, New Brentford
Holsworth Joshua (boarding), Drum lane, Old Brentford
INFANTS' SCHOOL, Old Brentford
James Eliza (day & brdng.) O. Brentfd
NATIONAL SCHOOL, Ham, New Brentford—James Biergine, master
Pickering Emma (preparatory), Butts, N. Brentford
Powell Sophia (boarding), Butts, N. Brentford
Seppings John, Old Brentford
Valentine Broughton, Butts, N. B.

ATTORNEYS.

Clark Geo. & John Jas. New Brentfrd
Fletcher Robert Thos. Butts, N. B.
Nicholas Alfred, Butts, New Brentfrd

AUCTIONEERS & APPRAISRS

Coombs Charles, New Brentford
Grocock Saml. (appraiser), New B.
King John, Old Brentford
Young John, Old Brentford

BAKERS & FLOUR DEALERS.

Bond James, Old Brentford
Boxall William (and corn dealer), New Brentford
Bradshaw Thomas, New Brentford
Briggs Sarah, Old Brentford
Carver John, Old Brentford
Clark William, Old Brentford
Dexter John, New Brentford
Eaton William, Old Brentford
Elgood Henry, New Brentford
Hope John, Old Brentford
King Wm. (muffin), Half acre, O. B.
Newins Henry, Old Brentford
Nuthall Thomas, Old Brentford
Purnell Samuel, Old Brentford
Rogers George, Old Brentford
Simmonds Chas. Wm. New Brentfrd
Stiff John, Old Brentford
Welch William, New Brentford

BARGE MASTERS AND LIGHTERMEN.

Baker John, Old Brentford
Banyon Robert, Old Brentford
Bourne William, New Brentford
Dale Joseph, New Brentford
Harris Joseph, Old Brentford
Layton Thomas, Old Brentford
Napper John, Old Brentford
Rogers Fras. & Son, New Brentford
Townsend Wm. George, Butts, N. B.
Winter Thomas, Old Brentford

BASKET MAKERS.

Bowden Thomas, Old Brentford
Dawes Mary, Old Brentford

BLACKSMITHS & FARRIERS.

Bailey Thos. & John, Old Brentford
Hinge John, New Brentford
Hockenhull Joseph, Old Brentford

BOOKSELLERS & STATIONRS

Bontems John Francis (& registrar), New Brentford
Murphy Chas. Jas. (& printer), New Brentford
Norbury Philip and Mary Ann (and printers), New Brentford
Over James, Old Brentford
Seppings John, Old Brentford
White Ann, Old Brentford
Woodbridge Stephn. New Brentford

BOOT AND SHOE MAKERS.

Ball James, Old Brentford
Boylett George, Old Brentford
Buttery Charles, New Brentford
Callis John, Old Brentford
Chown John, New Brentford
Cook Frederick, New Brentford
Cox Thomas George, Old Brentford
Dale James, Old Brentford
Edwards Eliz. (ladies'), Butts, N. B.
Gillham Henry, Old Brentford
Goldney Joseph, Old Brentford
Janaway Jonathan, Old Brentford
Lowe John, Boston rd. Old Brentfrd
Lowe Thomas, Old Brentford
Parsons Thomas, Old Brentford
Potter William, New Brentford
Sanders George, Old Brentford
Sanders Joseph, Old Brentford
Sanders William, New Brentford
Skemils Walter, Old Brentford
Swatton William, Boston rd. O. B.
White Henry, Old Brentford

BRAZIERS AND TIN-PLATE WORKERS.

Gray George, New Brentford
Hunter Alexander, Old Brentford
Searle Geo. Fulham, New Brentford
Stephenson Geo. & Son, New Brentfd
Tucker William, Old Brentford
Waters David, New Brentford

BREWERS.

Geary William, New Brentford
Hazard Jno. & Co. Royal brewery, O. B.

BRICKLAYRS & PLASTERERS

Alderson James, Old Brentford
Gardiner William, Old Brentford
Nottingham Joseph, Old Brentford
Penticost William, Old Brentford
Rogers Richard, Old Brentford
Waight David, Old Brentford

BUTCHERS.

Barns Ann & Diana (pork), New B.
Barns Wm. James, Old Brentford
Burbridge Thomas, Old Brentford
Eustance Wm. (pork) New Brentford
Fletcher John, Old Brentford
Flower William, New Brentford
Goring Robert, New Brentford
Lack George (pork), New Brentford
Kerr Jas. (& dairyman) Old Brentford
Machell Jas. New & Old Brentford
Plim Martin, New Brentford
Richardson Edward, Old Brentford
Shackell Edmund, Old Brentford
Smith William, Old Brentford
Tuffnell John, Old Brentford
Vaughan John, Old Brentford

CABINET & CHAIR MAKERS.

Dear Chas. & Son, Old Brentford
Heap Robert, New Brentford
Perrott Thos. (chair makr) Old Brentford

CARPENTERS, BUILDERS, AND UNDERTAKERS.

Brown John, New Brentford
Clutterbuck Edw. Butts, New Brentford
Davis Thos. Butts, New Brentford
Ezard Henry, Old Brentford
Figg John, Old Brentford
Greive Thomas, Old Brentford
Heap Robert, New Brentford
Lance Charles, New Brentford
Mabberly George, New Brentford
Thornton John, New Brentford
Winkworth John, New Brentford
Young John, Old Brentford

CHEESEMONGERS.

Barringer Samuel Wright, New Brentford
Best Abraham, New Brentford
Chandler George (& porkman), New Brentford
Glover Christopher and Son, New Brentford
Haynes Jacob, New Brentford

CHINA, GLASS, &c. DEALERS.

Christmas Elizabeth, New Brentford
Walkling James, New Brentford

CHYMISTS & DRUGGISTS.

Hammond William, New Brentford
Hazell Robert, New Brentford
Slark James. Old Brentford

CLOTHES DEALERS.

Ezard Henry, New Brentford
Hopkins Thomas, New Brentford
Martin James, Old Brentford
Rolls George (and shoe warehouse), New Brentford
Wood Jonah, New Brentford.

COACH BUILDERS.

Chitty James, Old Brentford
Dowden James, New Brentford
Thick Thomas, Old Brentford

COAL MERCHANTS AND DEALERS.

Andrews Geo. Wm. Old Brentford
Bourne William, New Brentford
Brown John, New Brentford
Clarke John (& lime) Old Brentford
Curtis William, New Brentford
Geary William, New Brentford
Grainger William, New Brentford
Gutteridge William, Old Brentford
Jupp William & Henry (& salt), Old Brentford
Layton Thomas, Old Brentford
Montgomrey Jas. & Son, Old Brentford
Townsend Wm. George, Butts, New Brentford
Stapleton Sarah (dealer) Old Brentfrd
Walker Robert, New Brentford
Warne John, Old Brentford
Welch William, New Brentford

CONFECTIONERS.

Boxall William, New Brentford
Cherry Jas. (wholesale) Nw Brentfrd
Chinery Jeremiah, Old Brentford
East Robert, Old Brentford
Pearse John, Old Brentford
Sleap Ann, Old Brentford

COOPERS.

Matthews John, New Brentford
Neville James, Old Brentford
Sanders Jas. (and brush dealer) New Brentford
Sansom James, Old Brentford

CORN MERCHANTS AND DEALERS.

Andrews Geo. Wm. Old Brentford
Bourne William, New Brentford
Brown John, New Brentford
Curtis William, New Brentford
Grainger William, New Brentford
Gutteridge William, Old Brentford
Jupp Wm. & Henry, Old Brentford
Layton Thomas, Old Brentford
Stapleton Sarah, Old Brentford
Warne John, Old Brentford

CURRIERS AND LEATHER CUTTERS.

Burness Joseph, Old Brentford
Lambert William, New Brentford
Sweet Thomas, Old Brentford
Wood Alexander, New Brentford

CUTLERS.

Barns William James, Old Brentford
Simpson George, New Brentford

DISTILLERS.

Booth Sir Felix & Co. Old Brentford

ESTATE AGENTS.

Grocock Samuel, New Brentford
Gutteridge William (and appraiser), Old Brentford
King John, Old Brentford

FIRE, &c. OFFICE AGENTS.

Alliance, John Winkworth, New Brentford
Atlas, Henry & John Sexton, New Brentford
British, Henry John Robinson, New Brentford
County (fire) & Provident (life), Abraham Best, New Brentford
Globe, Joseph Hill, Butts, New Brentford
Guardian, James Walkling, New Brentford
Licenced Victuallers' (General), John King, Old Brentford
Mutual, John Carver, Old Brentford
Phœnix, Matt. Gibson, Old Brentfrd
Royal Exchange, Philip & Mary Ann Norbury, New Brentford

FRUITERERS AND GREEN-GROCERS.

Brown Henry, New Brentford
Brown Richard, Old Brentford
Harris Alexander, New Brentford
Howard Sophia, New Brentford
Hugall William, New Brentford
Kayes Charles, New Brentford
Knight William, Old Brentford
Lake Mary, Old Brentford
Newman William, Old Brentford
Pearce James, New Brentford
Pearman Thomas, Old Brentford
Rackett James, New Brentford
Seymour John, Old Brentford

FURNITURE BROKERS.

Coombs Charles, New Brentford
Dear Charles & Son, Old Brentford
KilsbyWm. (& appraiser) OldBrentfd
King John, Old Brentford
Martin John, Old Brentford
Over James, Old Brentford
Radcliff Harriet, New Brentford
Taylor John, Old Brentford

GROCERS & TEA DEALERS.

(See also Shopkeepers, &c.)

Barringer Samuel Wright, New Brentford
Best Abraham, New Brentford
Briggs Daniel, New Brentford
Chandler George, New Brentford
Coles John Wm. New Brentford
Conaway James, Old Brentford
Dicken George, Old Brentford
Dicken William, Old Brentford
Evens Benjamin, Old Brentford
Glover Christopher & Son, New Brentford
Grist John, New Brentford
Hammond William, New Brentford
Layton George, Old Brentford
M'Gowran James, Old Brentford
Munn Jonathan, Old Brentford
Radcliffe Harriet, New Brentford
Round John, Old Brentford
Sansom James, Old Brentford
Senols & Barton, Old Brentford
Smallwood Samuel, New Brentford
Studley Richd. James, Old Brentford
Yeaxley George, New Brentford

HATTERS.

Baynton Edmund, New Brentford
Thomas William, Old Brentford

INNS.

Castle (and posting house), William Cullen, New Brentford
Royal Hotel, Jas. Stout, OldBrentfrd
Star and Garter, John & Danl. Grenaway Porter, Old Brentford
Three Pigeons, William Tinson, New Brentford

IRONMONGERS.

Searle Geo. Fulham, New Brentford
Stephenson George & Son, New Brentford
Tucker William, Old Brentford
Waters David, New Brentford

LINEN, &c. DRAPERS.

Beamish Isaac, Old Brentford
Bunting William, New Brentford
Chappell Henry, Old Brentford
M'Nea David, Old Brentford
Sexton Hy. & John, New Brentford
Walbran George, New Brentford
Williams Roger, New Brentford

MALTSTERS.

Grainger William, New Brentford
Jupp Wm. & Henry, Old Brentford
Warne John, Old Brentford

MARINE STORE DEALERS.

Goddard Samuel (and umbrella maker), New Brentford
Pearce Henry, Old Brentford

MARKET GARDENERS.

Allen Charles, Old Brentford
Bursell Richard, Old Brentford
Bursell Thomas, Old Brentford
Goldwin John, Old Brentford
Hall George, Old Brentford
Jones Samuel, Old Brentford
Malcolm Allen, Old Brentford
Meyers Judy, Boston road, Old Brentford
Newell Thomas, Boston road, Old Brentford
Story James, Old Brentford
Vaughan William, Old Brentford
Wallace Henry, Old Brentford

MATTRESS MAKERS.

Lyons Daniel, New Brentford
Prior Charles, Boston road, Old B.

MILLINERS & DRESS MAKRS.

Edwards Eliz. Butts, New Brentford
Figg Lydia, Old Brentford
Haswell Elizabeth, New Brentford
Hearn Sarah, New Brentford
Heath Mary Ann, New Brentford
Martin Maria, Old Brentford
Moulter Sarah, Boston road, Old B.
Pearse Emma, Old Brentford
Prior Harriet, Old Brentford
Shuckford Emily & Harriet (& lace dealers) New Brentford
Tilbury Mary, Old Brentford
Walters Elizabeth, Old Brentford

OIL AND COLOURMEN.

Hammond William, New Brentford
Hazell Robert, New Brentford
Hughes Henry, Old Brentford
Hughes Phillis, Old Brentford
Senols & Barton, Old Brentford
Tillyer Joseph, New Brentford

PAINTERS, PLUMBERS, AND GLAZIERS.

Adderley James, Old Brentford
Neill James, Old Brentford
Neill John, Old Brentford
Neill Richard, Old Brentford
Robinson Hy. John, New Brentford
Sweeper William, Old Brentford
Thorn Joseph, New Brentford
Yeaxley George (& paper hanger), New Brentford

PAWNBROKERS.

Burford John, Old Brentford
Dean Hannah, New Brentford
Jones John Wm. New Brentford
Potter William, Old Brentford

PERFUMERS AND HAIR DRESSERS.

Brooksby Thomas, New Brentford
Burnham Mary, Old Brentford
Matthews Stephen, Old Brentford
Melvin James, Old Brentford
Swapp George, New Brentford

POULTERERS.

Fricker William, Old Brentford
Penny George, New Brentford

RAG DEALERS.

Hughes Henry, Old Brentford
Hughes Phillis, Old Brentford

SADDLERS.

Botton Charles, Old Brentford
King William, New Brentford
Marsden Thomas, New Brentford
Quinion Joseph Geo. Old Brentford

SHOPKEEPERS & DEALRS IN GROCERIES & SUNDRIES.

Dale Henry, Old Brentford
Goldsbrough Emma, Old Brentford
Harper William, Old Brentford
Harris Henry, New Brentford
Herbert Ann, Old Brentford
Jacobs William, Old Brentford
Knight Martha, Old Brentford
Page Thomas, Old Brentford
Palmer Catherine, Old Brentford
Rogers George, Old Brentford
Williams James, Old Brentford

SMITHS & BELLHANGERS.

Searle Geo. Fulham, New Brentford
Stephenson George & Son, New Brentford
Tucker William, Old Brentford
Waters David, New Brentford

STAY MAKERS.

Briggs Susannah, New Brentford
Watson William, Old Brentford

STRAW HAT MAKERS.

Thornton Mary Ann, New Brentford
Wale Dinah, New Brentford

SURGEONS.

Bonney Francis, Old Brentford
Cooper George, New Brentford
Farrell John, New Brentford
Radcliffe Henry John, Butts, N. B.
Ralfs William, Old Brentford
Richards Henry, Old Brentford

TAILORS.

Bennett George, Old Brentford
Bond William Dodd, Old Brentford
Edenborough Wm. Boston road, O.B.
Ellis Joseph, New Brentford
Etherington J. Boston road, O. B.
Harris William Peet, Old Brentford
Hunt Charles, Boston road, O. B.
Ilsley Joseph, Old Brentford
Knight William, Old Brentford
Lowe John, New Brentford
Rapkin Richard, Boston road, O. B.
Sanders Thos. Tunstall, OldBrentford
Stacey Henry, Old Brentford
Sumner Thomas, Old Brentford
Warren Thomas, Old Brentford
Whitman Henry & Co. N. Brentford
Wood Jonah, New Brentford
Wright James, Old Brentford

TALLOW CHANDLERS.

Dale Henry, Old Brentford
Glover Christr. & Son, New Brentford
Round John, Old Brentford
Ruff John Dearle, New Brentford
Sage William (& wax), N. Brentford

TAVERNS & PUBLIC HOUSES.

Barge Aground, Wm. Perress, Old Brentfd
Black Boy & Still, John Blackman, New Brentford
Black Boys, Jas. Swithin Trimmer, New Brentford
Bull, James Starbuck, Old Brentford
Cannon, Mary Ann Dale, Old Brentford
CatherineWheel, Wm. Mantle, NewBrentfd
Drum, Thomas Begley, Old Brentford
Feathers, John Millar, Old Brentford
Fox & Hounds, Jas. Gascoine, Old Brentfd
George IV, John Stacey, Old Brentford
Half Moon & Seven Stars, Robert Pearce, Old Brentford
Hand & Flower, John Fisher, Old Brentford
King's Arms, Thos. Hoare, Old Brentford
Magpie & Crown, Geo. Boxall, NewBrentfd
Magpie and Stump, James Palmer, New Brentford
Marquess of Granby, Richard Smith, Old Brentford
One Tun, John Thick, Old Brentford
Red Lion, Sarah Pearce, New Brentford
Red Lion, Eliz. Saunders, Old Brentford
Running Horses, Francis Morum, Old Brentford
Salutation, William Crosby M'Nea, Old Brentford
Seven Stars, Arthur Winkley, Boston road, Old Brentford
Six Bells, Thomas Piper, New Brentford
Waggon and Horses, Ann Sibley, Old Brentford
Waterman's Arms, William Butler, Old Brentford
White Hart, Richd. Weston, Old Brentfrd
White Horse, Eliz. Barnes, New Brentfrd

TEA DEALERS.

Brown James (and draper), Old Brentford
Kelvie John, Old Brentford

TOBACCONISTS.

Ashley Lucy, Old Brentford
Evans John, Old Brentford
Herbert Ann, Old Brentford
Lance Charles, New Brentford
Neill Richard, Old Brentford
Nyren Michael, Old Brentford
Parsons Joseph, Old Brentford

TOY DEALERS.

Bontems John Francis, N. Brentford
Bryant Ann, New Brentford
Mabberly George, New Brentford
Sanders James, New Brentford
White Ann, Old Brentford

UNDERTAKERS—FURNISHNG

Coe John, Old Brentford
King John, Old Brentford
Thornton John, New Brentford
Winkworth John, New Brentford

UPHOLSTERERS.

Heap Robert, New Brentford
Kirk John, Old Brentford
Radcliff Harriet, New Brentford

WATCH & CLOCK MAKERS.

Bacon Thomas, Old Brentford
Honeybone Thos. (& jeweller), Old Brentford
Mann George, Boston road, O. B.
Upjohn James & Son (& jewellers), New Brentford

WHEELWRIGHTS.

Chitty James, Old Brentford
Dowden George, New Brentford
Thick John, Old Brentford [ford
Thick Thos. (and smith), Old Brent-

WINE & SPIRIT MERCHANTS

Stout James, Old Brentford
Tillyer Joseph, New Brentford

Miscellaneous.

Ackerman George, eating house, New Brentford [Brentford
Allen Wm. coach & chaise proprietor, Old
Brown Thomas, fishmonger, Old Brentfrd
Clark George, clerk to magistrates and Brentford union, New Brentford
DISPENSARY, New Brentford—Cooper and Farrell, surgeons
GAS WORKS, Old Brentford—Thomas Spinney and Son, managers
GRAND JUNCTION WATER WORKS, Old Brentford— — Mercer, clerk
Hill Joseph, secretary to the savings' bank, New Brentford [ford
Hughes Jas. sausage maker, Old Brent-
Jones William, bookbinder, Butts, N. B.
Lindley John, orange merchant & foreign fruiterer, New Brentford [Brentford
Manley Richd. coffee & dining rooms, New
MECHANICS' INSTITUTION, at Mr. Murphy's, New Brentford [Old Brentford
Montgomrey Jas. & Son, timber merchants,
Norman John, tripe dresser, Old Brentford
Norminton Francis, dyer, &c. Old Brentford
Price, Montague & Co. glass cutters, Old Brentford [New Brentford
Ralfe Thomas, inspector of weights, &c.
Ronalds Hugh & Son, nursery & seedsmen, New Brentford
Rowe Thomas B. & Laurence, soap and soda manufacturers, Old Brentford
Saunders John, veterinary surgeon, Old Brentford
SAVINGS' BANK, New Brentford (open every Monday from 12 till 2)—Joseph Hill, secretary
Shackle Thomas, window-blind maker and painter, Boston road, Old Brentford
Shambler John, fishmonger, New Brentford
Smith John, fellmonger and rope maker, New Brentford
Sweet John, stone mason, New Brentford
Wale Dinah, clog maker, New Brentford
Walkling James, bottle merchant, New Brentford
White Nathaniel Charles, egg and butter merchant, Old Brentford

COACHES, &c.

Calling at the Castle Inn, New Brentford.
To and from LONDON & the WEST OF ENGLAND, READING, HENLEY, WINDSOR, &c. *Coaches* continually during the day—also *Omnibuses* to and from LONDON, HOUNSLOW, ISLEWORTH, RICHMOND & TWICKENHAM, pass through almost every half hour—and —Attwell's *Omnibuses*, from his house, Old Brentford, several times a day.

CARRIERS.

To LONDON, EALING and places adjacent, Thomas Ivemey, from his house, Old Brentford, daily.

CONVEYANCE BY WATER.

To LONDON and various other parts, goods are forwarded from the Grand Junction wharf, daily.

CHISWICK, TURNHAM GREEN, LITTLE SUTTON,

AND STRAND ON THE GREEN.

CHISWICK is a neat and respectable village and parish, in the hundred of Ossulton, about five miles west from London; seated on the north bank of the Thames, and approaching to the great western road. The principal object of importance and attraction is Burlington House, the princely mansion and grounds of his Grace the Duke of Devonshire, which are situated in this parish, and are the admiration of visiters. The gardens of the horticultural society, occupying thirty-six acres of ground, are also here; they are laid out with exquisite taste, and stored with shrubs, plants, &c., rare and various; the entrance to the grounds is from Turnham Green. The church, dedicated to St. Nicholas, stands upon an eminence near to the river, and has a neat appearance; its interior possesses nothing remarkable, but the churchyard has some interest attached to it, from its containing the remains of the famed artists Loutherbourg and Hogarth, as also those of Lord Macartney, the ambassador to China. On Hogarth's tomb are some impressive and elegant lines, by the celebrated Garrick; and at the entrance of the churchyard are some verses, written by A. Murphy, the dramatist, on the son of Thompson. An extensive national school is established here; and there are two breweries, upon a respectable scale. Population of Chiswick and its several hamlets, in 1831, was 4,994.

TURNHAM GREEN is in the parish of Chiswick, on the great western road. Very little business is carried on here; but the houses are truly respectable, and chiefly inhabited by persons who have residences for trade in London, or by those retired from business.

LITTLE SUTTON and STRAND ON THE GREEN are also in the parish of Chiswick, and lie between Turnham Green and the Thames. The majority of the houses in these places are occupied by market gardeners; the ground is nearly all laid out in gardens, and their produce proportionably contribute to the supply of the London markets.

POST, CHISWICK, *Receiving-House* at Job Ives'.—Letters from HAMMERSMITH arrive every morning at eight, noon at twelve, afternoon at three and evening at six, and are despatched every morning at nine, afternoon at one and four and evening at eight.

POST OFFICE, TURNHAM GREEN, Godfrey John Baynes, *Post Master.*—Letters from LONDON arrive every morning (Sunday excepted) at half-past ten, afternoon at half-past two and five and night at nine, and are despatched four times a day.—Letters from the WEST OF ENGLAND arrive (from Hounslow and Kingston), every morning at seven, and are despatched every evening at half-past six.

NOBILITY, GENTRY AND CLERGY.

T. G. means TURNHAM GREEN.

Anderson Mr. John, Turnham Green
Arnott William, esq. Chiswick
Attwood Miss —, 7 Williams's terrace, Turnham Green
Aylmer Mr. John, Turnham Green
Beecher Mrs. Sophia, Williams' terrace, Turnham Green
Bifield William, esq. Chiswick
Blackmore Miss —, Stamford brook, Turnham Green [terrace
Bonnett Stephn. esq. Turnham Green
Bostock Mrs. Mary, King's row, T. G.
Bourke Mrs. Williams's terrace, T.G.
Bowerbank Rev. Thomas Frere, Vicarage house, Chiswick
Brande Miss S. W. Chiswick mall
Brown Thos. Pearce, Turnham Green
Bryan Mr. Robert, Turnham Green
Bryant Mr. John, Turnham Green
Buckmaster Mrs. Sarah, Turnham Grn
Bull Mrs. —, Turnham Green
Capps Mr. Henry, Turnham Green
Chambers John Caro, esq. Chiswick
Churton Mr. Wm. Sutton Court lodge
Collet Mrs. Mary, Turnham Green
Collinson Mr. Geo. Turnham Green
Costerd Miss Eliz. King's row, T. G.
Devonshire his Grace the Duke of, Burlington house, Chiswick
Dickinson Mr. Wm. Turnham Green
Edgell Miss Eliz. 1 Queen's row, T.G.
Farden Mr. Richd. Turnham Green
Fendall Mrs. 3 Chiswick place
Fletcher Joseph, esq. Chiswick
Freeman Jas. esq. Turnham Green
Frere Jno. esq. Stamford brook, T.G.
Ganham Mrs. —, Turnham Green
Gibson Fredk. esq. Turnham Green
Gillingham Miss, 2 Queen's row, T.G.
Glen Mrs. —, Turnham Green
Grant William, esq. Turnham Green
Griffiths Mr. Philip, Little Sutton
Grimsdale Miss —, King's row, T. G.
Hammett Mr. Wm. Turnham Green
Harman Mrs. —, 9 Williams's terrace, Turnham Green
Hay Mr. John, Turnham Green
Hemitage Col. —, Little Sutton house
Higgs Mrs. —, 4 Chiswick place
Hindley Mr. Chs. Turnham Green terr
Hoole James, esq. Turnham Green
Horne Rev. Thomas, D. D. Chiswick
How Thomas, esq. Turnham Green
Ince Mrs. —, Turnham Green
Jackson Mr. J. T. Turnham Green
Jarvis Mrs. Mary, Turnham Green
Johnson Col. —, Merton place, T. G.
Jupp Mr. Joseph, Turnham Green
King Mr. William, King's row, T.G.
Langslow Mr. Robt. Turnham Green terrace [terrace
Leach Stephen, esq. Turnham Green
Lewis Capt. —, Chiswick [Green
Lindley John, esq. Terrace, A[illegible]
Lines Mrs. —, Merton place, T.[illegible]
Loftus Mr. James, Chiswick [T.G.
London Miss Lucy, Merton cottage,
Lonsdale Richard, esq. St. Albans place, Turnham Green
Lovegrove Mrs. —, Turnham Green
Miller Rev. Edward, Chiswick
Monkhouse Jno. esq. Chiswick mall
Mott Mr. Thomas, Turnham Green
Mumford Mr. Chas. Turnham Green
Mundell Mr. John, Turnham Green
Neate Charles, esq. Mawson house, Chiswick [Turnham Green
Philpot Mrs. —, Williams' terrace,
Piper Mr. James, Chiswick
Ponting Mr. Danl. Turnham Green
Preston Mr. Wm. Turnham Green
Promell Mr. Jas. Turnham Green terr
Roberts Mr. Henry, 2 Chiswick place
Robinson Mr. John, Chiswick

NOBILITY, &c.—Continued.

Ronalds Mrs. —, Turnham Green
Rumbell Joseph, esq. Cranbourn-lodge, Turnham Green
Salisbury Mr. Darius, Turnham Green
Sharp Charles, esq. Chiswick mall
Simmons Mr. Wm. Turnham Green
Smith Mr. John, Turnham Green
Smith Rev. J. Jennings, Turnham Grn
Swindell Mr. John, 5 Williams' terrace, Turnham Green
Tapp Mr. Chas. Terrace house, T.G.
Tasker Mr. Joseph, Turnham Green
Towkey Mrs. Mary, Williams' terrace, Turnham Green
Travis Mr. William, Turnham Green
Walker Mr. William Falkner, Turnham Green [terrace
Wilson Mr. Wm. Turnham Green
Wood James, esq. Chiswick
Woolf Mrs. —, Turnham Green

ACADEMIES & SCHOOLS.

Not otherwise described are Boarding.

Allen Jno. Summerfield hse. Chiswick
Bland Maria (day), Turnham Green
Brasier Edmund, Bradmore house, Chiswick
British School, Strand on the Green—Benjamin Crabb, master; Sarah Crabb, mistress
British Schools (Hammersmith, Chiswick and Turnham Green), Chiswick lane—Wm. Begg, master; Louisa Begg, mistress
Chiswick National School, Turnham Green—Jas. Clark, master
Chiswick National School (girls'), Chiswick—Eliz. Churchill, mistress
Clements Benjamin, Belmont house Grammar school, Turnham Green
Dempster Mr. & Mrs. John (preparatory), Falkland hse. Turnham Grn
Dixon & Goodwin, Turnham Green terrace
Dodsworth Amelia, Camden house, Turnham Green [ham Green
Fores Emma, Portland house, Turn-
Gell Catherine, Turnham Green
Graham Misses (preparatory), Belgrave house, Turnham Green
Harrison William, Turnham Green Academy
Infants' School, Turnham Green—Amelia Weavell, mistress
King Joseph, Turnham Green
Ockerby Mrs. —, Chiswick mall
Pringle Matilda, Annandale house, Turnham Green [Green
Smith Rev. John Jennings, Turnham
Stillwell Ann (day), Turnham Green
Walker Henry (day), Turnham Green
Zealey Henry (day), Chiswick

ATTORNEYS.

[illegible]is Robert Fitz, Turnham Green
[illegible]lor Robert Williams' terrace, Turnham Green

BAKERS & FLOUR DEALERS.

Eaton William, Strand on the Green
Ives Job, Church st, Chiswick
Payne Robert, Turnham Green
Shore Samuel, Turnham Green
Smith Abrahm. Church st, Chiswick
Walter William, Chiswick
Ward John, Turnham Green
Williams James, Turnham Green
Wood John, Turnham Green

BARGE BUILDERS.

Blundell Chas. Walter, Strand on the Green [Green
Harradine Thos. Jos. Strand on the
Piper John, Chiswick
Richardson Jas. Strand on the Green
Sangster John, Strand on the Green

BLACKSMITHS.

Jacobs Joseph, Chiswick lane
Lobjoit Thomas Moses (and lock), Turnham Green [wick
Murrell Thomas (and white), Chis-
Newcomb Wm. Turnham Green
Snell Benjamin (and white) Strand on the Green
Thornton Isaac, Turnham Green

BOOT AND SHOE MAKERS.

Brown George, Chiswick
Cook Edmund, Church st, Chiswick
Cresswell James, Turnham Green
Dyer David, Turnham Green
Headley William, Turnham Green
King William, Turnham Green
Pickton Edwd. Strand on the Green
Smith Henry, Chiswick
Yeomans John, Turnham Green

BREWERS.

Sich John & Henry, Lamb brewery, Chiswick [wick
Thompson, Douglas & Co. (ale), Chis-

BRICKLAYRS & PLASTERERS

Adamson Ths. Henry, Turnham Green
Bray John, Strand on the Green
Evans William, Chiswick
Field Hugh, Turnham Green
Francis Charles, Turnham Green
Morrell Andrew, Turnham Green
Phillips Thomas, Turnham Green
Wright William, Chiswick

BUILDERS.

(See also Carpenters.)

Field Hugh, Turnham Green
Wright William, Chiswick

BUTCHERS.

Cook Thomas, Chiswick lane
Cristfield William, Turnham Green
Evans Edw. (pork), Turnham Green
Gibbs Edw. Astell, Church st, Chiswck
Groves Lewis, Turnham Green
Stock Chas. Planer, Turnham Green
Tayler Thomas, Turnham Green

CARPENTRS & UNDERTAKRS

Atkinson Thomas, Turnham Green
Barratt William, Turnham Green
Crow George, Chiswick mall
Edymann Charles, Turnham Green
Gale Wm. Richard, Turnham Green
Harris John Fras. Turnham Green
Jackson William, Turnham Green
Jefferys Samuel (and timber dealer), Chiswick
Stillwell George, Turnham Green

COACH BUILDERS.

Leversidge Joseph, Turnham Green
Whitlock Henry, Turnham Green

COAL MERCHANTS & DEALRS

Burford Daniel, Chiswick
Burford Joseph, Chiswick
Cook Arthur, Turnham Green
Hobbs William, Chiswick
Jefferys Wm. Thomas, Chiswick
Layton & Part, Turnham Green
Marshall Wm. Strand on the Green
Robinson Geo. Strand on the Green
Saunders John & Son, Strand on the Green
Ward John, Turnham Green

CORN CHANDLERS.

Cook Arthur, Turnham Green
Shore Samuel, Turnham Green
Ward John, Turnham Green
Wood John, Turnham Green

COWKEEPERS.

Bryant Joseph, Turnham Green
Burford Joseph, Chiswick
Stevens James, Turnham Green

CRICKET BAT MAKERS.

Clapshaw Charles, Turnham Green
Clapshaw Mark (& turner), Turnham Green

FRUITERERS.

Beston John, Turnham Green
Dyer David, Turnham Green

GROCERS & CHEESEMONGRS

(See also Shopkeepers, &c.)

Adey Thomas (& oilman), Turnham Green
Fielder James, Turnham Green
Plummerridge James, Chiswick lane
Potts Lawson, Chiswick
Voysey Thomas (& tallow chandler), Turnham Green

HABERDASHERS.

Aldridge Frances, Turnham Green
Smith Robert, Turnham Green

HAIR DREESRSS.

Edymann George Frederick (& perfumer), Turnham Green
Edymann Henry, Chiswick
Overton John, Turnham Green

LIBRARIES---CIRCULATING.

Baynes Godfrey Jno. Turnham Green
Smith James, Chiswick

LIGHTERMEN AND BARGE OWNERS.

Penn Philip, Chiswick mall
Saunders John & Son, Strand on the Green

MALTSTERS.

Light Daniel, Strand on the Green
Saunders John & Son, Strand on the Green
Sich John & Henry, Chiswick

MARINE STORE DEALERS.

Morrell Andrew, Turnham Green
Thornton Isaac, Turnham Green

MARKET GARDENERS.

Ashley Lucy, Strand on the Green
Baldwin James, Turnham Green
Bursill James, Turnham Green
Cock Wm. Hogarth lane, Chiswick
Dancer Francis, Turnham Green
Dancer William, Little Sutton
Dean Edward, Strand on the Green
Elliott Charles, Turnham Green
Fromow Ann, Little Sutton
Green Robert, Turnham Green
Hancock Cornelius, Strand on the G.
Hemmett Benjamin, Turnham Green
Howell & Piper, Chiswick
Jefferys Abraham, Turnham Green
Jefferys Harry, Turnham Green
Knevett Charles, Turnham Green
Matyear Geo. Hy. Turnham Green
Mercer Samuel, Chiswick
Mills William, Chiswick
Rance Henry, Chiswick
Smith William, Turnham Green
Vaughan Thomas, Turnham Green

MILLINERS & DRESS MAKRS.

Baynes Mrs. G. J. Turnham Green
Dean Harriet, Turnham Green
Hetherington Julia, Turnham Green
Jennings Mary, Turnham Green
Jones Jane (& straw bonnet), Turnham Green
Matthews Phœbe, Turnham Green
Williams Georgiana, Turnham Green

NURSERY & SEEDSMEN.

Fitzgerald David, Turnham Green
Graham Barnard John (& florist), Turnham Green

PLUMBERS, PAINTERS AND GLAZIERS.

Bint Edward, Turnham Green
Holmes Jno. & Wm. Turnham Green
James William Henry, Chiswick
Vellenoweth Wm. (painter), Strand on the Green

PRINTERS---LETTER-PRESS.

Baynes Godfrey John (& bookseller, stationer & binder), Turnham Green
Whittingham Charles, Chiswick mall

SHOPKEEPERS & DEALRS IN GROCERIES & SUNDRIES.
Ballard Lydia, Chiswick
Brown Alfred, Strand on the Green
Carloss John, Turnham Green
Creasey James Henry, Chiswick
Eden Charles, Turnham Green
Fitzgerald David, Turnham Green
Florey Charles, Chiswick
Gough George, Chiswick
Gough John, Chiswick
Gray Maria, Turnham Green
Harradine Thos. Strand on the Green
Hoare Martha, Strand on the Green
Iles Hannah, Turnham Green
Myers Robert, Turnham Green
Plunkett Bartholomew, Chiswick
Richardson John, Chiswick
Sweet Sarah, Turnham Green
Walker James, Turnham Green
White Richard, Chiswick
Williams James, Turnham Green
Wise Martha, Strand on the Green
Wiselthir Samuel, Turnham Green
Worley Philip, Turnham Green

SURGEONS.
Collier George Frederick, M.D. Turnham Green
Cox Wm. Wilson, Turnham Green
Dodsworth Frederick Christopher, Turnham Green
Eyre Charles Cocks, Turnham Green
Graham & Leigh, Turnham Green
Loadman Robert, Chiswick mall

TAILORS.
Cooper James, Chiswick
Gough William, Chiswick
Marriott Henry, Turnham Green
Smith William, Turnham Green
Whapshott George, Chiswick

TAVERNS & PUBLIC HOUSES.
Barley Mow, Wm. Minchin, Turnham Green
Bell and Crown, Ann White, Strand on the Green
Bull's Head, Frances Milross, Strand on the Green
Burlington Arms, James Woodhall, Church street, Chiswick
City Barge, James Richardson, Strand on the Green
Coach and Horses, Mary Buckingham, Turnham Green
Crown, Charlotte Jefferys, Turnham Green
Crown and Anchor, Thomas Botheroyd, Turnham Green
Duke of York, Daniel Burford, Chiswick
Feathers, Ann Smith, Chiswick
Fox & Hounds, Wm. Such, Chiswick la
George & Devonshire Arms, Thomas Honess, Chiswick
George the Fourth, James Nichols, Turnham Green
Indian Queen, William Vellenoweth, Strand on the Green
Lamb, William King, Chiswick
Old Pack Horse, Joseph Hersey, Turnham Green
Pack Horse and Talbot, Robert Stout, Turnham Green
Prince of Wales, George Battersby, Turnham Green
Queen's Head, John Mercer, Turnham Green
Red Lion, William Clary, Chiswick mall
Roebuck, George Ball, Turnham Green
Ship, John Smith, Strand on the Green
Windmill, Jas. Harmes, Turnham Green

TOY DEALERS.
Carter Ann, Turnham Green
Gray Maria, Turnham Green

WHEELWRIGHTS.
Bennett James (& smith), Turnham Green
Hasted James (& smith), Turnham Green
Lobjoit Thomas Moses, Turnham Green

WHIP MAKERS.
Penrose Thomas, Turnham Green
Stanley William, Turnham Green

Miscellaneous.
Dibbin Francis William, land surveyor, Chiswick
Dorey George, stone mason, Strand on the Green
Evans Edward, poulterer, Turnham Green
Fitkin Thos. saddler, &c. Turnham Green
Foster James, registrar, Turnham Green
Grant Thos. fishmonger, Turnham Green
Harrod George, cheese and butter factor, Turnham Green
HORTICULTURAL SOCIETYS' GARDENS, Turnham Green—Danl. Munro, gardener
Jones Sarah, china & glass dealer, Turnham Green
LUNATIC ASYLUM, Chiswick—James Bell, proprietor
Marshall William, fishmonger, Strand on the Green
Oliver Evan, cooper, Turnham Green
Powell Thomas, coach proprietor, Turnham Green
Robinson George, brick maker and lime & stone merchant & wharfinger, Strand on the Green
Robinson George, agent for the Atlas fire office, Strand on the Green
ROYAL VICTORIA ASYLUM, Chiswick mall—Ann Bourhill, mistress
Slee John, wine merchant, Chiswick mall
Watts Bennett, livery stable keeper and coach & fly owner, Chiswick
West George, furniture broker and house agent, Turnham Green

OMNIBUSES.
To LONDON, Geo. Cloud's *Omnibuses*, from the George the Fourth, every half-hour during the day.
To and from LONDON, BRENTFORD, HOUNSLOW, ISLEWORTH, &c. *Omnibuses* pass thro' Turnham Green, continually during the day.

CARRIERS.
To LONDON, Mary Jennings, Abel Chapman and Andrew Spragg, from their houses, Turnham Green, daily.

CLAPTON AND HIGH-HILL FERRY.

CLAPTON is a hamlet, in the parish of St. John, Hackney, and hundred of Ossulton, 3 miles N. E. from London, situated on the Lea, which river skirts the eastern side of the hamlet; it is divided into Upper and Lower Clapton, and extends from Hackney church to Stamford Hill. The houses are in general well built; and the inhabitants are supplied with water from a reservoir belonging to the East London Water-works Company. The London orphan asylum is an object of considerable notice here; it is a handsome brick erection, with stone columns and projecting wings; its benevolent arrangements afford maintenance and education to about 250 boys and 150 girls, destitute orphans; the cost of erecting the building was £25,000. and the establishment enjoys very high and extensive patronage. Clapton was the birth-place of the philanthropic Howard; and in the hamlet stands Brooke House, a mansion formerly belonging to the Earl of Warwick, now in the occupation of Dr. Munroe, as a lunatic asylum. The places of worship are a proprietary chapel, erected in 1777, and others for independents and Wesleyan methodists. There are national and infants' schools, and, at Lower Clapton, the Hackney grammar school, and Bishop Woods' alms-houses for ten poor widows.

About half a mile from Upper Clapton is HIGH-HILL FERRY, also a hamlet under Hackney; it is very pleasingly situated on the Lea river, and is not only the residence of many persons retired from trade, but is also a place of active business, and contains some respectable establishments for calico and silk printing. The returns of the population of Upper and Lower Clapton and High-hill Ferry are included in those of Hackney parish.

POST (within the limits of the LONDON twopenny post delivery).—*Receiving-Houses* at William Howard's, grocer, Hill street, UPPER CLAPTON; at William Charsley's, baker, LOWER CLAPTON; and at Robert Bailey's, greengrocer, LOWER CLAPTON.—Letters arrive from and are despatched to LONDON three times a day.

*** *The letters* L. C. *and* U. C. *attached to an address signify respectively* LOWER *and* UPPER CLAPTON.

GENTRY AND CLERGY.
Adderley Thos. esq. Upper Clapton
Adnams Mrs. Elizabeth, 7 Clapton place, Lower Clapton
Alderson Christr. esq. Lower Clapton
Allen Mrs. Mary, 2 Clapton square
Appach Thos. esq. Upper Clapton
Archer George, esq. Buccleugh terrace, Upper Clapton
Arthur Mrs. Anne, Lower Clapton
Ashpetel William Hurst, esq. 28 Clapton square
Aubert John Louis, esq. Summit cottage, U. C.
Baker Thos. esq. Willow cottage, U. C.
Ballance John, esq. Lower Clapton
Barber Alfred, esq. Upper Clapton
Barclay Mrs. —, Warwick road, U. C.
Barker Thos. esq. Stamford grove West, Upper Clapton
Barnett Mrs. Thos. Upper Clapton
Barr Jeremiah, esq. Upper Clapton
Barrett Rev. Joseph, Upper Clapton
Bartleet George, esq. Upper Clapton
Bartlett Nicholas, esq. 26 Clapton sq
Barton Mr. George, Stamford grove West, Upper Clapton
Barton Mr. Samuel, Lower Clapton
Bedwell Mr. L. B. Lower Clapton
Belisario the Misses, 5 Wickham place, Lower Clapton
Bell Mr. Alexander, Upper Clapton
Benson Mrs. —, 10 Clapton square
Berger John, esq. Lower Clapton
Berger Lewis, esq. 3 Clapton square
Birbridge Wm. esq. Laura place, L. C.
Birch Joseph, esq. Willow field cottage, Upper Clapton
Bird Wm. esq. Clapton terrace, U. C.
Birkett Mr. Daniel, Upper Clapton
Birkitt John, esq. Clapton terr. U. C.
Bischoff Chas. B. esq. Springfld, U. C.
Boult Mr. Thomas, Lower Clapton
Boyce Rev. John, High-hill Ferry
Boyd Mr. Christr. 8 Portland pl, L. C.
Bradock John, esq. Lower Clapton
Bray Mr. Jasper Selwin, 19 Clapton sq
Bromley Wm. esq. Stamford grv. U. C.
Bros Thos. esq. Springfld house, U. C.
Brown Mr. John, Upper Clapton
Brown Mr. Thomas, Lower Clapton
Bunyard Chs. esq. Buccleugh ter. U. C.
Burnell John, esq. Lower Clapton
Burton John, esq. Rose house, U. C.
Butler Mr. Charles, Upper Clapton
Capper John, esq. Clapton terrace, Upper Clapton
Casellaine Herminagold, esq. Lower Clapton
Cazenove James, esq. Lower Clapton
Cazenove Philip, esq. Upper Clapton
Charrington John, esq. Clapton com

GENTRY, &c.—*Continued.*

Child Samuel, esq. Lower Clapton
Chitty Charles, esq. Mount pleasant lane, Upper Clapton
Clark Mrs. Catherine, Upper Clapton
Clarke Henry, esq. Upper Clapton
Clements Jacob, esq. Lower Clapton
Clements Rev. James Crook, Lower Clapton [West, U. C.
Clemitson Peter, esq. Stamford grove
Coles Charles, esq. Upper Clapton
Collier Edmd. esq. Laura place, L. C.
Collins John, esq. Lea Bridge road
Cooper Francis, esq. 17 Clapton sq
Cotton Samuel, esq. Lower Clapton
Cotton William, esq. Upper Clapton
Crampton Jas. esq. 4 Clapton square
Craven Arthr. esq. Craven lodge, U.C.
Craven Mrs. Margaret, LowerClaptn
Davis Mrs. Maria, Upper Clapton
Davison Thomas Robinson, esq. 23 Clapton square [East, U. C.
Day Mrs. Agatha, Stamford grove
Deane Mr. George, 6 Clapton square
DeBerckhemMrs.Susan,Up.Clapton
Dodgson Robert, esq. Upper Clapton
Doherty Mr. James, Lower Clapton
Dorgan Lawrence, esq. Buccleugh terrace, Upper Clapton
Douler William, esq. Upper Clapton
Dover Mrs. Wm. 7 Clapton square
Duesbury Dr. —, Lower Clapton
Dutton Thos. esq. Clapton terr. U. C.
Eaton Miss Harriet, Clapton terrace
Echalaz Mrs. Mary, Lower Clapton
Edwards Chas.Thos. esq. Up.Clapton
Eicke Mrs.Catherine, Upper Clapton
Elliott Mr. Samuel, Upper Clapton
Exley John, esq. 15 Clapton square
Farrell the Misses, Lower Clapton
Fisher R. H. esq. Summit place, L. C.
Ford Edward, esq. Laura place, L. C.
Foster Joseph Talwin, esq. Springfield, U. C. [place, L. C.
Frampton Mrs. Thomas, 14 Portland
Francis Mrs. John, 5 Clapton square
Freez Philip, esq. Lower Clapton
Gatfield Mrs. Harriet, Stamford grove East, Upper Clapton
Gaveller Mrs. —, Lower Clapton
Giberne Mark, esq. Lower Clapton
Gibson Joseph, esq. Lower Clapton
Gillis Capt. —, Valentine house, U.C.
Goodall Robt. esq. 13 Portland pl. L.C.
Goodings William, esq. 14 Clapton sq
Gray Michael, esq. 6 Portland pl. L.C.
Greatorex Jer. esq. Springhill house
Green Alexr. esq. 7 Clapton square
Green James, esq. 4 Clapton square
Gregory Mark, esq. 4 Clapton pl, L.C.
Gregory Rev.Thomas, Upper Clapton
Griffiths Rev. Thos. 8 Clapton square
Grinly William, esq. Summit place, Clapton common
Grove John, esq. 4 Portland pl. L. C.
Guillemard Mrs. —, 24 Clapton sq
Hackblock Mrs. —, 2 Portland pl, L.C.
Hackblock John, esq. Lower Clapton
Hackblock Wm. esq. Summit place, Clapton common [square
Hamilton William, esq. 11 Clapton
Hancock Chas. esq. Wickham pl, L.C.
Hancock Mr. Richd. Lower Clapton
Hanks John, esq. Upper Clapton
Harrison the Misses, Buccleugh terrace, Upper Clapton
Havenith Leon, esq. Laura place, L.C.
Hawke Jno. esq. 7 Portland place, L.C.
Heathcote Rev. Charles John, Parsonage, Upper Clapton
Heaviside Thos. esq. Lower Clapton
Hensley Chas. esq. Lower Clapton
Holmes Mrs. Eliz. Upper Clapton
HopgoodThos. esq. Buccleugh ter. U.C.
Horsten John, esq. Lower Clapton
HoskinsCapt.Thos. 20 Clapton square
HumphreysJohn, esq. UpperClapton
Hunt Mrs. Maria, Lower Clapton
Hunter James C. esq. Stamford grove East, Upper Clapton
Hutchins Mrs. Eliz. Lower Clapton
Jacobson Howard, esq. Stamford grove West, Upper Clapton
Jacombe John, esq. Clapton terr. U.C.
James Mrs. James, 2 Clapton pl, L.C.
James Louis, esq. Stamford grove West, Upper Clapton
Johnson George, esq. Upper Clapton
Johnson Mrs. Mary, Upper Clapton
Johnstone William, esq. Buccleugh terrace, Upper Clapton
Jones J. esq. Upper Clapton
Jordan Wm. James, esq. High bridge
Jordein Mr. Inglis, Upper Clapton
JubbMrs.Ann, Wickham place, L. C.
Kent Wm. A. esq. Laura place, L.C.
Laing Jas. esq. Buccleugh terr. U.C.
Lalor John, esq. 5 Clapton square
Lancaster Mr. Wm. Upper Clapton
Lane Jas. esq. Arbutus place, U. C.
Lawrence Chas. esq. Lower Clapton
Lecesne Mr. Louis, Upper Clapton
Lee Mrs. Elizabeth, 9 Clapton square
Leigh Mr. John Porter, Lwr. Clapton
Lepine John, esq. Springfield, U.C.
Levine Mr. Henry, Lower Clapton
Lewes Mr. Benj. Upper Clapton
Lloyd Thomas, esq. Clapton terrace
Lucas Mrs. —, Grove, Upper Clapton
Lucas Thomas, esq. Lower Clapton
Lynes Henry, esq. Lower Clapton
Mallison Mrs. —, Grove, Upper C.
Mann Mr. Christr. Lower Clapton
Marshall Lawrence, esq. Elm cottage, Upper Clapton
Marshall Wm. esq. Springfield, U.C.
Mather Rev. James, Clapton terrace
May William, esq. Laura place, L.C.
Merrett William, esq. Buccleugh terrace, Upper Clapton
Messer Mrs. Anna, Upper Clapton
Milne Josh. esq. Clapton terr. U. C.
Moens Jacob B. esq. Springfield
Morland Miss Ann, Lea bridge road
Morris Mrs. Colonel, Laura pl. L. C.
Moul James, esq. Springfield, U. C.
Mountague James, esq. Clapton common [place, L. C.
Mullens Wm. Herbert, esq. Wickham
Munt Mr. Richard, Lower Clapton
Musgrove John, esq. Lower Clapton
Nalder Francis. esq. 10 Portland place, Lower Clapton [L. C.
Nalder Frederick H. esq. Laura place,
Neal Saml. esq. Myrtle cottage, U. C.
Neilson Claude, esq. Summit house, Upper Clapton
Nicholson Mr. John, Upper Clapton
Nisbett Mrs. Mary, Upper Clapton
Norton Captain —, Stamford grove East, Upper Clapton
Old Mr. Thomas, 8 Clapton square
Oliver Mr. John Rixon, Upper C.
Ord Mr. John, Upper Clapton
Oughton Mrs. —, Lower Clapton
Oxley Mrs. —, Upper Clapton
Parnell Mr. Hugh J. R. Uppr. Clapton
Parr William, esq. Summit place, Clapton common
Paton Mrs. Wm. 12 Clapton square
Pearson Mrs. Constance, Up. Clapton
Poole Mr. John, Upper Clapton
Powell John Clarke, esq. Lr. Clapton
Powles Thomas, esq. Upper Clapton
Prellar Charles Augustus, esq. Upper Clapton [U. C.
Preston Jno. esq. Buccleugh terrace,
Price Jos. esq. Brook cottage, U. C.
Pullen Mr. Jno. S. esq. 25 Clapton sq
Pullen Mrs. Jos. 25 Clapton square
Reithmuller Mr. Christopher W. 27 Clapton square
Ricard Mr. Wm. 12 Portland pl. L.C.
Rogers Hy. esq. 10 Clapton square
Rohrs Chas. Wm. esq. Lwr. Clapton
Roper Mr. Samuel, 9 Clapton square
Rust Thomas Wills, esq. Buccleugh terrace, Upper Clapton
Rutt George, esq. Lower Clapton
Rutt Henry, esq. Lower Clapton
Rutter John, esq. Grove, Upper C.
Rutter Wm. esq. Warwick road, U.C.
Saunders Nathl. esq. 13 Clapton sq
Savage William, esq. Stamford grove East, Upper Clapton
Scott Benj. W. esq. Clapton common
Secretan Geo. esq. Laura place, L. C.
Sewell Isaac, esq. Lower Clapton
Sex Edward, esq. Upper Clapton
Sharp Mr. William, Upper Clapton
Sharwood Mr. Saml. Clapton commn
Shaw Robt. G. esq. Springfield, U.C.
Shee Jos. esq. Buccleugh terr, U. C.
Shepherd Geo. esq. Laura pl, L. C.
Siffken Mr. Henry Jacob, 18 Clapton square [L. C.
Smart Thomas, esq. 5 Portland place,
Smith Henley, esq. Spring cottage, Upper Clapton [U. C.
Smythers Mrs. Sophia, Bellevue ter.
Snaith Mrs. —, Lower Clapton
Soames Hy. A. esq. Upper Clapton
Squire George Frederick, esq. Buccleugh terrace, U. C. [Clapton
Stallard Saml. Frampton, esq. Upper
Starbuck Charles Frederick, esq. Upper Clapton
Steel Joseph, esq. Summit pl, U. C.
Syms Mrs. Jane, Summit place, U.C.
Tanner Jno. Jos. esq. Upper Clapton
Tanquary Thomas Butts, esq. Laura place, Lower Clapton
Taylor Geo. esq. Springfield, U. C.
Thackeray Saml. esq. Lower Clapton
Thompson the Misses Jane, Ann and Mary, Upper Clapton
Tidswell Samuel, esq. Upper Clapton
Toulmin Henry, esq. Mount Pleasant house, Upper Clapton
Tucker Henry, esq. Upper Clapton
Turner Skinner, esq. Lower Clapton
Tyssen John Robert Daniel, esq. Warwick lane, Upper Clapton
Van Somner Jas. esq. Uppr. Clapton
Vaux Mrs. Mary Ann, 21 Clapton sq
Walker George, esq. Upper Clapton
Walker Miss —, 22 Clapton square
Wallis Mrs. Susannah, Stamford grove East, Upper Clapton
Ward Mrs. —, 1 Clapton place, L. C.
Warren Miss S. Springfield, U. C.
Waterworth William, esq. 8 Clapton place, Lower Clapton
Weber Charles Frederick, esq. Upper Clapton [Clapton
Welton Rev. Thomas Summit pl, U.
Weston James, esq. Upper Clapton
Wheelwright Mrs. Jane Frances, Upper Clapton
Williams John, esq. Arbutus pl, U. C.
Williams Joseph Richard, esq. Lower Clapton [square
Willis Christopher, esq. 3 Clapton
Willis Jos. esq. 11 Portland pl, L. C.
Winter John, esq. 2 Clapton square
Wright Chas. esq. Laura place, L. C.
Wright James, esq. Upper Clapton
Wright William Consett, esq. Springfield cottage, Upper Clapton
Wynn George, esq. Upper Clapton

ACADEMIES & SCHOOLS.

Aird Donald, Clapton house school
Ashcombe Misses, Lower Clapton
Dodgson Thomas, Upper Clapton
Gorton Alice, Clapton terrace, U.C.

GRAMMAR SCHOOL (Hackney), Lower Clapton—Rev. W. B. Thomas, master [Clapton
Hicks Miss, Wickham place, Lower
Montaigne J. W. Upper Clapton
NATIONAL SCHOOLS, (boys' & girls'), Upper Clapton—Jno. Isaacs, master; Mary Dockrill and Grace Roberts, mistresses [L. Clapton
Prescod Susannah, Pond cottage,
Rippingham Mary, Warwick cottage, Upper Clapton
Sargant Mrs. —, 6 Clapton square
Sharp Elizabeth (young gent.'s), Springfield, Upper Clapton
Slater Anna, Lower Chapton
Warwick Misses, 1 Portland place, Lower Clapton [Clapton
Wellings Sarah & Catherine, Upper
Wood Misses, Upper Clapton
Wyett Ellen, Upper Clapton

ARTISTS.

Ball Isaac, Lower Clapton
Cost Henry, Lower Clapton
Hawkins George, Arbutus cottage, Upper Clapton [Clapton
Jones Thomas, Clapton place, Lower
Montaigne Wm. Jno. Upper Clapton

BAKERS & FLOUR DEALERS.

Barnard Wm. Hill st, Upper Clapton
Brown Matthew, Upper Clapton
Charsley William, Lower Clapton
Grimwood Alexander, Brook st, U.C.
James Charles, Lower Clapton
James George, 11 Clapton pl, L. C.
Underwood Edward, Wood st, U.C.
Watt James, Hill st, Upper Clapton

BARGE OWNERS.

Saunders T. & G. Lea bridge
Wicks William, Lea bridge wharf

BOOKSELLERS & STATIONRS

Ball Isaac, Lower Clapton
Dawes Hny. Hill st, Upper Clapton
Pickersgill Richard, Lower Clapton
Upcraft Louisa, Upper Clapton

BOOT AND SHOE MAKERS.

Alder Henry, Lower Clapton
Crook John, Upper Clapton
Hodges Jas. Wood st, Up. Clapton
Lewis John, Lea bridge road, Clapton
Owen Thos. (boot), Upper Clapton
Underwood William, Upper Clapton
Wood John, Clapton gate

BRICK MAKERS.

Lee Henry & John, Brickfields, High hill ferry
Rhodes Thos. & William, Brickfields

BRICKLAYERS.

Fieldwick William, Upper Clapton
Gray John, Lower Clapton

BUILDERS.

Boulton Fred. Brook st. Up.Clapton
England George, Lower Clapton
Fieldwick William, Upper Clapton
Rumens John, Lower Clapton
Snewin Philip, Upper Clapton
Snewin Thomas, Lea bridge road

BUTCHERS.

Hersent Thomas, Upper Clapton
Hunt Thomas, Upper Clapton
Robinson Henry, Lea bridge road
Slater Richard, Lower Clapton

CALICO & SILK PRINTERS.

Andrews David, High hill ferry
Birch William, High hill ferry
Peddington & Co. High hill ferry

CARPENTRS & UNDERTAKRS

Boulton Fred. Brook st. Up.Clapton
Dockerill William, Upper Clapton
England George, Lower Clapton
Monk Samuel (undertaker), Back lane, Lower Clapton
Rumens John, Lower Clapton
Rumens Wm. Back lane, Lwr. Clapton
Snewin Philip, Upper Clapton [ton
Snewin Thos. Lea bridge road, Clap-
Whales Joshua, Brook st, U. C.

CHESEMONGERS.

Homan Mary Ann, Lower Clapton
Wiggins John, Lower Clapton

COACH MASTERS.

Breach Jas. Hill st, Upper Clapton
Bryan Thomas, Clapton Common
Clarke William, Lower Clapton
Kendall George, Upper Clapton
Kerrison James, Upper Clapton
Martin Thomas, Lower Clapton
Newman James, Lower Clapton
Whitebread George & Charles, Lower Clapton

COAL MERCHANTS.

Farmery Mariena, Upper Clapton
Leigh John & Co. Lea bridge
Looe Martin, Spring hill, U. C.
Wicks William, Lea bridge

CORN DEALERS.

Digby Thomas, Lower Clapton
Kerrison James, Upper Clapton
Scriven Thomas, Brook st, U. C.

DYERS.

Baker George (& calenderer), High hill ferry
Eness Samuel, Lower Clapton
Whipp William, Brook st, Clapton

FRUITERERS AND GREENGROCERRS.

Bailey Robert, Lower Clapton
Choat Edward, Lower Clapton
Curry George, Wood st, U. C.
Dodds Cuthbert, Brook st, U. C.
Fordham George, Hill st, U. C.
Foster William, Clapton place, L. C.
Haydon William, Lower Clapton
Muncey Charles, Back lane, L. C.

GARDENERS & FLORISTS.

Bailey Thomas, Upper Clapton
Batten James, Brook st, U. C.
Curry James, Brook st, U. C.
Lowe H. & Co. (and nurserymen), Upper Clapton
Parker Robert, Lower Clapton

GROCERS AND DEABERS IN SUNDRIES.

Clapham James, Clapton gate
Furley Thomas, Upper Clapton
Hickman Frederick, Upper Clapton
Howard Wm. Hill st, Upper Clapton
Reynold William, Upper Clapton

HAIR DRESSERS.

Puddefoot Walter, Upper Clapton
Scamer Rayfield, Back lane, L. C.
Ward Richard, Clapton gate
White William, Brook st, U. C.

INNS & PUBLIC HOUSES.

British Oak, Stephen Murrell, Upper Clapton [Clapton
Crooked Billet, John Drew, Upper
Duke of Clarence, Fras. Wm. Gentry, Back lane, Lower Clapton
Duke of York, Richard Horsay, Caroline st, Upper Clapton
Fountain, George & Charles Whitebread, Lower Clapton
Jolly Anglers, Wm. Wicks, Lea bridge
Old King's Head, William Niblett, Upper Clapton [ferry house
Mount Pleasant, Hy. Watts, High-hill
Royal Sovereign, Thomas Lunn, Brook st, U. C. [Clapton
White Hart, John Horn, Lower
White Swan, George Kendall, Upper Clapton [Clapton
Windsor Castle, Robt. King, Lower

IRONMONGERS.

Harries John, Upper Clapton
Carmichael John, Hill st, U. C.

LINEN DRAPERS.

Debenham Robert, Upper Clapton
Holmes Rebecca, Lower Clapton
Munday Joseph, Upper Clapton

LIVERY STABLE KEEPERS.

Hill John, Back lane, Lower Clapton
Martin Thomas, Lower Clapton

MILLINERS & DRESS MAKRS.

Ashton Louisa & Emily, Hill st, U.C.
Bailey Sarah, Lower Clapton
Campbell Martha, Clapton pl. L. C.
Cox Ann, Back lane, Lower Clapton
Gibbins Charlotte, Back lane, L. C.
Nowland Louisa, Upper Clapton
Patrick Mary, Hill st, Upper Clapton
Wheddon Caroline, Clapton place
Wollard Eliza & Elizth. Lwr Clapton
Yerworth Theodosia, Back lane, L.C.

PAINTERS, PLUMBERS AND GLAZIERS.

Barber John & Wm. Upper Clapton
Cook Thos. Wood st, Upper Clapton
Kingaby Chas. Lea bridge rd, Clapton
Showell Edward, Upper Clapton
Trayhorn Robert, Upper Clapton

SADDLERS.

Pelling John, Clapton place, L. C.
Woollard Edward, Lower Clapton

SURGEONS.

Barff Fredk. 3 Portland place, L.C.
Garrod Saml. Jos. 3 Clapton pl, L. C.
Jones Jno. 9 Buccleugh terrace, U.C.
Toulmin Francis, Lower Clapton
Toulmin Frederick, Upper Clapton
Welch Ryder, Upper Clapton

TAILORS.

Brown John & Son, Lower Clapton
Chambers George, Back lane, L. C.
Pratt William, Lower Clapton
Sayer George, Upper Clapton
Tuck John, Back lane, LowerClapton

TEACHERS OF MUSIC AND DANCING.

Botcherby George, Lower Clapton
Rogers Charles, Lower Clapton

WHITESMITHS.

Carmichael John, Hill st, U. C.
Carmichael John, Lower Clapton

Miscellaneous.

Ashton Louisa & Emily, baby linen warehouse, Hill st, Upper Clapton
Bacon Jas. smith & farrier, Upper Clapton
Ballard John, carrier, Upper Clapton
Boston Joseph, veterinary surgeon, Upper Clapton [Lower Clapton
Daniell William, collector, Down terrace,
Dove Thomas, piano forte maker, Upper Clapton [Clapton
Eness Mary Ann, straw hat maker, Lower
Fieldwick Jno. wheelwright, Lower Claptn
Fletcher Jas. upholsterer, Back lane, L. C.
Garva James, chymist & druggist, Lower Clapton [ferry
Harrington William, boat owner, High-hill
Harvey Thos. fishmonger, Lower Clapton
LONDON ORPHAN ASYLUM, Lower Clapton—Rev. Robert Heath, head master; Ann Freeman, mistress
LUNATIC ASYLUM (Dr. Munroe's), Brook house, L. C. [Lower Clapton
Middleton William, tea and coffee dealer,
Montaigne John Wm. registrar of births, deaths and marriages, Upper Clapton
Morrice Geo. cabinet maker & upholsterer, Upper Clapton [Upper Clapton
Moseley Francis, china and glass dealer,
Renshaw Ann, teacher, Upper Clapton
Rumbal Thos. cowkeeper, Upper Clapton
Snewin Philip, jun. agent to the Imperial fire office, Upper Clayton
Snewin Richd. house agent, Lower Clapton
Walker Henry, oilman, Lower Clapton

COACHES.

To LONDON, *Coaches* and *Omnibuses*, every quarter of an hour.

EALING AND LITTLE EALING.

EALING is a village, in a very populous parish (which also contains Old Brentford), in the hundred of Ossulton. The village is situated near the Uxbridge road, 9 miles S. S. E. from that town, about 6¼ W. from London, and on the line of the Great Western railway, which passes on the north side of the village; it contains, with its immediate neighbourhood, many handsome villas and pleasant seats, with several very respectable school establishments. At Castlebar Park, in this parish, the Duke and Dutchess of Kent resided for some time. The church, dedicated to St. Mary, is a neat brick edifice, with a square tower and turret; the living is a vicarage, in the patronage of the Bishop of London; the Rev. John Smith is the present incumbent. John Horne Tooke, author of the 'Diversions of Purley,' and the celebrated Mrs. Trimmer, were interred in the cemetery of this church. Here are two schools, liberally supported, and conducted upon the national system, for children of both sexes, some of whom are annually clothed; there are also alms-houses, and a workhouse for the parish poor.—LITTLE EALING contains but few residences; these are mostly situated between Ealing and Brentford. A pleasure fair is held at Ealing on the 24th of June and two following days. The entire parish, including Old Brentford, contained, according to the returns for 1831, 7,783 inhabitants.

POST OFFICE, EALING, Frederick Blake, *Post Master*, and a *Receiving-House* at Phœbe Lawford's.—Letters arrive from and are despatched to LONDON three times a day.

*** *The names without address are in* EALING.

NOBILITY, GENTRY AND CLERGY.

Buckland R. esq. Ealing
Byron the Hon. Lady, Fordoak
Carbonell Colonel —, Ealing
Carr Lady —, Ealing common
Clark Robert, esq. Ealing
Collis Henry, esq. Castlebar hill
Cuthbertson Miss, Ealing
Douglas James, esq. Ealing
Evans George, esq. Ealing
Heddy William, esq. Ealing
Hemmings James, esq. Ealing
Holt Joseph, esq. Ealing
Ibbotson John, esq. Ealing green
Lawrence—, esq. M.D. Lit. Ealing park
Lawson Mrs. —, Ealing
Lemond Sir James, Drayton green
Lindsey Rev. J. Ealing green
Littlewood James, esq. Ealing
Minton Samuel, esq. Ealing
Morse Edward, esq. Drayton green
Penn Henry, esq. Ealing
Simpkins Jas. esq. Ealing common
Sleap Mr. Jonathan Thos. Ealing grn
Raymond Jas. esq. Ealing common
Repton Rev. Edward, Drayton green
Roberts Mrs. —, Ealing
Rogers William, esq. Ealing
Rothschild Madame —, Gunsbury
Seymour Lady —, Little Boston house, Little Ealing
Smallman Mrs. Eliz. Ealing common
Smith Rev. John, Ealing
Strudwick James, esq. Ealing
Trye Mrs. Anne, Ealing
Wetherall General Sir Francis Augustus, Ealing
Wood George, esq. Hanger hill
Wood James, esq. Hanger hill
Wood Thomas, esq. Castlebar hill
Wyley William, esq. Cartlebar park

ACADEMIES AND SCHOOLS.
Not otherwise described are Day Schools.

Atlee Charles, Ealing grove
Atlee Miss Mary, Ealing green
Birkett Joseph (boarding), Ealing
Chignell Mary (boarding),
Helm Joseph, Ealing grove
INFANTS' SCHOOL, Ealing—Mrs. Green, mistress
Lovegrove Misses (boarding)
Lovegrove Thomas (boarding)
NATIONAL SCHOOL, Miss Walker, mistress
NATIONAL SCHOOL, William Pearce, master; Mary Pearce, mistress
Nicholas Francis (boarding)
Ray William, Thorn house academy
Robinson Mary Ann (boarding), Little Ealing
Trehern Mrs. (boarding)

BAKERS.

Eden Charles
Goodrich Richard
Long Edward
Walter Thomas

BLACKSMITHS.

Atlee Thomas
Hinge John
Rackliff Daniel

BOOT AND SHOE MAKERS.

Chard Richard
Cope Henry
Franklin George
Jones George
Mumford John
Porter Henry
Stemp Stephen
Whitley Thomas

BRICKLAYERS.

Hancock Henry (& builder)
Payne Robert Michael

BUTCHERS.

Chambers William
Goodwin Thomas
Oliver John
Selmes Alexander
Tompkins Ann

CARPENTERS.

Dickins James, Ealing grove
Grover James (& builder)
Nye Thomas (& builder)
Wecklin William Home

CHINA & GLASS DEALERS.

Blake Frederick
Dorchester Ann

CONFECTIONERS.

Knight James
Luck Jonathan

CORN DEALERS.

Goodrich Richard
Knight James

GROCERS AND DEALERS IN SUNDRIES.

Atlee Mary Eliz.
Blake Frederick
Dorchester Ann
Haines John
Jones Nathaniel
Knight James
M'Nair James
Pain Mary
Sheargold Richd.
Stevens John
Tidy William
Wallace William
Walter Thomas
Yeates James

INNS & PUBLIC HOUSES.

Bell, William Williams
Castle, John Tickner
Coach & Horses, John Dalton
Feathers, Edwin Slark
Fox & Goose, Jas. Kidney, Hanger la
Green Man, Samuel Tompkins
Horse & Groom, Richard Norden
King's Arms, William Goodman, Ealing grove
New Inn (& posting house), John Skoyles
Old Hat, James Nettleton
Old Hat (original, & commercial inn), James Price
Plough, Trever Evans, Little Ealing
Red Lion, Charles Mathews
Rose & Crown, Henry Mathews

LINEN DRAPERS.

Fountain Abraham
Wyman Robert

MARKET GARDENERS.

Knevett Samuel
Mulcock Thomas, *Grove*
Rance Henry
Thompson John
Wells Henry

MILLINERS.

Allen Sarah (and dress)
Harris Abigail (straw hat)
Jones Miss (and dress)
Moon John (straw hat)
Searle A. & S. (and dress)

NURSERY & SEEDSMEN.

Mountjoy Richard & Son, Hanwell nursery, near the Old Hats, Ealing

PLUMBERS, PAINTERS, AND GLAZIERS.

Fidler Thomas
Hawkins James
Moore James
Thorn Joseph

SADDLERS AND HARNESS MAKERS.

Colley Robert, Ealing common
Towers George

SURGEONS.

Dickinson George, Ealing green
Tattersall James, M. D.
Wilkins Henry

TAILORS.

Carter John
Montgomery Thomas
Price William

WHEELWRIGHTS.

Cutting James
Newton James

Miscellaneous.

Atlee Charles, parish clerk
Baker William Abee, tea dealer
Evans Thomas, greengrocer
Fletcher John, bookseller & stationer
Grover James, fire office agent
Hayles Benjamin, druggist and oilman
Jackson Geo. composition manufacturer
Taylor Edward, hair dresser
Taylor Thomas, cowkeeper
WORKHOUSE, Ealing—John Frost, master; Elizabeth Frost, mistress

COACHES & OMNIBUSES.

To LONDON, *Coaches* and *Omnibuses*, from the New Inn, Ealing, several times during the day; and *Coaches*, to and from UXBRIDGE and WYCOMBE, pass through daily.

RAILWAY CONVEYANCE.

To LONDON (short trains), every morning (Sunday excepted), at eight, and twenty minutes before nine, forenoon at eleven, afternoon at three, and evening at seven. On Sunday at half-past eight in the morning, and half-past eight in the evening.

To MAIDENHEAD and SLOUGH, a train every evening at six, and on Sunday an additional train at eight in the morning.

*** The hours of the *trains* starting will be subject to alteration, as the line progresses towards completion.

CARRIERS.

To LONDON, Henry Reynolds and Daniel Dunce, from their houses, Ealing, daily; and several other *Carriers* to and from LONDON, UXBRIDGE and WYCOMBE, pass through daily.

EDGWARE AND GREAT AND LITTLE STANMORE.

EDGWARE, once a market town, is in the parish of its name and hundred of Gore, eight miles from the western extremity of Oxford-street, London—situated on the road to St. Albans, and until of late years was a place of prosperous thoroughfare. The agreeable scenery by which it is surrounded, and the excellence of the roads leading to it, also rendered the village attractive as a residence for respectable families. The western side of its principal street is in the parish of LITTLE STANMORE, where, in the early part of the eighteenth century, James Duke of Chandos erected his magnificent palace of 'Canons,' and resided in a style of regal splendour; the sum of £250,000. is said to have been expended upon its erection; and so extravagant was the outlay upon its embellishment that, as it is recorded, the locks and hinges of the doors were of silver. After the death of the duke this noble edifice was taken down, and sold piecemeal: the columns formed part of the portico of Wanstead House, which has shared the same fate (as noticed at page 164); the marble staircase was adjusted in the Earl of Chesterfield's mansion in Mayfair, and the admired statue of George I ornaments the area of Leicester-square. Edgware is within the jurisdiction of a court of requests, holden at Brentford and Uxbridge, for the recovery of debts under forty shillings; petty sessions are held here for the division, and courts baron and leet annually; and this is one of the polling stations at the election of county representatives.

The places of worship are the parish church, dedicated to Saint Margaret, and a chapel for independents. The parish church of Little Stanmore, dedicated to St. Lawrence, is well worthy of inspection; it was rebuilt about the beginning of the last century by the Duke of Chandos, who devoted a large sum to the decoration of the ceiling and walls, and the pictorial embellishments of the altar, which were executed by first-rate artists. Handel, who resided at Canons as chapel master, composed, it is said, his sacred drama of 'Esther' for the consecration of this church; and in 1790 a grand concert of sacred music was performed within its walls, to the honour of this great composer. The place of sepulture of the Chandos family is in this church, and over the vault is a monument to the first Duke of Chandos. The principal charities supported in Edgware are a well maintained free school and two sets of alms-houses; of the latter, those erected by Charles Day, Esq., in 1828, are liberally endowed, and consist of eight tenements for tradesmen's widows; the structure, which adds to the pleasing appearance of the village, cost £2,000. when completed. An annual fair is held on the first Wednesday, Thursday and Friday in August, for cattle and toys; on the two last days races are held, which in general are well attended. The parish (exclusive of that part in the parish of Little Stanmore), contained, by the returns for 1831, 591 inhabitants; the population of Little Stanmore, at the same period, was 876.

Two miles from Edgware, in the same hundred, is GREAT STANMORE, a genteel village and parish. The church, dedicated to Saint John the Baptist, contains a magnificent tomb to the memory of Sir John Wolstenholme, Knight, at whose expense the church was built: the benefice is a rectory, in the presentation of George Harley Drummond, Esq., and present incumbency of the Rev. A. R. Chauvell. There is an excellent national school for twenty boys and forty girls, who are clothed and educated. It was at this village that the meeting of George IV (then Prince Regent), and the Emperor of Russia and King of Prussia, with Lous XVIII, took place, after the final overthrow of Bonaparte. The parish of Stanmore, in 1831, contained 1,144 inhabitants.

POST OFFICE, EDGWARE, Frederick Tootell, *Post Master*.—Letters from LONDON arrive every forenoon at half-past eleven, afternoon at half-past five and night at half-past nine, and are despatched every morning at half-past five and half-past nine and afternoon at half-past three.

POST OFFICE, STANMORE, Henry Seabrook, *Post Master*.—Letters from LONDON arrive every afternoon at one, evening at seven and night at ten, and are despatched every morning at half-past five and eight, afternoon at three and evening at seven.

NOBILITY, GENTRY AND CLERGY.

Abbott Wm. esq. Hermitage, Stanmore [priory
Abercorn the Marquess of, Bentley
Barron Rev. John Augustus, A. M. Stanmore [Edgware
Carter Thomas, esq. Brockley hill,
Chauvel Rev. Arthur Robinson, Stanmore [more
Clutterbuck Peter, esq. Grove, Stan-
Day Mrs. —, Hill house, Edgware
Drummond George Harley, esq. Stanmore
Fiott Rev. Nicholas, Edgware
Hooper George, esq. Stanmore
Ledger Matt. esq. Newlands, Edgware
Loosley Richard, esq. Edgware
Lushington Charles, esq. Edgware
Majoribanks Edwd. esq. Stanmore
Martin Miss —, Stanmore
Mayne Capt. —, Stanmore
Mutter Rev. George, Little Stanmore
Norton John, esq. Stone grove, Edgware [Edgware
Phillimore Wm. esq. Deacon's hill,
Plumer Lady —, Canons, Edgware
Plumer Thomas Hall, esq. South Lodge, Canons, Edgware
Rice Edward, esq. Stanmore
Rice Miss —, Stanmore
Savery N. N. esq. Newlands, Edgware
Scott Mr. George E. Stanmore
Sladen J. esq. South Lodge, Edgware
South Mr. Thomas, Stanmore
Smirke Sir Robert, Stanmore
Smith Rev. Edwd. John, Stanmore
Taylor Capt. —, Stanmore
Teed Thomas, esq. Stanmore
Tennent Colonel —, Stanmore
Tootell Mr. Wm. S. (conveyancer), Edgware [Edgware
Wheldon Thos. esq. Crabtree orchard,
Williams Mrs. John, Stanmore
Willson Mrs. —, Stanmore [ware
Wylde Henry, esq. Stone grove, Edg-

ACADEMIES & SCHOOLS.

Barron Rev. John Augustus (boarding), Stanmore
Cole William (boarding), Edgware
FREE SCHOOL (boys') Edgware—Charles Pantyn, master
George Edward (boarding), Edgware
NATIONAL SCHOOLS (boys' & girls'), Stanmore — Mr. Brook, master; Mrs. Brook, mistress
Scott Mrs. (boarding), Edgware
Seabrook Mrs. J. (brdng.) Stanmore
Smith Rev. E. J. (boarding) Stanmore

BAKERS.

Hawkes William, Stanmore
King John, Edgware
Moss Benjamin, Stanmore
Royer Richard, Edgware
Sexton John, Stanmore
Spencer Mary, Stanmore
White Daniel, Edgware

BLACKSMITHS.

Butt Mason, Edgware
Franklin James, Stanmore
Garrett Robert, Stanmore
Hinge William, Edgware

BOOKSELLERS & STATIONRS.

Greene Alfred, jun. (and printer and toy dealer), Stanmore
Greene Alfred Richard, Edgware
Rust Henry, Edgware

BOOT AND SHOE MAKERS.

Allen William, Stanmore
Bruton William, Edgware
George Joseph, Stanmore
Hills John, Stanmore
Knight William, Stanmore
Reynolds Henry, Stanmore
Saint Thomas, Stanmore
Sutherland William, Edgware
Watkins Robert, Edgware
Woodstock Eliza, Edgware

BREWER.

Clutterbuck Thomas (and maltster), Stanmore

BRICKLAYERS.

Humphrey Thomas, Stanmore
Stovell Thomas, Edgware
Wager William, Edgware

BUTCHERS.

Dracott William, Stanmore
Fenn William, Edgware
Gibbons Joseph, Edgware
Ginger John, Stanmore
Ginger Joseph, Edgware
Ham Charles, jun. Edgware
Hawkes Robert, Stanmore
Sexton Charles, Stanmore

CARPENTERS & UNDERTKRS.

Bailey James, Stanmore
Eyles William, Stanmore
Fassnidge Walter, Edgware
Ham Charles, Edgware
Jordan George, Edgware
Kirby George (and timber dealer), Stanmore [Stanmore
Wilson John (and timber dealer),

COAL MERCHANTS.

Gough John, Stanmore
Hunt Thomas Brown, Edgware
Mortimer Joseph, Stanmore
Seabrook Henry (and tallow chandler), Stanmore
Tootell Frederick, Edgware

CORN DEALERS.

Greene Alfred Richard, Edgware
King John, Edgware
Moss Benjamin, Stanmore
Royer Richard, Edgware
Tootell Frederick, Edgware
White Daniel, Edgware

FIRE, &c. OFFICE AGENTS.

COUNTY (fire) & PROVIDENT (life), Thomas Liman, Stanmore
FREEMASON'S (life), Alfred Greene, Stanmore
GUARDIAN, Henry Seabrook, Stanmore
IMPERIAL, Alfred Richard Greene, Edgware
NORWICH UNION, George Jordan, Edgware
PROTECTOR, Chas. Pantyn, Edgware

GROCERS & TEA DEALERS.

(See also Shopkeepers, &c.)

Gough John, Edgware
Greene Alfred Richard (and stamp office), Edgware
Greig Charles, Edgware
Mortimer Joseph, Stanmore
Rust Henry, Edgware
Seabrook Henry, Stanmore

HAIR DRESSERS.

Barrett John, Stanmore
Stone William (and leather cutter), Edgware

INNS.

Abercorn Arms (and posting house), John Seabrook, Stanmore
Chandos Arms (and excise office), Elizabeth Perfect, Edgware
White Hart (and posting house), Robert Cribb, Edgware

IRONMONGERS.

Chandler Benjamin, Stanmore
Garrett Robert, Stanmore
Jordan George, Edgware

LINEN DRAPERS.

Brown Elizabeth, Stanmore
French William, Edgware
Godwin William, Stanmore
Grainge William, Edgware
Pegler Francis John, Stanmore

MILLINERS AND DRESS MAKERS.

Brown Elizabeth, Stanmore
Rodway Mary, Edgware

PLUMBERS, PAINTERS, &c.

Balderston James, Stanmore
Bodimeade William, Edgware
Hinton Vincent, Edgware
Hobday James, Stanmore
Read John, Stanmore

SADDLERS.

Ashby Sarah, Edgware
Stanford Henry, Stanmore

SHOPKEEPERS & DEALRS IN GROCERIES & SUNDRIES.

Ballard William, Edgware
Bone Mary Ann, Edgware
Gonm George, Stanmore
Hall Isaac, Edgware
Poulter William, Edgware
Saunders John, Stanmore
Stone Betsy, Edgware
Willoughby Joseph, Stanmore

SURGEONS.

Andrews & Rogers, Stanmore
Foote William, Edgware
Gatley J. R. Edgware
Noverre Arthur, Stanmore

TAILORS.

Fenn Thomas, Edgware
Hargood John, Stanmore
Hone William, Edgware
Lyne William, Edgware
Pyle Mark, Stanmore

TAVERNS & PUBLIC HOUSES.

Boot, John Tattersay, Edgware
Crown, Elizbth. Jane Lawford, Stanmore
George, William Fenn, Edgware
Masons' Arms, Mary Fenn, Edgware
Vine, Elizabeth Stonhill, Stanmore
White Lion, Abraham Smith, Edgware

WHEELWRIGHTS.

Jordan George, Edgware
Robins Charles, Stanmore
Stanton John, Edgware

Miscellaneous.

Bottoms Samuel, fishmonger, Stanmore
Cross Joseph, basket maker, Edgware
Doery Wm. coach proprietor, Stanmore
Greene Alfred, registrar of births and deaths, Stanmore
Hinton Sarah, straw hat maker, Edgware
King Francis and Son, veterinary surgeons, Stanmore
Morgan Robert, nurseryman, &c. Stone grove, Edgware
Pegler Chas. surveyor of taxes, Stanmore
Penning D. inspector of taxes, Stanmore
Potten Richard, gardener and seedsman, Stanmore
Ruault Monsieur, professor of French, Stanmore
Tomlin Susan, poulterer, Edgware
Vialls Benj. watch, &c. maker, Stanmore
Woodcock John, fishmonger, Edgware

COACHES,

Passing through Edgware.

To LONDON, a *Coach* (from Shenley) every morning (Sunday excepted) at half-past nine—a *Coach* (from St. Albans) calls at the White Hart, every forenoon at half-past ten—the *Despatch* (from Aylesbury) every day at half-past twelve—a *Coach* (from Hemel Hempstead) calls at the Chandos Arms, every afternoon at five—and a *Coach*, from the Abercorn Arms Inn, Stanmore, every morning at eight and afternoon at five.

To AYLESBURY, the *Despatch* (from London) calls at the Chandos Arms, every afternoon at four; goes through Watford, Berkhampstead and Tring.

To HEMEL HEMPSTEAD, a *Coach* (from London) calls at the Chandos Arms, every morning at half-past nine; goes through, Bushey and Watford.

To ST. ALBANS, a *Coach* (from London) calls at the White Hart, every afternoon (Sunday excepted) at four.

To SHENLEY, a *Coach* (from London) calls at the White Hart, every afternoon at half-past five.

CARRIERS.

To LONDON, Benjamin Hawkes, jun. from his house, Stanmore, daily—Thos. Cole, from Watford, twice a week.

EDMONTON

IS a village and parish, in the hundred of its name, about six miles north from London and four from Enfield; situated on the high road to Hertford, along which it extends for upwards of a mile. The new river winds through several parts of the parish, imparting a pleasing and picturesque effect to the pleasure grounds and meadows through which it passes. Besides the dwellings occupied by persons in trade, the village contains several ranges of respectable houses, and in detatched situations many elegant mansions and handsome villas; there are also several boarding schools of the most respectable class, this vicinage being deemed particularly salubrious. The village is efficiently lighted with gas, and amply supplied with water; and in point of trade it enjoys no mean consideration: that in timber is extensive, being carried on by means of the Lea navigation, which passes within three quarters of a mile of the village—the principal merchants in this branch are the Messrs. Corker; there is also an old established concern for the manufactory of coaches, which employs many hands. Petty sessions for the division are held at one of the principal inns every alternate Friday; a court leet and baron annually in Whitsun week, and the parish is within the jurisdiction of a court of requests at Enfield, for the recovery of debts under 40*s*. This place has been noted for some singular, deplorable and ludicrous circumstances:—'Bury Hall,' the seat of the regicide president Bradshaw, retains many of its original features. Peter Fabel, a learned man and reputed conjuror was born here; and upon some of his alleged exploits was founded a drama, produced about the year 1490, called 'The Merry Devil of Edmonton.' An occurrence here also gave rise to a tragedy, founded on the history of an unfortunate woman who, in 1621, was executed for witchcraft! And in later times it has been celebrated as the scene of Cowper's popular ballad of 'John Gilpin,' and the 'Bell' Inn has a sign painting, delineating the return of the equestrian from Ware.

The places of worship are the parish church, dedicated to All Saints (a modern brick structure, with an old embattled tower); Weld chapel of ease, in Southgate-street; another, dedicated to St. Paul, situated on Winchmore Hill; and others for baptists, independents, Wesleyan methodists and the society of friends. There are several charity schools, well supported by subscriptions, donations and legacies; that upon the national plan imparts instruction to upwards of 300 children. There is also a fund for apprenticing children, and some benefactions to the poor. Fairs are held annually in the beginning of September, at Southgate, in this parish, for toys and pleasure. Population, in 1831, 8,912.

POST OFFICE, Fore street, Thomas Corker, *Post Master*.—Letters from LONDON arrive every morning at half-past ten, afternoon at half-past two and half-past five and night at nine, and are despatched every morning at five and half-past nine and afternoon at half-past one and half-past four.

GENTRY & CLERGY.

Adams Charles Henry, esq. Lower Edmonton
Andrews Chas. Weston, esq. Lower Edmonton
Ansell Mrs. —, Fore st
Baker John, esq. 2 Angel place
Baker John, esq. Parade
Baker William, esq. 7 Parade
Barker William, esq. Fore st
Blyth Andrew, esq. Fore st
Brown Mrs. Isabella, 7 Angel place
Brown Mr. Thomas, Fore st
Burgess Mrs. —, 5 Parade
Burls Mrs. W. Lower Edmonton
Burn John, esq. Fore st
Campbell Mrs. Chas. Lower Edmonton
Carr Mrs. —, Lower Edmonton
Chapman John, esq. Fore st

Chapple John Abraham, esq. Lower Edmonton
Chubb Mrs. Elizabeth, Fore st
Clare A. esq. Tanner's end
Clarke Wm. esq. Lower Edmonton
Collet Richard, esq. Fore st
Connell —, esq. Fore st
Cornwall Mrs. —, 9 Parade
Druce the Misses, 1 Angel place
Drury Mr. Meeson, Fore st
Dyke Wm. esq. Lower Edmonton
Eaton Mrs. —, Fore st
Emeree William, esq. Fore st
Eldred Thomas, esq. Fore st
Fardell Mrs. Mary, Fore st
Fellowe Rice Geo. esq. Tanner's end
Fenning Mrs. —, Lower Edmonton
Field Edwd. esq. Lower Edmonton
Field Edward John, esq. Lower Edmonton [place
Fielder Mr. John William, 5 Angel
Flanders Wm. Thomas, esq. Fore st
Galloway George, esq. Fore st
Goff Daniel, esq. Lower Edmonton
Gordon Alexander, esq. Fore st
Gosset Robert Newbury, esq. Lower Edmonton
Gould Mrs. Mary, Fore st
Gray Benjamin, esq. Angel place
Grover John, esq. 10 Parade
Guillouneau Geo. esq. Causeware hall
Harding Mr. Robert, 4 Angel place
Heaver Thos. esq. Lower Edmonton
Henderson Miss —, Fore st
Hewling Rev. Geo. Robert, Fore st
Hinton Wm. esq. Lower Edmonton
Hodges Mr. J. M. Fore st [ton
Holt Jos. Simons, esq. Lwr. Edmon-
Horne Mrs. —, Fore st
Horns Mrs. Caroline, Fore st
Humphrey Mrs. —, Fore st
Humphreys Miss —, Fore st
Johnson Chas. esq. Tanner's end
Jones Mr. Wm. (attorney), Fore st
King Thos. esq. Lower Edmonton
King William, esq. Fore st
Knight Thos. esq. Lower Edmonton
Kolle John, esq. Lower Edmonton
Leggetter John, esq. Fore st [ton
Lingford the Misses, Lower Edmon-
Lomas William, esq. Fore st
Lowe John, esq. Fore st [ton
Martin Edwd. H. esq. Lower Edmon-
Mercer Miss —, 8 Parade [monton
Mores Edwd. Rowe, esq. Lower Ed-
Munt Mrs. —, Fore st
Mushet Mrs. —, Milfield house
Nash Mrs. Susanna, Lower Edmonton
Nicholson Mrs. —, Fore st
Parkinson Jno. esq. Lower Edmonton
Parrott Mr. Robert, Fore st
Peppin Thos. esq. Lower Edmonton
Pitt James, esq. Fore st
Pottell Mr. Wm. Lower Edmonton
Powell Mrs. —, Fore st
Price Charles, esq. Fore st
Pryor Mrs. —, 4 Parade
Ray Mrs. Ann, Tanner's end
Reynolds Mr. James, 6 Angel place
Robinson E. esq. Parade
Roscow Samuel, esq. Fore st
Ross Captain Robert, Marsh side
Routh Fras. G. esq. Lower Edmonton
Salmon Mrs. —, Bury st
Sawyer John, esq. Lower Edmonton
Selby Mr. —, Lower Edmonton
Sillis the Misses, Lower Edmonton
Slatcher Miss Mary, Angel place
Smyth J. E. T. esq. Wirehall cottage
Snell John, esq. Fore st
Soames James, esq. Tanner's end
Solomons Henry, esq. Fore st
Soper James, esq. Church st
Soper John, esq. Bury st
Stratton Mrs. —, Fore st
Symondson Wm. esq. Lwr. Edmonton
Tate Rev. James, Vicarage, Lower Edmonton
Tate Rev. Thomas, Vicarage, Lower Edmonton
Tatham John, esq. 6 Parade
Taylor Edwd. esq. Lower Edmonton
Taylor Wm. esq. Lower Edmonton
Tyrie David, esq. Fore st
Ward Mr. —, Lower Edmonton
West Mrs. —, Fore st
Wheeler Mr. —, Lower Edmonton
Whitehead John Wm. esq. Hide lane
Willis John, esq. Fore st
Williams Mrs. Gregory, Bury hall
Wilkinson Mrs. Sarah, Lower Edmonton
Wilson Capt. John Henry, Fore st
Worsley Charles, esq. Paul house
Zinzan Robert, esq. 3 Angel place

ACADEMIES AND SCHOOLS.
Not otherwise described are Boarding.

Allen Charlotte (day) Lwr. Edmonton
CHARITY SCHOOL, Lower Edmonton —Mary Boon, mistress
Collins Thos. (day), Lower Edmonton
Connell Ann (day), Fore st
Eady Manasseh Phillips, Bridport hall
Firminger Thomas, Bury st
Gordon Alexander, Manor house
Hind Rachael, Fore st
Jennings Ann, Fore st
LATYMER'S CHARITY, Lower Edmonton—Chas. Hy. Adams, master
Markham Elizabeth, 1 Parade
Markham Robert (day), 1 Parade
NATIONAL SCHOOL, Lower Edmonton—Edward Boon, master
Parkins Miss, 3 Parade
Pike Miss, Lower Edmonton
Ross John, Fore st
Vincent James, Lower Edmonton
White David James, College house

BAKERS & FLOUR DEALERS.

Cooper Samuel, Lower Edmonton
Duckworth Richard, Silver st
Frost Samuel, Fore st
Glasscock John, Fore st
Hogben John, Lower Edmonton
Marriott John, Lower Edmonton
Mason Joseph, Fore st
Smart Samuel, Fore st
Wood George, Fore st

BARGE OWNERS & WHARFINGERS.

Lewis Walter, Waterside
Rowley William, Silver st
Wicks Benjamin, New ferry

BASKET MAKERS.

Cripps Thomas, Fore st
Potts Thomas Alfred, Fore st

BLACKSMITHS & FARRIERS.

Allen John, Union square
Holyoak Jonathn. Lower Edmonton
Pratt Luke, Lower Edmonton
Sergent Joseph, Lower Edmonton
Stanley Thomas, Silver st

BOOKSELLERS & STATIONRS.

Green John Wm. Lower Edmonton
Rowley Benjamin, Fore st

BOOT & SHOE MAKERS.

Challis James, Fore st
Clark James, Lower Edmonton
Cock Benjamin, Lower Edmonton
Field William, Fore st
Kerry James, Lower Edmonton
Offwood Thomas, Fore st
Saltmarsh Henry, Lower Edmonton
Streck Alexander, Fore st

BRICKLAYERS & BUILDERS.
(See also Carpenters.)

Downing William, Lower Edmonton
Grand Joseph, Fore st
Paine William, Union square
Rowley John Wright, Fore st

BUTCHERS.

Brown Eliz. (pork), Lower Edmonton
Clinker William, Fore st
Dickinson Peter, Lower Edmonton
Gilderson Wm. Lower Edmonton
Hughes Charles, Fore st
Stanley John Hughes, Fore st
Turner Philip, Lower Edmonton
Witham Mary, Fore st

CARPENTERS, BUILDERS & UNDERTAKERS.

Barker George, Lower Edmonton
Brand Richard, Lower Edmonton
Corker George & Thomas, Fore st
Lawrance Randall, Silver st
Sanderson George, Fore st
Skilton Thomas, Lower Edmonton

CHYMISTS AND DRUGGISTS.

Dowden Edward, Lower Edmonton
Wilkinson Thomas, Fore st

CLOTHES DEALERS.

Hart Aaron, Fore st
Jones Henry, Fore st
Sheath Nathaniel, Fore st

COACH BUILDER.

Booker Eleazer, Fore st

COACH MASTERS.

Matthews Wm. Lower Edmonton
Matthews Wm. jun. Lwr. Edmonton
Willis John, Lower Edmonton
Winder Robert, Lower Edmonton

COAL MERCHANTS.

Beaton Andrew, Fore st
Burton Henry, Fore st
Collins Thomas, Lower Edmonton
Dickson Henry, Fore st
Heath William, Fore st
Lee Goodall, Fore st
Rowley William, Silver st

CORN CHANDLERS.

Clinker Isaac, Fore st
Clinker Martha, Fore st
Copland Thomas Cooke, Fore st
Fryer Henry, Lower Edmonton
Heath William, Fore st
Rowley William, Silver st

DYERS.

Cranston William, Fore st
Farrenberg John, Fore st

FIRE, &c. OFFICE AGENTS.

ATLAS, Andrew Beaton, Fore st
NORWICH UNION, John Brown, Lower Edmonton
PHŒNIX, Jas. Billingay, Fore st [st
ROYAL EXCHANGE, Benj. Rowley, Fore
SUN, George Corker, Fore st

FRUITERERS.

Jefkins Henry, Lower Edmonton
Phillips Jacob (& confectionr.) Fore st

FURNITURE BROKERS.

Aylin Benjamin, Fore st
Burton John Pritchard, Fore st
Rodds John (cabinet maker), Fore st

GROCERS & TEA DEALERS.
(See also Shopkeepers, &c.)

Beaton Mary and William, Fore st
Beckett Edward, Fore st
Dickinson Chas. Lower Edmonton
Dickson Henry (& tallow chandler, oilman & cheesemonger), Fore st
Groves Henry, Lower Edmonton
Hickman Frederick, Fore st
Kempton Elizabeth, Lwr. Edmonton
Thorn Thomas, Lower Edmonton

HAIR DRESSERS.

Garnett James, Silver st
Hayhow Eliz. Lower Edmonton

INNS & POSTING HOUSES.

Angel, George Boyd, Fore st
Bell, Mary Ann Gardner, Fore st

LINEN DRAPERS.
Beck John, Lower Edmonton
Nunneley Edward Coleman, Fore st
Revill Matthew, Fore st
Udall Robert, Fore st

MARKET GARDENERS.
Brown Samuel, Lower Edmonton
Chapple John, Bury st
Jefkins Henry, Lower Edmonton
Lashwood James, Tanner's end
May James, Tanner's end
Pennett Henry, Fore st.
Read Stephen, Hide
Sawyer Samuel, Hide
Vardon John, Bury st

MILLINERS & DRESS MAKRS.
Bygrave Sarah, Lower Edmonton
Liberty H. Lower Edmonton
Mitchell Emily, Fore st
Sell Ann, Lower Edmonton

NURSERY & SEEDSMEN.
Hardy John, Silver st
Hardy William, Silver st
Page Thomas, Fore st

PAINTERS, PLUMBERS AND GLAZIERS.
Brown John, Lower Edmonton
Brown Mary, Lower Edmonton
Brown Samuel, Fore st
Harding Robert, Fore st
Hogg Arthur, Lower Edmonton
Mander Edward, Lower Edmonton
Scott Alexander, Silver st
Tilley John, Lower Edmonton
Wall John Grimley, Fore st

SADDLERS AND HARNESS MAKERS.
Callacott William, Lower Edmonton
Cooley Richard, Fore st
Spendlove Robert, Fore st
Wescombe John, Fore st

SHOPKEEPERS & DEALRS IN GROCERS & SUNDRIES.
Allard James, Tanner's end
Barnard George, Fore st
Brand Richard, Lower Edmonton
Cropley Samuel, Claremont st
Downes Caroline (shoe warehouse), Fore street
Hall George, Fore st
Jennings Elizabeth, Fore st
Kerry James, Lower Edmonton
Kerry Susan, Fore st
Nelson John, Fore st
Tilley John, Lower Edmonton

STAY MAKERS.
Evans Elizabeth, Lower Edmonton
Pearson Ann, Lower Edmonton

STRAW HAT MAKERS.
Moston Jane, Lower Edmonton
Scott Elizabeth, Silver st

SURGEONS.
Fry Arthur, Fore st
Hammond & Biddle, Lower Edmonton
Nias Henry, Fore st

TAILORS.
Cranston John, Fore st
Davis Joseph, Fore st
FrostickWilliam Boswell, LowerEdmonton
Kerry John, Fore st
Viton John, Lower Edmonton
WinterburnThomas, LowerEdmontn
Woods James, Lower Edmonton

TAVERNS & PUBLIC HOUSES.
Bull, Martha Percival, Tanner's end
Cock, George Tucker, Houndsfield
Cross Keys, JamesSleigh, LowerEdmonton
Golden Fleece, Robert Wm. Reed, Fore st
Golden Lion, Thomas Clapham, Lower Edmonton
Horse & Groom, Thomas Moreton, Lower Edmonton
Jolly Farmer, JohnCamp, LowerEdmonton
King's Head, John Docking, LwrEdmontn
New Ferry, Benjamin Wicks, Cook's ferry
OverthrownCart, IsaacHodgkinson, Marsh side
Rose & Crown, Benjamin Dymant, Lower Edmonton
Stag & Hounds, William Willis, Bury st
Three Tuns, John Wescombe, Fore st
Two Brewers, John Canning, Tanner's end

TIMBER & DEAL MERCHNTS.
Corker George & Thomas, Fore st

WATCH MAKERS.
Ballard Henry, Fore st
Higgins Andrew, Fore st

WHEELWRIGHTS.
Collins John, Water lane
Gudgeon Thomas, Lower Edmonton
Hagger Benjamin, Lower Edmonton

Miscellaneous.
Billingay James, ironmonger, &c. Fore st
Burrell Jas. whip maker, Lower Edmonton
Clarkson William, cutler, Fore st
Coventry George, paper hanger, Fore st
Fearby John Wilson, brush maker, Lower Edmonton
Goodman Thomas, miller, Tanner's end
Gossett Robert, surveyor, Fore st
Graham Robert, hardwareman, Lower Edmonton
Mares Frederick, music teacher, Lower Edmonton
Martin Thomas, pawnbroker, Fore st
Mills John, cooper, Lower Edmonton
Pomfret John, poulterer, Fore st
Potts Stephen, china & glass dealer, Fore st
Richardson William, stone mason, Fore st
Robertson William, piano-forte maker, Fore st
Rogers William Henry, haberdasher, Lower Edmonton
SAVINGS' BANK, Bridge cottage—Daniel Judd, actuary
STATION HOUSE, Lower Edmonton—Robert Parker, keeper
Tilley George, locksmith, Lower Edmonton
UNION POORHOUSE, Lower Edmonton—Mr. Lamb, master; John Adlington, relieving officer
Watts Richard, type founder & printers' ink maker, Bury st

OMNIBUSES,
To LONDON, from the King's Head, Rose and Crown and Angel, every half-hour, from half-past seven in the morning until eight at night.

CARRIERS.
To LONDON, James Cowling, Daniel Robins, Ann Shadbolt & Richard Pepper, from their houses, daily.

ENFIELD AND NEIGHBOURHOOD.

ENFIELD, once a market town, is in the parish of its name and hundred of Edmonton, 10 miles N.E. from London and about two and a half from Edmonton—situated on the west of the road from the metropolis to Ware, in Hertfordshire. Prior to the Norman invasion Enfield was called *Infen* or *Enfen*, from the fens which surrounded it; but in Domesday-book it is designated *Enfelde*, from which arose its present name. The town consists chiefly of two streets, in which are a number of handsome dwellings; and the inhabitants are amply supplied with water from excellent springs. The character for healthfulness which this part of the country has long maintained, together with the general respectability of the neighbourhood, may in a great measure account for the numerous boarding-schools, for youth of both sexes, established in the village and its vicinity. An ancient building, called the Palace (in which, it is said, Edward VI held his court), now occupied as an academy, stands nearly opposite to the church: one of the rooms is wainscoted with fine English oak, and the ceiling is ornamented; over the mantle-piece are the arms of England and France, excellently carved; this must, in its day, have been an exquisite piece of workmanship—it is still in good preservation. In a field at the rear of the house is the famed cedar tree, planted about the year 1666, measuring nineteen feet in circumference at three feet from the ground. The celebrated Enfield Chase forms one of the boundaries of the town; at the time of its enclosure 7,032 acres were allotted to it. A handsome stone cross embellishes the market-place, on which is engraven the dates of the various charters granted for the holding of fairs and markets: an attempt was lately made to re-establish the market, which had been long discontinued; but, from different causes, it proved abortive. Previous to the decay of the market the tanning business was spiritedly carried on and supported; the only manufacturing establishments at present here are one for crape, and another, under government, for the supply of small-arms, but not extensive. The crown, in right of the dutchy of Lancaster, possesses the manor, and courts leet and baron are held annually at the 'King's Head' inn; a court of requests is likewise held, at the same place, on the last Tuesday in every month, for the recovery of debts under 40*s*.

The parish church of St. Andrew is an ancient structure, with a low square embattled tower; it contains many antique and several superb monuments, eminently deserving the attention of the stranger: the benefice is a vicarage, in the patronage of the master and fellows of Trinity college, Cambridge. There are also St. James' and Jesus' chapels of ease: the latter, at Forty Hill, was erected by and endowed at the sole expense of Christian Paul Meyer, Esq.; the appointment of the minister is vested in the vicar, and the whole of the sittings are free. There is, also, Christ church, a beautiful edifice, recently erected at Cockfosters, the western extremity of the parish, at the expense of Robert Lee Cooper Bevan, Esq., of Trent Park. There are places of worship for baptists, independents, Wesleyan methodists and presbyterians. At Chase side is a school, erected in 1838, conducted upon the principles of the British and Foreign School Society. A free grammar school, a school of industry, one for infants, apprenticeship funds, a lying-in institution, alms-houses, and several bequests for the relief of the poor, comprise the established charities. The country around Enfield, towards Southgate particularly, is truly delightful, and rural villas embellish the lovely scenery. East Lodge was the country seat of Charles I, and South Lodge was the favourite residence of the Earl of Chatham. Fairs are held, on the 23rd September for toys, &c., and on the 30th November for cattle. Population of the parish, in 1831, 8,812 persons.

POST OFFICE, Thomas Jelly, *Post Master*.—Letters from LONDON arrive every morning at nine and ten, afternoon at three and evening at six, and are despatched at the same hours.—Letters from the North arrive every morning at nine, and are despatched every evening at six.

GENTRY AND CLERGY.

Adams —, esq. Chase side
Addington Luke, esq. Chase side
Angerstein Frederick, esq. Hill lodge, Clay hill
Archer John, esq. Chase side
Barnes Lady —, Beech hill
Bennett J. esq. Enfield wash
Bevan David, esq. Belmont
Bevan Robt. Lee Cooper, esq. Trent park
BowlesHy.Carrington,esq.Bull's crss
Browning Richard, esq. Chase side
Browning Thomas, esq. Chase side
Burgess Wm. esq. Enfield highway
Burnham Thomas, esq. Baker st
Capes George, esq. Baker st
Challis Thomas, esq. Baker st
Childs Mrs. Gough park, Forty hill
Clulow Wm. Whitakr. esq. Enfield wash
Connop Major —, Durant's
Connop Woodham, esq. Durant's harbour
Cresswell Rev. Daniel, D. D. Silver st
Davies Rev. Samuel A. Holly bush
Dear Charles, esq. Baker st
Dixon John, esq. Forty hill
Dobson Thomas, esq. Forty hill
Drake —, esq. Enfield highway
Elmore W. C. esq. Enfield wash
Elphinstone Hon. Mrs. —, East lodge
Everett Wm. esq. Chase side house
Fagg Thomas, esq. Chase side
Fauntleroy Robert, esq. Clay hill
Fosbroke Rev. —, Chase side
Gisler Mrs. —, Turkey st
Green —, esq. Hadley common
Harman Edward, esq. Clay hill
Harper Chas. David, esq. Chase side
Harper William, esq. Chase side
Harrison Daniel, esq. Chase side
Hartley John, esq. Silver st
Holt Capt. Francis, Baker st
Jones Rev. Thos. Enfield highway
Kelham Mrs. —, London lane
Lachlan —, esq. Chase side
Lewis Mrs. E. Old Park
Linwood William, esq. Forty hill
Lochner Capt. —, Forty hill
Maples Mrs. —, Baker st
Mark William, esq. Silver st
Martin Mrs. —, Chase side
Martin Col. Thomas, Baker st
May Dr. Thomas, Enfield
Meyer James, esq. Forty hill
Monk Mrs. —, Enfield
Mott Richard, esq. Chase side
Noble Mark, esq. Chase side
Noble Thomas, esq. Chase side
Palk Lady Elizabeth, Rectory house
Palmer Richard, esq. Ridgway oaks
Paris Thomas, esq. Chase side
Pateshall P. esq. Turkey st
Porter Mrs. —, Chase side
Rahn Dr. —, Chase side
Riddell John, esq. Windmill hill
Riddell Mrs. Rose, Windmill hill
Russell Rev. John, Forty hill
Sarel Andrew Lovering, esq. Turkey st
Seward Charles, esq. Chase side
Sherwin Mrs. —, Silver st
Stevens Joseph Jones, esq. Enfield wash
Strange John, esq. Silver st
Stratton Henry, esq. Baker st
Thompson Mrs. —, Baker st
Toogood Miss —, Forty hill
Townsend Miss —, Baker st
Tucker Benjamin, esq. Clay hill
Welbank Richard, esq. Clay hill
White Thos. Holt, esq. Chase lodge
Wilkinson Abrhm. esq. White webbs
Williams Benjamin, esq. Baker st
Williams Edward, esq. Chase side
Wright Chas. esq. Enfield highway

ACADEMIES AND SCHOOLS.

Not otherwise described are Day Schools.

Albert William, Baker st
Blake Elizabeth, Enfield
BRITISH SCHOOL, Chase side—Henry Wakley, master; Sarah Robinson, mistress
Cheney Ann (boarding), Baker st
Fielding Thomas, Enfield highway
FREE GRAMMAR SCHOOL, Church yard—James Emery, master
Freeman Stephen (brding.) Baker st
Gotty Margaret (brding.) Chase side
Hainworth Wm. Nag's Head lane
Hardy Mary Ann, Enfield wash
Lake & Dorey (ladies' boarding), Chase side
May Dr. Thos. (boarding), Enfield
NATIONAL SCHOOL, Enfield highway—George Turner, master; Emma Andrews, mistress
Rignall John Riley, Silver st
Ruston Miss (boarding), Enfield
SCHOOL OF INDUSTRY, Church yard—Sarah Young, mistress
Weare Thomas (boarding), Baker st

ATTORNEYS.

Lucena Stephen Lancaster, Enfield
Sawyer & Beckett, Silver st
Sawyer Henry (and clerk to magistrates, & deputy coroner), Silver st

AUCTIONEERS & APPRAISRS.

Barrow Thomas T. Baker st
Compton Thos. (and land and timber surveyor), Enfield
Leifchild William, Baker st
Richards & Strick, Baker st

BAKERS & FLOUR DEALERS.

Cox John William, Chase side
Green Edward, Enfield wash
Hicks Henry, Chase side
Hoy William, Enfield highway
Hubbard Jos. (gingerbread), Baker st
Jelly Joseph, Silver st
Jelly Thomas, Enfield
Meed Daniel, Forty hill
Silver Charles, Enfield highway
Skingsley Henry, New lane
Townsend Daniel, Enfield
Young Samuel, Baker st

BLACKSMITHS & FARRIERS.

Bird John, Enfield highway
Merison Mark, Baker st
Parbery Thomas, Nag's Head lane
Potts Joseph, Baker st
Searle William, Windmill hill
Stoton Thomas, Enfield highway
Swain Edward, Baker st

BOOT AND SHOE MAKERS.

Bliss Thomas, Chase side
Brown George, Baker st
Bucknell Robert, Baker st
Carruthers John, Chase side
Cornish John, Enfield highway
Dell John, Baker st
Draper David, Chase side
Gunner William, Enfield highway
Harnett John, Market place
Leech Charles Edward, Chase side
Manning John, Silver st
March John, Enfield
Packer Moses, Silver st
Prime William, Forty hill
Staker William, Chase side
Stilwell Richard, Windmill hill

BRAZIERS AND TINMEN.

Colby Joseph, Baker st
Errington Edward, Baker st
Grimbly Robert, Chase side

BREWERS.

Brailsford Richard, Baker st
Eisdells & Martin, Chase side
Wheelwright John, Enfield highway

BRICKLAYERS.

Bennett William, Enfield highway
Evans William, Chase side
Mitchell John, Silver st
Patman John Prior, Enfield

BUTCHERS.

Belsham Joseph, Enfield highway
Castle John, Windmill hill
Gocher Jacob, Baker st
Herbert William, Enfield wash
Hollingsworth Daniel, Baker st
Jones William, Baker st
Lee William (pork), Silver st
Pennyfather John, Chase side
Price Thomas, Enfield highway
Taylor James, Enfield
Taylor James Thomas, Enfield
Taylor Thomas Forman, Enfield
Young Walter, Baker st

CARPENTERS, &c.

Bilton William, Silver st
Carpenter Jesse (and upholsterer and undertaker)
Corne Robert, Baker st
Draper Henry (builder), Silver st
Forster Thomas, Silver st
Graystone Ebenezer, Chase side
Hammond Charles Haws, Baker st
Hill John, Forty hill
Smith George, Baker st
Smith William, Baker st

CHYMISTS AND DRUGGISTS.

Smartt George Lifford, Baker st
Tuff John (and oil and colourman), Enfield

COACH PROPRIETORS.

Glover John, Baker st
Glover Thomas, Market place
Guiver Jasper, Enfield highway

COAL & CORN MERCHANTS AND DEALERS.

Cox William, Chase side
Deane Robert, Enfield wash
Reynolds Thomas, Forty hill
Stalley John, Silver st
Warren William, Enfield wash
Taylor Thomas, Chase side

CONFECTIONERS.

Alsop George, Enfield
Gibbon Ebenezer, Enfield

COOPERS.

Sheffield Thomas, Chase side
Taylor Mary, Baker st
Wingrove James, Baker st

FIRE, &c. OFFICE AGENTS.

ALLIANCE, Jas. Emery, Church yard
GLOBE, Thomas Compton, Enfield
GUARDIAN, Stephen Lancaster Lucena, Enfield
PHŒNIX, Charles Smith, Baker st
ROYAL EXCHANGE, John Prior Patman, Enfield

GROCERS & TEA DEALERS.

(See also Shopkeepers, &c.)

Barnett Samuel, Baker st
Dickson Henry, Enfield
Lake William, Enfield
Lyne John, Baker st
Stalley John, Silver st
Taylor Thomas, Chase side
Terry Edward,

HAIR DRESSERS.

Belcher Thomas, Enfield highway
Coles Charles, Silver st
Duffey Matthew, Enfield
Pawley William, Baker st

INNS.
Goat (and posting house), Thomas Reynolds, Forty hill
Greyhound (& posting house), Geo. Holt, Enfield
King's Head, Wm. Glover, Market place

LINEN DRAPERS.
Hammond Thomas, Baker st
Luttman John, Enfield
Riches George, Baker st
Shave George, Enfield

MARKET GARDENERS.
Baxter Henry, Baker st
Coomes Samuel, Baker st
Coomes Sarah, Baker st
Cracknell John, Baker st
Cracknell William, Bull's cross
Mitchell William, Enfield highway
Wilson George, Enfield highway
Wilson Josiah, Enfield highway
Winterborn Joseph, London lane
Woodhouse Joseph, Baker st

MILLINERS AND DRESS MAKERS.
Fox Sarah, Enfield
Graves Mary, Enfield
Leech Mary and Lucy, Enfield

NURSERY & SEEDSMEN.
Johnson Isaac, Chase side
Joyning Robert, Enfield wash
Meikle George, Enfield
Robinson Edward, Chase side
Rowsell Peter, Holly bush

PAINTERS, PLUMBERS AND GLAZIERS.
Butcher John, Chase side
Cutbush Thomas, Enfield
Hill John, Forty hill
Hobbs William, Enfield
Matthews Chamberlain, Baker st
Matthews Joseph, Baker st

POULTERERS.
Game James, Baker st
Wall Lucy, Enfield

SADDLERS AND HARNESS MAKERS.
Crossingham Stephn. Enfield highwy
Grout Thomas, Silver st
Phipps George, Enfield
Smith William, Enfield highway

SHOPKEEPERS & DEALRS IN GROCERIES & SUNDRIES.
Allen Charles, Baker st
Ansell Anne, Enfield highway
Baxter Henry, Baker st
Boswell Thomas, Chase side
Chase Francis, Holly bush
Cocher John, Enfield highway
Davies Hugh, Enfield highway
Dean Robert, Enfield wash
Dodsworth Thomas, Enfield wash
Draper David, Chase side
Ewington John, Chase side
Hasler Mary, Forty hill
Jude Ann, Chase side
Margetson Elizabeth, Chase side
Parker Ann, Enfield wash
Pasfield John, Chase side
Sheffield Martha, Enfield
Smith James, Enfield highway
Wallis Thomas, Enfield wash
Warren Richard, Enfield highway
Warren William, Enfield wash
Wilkinson John, Enfield wash

STRAW HAT MAKERS.
Bibbey Ann, Market place
Britten Harriet, Enfield highway
Chester Ann, Holly bush
Coventry Elizabeth, Enfield
Smith Lydia, Baker st

SURGEONS.
Asbury Jacob Vale, Silver st
Holt William Henry, Baker st
Jameson John, Enfield highway
Millar John, Baker st
Tate Robert, Enfield highway

TAILORS.
Boswell Thomas, Chase side
Coles Henry, Baker st
Coles William, Enfield
Cracknell Charles, Church lane
Deller John, London lane
Guiver John, Enfield highway
Ravenhill Samuel, Enfield highway
Rumney James, Baker st
Taylor Thomas, Baker st
Westmoreland John, Silver st

TAVERNS & PUBLIC HOUSES.
Bell, Thomas Evans, Baker st
Bell, Francis Robinson, Enfield wash
Black Horse, Wm. Walpole, Enfield highwy
Canteen, Thomas Martin, Enfield loch
Crown and Three Horse Shoes, James Jarvis, Chase side
George Inn, Robert Mathison, Enfield
Holly Bush, Grace Brewer, Holly bush
King's Arms, Augusts. Aves, Enfield highwy
Nag's Head, William Hall, Enfield
Old Bull, John Herbert, Bull's cross
Old Sarjeant, Daniel Webb, Parsonage lane
Plough, William Brown, Turkey st
Red Lion, Fredk. Amey, Enfield highway
Rising Sun, William Jordan, Chase side
Rose & Crown, Martin Williams, Enfield highway
Rummer, William Camfield (& horse dealer) [Enfield
Sun & Woolpack, Jno. Gilbert, Enfield wash
Wheat Sheaf, William Henry Ade, Baker st
White Lion, Jasper Guiver, Enfield highwy

TOY DEALERS.
Fox Rebecca, Silver st
Lake Mary, Enfield
Leech Mary, Enfield

WATCH AND CLOCK MAKERS
Harwood Frederick, Baker st
Ridley Thomas, Silver st

WHEELWRIGHTS.
Etteridge Thomas, Enfield wash
Hall Edward, Enfield highway
How James, Enfield highway
Merison Mark, Forty hill
Parsons George, Enfield wash
Wren Samuel, Baker st

WINE & SPIRIT MERCHANT.
Smith Charles, Baker st

Miscellaneous.
Armer Thomas, whitesmith, Baker st
Barrow Thomas Taylor, bookseller, &c. Baker st
Battaglia Theodore, professor of languages, Enfield highway
Capes George, registrar of births & deaths, Baker st
Colby Joseph, ironmonger, Baker st
Corne Robert, hatter, Baker st
Drane William George, fruiterer, Enfield
Ewington John, furniture broker, Baker st
Gofton William, clothes dealer, Silver st
GOVERNMENT ARMORY, Enfield loch—George Lovell, superintendent
Hobson Aaron, stone mason, London lane
Leach Maria Elizabeth, teacher of music, Silver st
Logsdon Joel, coach maker, Enfield
Nunn Joshua, leather cutter, Enfield
Prior William, carver & gilder, Baker st
Reynolds Thomas, proprietor of the specific for gout and rheumatism, Enfield
Searle John, basket maker, Chase side
SHOREDITCH WORKHOUSE (for children), Baker st—William Hawes, master
WORKHOUSE, Chase side—Henry Edward Parker, master
Young Henry, road surveyor, Enfield

OMNIBUSES.
To LONDON, — Glover's *Omnibuses*, from the King's Head, Enfield, every morning at half-past seven and half-past eight, forenoon at ten and afternoon at two and four—and from the White Lion and Bell, Enfield highway, every morning at eight and half-past eight and afternoon at three, four & half-past five.

CARRIERS.
To LONDON, Thomas Young, Edward Anderson and Joseph Moore, daily.

FINCHLEY, HENDON AND NEIGHBOURHOODS.

FINCHLEY village and parish are in the Finsbury division of the hundred of Ossulton, the former being seven miles N. N. W. from London; the parish is nearly eighteen miles in circumference. The great north-western road, through Highgate, passes to the east of the parish church, and is joined by another road from Saint John's wood, Paddington; several other roads have been formed across Finchley common, which formerly comprised upwards of one thousand acres, now nearly all enclosed. On this spot General Monk drew up his army in 1660; and here, in 1780, an encampment was formed after the riots promoted by Lord George Gordon. The church, dedicated to St. Mary, is a stone edifice, in the later style of English architecture, and contains several ancient monuments; the benefice is a rectory, in the gift of the see of London; the present incumbent is the Rev. Ralph Worsley. The other places of worship are a chapel of ease at Whetstone, and others for independents and Wesleyan methodists. A school, supported by public subscription, and six alms-houses, comprise the charities. A market for pigs, held on Monday, was formerly numerously attended; it has long been on the decline—the little business now done is transacted at the 'George' inn. The parish of Finchley contained, by the last returns, 3,210 inhabitants.

HENDON is a village and parish in the hundred of Gore—the former seven miles N. W. from London, and the latter adjoining Finchley parish. The village, though irregularly built, occupies an agreeable situation, on an eminence in a small vale, watered by the river Brent, over which is a stone bridge; the environs are pleasant, presenting many rural walks and fine scenery, adorned with handsome villas. The places of worship are, the parish church, dedicated to Saint Mary; a new one, at Mill-hill, completed at the expense of the late William Wilberforce, Esq.; and chapels for baptists, independents and Wesleyan methodists. Two schools upon the national system, and Daniels' alms-houses for six poor men and four women, are the public charities: one of the school-rooms is erected upon a piece of ground presented by David Garrick, Esq., the celebrated actor, who was lord of the manor, in the year 1766. The parish, which is extensive, contained, at the period of the last census, 3,110 inhabitants.

POST OFFICE, Church end, FINCHLEY, John Bailey, *Post Master.*—Letters from LONDON arrive every morning at nine, afternoon at one and evening at seven, and are despatched every morning at nine and afternoon at four.

POST OFFICE, FINCHLEY COMMON, Robert Stephens, *Post Master.*—Letters from LONDON arrive every forenoon at a quarter before ten and afternoon at five, and are despatched every morning at half-past nine and afternoon at half-past four.—Letters are despatched (by penny post) to BARNET every evening at seven.

POST OFFICE, Brent street, HENDON, Robert Young, *Post Master.*—Letters from LONDON, &c. arrive every morning at eight, noon at twelve and night at eight, and are despatched every morning at nine and afternoon at four.

*** *The letters* F., F. C. *and* H. *attached to an address signify respectively* FINCHLEY, FINCHLEY COMMON *and* HENDON.

NOBILITY, GENTRY, AND CLERGY.

AckermanMr.Isaac,Finchleycommn
Allen Mr. Robt. Golder's green, H.
Andrews Mr. Jos. Finchley common
Andrews Mr.Thos. Finchley common
Bacon John, esq. Fryern watch
Balls Mr. James, Finchley lodge
Bamford Capt. —, Collin Deep, H.
Barker Mr. Wm. East end, Finchley
Barron Mr. Henry, Park farm, F.
Belcher Mr. Thomas, East end, F.
Block Mr. James, Brent lodge, F.
Briant Mrs. —, Mill hill, Hendon
Brown Rev. Joseph, Mill hill, H.
Burls Mr. William, Brent lodge, H.
Butler Edwd. Robt. esq. East end, F.
Butler Mr. Thos. Ballard's lane, F.
Chapell Mr. George, Fryern park
Chaplin Mr. Wm. Courthouse farm, Nether st, Finchley
Claridge Mr. Robert Allen, Church end, F.
ComptonMr.Jermh.Commonside,F.
Cookes Mrs. Ann, Nether st, F.
CooperMr.IsaacSutton,nr.Tollbar,F.
Courtney Mr. F. B. Ballard's lane, F.
Crowen Mr. —, Fryern park
Cugnoni James, esq. M.D. Whetstone
Cullum Mr. Samuel, East end, F.
Dignum Mr. Philip Jas. Fryern park
Dixon Mr. Richard, Oak lodge, F.
English Mrs. Susanna B. East end, F.
Fanning Mr. William, Elm place, F.
Field Mr. Geo.Ventris, Park place,F.
Ford Mr. Thomas, Common side
Frost Mr. Henry, Common side
Gaddesden Mr.Roger,Burroughs, H.
Gammell Mr.—, Bellevue cottage, F.
Gibbs Mr. —, Fryern park
Gilbert Mr. Wm. Finchley common
Grisewood Mrs.Eleanor, East end, F.
Hankey Mrs. Isabella, Grass farm, F.
Harding Mr. Joseph, East end, F.
Hooper Mr. Wm. Ballard's lane, F.
Hughes Mr. Richard, East end, F.
Hunter Mr. David, East end cottage
Innis Capt. John, Mill hill, Hendon
Jarman Mr. —, Fryern park
Kingston Mr.Valentn.Fallow corner, F.
Knight Mr. Valentine, East end, F.
Lambert Wm. esq. Woodhouses, F.
Lermitte Jas. esq. near Finchley C.
Monro Mr. Jas. East end, Finchley
Morrison Mr. Charles, Strawberry vale, F. C.
Morwood Mrs. Chas. Smart's place, East end, F.
Musson Mr. —, Ballard's lane, F.
Nelson William, esq. Finchley lodge
Orchard Thos. esq. Finchley common
Penny Mr. —, Ballard's lane, F.
Platt Mr. —, Ballard's lane, Finchley
Pouncy Mr. John Wm. East end, F.
Prince Mr. Daniel, Brent st, Hendon
Raphael Mr.Lewis,Golder's green, H.
Ray Mrs. Ann, East end, Finchley
Reeder Henry, esq. M.D. East end, F.
ReeveMr.Jno.Wm. Finchley commn
Rew Mr. William Pell, East end, F.
Rhodes Abrhm. R. esq. Mill hill, H.
Roscoe Robert, esq. Church end, F.
Roscoe Mr. Robt. Finchley common
Rouse Mr. Edwd. Finchley common
Ryder Mr. Thomas, Parson st, H.
Salvin Anthony, esq. Elmshurst, F.
Sauer—, esq.Horseshoe bottom,F.C.
Shuter John, esq. Mill hill, Hendon
Simpson Mrs. Eliz. Bow cottage, F.
Spencer Mr. John, Fallow corner, F.
Stanton Mr. Stephen, Page st, H.
Sykes Mr. —, Fryern park
Taylor Mr. John, Fallow corner, F.
Tenterden Rt. Hon. Lord, Hendon pl
TillettMr.John, Park place, near F.C.
Todd Mr. Jno. Cold Arbor place, F.C.
Tomlinson Mr. H. B. Finchley comn
Trewhett Mr. George, Long lodge, Nether st, Finchley
Ware Mr. Samuel, Hendon hall
Warren Mr. Robert, Mill hill, H.
Webster Mr. Edward Webster Bullock, Church yard, Hendon
Wheeler Mr. Gervas, Nether st, F.
Williams Rev. Theodore, Hendon
Wimbush Samuel, esq. Finchley
Wood Mr. Alexr. Finchley lodge
Worsley Rev. Ralph, Nether st, F.

ACADEMIES & SCHOOLS.

Not otherwise described are Day Schools.

Bolton Horatio Nelson, Woodland house, East end, F.
Cousins Fredk. (boarding), Ballard's lane, F.
Cousins Misses (boarding), Ballard's lane, Finchley
Gee Mrs. (boarding), Brent st, H.
Gowring JohnWm. Geo. (boarding), Nether st, F.
LockwoodWm.(boardg.) Burroughs, Hendon
NATIONAL SCHOOL, Church end, Finchley—Wm. Joyner, master; Ann Mills, mistress
PAROCHIAL SCHOOL, Church lane, Hendon—William Charsley, master; Miss Harrington, mistress
Smith John Stantial (boarding), Terrace house, Common side
Thompson Clara, Strawberry place, Finchley C.
Worsley Rev. Henry, LL.D. (boardg), Manor house, F.

BAKERS.

Bailey John, Church end, Finchley
Bean Ann, Bull's lane, Finchley
Boond Robert, Mill hill, Hendon
Buckell William, Mill hill, Hendon
Clark Samuel, Burroughs, Hendon
Hearn William, Church end, Hendon
Pooley Ann, Hog market, Finchley
Salsbury William, Brent st, Hendon
Slough John, Lodge lane, F. C.
Wand Edwd. Trusthard, East end, F.

BLACKSMITHS & FARRIERS.

Armitage John, Brent st. Hendon.
Dodd James, East end, Finchley
Humphreys Elizabeth, Lodge lane
Irons Edward, Finchley common
James Benjamin (and bell hanger), Church end, Finchley
Jones John, the Hyde, Hendon
Lodge John, Mill hill, Hendon
Suckling Josiah, Brent st, Hendon

BOOT & SHOE MAKERS.

Audsley Thomas, Church end, F.
Bray George, Lodge lane, F. C.
Chipp William, Cuckold's haven, F.
Freeman John, East end, Finchley
Frost Thomas, Hog market, Finchley
Gale Richard, Finchley common
Green George, Brent st, Hendon
Mott Joseph, Bull's lane, Finchley
Pain George, Ballard's lane, Finchley
Williams Richard, Lodge lane, F.
Woodstock James, Burroughs, H.

BRICKLAYERS.

Nicholl Thos. Parson st, H.
Plowman Mark (& builder), East end, F.
Russell Mary, Finchley common
Steward Geo. Brent st, H.
Wood Jas. (& auctioneer), Mill hill, H.

BUTCHERS.

Attkins Samuel, East end, Finchley
Barnes John, Brent st, Hendon
Bryant Isaac (& pork), Burroughs, H.
Bush James, North end, Finchley
Claridge Edward, Hog market, F.
Howard Robert, Burroughs, Hendon
Laman John, East end, Finchley
London Wm. Burroughs, Hendon
Richardson William, the Hyde
Satchell Thomas, Mill hill, Hendon
Summerlin Thomas, Church end, F.
Wright William, Church end, F.

CARPENTERS.

Allpress Philip, East end, Finchley
Fleurriet Dav. (& builder), Brent st, H.
Freemantle Moses, Church end, F.
Legg Richard, Church end, Finchley
Malkin Henry, Parsons st, Hendon
Oldfield Charles, the Hyde
Poyser Robert (& builder), Brent st, H.
Russell Richd. near Finchley commn
Skillman William, Mill hill, Hendon

COAL DEALERS.

Jones John (& corn), Lodge la. F. C.
Malkin Henry, Parsons st, Hendon
Slough John, Lodge lane, F. C.
Stevenson John, Hog market, F.
Young Robert, Brent st, Hendon

GARDENERS.

Butler Walter, Lodge lane, F. C.
Evans Evan, Church end, Finchley
Franklin James (& seedsman) Church end, Finchley
Milne William (& nursery & seedsman), F. C.

GROCERS AND DEALERS IN SUNDRIES.

Burton William, Brent st, Hendon
Conner Robert, Finchley Common
Dell Joseph, Hog market, Finchley
Drew Cecilia & H. Church end
Evans Evan, Church end, Finchley
Foskett William, High road, F. C.
Hayes Robert, Cuckold's haven
Howard Robert, Burroughs, Hendon
Jones John, Lodge lane, F. C.
Kerridge Francis, Ballard's lane, F.
Kitchener Samuel, Mill hill, Hendon
Pope James, Church end, Finchley
Randell John, East end, Finchley
Slough John, Lodge lane, F. C.
Smart John, Brent st, Hendon
Stephens Robert (& fire office agent), East end, Finchley
Tattam John, Hog market, Finchley
Taunton John, Golder's green, H.
Welsh John, Burroughs, Hendon
Young Robert, Brent st, Hendon

HABERDASHERS.

Craig Samuel F. East end, F.
Robbins Eliza (& milliner), Brent st, H.

PLUMBERS, PAINTERS AND GLAZIERS.

Graves George, near Red Lion, F. C.
Hudgell John, Brent st, Hendon

PLUMBERS, &c.—Continued.
Hudson John, Burroughs, Hendon
Jones Thomas, Church end, Hendon
Nash Thomas, Church end, Finchley
Taunton John, Golder's green, H.
Worley John, East end, Finchley

SADDLERS.
Kimpton John, Finchley common
Kimpton John, Brent st, Hendon

SURGEONS.
Corrie James, East end, Finchley
Harrison John, Finchley common
Holgate John Wyndham, Brent st, H.
White John, Finchley common

TAILORS.
Burgess James, Mill hill
Davies John, East end, Finchley
Johnson William, Mill hill, Hendon
Lawrance Aaron, East end, Finchley
Meany Andrew, East end, Finchley
Prior Thomas, Burroughs, Hendon
Ridenton William, Finchley commn
Tow James Abel, Brent st, Hendon
Ward Thomas (& draper), Ballard's lane, Finchley
Wrigglesworth John, Bull's lane, F.

TAVERNS & PUBLIC HOUSES.
Adam & Eve, John Hamilton, Mill hill, H.
Angel & Crown, Jas. Lemaire, Mill hill, H.
Bald-faced Stag, Jno. Moore, Finchley com
Bell, Charles Thomas Davies, Brent st, H.
Five Bells, Richard Wisdom, East end, F.
George, Abraham Schofield, East end, F.
Green Man, Chas. Spelt, Finchley commn
Greyhound, Wm. Winfield, Church end, H
Hammers, Geo. Johnson, Mill hill [F.
King of Prussia, John Boyce, Church end,
King's Head, Jacob Hemmy, Mill hill, H.
Plough, Wm. Willison, Mill hill, Hendon
Queen's Head Inn, James Love, Church end, Finchley
Red Lion, Sarah and Sarah Muggeridge, near Hog market, Finchley
Sun, Thomas Ralph, Highwood hill, H.
Swan, John Taunton, Golder's green, H.
Swan-with-Two-Necks, Catherine Baker, Finchley common [Finchley comn
Swan-with-Two-Nicks, William Carter,
Three Crowns, Pearce & Ray, Highwood hill, Hendon [common
Torrington Arms, George Osman, Finchley
Welsh Harp, Benj. Flurry, Edgware road
White Bear, John Perkins, Burroughs, H.
White Lion, Neat Ladd, Finchley common

WHEELWRIGHTS.
Lee Halsey, Finchley common
Marsh John, the Hole, Hendon
Taylor George, Brent st, Hendon
Wise William, Finchley common

Miscellaneous.
Beal William, parchment manufacturer, Tinker's bottom, Finchley
Beavis John, dairyman, East end, Finchley
Charsley William, registrar of births and deaths, Church lane, Hendon [corner
Cobley Wm. clerk of the market, Fallows
Crooks Lucy, dress maker, East end, F.
Earl Thomas, hair dresser, Brent st, H.
Holden Thos. dairyman, Finchley commn
Howell Geo. drawing master, Finchley C.
Hutton Anthony, furniture broker, &c. East end, Finchley
Jones Mary, draper, &c. Church end, F.
Marshall William, furniture broker, Finchley common [end, F.
Santer & Barrow, beast salesmen, East
Skaife John S. clerk to the magistrates, Cherrytree hill, Finchley
Smart Nevil, brick maker, Finchley comn
Warren Thomas, cooper, Parson's st, H.
Woolley William, coach proprietor, &c. Mill hill, Hendon

COACHES & OMNIBUSES.
To LONDON, Ellis' *Coaches*, from the Queen's Head, Finchley, every morning at a quarter before nine—Robinson's *Coaches*, from the Torrington Arms, Finchley common, every morning (Sunday excepted) at half-past eight, and on Sunday evening at seven—Woolley's *Coaches*, from Mill hill, every morning at eight and evening at seven; go thro' Hendon—and Philip Smith's *Omnibus*, from the George and Five Bells Inn, Finchley, every morning (Sunday excepted) at half-past nine, afternoon at one and evening at half-past six, and on Sunday evening at half-past seven.
⁎ For other Coaches passing over Finchley common, see BARNET, page 184.

CARRIERS.
To LONDON, Charles Drewell, from Ballard's lane, Finchley, Robert Brettell, from Mill hill, goes thro Hendon, and P. Hampton, from Finchley common, every morning (Sunday excepted)

FULHAM,

WITH PARSON'S GREEN, WALHAM GREEN, NORTH END (OR ST. JOHN'S) & NEIGHBOURHOODS.

FULHAM is a parish and village in the hundred of Ossulton, four miles s. w. by w. from Hyde Park Corner; situated on the north bank of the Thames, and connected with Putney, in Surrey, by a wooden bridge over the river. This is a populous parish, and comprises Walham Green, Parson's Green and North End, or St. John's, and formerly Hammersmith, which has lately been separated from Fulham and erected into a distinct parish. The earliest mention we find made of Fulham, occurs in a grant of the manor by Tyrhtilus, bishop of Hereford, to Erkenwald, bishop of London, and his successors, about the year 691; in which grant it is called *Fulanham;* other authorities have named it *Fullonham, Fullenham,* and *Foulham.* In the vicinity of Fulham are several extensive nursery grounds, and much of the land is occupied by market gardeners. A manufactory for earthenware, in imitation of porcelain, was established here so far back as 1684; but the fine manufacture has been superseded by that of jars, pots, &c. of stone-ware. The place is well lighted with gas, from works situated at Sand's end, at the extremity of the parish.

The parish church of All Saints stands near the water side, and is an ancient stone building, consisting of a nave, chancel, and two aisles; at the west end is a handsome Gothic tower, 95 feet in height (built, it is conjectured, about the 14th century), containing a set of excellent bells. The living comprises a rectory and vicarage; the former is a sinecure, in the patronage of the bishop of London, and the latter in the presentation of the rector; the Rev. George Robert Baker is the incumbent, and the Rev. J. W. North the present curate. Besides the church, there are places of worship for various religious classes. A school has been erected here, at the expense of £600., in which children (80 of whom are clothed) are educated upon the system of Dr. Bell; there are likewise an infants' school, twelve almshouses for poor widows, and a union poorhouse. The bishop of London's palace, situated on the bank of of the Thames, is a brick edifice, and consists of two courts; the principal entrance into the great quadrangle is on the west side, through an arched gateway: it was built by bishop Fitzjames, in the reign of Henry VII; no curiosity is excited by its outward appearance, nor does it, indeed, internally possess any object to gratify the traveller's research; the building, with the grounds, embrace about 37 acres, and the whole is surrounded by a moat, over which are two bridges. There are numerous beautiful residences seated along the banks of the Thames, in the immediate vicinage of Fulham; and the approach to the village by water presents a rich variety of elegant seats, gardens, and plantations, the entire combining to produce a delightful landscape of highly refined scenery. The parish of Fulham contained, by the returns for 1831, 7,317 inhabitants.

PARSON'S GREEN, is a pleasant village in the parish of Fulham, and derives its name from the Rectory-house, which stands on the west side of the green; it lies about midway between Fulham and Walham Green, and stages are constantly passing through it. Many good residences and several respectable school establishments are in this neighbourhood. A fair was formerly held here on the 17th of August, but it has been discontinued for some years.

WALHAM GREEN, in the same parish as Parson's Green, was formerly called *Wendon Green,* and was afterwards varied to *Wandon, Wansdon, Wandham,* and *Walham Green,* by which latter appellation it is now recognized. It consists principally of one main street, which branches off into the high road to London. The population of late years has much increased, which has rendered the erection of a chapel of ease necessary, and a neat structure was completed in 1828; it contains a beautiful window of stained glass, the subject of which is the Transfiguration. There are also two chapels for dissenters, and a national and infants' schools for children of both sexes. In the neighbourhood are several superior boarding schools.

NORTH END, or ST. JOHN'S, in the same parish, extends from Walham Green to Hammersmith, and contains some very handsome dwellings. In this hamlet are two private establishments, ('Normand House' and 'Beaufort House,') for the reception of insane persons. A large ale brewery, called the 'North End Brewery,' is situated on the Kensington side of the village.

POST, *Receiving-Houses* at William Sadler's, High street, FULHAM; at Robert Crunder's, shopkeeper, PARSON'S GREEN; and at Charles Griffin's, WALHAM GREEN.—Letters from LONDON arrive every morning at half-past nine, afternoon at half-past one, half-past two and half-past four, and are despatched every morning at half-past ten, afternoon at half-past two and half-past five and night at half-past seven.

*** *The names are in* FULHAM *when the streets only and not the village are mentioned.*

NOBILITY, GENTRY AND CLERGY.

Aldred Richd. esq. Wansdown house
Andrews Mr. John, Ivy lodge, Fulham road
Arnold Mr. W. J. D. 5 Stamford villas
Atkins Mrs. —, Stamford house
Austin Mrs. —, 10 Elysium row, King's road
Bagshaw Mrs. —, North end terrace
Baker Rev. Robt. Geo. Church row
Barnard Mrs. Mary, Fulham house
Barnes Robert, esq. 1 Hermitage cottages, St. John's
Beckford Wm. esq. Peterboro house
Belfield Thos. esq. Parson's Green
Blachford John, esq. North End
Bloomfield the Right Hon. Lord Bishop of London, Fulham palace
Burchell William, esq. Churchfield house, King's road
Brock Edward, esq. St. John's
Bunnett Mr. George, Church row
Byham Mr. William, St. John's
Caddell Rev. Henry, 3 Hermitage cottages, St. John's
Carlton Thos. esq. Parson's Green
Catley Stephen Reed, esq. Grove bnk
Caufield Mr. —, Heckfield cottage
Chadd George, esq. Willow bank house, Fulham
Champion George, esq. Dorset villa
Coates Benj. esq. Walham Green
Collett Kenrick, esq. Holcroft house, Fulham
Collins Captain Charles, Pomona place, King's road
Collins Mrs. Mary, North End
Coomes John, esq. St. John's villa
Croker Mr. Thomas Crofton, Rosamond's bower, Parson's Green
Curzon Hon. Sidney Roper, the Hermitage, St. John's
Dale Joseph, esq. Kensington hall,
Daniels John, esq. East end house, Parson's Green
Daubeney Mrs. —, Pomona pl, King's road
Dawson Capt. —, North End cottage
De Lattre John M. esq. St. John's villa
Down Thos. Thornton, esq. St. John's
Edmonds John Thomas, esq. Rose cottage
Ekins Mrs. —, 2 Hermitage cottage, St. John's
Feuilade Geo. R. esq. Rose cottage, St. John's
Franklin Mr. Jos. Walham Green
Galliny Mr. Arthur, St. John's
Gerrard Mr. Lund, St. John's
Gillow Mrs. —, St. John's
Green Mrs. Eliz. 4 Stamford villas
Harcourt George V. esq. M. P. Broom house
Harding Mr. Wm. Tyfyree cottages, St. John's
Hatton Mr. George, St. John's
Higgins Captain —, Pomona place, King's road
Howard Mrs. —, Church row
Hullmandell Mr. Charles, Acacia cottage, Parson's cross
Hunt Jno. esq. 1 Myrtle pl, St. John's
Keates Mr. —, Parson's Green
Kender William, esq. Purser's cross
King Charles, esq. Craven cottage
King Mr. Fredk. Parson's Green lane
King Mrs. Hannah, 23 Stamford villas
Kitchener Mr. Thomas, St. John's
Lamb Mrs. Elizabeth, North End
Laurie John, esq. Munster house
Layton James, esq. Parson's Green
Lee Mr. Charles, Stamford villa
Londonderry the Most Noble the Marquess of, Rosebank cottage
Ludlam Mrs. M. North End
M'Adams Mrs. —, Walham Green
M'Naier Mrs. —, St. John's
Malcolm Lady, Mulgrave house
Markes Mr. R. Parson's Green
Miller Thomas, esq. Andover house, King's road
Mills G. G. esq. North End terrace
Mist Thos. esq. Parson's Green lane
Montgomery Mrs. 2 Myrtle place, St. John's
Mundell John, esq. Buff cottage, Walham Green
Nash Thomas, esq. St. John's
Nepean Rev. Evan, Grove house, Fulham
Nicholson Mr. William, 8 Stamford villas
Norford Miss —, Church row
Norris the Right Hon. Lord, Broom house
North Rev. J. W. Church row
Osborne Miss —, 7 Elysium row, King's road
Pailey Thos. esq. Percy cross house
Pain Edward, esq. St. John's
Pain John, esq. 4 Hermitage cottage, St. John's
Palmer John Horseley, esq. Thirlingham cottage
Palmer Mr. James Fredk. Burwood
Panter John Leech, esq. Walham Green
Pearce Mrs. Vine cottage, Sand's end
Patterson Miss —, Parson's Green
Porter Miss Ann, Church st
Powell John esq. Park house
Ravensworth the Right Hon. Lord, Purser's cross
Rice Mrs. —, Stamford villas
Richardson Thos. esq. Park cottage
Robertson Mrs. —, 9 Elysium row, King's road
Roe Thomas, esq. Church row
Scargill Mrs. Mary Ann, North End terrace
Shelley Sir John, Ivy cottage, King's road
Simpson Mr. Geo. Parson's Green
Smart Mr. James, Broom lane
Smith Mrs. —, Colehill lodge
Smith Miss Sarah, St. John's
Southcott Mrs. —, Church row
Sparkes Mr. Richard A. North End
Stevens Miss Ann, Hermitage lodge
Stevens Francis, esq. St. John's
Street Mr. George, 10 Stamford st
Sullivan Laurence, esq. Broom house
Syms Mrs. Frances, 4 Elysium row, King's road
Taylor Mr. Edward, St. John's
Thomas Mr. John, Bellevue cottage, King's road
Walford Mrs. —, Bellevue lodge, King's road
Wall Mr. James, St. John's
Wall Mr. John, Tyfyree cottage, St. John's
Warwick Benjamin, esq. Victoria house, St. John's
Waters Mr. Samuel Reeve, 2 Stamford villas
Watson Mrs. —, 8 Elysium row, King's road
Weightson Robert, esq. Mallore cottage
Weston Mrs. —, North End terrace
White Charles Edward, esq. Lindon house, High st
Wild James, esq. North End
Wood Thos. Jones, esq. St. John's
Wood Rev. William, Fulham fields
Woolmer Sherley, esq. Elysium villa, King's road
Wright Mr. James, Walham Green
Wright Mr. John, Pomona place, King's road

ACADEMIES & SCHOOLS.

Marked thus * are Ladies', and thus † are Gentlemen's Boarding.
Not otherwise described are Day Schools.

*Batsford Ann (gent.'s preparatory), Church row
*Butler Jane, Melville house, North End
Faulkner Charlotte (boarding & day), Walham Green
*Gifford Mrs. —, Parson's Green
*†Hackman Graham & Thomas, Fulham road
Hurst Eliza, Parson's Green
INFANTS' SCHOOL, Church st—Mary Ann Janes, mistress
INFANTS' SCHOOL, Walham Green—Sarah Wood, mistress
*King Harriet & Maria, Bridge st
Learmouth Charlotte Ann, High st
Morris Harriet, High st
NATIONAL SCHOOL, (boys' & girls'), Church st—Wm. Popple, master; Frances Raymond Moye, mistress
NATIONAL SCHOOL, Walham Green—Robert Garland, master; Mary Ann Custance, mistress
Nicholls William (evening), High st
†Roach Charles, Rectory house, Parson's Green
†Roy Rev. Robert & Edward Nash, Burlington road
*Smith Eliza, Fulham
Wells William, Walham Green

ARCHITECTS & SURVEYORS.

Gifford Edward, King's road
Nicholls Wm. High st
Winterbottom and Sands, Walham Green

ATTORNEYS.

Draper Carter, Purser's cross
Thompson Matthew, 1 Stamford villa, Walham Green

BAKERS.

Griffin Charles, Walham Green
Guillan Robt. John, Walham Green
Harvey William, High st
Haydon Robert, Parson's Green
Maunder James, Walham Green
Maunder John, North End
Strutton George, King's road
Trier Fanny, Parson's Green
Watts Charles, High st

BASKET MAKERS.

Sexton Samuel, Walham Green
Walden Samuel, Walham Green

BLACKING MANUFACTURER.

Wilbeam John Jackson, Walham Green

BLACKSMITHS & FARRIERS.

Hallett William, Bridge st
Lewis Joseph, Walham Green
Potter Thomas, King's road
Veness David & Sons, Fulham road

BOOT & SHOE MAKERS.

Ayres James, Burlington road
Carter John, Walham Green
Coleman William, High st
Davey James, Parson's Green lane
Eldridge Christopher (and leather cutter), Walham Green
Eldridge Thomas, Walham Green
Jackson George, Walham Green
Jordan James, King's road
Lucas Henry, North End
Pickton Edward, High st
Richmond Henry Wm. Walham Green
Richmond William, High st
Smith John, Walham Green
Smithers George, Parson's Green
Wright Benjn. Thomas, Church st
Wright James, High st

BREWERS.

Bell William, Parson's Green
Ford Edward, High st
Quaife & Tyrrell, North End brewery

BRICKLAYERS, PLASTERERS AND BUILDERS.
Coomer William, Walham Green
Dawson John, Church st
Faulkner John, King's road
Mullinger George, North End
Wells Catherine, Walham Green

BUTCHERS.
Collins Charles, Walham Green
Collins Henry, Walham Green
Flicker William, Church st
Hunt William, Parson's Green lane
Knight John, Walham Green
Knight Samuel, High st
Seaton William, Walham Green
Smith John (pork), High st
Watts Alfred, Church st

CABINET MAKERS AND UPHOLSTERERS.
Davis Benjamin (and carver and gilder), High st
Davis John, Church st

CARPENTERS & BUILDERS.
(See also Bricklayers and Builders.)
Faulkner Frederick, King's road
King James, Walham Green
Plaw William (and rustic chair maker), King's road
Potter William, Church st
Russell Thomas, North End
Shail Daniel, Walham Green
Stedman James, North End
Wilcox Richard, High st

COAL MERCHANTS.
Marked thus * are also Lightermen.
Bullen Henry, Crabtree
ChasemoreWm.(& timber),Burlington rd
*Millett Giles (and sand), High st
*Mitchell Dennis, Parson's Green
Osborne Henry & Co. St. John's wharf, Stamford bridge
*Quinton Edward, High st

COOPERS.
Dobson Geo. Joshua, Walham Green
Freeman David, High st

CORN DEALERS.
Caird Alexander, Walham Green
Hutchinson Andrew, King's road
Maunder James, Walham Green
Maunder John, North End
Watts Charles, High st

COWKEEPERS.
Burgess Daniel, King's road
Chandler John, Walham Green
Deacon Thomas, Walham Green
Hill William, Walham Green
Howes Richard, Parson's Green
Ive Samuel, London road
Kenton Francis, Burlington road
Willer Richard, King's road

FIRE, &c. OFFICE AGENTS.
BRITISH (fire) and WESTMINSTER (life), John Butt, Walham Green
PHŒNIX, Daniel Allsop, High st
ROYAL EXCHANGE, John Potts, Walham Green

FURNITURE BROKERS.
Jackson William (and appraiser), Walham Green
Jones John, Walham Green

GLASS & CHINA DEALERS.
Mercer James, Walham Green
Pitts William, High st

GREENGROCERS AND COAL DEALERS.
Chambers Robert, Walham Green
Hutten James, Walham Green
Nadauld Richard, Bridge st
Nicholls William, High st
Salter Edward, North End

GROCERS & CHEESEMNGRS.
(See also Shopkeepers, &c)
Burt Richard, Walham Green
Freeth Henry (and oil and Italian warehouse), Church st
Hastings Richard, Church st
Hulme Mary, High st
Martin John, High st
Mercer James, Walham Green
Potts John, Walham Green
Stocking Fredk. Jas. Walham Green
Strutton George, King's road
Wackrill George, Walham Green
Weaver Isaac (& poulterer), High st
Wilbeam John Jackson, Walham Green

HAIR DRESSERS AND PERFUMERS.
Clements William, Walham Green
Lavis John, High st
Wakeford Charles (and toy dealer), High st

IRONMONGERS.
Cook John, Church st
Marchant William, Walham Green

LIBRARIES.
Clements William, Walham Green
Jones Parkins, High st

LINEN DRAPERS, &c.
Bentley Bryan, Walham Green
North Charles, Walham Green
Wilshin John, High st

LUNATIC ASYLUMS— PRIVATE.
Mence Mrs. & Miss Pierce (Charles Mence, trustee), Beaufort house, North End
Talfourd Ann, Normand house, North End

MALTSTERS.
Goslin & Down, North End
Goslin Edward, North End
Poole Samuel Gore, Walham Green
Randell John, Church st

MARINE STORE DEALERS.
Bond Jonathan, High st
Chambers Robert, Walham Green
Emmett William, Walham Green

MARKET GARDENERS.
Adams James, Fulham fields
Ayres William, Fulham fields
Bagley Charles, Sand's end
Bagley George, Fulham road
Bagley William, Fulham fields
Bagley Wm. & Joshua, Fulham fields
Bower George, Crabtree
Broadbent Samuel, Sand's end
Chalk Solomon, Fulham fields
Chandler John, Walham Green
Clarence John, North End
Coomer Richard, Fulham fields
Crouch John, Fulham fields
Culver William, Fulham fields
Dancer Alexander, Fulham road
Fitch Daniel, Henry & Wm., Broomhouse, Parson's Green
Fuller Thomas, North End
Goater Thomas, Fulham fields
Harwood Ann, Sand's end lane
Matyear Robert, Fulham road
Matyear William, Crabtree
Moore George Colton, North End
Parry Walter, King's road
Perry Richard, Broom house
Poupart James, London road
Ratty Paul, North End
Salter James, North End
Stanley William, North End
Steel Richard, Fulham fields
Styles Henry, North End
Taylor Mary, Hammersmith road
Tims Thomas, North End
Turner Wm. Lower Richmond road
Warner Henry, Hammersmith road
Wilcox Frederick, Fulham fields
Yeldham Joseph, Fulham fields

MILLINERS AND DRESS MAKERS.
Deacon Charlotte, Walham Green
Dealy Diana, Walham Green
Filewood Diana, Walham Green
Spurway Susannah, High st
Trier Miss, Parson's Green
Watts Eliz. Church row
Wilson Harriet & Rebecca, Walham Green

NURSERY & SEEDSMEN.
Dancer Alexander, Fulham road
Fitch Danl.Hy.&Wm.Parson's Green
Whitley & Osborn, King's road

OMNIBUS PROPRIETORS.
Bartlett Thomas, Walham Green
Blanch William, Walham Green
Coggan Thomas, Bridge st
Kempshall John, Church st
King William, Fulham fields
Patey James, Church st
Pickard John Samuel, Church st
Webb George & Co. Burlington road

PAINTERS, PLUMBERS AND GLAZIERS.
Alsop Daniel, High st
Doulton James, Walham Green
Gattrell Joseph, Parson's Green
Jones Parkins (& zinc works), High st
Jones Thomas, King's road
Lane Daniel, Fulham fields
Parker Edward, North End
Pocock Edward, King's road
Scott William, Walham Green

PAPER HANGERS.
Alsop Daniel, High st
Davis Benjamin, High st
Jonas Joseph, Walham Green
Jones Parkins, High st
Parker Edward, North End

SADDLERS AND HARNESS MAKERS.
Burton Henry, Church st
Kippen Joseph, Walham Green
Langdon Sarah, Walham Green

SHOPKEEPERS & DEALRS IN GROCERIES & SUNDRIES.
Ashby Fanny, North End
Bower Christopher, Parson's Green
Bohne Jno. High st, & at Walham Grn
Boughton Thomas, North End
Cane John, Sand's end
Chipperton John, North End
Cowley Charles, North End
Crunden Robert, Parson's Green
Grimson Edmund, High st
Hailing Mary, Sand's end
Harris Thomas, High st
Jerrett John, Parson's Green
Mitchell Dennis, Parson's Green
Russell Thomas, North End
Sadler William, High st
Search Frederick, Walham Green
Sanders Richard, Walham Green
Smallwood George, Sand's end
Stanbury Eliza, Walham Green
Small William, Parson's Green lane
Thompson John, Walham Green
Walker John, High st

STATIONERS.
Banks John (& news agent), High st
Jones Parkins, High st
Lavis John (and toy dealer), High st

STRAW HAT MAKERS.
Bentley Bryan, Walham Green
Cotton Susannah, High st
Jonas Elizabeth, Walham Green
Parnell Mary, High st
Wells Catherine, Walham Green

SURGEONS.
Atkins William E. Church row
Holmes Joseph, Bridge st
Rouse Robert, Walham Green
Ryle John Hood, Walham Green
Waring John Arthur, Parsons Green

SURVEYORS.
See Architects and Surveyors.

TAILORS.
Bower Christopher, Parson's Green
Cannon Edward, Walham Green

Dobson Henry, Walham Green
Griffin George, Walham Green
Grimson Samuel, High st
Hackman Henry (& draper), High st
Marrott Robert, Walham Green
Perriam James, High st
Scott William, Walham Green
Watts Edmund, High st
Wilcox Thomas, High st

TAVERNS & PUBLIC HOUSES.

Cock, Edward Sadler, Walham Green
Crabtree House, Henry Bullen, Crabtree
Crown, Emma Marshall, North End
Duke's Head, Rees Price, Parson's Green
Eight Bells, Thomas Coggan, Bridge st
George, William Blanch, Walham Green
Golden Lion, William Watts, High st
Greyhound, Lambert Tinkler, Fulham fields
Hand of Flowers, John Tiver, Sand's end
King's Arms, Samuel Smith, Church st
King's Head, Jonathan Thurlow, High st
King's Head, William Wells, Walham Green
Lillie Arms, John Crow, North End
Peterborough Arms, John Crooks, King's rd
Red Lion, Sarah Parslow, Walham Green
Rose, Thomas David Cowtrick, Sand's end
Seven Stars, James Stratten, North End
Ship, Joseph Landon, Church st
Swan, Ann Rowe, Bridge st
Three Compasses, Samuel South, High st
Three Kings, Harriet Pritchard, North End
Wheat Sheaf, Wm. Depledge, Purser's cross
White Hart, Sarah Bayford, Walham Green
White Horse, George Pitts, Parson's Green
White Lion, Charles Vine, Walham Green
White Swan, Chs. Osborne Hart, Walham G.

TIN-PLATE WORKERS.

Clark Robert, Walham Green
Collins Charles, Walham Green
Cook John, Church st
Osborn William Thomas (& brazier), High st

WHEELWRIGHTS.

Hallett William (and coach maker), Bridge st
Jones John, Walham Green
Nash William, North End
Sanders Richard, Walham Green
Wilcox James, Purser's cross

WHITESMITHS AND BELL-HANGERS.

Clark Robert, Walham Green
Hudnott Edward, Bridge st
Marchant Thomas, Walham Green
Marchant William, Walham Green
Potter Thomas, King's road

Miscellaneous.

Coleman Mary, confectioner, High st
Davis Thos. clothes salesman, King's road
Exton William, tobacconist, Walham Green
FRIENDLY SOCIETY, Church street—William Popple, secretary
Gosling Thomas, poulterer, Walham Green
Hackman Thomas, registrar of births and deaths and vestry clerk, Fulham road
Honer Elizabeth, dyer, Parson's Green
Honer George, printer, Parson's Green
IMPERIAL GAS WORKS, Sand's end—Joseph Mewdle, clerk
Jordan Sarah, stay maker, Church st
Martin Robert, British wine dealer, Walham Green
Moore George, tobacco-pipe maker, Walham Green
Newman Thomas, tobacconist, High st
Perry Edmd. stone mason, Walham Green
Phelps John, fishmonger, High st
Potts John, undertaker, Walham Green
Sadler Edward, engineer and millwright, Walham Green
SAVINGS' BANK, Church street—Thomas Hackman, secretary
Sawyer Henry, clothes dealer, Walham Green
Steedman Eliz. Martha, druggist, High st
UNION WORKHOUSE, High st—George Stovell, master; Mary Stovell, mistress
White Charles, stone potter, Church st
Wrightson William, watch & clock maker, Walham Green

COACHES,

To & from LONDON, PORTSMOUTH, GUILDFORD and CHICHESTER, pass through Fulham, Parson's Green and Walham Green continually.

OMNIBUSES.

To LONDON, from the Eight Bells, Bridge st, Ship, Church st, and the George, Walham Green, every quarter of an hour.

CARRIERS.

To LONDON, John Prosser, from Fulham road, and John North and James Baker, from Parson's Green, daily.

CONVEYANCE BY WATER.

To LONDON, Jos. Powell's *Boat*, daily.

HAMMERSMITH

IS a highly respectable and populous village, and has lately been erected into a distinct parish, previous to which it was a chapelry in the parish of Fulham; it is in the Kensington division of the hundred of Ossulton, about three miles and a half from Hyde Park Corner; situated on the great western road—its buildings reaching, on its eastern extremity, almost to Kensington, and forming one of the most populous appendages to the western part of the metropolis. In claiming historical celebrity, Hammersmith may record the quartering of Earl Fairfax's army, in 1647, pending the propositions between Charles I and the parliament: here, too, was the spot chosen by Sindercourt for his intended assassination of Oliver Cromwell, as he passed from Hampton Court to Whitehall. At this place is an ancient convent of English Benedictines, which escaped the general destruction of religious houses, owing to its want of endowment: the order was founded by Saint Benedict in 516; of this order there have been four emperors, twelve empresses, forty-six kings and fifty-two queens. The village is pleasantly seated on the northern bank of the Thames, and the principal street extends along the line of the turnpike road; the houses are in general of respectable appearance, and those of modern erection are numerous and handsome: in the environs, particularly towards the river, seats and villas meet the eye in every direction; and the nurseries and garden grounds occupy a very considerable acreage of land, equally productive and profitable. Hammersmith, within a small space of time, has received very important improvements: the streets are now well paved, and lighted with gas, and the inhabitants are supplied with water by the West Middlesex Company. As the suspension bridge over the Thames is, however, the improvement of greatest magnitude, a particular notice may be deemed necessary:—The first stone was laid by his royal highness the Duke of Sussex on the 7th of May, 1825, and the bridge was opened to the public on the 6th of October, 1827; the cost of the work, when completed, was about £45,000. The bridge is formed by piers on shore, and two stone towers rising from the bed of the river; the chains, suspended from the towers and secured to the piers, support the roadway, running through arches in the towers fourteen feet wide. The dimensions of the bridge are—waterway between the suspension towers, four hundred feet; distance between the tower and pier, on the Middlesex side, one hundred and forty-two feet eleven inches; distance between the tower and pier, on the Surrey side, one hundred and forty-five feet six inches. The chains stretching from the shore piers support a road-way of six hundred and eighty-eight feet eight inches; width of the carriage-way, twenty feet—of the footway on each side, five feet; extreme length, from the back of the piers on shore, eight hundred and twenty-two feet eight inches. The suspension towers are constructed of stone, and designed as archways of the Tuscan order; the approaches on both sides are provided with octagonal lodges, or toll-houses. A creek, which extends from the Thames to the village, is navigable for barges. Petty sessions for the Kensington division are held here weekly, and courts leet and baron at Easter and in November. Hammersmith is within the limits of the new metropolitan police establishment; and the court of requests held in Kingsgate-street, London, includes this place within its jurisdiction.

The places for divine worship consist of Saint Paul's church, near the Broadway; St. Peter's, in the square of its name; St. Mary's chapel; one chapel for baptists, two for independents, one for Wesleyan methodists, a meeting-house for the society of friends, and a Roman catholic chapel. The church of St. Paul, erected in 1631, is a spacious edifice of brick, with a square tower. St. Peter's church is a handsome structure, in the Grecian style of architecture; the site was presented by George Scott, Esq., and the cost, amounting to £12,223. 8*s.* 4*d.*, was defrayed by the parliamentary commissioners; its erection was commenced in 1827, and it was consecrated on the 15th October, 1829, by the bishop of London; it contains upwards of 1,570 sittings, 600 of which are free. The livings of both churches are curacies, in the patronage of the see of London; that of St. Mary's chapel is a donative, in the gift of the Hunt family, one of whom, the late Richard Hunt, Esq., erected the chapel at his sole expense. Among the many valuable and benevolent institutions in Hammersmith is that endowed in 1624 by Edward Latymer, Esq., who bequeathed thirty-five acres of land, the rent to be appropriated to clothing six poor men, and educating and clothing six poor boys: in 1679 the produce was £68. 15*s.*, and in 1825 it was £507. 16*s.*; the income from the property having thus increased, the trustees are now enabled to clothe thirty men, and educate and clothe eighty boys; the dress of the men and boys is dictated by the will of the founder. A school for the education of fifty girls is supported by voluntary subscription; and in a Sunday school, instituted in 1787, about two hundred children receive instruction. At Brook-green there are alms-houses for four poor widows; and in the village a mechanics' institution and a savings' bank have been established with complete success. In 1831 Hammersmith (being then a chapelry under Fulham parish) contained a population of 10,222 inhabitants.

POST, *Receiving-Houses* at David Lloyd's, Dorcas terrace; at James Russell's, Broadway; at Elizabeth Read's, 8 Dorvill's row; and at Mary Ann Woodhouse's, King street.—Letters from all parts arrive every morning (Sunday excepted) at nine, afternoon at one and four and night at eight, and are despatched every morning at nine and afternoon at one and four.—Letters from the WEST OF ENGLAND arrive every morning at seven, and are despatched to HOUNSLOW every evening at twenty minutes before seven.

GENTRY & CLERGY.

Adams Mr. Richd, 8 St. Peter's terr
Ager Mr. John Saml. 9 Portland pl
Aldridge Mr. John, King st
Alexander Geo. esq. M.D. Queen st
Bathurst Mr. Lonsdale, 12 Vale place
Belmont Mr. —, King st
Bifield George, esq. St. Peter's sq
Blockey Mr. J. 4 Montague place
Bowler Mrs. —, 2 Montague place
Brayne Mr. Joseph, Webb's lane
Brooks Mr. James, South st
Brown Mrs. Charlotte, 9 Portland pl
Burch Mr. —, 4 St. Peter's terrace
Burke Mrs. Susannah Mary, 8 Portland place
Bush Mr. Michael, 5 Portland place
Cadbury Stphn. esq. 24 St. Peter's sq
Campton Miss —, 8 Portland place
Carr Miss Martha, Grove place
Carr Mrs. William, 17 St. Peter's sq
Casse Mrs. —, Upper mall
Chamberlain Mr. Wm. 19 Vale place
Chapman Mrs. —, 8 Vale place
Chappel Mrs. —, Victoria terrace
Cherrell Mr. James, 1 Westcroft pl
Chipp Mrs. Elizabeth, 6 Vale place
Chisholme Rev. George, D.D. 1 Theresa terrace
Christian Mr. Edward, 5 Vale place
Clark Miss —, Sussex place
Clow Mr. Thomas, Webb's lane
Coleman Mr. John, 9 Vale place
Cooper Mr. Henry, 3 Vale place
Copeland Mrs. Lucy, Sussex house, Fulham road
Cumming Rev. John, Albion place
Dawson Mrs. Ann, 2 Theresa terrace
Dawson Mrs. Louisa, 7 James place
De Castro Danl. esq. 10 Theresa terr
De Castro Danl. esq. 1 St. Peter's sq
Dixon Henry, esq. Middle mall
Doo George, esq. 29 St. Peter's sq
Dyer George, esq. Upper mall
Edwards Mr. John, King st
Elwell Mr. Richard, Queen st
Farthing Mr. Jas. 4 Brook green terr
Fenn Miss —, 3 Theresa terrace
Fielder Mr. William, 18 Vale place
Filby Mr. William, 1 St. Peter's terr
Freeman Mrs. Mary, St. Peter's place
Freeman Mr. —, Upper mall
Gibbs Mr. —, 9 St. Peter's terrace
Gibson Mr. Samuel, 6 St. Peter's terr
Gough Mrs. Ann, Middle mall
Grace Charles, esq. Middle mall
Green Mr. Jas. Brandenburgh place
Green Robert, esq. Brook green
Griffin Alfred, esq. Upper mall
Hamilton Thomas, esq. Upper mall
Hanington Miss Rachael, Upper mall
Hanson John, esq. Middle mall
Harmond the Misses, 2 St. Albans terr
Harris Mr. Henry George, 3 Lower Brook green terrace
Harrison Mr. —, Brook green terrace
Haslam Mrs. Eliza, 16 St. Peter's sq
Haverfield Rev. T. T. 25 St. Peter's sq
Hawkins Mr. Henry, Montague house, King st
Henley Mrs. Clara, 2 Vale place
Hibbard Mr. —, 16 Vale place
Hilditch Mrs. Sarah, 1 Brook green ter
Hill Mr. James, 5 Lower Brook green terrace
Hill Thomas, esq. Hope cottage, St. Peters
Holbeck Mrs. —, James place
Holbeck Mr. Louis, James place
Holtaway Mrs. W. 3 Westcroft place
Hooper Mr. Henry, Caroline place
Hopwood Mrs. Maria, Albion place
Horwell William, esq. Brook green
Howard Mrs. —, 3 St. Peter's square
Howett Jos. Chas. esq. 6 St. Peter's sq
Hunt Charles, esq. Brook green
Hunter Mr. James, 1 Montague place
Hunter Mr. John, 6 Theresa terrace
Hurst Mrs. Elizabeth, 4 Lower Brook green terrace
Hurtson Mr. —, 5 St. Peter's sq
Hyde Rev. William, 7 Portland place
Jacobs Mrs. B. King st
Jelly Mr. John, Victoria terrace
Jelly Miss Sarah, 2 Brook green terr
Jones John, esq. Middle mall
Katterns Rev. D. Queen st
King Charles, esq. 18 St. Peter's sq
King David, esq. St. Peter's square
King William, esq. Hamlet house, King st
Lacelles Mrs. —, 6 Lower Brook green terrace
Legg Mr. Richd. Henry, 17 Vale place
Lepip[illegible] Peter, Brandenburgh pl
Leslie Lewis, esq. Upper mall
Logan Miss —, Victoria terrace
Lovelace Mr. George, 6 Montague pl
Maclean Mrs. Mary, 27 St. Peter's sq
Mallam George, esq. Upper mall
Mansell Mr. Wm. 5 St. Peter's terr
Maston Robert, esq. 2 St. Peter's sq
Mattey Mr. Bernard, Brook green
Milbourne Thomas, esq. 4 Theresa terrace
Mout Mrs. Mary Ann, Brandenburgh place
Moyes Mrs. Hannah P. Brook green
Naylor Mr. Thos. 8 Theresa terrace
Nicholls Mr. —, Queen st
Nooth Capt. Hy. Steph. 20 St. Peter's sq
Oliver Mr. —, Brook green
Osborne Mrs. —, 3 Portland place
Park Mrs. —, Albion place, Brook green
Parkinson Rev. Richard, 11 St. Albans terrace
Parrin Rev. Alfred, St. Peter's sq
Parry Richard, esq. St. Peter's sq
Peglino John B. esq. Brook green
Phillips Mr. Samuel, Tunwell lodge, St. Peter's
Pierce Mr. J. Victoria terrace
Poole Mr. John, 3 St. Peter's terrace
Raggett Mr. Chas. 12 St. Peter's terr
Ratford Mrs. —, 11 Theresa terrace
Robarts the Misses, 3 St. Albans terr
Robins William, esq. 22 St. Peter's sq
Ross Mrs. —, 5 Serampore place
Samuels Mr. John, 15 Vale place
Sandle Mr. Joseph, Grove place
Scoles Mr. John, 5 Theresa terrace
Scott Geo. esq. Raven court, King st
Scott Mr. James, Brook green
Scott Mrs. Sarah, Middle mall
Seater Mrs. —, 9 Theresa terrace
Shackle William, esq. King st
Smith Mr. —, Upper mall
Smith Mrs. Eliza, 2 St. Peter's terr
Smith Mr. John, Brook green
Smith Mr. Thomas, 4 Vale place
Spike Richard, esq. King st
Stagg Mrs. —, 27 St. Peter's square
Stevenson Mrs. Isabella, 4 St. Albans terrace
Taber Mr. Robert, Brook green
Taylor Mr. Elisha, Brook green
Tillott Mr. John, Brook green
Travers Henry Thomas, esq. 10 St. Albans terrace
Walford Mr. Arthur, Grove place
Walker Mr. John, 1 Vale place
Wallis Mr. Thomas, North place
Walsh Mrs. E. 4 Vale place
Walther the Misses, 2 Westcroft pl
Walton Mr. William, Fulham road
Watts Mrs. Webb's lane
Weatherall Thomas, esq. Beecham lodge
Webster Mr. Benjamin, Montague pl
Wells Rev. John, 7 Vale place
Westley Mr. Fred. Brook green lane
Whitrow Mrs. Mary, Webb's lane
Wichell Charles, esq. 12 Theresa terrace
Wickham Rev. Edward, Eagle house, Brook green
Wiggins William, esq. Middle mall
Wilger Christopher, esq.
Wilkinson Mr. Jeffreys, 6 Portland place
Williams Mr. Thomas, Brook green
Willis Mr. Joseph, Brook green
Wright Mrs. Ann, 1 Portland place
Wright Mr. Payne, Trevor house, George st

ACADEMIES AND SCHOOLS.

Marked thus * are Ladies', and thus † are Gentlemen's Boarding.
Not otherwise described are Day Schools.

†Allen Jos. Bridge house academy
Alloms Ann, St. Peter's square
*Andrews Miss —, 4 St. Peter's sq
Atkins Elizabeth, 19 Dorvill row
*Bailey Elizabeth & Mary, Brunswick house, near Hammersmith gate
CATHOLIC CHARITY SCHOOL, Brook green—Ann Banks, mistress
*Clifton Elizabeth, 7 Theresa terrace
†Cohen Isaac, Holland house, Middle mall
*Cohen Louisa, Holland house, Middle mall
Cork Fanny (preparatry), Dorcas terr
*Cox Misses, Montague house, Brook green lane
*Edwards Mrs. and Misses, Broadway
FEMALE CHARITY SCHOOL, Churchyard—Catherine Pritchard, mistress
†Forster Frederick, Gordon house, Queen st
*Fryer Misses, Cedars, Hammersmith
†Furners Wm. (& day), St. Peter's sq
Gearing Sarah Ann, George st
*Gray Mrs. (catholic), Brook green house
*Halley & Mair, King st
†Hanningham & Omeahr, Mansion house, King st
Harland Amelia, Bridge road
Higs Penelope (preparatory for young gents.), Albion house, St. Peter's sq
†Hoare William, Burlington house
†Hunt Thos. Kent house, Lower mall
LATYMER'S FREE SCHOOL, Churchyard—Joseph Millward, master
*Levesque Misses, Webb's lane
Millward Mrs. —, Brook green lane
Minchin Mrs. & Miss, 5 Dorvill row
Palmer Margaret, South st
†Peel & Leeson, Cumberland house, Fulham road
*Petch Miss, Grove hall, King st
*Richardson Mrs. W. Portland house, 4 Portland place
*Roberts Mrs. —, Brook green
*Robertson Mary, 23 St. Peter's sq
ST. MARY'S CHARITY SCHOOL, Hammersmith road—William Gillham, master; Mary Ann Gillham, mistrss
SCHOOL OF INDUSTRY, Dorvill row—Charlotte Weavell, mistress
*Selby Mrs. —, (convent), King st
Stapleton Mary Ann, King st
†Stevens Thomas, Broadway house, Broadway
*Strong Esther, Brook green
†Walker William, Albion house, Webb's lane

Ward Sarah, King st [Brook green
†Wickham Rev. Edward, Eagle house,
Wickstead Mary, Dorcas terrace
*Wright Misses, Sudbury hse, King st

AGENTS.

Marked thus * are House Agents.
(See also Fire, &c. Office Agents.)

*Brown Charles, Westcroft place
Coles Joseph (for Guinness's porter and bottled ale), Broadway
*Gardner Edward, North place,
*Garrod James, King st
Holmer John (for Palmer & Co.'s patent candle lamp), King st
Johnston Laing (for Guinness's porter), King st
*Rainbow Ephraim, King st
Reeves Daniel (general), Waterloo st
*Stanham George, 20 Vale place
*Wilson John Thomson, Vale place, near Hammersmith gate
Wright John (for the Brentford Gas Co. and Palmer & Co.'s patent candle lamp), Hammersmith gate
Yorston Charles (for newspapers), 18 Dorvill row

ARCHITECTS & SURVEYORS.

Gardner Edward, North place
Garrod James, King st

ATTORNEYS.

Bird James, Sussex place [lane
Jones Thomas, Paradise row, Webb's
Lonsdale Richard, 1 St. Albans place
Naylor Elisha, 1 George place
Watson Robert & Sons, King st

AUCTIONEERS.

Gardner Edward, North place
Gomme James Chettle, King st

BAKERS & FLOUR DEALERS.

Bailey David, Upper mall
Beall Felix, 7 Angel terrace
Bosworth Charles, Dorcas terrace
Bransgrove George, Fulham road
Brown Thomas, Dorcas terrace
Chapman Hannah, Queen st
Chaundy Philip, Queen st
Clark William, 1 Brook green terr
Clements James, Waterloo st
Coulson Daniel, King st
Croxford Newman, King st
Day Susanna, Upper mall
Dobson Henry, King st
Eves Spencer, King st
Howe William, Hammersmith terr
Morison William, Broadway
Payne Albert Christophr. 11 Sussex pl
Philp Daniel, Grove place [gate
Rogers Roger, near Hammersmith
Shore Wm. Henry, St. Peter's place
Skelton James, St. Peter's place
Smith John (& corn dealer), King st
Smith Richard, King st
Wimpey Charles, Queen st

BASKET MAKERS.

Hamlin John, King st [lane
Spencer Benj. (& mat) Brook green
Warner Mrs. —, King st
Welch Sarah, Waterloo st

BLACKSMITHS.

Bennett Walter, King st
Cannon William, Creek wharf
Gibson John, King st
Read Daniel, Brook green
Smith Isaac (and farrier), King st
Walker Richard, Lower mall
Wright John, Hammersmith gate

BLEACHERS & CALENDRERS.

M'Culloch Andrew & Sons, Spring vale, and at *Lyons, France*

BOAT & BARGE BUILDERS.

Biffen John, Lower mall
Chandler Joseph, High bridge
Sawyer Thomas, Upper mall

BOOKSELLERS & STATIONRS.

Barker Frederick (and bookbinder), Dorcas terrace
Froy William, 11 Dorvill row
Hambridge William, King st [race
Page Edw. (& bookbinder) 9 Angel ter-
Rayner Charles, Smith, King st
Read Elizabeth, 8 Dorvill row
Walker Charlotte (and bookbinder), 7 Angel terrace
Wood Nancy, King st

BOOT & SHOE MAKERS.

Aldridge Thomas, Brook green lane
Appleford John Wm. 17 Dorvill row
Argent William, Broadway
Ashfield George, St. Peter's place
Ballinger George, 24 Dorvill row
Candy John Marmaduke, 4 Angel terr
Cavanagh Michael, King st
Creed Edward, Fulham road
Davis Jane, King st
Dockerill William, Chapel st
Dunning John, Fulham road
Forrest William, Waterloo st
Green William, St. Peter's place
Gumm William, Brook green lane
Henley James, South st
Honnor William, 22 Dorvill row
Jessmey George, Hammersmith road
Maishman Isaac, 7 Webb's lane
Middleton John, Middle mall
Mussared William, Broadway
Othen Charles, Brook green
Otterway William, Chapel st
Phillips Benjamin, King st
Pidgeon Isaac, Webb's lane
Reardon John, King st
Rumbell Henry, King st
Stapleton George, King st
Talbot Philip, George st
Whiffing Charles, Waterloo st

BRAZIERS AND TINMEN.

Greenhalgh John, 5 Dorvill row
Holmer John, King st
Jordan Thomas, King st
Olive James, Broadway
Wright John, Hammersmith gate

BRICK MAKERS.

Bird George William & Son, Brook green, and at 7½ Thayer st, *London*
Payne Henry, Devonshire st

BRICKLAYERS & PLASTRERS

Beagley John, Waterloo st
Chamberlain Thomas, King st
Cole Frederick Wm. St. Peter's place
Dowell David, 2 Dorvill row
Fitzwater George, St. Peter's place
Lee Joseph, Angel lane
M'Loughlin James, North place
Mansell Jane, George st
Millwood Edward William, King st
Millwood James, Brook green
Prior William, Chapel st
Slade James, Victoria place
Westmore Timothy, Fulham road
Wilson John Thompson, Vale place, near Hammersmith gate

BUILDERS.

(See also Carpenters & Undertakers.)

Bird George William & Son, Brook green, and 7½ Thayer st, *London*
Brown Charles, Westcroft place
Burley George, Bridge road
Carter Henry, Bridge road
Gomme James, King st
Gomme James Chettle, King st
Millwood Edward William, King st
Payne Henry, Devonshire st
Slade James, Victoria place
Webb James, Webb's lane
Wilson John Thompson, Vale place, near Hammersmith gate

BUTCHERS.

Cartwright Thomas, King st
Cutler Dennis, King st
Day John, King st
Deacon John, King st
Fallover William, Broadway [gate
Fazen Daniel, near Hammersmith
Gurney John, Queen st
Portlock William Arnold, King st
Rimell William, King st [terrace
Rippington Richd. nr Hammersmith
Saunders James, King st
Walker Mrs. King st

CABINET MAKERS AND UPHOLSTERERS.

Bannard Jno. Henrietta pl. High brdge
Barker James, King st
Bland Henry Nicholas, King st
Bond Stephen Griffiths, Dorcas terr
Eaton James, King st
Mitchell Thomas Reynold, King st
Webster George, King st

CARPENTRS & UNDERTAKRS.

(See also Builders.)

Almond John, King st
Atkinson Walter, Queen st
Bland Robert, Broadway
Carter Henry, Bridge road
Chamberlain Henry, King st
Clark Manoah, Webb's lane
Clark William, Webb's lane
Cockett Mary, Queen st
Draper Henry, Grove place
Draper John, St. Peter's place
Eyles James, Waterloo st
Eyles Joseph, Caroline place
Gomme James Chettle, King st
Herring John, King st [bridge
Hopkins John, Henrietta place, High
Mitchell Thomas Reynold, King st
Moody Thomas, King st
Pither John, King st
Randell John, Bridge road
Rimell Valentine, King st
Shoobridge Charles, King st
Stanham George, 20 Vale place
Stedham James, North place
Webb James, Webb's lane

CARVERS AND GILDERS.

Froy William, 11 Dorvill row
Luck William, King st

CHEESEMONGERS.

(See also Grocers.)

Kilbey George, King st
Salter William Davis, King st

CHINA & GLASS DEALERS.

Lloyd David, Dorcas terrace
Munday Mathias & Ann, Broadway
Pegg James, King st
Tonge George, King st

CHYMISTS AND DRUGGISTS.

Adams Francis, King st
Batchelor Fredk. & Co. Broadway
Driver Samuel Neal, King st
Greeves John, King st
Horton F. W. Dorcas terrace
Reboul Anthony Michael, King st
Warner Henry, 5 Angel terrace
White John Lewis & Co. King st
Wright & Collick (and manufacturing chymists), King st

CLOTHES SALESMEN.

Bennett Sarah, King st
Down John, King st
Glayne Isaac, King st
Haine Matthew, King st
Levy Solomon, Waterloo st
Martin William, Webb's lane
Reeve John (and hatter), King st

COAL MERCHANTS & DEALRS.

Chapman Hannah, Queen st
Cockett Mary, Queen st
Cromwell James (and hop), King st
Eames Daniel, King st
Farlow Isaac, Brook green

COAL MERCHANTS, &c.—Contd.
Hall John, Ebenezer place
Hambridge Richard, Queen st
Pamphilon Martha, Broadway
Philp David, Hope wharf, Hammersmith terrace
Porter William, Queen st
Sawyer Thomas, Upper mall
Strother Joseph, Creek wharf [terr
Wakeman Wm. near Hammersmith
Weston William, King st
Wilson John Thompson, Vale place, near Hammersmith gate
Young John, 5 St. Albans terrace

CONFECTIONERS.
BridgmanMary,nr Hammersmith gte
Churchman Andrew, 3 Dorvill row
Dearn Ann, King st
Goodwin Richard, King st
Haynes Samuel, King st
Kingham Robert, King st [place
Schmae Edwd. & William, 23 Vale

COOPERS.
Flux William, King st
Speer Richard (and turner), King st

CORN DEALERS.
Field John Kemble, King st
Skelton James, St. Peter's place
Smith William, Broadway

COWKEEPERS.
Anstiss Joseph, Webb's lane
Anstiss Thomas, Webb's lane
Davies William, New road
Ford John, Brook green
Goddard Thomas, Webb's lane
Hitchcock John, Brook green
Lambert Saml. Trafalgar st [lane
Meacock Wm. & John, Brook green
Millwood James, Brook green
Saunders Sarah, King st
Townsend James, South st
Yeldham Isaac, Waterloo st

CURRIERS & LEATHER CUTTERS.
Braithwaite John, King st
Seager Thomas, 2 Angel terrace

DYERS AND SCOURERS.
Clarke William, King st
Lance Richard & Son, Dorcas terrace
Warne John, 7Bridge st, High bridge

FIRE, &c. OFFICE AGENTS.
County (fire) & Provident (life), James Russell, Broadway
Globe, Daniel Eames, King st
Guardian, Joseph Strother, King st
Norwich Union, John Herring, King st
Protestant Dissenters', Edward Page, 9 Angel terrace [King st
Royal Exchange, James Gomme,
Sun, Wm. Pater, King st [terrace
York, Charles Wheatley, 2 Angel

FISHMONGERS.
Denney Ann, King st
Gibson Moses, King st

FLORISTS AND SEEDSMEN.
(See also Nursery and Seedsmen.)
Ackland Joseph, King st
Colley & Hill, King st
Gyett John, Dorvill row

FRUITERERS AND GREEN-GROCERS.
Butlin Jane, 24 Vale place
Cook James, (& ginger beer manufacturer), King st
Cordrey Sarah, Brook green lane
Cox James, King st
Cunningham Henry, King st
Davie David, King st
Denman Henry, 21 Dorvill row
Fround Robert, George st
Gale John, King st
Gould Abraham (& brush dealer), King st [gate
Harman John, near Hammersmith
Hull Robert, Queen st
Instone Benjamin, King st
Knevett Thomas, 21 St. Peter's place
Newton John, King st
Reeves Daniel, King st
Smith Thomas, Hammersmith road
Webb George, St. Peter's place
Weston William, King st

FURNITURE BROKERS.
Anthony William, King st
Bannard John, Henrietta place, Upper mall [st
Callis Richd. jun. (& appraiser), King
Chamberlain Henry, King st
Eaton James (& appraiser), King st
Eyles James, Waterloo st
Fricker William, King st
Longley Edward (& bedstead maker), 4 Dorvill row
Norden Abraham, King st [st
Rainbow Ephm. (& appraiser), King

GROCERS & CHEESEMONGRS
(See also Shopkeepers.)
Archer William, 3 Angel terrace
Bown John, King st
Brown William, Webb's lane
Donaldson Jas. 2 Brook green terr
Goodrich Simon, King st
Griggs Robert, Victoria place
Hicks Benjamin Edward, Broadway
Hubbard Samuel, Broadway
Jackson James, 6 Dorvill row
Jennings Edward, King st
Litchford Charles, King st
Lloyd David, Dorcas terrace
M'Gowran Francis (& oil, lead, glass & colour warehouse), King st
Pater William, King st
Pocock Samuel, Broadway
Redman Henry John, King st
Reed Walter, North place
Russell James, Broadway
Saw Robert, King st
Smith William, Queen st
Stanham George, 20 Vale place
Strong Richard, King st
Thompson John, King st
Tipper William, Broadway
Tonge George, King st
Young John, 5 St. Albans terrace

HABERDASHERS.
Barker John Dyke, King st
Barker John Robt. Edwd. King st
Bond Ann (& child bed linen warehouse), near Hammersmith gate
Claney Harriet, 6 Angel terrace
Harrison Saml. (& tea dealer), King st
Wells George William, Broadway

HAIR DRESSERS.
Adams George, King st
Bennett George James, King st
Edwards Jas. nr. Hammersmith gate
Elliott James, King st
Gayleard Thomas, Broadway
Johnson William, 13 Dorvill row
Powell Thomas, King st
Reynolds James, Queen st
Whiffing Charles, Waterloo st

HAT MANUFACTURERS.
Jennings William Vinson, King st
Palmer Samuel, 8 Angel terrace, and 85 Strand, *London*

IRONMONGERS.
Bryceson William, Westcroft place
Holmer John, King st
Jordan Thomas, King st [st
Pegg James (& rag merchant), King
Wright John (& gas fitter), Hammersmith gate

JEWELLERS.
Cole Catherine, 6 Angel terrace
Hambridge William, King st
Prime John, 9 Dorvill row

LIBRARIES—CIRCULATING.
Barker Frederick, Dorcas terrace
Rayner Charles Smith, King st
Read Elizabeth, 8 Dorvill row
Wood Nancy, King st

LIGHTERMEN AND BARGE OWNERS.
Adams Robert, Lower mall
Quinton Sarah, 7 Sussex place
Redknap Joseph, Bridge place

LINEN DRAPERS.
Akhurst William, Broadway
Filbey William, 10 Angel terrace
Hutchinson Henry, Westcroft place
Loudonsack Frederick Wm. King st
Lovely William, King st
Masters Richard, Broadway
Millar Robert James, King st
Smee & Wiltshire (and outfitters), Queen st
Wells George William, Broadway
Whiteman William, 5 Angel terrace
Wingrove & Walker, King st and Westcroft place

LIVERY STABLE KEEPERS.
Battersby Charles, Broadway
Beazley George, King st
Brownjohn James, King st
Martin William, Bridge road
Miller Margaret, King st
Pigot Squire, King st [gate
RichardsonFrederick,Hammersmith
Smith John (& coach proprietor), King st [smith gate
Wheeler William, near Hammer-

LUNATIC ASYLUMS—PRIVATE.
Mercer Thomas, the Retreat, King st
Mullins George (& surgeon), Hope house, Brook green

MALTSTERS.
Cromwell James, King st [mall
Sich Thos. & Henry, West end, Upper
Smith Wm. River side, Upper mall

MARINE STORE DEALERS.
Bolton William, King st
Hambridge William, Upper mall
Pegg James, King st

MARKET GARDENERS.
Bacchus Jas. New road, Starch grn
Brown William, Starch green
Burnham Rebecca, Fulham road
Clark James, Starch green
Day John, Starch green
Dedman Thomas, Redcow lane
Dobson George, Angel lane
Green Philip, Brook green
Gyett John, Dorvill row
Hodges Robert, Starch green
Lee Edward, Bradmore lane
Martin Henry, Starch green
Master Reuben, Hammersmith road
Millwood James, Brook green
Roberts Wm. Hammersmith road
Wells William, Brook green

MILLINERS & DRESS MAKRS.
Claney Harriet, 6 Angel terrace
Glaysher Maria, King st
Hockley Mary, St. Peter's place
Horton Eliza, King st
Hutchings Sarah, Bridge road
Lucas Mary Ann, Brook green lane
Machell Mary, 1 Angel terrace
Millwood Elizabeth, King st
Parr Sophia, Waterloo st
Smith Sarah, Brook green lane
Sparham Ann, 7 Dorvill row [pl
Strickland Mary Ann, 16 St. Peter's
Taylor & Evans, Angel lane
Welchman & Underwood, King st
White H. & E. 2 Angel terrace
White Jane, George st
Willis Mary, Queen st

NURSERY & SEEDSMEN.
Ackland Joseph, King st
Colley & Hill, King st
Lee John & Co. Hammersmith road

OIL AND COLOURMEN.
M'Gowran Francis, King st
Reeves William, King st
Russell James, Broadway

OMNIBUS PROPRIETORS.
Ashton Thomas, King st
Cloud George, King st
Danby Thomas, Brook green lane
Hardwick John, 18 South st
Mitchell Ann, King st

PAINTERS---HOUSE, &c.
(See also Plumbers, &c.)
Brown George, George st
Greenhead Jno. (ornamental), Dorcas terr
Smith John (coach), King st

PAPER HANGERS.
Eyles James, Waterloo st
Gooding Wm. Thos. 10 Dorvill row

PAWNBROKERS.
Aldous James, King st
Watts Edward, 3 Angel terrace
Woods Edward De Lima, King st

PLUMBERS, PAINTERS AND GLAZIERS.
Barry Richard, Dorcas terrace
Chalk George, King st
Charlton William, Brook green lane
Clark Fredk. (& lead works), King st
Felthouse George, 6 Dorcas terrace
Friberg John, Brook green lane
Gooding Wm. Thos. 10 Dorvill row
Holmes Eleanor, King st
Jones John, 15 Dorvill row
Reeves Wm. (& glass cutter), King st
Saunders William, King st
Thorn Thomas, King st
Wescombe Thomas, Victoria place

POULTERERS AND PORK BUTCHERS.
Gale John, King st
Greenhead John, Dorcas terrace
Kilbey George, King st
Nokes William, King st
Richards Edward, 1 Dorvill row
Senior Charles, Westcroft place

PRINTERS---LETTER-PRESS.
Crosier Henry, Broadway
Page Edward, 9 Angel terrace
Rayner Charles Smith, King st

PROFESSORS & TEACHERS.
Clifton John (music), 7 Theresa terr
Gearing John (drawing), George st
Grathern William (music), 4 Serampore terrace
Lee Benjamin (portrait painter), King st
Myers Philip James (harp), Grove pl
Shaw Chas. (drawing), North place

SADDLERS AND HARNESS MAKERS.
Day William, King st
Harding Richard, King st
Hockley Samuel, St. Peter's place
Sharp Joseph, King st

SHOPKEEPERS & DEALRS IN GROCERIES & SUNDRIES.
Andrews Joseph, King st
Ashfield George, St. Peter's place
Bailey David, Upper mall
Bannard John, Henrietta place
Bennett Walter, King st
Carlton Stephen, King st
Clark William, Upper mall
Cook Charles, King st
Cooper Thomas, Fulham road
Cousins Charles, Queen st
Gilbey William, 20 Dorvill row
Graham Thomas, Middle mall
Newman Sarah, Fulham road
Parker George Henry, George st
Phipps Martha, Queen st
Porter William, Queen st
Pruden Edward, Brook green
Read Daniel, Brook green
Ryland Eliza, nr Hammersmith gate
Taylor John, King st
Weller Mary Ann, George st
Wellesley Henry, King st
Woodhouse Mary Ann, King st
Woolley Jno. Hammersmith terrace

STAY MAKERS.
Tagg Mrs. King st
Taylor & Evans, Angel place

STONE MASONS.
Fry John, King st
Millwood Geo. (and statuary), King st

STRAW HAT MAKERS.
Clements Emma F. King st
Dowell Ann, Dorvill row
Eyles Hannah & Caroline, King st
Overy Sophia, King st
Peat James (and presser), King st

SURGEONS.
Betts John, Grove place
Bowling and Pickering, King st
Brown John, King st
Dewsnap Mark, King st
Horton F. W. Dorcas terrace
Iago Fras. Robert, Hammersmith rd
Loader Robert, 1 St. Albans terrace
Mullins Geo. Hope house, Brook grn
Perfect Thos. William Chamberlain (& registrar of births and deaths), Hammersmith terrace
Pratt Henry, Dorcas terrace
Roy Danl. Thos. (& registrar), Broadway
Russell James, Munden terrace
Simpson William, Queen st

TAILORS.
Baker John, Brook green
Barge H. R. St. Peter's place
Buckingham Thomas, North place
Butler Daniel (& clothier), King st
Coleman George, St. Peter's place
Clements Henry & Chas. Edward, 11 Angel terrace
Farr James, George st
Fowell John, Queen st
Henney George, Dorcas terrace
Hunt Henry, King st
Hunt Henry, Broadway
Hutchings William, Bridge road
Jarvis John, Waterloo st
Jennings Wm. 23 St. Peter's place
Kinton Margaret (and shoe warehouse), King st
Pyke & Lyme, King st
Scott Timothy, King st
Seabrook Robert, St. Peter's place
Seaward Thomas, King st
Swinson James, King st
White James, 16 Dorvill row
White John Barlow, King st

TALLOW CHANDLERS.
Parkinson Jno. & Thos. (wax bleachrs.) Grove place, & Skinner st, *London*
Pater William, King st
Russell James, Broadway

TAVERNS & PUBLIC HOUSES.
Angel, William Nabden, 1 Angel terrace
Bell and Anchor, Frederick Richardson, Hammersmith gate
Black Bull, John Daly, King st
Black Lion, John Rainbow, St. Peter's place
Britannia, Robert Paris, Fulham road
Cannon, William Potter, Queen st
Chaise and Horses, John Wolfe, King st
City Arms Tavern, William Hetherington, Lower mall
Cock and Magpie, Thomas English, King st
Cross Keys, Thos. Gore, St. Peter's place
Dove, Thomas Sawyer, Upper mall
Duke of Sussex, William Martin, Victoria terrace, Bridge road
George, Charles Battersby, Broadway
Half Moon and Seven Stars, William Taylor, Starch green
Hampshire Hog, Richard Rimell, King st
Hand & Flower, Thomas Steele, 25 Vale place, Hammersmith road
Hop Poles, George Wm. Howse, King st
Hope & Anchor, John Thomas, Waterloo st
Jolly Gardeners, Wm. Weatherly, Brook grn
Maltman & Shovel, Jno. Pampilon, King st
Nag's Head, Joseph Coxen, King st
Old Ship, Hercules Wright, Upper mall
Plough & Harrow, George Day, King st
Queen's Head, Isaac Farlow, Brook green
Raven, Thomas Shackell, New road
Red Cow, Stephen Eeles, King st
Red Lion, William Pring, Lower mall
Rose & Crown, Noble Bullen, King st
Salutation, Thomas Ashton, King st
Ship, Elizabeth Tibballs, Bridge road
Six Bells, John Hill, Queen st
Suspension Bridge, Wm. Bacchus, King st
Sussex Arms, Isaac Ainsworth, Broadway
Swan, Squire Pigot, King st
Thatched House, Chas. Lingard, Webb's lane
Three Jolly Gardeners, Wm. Cripps, King st
White Bear, John Meacock, King st
White Hart, James Brownjohn, King st
Windsor Castle, George Beazley, King st

TIMBER MERCHANTS.
Philp David, Hope wharf, Hammersmith terrace
Rimell Valentine (and cement merchant & wharfinger), Creek wharf, King street

TOBACCONISTS.
Chandler Wm. nr Hammersmith gate
Elliott James, King st
Gayleard Thomas, Broadway
Haggerstone Robert, King st
King Henry, King st
Livermore Mary, King st
Skinner Elizabeth, King st

TOY DEALERS.
Chappell Wm. (and brush), King st
Ferguson Jos. (& trunk makr.) King st
Haggerstone Robert, King st
Hambridge William, King st
Walker Charlotte, 7 Angel terrace
Wood Nancy, King st

VARNISH MANUFACTURERS.
Strong Alfred Richard & Frederick George, Brook green
Wright & Collick, King st

WATCH MAKERS.
Durrant Thomas, King st
Prime John, 9 Dorvill row
Wheatley Charles, 2 Angel terrace

WHEELWRIGHTS.
Cunnington Thos. Brook green lane
Morgan James, Bridge road

WHITESMITHS AND BELL-HANGERS.
Bailey Wm. near Hammersmith gate
Bryceson William (& iron bedstead maker), King st
Court Stephen, Westcroft place
Glaysher John, King st
Holmer John, King st
Jordan Thomas, King st
Miller Edward, Chapel st
Perry Phineas, St. Peter's pl
Walker Richd. Providence pl. Upper mall
Wright John (and manufacturer of malt kiln plates and improved hot air furnaces), Hammersmith gate

WINDOW BLIND MAKERS.
Aldridge John (and rustic chair maker), Dorcas terrace
Eyles James, Waterloo st
Smith George, King st

WINE & SPIRIT MERCHANTS
Johnston Laing, King st
Morecraft William John, Grove place

Miscellaneous.
Brun Peter, picture dealer, Dorcas terrace
Caplin William, whip maker, King st
Cayley Sarah, fringe and tassel manufacturer, & Berlin wool repository, King st
Churchman Andrew, ginger beer maker, Dorvill row
Clark M. umbrella maker, Middle mall
Cole Thomas, sexton, St. Peter's place

MISCELLANEOUS—*Continued.*
Cromwell James, brewer, King st
Dowell Ann, furrier, 2 Dorvill row
HAMMERSMITH BRIDGE COMPY. Bridge road—G. W. Jones, secretary
Hoof Thomas, well sinker, Bridge road
Hoof William, road contractor, Brook grn
Longley & Sutton, garden and Windsor chair makers, King st
Longley Edward, jun. turner, 4 Dorvill [row
Miller Thomas, coach builder, King st
OliverHenry,writer & grainer,Webb's lane
Perry William, goldbeater, Waterloo st
Petitpierre Mary, German and fancy wool repository, Albion place
Phillips Edw. rope & twine dealer, King [st
POLICE STATION, Brook green—David Williamson, superintendent
SAVINGS' BANK, Broadway—James Russell, secretary
Scannell J. plasterer, Salem place
Spiegelhalder G. clock maker, Broadway
Swinson Thomas, dentist, 12 Dorvill row
Thomas Richard, comb maker, King st
Vile William, lime merchant, Creek wharf
Waller Wm. Hy. steam saw mills, King st
WEST MIDDLESEX WATER WORKS—Matthew R. Knight, secretary
Weving Thomas, dining rooms, King st
WORKHOUSE, King st—Thomas Preice, governor

OMNIBUSES.

To LONDON, George Cloud's *Omnibuses*, from the Prince of Wales, Turnham green, every half-hour during the day—John Hardwick's, from the Plough and Harrow, Hammersmith, every forenoon at half-past nine and half-past ten, afternoon at a quarter before two and evening at half-past seven—Ann Mitchell's, from the Windsor Castle, twice a day—Thos. Danby's, from the White Hart & Thos. Ashton's, from the Salutation, three times a day, and—Chancellor's, several times a day.

CARRIERS.

To LONDON, Elizabeth Pope and Son, from King street, and John Brown, from George street, every morning.

Numerous *Coaches* and *Carriers* to and from LONDON & places on the GREAT WESTERN ROAD, are continually passing through Hammersmith.

HAMPSTEAD AND NEIGHBOURHOOD.

HAMPSTEAD is a large and respectable populous village and parish, in the Holborn division of the hundred of Ossulton, 4 miles N. W. from London—situated on the southern acclivity of a hill. Previous to the year 1598 (when it was constituted a distinct parish), this place was but an inconsiderable hamlet to Hendon. On the summit of the hill is Hampstead Heath, commanding, from many points, prospects extensive, varied and beautiful, including the metropolis and the surrounding country; the scenery on all sides is eminently picturesque, agreeably diversified with wood-clad hills and broken grounds, extensive meadows and retired vales, frequently relieved by noble mansions, elegant villas and rural cottages. The medicinal springs of Hampstead were formerly in high estimation; at the present time, however, though their virtues remain, it is more regarded as a salubrious and pleasant place of residence and relaxation than resorted to for its waters. Many eminent men have selected this village and its vicinage for their domicile: on the left of the entrance to the village from London is a large square mansion, once the residence of Sir Harry Vane, who was signalized by his opposition to the measures of Cromwell, and was arrested in this house. The 'Upper Flask' is mentioned in Richardson's 'Clarissa,' and it was also the place of meeting of the famous 'Kit-Kat' club; it was occupied by the celebrated George Alexander Stevens until his death, and is now the residence of Thomas Sheppard, Esq. M.P. In a small house on Haverstock Hill died the witty and profligate Sir Charles Sedley; and the same dwelling was occupied, for a short time, by Sir Richard Steele, the highly distinguished essayist and contemporary of Addison.

The church, dedicated to Saint John, is a neat brick edifice, and contains some interesting monuments: one of these, to the memory of Lady Erskine, beautifully executed by Bacon the younger, will particularly attract notice; so will those, also, to Sir James Macintosh; of Harrison, inventor of the longitude time-piece; Carter, the antiquary and architect; and Charles Incledon, the celebrated vocalist. The benefice is a perpetual curacy, in the presentation of Sir Thos. Maryon Wilson, Bart., lord of the manor, and present incumbency of the Rev. Samuel White, D. D. The other places of worship are Hampstead chapel, in Well-walk; St. John's, on Downshire-hill (proprietory chapels); and chapels for baptists, unitarians, primitive and Wesleyan methodists, and Roman catholics. The charities comprise national and Sunday schools, and others supported by subscription; apprenticeship funds, and some humane bequests for the mitigation of distress. In the reign of William III, the election of representatives for the county took place on Hampstead Heath; in 1701 the ceremony was removed to Brentford, from which the return still continues to be made. The parish of Hampstead St. John contained, by the returns in 1831, 8,588 inhabitants; and in 1839 the population was estimated to have increased to about 12,000.

POST OFFICE, High street, Eleanor Lovell, *Post Mistress* (and stamp distributer).—Letters from LONDON arrive every morning at eight, forenoon at eleven and afternoon at two and five, and are despatched every morning at six and nine and afternoon at two and half-past four.—Letters for the North are despatched every evening at six.

NOBILITY, GENTRY AND CLERGY.

A'Beckett Mr. Wm. Haverstock hill
Allen Mr. Jno. Wm. 3 Haverstock terr
Allen Mr. Richard, Pond st
Ansell Mr. Thomas, High st
Aplin Mr. Benjamin, Downshire hill
A'Price Sir Thos. bart. Gangmore hse
Atkinson Beamont, esq. South grove
Ayre Rev. John, High st
Bailey Charles, esq. Grove house
Bailey Miss Johanna, Windmill hill
Bakewell Mr. Frederick Collier, 6 Haverstock terrace
Bakewell Mr. Robert, 18 Downshire [hill
Ball William, esq. Heath st
Ballantine Mrs. Wm. Church row
Ballantine Mr. Wm. jun. Church row
Barnewall Henry, esq. Oak cottage
Basilico Mr. Andrew, Haverstock hill
Battley Richard, Esq. Pond st
Baxendale Lloyd Salisbury, esq. Whetherall house
Beattie William, esq. M. D. Rose villa
Beaver Richard, esq. 6 Pond st
Beechcroft Mr. Rd. Whetherall cottge
Bencroft Mrs. Sarah, High st
Bigg John, esq. West end
Blackwood Arthur Johnstone, esq. Roslyn lodge
Blissett William, esq. Manor house, [Downshire hill
Blunt Mrs. Catherine, Bartrams
Bockett Daniel Smith, esq. Pond st
Bodkin William Henry, esq. Hampstead heath
Bosanquet Chas. esq. the Firs, Hamp- [stead heath
Boult Miss Eliza, 41 Downshire hill
Bradford Robert, esq. near Well walk
Bradney Mrs. Sarah, Woodbine cottge
Bradshaw Jno. esq. Bodenham cottge
Briggs Mr. Samuel, England's lane
Brooks Wm. esq. White house, Pond st
Burgess Mr. Hy. 48 Downshire hill
Burgess Mr. Hy. Weech, West end
Burgh Rev. Allatson, Well walk
Burke Mr. Thomas Haviland, Hampstead heath
Burn Mr. James, Haverstock hill
Bush Mr. John, Whetherall cottage
Butcher Mr. Wm. Haverstock hill
Cameron John Campbell, esq. Hampstead heath
Carlile James Emlyn, esq. High st
Castleden Rev. James, Hollybush hill
Cavendish Hon. Augustus, Haverstock terrace
Chester Miss —, Wentworth place
Chester Ed. Yates, esq. Lawn cottage
Claypon Bartw. esq. Branchhill house
Claypon Joseph, esq. Nine elms
Clowser Edward Page, esq. Mount lodge
Cole Benjamin, esq. Frognal
Cooke Captain John, High st
Coombs Mrs. —, Downshire hill
Cooper Chas. esq. Whetherall place
Corfield Mr. George, Haverstock hill
Criswick Mr. James, Southend green
Crofton Anthony, esq. Hollybush hill
Darley Mr. George, Holly place
Davenport Burrage, esq. Church row
Davis Richd. Hart, esq. Mount grove
Dawson Mr. Benjn. Hollybush hill
Delamain Mr. Hy. Ferdinand, John st
Edwards Mr. James, Haverstock hill
Elley Charles, esq. 9 Well walk
Ennos John, esq. Roslyn st
Erle Mrs. —, North end
Espinasse James, esq. Grove place
Evans Rev. James H. the Heath
Evans Joshua, esq. Golder's hill
Falkner Frederick, esq. 6 Well walk
Fearon Henry Bradshaw, esq. Hampstead heath
Fentham Thomas, esq. West end
Field Mr. Edw. Wilkins, Windmill hill
Field Ts. Meyrick, esq. Haverstock hill
Finch Miss —, High st
Firth Richard, esq. Elm row
Forbes John Hopton, esq. North end
Forman Robert, esq. Wynford house
Foster Matthew, esq. Bellesize villa
Freeman Thomas, esq. Grove place
Freshfield Chas. Kaye, esq. Vale of health
Galloway Rt. Hon. Countess Dowager, [Roslyn house
Garratt Wm. Albin, esq. North end
Giles Jas. Sharp, esq. Hampstead road
Gill Mr. Henry, Haverstock hill

Greaves Mrs. Mary Ann, Holly cottage
Gregory Mr. Chas. Haverstock hill
Griffiths Mr. Edwd. 50 Downshire hill
Gylby Jno. Parker, esq. Haverstock hill
Hamilton Mr. George, John st
Hamilton Mr. Wm. Haverstock hill
Hammond Henry, esq. Heath st
Handley Mr. Charles, Lower heath
Hankinson Rev. Robt. Edw. Elm row
Hardy Mrs. —, Downshire hill
Harrison Geo. Wm. esq. Claremont cottage [Snowdon house
Harrison John Fairweather, esq.
Harvey Edmd. esq. Hampstead heath
Herring Thomas, esq. Bellesize
Hetherington Miss —, Frognal
Highmore Anthony, esq. Roslyn st
Hill Matthew Davenport, esq. Vale of health [heath
Hoare Mrs. Hannah, Hampstead
Hoare John Gurney, esq. Heath end
Hoare Joseph, esq. North end
Hoare Saml. esq. North end [nal
Hodgson Jno. esq. Laurel lodge, Frog-
Holford Mrs. Mary Ann, Grove house
Hollingworth Rev. Dr. John Banks, Haverstock hill
Holmes Mr. Nathaniel Reynolds, Lower heath [place
Holworthy Rev. Chas. B.A. Whetherall
Houlditch Richard, esq. Pond st
Hudson Mr. Geo. West end cottage
Hughes Mrs. —, Pilgrim's cottage
Hughes Mr. Wm. jun. Lower heath
Hutchinson Mr. Wm. Haverstock hill
Innes Mr. John William, Roslyn st
Jackson Hugh, esq. the Terrace
James Mrs. —, Valemount cottage
James John, esq. Roslyn st
Jeffries Mrs. Lucy, 44 Downshire hill
Jennings Rev. Philip, D. D. Pond st
Johnson Mrs. Esther, 8 Well walk
Jones Mr. Henry Montray, John st
Jones William, esq. Downshire hill
Jowett Henry, esq. Church row
Kelly Jno. esq. Grove cottage, Frognal
Kemp Mrs. —, Pilgrim's cottage
Kennerley Charles, esq. 9 Pond st
Kenrick Rev. R. G. Downshire hill
Kerrison Rt. Masters, esq. M.D. Frognal
Key Sir John, bart. Church row
Keys Miss Sarah, Greenhill, High st
Kibblewhite James, esq. West end
Kilburn Mrs. Eliz. Bartram's house
Kinder Mr. Henry, Windmill hill
Lake Mr. Wm. Edward, 4 Well walk
Lang Thomas, esq. Bellesize lane
Lawes William C. H. esq. 3 Pond st
Leech John, esq. West end
Lescher Joseph Sydney, esq. Pond st
Levett Rev. Edward, the Terrace
Lindsay Mr. James, Well walk
Longman Ths. Norton, esq. Greenhill
Loveday Mr. Arthur, 24 Church row
Lownds Thomas, esq. Upper terrace
Lund John, esq. Haverstock lodge
M'Donald Francis, esq. Bellevue
MacEnnis Genl. —, Hampstead heath
Mallett John Lewis, esq. Bellemont
Mansfield Rt. Hon. Earl, Ken wood
Martin Mr. Robert, Heath st
Maynard Mr. Henry, Haverstock hill
Maynard Mr. Thomas, Frognal rise
Mayo Miss Elizabeth, Bellesize lane
Meeres Mr. Nathaniel, 10 Well walk
Melville Jas. Cosmo, esq. Cannon hse
Menet Mrs. Mary, Frognal
Miles John, esq. West end
Moore Mrs Mary Ann, Bellevue cottge
Munroe Geo. esq. Cobourg cottage
Murdoch Jas. Gordon, esq. Frognal
Neave Sir Thos. bart. Oakhill lodge
Nelson John, esq. Baumur house
Nevinson Edwd. Hy. esq. Pilgrim's hse
Nicholls Mr. Chas. Haverstock hill
Ord General James, West end house
Osborne Lord Sidney, Golder's hill
Page Mr. Thomas, Frognal
Palgrave Sir Francis, Hampstead grn
Papps Mr. George, Downshire hill
Park John Ranicar, esq. M.D. John st
Paton Mrs. Mary, Whetherall house
Paxon Mr. George High st
Paxon Mr. Geo. H. New end square
Payne Mr. William, Frognal
Pearse Jno. Meriscoe, esq. the Terrace
Perryman Mr. Edwd. Britannia cottge
Pettit Mrs. Rachael, South end green
Phillips Mr. Jonathan, Gardnor house
Plank Mr. Henry, Downshire hill
Platt Thomas Pell, esq. Child's hill
Powell David, esq. Heath lodge
Pownall Wm. esq. Hampstead square
Prance Mr. Miles Hammett, 2 Haverstock terrace
Prance Robert, esq. Sidney house
Pratt Samuel, esq. Lower heath
Pryor Mrs. Hannah, Heath house
Pryor Marlborough, esq. Fowley house
Purton William. esq. Squire's mount
Ramsay Mr. Alexander, North end
Reid Thos. Whitehead, esq. High st
Reve Mrs. Sarah, 3 Well walk
Reynolds John Stuckey, esq. Hampstead heath
Rhodes Miss —, 14 Church row
Rigge Mr. Henry, Haverstock hill
Robinson Miss —, High st
Rochfort Walter, esq. Lower Russel house [heath
Rogers Mrs. Georgiana, Hampstead
Roper Thomas, esq. Roslyn st
St. John Mr. —, West end
Salisbury Mr. Richd. Whetherall place
Scott John, esq. St. Ann's cottage
Sellon Miss —, New end
Sewell John, esq. Sydney cottage
Shaw Thomas, esq. 8 Pond st
Sheppard Thos. esq. M.P. Lawn house
Shout Mr. Robt. West end [hall
Sidebottom Edw. Venner, esq. Cannon
Sims William, esq. North end
Slater Miss Anna Maria, Elm row
Slater Miss Sarah, Church row
Stephenson Robt. esq. Haverstock hill
Stinton Joseph, esq. Bellesize lane
Stone Mr. Robert, Frognal
Sulivan Cornelius Patrick, esq. Frognal
Tate Mrs. Mary, Hampstead heath
Tatham Joseph, esq. Church row
Tatham Mrs. Mary Ann, 45 Downshire hill
Taylor David, esq. Bellevue
Thompson John, esq. Priory, Frognal
Thwaits Mr. John Alexr. Well walk
Tindal Sir Nicholas Conyngham, Erskine house, Hampstead heath
Toller Edwd. esq. Hampstead heath
Toller Edward, jun. esq. Church row
Toller Thos. esq. Hampstead heath
Vizard William, esq. Pond st
Wainwright Geo. Wm. esq. Poplar hse
Walker Lawrnce. esq. Bellesize cottge
Ward William, esq. Netley cottage
Wardell John Lloyd, esq. North end
Webster Mr. Alexander, New end
Welland Mr. James, Surrey cottage
White Henry, esq. the Mount
White Jno. North, esq. Manor house, Frognal [grove
White Rev. Samuel, D. D. Montagu
Widger Mr. Giles, Haverstock hill
Wilkinson Mr. Thomas, Frognal
Williams John, esq. Bellevue
Wilshen Miss Ann, 5 Well walk
Winbolt Mrs. —, North end
Windle William, esq. Milford house
Winfield William, esq. Bartrams
Wing Thomas, esq. Coburg house
Wood Mr. Basil George, Pond st
Wood Mr. George, Haverstock hill
Wood Western, esq. Kent cottage
Woodroffe Wm. esq. Montague grove
Woollaston Mrs. —, Roslyn st
Worsley Philip, esq. Vale of health
Wright John, esq. Bellesize park

ACADEMIES & SCHOOLS.

Not otherwise described are Day Schools.

Boswell Judith (preparatory), Haverstock hill
Brooks Thos. Upper terrace [house
Butt Rev. Jno. (boarding) North end
CATHOLIC SUBSCRIPTION (girls), Holly place—Jane M'Carty, mistrss
Champney Mary (brdg.), Lower terr
Chittenden Margaret, Heath st
Clarke Sarah, 10 New end
Crow Libraire, 2 New end square
Curryer Ann (boarding and day), Heath mount
Curryer William, Stamford lodge
Dawson Mrs. B. (boarding) Mount
Edwards & Nicholson (gent.'s catholic preparatory), Church row
Godsman Jane (boarding), Upper Russell house
Hessey James A. (boarding) High st
INDUSTRIAL SCHOOL (boys), Church place—John Death, master
INFANTS' SCHOOL, New end—Jos. Slocombe, master; Sarah Slocombe, mistress
Koller Elizabeth, Perrin's court
Lawrence Jno. M.A. (brdg.) Heath mnt
Lewis Sarah (boarding), Heath st
Matthews Misses (boarding), Frognal
NATIONAL SCHOOL, New end—Mr. Jones, master
Nelson Misses (boarding), High st
Noble Sophia (brdg.) Elizabeth house
Parker Ann Mary (brdg.) Rose cottge
Pridmore Eliz. (brdg. & day), High st
Richardson Philip, Heath st [row
Shingleton William (brdg.) Church
Simmons Wm. Henry, Flask walk
Solomon Eliz. (Jews' ladies' boarding) New end square [st
Stodart Mary Ann (boarding), Roslyn
Strafford Harriet (bdg.) Church row
Strudwick Edmd. Peter, 11 New end
Wood Jane (preptry.) Downshire hill
Wright Ann, South end green

AUCTIONEERS & APPRAISRS.

Green Wm. (& undertaker), Downshire hill [High st
Paxon Wm. & Henry (& undertakers)
Sinton George, Haverstock hill

BAKERS.

Buckle Joseph, High st
Burck Andrew, High st
Evans Samuel, High st
Fleck John, High st
Forrester James, High st
Gamble Richard, Heath st
Gilson Nathaniel, Downshire hill
Kent James, West end
Peat Thomas, Heath st
Southey William, New end
Steuart John, Heath st

BLACKSMITHS & FARRIERS.

Dickson John, Church lane
Graveney Sarah, New end
Hately James, Heath st [yard
Hately James, jun. Yorkshire Grey
Hazard Richard, Golden square
Keith Robt. (& whitesmith), High st
Peacock James, Roslyn st
Watson George, Heath st

BOOKSELLERS & STATIONRS.

Lindsey Senthill (and newsman), High st [Heath st
Richardson Philip (and bazaar),
Shaw Thomas, (and engraver and printer), Heath st [st
Smith David (printer & library), High

BOOT & SHOE MAKERS.

Ashenden James, Heath st
Cook Robert, Heath st
Cooper John, Flask walk
Disney Francis, Heath st
Dixon John, High st
Gundry & Sons, High st
Henley William, Flask walk
Humphrys Thomas, Roslyn st
Jackson George (& leather cutter), New end
Knobbs James (& India rubber golosh manufacturer), Roslyn st
Lowe Thomas, Heath st
Randall Henry, Flask walk
Simmonds James, Hollybush hill
Tillyard Jos. Perrin's court, High st
White Thomas, New end

BRICKLAYERS, PLASTERERS AND SLATERS.

Clowser George Henry, Flask walk
Field John (& builder), Heath st
Hedges John, Lower heath
Kerrison John (& builder), Perrin's court
Peppiat Pearcey, Bradley's buildings
Satterthwaite James, 4 New end

BUTCHERS.

Bartington George, Flask walk
Brittan William, Heath st
Cooke William, Roslyn st
Cunnington Thomas (& meat salesman to Her Majesty), High st
Davies Thomas, New end
Griffin Benjamin, High st
Griffin William, Flask walk
Kerridge William, Heath st
Pritchard Daniel (& pork), New end
Smith John, High st

CABINET MAKERS AND UPHOLSTERERS.

Ekins Shadrach (& wire worker), High st
Farrington John, Heath st
Nash Henry, Downshire hill
Sell John, Heath st
Vile Joseph, Roslyn st

CARPENTERS AND UNDERTAKERS.

Marked thus * are also Builders.

Arnold John, end of Well walk
*Ashenden John & Richd. Heath st
Batchelour William, High st
Billing Edward, West end
*Clowser George Henry, Flask walk
Dearman Edward, 25 Flask walk
Hunt James, Hampstead road
*Johnson Wm. St. John's cottage, Lower heath
Kerrison Jno. Perrin's court, High st
Nash Henry, John st, Downshire hill
*Neal Jno. (& undertaker to the Edmonton union), Yorkshire Grey yd
*Nicholas James, 16 Flask walk
Nightingale William, Church lane
*Paxon James, Bradley's buildings
Sell John, Heath st
*Smith James, High st
Taylor John Robt. & Jesse, Church row
Vile Joseph, Roslyn st
Watson Thomas, Squire's mount
Wright Richard, South end green

CHEESEMONGERS AND PORKMEN.

(See also Grocers; and also Shopkeepers.)

Collins William (porkman), Heath st
Martin Richard, High st.
Pluckwell Robert, Flask walk

CHINA, GLASS, &c. DEALERS.

Cook Ann, Heath st
Prince George, High st
Satterthwaite James, 4 New end
Threadgold Ralph, Downshire hill

CHYMISTS & DRUGGISTS.

Anderson George, Roslyn st
Gallard William, High st
Morton Thomas, Heath st
Smith James, High st

CLOTHES DEALERS.

Randall Henry, Flask walk
Simmons Israel, Roslyn st

COACH BUILDERS.

Mynott Edward, High st
Stone Henry, New end square

COACH PROPRIETORS.

Hamilton Alexander, High st
Woolley William, High st

COAL MERCHANTS.

Crowson John, Holly bush hill
Hamilton Alexander, High st
Livock John, Heath st
Suter Alfred, Heath st

CONFECTIONERS.

Howse John, High st
Mose Sarah, High st

COOPERS.

Phillips Daniel, High st
Sharpe William, Church lane

CORN DEALERS.

Crowson Joen, Holly bush hill
Hamilton Alexander, High st
Smith James, New end
Suter Alfred (& seedsman), Heath st

COW KEEPERS.

Bates John, Frognal
Bearden John, Grove place
Castleman Lawrence, South end grn. and 42½ Clipstone st, *London*
Collins William, Heath st
Culverhouse John, New end
Griffin William, Flask walk
Harrington John, Shoot-up-hill lane
Hayter Ephraim, Flask walk
Randall Henry, Branch hill
Riddall John, Golden square
Roach John, New end
Tibbles Joseph, Roslyn st
Tooley Henry, Back lane, Flask walk

FIRE, &c. OFFICE AGENTS.

ALLIANCE, Francis Jonathan Rowbotham, jun. High st
ATLAS, Wm. Green, Downshire hill
BRITISH, James Poulter, High st
LICENSED VICTUALLERS' (fire & life), Senthill Lindsey, High st
PHŒNIX, John Field, Heath st
ROYAL EXCHANGE, Samuel Evans, High street
SCOTTISH UNION, Geo. Edwd. Smith, High st
SUN, Wm. Henry James, 4 New end
YORK and LONDON, Henry Handy, Heath st

FISHMONGERS.

Hearn Anthony, Heath st
Lee James, Heath st
Price Edward, Church place

FRUITERERS AND GREENGROCERS.

Edwards John, Roslyn st
Eldridge John, High st
Hopkins Henry, Heath st
Lawrance William, Heath st
Mayo William, Heath st
North George, Flask walk
Reeves James, Roslyn st
Shurety John, High st
Smith Samuel, Yorkshire Grey yard
Steptoe William, Heath st

FURNITURE BROKERS.

Batchelour William, High st
Farrington John, Heath st
James George, Holly bush hill
Sell John, Heath st

GROCERS, TEA DEALERS & CHEESEMONGERS.

(See also Cheesemongers; and also Shopkeepers.)

Ashby George Payne, High st
Garrett William, Heath st
King William, High st
Miller Charles, High st
Newton George, Heath st
Pannell Robert, Heath st
Poulter James, High st
Prince Edward, Hampstead road
Prince George, High st
Thompson Thomas, High st
Threadgold Ralph, 31 Downshire hill
Ware Mary, High st
Wright James, Roslyn st

HAIR DRESSERS AND PERFUMERS.

Crabb John, High st
Dorman Richard, Heath st
Randall Henry, Flask walk
Raysin Lucy, Holly bush hill
Smith Daniel, High st

HOUSE & ESTATE AGENTS.

Green William, Downshire hill
James George, Holly bush hill
Paxon William & Henry, High st
Robotham Francis Jonathan, junr. (estate), High st

IRONMONGERS & BRAZIERS.

Fearnley John, High st
Hately James, Heath st
Keith Robert, High st
Watson Geo. (furnishing), Heath st

LANDAU, FLY, &c. OWNERS—FOR HIRE.

Chapman James, North end
Dowse William, Flask walk
Gornall James, Well walk
Hamilton Alexander (& post chaises and horses), High st
Nevill William, Downshire hill
Nightingale Wm. jun. Church row
Pope John, Heath st
Smith John, Church lane
Woolley William, High st

LIBRARIES.

Crabbe Joseph, Haverstock hill
PUBLIC LIBRARY, Flask walk—Sarah Dearman, librarian
Shaw James, Heath st
Smith David, High st

LINEN DRAPERS & HOSIERS.

Evans Thomas Andrews, High st
Munday John, Heath st
Reed William, High st
Wilcocks John, High st

LIVERY STABLE KEEPERS.

Ayres Thomas (the Castle), Heath
Dowze William, Flask walk
End James, Downshire hill
Gornall James, Well walk
Groves James, High st
Hamilton Alexander, High st
Healey Francis, Haverstock hill
Nevile William, Downshire hill

LOCKSMITHS AND BELLHANGERS.

Frith Peter, High st
Hately James, jun. Yorkshire Grey yd

MARBLE MASONS.

Clowser George Henry, Flask walk
Field John, Heath st

MARINE STORE DEALERS.

Davies John, New end
Pope John, Heath st
Raimond Benjamin, Roslyn st
Wheatley Robert, New end

MILLINERS & DRESS MAKRS.

Baldock Mrs. Flask walk
Bones Martha, High st
Dennen Eliza, Heath st
Fenton Mary Ann, Heath st

Fuller Martha & Elizbth. Flask walk
Gumbleton Mary & Elizbth. Heath st
Hollingsworth Sarah, Flask walk
HumphreyMartha,Vine hse,New end
Kelly Sarah, New end
Morris Lucretia, Heath st
Nisbet Charlotte, High st
Pedden Mary, Roslyn st
Reed Elizabeth, High st
Simons Louisa, High st
Swepson Sarah, top of Church row
Ware Harriet, Hampstead square

NURSERY & SEEDSMEN.

Brown Thomas, Bedford nursery, Hampstead road
Campbell George(& florist),Heath st
LoudonRobt.Church row & Well wlk
Sinton George, Haverstock hill
Ward John, Grove place
Welland James, Devonshire hill

PAPER HANGERS.

Green William (and undertaker), Downshire hill
Langmead William, High st
Moseley John, Heath st
Paxon Wm. & Hy. (& upholsterers) High st

PLUMBERS, PAINTERS AND GLAZIERS.

Mallard Richard, Heath st
Nash William, Roslyn st
Paxon Francis, High st
Spencely John, 1 Alpha pl, New end
Swift James F. Roslyn st
Turner William Farrant, High st
Ware Richard, Heath st

POULTERERS AND DEALERS IN GAME.

Alexander Thomas, Roslyn st
Draper Joseph, Flask walk
Hogg William, High st
Pritchard Daniel, New end
Squires John, Heath st

PROFESSORS & TEACHERS.

Abbott Edw. F. (drawing) the Grove
Akers Jno. (drawing) Pilgrim's lane
Cooper Thomas (portrait), Heath st
Cox Charles (music) High st
Dawson Benj. (drawing) Holly bush hill
Firth Richard A. (music) Elm row
Sclous Henry C. (drawing) John st
WebsterAlex.(writing,&c.)Flask wk

SADDLERS.

Chovil William, Church lane
Clarke Joseph, High st

SHOPKEEPERS & DEALRS IN GROCERIES & SUNDRIES.

Ambridge Wm. Alexr. North end
Armes George, Flask walk
Butcher Elizabeth, New end
Clews William, Heath st
Culverhouse John, New end
Dairy William, Haverstock hill
Eldridge James, New end
Ely William, Heath st
Ephgrave John, Church place
Felton Ann, West end
Green George, Flask walk
Gunby Henry John, Flask walk
Hathaway Thomas, West end
Jennings Timothy, South end green
Lucas Thomas, Church lane
Preston Thomas, 9 New end
Ricketts Henry, Southend green
Smith John, New end
Symmons George, Yorkshire Grey yard
Winsbury Mary, Roslyn st

STRAW HAT MAKERS.

Bransgrove & Nelms, 4 New end
Gumbleton Mary & Eliz. Heath st
Hayes Emma, Flask walk
Peacock Elizabeth, near Heath st
Phillips Frances, Roslyn st
Reed Elizabeth, High st

SURGEONS.

Davis Thomas, High st
Evans & Haines, near Heath st
Lord Chas. Francis James, High st
Shaw William, High st

TAILORS.

Allen William, West end
Bankes Joseph, New end
Barnes John, Flask walk
Bowmaker Joshua, High st
Brett Wm. Perrin's court, High st
Dowse James, Heath st
Fenn Joseph, High st
Fenton John, Heath st
Kirby George, New end
Nightingale Mary, Heath st
Self James, Heath st
Self Robert, Heath st
Shingler Thomas, High st
Shingler William, High st

TAVERNS & PUBLIC HOUSES.

Bird in Hand, Charles Franklin, High st
Black Boy & Still, William Male, High st
Bull & Bush, John Hare, North end
Castle, Elizabeth Burgess, Child's hill
Coach & Horses, William Eagle, Heath st
Cock & Crown, Thomas Parker, High st
Cock & Hoop, William Jordan, West end
Duke of Hamilton, James Smith, New end
Flask, Henry Haward, Flask walk
Freemasons' Arms, James End, Downshire hill
George, George Diller, Haverstock hill
Green Man, James Carpenter, Well walk
Hare & Hounds, Joseph Mallen, North end
Hawk, Thomas Marsden, New end square
Holly Bush, Thomas Buck, Holly bush hill
Horse & Groom, William Hughes, Heath st
Jack Straw's Castle, Thomas Ayres, Hampstead heath
King of Bohemia, Philip Ridout, High st
Load of Hay, Robt. Haward, Haverstock hill
Nag's Head, Rosemary Wickham, Heath st
Red Lion, William Mattison, Redlion hill
Spaniards, John Chapman, Highgate road
Three Horse Shoes, Robert Ware, High st
White Bear, Samuel Titmuss, New end
White Horse, Matthew Maynard, South end green
William IV, Thomas Stout, High st
Yorkshire Grey, John Neal (Edinburgh ale), Yorkshire Grey yard

TOBACCO PIPE MAKERS.

Monks Wm. Johnson's yard, High st
Oakley William, Squire's mount

TOBACCONISTS.

Hankins Mary (& wax, &c. chandler), Heath st
Milton Robert, (& leather cutter), Perrin's court

TOY DEALERS.

Crabbe Joseph (& fancy stationer), Haverstock hill
Lovell Eleanor (& fancy stationer), Post office, High st
Phillips John James, Heath st
Taylor Eliza, Yorkshire Grey yard

WATCH MAKERS AND JEWELLERS.

Handy Henry, Heath st
Judge Thomas (& working jeweller), Flask walk
Robotham Francis J. High st

WHEELWRIGHTS.

Mynott Edward, High st
Payne Jonathan, Branch hill
Stone Henry, New end square

WHITESMITHS & BRAZIERS.

Frith Philip, High st
Hately James, Heath st
Keith Robert, High st
Watson Geo. (& gas fitter), Heath st

Miscellaneous.

AdamsChs.relieving officer,Holly bush hill
Buckland Thomas, brewer, Hampstead brewery, High st
Caughlin Thomas, turncock, South end
Dailey Michael, dyer, &c. Roslyn st
Geeves Ann, upholsterer, Church lane
Goodair Hugh, hatter, Heath st
HAMPSTEAD WATER WORKS, Pond st
Hunt Frederick,undertaker,Perrin's court
Langmead Wm. carver & gilder, High st
MingRobert,basket&mat maker, Heath st
Morris Lucretia, stay maker, Heath st
MoseleyJno.working upholsterer,Heath st
Phillips John, appraiser, &c. Flask walk
POLICE STATION, 1 Heath street—James Dawkins, inspector
Pritchard Daniel, ham & beef shop, New end
Robotham FrancisJonathan,jun. collector of queen's taxes & highway rate, actuary to the savings' bank, & registrar of births, marriages and deaths, High st
SAVINGS' BANK, 12 New end (open on Saturday evening from 7 to 9)—Francis Jonathan Robotham, actuary
Stevenson Samuel, bailiff of the manor, Church row
UNION POORHOUSE, New end—William Barrolough, master; Eliz. Barrolough, mistress

COACHES & OMNIBUSES.

To LONDON, Woolley's *Coach* (from Hendon) calls at the office, High st, every morning at half-past nine—Hamilton's *Coaches* and *Omnibuses* and other *Omnibuses*, from the office, High street, and Jack Straw's Castle, every hour from eight in the morning till nine at night.

To HENDON, Woolley's *Coach* (from London) calls at the office, High street, every morning at half-past nine.

CARRIERS.

To LONDON, the London Parcel Delivery Company, from William Garrett's, grocer, Heath st, every morning at a quarter before ten, afternoon at a quarter before three & evening at seven—James Fosket, from Holly bush hill; Robert Foskett, from 13 Flash walk; Robert Spencer, from the Yorkshire Grey yard; James Taylor, from High street; and James Tooby, from Perrin's court, all daily.

HAMPTON, HAMPTON COURT, HAMPTON WICK,

NEW HAMPTON, HANWORTH AND NEIGHBOURHOODS.

HAMPTON is a genteel and pleasant village, on the north bank of the Thames, in the parish of its name and hundred of Spelthorne, distant from London about twelve miles and from Kingston two. It is one of those many delightful places to which, in the summer season, the denizens of 'the great city' feel happy in making excursions; and the angler, too, here finds good sport, as the river about this part abounds with fish. Amongst the numerous beautiful seats with which this charming neighbourhood is embellished, the villa in which the celebrated Garrick resided may be particularly noticed: in a small temple on the lawn, dedicated to Shakspeare, he placed a statue of our inimitable bard, which Mrs. Garrick, after the decease of the great actor, presented to the British museum—Mr. Carr, the late proprietor of the mansion, however, very judiciously substituted another for it. Opposite to Hampton is Moulsey Hurst, often the scene of pugilistic contests, and where races, also, are held annually in June, when the queen presents a plate of £100. value. The church, dedicated to the Blessed Virgin, having long approached to dilapidation, was taken down at the commencement of 1830;

and on the 15th of April, in that year, the first stone of a new edifice was laid. The present is an elegant structure: the estimated cost was £8,000., towards which George IV contributed £2,000, and the remainder was defrayed by the church commissioners and the parish; the organ was presented by his late majesty, the chandeliers, branches, &c., by the present queen dowager, and the eight bells were recast by subscription amongst the parishioners. The benefice is a vicarage, in the gift of the crown; the Rev. S. J. Goodenough is the incumbent, and the Rev. John Johnstone is the present curate. The parish of Hampton (exclusive of Hampton Wick,) contained, by the last returns, 2,529 inhabitants.

HAMPTON COURT is about a mile from Hampton, and derives its principal consequence from the palace being situated in it. This magnificent and extensive edifice was built by William III, upon the site of a former one erected by Cardinal Wolsey; it is generally occupied by nobility and others holding offices under government, except the principal suite of rooms, which may be inspected by the public; they contain many admired and valuable paintings (including the famed portraits of the beauties of the court of Charles II), some fine pieces of tapestry, and other rare specimens of taste and antiquity, which have at all times attracted the attention of the *virtuoso*. The gardens are extensive: in the greenhouse may be seen a grape vine, said to be the largest in this country, and which in one season produced two thousand two hundred and seventy-two bunches, weighing eighteen cwt.; the fruit goes to the royal table. At the entrance of the gardens is a maze, which furnishes much amusement to those who thread its alleys, and are not acquainted with the secret by which its centre is gained and egress from it accomplished. The visiter or traveller, in coming from Teddington to this place, may pass through Bushey Park, which is a royal demesne—a privilege obtained by Timothy Bennett, a shoemaker, of Hampton Wick, in 1752. This delightful seat is now the country residence of the dowager queen Adelaide.

HAMPTON WICK is a hamlet in Hampton parish, yet distinct as regards maintaining its own poor; it is three miles from Hampton and the like distance from Twickenham, situated on the banks of the Thames, over which there is a stone bridge communicating with Kingston; the first stone was laid by the late Lord Liverpool, in 1825. A new episcopal chapel has been erected here, at the expense of about £4,000, defrayed by the church commissioners. Population, in 1831, 1,463.

About one mile from Hampton, in that parish, is NEW or EAST HAMPTON, a small village, and, as its name implies, of modern date.

HANWORTH, a small parish and village, is about one mile from Hampton and three from Hownslow. A neat church, dedicated to St. George, was a few years since erected in the park, at the cost of £5,000.; Mr. Wyatt was the architect. Hanworth park was some time ago in the possession of the Duke of St. Albans, but is now the property of Henry Perkins, Esq. Thomas Killigrew, a wit, dramatist and courtier in the reign of Charles II, is said to have been born at Hanworth. Population, 671.

POST OFFICE, HAMPTON, William Downton, *Post Master*.—Letters from LONDON arrive every morning at eight, noon at twelve and evening at six, and are despatched every morning at half-past eight and afternoon at half-past three.

POST OFFICE, HAMPTON COURT, Robert Evans, *Post Master*.—Letters from LONDON arrive every morning at nine, afternoon at half-past twelve and evening at seven, and are despatched every morning at eight and afternoon at three.

POST, HAMPTON WICK, *Receiving-House* at James Ruff's, grocer, &c.—Letters to all parts are despatched every morning at half-past seven and afternoon at two.

ROYALTY, NOBILITY, GENTRY AND CLERGY.

Her Majesty the Queen Dowager, Bushey park [Home park
Albemarle the Right Hon. Lord,
Archer Mrs. —, Hampton Court
Bailey Miss —, Hampton Court grn
Bainbridge Mrs. —, Hampton Court palace [palace
Barne Mrs. —, Hampton Court
Barton Wm. Hy. esq. Bushey park
Bayly Lady Sarah, Hampton Court palace [Court palace
Beresford Lady Frances, Hampton
Biggs Mrs. —, Hampton Court
Biggs Henry, esq. Hampton Court
Bohem Mrs. —, Hampton Court pal
Borthwick Peter, esq. Hampton
Bowator Sir Edward, Hampton Court green [lace
Boyde Miss —, Hampton Court pa-
Boyle Lady—, Hampton Court palace
Buckland Mrs. —, Hampton
Burnett Thomas, esq. Hanworth
Campbell Jas. esq. Hampton Court gn
Charrington Augustus, esq. Hampton
Chester Miss—, Hampton Court pal
Cottin Colonel, Hampton Court pal
Cumberland Lady Albina, Hampton Court palace [palace
Cuthbert Capt. —, Hampton Court
DeBlacquiere Lady, Hampton Court palace [Bushey park
Denbigh the Right Hon. Lord,
Devonshire Jno. Kent, esq. Hampton
Durnford Rev. —, Hanworth [lace
Eden Miss —, Hampton Court pa-
Eden Mrs. —, Hampton Court palace
Erne the Countess of, Hampton Court palace [Court palace
Farquier Mrs. & the Misses, Hampton
Fitzgerald Mrs.—, Hampton Court pal
Fletcher Samuel, esq. East Hampton
Fortnum Richd. esq. Hampton Wick
Goodenough Rev. Samuel James, Hampton
Goodricke the Hon. Lady, Hampton
Hetherington Joel, esq. Hampton Crt
Hildyard Mrs. Hampton Court palace
Hoste Lady Harriet, Hampton Court palace
Hulme Mrs. —, Hampton Wick
Jackson William, esq. the Castle house, Hampton [green
Jesse Edward, esq. Hampton Court
Johnstone Rev. John, Hampton
Kent Francis Jackson, esq. Castle house, Hampton
King Mrs. —, Hampton
Kirkman Sir John, Hampton
Linfield Mrs. —, Hampton Wick
Lloyd Mrs. —, Hampton
Lynn Rev. George Goodenough, Hampton Wick
Marlborough her Grace the Dutchess of, Hampton Court palace [lace
Monk Lady Eliz. Hampton Court pa-
Montgomery Lady, Hampton Court palace [Home park
Moore Mrs. General —, Pavilion,
Moore Mrs.—, Hampton Court palace
Morgan Mrs. Col. Hampton Court grn
Nichols Charles Geo. esq. Hampton
O'Grady Hon. Col. Hampton Court green [palace
Paget Hon. Berkeley, Hampton Court
Pakington Miss —, Hampton Court
Pechell Sir John Brooke, Hampton Court palace [palace
Pechell Dowagr. Lady, Hampton Court
Perkins Henry, esq. Hanworth park
Ponsonby Lady Emma, Hampton Court palace
Ponsonby Mrs. —, Hampton
Reynett Miss —, Hampton Court palace [palace
Reynett Sir James, Hampton Court
Rich Captain, R. N. Hampton Wick
Secker Miss —, Hampton
Seymour Lord Geo. Hampton Court palace [palace
Seymour Sir George, Hampton Court
Seymour Sir Horace, Hampton Court palace [palace
Sheridan Mrs. —, Hampton Court
Siddell Miss—, Hampton Court palace
Slade Rev. H. R. Hampton
Smart Miss—, Hampton Court palace
Smith Lady Ann Culling, Hampton Court palace
Stapleton Hon. Mrs. —, Hampton Court palace
Stevens John, esq. East Hampton
Stewart Miss—, Hampton Court pal
Talbot Mrs. R. Hampton Court palace
Thornhill Miss —, Hampton Court
Thoroton Miss —, Hampton Court palace
Thresher John, esq. Hampton
Vesey Mrs.—, Hampton Court palace
Vixon Mr. —, Hampton Common
Walpole the Misses, Hampton Court palace [green
Wheatley Sir Henry, Hampton Court
Witched Admiral Sir James, Hampton Court palace
Wise Miss —, Hampton [lace
Wright Mrs. —, Hampton Court pa-
Yates Osborn, esq. Hampton Court

ACADEMIES & SCHOOLS.

Not otherwise described are Boarding.

Barnes Riley (and registrar), Hampton Wick [ton
Berryman & Francis (ladies'), Hamp-
Berryman Jane, Hampton
CHARITY SCHOOL (girls'), Hampton Wick—Mrs. Keyworth, mistress
Fenner Charles, Hampton Wick
FREE GRAMMAR SCHOOL, Hampton —George Bridges, master
INFANTS' SCHOOL, Hampton—
Mills John Edward, Hampton
SCHOOL OF INDUSTRY, Hampton—Mrs. Faulkner, mistress
Slade Rev. H. R. Hampton Court
Slow Miss, Hampton Wick
Walton Wm. (classical), Hampton

ATTORNEYS.
Guy John, Hampton Wick
Kent Francis Jackson, Hampton

BAKERS & FLOUR DEALERS.
BennThos.(&confectioner),Hamptn
Berryman —, Hampton
Bishop Mary, Hanworth
Chamney Thomas (& confectioner), Hampton Court palace
Dobson John, Hampton Wick
Downton William, Hampton
Ford William, Hampton Court
Hammond Edward, Hampton
Hill James, Hampton Wick
Payne Samuel, Hanworth
Smith & James, Hampton Wick
Twallin Henry, New Hampton

BLACKSMITHS & FARRIERS.
Allibon Henry, Hanworth
Dormer John, Hampton
Gatfield Daniel, Hanworth
Goldring George, Hampton Court
Payne William, New Hampton
Stanton —, Hanworth
Wernham William, Hampton Wick
Wood John, Hampton Court

BOOKSELLERS & STATIONRS.
Kensett Hannah (and dealer in Berlin wool), Hampton Wick
Russell John (& library), Hampton

BOOT & SHOE MAKERS.
Child Michael, Hampton
Cook James, Hanworth
Crick Wm. Hampton
Finis John (& leather cutter),Hampton Wick
Harris William, Hampton
Holmes George, New Hampton
Hussey William, New Hampton
Lewcock George, New Hampton
Lewcock John, Hampton
Minton Robert, Hampton Wick
Pigrum William, Hampton Wick
Powell Thomas, Hampton Wick
Sawyer James, Hampton Wick
Schlenker Casper, Hampton
Thornton Thomas, Hampton
Turk William, Hampton Wick
Walker Joseph, Hampton Court

BRICKLAYERS.
Jacobs William, Hanworth
Poulton William, Hampton Wick
Rhodes Richd.(& builder), Hampton
Watson William, Hampton
Wixen John, Hampton

BUTCHERS.
Coxen Richard, Hanworth
Elphick Job, Hampton Wick
Fisher Edward, New Hampton
Hitching William, Hampton Wick
How Daniel, New Hampton
Ive John, Hampton Court
Jenkins George, Hampton Wick
Lawrence Sarah, Hampton
Paris James (pork), Hampton
Peters Henry, Hampton
Turner James, Hampton Court

CARPENTERS & BUILDERS.
Annett James, Hampton
Austin William, New Hampton
Belchamber Robert, Hampton Wick
Bushell Robert, Hanworth
Butler Edward, New Hampton
Cottrell Charles, Hampton Court
Davis John, New Hampton
HawkridgeJohnWm.HamptonWick
HeadlandGeo.Welch,HamptonWick
King Robert, Hampton Court
Mansell Charles, Hampton
Morten Henry, Hampton Wick
Reah Robert, Hampton Wick
Walker James, Hampton Wick

CHINA, GLASS, &c. DEALERS.
Cox William, Hampton
Hall John, Hampton
Reed Wm. (& marine store dealer), Hampton Wick
Wright Susannah, Hampton

CHYMISTS & DRUGGISTS.
Benbow George, Hampton
Freemantle William, New Hampton
Hampton Edward, Hampton Wick

COACH MAKERS.
Bonner Henry, Hampton Wick
Lockett Benj. Henry, Hampton Wick

COACH PROPRIETORS.
Roach James, Hampton
Row Henry (and fly and landau), Hampton Court

COAL & CORN MERCHANTS AND DEALERS.
Andrews Andrew, New Hampton
Ball Robert, Hampton Wick
Barker Wm. (coal), Hampton Wick
Goodall Thomas, New Hampton
South James, Hampton
Thompson Thomas, Hampton Wick
Wells Chas. (& mealman), Hampton
Wells Frederick, Hampton
Wood Peter, Hampton Court green

DRESS MAKERS & MILLINRS.
Fitzgerald Mary, Hampton Court
Palmer Emma, Hampton Wick
Purchase —, Hanworth
Rigden & Tomlin, Hampton Wick
Saunders Hannah, Hampton
Watson Elizabeth, Hampton
Weston Sarah, Hampton Wick

FISHING TACKLE DEALERS.
Benn William, Hampton
Walter John Bartlett, Hampton
Wignall Henry, Hampton Court

FISHMONGERS.
Coombes Edwin, Hampton
Ruff Henry, Hampton

FRUITERERS.
Abbett Sarah, Hampton
Chitts Sarah, Hampton Wick
King John, Hampton Wick

GROCERS & CHEESEMONGRS
Aris Sarah, New Hampton
Cox William, Hampton
Downton William, Hampton
Evans Robert, Hampton Court
James Edward, Hampton Wick
Ruff James, Hampton Wick
Sharland Thomas, New Hampton
Twemlow William, New Hampton

INNS.
Bell, Mary Bigbee, Hampton
King's Arms, Samuel Redford (and post master by appointment to her Majesty and the Queen Dowager), adjoining the Royal palace and gardens, and opposite Bushey park, Hampton Court
Mitre, William Goodman (late occupant of the celebrated Toy Inn), foot of Hampton Court bridge
New Toy, William Squires, Hampton Court
Red Lion, Patty Lawrence, Hampton

LINEN DRAPERS.
Abbett George, Hampton
Ford William, New Hampton
Harris William, Hampton
Rigden William, Hampton Wick
Sanders Charles Hampton

LOCKSMITHS & BELLHANGRS
Fell Frederick, Hampton
White J. Hampton Wick

MALTSTERS.
Bowyer Thomas, Hampton Wick
Galley Elizabeth, Hampton Wick
Smith Richard, Hampton Wick

MILLERS AND MEALMEN.
Baker John, New Hampton
Turvill Richard, New Hampton

MUSIC TEACHERS.
Fitzgerald William, Hampton Court
Salisbury John James (& organist of Hampton church), Hampton

PAINTERS, GLAZIERS, &c.
Francis Thomas, Hampton
Jones George, Hampton Wick
Jones George, jun. (and agent to Sun fire office), Hampton
Parsons Mrs. —, Hampton
Rhodes Robert, Hampton
Walton James, Hampton Court
Wright Alfred, Hampton Wick

PERFUMERS.
Cheek Frederick, Hampton
Fitzgerald Mary (& stationer), Hampton Court
Regester Benjamin, Hampton Wick
Stacey Stephen Richard (& cupper), Hampton Court

POULTERERS AND GAME DEALERS.
Parsons James, Hampton Court
South James, Hampton

SHOPKEEPERS & DEALRS IN GROCERIES & SUNDRIES.
Arters James, Hampton Wick
Bishop Mary, Hanworth
Bonner Henry, Hampton Wick
Cox Thomas, Hanworth
Eldridge Thomas (and coal dealer), Hampton Wick
Hussey William, New Hampton
Steadman John, Hampton
Thomas William, Hampton
Williams Walter, Hanworth
Wright Susannah, Hampton

STAY MAKERS.
Gallard Esther, Hampton
Money Mary, Hampton Wick

STRAW HAT MAKERS.
Stovell Elizabeth, Hampton
Weller Ann, Hampton Wick

SURGEONS.
Baker Francis, Hampton Court
Cullen William Hy. Hampton Court
Holberton Thomas Henry, Hampton
Jepson Henry, Hampton

TAILORS.
Abbett George, Hampton
Butler Chas. (& hatter), New Hampton
Chapman Thos. (& hatter), Hampton
Grossmith Robert, Hampton Wick
Harwood Wm. & Son, Hampton Court
Legg William, Hampton Wick
Moon George, (& hatter), Hampton
Sanders Charles, Hampton

TAVERNS & PUBLIC HOUSES.
Brown Bear, John Chantrell, Hanworth
Canteen, Wm. Cleave, Hampton Court yd
Crown, Charles Cook, Hampton
Duke of Clarence, Lucy Lodge, New Hampton
Duke of Wellington, Henry John Coltmar, New Hampton
Jolly Coopers, James Harris, Hampton
King's Arms Tap, Wm. Hawes, Hampton Ct
Maidenhead, Christopher Fell, Hampton
Rose & Crown, John Buggs, Hampton Wick
Swan, James Blackwell, Hanworth
Swan, William Marshall, Hampton Wick
White Hart, Thomas Downer, Hampton
White Hart, Edward Evans, Hampton Wick
White Horse, Letitia Parkin, Hamptn Wick
White Horse, Leonard Windsor, Hampton

TOY DEALERS.
Crick William, Hampton
Walsh Jane, Hampton

Miscellaneous.
Ayliff William, brazier, Hampton Wick
Benn Abraham, horse dealer, Hanworth
Children Robert, printer, New Hampton
Crabe —, clerk of the works, Hampton Court palace
Eales William, wheelwright, Hanworth
Farey William, cooper, New Hampton
Fletcher Charles, saddler, Hampton Court
Fisher George, parish clerk, Hampton
Harris Chas. marine store dealer, Hampton

MISCELLANEOUS—Continued.

Kensett Hannah, ink and blacking manufacturer, Hampton Wick
Lemmon Orange, gun and watch maker, Hampton Wick [New Hampton
Martin Thomas, gate and hurdle maker,
Mason George, stone mason, Hampton
Mawson John, seedsman, New Hampton
Middleham Jno. tobacconist, Hamptn Wick
Napp Richd. landau & fly owner, Hampton
Parsons Benjamin, wheelwright, Hampton
Rolfe & Stowell, brewers, Hampton
Ruff John, wax & tallow chandler, Hampton
Russell John, sexton, Hampton
Smith Isaac, dairyman, Hampton
Tollman George, licensed to let horses for hire, New Hampton
Walker Henry, surveyor, Hampton Wick
Wright Alfred, chapel clerk, Hamptn Wick

COACHES & OMNIBUSES.

To LONDON, a *Coach* (from Chertsey) calls at the Mitre Inn, Hampton Court bridge, every morning (Sunday excepted) at nine—*Coaches* and *Omnibuses*, from the King's Arms Inn, Hampton Court, every hour during the day—& *Coaches* to and from LONDON & SUNBURY pass through Hampton Court six times a day.

To CHERTSEY, a *Coach* (from London) calls at the Mitre, every evening (Sunday excepted) at six—and *Omnibuses* from the Bell Inn, Hampton, every morning at half-past eight, half-past nine and half-past ten, afternoon at half-past two and four and evening at six.

RAILWAY CONVEYANCE.

Omnibuses to the SOUTHAMPTON RAILWAY (two miles and a half from Hampton), to meet the trains (*fare, sixpence.*)

CARRIERS.

To LONDON, Elizabeth Wooldridge, from Hampton, every Monday, Wednesday and Friday—and Thomas Wooldridge, every Tuesday, Thursday & Sat.

HANWELL

IS a small respectable village in the parish of its name and hundred of Elthorne, eight miles west of London; it stands on the road to Uxbridge, and on the line of the Great Western railway, which is carried over the turnpike road here by an archway; and there is a station belonging to the company at the village. The air of this neighbourhood is considered exceedingly pure, and the country around remarkably pleasant—circumstances which have induced several families of distinction to adopt it as their residence; the village likewise possesses several good inns, among which the 'Duke of York' affords excellent accommodation for the commercial traveller. The church, dedicated to St. Mary, is a small brick edifice, rebuilt in 1781; it does not present anything that merits description, but it contains the remains of Jonas Hanway, a celebrated traveller and philanthropist, who died in 1786: the benefice is a rectory, in the gift of the see of London. There is a chapel for independents; also a school, now conducted upon the national plan, principally supported from a rental of lands, bequeathed in 1484 by a Mr. William Hobayne. The parish contained, in 1831, 1,213 inhabitants.

POST OFFICE, John Butler, *Post Master.*—Letters from LONDON arrive and are despatched (by foot post through Brentford) every morning at eight, noon at twelve, afternoon at three and evening at eight.

GENTRY AND CLERGY.

Ankins Joseph, esq.
Atley Mr. William
Baillie George, esq. Hanwell grove
Bridges George, esq. Brent lodge
Compson Joseph Nathaniel, esq.
Emmerton Rev. James Alexander
Gooch Mr. Albert, Park cottage
Haffender Mr. Thomas (surgeon)
Hodges Benjamin George, esq.
Johnson William, esq. Lawn house
Ladley John, esq.
Littleboy James, esq.
Margetts Peck, esq.
Marriott Robert, esq.
Sheringham John, esq. Kent lodge
Smith Jno. esq. the Briers [house
Spearman Alex. Young, esq. Spring
Swann Mrs. Sarah
Turner Charles, esq. Hanwell park
Walmsley Rev. Tindal Thompson, D.D. Hanwell rectory [tage
Woodroffe Mrs. Susan, Hanwell cot-
Young Mrs. and Miss —

ACADEMIES AND SCHOOLS.

Emmerton Rev. Jas. Alex. (boardg.)
NATIONAL SCHOOL—Wm. Weston, master; Lucy Weston, mistress
Taylor James (day)

INNS & PUBLIC HOUSES.

Duke of York (commercial & coach office), George Tyrrell [Holt
King's Arms (commercial), Elizabeth
Royal Victoria, Charles Brown
Wharncliffe Viaduct, William James Cockerill

SHOPKEEPERS, TRADERS, &c.

Abbott James Andrews, carpenter, and corn and coal merchant
Allen Arthur, grocer
Andrews James, painter & glazier
Attwell George, hair dresser
Bailey Edmund, carpenter
Bailey William, fishmonger [clerk
Batty Charles, bricklayer and parish
Butler John, baker
Carter Thomas, tailor
Chamberlaine George, baker
Chandler William, dairyman
Chilton William, butcher
Cockerill William James, licenced to let horses and gigs
Coleman John, bricklayer
Coleman Sarah, straw hat maker
Corby James, baker
Evans Sophia, druggist
Filbey George, bricklayer [scourer
Garrard Charles Venables, dyer and
Gladman John, painter and glazier
Goring Henry, butcher
Harding Samuel, boot & shoemaker
Hitchcock William, carpenter
Leggett Cornelius, blacksmith
Lovegrove Geo. grocer & tea dealer
Magnell Mrs. —, private lunatic asylum, Hanwell
Minton Thomas, boot & shoemaker
Neill William, dairyman
Palmer John, grocer and tea dealer
Rowles Robert, butcher and grocer
Sims Honor Amelia, grocer
South William, smith and farrier
Swinbank James, tailor
Tyrrell Geo. wine & spirit merchant, and licensed to let horses and gigs
Weblin Aaron, boot and shoemaker and grocer
White William, boot and shoemaker
Wood Mrs. —, private lunatic asylum, Hanwell [store dealer
Woolley Richard, brazier and marine
Yeoman William, tailor

COACHES.

To and from LONDON, UXBRIDGE, HIGH WYCOMBE, OXFORD, CHELTENHAM, and WORCESTER, call at the Duke of York Inn, daily.

RAILWAY CONVEYANCE.

ON THE GREAT WESTERN LINE.

To LONDON, *trains*, from the Hanwell Station, every morning at eight, forenoon at eleven, afternoon at three and evening at seven.

To MAIDENHEAD & SLOUGH, *trains*, every morning at half-past nine, afternoon at half-past one and half-past four, and evening at half-past eight.

CARRIERS.

To LONDON, George Chad, from his house, every Monday, Wednesday and Friday; and carriers to and from LONDON, UXBRIDGE, HIGH WYCOMBE and OXFORD, pass through daily.

HAREFIELD, ICKENHAM AND RUISLIP.

HAREFIELD is a village and parish in the hundred of Elthorne, four miles north from Uxbridge; the parish is bounded on the west by the river Colne, and the Grand Junction canal passes through it. Authentic records demonstrate that this is a place of considerable antiquity, and, in former times, of some consequence: in Domesday-book the name is written *Herefelle;* and it is said to have obtained its present appellation from the abundance of hares found in this vicinage. The privileges of this manor are as extraordinary as they are ancient, and those of the persons born within it rather extensive: the latter are exempt from toll at markets and fairs, and are free of every town in England (London excepted); the lord of the manor is considered a lay bishop, and has jurisdiction here to the exclusion of all other spiritual advisers! The present lord of the manor is C. N. Newdigate, Esq. The church, dedicated to the Virgin Mary, contains several monuments to the long-established family of Newdigate, and a superb one to the memory of Alice Countess of Derby, who, about the year 1636, founded and endowed alms-houses for six poor widows, now fallen to decay; there are some other memorials of considerable sculptural excellence, and the elaborately carved reading-desk attracts much attention. A small pleasure fair is held on the 23rd of April. In 1831 the parish contained 1,285 inhabitants.

About two miles and a half from Uxbridge is ICKENHAM, a very small village and parish, presenting nothing deserving of notice but the eminently beautiful seat of T. T. Clarke, Esq.; the mansion was erected in the reign of Charles I, and is supposed to have been occasionally occupied by him during his contention with the parliament. The church is dedicated to St. Giles; the living is a rectory, in the presentation of Mr. Clarke, and present incumbency of the Rev. John Addison. A cattle fair is held on the 30th April, and one for pleasure on the 4th June. The parish contains only 297 inhabitants.

RUISLIP is a village and parish in the same hundred as Harefield, about three miles and a half from that village. The Grand Junction canal company have a large sheet of water (covering one hundred acres) in this parish, for supplying the branch of the canal that leads to Paddington. The church, dedicated to St. Martin, is a venerable structure, of Gothic architecture, and stands in a retired and pleasant situation; the benefice is a vicarage, in the gift of the dean and canons of Windsor. Ralph Deane, Esq., is lord of the manor, and holds a court leet annually. A small pleasure fair is held here on the 31st of May.—By the returns of 1831 the parish of Ruislip contained 1,197 inhabitants.

POST OFFICE, HAREFIELD, Henry Hart, *Post Master*.—Letters from LONDON and all parts arrive every morning (Monday excepted) at eight, and are despatched every afternoon at three.

GENTRY AND CLERGY.

Addison Rev. John, Ickenham
Bab Mrs. —, Harefield
Clarke Thomas Truesdale, esq. Ickenham
Clarke Ths. Truesdale, esq. jun. Ruislip
Crespigny Philip, esq. Harefield
Deane Ralph, esq. Ruislip
Ewer Mr. James, Ruislip
Fuller Sir Joseph, Ruislip
Gardner Henry, esq. Ruislip
Gell John Henry, Ickenham
Haines Wm. Felix, esq. Harefield park
Inglestone Mrs. —, Ruislip
Lightfoot Rev. John, Harefield
Maydonton Mrs. —, Ruislip
Morgan Stephen, esq. Harefield grove
Newdigate Charles Newdigate, esq. Harefield place
Packe Rev. Christopher, Ruislip
Paton Mr. —, Harefield
Slack Saml. esq. Sidney lodge, Harefield
Spedding Benjamin, esq. Harefield
Sombs Mr. Nathaniel, Ruislip
Stone Mr. Orlando, Ruislip
Street Mrs. Harefield
Tyte Captain William R. Ruislip
Wardell Thomas, esq. Ickenham
Webb Rev. —, Harefield
Williamson Mr. Ths. (surgeon), Harefield

ACADEMIES.

Collett Thomas (day), Ickenham
Esther Mrs. —, (day), Ickenham
HAREFIELD SCHOOL—Saml. Smith, master; Mary Ann Smith, mistress

BAKERS.

Homewood Thomas, Ickenham
Newman Thomas, Ruislip
Thompson Richard, Harefield
Weedon Thomas, Harefield

BOOT & SHOE MAKERS.

Bryant John, Harefield
Butler John, Ickenham
Butler Stephen, Ickenham
Foster Philip, Harefield
Grigg John, Ruislip
Hawkins John, Harefield
Hinson John, Harefield
Rogers James, Harefield

BRICKLAYERS.

Hester Giles, Ickenham
Page John, Ruislip
Poulton Richard, Ruislip

BUTCHERS.

Collett William, Harefield
Ratcliff John, Harefield
Ratcliff Matthew, Ruislip
Treadaway William, Ickenham

CARPENTERS.

Cooper William, Ickenham
Weedon George, Harefield

CORN DEALERS.

Goodman Hy. (& maltster), Harefield
Tucker William, Hill end, Harefield

GROCERS AND DEALERS IN SUNDRIES.

Beach Richard, Ruislip
Cockman James, Harefield
Collett Robert Henry, Harefield
Crook James, Harefield
Hollywood Daniel (& draper), Ickenham
Homewood Thomas, Ickenham
Honeybourn Fanny, Harefield
Lake George, Harefield
Pear Selina, Harefield
Ratcliff Richard, Harefield
Tucker William, Hill end, Harefield

SMITHS.

Baldwin Henry, Ruislip
Filkins Charles, Harefield
Hibbart John, Harefield
Montague Thos. William, Ickenham
Page William, Ruislip
Wild John, Harefield

TAILORS.

Hale Henry John, Harefield
Newcombe Joseph, Harefield

TAVERNS & PUBLIC HOUSES.

Black Horse, Hannah Smith, Ruislip
Coach and Horses, William Treadaway, Ickenham
Cricketters, Stephen Wise, Harefield
George, Elizabeth Ratcliff, Ruislip
King's Arms, John Ratcliff, Harefield
Six Bells, George Ive, Ruislip
Sun and Ship, George Green, Ruislip
True Lover's Knot, James Weatherley, Ruislip
White Horse, George Weedon, Harefield
White Swan, James Godleman, Ruislip

WHEELWRIGHTS.

Atkins William, Harefield
Barringer Daniel, Ruislip
Mattheson Daniel, Ruislip
Rich William, Harefield

Miscellaneous.

Cooper Samuel, lime burner and coal dealer, Harefield
Hone George, timber dealer, Harefield
MINES ROYAL COPPER COMPANY, Harefield—Benjamin Spedding, secretary
Newcombe Joseph, parish clerk, Harefield
Saich William, saddler, Ruislip
Williamson Hny. livery stables, Harefield

COACH.

A *Coach*, from Harefield, every morning, (Sunday excepted) at half-past nine, to meet Joseph Tollett's coach to London.

CARRIER.

To LONDON, William Gates, from his house Harefield, every Thursday morning; goes through Ruislip and Stanmore.

HARMONDSWORTH, LONGFORD, SIPSON,

WEST DRAYTON AND NEIGHBOURHOODS.

HARMONDSWORTH is a village and parish, in the hundred of Elthorne, four miles S. from Uxbridge, and nearly three E. by N. from Golnbrooke. There is a cotton weaving concern lately established here, but the majority of the inhabitants of the parish are employed in agriculture. The church, dedicated to St. Mary, is an ancient edifice, having a doorway in the Norman style of architecture, and a western tower with angular turrets and battlements: the living is a vicarage consolidated with that of West Drayton, in the gift of Hubert de Burgh, Esq.; the Rev. Frederick Tompkins, D.D. is the present incumbent. The parish contained, by the last returns, 1,276 inhabitants.

About half a mile from Harmondsworth, in that parish, is the hamlet of LONGFORD, situated on the main road to Bath and Oxford, and consequently a place of considerable thoroughfare. A few years since extensive print works were in operation here: but these have now ceased, and no particular trade is attached to the hamlet.

Situated between Longford and West Drayton is SIPSON, another hamlet in the parish of Harmondsworth. The dwellings in this place are but few, and those of rather mean appearance.

WEST DRAYTON is a village and parish, in the same hundred as Harmondsworth, one mile from that village and about the same distance from Longford.—The church, dedicated to St. Martin, has an embattled tower at the west end, and contains a font curiously sculptured in compartments. The Grand Junction canal passes through this parish; and close to the village is a station of the Great Western Railway Company, called the 'West Drayton Station,' though locally situated in Hillingdon parish. Population, in 1831, 662.

POST, HARMONDSWORTH, *Receiving-House* at the Five Bells.—Letters from all parts arrive (from Hounslow) every morning at half-past nine, and are despatched every afternoon at half-past three.

POST, WEST DRAYTON, *Receiving-House* at the Swan.—Letters from UXBRIDGE arrive every morning at ten, and are despatched every afternoon at three.

GENTRY AND CLERGY.

French Miss Sarah, West Drayton
Gaches Mr. Raymond (surgeon), West Drayton
Harabin Miss Elizabeth, Drayton house
Huble William, esq. West Drayton
Jaquet Mr. Jas. Henry, West Drayton
Lowden Capt. —, West Drayton
Poole —, esq. West Drayton hall
Smith Henry, esq. Harmondsworth
Tiercelin Jno. Jos. esq. West Drayton
Tompkins Rev. Frederick, D.D. Harmondsworth

BAKERS & FLOUR DEALERS.

Appleton Henry, Sipson
Cogdell Elizabeth, Harmondsworth
Gilbert Joseph, West Drayton
Hawtree Henry, West Drayton
Hawtree James, Harmondsworth
Rolfe Robert, West Drayton

BLACKSMITHS.

Malling John, Harmondsworth
Watts Ann, West Drayton

BOOT AND SHOE MAKERS.
Bagley James, Sipson
Houlton Joseph, West Drayton
Lintill John, West Drayton
Williams James, West Drayton

BREWERS.
Hatchett John, West Drayton
Lloyd Jephtha, West Drayton

BUTCHERS.
Jones Thomas, Harmondsworth
Ratcliff Ralph, West Drayton
Ratcliff William, West Drayton
West Nathaniel, West Drayton

GROCERS AND DEALERS IN SUNDRIES.
Gilbert Joseph, West Drayton
Grey James, Sipson
Hawtree James, Harmondsworth
Haynes John, West Drayton
Sidwell Samuel (& carpenter), West Drayton
Stanbrook William, Harmondsworth
Starns James (and draper), Sipson

MALTSTERS.
Lloyd Jephtha, West Drayton
Thatcher James, West Drayton

MARKET GARDENERS.
Bagley Warwick, West Drayton
Colley Richard, Harmondsworth
Cooper John, Sipson

TAVERNS & PUBLIC HOUSES.
Crown, John Nelson, West Drayton
Five Bells, Miriam Brookman, Harmondsworth
King's Arms, William Godfrey, Longford
King's Head, Peggy Bedford, Longford
King's Head, Ralph Pizzey, West Drayton
Magpies, John Evans, Sipson green
Six Bells, Jane Miller, West Drayton
Sun, John Wyatt, Harmondsworth
Swan, Thomas Seddon, West Drayton
White Horse, James Spratley, Longford

WHEELWRIGHTS.
Passingham Wm. Harmondsworth
Wells William, West Drayton

Miscellaneous.
Appleton William, fruiterer and greengrocer, Sipson
Bryan William, hay dealer, Longford
Hood Thomas, builder, West Drayton
Mercer Daniel and Richard, millers and paper makers, West Drayton
Mills William, cotton weaver, Harmondsworth
Springall Wm. bricklayer, West Drayton
Taplin Joseph, coal & corn merchant, West Drayton
Tillyer James and Richard, farmers, Harmondsworth
Watkins Stephen, brick maker, West Drayton
Wright James Edwin, seed crusher, West Drayton
Wyett Elizabeth, milliner, West Drayton

RAILWAY CONVEYANCE.

BY THE GREAT WESTERN LINE.

To LONDON, *Trains*, every morning (Sunday excepted) at twenty minutes past nine; twenty minutes past twelve noon; and twenty minutes past five afternoon. On *Sundays*, two *Trains* only, viz. at twenty minutes past nine in the morning & twenty minutes past five in the evening.

To MAIDENHEAD and SLOUGH, *Trains*, every morning (Sunday excepted) at ten, noon at twelve and afternoon at five. On *Sundays*, two *Trains* only, viz. at half-past eight in the morning and five in the afternoon.—John Smith, agent, at West Drayton station.

To and from UXBRIDGE and DRAYTON, Tollitt's *Coach*, to meet the railway trains.

CARRIERS.

To and from LONDON and the West, *Waggons* and *Carriers* pass through Longford, daily.

To UXBRIDGE, Whitten's *Cart*, from West Drayton, daily.

HARROW, GREENFORD AND NORTHOLT.

HARROW, formerly a market town, is in the parish of its name and hundred of Gore—situated nearly ten miles N. W. by W. from London, upon a hill, one of the highest in the county, and thence generally designated 'Harrow-on-the-Hill.' The London and Birmingham railway passes within about a mile and a half of the village. Harrow derives almost its sole importance from its school, which has long maintained its distinguished rank; in it the sons of nobility, and members of other families of high distinction and fortune, have received their education; and the brilliant career of some of the greatest men that have figured in the church, the state, or in arms, may be ascribed to their several studies at HARROW SCHOOL. It was founded by John Lyon, of Preston (a neighbouring hamlet), in the reign of Elizabeth: amongst the statutes, which were drawn up by the founder, archery was especially enjoined as one of the amusements of the students; and formerly, on the 1st of August, a trial of skill took place in that exercise, when the best marksman was presented with a silver arrow: some ancient customs and ceremonies are still observed. The trade of the place is in a great measure dependent upon this establishment; but it is likewise much resorted to by strangers, either attracted hither upon some holiday occasion, or to enjoy the fine views and general beauty of the surrounding scenery. Families of the highest order and greatest opulence choose Harrow and its neighbourhood as their residence; and several elegant seats and mansions add to the embellishments of the adjacent country. There are two principal inns, which are entitled to notice for the comfortable accommodation they afford; the 'King's Head,' especially, is a superior commercial house, as well as a posting establishment. The church, dedicated to Saint Mary, and situated on the hill, is a commodious structure, with a tower at the west end, surmounted by a lofty spire and a curious Norman doorway: the prospect from the summit of the tower is grand, picturesque and very extensive; the edifice itself is a commanding object for many miles around. At Pinner, in this parish, is a chapel of ease; and there are places of worship for baptists and Wesleyan methodists. Besides the grammar school there is a charity school with a small endowment, and one upon the national plan. At the extremity of the parish, towards Stanmore, is Bentley Priory, the splendid mansion and seat of the Marquess of Abercorn. A charter for holding a market on Monday, and an annual fair, was granted to this place by Henry III; the market has been discontinued, but the fair is held on the first Monday in August. The parish of Harrow (including the hamlet of Weald and Greenhill,) contained, at the census for 1831, 3,861 inhabitants.

Two miles and a half from Harrow, and four and a half N. by E. from Hounslow, in the hundred of Elthorne, stands the village of GREENFORD, in a pleasant situation, and surrounded by many genteel residences. The church, dedicated to the Holy Cross, has a handsome appearance, and stained glass ornaments some of the windows; the living is a rectory, in the patronage of the provost and fellows of King's college, Cambridge. A chapel for baptists, and a school upon the national plan, are in the parish. Population, in 1831, 477.

NORTHOLT is a village and parish in the same hundred as Greenford, situated between that village and Harrow. The church, a small neat edifice, dedicated to St. Mary, stands on an acclivity commanding some very pleasing scenery; the benefice is a vicarage, in the presentation of the see of London. Population, 447.

POST OFFICE, HARROW, James Winkley, *Post Master.*—Letters from LONDON arrive every forenoon (Sunday excepted) at half-past eleven and afternoon at half-past five, and are despatched every morning at nine and afternoon at four.

POST OFFICE, GREENFORD, John Sayer, *Post Master.*—Letters from all parts arrive (by foot post from Stanwell) every morning at eight and noon at twelve, and are despatched every morning at seven and and afternoon at a quarter past two.

NOBILITY, GENTRY AND CLERGY.
Abercorn the Most Noble the Marquess of, Bentley priory, Harrow
Brown Jno. esq. Sudbury hill house
Clark Andrew, esq. Greenford place
Colenson J. W. esq. B. A. Harrow
Copeland John, esq. Sudbury lodge
Cunningham Rev. John, Julian hill, Harrow
Dakins Rev. John, Greenford
Dillon Doctor —, Harrow
Drury Rev. Henry, Harrow
Ewart Mrs. Caroline, Harrow
Ferres William, esq. Harrow
Gibb James Francis, esq. Greenford
Gray Rev. Jno. Edwd. Whimbley park
Greenhill Mr. James, Harrow
Harris G. F. esq. M. A. Harrow
Hinxman John, esq. Sudbury grove
Hulcott James, esq. Sudbury
Judd Mrs. —, Harrow
Leighton Sir James, Greenford
Lewis Miss —, Aspen lodge
Lindus Wm. esq. Egremont cottage
Marillier J. W. esq. Harrow
Marillier Jacob Francis, esq. Harrow
Murray Rev. Edward, Northolt
Oxenham Rev. W. M. A. Harrow
Phelps Rev. William W. Harrow
Ravener Mr. George, Greenford
Steel Rev. T. H. M. A. Harrow
Smith Mr. William, Harrow
Thornton Sir William, Greenford
Tompkins Rev. John, Greenford
Webster George, esq. Sudbury priory
Wilkins Hy. esq. the Mount, Harrow
Wilkinson George Hy. esq. Harrow
Wilkinson Rev. William Francis, Harrow
Wordsworth Rev. Christopher, D. D. Harrow

ACADEMIES & SCHOOLS.
HARROW GRAMMAR SCHOOL:—
Rev. Christr. Wordsworth, D. D. *fellow of Trinity col. Cambridge, head master.*
Rev. Henry Drury, M. A. *under master.*
Rev. W. Oxenham, M. A. *assistant mastr.*
Rev. W. W. Phelps, M. A. *assistant master.*
Rev. T. H. Steel, M. A. *fellow of Trin. college, Cambridge, assistant master.*
G. F. Harris, esq. M. A. *fellow of Trinity college, Cambridge, assistant master.*
J. W. Colenso, esq. B. A. *fellow of St. John's college, Cambridge, assistant master for mathematics.*
J. W. Marillier, esq. *French master.*
Jacob Francis Marillier, esq. *mathematical assistant master.*
H. Angelo, esq. *fencing master.*

CHARITY SCHOOL, Greenford—John Sayer, master
Longworth Rebecca (day), Harrow
Longworthy William (day), Harrow
Michod John (day), Harrow
NATIONAL SCHOOL, Northolt—Mrs. Nunn, mistress
NATIONAL SCHOOLS, Harrow—John Carter, master; Ann Smith, mistrss
Sandiland Miss (boarding), Harrow

BAKERS.
Armstrong Wm. Duncan, Harrow
Bradshaw George, Greenford
Dean James, Northolt
Fuller Elizabeth, Harrow
Harris Ambrose, Harrow
Reid John, Harrow
Smith William, Harrow
Woodward Thomas, Harrow

BLACKSMITHS & FARRIERS.
Chapman James, Harrow
Hawkins John, Northolt
Hinge Sarah, Greenford
Slade William, Harrow
Thompson William, Northolt

BOOKSELLERS & STATIONRS
Baker Hannah, Harrow
Warren John, Harrow

BOOT & SHOE MAKERS.
Balding Thomas, Greenford
Brownrigg Sophia, Harrow
Burgis Joseph, Harrow
Chatham William, Harrow
Dear James, Harrow
Dixon Henry, Harrow
Lester Richard, Northolt
Parsons Henry, Harrow
Powell Ann, Harrow
Powell Edward, Harrow
Skeggs Abraham, Harrow

BRICKLAYERS.
Chapman R. & Co. Harrow
Martin William, Harrow
Stevens John (horses for hire), Harrow

BUTCHERS.
Ballard John, Harrow Weald
Hitchcock Thomas, Greenford
Hodsdon Thomas, Harrow
Kench Joseph, Harrow
Walker Joseph, Harrow
Walker Thomas, Harrow

CARPENTERS.
Buckingham Charles, Harrow
Kench Thomas, Harrow
Parsons Rhoades, Harrow
Watkins Hugh, Harrow
Woodbridge John, Harrow

COAL MERCHANTS.
Allen Harriet, Greenford wharf
Armstrong William Duncan (and corn), Harrow
Farmborough Joseph, Harrow
Neary James, Harrow

FIRE, &c. OFFICE AGENTS.
COUNTY, William Winkley (& deputy registrar), Harrow
PHŒNIX, Henry Ferdinando Bowen (and chymist), Harrow

GROCERS AND DEALERS IN SUNDRIES.
Babb William, Harrow
Bailey William, Sudbury
Bell John, Harrow
Bird Isaac, Harrow
Bowen George Harrow
Bradshaw George, Greenford
Clark Mary, Harrow
Dean James, Northolt
Farmborough Joseph, Harrow
Farmborough Joseph, jun. Harrow
Harris Ambrose, Greenford green
Harris Frances, Greenford green
Hawkins William, Northolt
Kench Joseph, Harrow
King William, Greenford
Neary James, Harrow
Parsons Rhoades, Harrow
Reynolds Philip, Harrow
Royston John, Harrow
Stevens Zachariah, Harrow
Vincent Thomas, Northolt
Watkins Hugh, Harrow
Winter Richard, Harrow
Woodward Thomas, Harrow

INNS.
Crown & Anchor (and coach office), John Bliss, Harrow
King's Head (and posting and commercial), James Lawes, Harrow

LINEN DRAPERS.
Blake Joseph, Harrow
Brownrigg Samuel, Harrow
Watkins Hugh, Harrow

NURSERY AND SEEDSMEN.
Green William, Sudbury
Sellwood John, Harrow

PASTRYCOOKS.
Bird Isaac, Harrow
Clark Mary, Harrow
Crane Rebecca (& tea dealer), Harrow
Greenhill Maria, Harrow
Parsons Rhoades, Harrow
Wilkins James, Harrow

PLUMBERS, PAINTERS, &c.
Baldwin David, Harrow
Baldwin Samuel, Harrow
Bliss & Arnold, Harrow
Clowes James, Harrow
Hudson Thomas, Harrow

SADDLERS AND HARNESS MAKERS.
Row James, Harrow
Way Henry John, Harrow

STATIONERS & HATTERS.
Arnold William (& glover), Harrow
Brownrigg Samuel, Harrow
Pope Joseph, Harrow

STRAW HAT MAKERS.
Carter Susannah, Harrow
Chatham Hannah, Harrow
Farmborough Eliza (& milliner) Harrow
Lambird Hannah, Harrow
Reed Mary Ann, Harrow

SURGEONS.
Bowen Benjamin, Harrow
Bowen Frederick, jun. Harrow
Hewlett Thomas, Harrow

TAILORS.
Smith Thomas, Harrow
Sweetman William, Greenford
Tillyard George, Harrow
Timberlake William, Harrow
Winkley James & William, Harrow
Woodbridge William, Harrow

TAVERNS & PUBLIC HOUSES.
Bell, John Leach, Harrow Weald green
Black Horse, Ambrose Harris, Greenford
Black Horse, Harry Wellum, Sudbury
Castle, James Walker, Harrow
Crown, Henry Beasley, Harrow
Crown, James Hitchcock, Northolt
Hare, John Foskett, Harrow Weald
Hare and Hounds, Elijah Oliver, Northolt
Marquess of Granby, Jno. Trussell, Greenhill
Mitre, Richard Luckett, Sudbury
Plough, George Saunders, Northolt
Queen's Arms, Francis Russell, Greenhill
Red Lion, Thomas Coles, Greenford
Red Lion, William Smith, Harrow Weald
Seven Balls, John Ballard, Harrow Weald
Swan, James Ward, Harrow
Three Horse Shoes, James Green, Harrow
White Hart, Thomas Vincent, Northolt
Windmill, William Davison, Harrow

WATCH & CLOCK MAKERS.
Johnson Samuel, Harrow
Moses Samuel, Harrow

WHEELWRIGHTS.
Page Wm. (& undertaker), Harrow
Reed Richard, Greenford

Miscellaneous.
Names without address are in HARROW.
Boswell George, brazier, &c.
Boulton Mary, milliner, &c.
Carter John, glass dealer
Chapman James, ironmonger and smith
Goshawk Edmund, hair dresser and bird preserver
Sandilands James, cabinet maker
Sayer John, parish clerk, Greenford
Warner William, fishmonger
Westmore Ann, hosier
Winkley F. registrar

COACH.
To LONDON, a *Coach* (from Pinner), calls at the Crown & Anchor, Harrow, every morning at eight, and to PINNER, the same *Coach*, every evening at six.

RAILWAY CONVEYANCE.
To LONDON & BIRMINGHAM, *Trains* pass on this line about a mile and a half from Harrow, several times a day.

CARRIER.
To LONDON, William Hudson, from his house, Harrow, every Tuesday Thursday and Friday.

HAYES, NORWOOD, SOUTHALL & NEIGHBOURHOODS.

HAYES is a village and parish, in the hundred of Elthorne, 12 miles from London and somewhat more than three from Uxbridge. The village has no pretensions to uniformity, and a great portion of the dwellings are detached, the situation however is remarkably pleasant—about Wood End particulary so, and in this part are many highly respectable families. The only article manufactured is candles, at Wood End Green. The church, which is dedicated to St. Mary, is an ancient edifice, and contains some monuments sufficiently denoting its antiquity; it has a low square tower, in the early style of English architecture; and the chancel windows contain some armorial bearings in stained glass. The living comprises a rectory (which is a sinecure) and a vicarage, with the perpetual curacy of Norwood, in the patronage of the Hambrough family; the Rev. J. N. Freeman is the present incumbent. A pleasure fair is held here on the 11th of June. The parish contained, by the last census, 1,575 inhabitants.

NORWOOD is a precinct and parochial chapelry, in the same hundred as Hayes, about 2½ miles N.W. from Hounslow; pleasantly situated between the great western line of road and that leading to Uxbridge, and near to the bank of the Grand Junction canal. It contains a neat episcopal chapel, the living of which is annexed to that of Hayes; the present curate is the Rev. Edward Moore. The only articles of manufacture here, are those of oil and Roman vitriol. The chapelry, including Southall, contained, in 1831, 1,320 inhabitants.

SOUTHALL is a village, in the precinct of Norwood, about two miles north therefrom; pleasantly situated on the road to Uxbridge, from which town it is distant about 5½ miles. The neighbourhood of Southall is exceedingly respectable; and the village itself is one of considerable thoroughfare, but it possesses no particular trade; there is, however, a large stock market held every Wednesday, which is well attended by purchasers from the metropolis; there are likewise two annual fairs, one at Easter and one at Michaelmas. A county lunatic asylum is in this place: those of the unfortunate inmates who are capable of application are employed in various trades, and there are at times upwards of one thousand in the establishment. Here is also a private lunatic asylum, delightfully situated at Southall park, conducted by the proprietor, Sir William Charles Ellis. The population is returned with Norwood.

POST OFFICE, SOUTHALL, William Humber, *Post Master.*—Letters from LONDON arrive every afternoon at one and night at twenty minutes past eight, and are despatched every morning at half-past five and afternoon at half-past three.—Letters from WORCESTER arrive every morning at half-past five, and are despatched every night at half-past nine.

POST, HAYES, *Receiving-Houses* at Thomas Clarke's, grocer, and at Sophia Dance's, White Hart.—Letters from all parts arrive (from Southall) every morning at nine, and are despatched every evening at six.

NOBILITY, GENTRY AND CLERGY.

Armstrong Benjamin John, esq. Southall green
Back James, esq. Hayes
Bailey Mrs. —, Wood End green
Bignell Richd. esq. Hayes
Bradbury Mrs. Susannah, Wood End green
Briggs Edwd. esq. Park house, Hayes
Burt Rev. John, Southall green
Cain Thomas, esq. Norwood green
Chadwick Mr. Benj. (surgeon), Hayes
Cogger Mrs. —, Hayes
Coleraine Lady —, Hayes
Eddy Thomas, esq. Hayes
Ellis Sir Wm. Charles, Southall park
Emersly Mrs. —, Hayes
Eves George, esq. Hayes
Freeman Rev. John Neville, Hayes
Grant Colonel —, Hayes park
Hayes William, esq. Southall
Hurley Alfred William, esq. Springwell cottage, Hayes
Jersey the Earl of, Osterly park
Laws Mrs. —, Southall
M'Neill Forbes, esq. Grove lodge
Marsden Mr. Thomas C. Hayes
Mason Hy. Batt, esq. Wood End green
Moore Rev. Edward, Norwood green
Neale Mrs. —, Hayes
Parker Mr. —, Southall
Pedler Miss —, Hayes
Phelps Henry, esq. Southall
Shackle Edwd. esq. Hayes
Sturmer Rev. Frederick, Wood End green
Thackthwaite Miss —, Norwood grn
Thompson Mrs. Ann, Hayes
Walker William, esq. Townsend lodge, Southall
Weatherley Mrs. —, Hayes
Wilshin Mr. Andw. Hayes
Winfield Mrs. Harriet, Wood End green
Wood Miss —, Hayes
Wood Samuel, esq. Hayes
Woodward John, esq. Hayes

ACADEMIES AND SCHOOLS.

Fleet Joseph (day & boarding), Wood End green
FREE SCHOOL, Norwood green—John Vincent, master; Mary Ann Vincent, mistress
Honothorn John (day), Norwood green
NATIONAL SCHOOL, Wood End green—George Lamb, master; Mary Lamb, mistress
Thomas Mrs. Wood End green

BAKERS.

Ambridge James, Hayes
Austin Edward, Southall
Birch Robert, Norwood green
Gray Charles, Hayes
Smith John, Hayes
West John, Southall
Woodruff Stephen, Hayes

BLACKSMITHS.

Burt George, Southall green
Green George, Hayes
Herridge Leonard, Hayes
Hewins Samuel, Hayes
Stevens Richard, Southall

BOOT AND SHOE MAKERS.

Baker Henry, Hayes
Batten Robert, Hayes
Chapman George, Wood End green
Dimock Thomas, Southall
Grenville Frederick, Hayes
Grenville Robert, Hayes
Hibbard George, Southall
Masters Thomas, Wood End green
Rogers Francis, Southall
Sims Edward, Norwood green
Tompkins William, Norwood green
Watkins George, Yeading

BREWERS.

Kemp & Heron, Hayes

BRICKLAYERS.

Baldwin James, Hayes
Chuter William, Hayes
Folley William, Hayes
Over Thomas, Southall

BUTCHERS.

Gray Charles, Wood End green
Harper Thomas, Southall green
Hill John, Southall
Ratcliff Thomas, Wood End green

CARPENTERS.

Brown John, Norwood green
Brown John, jun. (& timber dealer), Hayes
Brown Mary, Southall
Hunt John, Hayes
Lane William, Wood End green
Reynolds Christopher, Norwood grn
Toovey James, Hayes

CATTLE SALESMEN.

Fairbrother Edmund, Southall
Mills William, Southall
Savage Robert, Hayes
Welch Alfred, Southall

COAL MERCHANTS.

Bradbury Thomas (and tallow chandler), Wood End green
Maynard George, Hayes
Morten William, Hayes

CORN CHANDLERS.

Maynard George, Hayes
Morten William, Hayes
West John, Southall

GROCERS AND DEALERS IN SUNDRIES.

Austin Edward, Southall
Baker William, Southall green
Chapman Amelia, Wood End green
Clarke Thomas (and druggist & fire office agent), Hayes
Dodd Benjamin, Hayes
Edwards John, Wood End green
Ewer Henry, Southall
Goldsbury Samuel, Southall
Hall Thomas, Hayes
Harper Thomas, Southall green
Reynolds Christopher, Norwood grn
Rogers Francis, Southall
Sexton Robert (& fruiterer), Hayes
Smith John, Hayes
Weedon Thomas, Southall

INNS & PUBLIC HOUSES.

Adam & Eve, Joseph Baylis, Hayes
Angel, Thomas Robottom, Hayes
George & Dragon, Levi Puddifoot, Southall green
King of Prussia, Mary Hands, Southall
Plough, Geo. Warby, Norwood green
Red Lion (and posting house & post office), William Humber, Southall
Three Tuns, John Carruthers, Southall green
Waggon & Horses, John Burdett, Hayes
White Hart, Sophia Dance, Hayes
White Hart (and coach office), Edward Nash, Southall
Wolf, Mary Ann Bliss, Norwood green

LUNATIC ASYLUMS.

PRIVATE ASYLUM, Southall park—Sir Wm. Charles Ellis, proprietor
SOUTHALL, OR COUNTY ASYLUM—John Gideon Van Millengen, M.D. governor.

MALTSTERS.

Kemp & Heron, Hayes
Maynard George, Hayes
Morten William, Hayes

PLUMBER, PAINTER AND GLAZIER.

Bird Geo. Christophr. Norwood green

SADDLERS.

Jacobs Edward, Hayes
Quinion Thomas, Southall

SURVEYORS.

Newman Henry Thomas, Southall
Trumper James, Southall

TAILORS.

Dowman John (and draper and clothier), Hayes
Miller Thomas, Norwood green

WHEELWRIGHTS.

Barton William, Hayes
Brown John, Norwood green
Brown John (and smith), Hayes
Carter Francis, Hayes
Reed William, Southall

Miscellaneous.

Clarke Ann, linen draper, Hayes
Dobbs Henry, oil and Roman vitriol manufacturer, Norwood green
Harradine John, boat builder, Norwood green
Lacey Joseph, brazier and tinman, Hayes
Oldacre Chas. livery stable keeper, Hayes
Shurley Frederick, registrar, Hayes
Symonds Robert, miller, Norwood green
Westbrook Henry Edward, wharfinger & brick maker, Norwood grn & at *Heston*

COACHES AND CARRIERS, To and from LONDON, WORCESTER, CHELTENHAM, GLOUCESTER, OXFORD, and HIGH WYCOMBE, pass through Hayes and Southall, daily.

HIGHGATE

IS a chapelry, partly in the parish of St. Pancras, but chiefly in that of Hornsey, in the hundred of Ossulton. The village is said to have received its name from the toll-gate, erected on the brow of the hill (near the site of an ancient hermitage,) by one of the bishops of London, on the formation of a new road leading from the metropolis towards the north of England. The hill on which Highgate stands is four hundred feet above the summit of St. Paul's cathedral, and consequently affords many extensive and beautiful prospects of London and the neighbouring country. Norden, in speaking of this village, says—'It is a most pleasant dwelling, yet not so pleasant as healthful: for the expert inhabitants there report that divers who have been long visited with sicknesse, not curable by physicke, have in a short time repayred their health by that sweete salutarie aire.' The old north road to Barnet lay through Tallingdon lane, Hornsey park, Whetstone, &c., and in winter was almost impassable: this incommodious thoroughfare was superseded by a line of road laid out by the county, with the active co-operation of the bishop of London (before noticed), beginning at Highgate-hill; travellers and visiters to the metropolis now, however, generally prefer what is termed the 'archway' road to that surmounting the hill, the former being a route much more convenient and agreeable; this improvement is one worthy of particular notice, as it combines ornament with utility. The undertaking was of a stupendous character, and many difficulties opposed its completion. The original plan was to form a tunnel, three hundred yards in length, through the centre of the hill: upwards of one hundred and thirty yards were completed, when, on the 13th of April, 1812, when the workmen happily had withdrawn to dinner, the entire of the superincumbent body fell in with an astounding crash; the design was then necessarily altered, and the present arch and line of road substituted. The destruction of the tunnel was immediately seized upon as the groundwork of a comic piece, entitled the 'Highgate Tunnel, or the Secret Arch,' introduced at the Haymarket theatre. Highgate, within the last twenty years, notwithstanding the numerical decrease of passengers, has kept pace with the most prosperous suburban villages of the capital, both in general appearance and increase of population; this improvement is to be ascribed solely to the acknowledged salubrity and natural attractions of its situation. The only manufacture is that of soda water, carried on upon a very extensive scale by Mr. Dunn, at the pharmaceutical laboratory. At the 'Fox and Crown' tavern, on the road leading from Highgate to Kentish Town, appears the following inscription: 'this coat of arms is a grant from Queen Victoria to John Turner, for services rendered when in danger travelling down this hill, July 6th, 1837.' The custom of imposing a nugatory oath upon all strangers on their first entering Highgate has given way before the more improved manners of the age: a pair of horns, upon which the oath was administered, was formerly kept at each of the public houses; and persons willing to officiate at the ridiculous ceremony may still be found, but these are follies of a past age, when boisterous merriment was taken as happiness.

The new church and cemetery are striking improvements to Highgate; towards the erection of the former the sum of £5,000. was contributed by the church commissioners. It is a handsome structure, surmounted by a lofty spire; and a more beautiful site than that chosen for it, or a style of architecture more appropriate to its situation, cannot be well conceived: the interior is eminently neat and commodious, and the entire presents a creditable testimonial of the taste and judgment of the architect, Mr. L. Vulliamy; it is sufficiently capacious for a congregation of fifteen hundred persons, and has five hundred free sittings. The living has been constituted a consolidated chapelry, and the patronage vested in the metropolitan see; the minister is the Rev. T. H. Cawston, who is assisted by the Rev. O. Reynolds. The old chapel of ease, which formerly stood near the gatehouse, was taken down after the consecration of the new edifice. The cemetery occupies the acclivity of the hill below the church, and is ornamentally planted with trees, shrubs and flowers; a considerable portion of the ground is enclosed, and contains crypts or catacombs, the entrance to which is constructed in the Egyptian style. Both church and cemetery, indeed, well deserve the admiration they have obtained. The other places of worship are for baptists and independents. A free grammar school (founded by Sir Roger Chomeley), a school for twenty-six girls, the greater number of whom are clothed, national and infants' schools, twelve almshouses and several minor charities, attest the benevolent disposition of the inhabitants. In January, 1839, a literary and scientific institution was established here, under the most favourable auspices; and it is in contemplation to erect a building which shall at once be suitable to the purposes of the institution, and present an architectural ornament to the place. In the same year an horticultural society was established, and a savings' bank opened. The population of Highgate, at the census taken in 1831, was made up with the respective parishes in which it is locally situated; it is pretty accurately ascertained, however, that the number of inhabitants in the village at that period amounted to about 4,000; and it is apparent, from the erection of a great number of new mansions, inhabited by wealthy citizens from London, that the amount is now much augmented.

POST OFFICE, High street, Thomas Henry Dunn, *Post Master*.—Letters from LONDON arrive every morning at eight, forenoon at eleven and afternoon at two and five, and are despatched every morning at half-past nine, afternoon at two and half-past four and night at nine.—Letters for the Northern mails and for SCOTLAND and IRELAND are despatched to Barnet every evening at half-past six.

NOBILITY, GENTRY AND CLERGY.

Banfield Mr. John, Southwood lane
Barclay John, esq. Hornsey lane
Barron William, esq. Highgate hill
Basevi Nathaniel, esq. Fitzroy farm, Highgate
Basevi William, esq. Fitzroy farm, Highgate
Bassett Henry, esq. Highgate hill
Beauchamp Mr. Wm. Hornsey lane
Bedgegood Thos. esq. Hornsey lane
Belcher William, esq. Highgate
Bland Jos. esq. Rose cottge. Highgate
Blessley Rev. Robert, North hill
Block Allen, esq. the Grove, Highgte
Bloxam Charles, esq. Hornsey lane
Bloxam Miss Louisa, South grove
Bousfield Mr. Thos. Highgate commn
Browning Mrs. Eliz. Hornsey lane
Bult Mr. Samuel, Hornsey lane
Causton Rev. Thomas Henry, M. A. South grove
Chamberlayne Philip, esq. 6 Holly terrace
Chester Harry, esq. South grove
Churchill Mrs. Susannah, High st
Clarke Thomas, esq. Highgate hill
Collingridge Thos. esq. Highgate hill
Colson Mr. Robert, Highgate commn
Cooke Mrs. Mary, Southwood lane
Cooper William Dodge Cooper, esq. (magistrate), Park house
Cralland Mr. James, Hornsey lane
Crawley Charles, esq. Fitzroy farm, Highgate
Crawley George, esq. Fitzroy farm, Highgate
Crew William, esq. North hill
Crosley Mr. Samuel, Hornsey lane
Cross Mr. Joseph, South grove
Davies Mrs. Eliz. Highgate common
Dear Mr. James, Hornsey lane
Dickinson Thos. esq. Hornsey lane
Dixey Mr. Edward, North hill
Dixey Mrs. George, North hill
Doxey Joseph, esq. 5 Holly terrace
Eldred Wm. esq. Railfall, North rd
Evans Mrs. —, Woodbine cottage, North hill
Farrar F. esq. Highgate rise
Fennell Mr. Samuel, Hornsey lane
Fernee Mr. Thomas, Southwood lane
Fisher William, esq. 8 Holly terrace
Gardiner Joseph, esq. High st
Garrard Sebastian, esq. Little Priory, Highgate common
Gatty George, esq. Southwood lane
Godfrey Joseph, esq. High st
Grayhurst Michael, esq. the Grove, Highgate
Green Mr. Charles, North hill
Griffiths Charles, esq. North hill
Hale Mrs. Elizabth. Southwood lane
Harrison George, esq. Highgate hill
Harriss Miss —, Southwood terrace
Hazlewood Lewis, esq. Archway road
Hill S. H. esq. High st
Hine Mr. J. H. Southwood terrace
Holm Mr. John, High st
Hooper R. V. esq. Southwood lane
Horwood Mr. T. R. Highgate commn
Howe Thos. esq. Lauderdale house
Hunt Wm. Andrews, esq. North hill
Ingram Capt. J. the Ponds
Janson Mr. —, Wood lane, Highgate common
Johnson Adolphus Pugh, esq. Bank, Highgate
Jones John, esq. High st
Jones Mrs. Louisa, the Grove, Highgate
Judkin Rev. H. 6 Holly terrace

NOBILITY, &c.—*Continued.*

Keith Thos. Hilton, esq. Southwood la
Kinderley Geo. esq. the Grove, Highgte
Knight Chas. esq. Ivy house, High st
Longman Mrs. Judith, Southwood hse
Lynn Mrs. Sarah, Hornsey lane
M'Laughlin Mr. Jas. Southwood terr
Maillard Mr. Parnell R. Southwood la
Mallalieu Alfred, esq. Bank, Highgte
Martineau Jos. esq. Elm lodge, Highgte
Melton Mrs. Mary, Southwood lane
Methley Mrs. —, Hornsey lane
Milne Mrs. James, 9 Holly terrace
Mitchell Mr. Jno. M. D. Prospect terr
Mitchell Wm. esq. Southwood lane
Molesworth Capt. —, R.N. North hill
Morewood George, esq. the Grove
Nettlefold J. S. esq. North hill
Nicholls James, esq. 4 Holly terrace
Nicholson Wm. esq. Hornsey lane
Owen Mrs. Geo. Drake's pl. North hill
Parker Hy. esq. South grove, Highgate
Parry John, esq. North hill
Peacock J. M. esq. Bellevue house, Hornsey lane
Phelp John, esq. North hill
Pitcher Mr. Wm. Henry, Southwood hill cottage [Hornsey lane
Poland Peter, esq. Farquhar house,
Prosser Mrs. Wm. the Grove, Highgate
Puckle Edward, esq. Southwood ldge
Raine Mr. Thompson, 7 Holly terrace
Redmayne Giles, esq. Winchester hall
Reynolds Rev. O. Southwood terrace
Richards Mr. Benj. Southwood terr
Rippon Thomas, esq. Hornsey lane
Rougemont Mrs. —, South grove
Rougemont Denis Alexander, esq. Bank, Highgate [hill
Rougemont Mrs. Frances, Highgate
Ryall James, esq. Southwood lane
Sadler Mrs. Sarah, Park pl. North hill
St. Albans his Grace the Duke of, Holly lodge [Highgate
Saltwell Wm. Henry, esq. the Grove,
Scott Rev. William, Bank, Highgate
Shultes Henry, esq. Hornsey lane
Smith Geo. esq. the Grove, Highgate
Smith Mr. John, North hill
Snow Miss —, Hornsey lane [terr
Southgate Jas. Webb, esq. 3 Holly
Squance Miss —, 2 Holly terrace
Squance Barry P. esq. 2 Holly terr
Stedman Mr. —, Drake's pl. North hill
Stringer Mr. George, Ivy cottage
Tatham John, esq. Highgate hill
Tatham Meaburn, esq. Merton lodge
Tatham Thos. Trevor, esq. North hill
Taylor Mr. Henry, Highgate commn
Thomas John, esq. High st
Thompson Mr. F. Bank, Highgate
Thompson Jos. esq. Bank, Highgate
Thorpe Mr. —, Bank, Highgate
Throgmorton Mrs. —, Hornsey lane
Thrusfield Mrs. Eleanor, Southwood terrace
Truefit Peter, esq. High st
Venn Rev. Henry, Hornsey lane
Wakefield Wm. Steir, esq. the Grove
Walker Mrs. —, Highgate hill
Warter H. D. esq. the Grove
Waters T. M. esq. Highgate lodge
Webb Mrs. Ann, Southwood lane
Wells Jonas S. esq. Bank, Highgate
Whittaker Mrs. —, Hornsey lane
Whittaker Edwd. esq. Southwood la
Withers Mr. Robert, Wood lane, Highgate common [North hill
Wood Roger, esq. Woodland cottage,
Woodward Mr. Wm. Highgate hill
Yarnold Mrs. —, Hornsey lane

ACADEMIES & SCHOOLS.

Not otherwise described are Boarding.

Addison William, Cromwell house
Cahusac Sophia, Hornsey lane
Chipperfield Rev. Thos. the Ponds
Clarke Charles C. (day and private), High st [Highgate hill
Dennett Miss (dancing), Grove cottge.
Fenner Zachariah (boarding & day), the Grove, Highgate
GRAMMAR SCHOOL, High st—Rev. John B. Dyne, M.A. master
Grignon & Hull, South grove
INFANTS' SCHOOL (day and Sunday), Castle yard—Sarah Simmonds, mistress [Bank
Kieckhoefer Mrs. G. (preparatory),
Lewis Mrs. North hill
NATIONAL SCHOOL, Southwood lane —John Pettet, master
Neumegen Leopold (Jews, boarding), the Ponds [lane
Norton Mrs. (preparatory), Hornsey
Page Harriet (music), Southwood terr
Porter Mary Ann, North hill
Reid Ann (preparatory), North hill
Russell Sarah, Hornsey lane
Siddle Mrs. (day), Southwood lane
Southgate Thomas Bishop (music), Hornsey lane [Prospect terr
Warren Charlotte (preparatory), 2
Watson Alice (brdng. & day), High st

AUCTIONEERS.

Prickett Geo. (& surveyor), High st
Sadleir Thomas (and furniture warehouse and upholsterer), High st

BAKERS & FLOUR DEALERS.

Atkins John, High st
Burke Elizabeth, High st
Cole Joseph, High st
Fisher John (and biscuit), the Ponds
Fitch Thomas, High st
Freeman Robert, High st
Gozzard Charlotte, High st
Hamp George, North hill
Morgan Thomas, High st

BLACKSMITHS & FARRIERS.

Attkins Thomas, High st
Boston Mary & Son, Townshend's yard, High st
Dodd John, High st
Learman John, High st

BOOKSELLERS, STATIONERS & LIBRARIES.

Broadbent Catherine, London house, High st
Savage Celia S. & E. (fancy stationers—late Bage), High st

BOOT & SHOE MAKERS.

Andrews John, North hill
Barnard John, the Ponds
Blanche James, High st
Endersby Richard, High st
Hunter Robert, High st
Morgan William, High st
Potter William, High st
Reading John, High st
Stone Henry Richard, High st
Taylor William, corner of Hampstead lane
Webb & Lawrance, High st

BRICK & TILE MAKERS.

Colson Thos. & Wm. Archway road

BRICKLAYERS.

Covington Joseph, High st
Townshend Thos. (& builder) High st
Warr James, York buildings, High st

BUTCHERS.

Attkins Etty, High st
Attkins James (pork), High st
Chapman Edward, High st
Pritchard Henry, High st
Symonds Henry, the Ponds

CABINET MAKER AND UPHOLSTERER.

Sadleir Thomas (and undertaker), High st

CARPENTERS, BUILDERS & UNDERTAKERS.

Broadbent Thomas, High st
Burr John, High st
French John, High st
Ginn Thomas, High st
Harrmann Frederick, High st

CARVERS, GILDERS AND PAPER HANGERS.

Hine Robert, High st
Wood Joseph, North hill

CHYMIST AND DRUGGIST.

Dunn Thomas Henry (& manufacturing chymist), High st

CLOTHES DEALERS.

Cooper John (& rags), High st
Endersby Richard, High st
Morris Elizabeth, High st
Tranfield Hannah, High st

COAL DEALERS.

Bew George, North hill
Bullen John, High st
Fleming Thomas, High st
Lea Thomas, North hill
Row William, High st
Toyne William, North hill
White John, North hill

CORN, &c. DEALERS.

Griffiths William (& malt & hops), High st
Row William, High st

COW KEEPERS.

Allcock Thomas, High st
Attkins Samuel, Highgate hill
Bew George, North hill
Fernee John, the Ponds
Johnson John, Manor farm
Odell William, North hill
Simmonds Wm. Highgate common
Turner Ann, Hornsey lane
Upton Ann, High st

CURRIERS AND LEATHER CUTTERS.

Dennis John, High st
Endersby Richard, High st

EATING HOUSE KEEPERS.

Back James, High st
Barnes William, Grove st

FIRE, &c. OFFICE AGENTS.

BRITISH (fire) and WESTMINSTER (life), Abraham Eagles, High st
GLOBE, Thomas Sadleir, High st
GUARDIAN, Wm. Jos. Cooze, High st
NORWICH UNION, John Worley, Southwood lane [High st
ROYAL EXCHANGE, Thos. Broadbent,
YORK and NORTH of ENGLAND, Joseph Humphrey, High st

FISHMONGERS AND POULTERERS.

Clark John Matthias, High st
Norman William, High st

FRUITERERS AND GREENGROCERS.

Brown Elizabeth, High st
Danes Thomas, High st
Keeble Thomas (grower), High st
White Henry, High st

GROCERS & TEA DEALERS.

(See also Shopkeepers, &c.)

Arthur Tryphena (& tobacconist), High st
Attkins Benjamin, High st
Bullen John (& glass, &c.) High st
Clarke Joseph (& oilman), High st
Fleming Stephen, North hill
Fleming Thomas, High st
Groves Charles and John (& cheesemongers, oilmen, & tallow chandlers), High st
Hansford William Gregory, High st
Humphrey Joseph, High st
Newman Jno. near the Angel, Ponds

Toyne William, North hill
White John, North hill

HAIR DRESSERS.

Golden John, High st.
Goode Henry, High st

INNS AND PUBLIC HOUSES.

Angel, George Fenner, High st [st
Bell & Horns, Richard Young, High
Bull, John Pickering, North hill
Castle, Emily Barnes, High st [st
Cooper's Arms, Wm. Williams, High
Duke'sHead, AnsonWaldron, High st
Flask, William Nash, the Grove
Fox & Crown, John Turner, Highgate hill West [High st
Gate House Hotel, Robert Rogers,
Green Dragon, Jno. Watkins, High st
Mitre, Wm. Grove, High st [hill
Old Crown, Geo. Pittman, Highgate
Red Lion, William Ivens, High st
Red Lion & Sun, Ann Upton (and brewer), High st
Rose & Crown, John Bean, Prospect house, High st [North hill
Wellington, Eleanor Frost, foot of
Woodman, Charles Fred. Ramsway, Archway road
Wrestlers, SusannahWatson, High st

IRONMONGERS, SMITHS & BRAZIERS.

Attkins Thomas, High st
Boston Mary & Son, Townshend's yard, High st
Janes James, High st [High st
Thompson John, (and tinman, &c.)

LANDAU, FLY, &c. OWNERS FOR HIRE.

Covington Joseph, Muswell hill road
Gardner Thomas, High st
Hale Abraham, the Grove
Hickenbottom Stephen (omnibus), the Grove
Hughes Joseph, Duke's Head yard
Rogers James, Hornsey lane
Wiber J. & C. (omnibus), Castle yard

LINEN DRAPERS.

Drake Joseph, High st
Martin Thomas, High st
Palmer Philip, High st

MILLINERS & DRESS MAKRS

Dutton Emma, High st
Harding Frances, High st
Illidge Isabel, High st
Jolliffe Ann, Southwood lane corner
Sherrard Jane, the Ponds
Sims Catherine Louisa, North place
Smith Sarah & Mary Anne, Southwood lane
Snow & Barnard, High st

NURSERYMEN, SEEDSMEN AND FLORISTS.

Cutbush William, South grove
Eagles Abraham, High st
Stein Peter, Grove nursery

PAINTERS, PLUMBERS AND GLAZIERS.

Cooze William Joseph, High st
Manton George, High st
Martin Robert, North hill
Redfern Mary, High st
Sims James Hall, High st
Worley John, Southwood lane

PASTRYCOOKS AND CONFECTIONERS.

Atkins John, High st
Jennings Samuel, High st
Wooder William, High st

SADDLERS AND HARNESS MAKERS.

Cooper Thomas Dawes, High st
Kimpton Jane, High st

SHOPKEEPERS & DEALRS IN GROCERIES & SUNDRIES.

Endersby Richard, jun. Hornsey lane
Gozzard Charlotte, High st
Jennings Samuel, High st
Johnson Thomas, Archway road
Middlemiss Mary, High st
Sims Thomas Whitlow, North hill
Strong Robert, North hill

SODA WATER MANUFACTRER

Dunn Thomas Henry, Laboratory, High st

STAY MAKERS.

Harman Sarah Bower, High st
Snow & Barnard, High st

STONE MASONS.

Cansick Harker, Southwood lane
Townshend Thomas, High st

STRAW HAT MAKERS.

Ashenden Sarah, High st
Broadbent Sarah, High st
Clark Mary, High st
Middleton Mary, High st

SURGEONS.

Dobson John H. Hornsey lane
Gillmann & Moger, the Grove
Richardson Wm. Thos. Highgate hill
Snow Bernard Geary, Highgate hill
Wetherell Nathl. Thos. nr the Grove

TAILORS.

Fardoe Joseph, High st
Harrington Richard, High st
Holston James, High st
Hornell John, High st
Pitkin James, High st
Pringle Thomas, High st
Proughten George, High st
Traher Richard, High st

TOY DEALERS.

Broadbent Catherine, High st
Jennings Samuel, High st
Keeys Samuel, High st
Savage Celia S. & E. High st
Sims Mary, Southwood lane

WATCH AND CLOCK MAKERS

Aumonier Henry (& jeweller), High st
Ebdon Joseph, High st

WINE & SPIRIT MERCHANTS

Groves Charles & John (British wines), High st
Lacugne A. (foreign) North hill

Miscellaneous.

Andrews George, tobacco pipe maker, Muswell hill road [hill
Baker William, farmer and drover, North
Crump Rd. brush makr. & undertkr. High st
Franks James, newsvender, &c. the Ponds
Johnston Andrew, wheelwright and general smith, High st [yard
Jones William, coach painter, &c. Stable
LITERARY & SCIENTIFIC INSTITUTION, Henry Chester, esq. president
Morris John, device manufacturer, High st
SAVINGS' BANK—(open every Saturday evening from 7 till 9)
Spiller Catherine & Co. dealers in medicines, Archway road
Stevens William, cooper, &c. High st

COACHES,

To and from LONDON and the NORTH, pass the Wellington Inn, foot of North hill, and the Woodman Inn, Archway road, continually during the day & night.

OMNIBUSES.

To LONDON, Hickinbottom's *Omnibuses*, from Hall's office, near the Gatehouse, every morning (Sunday excepted), at nine and ten, afternoon at two, and evening at seven, and on Sunday at the three latter hours; — Smith, from Castle yard, every morning (Sunday excepted), at ten, afternoon at two, and evening at seven, and on Sundays at the two first named hours, and evening at eight; and — Weber, from the Castle yard, every morning (Sunday excepted), at ten, and evening at six, and on Sundays at half-past nine in the morning, and evening at eight.

CARRIERS.

DAILY, SUNDAY EXCEPTED.

To LONDON, the London Parcels' Delivery Company, from the Post office, High street, morning at ten, afternoon at three, and evening at eight.

To LONDON, John Bell, jun. from High st, morning at half-past ten—William Cokeham, from North hill, morning at ten and afternoon at two—and John Petit, from High street, at twelve at noon.

HORNSEY, CROUCH END AND MUSWELL HILL.

HORNSEY is a village and parish in the hundred of Ossulton, about six miles N. W. from the 'Standard,' in Cornhill—agreeably situated in a vale, through which flows the New river, and environed by hills commanding prospects as beautiful as they are extensive, including various views of the metropolis and the surrounding country. This place was in former times designated *Haringay Forest*, and from a remote period has belonged to the see of London, whose bishops had formerly a park here. The mansion of Haringay is situate in the Green lanes leading to Southgate, and was occupied for more than half a century by the late Edward Gray, Esq., who died in September, 1838. The parish includes the hamlets of CROUCH END, MUSWELL HILL and STROUD GREEN, and the principal portion of the town of Highgate. The places of worship are the parish church, and a chapel of ease (formerly baptist) under the establishment: the greater part of the church and its tower are of considerable antiquity, and, having recently been repaired and ornamented, its appearance is highly pleasing; it is partially covered with ivy, amongst which numerous nests of birds may be distinctly observed. There are two charity schools—one upon the national plan for sixty boys, who are clothed, and another for fifty girls; also several benefactions for apprenticing boys, and for other charitable purposes. The hospital and dairy farm of the knights of St. John of Jerusalem, the wells of which still retain a reputation for medical efficacy, were situated here; and at Muswell Hill was formerly a chapel, dedicated to the Virgin Mary, much resorted to by pilgrims prior to the reformation: from the summit of this eminence visiters enjoy an extensive landscape over the metropolis, and the counties of Essex, Kent and Surrey. This neighbourhood is considered one of the most agreeable round London, and is inhabited by persons of the first respectability. Lands, held under the lord of the manor, descend in common to all the sons or daughters of a customary tenant. The jurisdiction of the court of requests, held in Kingsgate-street, London, extends over Hornsey parish; the population of which amounted, in 1831, to 4,856 persons, and it is now estimated at nearly 7,000.

POST OFFICE, near the Church, HORNSEY, Thomas Grimes, *Post Master.*—Letters from LONDON and all parts arrive every morning at nine, noon at twelve, afternoon at four and evening at seven, and are despatched every morning at nine and afternoon at one and four.

POST OFFICE, opposite the King's Head Inn, CROUCH END, George Ives, *Post Master.*—Letters from LONDON, &c. arrive every morning at nine, forenoon at eleven, afternoon at three and evening at six, and are despatched every morning at nine and afternoon at half-past one and four.

POST OFFICE, near the Green Man Inn, MUSWELL HILL, Mary Anderson, *Post Mistress.*—Letters from LONDON and all parts arrive every morning at eight, noon at twelve, afternoon at three and evening at six, and are despatched every morning at a quarter past eight and afternoon at four.

GENTRY AND CLERGY.

Angell William Sandy, esq. Tottenham lane, Hornsey [Hill
Attwood Matthias, esq. M.P. Muswell
Attwood Matthias, esq. Muswell Hill
Barnes Mr. William, Middle lane
Bell Thomas, esq. Hornsey
Billing —, esq. M.D. Hornsey
Booth John Gillyat, esq. Crouch hall
Bourdillon —, esq. Grove hse, Hornsy
Bradshaw Joseph H. esq. Hornsey
Buckton Geo. esq. Oakfield, Crouch hil
Chapman Thory, esq. Crouch hill
Coleman John, esq. Crouch End
Corunthwaite Tully Joseph, esq. Crouch End [End
Cornthwaite Rev. Tully, jun. Crouch
Cutler John, esq. Tottenham lane
Danvers Frederick S. esq. Priory lodge
Dickinson John, esq. Crouch hill
Dyer George, esq. Crouch End
Eady William, esq. Tottenham lane
Ewart James, esq. Muswell Hill
Eykyn Richard, esq. Crouch End
Fletcher Francis, esq. Crouch hall
Fuller Mrs. Fanny, Hornsey
Geddes George, esq. Tottenham lane
Gibbons John, esq. Crouch End
Gurney Sidney, esq. Crouch End
Hamilton Mrs. Eliz. Tottenham lane
Hands Mr. Benjn. (surgeon), Hornsey
Harvey Rev. Richard, Rectory
Haygarth Rev. Richard, Muswell Hill
Hitchcock —, esq. Tottenham lane
Houston Mrs. Eliz. Tottenham lane
Kilgour Geo. Henry, esq. Muswell Hill
Latter Mr. —, Hornsey [lodge
Lawrence Benjn. esq. Campsbourne
Maples T. Fredk. esq. Crouch End
Marshall Richard, esq. Muswell Hill
Martineau Miss M. Crouch hall
Mavor Mr. William, Crouch End
Moreton William, esq. Hornsey
Moreton William H. esq. Hornsey
Moulton Mr. Charles, Muswell Hill
Orchard Wm. esq. Middle lane, Hornsy
Rowley Mr. Thomas, Middle lane
Saunders —, esq. Bemerton villa,
Soulby Mrs. —, Crouch End
Spooner Mrs. Mary, Hornsey [Hill
Taylor Jno. esq. Holland hse, Crouch
Taylor John, esq. Tottenham lane
Thrupp Henry Joseph, esq. Hornsey
Vyse F. A. esq. Hornsey
Warner George, esq. Priory
Warner Henry, esq. Priory
Warner Redstone, esq. Priory
Wells Mr. Jno. Stroud Green, Hornsey
Whitworth Mr. Wm. Tottenham lane
Wilkinson Mr. Charles, Hornsey
Williams Mr. Rd. Stroud Green, Hrnsy
Wood E. H. esq. Muswell Hill
Woolcott Mr. George, Muswell Hill

ACADEMIES & SCHOOLS.

Lobb the Misses (ladies' boarding), Crouch end [Muswell Hill
Meeres Martin (gent.'s boarding),
Saunders the Misses (prepy), Hornsey
Smith Wm. (gent.'s bdg), Crouch End

TAVERNS & PUBLIC HOUSES.

Green Man, Catherine Hawkins, Muswell Hill
Hope & Anchor, Joseph Ebdon, Hornsey
Hornsey Wood house, Charles Bradbroke, Hornsey Wood tea gardens [End
King's Head, Charles Proughten, Crouch
Manor House, William Tomlinson, Green lanes [Hornsey
Nightingale, John Ebdon, New River side,
Sluice House (or Eel-pie House), Charles Saffrey, near Hornsey Wood
Three Compasses, Radford and Winks, Hornsey

SHOPKEEPERS, TRADERS, &c.

The names without address are in Hornsey.

Anderson Mary, grocer, Muswell Hill
Bayley William, shoemaker
Brett James, bricklayer, Crouch End
Bumpstead John, painter & glazier, Crouch End [Muswell Hill
Chamlett Mrs. T. grocer, &c. Back hill,
Clark John, carpenter, Crouch End
Cooper William, smith and farrier
Davies Chas. linen draper, Crouch End
Dean John, shoemaker, Crouch End
Eames William, carpenter & wheelwright [place
Ebdon John, carpenter, Nightingale
Elder William, bricklayer
Grimes Thos. grocer, near the Church
Guley William, posting & fly master
Howard Mary E. baker, &c.
Ives George, baker, Crouch End
Litten John, shoemaker
Marshall Geo. carpenter & builder
Moyes Sarah, blacksmith & farrier
Norris Richard, shoemaker
Proughten James, builder and bricklayer, Crouch End
Riseley Hannah, corn chandler and baker, Muswell Hill [End
Robinson Edward, saddler, Crouch
Saffrey Charles, wine and spirit merchant, near Hornsey wood
Smeton John, butcher
Turnbull James, grocer, Crouch End
Webb William, butcher, Crouch End
Whitton William, coal merchant, Muswell Hill
Wright Joseph, coal merchant

OMNIBUSES.

To LONDON, Robert Baker, Edward Robinson, and Edmund Vass's *Omnibuses*, every morning at a quarter before and a quarter past nine, and a quarter before ten, two afternoon, and at a quarter past seven evening.

CARRIERS.

To LONDON, William Greaves, Thomas Greaves, and Joseph Wright, from Muswell Hill, daily at twelve noon.

HOUNSLOW, HESTON, CRANFORD BRIDGE,

HARLINGTON AND NEIGHBOURHOODS.

HOUNSLOW (formerly a market town) is a chapelry, partly in the parish of Isleworth, but chiefly in that of Heston—ten miles W.S.W. from London and six E.N.E. from Staines; situated upon the edge of the Heath of its name. It is a place of distinguished thoroughfare, the great western and Bath roads uniting here; and it is frequently favoured by the presence of royalty, this being the station where a relay of horses is kept ready for her Majesty, on her way to and from the palace at Windsor; the horses are furnished either from the 'Red Lion' or the 'Rose and Crown' inns, both superior posting establishments, the former being also the commercial house. Gunpowder is manufactured extensively at the mills in this neighbourhood. A priory of the order of the Holy Trinity formerly existed here, the chapel attached to which was converted into a chapel of ease to Heston; there is likewise a chapel for methodists. In 1686, after the suppression of the Duke of Monmouth's rebellion, James II formed an encampment on the heath, and granted the privilege of holding a market thereon, as long as the encampment should continue and during any future one, but no market has been held within the last thirty years; to effect its revival, however, it is understood some measures are in contemplation, and the situation is well adapted for the proper support of one; it is also meditated to constitute it a distinct parish, as far as regards ecclesiastical affairs. About fifty years since there were erected on the heath barracks for cavalry, which afford accommodation for nearly 400 men and their horses. The ancient chapel of the priory (before mentioned) was taken down in June, 1828, and a new church erected on its site at an expense of £5,300. partly defrayed by the church commissioners, and the remainder by voluntary contribution; it is a handsome structure, in the modern English style of architecture, with a low spire and two turrets. Independents, and Wesleyan and primitive methodists, have a chapel each. There is an excellent school, for one hundred boys and one hundred girls, supported by subscription. Fairs are annually held on the first Monday after Whit-Monday and the first Monday after New Michaelmas-day. The population of Hounslow is returned with that of the two parishes in which it is locally situate.

About a mile and a half from Hounslow is the village of HESTON, in a populous parish of its name. There are gunpowder works in the parish, but the majority of the inhabitants are engaged in agriculture. The soil of this district produces wheat of superior quality, and in the reign of Elizabeth (according to Norden) it was used for the bread of the royal table. The church, dedicated to St. Leonard, is a small building, and for a long time was found inadequate to the accommodation of the parishioners, but some years since it received an addition of upwards of two hundred sittings. In this sanctuary are interred the remains of Sir Joseph Banks, president of the royal society, and those of his lady. A parochial school for children of both sexes, supported chiefly by contributions, is the only charity. The parish (including part of Hounslow chapelry) contained, when the census was taken in 1831, 3,110 inhabitants.

Three miles from Hounslow is CRANFORD BRIDGE, a village in the parish of Cranford and hundred of Elthorne—situated on the great Bath road, and on the bank of the river Colne, which is crossed by a bridge; hence the name of the village. Cranford Park, the admired seat of the Countess of Berkeley, is the principal object of attraction to this place: her ladyship presents to the parish benefice, which is a rectory; the church is dedicated to St. Dunstan. Population, in 1831, 377.

In the same hundred as Cranford Bridge, one mile from that village and four from Hounslow, is HARLINGTON, or *Arlington*, village and parish. The church, dedicated to St. Peter and St. Paul, is built of stone; its porch is admitted to be a beautiful specimen of Norman architecture: the living, a rectory, is in the patronage and incumbency of the Rev. Edward Davidson, and the Rev. L. C. Booth is his curate. The baptists have a large chapel here. A fair is held on the 21st May. The family of Bennett takes the titles of baron and earl from this place. Population of the parish, in 1831, 648.

POST OFFICE, HOUNSLOW, Ann Butler, *Post Mistress.*—Letters from LONDON arrive and are despatched (by threepenny post) three times a day; also arrive by the Gloucester mail every evening (Sunday excepted) at half-past nine, and are despatched every morning at six.—Letters from all parts of the West arrive every morning at six, and are despatched every night at half-past nine.

POST, HESTON, *Receiving-House* at the Rose and Crown.—Letters arrive from and are despatched to HOUNSLOW three times a day.

POST, *Receiving-Houses* at the White Hart Inn, CRANFORD BRIDGE; and at the Lion, HARLINGTON.—Letters from HOUNSLOW arrive every morning at eight, and are despatched every afternoon at four.

NOBILITY, GENTRY, AND CLERGY.

Astell Edward, esq. Hounslow
Benson Rev. Joseph, D.D. Hounslow
Berkeley the Countess Dowager, Cranford park
Berkeley Right Hon. Moreton, Cranford park
Booth Rev. Leeds Comyns, Harlington
Brooks Captain —, Bath road
Brown William, esq. Harlington
Cane Thomas, esq. Norwood green
Cane William, esq. Cranford
Cole William, esq. Sutton
Cooper James, esq. Cranford
Cox John, esq. Cranford
Ensor James, esq. Hounslow heath
Fraser Mrs. —, Fern cottage, Heston
Freemantle Colonel —, Cranford
George Rev. Jonathan, Harlington
Gooding Captain —, Bath road
Graham Mrs. —, Cranford
Graham Frederick, esq. Cranford
Graham James, esq. Cranford
Harvey Lester, esq. Hounslow
Hawley Mr. William, Harlington
Henley Mr. Jas. Bell road, Hounslow
Hicks Rev. J. Cranford
Hinds Mr. William, Harlington
Hogarth John, esq. Heston hall
Hope Richard, esq. Brentford road
How Mrs. —, Lampton
Humphrey James, esq. Bath road
Lonsdale Rev. W. M.A. Hounslow
Magnell Mrs. —, Cranford
Marshall Thos. esq. Smallbury green
Neville Mrs. —, Heston
Newman David, esq. Heston
Palmer Mrs. Mary, Hounslow
Phillips Miss —, Bath road
Poulton John, esq. Staines road
Pownall Henry, esq. Spring grove
Raper Mr. James, Bath road
Rippon John Jas. esq. Hounslow heath
Rogers Mrs. Ann, Harlington
Serle Edward, esq. Bath road
Smith Henry Webb, esq. Bath road
Sparks Mr. Joseph, Harlington
Sparks Mr. Ralph, Harlington
Sprang Mr. John, Harlington
Stewart Mr. James, Sutton
Sutton Coles, esq. Heston
Taylor Richard, esq. Hounslow heath
Travers Capt. Nicholas, barrack mastr
Trimmer Rev. Henry Scott, Heston
Weston Mr. John, Harlington
Whiting John, esq. Heston villa
Wingfield Captain —, Sutton

ACADEMIES & SCHOOLS.

Not otherwise described are Day Schools.

Burgoyne Priscilla, Staines road
Cooper Miss, Hounslow
Dixon Sophia, Hounslow
Filbey Misses (day & boardg), Hounslow
Hauge Eliz. (day & boardg), Bath road
Newman Chales, Harlington
Ragsdell Miss (day & boarding), Harlington
Skally & Londsdale (bdg), Albemarle house, Hounslow
Tolley William, Hounslow
Webster Wm. (boarding), Harlington
Welsh Francis (boarding), Cranford

AUCTIONEERS & APPRAISRS.

Parnham James, Staines road
Peisley John (and land and estate agent), Hounslow
White Francis, Hounslow

BAKERS & FLOUR DEALERS.

Booker Henry, Cranford
Brett Starmer, Heston
Cooper Richard, Hounslow heath
Cottrell Edwd. (& biscuit), Hounslow
Friberg James, Hounslow
Lewis William, Heston
Loder Jesse, Hounslow
Long James (and biscuit), Hounslow
Marshall Rd. & Son (& biscuit), Heston
New Ann, Hounslow
Pearce Charles, Staines road
Philp Alfred, Harlington
Philp John, Harlington
Sargeant Wm. Staines road
Slark Edmd. Church parade, Hounslow
Tillyer Jacob, Harlington
Willis John (& biscuit), Hounslow

BLACKSMITHS & FARRIERS.

Boughton Peter, Hounslow
Carter William, Hounslow
Francis John, Cranford
Hinge Mrs. Hounslow
Mallings William, Harlington
Webb Robert, Heston
Webb Thomas, Cranford

BOOKSELLER & STATIONER.

Gotelee John (& printer & circulating library), Church parade, Hounslow

BOOT & SHOE MAKERS.

Basley John, Hounslow
Batchelor James, Hounslow
Brooks William, Hounslow heath
Cahnon Isaac, Hounslow
Drinkwater William, Harlington
Fullbrook Felix, Hounslow
Gray Henry, Staines road
Higgins George, Hounslow
Lambon James, Heston
Rawlinson Joseph, Hounslow
Smith George, Harlington
Smith John, Harlington
Stevens William, Hounslow
Strong William, Harlington
Tompkins William, Hounslow
Ward George, Hounslow
Williams Charles, Hounslow

BRAZIERS AND TINMEN.

Appleton John, Hounslow
Atkins Joseph (and zinc), Hounslow

BRICKLAYERS.

Basent Jas. (& plasterer), Staines rd
Burchett Edward & Son, Hounslow
Burgess John, Harlington
Littlewood Thomas, Staines road

BUTCHERS.

Arnold Benjamin, Hounslow
Cranage William, Hounslow
Filbey Robert, Hounslow
Finch George, Hounslow
Furnell Thomas, Hounslow
Green Joseph, Staines road
Hewett Robert, Hounslow
Hughes James, Harlington
Jeffs James, Hounslow
Lingood James, Heston
Philp Shadrach, Harlington
Shervill James, Hounslow
Stodgell William, Hounslow
Yates Frances (pork), Hounslow

CARPENTRS & UNDERTAKRS.

Bennett George, Staines road
Gallup Richard, Hounslow
Hanson Cornelius, Lampton
Hiscock Thomas, Hownslow
Sidwell Thomas, Cranford
Springall Joseph, Hounslow

CHYMISTS & DRUGGISTS.

Kent John (and oilman), Hounslow
Ward James, Church parade

COAL MERCHANTS & DEALRS

Brumbridge George Bartholomew, Staines road
Friberg James, Hounslow
Jeffs James, Hounslow
Jennings Robert, Hounslow
Marshall Richard & Son, Heston
Sharp Daniel, Harlington.
Stockbridge Francis, Hounslow
Willis John, Hounslow

COOPERS.

Anstead Jno. (& net maker) Hounslw
Blewchamp John, Hounslow

CORN DEALERS.

Ades James (& flour), Hounslow
Bendall Thos. (& seedsman) Hounslw
Brumbridge George Bartholomew (and miller), Staines road
Friberg James, Hounslow
Jeffs James, Hounslow
Jennings Robert, Hounslow
Marshall Richard & Son, Heston
Willis John, Hounslow

FIRE, &c. OFFICE AGENTS.

ALLIANCE, Benj. Draper, Hounslow
GLOBE, John Peisley, Hounslow
GUARDIAN, Robt. Jennings, Hounslw
NORWICH UNION, James Ward, Church parade, Hounslow
ROYAL EXCHANGE, Ann Butler,
SUN, John Gotelee, Church parade, Hounslow; Danl. Sharp, Harlingtn

GROCERS & CHEESEMONGRS.
(See also Shopkeepers, &c.)
Goatley John, Hounslow
Green John Vanham, Church parade, Hounslow
Harding William, Heston
Lewis Henry, Hounslow
Sambrook Samuel, Hounslow
Stacey William, Hounslow
Watson William, Hounslow
White John & Francis & Edwin (& tallow chandlers), Hounslow
Willis Thomas, Hounslow

HAIR DRESSERS.
Church Joseph, Hounslow
Lower Ann, Hounslow
Taylor Samuel, Hounslow

HORSE DEALERS.
Benn Charles & Son, Cranford
Saben William, Hounslow
Statsbury John, Brentford road

INNS—POSTING.
George (and commercial) Stephen Coomes, Hounslow
Red Lion & Commercial Inn, John Lawless (post master to Her Majesty), Hounslow
Rose & Crown, Robert Blizard (and post master by appointment to Her Majesty and the Queen Dowager), Hounslow
White Hart, Geo. Bailey, Cranford bridge

IRONMONGERS.
Appleton John, Hounslow
Gay Mary, Hounslow
Jefferson Robert Beale, Hounslow

LEATHER CUTTERS.
Farrell John, Hounslow
Jeffs James, Hounslow

LINEN DRAPERS.
Beauchamp Richard, Hounslow
Crisp Alfred, Hounslow
Stuart Wm. Church parade, Hounslow

MARINE STORE DEALERS.
Cox Ann, Hounslow
Tilley Mary, Hounslow

MARKET GARDENERS.
Barnham James, Feltham
Beach James, Hounslow
Benham Jos. Staines road, Hounslow
Coleman John, Harlington
Edwards Elias, Harlington
Hatchman Wm. Harlington
HumphreyJno. (&seedsman) Hounslow
Hunt John, Harlington
Jessop Joseph, Harlington
M'Combie Geo. Bath road, Hounslow
Newman Matthew, Harlington
Philp Benjamin Batten, Harlington
Philp Richard Wickliffe, Harlington
Raper John, Harlington
Rolfe Thomas, Harlington
Salmon Frederick, Sutton
Tattersall George, Harlington

MILLINERS & DRESS MAKRS.
Derham Mary, Harlington
Gatfield Mary, Hounslow
Holmes Ann (& lace dealer) Hounslow
Morris Eliza, Harlington
Paine Ann, Hounslow
Rawlinson Elizabeth, Hounslow
Shepard Sarah, Hounslow
Warden Susannah, Hounslow
Wells Jane, Hounslow

PLUMBERS, PAINTERS AND GLAZIERS.
Cave James (painter), Hounslow
Commins William, Hounslow
Draper Benjamin, Hounslow
Lofting John, Hounslow
Morris Thomas, Hounslow
Ogilvie William, Hounslow

POULTERERS.
Burchett William, Hounslow
Coleman William, Hounslow

SADDLERS AND HARNESS MAKERS.
Eycars Samuel, Hounslow
Gay Geo. (& rope & twine) Hounslow
Holloway Ann, Hounslow
Holloway Robert, Hounslow

SHOPKEEPERS & DEALRS IN GROCERIES & SUNDRIES.
Bexley Mary, Harlington
Cooper Richard, Hounslow heath
Hill William, Staines road
Lanham John, Staines road
Maberly Augustin Wm. Hounslow
Neller James, Harlington
Powell George, Heston
Rayment Richard, Harlington
Sharp Daniel, Harlington
Sidwell Thomas, Cranford
Stacey Caleb, Staines road
Temple William, Heston
West Augustus, Staines road
Williams Daniel, Hounslow

STRAW HAT MAKERS.
Packer Mrs. Harlington
Shephard Sarah, Hounslow
Vidler Ann & Mary, Hounslow
West Sarah, Hounslow

SURGEONS.
Camden George James Stredwick, Hounslow
Frogley Ralph Allen, Hounslow
Knevett Charles, Hounslow

SURVEYORS.
Newman Charles, Harlington
Peisley John, Hounslow

TAILORS.
Bradley Jonathan, Hounslow
Derham Robert, Harlington
Filbey Joseph, Hounslow
Grubb William, Hounslow
M'Rae George, Bath road
M'Rae Peter, Hounslow
Philp Thomas, Harlington
Pleasants Henry, Staines road
Tidbury William, Staines road
Titcombe Joseph, Hounslow
White Thomas, Harlington

TAVERNS & PUBLIC HOUSES.
Bell, John Brunsden, Hounslow
Berkeley Arms, John Green, Cranford bridge
Black Horse, James Berry, Heston
Chaise & Horses, Wm. Heath, Hounslow
Coach & Horses, Charles Compton, Harlington
Coach & Horses, Rebecca Ann Woodward, Hounslow
Cricketers, William Curtis, Staines road
Cross Lances, Dodds Vickers, Hounslow
Crown, John Edwards, Harlington
Crown & Cushion, Jas. Merriott, Hounslow
Duke of Wellington, William Woodbridge, Staines road
George the Fourth, Hannah Baker, Staines road
George (Tap) William Froome, Hounslow
King's Arms, James Binfield, Hounslow
King's Head, Clarinda Powell, Hounslow
Lion, Daniel Sharp, Harlington
Lion & Lamb, James Curtis, Hounslow
Marquess of Granby, Jno. Patfield, Hounslw
Nag's Head, Joseph Newcomb, Hounslow
Prince Regent, Eliz. Stodgell, Hounslow
Queen's Head, Thomas Hall, Heston
Red Lion (Tap) John Batten, Hounslow
Rose & Crown, Edwin Cook, Heston
Rose and Crown (Tap) John Garrett, Hounslow
Tankerville Arms, My. Johnson, Hounslow
Ship, Thomas West, Hounslow
White Bear, Jos. Percival Perman, Hounslow
White Hart, William Walker, Harlington

TOY DEALER.
Gotelee John, Church parade, Hounslow

VETERINARY SURGEONS.
Boughton Peter, Hounslow
Carter William, Hounslow

WATCH & CLOCK MAKERS.
Freebody Thomas, Hounslow
Newcomb Joseph, Hounslow

WHEELWRIGHTS.
Gurney William, Staines road
James Thomas, Hounslow
Musto Henry, Harlington
Tillier Philip, Harlington

WINE & SPIRIT MERCHANTS.
Blizard Robert, Hounslow
Jennings Robert, London road
Lawless John, Hounslow

Miscellaneous.
Adams William, fishmonger, Hounslow
Barber Wm. hat manufacturer, Hounslow
Beale Moses, clothes dealer, Hounslow
Bristow Thomas, coach maker, Hounslow
Chandler Percival, coach & sign painter, Hounslow
Cook John, basket maker, Hounslow
Curtiss & Harvey, gunpowder manufacturers, Hounslow heath
Daws Robert, patent recumbent chair manufacturer, Harlington
Hill Amelia, stay maker, Hounslow
Jackson John Hy, pawnbroker, Hounslow
Lane John, nursery & seedsman, Staines road
Luffman Joseph, butter and egg dealer, Hounslow
Martin William, cowkeeper, Bath road
Robinson Elizabeth & Sarah, glass and china dealers, Hounslow
Smith Jas. fishmonger & fruiterer, Hounslow
Spencer Lucy, clothes dealer, Hounslow
Staff Simon, canvass manufactr. Bath rd
Stevens William, tobacconist, Hounslow
Stokes James, artist, Hounslow
Such James, furniture broker, Hounslow
Taylor James, locksmith and bellhanger, Hounslow
Tucker John, millwright, &c. Harlington
Westbrook Henry and Edward, brick makers, Heston
Woods Thos. cabinet maker, Church parade, Hounslow

COACHES & OMNIBUSES.
To LONDON, John Brunsden's *Omnibuses*, from the Bell Inn, Hounslow, three times a day, and *Coaches* to and from London and all parts of the West of England, pass thro' Hounslow, daily.

CARRIERS.
To LONDON (all parts of), Thomas Searle, James Smith & William Lovegrove, from Hounslow, daily, and Daniel Sharp, from his house, Harlington, twice a week.
Besides the above, *Carriers*, to and from London and all parts of the West, pass through Hounslow, daily.

ISLEWORTH

IS a village, in the parish and hundred of its name; nearly nine miles W. S. W. from Hyde Park Corner, about one mile from Richmond, and five from Kingston, in Surrey; delightfully situated on the northern bank of the Thames. The parish is bounded on its eastern side by the Grand Junction canal, and separated from Brentford by the river Brent; from hence to that town the stranger may enjoy a most delightful walk through the Duke of Northumberland's park, and immediately past the princely mansion of Sion House. The village consists of one principal street, well lighted with gas, and the houses are in general respectable and well built; the environs are rich in beautiful scenery, on both banks of the river—being embellished with elegant mansions, pleasure grounds and shrubberies. A very considerable portion of the land in the neighbourhood is cultivated by market gardeners, who send their produce to the London markets; and some of the finest fruits and vegetables are reared from the gardens here. Calico printing was formerly carried on at this place to a considerable extent, but this branch has ceased to exist for some years; the principal mills now are for flour, worked by the Colne stream; there is a large brewery in the village, and Roman cement and whiting is manufactured largely.

The places of worship are the parish church, a chapel for Wesleyan methodists, another for Roman catholics, and a friends' meeting-house. The church, which is dedicated to All Saints, occupies an elevated situation near the margin of the Thames, and from the river forms a conspicuous and interesting feature in the landscape; the body is of brick, but the tower is of stone—and, being overspread with ivy, presents a very picturesque appearance. The interior contains several very handsome monuments, some of which are highly attractive. The living is a vicarage, in the patronage of the dean and canons of Windsor; the present incumbent is the Rev. Henry Glossop. The charities are, a national school for boys and girls, a Sunday school, and one for infants; the first is well supported by endowments, and the two latter by subscriptions; also almshouses, founded by Mrs. Ann Tolson, for six aged unmarried men, and the like number of aged widows or maidens; others by Mrs. Mary Bell, for six aged women; and another for six poor women, founded by Sir Thomas Ingram. The entire parish (including part of Hounslow) contained, by the parliamentary returns for 1831, 5,590 inhabitants.

POST OFFICE, Square, Henry Quarman, *Post Master.*—Letters from LONDON arrive every morning (Sunday excepted) at eight, forenoon at eleven, afternoon at three and evening at six, and are despatched every morning at eight, noon at twelve, afternoon at three and evening at six.

NOBILITY, GENTRY AND CLERGY.

Ailsa the Most Noble the Marquess of, St. Margaret's, Isleworth
Allen Lady Frances, Somerset cottage, North st
Angus Mrs. Isabella, Church st
Bennett James, esq. North st
Caulier Mr. Joseph, Thames cottage
Clark George, esq. Sion place
Clark John James, esq. Sion place
Cooper the Dowager Lady, Isleworth house
Cridland Mr. Henry, Brentford end
Douglas Miss —, Rectory house, Isleworth
Drinkwater Miss Mercy, London road
Farnell Miss —, Gumley row
Farnell Mr. Henry (attorney), Holland house
Featherstonehaugh Mrs. —, Sion place
Field Geo. esq. Marlborough cottage
Filer Mrs. —, South st
Fisher Mrs. —, London road
Gee Mrs. —, Worton lane
Giblin Miss —, Isleworth
Gleney George, esq. Worton lodge
Glossop Rev. Henry, Church st
Gordon Lord F. Frederick, Railes head house
Gostling George, esq. Whitton
Hodgson Miss —, Brentford end
Hope Richard, esq. Smallberry green
James Rev. John B. M.D. Gumley row
Leman Mrs. Christian, Brentford road
Mills Mr. George, Church st
Northall Miss Amelia, North st
Northumberland His Grace the Duke of, Sion house
Passingham Miss —, South st
Pownall Henry, esq. Spring grove
Sermon Mrs. —, London road
Shea Mrs. —, Roman Catholic chapel
Stanbrough Mr. Jas. Wm. Church st
Story Mr. Wm. Henry, Hedden house
Thompson Mrs. Elizbth. Gumley row
Wallinger Mrs. Sarah, Richmond road
Wareing Rev. Anthony, near Shrewsbury wharf
Williams Samuel, esq. Gumley house
Wilthien Miss —, Twickenham road

ACADEMIES & SCHOOLS.

Not otherwise described are Boarding.

Dixon Henry (day and boarding), Twickenham road
Kenden Mrs. & Miss, Church st
Lane Misses, Sion lodge
NATIONAL SCHOOL, Square—Moses Adams, mastr; Eliza Adams, mistrss
Rance James (day), Square
Thomas Ann, Porch house
Thompson Elizabeth (day), Richmond road
Winkworth William (day), Church st

AUCTIONEERS.

Grimault John, Brentford end
Warren William Thos. Worton lane

BAKERS.

Banyon Thomas, Brentford end
Chapman Joseph, South st
Imrie George, South st
King Jonathan, Swan st
Piper James, Brentford end
Saunders Charles (muffin), South st
Slocombe John, Swan st
Smith Edward, South st
Woolven Henry, South st

BASKET MAKERS.

Cole George, South st
Wheatley George, Brentford end

BOOKSELLERS & STATIONRS

Durban John, Brentford end
Thompson William Shore (and perfumer), Square

BOOT AND SHOE MAKERS.

Allistone A. Worton lane
Barnard William, South st
Bass Robert, Brentford end
Bowden William, Brentford end
Brett William, Linkfield place
Campbell Mary, Square
Cook William, Brentford end
Crawther Jacob, Square
Dawes Thomas, South st
Denyer James, Brentford end
Gardner William, South st
Higgins Edmund, Brentford end
Jackson James Thos. Brentford end
May William, Brentford end
Maynard Robert, Brentford end
Murray William, South st
Riminton John, South st

BREWERS.

Farnell John & Charles & William T. Isleworth

BRICKLAYRS & PLASTERERS

Bardrick Thos. (plasterer), Church st
Burchett Geo. Northumberland terr
Pope Jonathan, South st
Rathing George, Church st
Smith William, South st

BUTCHERS.

Crowther Jacob (pork), Square
Dicken John, Brentford end
Lawrence William, Square
Lee Edward, South st
Paine Edward, South st
Rowles Matthew, Square
Sage John (pork), South st
Temple William, Church st

CARPENTERS & UNDERTAKRS

Atlee William & Sons, Square
Baylis John, South st
Pink Charles, South st
Walker John, Worton lane
Wiles James, Square
Winkworth Robert, Square

CHINA, GLASS, &c. DEALERS.

Attlee William, jun. South st
Young Benjamin, South st

CHYMISTS AND DRUGGISTS.

Thompson William Shore (and confectioner), Square
Viney David (and oil & colourman), South st

COACH PROPRIETORS.

Blackwell William, Brentford end
Limpus Henry, Brentford end
Limpus Joseph, South st
Swait John, South st

COAL MERCHANTS AND DEALERS.

Beck Edward (and lime and slate), Shrewsbury wharf
Brown James, Brentford end
Fowler Wm. Henry, Brentford end
Imrie George, South st
Killick Henry (and lead merchant), Brentford end
Smith Edward, South st
Smith James, Church st
Stanbrough James & C. H. Phœnix wharf
Styles Samuel, Railes head

CONFECTIONERS.

King Jonathan, Swan st
Slocombe John, Swan st
Thompson William Shore, Square

COOPERS.

Morgan Jno. (& turner) Brentford end
Neville James, Square

CORN FACTORS & DEALERS.

Beck Edward (& maltster), Shrewsbury wharf
Brown James, Brentford end
Gold William, Brentford end
Smith Edward, South st
Smith James (& wharfinger), Church street
Stanbrough James & C. H. Phœnix wharf
Stedman Hy. (& mealman) London rd

COW KEEPERS.

Brown Mrs. Worton lane
Checkley William, South st
Collin James, Smallberry green
Crowther Jacob, Square
Norris James, Sion hill
Temple William, Church st

FIRE, &c. OFFICE AGENTS.

BRITISH (fire) & WESTMINSTER (life), Benj. Young, jun. South st
PHŒNIX, Henry Quarman, Square

FRUITERERS AND GREENGROCERS.

Drewett William, South st
Eggar Jane, Swan st
Love James, Church st

GLOVERS.

Large Joseph, Brentford end
Sellwood William, Brentford end

GROCERS & CHEESEMONGRS

(See also Shopkeepers, &c.)

Barker William, South st
Dicken Joseph, Brentford end
Jones William, Church st
Norfolk John, South st
Quarman Henry, Square
Rance James, Square
Smith Edward, South st
Temple Elizabeth, Twickenham rd
Temple William, Church st
Viney David, South st
Young Benjamin, South st

LIGHTERMEN AND WHARFINGERS.

Beck Edward, Shrewsbury wharf
Cuseley James, Church st
Fowler Wm. Henry, Northumberland wharf, Brentford end
Love Thomas, Church st
Smith James, Church st
Styles Samuel, Railes head
Wapshott Thomas, Square

LINEN AND WOOLLEN DRAPERS.

Humphrey Philip, South st
Key William, Twickenham road

MARKET GARDENERS.

Beach Mrs. London road
Benham Charles, Worton lane
Chapman Charles, Brentford road
Chapman John, Sion hill
Clark William Minshon, Twickenham road
Cox Ann, Twickenham road
Flint Mrs. Church st
Gardner George, Smallberry green
Gardner John, Smallberry green
Goodenough Fras. Brazil mill lane
Jacobs William, London road
Jones William, Luck lane
Kendall Richard, Twickenham road
Kendall William, Worton
Knevett Henry, Twickenham road
Knevett Thomas, Whitton
Lewis Llewelyn, Worton lane
Mann Edward, Twickenham road
Mann William, Mogden
Norris James, Sion hill
Poole William, Worton lane
Portsmouth George, Linkfield lane
Powell William, Worton lane
Pratt John, Worton lane
Purrott Thomas, South st
Richardson George, North st
Richens James, London road
Roper James, Twickenham road
Stanbrough C. H. London road
Trumper Robert, Sion hill
Warren Wm. Thomas, Worton lane
Wilmot John, Brentford road

MILLERS.

Kidd Samuel, Church st
Stanbrough James, Phœnix wharf

MILLINERS AND DRESS AND STRAW HAT MAKERS.

Anstead Ann, Square
Bruckland Matilda, Linkfield place
Clements Elizabeth, South st
Hofnell Miss M. London road
Jaques Mary Ann, Brentford end
Newman Mrs. South st
Palmer Mary Ann, South st
Penny Jane, Phœnix row
Pindur Mary, North st
Rance Mrs. Square
Shepherd Rebecca, South st

PAINTERS, PLUMBERS AND GLAZIERS.

Corby Jonathan George, South st
Hoane Joseph, Brentford end
Milliner James, South st
Neale James, Worton lane
Woods Henry, Square

PERFUMERS AND HAIR CUTTERS.

Church Thomas, Brentford end
Clements Henry, South st
Clements John, Square

PRINTERS---LETTER-PRESS.

Adam Moses (& lithographic) Square
Hodgson Orlando, Worton lane

PROFESSORS & TEACHERS.

Kindon Henry (dancing), Church st
Limpus Richd. (music), Linkfield pl

ROMAN CEMENT MANFCTRS.

Ashby William & Son (and plaster of Paris and whiting manufacturers and lime burners), Isleworth

SHOPKEEPERS & DEALRS IN GROCERIES & SUNDRIES.

Dilnutt John, Worton lane
Druce Benjamin, Linkfield place
Goodman John, Brentford end
Goulding Frances, Worton lane
Grimshaw Sarah, South st
Harris Rebecca, South st
Hitchman Harriet, Church st
Price James, South st
Rowles Matthew, Square
Sage James, South st
Smedley Charlotte, Railes head
Toyne George, Smallberry green
Winkworth Robert, Swan st

SMITHS.

Beck George, South st
Boughton William, Brentford road
Hood John (& gun smith), South st
Perry Charles, Brentford end
Smith Charles (& tinman), South st
Smith William (and ironmonger), Church st
Stilwell William, North st
Stinton James, South st
Wadey Elias, London

SURGEONS.

Barry & Case, London road
Day, Day & Mackinlay, Square

SURVEYORS---LAND.

Adams Moses (and tythe surveyor), Square
Warren William Thomas, Worton la

TAILORS.

Fisher John & William, South st
Hopkins James, Church st
Hopkins Joseph, Brentford end
Poor John, South st
Poore Thomas, South st

TALLOW CHANDLERS.

Dicken Joseph, Brentford end
Young Benjamin, South st

TAVERNS & PUBLIC HOUSES.

Angel, Samuel Jones, Brentford end
Bell, William English, Square
Castle, Henry Athee, South st
Castle, John Taylor, Smallberry green
Chequers, Thomas Halford, London road
Coach & Horses, Edwd. Bird, Worton lane
Coach & Horses, Wm. Breakwell, Brentford road
Coach & Horses, Samuel Styles, Richmond road
George, Charles Butler, South st
George & Dragon, Benjamin Millard, Brentford end
Half Moon and Crown, Mary Wetherly, Brentford end
King's Arms, John Leader, South st
London Apprentice, Jno. Downer, Church st
Northumberland Arms (& commercial inn), Joseph Griffin, Square
Orange Tree, Thos. Buckman, Church st
Rose & Crown, Margaret Carter, Brentford road
Royal Oak, John Farlar Nicholls, Worton lane
Swan, William Grover, Swan st
Waterman's Arms, James Finn, Square

TIMBER MERCHANTS.

Beck Edward, Shrewsbury wharf
Dowson Joseph & Co. Grand Junction wharf

WATCH AND CLOCK MAKERS

Edmonds Richard, Brentford end
Elsdon William, Square

WHEELWRIGHTS.

Gaylor James (and hurdle maker), Brentford end
Ravenhill Chas. Twickenham road
Wadey Elias (& smith), London rd

Miscellaneous.

Barber Saml. & Son, hatters, Brentford end
BILLIARD ROOMS, Square, Joseph Griffin, proprietor
Bunce William John, pink dye manufacturer, nr Isleworth house, Richmond rd
Emmerson George, rope & sail maker, Brentford end
Esden James & Son, slaters, Linkfield pl
Fishlock Wm. marine store dealer, South st
Franklin James, stone mason, South st
Holloway Ann, saddler, Swan st
Humphrey Philip, pawnbroker, South st
Jaques Richard, umbrella maker, Brentford end
Lewis Llewelyn, registrar, Worton lane
Norminton John, dyer, Church st
Penny Wm. chair maker, Brentford end
Sansom Jos. marine store dealer, Swan st
Thompson William Shore, toy dealer and cutler, Square
UNION WORKHOUSE, London road, Mr. Brown, master
Winkworth Wm. deputy registrar, Church st

OMNIBUSES.

To LONDON, *Omnibuses* from the Northumberland Arms, Square, and the George Inn, South st, almost every hour from eight in the morning till six in the evening.
To HOUNSLOW, several times during the day.

CARRIERS.

To LONDON, Thomas Winkworth, from his house, South st, daily.

CONVEYANCE BY WATER.

To LONDON, Robert Tyrrell & William Timms, to the City, and Hungerford market daily.

KILBURN

IS a hamlet, partly in the parish of St. John, Hampstead, and partly in that of Wilsdon, three miles W.N.W. of London; situated on the road to Edgware, in a rural and healthful part. This village of late years has much increased in population and respectability, many beautiful villas and houses have been erected in and around it; and the pleasant distance which it is from the metroplis, joined to the constant accommodation of conveyances, have rendered it a desirable place of residence to persons having establishments of business in town. The London and Birmingham railway passes under the main street of the village. Kilburn is said to derive its name from *Cold bourne*, a stream which has its rise near West-end, and, passing through here to Bayswater, and thence to the Serpentine in Hyde park, flows through Ranelagh into the Thames. Here was formerly a nunnery of the order of St. Benedict; there are no remains of the priory, but its site is still pointed out in the Abbey fields, near to the tea-drinking house called Kilburn Wells, where is also a mineral spring, the waters of which possess highly aperient properties, and were, at one time, much resorted to. A chapel of ease, of which the Rev. W. S. Hancock is minister; and a charity school for boys and girls, supported by subscription, are in the village,—the population of which is returned with the parishes above-mentioned.

POST OFFICE, near the Black Lion, Main street.—Letters from LONDON, &c. arrive every forenoon at eleven, afternoon at three and evening at six, and are despatched every morning at ten and afternoon at two & five.

NOBILITY, GENTRY AND CLERGY.

Anderson Mrs. —, Mapesbury
Athol his Grace the Duke of, 1 Greville place
Ball J. esq. Greville place
Boyes Mrs. —, Langford place
Brooks Mrs. Mary, 1 Prospect place
Bullock Mrs. —, Kilburn priory
Burnett Benjamin, esq. 6 Waterloo
Carling Mrs. —, Greville place
Cartwright Mr. Frank, St. Margaret's cottage
Chater Mrs. N. 2 Waterloo
Conyngham the Right Hon. Marchioness, Kilburn house
Cooper Mr. John, 6 Greville place
Coverdale John, esq. Oak lodge
Dalphin Mrs. —, Kilburn
Devon Mrs. M. Waterloo cottage
Dickins Mrs. —, Kilburn priory
Dickinson Jos. esq. 4 Prospect place
Dickinson the Misses, Chapel terrace
Edlin Robert, esq. 7 Chapel terrace
Edwards Mr. —, Greville place
Fallows John, esq. Exmouth cottage
Forster Mr. Thos. Howard lodge
Frankham the Misses, York cottage
Franklin William, esq. Kilburn
Froggatt John, esq. Shootup hill
Gostling Chas. esq. Old Abbey cottage
Greeves William R. esq. 3 Waterloo
Grieve Mrs. —, 5 Waterloo place
Gurney Rev. William, Elmtree house
Gurr Mr. John (surgeon), Kilburn
Hancock Samuel, esq. Waterloo
Hancock Rev. Wm. S. York cottage
Harris Mr. Thomas, Cromer cottage
Hawkins Thos. esq. West end cottage
Higgins Mr. Thomas, West end lane
Kent Mr. Thos. (surgeon) Sydney terr
Keys Mrs. Eliz. Beaufain cottage
Langley — esq. Chapel terrace
Mackintosh John, esq. Oakland house, Cricklewood
Maples Capt. —, R.N. 3 Kilburn priory
Mayo Newman, esq. 5 Greville place
Mortimer Edw. esq. 5 Greville place
Mortimer Thos. Hill, esq. 4 Greville pl
Pyne William, esq. Ride cottage
Radford William, esq. Kilburn lodge
Robinson G. B. esq. 3 Greville place
Salter Mr. John, Kilburn
Salusbury Lady —, Elm lodge
Sanderson Chas. esq. Kilburn lodge
Sanderson Mr. Thomas Mark, St. Mildred's cottage
Shaw Mr. Benjamin, Priory cottage
Smyth Mr. Henry, Sydney terrace
Southey J. esq. Waterloo
Spratt Mr. Charles, Kilburn cottage
Symmons Mrs. General, 5 Kilburn priory
Thickbroom John D. esq. Prospect place
Thompson John, esq. Elm cottage
Tribe Thomas, esq. Greville place
Verey Mrs. Mary, 6 Chapel terrace
Watson Mrs. —, 6 Kilburn priory
Watson Chas. esq. Lausanne cottage
Webster Mr. Thomas, Prospect place
Westall Mrs. —, Chapel terrace
Wilson Mrs. —, 4 Kilburn priory
Woollam Mr. —, Exmouth lodge
Wybrow William, esq. Gothic house

ACADEMIES & SCHOOLS.

Not otherwise described are Boarding.

Chapman John, Priory
Gibletts Misses, Greville place
Hodgkinson Enoch, Cricklewood
Lancaster Eliza & Jane, Sidmouth cottage
NATIONAL SCHOOL (boys & girls)—Robert Hickman, master; Mary Hickman, mistress
Scarborough Henrietta, Royston hall
Smith Mrs. — (day), Kilburn

INNS AND PUBLIC HOUSES.

Bell (Kilburn Wells), William Plumridge, Kilburn
Black Lion, Nathaniel Hardy
Cock, Henry M'Dermott
Crown, Edward Wardley, Cricklewood
Red Lion (& tea gardens), Mary Pope

SHOPKEEPERS & TRADERS.

Arnold John, shoemaker
Baldwin Frances, straw hat maker
Baldwin Wm. Ormond, plumber, &c.
Brown Benj. carpentr, &c. West end la
Brown Geo. shopkeeper & fly owner
Butcher Henry, plumber and glazier
Cartwright Francis, tailor
Chamberlayne John, shoemaker
Charsley John, painter and glazier
Clarke Jno. grocer, cheesemongr, &c.
Cowne Samuel, surgeon
Debenham Frederick, baker and post office
Ede Geo. & Charles, blacksmiths and farriers [near the Turnpike
Farrant John, gardener and florist,
Gardner William, shoemaker
Goddard Henry, plumber, &c.
Hale Robert, butcher
Hale Wm. miller and corn dealer, Windmill [and seedsmen
Henderson Andrew & Son, nursery
Hill James, shoemaker
Holloway Thomas, shoemaker
Ives Wm. bricklayer, West end lane
Jack David, baker
Luxton James, bricklayer & plasterer
Marnham James, corn & coal dealer
Mitchell Matthew, carman, &c.
Muncey Charles, dairyman
Murch Richard, tailor
Newman Joseph, butcher
Pearce John, tailor
Pink Francis, carpenter and builder
Prior Saml. rustic chair, &c. maker, Cricklewood [porkman
Roberts William, cheesemonger and
Searles William, shopkeeper
Stanford Joseph, saddler
Sterling Henry, dairyman [dealer
Stutley Henry, grocer, draper & glass
Vere Jno. Holton, grocer & coal dealr
Vere William, carpenter, undertaker and house agent
Vere William & George, ale & porter brewers, Kilburn brewery
Williams Charles, dairyman
Woollams William, paper hanger

COACHES & OMNIBUSES.

To LONDON, Trevitt's *Omnibuses*, from the Black Lion, Kilburn, every morning at nine, twelve at noon, afternoon at a quarter before three and half-past five, and evening quarter before eight.

To and from LONDON, AYLESBURY, EDGWARE, ELSTREE, &c. *Coaches* pass through Kilburn daily.

CARRIERS.

To LONDON, Elizabeth Bridges, from West end lane, every morning at ten.

PINNER

IS a village and parish, in the hundred of Gore; 13 miles N. W. from London and 2½ N.N.W. from Harrow; situated in a fine open part of the country. It is a place of no trade but that immediately necessary for its inhabitants, and consequently without interest to the commercial traveller. At this place died, in 1798, Mr. John Zephaniah Howell, who had been governor of Bengal, and who published a curious and interesting account of his confinement, with many other persons, in the 'black-hole at Calcutta.' The church, dedicated to St. John the Baptist, and situated at the extremity of the village, on an elevated site, is a large antique edifice, chiefly built of flint: it contains a font, in high estimation as a curious and rare specimen of antiquity; and the stained glass of the windows is noticed as a peculiarly fine sample of that art in the early ages. The living is a perpetual curacy, in the gift of the vicar of Harrow. Pinner received from Edward III the grant of a weekly market and two annual fairs; the former has been entirely discontinued, and the latter are falling into disuse. The parish contained, by the returns for 1831, 1,270 inhabitants.

POST OFFICE, Matthew Cook, *Post Master.*—Letters from LONDON arrive (by foot post from Watford) every morning at nine, and are despatched every afternoon at five.

GENTRY AND CLERGY.

Abbs Major William
Beauclerk John, esq.
Boyd Mr. William
Burrows Rev. Thomas
Carr Ralph, esq.
Doogood Mr. William
Ellis John, esq.
Ewer Mrs. Thomas
Garrard Mr. James
Graham Nathaniel, esq.
Hill Mr. Thomas
Howard Mrs. —
Kelly Mr. Hubert (surgeon)
Kilbey Mrs. M.
Lawrence Mrs. —
Milman Sir William
Pell Lady —
Pye Mrs. —
Randall John, esq.
Soames Mrs. —
Thompson Mr. John
Tilbury John, esq.
Turner Mrs. Harriet
Walkden Mr. Richard
Woolfrey Mr. James

ACADEMIES.

Pay Catherine Mary (ladies' brdng.)
Richardson George (boys' day)

INNS & PUBLIC HOUSES.

Bell, Wm. Freeman, Pinner common
Crown, William Ginger
George, William Whittick
Queen's Head, Harry Mayo
Red Lion, William Gunn

SHOPKEEPERS & TRADERS.

Baker Sarah, dress maker
Baker William, parish clerk and collector of Queen's taxes
Banks John, grocer and rope maker
Beaumont John, wheelwright
Bedford James, tailor
Bradbury Jacob, baker [seller
Church Abraham, draper and bookseller
Churchill Caroline, dress maker
Cook Mathew, grocer and baker
Crutch Sophia, grocer [grocer
Crutch Wm. ironmonger, smith and
Dear Samuel, blacksmith
Doney George, bricklayer
Gladman James, shoemaker
Gude Thomas, plumber and painter
Higgs Joseph, shopkeeper

SHOPKEEPERS, &c.—*Continued.*
Hodgett Henry, shoemaker
Jaques John, miller
Kerley John, butcher
Kilby Joseph, plumber, &c.
Moores William, grocer
Murch Daniel, tailor
Murch Henry, tailor
Poulton William, carpenter
Tull Elizabeth, straw hat maker
Tull Thomas, grocer and shoemaker
Webb Mary, grocer, baker, & draper
White Vincent, builder, &c.
Woodbridge Charles, builder, &c.

COACH.

To LONDON, the *Comet*, from the Queen's Head, every morning (Sun. excepted), at eight, and on Sundays at a quarter before five in the evening.

CARRIERS.

To LONDON, James Garraway, every Tuesday, Thursday and Saturday; and Thomas Ashby, every Wednesday and Saturday.
To UXBRIDGE, Thomas Ashby, every Thursday.
To WATFORD, Joseph Higgs, every Tuesday.

PONDERS END

IS a hamlet in the parish of Enfield, about two miles from that place and eight miles and a half N. N. E. from London, situate on the road to Cambridge; it is a place of great thoroughfare, and the neighbourhood is very respectable. A manufactory for crape employs a number of hands here, and there is a large flour mill. The Lea navigation passes within a mile of the village. A chapel for independents is the only place of worship here. The population is included in the returns for Enfield parish.

POST, *Receiving-House* at Thomas Brading's.—Letters arrive from and are forwarded to ENFIELD two or three times a day.

GENTRY & CLERGY.
Baylis John, esq. South st
Clark John, esq. Ponders End
Coombs John, Scotland green
Croshaw Charles, esq. Scotland grn
Ellis Mrs. —, Ponders End
Farmer Mrs. Ellen, Ponders End
George Augustin, esq. Ponders mills
Hawes Samuel, esq. Ponders End
Naylor Thomas, esq. Boundary place
Nicholls Rev. —, Ponders End
Potter John Dell, esq. South st
Symonds Wm. esq. Boundary place
Waller William, esq. Ponders End
Wilsden Rev. —, Ponders End
Wilson William, esq. Ponders End
Witton Mrs. —, Ponders End
Wright Edwd. esq. Boundary house

ACADEMIES & SCHOOLS.
Barker Concordia & Louisa
Barker John Thomas
Clarke Mrs. John (boarding & day)
Ferry John M. (boarding & day), Providence house
INFANTS' SCHOOL--Mary Blyth, mistress
Pettitt Mary

PUBLIC HOUSES.
Falcon, Joseph Evans, South st
Goat, Joseph Coomes
Two Brewers, John Bennett
White Hart, John Kent

SHOPKEEPERS & TRADERS.
Andrews William, cooper
Barker John Thomas, druggist
Bliss Thomas, shoe maker
Brading Thomas, grocer
Catley Charles, cow leech
Cock Benjamin, shoe maker
Coomes Joseph, fire office agent
Dexter James, saddler
Downing John, bricklayer
Farmer Wm. miller, Ponders mills
Field Jeremiah, carpenter & builder
Garment John, grocer, South st
Grout & Co. crape manufacturers, South st
Guiver Henry, tailor
Ives Thomas Paine, barge owner, South st
Judd Thomas, barge owner, South st
Kelly Samuel, shoe maker
Kent James, butcher
Kied Thomas, brewer & beer retailer, Scotland green
King George Augustus, market gardener, Scotland green
Lord William, grocer
Mather Robert, coal dealer
Mould Lestock, builder
Naylor Leeds, coal merchant
Naylor William Baker & Son, wine and spirit merchant
Newman Nathl. painter & glazier
Poyser Daniel, wheelwright
Poyser Henry, brewer
Prime Thomas, blacksmith
Prior George, linen draper
Riseley Susannah, linen draper
Stevens Eleanor, straw hat maker
Stevens Thomas Edmund, tailor
Talboot Thedorus, baker
Taylor Henry, butcher
Thirgood Joseph, market gardener
Wadsworth Wm. grocer, South st
Webb George, market gardener
Westley Charles, baker
Whitehead Thos. barge owner, South st
Willis John, shoe maker
Wood Joseph, carpenter
Wright William, coach proprietor, Scotland green

COACHES & OMNIBUSES.

To LONDON, an *Omnibus*, every morning at eight, & afternoon at half-past two.
To and from LONDON, CAMBRIDGE, HERTFORD, LYNN, WARE, &c. *Coaches* pass through daily.

CARRIERS.

To and from LONDON, UXBRIDGE, and WATFORD, pass through daily.

SOUTHGATE AND WINCHMORE HILL.

SOUTHGATE is a genteel village in the parish and hundred of Edmonton, seven miles N. by W. from London, three from Edmonton and about three and a half from Enfield—situate at the extremity of Enfield Chase, from which circumstance may be deduced its name, as having formed the southern entrance to that celebrated tract of land. Many beautiful seats, elegant mansions and neat villas embellish the neighbourhood; the parks, as well as the country round, are finely wooded. The New river passes close to one end of the village, and tends at once to the convenience of the inhabitants and the improvement of the naturally pleasing appearance of the place. The places of worship are a chapel of ease to Edmonton, and one for independents. A school was founded here by John Walker, Esq., upon the Lancasterian plan, and is now supported by his widow; nine boys and the same number of girls of the school are clothed, by means of a bequest made by Mrs. Cowley. In a field contiguous to the village several pieces of cannon were found, and a military gorget that belonged to Oliver Cromwell—his initials on it, is formed by jewels, handsomely inlaid; this interesting relic is now in the British museum. Two small fairs are held annually, one on Holy Thursday, and the other early in the month of September. Population is returned with Edmonton.

Two miles from Southgate, the like distance from Edmonton, and eight north from London, is the respectable village of WINCHMORE HILL, situated, as its name implies, upon an eminence, the views from whence embrace a most extensive range of delightful country, decorated by tasteful residences. A chapel of ease to Edmonton was a few years since erected here; and the independents have two chapels and the society of friends one. The population is returned with Edmonton.

POST, *Receiving-Houses* at SOUTHGATE and WINCHMORE HILL.—Letters arrive from and are despatched to LONDON twice a day.

GENTRY & CLERGY.
Austin J. J. esq. Winchmore Hill
Beorton Mr. —, Southgate
Blinkhorn —, esq. Bowes
Booth Joseph, esq. Winchmore Hill
Busk E. esq. Winchmore Hill
Butler J. L. esq. Southgate
Carrick Mrs. —, Southgate
Carter Mr. —, Winchmore Hill
Child Richard, esq. Winchmore Hill
Coster Thomas, esq. Bowes
Curtis George, esq. Southgate
Curtis T. A. esq. Southgate
Curtis Thomas, esq. Palmer's green
East Sir Edward, Southgate
Edgecombe Mrs. —, Southgate
Eykyn Mrs. —, Southgate
Firth Peter Pope, esq. Winchmore Hill
Gibbons S. esq. Winchmore Hill
Griffiths Miss —, Winchmore Hill
Hoggart C. L. esq. Winchmore Hill
Johnson E. esq. Winchmore Hill
Jones Mrs. —, Winchmore Hill
Langton Mr. —, Southgate
Macaughty —, esq. Southgate
Mason Major —, Southgate
May Mrs. —, Winchmore Hill
Mellish Raphael, esq. Bush hill
Middleton Mr. —, Southgate
Pawling Rev. —, Palmer's green
Pearson —, esq. Winchmore Hill
Powys H. P. esq. Southgate
Radford J. esq. Winchmore Hill
Sadler Mr. —, Southgate
Sale Rev. —, Southgate
Schnider J. esq. Southgate
Simmons Mrs. —, Winchmore Hill
Smith Captain —, Southgate
Starkey Mr. William, Bowes

Taylor Mrs. —, Southgate
Thompson Mrs. —, Winchmore Hill
Todd Mrs. —, Winchmore Hill
Turner Sharron, esq. Winchmore Hill
Wade Mr. John, Winchmore Hill
Wadmore J. esq. Southgate
Walker Mrs. —, Southgate
Walker J. esq. Southgate
Warren Rev. Edwd. Winchmore Hill
Watson J. H. esq. Southgate
Whitehead John, esq. Palmer's green
Wild Benjamin, esq. Bowes
Wilkinson Jacob, esq. Southgate
Wright Miss —, Winchmore Hill
Yellowley Mrs. —, Winchmore Hill

ACADEMIES & SCHOOLS.

Blagden Robert, Southgate
MRS. WALKER'S CHARITY SCHOOL, Southgate — Matthew Morton, master; Mrs. Morton, mistress
Pawling Rev. —, Palmer's green
Robson Mrs. —, Winchmore Hill
Rumsey Mr. J. R. Southgate
Skinner Mary, Winchmore Hill

AUCTIONEERS & APPRAISRS.

Jones John, Winchmore Hill
Udall & Co. Winchmore Hill

BAKERS & FLOUR DEALERS.

Catchpool John, Winchmore Hill
Conisbie George, Southgate
Hanscombe John, Southgate
Howard Richard Thomas, Southgate
Howson & Mitchell, Winchmore Hill

BLACKSMITHS.

Balaam George, Southgate
Burton John, Winchmore hill
Gladwin William, Southgate

BOOT & SHOE MAKERS.

Crane William, Southgate
Forster John, Winchmore Hill
Fullaway John, Southgate
Harwood Richard, Winchmore Hill
James John, Southgate
King John, Winchmore Hill

BRAZIERS AND TINMEN.

Cowles Richard, Winchmore Hill
Gurney William, Southgate

BUTCHERS.

Earle John, Southgate
Horsey William, Winchmore Hill
Lowen & Vincent, Southgate
Suter & Druce, Southgate

CARPENTERS.

Allen Edward, Winchmore Hill
Cole John, Southgate
Kerry John, Southgate
Sell John, Winchmore Hill
Wilkinson Thomas, Southgate

COAL AND CORN DEALERS.

Catchpool John, Winchmore Hill
Ellis Abel, Southgate
Long Ann & Son, Southgate
Morris John, Winchmore Hill
Surry Thomas, Southgate

GROCERS AND DEALERS IN SUNDRIES.

Evenett William, Southgate
Lewis George, Southgate
Long Ann & Son, Southgate
Udall & Ostliffe, Winchmore Hill

INNS & PUBLIC HOUSES.

Cherry Tree, Henry Eaton, Southgate
Crown, Joseph Hoy, Southgate
Fox, Harriet Webb, Palmer's green
Green Dragon, John Tatem, Winchmore Hill
King's Head, Edw. Flowerday, Winchmore Hill
Orange Tree, Ann Clarke, Highfield rw
Stag & Hounds, Wm. Wills, Bury st

LINEN, &c. DRAPERS.

Goodman Richard, Southgate
Howell —, Southgate
Udall & Ostliffe, Winchmore Hill

MILLINERS & DRESS MAKRS

Binsted & Felwick, Winchmore Hill
Gates Sophia, Southgate
Lowing Harriet, Winchmore Hill
Thomas Elizabeth, Winchmore Hill

PAINTERS AND GLAZIERS.

Riley Richard, Winchmore Hill
Skikelthorpe Edward, Southgate

SURGEONS.

Hammond & Ward, Southgate
Radford Charles, Winchmore Hill
Wilkinson Charles, Southgate

TAILORS.

Bedford John, Southgate
Corsone Alex. Winchmore Hill
Province Richard, Winchmore Hill

WHEELWRIGHTS.

Gudgin George, Southgate
Jones John, Palmer's green
Mayes Richard, Southgate

Miscellaneous

Auty Joseph, chair maker, Southgate
Cuthbert James, nurseryman, Southgate
Gates William, plasterer, Southgate
Hill Anthony, brewer, Southgate
Linwood Margaret, bricklayer, Southgate
Simmons Abraham, fishmonger, Southgate
Tarrant William, saddler, Southgate

COACHES.

To LONDON, every morning, at eight and half-past eight, and every afternoon at five.

CARRIERS.

To LONDON, William Luck, — Eaton, and — Reeve, daily.

STAINES,

WITH THE VILLAGES OF ASHFORD, LALEHAM, FELTHAM, LITTLETON, BEDFONT, STANWELL, COLNBROOK AND NEIGHBOURHOODS.

STAINES is a respectable market town and parish in the hundred of Spelthorne, 16 miles W.S.W. from London and 10 W.S.W. from Brentford, situated on the north bank of the Thames. Its name is said to be derived from the boundary stone, marking the jurisdiction of the lord mayor of London as conservator of the river; the stone is placed a little above the bridge, and on it is inscribed, 'God preserve the City of London—A.D. 1284.' It formerly was customary for the metropolitan chief magistrate to come up the Thames in state, twice a year, to this boundary stone; but the practice has for a long time been discontinued. Edward the Confessor, in 1066, granted the manor and rectory of Staines to the abbot and convent of Westminster; after the dissolution of religious houses, particularly from the time of James I, it had various possessors. At a remote period a forest extended from hence to Hounslow; but for centuries it has been parcelled off for divers purposes. Within the last twenty years the town has received material improvements: it principally consists of one wide street, containing some good houses, terminating at the river Thames, across which a handsome stone bridge has superseded the old iron one; and a new street has been formed on a line with the bridge, which presents a very pleasing entrance to the town from Egham; the streets and shops are well lighted by gas, from works established in 1833. The trade of Staines is chiefly of a local nature, although there are some mills for grinding corn, and one for the manufacture of mustard. Its government is vested in two constables and four headboroughs, nominated by the leet jury and sworn in before the lord of the manor at his court leet. The places of worship are the parish church, and chapels for baptists, independents and the society of friends; the latter form a numerous and respectable proportion of the inhabitants of Staines. The church, dedicated to St. Mary, was erected by Inigo Jones in 1631, and was rebuilt a few years since; it is a neat brick edifice, with a square embattled tower, surmounted by stone pinnacles at each corner; the interior is handsomely fitted up, and the sittings most judiciously arranged: the benefice is a vicarage, with the perpetual curacies of Ashford and Laleham annexed, in the gift of the crown, and incumbency of the Rev. Robert Govett. There are free schools for boys and girls upon the national and Lancasterian systems, one for infants, and a school of industry; the poor are benefited by various donations in bread, clothing, &c. In this parish, and in the occupation of the widow of the late Lieutenant-Colonel Carmichael, is Duncroft House, in which King John is said to have slept after signing *Magna Charta* at Runymede. The market is held on Friday, and the annual fairs on the 11th of May and 19th of September. The parish, at the census of 1831, contained 2,486 inhabitants. [For the population of the several following parishes, *see* paragraph after STANWELL.]

About a mile and a half from Staines is the small and unimportant village of ASHFORD, containing the pretty but diminutive parish church, dedicated to St. Michael, in which service is performed on alternate Sundays with LALEHAM, which village is about two miles from Ashford and the like distance from Staines. The church of Laleham, dedicated to All Saints, is a low fabric with a square tower; the living is a perpetual curacy, annexed to the vicarage of Staines.

One mile from Ashford and three from Staines is FELTHAM village, long and straggling, without any pretension to uniformity or claim to beauty; a part of the village occupies very high ground, equal in altitude to Richmond Hill: the inhabitants consist chiefly of market gardeners and farmers, and there is a manufactory of candles on an extensive scale. The church, dedicated to St. Dunstan, is a small plain brick edifice—the living a discharged vicarage, in the gift (or was lately), of the Morris family.

Two miles from Laleham is the small parish of LITTLETON. It contains a church, dedicated to St. Michael, and a free school; but no trades are carried on here, save the solitary one of a blacksmith—nor is there a public house in the parish. The benefice is a rectory, in the presentation of Thomas Wood, Esq. M.P., to whom, indeed, nearly all the parish belongs.

Three miles E. N. E. from Staines, lying on the great western road, is the small and agreeable village of BEDFONT, or EAST BEDFONT. The church, dedicated to St. Mary, is a small building, possessing nothing attractive. In front of it, however, are two yew trees, deserving of observation on account of the care that has evidently been taken in their training: on one is cut '1704,' and on the other, the letters 'J. H., J. G., R. T.,' initials of persons serving as churchwardens at the time they were planted. The living is a vicarage, in the patronage of the bishop of London, and present incumbency of the Rev. Robert Jones, D. D. Bedfont is a polling station at the election of representatives for the county.

Two miles from Bedfont and the like distance from Staines is STANWELL village and parish; the latter is somewhat extensive; the village is very neat, and its inhabitants of a respectable class. The church, dedicated to St. Mary, is in the later English style of architecture; the benefice, a discharged vicarage, is in the gift of the crown. A chapel for independents, and a free school for boys (the latter founded about the year 1624, as appears by an inscription in front of the building), are in the village. In this parish is the chapelry of COLNBROOK (formerly a market town), situated on the river Colne, from which it derives its name. The village consists principally of one long street, the houses of which, for the most part, are neatly built, and of respectable appearance. The trade chiefly arises from its situation as a great thoroughfare, and there is a paper mill in the vicinity. The chapel, a neat modern edifice, is dedicated to St. Mary. The market has for many years been discontinued; but there are two fairs held annually—one on the 5th of April, the other on the 3rd of May, for cattle and horses.

The foregoing parishes are all locally situated in the hundred of Spelthorne; and their population, according to the census of 1831, was as follows:—ASHFORD, 458; LALEHAM, 588; FELTHAM, 924; LITTLETON, 134; BEDFONT (with HATTON), 968; STANWELL (with COLNBROOK), 1,386.

POST OFFICE, High street, STAINES, Mary Evitts, *Post Mistress.*—Letters from LONDON arrive every morning at six, and are despatched every night at ten minutes before eight.—Letters from BRACKNELL, WOKINGHAM and READING arrive every evening at seven, and are despatched every morning at half-past six.—Letters from WINDSOR arrive every evening at seven, and are despatched every morning at half-past six.

Receiving-Houses at the Three Horse Shoes, LALEHAM; at the Black Dog, BEDFONT; at Joseph Potier's, FELTHAM; and at David Cragington's, STANWELL.—From all which places letters are despatched to STAINES every afternoon.

NOBILITY, GENTRY AND CLERGY.

Ascough Mrs. —, London road
Ashby Mrs. Frances, High st
Barber Miss —, Stanwell moor
Barriss William, esq. Laleham
Bockett Rev. Benjamin, Feltham
Brigham Wm. esq. Knowle green hse
Buckland Rev. John, Laleham
Burrell the Hon. Lindsey, Laleham
Cadbury Mr. James, Feltham hill
Carmichael Mrs. Col. Duncroft house
Cobb Mr. William, Stanwell
Edgell Rev. John, Stanwell
Ellis Captain —, Stanwell
Englehart George, esq. Bedfont
Fowler Mrs. —, High st
Gibbons John, esq. Stanwell
Gibbons Sir John, Stanwell park
Goring Mr. Thomas, High st
Govett Rev. Robert, Staines
Hagen Miss —, Knowle green
Hagen Mr. Thomas, Stanwell
Hall Mrs. —, High st
Harding Sir Henry, Littleton
Harris Mrs. —, Laleham road
Harrison Mrs. & Miss, Laleham
Hatchett Mr. Richard, Bedfont
Heath Mr. Robert, Stanwell moor
Heath Mr. Thomas, Stanwell
Hedge Mrs. Elizabeth, High st
Hitchcock Mr. William, Stanwell
Holland Captain —, Staines moor
Irving John, esq. M. P. Ashford
Jennings Mr. William, Knowle grn
Jones Rev. Robert, D. D. Bedfont
Lawless Mr. James, Knowle green
Leno Mr. Matthew, Laleham road
Lucan the Earl of, Laleham house
Maddeford Mrs. —, Staines
Mangles Mrs. Mary, Laleham
Mitchiner Mr. James Hales, High st
Pearse Mr. Fredk. Wm. Knowle grn
Pope Miss Margaret, High st
Raddick Captain —, Feltham hill
Reed William, esq. Bedfont
Reynolds Mr. John, Knowle green
Seagall Mr. George, Ashford
Seaman George, esq. Laleham
Sexton Mr. Henry, Stanwell
Seymour Mr. Watson, London road
Sheffield Mr. J. Feltham hill
Shells Frederick, esq. Feltham hall
Sherbourn Mr. Francis, Bedfont
Simmonds John, esq. M. D. High st
Stevens Miss —, Church st
Sulivan Robert, esq. Ashford
Thackarah George, esq. Feltham pl
Treble Mr. John, Knowle green
Vale Rev. Edward, Feltham
Williams Captain —, Stanwell
Wood Capt. Thomas, M. P. Littleton
Wood Col. Thomas, M. P. Littleton

ACADEMIES & SCHOOLS.
Not otherwise described are Day Schools.

Allcot Charles, Feltham
Bennett Eliza (boarding), Church st
Bennett George (boarding), High st
Buckland Rev. Jno. (brding.) Laleham
CHARITY SCHOOL, Ashford—Mrs. Goodenough, mistress
Eastgate Ann, Laleham
Fenton Ann (gent.'s preparatory), Laleham
FREE SCHOOL, Stanwell—Thomas Webb, master
INFANTS' SCHOOL, Church st—Mrs. Jenkins, mistress
INFANTS' SCHOOL, Ashford—Mrs. Purser, mistress
INFANTS' SCHOOL, Stanwell—Ann Cragington, mistress
Jefferson Thomas (day & boarding), High st
LANCASTERIAN, Church st—Mr. Robinson, master
Mewes Ann, Laleham
Ollive & Billinghurst (ladies' boarding), High st
Philips Miss, Feltham
SCHOOL OF INDUSTRY, Laleham road—Mary Brown, mistress
Stackhouse Rachael (boarding) High st

ATTORNEYS.

Horne Randolph, Clarence st
Richings Thomas, Thames cottage, Laleham road

AUCTIONEERS & APPRAISRS.

Adams Jas. (& valuer), Clarence st
Baker James, High st
Stephens James, High st
Stephens Thos. Wm. jun. High st
Wagner Jno. (& surveyer), Clarence st

BAKERS & FLOUR DEALERS.

Armstrong William, Feltham
Booker William, Church st
Fitzwater James, Laleham
Freeman William, Stanwell
King Isaac, High st
Merrick Joseph, Ashford
Powell William, High st
Riddington Thomas, High st
Rokes Saml. (& corn dealer), High st
Smith Joseph, High st
Stockwell Jonathan, Feltham
Taylor Elizabeth, Stanwell
Tilly John, High st
Verrey Charlotte, Laleham
Westbrook William, Bedfont

BANKERS.

Ashby Thomas, Henry, Charles, Frederick & Skidmore, High st—(draw on Williams, & Co. London)
SAVINGS' BANK, Church st—(open every Monday from 12 till 2)—James H. Mitchener, secretary

BARGE OWNERS.

Ashby Skidmore & John, Staines wharf, Church st
Clark James, High st

BLACK AND WHITESMITHS.

Beldam Robert, Feltham
Burchett James, Laleham
Coles Richard, Bedfont
Edwards William, Feltham
Hayter Charles, High st
Hayter Elizabeth, High st
Lintott Nichols, Stanwell
Pike Mark, Church st
Purser Edward, Littleton
Purser John, Ashford
Rackliffe Daniel, Hatton
Silver John, Bedfont

BOOKSELLERS & STATIONRS.

Hayter William High st
Norris Jane (& library), Clarence st
Wilmhurst Harriet & Eliz. High st

BOOT & SHOE MAKERS.

Banham Noah, Stanwell
Carruthers Edward, High st
Cooper Solomon, Laleham
Cragington David, Stanwell
Eastgate Alexander, Ashford
Fitzwater John C. Laleham
Gubbins Thomas, Church st
Hayter Richd. (& china dealer), High st
Jones James, Hatton
Keen Lawrence, Stanwell
King Thomas, High st
Page Henry, Clarence st
Pope William, Bedfont
Robinson John, Bedfont
Roe Geo. (& leather cutter), High st
Russell Thomas, Stanwell
Sherwood Edward, Church st
Stanbridge William, High st
Thomas John, Bedfont
Wigley William, High st
Young Constantine John, Church st

BREWERS.

Ashby Hny. Chas. & Fred. Church st
Chandler Thos. & William, Laleham
Deane Edmund, Feltham
Harris Thos. & John, Knowle green
Lawrence James, White Hart Inn, Colnbrook

BRICKLAYERS.

Jacobs Edward, Ashford
Kent William, Church st

Lodge William, Feltham
Mole Henry, Stanwell
Osman Thomas, Laleham
Parry John, Laleham
Pope Joseph, Feltham
Powell George, Stanwell
Taylor William (& slater), High st

BUTCHERS.

Champion Jesse, Bedfont
Cooper Thomas, High st
Cushen Thomas, High st
French John, Feltham
Goring John, High st
Hicks John, Laleham
Holmes Thomas & Richard, Feltham
Layton George, Laleham
Lintott James, High st
Lintott William, Stanwell
Willoughby Thomas, High st

CABINET MAKERS AND UPHOLSTERERS.

Adams James (and land and estate agent), Clarence st
Atkinson Daniel, High st
Richardson Henry (and undertaker), Ashford

CARPENTERS & BUILDERS.

Allman John, High st
Clarke Henry, High st
Cousins William, Church st
Dexter Edward, Church st
Latham William, Ashford
Lintill George, Stanwell
Richardson Henry, Ashford
Sidwell Robert & Thomas, Stanwell
White Josiah, Laleham

CATTLE DEALERS.

Cornish Robert, Laleham
Deale Charles & Robert, Laleham
Merrick Edward, Stanwell
Merrick John, Stanwell

CHYMISTS AND DRUGGISTS.

Chandler John, High st
Dodd Elijah, High st
Hodder Henry (& oil & colourman), High st

COACH BUILDERS.

Pasmore Ephraim, High st
Tyler Henry, Bedfont

COACH PROPRIETORS.

Fagg Alfred, Bedfont
Neesham John, Laleham
Sherley William, Bedfont gate

COAL & CORN MERCHANTS.

Ashby Skidmore & John (and stone, cement, & salt wharf), Church st
Deane Edmund, Feltham
Dexter Thomas (and seed), High st
Holgate William, High st

FIRE, &c. OFFICE AGENTS.

Atlas, William Booker, Church st
British Commercial, Randolph Horne, Clarence st
County (fire) & Provident (life), Joseph Kent, High st
Imperial, William Brown, High st
Norwich, James Baker, High st
Phœnix, Randlph. Horne, Clarence st
Royal Exchange, William B. Byng, High st
Sun, James Adams, Clarence st

FRUITERERS.

Beard Ellis, High st
Critcher Robert, High st

GROCERS & CHEESEMONGRS

(See also Shopkeepers, &c.)

Atkins William, High st
Best John, Stanwell
Blackwell Thomas (and porkman), High st
Claridge Robert, High st
Jackson James (and dealer in British wines), High st
Kent Joseph, High st
Robinson Philip, Feltham
Taylor Elizabeth, Stanwell
Taylor James, High st
Treble John, Church st

HAIR DRESSERS.

Nash Edward, High st
Rushforth James, Clarence st

HATTERS.

Holder John (manufactr.) Church st
Jones James, High st
Pott Francis, High st
Wigley William, High st

HORSE DEALER.

Sherley William (and stock valuer), Bedfont gate

INNS—POSTING.

Angel & Crown, John Wayt, High st
Black Dog, Edward Walker, Bedfont
Bush & Clarence Hotel, John Collins (and post master by appointment to Her Majesty), Clarence st
New Inn, Chas. Rattew, Bedfont gate
White Hart, Jas. Lawrence, Colnbrook

IRONMONGERS.

Ashby Edward (and bell hanger and brazier), High st
Hayter Charles, High st
Spencer John, High st

LINEN, &c. DRAPERS.

Best John, Stanwell
Budd H. & E. Bedfont
Jones James, High st
Lane James, Clarence st
Mole Henry, Stanwell
Morford Robert, High st
Palmer & Clarke, Clarence st
Robinson Philip, Feltham

MALTSTERS.

Chandler Thos. & William, Laleham
Harris Thos. & John, Knowle green
Keene John, Chapel st

MARKET GARDENERS.

Austin William, Bedfont
Cromwell John, Feltham
Gardner George, Feltham

MILLERS & MEALMEN.

Carpenter Henry, Stanwell moor
Finch, Rickman, & Finch (and mustard manufacturers), Church st
Murrell Wm. Hale mill, Church st
Watson Alexander, Stanwell moor

MILLINERS & STRAW HAT MAKERS.

Budd H. and E. Bedfont
Cranmer Hannah, Church st
Grave Mary Ann, High st
Palmer & Clarke, Clarence st

NURSERY & SEEDSMEN.

Bartlett George, Clarence st
Collins John, High st

PAINTERS AND GLAZIERS.

Boulter John, High st
Greener Joseph, Church st
Pearse Ann, High st
Thorpe Robert, Feltham
Young George, Chapel place

PRINTERS—LETTER-PRESS.

Norris Jane, Clarence st
Watkins Wm. (& bookbinder), High st

SADDLERS.

Croxford Christopher, High st
Denyer Edmund, High st
Elborough Richard, Bedfont

SHOPKEEPERS & DEALRS IN GROCERIES & SUNDRIES.

Blithman Thomas, High st
Bolton John, Knowle green
Brewer John, Ashford
Charlton Ann, Church st
Cousins Samuel, High st
Edwards Edward, Knowle green
Edwards William, Feltham
Fitzwater James, Laleham
Lodge William, Feltham
Mole Henry, Stanwell
Newman William, Ashford
Powell William, High st
Prior Elizabeth, Bedfont
Richardson Sarah, Bedfont
Smith Mary Ann, Knowle green
Verrey Charlotte, Laleham
Waters William Henry, Church st
Westbrook William, Bedfont
Whitticks Henry, Feltham
Wild John, Feltham
Woding Mary, Laleham

SURGEONS.

Baker Jas. (& registrar), Clarence st
Curtis Frederick, High st
Heale James Newton, High st
Langridge John, High st
Watson Benjamin, High st

TAILORS.

Beauchamp John, Laleham
Dormer Thomas, Stanwell
Goring Thomas, High st
Green Henry, High st
Johnson James, Feltham
Paull William, Church st
Pott Francis, High st
Scott Thomas, Church st
Toplis John, Feltham
Vercoe William, Church st

TALLOW CHANDLERS.

Dearle Wm. (& cart grease), High st
Toussaint Joseph & Son, Feltham

TAVERNS & PUBLIC HOUSES.

Anchor, John Lintill, Stanwell moor
Bell, George Gammon, Bedfont
Blue Anchor, William Yarnall, High st
Catherine Wheel, Richd. Bates, Colnbrook
Cock, George Berryman, Church st
Crooked Billet, Saml. Hedge, London rd
Crown, Joseph Vincent, West Bedfont
Crown & Anchor, George Collins, High st
Duke of Wellington, Ann Henwood, Hatton
Duke's Head, Henry Tyler, Bedfont
Feathers, James Stratton, Laleham
Five Bells, George Lintill, Stanwell
Greyhound, William Hutt, High st
King's Head, Alexander Eastgate, Ashford
Pack Horse, Henry Handover, Laleham rd
Phœnix, William Walker, Church st
Punch Bowl, Eliz. Courteney, nr. Colnbrook
Red Lion, John French, Feltham
Rose & Crown, James Jardine, Feltham
Stag & Hounds, Wm. Sparkes, London rd
Star, Mary Savage, Colnbrook
Swan, George Ager, Stanwell
Three Horse Shoes, John Dyos, Laleham
Three Tuns, Joseph Staples, High st
White Lion, John Yeldham, High st

TOY DEALERS.

Norris Jane, Clarence st
Wilmhurst Harriet & Eliz. High st

VETERINARY SURGEONS.

Gunner Charles, High st
Simmonds Winstone, High st

WATCH & CLOCK MAKERS.

Johnston David, High st
Wood William Henry, High st

WHARFINGERS.

Ashby Skidmore and John, Staines wharf, Church st

WHEELWRIGHTS.

Heath Robert, Stanwell
Johnson Wm. Common lane, Staines
Latham William, Ashford
Markwick John, Bedfont
Simmonds Henry, Knowle green

Miscellaneous.

Adams Jas. high constable, Clarence st
Ashby Henry & Co. wine & spirit merchants, High st
Barnes Thomas, whip thong maker, Poyle, Colnbrook
Barney William, breeches maker, High st
Bible Depository High st—Rev. Robert Govett, secretary
Brace Moses, basket maker, High st
Gillott George, working cutler, High st
Graves William, cowkeeper, Shooting off
Horne Henry, relieving officer, Knowle green
Horne Randolph, clerk to Staines Union, Clarence st
Ibbotson Richd. & Percy, paper makers, Poyle mill, near Colnbrook
Jenkins Maria, dyer & scourer, High st
Osman William, basket maker, High st
Potiers Joseph, poulterer, Feltham
Russen Rosina, dyer & scourer, High st
Seabrook Richard, cowkeeper, Church st
Sexton William, gardener, Church st

MISCELLANEOUS—*Continued.*
Sidwell Robert, parish clerk, Stanwell
Squibb John, stonemason, Black Boy lane
Stapleton Wm. fishmonger & poulterer, High st
Stephens Thomas Wm. furniture broker, [High st
Strange Thomas, cooper, Church st
WORKHOUSE, Stanwell—Thos. Tindall, master; Mrs. Tindall, matron
Yeaxley Wm, carver & gilder, Clarence st

COACHES.

The following Coaches call at the Bush and Clarence Hotel *and the* Angel & Crown Inn *unless otherwise expressed.*

To LONDON, *Coaches*, from Englefield Green, every morning (Sunday excepted) at nine—a *Coach*, from Blackwater, at ten—the *Old North Devon*, from Barnstaple, and the *Defiance*, from Exeter, at half-past ten—*Coaches*, from Reading, every afternoon at two, three and five—and another, every Monday, Wednesday and Friday forenoon at half-past eleven.

To LONDON, a *Coach*, from Sunninghill, and a *Coach*, from the Three Horse Shoes, Laleham, call at the Bush and Clarence Hotel, every morning (Sunday excepted) at eight—the *Telegraph* (from Southampton) calls at the New Inn, Bedfont gate, every evening at six—and a *Coach* (from Odiham & Basingstoke) calls at the Duke's Head, every Monday, Wednesday and Friday afternoon at two.

The following Coaches are from LONDON, *and call at the two Inns above mentioned unless otherwise expressed.*

To BARNSTAPLE, the *Old North Devon*, every evening at half-past six.

To BLACKWATER, a *Coach*, every evening (Sunday excepted) at six.

To ENGLEFIELD GREEN, *Coaches*, every forenoon at eleven, afternoon at half-past five & evening at seven & eight.

To EXETER, the *Defiance*, every evening at six.

To ODIHAM and BASINGSTOKE, a *Coach*, calls at the Duke's Head, Bedfont, every Tuesday, Thursday & Saturday forenoon at eleven.

To READING, *Coaches*, daily (Sunday excepted) at twelve and afternoon at five, and every Tuesday, Thursday & Saturday afternoon at half-past two.

To SOUTHAMPTON, the *Telegraph*, calls at the New Inn, Bedfont gate, every morning (Sunday excepted) at ten.

To SUNNINGHILL, a *Coach*, every evening (Sunday excepted) at five.

OMNIBUSES.

To LONDON, an *Omnibus*, from the White Lion, every morning (Sunday excepted) at eight, and another (from Egham) at half-past seven.

To EGHAM, an *Omnibus* (from London) calls at the White Lion, every evening.

CARRIERS.

To LONDON, — Russell's *Waggons*, pass Bedfont gate, daily; — Lampert, every Monday, Thursday & Friday—Thomas Dexter, from High street, every Monday, Wednesday and Friday—and Joseph Phillips & Timothy Strange, from their houses, Staines, every Monday & Thurs.

To EXETER, — Russell's *Waggons*, pass Bedfont gate, daily.

To FARNHAM, — Lampert's *Waggons*, pass Bedfont gate, every Tuesday, Friday and Saturday.

To HARTLEY ROW, *Waggons*, pass Bedfont gate, every Tuesday & Friday.

*** As the *Great Western* and the *Southampton Railways* progress, the number of Coaches and Carriers passing upon the western line of road will suffer diminution, and the time of the various Coaches will be subject to alteration.

STOKE NEWINGTON AND STAMFORD HILL.

STOKE NEWINGTON is a village and parish in the Finsbury division of the hundred of Ossulton; about three miles N.E. from London and two from Edmonton—situate on the high road to Cambridge, and adjoining the parish of Hackney. It principally consists of a long street, extending from Kingsland road to Stamford Hill, and another branching off to the church; these streets are macadamised, and lighted with gas; and the inhabitants are supplied with water by the New River Company, who formed a reservoir here, covering sixty-three acres of land. Besides the regular streets there are numerous neat detached residences, and some extensive nursery grounds; and the entire neighbourhood is eminently respectable. There is no particular manufacture attached to the village; its trade depends on the resident population, assisted in some degree by its thoroughfare situation on a great public road. Considerable improvements have lately been made in this suburban district; one of the most conspicuous additions is the new cemetery, now forming by a company, and called 'Abney Park Cemetery;' it is approached from Church-street, in the village, and from the High-street leading to Stamford Hill; the area comprises about thirty-five acres, which are tastefully laid out and planted with evergreens. The church, dedicated to Saint Mary, is a low structure, re-erected in 1563; very material additions, comprising a new steeple to the tower and a new gallery to the interior, were made to it a few years since; it contains several elegant monuments: the benefice is a rectory, in the patronage of the prebendary of Newington in St. Paul's cathedral, London. Independents, unitarians and the society of friends have chapels. Charity schools for children of both sexes are amply supported, some by bequests and others by subscriptions and donations—to one of these an apprenticeship fund is attached; there are also several minor charities for the benefit of the poor of the parish. Queen Anne Boleyn had a house on Newington-green, believed to have been on the same site as that now occupied by Thomas Garratt, Esquire. Near the church is a walk, termed 'Queen Elizabeth's walk;' and it was here that that princess's favourite, Dudley Earl of Leicester, generally resided. Dr. Isaac Watts dwelt in this parish for some years, and in it he penned his much-admired hymns—he died on the 25th November, 1748. Daniel Defoe, the author of 'Robinson Crusoe,' and some other ingenious works—Thomas Day, author of 'Sandford and Merton'—and that ornament to human nature, the philanthropic Howard, were among the number of eminent men who made Newington their home. In 1831 the parish of St. Mary, Stoke Newington, contained 3,480 inhabitants, which number has since very considerably increased.

About three miles and a half north-east from London, situated between Stoke Newington and Tottenham, is the beautiful and highly respectable village of STAMFORD HILL. It is composed principally of handsome genteel private houses, occupied by persons who either have trade establishments elsewhere or have retired from business; many families of distinction, too, have elegant seats and tasteful vilas in the immediate vicinity: altogether the appearance of the place is very superior to that of the greater number of villages closely connected with the metropolis; and the constant succession of carriages of every description is at once convenient to the inhabitants, and diffuses a pleasing air of animation. A chapel of ease is the only place of worship.

POST OFFICE, High street, STOKE NEWINGTON, Thomas Driver, *Post Master.*—Letters from LONDON, &c. arrive every morning at half-past eight, forenoon at eleven, afternoon at three and evening at six, and are despatched every morning at ten, afternoon at two and five and night at eight.—Letters are despatched to TOTTENHAM, EDMONTON, and ENFIELD every morning at ten and afternoon at four; and to WALTHAM CROSS and the North every evening at six.

*** *The letters* S. N. *attached to an address signify* STOKE NEWINGTON.

GENTRY AND CLERGY.
Acroyd Mr. Robt. 38 Nelson terr. S.N.
Adamthwaite Jno. A. esq. Green lanes
Alexander Mrs. Ann, Church st, S.N.
Alexander Geo. W. esq. Church st, S.N
Allen Mr. Wm. 38 Newington green
Allen Wm. esq. Paradise row, S. N.
Andrew Mr. Thos. 18 Shacklewell lane
Aspin Mr. Jehoshaphat, 24 Newington green [Green lanes
Atkinson William, esq. Paradise place,
Barclay Mr. Robert, 1 Rectory place, Shacklewell road [lewell lane
Barlow Thos. esq. White cottg. Shack-
Bates Mrs. Jane, 30 Nelson terr, S.N.
Beetham William, esq. Paradise row
Bennett —, esq. Caledonian cott. S.N.
Bennett Mr. Rd. 8 Newington green
Betteley Samuel, esq. Green lanes
Birch Rev. Edw. M.A. Shacklewell road
Bircheno Mrs. —, Park st, S. N.
Bishop Miss —, Paradise row [S.N.
Brooks Miss Jane, 2 Coronation place,
Browning Mr. William Hardwick, 10 Newington green
Bumpstead Mrs. —, Albion road, S.N.
Burrows Jer. esq. 17 Newington green
Burton Capt. James, Amherst place, Shacklewell road [road
Campbell Rev. John, Shacklewell
Chubb Mr. Jno. 39 Newington green
Clarke Mr. Robt. 12 Newington green
Clissold Rev. Augustus, Paradise house, Stoke Newington
Cohen Mr. Aaron, Shacklewell green
Coldrey Mr. Thos. 42 Newington green
Cooke Mr. Horatio Nelson, 37 Nelson terrace
Cooper Mr. John, Shacklewell green
Cooper Miss Mary, 16 Newington green [Shacklewell road
Cox Rev. John, 2 Down cottages,
Davies Mrs. Sarah, 44 Newington grn
De la Chaumetta Mrs. —, Albion road
Dixon Mrs. Eliz. Stoke Newington road [Shacklewell road
Donnison John, esq. 1 Down cottages,
Dudley William, esq. Nelson terrace
Dutton Mr. Matthew, Church st
Ellwood Mr. Jno. 10 Coronation place
Elmenhorst Mr. Theodore, Nelson ter

Emery Mr. Peter, 43 Newington green
Fincham Mrs. Edw. Shacklewell lane
Fleetwood Mr. Chs Shacklewell lane
Foster Mrs. Martha, 40 Nelson terrace
Gardiner Mr. William, Paradise row
Garratt Mrs. Mary, 3 Newington green
Garratt Thos. esq. 2 Newington green
Gilmore Mr. Mungo, Stamford Hill
Glass Mr. Chas. opposite the Church yard, Church st [S.N.
Gowar Mr. Saml 1 Wellington place,
Grant Mr. Alex. nr Newington green
Grant Mr. James, Sister's cottage, Stoke Newington road [lane
Green Mr. Robert, 14 Shacklewell
Greenland Mr. Alfred, 2 Rectory place, Shacklewell lane
Guy Mr. Richard B. Albion road
Hall Benjamin, esq. Church st
Hancock Charles, esq. Green lane
Hanley Wm. esq. 20 Newington green
Harris Edward, esq. Paradise row
Harrison Geo. esq. Trafalgar house, Shacklewell lane
Harrison Swainston, esq. 4 Down cottages, Shacklewell road
Hassell Mr. Thomas Benjamin, 35 Newington green [green
Haywood William, esq. 7 Newington
Heale Mrs. Christiana, 45 Newingtn gn
Hindle Jno. esq. Truman place, S.N.
Hobson Joshua, esq. Stamford Hill
Hobson William, esq. Markfield, Stamford Hill [place, S.N.
Hogben Mr. Henry, 11 Wellington
Hughes Mr. Wm. Stoke Newington rd
Hunt Mrs. Margaret, 41 Newington green [lewell green
Hunt Mr. Wm. Manor house, Shack-
Hurel Mr. Chas. 13 Newington green
Huxley Mr. Jas. 14 Newington green
Huxley Mr. Thomas, Rectory place, Shacklewell road
Janson Joseph, esq. Church st
Janson Mrs. Sarah, Church st
Jefferson Rev. John, Church st, S.N.
Johnson Mr. Wm. 46 Newington grn
Jones R. L. esq. Stamford Hill
Jones Mr. Wm. 22 Newington green
Kitchener Robt. J. esq. Nelson terrace
Lafargue Mrs. Josepha, Stoke Newington road
Lake Mr. Geo. 25 Newington green
Langton David, esq. Lordship terrace
Lewis Mr. Thomas, Albion road
Lister Miss Eliz. Wellington road, S.N.
Maltby Thomas James, esq. 34 Newington green [green
Marshall Mrs. Mary, 18 Newington
Morgan Mrs. —, Paradise row
Morrison Mrs. Eliza, Stoke Newington road [terrace
Mountford Mrs. Sarah, 29 Nelson
Nash Mr. Thomas, 29 Newington grn
Nicholson Mr. James, Wellington place, Shacklewell road
Oldham Joseph, esq. Stamford Hill
Pearson John, esq. Nelson terrace
Pellatt Mill, esq. Shacklewell road
Perkins Mr. James, York house, Shacklewell green
Phillips Mr. John, 6 Newington grn
Pim William, esq. High houses, S.N.
Pitman Mr. Wm. 19 Newington grn
Povah Rev. Richd. 23 Newington grn
Powell Thos. esq. Woodbury down
Prior Mr. Thos. Robt. 17 Shacklewell la
Pyne Mr. Peter, Stoke Newington rd
Ralfe Robert, esq. 6 Down cottages, Shacklewell road
Richardson Mr. William, Rectory place, Shacklewell road
Riley Benjamin, esq. Green lanes
Rippon Mr. John B. Shacklewell gn
Robinson Mr. Charles, Stoke Newington road
Robinson Mr. Joseph, Middleton cottage, Stoke Newington road
Robson Mr. N. 4 Shacklewell lane
Rogers Mr. Erastus, Brunswick grove
Rogers Mr. Robert W. J. 28 Newington green [green
Rotton Mr. John, 32 Newington
Rouse Henry, esq. Stamford Hill
Rudd Thos. esq. 1 Newington green
Scott Mrs. —; Albion road [race
Seymer Mr. Thomas, 33 Nelson ter-
Sharpe the Misses, Amherst place
Simmons Mr. Edw., S. Newingtn rd
Smith Mr. Leapidge, Rectory cottage, Shacklewell road [race
Smith Mr. Richard, 23 Nelson ter-
Springsguth Mr. Samuel, jun. Shacklewell green [green
Starey Mr. Benjamin, 15 Newington
State Mr. Opie, Church st, S. N.
Strong Mr. Jos. 33 Newington green
Taylor Rev. A. W. Church st, S. N.
Taylor Mr. James, 36 Nelson terrace
Truman Mr. Thos. 31 Nelson terrace
Tuohy Mr. Jos. 40 Newington green
Washington Mr. Thos. 39 Nelson terr
Wilks Mr. Robt. 36 Newington grn
Williams Jos. esq. 2 Shacklewell lane
Wilson Mr. David, Stamford Hill
Wilson Josiah, esq. Stonard hse, S.N.
Winch Mr. Wm. 31 Newington green
Wood Mr. Wm. Shacklewell green
Woodley Captain Wm. Green lanes

ACADEMIES & SCHOOLS.

Not otherwise described are Boarding.

Balls Orlando, Shacklewell green Academy
Bott Thomas (languages), Stoke Newington road [Hill
Clements James (& day), Stamford
Dodd John Robert, Church row
Dutton Miss (preparatory), Church st
Evison Mrs. & Mary, 10 Sandford place, Newington common
Giles Eliz. Ann & Cath. Church st
Green Francis (day), High st
Harford James Unwin (boarding and day), 30 Nelson terrace
Hornblower Miss, Stamford Hill
Jones Charlotte, Stoke Newington rd
LANCASTERIAN, near Stamford Hill bridge—James Bonwick, master; Harriet Abraims, mistress
Le Mare Robert, Stamford Hill [st
Mackenzie Clement Hy. (day) Church
Masters Eliz. (day), High st, S. N.
Miles Mrs. Palatine houses
NATIONAL SCHOOL, Church rw—Chs. Beavitt, master; Ann Hyde, mistrss
NEWINGTON AND KINGSLAND BRITISH SCHOOLS, Cock & Castle lane —George Poole, master; Ann Blythman, mistress
Niass Jane (gent.'s preparatory), 26 Nelson terrace
Parker Thomas, Church row
Peil Lydia, Vittoria place, S. N.
Phillips Amelia, Stoke Newington rd
Pike Rev. Godfrey Theopls. Church st
Sansbury Maria, 37 Newington green
Shaw Louisa (French language), Palatine houses
Shephard Misses, Church st
Softley Willam, Stoke Newington rd
Springsguth Ann & Mary (music), Shacklewell green
Sweetapple Miss (friends), Church st
Thorogood Miss, Lordship terrace
Todd Mrs. (preparatry), Lordship terr
Van de Linde Rev. Gerard (French and English), Bellevue house, Wellington road, S. N.
Wallace George, Paradise row
Webb Emma, Jane & Martha, 2 Wellington place, S. N. [S. N.
Woodrooffe Maria, 3 Wellington pl,

BAKERS & FLOUR DEALERS.

Ashton Ann, Stamford Hill
Bostel Thomas Taylor, 1 Palatine houses, Stoke Newington
Burgess Jane & Son, Shacklewell la
Carter John, High st, S. N.
Clarke Thomas, High st, S. N.
Dickie Charles, High st, S. N.
Engisch Christian, High st, S. N.
Fordham Maria, High st, S. N.
Griffin John, Stoke Newington road
James Samuel, 36 Church st, S. N.
Kemp Peter, 30 Newington green
Last George, High st, S. N.
Packman Richd. Stoke Newington rd
Turney Geo. 4 Gloucester pl, S.N. road
Walton Lucy, Stoke Newington road
Watt James, Hill st, Stamford Hill

BASKET MAKERS.

Boast Samuel, High st, S. N.
Denyer Francis, High st, S. N. [S.N.
Livermore Jos. York place, High st,

BLACKSMITHS & FARRIERS.

Carvey John, Sandford lane, S. N.
Trower Richard, Back road
Whitmore John (and locksmith and bellhanger), High st, S. N.

BOOKSELLERS & STATIONRS.

Herbert Daniel (& printer, binder and library), Stoke Newington road
Masters Joseph, 5 Church st
Miller Charles (& printer), Church st
Paterson Ann, 14 Vittoria place, Church st, S. N. [S. N.
Secretan John (and library), High st,
Wales Rd. (& general fancy resository & news agent), 1 Church st, S. N.

BOOT & SHOE MAKERS.

Bale Edmund, Stoke Newington road
Blackeby Wm. Stoke Newington road
Bridge Saml. Geo. Stamford Hill brdge
Broadhurst Thomas, High st, S. N.
Clapp William (and leather cutter), High st, Stoke Newington
Clarke William, 3 John st, S. N.
Davidge James, High st, S. N.
Dell Samuel, 2 Church st, S. N.
Dim Geo. 1 Park st, Church st, S. N.
Eldred Thomas, 1 Caroline place, Newington common [road
Francis Benjamin, Stoke Newington
Griffiths Thomas, Stamford Hill
Hale James, 12 Church row, S. N.
Jones James, 16 Church st, S. N.
Kippist George, Meadow st, S. N.
Pattison Joshua, High st, S. N.
Potter Henry, High st, S. N.
Smith John, 3 Church st, S. N.
Vanderberg Joseph, Shacklewell lane
Walker Thos. near Newington green
Wasp Mary, High st, S. N.
Whittenbury Joseph, Rochester terrace, High st, S. N. [lane
Wood Thomas, corner of Shacklewell
Wood Thos. jun. 5 Wellington place

BREWERS.

Knight William, High st, S. N.
M'Leod Bentley George More and Edward, Stamford Hill

BRICK MAKERS & BUILDERS.

Catling James & Son, Stoke Newington road & *Tottenham* [S. N.
Rhodes Thos. & Wm. Prospect place,
Sandars Thomas, Shacklewell lane
Smith Benjamin, 15 Shacklewell lane
Webb Robert & Geo. Coach & Horses lane, Stoke Newington
Webb Robt. Wm. & George, Coach and Horses lane, S. N.
Widdows Thomas, Church st, S. N.

BRICKLAYERS, &c.

Binnings George, High st, S. N.
Catling James & Son, Stoke Newington road, and at *Tottenham*
Clarke Benj. 4 Palatine houses, S.N.

BRICKLAYERS, &c.—Continued.
Jones William (and builder), Chapel road, Stamford Hill [S. N.
Paul Geo. Edward's lane, Church st,
Robson William, Church st, S. N.
Workman John, Stamford Hill

BUTCHERS.
Brampton Samuel, High st
Carr John Wilson, High st, S. N.
Chinner Charles, High st. S. N.
Feast Sarah, Church st, S. N.
Greedus Philip, High st, S.N.
Grocott Jos. Stoke Newington road
Hill Wm. High st, S. N. [S. N.
Messenger James, 43 Nelson terrace,
Phillips Thomas, York place, High st
Raynar John, Shacklewell lane
Sadler William, High st, S. N.
Sweet Thomas, 33 Church st, S. N.
TrenholmThos.6Palatine houses,S.N
TriggRuth,Stamford Hill bridge,S.N.

CARPENTRS & UNDERTAKRS.
Blackall Saml. 2 Nelson terrace, S.N.
ChildsRobt.2Ross place, High st,S.N.
Clarke Edward, Church st, S. N.
Clarke George, Stamford Hill
Clarke John Hayhow, Nursery place
Clarke Joshua, High st, S. N.
Coal William, High st, S. N.
Coulson Henry, Wellington st, S. N.
Cuthbert Charles, High st, S. N.
Dore Joseph, 41 Nelson terrace
Foster John, 20 Church st, S. N.
Inwood William, Newington green
Iszard Meshach, High st, S. N.
Knowles Thomas, Shacklewell lane
Lamb William, Stamford Hill
Lewis David,Chapel rd, Stamford Hill
Monk Robert, 1 Red Lion lane, S. N.
Prior Wm. Stoke Newington road
Provis Joseph Edward (and window blind maker), 4 Tyson road, S. N.
Saunders George, Church row
Silvester Solomon, High st, S. N.
Sutton John, 35 Church st, S. N.
WiddowsThomas(&builder),Church st, Stoke Newington

CARVERS & GILDERS.
Luck William, High st, S. N.
Wells —, York place, High st

CHEESEMONGERS.
Allen Wm. Woodgate, 3 Church st
Carr William, High st
Crossley John & Richard, High st
Dalton Francis, 10 and 11 Carlton place, High st, Stoke Newington
Gantley John, 7 Church st, S. N.
Mills Robert, High st, S. N.
Purssord Frederick, 2 High st, S. N.
Taylor Thos. Jarman, Palatine houses

CHINA, GLASS, &c. DEALERS.
Cooper Thomas, 1 High st, S.N.
Hillum John, Church st, S.N.
Rawlins John, High st, S. N.

CHYMISTS & DRUGGISTS.
Stevens Henry, High st, S.N.
Westbrook John, High st, S.N.

COACH MAKERS.
Bressey Robt. Nathaniel, 3 High st, Stoke Newington road
Draper Jabez, 15 Victoria place,S.N.

COACH MASTERS.
Eldridge James, 19 Church st
Hunt Thomas, Church st, S.N.
Lapwood Edward, Coach and Horses lane, Newington green
Low Stephen, Wellington st, S.N.
Sumpter George, Stamford Hill
Willan Leonard, High st, S.N.
Wombwell Maria, Lordship road

COAL MERCHANTS.
Allen William W. 3 Church st
Bryant Lewis, Stamford Hill
Harwood Wm, York place, High st
Rogers Joseph G. High st, S.N.
Telfer George, 4 Newington green

CONFECTIONERS.
Carpenter James, High st, S.N.
Carter John, High st, S.N. [road
Streete Samuel, Stoke Newington
Volckman Francis, High st, S. N.
Walton Lucy, Stoke Newington road

COOPERS.
Knight William, High st, S.N.
Rose Edmund C.(wine) High st,S.N.

CORN CHANDLERS.
Burgess John Funston, High st,S.N.
Love William, High st, S.N. [S.N.
Rogers Jos.G.(& seedsman) High st,

COW KEEPERS.
Doggett James, Shacklewell lane
English William, High st, S.N.
Lock John, Church st, S.N.
Low Stephen, Wellington st, S.N.
Stapleton Jno. Gillard, Newington common, S.N. [Church st
Wombwell Mary, Lordship road,

DYERS & SCOURERS.
Briggs John, Brunswick place, S.N.
King Wm. Nursery place, S.N.

FIRE, &c. OFFICE AGENTS.
GLOBE, Thomas Driver, High st
NATIONAL PROVIDENT, Ths. Cooper, High st, S.N. [High st
PROTECTOR, Frederick Purssord,
WEST MIDDLESEX, William B.Webster, High st, Stoke Newington

FRUITERERS AND GREENGROCERS.
Blaxter William, 7 Church st, S.N.
Davenport Thomas, High st, S. N.
Eaton John, High st, S.N.
Lock John, Church st, S.N.
Reynolds Saml.22 Coronation pl.S.N.
Rumball Rebecca, High st, S. N.
Waters James, High st
Wilkins James, High st, S. N.

FURNITURE BROKERS.
Bond Henry, 46 Nelson terrace
Childs Robert,2 Ross pl.High st, S.N.
Dockrell Wm. York pl. High st, S.N.
Parker Thomas, High st, S. N.
Saffery Mary Ann, High st, S. N.
Wilson William, High st, S. N.

GARDENERS.
Argent Chas. 12 Park st, Church st
Burns Wm, Red Lion lane, Church st
Gill Thomas, Stamford Hill

GROCERS & TEA DEALERS.
(See also Shopkeepers, &c.)
AllenWm.Woodgate,3Church st,S.N
Butcher Charles, Stamford Hill
Dalton Francis, 10 & 11 Carlton pl
Driver Thomas, High st, S. N.
Dyall John, High st, Stoke Newingtn
Fay James, Church st
Hensley Fred. James, High st, S. N.
Hunt Thomas, Church st, S. N.
Iszard Meshach, High st, S. N.
Jobson John, High st, S. N.
Lawrence Lawrence, 3 High st
Linton Miles, 6 Church st, S. N.
Meredith Charles, S.Newington road
Mills Robert, High st, S. N.
Peppercorn Thomas, Church st, S.N.
Rumball Samuel, Stamford Hill
Springsguth Matthw. Shacklewell la
Taylor Thomas Jarman, 2 Palatine houses, Stoke Newington
Wright Maria, Stoke Newington road

HABERDASHERS.
Christmas John, 7 Palatine houses
Papprill William, Shacklewell lane

HAIR DRESSERS.
Dimond William, 2 Park st
Eaton Chas. York pl. High st, S. N.
Fletcher George, High st, S. N.
Tucker Rebecca, 4 Church st

IRONMONGERS.
Walker James, 17 High st, S. N.
Whitmore John, Stamford Hill brdge

LAND & HOUSE AGENTS.
Catling James & Son, Stoke Newington road and *Tottenham*

LINEN DRAPERS, HABERDASHERS, &c.
Balle William, High st, S. N. [S.N.
Cockett Adolphus Horatio, High st,
Dunthorne Edward, High st, S. N.
Hunton Fulleretta & Joseph, Church st, Stoke Newington
James Richard, High st, S. N.
Levitt Thomas & Thomas, Church st, Stoke Newington [road
Roberts Edward, Stoke Newington

MILLINERS & DRESS MAKRS.
Balle Mrs. W. High st, S. N.
Brown Charlotte, 1 Prospect terrace, Stoke Newington [S. N.
EllwoodHarriet,15 Coronation place,
Ottley Charlotte, High st, S. N.
Prior Mary A. 4 Prospect terrace
Rumball Sophia, Stamford Hill
Smith MaryAnn,15 Shacklewell lane
Strutton Mrs. —, High st, S. N.
Webster Phillis, High st, S. N.
Young William, 16 Park st

NUSERYMEN.
Adamson William & Son (and fruit growers and market gardeners), Stoke Newington common and Stamford Hill
Clayden John, 2 Wellington st, S.N.
Franklin Richard, Down cottages, Shacklewell lane
Gellan Thomas, Shacklewell lane
Lucking Wm. Sandford's lane, S.N.
Mackay Robert, Eden nursery, High st, Stoke Newington
Milne John (and florist), Albion road
Ross John, Caledonian nursery, S.N.
Watts William, High st, S.N.

OIL AND COLOURMEN.
Driver Thomas, High st, S. N.
Jones Thomas Jephtha, High st, S.N.
Rumball Samuel, Stamford Hill
Sharman William, 44 Nelson terrace

PAINTERS, PLUMBERS, AND GLAZIERS.
Armitage Wm.Jos.34 Church st,S.N.
Bishop Charles, Stamford Hill
Broadbridge Charles, Church st,S.N.
Broadbridge Thomas, Church st,S.N.
Stansfield John, High st, S. N.
Weymark Richard, Sidney row, Stamford Hill
Whincop George, High st, S. N.
Young Peter, High st, S. N.

RAG MERCHANTS.
Boothey Ann, High st, Stoke N.
Tollady Charles, High st, Stoke N.

SADDLERS.
Allen Thomas, Stamford Hill
Haynes Wm. Stoke Newington road
Shaw Sarah, High st, StokeNewingtn

SHOPKEEPERS & DEALRS IN GROCERIES & SUNDRIES.
Arber Joseph, Stamford Hill bridge
Baddeley Joseph, Shacklewell lane
Chandler Ann, Church st, Stoke N.
Chase William, Meadow st, S. N.
Clarke Job, Church st, Stoke N.
Dawson Geo. Stamford Hill bridge
Dowsett Wm. Stamford Hill bridge
Fay Jas. Church st, Stoke Newingtn
Field Geo. High st, Stoke Newington
Goulden Benj. Stoke Newington rd
Hillum Mary, Church st, Stoke N.
Jeffery John Isaac, 23 Great Bowling green st, Stoke Newington
Jobson John, High st [ton
Jones John, High st, Stoke Newing-
Lapwood Edwd. nr Newington green
Marshall Robt. 1 Meadow st, S. N.
Pain Fanny and Elizbth. 1 Sidney row, Stamford Hill [ton
Polley John, High st, Stoke Newing-

Reynolds Samuel, High st, Stoke N.
Richards Samuel, High st, Stoke N.
Rumball Samuel, Stamford Hill
Smith James, Sandford's lane, S. N.
Ward Robert, 14 Margaret st, Stamford Hill
Webster Jos. 1 Frederick pl. Shacklewell green
Wilson Edward, Stamford Hill

STAY MAKERS.

Giles Richd. Rochester terr. High st
Lydamont Sarah, York place, S. N.
Tallon Elizabeth, High st, S. N.
Thurlow Maria, High st, Stoke N.

STONEMASONS.

Cusworth John, Stamford Hill
Heath Hannah, York pl. High st, S.N.

STRAW HAT MAKERS.

Cole Elizabeth, Church st, S.N.
Morrison Martha, 7 Union st, S. N.
Ottley Charlotte, High st, S. N.
Simpson Jas. Stoke Newington road
Thurlow Frederick, High st, S. N.
Walsh George, Stamford Hill

SURGEONS.

Battye Thomas, 8 Newington green
Bishop John Dommett, 5 Rochester terrace, High st, S. N.
Bond Edw. Thornley, Church st, S. N.
Burge Frederick, 2 Albion cottages
Foster Wm. Penn, Church st, S. N.
Price John Cook, Stamford Hill
Renton Jas. Chas. 24 Nelson terrace
Reynolds & Brett, High st, S. N.
Robinson William B. (& registrar of births & deaths), Shacklewell la
Robinson William H. (and deputy registrar), Shacklewell lane
Spencer Wm. Thos. 25 Nelson terr

TAILORS.

Clay Saml. 5 Diapason row, High st
Dore James, 41 Nelson terrace
Honor Wm. Thomas, High st, S. N.
Lyons Benjamin, High st, S. N.
Murrell Thomas, Church st, S. N.
Secar Thomas, High st, S. N.
Seymour John, Church st, S. N.
Smith William, 4 Church st, S. N.
Wright James, High st, S. N.

TAVERNS & PUBLIC HOUSES.

Amherst Arms, Thomas Warrington, Shacklewell road
Birdcage, Samuel Gill, Stamford Hill
Black Bull, Thomas King, High st, S. N.
British Oak, Stephen Murrell, Grove lane, Stamford Hill
Coach & Horses, Thos. Dean, High st, S. N.
Coach & Horses, George Main, Coach & Horses lane
Cock & Castle, Robert Harrington, Cock and Castle lane
Falcon, William Drury, Church st, S. N.
Green Man (and tea gardens), Eliz. Long, Shacklewell lane
Fox, Phœbe Richardson, Back road
Hare & Hounds, Eliz. Bellew, Palatine houses, S. N.
Old Turnpike House, Sarah Brant, Stamford Hill
Red Lion, James Flack, Church st, S. N.
Rochester Castle, Robt. James, High st, S.N.
Rose & Crown, John Baker, Church st, S.N.
Three Crowns, Geo. Moade, High st, S. N.
Three Jolly Butchers, William Barker, High st, Stoke Newington
Victoria, — Haines, High st, Stoke Newington
Weavers' Arms, Joseph James, foot of Stamford Hill
Weavers' Arms, Michl. Starkey, near Newington green
White Hart, Saml. Kingston, High st, S.N.

TOBACCONISTS.

Dunthorne Moses, Stoke Newington road
Heath John, York place, Stoke Newington
Secretan Jno. Francis, High st, S. N.
Smith Margaret, 5 Church st, S. N.

TOY DEALERS.

Bulgin Clarissa Lucy, Stamford Hill
Harford John F. High st, S. N.
Miller Charles, Church st, S. N.
Parker Ann, High st, S. N.
Pitchforth Charles (& wire worker), High st, Stoke Newington
Robson William, Church st, S. N.

WATCH & CLOCK MAKERS.

Archer Thos. Stoke Newington road
Webster Wm. Bennett, High st, S. N.

WHEELWRIGHTS.

Rendall James, Nursery place
Ward William, Tyson road, S. N.

Miscellaneous.

Barker Charles, poulterer, High st. S. N.
Bell William, jeweller, Stamford Hill
Church Edward, piano, &c. tuner, Stoke Newington road
Comley William, dentist & cupper, Stoke Newington road
Crosland John, vestry clerk, Church st, S.N.
Daniels William, collector of poor rates, Down's terrace
Day William & Son, auctioneers & surveyors, 34 Nelson terrace
DISPENSARY, High st, S.N.—Mr. Claudius Miller, resident medical officer, York pl
Dockerell William, dealer in building materials, High st, S. N.
Featherstone Maria, wardrobe dealer, High st, S.N.
Gretton Thomas, chaser, 42 Nelson terrace
INVALID ASYLUM, High st, S. N.—Mrs. Mary Busby, matron
Jones Edmund, clothier, High st, S. N.
Joselin Richd. hatter, &c. Church st, S. N.
Kennedy Lawrence, silversmith & pawnbroker, 1 Rochester terrace, S. N.
King Charles, eating-house, High st, S. N.
Law John A. artist, Church st, S. N.
Nalders, Spall & Hardisty, glove manufacturers, near Shacklewell lane
POLICE DIVISION (N. Islington) Barret grove—James Johnston, superintendent
Prestage Thos. fishmonger, High st, S. N.
Rose E. C. brush & matting warehouse, High st, Stoke Newington
SAVINGS' BANK, High st, S. N.—Edwin Symons, actuary
Sear Thomas, brush, patten & clog maker, High st, S. N.
Spottiswoode Andrew, queen's printer, Bible office, Shacklewell
Tegg George, veterinary surgeon, Stamford Hill
Wells George William, window blind maker, High st
Wyles Thos. dairyman, Stoke Newington road
Yardley William, registrar of births and deaths, Nelson terrace, S. N.

COACHES,

To and from LONDON, and the North and Eastern part of the Kingdom, pass thro' Stoke Newington almost hourly, but do not stop at any of the Inns.

OMNIBUSES & FLYS.

To LONDON, Willan's *Omnibuses*, from the Coach & Horses, High st, and the Falcon, Church st—Hunt's and Spink's, from the Three Crowns, corner of Church st, & the Rose & Crown, Church st, every half-hour from eight in the morning until ten at night—and Geo. Sumpter's, from Stamford Hill, every hour from eight in the morning until nine at night.

To LONDON, James Eldridge's *Flys*, from 19 Church st, every morning at a quarter before nine, forenoon at eleven & afternoon at a quarter before two and a quarter before five—& James Ransom's *Flys*, from the Three Crowns & Rose & Crown, Church st, every morning at half-past eight, forenoon at eleven and afternoon at three and five; go through Islington.

CARRIERS,

To LONDON, the London Parcels Delivery Company, from Thomas Driver's, Post office, High street, every morning (Sunday excepted) at ten, afternoon at three, and evening at seven.

To LONDON, James Lowe's *Cart*, from 10 John st, and Richard Wells, from 5 Palatine houses, daily (Sunday excepted.)

SUNBURY, SHEPPERTON, LOWER & UPPER HALLIFORD,

CHARLTON AND NEIGHBOURHOODS.

SUNBURY is a respectable village and parish in the hundred of Spelthorne, about 15 miles s. w. from London, equi-distant (about five miles) from Chertsey, Esher, Hounslow and Staines, and two from Hampton; pleasantly situated near to the Thames, and in a neighbourhood remarkable for the number of handsome seats and mansions; amongst these is one formerly possessed by the Earl of Pomfret, then noticed as an epitome of the *façade* at Hampton Court (and often described as a miniature of that ancient palace); it has been materially altered, and is now the property of Richardson Purves, Esq. The church, dedicated to St. Mary, is a brick structure, erected in 1752, and comprises a nave, chancel and north aisle, with galleries and an organ-loft, and a square tower, surmounted by a cupola: from its summit the view is very extensive, and embraces Windsor Castle, St. Paul's, Hampton Court and its palace, Bushey Park, Claremont, &c. The living is a vicarage, in the gift of the dean and chapter of St. Paul's; the present incumbent is the Rev. James Cowe, and the Rev. Charles Moffat is his present curate. The charities comprise a national school for boys and girls, four alms-houses and a workhouse. Two small fairs are held, on Shrove-Tuesday and the Wednesday in Whitsun week, for toys, &c. In 1831 the parish contained 1,863 inhabitants.

In the same hundred as Sunbury, about two miles from that village, on the road to Chertsey, is the village of SHEPPERTON, in the parish of its name. It is a place possessing nothing worthy of remark, as regards either trade or curiosity. It contains a small church, dedicated to St. Nicholas, and a national school for boys and girls, erected in 1833, supported by voluntary contributions. Population of the parish, at the last census, 847.

In the parish of Shepperton are the hamlets of UPPER and LOWER HALLIFORD, the latter situate on the north bank of the Thames, and supposed to derive its name from an ancient *ford* here, by means of which Julius Cæsar crossed the river when he fought a battle with the Britons in this neighbourhood—a circumstance that has received confirmation from the number of Roman weapons found in and about the hamlet at different periods. The population is returned with Shepperton.

POST OFFICE, SUNBURY, Louisa Ruff, *Post Mistress.*—Letters from LONDON arrive every morning at ten and afternoon at one, and are despatched every morning at seven and afternoon at three.

POST, LOWER HALLIFORD, *Receiving-House* at James Tilleard's, grocer.—Letters for LONDON and all parts are despatched to Esher every afternoon at four.

GENTRY & CLERGY.

Adcock Wm. Robt. esq. Shepperton
Batty Captain —, Charlton
Bishop John, esq. Sunbury
Carpenter Capt. Digby Thomas, Hawk house, Sunbury
Carruthers James, esq. Lower Halliford
Cobbett William, esq. Sunbury
Collingridge John, esq. Sunbury villa
Cooper Samuel, esq. Shepperton
Cowe Rev. James, Sunbury vicarage
Crump Miss H. Sunbury
Dabbs John, esq. Thames bank house, Sunbury
Douglas Miss —, Lower Halliford
Douglas Miss —, Sunbury
Everard Mrs. —, Halliford house, Sunbury
Gibbons Robt. F. esq. Lower Halliford
Graham Mrs. General, Sunbury
Hankins Colonel —, Sunbury
Hayes Thos. esq. Darby house, Sunbury
Hedges Killingsworth Richard, esq. Sunbury
Hetherington Capt. Edward, Charlton
Hubbard Mrs. Tabitha, Sunbury
Iveson John, esq. Lower Halliford
Jones Mrs. Elizbeth, Upper Halliford
King Mr. Thomas, Upper Halliford
Lahee James, esq. Upper Halliford
Landon Captain Samuel, Sunbury
Marryott William, esq. Sunbury
Matheson Mr. Daniel, Sunbury
Mather Mr. John, Sunbury
Mitchison John, esq. Sunbury
Moffat Rev. Charles, Sunbury
Oliver Lionel, esq. Sunbury
Palmer Mr. Mark, Lower Halliford
Payne Sir Charles, Sunbury
Peacock Thos. esq. Lower Halliford
Pemberton Mrs. —, Sunbury
Pickering Miss —, Shepperton
Porter Edwd. esq. Sunbury common
Purves Richardson, esq. Sunbury place
Raphael Lewis, esq. Kempton park, Sunbury
Rosewell Mr. Thomas, Lower Halliford
Russell the Misses, Shepperton
Russell Rev. William, Rectory house, Shepperton
Scott James, esq. Shepperton
Simpson Mrs. —, Sunbury
Steward Thos. esq. Lower Halliford
Todd Richard, esq. Clock house, Upper Halliford
Tull Samuel, esq. Charlton park
Turner Joseph, esq. Sunbury
Underwood Edmd. esq. Shepperton
Wall Rev. Danl. Henry, Sunbury lodge
Wells Mrs. —, Lower Halliford
Weightman William Alexander, esq. Spelthorne grove, Sunbury
West Rev. Isaac, Sunbury

ACADEMIES AND SCHOOLS.

Bolt William (boarding), Sunbury
Hawkes Lucy (day), Sunbury
INFANTS' SCHOOL, Sunbury—Charlotte Gunyon, mistress
NATIONAL SCHOOL, Shepperton—William Trott, master; Alice Danby, mistress
NATIONAL SCHOOL, Sunbury—John Anning, master; Jane Leggett, mistress
Oborn Stephen (day,) Sunbury
Spowers Geo. P. (boarding), Sunbury

BAKERS & FLOUR DEALERS.

Baker John, Sunbury
Bishop Eliza, Sunbury
Brett Wm. Shepperton
Foster John (& biscuit), Upper Halliford
James John & Son, Sunbury
Moore James, Lower Halliford
Ruff Louisa, Sunbury
Strudwick John, Shepperton

BLACKSMITHS & FARRIERS.

Champion James, Shepperton
Every William, Sunbury
Humphreys John, Sunbury

BOOT AND SHOE MAKERS.

Berryman James, Shepperton
Collins George, Sunbury
Cox George, Sunbury
Danby George, Shepperton
Goddard James, Sunbury
Goldhawk John, Shepperton
Heath James, Sunbury
Nash Nicholas, Sunbury
Nash William, Sunbury
Saunders William, Sunbury
Scott William, Shepperton
Wilkins Wm. (& leather cutter), Sunbury

BREWERS.

King John, Sunbury
Puffett Richard, Upper Halliford

BRICKLAYRS & PLASTERERS.

Burt John, Sunbury
Clemons John (& plasterer), Sunbury
Green Charles, Sunbury
Jacob James (and slater), Sunbury
King William, Lower Halliford
Strong John, Shepperton

BUTCHERS.

Bishop William (pork), Sunbury
Bolton James, Sunbury
Clark William, Shepperton
Smith John, Sunbury
Turner John, Sunbury
Vincent William, Shepperton

CARPENTERS & BUILDERS.

Annett Thomas, Sunbury
Annett Thomas, jun. Sunbury
Bliss John, Sunbury
Dove John Frederick, Sunbury
Sanders Henry, Lower Halliford

COAL & CORN MERCHANTS.

Grove James, Sunbury
James John & Son (& seed), Sunbury
Stone Robert, Lower Halliford
Vincent William, Shepperton
Winch John, Sunbury

DRESS MAKERS.

Burt Mary, Sunbury
Clemons Mrs. Sunbury
Cotsford Susan, Sunbury
Darbon Susan, Sunbury
Giles Mary, Sunbury
Graham Ann, Sunbury
Oborn Sarah (and straw hat maker), Sunbury
Rogers Ann, Sunbury

FIRE, &c. OFFICE AGENTS.

KENT, William Jacob, Sunbury
PHŒNIX, Wm. Thos. Collins, Sunbury

FISHMONGERS.

Bennett Thomas, Sunbury
Clark James (& poulterer), Sunbury
Perdue Henry, Shepperton
Ruff William, Sunbury
Stapleton William, Sunbury

FRUITERERS.

Goodman George, Sunbury
Scarlett William, Sunbury
Westbrook James, Sunbury

GROCERS AND DEALERS IN SUNDRIES.

Alder William, Shepperton
Claridge Wm. Shepperton
Collins George, (and fishing tackle), Sunbury
Grove James, Sunbury
Hayward Jas. (& china dealer), Sunbury
Newbury Geo. (& ironmngr), Sunbury
Oborn Thomas, Sunbury
Pearce Ann, Sunbury
Ruff Louisa, Sunbury
Smith John, Upper Halliford
Smith John, Sunbury
Strong John, Shepperton
Tilleard James, Lower Halliford
Vincent William, Shepperton

INNS.

Anchor, George Tebbutt, Shepperton
Flower Pot (and posting house), John Curtis Worthington, Sunbury

LINEN DRAPERS.

Bright George, Shepperton
Collins Wm. Ths. (& stamp office), Sunbury
Newbury George, Sunbury
Oborn Thomas, Sunbury
Strong John, Shepperton

MALTSTERS.

King John, Sunbury
Puffett Richard, Upper Halliford
Reid Neville, Lower Halliford
Winch John, Sunbury

MARKET GARDENERS.

Leonard Edward, Charlton
Voller Thomas, Upper Sunbury
Willmer John Thomas (and nurseryman and florist), Sunbury common

PAINTERS, PLUMBERS, &c.

Raven William, Lower Halliford
Slatter Richard, Sunbury
Wilder & French, Sunbury

ROPE MAKERS.

Tidy Jas. (& mat & basket), Sunbury
Tilleard Mrs. Lower Halliford

SADDLERS.

Fowler Richard, Shepperton
Giles George, Sunbury
Rance David, Shepperton

SURGEONS.

Broxholm Rbt. (& registrar), Sunbury
Gilchrist Charles Dobree, Sunbury

TAILORS.

Bolton John, Sunbury
Bright George, Shepperton
Burchett William & Son, Sunbury
Read Charles, Sunbury
Wake John (and hatter), Sunbury

TAVERNS & PUBLIC HOUSES.

Bull, Benjamin Deller, Shepperton
Castle, John Ford, Sunbury
Crown, Thomas Downton, Shepperton
George, William Mills, Sunbury
Goat, Benjamin Collyer, Upper Halliford
King's Head, Robert Stevens, Shepperton
Magpie, William Nalder, Sunbury
Red Lion, James Dearman, Lower Halliford
Ship, Robert Stone, Lower Halliford
Three Fishes, John Bennett, Sunbury
Traveller's Friend, James Grove, Sunbury common
White Horse, Edward Stroud, Sunbury

WHEELWRIGHTS.

North Daniel, Shepperton green
Stroud Thomas, Sunbury

Miscellaneous.

Andrews John, cooper, Lower Halliford
Anning John, vestry clerk, Sunbury
Bellord Thomas, stay maker, &c. Sunbury
Broxholm G. R. deputy registrar, Sunbury
Collins William, parish clerk, Sunbury
Holland Thomas, mealman, Sunbury
Hunt Thos. ironmonger & smith, Sunbury
Kellick William, miller, Sunbury common
Layton Frederic, furniture broker, Sunbury
Lestone James, hair dresser, Sunbury
Roake Edmd. cattle salesmn, Lwr Halliford
Rolls William, cattle dealer, Sunbury
Sanderson James, surveyor, Sunbury
Wilkins William, tea dealer, Sunbury
Wood Thomas James, watch and clock maker and working jeweller, Sunbury
WORKHOUSE, Sunbury common—George Stolworthy, governor

COACHES.

To LONDON, *Coaches*, from the Flower Pot Inn, Sunbury, every morning at a quarter before eight and half-past nine, forenoon at eleven, afternoon at a quarter before 3 & evening at a quarter before 6.

CARRIER.

To LONDON, Anthony Jordan, from Sunbury, every Tuesday & Friday evening—calls at the Rose Inn, Smithfield; Saracen's Head, Skinner st; Spotted Dog, Strand; & White Bear, Spread Eagle and Old White Horse Cellar, Piccadilly.

TOTTENHAM,

OR, as it is commonly called, TOTTENHAM HIGH CROSS, is a village and parish in the hundred of Edmonton; the parish comprising the several divisions of 'High Cross,' 'Lower' 'Middle,' and 'Wood Green' Wards. The village is five miles N.E. from London, and consists chiefly of one long street, the buildings forming which are irregularly arranged on the line of road leading from London to Cambridge. In domesday-book it is written *Totehám*, said to be derived from the Saxon words *Toten* and *Ham*—and its adjunct from a *high cross* of wood, which formerly surmounted the church tower, visible for many miles round. The present cross, near Tottenham green, which has superseded the original one of wood, is an octangular brick column, erected in 1600, and repaired and decorated with various architectural embellishments in 1809. Tottenham and its vicinage are embellished with many handsome mansions and villas, interspersed with gardens, and numerous families of opulence are residents. The village is lighted with gas, and well watered by several fountains produced by boring; a stream, once the river Moselle, passes through the parish, and empties itself into the river Lea, and the latter is navigable to this place; the New River likewise passes through Tottenham, and an extensive reservoir is formed to add to its waters. This is not a place distinguished for manufactures or particular trade, the latter being confined to the supply of its inhabitants with general commodities, and the former consisting chiefly of the manufacture of crape (for which there is one establishment) and of brown earthenware and tiles, with some extensive oil and flour mills. The civil government of the parish is vested in two churchwardens, four overseers, one vestry clerk, two surveyors of the highways, and one sexton, who is constable.

The places of worship are the parish church, a new chapel of ease, and chapels for baptists, Wesleyan methodists, Roman catholics and the society of friends. The church, which is dedicated to Allhallows, and stands about a quarter of a mile west of the high road, is in the later style of English architecture, with a square embattled tower, covered with ivy; this church was repaired in 1816, at an expense of £3,000. The new church, or Trinity chapel of ease, is on Tottenham green, and was erected in 1829, at an expense of £5,000. defrayed partly from the fund of the church commissioners, and the remainder by subscriptions; it is a handsome Gothic structure, with a clock fronting the high road, and contains 800 sittings, of which nearly half that number are free. The living of Tottenham is a vicarage, in the gift of the dean and chapter of St. Paul's. The charities of Tottenham are tolerably extensive, and comprise several scholastic establishments and almshouses, all well endowed; amongst the former are blue and green coat schools, and a free grammar school, founded by the Dutchess of Somerset in 1686, for forty boys; there are also some benefit societies, a charity for lying-in women, and a savings' bank. At a short distance from the high road is 'Bruce Castle,' a mansion rebuilt in the 17th century on the site of an ancient castellated edifice, erected in the reign of Henry VIII: the present building is now occupied as a school, and a detached brick tower (which covers a deep well) is the only remaining vestige of the ancient structure. In the parish is a well, the water of which is similar in its properties to that at Cheltenham: likewise a spring, called 'Ladies' Well, of reputed efficacy for disorders in the eyes,—and it is asserted that this water never freezes. The parish contained, by the returns for 1831, 6,937 inhabitants.

POST OFFICE, High Cross ward, William Colyer, *Post Master.*—Letters from LONDON arrive every morning at half-past ten, afternoon at two and five and night at half-past eight, and are despatched every morning at eight and ten, afternoon at half-past one and five and evening at half-past seven.

GENTRY AND CLERGY.

Addis Miss Mary, Lower ward
Ansell Mr. Charles, Lower ward
Austin Mr. John, Wood Green ward
Babington Mrs. —, High Cross ward
Back Mr. —, Wood Green ward
Back John, esq. Middle ward
Bacon Mr. Huntley, Wood Green ward
Bailey Mrs. Eliz. High Cross ward
Ball Mr. William, Middle ward
Barber Mr. Richard, Middle ward
Barnes Mr. —, Wood Green ward
Beadnell Mr. John, High Cross ward
Beale Mr. Henry, High Cross ward
Beard Mrs. —, High Cross ward
Beaumont Mr. —, Wood Green ward
Beer Mr. Wm. Middle ward
Berminster Mr. Wm. Walter, Middle ward
Bevan Mr. Paul, High Cross ward
Biggins Mrs. Sarah, Lower ward
Breffitt Geo. esq. High Cross ward
Brooksbank Mr. Thos. Lower ward
Buckworth Mrs. Mary, Lower ward
Chapman Mr. William, Lower ward
Cheeseman Mrs. Ann, Lower ward
Clarkson Fred. esq. Wood Green ward
Cock Mr. John, Middle ward
Collier Miss Jane, Middle ward
Collins Chas. Jas. esq. High Cross ward
Constantine Mrs. Ann, Middle ward
Cook Mr. —, High Cross ward
Cooper Mrs. —, High Cross ward
Cooper Mr. James, Wood Green ward
Cooper Mr. Thos. High Cross ward
Corney Mr. Ed. Bland, High Cross wrd
Cosbie Mr. —, Wood Green ward
Dalby Mrs. —, Lower ward
Daniel Mr. —, Middle ward
Davis Rev. J. J. Middle ward
Dawson Mr. Roger, Lower ward
De Witte Mrs. —, Middle ward
Dermer Miss D. S. High Cross ward
Dobson Mr. —, Middle ward
Dodd Mr. William, Middle ward
Done Mrs. —, High Cross ward
Dunster Rev. —, Lower ward
Dunster Mr. Henry, Middle ward
Durant Mr. Geo. High Cross ward
Ellis Mr. —, Wood Green ward
Ewart Rev. Thos. Henry, Middle ward
Faulkner Geo. esq. Wood Green ward
Fletcher Mr. Joseph, Middle ward
Flight Mr. Thomas, Middle ward
Flowers Mrs. —, Middle ward
Forster Miss Elizabeth, Lower ward
Forster Mr. Josiah, High Cross ward
Forster Mr. Robt. High Cross ward
Fowler Thomas, esq. Middle ward
Fox Mr. —, Middle ward
Fox Mr. Francis, Middle ward
Fox Mr. Wm. Michael, Lower ward
Freeman Mrs. E. L. Lower ward
French Mr. Joseph, High Cross ward
Fyfe Mr. —, Wood Green ward
Garman Mr. Thomas, Lower ward
Garth Mr. Thos. A. High Cross ward
Gatfield Mr. Chas. High Cross ward
Gibbin Mr. John, High Cross ward
Gibbs John, esq. Wood Green ward
Gibson Thos. esq. High Cross ward
Gibson Mr. William, Lower ward
Greaves Miss Martha, Middle ward
Green Mr. Thos. Wood Green ward
Gresham Miss —, Middle ward
Harman —, esq. High Cross ward
Harend Mr. James, Lower ward
Harris Mrs. —, Lower ward
Harris Mr. Anthony, Lower ward
Harris Mr. Thomas, Lower ward
Harvey Mrs. —, Middle ward
Hicks Mrs. —, High Cross ward
Hobson Wm. esq. High Cross ward
Hodgkin Mr. John, Middle ward
Holbrook James, esq. Middle ward
Holt Mrs. —, Middle ward
Holt the Misses, Middle ward
Horne Miss Martha, Middle ward
Howard Mrs. Elizabeth, Middle ward
Howard Mr. John, Middle ward
Howard Mr. Robert, Middle ward
Howard Thos. esq. Middle ward
Howell Mr. William, Middle ward
Hunt Mr. Philip Thos. High Cross wrd
Huskisson Mr. S. M. Middle ward
Janson Mrs. —, Lower ward
Janson Mr. Halsey, High Cross ward
Janson Mr. William, Middle ward
Janson Mr. Wm. jun. High Cross ward
Johnson Mr. Andw. High Cross wrd
Johnson Mr. Ebenzr. High Cross ward
Johnson Mr. John, Middle ward
Johnson Mr. Patk. Wood Green ward
Keeling Mr. John, Middle ward
King Mr. James, Lower ward
Kirby Mr. Wm. Wood Green ward
Knott Mrs. —, Middle ward
Lane Mrs. Ruth, Lower ward
Laundy Mr. Joseph, Middle ward
Lawford John, esq. Wood Green ward
Lennox Geo. Wm. esq. Wood Gn. ward
Lindo Mr. —, Wood Green ward
Lowe Mrs. Eleanor, High Cross ward
M'Ghie Mr. B. A. High Cross ward
M'Math Mr. Andrew, Middle ward
Marshall Mr. John, Middle ward
Marshall Mr. John, High Cross ward
Maud Mrs. —, Lower ward
Mercier Francis, esq. Wood Green ward
Messer Mr. Josiah, Middle ward
Mills Mr. John, Wood Green ward
Mortlock Mrs. High Cross ward
Overend Mrs. —, Wood Green ward
Owen Mr. Thos. Wood Green ward
Parker Mrs. Charlotte, High Cross wrd
Perkin Miss —, Middle ward
Petersdorff Mr. —, Middle ward
Phillips Mrs. Elizabeth, Middle ward
Phillips Mr. John, Wood Green ward
Pifford Mr. J. G. Lower ward
Pinkerton Mrs. Ann, Lower ward
Porter Mr. George, Middle ward
Potter Miss —, High Cross ward
Powell Rev. Dav. Thos. High Cross wrd
Powmal Mr. —, Wood Green ward
Pownall Mr. Chas. Wood Green ward

GENTRY, &c.—*Continued.*
Pownall Mr. James, High Cross ward
Pryor Mrs. Elizabeth, Middle ward
Rhodes Thos. esq. Wood Green ward
Rickman Mr. S. P. High Cross ward
Rigge Mr. John, Middle ward
Robinson Dr. William, Lower ward
Row Mr. James, High Cross ward
Rowney Mrs. —, Lower ward
Rumfitt Mr. Charles, Middle ward
Saunderson John, esq. Middle ward
Scales Mr. John, Wood Green ward
Scambler Mr. Hny. Wood Green wrd
Shadbolt Mr. Chas. High Cross ward
Shadbolt Mr. Chs. jun. High Cross wrd
Sherrer Mr. John, Lower ward
Shippen Mr. Peter, Middle ward
Shuttleworth Mr. George Edmund, High Cross ward
Smale Mr. Henry Lewis, Lower ward
Soames Charles, esq. Lower ward
Squires Miss —, High Cross ward
Stacy Miss —, Middle ward
Stacy Mr. George, Middle ward
Staples Mr. Samuel, Middle ward
Stevenson Mr. John, Lower ward
Stonard Mrs. —, Lower ward
Swinscow Mr. —, Lower ward
Tasker Miss —, Middle ward
Telford Mrs. —, High Cross ward
Thompson Miss —, High Cross ward
Thompson Rev. Geo. High Cross ward
Thompson Mr. James, Lower ward
Thompson Jno. esq. High Cross ward
Timbrell Mr. Andrew, Middle ward
Townend Mr. Jno. High Cross ward
Vaux Rev. Edward, Lower ward
Vernom Mr. —, Lower ward
Walker Mr. Geo. Wood Green ward
Walstab A. G. esq. High Cross ward
Wansey —, esq. Wood Green ward
Ward W. esq. High Cross ward
Warmington Mr. Jas. Middle ward
Waud Christr. esq. High Cross ward
Webb Mr. Benj. High Cross ward
Webster Miss E. Middle ward
Whitaker Mr. —, Middle ward
Whiting Mrs. C. Middle ward
Whittle Mr. —, Wood Green ward
Wigglesworth Mrs. —, Middle ward
Wilkins Geo. esq. High Cross ward
Wilkinson Mrs. Mary, High Cross wrd
Williams Mrs. —, Lower ward
Williams Thomas, esq. Middle ward
Wilson Mr. —, Middle ward
Windus Benjamin Godfrey, esq. High Cross ward
Winsor Mr. —, Wood Green ward
Wollaston Richd. esq. High Cross wrd
Woolley Mr. —, Wood Green ward
Wright Wm. esq. Lower ward park
Yates Mr. —, Middle ward

ACADEMIES AND SCHOOLS.
Not otherwise described are Boarding.
Baird James (day), High Cross ward
Barge Mary and Agnes, Middle ward
BLUE COAT SCHOOL (girls'), Middle ward—Mary Burnett, mistress
Craden —, Sherbro' house
Cuttell Miss, Wood Green
FREE GRAMMAR SCHOOL, High Cross ward—Lancaster Rickards, master
Glynes Louisa (preparty.) Lower ward
Hill Brothers, Middle ward
Holmes Jas. (day), High Cross ward
LANCASTERIAN SCHOOL (girls'), Middle ward—My. Eliz. Cooper, mstrss
LANCASTERIAN SCHOOL (boys'), Church road—Geo. Ross, master
Middlecoat Mary, Bruce terrace
Moore Sarah, Lower road
Murray James, White Hart lane
Pike Wilberforce, Comb's croft house
QUAKERS' COLLEGE—Thos. Binns, master
ROMAN CATHOLIC SCHOOL, White Hart lane; — Murphy, master
SCHOOL OF INDUSTRY, High Cross ward—Elizabeth Harris, mistress
Watkins Amelia, White Hart lane
Youle Peter, High Cross ward

AUCTIONEERS & APPRAISERS.
Gasson James, Middle ward
Richards Samuel, Lower ward
Shuttleworth Geo. E. Tottenhm green
Whybro Edward, Tottenham green

BAKERS & FLOUR DEALERS.
Appleton Robert, High Cross lane
Ashcroft Ebenezer, High Cross lane
Gardiner Alexander, Lower ward
Goodman Thomas, Middle ward
Hood Thomas, High Cross ward
Kent Edward, Church road
Langran Joseph, Lower ward
Moore William, High Cross ward
Peart Thomas, Middle ward
Scott David, Middle ward
Smith Charles, Middle ward
Vass John Dickinson, Lower ward
Wilson Thomas, West green
Wright Joseph, High Cross ward

BLACKSMITHS & FARRIERS.
Balaam William, Marsh lane
Humphriss Edwd. High Cross ward
Leggett John, Middle ward
Mould John, Lower ward
Turner Charles, Middle ward
Turner John (& veterinary surgeon), High Cross ward
Wood Peregrin (and locksmith), Middle ward

BOOT & SHOE MAKERS.
Allard William, Lower ward
Challis William, High Cross lane
Colcock Robert, Middle ward
Dickinson John, High Cross ward
Finney Thos. Stephen, Middle ward
Francis Thomas, Middle ward
Griffiths James, Middle ward
Harding George, Middle ward
Huggins John, Middle ward
Humphreys John, Lower ward
Knott Thomas, High Cross lane
Leakey John, Middle ward
Leakey Joseph, Middle ward
Morgan Richard, High Cross ward
Pickett Wm. & Eliz. High Cross ward
Renwick John, High Cross ward
Spencer Samuel, High Cross ward
Spooner Robert, Lower ward
Tansley Frederick, Middle ward

BRAZIERS AND TINMEN.
Moore George, Middle ward
Tilley Thomas, Lower road

BREWERS.
Chalkley George, jun. Lower ward
Clark John, High Cross ward
Clark Thomas, Church road
Freeman Jeremiah, Middle ward
Haddan William John, Middle ward

BRICK MAKERS.
Forster Robert, Middle ward
Sanders Thomas, Middle ward
Scales William, Wood Green ward

BRICKLAYERS & BUILDERS.
(See also Carpenters, &c.)
Brooks George, Middle ward
Catling James, High Cross ward
Catling Michael, West green
Clarke Rachael, Middle ward
Miers Abraham, Middle ward
Paine William, Lower ward
Sanders Thomas, Middle ward

BUTCHERS.
Aris Thomas, High Cross lane
Boon John, Middle ward
Chace John, High Cross lane
Curling Thomas, Lower ward
Hazell James, Lower ward
Martin Richard, High Cross ward
Sheward John, High Cross ward
Smith John, Middle ward
Tuck Geo. Storey, High Cross ward
Waland James, Church road

CABINET MAKERS.
Burton James, Middle ward
Dennison James, High Cross ward
Richards Samuel, Lower Ward

CARPENTERS, BUILDERS, AND UNDERTAKERS.
Adlington John, Middle ward
Ashwell Thomas, High Cross ward
Chalkley George, Lower ward
Cole Edmund John, Wood green
Davies William, High Cross ward
Fidler Edward, Middle ward
Howse William, Middle ward
Huggins Edward, West green
Humphreys Thomas, Middle ward
Seagoe Robert, Lower ward
Stickley James, High Cross ward
Thomas Daniel, Wood green ward
Wright Edward, White Hart lane

CHEESEMONGERS.
Garman Geo. & Wm. High Cross ward
Ives William, Middle ward
Mole James, Lower ward

CHINA, GLASS, &c. DEALERS.
Bower William, Middle ward
Garman Wm. & George, Marsh lane
Ives William, Middle ward
Tuck Charles, High Cross ward

CHYMISTS & DRUGGISTS.
Brickwell James, Middle ward
Shillitoe Thomas, Middle ward
Silver Daniel, Middle ward
Wall William, Lower ward

COACH BUILDERS.
Glover William, Middle ward
Smith William, Lower ward
Whitehead George, High Cross ward

COACH PROPRIETORS.
Hunt Henry, High Cross ward
Isaac Sarah & Joseph, Lower ward
St. John Josiah, Lower ward

COOPERS.
Cozens Joseph, Middle ward
Hasted James, Lower ward

CORN & COAL CHANDLERS.
Bell Ed. (merchnt.) Tottenham mills
Collins Joseph, Middle ward
Cook Thomas, Lower ward
Goddard Isaac, High Cross ward
Hadlow John, Middle ward
Masons William, Lower ward
Pryer William, Lower ward
Smith Charles, Middle ward
Zinzell James (coal), Lower ward

CRAPE MANUFACTURERS.
Baylis & Co. Church road

FIRE, &c. OFFICE AGENTS.
GUARDIAN, Thomas Shillitoe, Middle ward
IMPERIAL, William Woollaston Reid, High Cross ward
NORWICH, William Edmunds, Middle ward
PHŒNIX, Thomas Newson, Middle ward

FRUITERERS AND GREEN-GROCERS.
Burgin Ann, Lower ward
Davis Robert, Middle ward
Levy Alexander, High Cross ward
Quittenlor Edward, High Cross ward
Studman Thomas, High Cross ward

GARDENERS.
Burgin Ann, Lower ward
Pennett George, Middle ward

GROCERS & TEA DEALERS.
(See also Shopkeepers.)
Banks Samuel, Middle ward
Bland George, Middle ward
Burton Henry William, Lower ward
Clarke Charles, Lower ward
Colyer William, High Cross ward
Copeland Joseph, Lower ward

Fitkin John, High Cross ward
Francis Joseph, Middle ward
Garman William & George, High Cross ward [Middle ward
Ives William (and cheesemonger),
Johnson George, Middle ward
Linton Miles, Lower ward
Phillips Edward, High Cross ward
Reid Wm. Woollaston, High Cross wrd
Topping George, High Cross ward

HAIR DRESSERS.

Bell John, Middle ward
Carter Thomas, Lower ward
Ingram John, Lower ward
Pluckwell Henry Jas. Middle ward
Rodwell Edmund, Middle ward
Warren Robert, High Cross ward

IRONMONGERS.

Tilley Thomas, Lower ward
Turner John, High Cross ward

LEATHER CUTTERS.

Carter William, Lower ward [ward
Mitchell Edward (& currier), Middle

LINEN DRAPERS.

Cove Henry, Middle ward
Ellis Mary, High Cross ward
Hancock John, Middle ward [ward
Moody Francis Herbert, High Cross
Stephenson John, Middle ward
Wright William, Lower ward

MILLER.

Bell Edward, Tottenham mills

MILLINERS & DRESS MAKRS.

Beaton Emma, White Hart lane
Claxton Mary Ann, Middle ward
Harris Mary, Church road [ward
Harvey Amelia & Cordelia, Middle
Holt Ann, Lower ward
King Susan, Lower ward
Leak Margaret, Middle ward
Ovenall Maria, Lower ward
Stephenson Hannah Jane, High Cross ward [ward
Whitmore Elizabeth, High Cross

OIL MILLS.

Bell Edward, Tottenham mills

PAINTERS, PLUMBERS, AND GLAZIERS.

Archer Catherine, Middle ward
Burkett Charles, Lower ward
Hackwell John, Middle ward
Hunning George, Middle ward
Spurway Wm. Geo. High Cross ward
Wharton & Son, Middle ward
Wharton James, High Cross ward

PASTRYCOOKS.

Goodman Joyce, Lower ward
Peart Thomas, Middle ward

PLASTERERS.

Goodacre William, High Cross ward
Pulham James (& modeller), Lower ward

POULTERERS.

Hayes John, Lower ward
Pomfret John, Lower ward

SADDLERS AND HARNESS MAKERS.

Coote Joseph, Lower ward
Dickey John, Middle ward

SHOPKEEPERS & DEALRS IN GROCERIES & SUNDRIES.

Asten John, Lower ward
Bower William, Middle ward
Charlwood Wm. High Cross ward
Giles Robert, Middle ward
Hankin Ann, Middle ward
Hedges Mary, Middle ward
Jackson Mary, White Hart lane
Jennings George, High Cross ward
Lewis William, Church road
Lewis William, James' place
Oakman William, High Cross ward
Taylor James, Church road
Ward George, Middle ward
Weston Matthew, High Cross ward
White Mary Ann, Lower ward

STATIONERS.

Coventry Geo. (& printer), Lowr wrd
Hunnings William Butters (and printer), Middle ward
Wood Sarah, High Cross ward

STRAW HAT MAKERS.

Adcock Sophia, Middle ward
Mason Mary, Lower ward

SURGEONS.

Hall John, Middle ward
May Edward Curtis, High Cross wrd
Moon William, Lower ward
Pett Alfred, Lower ward
Wollaston Robert, Middle ward

SURVEYORS.

Barrett William, Middle ward
Sanders Thomas, Middle ward
Whybro Edward, Tottenham green

TAILORS.

Adcock Daniel, Middle ward
Beaton Wm. Hy. White Hart lane
Edmunds William, Middle ward
Fowles James, Middle ward
Harvey Henry, Middle ward
Lloyd Samuel, Lower ward
Mason William, High Cross ward
Palmer James, Lower ward
Rogers John, High Cross ward
Selman Joseph, Lower ward
Stacey William, Church road

TALLOW CHANDLERS.

Burgess Sarah, Lower ward
Clarke Charles, Lower ward
Johnson George, Middle ward

TAVERNS & PUBLIC HOUSES.

Bell & Hare, Saml. Mitchell, Middle ward
Black Boy, Chas. Chance, West green
Bull, James Martin, High Cross ward
Coach & Horses, Wm. Sargant, Lower wrd.
George & Vulture, John Fox, Middle ward
Plough, John Brooks, Middle ward
Queen's Head, Tho. Wright, Wood green
Red Lion, Frederick Dubois, Middle ward
Roebuck, James Quelch, Lower ward
Rose & Crown, Jas. Aylott, High Cross wrd
Ship, David Harland, Middle ward
Swan, George Downes, High Cross ward
Three Compasses, John Pratt, White Hart lane [Wood green
Three Jolly Butchers, Alexander Watson,
Waggon & Horses, Chs. Lucas, Lower wrd
White Hart, Wm. Boulter, Lower ward
White Hart, Sml. Patrick, High Cross wrd

TOY DEALERS.

Bishop Henry, Middle ward
Bodle Susanna, Middle ward

UPHOLSTERERS.

Christie James, Middle ward
Gasson James, Middle ward
Richards Samuel, Lower ward
Robinson James, Middle ward

WATCH & CLOCK MAKERS.

Cosher Thomas, Middle ward
Newsom Thomas, Middle ward
Norton Charles, Middle ward

WELL SINKER & BORER.

Clark Thomas, corner of Marsh lane, Lower ward

WHEELWRIGHTS.

Fidler Edward, Middle ward
Moulding John, Middle ward
Perrin Alexander, High Cross ward
Stacy Richard, Lower ward
Tatum John, High Cross ward

WINE MERCHANTS.

Culff Margaret, High Cross ward
Wiglesworth Eliz. (& spirit) Lwr. ward

Miscellaneous.

Barrett Wm. conveyancer, Middle ward
Barton Philip Henry, teacher of the piano, High Cross ward [ward
Brown James. furniture broker, Lower
Campbell William, window blind maker and coach joiner, Lower ward
Castleton John, stonemason, Middle ward
Coleman Chas. nurseryman, Lower ward
Elliott Paul, glass cutter, Lower ward
Fulloon Robt. Dod, solicitor, Lower ward
London Caoutchouc Company, manufacturers of patent ropes and waterproof cloth, Middle ward [ward
Randell James, brush maker, High Cross
Savings' Bank, High Cross ward—Lancaster Rickards, secretary [ward
Thorne Mary, oil and colour shop, Lower
Tomlinson & Russell, pawnbrokers, Middle ward [ward
Wadkins John, clothes salesman, Lower
Wilson Henry, hat maker, Lower ward

COACHES.

To LONDON, from St. John's and Isaac's Offices, and the Rose & Crown, Ship and the Swan, *Coaches* every half hour, from half-past seven in the morning until nine at night.

To & from London, Cambridge, Hertford, Lynn, York, &c., *Coaches* pass through daily.

CARRIERS.

To LONDON, Edward Oakley and — Hartley, daily.

TWICKENHAM AND TEDDINGTON.

TWICKENHAM is a village and parish in the hundred of Isleworth, about ten miles west of Hyde Park Corner—delightfully situated on the western bank of the Thames, on the road from London through Isleworth, or Richmond to Hampton Court. Its name was formerly written *Twicknam*, referring to its position between two streams or brooks that flow into the Thames at each end of the village. Twickenham is a place of some antiquity, mention being made of it in the records kept by the monks of Canterbury as having been given to the bishop of that see, in the eighth century, by King Offa; it has likewise long been noted as the retreat and residence of the statesman and the scholar; while the loveliness of its situation, the uniform neatness of the village and healthfulness of its air, joined to the convenient distance at which it lies from the metropolis, make it much resorted to at almost all seasons of the year, and essentially contribute to its prosperity. The princely mansion of Strawberry Hill, once the residence of Sir Robert Walpole (now occupied by Earl Waldegrave), is seen to great advantage from the river; and the vicinage of Twickenham is adorned throughout by a number of beautiful seats and tasteful villas: amongst the latter is the one once occupied by that favourite of the muses, Pope, who lived and died here; it is still shewn to the inquiring stranger, but it has been much enlarged, and presents not the same appearance as when possessed by its original classic owner. The celebrated grotto is no longer remarkable for aught, save that it was erected under the immediate direction of the bard; unsparing time, and the pardonable thefts of his admirers, have combined to deprive it of nearly all its peculiar features. Cross Deep Lodge, the residence of Richard Hunt Matthews, Esq., is another beautiful seat. At the western extremity of this (as it may be termed) classic village, the Thames intersects by its silver streams many a verdant spot, and, while it forms numerous little islands, seems to linger, as if unwilling to quit the enchanting scene. The principal branches of trade here are oil-mills on Twickenham common, and some large breweries; the most extensive of the latter is that belonging to Messrs. Cole and Co. The places of worship are the parish church, Montpelier chapel of ease, and a chapel each for independents and Wesleyan methodists. The church, dedicated to Saint Mary, stands near the river, and is a neat brick structure, of the Doric order, with an ancient embattled tower; it contains many highly interesting monuments and memorials; Bishop Warburton erected one to the memory of Pope, with the poet's bust in white marble; it is placed over the gallery on the north wall, with the following inscription:—

'Alexander Pope, M. H. Gulielmus Episcopus
Glocestriensis amicitiæ causa fac cur, 1761.
Poeta loquitur.
For one who would not be buried in Westminster Abbey.
Heroes and kings, your distance keep,
In peace let one poor poet sleep,
Who never flatter'd folks like you—
Let Horace blush, and Virgil too!'

A monument to Mrs. Clive, the celebrated actress, is also in this church. The benefice is a vicarage, in the presentation of the dean and canons of Windsor, and present incumbency of the Rev. Charles Proby. The principal charity is a school, liberally supported, and conducted upon the national system, in which are instructed one hundred and ten boys, of whom thirty annually receive clothing. Fairs, for toys, &c., are held on Holy Thursday and following day, and on the 9th and 10th of August. The population of the parish, by the returns for 1831, amounted to 4,571.

About two miles from Twickenham, in the hundred of Spelthorne, is the village of TEDDINGTON, most pleasantly seated close to the banks of the Thames, and on the road to Hampton Court through Bushey Park. The name is supposed to be derived from the Saxon word *Tydenton*, signifying 'the ending of the tide,' which does not flow above this place. The celebrated quaker, William Penn, resided here for some time; the letter wherein he clears himself of the charge of papistry is dated from Teddington, October 24, 1688. The church, dedicated to St. Mary, stands near the Thames, and is a small brick structure, with a low square tower; this tower, and the east window, have the features of antiquity; but the other part of the fabric is more modern, and the present belfry was constructed not many years since. In this church are interred the remains of the distinguished Dr. Stephen Hales; and on the north-east wall is a monument (date 18th October, 1720,) to the once famed actress, Margaret Woffington; likewise a monument to Sir Orlando Bridgeman, an eminent lawyer, who died in 1674. There is a small school here for instructing girls in knitting and reading, founded by Lady Bridgeman; and a few years since was erected a parochial schoolhouse, towards the cost of which the Queen Dowager contributed £100. and Joseph Strachan, Esq. £50. An extensive wax bleaching concern is carried on here. In 1831 the parish contained 895 inhabitants.

POST OFFICE, King street, TWICKENHAM, William Curtis, *Post Master.*—Letters from LONDON arrive and are despatched four times a day.—Letters from all parts of the West arrive (from Hounslow and Kingston) every morning at seven, and are despatched every evening at half-past seven.

POST, TEDDINGTON, *Receiving-House* at Edward Abbett's, baker.—Letters from all parts arrive (from Twickenham) three times a day, and are despatched every morning at eight and afternoon at three.

NOBILITY, GENTRY AND CLERGY.

Alldridge H. Wm. esq. Twickenham common
Alley John Henry, esq. (barrister), Twickenham green
Ansell Richard, esq. Gifford lodge
Ashbridge Mr. Jeremiah, Twickenham common
Atterbury Mrs. —, Twickenham common
Barclay Alexander, esq. Teddington
Barnard George, esq. Cross Deep
Bateman Lieut.-Col. Twickenham common
Benson Thomas Starling, esq. Manor house, Teddington
Borland Jas. esq. M. D. Teddington
Bowles Miss —, Teddington
Brassey Richard John, esq. Montpelier row
Brent Timothy, esq. Little Marble hill
Briscoe John J. esq. M. P. Cross Deep
Brome Jno. esq. Teddington house
Budgen Captain —, King st
Burdett Wm. Jones, esq. Compt hall
Burt Mrs. —, 1 Montpelier row
Bush the Misses, Twickenham park
Butcher Mr. —, Richmond road
Byng the Misses, Waterside
Calvert Mrs. —, Whitton
Cambridge the Venerable Archdeacon, Waterside
Carter Mr. C. (attorney), Waterside
Caulfield Captain —, Twickenham common
Clay William, esq. M. P. Fullwell lodge, Twickenham common
Collard Capt. Valen. R. N. Teddington
Cotter Mr. John, Teddington
Crole Daniel, esq. Cross Deep
Crow Mr. F. York lodge
Davies Miss —, Spackman's buildings
Davies Mrs. —, Little Strawberry hill
Davies Mr. Jas. Spackman's buildings
Dean John, esq. 11 Sion row
De Stark Capt. —, Montpelier row
Devon Charles, esq. Teddington pl
Edwards Mr. James, Teddington
Espinasse Colonel —, Eatham lodge
Fonblanque John, esq. Amyard house, Isleworth lane
Forsyth Wm. esq. Richmond road
Foy Mrs. —, Crown lane
Fuller Mr. John, Teddington
Gompertz Abrm. esq. Montpelier row
Gostling George, esq. Whitton
Green the Misses, Montpelier row
Hampston Chas. Jas. esq. Heath lane
Hardesty Mrs. —, Teddington
Harriott Major T. J. Heath lane
Hathaway W. S. esq. Teddington
Hawkins Henry, esq. 2 Sion row
Haynes George, esq. Richmond road
Hedding Wm. Levitt, esq. Teddington
Herbert Mrs. —, Back lane
Hunt Henry, esq. Isleworth lane
Jakes Mr. Thos. Twickenham green
Johnstone Sir Alex. Richmond road
Jullian Mrs. —, Teddington
Kirkman Mrs. —, 6 Sion row
Leach Alexander, esq. Heath lane
Lee Miss —, 5 Sion row
Lind Francis, esq. Cross Deep
Lloyd James, esq. Gothic villa
Lloyd Rev. John Henry, Teddington
Lockwood Mr. Thomas, 4 Sion row
Lyster Mrs. General, London road
Mackewen Mr. James, Richmond rd
Matthews Richard Hunt, esq. Cross Deep lodge
Mercer the Misses, Teddington
Moore Mrs. Henrietta, Waterside
Moore Miss —, Teddington
Mortimer Mrs. —, Twickenham common
Moxon Thomas, esq. Twickenham lodge
Murray Alexander, esq. Water side
Murray C. K. esq. Church yard
Nicholson Rev. Hy. D. D. London rd
Peel Colonel J. Marble hill
Pettingal Rev. C. T. Heath lane
Porter Miss Ann, London road
Proby Mrs. —, Grove cottage
Proby Rev. Charles, Church yard
Ramsden Captain —, London road
Reed Miss —, London road
Robards Wm. esq. Montpelier row
Robinson Mrs. —, Teddington
Ross William, esq. Pond house
Rosser J. esq. Twickenham common
Rumnell William, esq. 1 Sion row
Scott Mrs. —, Heath lane
Sharp Capt. Henry Jelf, Waterside
Shoemack —, esq. Teddington
Shore Sir Robert, Hampton road
Skrine Rev. John Harcourt, Rose cottage, Teddington
Sneyd Mrs. —, King st
Strachan Jas. Morgan, Teddington grove
Taylor Mrs. Fras. Montpelier row
Turnour Lady Jane, Laurel lodge, Heath lane
Twining Miss —, London road
Waldegrave the Right Hon. Earl, Strawberry hill
Warwick the Misses, Waterside
Washington Mr. —, Cross Deep
Watson Mr. —, Montpelier row
Weaver Mrs. Ann, Church st
Wells Mr. William, London road
West Capt. —, R. N. Teddington
White Mrs. —, Park villas
Wilkie Rev. James, A. M. London rd
Wilkinson Mr. William, Teddington
Williams Capt. —, R. N. Teddington
Williams Jas. esq. Sandy Coomb lodge
Winthorp Mrs. Ann, 3 Sion row
Woolnough Capt. Joseph Chappell, R. N. K. H. Waterside
Wray Rev. Edwd. Twickenham green

ACADEMIES AND SCHOOLS.
Not otherwise described are Boarding.

Acton Miss, Feversham house, Teddington
CHARITY SCHOOL, Waterside—Wm. Seymour, master; Mrs. Seymour, mistress
Childs William (day), Heath lane
Chowne Miss Eliza, Holly house, Twickenham road
Nicholson Rev. Henry, D.D. London road
PAROCHIAL SCHOOL, Teddington—Mr. Whipple, master
Pettingal Rev. Chas. Thomas, Heath lane
Robson Mrs. Frances, Walnut Tree house Academy, London road
Sandoz Philip, Church st
Wilkie Rev. James, A. M. London rd

BAKERS & FLOUR DEALERS.

Abbett Edward, Teddington
Baker George, Church st

Chamberlaine Jas. Twickenham grn
Collis John, Teddington [green
Harrison John Davies, Twickenham
Kirby John Eling, Richmond road
Lemon William, Teddington
Merry Edward, King st
Searle James, Church st
Searle William, Heath lane

BLACKSMITHS & FARRIERS.

Barrett Richard, London road
Chapman Ann, Church st
Davies Harrison, Back lane
Gatfield William, Heath lane
Rogers Ann, Heath lane
Whitman William, Teddington

BOOKSELLERS, STATIONERS AND PRINTERS.

Curtis William, King st
Seymour William, Church st

BOOT AND SHOE MAKERS.

Baker Edmnd. (& umbrella), Heath la
Cogswell Thomas, London road
Collett Allen, Chappell row
Colley George, Teddington
Edwards James, London road
Idle John, Richmond road
Kipps Edward, Teddington [lane
Leake Wm. (& leather cutter), Heath
Mesley Samuel, Church st
Missen James, Church st
Murray Charles, Church st
Redknap Enos, Church st
Simmons James, Twickenham green
Whale George, King st
Wilkins Charles, Twickenham green

BRAZIERS AND TIN-PLATE WORKERS.

Chapman Ann, Church st
George Ann and Son, Church st
Smith Thomas (& gas fitter), King st

BREWERS.

Bowyer Thomas, London road
Chamberlaine James, jun. Twickenham green [don road
Cole George Beauchamp & Co. Lon-
Fisher Robt. (& cooper), London rd
Saunders Edwd. Twickenham green
Tutton John, Richmond road
Withers Henry, Chappell row

BRICKLAYERS.

Marlow Wm. Twickenham common
Taylor Arthur, Richmond road

BUTCHERS.

BarnesJos. (pork), Twickenhm green
Candler John (pork), Church st
Goodchild John, Church st
Green Joseph, Twickenham green
Holton Benjamin, Church st
Lawrence Robt. Twickenham green
Porter William (& pork), Teddington
Price William, Heath lane
Rowles George, King st
Stodwell John Matthew, Church st
Wade Joseph Harper, Teddington
Way William, Church st
Withers William, London road

CABINET MAKERS AND UPHOLSTERERS.

Anderson Robert (& paper hanger), Back lane
Dunn Joseph, London road
Jones Joseph, King st
Rivers George, London road

CARPENTERS, BUILDERS & UNDERTAKERS.

Burchett Ann Elizabeth, Church st
Cockrell Stephen (& house agent), Twickenham
Cooper William White, King st
Goodfellow Jas. Sandy Coomb lane
Holmes Thomas, Church st
Neighbour Edw. Henry, Chapel row
Parpworth Radford (& house agent), Twickenham green
Todd Henry, Heath lane
Whittle Oliver, Twickenham green
Wright Horace, Teddington

CHINA, GLASS, &c. DEALERS.

Morton Eleanor Harriet, Church st
Smith George, Twickenham green
Weston Flora, Church st

CHYMISTS AND DRUGGISTS.

Parrott Augustus Alfred, Church st
Routh Oswald Foster, King st
Wheeler Robert, King st

COACH, LANDAU AND FLY OWNERS.

Berkshire Peter, Montpelier row
Tapps John, King st
Willis William, King st

COACH MAKERS.

Oliver George Augustus (to Her Majesty), London road
Smith & Hasted, Richmond road

COAL DEALERS.

Bowyer Thos. London road [green
Chamberlaine Jas. jun. Twickenham
Kirby John Eling (and lighterman), Richmond road

CORN DEALERS.

Bowyer Thomas, London road
Collis John, Teddington [road
Peters Geo. (& malt & hop) Richmond
Turner Lydia (and seed), King st

FIRE, &c. OFFICE AGENTS.

ATLAS, William Holmes, Church st
BRITISH, Henry Todd, Heath lane
IMPERIAL, William Curtis, King st
PHŒNIX, Steph. Cockrell, Teddingtn
SUN, William Seymour, Church st

FISHMONGERS.

Auger Richard, King st
Coxen Mary, Church st
Harris Barnett, Church st
Harris John, Teddington

FRUITERERS.

Avis Richard, King st
Hamblen Stephen, Church st
Moscrop Robert, Teddington
Pickle John, Heath lane
Seth John, Church st
Smith Richard, Richmond road

FURNITURE BROKERS.

Ives George, Heath lane
Ives George, jun. (and auctioneer) Heath lane

GROCERS, TEA DEALERS & CHEESEMONGERS.

(See also Shopkeepers.)

Abbett Edward, Teddington
Bridges Edward, Church st
Cooper William White, King st
Folley James, Heath lane
Holmes William, Church st
Kirkman Christopher, King st
Leverett Edward, Teddington
Simmons James, Teddington
Smith Samuel, Church st
Toone Edward, King st
Wall William, Church st
Wheeler Daniel, 8 Sion row

HAIR DRESSERS.

Etherington John Bullen, King st
Lupton Richard, Church st
Meads John Wilson, Teddington
Peek John, Church st

IRONMONGERS & SMITHS.

Chapman Ann, Church st
George Ann & Son, Church st
Smith Thomas, King st

LINEN, &c. DRAPERS.

Baldry James, Twickenham green
Carpenter Ann, London road
Lemon Martin, Teddington
Molteno Wm. Henry, Church st
Page John, London road
Powell Hector, Church st
Simmons James, Teddington
Tapps Thomas, London road

MALTSTERS.

Bowyer Thos. London road [road
Cole Geo. Beauchamp & Co. London
Saunders Edwd. Twickenham green
Saunders Mary, Twickenham green

MARKET GARDENERS.

Geary James, London road
Goswell William, Richmond road
M'Combie Joseph, Back lane
May John, Twickenham green
Peake William, Isleworth lane
Pickle John, Heath lane
Richardson James, Teddington
Richardson John, London road
Seth John, Church st
Smith Richard, Richmond road
Smith Wm. Geo. Twickenham green
Stonely Henry, Richmond road

MILLINERS, DRESS MAKERS AND HABERDASHERS.

Allnutt Mrs. the Cross, Twickenham common
Lavin Miss, Heath lane
Redknap Eliza, Church st

PAINTERS, PLUMBERS AND GLAZIERS.

Allnutt William Henry, London road
Collett Isaac, King st
Ewington George, London road
GinmanNicholas, Twickenham green
Lovegrove John Garland, Church st
Rice Richard, Teddington
Selfe Henry, Teddington

SADDLERS.

Castle Charles, Church st
Cole Samuel, Teddington
Dale Allen, King st

SEED CRUSHERS.

Allan & Pitcairn, Twickenham green mills

SHOPKEEPERS & DEALRS IN GROCERIES & SUNDRIES.

Avis Sarah, Richmond road
Baldry James, Twickenham green
Carpenter Ann, London road
Collis John, Teddington
Cross George, Heath lane
Fanthum Wm. Twickenham green
Gunn Mary, Chapel row
Harris Mary, Twickenham green
HarrisonJno. Davies, Twickenham gn
Harrow James, Richmond road
Hysell Mary, Teddington
Jackson Jemima, London road
James Thomas, Heath lane
Jenkins Joseph, Twickenham green
Lemon William, Teddington
Walker David, Twickenham green
Wheeler Wm. Twickenham green
Wilkes Mary, Twickenham green

STRAW HAT MAKERS.

Baker Mary Ann, Heath lane
Etherington Hester, King st
Holton Harriet, Church st
Maycock Elizabeth, Church st
Slight Harriet, Chappell row

SURGEONS.

Barry Henry, Richmond road
Clark Charles C. Back lane
Litchfield Thomas, Heath lane
Martin Charles, Heath lane
Simoens Jeronimo, King st
Thompson John, Teddington

SURVEYORS.

Allnutt William Henry, London road
ChildsWm. (land & timber), Heath la

TAILORS.

Ayliffe John, Church st
Bowyer James (& hatter), King st
Brewer James, Twickenham green
Chamberlin Jas. Twickenham green
Enticknap William, London road
Erricker John, Teddington
Green Joseph, Twickenham green
Harris Henry, Church st
Parslow Philip, Teddington

TAVERNS & PUBLIC HOUSES.

Black Dog, Mary Kinggett, London road
Clarence Arms, John Royal, Teddington
Crown, Sarah Clark, Richmond road
Duke of York, Mary Ann Charlesworth, London road
Duke's Head, Thomas Webster Hearne, Twickenham green
Eight Bells, Joseph Ingram, Bell lane
Fox, Thomas Prosser, Church st
George & Dragon, Amy Maddock, King st
Horse&Groom, FerdinandGoodale, King st
King's Head, James Green, Teddington
King's Head (posting and commercial), William Willis, King st
PrinceBlucher, William Richards, Twickenham green
Red Lion, William Heirons, Twickenham [green
RoyalOak, Christiana Moscrop, Teddintn
Royal Oak, Rachael Wicks, Richmond rd
Three Kings, William Baldry, Heath lane
Three Tuns, Charles May, London road
Two Sawyers, Martha Griffin, Church st
White Swan, Sarah Pines, Water side

WAX & TALLOW CHANDLERS.

Barclay Alexander (& wax bleacher), Teddington
Holmes William, Church st
Regent Richd. (& tobacconist), King [st

Miscellaneous.

Ayliffe John, toy dealer & tobacconist, Church st
Barnes Joseph, cutler, Twickenham green
Beale Joshua, watch maker, King st
Coster Daniel, marine store dealer, Twickenham green
Foot Richard, poulterer, London road
Gooch James, registrar, Heath lane
Laing Robert, nurseryman, Richmond rd
Lamb John, parish clerk, Church st
Mason Mary, stone mason, Heath lane
May John, farmer, Twickenham green
May William, farmer, Twickenham
ROYAL HUMANE SOCIETY'S RECEIVING HOUSE, at the White Swan, Waterside
Russen Sarah, dyer, Richmond road
Simmonds James, veterinary surgeon, Twickenham green [Heath lane
Staples Sarah, butter and cheese factor,
Stuckey William, wheelwright, Twickenham green [London road
Warren John, wine & spirit merchant,

COACHES & OMNIBUSES.

To and from LONDON, *Coaches* call at the King's Head Inn, Twickenham, almost every half hour during the day.
To RICHMOND, *Omnibuses* every hour.
To SUNBURY, *Coaches*, from the King's Head Inn, three times a day.

CARRIERS.

To LONDON, Henry Jackson & Thomas Webb, from their houses, Twickenham, daily—and Henry Gildon, from Bell lane, every Monday, Wednesday, and Friday.

CONVEYANCE BY WATER.

To LONDON, Robt. Gildon, & Geo. Redknap, from Bell lane, three times a week.

UXBRIDGE,

WITH THE VILLAGES OF COWLEY & GREAT & LITTLE HILLINGDON & NEIGHBOURHOODS.

UXBRIDGE is a market town and chapelry in the parish of Hillingdon and hundred of Elthorne, 15 miles W. by N. from London—situated at the north-western extremity of the county of Middlesex, and on the high road from London to Oxford. The ancient name of this place was *Oxebreuge* or *Woxbrigge*, afterwards varied to *Waxbridge*, *Woxbridge* and *Oxbridge*, whence the transition to its present appellation was imperceptible. The town was founded, probably, about the time of Alfred; it was surrounded by a ditch, and the whole site then comprised about eighty-five acres; as a frontier station it was important under the feudal system, and there is every indication of its having been fortified at an early period of our history. The present town, which occupies a gentle acclivity on the bank of the Colne, is well paved, lighted with gas, and supplied with water from numerous wells. The general trade of the place is very considerable, and under the title of manufactures may be comprised the making of agricultural implements, Windsor and fancy chairs, great quantities of bricks, rickcloth, and rope and twine; there are also some breweries, oil-mills and maltings; but its great and staple trade is that in corn and flour, for which it has long been noted; the mills employed in the flour trade are numerous, and of great power. The facilities afforded by the river Colne for the erection of machinery, and by the Grand Junction canal for water carriage, have rendered Uxbridge remarkably prominent in this branch of commerce. Its leading thoroughfare situation likewise adds to its prosperity, and the inns and taverns present very superior accommodation alike for the posting and commercial traveller. The 'Crown' inn, near the bridge, is famed in history as the house in which Charles I held the negociations, in 1645, to take into consideration the grievances of Scotland and the entire nation; the room in which the treaty was concluded is now the dining-room of the inn, and is preserved in its original state. In 1647 the head-quarters of the parliamentary army were established here, and a garrison was kept in the town so late as the year 1689. The municipal government of Uxbridge is vested in one high constable and three assistants, with four headboroughs. A petty sessions is held, by a bench of county magistrates, on the first and third Monday in every month; and on the first Wednesday monthly a county court, for the recovery of debts under 40*s*., sits at the 'George' inn. The old market house, built in 1561, was removed by act of parliament in 1785, and the present erected, at an expense of nearly £3,000.; it is a commodious building, one hundred and forty feet in length and forty-nine in width, constructed of brick, and supported on fifty-one wooden columns, with several spacious apartments, appropriated to various purposes. Uxbridge confers the inferior title of earl on the Marquess of Anglesey.

The places of worship are the church (or rather chapel of ease to Hillingdon), and chapels for independents, baptists, Wesleyan methodists and unitarians. The church, dedicated to St. Margaret, stands behind the market house; it is composed of brick and flint, and its architecture that of the later English style, with a low square tower; the interior contains an ancient octagonal stone font, and a few elegant monuments. The living is a perpetual curacy, in the archdeaconry of Middlesex and diocess of London; and in the patronage of the trustees of G. Townsend, Esq., who are to present a fellow of Pembroke college, Oxford; the present officiating minister is the Rev. Charles Parker Price. The principal charities established in Uxbridge are some excellent free schools—one particularly, conducted on the national plan, imparts instruction to upwards of one hundred boys; there are others for girls, and one of industry. An apprenticeship fund, and some benevolent bequests for the assistance of the aged and infirm, are the minor charities. The market days are Thursday and Saturday, the former a large corn market, and the latter for general commodities. Fairs are held on 25th March, 31st July, 29th September and 11th October, the two latter now observed chiefly as statute fairs: on the 1st of August is a considerable show of wool. The chapelry (or town) of Uxbridge contained, by the returns for 1831, 3,043 inhabitants.

About one mile from Uxbridge, in the same hundred, is COWLEY village and parish, surrounded by the parish of Hillingdon. It has a small but neat church, in the cemetery of which are interred the remains of the once celebrated and no less unfortunate Dr. Dodd. The trade of Cowley partakes of the character most prominent in that of Uxbridge, there being many corn mills; tanning is the next leading branch, and is carried on very extensively. Population of the parish, in 1831, 315.

HILLINGDON is a parish, comprising the two villages of Great and Little Hillingdon and the chapelry of Uxbridge. In the church-yard of Great Hillingdon is a remarkable high yew tree, which, by the parish book, appears to be upwards of two hundred years old. The Dean of Carlisle, who is the rector of the parish, has a handsome mansion in the village. Hillingdon House which is adjacent, is the seat of R. H. Cox, Esq. (of the, firm of Greenwood, Cox and Co., of London); the grounds are highly picturesque, beautifully disposed, and enriched with a fine sheet of water: this demesne was formerly in the possession of the Marchioness of Rockingham. Besides these admired residences, there are others in the neighbourhood belonging to persons of distinction. The church, dedicated to St. John the Baptist, is principally in the later English style of architecture, with an embattled tower at the western end. Among other monuments that impart interest to the interior is a very fine one to the memory of Henry Earl of Uxbridge. In the church-yard is the tomb of John Rich, a celebrated comedian, who died in 1761. The benefice is a discharged vicarage, in the presentation of the bishop of London. An annual fair, for pleasure, is held here on the 16th of May. The parish of Hillingdon contained, at the census of 1831 (exclusive of the chapelry of Uxbridge,) 3,842 inhabitants.

POST OFFICE, High street, UXBRIDGE, William Lake, *Post Master*.—Letters from LONDON arrive (by the Worcester mail) every night at ten, and are despatched every morning at half-past four.—Letters from the West arrive every morning at half-past four, and are despatched every night at ten.

POST, GREAT HILLINGDON, *Receiving-House* at Benjamin Betteridge's.—Letters are despatched to UXBRIDGE every night at eight.

NOBILITY, GENTRY AND CLERGY.

Beasley Thomas, esq. LL. D. High st
Benham Mr. Ebenezer, Hertford terrace
Benson Mrs. —, New crofts, Hillingdon
Bent Thomas, esq. Great Hillingdon
Blount Mrs. Elizab. Hillingdon end
Brew Captain —, Hillingdon end
Brown Mrs. Sarah, Hillingdon end
Burr William, esq. Cowley hall
Campbell Rev. Henry, Cowley
Chippendale John, esq. the Lodge
Cox Rd. Henry, esq. Hillingdon house
Dagnell Thomas, esq. Cowley
Davidson Mrs. Mary, Hillingdon end
De Salis Dowager Countess, Dawley lodge
De Salis the Honble. Count Fane, High st
Edes the Misses, Uxbridge common
Elliott Mr. William, Hillingdon end
Fassnidge Mrs. Mary, High st
Fuller Miss —, Great Hillingdon
Gardiner Ths. esq. Claremont cottage
Grainge Mrs. Eliz. Hillingdon end
Grenville Algernon, esq. Uxbridge common
Hale George, esq. Vineyard, Hillingdon end
Hale Rev. George Carpenter, Great Hillingdon
Harley Hon. Miss, Cowley rectory
Harris James S. A. esq. High st
Hartwell Mrs. —, High st
Heming Richd. esq. Great Hillingdon
Hesilrige Lady Maynard, Gt. Hillingdn
Hilliard Rev. John, Cowley house
Hodgson Rev. Bilbey P. Gt. Hillingdon
Hull Mrs. Anna, High st
James William, esq. Cowley
Johnson Mrs. Elizabeth, High st
Lee Mrs. Harriet, Hillingdon end
Mills Charles, esq. Little Hillingdon
Morten Mr. Ts. Pield heath, Hillingdn
Price Rev. Chas. Parker, Parsonage hse
Rolfe Mrs. Susannah, Hillingdon end
Rutter Mr. Daniel, Montague house, Uxbridge common
Rutter Mr. Joseph, Great Hillingdon
Saltonstall Mrs. Mary, Little Hillingdn
Sherwin Mrs. Ann, Hillingdon end
Sims Rev. William Francis, High st
Smith Mrs. Catherine, High st
Spooner John, esq. Hillingdon court
Stamper Rev. Thos. G. Hillingdon end
Stevens Ralph, esq. High st
Stuart Major —, Hillingdon grove
Walford Mr. Robert, Hillingdon end
Webb Mrs. Little Hillingdon
Wentworth Mr. Philip, High st
Willan Rd. esq. the Grange, Hillingdon
Williams Thomas, esq. Cowley grove
Wilshin Mrs. Grace, Colham green
Wiseman Sir William S. bart. Hillingdon end

ACADEMIES AND SCHOOLS.

Not otherwise described are Boarding.

Bingham Mrs. Harris's place
BRITISH SCHOOL, Cowley road—George M'Cowen, master
Clinton Elizabeth (day), High st
Dry Wm. Rectory house, Gt. Hillingdn
Geary the Misses, Hillingdon end
HILLINGDON & DRAYTON SCHOOLS—John Hedgecock, master; Jane Sherley, mistress
INFANTS' SCHOOL, Cowley—Mrs. Perryman, mistress
Jones & Parry (ladies'), Hillingdon end
Mann Misses, Cedar house, Great Hillingdon
Moore Sarah, Hillingdon end
Smart Fred. (day), Vine street terrace
Tew Jane (day), Cowley
UXBRIDGE SCHOOL, High st—Thos. Beasley, LL D. head master; Rev. William F. Sims, second master
Wilkinson Robert, Cave house academy, High st—preparatory department by Mrs. Wilkinson

ATTORNEYS.

Geary Henry, jun. High st
Norton Henry (& vestry clerk), High st
Riches & Woodbridge (and clerks to magistrates), High st
Watford Thomas Witts, Hillingdon end
Woolls Edward, High st

AUCTIONEERS & APPRAISRS.

Attwell William, London st
Heron & Son, High st
Moore Geo. B. (appraiser), High st
Morten Thomas, Hillingdon end
Murray Thomas, High st
Stransom William, London st

BAKERS & FLOUR DEALERS.

Adwell Thomas, Windsor st
Austin George, Windsor st
Ball James, King st, Uxbridge moor
Crockett William, Uxbridge moor
Davis William, Great Hillingdon
Deane Wm. Frederick, Windsor st
Fletcher William, Hillingdon end
Grange Thomas, High st
Homewood Spencer, High st
Hyde George Henry, High st
Jarvis Robert, Great Hillingdon
Nash John, High st
Nash William, London st
Pickett George, Cowley
Savery Charles, Great Hillingdon

BANKERS.

Hull, Smith & Co. High st—(draw on Sir R. C. Glyn & Co. London)
SAVINGS' BANK, Public Rooms, Uxbridge—(open every Tuesday from 12 till 2)—Henry Norton, secretary

BLACKSMITHS.

(See also Whitesmiths.)

Bunce James, Great Hillingdon
Harris Jos. nr Grand Junction wharf
Littleford George, Vine st
Stevens Thomas, Uxbridge moor
Stevens William, High st
Winter John, Cowley

BOOKSELLERS & STATIONRS.

Cosier Henry Grimsdell, London st
Grainge Robt. Wyatt & Thos. Wyatt, High st
Lake Wm. (& library & newsvender), High st

BOOT & SHOE MAKERS.

Baker Frederick, Cowley
Brickwell John, London st
Betteridge Benj. Great Hillingdon
Cove Thomas, London st
Cove Timothy, High st
Darvill William, High st
Dean John, High st
Dean William, Windsor st
Dix Joseph (and hatter), High st
Dunton George, Cowley
Hunt Edward, Vine st
Milton Robert, Windsor st
Morris Josiah, Windsor st
Payne John, Windsor st
Stevens Robert, Vine street terrace
Stevens William, Chapel row
Tribe Thomas and John, London st
Turton James, Cowley
Wheeler Charles, High st
Wright George, Cowley road

BRAZIERS AND TINMEN.

Bailey John, High st
Grainge Henry and Daniel, High st
Greenville Jos. Rockingham terrace

BREWERS.

Harman George, High st
Shackle Thomas, London st

BRICK & TILE MAKERS.

Bennett James, Hillingdon
Heron William and Co. High st
Keen Stephen, Hillingdon
Portsmouth Timothy, Hillingdon
Rutty John, Hillingdon
Stapleton George, Hillingdon
Stroud James & Abraham, Hillingdon

BRICKLAYRS & PLASTERERS.

Hardy Thomas, Cowley
Page Daniel and Sons, Windsor st
Roffe Thomas, Great Hillingdon
Shoppee Joseph, High st
Taylor Thomas, Hillingdon end

BUTCHERS.

Batten Joseph, Vine street terrace
Farrant John, Windsor street green
Funge Thos. Chapel row, Windsor st
Garrett John, Windsor st
Maydon Thomas, Uxbridge moor
Piercy Richard, Cowley
Ratcliff Thomas, Great Hillingdon
Raveny Elizabeth, Windsor st
Roadnight Joseph, Hillingdon end
Russell Sarah, Windsor st
Shaw James, Windsor st
Shrimpton Job, London st
Silver George Allen, Windsor st
Turpin George, London st
Webb Thomas, High st
West Nathaniel, Cowley

CABINET MAKERS AND UPHOLSTERERS

Dunham Richard, Uxbridge moor
Fassnidge James, Hillingdon end
Moore George B. High st
Morten Henry, Hillingdon end
Stransom William, London st

CARPENTRS & BUILDERS.

Dunham Richard, Uxbridge moor
Fassnidge James, Hillingdon end
Fearn & Williams, Windsor st
Hardy Thomas, Cowley
Morten Henry, Hillingdon end
Murray Charles, High st
Page Daniel and Sons, Windsor st
Reid George, Great Hillingdon
Shoppee Joseph, High st

CHAIR MAKERS—WINDSOR.

Prior John, Hillingdon end
Prior Robert, Hillingdon end

CHYMISTS & DRUGGISTS.

Chambers William, London st
Norton Robert, High st
Pullin Henry, London st
Rayner John, High st

CLOTHES DEALERS.

Hopkins William Henry, High st
King John, Windsor st
Milton Robert, Windsor st
Perry Timothy, Windsor st
Tew Joseph, High st

COACH BUILDERS.

Hood Edward, High st
Lovell Charles, Hillingdon end

COACH PROPRIETORS.

Allen Joseph, High st
Tollit William, High st
Tollit William, jun. High st

COAL MERCHANTS & DEALRS

Ball James, King st, Uxbridge moor
East William, London st
Elliott Thomas, Crown wharf
Grange Thomas, High st
Heron Geo. Hy. High st
Hull John (& corn merchnt), Treaty wharf
Lightfoot William Burton, Cowley
Murray Thomas, High st
Norton Wm. jun. Buckinghamshire wharf

COAL MERCHANTS, &c.—Contd.
Osborne Thos. (& slate), High st
Perkins Hy. Grand Junction wharf
Powell John (dealer), High st
Smith William (dealer), Windsor street green
Watts Wm. Moor wharf, Uxbridge moor
Willans George, Cowley
Willans James, Cowley lock

CONFECTIONERS.
Jephs Francis Ford, High st
Marsham Charles, High st
Nash William, London st

COOPERS.
Harman William, Windsor st
Lovell John, Windsor st

CORN CHANDLERS.
Adams Henry, High st
Austin George, Windsor st
Basset William, Uxbridge moor
Beach John, Vine street terrace
Busbey Christopher, Windsor st
Coster Charles, High st
Dwight William High st
Grimsdale Thos. Morten, London st
Humphreys George, Cowley
Savery Charles, Great Hillingdon
Willans James, Cowley lock

CORN MERCHANTS.
See Millers.

CURRIERS.
East William, London st
Elliot Thomas, Crown wharf
Hill William, High st

FELLMONGERS AND WOOL-STAPLERS.
Line William (& parchment maker), Uxbridge moor
Tribe Bernard John, London st

FIRE, &c. OFFICE AGENTS.
Alliance, Edward Woolls, High st
Atlas, Thomas Murray, High st
British, Edw. Thos. Angell, High st
County (fire) & Provident (life), Henry Norton, High st
Essex Economic, Spencer Homewood, High st
General Benefit, William Attwell, London st
Globe, William Lake, High st
National, Henry Grimsdale Cosier, London st
Phœnix, Robert Austin, London st
Royal Exchange, Thomas Gilby, High st
Sun, William Goodman, High st

FISHMONGERS.
Bennett Michael, High st
Hughes Edward, London st

FRUITERERS AND GREEN-GROCERS.
Ashton John, Windsor st
Dwight William, High st
Jones Mary, London st

FURNITURE BROKERS.
Dunham Richard, Uxbridge moor
Mason Samuel, Hillingdon end
Stransom William, London st

GLASS & CHINA DEALERS.
Baker James, High st
Holden William, Windsor st
Mason Samuel, Hillingdon end

GROCERS & TEA DEALERS.
(See also Shopkeepers.)
Baynham William, Windsor st
Bonsey Richard, Great Hillingdon
Bray Richard, High st
Cockman James, Windsor st
Gilby Thomas, High st
Hall Thomas & Son, Windsor st
Hetherington George Budd, High st
Hogg George, Chapel st
James Charles Clement, London st
Kemp John Fox, High st
Smith John, Great Hillingdon
Warren George (and cheesemonger), High st
Webster Charles, High st

GUNSMITHS.
Niebour Charles, London st
Strickland William, London st

HURDLE MAKERS.
Barnett Jas. near Hillingdon turnpike
Barnett James, jun. Cowley road
Page Daniel and Sons (and rake), Windsor st
Prior John, Hillingdon end
Prior Robert, Hillingdon end

INNS.
Chequers, Joseph Allen, High st
Crown and Old Treaty House (and posting and commercial), Charlotte Langstone, High st
De Burgh Arms, Joseph Cole, near West Drayton station, Hillingdon
George, John Money, High st
Grapes, Benj. Drinkwater, London st
King's Arms, Edward Clarke (and coach office), London st
Ram, James Chapman, High st
Red Lion, Francis Lloyd, Great Hillingdon
Three Tuns, Henry Foster, London st
White Horse, (and posting and commercial & assembly rooms), Sarah and William Trehern, High st

IRONMONGERS.
Bailey John, High st
Grainge Henry & Daniel, High st
Grainge Robert Wyatt and Thomas Wyatt, High st
Stacey James (and iron founder), High st

LINEN DRAPERS.
Angell Edward Thomas, High st
Bridger William, High st
Ellis Thomas (and furrier), High st
Goodman William, High st
Johnson Thomas & Son, High st
Lottimer & Dalgliesh, High st
Moore Thomas, London st
Tew Joseph, High st

MALTSTERS.
Brown Edward (& corn merchant), London st
Grimsdale Thomas Morten (& mustard maker), London st
Lightfoot William Burton, Cowley
Shackle Thomas, London st

MARINE STORE DEALERS.
Marlow Thomas, Hillingdon end
Stevens Thos. King st, Uxbridge moor

MARQUEE, & RICK & WAGGON CLOTH & SACK MANUFCTRS.
Brownie & Son (by appointment to Her Majesty & the Royal Family), High st
Redford Lucy, High st

MILLERS, MEALMEN, AND CORN MERCHANTS.
Austin Jno. Rabb's mill, Cowley road
Benbow Richard, Cowley hall mill, Hillingdon
Fell Jno. Hermitage, Uxbridge common
Fell Rd. Bellmont, Uxbridge common
Fountain Edwd. & John, Fountain's mill, Hillingdon, & Troy mill, *Herts.*
Geary Henry, High st
Homewood Spencer, High st, & Upper Colham mill, Uxbridge moor
Hull Samuel, High st, and Colham mills, Hillingdon
Hull Wm. & Henry, High st, & Denham mills
Mercer Jno. & Hy. High st, Town mills
Norman James, High st
Smith Thos. & Wm. F. Colham mills
Stevens Henry Jas. near High bridge
Tate Robt. jun. Upper Colham mills

MILLINERS & DRESS MAKRS.
Badham Ann, Vine st
Bassett Mary Ann, Uxbridge moor
Bayles Elizabeth, Hillingdon
Best & Tribe, Hillingdon end
Burgess Elizabeth, High st
Dainty Mary Ann, Chapel st
Edwards Eliz. Vine street terrace
Filbey Miss, Windsor st
Hardman Maria, London st
Marchmount Mary, Windsor st
Pakeman Jane, London st
Ratcliffe A. & M. Vine st
Sturgess Mary, Windsor st

NURSERY AND SEEDSMEN.
Brown & Attwell, Hillingdon end
Wall Thomas, Hillingdon end

OIL AND COLOURMEN.
Chambers William, London st
Rayner John, High st
Heron Christopher, London st

OIL CAKE & BONE MANURE MANUFACTURERS.
Rayner Brothers, Upper Colham mill, Uxbridge moor; office, High st

PAINTERS, PLUMBERS, &c.
Burgiss Wm. John (& gilder), High st
Gigg Henry, Windsor st
Hailey Ephraim, High st
Kearley William, Hillingdon end
Lee Thomas, London st
Pettingell Jos. Rockingham terrace
Rawlinson Ann, London st
Tollit Charles (painter), High st
Weedon George (painter), High st

PATTEN MAKERS.
Lowe Joseph, High st
Wake Edward, High st

PERFUMERS AND HAIR DRESSERS.
Bryning William, London st
Hardman James, London st
Redrup John, Windsor st
Sparkhall & Mitchell, Windsor st
Walker Thomas, High st

POULTERERS.
Bainbridge William, London st
Nicholls George, High st

PRINTERS—LETTER-PRESS.
Cosier Henry G. London st
Lake William (and engraver), High st

PROFESSORS & TEACHERS OF MUSIC.
Birch John T. Cowley road
Niebour Geo. Henry, Uxbridge moor
Pontyfex William, London st

ROPE AND TWINE MANUFACTURERS.
Aspray Thomas (& sack), Cowley
Brownie & Son, High st
Dean Daniel, Great Hillingdon
Redford Lucy, High st

SADDLERS AND HARNESS MAKERS.
Clarke William, Great Hillingdon
Hutson Giles Bell, High st
Ingram William, London st
Masters George, High st
Thonger John, High st
Watkins Thomas, Great Hillingdon

SHOPKEEPERS & DEALERS IN GROCERS & SUNDRIES.
Ayers Thomas, Uxbridge moor
Bigg William Henry, London st
Birch Edmund, Hillingdon
Bowman George, Cowley
Brotherton Benj. Hillingdon end
Brown William, Uxbridge moor
Clayton William, Hillingdon
Farrant John, Windsor st
Grimshaw William, Windsor st
Harrison James, Windsor st
Haynes James, Cowley
Herbert John, Cowley

Poulton Thomas, Vine st
Salter James, Hillingdon
Saunders William, Hillingdon
Smith James, Hillingdon
Smithers John, Hillingdon
Stanley Thomas, Cowley
Stephens Rebecca, Windsor st
Thornton Joseph, Hillingdon
Turton James, Cowley
Willans James, Cowley lock

STONE & MARBLE MASONS.

Burgiss Edward, High st
Tomlinson John, Hillingdon end

STRAW HAT MAKERS.

Best & Tribe, Hillingdon end
Dainty Mary Ann, Chapel st
Ellis Thomas, High st [moor
Godleman Mary, Moorhall, Uxbridge
King Mary, Windsor st
Pakeman Jane, London st

SURGEONS.

Blount Samuel, High st
James & Bullock, High st
Macnamara Daniel, Hillingdon end
Norton Robert, High st
Patten Charles, High st
Rayner Matthew, High st
Rayner William, London st
Stilwell James, Hillingdon end

SURVEYORS---LAND.

Hughes Edward, London st
Murray Thomas (& timber), High st
Tyerman Thomas (& architect), Hillingdon end
Willans John Allnutt, Cowley

TAILORS.

Birch John, London st
Birch William Henry, High st
Brown Wm. (& glover), Windsor st
Brown Wm. Charles, High st [st
Brown Wm. jun. (glover), Windsor
Clinton Richard, High st
Corden Joseph, Cowley [don st
Davies Richd. (& pawnbroker), Lon-
Eaglestone William, Great Hillingdon
Pakeman John, London st
Perry Timothy, Windsor st
Prior William, Hillingdon end
Stransom John, London st [moor
Strickland John, King st, Uxbridge

TALLOW CHANDLERS.

Cockman James, Windsor st
Gilby Thomas, High st
Hetherington George Budd, High st
Webster Charles, High st

TANNERS.

Darvill James, High st
Hole Charles, Cowley

TAVERNS & PUBLIC HOUSES.

Bell, John Keen, High st
Bells, Jemima Griffiths, Hillingdon end
Castle, John Hollis, Windsor st [sor st
Catherine Wheel, Geo. Colebrook, Wind-
Crown, John Newton, Cowley
Crown & Sceptre, William Bunce, High st
Dolphin, Jeremiah Packer, Uxbridge moor
Falcon, William Hall, High st
Feathers, Thomas Holden, High st
Fox, John Mathews, Cowley
General Elliott, Richard Dunham, Uxbridge moor [don end
Green Dragon, Stepn. Cowdery, Hilling-
Green Man, James Johnson, near Hillingdon turnpike
New Inn, Wm. Buckingham Windsor st
Packet Boat, George Willans, Cowley
Queen's Head (late Jolly Ostler), Richard Green, Windsor st
Red Lion, Thomas Johnson, High st
Rose & Crown, James Janes, London st
Royal Standard, William & Zachariah Hollier, Hillingdon turnpike
Sun, William Cherry, High st [Bridge
Swan & Bottle, David Neale, near the
Three Legs, Mary Ann Davis, Windsor st.
Vine, Mary Crutchley, Great Hillingdon
Wellington Arms, James William Giles, Vine street terrace

TIMBER MERCHANTS.

Elliot Thomas, Crown wharf
Grange Thomas, High st [moor
Mason Chas. Algiers wharf, Uxbridge
Osborne Thomas, High st
Roffe Wm. Buckinghamshire wharf

TURNERS IN WOOD.

Prior John, Hillingdon end
Prior Robert, Hillingdon end
Wake Andw. (& brush maker), High st
Watts William, Moor wharf

UNDERTAKERS.

Angell Edward Thomas, High st
Goodman William, High st
Hardy Thos. (& paper hanger), Cowley
Page Daniel & Sons, Windsor st
Murray Charles, High st
Shoppee Joseph, High st
Stransom William, London st

VETERINARY SURGEONS.

Fassnidge William, High st
Marlin John, High st

WATCH AND CLOCK MAKERS

Attwell William, London st
Guildford & Kirby, High st
Kember Richard, London st

WELL BORERS.

Page Daniel & Sons, Windsor st

WHARFINGERS.

Brownie & Son, High st
Elliot Thomas, Crown wharf
Hull John, Treaty wharf [moor
Mason Chas. Algiers wharf, Uxbridge
Perkins Henry, Grand Junction whrf
Tomlinson Jno. Uxbridge moor whrf
Watts Wm. Moor whrf. Uxbridge mr

WHEELWRIGHTS.

Emmerton John, Hillingdon
Gibbs Joseph, Cowley
Hood Edward, High st [moor
Mason Chas. Algiers wharf, Uxbridge
Sherwin George, Hillingdon end

WHITESMITHS.

Alport Edward, Windsor st
Arthur John, Hillingdon end
Bailey John, High st
Grainge Henry and Daniel, High st
Horth Richard, Windsor st

WINE & SPIRIT MERCHANTS

Chambers William, London st
Heron George Henry, High st
Murray Thomas, High st
Trehern William, High st

Miscellaneous.

Allen William, esq. collector, High st
Austin Robert, hatter and tobacconist, London st [don st
Batte Obadiah, livery stable keeper, Lon-
Best William, Roman cement dealer and glue manufacturer, High st
Excise Office, at Mr. Spivey's, High st
Farrant Jno. bailiff for county, Windsor st
Fletcher William, trunk maker, Vine st
Gouldsmith Samuel, dyer, Hillingdon end
Grand Junction Canal Office, Cowley lock—James Roadnight, clerk
Hardman James, toy dealer, London st
Heron Christopher, bottled ale & porter merchant, London st [Hillingdon
Hibbert Thos. horse dealer, Gould green,
Holland John, surveyor of Grand Junction Canal, Yiewsley
Kellaway Mary, dining rooms, Hillingdon
Lowe Harriet, umbrella maker, High st
Lunatic Asylum (private), Moorcroft House, Hillingdon—James Stilwell, proprietor
Murray Charles, inspector of corn returns and high constable, High st
Police Station, Windsor st—David Cooper, superintendent sergeant
Riches & Woodbridge, clerks to commissioners for paving, &c. High st
Smith Robert, tobacco pipe maker, King st
Smith Saml. sieve, &c. maker, Windsor st
Stacy James, proprietor of the Gas Works Cowley road
Taylor John, cutler, Windsor st
Union Poor House, Hillingdon heath—William Weekley, master
Walding Sarah, net maker, High st
Woodbridge Charles, clerk to Board of Guardians, High st
Youens Robert, basket maker, Windsor st

COACHES.

The following Coaches call at the King's Arms, *unless otherwise expressed.*

To LONDON, the *Royal Mail*, from Worcester, every afternoon at half-past four—the *Champion*, from Gloucester, every morning at six—the *Sovereign*, from Cheltenham, at the same hour—the *Blenheim*, from Oxford, every afternoon at half-past two—the *Monarch*, from Worcester, every morning (Sunday excepted) at half-past nine—Hart's *Coach*, from High Wycombe, every morning at half-past ten—the *Age*, from Oxford, every afternoon at three—and Joseph Tollit's *Coaches*, every morning (Sunday and Monday excepted) at half-past ten, and on Sunday evening at five and Monday morning at half-past seven.

To LONDON, a *Coach*, from William Tollit, senior's office, every afternoon at three—William Tollit, junior's *Coach* every morning (Sunday excepted) at eight—a *Coach*, from the Chequers, every Sunday morning at seven and afternoon at five—the *Comet*, from Leamington, calls at the White Horse, every morning at six, and the *Sovereign*, every afternoon at half-past five—a *Coach*, from Wendover, every morning (Sunday excepted) at half-past nine—a *Coach*, from Amersham, calls at the Chequers, every morning (Sunday excepted) at eight—the *Retaliator*, from Cheltenham, calls at the Three Tuns, every evening (Sunday excepted) at half-past five—and the *Safety*, from Thame, calls at the George, every Monday, Wednes. & Fri. morning.

All the above Coaches go through Hayes, Southall and Hanwell.

The following are from London.

To AMERSHAM, a *Coach* calls at the Chequers, every evening (Sunday excepted) at half-past six.

To CHELTENHAM, the *Sovereign*, every morning (Sunday excepted) at nine—and the *Regulator* and the *Retaliator*, at ten; both go through High Wycombe and Oxford.

To GLOUCESTER, the *Champion*, every evening (Sunday excepted) at half-past six; goes through Beaconsfield, High Wycombe, &c.

To HAREFIELD, a *Coach*, from the Falcon, every evening (Sunday excepted) at half-past five.

To HIGH WYCOMBE, a *Coach* calls at the Falcon, every day (Sunday excepted) at twelve—and Joseph Tollit's and Joseph Hart's *Coaches*, from the King's Arms, every evening at half-past five; all go through Beaconsfield and Loudwater.

To LEAMINGTON, the *Sovereign* calls at the King's Arms, every forenoon at eleven—and the *Comet* calls at the White Horse, every night (Sunday excepted) at eight.

To OXFORD, the *Age*, every afternoon at three—and the *Blenheim*, every day (Sunday excepted) at twelve; both go through Beaconsfield & High Wycombe.

To THAME, the *Safety* calls at the George, every Tuesday, Thursday and Saturday forenoon at eleven; goes thro' Beaconsfield, High Wycombe & Risboro'.

To WENDOVER, a *Coach*, every afternoon (Sunday excepted) at half-past four; goes thro' Amersham & Missenden.

To WORCESTER, the *Royal Mail*, every night at ten—& the *Monarch*, at seven; both go through Beaconsfield, High Wycombe and Oxford.

OMNIBUSES.

To LONDON, an *Omnibus* (from Thame) calls at the Falcon, every Monday, Wednesday and Friday.

To THAME, an *Omnibus* (from London) calls at the Falcon, every Tuesday, Thursday & Saturday forenoon at eleven.

CARRIERS.

To LONDON, Budd & Co. Joseph Johnson, Richard Andrews, Richard Crockford, Gilbert & Haynes, Joseph Jolly, and Beasley & Gilbert, all daily—the Commercial Company's *Waggons*, four times a week—John Ward and Richard Dawes, three times a week—& Richard Howland, every Wednesday, Fri. & Sat.

To LONDON, William Abbott, William Rackley, Richard Crockett, Jas. Groves, and William Pedder, every Monday and Thursday—Thomas Greenfield, every Monday and Friday—William Dancer, every Tuesday & Friday—Christopher Baker, every Tuesday and Saturday—Thomas Johnson & John Hatton, every Sunday & Wednesday—Michael Horton and Thomas Golby, every Sunday—Richard Andrews and William Atkins, every Monday—Wm. Lever & Symonds Franklin, every Wednesday—Joseph Tranter & John Shelton, every Thursday—and William Willson and John Baker, every Friday.

To AMERSHAM, William Rackley and Richard Crockett, every Wed. & Sat.

To BANBURY and BUCKINGHAM, Thomas Golby's *Waggons*, every Tues.

To BEACONSFIELD, Jas. Groves, every Tuesday and Saturday—and William Greenfield, every Sunday & Wednesday.

To BICESTER, Symonds Franklin's *Waggon*, every Friday.

To CHELTENHAM, Gilbert & Haynes' *Waggons*, daily—and Richard Dawes, every Sunday, Tuesday & Thursday.

To CHIPPING NORTON, John Ward's *Waggons*, every Sunday, Tues. & Thurs.

To CIRENCESTER, Budd & Company's *Waggons*, daily.

To HADDENHAM, Michael Horton & William Lever, every Tuesday—and William Wilson, every Saturday.

To HIGH WYCOMBE, William Dancer, every Wednesday & Saturday—William Abbott, every Wednesday and Friday—and Richard Atkins, every Wednesday.

To KINGSTON, John Hatton's *Waggons*, every Tuesday and Friday.

To LOUDWATER, Jas. Goulding, every Wednes. & Sat.

To MISSENDEN, William Pedder, every Wednes. & Sat.

To OXFORD, the Commercial Company's *Waggons*, every Sunday, Monday, Wednesday and Saturday.

To STOKE, Christopher Baker, every Wednesday & Sat.

To STOKENCHURCH, Joseph Tranter, every Sat.

To THAME, Richard Howland, every Sunday, Tues. and Fri.

To WATLINGTON, John Shelton, every Thurs.

To WINDSOR, IVER and SLOUGH, John Hampton, every Tues. Thurs. & Sat.

To WOODSTOCK, Thomas Johnson, every Tuesday and Friday.

To WORCESTER and BIRMINGHAM Joseph Jolly's *Waggons*, daily.

CONVEYANCE BY WATER.

To LONDON—and goods also forwarded to all parts of the kingdom, from John Watts' and John Tomlinson's wharfs, Uxbridge moor.

To AYLESBURY, a *Barge*, from Treaty wharf, every Thursday.

WILSDON, KINGSBURY AND NEIGHBOURHOODS.

WILSDON, or *Willesden*, is a neat and retired little village, in the parish of its name and hundred of Ossulton, about five miles W. N. W. from Tyburn turnpike; pleasantly situated on the small river Brent, and a branch from the Grand Junction canal crosses a part of the parish. The places of worship are the parish church, dedicated to St. Mary, and a chapel for dissenters. The charities comprise five almshouses, and a school supported by subscriptions. The living is a vicarage, in the presentation of the dean and chapter of St. Paul's; the Rev. Henry John Knappe is the present incumbent, and his curate the Rev. Thomas R. White. There are two fairs, one on Holy Thursday, the other on St. James's day. The parish of Wilsdon contained, by the government returns for 1831, 1,876 inhabitants.

Two miles north from Wilsdon, in the hundred of Gore, is the village of KINGSBURY, possessing nothing worthy of particular remark—its principal recommendation being the salubrity of the air, and the cheerful and rural scenery of the neighbourhood. The church, which is dedicated to St. Andrew, is an edifice of very humble appearance; the living is a perpetual curacy, in the patronage of the dean and chapter of St. Paul's. The population of this parish, according to the last returns, was 463.

POST OFFICE, WILSDON, Edward Brown, *Post Master.*—Letters from LONDON and all parts arrive every forenoon at eleven and afternoon at five, and are despatched every morning at ten and afternoon at five.

POST, KINGSBURY, *Receiving-House* at the King's Arms.—Letters from LONDON arrive every night at nine, and are despatched every morning.

GENTRY AND CLERGY.

Anderson William, esq. Mapesbury house, Wilsdon
Baker Mr. Thos. Kingsbury
Bean Wm. esq. Rectory house, Wilsdon
Bond Capt. Mount pleasant, Kingsbry
Closier George, esq. Kingsbury
Colley Mr. George, Kingsbury
Collins Barnett, esq. Kingsbury
Cooper Edward Joshua, esq. M. P. Bransbury house, Wilsdon
Cullum Mr. James, Wilsdon
Dickinson Mr. William, Wilsdon
Elmore John, esq. Neasdon
Field Mr. John, Kingsbury
Field Mr. William, Kingsbury
Finch Mrs. —, Wilsdon
French Mr. Jno. Black pot hill, Kingsbury
Hall Mrs. —, Wilsdon
Hare John, esq. Kingsbury
Harpley Mrs. —, Kingsbury
Harris Thos. esq. Grove farm, Kingsbury
Knapp Rev. Hy. John, M.A. Wilsdon
Manning Mr. James, Chalk Hill house, Kingsbury
Newman Robert, esq. Wilsdon
Nicoll Joseph, esq. Neasdon
Nicoll Mr. William, Kingsbury
Ponsford Mr. William, Kingsbury
Rust Mr. William, Kingsbury
Sellon William, esq. Harlesdon green
Silbey Robert, esq. Kingsbury
Stubbs Francis, esq. Kingsbury
Thompson Mr. Wm. Bush cottage, Kingsbury
Vouillon Monsieur, Wilsdon
White Rev. Thos. Reader, M.A. Wilsdon

INNS & PUBLIC HOUSES.

Crown, Wm. Gore, Harlesdon green
Green Man, Jacob Burch, Harlesdon green
King's Arms, Thos. Head, Kingsbury
Plough, Thomas Holden, Kingsbury
Red Lion, Charlotte Harding, Kingsbury
Royal Oak, George Melville, Harlesdon green
Six Bells, Thos. Odell, Wilsdon
Spotted Dog, Jas. Twyford, Wilsdon
Spotted Dog, Jos. Twyford, Neasdon
White Hart, James Parry, Wilsdon

SHOPKEEPERS & TRADERS.

Allen Hudson, tailor, Kingsbury
Benstead Thos. master of National School, Wilsdon
Brown Edward, carpenter and timber dealer, Wilsdon
Butcher Charles, grocer, Harlesdon green
Chad Thomas, grocer, Kingsbury
Chandler Wm. bricklayer, Wilsdon
Dawson Robert, grocer and shoemaker, Harlesdon green
Griffin Robt. baker, Harlesdon green
Hale Robert, butcher, Kingsbury
Hendry Alexander, grocer & butcher, Wilsdon
Holford Andrew, boot and shoemaker, Wilsdon
Jackman Geo. blacksmith, Neasdon
Mead James, wheelwright, Harlesdon green
Norris Geo. wheelwright, Kingsbury
Odell Thos. painter & glazier, Wilsdon
Parsons Charles, shoemaker, Harlesdon green
Richardson Jas. grocer, Kingsbury
Salmon Hy. tailor, Harlesdon green
Vogler Edward, nurseryman, Harlesdon green
Ward Thomas, blacksmith, Harlesdon green
Wood Thomas, baker and corn dealer, Kingsbury

COACHES.

To LONDON, a *Coach* (from Harrow) passes through Harlesdon Green every morning (Sunday excepted) at half-past nine, and returns in the evening at four.

To and from LONDON, WATFORD and ST. ALBANS, *Coaches* pass thro' Kingsbury daily.

CARRIERS.

To and from LONDON and HARROW, *Carriers* pass through Harlesdon Green three times a week.

To and from STANMORE and WATFORD, *Carriers* pass through Kingsbury daily.